TRANSNATIONAL CIVIL LITIGATION

■ ■ ■

By

Joachim Zekoll
University Professor
Chair of Private Law, Procedure and Comparative Law
Johann Wolfgang Goethe Universität, Frankfurt

Michael Collins
Joseph M. Hartfield Professor
University of Virginia School of Law

George Rutherglen
John Barbee Minor Distinguished Professor
University of Virginia School of Law

AMERICAN CASEBOOK SERIES®

WEST.

Mat # **40889873**

American Casebook Series is a trademark registered in the U.S. Patent and Trademark Office.

© 2013 LEG, Inc. d/b/a West Academic Publishing
    610 Opperman Drive
    St. Paul, MN 55123
    1-800-313-9378
Printed in the United States of America

ISBN: 978-0-314-90813-1

TO

BIRGIT & CHRISTINA
J.E.Z.

JESSICA
G.A.R.

ANNIE
M.G.C.

PREFACE

Globalization has turned transnational civil litigation—once a niche topic—into a burgeoning field that has become an integral part of the practice of U.S. lawyers. This casebook focuses primarily on international civil litigation as it impacts U.S. courts, U.S. litigants and U.S. judgments. We have chosen this focus because American lawyers will typically encounter the problems of transnational litigation in U.S. courts involving domestic parties and a foreign party or transaction. This focus notwithstanding, the book's purpose is also to sensitize U.S. students to radically different perceptions of procedural fairness as they prevail outside the United States. Areas in which American lawyers are particularly likely to encounter transnational litigation problems outside the U.S. include the service of process and judicial documents abroad, discovery abroad in connection with U.S. litigation, and the enforcement of U.S. judgments abroad. In many respects, American rules governing these areas differ sharply from their foreign counterparts. Service of process, often informally effected in the United States by private parties, is considered a task of sovereign authority in many foreign nations. The largely unlimited and party-driven access to evidence, a lynchpin of U.S. domestic discovery proceedings, is unknown elsewhere. And 6- or 7-digit awards for pain and suffering, as well as treble and punitive damages are considered unacceptable windfalls to private litigants in most of the rest of the world. Consequently, American judgments containing such awards against foreign defendants (and others) are rarely enforceable outside the United States.

In addition to these areas which cause and force American lawyers to recognize and proactively address conflicting foreign preferences and preoccupations, there are many other facets of transnational civil litigation in the U.S. that produce regulatory clashes with foreign rules and expectations. These include the exercise of long-arm jurisdiction over foreign parties having perhaps minimal contacts with the American forum, antisuit injunctions issued by U.S. courts against foreign litigation and by foreign courts against U.S. litigation, as well as the extraterritorial application of U.S. law to conduct occurring abroad but affecting domestic American interests, and the status and treatment of choice of forum and choice of law agreements here and abroad.

The chief purpose of this book is to provide a readily accessible teaching tool for those who may be considering a civil procedure course with a transnational perspective—particularly current teachers of civil procedure who may have no specific background in the field of transnational litigation. We also hope that more seasoned teachers of courses in international civil procedure and international business transactions may be attracted by this book. And although we have made ample use of secondary sources and scholarship, we have tried to avoid the temptation to have the book serve as a treatise rather than a teaching tool. Where appropriate, we have included links to relevant websites, and we have also included an Appendix for some of the documents that we more frequently reference in the text. We are also aware that as this book goes into production, the Supreme Court's decision in Kiobel v. Royal Dutch Petroleum Co., 621 F.3d 111 (CA2 2010), cert. granted, 565 U.S. ___ (2011) (reargued October 2012), looms on the horizon, and has the potential to reshape litigation under the Alien Tort Statute—as discussed in Chapter 2. We will provide an update in connection with the *Kiobel* decision once it is made.

Although our emphasis throughout the book remains on U.S. perspectives and procedural tools to solve problems in U.S.-based transnational civil litigation, we have added examples of the way in which many of the issues discussed in the book are handled in foreign legal systems. The foreign court opinions and legal materials that we have selected illustrate how foreign judges cope with U.S. law and how foreign legislatures address transnational legal questions. Thus, the book undertakes an effort, albeit a modest one, to add a comparative perspective that we hope will help students better understand foreign approaches in a variety of transnational litigation settings. While the acquisition of knowledge in foreign law will necessarily remain limited, we hope that students will at least be in a position to share, in the end, Judge Cardozo's conviction that he expressed almost 100 years ago: "We are not so provincial as to say that every solution of a problem is wrong because we deal with it otherwise at home." Loucks v. Standard Oil Co of New York, 224 N.Y. 99, 111 (N.Y. 1918).

J.E.Z.
Frankfurt am Main, Germany

M.G.C.
Charlottesville, Virginia

G.A.R.
Charlottesville, Virginia

March 15, 2013

ACKNOWLEDGMENTS

We wish to thank Matthias Reimann and his publisher for permission to include portions of his book, Matthias Reimann, Conflict of Laws in Western Europe: A Guide Through The Jungle (Transnational Publishers, 1995). We also thank our friends and colleagues for their helpful comments and suggestions. We also acknowledge the able research assistance of UVA law students Marta Cook and Jordan Miller, and of Michael Schulz who is based in Frankfurt, Germany. Finally, preparation of this book in camera-ready form would not have been possible without the excellent assistance of Lisa Lambert. For any errors, we alone are responsible.

SUMMARY OF CONTENTS

Preface V
Acknowledgments VII
Table of Contents XIII
Table of Cases XXIII

CHAPTER 1.   Personal Jurisdiction and Forum Selection................................. 1

Section
A.   **Introduction**.. 1
B.   **Specific Jurisdiction**.. 3
C.   **General Jurisdiction** 43
      Note on "Doing Business" as a Basis for Jurisdiction
      over Foreign Parties 55
D.   **Transient Jurisdiction** 58
      A Comparative Note on Transient Jurisdiction.................................... 62
E.   **The Reach of Process** 62
F.   **Litigating Personal Jurisdiction** 73
G.   **Personal Jurisdiction in Europe: The Brussels Convention
      and Regulation** 79
H.   **Attachment and Global Assets**... 99
I.   **Forum Selection Clauses** 114
      Note on the Hague Choice of Court Convention 137
      Note on Forum Selection Clauses Under E.U. Law........................... 138

CHAPTER 2.   Subject Matter Jurisdiction 141

Section
A.   **Introduction**.. 141
B.   **Alienage and Diversity Jurisdiction** 142
      1.   *Citizens or Subjects of Foreign States* 142
      2.   *Permanent Resident Aliens and Alienage Jurisdiction*............... 155
      3.   *Foreign Corporations and Diversity* 160
            Note on Removal to Federal Court... 161
C.   **Cases Arising Under Federal Law**... 162
      1.   *Human Rights Litigation under the Alien Tort Statute* 163
      2.   *Claims under the Torture Victim Protection Act* 182
      3.   *Claims under the Anti-Terrorism Act of 1990* 184
      4.   *Suability of Private Actors and Related Matters* 184
      5.   *Cases Implicating Foreign Policy Concerns* 196
            Note on "Universal Jurisdiction"... 204
      6.   *Cases Arising Under Treaties* 205
D.   **Venue and Alien Defendants**... 218

1.   *Venue in Suits Against Aliens* 218
2.   *Venue in Suits Against Alien and Non-Alien Defendants* 219
3.   *Fallback Venue* 219
4.   *Transfer of Venue* 219
5.   *Transfer of Venue versus Forum Non Conveniens* 220
      Note on the Sequencing of Jurisdictional
      and Related Objections 221

CHAPTER 3.   Suits Against Foreign Sovereigns 223

Section
A.   The Foreign Sovereign Immunities Act 223
1.   *Origins and Structure* 223
2.   *Constitutionality* 225
3.   *Scope* 235
4.   *Exceptions to Sovereign Immunity* 255
B.   The Act of State Doctrine 291

CHAPTER 4.   Service of Process 321

Section
A.   Service on Foreign Defendants Under the Federal Rules 321
1.   *Waiver of Service* 321
2.   *Absent a Waiver of Service* 322
      (a) Serving Foreign Defendants within a U.S.
           Federal Judicial District 322
      (b) Serving Foreign Defendants in a Foreign
           Country 323
B.   Service Under the Hague Convention 324
C.   Coordinating the Hague Convention and the Federal Rules 325
D.   Determining the Applicability of the Hague Convention 337
      Note on Service of Process within the E.U. 350
E.   Service in Violation of Foreign Law 350
1.   *Introduction* 350
2.   *Article 13 of the Hague Service Convention* 352
3.   *Statutory Construction and U.S. Service Provisions* 359
F.   Service on Foreign States, Agencies and Instrumentalities 361

CHAPTER 5.   Parallel Litigation 371

Section
A.   International Forum Non Conveniens 371
      A Comparative Note on Forum Non Conveniens 395
B.   Abstention (*Lis Pendens*) and Parallel Litigation 398
      Background Note on Abstention and Parallel Litigation in the
      Purely Domestic (U.S.) Setting 399
      A Comparative Note on Lis Pendens 412

Note on the Hague Choice of Court Convention 414

C. **International Antisuit Injunctions and Parallel Litigation** 415

    1. *Approach(es) of U.S. Courts* 415

    2. *Approach(es) of European Courts* 433

CHAPTER 6. Taking Evidence Abroad 449

Section

A. **Introduction** 449

    1. *An Overview of Discovery in American Courts* 449

    2. *Foreign Methods of Obtaining Evidence* 451

    3. *American Discovery and Foreign Perceptions* 452

B. **The Hague Evidence Convention** 453

    1. *Overview of the Hague Evidence Convention*

       Procedures 453

    2. *Privileges Against Testifying Under the Convention* 454

    3. *Subject Matter Scope of the Hague Evidence Convention* 455

    4. *The Exclusion of Pretrial Discovery Documents* 456

    5. *The Exclusivity of the Hague Evidence Convention* 457

C. **U.S. Discovery Conducted Abroad** 471

    A Case Illustration 471

D. **The Personal Jurisdiction Requirement** 473

    1. *Nonparty Witnesses* 473

    2. *Jurisdictional Discovery* 473

E. **Post-*Aérospatiale* Decisional Law** 474

F. **Foreign Blocking Statutes** 481

G. **U.S. Discovery and Evidence Production for Foreign**

    and International Tribunals 496

CHAPTER 7. International Litigation and Choice of Law 511

Section

A. **An Overview of American Choice of Law** 511

    1. *Traditional Choice of Law Rules* 511

    2. *Interest Analysis and the Conflicts of Revolution* 514

    3. *The Restatement (Second) of Conflict Laws* 516

B. **American Choice of Law in the Transnational Setting** 518

C. **Constitutional Limits on American Choice of Law** 526

D. **International Choice of Law Clauses** 533

    1. *Validating and Interpreting Choice of Law Clauses* 534

    2. *The Interrelationship between Choice of Law and*

       Choice of Forum Clauses 546

E. **The European Perspective on Choice of Law** 554

    Matthias Reimann, Conflict of Laws in Western

    Europe 3-17 (1995) 555

    Note on Subsequent Developments in the European Union 560

    Article 6, Rome I Regulation 561

Article 14, Rome II Regulation 562

F.   **The Extraterritorial Application of U.S. Statutes**.............. 563

     1.   *Extraterritorial Reach of U.S. Antitrust Laws* 564

     2.   *A Comparative Perspective on Extraterritoriality* 590

     3.   *The Extraterritorial Reach of Federal Securities Laws* 603

CHAPTER 8.   Recognition and Enforcement of Judgments 617

Section

A.   **Introduction** 617

B.   **Enforcing Foreign Judgments In the**
     U.S.--Basic Considerations................................... 621

     1.   *Traditional Approaches and the Regime of Comity* 621

     2.   *The Source of law Governing Enforcement of*
          Foreign Judgments in U.S. Courts 627

     3.   *Introduction to Current Approaches Under State Law* 632
          Uniform Foreign-Country Money Judgments
          Recognition Act 633

C.   **Foreign Judgments and the Requirements of Personal**
     Jurisdiction   636

D.   **Foreign Judgments Raising Domestic (U.S.) Public Policy**
     Concerns.. 651

     1.   *Concerns Regarding Substantive Law*........................... 651
          The SPEECH Act of 2010................................... 663

     2.   *Concerns Regarding Fair Procedures* 666
          Note on U.S. Recognition of Foreign
          Tax and Penal Judgments................................... 672

E.   **U.S. Judgments and Foreign Public Policy Concerns**........... 673

F.   **Judgment Recognition Under European Union Law** 684
     Brussels Regulation Arts. 34-35 685

CHAPTER 9.   International Arbitration... 693

Section

A.   **Introduction** 693

B.   **Claims Subject to Arbitration** 695

C.   **Enforcement of Arbitration Awards**............................. 704

D.   **Antisuit Injunctions in Aid of Arbitration**...................... 723

APPENDICES.   737

A.   **The Hague Service Convention** 737

B.   **The Hague Evidence Convention** 742

C.   **The Hague Choice of Court Convention**........................ 748

D.   **The Brussels Regulation (EC Regulation 44/2001)** 758

E.   **The New York Convention** 771

F.   **The Foreign Sovereign Immunities Act of 1976**................ 776

TABLE OF CONTENTS

PREFACE V
ACKNOWLEDGMENTS VII
SUMMARY OF CONTENTS IX
TABLE OF CASES XXIII

CHAPTER 1. Personal Jurisdiction and Forum Selection................................ 1

Section
A. **Introduction**... 1
B. **Specific Jurisdiction**... 3
    Asahi Metal Industry Co., Ltd. v. Superior Court 3
    Notes and Questions for Discussion 10
    J. McIntyre Machinery, Ltd. v. Nicastro 14
    Notes and Questions for Discussion 26
    Wien Air Alaska, Inc. v. Brandt... 29
    Notes and Questions for Discussion 36
    Yahoo! Inc. v. La Ligue Contre Le Racisme
    et L'Antisemitisme 36
    Cannon Mfg. Co. v. Cudahy Packing Co. 42
C. **General Jurisdiction** 43
    Goodyear Dunlop Tires Operations, S.A. v. Brown................ 44
    Notes and Questions for Discussion 50
    Helicopteros Nacionales De Columbia, S.A. v. Hall 51
    Bauman v. DaimlerChrysler Corp. 53
    Note on "Doing Business" as a Basis for Jurisdiction
    Over Foreign Parties 55
D. **Transient Jurisdiction** 58
    Burnham v. Superior Court.. 58
    Notes and Questions for Discussion 61
    A Comparative Note on Transient Jurisdiction............................. 62
E. **The Reach of Process**.. 62
    Capital Int'l, Ltd. v. Rudolff & Co., Ltd. 63
    United States v. Swiss American Bank, Ltd. 64
    Notes and Questions for Discussion 71
F. **Litigating Personal Jurisdiction** 73
    **Insurance Corp. of Ireland, Ltd. v. Compagnie des
    Bauxites de Guinée**.. 73
    Notes and Questions for Discussion 78
G. **Personal Jurisdiction in Europe: The Brussels Convention
    and Regulation** 79
    Johann Gruber v. Bay Wa AG 82
    Notes and Questions for Discussion 89
    Shevill v. Presse Alliance SA 91

Notes and Questions for Discussion 95
eDate Advertising GmbH v. X, and Martinez v. MGN, Ltd. 96
Notes and Questions for Discussion 98
H. **Attachment and Global Assets** 99
Shaffer v. Heitner 100
Grupo Mexicano de Desarrollo, S.A. v. Alliance Bond Fund, Inc. 102
Notes and Questions for Discussion 111
Mareva Compania Naviera S.A. v. Int'l Bulkcarriers S.A. 113
I. **Forum Selection Clauses** 114
The Bremen v. Zapata Off-Shore Co. 114
Notes and Questions for Discussion 122
Carnival Cruise Lines, Inc. v. Shute 122
Richards v. Lloyd's of London 126
Notes and Questions for Discussion 133
Lauro Lines s.r.l. v. Chasser 135
Note on the Hague Choice of Court Convention 137
Note on Forum Selection Clauses Under E.U. Law 138

CHAPTER 2.   Subject Matter Jurisdiction 141

Section
A. **Introduction** 141
B. **Alienage and Diversity Jurisdiction** 142
    1. *Citizens or Subjects of Foreign States* 142
        Chase Bank v. Traffic Stream (BVI)
        Infrastructure Ltd. 143
        Sadat v. Mertes 145
        Notes and Questions for Discussion 152
        Hodgson v. Bowerbank 154
        Notes and Questions for Discussion 154
    2. *Permanent Resident Aliens and Alienage Jurisdiction* 155
        Antonier v. Miller 156
        Notes and Questions for Discussion 158
    3. *Foreign Corporations and Diversity* 160
        Note on Removal to Federal Court 161
C. **Cases Arising Under Federal Law** 162
    1. *Human Rights Litigation under the Alien Tort Statute* 163
        Filartiga v. Pena-Irala 164
        Tel-Oren v. Libyan Arab Republic 166
        Sosa v. Alvarez-Machain 167
        Notes and Questions for Discussion 180
    2. *Claims under the Torture Victim Protection Act* 182
        Mohamad v. Palestinian Authority 183
    3. *Claims under the Anti-Terrorism Act of 1990* 184
    4. *Suability of Private Actors and Related Matters* 184
        Kadic v. Karadzic 185
        Notes and Questions for Discussion 194

             Kiobel v. Royal Dutch Petroleum Co. 196
     5.   *Cases Implicating Foreign Policy Concerns* 196
             Patrickson v. Dole Food Co.... 197
             Notes and Questions for Discussion 203
             Note on "Universal Jurisdiction"... 204
     6.   *Cases Arising Under Treaties*... 205
             Benjamins v. British European Airways 206
             Narkiewicz-Laine v. Scandanavian Airlines Sytems 214
             Notes and Questions for Discussion 216
D.   **Venue and Alien Defendants**.. 218
     1.   *Venue in Suits Against Aliens* 218
     2.   *Venue in Suits Against Alien and Non-Alien Defendants* 219
     3.   *Fallback Venue* 219
     4.   *Transfer of Venue* 219
     5.   *Transfer of Venue versus Forum Non Conveniens* 220
    Note on the Sequencing of Jurisdictional
    and Related Objections 221

CHAPTER 3.   **Suits Against Foreign Sovereigns** 223

Section
A.   **The Foreign Sovereign Immunities Act** 223
     1.   *Origins and Structure* 223
     2.   *Constitutionality* 225
             Verlinden, B.V. v. Central Bank of Nigeria............................ 225
             Notes and Questions for Discussion 231
     3.   *Scope* 235
             Argentine Republic v. Amerada Hess Shipping Corp. 235
             Notes and Questions for Discussion 242
             Republic of Austria v. Altmann... 243
             Dole Food Co. v. Patrickson.. 245
             Notes and Questions for Discussion 251
     4.   *Exceptions to Sovereign Immunity*... 255
             Republic of Argentina v. Weltover, Inc. 255
             Notes and Questions for Discussion 261
             Saudi Arabia v. Nelson.. 264
             Notes and Questions for Discussion 273
             Cicippio-Puleo v. Islamic Republican of Iran 276
             Notes and Questions for Discussion 281
             Zappia Middle East Constr. Co. v. Emirate of Abu Dhabi..... 285
             Notes and Questions for Discussion 289
B.   **The Act of State Doctrine**.. 291
    Banco Nacional de Cuba v. Sabbatino 291
    Notes and Questions for Discussion 301
    Alfred Dunhill of London, Inc. v. Republic of Cuba............... 304
    Notes and Questions for Discussion 310
    W.S. Kirkpatrick & Co., Inc. v. Environmental

Tectonics Corp., Int'l 313
        Notes and Questions for Discussion 316

CHAPTER 4.   **Service of Process** 321

Section
A.   **Service on Foreign Defendants Under the Federal Rules** 321
      1.   *Waiver of Service* 321
      2.   *Absent a Waiver of Service* 322
           (a)   Serving Foreign Defendants within a U.S.
               Federal Judicial District 322
           (b)   Serving Foreign Defendants in a Foreign
               Country 323
B.   **Service Under the Hague Convention** 324
C.   **Coordinating the Hague Convention and the Federal Rules** 325
    Bankston v. Toyota Motor Corp. 326
    Brockmeyer v. May 328
    Notes and Questions for Discussion 336
D.   **Determining the Applicability of the Hague Convention** 337
    Volkswagenwerk Aktiengesellschaft v. Schlunk 338
    Notes and Questions for Discussion 348
    Note on Service of Process within the E.U. 350
E.   **Service in Violation of Foreign Law** 350
      1.   *Introduction* 350
      2.   *Article 13 of the Hague Service Convention* 352
          Proceedings Concerning the Constitutional
          Complaint of L. . . .GmbH 352
          Notes and Questions for Discussion 358
      3.   *Statutory Construction and U.S. Service Provisions* ... 359
          F.T.C. v. Compagnie de Saint-Gobain-Pont-à-Mousson 360
F.   **Service on Foreign States, Agencies and Instrumentalities** 361
    Transaero, Inc. v. La Fuerza Aerea Boliviana 361
    Notes and Questions for Discussion 369

CHAPTER 5.   **Parallel Litigation** 371

Section
A.   **International Forum Non Conveniens** 371
    Piper Aircraft Co. v. Reyno 372
    Notes and Questions for Discussion 381
    In re Union Carbide Gas Plant Disaster 383
    Guidi v. Inter-Continental Hotels, Corp. 385
    Notes and Questions for Discussion 390
    Iragorri v. United Technologies Corp., ... 391
    A Comparative Note on Forum Non Conveniens 395
    Owusu v. Jackson 396

B.   **Abstention (Lis Pendens) and Parallel Litigation** 398
      Background Note on Abstention and Parallel Litigation in the
      Purely Domestic (U.S.) Setting 399
      Colorado River Water Conservation Dist. v. United States 400
      **Royal and Sun Alliance ins. Co. of Canada
      v. Century Int'l Arms, Inc.** 403
      Notes and Questions for Discussion 410
      A Comparative Note on Lis Pendens 412
      Note on the Hague Choice of Court Convention 414
C.   **International Antisuit Injunctions and Parallel Litigation** 415
      1.   *Approach(es) of U.S. Courts* 415
            Kaepa, Inc. v. Achilles Corp. 415
            **Quaak v. Klynveld Peat Marwick Goerdeler
            Bedrijfsrevisoren** 423
            Notes and Questions for Discussion 431
            Laker Airways Ltd. v. Sabena, Belgian World Airlines 431
      2.   *Approach(es) of European Courts* 433
            **Gregory Paul Turner v. Felix Fareed Ismail Grovit and
            Others** 433
            Notes and Questions for Discussion 436
            Airbus Industrie G.I.E. v. Patel 437
            Notes and Questions for Discussion 446

CHAPTER 6.   Taking Evidence Abroad 449

Section
A.   **Introduction** 449
      1.   *An Overview of Discovery in American Courts* 449
      2.   *Foreign Methods of Obtaining Evidence* 451
      3.   *American Discovery and Foreign Perceptions* 452
B.   **The Hague Evidence Convention** 453
      1.   *Overview of the Hague Evidence Convention
            Procedures* 453
      2.   *Privileges Against Testifying Under the Convention* 454
      3.   *Subject Matter Scope of the Hague Evidence Convention* 455
      4.   *The Exclusion of Pretrial Discovery Documents* 456
      5.   *The Exclusivity of the Hague Evidence Convention* 457
            **Société Nationale Industrielle
            Aérospatiale v. U.S. District Court** 458
            Notes and Questions for Discussion 468
C.   **U.S. Discovery Conducted Abroad** 471
      A Case Illustration 471
D.   **The Personal Jurisdiction Requirement** 473
      1.   *Nonparty Witnesses* 473
      2.   *Jurisdictional Discovery* 473
E.   **Post-Aérospatiale Decisional Law** 474
      Valois of America, Inc. v. Risdon Corp. 475

Notes and Questions for Discussion 479

F.   **Foreign Blocking Statutes** 481
       Société Internationale Pour Participations Industrielles et
       Commerciales, S.A. v. Rogers 483
       Notes and Questions for Discussion 487
       Richmark Corp. v. Timber Falling Consultants 489
       In re **Marc Rich & Co. A.G.** 491
       Notes and Questions for Discussion 493

G.   **U.S. Discovery and Evidence Production for Foreign**
       and International Tribunals 496
       Intel Corp. v. Advanced Micro Devices, Inc. 497
       Notes and Questions for Discussion 505
       In re Application for an Order Permitting
       Metallgesellschaft AG to take Discovery 506
       Notes and Questions for Discussion 509

CHAPTER 7.   International Litigation and Choice of Law 511

Section
A.   **An Overview of American Choice of Law** 511
       1.   *Traditional Choice of Law Rules* 511
       2.   *Interest Analysis and the Conflicts of Revolution* 514
       3.   *The Restatement (Second) of Conflict Laws* 516
B.   **American Choice of Law in the Transnational Setting** 518
       Spinozzi v. ITT Sheraton Corp. 519
       Notes and Questions for Discussion 524
C.   **Constitutional Limits on American Choice of Law** 526
       Home Insurance Co. v. Dick 527
       Notes and Questions for Discussion 531
D.   **International Choice of Law Clauses** 533
       1.   *Validating and Interpreting Choice of Law Clauses* 534
              Nedlloyd Lines B.V. v. Seawinds Ltd. 535
              Notes and Questions for Discussion 542
       2.   *The Interrelationship between Choice of Law and*
              Choice of Forum Clauses 546
              Albemarle Corp. v. AstraZenica U.K., Ltd. 546
              Notes and Questions for Discussion 553
E.   **The European Perspective on Choice of Law** 554
       Matthias Reimann, Conflict of Laws in Western
       Europe 3-17 (1995) 555
       Note on Subsequent Developments in the European Union 560
       Article 6, Rome I Regulation 561
       Article 14, Rome II Regulation 562
F.   **The Extraterritorial Application of U.S. Statutes** 563
       1.   *Extraterritorial Reach of U.S. Antitrust Laws* 564
              American Banana Co. v. United Fruit Co. 564
              Notes and Questions for Discussion 567

United States v. Aluminum Co. of America 568
Notes and Questions for Discussion 571
**Timberlane Lumber Co. v. Bank of
America N.T. & S.A.** 572
Notes and Questions for Discussion 575
**Restatement (Third) of Foreign Relations Law
of The United States §§ 402 & 403** 576
Hartford Fire Ins. Co. v. California 578
Notes and Questions for Discussion 586

2.   *A Comparative Perspective on Extraterritoriality* 590
**Ahlström Osakeyhtiö et al. v. Commission of
the European Communities** 590
Notes and Questions for Discussion 594
Hoffman-La Roche, Ltd. v. Empagran, S.A. 595
Notes and Questions for Discussion 601

3.   *The Extraterritorial Reach of Federal Securities Laws* 603
Morrison v. National Australia Bank Ltd. 604
Notes and Questions for Discussion 615

CHAPTER 8.   Recognition and Enforcement of Judgments 617

Section

A.   Introduction 617
**B.   Enforcing Foreign Judgments In the
U.S.--Basic Considerations** 621

1.   *Traditional Approaches and the Regime of Comity* 621
Hilton v. Guyot 621
Notes and Questions for Discussion 625

2.   *The Source of law Governing Enforcement of
Foreign Judgments in U.S. Courts* 627
Johnston v. Compagnie Génerale Transatlantique 627
Notes and Questions for Discussion 630

3.   *Introduction to Current Approaches Under State Law* 632
**Uniform Foreign-Country Money Judgments
Recognition Act** 633
Notes and Questions for Discussion 635

**C.   Foreign Judgments and the Requirements of Personal
Jurisdiction** 636
Evans Cabinet Corp. v. Kitchen Int'l, Inc. 636
Notes and Questions for Discussion 641
Somportex Ltd. v. Philadelphia Chewing Gum Corp. 643
Notes and Questions for Discussion 650

**D.   Foreign Judgments Raising Domestic (U.S.) Public Policy
Concerns** 651

1.   *Concerns Regarding Substantive Law* 651
Southwest Livestock & Trucking Co. v. Ramon 651
Notes and Questions for Discussion 654
Telnikoff v. Matusevitch 656

		Notes and Questions for Discussion	661
		Bachchan v. India Abroad Publications Inc.	662
		The SPEECH Act of 2010	663
		Yahoo! Inc. v. La Ligue Contre le Racisme et L'Antisemitisme	664
	2.	*Concerns Regarding Fair Procedures*	666
		The Society of Lloyd's v. Ashenden	666
		Notes and Questions for Discussion	671
		Note on U.S. Recognition of Foreign Tax and Penal Judgments	672
E.		**U.S. Judgments and Foreign Public Policy Concerns**	673
		German Code of Civil Procedure [ZPO] §328	674
		***Re* the Enforcement of a U.S. Judgment**	675
		Notes and Questions for Discussion	679
		***Re* the Enforcement of a U.S. Judgment**	680
		Notes and Questions for Discussion	682
F.		**Judgment Recognition Under European Union Law**	684
		Brussels Regulation Arts. 34-35	685
		Krombach v. Bamberski	686
		Notes and Questions for Discussion	689

CHAPTER 9.	**International Arbitration**	693

Section

A.	**Introduction**	693
B.	**Claims Subject to Arbitration**	695
	Vimar Seguros y Reaseguros, S.A. v. M/V Sky Reefer	695
	Notes and Questions for Discussion	702
C.	**Enforcement of Arbitration Awards**	704
	Parsons & Whittemore Overseas Co., Inc. v. Société Général de l'Industrie du Papier	704
	Notes and Questions for Discussion	711
	Baxter International, Inc. v. Abbott Laboratories	716
	Notes and Questions for Discussion	721
D.	**Antisuit Injunctions in Aid of Arbitration**	723
	Paramedics Electromedicina, Ltda. v. GE Medical Information Technologies, Inc.	723
	Notes and Questions for Discussion	729
	Allianz SpA, and Generali Assicurazioni Generali SpA v. West Tankers, Inc.	730
	Notes and Questions for Discussion	734

APPENDICES.		737

A.	**The Hague Service Convention**	737
B.	**The Hague Evidence Convention**	742
C.	**The Hague Choice of Court Convention**	748

D.   **The Brussels Regulation (EC Regulation 44/2001)** 758

E.   **The New York Convention**.. 771

F.   **The Foreign Sovereign Immunities Act of 1976** 776

TABLE OF CASES

Principal cases are in italic type. Non-principal cases are in roman type. References are to pages.

A. Ahlström Osakeyhtiö et al. v. Commission of the European Communities, 590

AAR Int'l, Inc. v. Nimelias Enters. S.A., 134

Abbott Labs. v. Takeda Pharm. Co., 125

Ackermann v. Levine, 655

Afram Export Corp. v. Metallurgiki Halyps, S.A., 42

Air Crash at Taipei Taiwan on October 31, 2000, *In re*, 482

Air Crash Disaster Near New Orleans, La., *In re*, 393

Airbus Industrie G.I.E. v. Patel, 437

Alabama Great Southern Railway Co. v. Carroll, 512

Alaska Packers Ass'n v. Indus. Acc. Comm'n, 532

Albemarle Corp. v. AstraZenica U.K., Ltd., 126, *546*

Alfadda v. Fenn, 393

Alfred Dunhill of London, Inc. v. Republic of Cuba, 304

Allgeyer v. Louisiana, 531

Alliance Bond Fund, Inc. v. Grupo Mexicano de Desarrollo, S.A., 112

Allianz SpA, & Generali Assicurazioni Generali SpA v. West Tankers Inc., 730

Allstate Ins. Co. v. Hague, 532

Altmann, Republic of Austria v., 243

Aluminum Co. of America, United States v., 481, *568*

Amchem Prods., Inc. v. British Columbia (Workers' Compen. Bd.), 446

American Banana Co. v. United Fruit Co., 564

American Dredging Co. v. Miller, 393

Amoco Egypt Oil Co. v. Leonis Nav. Co., 55

Amoco Overseas Oil Co. v. Compagnie Nationale Algerienne de Navigation, 101

Amusement Equipment, Inc. v. Mordelt, 61

Anschuetz & Co., GmbH, *In re*, 473

Antonier v. Miller, 156

Apollon, The, 563

Application for an Order Permitting Metallgesellschaft AG to Take Discovery, In re, 506

Argentine Republic v. Amerada Hess Shipping Corp., 181, *235*

Aristech Chemical Int'l Ltd. v. Acrylic Fabricators Ltd., 11

Asahi Metal Industry Co. v. Superior Court, 3, 28, 533

AT&T Mobility LLC v. Concepcion, 702, 713

"Atlantic Star," Owners of the Motor Vessel v. "Bona Spes," Owners of the Motor Vessel, 396

Automotive Refinishing Paint Antitrust Litig., *In re*, 474

AVC Nederland B.V. v. Atrium Inv. Partnership, 134

Babcock v. Jackson, 514

Bachchan v. India Abroad Publications Inc., 662

Baker v. General Motors Corp., 403

Baldwin v. Iowa State Traveling Men's Association, 650

Banco Nacional de Cuba v. Farr, 302

Banco Nacional de Cuba v. Sabbatino, 197, *291*

Bankston v. Toyota Motor Corp., 326

Banque Libanaise Pour Le Commerce v. Khreich, 631

Barone v. Rich Bros. Interstate Display Fireworks Co., 13

Bauman v. DaimlerChrysler Corp., 53

Baxter International, Inc. v. Abbott Labs., 716

Beaty, Republic of Iraq v., 283

Bendix Autolite Corp. v. Midwesco Enters., 51

Beneficial Nat'l Bank v. Anderson, 203

Benjamins v. British European Airways, 206

Benton Graphics v. Uddelholm Corp., 480

Berizzi Bros. Co. v. S.S. Pesaro, 223

Bernhard v. Harrah's Club, 516

Bernkrant v. Fowler, 516

Bhatnagar v. Surrendra Overseas Ltd., 382

BMW of North America, Inc. v. Gore, 683

Boit v. Gar-Tec Products, Inc., 12

Bradford Elec. Light Co. v. Clapper, 527

Bremen, The v. Zapata Off-Shore Co., 114, 545, 702

Brillhart v. Excess Ins. Co., 401

Brockmeyer v. May, 328

Broderick v. Rosner, 626

Bryant v. Finnish Nat'l Airline, 55

Burger King Corp. v. Rudzewicz, 10, 36, 40

Burnham v. Superior Court, 58

Calavo Growers of Cal. v. Generali Belgium, 391

Calder v. Jones, 36

Cannon Mfg. Co. v. Cudahy Packing Co., 42

Capital Currency Exchange, N.V. v. National Westminster Bank PLC, 393

Carnival Cruise Lines, Inc. v. Shute, 122, 139

Carolina Power & Light Co. v. Uranex, 101, 111, 715

Chae Chan Ping v. United States, 632

Chevron Corp. v. Naranjo, 665

China Trade & Dev. Corp. v. M.V. Choong Yong, 432

Chinese Manufactured Drywall Products Liability Litigation, *In re*, 27

CIBC Mellon Trust Co. v. Mora Hotel Corp., 655

Cicippio-Puleo v. Islamic Republic of Iran, 276

Coakes v. Arabian American Oil Co., 383

Cohen v. Beneficial Indus. Loan Corp., 79, 112

Colorado River Water Conservation Dist. v. United States, 400

Commodity Futures Trading Comm'n v. Nahas, 360

Compania de Gas de Nuevo Laredo, S.A. v. Entex, Inc., 303

Conax Florida Corp. v. Astrium, Ltd., 349

Connelly v. R.T.Z. Corp., 396

Coury v. Prot, 153

CSR Ltd. v. Cigna Ins. Australia Ltd., 447

Cuba R.R. v. Crosby, 513

Day & Zimmerman, Inc. v. Challoner, 518

De Melo v. Lederle Labs., 382

Decision of the Federal Constitutional Court, December 7, 1994, 456

Decision of the Munich Court of Appeals, May 9, 1989, 456

Decision of the Munich Court of Appeals, November 27, 1980, 456

DeSantis v. Wackenhut Corp., 544, 653

Diggs v. Richardson, 206

Doe I v. Unocal Corp., 195, 196

Doe v. Exxon Mobil Corp., 195

Dole Food Co. v. Patrickson, 245

Donovan v. City of Dallas, 400

Dow Chemical Co. v. Alfaro, 393

Dow Jones & Co. v. Harrods, Ltd., 665

Durfee v. Duke, 650

eDate Advertising GmbH v. X, 96

EEOC v. Waffle House, 714

Ehrenfeld v. Mafouz, 40

El Al Israel Airlines, Ltd. v. Tsui Yuan Tseng, 217

Empire Healthchoice Assur., Inc. v. McVeigh, 203

Erich Gasser GmbH v. MISAT s.r.l., 413

Erie Railroad Co. v. Tompkins, 112, 124, 165, 518, 554, 627

Euromepa, S.A. v. R. Esmerian. Inc., 510

Evans Cabinet Corp. v. Kitchen Int'l, Inc., 636

Evans Transp. Co. v. Scullin Steel Co., 411

Ex parte Pope Chevrolet, Inc., 13

Exxon Shipping Co. v. Baker, 683

Eze v. Yellow Cab Co., 153

F. Hoffman-LaRoche Ltd. v. Empagran, S.A., 575, *595*

F.T.C. v. Compagnie de Saint-Gobain-Pont-à-Mousson, 360

Falkirk Min. Co. v. Japan Steel Works, Ltd., 13

Fauntleroy v. Lum, 618

Ferdinand Marcos, *In re* Estate of, 111

Filartiga v. Pena-Irala, 164

Finanz AG Zurich v. Banco Economico S.A., 113

Finova Capital Corp. v. Ryan Helicopters U.S.A., Inc., 406

First National City Bank v. Banco Nacional de Cuba, 303

First National City Bank, United States v., 495

Fleming v. Yamaha Motor Corp., USA, 349

Flores v. Southern Peru Copper Corp., 195

Franchise Tax Bd. v. Constr. Laborers

Vacation Trust, 163

Frummer v. Hilton Hotels, Int'l, Inc., 55, 56

Garcia v. Chase Manhattan Bank, N.A., 311

Gator.com Corp. v. L.L. Bean, Inc., 55

Gianoli, *In re* Application of, 510

Gilbertson, Her Majesty the Queen in Right of the Province of British Columbia v., 672

Gilmer v. Interstate/Johnson Lane Corp., 702

Glen v. Club Mediterranee, S.A., 310

Goldhammer v. Dunkin' Donuts, Inc., 412

Goodyear Dunlop Tires Operations, S.A. v. Brown, 44, 72

Go-Video, Inc. v. Akai Elec. Co., 62

Grable & Sons Metal Prods., Inc. v. Darue Engineering & Mfg., 203

Grace v. McArthur, 61

Graco, Inc. v. Kremlin, Inc., 472

Gregory Paul Turner v. Felix Fareed Ismail Grovit & Others, 433

Griffin v. Griffin, 618

Grupo Mexicano de Desarrollo, S.A. v. Alliance Bond Fund, Inc., 102

Guardian Insurance Co. v. Bain Hogg International Ltd., 642

Gucci America, Inc. v. Weixing Li, 113

Guidi v. Inter-Continental Hotels, Corp., 385

Gulf Oil Corp. v. Gilbert, 220

H. Heller & Co. v. Nocacor Chemicals Ltd., 56

Hafer v. Melo, 253

Hanna v. Plumer, 554

Hargrave v. Fibreboard Corp., 42

Harris Rutsky & Co. Ins. Servs., Inc. v. Bell & Clements Ltd., 36

Hartford Fire Ins. Co. v. California, 482, *578*

Haumschild v. Continental Cas. Co., 512

Helicopteros Nacionales de Columbia, S.A. v. Hall, 51

Hendrikman & Feyen v. Magenta Druck & Verlag, 690

Her Majesty the Queen in Right of the Province of British Columbia v. Gilbertson., 672

Hertz Corp. v. Friend, 160

Hidden Brook Air, Inc. v. Thabet Aviation Int'l, Inc., 526

Hilton v. Guyot, 575, *621*

Hodgson v. Bowerbank, *154*, 181

Hoffmann v. Krieg, 690

Home Insurance Co. v. Dick, *527*

Howe v. Goldcorp Investments Ltd., 393

Hudson v. Hermann Pfauter GmbH & Co., 479, 481

Husa v. Laboratories Servier SA, 479, 481

IIT v. Vencap, Ltd., 164

Illinois v. City of Milwaukee, 197

In re Air Crash at Taipei, Taiwan on October 31, 2000, 482

In re Air Crash Disaster Near New Orleans, La., 393

In re Anschuetz & Co., GmbH, 473

In re Application for an Order Permitting Metallgesellschaft AG to Take Discovery, *506*

In re Application of Gianoli, 510

In re Application of Malev Hungarian Airlines, 510

In re Application of Schmitz, 510

In re Automotive Refinishing Paint Antitrust Litig., 474

In re Chinese Manufactured Drywall Products Liability Litigation, 27

In re Estate of Ferdinand Marcos, 111

In re Marc Rich & Co. A.G., *491*

In re South African Apartheid Litigation, 195

In re Treco, 671

In re Union Carbide Gas Plant Disaster, 383

In re Union Carbide Gas Plant Disaster at Bhopal, India, 382

In re Uranium Antitrust Litigation, 577

In re Vitamins Antitrust Litigation, 474, 480

Indasu Int'l, C.A. v. Citibank, N.A., 394

Ins. Corp. of Ireland, Ltd. v. Compagnie des Bauxites de Guinée, *73*, 473, 643

Intec USA, LLC v. Engle, 159

Intel Corp. v. Advanced Micro Devices, Inc., *497*

Interamerican Refining Corp. v. Texaco Maracaibo, Inc., 493

Intercontinental Credit Corporation v. Roth, 473

International Shoe Co. v. Washington, 3, 56

International Trading & Indus. Inv. Co. v. DynCorp Aerospace Technology, 712

IntraComm, Inc. v. Bajaj, 125

Iragorri v. United Technologies Corp., 391

J. McIntyre Machinery v. Nicastro, *13*, 72

Jackson v. The Archimedes, 568

Jerguson v. Blue Dot Inv., Inc., 160

Johann Gruber v. Bay Wa AG, *82*

John Sanderson & Co. (Wool) v. Ludlow Jute Co., 631

Johnston v. Chief Constable of the Royal Ulster Constabulary, 690

Johnston v. Compagnie Générale Transatlantique. 627

JPMorgan Chase Bank v. Traffic Stream (BVI) Infrastructure Ltd., 143, 160

Kadic v. Karadzic, 61, 181, *185*

Kaepa, Inc. v. Achilles Corp., *415*

Keeton v. Hustler Magazine, Inc., 95

Kerotest Mfg. Co. v. C-O-Two Fire Equipment Co., 402

Kiobel v. Royal Dutch Petroleum Co., 196

Klaxon Co. v. Stentor Electric Mfg. Co., 392, 518

Klinghoffer v. S.N.C. Lauro Lines, 55

Knight v. Ford Motor Co., 474

Koster v. Automark Indus., Inc., 641

Krombach v. Bamberski, 686

L. . . GmbH, Proceedings Concerning the Constitutional Complaint of, 352

Lacey v. Cessna Aircraft Co., 384

Lagstein v. Certain Underwriters at Lloyd's, London, 712

Laker Airways Ltd. v. Pan American World Airways, 393

Laker Airways Ltd. v. Sabena, Belgian World Airlines, 431, 432

Lakin v. Prudential Securities, 55

Laminoirs-Trefileries-Cableries de Lens, SA v. Southwire Co., 722

Lauro Lines s.r.l. v. Chasser, 135, 394

LFC Lessors, Inc. v. Pacific Sewer Maintenance Corp., 134

Lipcon v. Underwriters at Lloyd's of London, 125, 134

Lister v. Marangoni Meccanica S.p.A., 13

Lobo v. Celebrity Cruises, Inc., 337

Lockman Foundation v. Evangelical Alliance Mission, 382

Loucks v. Standard Oil Co. of New York, 513, 655, 711

Malev Hungarian Airlines, *In re* Application of, 510

Marc Rich & Co. A.G., In re, 491

Marcos, Republic of the Philippines v., 197

Mareva Compania Naviera S.A. v. Int'l Bulkcarriers S.A., 113

Marks v. United States, 27

Martinez v. MGN, Ltd., 96

MAS Capital, Inc. v. Biodelivery Sciences Int'l, Inc., 161

McCord v. Jet Spray Int'l Corp., 655

McCreary Tire & Rubber Co. v. CEAT S.p.A, 715

McGee v. International Life Ins. Co., 41

MeadWestvaco Corp. v. Rexam PLC, 474

Mesa v. California, 232

Metropolitan Life Ins. Co. v. Taylor, 203

Mid-America Tablewares, Inc. v. Mogi Trading Co., 41

Mikerina v. Delta Air Lines, Inc., 218

Milliken v. Meyer, 50

Milwaukee County v. M.E. White Co., 672

Ministry of Defense and Support v. Elahi, 283

Mitsubishi Motors Corp. v. Soler Chrysler-Plymouth, Inc., 545, 704, 713

Mohamad v. Palestinian Authority, 183, 196

Molinos Valle del Cibao, C. por A. v. Lama, 153

Moore v. Mitchell, 673

Morrison v. National Australia Bank Ltd., 604

Murray v. The Schooner Charming Betsy, 233, 352

Narkiewicz-Laine v. Scandanavian Airlines Systems, 214

Nat'l Steam-Ship Co. v. Tugman, 160

Nedlloyd Lines B.V. v. Seawinds Ltd., 535

Neuchatel Swiss Gen. Ins. Co. v. Lufthansa Airlines, 410, 412

New York Life Ins. Co. v. Dodge, 531

Nichols v. G.D. Searle & Co., 55

O'Neill v. St. Jude Medical, Inc., 204

Omni Capital Int'l, Ltd. v. Rudolff & Co., 63

Ontario, Inc. v. World Imports U.S.A., Inc., 412

Osborn v. Bank of the United States, 232

Owusu v. Jackson, 396

Pacheco de Perez v. AT&T Co., 204

Pacific Employers Ins. Co. v. Indus. Acc. Comm'n, 532

Paquete Habana, The, 164, 165

Paramedics Electromedicina Comercial, Ltda. V. GE Medical Systems Information Technologies, Inc., 723

Parsons & Whittemore Overseas Co. v. Société Genérale de L'Industrie du Papier (RATKA), 620, 704

Parsons Steel v. First Alabama Bank, 437

Patrickson v. Dole Food Co., 197

Pennoyer v. Neff, 3, 531

Pennzoil Prods. Co. v. Colelli & Assoc., Inc., 13

Perkins v. Benguet Consol. Mining Co., 50

Philadelphia Gear Corp. v. American Pfauter Corp., 457

Philadelphia Newspapers, Inc. v. Hepps, 662

Phillip Morris USA v. Williams, 683

Phillips Petroleum Co. v. Shutts, 533

Pinker v. Roche Holdings, Ltd., 72

Piper Aircraft Company v. Reyno, 372, 383

Pollux Holding Ltd. v. Chase Manhattan Bank, 391

Pope Chevrolet, Inc., *Ex parte*, 13

Presbyterian Church of Sudan v. Talisman Energy, Inc., 56, 195, 196

Prewitt Enters. v. OPEC, 352

Quaak v. Klynveld Peat Marwick Goerdeler Bedrijfsrevisoren, 423

Quackenbush v. Allstate Ins. Co., 401

Quantum Corp. Funding, Ltd. v. Assist You Home Servs. of Va., 113

Rationis Enterprises Inc. of Panama v. Hyundai Mipo Dockyard Co., 526

Ratliff v. Cooper Labs., Inc., 50

Re the Enforcement of a U.S. Judgment, 675

Re the Enforcement of a U.S. Judgment II, 680

Remington Products, Inc. v. North American Philips Corp., 493

Republic of Argentina v. Weltover, Inc., 255, 311

Republic of Austria v. Altmann, 243

Republic of Iraq v. Beaty, 283

Republic of the Philippines v. Marcos, 197

Rich v. KIS California, Inc., 474, 479

Richards v. Lloyd's of London, 126, 545

Richmark Corp. v. Timber Falling Consultants, 489

Rio Properties, Inc. v. Rio International Interlink, 351

Rodriguez v. Fullerton Tires Corp. v. Custom Metal Spinning Corp., 12

Royal and Sun Alliance Ins. Co. of Canada v. Century Int'l Arms, Inc., 403

Royal Bed & Spring Co. v. Famossul Industria e Commercia de Movies Ltda., 124

Ruhrgas AG v. Marathon Oil Co., 159, 221

Russell Brands, LLC v. GVD Int'l Trading S.A., 350

Ruston Gas Turbines, Inc. v. Donaldson Co., 13

Saadeh v. Farouki, 159

Sadat v. Mertes, 145

Samantar v. Yousef, 252

Santissima Trinidad, The, 243

Sarl Louis Feraud Int'l v. Viewfinder, Inc., 662

Saudi Arabia v. Nelson, 254, 264, 317

Scherk v. Alberto-Culver Co., 702

Schmitz, *In re* Application of, 510

Schoenbaum v. Firstbrook, 604

Schooner Exchange, The v. McFadden, 223

Semmes Motors, Inc. v. Ford Motor Co., 402

Shaffer v. Heitner, 58, 100, 113, 311

Shevill v. Presse Alliance SA, 91

Siedler v. Jacobsen, 642

Siegelman v. Cunard White Star Ltd., 534

Siemer v. Learjet Acquisition Corp., 61

Sinaltrainal v. Coca-Cola Co., 195

Singh v. Daimler-Benz AG, 158

Sinochem Int'l Co. Ltd. v. Malaysia Int'l Shipping Corp., 221, 394

Smith Kline & French Labs. Ltd. v. Bloch, 381

Société Internationale Pour Participations Industrielles et Commerciales, S.A. v. Rogers, 483

Société Nationale Industrielle Aérospatiale v. U.S. District Court, 348, 458, 479, 483

Society of Lloyd's, The v. Ashenden, 666

Solimene v. B. Grauel & Co., K.G., 679

Somportex Ltd. v. Philadelphia Chewing Gum Corp., 643

Sosa v. Alvarez-Machain, 167, 183

South African Apartheid Litigation, In re, 195

Southwest Livestock & Trucking Co. v. Ramon, 651

Spinozzi v. ITT Sheraton Corp., 519

SS Lotus-France v. Turkey, The Case of the, 563

State Farm Fire & Cas. Co. v. Tashire, 153

State Farm Mutual Automobile Ins. Co. v. Campbell, 95, 683

Steel Co. v. Citizens for a Better Environment, 221

Stewart Organization, Inc. v. Ricoh Corp., 123, 134, 392

Strawbridge v. Curtiss, 142, 153

Success Motivation Inst. of Japan Ltd. v. Success Motivation Institute, Inc., 630

Sung Hwan Co. v. Rite Aid Corp., 655

Swiss American Bank, Ltd., United States v., 64

Tafflin v. Levitt, 217

Tahan v. Hodgson, 631

Tele-Save Merchandising Co. v. Consumers Distributors Co., 544

Telnikoff v. Matusevitch, 656

Tel-Oren v. Libyan Arab Republic, 166

Thornton, United States v., 111

Timberlane Lumber Co. v. Bank of America N.T. & S.A., 572

Torres v. Southern Peru Copper Corp., 161, 195, 196, 204

Townsend v. Sears, Roebuck & Co., 517

Transaero, Inc. v. La Fuerza Aerea Boliviana, 361

Treco, *In re*, 671

Trugman-Nash, Inc. v. New Zealand Dairy Board, 493

Turner Entertainment Co. v. Degeto Film GmbH, 411, 412

Umana v. SCM S.p.A., 457

Umbenhauer v. Woog, 351

Underhill v. Hernandez, 254

Union Carbide Gas Plant Disaster at Bhopal, India, *In re*, 382

Union Carbide Gas Plant Disaster, *In re*, 383

United Mine Workers, United States v., 703

United States v. Aluminum Co. of America, 481, 568

United States v. First National City Bank, 495

United States v. Swiss American Bank, Ltd., 64

United States v. Thornton, 111

United States v. United Mine Workers, 703

United Steelworkers v. Enterprise Wheel & Car Corp., 714

Uranium Antitrust Litigation, *In re*, 577

Vagenas v. Continental Gin Co, 619

Valois of America, Inc. v. Risdon Corp., 475

Van Cauwenberghe v. Baird, 79, 394

Van Dusen v. Barrack, 220, 372

Verlinden B.V. v. Central Bank of Nigeria, 163, *225*

Victrix Steamship Co. S.A. v. Salen Dry Cargo A.B., 713

Vimar Seguros y Reaseguros, S.A. v. M/V Sky Reefer, 134, *695*

Vitamins Antitrust Litigation, *In re*, 474, 480

Voice Systems Marketing Co. v. Appropriate Technology Corp., 61

Volkswagenwerk Aktiengesellschaft v. Schlunk, 338

Volkswagenwerk, A.G. v. Superior Court, 471

W.S. Kirkpatrick & Co. v. Environmental Tectonics Corp., 313

Walton v. Arabian American Oil Co., 525

Washington Equip. Mfg. Co. v. Concrete Placing Co., 50

Weltover, Inc., Republic of Argentina v., 255, 311

White v. Kenneth Warren & Son, Ltd., 489

Whitney v. Robertson, 218

Wien Air Alaska, Inc. v. Brandt, 29

Wiles v. Morita Iron Works Co., 12, 13

Wilson v. Lufthansa German Airlines, 457

Wilton v. Seven Falls Co., 401

Wiwa v. Royal Dutch Petroleum Co., 55

Wong v. PartyGaming Ltd., 124

World-Wide Volkswagen Corp. v. Woodson, 11, 618

Yahoo!, Inc. v. La Ligue Contre Le Racisme et L'Antisemitisme, 36, 99, 664

Yavuz v. 61 MM, Ltd., 126

Young v. New Haven Advocate, 99

Zappia Middle East Constr. Co. v. Emirate of Abu Dhabi, 285

Zicherman v. Korean Air Lines Co., 216

Zippo Mfg. Co. v. Zippo Dot Com, Inc., 99

Zschernig v. Miller, 632

TRANSNATIONAL CIVIL LITIGATION

CASES AND MATERIALS

CHAPTER 1

Personal Jurisdiction and Forum Selection

A. INTRODUCTION

Determining the proper court(s) in which a lawsuit may be brought is an initial consideration in all litigation. But it is of particular significance in international civil litigation. A court's ability to hear a dispute and enter a valid judgment is thought to consist of two elements—the ability to reach out to a defendant and enter a judgment against him that will be binding, and the ability of the court to hear the particular kind of dispute that has been brought before it. Although both are aspects of jurisdiction, the former comes under the label of personal jurisdiction, the latter, subject matter jurisdiction. Both concepts are discussed in this chapter as they relate to international civil litigation.

Choice of forum is a matter of concern to litigants and their attorneys because, in addition to questions of convenience, they perceive that the choice of decisionmaker can affect the outcome. This is particularly true in litigation that involves litigants from different countries. Outcome can be affected for example, because different courts may choose to apply different substantive law, different procedures, or because of the possible bias against the outsider and in favor of the insider who also enjoys the home-field advantage of operating in a familiar legal system. Foreign defendants sued in the United States may encounter such unfamiliar procedures such as juries, class actions, and wide-ranging discovery. See Stephen B. Burbank, *Jurisdictional Equilibration, the Proposed Hague Convention and Progress in National Law*, 49 Am. J. Comp. L. 203, 242 (2001) (noting that the U.S. legal system is distinctive as much for its procedural as its substantive rules, yet noting that recent U.S. procedural developments may make matters marginally less problematic for foreign defendants).

Although jurisdictional considerations tend to focus on the commencement of a lawsuit, they also have an eye toward the conclusion of litigation. As discussed in Chapter 8, only a judgment recognized as jurisdictionally valid will be enforceable, should enforcement become an issue. Within the confines of a single domestic regime such as the U.S. where the courts of different states recognize roughly similar grounds for the assertion of jurisdiction, matters are less complicated than they are in a transnational setting in which different jurisdictions may recognize different standards for the valid assertion of jurisdiction. Indeed, the difficulties are sufficiently great that international agreements and treaties have been entered into and others remain on the drawing board that would streamline and limit the available bases for jurisdiction among signatory countries, largely for the purposes of making international judgment recognition more predictable.

Jurisdictional concerns also play a role long before any litigation occurs. Parties may wish to plan their activities and structure their operations in such a way as to be able to predict where litigation can take place if a dispute should arise from their activities. This is particularly true in a global economic setting in which commercial actors operate across borders and in different legal systems. Sometimes this planning may take the form of contractual agreements regarding the applicable forum and/or the applicable law. We address contractual forum selection in Section I, below; and we address choice of law clauses in Chapter 7. But the first parts of this chapter address the problems of personal jurisdiction when no contractual forum choice has been made.

Within the U.S., jurisdictional considerations have both a constitutional and subconstitutional dimension. Personal jurisdiction over a non resident or foreign defendant ordinarily requires statutory authorization from the relevant state in whose courts the lawsuit is brought. Such authorization generally takes the form of a "long-arm" statute permitting a judicial system to reach out to persons beyond its borders. For most litigation involving foreign parties, this means that litigants must look initially to the 50 different state long-arm statutes. Even when litigation is brought in a federal court, it is ordinarily the case that the court's reach will be limited by the long-arm statute of the state in which it sits. See Rule 4(k)(1)(A), Fed. R. Civ. P. Indeed, the state long arm is the default rule in federal court under even if the claim arises under federal law. Id. Nevertheless, for some claims governed by federal law, a federal long-arm statute may be applicable; and when it is, its reach may be broader than the state court's. See Rule 4(k)(1)(C). And it may also be possible for a plaintiff to secure statutory jurisdiction in a federal court based on the defendant's relationship with the U.S. in the aggregate under Rule 4(k)(2) for claims arising under federal law—a topic that we discuss in Section E of this chapter.

In addition, as just noted, constitutional considerations under the Fourteenth Amendment's Due Process Clause operate as an outside limit on all exercises of personal jurisdiction by state courts, even when jurisdiction is statutorily authorized. And when suit is brought in a federal court (and absent a federal long arm or the applicability of Rule 4(k)(2)), the federal court is ordinarily limited by the same due process limits that would be applicable to the state in which it sits. In sum, plaintiffs may attempt to bring suit in any U.S. forum in which these statutory and constitutional prerequisites are met, whether the plaintiff (or defendant) is domestic or foreign, and whether the events sued over occurred here or abroad.

Nevertheless, there are additional filters that further refine the proper forum choice. Within the U.S., considerations of subject matter jurisdiction may determine whether the suit can go forward in a federal as opposed to a state court, although state court subject matter jurisdiction is generally unlimited while federal court subject matter jurisdiction is not. And even within a proper court system, state and federal venue rules may further limit the choice of courts within which suit may be brought, as noted in Chapter 2, Section D.

Satisfying personal and subject matter jurisdiction as well as venue may not be the end of the inquiry, however, since courts may sometimes exercise their discretion to decline to hear a given case, either through statutory provisions for transfer of venue to another court within the relevant jurisdiction, or through dismissal on *forum non conveniens* grounds in favor of a substantially preferable forum. As discussed below, when suit is brought in or removed to a federal court, *forum non conveniens* inevitably implicates dismissal in favor of having litigation go forward in a foreign rather than a U.S. jurisdiction. *Forum non conveniens* dismissals are briefly noted in this chapter, but they are more fully considered in Chapter 5.

B. SPECIFIC JURISDICTION

The starting point for the exercise of personal jurisdiction in American courts in the transnational setting is the same as it is in the domestic setting. The modern era of personal jurisdiction begins with International Shoe Co. v. Washington, 326 U.S. 310 (1945). There the Court declared that a state may constitutionally exercise jurisdiction over a non resident defendant provided he has "certain minimum contacts with it such that the maintenance of the suit does not offend traditional notions of fair play and substantial justice." Id. at 316. Due process, said the Court, "does not contemplate that a state may make a binding judgment in personam against an individual or corporate defendant with which the state has no contacts, ties, or relations." Id. at 319. In so concluding, the Court reiterated what it had first declared in Pennoyer v. Neff, 95 U.S. 714 (1877)—that a state's assertion of personal jurisdiction is limited by the Due Process Clause of the Fourteenth Amendment. Yet *International Shoe* also departed from the traditional territorialist perspective of *Pennoyer* that had focused primarily on the physical presence of the defendant within the jurisdiction, or the defendant's consent to jurisdiction, or the presence of property in the forum. As discussed below, these traditional bases of jurisdiction still survive in one form or another, as curtailed, refined, and supplemented by *International Shoe* and its progeny. But instead of deploying due process primarily as a limit on extraterritorial exertions of state power, *International Shoe* read due process as imposing a reasonableness requirement on a state's exercise of jurisdiction. The decision that follows represents one effort by the Supreme Court to apply the general principles of *International Shoe* (and its progeny) to the international civil litigation setting in a product liability case.

Asahi Metal Industry Co., Ltd. v. Superior Court

Supreme Court of the United States, 1987.
480 U.S. 102.

JUSTICE O'CONNOR announced the judgment of the Court and delivered the unanimous opinion of the Court with respect to Part I, the opinion of the Court with respect to Part II-B, in which the CHIEF JUSTICE, JUSTICE BRENNAN, JUSTICE WHITE, JUSTICE MARSHALL, JUSTICE BLACKMUN, JUSTICE POWELL, and JUSTICE STEVENS join, and an opinion with respect to Parts II-A and III, in which the CHIEF JUSTICE, JUSTICE POWELL, and JUSTICE SCALIA join.

[The plaintiff, Gary Zurcher, was severely injured in a motorcycle accident in 1978 when one of his tires blew out on a California freeway. Zurcher, a Californian, brought a product liability action in the California state courts against various defendants, including the manufacturer of the motorcycle and Cheng Shin Rubber Industry Co.—the Taiwanese manufacturer of an allegedly defective tire tube. Cheng Shin then brought a third-party complaint against Asahi, the Japanese manufacturer of the valve assembly for the tube. Zurcher brought no claim against Asahi, however, and settled with Cheng Shin and the remaining defendants. Asahi moved to dismiss the third-party action brought against it by Cheng Shin arguing that the California courts lacked personal jurisdiction over it.]

[Asahi] manufactures tire valve assemblies in Japan and sells the assemblies to Cheng Shin, and to several other tire manufacturers, for use as components in finished tire tubes. * * * Cheng Shin bought and incorporated into its tire tubes [anywhere from 100,000 to 500,000 assemblies annually between 1978 and 1982]. Sales to Cheng Shin accounted for 1.24 percent of Asahi's income in 1982 and 0.44 percent in 1982 Cheng Shin alleged that approximately 20% of its sales in the United States are in California. Cheng Shin purchases valve assemblies from other suppliers as well, and sells finished tubes throughout the world.

In 1983 an attorney for Cheng Shin conducted an informal examination of the value stems of the tire tubes sold in one cyclery in Solano County. The attorney declared that of the approximately 115 tire tubes in the store, 97 were purportedly manufactured in Japan or Taiwan, and of those 97, 21 valve stems were marked with the circled letter "A", apparently Asahi's trademark. Of the 21 Asahi valve stems, 12 were incorporated into Cheng Shin tire tubes. The store contained 41 other Cheng Shin tubes that incorporated the valve assemblies of other manufacturers. * * * An affidavit of a manager of Cheng Shin whose duties included the purchasing of component parts stated: "In discussions with Asahi regarding the purchase of valve stem assemblies the fact that my Company sells tubes throughout the world and specifically the United States has been discussed. I am informed and believe that Asahi was fully aware that valve stem assemblies sold to my Company and to others would end up throughout the United States and in California." An affidavit of the president of Asahi, on the other hand, declared that Asahi "has never contemplated that its limited sales of tire valves to Cheng Shin in Taiwan would subject it to lawsuits in California." The record does not include any contract between Cheng Shin and Asahi.

Primarily on the basis of the above information, the Superior Court denied the motion to quash the summons stating: "Asahi obviously does business on an international scale. It is not unreasonable that they defend claims of defect in their product on an international scale." [The California Supreme Court upheld personal jurisdiction over Asahi. 39 Cal.3d 35, 702 P.2d 543 (1985).]

II

A

The Due Process Clause of the Fourteenth Amendment limits the power of a state court to exert personal jurisdiction over a nonresident defendant. "[T]he constitutional touchstone" of the determination whether an exercise of personal jurisdiction comports with due process "remains whether the defendant purposefully established 'minimum contacts' in the forum State." Burger King Corp. v. Rudzewicz, 471 U.S. 462, 474 (1985). Most recently we have reaffirmed the oft-quoted reasoning of Hanson v. Denckla, 357 U.S. 235, 253 (1958), that minimum contacts must have a basis in "some act by which the defendant purposefully avails itself of the privilege of conducting activities within the forum State, thus invoking the benefits and protections of its laws." *Burger King*, 471 U.S., at 475. "Jurisdiction is proper . . . where the contacts proximately result from actions by the defendant *himself* that create a 'substantial connection' with the forum State." Ibid; quoting McGee v. International Life Insurance Co., 355 U.S. 220, 223 (1957) (emphasis in original).

Applying the principle that minimum contacts must be based on an act of the defendant, the Court in World-Wide Volkswagen Corp. v. Woodson, 444 U.S. 286 (1980), rejected the assertion that a *consumer's* unilateral act of bringing the defendant's product into the forum State was a sufficient constitutional basis for personal jurisdiction over the defendant. * * *

Since *World-Wide Volkswagen,* lower courts have been confronted with cases in which the defendant acted by placing a product in the stream of commerce, and the stream eventually swept defendant's product into the forum State, but the defendant did nothing else to purposefully avail itself of the market in the forum State. Some courts have understood the Due Process Clause, as interpreted in *World-Wide Volkswagen,* to allow an exercise of personal jurisdiction to be based on no more than the defendant's act of placing the product in the stream of commerce. Other courts have understood the Due Process Clause and the above-quoted language in *World-Wide Volkswagen* to require the action of the defendant to be more purposefully directed at the forum State than the mere act of placing a product in the stream of commerce.

The reasoning of the Supreme Court of California in the present case illustrates the former interpretation of *World-Wide Volkswagen.* The Supreme Court of California held that, because the stream of commerce eventually brought some valves Asahi sold Cheng Shin into California, Asahi's awareness that its valves would be sold in California was sufficient to permit California to exercise jurisdiction over Asahi consistent with the requirements of the Due Process Clause. The Supreme Court of California's position was consistent with those courts that have held that mere foreseeability or awareness was a constitutionally sufficient basis for personal jurisdiction if the defendant's product made its way into the forum State while still in the stream of commerce.

Other courts, however, have understood the Due Process Clause to require something more than that the defendant was aware of its product's entry into the forum State through the stream of commerce in order for the State to exert jurisdiction over the defendant. * * *

We now find this latter position to be consonant with the requirements of due process. The "substantial connection" between the defendant and the forum State necessary for a finding of minimum contacts must come about by *an action of the defendant purposefully directed toward the forum State.* * * * The placement of a product into the stream of commerce, without more, is not an act of the defendant purposefully directed toward the forum State. Additional conduct of the defendant may indicate an intent or purpose to serve the market in the forum State, for example, designing the product for the market in the forum State, advertising in the forum State, establishing channels for providing regular advice to customers in the forum State, or marketing the product through a distributor who has agreed to serve as the sales agent in the forum State. But a defendant's awareness that the stream of commerce may or will sweep the product into the forum State does not convert the mere act of placing the product into the stream into an act purposefully directed toward the forum State.

Assuming, *arguendo,* that respondents have established Asahi's awareness that some of the valves sold to Cheng Shin would be incorporated into tire tubes sold in California, respondents have not demonstrated any action by Asahi to purposefully avail itself of the California market. Asahi does not do business in California. It has no office, agents, employees, or property in California. It does not advertise or otherwise solicit business in California. It did not create, control, or employ the distribution system that brought its valves to California. * * * There is no evidence that Asahi designed its product in anticipation of sales in California. * * * On the basis of these facts, the exertion of personal jurisdiction over Asahi by the Superior Court of California exceeds the limits of Due Process.

B

The strictures of the Due Process Clause forbid a state court from exercising personal jurisdiction over Asahi under circumstances that would offend "traditional notions of fair play and substantial justice." *International Shoe Co.*, 326 U.S., at 316.

We have previously explained that the determination of the reasonableness of the exercise of jurisdiction in each case will depend on an evaluation of several factors. A court must consider the burden on the defendant, the interests of the forum state, and the plaintiff's interest in obtaining relief. It must also weigh in its determination "the interstate judicial system's interest in obtaining the most efficient resolution of controversies; and the shared interest of the several States in furthering fundamental substantive social policies." *World-Wide Volkswagen*, 444 U.S., at 292.

A consideration of these factors in the present case clearly reveals the unreasonableness of the assertion of jurisdiction over Asahi, even apart from the question of the placement of goods in the stream of commerce.

Certainly the burden on the defendant in this case is severe. Asahi has been commanded by the Supreme Court of California not only to traverse the distance between Asahi's headquarters in Japan and the Superior Court of California in and for the County of Solano, but also to submit its dispute with Cheng Shin to a foreign nation's judicial system. The unique burdens placed upon one who must defend oneself in a foreign legal system should have significant weight in assessing the reasonableness of stretching the long arm of personal jurisdiction over national borders.

When minimum contacts have been established, often the interests of the plaintiff and the forum in the exercise of jurisdiction will justify even the serious burdens placed on the alien defendant. In the present case, however, the interests of the plaintiff and the forum in California's assertion of jurisdiction over Asahi are slight. All that remains is a claim for indemnification asserted by Cheng Shin, a Taiwanese corporation, against Asahi. The transaction on which the indemnification claim is based took place in Taiwan; Asahi's components were shipped from Japan to Taiwan. Cheng Shin has not demonstrated that it is more convenient for it to litigate its indemnification claim against Asahi in California rather than in Taiwan or Japan.

Because the plaintiff [Cheng Shin—eds.] is not a California resident, California's legitimate interests in the dispute have considerably diminished. The Supreme Court of California argued that the State had an interest in "protecting its consumers by ensuring that foreign manufacturers comply with the state's safety standards." The State Supreme Court's definition of California's interest, however, was overly broad. The dispute between Cheng Shin and Asahi is primarily about indemnification rather than safety standards. Moreover, it is not at all clear at this point that California law should govern the question whether a Japanese corporation should indemnify a Taiwanese corporation on the basis of a sale made in Taiwan and a shipment of goods from Japan to Taiwan. The possibility of being haled into a California court as a result of an accident involving Asahi's components undoubtedly creates an additional deterrent to the manufacture of unsafe components; however, similar pressures will be placed on Asahi by the purchasers of its components as long as those who use Asahi components in their final products, and sell those products in California, are subject to the application of California tort law.

World-Wide Volkswagen also admonished courts to take into consideration the interests of the "several States," in addition to the forum state, in the efficient judicial resolution of the dispute and the advancement of substantive policies. In the present case, this advice calls for a court to consider the procedural and substantive policies of other nations whose interests are affected by the assertion of jurisdiction by the California court. The procedural and substantive interests of other nations in a state court's assertion of jurisdiction over an alien defendant will differ from case to case. In every case, however, those interests, as well as the Federal Government's interest in its foreign relations policies, will be best served by a careful inquiry into the reasonableness of the assertion of jurisdiction in the particular case, and an unwillingness to find the serious burdens on an alien defendant outweighed by minimal interests on the part of the plaintiff or the forum State. "Great care and reserve should be exercised when extending our notions of personal jurisdiction into the international field." United States v. First National City Bank, 379 U.S. 378, 404 (1965) (Harlan, J., dissenting).

Considering the international context, the heavy burden on the alien defendant, and the slight interests of the plaintiff and the forum State, the exercise of personal jurisdiction by a California court over Asahi in this instance would be unreasonable and unfair.

JUSTICE BRENNAN, with whom JUSTICE WHITE, JUSTICE MARSHALL and JUSTICE BLACKMUN join, concurring in part and in the judgment.

I do not agree with the plurality's interpretation of the stream-of-commerce theory, nor with its conclusion that Asahi did not "purposely avail itself of the California market." I do agree, however, with the Court's conclusion in Part II-B that the exercise of personal jurisdiction over Asahi in this case would not comport with "fair play and substantial justice[.]" This is one of those rare cases in which "minimum requirements inherent in the concept of 'fair play and substantial justice' defeat the reasonableness of jurisdiction even [though] the defendant has purposefully engaged in forum activities." Burger King Corp. v. Rudzewicz, 471 U.S. 462, 477-478 (1985). I therefore join Parts I and II-B of the Court's opinion, and write separately to explain my disagreement with Part II-A.

* * * The stream of commerce refers not to unpredictable currents or eddies, but to the regular and anticipated flow of products from manufacture to distribution to retail sale. As long as a participant in this process is aware that the final product is being marketed in the forum State, the possibility of a lawsuit there cannot come as a surprise. Nor will the litigation present a burden for which there is no corresponding benefit. A defendant who has placed goods in the stream of commerce benefits economically from the retail sale of the final product in the forum State, and indirectly benefits from the State's laws that regulate and facilitate commercial activity. These benefits accrue regardless of whether that participant directly conducts business in the forum State, or engages in additional conduct directed toward that State. Accordingly, most courts and commentators have found that jurisdiction premised on the placement of a product into the stream of commerce is consistent with the Due Process Clause, and have not required a showing of additional conduct.

[The plurality's] endorsement * * * of what appears to be the minority view among Federal Courts of Appeals represents a marked retreat from its analysis in World-Wide Volkswagen v. Woodson, 444 U.S. 286 (1980). In that case, "respondents [sought] to base jurisdiction on one, isolated occurrence and whatever inferences can be drawn therefrom: the fortuitous circumstance that a single Audi automobile, sold in New York to New York residents, happened to suffer an accident while passing through Oklahoma." The Court held that the possibility of an accident in Oklahoma, while to some extent foreseeable in light of the inherent mobility of the automobile, was not enough to establish minimum contacts between the forum State and the retailer or distributor. The Court then carefully explained:

> "[T]his is not to say, of course, that foreseeability is wholly irrelevant. But the foreseeability that is critical to due process analysis is not the mere likelihood that a product will find its way into the forum State. Rather, it is that the defendant's conduct and connection with the forum State are such that he should reasonably anticipate being haled into Court there."

The Court reasoned that when a corporation may reasonably anticipate litigation in a particular forum, it cannot claim that such litigation is unjust or unfair, because it "can act to alleviate the risk of burdensome litigation by procuring insurance, passing the expected costs on to consumers, or, if the risks are too great, severing its connection with the State." 444 U.S. at 297.

To illustrate the point, the Court contrasted the foreseeability of litigation in a State to which a consumer fortuitously transports a defendant's product (insufficient contacts) with the foreseeability of litigation in a State where the defendant's product was regularly sold (sufficient contacts). The Court stated:

> "Hence if the sale of a product of a manufacturer or distributor such as Audi or Volkswagen is not simply an isolated occurrence, but arises from the efforts of the manufacturer or distributor to serve, directly or indirectly, the market for its product in other States, it is not unreasonable to subject it to suit in one of those States if its allegedly defective merchandise has there been the source of injury to its owner or to others. The forum State does not exceed its powers under the Due Process Clause if it asserts personal jurisdiction over a corporation that delivers its products into the stream of commerce with the expectation that they will be purchased by consumers in the forum State." Id., at 297-298.

The Court concluded its illustration by referring to Gray v. American Radiator & Standard Sanitary Corp., 22 Ill. 2d 432, 176 N. E. 2d 761 (1961), a well-known stream-of-commerce case in which the Illinois Supreme Court applied the theory to assert jurisdiction over a component-parts manufacturer that sold no components directly in Illinois, but did sell them to a manufacturer who incorporated them into a final product that was sold in Illinois.

The Court in *World-Wide Volkswagen* thus took great care to distinguish "between a case involving goods which reach a distant State through a chain of distribution and a case involving goods which reach the same State because a consumer * * * took them there." 444 U.S., at 306-307 (Brennan, J., dissenting). The California Supreme Court took note of this distinction, and correctly concluded that our holding in *World-Wide Volkswagen* preserved the stream-of-commerce theory.

In this case, the facts found by the California Supreme Court support its finding of minimum contacts. The Court found that "[al]though Asahi did not design or control the system of distribution that carried its valve assemblies into California, Asahi was aware of the distribution system's operation, and it knew that it would benefit economically from the sale in California of products incorporating its components." Accordingly, I cannot join the plurality's determination that Asahi's regular and extensive sales of component parts to a manufacturer it knew was making regular sales of the final product in California is insufficient to establish minimum contacts with California.

Justice Stevens, with whom Justice White and Justice Blackmun join, concurring in part and concurring in the judgment.

The judgment of the Supreme Court of California should be reversed for the reasons stated in Part II-B of the Court's opinion. While I join Parts I and II-B, I do not join Part II-A for two reasons. First, it is not necessary to the Court's decision. * * * [T]his case fits within the rule that "minimum requirements inherent in the concept of 'fair play and substantial justice' may defeat the reasonableness of jurisdiction even if the defendant has purposefully engaged in forum activities." *Burger King*, 471 U.S., at 477-478 (quoting International Shoe Co. v. Washington, 326 U.S. 310, 320 (1945)). Accordingly, I see no reason in this case for the Court to articulate "purposeful direction" or any other test as the nexus between an act of a defendant and the forum State that is necessary to establish minimum contacts.

Second, even assuming that the test ought to be formulated here, Part II-A misapplies it to the facts of this case. The Court seems to assume that an unwavering line can be drawn between "mere awareness" that a component will find its way into the forum State and "purposeful availment" of the forum's market. Over the course of its dealings with Cheng Shin, Asahi has arguably engaged in a higher quantum of conduct than "[t]he placement of a product into the stream of commerce, without more. . . ." Whether or not this conduct rises to the level of purposeful availment requires a constitutional determination that is affected by the volume, the value, and the hazardous character of the components. In most circumstances I would be inclined to conclude that a regular course of dealing that results in deliveries of over 100,000 units annually over a period of several years would constitute "purposeful availment" even though the item delivered to the forum State was a standard product marketed throughout the world.

NOTES AND QUESTIONS FOR DISCUSSION

1. The Court in *Asahi* was unable to agree on whether "minimum contacts" were present. But it was close to unanimous in finding that the exercise of jurisdiction over Asahi would be "unreasonable and unfair" and thus violative of due process. In so doing, the Court makes clear that, even if minimum contacts are present, the reasonableness of the exercise of personal jurisdiction is part of the constitutional calculus. But wasn't the minimum contacts inquiry of *International Shoe* supposed to be the proxy for determining whether the exercise of jurisdiction over a nonresident defendant was unreasonable and unfair?

2. Note that *Asahi* did not invent its reasonableness inquiry to deal specifically with the foreign defendant or the problem of transnational litigation. The Court had earlier applied it in the purely domestic setting and suggested that whereas the plaintiff would generally bear the burden of proving minimum contacts, the defendant would bear the burden of showing unfairness. See Burger King Corp. v. Rudzewicz, 471 U.S. 462, 476 (1985). Nevertheless, the outcome of the reasonableness analysis in *Asahi* greatly hinged on the fact it was a *foreign* defendant who has been haled into a U.S. court—from the defendant's perspective, a foreign legal system—and who was objecting to personal jurisdiction. Moreover, "foreignness" seems to be an important factor in finding the exercise of jurisdiction unreasonable in a number of post-*Asahi* cases. See Linda J. Silberman, Goodyear *and* Nicastro: *Observations from a Transnational and Comparative Perspective*, 63 S.C.L. Rev. 591, 594 & n.27 (2012). To what extent did the reasonableness decision in *Asahi* also turn on the fact that the entire indemnity dispute—indeed, the only remaining dispute—was between two foreign parties? The plaintiff Zurcher did not assert a claim directly against Asahi. If he had, or if he had not settled with Cheng Shin, would either of those events have made the fairness inquiry come out differently?

3. Consider the transnational dimension of *Asahi* and what it is that makes a U.S. forum so potentially problematic from the perspective of a foreign litigant, especially a foreign defendant. In the U.S., unlike in most countries, the fact-finder in civil cases is likely to be a jury. This might be thought both to add to the uncertainty of outcomes while at the same time presenting the possibility of higher awards of damages than might otherwise be forthcoming from a judge. Although there are mechanisms to police for excessive verdicts, they are indirect and operate only at the outside limits of permissible verdicts. In addition, and unlike in most other countries, there is the possibility of punitive damages in U.S. tort cases, also awardable by the jury, but also subject to scrutiny by the court at the margins. Furthermore, pre-trial discovery is much more free-wheeling in the U.S., and it is conducted with only modest involvement by the court. And as discussed in Chapter 8, choice of law in the U.S. presents a highly unpredictable system in which the law of any potentially interested state might apply, and Supreme Court review of choice of law questions is notoriously min-imalist. Last but not least, class actions are commonplace in U.S. courts.

4. Test your understanding of the weight that the "foreign defendant" factor carries by reconsidering the outcome had Asahi been a U.S. company (based in Pennsylvania), and Cheng Shin a U.S. company (based in Ohio). All other facts being the same, isn't it doubtful that fairness concerns would tilt against person-al jurisdiction over Asahi in the third-party action by Cheng Shin? Pennsylvania is a long way from California, but not as far as is Japan; and more importantly, the legal system of the two states is fundamentally alike. In this regard, note that some courts have concluded that litigation in the U.S. can be less problematic for defendants from some nearby countries, such as Canada, whose legal system also has similar roots. See, e.g., Aristech Chemical Int'l Ltd. v. Acrylic Fabrica-tors Ltd., 138 F.3d 625 (6th Cir. 1998).

5. Cheng Shin did not object to personal jurisdiction in the California courts. Was the personal jurisdiction case against Cheng Shin (in Zurcher's suit) easier than that against Asahi? Indeed, Cheng Shin—a foreign party—affirmatively wanted to have its third-party action against Asahi go forward in California. Why? Although the record is unclear on the point, California law might have supplied the relevant principle for indemnity and contribution in the product lia-bility case against Cheng Shin, absent a contract between the two. Should the difficulty (or impossibility) of obtaining indemnity and contribution outside the U.S. (for example, on an underlying strict product liability claim) matter to the fairness analysis over a third-party such as Asahi?

6. Unlike with the reasonableness/fairness question in *Asahi*, there is no major-ity on any particular approach to the minimum contacts question. The opinions differ primarily on what showing it takes to establish that the suit arises out of activities that were "purposefully directed" toward the forum state. (As the opin-ions note, the purposeful-availment requirement was clearly made part of the *International Shoe* minimum contacts analysis in World-Wide Volkswagen Corp. v. Woodson, 444 U.S. 286 (1980)). Post-*Asahi*, lower courts, especially in product liability cases, sought to characterize Justice Brennan's opinion for four

Justices as involving a pure "stream of commerce" theory, and Justice O'Connor's as calling for a kind of "stream of commerce plus." Are those short-hand characterizations accurate?

Note that Justice Brennan's own stream-of-commerce approach has important qualifications. As he put it: "The stream of commerce refers not to unpredictable currents or eddies, but to the regular and anticipated flow of products from manufacturers to distribution to retail sale. As long as a participant in this process is aware that the final product is being marketed in the forum State, the possibility of a lawsuit there cannot come as a surprise." *Asahi*, 438 U.S. at 117. Thus, even he would appear to require something more than a showing that an isolated product, transported through commercial channels, happened to end up where it did, causing injury. Moreover, he appears to require some level of awareness on the part of the manufacturer as to where the final product is marketed. See Wiles v. Morita Iron Works Co., Ltd., 530 N.E.2d 1382, 1389 (Ill. 1988) (reading Brennan's opinion in *Asahi* to require "at a *minimum*" such actual knowledge). Is this not also a kind of "stream-of-commerce plus" approach?

In addition, consider the "additional conduct" that Justice O'Connor seems to call for to establish purposeful availment, beyond the placing of a product into the stream of commerce. "[D]esigning the product for the market in the forum state" or "advertising" there, or "marketing the product through a distributor who has agreed to serve as the sales agent," were all mentioned in *World-Wide Volkswagen* as bearing on when a seller of goods might be found to be subject to the personal jurisdiction of a particular forum. Are the considerations that are relevant to finding purposeful availment on the part of *sellers* of products the same as those for manufacturers, or component manufacturers? By definition, many component manufactures will rely on others to do the direct marketing, the advertising and distribution. Consequently, won't many component manufacturers, as opposed to final product manufacturers (or sellers), frequently fail to satisfy the kinds of "additional conduct" called for by Justice O'Connor? Should such component manufacturers, particularly foreign part manufacturers, be harder to reach in a U.S. forum even for accidents that occur here? Note that in *World-Wide Volkswagen* itself, the German manufacturer of the car involved in the accident on an Oklahoma highway did not pursue its objection to personal jurisdiction of the Oklahoma courts; only the car's New York seller did, along with the regional distributor.

7. As Justice O'Connor notes, there was lower court disagreement about the minimum contacts/purposeful availment analysis of *World-Wide Volkswagen*. Similar disarray set in over *Asahi* in both transnational and domestic civil litigation. (Nor is it clear that the Court's latest effort in J. McIntyre Machinery v. Nicastro, 131 S.Ct. 2780 (2011) [set out below] has eased the confusion.) The lower court approaches tend to resemble the various strands in *Asahi* itself.

- For example, in Boit v. Gar-Tec Products, Inc., 967 F.2d 671 (1st Cir. 1992), the First Circuit concluded in a products liability action that there was no personal jurisdiction over a foreign manufacturer when there was no evidence that it intended to serve the forum's market through an intervening purchaser or otherwise. See id. at 683 (endorsing Justice O'Connor's *Asahi* plurality); see also Rodriguez v. Fullerton Tires Corp.

v. Custom Metal Spinning Corp., 115 F.3d 81, 85 (1st Cir. 1997) (same)
Falkirk Min. Co. v. Japan Steel Works, Ltd., 906 F.2d 369, 374-75 (8th
Cir. 1990) (same).

- Other courts took a different view. Some of them stitched together the
  opinion of Justice Brennan in *Asahi*, who wrote for three other Justices
  on the minimum contacts question, with the opinion of Justice Stevens.
  While Justice Stevens did not join either of the other two *Asahi* opinions
  on the minimum contacts question, his opinion stated that purposeful
  availment "requires a constitutional determination that is affected by the
  volume, the value, and the hazardous character of the components," and
  seemed inclined to think that perhaps that standard had been met in *Asahi*. See, e.g., Barone v. Rich Bros. Interstate Display Fireworks Co., 25
  F.3d 610, 614-15 (8th Cir. 1994) ("Should one engage in vote counting,
  which we are loathe to do, it appears that five justices agreed that continuous placement of a significant number of products into the stream of
  commerce with knowledge that the product would be distributed into the
  forum state represents sufficient minimum contacts to satisfy due process."); *Ex parte* Pope Chevrolet, Inc., 555 So.2d 109, 112 (Ala. 1989)
  (making similar calculation).

- Still other courts put aside all of the minimum contacts opinions in *Asahi*, on the theory that there was no majority for any one approach. See,
  e.g., Ruston Gas Turbines, Inc. v. Donaldson Co., Inc., 9 F.3d 415, 419-
  20 (5th Cir. 1993) (purporting to rely on the Supreme Court's (and its
  own) pre-*Asahi* authority regarding stream-of-commerce analysis); cf.
  Pennzoil Prods. Co. v. Colelli & Assoc., Inc., 149 F.3d 197, 206-07 (3d
  Cir. 1998) (finding that personal jurisdiction would be acceptable insofar as it met both of the tests in *Asahi*).

Whatever view of *Asahi* the lower courts may have taken, many have expressed exasperation. See Lister v. Marangoni Meccanica S.p.A., 728 F. Supp.
1524, 1527 (D. Utah) (1990) (lamenting "quandary" in which lower courts have
been left following *Asahi*); Wiles v. Morita Iron Works Co., Ltd., 530 N.E.2d
1382, 1388 (Ill. 1988) (noting confusion generated by the "extremely balkanized
opinion" in *Asahi*). See also Joachim Zekoll, *The Role and Status of American
Law in the Hague Judgments Conventions Project*, 61 Alb. L. Rev. 1283, 1298
(1998) (voicing the frustrations of the international community). For a sampling
of the vast commentary on *Asahi*, both in the purely domestic and international
setting, see, e.g., Diane S. Kaplan, *Paddling Up the Wrong Stream: Why the
Stream of Commerce Theory is not part of Minimum Contacts Doctrine*, 55 Bay-
lor L. Rev. 503, 570 (2003); Christine M. Wiseman, *Reconstructing the Citadel:
The Advent of Jurisdictional Privity*, 54 Ohio St. L.J. 403 (1993); Russell J.
Weintraub, *Asahi Sends Personal Jurisdiction Down the Tubes*, 23 Texas Int'l
L.J. 55 (1988); R. Lawrence Dessem, *Personal Jurisdiction after Asahi: The
Other (International) Shoe Drops*, 55 Tenn. L. Rev. 41 (1987); Earl Maltz, *Un-
raveling the Conundrum of the Law of Personal Jurisdiction*, 1987 Duke L.J.
669.

The Supreme Court did not revisit the issue it left unresolved in *Asahi* until the 2011 decision below. And yet the opinion did nothing to reduce, let alone resolve, the uncertainty.

J. McIntyre Machinery, Ltd. v. Nicastro

Supreme Court of the United States, 2011.

131 S.Ct. 2780.

JUSTICE KENNEDY announced the judgment of the Court and delivered an opinion, in which THE CHIEF JUSTICE, JUSTICE SCALIA, and JUSTICE THOMAS join.

Whether a person or entity is subject to the jurisdiction of a state court despite not having been present in the State either at the time of suit or at the time of the alleged injury, and despite not having consented to the exercise of jurisdiction, is a question that arises with great frequency in the routine course of litigation. The rules and standards for determining when a State does or does not have jurisdiction over an absent party have been unclear because of decades-old questions left open in Asahi Metal Industry Co. v. Superior Court of Cal., 480 U.S. 102 (1987).

Here, the Supreme Court of New Jersey, relying in part on *Asahi,* held that New Jersey's courts can exercise jurisdiction over a foreign manufacturer of a product so long as the manufacturer "knows or reasonably should know that its products are distributed through a nationwide distribution system that might lead to those products being sold in any of the fifty states." Applying that test, the court concluded that a British manufacturer of scrap metal machines was subject to jurisdiction in New Jersey, even though at no time had it advertised in, sent goods to, or in any relevant sense targeted the State.

That decision cannot be sustained. Although the New Jersey Supreme Court issued an extensive opinion with careful attention to this Court's cases and to its own precedent, the "stream of commerce" metaphor carried the decision far afield. Due process protects the defendant's right not to be coerced except by lawful judicial power. As a general rule, the exercise of judicial power is not lawful unless the defendant "purposefully avails itself of the privilege of conducting activities within the forum State, thus invoking the benefits and protections of its laws." Hanson v. Denckla, 357 U.S. 235 (1958). There may be exceptions, say, for instance, in cases involving an intentional tort. But the general rule is applicable in this products-liability case, and the so-called "stream-of-commerce" doctrine cannot displace it.

I

This case arises from a products-liability suit filed in New Jersey state court. Robert Nicastro seriously injured his hand while using a metal-shearing machine manufactured by J. McIntyre Machinery, Ltd. (J. McIntyre). The accident occurred in New Jersey, but the machine was manufactured in England, where J. McIntyre is incorporated and operates. The question here is whether the New Jersey courts have jurisdiction over J. McIntyre, notwithstanding the fact that the company at no time either marketed goods in the State or shipped them there. Nicastro was a plaintiff in the New Jersey trial court and is the respondent here; J. McIntyre was a defendant and is now the petitioner.

At oral argument in this Court, Nicastro's counsel stressed three primary facts in defense of New Jersey's assertion of jurisdiction over J. McIntyre.

First, an independent company agreed to sell J. McIntyre's machines in the United States. J. McIntyre itself did not sell its machines to buyers in this country beyond the U.S. distributor, and there is no allegation that the distributor was under J. McIntyre's control.

Second, J. McIntyre officials attended annual conventions for the scrap recycling industry to advertise J. McIntyre's machines alongside the distributor. The conventions took place in various States, but never in New Jersey.

Third, no more than four machines (the record suggests only one), including the machine that caused the injuries that are the basis for this suit, ended up in New Jersey.

In addition to these facts emphasized by petitioner, the New Jersey Supreme Court noted that J. McIntyre held both United States and European patents on its recycling technology. It also noted that the U.S. distributor structured its advertising and sales efforts in accordance with J. McIntyre's direction and guidance whenever possible, and that at least some of the machines were sold on consignment to the distributor.

In light of these facts, the New Jersey Supreme Court concluded that New Jersey courts could exercise jurisdiction over petitioner without contravention of the Due Process Clause. Jurisdiction was proper, in that court's view, because the injury occurred in New Jersey; because petitioner knew or reasonably should have known "that its products are distributed through a nationwide distribution system that might lead to those products being sold in any of the fifty states"; and because petitioner failed to "take some reasonable step to prevent the distribution of its products in this State."

Both the New Jersey Supreme Court's holding and its account of what it called "the stream-of-commerce doctrine of jurisdiction," were incorrect, however. This Court's *Asahi* decision may be responsible in part for that court's error regarding the stream of commerce, and this case presents an opportunity to provide greater clarity.

II

The Due Process Clause protects an individual's right to be deprived of life, liberty, or property only by the exercise of lawful power. This is no less true with respect to the power of a sovereign to resolve disputes through judicial process than with respect to the power of a sovereign to prescribe rules of conduct for those within its sphere. * * *

A court may subject a defendant to judgment only when the defendant has sufficient contacts with the sovereign "such that the maintenance of the suit does not offend traditional notions of fair play and substantial justice." International Shoe Co. v. Washington, 326 U.S. 310 (1945). Freeform notions of fundamental fairness divorced from traditional practice cannot transform a judgment rendered in the absence of authority into law. As a general rule, the sovereign's exercise of power requires some act by which the defendant "purposefully avails itself of the privilege of conducting activities within the forum State, thus invoking the benefits and protections of its laws," *Hanson,* though in some cases, as with an intentional tort, the defendant might well fall within the State's authority by reason of his attempt to obstruct its laws. In products-liability cases like this one, it is the defendant's purposeful availment that makes jurisdiction consistent with "traditional notions of fair play and substantial justice."

A person may submit to a State's authority in a number of ways. There is, of course, explicit consent. E.g., Insurance Corp. of Ireland v. Compagnie des Bauxites de Guinée, 456 U.S. 694 (1982). Presence within a State at the time suit commences through service of process is another example. See Burnham v. Superior Court, 495 U.S. 604 (1990). Citizenship or domicile—or, by analogy, incorporation or principal place of business for corporation—also indicates general submission to a State's powers. Goodyear Dunlop Tires Operations, S.A. v. Brown [131 S.Ct. 2846 (2011)]. Each of these examples reveals circumstances, or a course of conduct, from which it is proper to infer an intention to benefit from and thus an intention to submit to the laws of the forum State. Cf. Burger King Corp. v. Rudzewicz, 471 U.S. 462 (1985). These examples support exercise of the general jurisdiction of the State's courts and allow the State to resolve both matters that originate within the State and those based on activities and events elsewhere. Helicopteros Nacionales de Colombia, S.A. v. Hall, 466 U.S. 408 (1984). By contrast, those who live or operate primarily outside a State have a due process right not to be subjected to judgment in its courts as a general matter.

There is also a more limited form of submission to a State's authority for disputes that "arise out of or are connected with the activities within the state." *International Shoe.* Where a defendant "purposefully avails itself of the privilege of conducting activities within the forum State, thus invoking the benefits and protections of its laws," *Hanson,* it submits to the judicial power of an otherwise foreign sovereign to the extent that power is exercised in connection with the defendant's activities touching on the State. In other words, submission through contact with and activity directed at a sovereign may justify specific jurisdiction "in a suit arising out of or related to the defendant's contacts with the forum." *Helicopteros*; see also *Goodyear.*

The imprecision arising from *Asahi,* for the most part, results from its statement of the relation between jurisdiction and the "stream of commerce." The stream of commerce, like other metaphors, has its deficiencies as well as its utility. It refers to the movement of goods from manufacturers through distributors to consumers, yet beyond that descriptive purpose its meaning is far from exact. This Court has stated that a defendant's placing goods into the stream of commerce "with the expectation that they will be purchased by consumers within the forum State" may indicate purposeful availment. World-Wide Volkswagen Corp. v. Woodson, 440 U.S. 286 (1980). But that statement does not amend the general rule of personal jurisdiction. It merely observes that a defendant may in an appropriate case be subject to jurisdiction without entering the forum—itself an unexceptional proposition—as where manufacturers or distributors "seek to serve" a given State's market. The principal inquiry in cases of this sort is whether the defendant's activities manifest an intention to submit to the power of a sovereign. In other words, the defendant must "purposefully avai[l] itself of the privilege of conducting activities within the forum State, thus invoking the benefits and protections of its laws." Sometimes a defendant does so by sending its goods rather than its agents. The defendant's transmission of goods permits the exercise of jurisdiction only where the defendant can be said to have targeted the forum; as a general rule, it is not enough that the defendant might have predicted that its goods will reach the forum State.

In *Asahi,* an opinion by Justice Brennan for four Justices outlined a different approach. It discarded the central concept of sovereign authority in favor of considerations of fairness and foreseeability. As that concurrence contended, "jurisdiction premised on the placement of a product into the stream of commerce [without more] is consistent with the Due Process Clause," for "[a]s long as a participant in this process is aware that the final product is being marketed in the forum State, the possibility of a lawsuit there cannot come as a surprise." It was the premise of the concurring opinion that the defendant's ability to anticipate suit renders the assertion of jurisdiction fair. In this way, the opinion made foreseeability the touchstone of jurisdiction.

The standard set forth in Justice Brennan's concurrence was rejected in an opinion written by Justice O'Connor; but the relevant part of that opinion, too, commanded the assent of only four Justices, not a majority of the Court. That opinion stated: "The 'substantial connection' between the defendant and the forum State necessary for a finding of minimum contacts must come about by an action of the defendant purposefully directed toward the forum State. The placement of a product into the stream of commerce, without more, is not an act of the defendant purposefully directed toward the forum State."

Since *Asahi* was decided, the courts have sought to reconcile the competing opinions. But Justice Brennan's concurrence, advocating a rule based on general notions of fairness and foreseeability, is inconsistent with the premises of lawful judicial power. This Court's precedents make clear that it is the defendant's actions, not his expectations, that empower a State's courts to subject him to judgment.

The conclusion that jurisdiction is in the first instance a question of authority rather than fairness explains, for example, why the principal opinion in *Burnham* "conducted no independent inquiry into the desirability or fairness" of the rule that service of process within a State suffices to establish jurisdiction over an otherwise foreign defendant. As that opinion explained, "[t]he view developed early that each State had the power to hale before its courts any individual who could be found within its borders." Furthermore, were general fairness considerations the touchstone of jurisdiction, a lack of purposeful availment might be excused where carefully crafted judicial procedures could otherwise protect the defendant's interests, or where the plaintiff would suffer substantial hardship if forced to litigate in a foreign forum. That such considerations have not been deemed controlling is instructive. See, e.g., *World-Wide Volkswagen.*

Two principles are implicit in the foregoing. First, personal jurisdiction requires a forum-by-forum, or sovereign-by-sovereign, analysis. The question is whether a defendant has followed a course of conduct directed at the society or economy existing within the jurisdiction of a given sovereign, so that the sovereign has the power to subject the defendant to judgment concerning that conduct. Personal jurisdiction, of course, restricts "judicial power not as a matter of sovereignty, but as a matter of individual liberty," for due process protects the individual's right to be subject only to lawful power. *Insurance Corp.* But whether a judicial judgment is lawful depends on whether the sovereign has authority to render it.

The second principle is a corollary of the first. Because the United States is a distinct sovereign, a defendant may in principle be subject to the jurisdiction of the courts of the United States but not of any particular State. This is consistent with the premises and unique genius of our Constitution. * * * For jurisdiction, a litigant may have the requisite relationship with the United States Government but not with the government of any individual State. That would be an exceptional case, however. If the defendant is a domestic domiciliary, the courts of its home State are available and can exercise general jurisdiction. And if another State were to assert jurisdiction in an inappropriate case, it would upset the federal balance, which posits that each State has a sovereignty that is not subject to unlawful intrusion by other States. Furthermore, foreign corporations will often target or concentrate on particular States, subjecting them to specific jurisdiction in those forums.

It must be remembered, however, that although this case and *Asahi* both involve foreign manufacturers, the undesirable consequences of Justice Brennan's approach are no less significant for domestic producers. The owner of a small Florida farm might sell crops to a large nearby distributor, for example, who might then distribute them to grocers across the country. If foreseeability were the controlling criterion, the farmer could be sued in Alaska or any number of other States' courts without ever leaving town. And the issue of foreseeability may itself be contested so that significant expenses are incurred just on the preliminary issue of jurisdiction. Jurisdictional rules should avoid these costs whenever possible.

The conclusion that the authority to subject a defendant to judgment depends on purposeful availment, consistent with Justice O'Connor's opinion in *Asahi,* does not by itself resolve many difficult questions of jurisdiction that will arise in particular cases. The defendant's conduct and the economic realities of the market the defendant seeks to serve will differ across cases, and judicial exposition will, in common-law fashion, clarify the contours of that principle.

III

In this case, petitioner directed marketing and sales efforts at the United States. It may be that, assuming it were otherwise empowered to legislate on the subject, the Congress could authorize the exercise of jurisdiction in appropriate courts. That circumstance is not presented in this case, however, and it is neither necessary nor appropriate to address here any constitutional concerns that might be attendant to that exercise of power. Nor is it necessary to determine what substantive law might apply were Congress to authorize jurisdiction in a federal court in New Jersey. A sovereign's legislative authority to regulate conduct may present considerations different from those presented by its authority to subject a defendant to judgment in its courts. Here the question concerns the authority of a New Jersey state court to exercise jurisdiction, so it is petitioner's purposeful contacts with New Jersey, not with the United States, that alone are relevant.

Respondent has not established that J. McIntyre engaged in conduct purposefully directed at New Jersey. Recall that respondent's claim of jurisdiction centers on three facts: The distributor agreed to sell J. McIntyre's machines in the United States; J. McIntyre officials attended trade shows in several States but not in New Jersey; and up to four machines ended up in New Jersey. The British manufacturer had no office in New Jersey; it neither paid taxes nor owned property there; and it neither advertised in, nor sent any employees to, the State. Indeed, after discovery the trial court found that the "defendant does not have a single contact with New Jersey short of the machine in question ending up in this state." These facts may reveal an intent to serve the U.S. market, but they do not show that J. McIntyre purposefully availed itself of the New Jersey market.

It is notable that the New Jersey Supreme Court appears to agree, for it could "not find that J. McIntyre had a presence or minimum contacts in this State — in any jurisprudential sense — that would justify a New Jersey court to exercise jurisdiction in this case." The court nonetheless held that petitioner could be sued in New Jersey based on a "stream-of-commerce theory of jurisdiction." As discussed, however, the stream-of-commerce metaphor cannot supersede either the mandate of the Due Process Clause or the limits on judicial authority that Clause ensures. The New Jersey Supreme Court also cited "significant policy reasons" to justify its holding, including the State's "strong interest in protecting its citizens from defective products." That interest is doubtless strong, but the Constitution commands restraint before discarding liberty in the name of expediency.

Due process protects petitioner's right to be subject only to lawful authority. At no time did petitioner engage in any activities in New Jersey that reveal an intent to invoke or benefit from the protection of its laws. New Jersey is without power to adjudge the rights and liabilities of J. McIntyre, and its exercise of jurisdiction would violate due process. The contrary judgment of the New Jersey Supreme Court is *Reversed.*

JUSTICE BREYER, with whom JUSTICE ALITO joins, concurring in the judgment.

The Supreme Court of New Jersey adopted a broad understanding of the scope of personal jurisdiction based on its view that "[t]he increasingly fast-paced globalization of the world economy has removed national borders as barriers to trade." I do not doubt that there have been many recent changes in commerce and communication, many of which are not anticipated by our precedents. But this case does not present any of those issues. So I think it unwise to announce a rule of broad applicability without full consideration of the modern-day consequences.

In my view, the outcome of this case is determined by our precedents.

Based on the facts found by the New Jersey courts, respondent Robert Nicastro failed to meet his burden to demonstrate that it was constitutionally proper to exercise jurisdiction over petitioner J. McIntyre Machinery, Ltd. (British Manufacturer), a British firm that manufactures scrap-metal machines in Great Britain and sells them through an independent distributor in the United States (American Distributor). On that basis, I agree with the plurality that the contrary judgment of the Supreme Court of New Jersey should be reversed.

I

In asserting jurisdiction over the British Manufacturer, the Supreme Court of New Jersey relied most heavily on three primary facts as providing constitutionally sufficient "contacts" with New Jersey, thereby making it fundamentally fair to hale the British Manufacturer before its courts: (1) The American Distributor on one occasion sold and shipped one machine to a New Jersey customer, namely, Mr. Nicastro's employer, Mr. Curcio; (2) the British Manufacturer permitted, indeed wanted, its independent American Distributor to sell its machines to anyone in America willing to buy them; and (3) representatives of the British Manufacturer attended trade shows in "such cities as Chicago, Las Vegas, New Orleans, Orlando, San Diego, and San Francisco." In my view, these facts do not provide contacts between the British firm and the State of New Jersey constitutionally sufficient to support New Jersey's assertion of jurisdiction in this case.

None of our precedents finds that a single isolated sale, even if accompanied by the kind of sales effort indicated here, is sufficient. Rather, this Court's previous holdings suggest the contrary. The Court has held that a single sale to a customer who takes an accident-causing product to a different State (where the accident takes place) is not a sufficient basis for asserting jurisdiction. See *World-Wide Volkswagen*. And the Court, in separate opinions, has strongly suggested that a single sale of a product in a State does not constitute an adequate basis for asserting jurisdiction over an out-of-state defendant, even if that defendant places his goods in the stream of commerce, fully aware (and hoping) that such a sale will take place. See *Asahi* (opinion of O'Connor, J.) (requiring "something more" than simply placing "a product into the stream of commerce," even if defendant is "awar[e]" that the stream "may or will sweep the product into the forum State"); (Brennan, J., concurring in part and concurring in judgment) (jurisdiction should lie where a sale in a State is part of "the regular and anticipated flow" of commerce into the State, but not where that sale is only an "edd[y]," *i.e.,* an isolated occurrence); (Stevens, J., concurring in part and concurring in judgment) (indicating that "the volume, the value, and the hazardous character" of a good may affect the jurisdictional inquiry and emphasizing Asahi's "regular course of dealing").

Here, the relevant facts found by the New Jersey Supreme Court show no "regular . . . flow" or "regular course" of sales in New Jersey; and there is no "something more," such as special state-related design, advertising, advice, marketing, or anything else. Mr. Nicastro, who here bears the burden of proving jurisdiction, has shown no specific effort by the British Manufacturer to sell in New Jersey. He has introduced no list of potential New Jersey customers who might, for example, have regularly attended trade shows. And he has not otherwise shown that the British Manufacturer "purposefully avail[ed] itself of the privilege of conducting activities" within New Jersey, or that it delivered its goods in the stream of commerce "with the expectation that they will be purchased" by New Jersey users. *World-Wide Volkswagen.*

There may well have been other facts that Mr. Nicastro could have demonstrated in support of jurisdiction. And the dissent considers some of those facts (describing the size and scope of New Jersey's scrap-metal business). But the plaintiff bears the burden of establishing jurisdiction, and here I would take the facts precisely as the New Jersey Supreme Court stated them.

Accordingly, on the record present here, resolving this case requires no more than adhering to our precedents.

II

I would not go further. Because the incident at issue in this case does not implicate modern concerns, and because the factual record leaves many open questions, this is an unsuitable vehicle for making broad pronouncements that refashion basic jurisdictional rules.

A

The plurality seems to state strict rules that limit jurisdiction where a defendant does not "inten[d] to submit to the power of a sovereign" and cannot "be said to have targeted the forum." But what do those standards mean when a company targets the world by selling products from its Web site? And does it matter if, instead of shipping the products directly, a company consigns the products through an intermediary (say, Amazon.com) who then receives and fulfills the orders? And what if the company markets its products through popup advertisements that it knows will be viewed in a forum? Those issues have serious commercial consequences but are totally absent in this case.

B

But though I do not agree with the plurality's seemingly strict no-jurisdiction rule, I am not persuaded by the absolute approach adopted by the New Jersey Supreme Court and urged by respondent and his *amici.* Under that view, a producer is subject to jurisdiction for a products-liability action so long as it "knows or reasonably should know that its products are distributed through a nationwide distribution system that *might* lead to those products being sold in any of the fifty states." In the context of this case, I cannot agree.

For one thing, to adopt this view would abandon the heretofore accepted inquiry of whether, focusing upon the relationship between "the defendant, the *forum,* and the litigation," it is fair, in light of the defendant's contacts *with that forum,* to subject the defendant to suit there. *Shaffer v. Heitner.* It would ordinarily rest jurisdiction instead upon no more than the occurrence of a product-based accident in the forum State. But this Court has rejected the notion that a defendant's amenability to suit "travel[s] with the chattel." *World-Wide Volkswagen.*

For another, I cannot reconcile so automatic a rule with the constitutional demand for "minimum contacts" and "purposeful availment," each of which rest upon a particular notion of defendant-focused fairness. A rule like the New Jersey Supreme Court's would permit every State to assert jurisdiction in a products-liability suit against any domestic manufacturer who sells its products (made anywhere in the United States) to a national distributor, no matter how large or small the manufacturer, no matter how distant the forum, and no matter how few the number of items that end up in the particular forum at issue. What might appear fair in the case of a large manufacturer which specifically seeks, or expects, an equal-sized distributor to sell its product in a distant State might seem unfair in the case of a small manufacturer (say, an Appalachian potter) who sells his product (cups and saucers) exclusively to a large distributor, who resells a single item (a coffee mug) to a buyer from a distant State (Hawaii). I know too little about the range of these or in-between possibilities to abandon in favor of the more absolute rule what has previously been this Court's less absolute approach.

Further, the fact that the defendant is a foreign, rather than a domestic, manufacturer makes the basic fairness of an absolute rule yet more uncertain. I am again less certain than is the New Jersey Supreme Court that the nature of international commerce has changed so significantly as to require a new approach to personal jurisdiction.

It may be that a larger firm can readily "alleviate the risk of burdensome litigation by procuring insurance, passing the expected costs on to customers, or, if the risks are too great, severing its connection with the State." *World-Wide Volkswagen*. But manufacturers come in many shapes and sizes. It may be fundamentally unfair to require a small Egyptian shirt maker, a Brazilian manufacturing cooperative, or a Kenyan coffee farmer, selling its products through international distributors, to respond to products-liability tort suits in virtually every State in the United States, even those in respect to which the foreign firm has no connection at all but the sale of a single (allegedly defective) good. And a rule like the New Jersey Supreme Court suggests would require every product manufacturer, large or small, selling to American distributors to understand not only the tort law of every State, but also the wide variance in the way courts within different States apply that law

C

At a minimum, I would not work such a change to the law in the way either the plurality or the New Jersey Supreme Court suggests without a better understanding of the relevant contemporary commercial circumstances. Insofar as such considerations are relevant to any change in present law, they might be presented in a case (unlike the present one) in which the Solicitor General participates.

This case presents no such occasion, and so I again reiterate that I would adhere strictly to our precedents and the limited facts found by the New Jersey Supreme Court. And on those grounds, I do not think we can find jurisdiction in this case. Accordingly, though I agree with the plurality as to the outcome of this case, I concur only in the judgment of that opinion and not its reasoning.

JUSTICE GINSBURG, with whom JUSTICE SOTOMAYOR and JUSTICE KAGAN join, dissenting.

A foreign industrialist seeks to develop a market in the United States for machines it manufactures. It hopes to derive substantial revenue from sales it makes to United States purchasers. Where in the United States buyers reside does not matter to this manufacturer. Its goal is simply to sell as much as it can, wherever it can. It excludes no region or State from the market it wishes to reach. But, all things considered, it prefers to avoid products liability litigation in the United States. To that end, it engages a U.S. distributor to ship its machines stateside. Has it succeeded in escaping personal jurisdiction in a State where one of its products is sold and causes injury or even death to a local user?

Under this Court's pathmarking precedent in *International Shoe*, and subsequent decisions, one would expect the answer to be unequivocally, "No." But instead, six Justices of this Court, in divergent opinions, tell us that the manufacturer has avoided the jurisdiction of our state courts, except perhaps in States where its products are sold in sizeable quantities. * * *

I

* * * McIntyre UK representatives attended every ISRI [Institute of Scrap Metal Industries] convention from 1990 through 2005. These annual expositions were held in diverse venues across the United States * * *. McIntyre UK exhibited its products at ISRI trade shows, the company acknowledged, hoping to reach anyone interested in the machine from anywhere in the United States. * * *

From at least 1995 until 2001, McIntyre UK retained an Ohio-based company, McIntyre Machinery America, Ltd. (McIntyre America), as its exclusive distributor for the entire United States. Though similarly named, the two companies were separate and independent entities with no commonality of ownership or management. * * *

In a November 23, 1999 letter to McIntyre America, McIntyre UK's president spoke plainly about the manufacturer's objective in authorizing the exclusive distributorship: "All we wish to do is sell our products in the [United] States—and get paid!" * * * And in correspondence with McIntyre America, McIntyre UK noted that the manufacturer had products liability insurance coverage.

Over the years, McIntyre America distributed several McIntyre UK products to U.S. customers * * *. In promoting McIntyre UK's products at conventions and demonstration sites and in trade journal advertisements, McIntyre America looked to McIntyre UK for direction and guidance. To achieve McIntyre UK's objective, the two companies were acting closely in concert with each other. McIntyre UK never instructed its distributor to avoid certain States or regions of the country; rather, as just noted, the manufacturer engaged McIntyre America to attract customers from anywhere in the United States.

In sum, McIntyre UK's regular attendance and exhibitions at ISRI conventions was surely a purposeful step to reach customers for its products anywhere in the United States. At least as purposeful was McIntyre UK's engagement of McIntyre America as the conduit for sales of McIntyre UK's machines to buyers throughout the United States. Given McIntyre UK's endeavors to reach and profit from the United States market as a whole, Nicastro's suit, I would hold, has been brought in a forum entirely appropriate for the adjudication of his claim. He alleges that McIntyre UK's shear machine was defectively designed or manufactured and, as a result, caused injury to him at his workplace. The machine arrived in Nicastro's New Jersey workplace not randomly or fortuitously, but as a result of the U.S. connections and distribution system that McIntyre UK deliberately arranged. On what sensible view of the allocation of adjudicatory authority could the place of Nicastro's injury within the United States be deemed off limits for his products liability claim against a foreign manufacturer who targeted the United States (including all the States that constitute the Nation) as the territory it sought to develop?

II

* * *

Whatever the state of academic debate over the role of consent in modern jurisdictional doctrines, the plurality's notion that consent is the animating concept draws no support from controlling decisions of this Court. Quite the contrary, the Court has explained, a forum can exercise jurisdiction when its contacts with the controversy are sufficient; invocation of a fictitious consent, the Court has repeatedly said, is unnecessary and unhelpful. *See, e.g., Burger King Corp.* (Due Process Clause permits "forum . . . to assert specific jurisdiction over an out-of-state defendant who has not consented to suit there").[5]

III

This case is illustrative of marketing arrangements for sales in the United States common in today's commercial world.[6] A foreign-country manufacturer engages a U.S. company to promote and distribute the manufacturer's products, not in any particular State, but anywhere and everywhere in the United States the distributor can attract purchasers. The product proves defective and injures a user in the State where the user lives or works. Often, as here, the manufacturer will have liability insurance covering personal injuries caused by its products.

When industrial accidents happen, a long-arm statute in the State where the injury occurs generally permits assertion of jurisdiction, upon giving proper notice, over the foreign manufacturer. For example, the State's statute might provide, as does New York's long-arm statute, for the "exercise [of] personal jurisdiction over any non-domiciliary . . . who . . . "commits a tortious act without the state causing injury to person or property within the state, . . . if he . . . expects or should reasonably expect the act to have consequences in the state and derives substantial revenue from interstate or international commerce." * * * Or, the State might simply provide, as New Jersey does, for the exercise of jurisdiction "consistent with due process of law." * * *

The modern approach to jurisdiction over corporations and other legal entities, ushered in by *International Shoe,* gave prime place to reason and fairness.

---

[5] * * * The plurality's notion that jurisdiction over foreign corporations depends upon the defendant's "submission," seems scarcely different from the long-discredited fiction of implied consent. It bears emphasis that a majority of this Court's members do not share the plurality's view.

[6] New Jersey is the fourth-largest destination for manufactured commodities imported into the United States, after California, Texas, and New York.

Is it not fair and reasonable, given the mode of trading of which this case is an example, to require the international seller to defend at the place its products cause injury?[9] Do not litigational convenience and choice-of-law considerations point in that direction? On what measure of reason and fairness can it be considered undue to require McIntyre UK to defend in New Jersey as an incident of its efforts to develop a market for its industrial machines anywhere and everywhere in the United States? Is not the burden on McIntyre UK to defend in New Jersey fair, *i.e.,* a reasonable cost of transacting business internationally, in comparison to the burden on Nicastro to go to Nottingham, England to gain recompense for an injury he sustained using McIntyre's product at his workplace in Saddle Brook, New Jersey?

McIntyre UK dealt with the United States as a single market. Like most foreign manufacturers, it was concerned not with the prospect of suit in State X as opposed to State Y, but rather with its subjection to suit anywhere in the United States. * * * If McIntyre UK is answerable in the United States at all, is it not perfectly appropriate to permit the exercise of that jurisdiction at the place of injury?

In sum, McIntyre UK, by engaging McIntyre America to promote and sell its machines in the United States, "purposefully availed itself" of the United States market nationwide, not a market in a single State or a discrete collection of States. McIntyre UK thereby availed itself of the market of all States in which its products were sold by its exclusive distributor. "Th[e] 'purposeful availment' requirement," this Court has explained, simply "ensures that a defendant will not be haled into a jurisdiction solely as a result of 'random,' 'fortuitous,' or 'attenuated' contacts." *Burger King.* Adjudicatory authority is appropriately exercised where "actions by the defendant *himself*" give rise to the affiliation with the forum. *Ibid.* How could McIntyre UK not have intended, by its actions targeting a national market, to sell products in the fourth largest destination for imports among all States of the United States and the largest scrap metal market? * * *

IV

A

While this Court has not considered in any prior case the now-prevalent pattern presented here—a foreign-country manufacturer enlisting a U.S. distributor to develop a market in the United States for the manufacturer's products—none of the Court's decisions tug against the judgment made by the New Jersey Supreme Court. McIntyre contends otherwise, citing *World-Wide Volkswagen* and *Asahi.*

* * *

The decision [in *Asahi*] was not a close call. The Court had before it a foreign plaintiff, the Taiwanese manufacturer, and a foreign defendant, the Japa-

---

[9]   The plurality objects to a jurisdictional approach "divorced from traditional practice." But "the fundamental transformation of our national economy," this Court has recognized, warrants enlargement of "the permissible scope of state jurisdiction over foreign corporations and other nonresidents." McGee v. International Life Ins. Co., 355 U.S. 220 (1957).

nese valve-assembly maker, and the indemnification dispute concerned a trans-action between those parties that occurred abroad. All agreed on the bottom line: The Japanese valve-assembly manufacturer was not reasonably brought into the California courts to litigate a dispute with another foreign party over a transaction that took place outside the United States.

Given the confines of the controversy, the dueling opinions of Justice Brennan and Justice O'Connor were hardly necessary. How the Court would have "estimate[d] . . . the inconveniences," see *International Shoe,* had the injured Californian originally sued Asahi is a debatable question. Would this Court have given the same weight to the burdens on the foreign defendant had those been counterbalanced by the burdens litigating in Japan imposed on the local California plaintiff?

In any event, Asahi, unlike McIntyre UK, did not itself seek out customers in the United States, it engaged no distributor to promote its wares here, it appeared at no tradeshows in the United States, and, of course, it had no Web site advertising its products to the world. Moreover, Asahi was a component-part manufacturer with little control over the final destination of its products once they were delivered into the stream of commerce. It was important to the Court in *Asahi* that "those who use Asahi components in their final products, and sell those products in California, [would be] subject to the application of California tort law." To hold that *Asahi* controls this case would, to put it bluntly, be dead wrong.

B

The Court's judgment also puts United States plaintiffs at a disadvantage in comparison to similarly situated complainants elsewhere in the world. Of particular note, within the European Union, in which the United Kingdom is a participant, the jurisdiction New Jersey would have exercised is not at all exceptional. The European Regulation on Jurisdiction and the Recognition and Enforcement of Judgments provides for the exercise of specific jurisdiction "in matters relating to tort . . . in the courts for the place where the harmful event occurred." Council Reg. 44/2001, Art. 5, 2001 O.J. (L.12) 4. The European Court of Justice has interpreted this prescription to authorize jurisdiction either where the harmful act occurred or at the place of injury. See Handelskwekerij G.J. Bier B.V. v. Mines de Potasse d'Alsace S. A., 1976 E.C.R. 1735, 1748–1749.

* * *

For the reasons stated, I would hold McIntyre UK answerable in New Jersey for the harm Nicastro suffered at his workplace in that State using McIntyre UK's shearing machine. While I dissent from the Court's judgment, I take heart that the plurality opinion does not speak for the Court, for that opinion would take a giant step away from the "notions of fair play and substantial justice" underlying *International Shoe.*

NOTES AND QUESTIONS FOR DISCUSSION

1.   One might have supposed that the Court would take and resolve a case that would clear up the uncertainty generated by *Asahi.* What is the point of taking a case such as *Nicastro*, or—having taken the case and come to an impasse—going ahead and deciding it? Are litigants any better off now than they were after *Asahi*, a quarter century earlier? Do any of the *Asahi* formulations of the stream-of-commerce analysis have continuing force?

2. Justice Kennedy's plurality opinion arguably echoes Justice O'Connor's in *Asahi* in demanding something more than placement of a product in the stream of commerce with awareness of its ultimate destination. But what is one to make of his repeated reference to sovereignty concerns and his suggestion that the jurisdictional focus should be on the defendant's "submission" to state power? Are these, as Justice Ginsberg suggests in her dissent, a return to pre-*International Shoe* ways of thinking? Justice Ginsburg, by contrast, seems to focus on the contacts of McIntyre UK with the U.S. as a whole, rather than with a specific state, at least when it has dealt with a U.S. distributor and sells to any willing buyer in any of the states. Does her approach make more sense than the plurality's, at least when dealing with a foreign manufacturer like McIntyre UK? The concurring opinion of Justices Breyer and Alito is the narrower of the two opinions upholding jurisdiction, and is thus pivotal. "When a fragmented Court decides a case and no single rationale explaining the result enjoys the assent of five Justices, the holding of the Court may be viewed as that position taken by those Members who concurred in the judgments on the narrowest grounds . . . ." Marks v. United States, 430 U.S. 188, 993 (1977) (internal quotation omitted). But what precisely is the nature of their criticism of the plurality's opinion that this case does not involve "modern-day consequences"? For early commentary on *Nicastro*, see the collection of articles (mostly critical) by various authors in the Symposium, *Personal Jurisdiction for the Twenty-First Century: The Implications of* McIntyre *and* Goodyear Dunlop Tires, 63 S.C. L. Rev. 463-766 (2011).

3. *Nicastro,* like *Asahi,* involved an example of "specific jurisdiction"—where the purposefully directed activities of the defendant give rise to, or are sufficiently related to, the plaintiff's claim for relief. Given the variety of opinions generated by the two cases, how predictable will the minimum contacts inquiry now be, especially from the perspective of international actors? Note that because the concurring opinion would purport to leave matters as they were, and because theirs is arguably the controlling opinion, see Note 2, some courts have simply reverted to their post-*Asahi* precedents regarding personal jurisdiction. See, e.g., *In re* Chinese Manufactured Drywall Products Liability Litigation, 2012 U.S. Dist. LEXIS 124903 (E.D. La. Sept. 4, 2012) (reverting to controlling pre-*Nicastro* circuit court precedent).

Commercial actors—particularly international actors—want to be able to predict where they will have to defend litigation and are presumably willing to shape their behavior to achieve such predictability. At one level, there is uncertainty over the applicable state long-arm statute insofar as different states have approached the question of jurisdiction over nonresident defendants differently. And as *Asahi* and *Nicastro* show, there is also uncertainty at the constitutional level given the imprecision with which the minimum contacts inquiry has been stated and applied.

The uncertainty surrounding minimum contacts, however, is compounded still further by the considerably greater uncertainty regarding the reasonableness or fairness calculus—although the fairness inquiry tends to aid, not hurt nonresidents. See Kevin M. Clermont, *Jurisdictional Salvation and the Hague Treaty*, 85 Cornell L. Rev. 89, 105-106 (1999). (And note that the minimum contacts analysis in *Nicastro* does not appear to take account of the defendants' foreignness, unlike the reasonableness analysis applied in *Asahi*.) To be sure, fairness issues were not paramount in *Nicastro*, presumably because a majority found minimum contacts to be absent. On the other hand, Justice Ginsberg—who found minimum contacts—did not separately analyze the fairness factors, although (the absence of) fairness concerns are mentioned in the course of her dissent. Nevertheless, fairness issues and the uncertainty that surrounds them remain particularly significant in light of international comity concerns, since it remains unclear how such comity concerns ought to "count" in the fairness analysis. Much of the confusion undoubtedly resulted from the statement in *Asahi* that "Great care and reserve should be exercised when extending our notions of personal jurisdiction into the international field." *Asahi*, 480 U.S. at 115. Given the absence of any real guidance beyond *Asahi* on the reasonableness inquiry, however, lower courts will continue to wrestle with such language.

4.   As discussed at length in the materials at Section G, below, and as noted by Justice Ginsburg in her *Nicastro* dissent, the approach to personal jurisdiction of most European countries, and reflected in conventions and in regulations of the European Union, tends to be much more categorical than it is in the U.S. As such, it is thought to provide greater certainty and predictability regarding where suit can be brought than does the combination of long arm statutes and due process. The place of the injury, for example, is a standard basis for jurisdiction in the E.U. When you read those materials, consider whether the more categorical approach is also the more certain one. And consider as well Justice Ginsburg's suggestion that plaintiffs in the U.S. are disadvantaged compared to plaintiffs in Europe. Is the jurisdictional disadvantage for U.S. parties (if there is one) a more difficult burden than the substantive disadvantage that foreign defendants might face in the U.S.?

5.   Note finally that, unless the Supreme Court makes fundamental changes in its approach to due process, or abandons the enterprise altogether in the personal jurisdiction setting, some uncertainty seems inevitable even in the domestic (all-U.S.) setting. Is there any argument that Congress (or the Court) should alter the current approach to jurisdiction over foreign defendants, but perhaps not domestic defendants? See Silberman, 63 S.C. L. Rev. at 592, 604-06 (suggesting that a national contacts focus might be appropriate for exercises of specific jurisdiction). If the U.S. should be able to agree with other nations as to acceptable bases of jurisdiction, uncertainty could at least be reduced at the transnational level. Such a treaty would be binding on state and federal courts alike and would impact not just the resolution of jurisdictional questions in the first instance, but would provide a basis for recognition and enforcement of judgments that satisfied the treaty requirements.

Wien Air Alaska, Inc. v. Brandt

United States Court of Appeals, Fifth Circuit, 1999.
195 F.3d 208.

Higginbotham, Circuit Judge.

In this diversity case, we consider whether a foreign defendant's contacts with Texas are sufficient to confer personal jurisdiction under the Due Process Clause. Because we find sufficient minimum contacts exist and the assertion of jurisdiction would not be unfair or unreasonable, we Reverse the district court's dismissal and Remand for further proceedings consistent with this opinion.

I

Wien Air Alaska, Inc. (Wien Air) is an Alaskan corporation based in Texas, whose sole shareholder is Thor Tjontveit. Gerald I. Brandt is a citizen of the Federal Republic of Germany who provided his services as an attorney for Wien Air from approximately August 1989 to April 1991. Brandt originally visited Texas in 1989 to help Tjontveit acquire Wien Air, then conducted most of his business with Wien Air through foreign meetings, correspondence and communications to Texas, and a final set of meetings in Texas in April 1991.

Wien Air was in the business of leasing U.S. aircraft and planned to expand into Eastern Europe. Brandt helped Wien Air develop this plan. On September 29, 1990, Wien Air authorized Brandt to form two German companies to maintain airport facilities in Germany. Late that year, Wien Air learned that Brandt's law partner, Hubertus Kestler, represented another airline company, GAC Trans-Air Carrier Lease GmbH Flugzeugleasing (GAC) and its sole shareholder Stephan Grzimek. Kestler was developing a plan for GAC that competed with Wien Air's plans.

Brandt told Wien Air that he represented only Wien Air's interests and suggested that Wien Air might be able to purchase GAC because of GAC's financial problems, provided Wien Air sold GAC some airplanes first. Tjontveit proposed to buy GAC and Brandt told Tjontveit on January 3, 1991 that GAC would accept Tjontveit's offer if Tjontveit would pay $ 1.3 million earnest money to Brandt, toward the full price of 5 million deutsche marks (DM). Acceptances of this offer were exchanged during February and March 1991.

At the same time, Brandt arranged for Wien Air to purchase a 25% stake in Flugservice Berlin (FSB), a company owned by the former East German Airlines. On February 25, 1991, in Germany, a document was prepared, signed, and notarized, which supposedly created a new company, Neue Flugservice und Development Berlin GmbH (NFSB), as a holding company for the FSB purchase. Stock in NFSB was never turned over to Wien Air. Only in October of 1993 was it discovered by Ms. Long, an employee of Wien Air, that Brandt owned the FSB stock himself and had acquired the interest March 1, 1991.

Tjontveit met Brandt in Germany on March 11, 1991 to close Wien Air's purchase of GAC and Wien Air's sale of aircraft to GAC, but GAC stock was not delivered and the transaction did not close. Brandt's law partner Kestler, however, allegedly withdrew DM 5 million from Wien Air's bank in Germany that day without Tjontveit's knowledge or permission, using a power of attorney given to Kestler by Wien Air at Brandt's request.

Brandt prepared a new document, confirming the GAC deal, signed by GAC, notarized by Ms. Long, which set a new closing date for the sale: March 26, 1991. Later, Brandt would tell Wien Air that this document was unenforceable under German law because it was not notarized by a German notary. At that time, Brandt told Tjontveit to go to Iceland on March 25, 1991 to close the GAC transaction. Tjontveit went there, but neither Brandt nor GAC appeared. Brandt called and said closing would occur instead in mid-April 1991. On March 28, 1991 and April 2, 1991, Brandt wrote Tjontveit in Texas promising that all transactions would be completed as intended.

On April 6, 1991, Tjontveit terminated Brandt's services for himself and Wien Air, and on April 10, 1991, Tjontveit told Brandt that Wien Air had retained another lawyer as counsel and warned Brandt not to transfer or vote shares of FSB. Tjontveit then asked Brandt to return Wien Air's power of attorney and to take no further actions until instructed. Tjontveit stated, however, that he was not terminating Brandt as an attorney, but wanted to continue the relation once the GAC situation was resolved.

The GAC deal did not close on April 15, 1991. The next day, Brandt called Tjontveit in Texas to again promise that the GAC deal would close. Brandt said he would come to Texas to close all outstanding matters on April 21 and 22, 1991.

Meetings in Texas on April 21 and 22 occurred with both Brandt and Tjontveit present. At these meetings, Brandt stated the following: (1) Brandt would complete the German registration process for the two Wien Air subsidiaries; (2) FSB stock belonged to Wien Air, but Brandt held it in trust for Wien Air; (3) Brandt would return all of Wien Air's documents and all valuable personal property of Tjontveit; (4) Brandt would go back to Germany and determine the status of FSB and report back to Wien Air; and (5) Brandt was still acting as Wien Air's attorney.

Brandt did not disclose that he had appropriated the interest in FSB to himself or explain what had happened to the DM 5 million Kestler had taken. Brandt then demanded DM 1.3 million for past services. Wien Air agreed to pay this based on the above promises and representations, signing a document in German allowing Brandt to withdraw the money from a Wien Air account in Germany.

Finally, on May 9, 1991, in New York, Brandt announced the GAC deal would not close and GAC stock would not be delivered. He explained that the document evidencing that deal was not binding because it had not been notarized by a German notary. Brandt said he did not represent Wien Air or Tjontveit, but only represented GAC.

Wien Air brought suit in Texas state court alleging fraud, fraudulent inducement, and breach of contract and fiduciary duties. The case was removed to federal court. Brandt sought dismissal asserting lack of personal jurisdiction and forum non conveniens. The district court did not hold an evidentiary hearing but based its decisions on the affidavits and pleadings of the parties. The court granted dismissal, holding that Wien Air was unable to make a prima facie showing that the defendant had the necessary minimum contacts with Texas to support specific jurisdiction. We REVERSE the dismissal because we find that the defendant's contacts with Texas suffice to show the requisite minimum contacts and that the assertion would not be unfair or unreasonable. The issue of forum non conveniens was not raised on appeal and we do not consider it.

II

Wien Air seeks to establish jurisdiction over Brandt under the Texas long arm statute, which Texas construes to extend to the limits of due process. See Schlobohm v. Schapiro, 784 S.W.2d 355, 357 (Tex. 1990)[.] Obtaining personal jurisdiction over a non-resident of a state is constitutionally permissible if the nonresident "purposefully availed himself of the benefits and protections" of Texas by establishing "minimum contacts" with Texas such that the defendant could "reasonably anticipate[] being haled into court in the forum state" and the exercise of jurisdiction does not offend "traditional notions of fair play and substantial justice." Holt Oil & Gas Corp. v. Harvey, 801 F.2d 773, 777 (5th Cir. 1987); Wilson v. Belin, 20 F.3d 644, 647 (5th Cir. 1994).

At issue is whether Brandt's contacts with Texas are sufficient to support an assertion of personal jurisdiction. Because the district court did not hold an evidentiary hearing on the issue of jurisdiction, Wien Air need only establish a prima facie case. See *Wilson*, 20 F.3d at 648. Where the facts are not in dispute, the review of the district court's determination of personal jurisdiction is de novo. Id. at 647-48. Where facts are disputed, the plaintiff presenting a prima facie case is entitled to have the conflicts resolved in his favor. See Felch v. Transportes Lar-Mex SA De CV, 92 F.3d 320, 327 (5th Cir. 1996). The district court concluded that while Brandt "had contact with Wien Air in Texas on several occasions, those contacts related to and developed out of an ongoing relationship between the parties established in Germany and do not establish that Brandt purposefully availed himself of the benefits and protections of Texas law." Even if the parties formed their relationship in Germany, however, a single act by Brandt directed toward Texas that gives rise to a cause of action by Wien Air can support a finding of minimum contacts. See Calder v. Jones, 465 U.S. 783 (1984); Ruston Gas Turbines, Inc. v. Donaldson Co., 9 F.3d 415, 419 (5th Cir. 1993).

In *Calder* minimum contacts were found when a journalist wrote a defamatory article in Florida which he knew would affect the plaintiff's reputation in California. The Court specifically found that the defendant had "expressly aimed" the tort at California. 465 U.S. at 789. The defendants in *Calder* analogized themselves to a welder who works on a boiler in Florida which later explodes in California. The defendants argued that jurisdiction over the welder would not be proper (even if allowable over the manufacturer) because the welder did not control where the manufacturer sold the boiler and the welder "derived no direct benefit" from such distant sales. Id. The Court rejected this analogy based on the fact that the defendants were charged with intentional, tortious conduct directed toward the forum state. In those circumstances, the defendants must "'reasonably anticipate being haled into court there' to answer for the truth of the statements made in their article." Id. at 790, 789-90.

This test applies outside the context of defamation, see Allred v. Peterson, 117 F.3d 278, 286-287 (5th Cir. 1997), although it has been remarked that the effects of defamation are more obviously felt in a foreign forum than the effects of other intentional torts. Id. at 287 (citing Wallace v. Herron, 778 F.2d 391, 395 (7th Cir. 1985)). The foreseeable effects of a tort "are to be assessed as *part* of the analysis of the defendant's relevant contacts with the forum." Id. (quoting *Wallace*, 778 F.2d at 395 (emphasis added)). Foreseeable injury alone is not sufficient to confer specific jurisdiction, absent the direction of specific acts toward the forum. See, e.g., Jobe v. ATR Marketing, Inc., 87 F.3d 751, 753-54 (5th Cir. 1996); Southmark Corp. v. Life Investors, Inc., 851 F.2d 763 (5th Cir. 1988).

According to the plaintiff's allegations, however, Brandt performed several tortious actions outside of Texas directed towards Wien Air in Texas. These actions had foreseeable effects in the forum and were directed at the forum. These contacts take the form of letters, faxes, and phone calls to Texas by Brandt whose contents contained fraudulent misrepresentations and promises and whose contents failed to disclose material information.

For example, Wien Air provides a sworn affidavit from its employee Ms. Long stating that numerous calls, letters and faxes were made by Brandt to Wien Air in Texas, and she avers that these calls contained the promises, assurances, and representations that are at the heart of the lawsuit. In her words, "Mr. Brandt told me by phone to Texas that the delivery of the GAC stock would occur on March 11, 1991." She also stated that

> [t]here were several times between late 1990 and late 1991 when Mr. Brandt called me either at my home in Texas or at the office in Texas, regarding these transactions. He called many times between late February, 1991 through April, 1991 and reassured me that a deal had been consummated, that the GAC would be delivered to Wien Air, and that the aircraft purchases would all close.

Brandt also performed services through these communications. For example, Long states that Brandt sent by fax a copy of a Notary Act he prepared, notarized by Kestler, which supposedly "constituted acceptance of an offer Mr. Tjontveit had made to buy 100 percent of the GAC stock from Mr. Grzimek" according to Brandt.

Another example provided by Wien Air is a letter sent from Brandt to Texas, dated April 2, 1991, in which Brandt states, with respect to the GAC deal: "You know, I'm always helping you where I can. Also in this special matter, we will find a solution, which will satisfy you. This I promised you." In another letter to Texas, dated March 28, 1991, Brandt states: "Mr. Grzimek couldn't reach you by phone and so he begged me to confirm, that all pending contracts between you and Wien Air Alaska and him and GAC are valid and will be fulfilled by him and GAC, when both parties fulfill their obligations."

Brandt disputes the number and content of the communications between Brandt and Wien Air in Texas. Brandt claims, for example, that there were few or no calls, and even if there were any, there is no evidence that their content related to or gave rise to any cause of action. At this stage, however, any conflict between the plaintiff and defendant with respect to the content and existence of these communications must be construed in favor of Wien Air. As such, the prima facie evidence indicates that Brandt directed affirmative misrepresentations and omissions to the plaintiff in Texas.

The defendant argues that communications directed into a forum standing alone are insufficient to support a finding of minimum contacts. See, e.g., Holt Oil & Gas Corp. v. Harvey, 801 F.2d 773, 778 (5th Cir. 1987); * * * Nationwide Mutual Ins. v. Tryg International Ins., 91 F.3d 790, 796 (6th Cir. 1996); Reynolds v. International Amateur Athletic Fed., 23 F.3d 1110, 1116 (6th Cir. 1994); FDIC v. Malmo, 939 F.2d 535 (8th Cir. 1991); Austad Co. v. Pennie & Edmonds, 823 F.2d 223 (8th Cir. 1987). Cf. Allred v. Moore & Peterson, 117 F.3d 278 (5th Cir. 1997) (service of process on plaintiff in forum insufficient to support personal jurisdiction in abuse of prosecution claim).

In all of these cases, however, the communications with the forum did not actually give rise to a cause of action. Instead, the communications merely solicited business from the forum, negotiated a contract, formed an initial attorney-client relationship, or involved services not alleged to form the basis of the complaint. These cases are thus distinguishable from the present case. When the actual content of communications with a forum gives rise to intentional tort causes of action, this alone constitutes purposeful availment. The defendant is purposefully availing himself of "the privilege of causing a consequence" in Texas. Cf. Serras v. First Tennessee Bank National Ass'n., 875 F.2d 1212 (6th Cir. 1989). It is of no use to say that the plaintiff "fortuitously" resided in Texas. See *Holt Oil*, 801 F.2d at 778. If this argument were valid in the tort context, the defendant could mail a bomb to a person in Texas but claim Texas had no jurisdiction because it was fortuitous that the victim's zip code was in Texas. It may have been fortuitous, but the tortious nature of the directed activity constitutes purposeful availment.

Of course, when a lawyer chooses to represent a client in another forum, that in itself does not confer personal jurisdiction if the claim does not arise from the lawyer's contacts with the forum. See *Austad*, 823 F.2d at 226. However, when the claim arises from a breach of fiduciary duty based on a failure to disclose material information, the fact that the lawyer continually communicated with the forum while steadfastly failing to disclose material information shows the purposeful direction of material omissions to the forum state. Cf. Diamond Mortgage Corp. v. Sugar, 913 F.2d 1233 (7th Cir. 1990). In *Diamond Mortgage*, attorneys failed to disclose conflicts of interests at the time in which they rendered some of their services within the state of Illinois, which the Seventh Circuit found sufficient for "arising under" jurisdiction under a state long-arm statute. Id. at 1245-46. The court also found the assertion of jurisdiction was constitutional under the Due Process Clause. See id. at 1247. The services were performed not only by visits to the forum, but also by letters and phone calls. Furthermore, the court noted that "the precise number of physical visits to Illinois * * * may be irrelevant," because "'it is an inescapable fact of modern commercial life that a substantial amount of business is transacted solely by mail and wire communications across state lines, thus obviating the need for physical presence within a State in which business is conducted.'" Id. (quoting *Burger King*) * * *. Cf. *Serras*, 875 F.2d at 1218 (rejecting in dictum as "feeble" the defendant's argument that "if it had a duty to disclose * * * , that duty could have been performed anywhere so that any failure to perform shouldn't be held to establish a Michigan contact," at least when the plaintiff had also alleged affirmative acts of misrepresentation in Michigan).

In addition to the communications Brandt directed into Texas from outside of Texas, Brandt also visited Texas during 1989 at which time he allegedly gained from Tjontveit the confidential information he would later use against Wien Air. He also met with Wien Air during April of 1991. During the April meeting, Brandt allegedly made misrepresentations regarding his continuing legal representation of Wien Air. Brandt, however, claims he was no longer Wien Air's attorney during this time period (and thus under no duties) because his services as company attorney were terminated on April 6, 1991, as pleaded in Wien Air's complaint.

Even if Brandt's services were terminated on April 6, 1991, the evidence shows that on April 10, Tjontveit stated that he was not halting Brandt's services except with respect to the GAC dispute. His letter to Brandt dated April 10 reads: "I want to make it clear that I am not discharging you as my attorney and I wish to continue our relationship as attorney and client." It continues to say "if we can settle the GAC dispute satisfactorily to both of us it is my wish that I can revoke this letter and we can reestablish our relationship as we did before this dispute arose."

Furthermore, at the April 22, 1991 meeting, Brandt demanded payment for past legal services for dates up to and including the meeting dates, indicating a continuing attorney relationship with Wien Air. Brandt also allegedly promised that he was still functioning as Wien Air's attorney at that meeting in Texas and also promised to complete legal work for Wien Air that he supposedly had already started. This also indicates that an attorney client relationship continued to exist.

An attorney-client relationship can be limited without canceling it, and even a terminated relationship can be resumed. Construing the facts most favorably to the plaintiff, this is what appears to have occurred. Furthermore, by virtue of his alleged misrepresentations, Brandt induced the plaintiff to sign a document allowing Brandt to withdraw nearly $ 1 million from a trust account in Germany. Brandt also failed to disclose information regarding the GAC deal, insofar as Brandt allegedly no longer represented Wien Air's interests.

According to the evidence, Wien Air relied to its detriment on such misrepresentations and omissions when it authorized Brandt to take even more of Wien Air's money with the hope that finally the GAC deal would close. Brandt claims that no material fraud or misrepresentations could have occurred at the April, 1991 meetings in Texas because all relevant contracts had already been entered into. Thus, none of his representations could have been relied upon in relation to the contracts, since they already were formed.

This does little to combat the claims of breach of contract with respect to fiduciary duty, however. Furthermore, the evidence shows that the GAC deal had not closed as of April 22, 1991. Given Brandt's assertion that the GAC contract was invalid, it does not behoove him to argue that it was already entered into. Construing the situation most favorably to the plaintiff, the parties appeared to have been continually modifying a deal whose terms had yet to become final until the April meetings. The fact that the defendant's partner may have already converted the entire purchase price of DM 5 million does not mean that Wien Air did not detrimentally rely on the defendant's representations in Texas in April: Wien Air authorized Brandt to receive an additional DM 1.3 million in order to close the GAC deal. Then, during the next month, Wien Air went to New York in hopes of closing this deal, only to be thwarted again. All of this shows detrimental reliance.

This case is most similar to Carteret Savings Bank, F.A. v. Shushan, 954 F.2d 141 (3rd Cir. 1992). *Carteret Savings* concerned misrepresentation and breach of fiduciary duty claims. Minimum contacts were found when the defendant directed letters and phone calls to the forum and then went to the forum for a final meeting in which he failed to advise his client of material facts regarding conflicts of interest. Id. at 149. Similar to the present case, the meeting in *Carteret Savings* was a meeting regarding a business transaction prior to the closing of the deal. Id. at 146, 149. Not only did the court in *Carteret Savings* find minimum contacts, but the court also found it insignificant that the defendant might have come to the forum at the request of the plaintiff or that the defendant might not have initially solicited the plaintiff's business. Id. 150. We likewise find irrelevant such allegations by the defendant. For all of these reasons, we find that Wien Air has established a prima facie case of minimum contacts over Brandt with respect to its claims for fraud, fraudulent inducement, breach of contract and breach of fiduciary duty.

Once a plaintiff has established minimum contacts, the burden shifts to the defendant to show the assertion of jurisdiction would be unfair. See Akro Corp. v. Luker, 45 F.3d 1541, 1547 (Fed. Cir. 1995). To show that an exercise of jurisdiction is unreasonable once minimum contacts are established, the defendant must make a "compelling case" against it. Burger King Corp v. Rudzewicz, 471 U.S. 462 (1985). It is rare to say the assertion is unfair after minimum contacts have been shown. *Akro*, 45 F.3d at 1549. The standards to be used are the "traditional notions of fair play and substantial justice." *Felch*, 92 F.3d at 323 (quoting *Wilson*, 20 F.3d at 647; Asahi Metal Indus. Co. v. Superior Court, 480 U.S. 102 (1987)). The interests to balance in this determination are the burden on the defendant having to litigate in the forum; the forum state's interests in the lawsuit; the plaintiff's interests in convenient and effective relief; the judicial system's interest in efficient resolution of controversies; and the state's shared interest in furthering fundamental social policies. See Ruston Gas Turbines, Inc. v. Donaldson Company, Inc., 9 F.3d 415, 421 (5th Cir. 1993).

If a cause of action for fraud committed against a resident of the forum is directly related to the tortious activities that give rise to personal jurisdiction, an exercise of jurisdiction likely comports with the due process clause, given the obvious interests of the plaintiff and the forum state. See, e.g., D.J. Investments, Inc. v. Metzeler Motorcycle Tire Agent Gregg, 754 F.2d 542 (5th Cir. 1985).

Brandt claims the assertion would be unfair and unreasonable because he is a German citizen, most of the witnesses are in Germany, the courts in the U.S. would not be able to subpoena the German witnesses, German law applies to all of the issues, the judicial system's interest in efficiency would dictate Germany should resolve this dispute, and Texas has no interest in the case. Wien Air's prima facie evidence disputes many of these assertions, especially the issue of where most of the witnesses reside and whether they would be available to testify.

Admittedly, litigation in the U.S. would place a burden on the defendant. However, once minimum contacts are established, the interests of the forum and the plaintiff justify even large burdens on the defendant. See *Asahi*, 480 U.S. at 115. Moreover, Texas clearly has an interest because the dispute involves a corporation whose principal place of business is in Texas, and the corporation allegedly was defrauded. This distinguishes *Asahi*, in which no California parties remained in the lawsuit by the time the issue of personal jurisdiction in California arose. See id. at 114.

Resolving the conflicts in a light most favorable to the plaintiff, we find no overwhelming burden to the defendant that outweighs the legitimate interests of the plaintiff and the forum state. At most Brandt demonstrates an inconvenience which would be equally felt by forcing the plaintiff to litigate in Germany. For all of these reasons, we hold that the assertion of jurisdiction over the defendant is fair and reasonable.

Reversed and Remanded.

NOTES AND QUESTIONS FOR DISCUSSION

1. The court in *Brandt* places a lot of emphasis on the fact that the plaintiff had alleged various *intentional* torts whose effects were aimed at the relevant jurisdiction. As such, it was able to take advantage of the "effects" test associated with defamation cases such as Calder v. Jones, 465 U.S. 783 (1984), where the Supreme Court focused on the defendant's intent to cause the plaintiff to suffer injury in a particular forum, even though other contacts with the forum were sparse. As summarized by the court in Harris Rutsky & Co. Ins. Servs., Inc. v. Bell & Clements Ltd., 328 F.3d 1122, 1131 (9th Cir. 2003): "[T]he purposeful availment test may also be satisfied if the defendant intentionally directed his [London-based] activities into the forum state. The 'effects' test—derived from [*Calder*]—may be satisfied if the defendant is alleged to have (1) committed an intentional act; (2) expressly aimed at the forum state; (3) causing harm, the brunt of which is suffered—and which the defendant knows is likely to be suffered—in the forum state." Was it necessary for the *Brandt* court to rely on *Calder* to find personal jurisdiction? Cf. Burger King Corp. v. Rudzewicz, 471 U.S. 462 (1985) (upholding jurisdiction over franchisee in franchise termination suit brought in franchisor's home state, even though most of the franchisee's business contacts were with the franchisor's local office in the franchisee's home state).

2. In **YAHOO! INC. v. LA LIGUE CONTRE LE RACISME ET L'ANTI-SEMITISME, 433 F.3d 1199 (9th Cir. 2006) (en banc),** a majority of judges on the Ninth Circuit concluded that California had personal jurisdiction, based largely on *Calder*, over French human rights groups that had obtained an injunction from a French court against a California-based internet service provider. La

Ligue [LICRA] and a like-minded group sought to prohibit Yahoo! from allowing internet access in France to Nazi memorabilia. The defendants' contacts with California were described as follows: "sending a cease and desist letter to Yahoo! at its headquarters in Santa Clara, California; serving process on Yahoo! in Santa Clara to commence the French suit; obtaining two interim orders from the French court; and serving the two orders on Yahoo! in Santa Clara." Id. at 1205. The majority discounted the letter and service of process as grounds for personal jurisdiction, but it found the legal relief sought in France more significant:

> The first * * * requirements are that [defendants] "have '(1) committed an intentional act, [which was] (2) expressly aimed at the forum state[.]'" * * * It is obvious that both requirements are satisfied. LICRA intentionally filed suit in the French court. Indeed, it had previously signaled its intent to file suit in its April 5 letter to Yahoo!. * * * Further, [defendant's] suit was expressly aimed at California. The suit sought, and the French court granted, orders directing Yahoo! to perform significant acts in California. It is of course true that the effect desired by the French court would be felt in France, but that does not change the fact that significant acts were to be performed in California. The servers that support Yahoo.com are located in California, and compliance with the French court's orders necessarily would require Yahoo! to make some changes to those servers. Further, to the extent that any financial penalty might be imposed pursuant to the French court's orders, the impact of that penalty would be felt by Yahoo! at its corporate headquarters in California.

> The [other] requirement is that [defendant's] acts "'cause harm that the defendant knows is likely to be suffered in the forum state.'" [citation omitted.] This requirement is somewhat problematic, for Yahoo! has not shown or even alleged any specific way in which it has altered its behavior in response to the French court's interim orders. Yahoo! changed its policy with respect to Yahoo.com after the French court's orders were entered, but Yahoo! has consistently maintained that the change was unrelated to the orders. Therefore, even if we were persuaded that Yahoo!'s change of policy harmed it in some way, Yahoo! itself has represented that such harm was not caused by any action of [defendant's]. Nor is it clear that, absent the interim orders, Yahoo! would change its policy in the future. Indeed, Yahoo! represented to us during oral argument that there is nothing that it would like to do, but is now refraining from doing, because of the interim orders.

> Yahoo!, however, points to the possibility that a substantial penalty will be assessed under the French court's November 20 interim order. It points in particular to the provision in that order specifying that the potential amount of the penalty increases by 100,000 Francs for every day that Yahoo! is in violation of the court's orders. Yahoo! represents to us that even now, after its change of policy, it is acting in plain violation of the orders. It contends that a declaratory judgment determining the enforceability by an American court of the French court's orders will allow it to determine an appropriate course of conduct with respect to the ac-

tivities in which it continues to engage. The district court found that, notwithstanding its new policy,

> the Yahoo.com auction site still offers certain items for sale (such as stamps, coins, and a copy of *Mein Kampf*) which *appear* to violate the French Order. While Yahoo! has removed the *Protocol of the Elders of Zion* from its auction site, it has not prevented access to numerous other sites which reasonably "may be construed as constituting an apology for Nazism or a contesting of Nazi crimes."

169 F. Supp. 2d at 1185 (emphasis added).

In both this court and the district court, [defendants] have represented that, in their view, Yahoo! is in what they call "substantial compliance" with the French court's orders. They have further represented that they will not seek enforcement of the penalty provision if Yahoo! continues its present level of compliance with the orders. However, [defendants] have stopped short of making a binding contractual commitment that they will not enforce the orders, and they have taken no action to have the orders withdrawn. As their counsel made clear at oral argument, [defendants] want to be able to return to the French court for enforcement if Yahoo! returns to its "old ways." For its part, while Yahoo! does not independently wish to take steps to comply more fully with the French court's orders, it states that it fears that it may be subject to a substantial (and increasing) fine if it does not. Yahoo! maintains that in these circumstances it has a legally cognizable interest in knowing whether the French court's orders are enforceable in this country.

In a specific jurisdiction inquiry, we consider the extent of the defendant's contacts with the forum and the degree to which the plaintiff's suit is related to those contacts. A strong showing on one axis will permit a lesser showing on the other. A single forum state contact can support jurisdiction if "the cause of action . . . arise[s] out of that particular purposeful contact of the defendant with the forum state." *See Lake v. Lake*, 817 F.2d 1416, 1421 (9th Cir. 1987). The case before us is the classic polar case for specific jurisdiction described in *International Shoe*, in which there are very few contacts but in which those few contacts are directly related to the suit. *See Int'l Shoe,* 326 U.S. at 318 ("Some single or occasional acts of the corporate agent in a state . . . because of their nature and quality and the circumstances of their commission, may be deemed sufficient to render the corporation liable to suit."). All of the contacts with the forum state in this case are either the interim orders themselves or contacts directly related to those orders.

[Defendants] have not sought enforcement of the French court's orders in this country, and they have stated that they will not seek enforcement or penalties so long as Yahoo! continues its current course of conduct. However, [defendants] have not sought to vacate the French court's orders, and it is at least possible that they might later seek enforcement based on a continuation of Yahoo!'s current conduct. Or more likely, they might seek enforcement if Yahoo! changes it conduct in the future. But even if [defendants] seek enforcement at some time in the future, and even if the French court finds a violation that warrants the imposition of a penalty, enforcement of that penalty is extremely unlikely in the United States. Enforcement is unlikely not because of the First Amendment, but rather because of the general principle of comity under which American courts do not enforce monetary fines or penalties awarded by foreign courts.

Finally, Yahoo! contends that it has a legally protected interest, based on the First Amendment, in continuing its current policy with respect to Nazi memorabilia and Holocaust-related anti-Semitic materials. Until that contention is endorsed by the judgment of an American court, it is only a contention. But even if the French court's orders are not enforced against Yahoo!, the very existence of those orders may be thought to cast a shadow on the legality of Yahoo!'s current policy.

It is a close question whether [defendants] are subject to personal jurisdiction in California in this suit. But considering the direct relationship between [defendants] contacts with the forum and the substance of the suit brought by Yahoo!, as well as the impact and potential impact of the French court's orders on Yahoo!, we hold that there is personal jurisdiction.

433 F.3d at 1209-11.

The court also noted that the "brunt" of the harmful affects did not need to have been felt in California, so long as "a jurisdictionally sufficient amount of harm is suffered" in-state. Although a majority of the judges of the en banc appeals court voted to uphold personal jurisdiction, a minority of judges thought that the case was not yet ripe given the uncertainty regarding future enforcement of any possible judgment. But that minority of judges, together with certain other judges—also in a minority on the personal jurisdiction question and who thought personal jurisdiction was lacking—formed a majority in favor of dismissal of the case.

3. Note that some states have expressly enabled their courts to reach foreign defamation judgment creditors as part of their long-arm statutes. New York's statute reads as follows:

N.Y. C.P.L.R. § 302(d). Foreign defamation judgment.

The courts of this state shall have personal jurisdiction over any person who obtains a judgment in a defamation proceeding outside the United States against any person who is a resident of New York or is a person or entity amenable to jurisdiction in New York who has assets in New York or may have to take actions in New York to comply with the judgment, for the purposes of rendering declaratory relief with respect to that person's liability for the judgment, and/or for the purpose of determining whether said judgment should be deemed non-recognizable pursuant to [§ 5304] of this chapter, to the fullest extent permitted by the United States constitution, provided:

1. the publication at issue was published in New York, and

> 2. that resident or person amenable to jurisdiction in New York (i) has assets in New York which might be used to satisfy the foreign defamation judgment, or (ii) may have to take actions in New York to comply with the foreign defamation judgment. * * *

The provision was designed to overrule the result in Ehrenfeld v. Mafouz, 518 F.3d 102 (2d Cir. 2008) (dismissing declaratory action to prohibit enforcement of foreign judgment for lack of personal jurisdiction over foreign defendant). Note that N.Y.C.P.L.R. § 5304 (referenced in § 302(d)) provides that a foreign libel or defamation judgment is unenforceable if it was rendered in a court system that provides fewer free speech protections to defendants than those under the U.S. or New York constitutions.

4. In addition, and as further discussed in Chapter 8, Congress has recently provided by statute for federal court declaratory judgment actions when a foreign defamation or libel judgment against a U.S. party fails to comply with relevant federal and state constitutional standards, as elsewhere set out in the statute. See 28 U.S.C. §§ 4101, et seq. (The SPEECH Act of 2010). Among other things, the statute purports to provide for a kind of nationwide jurisdiction in such declaratory actions over the defamation judgment plaintiff (as the declaratory judgment defendant):

> "Nationwide Service of Process—Where an action under this section is brought in a district court of the United States, process may be served in the judicial district where the case is brought or any other judicial district of the United States where the [declaratory] defendant may be found, resides, has an agent, or transacts business."

Id. at § 4104(b).

5. The cases discussed so far have focused on transnational claims arising under tort law. International contractual dealings may often involve a nonresident party's reaching out to a party in the U.S. to conduct business with it, thus making it possible to argue for specific jurisdiction in connection with litigation arising out of those purposeful commercial activities. Can a single *contract* between a resident of a state and a nonresident party be a sufficient *contact* to give the courts of the resident's state jurisdiction over the nonresident in the resident's suit for breach of contract? The Court in *Burger King, supra,* stated that:

> If the question is whether an individual's contract with an out of state party *alone* can automatically establish sufficient minimum contacts in the other party's home forum, we believe the answer is that it cannot. * * * [A] "contract" is "ordinarily but an intermediate step serving to tie up prior business negotiations with future consequences which themselves are the real objects of the business transaction." [Hoopeston Canning Co. v. Cullen, 318 U.S. 313, 316-17 (1943).] It is these factors— prior negotiations and contemplated future consequences, along with the terms of the contract and the parties' actual course of dealing—that must be evaluated in determining whether the defendant purposefully established minimum contacts within the forum.

Burger King, 471 U.S. at 478-79 (emphasis in original).

Yet even a single contract may be sufficient for jurisdictional purposes, at least when the contractual relationship is or has become an ongoing one. In McGee v. International Life Ins. Co., 355 U.S. 220 (1957), a purely domestic case, the Court upheld California's jurisdiction over an out of state insurance company based on single policy when the contract was delivered in California, premiums were mailed from there and the policy holder was resident of California. *McGee* stated, "it was sufficient for purposes of due process that the suit was based on a contract which had a substantial connection with that State."

6. In Mid-America Tablewares, Inc. v. Mogi Trading Co., Ltd., 100 F.3d 1353 (7th Cir. 1996), a Wisconsin business (Mid-America) sued Mogi, a Japanese corporation whose business was to source contracts for (i.e., arrange for the manufacture of) dinnerware manufactured in Japan. Plaintiff sued for breach of warranty after it was determined by the U.S. Food and Drug Administration (FDA) that the dinnerware obtained by Mogi for the plaintiff exceeded regulatory levels regarding lead content. Initially, it was the Mid-America who reached out to Mogi who then recommended use of a Japanese manufacturer and indicated that one of its personnel would visit Mid-America in the states, which he did. Shipment was made by Mogi to Mid-America in Wisconsin. Various communications were exchanged between the parties regarding the quantity, shipping and delivery plans for the dinnerware. Mogi also represented that the lead levels of the dinnerware would comply with U.S. guidelines.

> Mogi's contacts with Wisconsin can hardly be said to be random, fortuitous, or attenuated. First, it is undisputed that Mogi directed a number of faxes to Hemmerich [a Mid-American official] in Wisconsin. Mogi's faxes contained not only recommendations about sourcing the dinnerware and information about price, quantity, and shipping, but also specific representations and assurances about the quality of the dinnerware (most notably Mogi's representation that the dinnerware would comply with federal lead standards). Additionally, the record reveals that during this period of initial discussions, Mogi sent various sample products directly to Mid-America in Eau Claire [Wisconsin] via Federal Express or airmail for Hemmerich's inspection and approval. * * *

> The foregoing facts clearly establish that Mogi purposefully directed its efforts toward Mid-America in connection with the Harvest Festival dinnerware transaction. * * * The fact that Mogi engaged in this conduct through mail and telecommunications from abroad does not detract from the appropriateness of exercising personal jurisdiction over Mogi. "It is an inescapable fact of modern commercial life that a substantial amount of business is transacted solely by mail and wire communications across state lines, thus obviating the need for physical presence within a State in which business is conducted. So long as a commercial actor's efforts are 'purposefully directed' toward residents of another State, we have consistently rejected the notion that an absence of physical contacts can defeat personal jurisdiction there." *Burger King*, 471 U.S. at 476. * * * As this Court has repeatedly recognized, "a defendant's participation in substantial negotiations conducted in the forum state leading to the contract at issue is a significant basis for personal jurisdiction." Nucor Corp.

v. Aceros y Maquilas de Occidente, S.A. de C.V., 28 F.3d 572, 581 (7th Cir. 1994)[.] * * *

Mid-America, 100 F.3d at 1360-61.

The Seventh Circuit also found the exercise of jurisdiction reasonable, focusing particularly on the state's interest in resolving a breach of contract case premised on "the shipment of goods posing a serious health hazard in the State." See also, e.g., Afram Export Corp. v. Metallurgiki Halyps, S.A., 772 F.2d 1358 (7th Cir. 1985) (upholding jurisdiction in a breach of contract action against a Greek steelmaker who negotiated to purchase scrap metal from in-state seller via telephone and telex, and who sent an agent to inspect scrap prior to shipment who then refused shipment).

7.   In both contract and tort settings, questions often arise regarding when, if ever, a foreign parent company can be subject to personal jurisdiction in a state for actions (within the state) of a local subsidiary, perhaps even a wholly owned subsidiary. The converse question sometimes arises as well: When, if ever, will a U.S. parent be liable for actions (outside of the U.S.) of its foreign subsidiary? Traditionally, American courts have been prepared to respect corporate formalities, and absent a showing that the subsidiary is the "alter ego" of the parent, or that the parent or subsidiary is acting as the local agent of the other, a parent corporation will not be subject to the jurisdiction of a state simply because its subsidiary would be, nor vice-versa. See Restatement (Second) of Conflict of Laws § 52 (1971); cf. Hargrave v. Fibreboard Corp., 710 F.2d 1154, 1159 (5th Cir. 1983) (stating parent can be subject to jurisdiction when the "parent corporation exerts such domination and control over its subsidiary 'that they do not in reality constitute separate and distinct corporate entities'").

Justice Brandeis gave the Court's perspective in the pre-*International Shoe* decision of **CANNON MFG. CO. v. CUDAHY PACKING CO., 267 U.S. 333 (1925).** There, even though the nonresident parent wholly owned the subsidiary, and even though it "exert[ed] its control both commercially and financially in substantially the same way, and mainly though the same individuals, as it does over those selling branches or departments of its business not separately incorporated," the corporate forum was honored. Id. at 335. Its books were kept separate, formalities were observed, and the Court refused to impute the acts of the in-state subsidiary to the nonresident parent.

> The question is * * * whether the corporate separation carefully maintained must be ignored in determining the existence of jurisdiction. The defendant wanted to have business transactions with persons resident in North Carolina, but, for reasons satisfactory to itself, did not choose to enter the state in its corporate capacity. It might have conducted such business through an independent agency without subjecting itself to the jurisdiction. *Bank of America v. Whitney Central National Bank,* 261 U. S. 171. It preferred to employ a subsidiary corporation. Congress has not provided that a corporation of one state shall be amenable to suit in the federal court for another state in which the plaintiff resides whenever it employs a subsidiary corporation as the instrumentality for doing business therein. *Compare Lumiere v. Mae Edna Wilder,*

> *Inc.,* 261 U. S. 174, 177-178. That such use of a subsidiary does not necessarily subject the parent corporation to the jurisdiction was settled by *Conley v. Mathieson Alkali Works,* 190 U. S. 406, 409-411, *Peterson v. Chicago, Rock Island & Pacific Ry. Co.,* 205 U. S. 364, and *People's Tobacco Co., Ltd. v. American Tobacco Co.,* 246 U. S. 79, 246 U.S. 87. In the case at bar, the identity of interest may have been more complete and the exercise of control over the subsidiary more intimate, than in the three cases cited, but that fact has, in the absence of an applicable statute, no legal significance. The corporate separation, though perhaps merely formal, was real. It was not pure fiction. There is here no attempt to hold the defendant liable for an act or omission of its subsidiary, or to enforce as against the latter a liability of the defendant.

Id. at 336-37.

How should corporate independence be measured? And by whose law? One might suppose that the jurisdictional inquiry should be the same as the inquiry for purposes of liability—i.e., the corporate veil should be pierced for jurisdictional purposes only when it could be pierced for liability purposes as well. But unless the jurisdictional inquiry was provisionally easier to satisfy, the merits might never be reached. Has the *Cannon* standard been further relaxed now that the *degree* of control (see *Hargrave, supra*) may be relevant in the liability context even when corporate formalities have been scrupulously observed? Scholars appear to take different views on the subject. Compare, e.g., Lea Brilmayer & Kathleen Paisley, *Personal Jurisdiction and Substantive Legal Relations: Corporations, Conspiracies, and Agency*, 74 Cal. L. Rev. 1, 3 (1986) (indicating that *Cannon* has been undermined by subsequent lower court developments), with John A. Swain & Edwin E. Aguilar, *Piercing the Veil to Assert Personal Jurisdiction over Corporate Affiliates: An Empirical Study of the* Cannon *Doctrine*, 84 B.U. L. Rev. 445 (2004) (finding reports of *Cannon*'s demise to be premature). *Cannon* notwithstanding, *should* courts be more willing to scrutinize the question of corporate independence when dealing with foreign parents of foreign subsidiaries? We consider the question in somewhat greater detail in the section that follows.

C. GENERAL JURISDICTION

Consider the possibility that a plaintiff might attempt to assert jurisdiction based on a foreign defendant's contacts with a state, but when it cannot be readily argued that the contacts in question were ones that gave rise to the lawsuit. When there is little or no nexus between the contacts and the underlying litigation, consider what sort of showing the plaintiff should have to make as a precondition to the successful assertion of jurisdiction. Must they be pervasive—in the way that a resident of a state could be said to have pervasive contacts with it, or a corporation in its principal place of business? Or could a lesser showing suffice?

Goodyear Dunlop Tires Operations, S.A. v. Brown

Supreme Court of the United States, 2011.

131 S.Ct. 2846.

JUSTICE GINSBURG delivered the opinion of the Court.

This case concerns the jurisdiction of state courts over corporations organized and operating abroad. We address, in particular, this question: Are foreign subsidiaries of a United States parent corporation amenable to suit in state court on claims unrelated to any activity of the subsidiaries in the forum State?

A bus accident outside Paris that took the lives of two 13–year–old boys from North Carolina gave rise to the litigation we here consider. Attributing the accident to a defective tire manufactured in Turkey at the plant of a foreign subsidiary of The Goodyear Tire and Rubber Company (Goodyear USA), the boys' parents commenced an action for damages in a North Carolina state court; they named as defendants Goodyear USA, an Ohio corporation, and three of its subsidiaries, organized and operating, respectively, in Turkey, France, and Luxembourg. Goodyear USA, which had plants in North Carolina and regularly engaged in commercial activity there, did not contest the North Carolina court's jurisdiction over it; Goodyear USA's foreign subsidiaries, however, maintained that North Carolina lacked adjudicatory authority over them.

A state court's assertion of jurisdiction exposes defendants to the State's coercive power, and is therefore subject to review for compatibility with the Fourteenth Amendment's Due Process Clause. International Shoe Co. v. Washington, 326 U.S. 310 (1945) (assertion of jurisdiction over out-of-state corporation must comply with "traditional notions of fair play and substantial justice"). Opinions in the wake of the pathmarking *International Shoe* decision have differentiated between general or all-purpose jurisdiction, and specific or case-linked jurisdiction. Helicopteros Nacionales de Colombia, S.A. v. Hall, 466 U.S. 408, 414 nn. 8-9 (1984).

A court may assert general jurisdiction over foreign (sister-state or foreign-country) corporations to hear any and all claims against them when their affiliations with the State are so "continuous and systematic" as to render them essentially at home in the forum State. See *International Shoe*. Specific jurisdiction, on the other hand, depends on an affiliation between the forum and the underlying controversy, principally, activity or an occurrence that takes place in the forum State and is therefore subject to the State's regulation. In contrast to general, all-purpose jurisdiction, specific jurisdiction is confined to adjudication of issues deriving from, or connected with, the very controversy that establishes jurisdiction

Because the episode-in-suit, the bus accident, occurred in France, and the tire alleged to have caused the accident was manufactured and sold abroad, North Carolina courts lacked specific jurisdiction to adjudicate the controversy. The North Carolina Court of Appeals so acknowledged. Were the foreign subsidiaries nonetheless amenable to general jurisdiction in North Carolina courts? Confusing or blending general and specific jurisdictional inquiries, the North Carolina courts answered yes. Some of the tires made abroad by Goodyear's foreign subsidiaries, the North Carolina Court of Appeals stressed, had reached North Carolina through the stream of commerce; that connection, the Court of Appeals believed, gave North Carolina courts the handle needed for the exercise of general jurisdiction over the foreign corporations.

A connection so limited between the forum and the foreign corporation, we hold, is an inadequate basis for the exercise of general jurisdiction. Such a connection does not establish the "continuous and systematic" affiliation necessary to empower North Carolina courts to entertain claims unrelated to the foreign corporation's contacts with the State.

I

* * *

Goodyear Luxembourg Tires, SA (Goodyear Luxembourg), Goodyear Lastikleri T.A.S. (Goodyear Turkey), and Goodyear Dunlop Tires France, SA (Goodyear France), petitioners here, were named as defendants. Incorporated in Luxembourg, Turkey, and France, respectively, petitioners are indirect subsidiaries of Goodyear USA, an Ohio corporation also named as a defendant in the suit. Petitioners manufacture tires primarily for sale in European and Asian markets. Their tires differ in size and construction from tires ordinarily sold in the United States. They are designed to carry significantly heavier loads, and to serve under road conditions and speed limits in the manufacturers' primary markets.

In contrast to the parent company, Goodyear USA, which does not contest the North Carolina courts' personal jurisdiction over it, petitioners are not registered to do business in North Carolina. They have no place of business, employees, or bank accounts in North Carolina. They do not design, manufacture, or advertise their products in North Carolina. And they do not solicit business in North Carolina or themselves sell or ship tires to North Carolina customers. Even so, a small percentage of petitioners' tires (tens of thousands out of tens of millions manufactured between 2004 and 2007) were distributed within North Carolina by other Goodyear USA affiliates. These tires were typically custom ordered to equip specialized vehicles such as cement mixers, waste haulers, and boat and horse trailers. Petitioners state, and respondents do not here deny, that the type of tire involved in the accident, a Goodyear Regional RHS tire manufactured by Goodyear Turkey, was never distributed in North Carolina.

Petitioners moved to dismiss the claims against them for want of personal jurisdiction. The trial court denied the motion, and the North Carolina Court of Appeals affirmed. Acknowledging that the claims neither related to, nor arose from, petitioners' contacts with North Carolina, the Court of Appeals confined its analysis to "general rather than specific jurisdiction," which the court recognized required a "higher threshold" showing: A defendant must have "continuous and systematic contacts" with the forum. That threshold was crossed, the court determined, when petitioners placed their tires "in the stream of interstate commerce without any limitation on the extent to which those tires could be sold in North Carolina."

Nothing in the record, the court observed, indicated that petitioners "took any affirmative action to cause tires which they had manufactured to be shipped into North Carolina." The court found, however, that tires made by petitioners reached North Carolina as a consequence of a "highly-organized distribution process" involving other Goodyear USA subsidiaries. Petitioners, the court noted, made no attempt to keep these tires from reaching the North Carolina market. Indeed, the very tire involved in the accident, the court observed, conformed to tire standards established by the U.S. Department of Transportation and bore markings required for sale in the United States.[1] As further support, the court invoked North Carolina's interest in providing a forum in which its citizens are able to seek redress for their injuries, and noted the hardship North Carolina plaintiffs would experience were they required to litigate their claims in France, a country to which they have no ties. The North Carolina Supreme Court denied discretionary review.

We granted certiorari to decide whether the general jurisdiction the North Carolina courts asserted over petitioners is consistent with the Due Process Clause of the Fourteenth Amendment.

II

A

The Due Process Clause of the Fourteenth Amendment sets the outer boundaries of a state tribunal's authority to proceed against a defendant. Shaffer v. Heitner, 433 U.S. 186, 207 (1977). The canonical opinion in this area remains *International Shoe*, in which we held that a State may authorize its courts to exercise personal jurisdiction over an out-of-state defendant if the defendant has "certain minimum contacts with [the State] such that the maintenance of the suit does not offend 'traditional notions of fair play and substantial justice.'"

Endeavoring to give specific content to the "fair play and substantial justice" concept, the Court in International Shoe classified cases involving out-of-state corporate defendants. First, as in *International Shoe* itself, jurisdiction unquestionably could be asserted where the corporation's in-state activity is continuous and systematic and that activity gave rise to the episode-in-suit. Further, the Court observed, the commission of certain "single or occasional acts" in a State may be sufficient to render a corporation answerable in that State with respect to those acts, though not with respect to matters unrelated to the forum connections. The heading courts today use to encompass these two *International Shoe* categories is "specific jurisdiction." Adjudicatory authority is "specific" when the suit "aris[es] out of or relate[s] to the defendant's contacts with the forum." *Helicopteros*.

International Shoe distinguished from cases that fit within the "specific jurisdiction" categories, "instances in which the continuous corporate operations within a state [are] so substantial and of such a nature as to justify suit against it on causes of action arising from dealings entirely distinct from those activities." Adjudicatory authority so grounded is today called "general jurisdiction." *Heli-*

---

[1] Such markings do not necessarily show that any of the tires were destined for sale in the United States. To facilitate trade, the Solicitor General explained, the United States encourages other countries to treat compliance with Department of Transportation standards, including through use of DOT markings, as evidence that the products are safely manufactured.

copteros. For an individual, the paradigm forum for the exercise of general jurisdiction is the individual's domicile; for a corporation, it is an equivalent place, one in which the corporation is fairly regarded as at home.

Since *International Shoe*, this Court's decisions have elaborated primarily on circumstances that warrant the exercise of specific jurisdiction, particularly in cases involving "single or occasional acts" occurring or having their impact within the forum State. As a rule in these cases, this Court has inquired whether there was "some act by which the defendant purposefully avail[ed] itself of the privilege of conducting activities within the forum State, thus invoking the benefits and protections of its laws." Hanson v. Denckla, 357 U.S. 235, 253 (1958). See, e.g., World-Wide Volkswagen Corp. v. Woodson, 444 U.S. 286, 287 (1980) (Oklahoma court may not exercise personal jurisdiction "over a nonresident automobile retailer and its wholesale distributor in a products-liability action, when the defendants' only connection with Oklahoma is the fact that an automobile sold in New York to New York residents became involved in an accident in Oklahoma"); Burger King Corp. v. Rudzewicz, 471 U.S. 462, 474-75 (1985) (franchisor headquartered in Florida may maintain breach-of-contract action in Florida against Michigan franchisees, where agreement contemplated on-going interactions between franchisees and franchisor's headquarters); Asahi Metal Industry Co. v. Superior Court of Cal., 480 U.S. 102, 105 (1987) (Taiwanese tire manufacturer settled product liability action brought in California and sought indemnification there from Japanese valve assembly manufacturer; Japanese company's "mere awareness . . . that the components it manufactured, sold, and delivered outside the United States would reach the forum State in the stream of commerce" held insufficient to permit California court's adjudication of Taiwanese company's cross-complaint) (opinion of O'CONNOR, J.).

In only two decisions postdating *International Shoe*, has this Court considered whether an out-of-state corporate defendant's in-state contacts were sufficiently "continuous and systematic" to justify the exercise of general jurisdiction over claims unrelated to those contacts: Perkins v. Benguet Consol. Mining Co., 342 U.S. 437 (1952) (general jurisdiction appropriately exercised over Philippine corporation sued in Ohio, where the company's affairs were overseen during World War II); and *Helicopteros* (helicopter owned by Colombian corporation crashed in Peru; survivors of U.S. citizens who died in the crash, the Court held, could not maintain wrongful-death actions against the Colombian corporation in Texas, for the corporation's helicopter purchases and purchase-linked activity in Texas were insufficient to subject it to Texas court's general jurisdiction).

B

To justify the exercise of general jurisdiction over petitioners, the North Carolina courts relied on the petitioners' placement of their tires in the stream of commerce. The stream-of-commerce metaphor has been invoked frequently in lower court decisions permitting jurisdiction in products liability cases in which the product has traveled through an extensive chain of distribution before reaching the ultimate consumer. Typically, in such cases, a nonresident defendant, acting outside the forum, places in the stream of commerce a product that ultimately causes harm inside the forum.

Many States have enacted long-arm statutes authorizing courts to exercise specific jurisdiction over manufacturers when the events in suit, or some of them, occurred within the forum state. For example, the "Local Injury; Foreign Act" subsection of North Carolina's long-arm statute authorizes North Carolina courts to exercise personal jurisdiction in "any action claiming injury to person or property within this State arising out of [the defendant's] act or omission outside this State," if, "in addition, at or about the time of the injury, products manufactured by the defendant were used or consumed, within this State in the ordinary course of trade." As the North Carolina Court of Appeals recognized, this provision of the State's long-arm statute "does not apply to this case," for both the act alleged to have caused injury (the fabrication of the allegedly defective tire) and its impact (the accident) occurred outside the forum.[4]

The North Carolina court's stream-of-commerce analysis elided the essential difference between case-specific and all-purpose (general) jurisdiction. Flow of a manufacturer's products into the forum, we have explained, may bolster an affiliation germane to specific jurisdiction. See, e.g., *World-Wide Volkswagen* (where "the sale of a product . . . is not simply an isolated occurrence, but arises from the efforts of the manufacturer or distributor to serve . . . the market for its product in [several] States, it is not unreasonable to subject it to suit in one of those States if its allegedly defective merchandise *has there been the source of injury to its owner or to others*") (emphasis added). But ties serving to bolster the exercise of specific jurisdiction do not warrant a determination that, based on those ties, the forum has general jurisdiction over a defendant.

A corporation's "continuous activity of some sorts within a state," *International Shoe* instructed, "is not enough to support the demand that the corporation be amenable to suits unrelated to that activity." Our 1952 decision in *Perkins v. Benguet* remains "[t]he textbook case of general jurisdiction appropriately exercised over a foreign corporation that has not consented to suit in the forum."

Sued in Ohio, the defendant in Perkins was a Philippine mining corporation that had ceased activities in the Philippines during World War II. To the extent that the company was conducting any business during and immediately after the Japanese occupation of the Philippines, it was doing so in Ohio: the corporation's president maintained his office there, kept the company files in that office, and supervised from the Ohio office the necessarily limited wartime activities of the company. Although the claim-in-suit did not arise in Ohio, this Court ruled that it would not violate due process for Ohio to adjudicate the controversy.

We next addressed the exercise of general jurisdiction over an out-of-state corporation over three decades later, in *Helicopteros*. In that case, survivors of United States citizens who died in a helicopter crash in Peru instituted wrongful-death actions in a Texas state court against the owner and operator of the heli-

---

[4] The court instead relied on N.C. Gen.Stat. Ann. § 1–75.4(1)(d), which provides for jurisdiction "whether the claim arises within or without [the] State," when the defendant "[i]s engaged in substantial activity within this State, whether such activity is wholly interstate, intrastate, or otherwise." This provision, the North Carolina Supreme Court has held, was "intended to make available to the North Carolina courts the full jurisdictional powers permissible under federal due process." Dillon v. Numismatic Funding Corp., 291 N.C. 674, 676, 231 S.E.2d 629, 630 (1977).

copter, a Colombian corporation. The Colombian corporation had no place of business in Texas and was not licensed to do business there. "Basically, [the company's] contacts with Texas consisted of sending its chief executive officer to Houston for a contract-negotiation session; accepting into its New York bank account checks drawn on a Houston bank; purchasing helicopters, equipment, and training services from [a Texas enterprise] for substantial sums; and sending personnel to [Texas] for training." [*Id.*] These links to Texas, we determined, did not "constitute the kind of continuous and systematic general business contacts . . . found to exist in *Perkins*," and were insufficient to support the exercise of jurisdiction over a claim that neither "arose out of nor related to" the defendant's activities in Texas.

Helicopteros concluded that "mere purchases [made in the forum State], even if occurring at regular intervals, are not enough to warrant a State's assertion of [general] jurisdiction over a nonresident corporation in a cause of action not related to those purchase transactions." We see no reason to differentiate from the ties to Texas held insufficient in *Helicopteros*, the sales of petitioners' tires sporadically made in North Carolina through intermediaries. Under the sprawling view of general jurisdiction urged by respondents and embraced by the North Carolina Court of Appeals, any substantial manufacturer or seller of goods would be amenable to suit, on any claim for relief, wherever its products are distributed. But cf. *World-Wide Volkswagen* (every seller of chattels does not, by virtue of the sale, "appoint the chattel his agent for service of process").

Measured against *Helicopteros* and *Perkins*, North Carolina is not a forum in which it would be permissible to subject petitioners to general jurisdiction. Unlike the defendant in *Perkins*, whose sole wartime business activity was conducted in Ohio, petitioners are in no sense at home in North Carolina. Their attenuated connections to the State fall far short of the "the continuous and systematic general business contacts" necessary to empower North Carolina to entertain suit against them on claims unrelated to anything that connects them to the State. *Helicopteros*.[5]

Respondents belatedly assert a "single enterprise" theory, asking us to consolidate petitioners' ties to North Carolina with those of Goodyear USA and other Goodyear entities. In effect, respondents would have us pierce Goodyear corporate veils, at least for jurisdictional purposes. Neither below nor in their brief in opposition to the petition for certiorari did respondents urge disregard of petitioners' discrete status as subsidiaries and treatment of all Goodyear entities as a "unitary business," so that jurisdiction over the parent would draw in the subsidiaries as well.[6] Respondents have therefore forfeited this contention, and we do

---

[5]   * * * [T]he North Carolina Court of Appeals invoked the State's "well-recognized interest in providing a forum in which its citizens are able to seek redress for injuries that they have sustained." But general jurisdiction to adjudicate has in United States practice never been based on the plaintiff's relationship to the forum. There is nothing in our law comparable to article 14 of the Civil Code of France (1804) under which the French nationality of the plaintiff is a sufficient ground for jurisdiction. When a defendant's act outside the forum causes injury in the forum, by contrast, a plaintiff's residence in the forum may strengthen the case for the exercise of specific jurisdiction. See Calder v. Jones, 465 U.S. 783 (1984).

[6] In the brief they filed in the North Carolina Court of Appeals, respondents stated that petitioners

not address it. [Reversed.]

NOTES AND QUESTIONS FOR DISCUSSION

1.   Does the *Goodyear* opinion suggest that only those corporations that are either incorporated in, or have their principal place of business in, the forum state, will be sufficiently "at home" to be subject to general jurisdiction? See Allan R. Stein, *The Meaning of "Essentially at Home" in* Goodyear Dunlop, 63 S.C. L. Rev. 527, 531-32 (2012) (stating that this is "the clear implication" of the decision). Note that Justice Kennedy's *Nicastro* plurality appears to reads *Goodyear* in a similar manner, stating that a corporation's state of incorporation and principal place of business "indicates general submission to [that] State's powers." If that is a fair reading of *Goodyear*, then when—if ever—will it be possible to secure general jurisdiction in the U.S. over a foreign corporation?

2.   The classic example of an exercise of general jurisdiction in reference to an individual would be a suit brought in defendant's domicile. In the individual context, domicile is established by physical presence coupled with the intent to remain for the indefinite future. See Restatement (Second) of Conflict of Laws §§ 11-20 (1971). As the Court once stated, "Domicile in the state is alone sufficient to bring an absent defendant within the reach of the state's jurisdiction for purposes of a personal judgment[.]" Milliken v. Meyer, 311 U.S. 457, 462 (1940) (upholding jurisdiction over domiciliary of forum state, even though defendant was served outside of state). See also Mary Twitchell, *The Myth of General Jurisdiction*, 101 Harv. L. Rev. 610, 667-70 (1988).

3.   In the corporate context, general jurisdiction might be premised on the corporation's principal place of business or its headquarters, or its place(s) of incorporation. In Perkins v. Benguet Mining, 342 U.S. 437 (1952) (discussed in *Goodyear*), Ohio had all but become the wartime domicile of a Philippine corporation. It is hardly unfair that a defendant should be suable in its own corporate backyard, even if the events giving rise to the lawsuit may have occurred elsewhere. By contrast, simple registration to do business in a state should, by itself, be insufficient. See, e.g., Washington Equip. Mfg. Co. v. Concrete Placing Co., 931 P.2d 170 (Wash. Ct. App. 1997); see also Ratliff v. Cooper Labs., Inc. 444 F.2d 745, 748 (4th Cir.), cert. denied, 404 U.S. 948 (1971) (stating that being qualified to do business in a state is "of no special weight" in determining general personal jurisdiction over a corporation). In addition, constitutional problems might attend a state's insistence as a condition of doing business that an agent for service of process be appointed for anything other than lawsuits arising from in-state-related activities. See Bendix Autolite Corp. v. Midwesco Enterprises, 486 U.S. 888 (1988) (striking down, on dormant commerce clause grounds, state statute that required corporation's submission to general jurisdic-

---

were part of an "integrated world-wide efforts to design, manufacture, market and sell their tires in the United States, including in North Carolina." Read in context, that assertion was offered in support of a narrower proposition: The distribution of petitioners' tires in North Carolina, respondents maintained, demonstrated petitioners' own "calculated and deliberate efforts to take advantage of the North Carolina market." As already explained, even regularly occurring sales of a product in a State do not justify the exercise of jurisdiction over a claim unrelated to those sales.

tion of state as precondition to securing benefits of a local statute of limitations and avoid tolling). By use of the "at home" metaphor, has the *Goodyear* Court substituted for the older notion of "presence," a notion of domicile? See Steven B. Burbank, *International Civil Litigation in U.S. Courts: Becoming a Paper Tiger?* 33 U. Pa. J. Int'l L. 663, 670 (2012). Should anything *less* than a showing akin to that of an individual's domicile suffice for corporate general jurisdiction, given the far-ranging consequences associated with it? See "Note on 'Doing Business' as a Basis for General Jurisdiction," below.

4. *Goodyear* relied heavily on the Court's prior decision in the area of general jurisdiction in **HELICOPTEROS NACIONALES DE COLUMBIA, S.A. v. HALL, 466, U.S. 408 (1984).** In *Helicopteros*, suit was brought in Texas state courts by a widow suing for the wrongful death of her husband who died in a helicopter crash in Peru. At the time of his death, the decedent (a U.S. national) was working on the construction of a pipeline in South America. She sued three defendants. (1) Bell Helicopters, a Ft. Worth, Texas based corporation that made the helicopter that crashed and that trained the pilots; (2) WSH, the joint venture consisting of Texas citizens, that was doing the work on the pipeline; and (3) Helicol (Helicopteros Nacionales de Columbia), a Columbian corporation that provided the pilots and air taxi service for the project.

Plaintiff won a million dollar verdict against Helicol whose jurisdictional objections were rejected by the Texas courts, and Helicol appealed to the U.S. Supreme Court. Curiously, the plaintiff argued only that Helicol's contacts with Texas were sufficiently great that it could be sued there even if the claim did *not* arise out of or relate to Helicol's activities in Texas. Although the *Helicopteros* Court and the *Goodyear* Court both minimized Helicol's contacts with Texas, they were hardly inconsiderable.

- Helicol had purchased substantially all of its helicopter fleet in Ft. Worth, Texas.
- Helicol did a total of approximately $4,000,000 worth of business in Ft. Worth continuously from 1970 through 1976 as a purchaser not only of the helicopters, but of equipment parts and services (i.e., approximately $50,000/month over a seven year period).
- Helicol's CEO went to Houtston, Texas to negotiate with WSH, which resulted in the contract to provide helicopter service in question. In that contract, Helicol agreed to obtain liability insurance payable in U.S> dollars to cover a claim such as this.
- Helicol sent pilots to Fort Worth during the 1970-76 period to pick up helicopters and fly them back to Columbia. Helicol sent maintenance personnel as well as pilots to Fort Worth to be trained, and thus had employees in Texas continuously during that same six-year period.
- Helicol recived roughly $5,000,000 from WSH for their services which payments were made from a bank in Houston and deposited to Helicol's bank in New York.

- Helicol also directed a Houston Bank to make payments to Rocky Mountain Helicopters to lease a large helicopter capable of moving heavier loads for WSH.

The Supreme Court was unimpressed with the plaintiff's showing. It characterized the contacts as follows:

> * * * Basically, Helicol's contacts with Texas consisted of sending its chief executive officer to Houston for a contract-negotiation session, accepting into its New York bank account checks drawn on a Houston bank, purchasing helicopters, equipment, and training services from Bell Helicopter for substantial sums, and sending personnel to Bell's facilities in Fort Worth for training.
>
> The one trip to Houston by Helicol's chief executive officer for the purpose of negotiating the transportation-services contract with Consorcio/WSH cannot be described or regarded as a contact of a "continuous and systematic" nature, as *Perkins* described it, and thus cannot support an assertion of in personam jurisdiction over Helicol by a Texas court. Similarly, Helicol's acceptance from Consorcio/WSH of checks drawn on a Texas bank is of negligible significance for purposes of determining whether Helicol had sufficient contacts in Texas. * * *
>
> The Texas Supreme Court focused on the purchases and the related training trips in finding contacts sufficient to support an assertion of jurisdiction. We do not agree with that assessment, for the Court's opinion in Rosenberg Bros. & Co. v. Curtis Brown Co., 260 U.S. 516 (1923) (Brandeis, J., for a unanimous tribunal), makes clear that purchases and related trips, standing alone, are not a sufficient basis for a State's assertion of jurisdiction. * * *
>
> In accordance with *Rosenberg*, we hold that mere purchases, even if occurring at regular intervals, are not enough to warrant a State's assertion of in personam jurisdiction over a nonresident corporation in a cause of action not related to those purchase transactions. Nor can we conclude that the fact that Helicol sent personnel into Texas for training in connection with the purchase of helicopters and equipment in that State in any way enhanced the nature of Helicol's contacts with Texas. The training was a part of the package of goods and services purchased by Helicol from Bell Helicopter. The brief presence of Helicol employees in Texas for the purpose of attending the training sessions is no more a significant contact than were the trips to New York made by the buyer for the retail store in *Rosenberg.*

Helicopteros, 466 U.S. at 416-18.

5. Is the Court's characterization of Helicol's contacts with Texas fair to the facts? And isn't *Helicopteros* a far more difficult case than *Goodyear*? Understand the consequences of a finding of general jurisdiction. If contacts such as these in *Helicopteros* were enough to allow for the exercise of general jurisdiction in Texas over Helicol, then they would be sufficient to allow for personal jurisdiction in Texas over Helicol for any lawsuit against it arising anywhere in the world over anything. Indeed, that is what *general* jurisdiction is all about.

Perhaps these dramatic consequences were what led the Court in *Goodyear* to clarify that such jurisdiction could only be upheld in a forum in which the corporation was effectively "at home."

6. The Court in *Helicopteros* proceeds on the assumption that the defendant had argued only for "general" jurisdiction over Helicol in Texas, rather than "specific" jurisdiction. Would the outcome have been different had the plaintiff argued for specific jurisdiction? Suppose that the underlying suit had been brought against Helicol by Bell Helicopters for failure to pay for aircraft delivered by Bell pursuant to their contractual agreement. Would specific jurisdiction in Texas be any easier an argument at this point? Why?

7. As discussed more fully at Section E, below, it is possible, in a case arising under federal law, for a federal district court to assert good jurisdiction over a defendant who is not subject to the jurisdiction of any particular state, provided that it would not be inconsistent with the Constitution and federal law for them to be made a defendant. See Rule 4(k)(2), Fed. R. Civ. P. This provision has been read as allowing jurisdiction where the defendant's nationwide contacts would be sufficient to satisfy due process. Would such a provision be a basis for general jurisdiction in a district court, or is its focus specific jurisdiction? Or both?

8. Could the fact that a U.S. subsidiary of a foreign parent coporation was subject to general jurisdiction in a state ever make the foreign corporation similarly subject to general jurisdiction in that state? The problem is essentially the same problem as that briefly noted in the materials on specific jurisdiction: When if ever may courts ingore the corporate form for purposes of personal jurisdiction? In **Bauman v. DaimlerChrysler Corp., 644 F.3d 909 (9th Cir. 2011)**, a panel of the Ninth Circuit concluded that Mercedez-Benz Germany (DaimlerChrysler A.G.) was subject to the general jursidiction in California where its subsidiary, Mercedes-Benz USA, would have been subject to general jurisdiction in the state. The underlying suit was brought by a number of Argentinean citizens against DaimlerChrysler for human rights abuses alleged to have been perpetrated against them by another DaimlerChrysler subsidiary (Mercedez Benz Argentina) during Argentina's "dirty war" in the 1970s and '80s. The panel noted two ways in which corporate form could be ignored for jurisdictional purposes:

> Under the controlling law, if one of two *separate* tests is satisfied, we may find the necessary contacts to support the exercise of personal jurisdiction over a foreign parent company by virtue of its relationship to a subsidiary that has continual operations in the forum. The first test, not directly at issue here, is the "alter ego" test. It is predicated upon a showing of parental *control* over the subsidiary. The two prongs of the "alter ego" test are as follows: (1) that there is such unity of interest and ownership that the separate personalities of the two entities no longer exist and (2) that failure to disregard their separate identities would result in fraud or injustice. The first prong of this test has alternately been stated as requiring a showing that the parent controls the subsidiary to such a degree as to render the latter the mere instrumentality of the former.

* * * The second test, which is applicable here, is the "agency" test. That test is predicated upon a showing of the *special importance* of the services performed by the subsidiary:

> The agency test is satisfied by a showing that the subsidiary functions as the parent corporation's representative in that it performs services that are sufficiently important to the foreign corporation that if it did not have a *representative* to perform them, the corporation's own officials would undertake to perform substantially similar services.

Doe v. Unocal Corp., 248 F.3d 915, 928 (9th Cir. 2001).

* * * For the agency test, we ask: Are the services provided by [the U.S. subsidiary] sufficiently important to [the foreign parent] that, if [the subsidiary] went out of business, [the parent] would continue selling cars in this vast market either by selling them itself, or alternatively by selling them through a new representative? We answer this question in the affirmative. In addition, this test requires the plaintiffs to show an element of control, albeit not as much control as is required to satisfy the "alter ego" test.

Bauman, 644 F.3d at 920.

Does such an approach go too far? Consider the statement of the eight judges who dissented from the denial of rehearing en banc:

> As the Supreme Court recently reaffirmed, for a foreign corporation to be subject to general jurisdiction, its contacts with the forum state must be "so continuous and systematic as to render [it] essentially at home in the forum State." [*Goodyear*] * * *

> The panel's interpretation of the agency test is far too expansive and threatens to make innumerable foreign corporations unconstitutionally subject to general personal jurisdiction in our courts. Indeed, it is difficult to see what limits there are on the panel's formulation. Anything a corporation does through an independent contractor, subsidiary, or distributor is presumably something that the corporation would do "by other means" if the independent contractor, subsidiary, or distributor did not exist.

> * * * Moreover, our court now seemingly rejects respect for corporate separateness, a well-established "principle of corporate law deeply ingrained in our economic and legal systems." *United States v. Bestfoods,* 524 U.S. 51, 61 (1998) (internal quotation marks omitted). It is "[a] basic tenet of American corporate law . . . that the corporation and its shareholders are distinct entities," over which jurisdiction must be individually established. * * * "Where two corporations are in fact separate" * * * "permitting the activities of the subsidiary to be used as a basis for personal jurisdiction over the parent violates this principle and thus due process." * * * *cf. J. McIntyre Mach., Ltd. v. Nicastro,* 131 S. Ct. 2780, 2797 (2011) (Ginsburg, J., dissenting) ("A few points on which there should be no genuine debate bear statement at the outset. . . . [A]ll agree, [the parent company] surely is not subject to general (all-

purpose) jurisdiction in New Jersey courts, for that foreign-country corporation is hardly 'at home' in New Jersey.").

* * * In sum, Daimler is hardly "at home" in California when sued only for its Argentinian subsidiary's activities in Argentina. Our court's holding represents a breathtaking expansion of general personal jurisdiction, which is unwarranted in light of Supreme Court precedent, the precedent of our sister circuits, and our own precedents. Moreover, today's decision presents a gratuitous threat to our nation's economy, foreign relations, and international comity.

Bauman v. DaimlerChrysler Corp., 676 F.3d 774, 775-79 (O'Scannlain, J., dissenting). Is there any answer to the dissenters' argument that the panel decision is inconcistent with *Goodyear*? For a thorough (pre-*Goodyear*) exploration of the problem of basing jurisdiction on the activities of corporate subsidiaries and efforts to pierce the corporate veil, see Charles S. Baldwin IV, et al., International Civil Dispute Resolution 98-130 (2d ed. 2008).

*NOTE ON "DOING BUSINESS" AS A BASIS FOR JURISDICTION
OVER FOREIGN PARTIES*

Consistent with *Goodyear*, some courts had considered the barrier against finding sufficiently pervasive contacts to satisfy general jurisdiction to be fairly high. See, e.g., Nichols v. G.D. Searle & Co., 991 F.2d 1195, 1200 (4th Cir. 1993) (cautioning against a broad construction of general jurisdiction and rejecting general jurisdiction despite almost $13 million in sales to the forum and the presence of approximately twenty employees); Amoco Egypt Oil Co. v. Leonis Nav. Co., 1 F.3d 848, 851 (9th Cir. 1993) (noting that courts have regularly refused to find general jurisdiction "even where the [defendant's] contacts were quite extensive").

However—at least prior to *Goodyear*, and notwithstanding *Helicopteros*—other courts have been inclined to base a finding of general jurisdiction on evidence of "doing business" in the forum on something more than an irregular basis. See, e.g., Lakin v. Prudential Securities, 348 F.3d 704, 705 (8th Cir. 2003) (upholding general jurisdiction when defendant had home-equity loans and credit lines with in-state residents amounting to "one percent of their total loan portfolio"); Wiwa v. Royal Dutch Petroleum Co., 226 F.3d 88, 95 (2d Cir. 2000) (upholding doing-business analysis of pre-*Helicopteros* decision of Frummer v. Hilton Hotels Int'l, Inc., 19 N.Y.2d 533, 227 N.E.2d 851 (1967) [noted below], and finding "a fair measure of permanence and continuity"); Klinghoffer v. S.N.C. Lauro Lines, 937 F.2d 44 (2d Cir. 1991) (leaving open question whether Palestine Liberation Organization (P.L.O.) was "doing business" within New York where its owned a building, a car, a phone, and had a number of permanent employees; suit was a wrongful death action brought against the P.L.O. over an alleged act of terrorism in the Mediterranean); Bryant v. Finnish Nat'l Airline, 15 N.Y.2d 426, 208 N.E.2d 439 (N.Y. 1965) (office in forum staffed with a few employees was sufficient for general jurisdiction). See also Gator.com Corp. v. v. L.L. Bean, Inc., 341 F.3d 1072 (9th Cir. 2003) (finding general jurisdiction over L.L Bean in California based on internet and other sales), *vacated as moot*, 398 F.3d 1125 (9th Cir. 2005).

A number of these expansive doing-business decisions come from the federal and state courts in New York. Those courts have read the state's long-arm statute (C.P.L.R. §301) as purporting to confer general jurisdiction over defendants with "continuous and systematic" contacts with the state, and dubs such contacts as "doing business" in the state, sufficient to subject them to jurisdiction even on claims that do not arise out of their "doing business" within the state. Although the verbal formula ("continuous and systematic") may track language in *Helicopteros* and *Goodyear*, the real question, of course, is whether the Constitution countenances the exercise of general jurisdiction over a corporation when there are contacts sufficient to satisfy the New York statute. Invocation of the phrases "doing business" or "presence" adds nothing to that inquiry, and has the potential to confuse it. (Indeed, the phrase "continuous and systematic" comes from International Shoe Co. v. Washington, 326 U.S. 310 (1945), which indicated that such contacts would support *specific* jurisdiction when the cause of action arose from such contacts—as in *International Shoe* itself. *International Shoe* stated that general jurisdiction would be available only when there were "continuous corporate operations" that were "*so* substantial and of such a nature" as to justify such jurisdiction. Id. at 318 [emphasis added].)

Perhaps the high-water mark of general jurisdiction came in *Frummer v. Hilton Hotels, Int'l, supra.* There, the New York Court of Appeals concluded that it had general jurisdiction over Hilton Hotels Ltd., a British corporation, because affiliated corporations of the U.S. parent (Hilton Hotels Int'l) performed travel agent and public relations services for Hilton U.K. in New York. "As we have frequently observed, a foreign corporation is amenable to suit in our courts if it is 'engaged in such a continuous and systematic course of "doing business" here as to warrant a finding of its "presence" in this jurisdiction.'" 19 N.Y.2d at 536. Thus, the New York courts upheld their jurisdiction to hear the plaintiff's lawsuit arising from his slip and fall in the London Hilton. But even more, the court stated "Since . . . Hilton (U.K.) was 'doing business' in New York in the traditional sense and was validly served with process in London, as provided by [state] statute, our courts acquired 'personal jurisdiction over the corporation *for any cause of action asserted against it, no matter where the events occurred which gave rise to the cause of action.*'" (emphasis supplied). See also H. Heller & Co. v. Nocacor Chemicals Ltd., 726 F. Supp. 49 (S.D.N.Y 1988) (noting that a finding of "solicitation" will often require "little more" before "doing business" will be satisfied).

A similar expression of such broad jurisdiction may be also found in Presbyterian Church of Sudan v. Talisman Energy, Inc. 244 F. Supp. 2d 289 (S.D.N.Y. 2004):

> The continuous presence and substantial activities need not be conducted by the foreign corporation itself. Indeed, personal jurisdiction may be based upon activities performed on behalf of a foreign corporation by an agent:

> Under well-established New York law, a court of New York may assert jurisdiction over a foreign corporation when it affiliates itself with a New York representative entity and that New York representative renders services on behalf of the foreign corporation that go beyond mere solicitation and are sufficiently important to the foreign entity that the corporation itself would perform equivalent services if no agent were available.

[quoting Wiwa v. Royal Dutch Petroleum Co., 226 F.3d 88, 95 (2d Cir. 2000).] In order to come within the ambit of this rule, "a plaintiff need demonstrate neither a formal agency agreement, nor that the defendant exercised direct control over its putative agent." *Id.* (internal citations omitted). However, the agent must be primarily employed by the defendant and not be engaged in similar services for other clients. * * *

244 F. Supp. 2d at 329-30.

Does the fact that U.S. affiliates perform services for a foreign company suggest anything more than that the foreign company should be subject to personal jurisdiction for claims that arise out of those services performed? The premise of the old *Frummer* decision (and its progeny, such as *Talisman Energy*) was that domestic affiliates of Hilton (U.S.) did "all the business which Hilton (U.K.) could do were it here by its own officials." So what? If Hilton (U.K.) had done those services itself, would it have been subject to *general* jurisdiction in New York, and thus suable for anything it did anywhere? Perhaps the answer would be yes, as far as the New York state courts are concerned. But are these agency-theory decisions really consistent with *Goodyear* and *Helicopteros*? Was Talisman Energy "at home" in New York? One can only suppose that *Goodyear* has clipped the wings of the "doing business" model of general jurisdiction in New York (and perhaps elsewhere), but old habits are likely to die hard. If those wings have been clipped, is that a good thing? See Meir Feder, Goodyear*, "Home," and The Uncertain Future of Doing Business Jurisdiction*, 63 S.C. L. Rev. 671, (2012) (answering in the affirmative, and noting lower courts' expansive interpretations of doing business prior to *Goodyear*).

On the subject of general jurisdiction, see also the pre-*Goodyear* articles by Lonny S. Hoffman, *The Case Against Vicarious Jurisdiction*, 152 U. Pa. L. Rev. 1023, 1091-1092 (2004) (questioning *Frummer*'s agency analysis); Mary Twitchell, *Why We Keep Doing Business with Doing-Business Jurisdiction,* 2001 U. Chi. Legal F., 171, 172; B. Glenn George, *In Search of General Jurisdiction*, 64 Tul. L. Rev. 1097 (1990); and Lea Brilmayer, *A General Look at General Jurisdiction*, 66 Tex. L. Rev. 721 (1988).

The view from abroad. Many consider the doing-business brand of general jurisdiction as exorbitant—particularly as practiced by New York courts—and it is generally rejected in most non-U.S. jurisdictions. See, e.g., Kevin M. Clermont & John R. B. Palmer, *Exorbitant Jurisdiction*, 58 Me. L. Rev. 474 (2006). In negotiations over a possible treaty or convention respecting the cross-border enforceability of judgments, most participants were prepared to place judgments in which jurisdiction has been founded on "doing business" (unless the claim was "directly related" to those business activities) on a "black list." (Black-list judgments would not be entitled to enforcement because of the questionable assertion of jurisdiction that they involve.) The U.S., however, has resisted such efforts, even though it was the U.S. that sought a "mixed convention" in the first place—i.e., a convention that would list (on a "white list") automatically acceptable bases of jurisdiction for purposes of judgment enforcement; a "black list" as described above; and a "gray list" of jurisdictional bases that would leave enforcement of judgments to the discretion of the enforcement forum. Why do you suppose the U.S. and other countries are so far apart on this question? See generally Friedrich K. Juenger, *The American Law of General Jurisdiction*, 2001 U. Chi. Legal F. 141, 161-166. Will *Goodyear* put those fears to rest, or will foreign actors (and countries) reasonably entertain doubts whether lower courts in the U.S. will heed the Supreme Court's message? Note that the *Goodyear* decision brought the U.S. closer to the grounds for general jurisdiction recognized in the E.U. See below at Section G.

D. TRANSIENT JURISDICTION

A time-honored form of acquiring general jurisdiction over a nonresident defendant in English and U.S. courts has been personal service of process on the defendant within the jurisdiction in which suit has been filed. Despite the cloud of constitutional uncertainty that may have hovered over such exercise of judicial power after the Supreme Court's decision in Shaffer v. Heitner, 433 U.S. 186 (1977)—with its admonition that "all" exercises of jurisdiction should be tested by the minimum contacts standard—it survived more or less intact in **BURNHAM v. SUPERIOR COURT, 495 U.S. 604 (1990)**. Although there were differing constitutional rationales offered in *Burnham* for the propriety of such "tag" jurisdiction, it remains an option for securing personal jurisdiction over a foreign defendant in the U.S. Unfortunately, there was no majority opinion for upholding the particular exercise of transient jurisdiction.

Justice Scalia sought to reconcile tag jurisdiction with due process by focusing on the fact that such a means of acquiring jurisdiction would have been due process at the time of the ratification of the Fourteenth Amendment in 1868.

> Among the most firmly established principles of personal jurisdiction in American tradition is that the courts of a State have jurisdiction over nonresidents who are physically present in the State. The view developed early that each State had the power to hale before its courts any individual who could be found within its borders, and that once having acquired jurisdiction over such a person by properly serving him with process, the State could retain jurisdiction to enter judgment against him, no matter how fleeting his visit. See, e. g., Potter v. Allin, 2 Root 63, 67 (Conn. 1793); Barrell v. Benjamin, 15 Mass. 354 (1819). That view had antecedents in English common-law practice, which sometimes allowed "transitory" actions, arising out of events outside the country, to be maintained against seemingly nonresident defendants who were present in England. See, e.g., Mostyn v. Fabrigas, 98 Eng. Rep. 1021 (K.B. 1774); Cartwright v. Pettus, 22 Eng. Rep. 916 (Ch. 1675).

Justice Story believed the principle, which he traced to Roman origins, to be firmly grounded in English tradition: "[B]y the common law[,] personal actions, being transitory, may be brought in any place, where the party defendant may be found," for "every nation may * * * rightfully exercise jurisdiction over all persons within its domains." J. Story, Commentaries on the Conflict of Laws 554, 543 (1846). See also id., 530-538; Picquet v. Swan, supra, at 611-612 (Story, J.) ("Where a party is within a territory, he may justly be subjected to its process, and bound personally by the judgment pronounced, on such process, against him").

Recent scholarship has suggested that English tradition was not as clear as Story thought, * * * Accurate or not, however, judging by the evidence of contemporaneous or near-contemporaneous decisions, one must conclude that Story's understanding was shared by American courts at the crucial time for present purposes: 1868, when the Fourteenth Amendment was adopted. * * *

Despite this formidable body of precedent, petitioner contends, in reliance on our decisions applying the *International Shoe* standard, that in the absence of "continuous and systematic" contacts with the forum, a nonresident defendant can be subjected to judgment only as to matters that arise out of or relate to his contacts with the forum. This argument rests on a thorough misunderstanding of our cases. * * *

Nothing in *International Shoe* or the cases that have followed it, * * * offers support for the very different proposition petitioner seeks to establish today: that a defendant's presence in the forum is not only unnecessary to validate novel, nontraditional assertions of jurisdiction, but is itself no longer sufficient to establish jurisdiction. That proposition is unfaithful to both elementary logic and the foundations of our due process jurisprudence. The distinction between what is needed to support novel procedures and what is needed to sustain traditional ones is fundamental, as we observed over a century ago:

> "[A] process of law, which is not otherwise forbidden, must be taken to be due process of law, if it can show the sanction of settled usage both in England and in this country; but it by no means follows that nothing else can be due process of law. * * * [That which], in substance, has been immemorially the actual law of the land * * * therefor[e] is due process of law. But to hold that such a characteristic is essential to due process of law, would be to deny every quality of the law but its age, and to render it incapable of progress or improvement. It would be to stamp upon our jurisprudence the unchangeableness attributed to the laws of the Medes and Persians." Hurtado v. California, 110 U.S. 516, 528-529 (1884).

The short of the matter is that jurisdiction based on physical presence alone constitutes due process because it is one of the continuing traditions of our legal system that define the due process standard of "traditional notions of fair play and substantial justice." That standard was developed by analogy to "physical presence," and it would be perverse to say it could now be turned against that touchstone of jurisdiction.

Burnham, 495 U.S. at 610-19.

Justice Brennan sought to distance himself from Justice Scalia's opinion in *Burnham*, and was not prepared to conclude, as Justice Scalia seemed to be, that tag jurisdiction would always comport with due process. Instead, he concluded that, in the circumstances of the case before the Court, the exercise of tag jurisdiction comported with the reasonableness and fundamental fairness requirements of due process as contemporarily understood.

> I agree * * * that the Due Process Clause of the Fourteenth Amendment generally permits a state court to exercise jurisdiction over a defendant if he is served with process while voluntarily present in the forum State. I do not perceive the need, however, to decide that a jurisdictional rule that "'has been immemorially the actual law of the land,'" automatically comports with due process simply by virtue of its "pedigree." Although I agree that history is an important factor in establishing whether a jurisdictional rule satisfies due process requirements, I cannot agree that it is the only factor such that all traditional rules of jurisdiction are, ipso facto, forever constitutional. Unlike JUSTICE SCALIA, I would undertake an "independent inquiry into the * * * fairness of the prevailing in-state service rule." I therefore concur only in the judgment.

> I believe that the approach adopted by JUSTICE SCALIA's opinion today—reliance solely on historical pedigree—is foreclosed by our decisions in International Shoe Co. v. Washington, 326 U.S. 310 (1945), and Shaffer v. Heitner, 433 U.S. 186 (1977). In *International Shoe*, we held that a state court's assertion of personal jurisdiction does not violate the Due Process Clause if it is consistent with "'traditional notions of fair play and substantial justice.'" 326 U.S., at 316, quoting Milliken v. Meyer, 311 U.S. 457, 463 (1940). In *Shaffer*, we stated that "*all* assertions of state-court jurisdiction must be evaluated according to the standards set forth in *International Shoe* and its progeny." 433 U.S., at 212 (emphasis added). The critical insight of *Shaffer* is that all rules of jurisdiction, even ancient ones, must satisfy contemporary notions of due process. No longer were we content to limit our jurisdictional analysis to pronouncements that "[t]he foundation of jurisdiction is physical power," McDonald v. Mabee, 243 U.S. 90, 91 (1917), and that "every State possesses exclusive jurisdiction and sovereignty over persons and property within its territory." Pennoyer v. Neff, 95 U.S. 714, 722 (1878). While acknowledging that "history must be considered as supporting the proposition that jurisdiction based solely on the presence of property satisfied[d] the demands of due process," we found that this factor could not be "decisive." 433 U.S. at 211-12. We recognized that "'[t]raditional notions of fair play and substantial justice' can be as readily offended by the perpetuation of ancient forms that are no longer justified as by the adoption of new procedures that are inconsistent with the basic values of our constitutional heritage." Id., at 212 (citations omitted).

Id. at 628-30 (Brennan, J., concurring in the judgment).

The defendant's contacts with the relevant forum in *Burnham*, however, were few and far between, consisting only of a three day visit to see his estranged family. Nevertheless, Justice Brennan was prepared to uphold—as consistent with his understanding of contemporary notions of due process—the exercise of general jurisdiction over the defendant, thus leaving open the question of whether anything less would have sufficed.

NOTES AND QUESTIONS FOR DISCUSSION

1. Within the U.S., the main contemporary issue raised by transient (or tag) jurisdiction has had to do with the use of force and coercion to lure a party into a particular jurisdiction for purposes of service. See, e.g., Voice Systems Marketing Co. v. Appropriate Technology Corp., 153 F.R.D. 117, 119-20 (E.D. Mich. 1994) (quashing service when defendant was tricked into staying within the jurisdiction for an extra day, primarily so that plaintiff's attorney could arrange for service of newly filed complaint). And, of course, there are some colorful examples of applications of transient jurisdiction. See, e.g., Amusement Equipment, Inc. v. Mordelt, 779 F.2d 264 (5th Cir. 1985) (upholding tag jurisdiction in Louisiana in a suit brought by Florida corporation against a German defendant over a contract regarding a shipment of goods from Germany to Florida; German defendant was served with process while attending convention in New Orleans); Grace v. McArthur, 170 F. Supp. 442 (E.D. Ark. 1959) (upholding service in airplane over Arkansas airspace). There is doubt, however, whether corporations, as opposed to natural persons, are amenable to tag jurisdiction at all. See Siemer v. Learjet Acquisition Corp., 966 F.2d 179 (5th Cir. 1992), cert. denied, 506 U.S. 1080 (1993) (citing relevant authorities and stating: "To assert, as plainitffs do, that mere service on a corporate agent automatically confers general jurisdiction displays a fundamental misconception of corporate jurisdictional principles.").

2. One of the primary transnational uses of transient jurisdiction in U.S. courts today is in connection with human rights litigation. See, e.g., Kadic v. Karadzic, 70 F.3d 232 (2d Cir. 1995), in which the court upheld personal service in New York on a Serbian leader who was outside the Russian Embassy while visiting the United Nations. (We address the topic of civil litigation under the Alien Tort Statute and related provisions is taken up in Chapter 2.) Because the successful invocation of "tag" jurisdiction is a form of general jurisdiction, there need not be any relationship between the defendants contacts with the state in which he is tagged and the underlying action.

3. When general jurisdiction via tag is found to exist in an American jurisdiction, it might still be possible for the defendant to have the forum changed to another forum through assertion of transfer of venue in the proper case or *forum non conveniens*. See Chapter 5. Would such largely discretionary devices take care of any fairness problems associated with the broad assertion of general jurisdiction associated with tag? Should it matter whether the forum jurisdiction rarely or never applied *forum non conveniens* principles? Note that at least one country (France) has traditionally allowed for a kind of reverse general jurisdiction based on *the plaintiff's* French domicile, no matter what relationship the lawsuit or the defendant has to France (apart from the existence of a French plaintiff). See Friedrich K. Juenger, *A Hague Judgments Convention?*, 24 Brook. J. Int'l L. 111, 115 (1998) (noting the practice but questioning its impact). Is this sort of jurisdiction any worse than transient jurisdiction sanctioned by *Burnham*?

A COMPARATIVE NOTE ON TRANSIENT JURISDICTION

Interestingly, tag jurisdiction is not well received by many countries outside the U.S., most of which do not permit it as a matter of their own law. See Joachim Zekoll, *The Role and Status of American Law in the Hague Judgments Convention Project*, 61 Alb. L. Rev. 1283, 1296-97 (1998); Russell J. Weintraub, *An Objective Basis for Rejecting Transient Jurisdiction,* 22 Rutgers L.J. 611, 613-16 (1991); see also Restatement (Third) of Foreign Relations Law of the United States §421 & Reporters' Note 5 (1987) (declaring that transitory jurisdiction "is no longer acceptable under international law if that is the only basis for jurisdiction and the action in question is unrelated to that state"). Moreover, U.S. judgments based on tag or transent jurisdiction do not travel well across borders for purposes of recognition and enforcement. See Chapter 8. What do you suppose is the basis for the hostility to this sort of exercise of jurisdiction? The general unfairness associated with the potential "surprise" nature of such assertions of jurisdiction—particularly over foreign defendants? The possible unrelatedness of the forum to the underlying dispute? Its intellectual heritage in eroded notions of "territoriality"? See Juenger, *supra* (Note 3) at 160-161 & n.130 (noting that "tag jurisdiction was among the exorbitant exercises of jurisdiction that many would place on the proverbial 'blacklist'"); Clermont & Palmer, 58 Me. L. Rev. at 480-81.

E. THE REACH OF PROCESS

When suit is brought in state courts, state long-arm statutes limit the reach of those courts, as does the Due Process Clause of the Fourteenth Amendment. In federal courts, matters could theoretically be different, insofar as the relevant jurisdiction is the entire U.S rather than any one state. Thus, for example, Congress could (hypothetically) enact a federal cause of action and provide a statute permitting jurisdiction in a federal court in any one of the states. And the constitutional limits would be those imposed by the Due Process Clause of the Fifth Amendment. Congress has enacted such statutes, for example, with respect to certain defendants in connection with Antitrust actions, 15 U.S.C. §§ 22, 25; see Go-Video, Inc. v. Akai Elec. Co., Ltd., 885 F.2d 1406 (9th Cir. 1989)); civil RICO actions, 18 U.S.C. § 1965(d); and in connection with statutory interpleader, 28 U.S.C. §§ 1335, 2361. When such a statute exists, the Rules specifically provide for its applicability. See Rule 4(k)(1)(C). But for most federal causes of action, Congress has not provided such a statute.

Absent such a provision, federal courts are ordinarily under the same restrictions as a state court would be in the state in which the federal court sits.

See Rule 4(k)(1)(A) (allowing for jurisdiction over those who are "subject to the jurisdiction of a court of general jurisdiction in the state where the district court is located"). Note that the term "general jurisdiction" in the Rule does not refer to general *personal* jurisdiction; rather it refers to general *subject matter* jurisdiciton. In short, the jurisdictional reach of a federal court, and in the absence of a federal long arm, ordinarily extends no further than that of a state court in the state (with the exception of provisions providing for a 100-mile bulge for joinder of certain additional parties under Rules 14 and 19—see Rule 4(k)(1)(B)).

In **OMNI CAPITAL INT'L, LTD. v. RUDOLFF & CO., LTD., 484 U.S. 97 (1987)**, the Supreme Court made clear that federal courts could not supply their own judge-made nationwide service rules when Congress had failed to create one. Thus, foreign defendants who lacked contacts sufficient to bring them within the reach of a given state's jurisdiction but who may have had enough contacts with the U.S. as a whole to make personal jurisdiction over them in a federal court constitutional, could effectively escape responsibility for civil violations of certain provisions of the Commodities Exchange Act that lacked its own service provision. See *Omni Capital,* 484 U.S. at 105 n.8 (quoting former Fed. R. Civ. P. 4(e) (superseded by the 1993 amendments)).

Partially in response to *Omni Capital*, Rule 4 was revised. Current Rule 4(k)(2) reads as follows:

> **4(k)(2)–Federal Claim Outside State-Court Jurisdiction.** For a claim that arises under federal law, serving a summons or filing a waiver of service establishes personal jurisdiction over a defendant if:
>
> > (A) the defendant is not subject to jurisdiction in any state's courts of general jurisdiction; and
> >
> > (B) exercising jurisdiction is consistent with the United States Constitution and laws.

As explained by the Advisory Committee comments on the orignal 1993 revision of Rule 4(k)(2) (prior to stylistic revisions in the current version):

> This paragraph corrects a gap in the enforcement of federal law. Under the former rule, a problem was presented when the defendant was a non-resident of the United States having contacts with the United States sufficient to justify the application of United States law and to satisfy federal standards of forum selection, but having insufficient contact with any single state to support jurisdiction under state long-arm legislation or meet the requirements of the Fourteenth Amendment limitation on state court territorial jurisdiction. In such cases, the defendant was shielded from the enforcement of federal law by the fortuity of a favorable limitation on the power of state courts, which was incorporated into the federal practice by the former rule. In this respect, the revision responds to the suggestion of the Supreme Court made in *Omni Capital*.
>
> The provision thus seeks to provide for personal jurisdiction in a federal court over a defendant who has sufficient contacts with the

United States as a whole but who has insufficient contacts with any one state to allow for jurisdiction in any state. Yet it is triggered only when there is a claim arising under federal law and there is no federal long-arm statute providing for personal jurisdiction that would trump the 4(k)(1) default rule of borrowing state law. When a federal long-arm statute is available, Rule 4(k)(2) is inapplicable because it is unnecessary. See also Rule 4(k)(1) (providing for jurisdiction "when authorized by a statute of the United States").

The newer provision raises a number of questions, however. For example, how does one show the lack of jurisdiction in each and every one of the states, and who has to make that showing? Is such a showing addressed only to constitutional limits, or to state statutory limits as well? Assuming such a showing can be made, how does one assess the sufficiency of national contacts (consistent with Fifth Amendment due process) in a context in which minimum contacts do *not* exist with any one state (consistent with Fourteenth Amendment due process)? Consider the operation of this provision in the case that follows. Note that this decision was rendered under the initial post-*Omni Capital* revision of Rule 4, and prior to certain stylistic alterations.

United States v. Swiss American Bank, Ltd.

United States Court of Appeals, First Circuit, 1999.

191 F.3d 30.

SELYA, CIRCUIT JUDGE.

This appeal raises issues of first impression, requiring us to delineate the circumstances under which foreign corporations may be brought before the federal courts through the medium of a recently enacted provision of the Civil Rules.

[The U.S. filed civil proceedings in a federal court in Massachusetts against certain banks for breach of contract, unjust enrichment, and conversion in connection with an effort to recover assets accumulated by a convicted felon and later forfeited by him to the government pursuant to a plea bargain. Two of the banks, Swiss American Bank, Ltd., and Swiss American National Bank (collectively referred to as "Swiss American") were institutions organized under the laws of Antigua. A third bank, IMB, was organized under Swiss law and based in Geneva, Switzerland.

The felon, John Fitzgerald, had over $7,000,000 deposited with Swiss American, which were the fruits of criminal activity. Those funds were condemned and forfeited to the U.S. pursuant to a final order of forfeiture in a Massachusetts federal criminal proceeding against Fitzgerald. Although notified of the forfeiture proceedings, Swiss American apparently disbursed $5,000,000 of the funds to Antiguan authorities and confiscated the remainder. After being sued civilly by the United States on the various contractual claims, the defendant banks moved to dismiss for lack of personal jurisdiction, and the district court granted the motion. The United States appealed.] * * *

ANALYSIS

A. Personal Jurisdiction: An Overview.

It is common ground that, for a court to render a binding decision consonant with due process, it must have personal jurisdiction over the parties, that is, the power to require the parties to obey its decrees. * * * Here, the jurisdictional analysis depends upon whether any statute or rule authorizes the forum court to exercise its dominion over the defendants, and if so, whether the court's exercise of that jurisdiction would comport with due process.

The constitutional inquiry proceeds in three steps: relatedness, purposeful availment, and reasonableness.[3] At the first stage, the court must ask whether the claim at issue arises out of or is related to the defendant's conduct within the forum state. At the second step, the court must scrutinize the defendant's contacts with the forum state to determine whether those contacts constitute purposeful activity, such that being haled into court there would be foreseeable. Lastly, the Constitution imposes an overall reasonableness restraint on the exercise of personal jurisdiction. An exercise of personal jurisdiction thus complies with constitutional imperatives only if the defendant's contacts with the forum relate sufficiently to his claim, are minimally adequate to constitute purposeful availment, and render resolution of the dispute in the forum state reasonable.

These constitutional requirements comprise a final hurdle for an aspiring plaintiff. A court need not even consider them unless it possesses statutory authorization to exercise specific personal jurisdiction over defendants of the type that the plaintiff targets. This authorization may derive from a federal statute, see, e.g., 15 U.S.C. § 22 (providing for worldwide service of process on certain corporate antitrust defendants), or from a state statute of general application, see, e.g., Mass. Gen. Laws ch. 223A, § 3 (providing "long-arm" jurisdiction). A state long-arm statute furnishes a mechanism for obtaining personal jurisdiction in federal as well as state courts. See Fed. R. Civ. P. 4(k)(1)(A).

In limited circumstances, the requisite authorization can be provided by Rule 4(k)(2), which functions as a sort of federal long-arm statute. When a plaintiff depends upon this recently adopted rule to serve as the necessary statutory authorization for the exercise of specific personal jurisdiction, the constitutional requirements are the same as those limned above, but the analytic exercises are performed with reference to the United States as a whole, rather than with reference to a particular state. The defendant's national contacts take center stage because the rule applies only to situations in which federal courts draw jurisdictional authority from the federal sovereign (unreinforced by "borrowed" state statutes), and, thus, the applicable constitutional requirements devolve from the Fifth rather than the Fourteenth Amendment. * * *

With this general schematic in place, we proceed to consider the govern-

---

[3] Sometimes, a defendant's contacts with a state are so pervasive that a court in that state may exercise personal jurisdiction over it even in cases entirely unrelated to those contacts. See Helicopteros Nacionales de Colombia v. Hall, 466 U.S. 408, 414 n.9, 415-16 (1984); Donatelli v. National Hockey League, 893 F.2d 459, 462-63 (1st Cir. 1990). Because the government's claim in this case does not invoke this "general personal jurisdiction," we do not dwell on it.

ment's two suggested bases for the assertion of personal jurisdiction over the defendants in the District of Massachusetts: the Massachusetts long-arm statute, Mass. Gen. Laws ch. 223A, §§ 3(a) & (d), and Rule 4(k)(2). Our review of the district court's ruling in this respect is plenary. * * *

B. Massachusetts Long-Arm Jurisdiction

* * * Because the United States sued in the District of Massachusetts, Rule 4(k)(1)(A) permits recourse to the Massachusetts long-arm statute. The government directs our attention to two subsections of that law. We mull each in turn. * * *

2. Section 3(d). Section 3(d) of the Massachusetts long-arm statute authorizes personal jurisdiction over one who causes "tortious injury in this commonwealth by an act or omission outside this commonwealth if he regularly does or solicits business, or engages in any other persistent course of conduct, or derives substantial revenue from goods used or consumed or services rendered, in this commonwealth." Mass. Gen. Laws ch. 223, § 3(d). * * * [T]he claim lacks merit for two reasons.

First and foremost, there is no showing here that the United States suffered tortious injury in Massachusetts. The legal injury occasioned by the tort of conversion is deemed to occur where the actual conversion takes place. See Cycles, Ltd. v. W.J. Digby, Inc., 889 F.2d 612, 619 (5th Cir. 1989). In this instance, the bank accounts were depleted and the forfeited assets redirected in Antigua, and, thus, the claimed injury occurred there. See Wenz v. Memery Crystal, 55 F.3d 1503, 1507-1508 (10th Cir. 1995) (holding that, under a similar long-arm provision, the tortious injury underlying an action for conversion of funds from London accounts by London-based tortfeasors occurred in London). By like token, since the government's claim of unjust enrichment is essentially a claim for restitution based on the alleged conversion, see Restatement of the Law on Restitution, Quasi Contracts, and Constructive Trusts §128 (1937), the legal injury stemming from it also must be presumed to have taken place in Antigua.

To blunt the force of this reality, the government replies that the forfeiture order was issued in Massachusetts. Fair enough—but this fact at most demonstrates that, upon the occurrence of the alleged conversion and the consequent unjust enrichment, the United States felt the effects of a tortious injury in the forum state. See Carty v. Beech Aircraft Corp., 679 F.2d 1051, 1064-65 (3d Cir. 1982) (collecting cases that distinguish tortious injury from the resulting economic harms). And since section 3(d) requires that the injury itself occur in Massachusetts, and does not apply merely because the plaintiff feels the effects of a tortious injury there, see Crocker v. Hilton Int'l Barbados, Ltd., 976 F.2d 797, 799-800 (1st Cir. 1992); Cunningham v. Ardrox, Inc., 40 Mass. App. Ct. 279, 282-83, 663 N.E.2d 577 (1996); see also Friedr. Zoellner (N.Y) Corp. v. Tex Metals Co., 396 F.2d 300, 302-03 (2d Cir. 1968) (holding that a similar jurisdictional statute "is not satisfied by remote or consequential injuries [flowing from a conversion] which occurred in [the forum state]," notwithstanding that "the plaintiff is domiciled, incorporated or doing business in that state"), these observations effectively end the matter.

The second reason why the government's invocation of section 3(d) misfires, involves the statutory requirement that the plaintiff must show that the defendant derived substantial revenue from services rendered in Massachusetts. In this instance, Fitzgerald (the money launderer who generated the cash) journeyed to Antigua to open the subject accounts and transferred the funds to the Swiss American banks from other foreign locations. On these facts, the government's plea reduces to an assertion that the defendants derived substantial revenue from within the commonwealth because the deposits originated with a Massachusetts resident. The statute specifies that substantial revenue must be derived from services which are "rendered * * * in" Massachusetts, Mass. Gen. Laws ch. 223(A), § 3(d), and the residency connection, standing alone, is simply too attenuated to satisfy this benchmark. For aught that appears, any services rendered by the defendants in the instant case were rendered in Antigua.

Inasmuch as the government has not met either of the dispositive criteria for authorization of personal jurisdiction under section 3(d), we uphold the district court's ruling that personal jurisdiction cannot be premised on the Massachusetts long-arm statute.

C. Jurisdiction Under Rule 4(k)(2).

* * * The rule's fabric contains three strands: (1) the plaintiff's claim must be one arising under federal law; (2) the putative defendant must be beyond the jurisdictional reach of any state court of general jurisdiction; and (3) the federal courts' exercise of personal jurisdiction over the defendant must not offend the Constitution or other federal law. * * *

1. *The Negation Requirement.* By its terms, Rule 4(k)(2) requires that the putative defendant not be subject to jurisdiction in any state court of general jurisdiction. The government argues that this requirement encompasses both subject matter and personal jurisdiction, and that, therefore, it can satisfy the negation requirement simply by showing that the state courts have no subject matter jurisdiction over a particular cause of action. Building on this porous foundation, the government then argues that 28 U.S.C. § 1345—the statute under which it brought this suit—grants exclusive subject matter jurisdiction to the federal courts.[5]

We find this reasoning unconvincing. Whether or not section 1345 provides an exclusive grant of subject matter jurisdiction—a matter on which we take no view—we nonetheless consider it pellucid that Rule 4(k)(2)'s reference to defendants who are "not subject to the jurisdiction * * * " refers to the absence of personal jurisdiction. We explain briefly.

Service is the traditional means by which a court establishes personal jurisdiction over a defendant. See *Burnham [v. Superior Court],* 495 U.S. at 610-11. Section (k) of Rule 4 governs the circumstances in which service (or waiver of service) will suffice to confer personal jurisdiction. The rule's two subsections both speak of the means by which "jurisdiction over the person" of a defendant

---

[5] The statute [28 U S.C. § 1345] reads in pertinent part: "Except as otherwise provided by Act of Congress, the district courts shall have original jurisdiction of all civil actions, suits or proceedings commenced by the United States . . . ."

can be established. See Fed. R. Civ. P. 4(k)(1)-(2). In this setting, it strains credulity to suggest that the mention of the unmodified word "jurisdiction" should be construed as anything other than a reference to "personal jurisdiction," when that understanding of the term makes reasonable sense in application (as it does here). It is, therefore, unsurprising that courts and commentators consistently have construed Rule 4(k)(2)'s allusion to the "jurisdiction" of the state courts to relate to personal jurisdiction. See, e.g., World Tanker Carriers Corp. v. MV Ya Mawlaya, 99 F.3d 717, 720 (5th Cir. 1996); * * *.

We hold, * * * that the absence of state court subject matter jurisdiction does not enter into the negation equation.

The government's better argument is that its case falls within the limits of Rule 4(k)(2) even when the rule is interpreted—as it must be—to require negation of personal jurisdiction over the defendant in any state court. The defendants' rejoinder is that, while the government alleged in its complaint that Rule 4(k)(2) supplied the necessary means for obtaining personal jurisdiction, it failed to plead or prove facts demonstrating the absence of personal jurisdiction over the defendants throughout the fifty states. This thrust and parry raises an issue of first impression concerning the order and allocation of proof in respect to Rule 4(k)(2)'s negation requirement, for no appellate court has offered a clear resolution of that problem. In a world of exponential growth in international transactions, the practical importance of this issue looms large.

The defendants (and the district court) certainly are correct in their insistence that a plaintiff ordinarily must shoulder the burden of proving personal jurisdiction over the defendant. Some district courts, relying on this shibboleth, have assigned outright to plaintiffs the burden of proving the Rule 4(k)(2) negation requirement. This paradigm in effect requires a plaintiff to prove a negative fifty times over—an epistemological quandary which is compounded by the fact that the defendant typically controls much of the information needed to determine the existence and/or magnitude of its contacts with any given jurisdiction. There is a corresponding problem with assigning the burden of proof on the Rule 4(k)(2) negation requirement to defendants: doing so threatens to place a defendant in a "Catch-22" situation, forcing it to choose between conceding its potential amenability to suit in federal court (by denying that any state court has jurisdiction over it) or conceding its potential amenability to suit in some identified state court. See Dora A. Corby, Comment, *Putting Personal Jurisdiction Within Reach: Just What Has Rule 4(k)(2) Done for the Personal Jurisdiction of Federal Courts?, 30* McGeorge L. Rev. 167, 196 (1998).

Faced with such dilemmas, courts historically have tailored special burden-of-proof regimes for specific classes of cases in order to strike an equitable balance. Cf., e.g., McDonnell Douglas Corp. v. Green, 411 U.S. 792, 802-05 (1973). We believe that Rule 4(k)(2) is fertile territory for such an innovation. The architects of the rule—and Congress, by adopting it—clearly intended to close the gap identified by the *Omni* Court and to ensure that persons whose contacts with this country exceeded the constitutional minimum could not easily evade civil liability in the American justice system. At the same time, however, the drafters also wrote the rule to preserve the established modalities for obtaining personal jurisdiction previously available under Rule 4(k)(1)(A) as the primary avenue to service on foreign defendants. The desire to achieve this secondary purpose led the authors of the rule to restrict its reach to those defendants with sufficient nationwide contacts to subject them to federal jurisdiction, but whose contacts were too exiguous to permit any state court to exercise personal jurisdiction over them. Viewed in this light, the application of traditional burden-of-proof principles to Rule 4(k)(2) cases not only would be inequitable, but also would shield foreign defendants who were constitutionally within the reach of federal courts from the exercise of personal jurisdiction, and, thus, thwart the core purpose that underlies the rule.

In our view, this core purpose can be achieved much more salubriously by crafting a special burden-shifting framework. To accomplish the desired end without placing the judicial thumb too heavily on the scale, we will not assign the burden of proof on the negation issue to either party in a monolithic fashion. We prefer instead to draw upon the burden-shifting arrangement devised by the Court to cope with somewhat analogous problems of proof in the discrimination context. We etch the contours of this proposed standard in detail below.

We hold that a plaintiff who seeks to invoke Rule 4(k)(2) must make a prima facie case for the applicability of the rule. This includes a tripartite showing (1) that the claim asserted arises under federal law, (2) that personal jurisdiction is not available under any situation-specific federal statute, and (3) that the putative defendant's contacts with the nation as a whole suffice to satisfy the applicable constitutional requirements. The plaintiff, moreover, must certify that, based on the information that is readily available to the plaintiff and his counsel, the defendant is not subject to suit in the courts of general jurisdiction of any state. If the plaintiff makes out his prima facie case, the burden shifts to the defendant to produce evidence which, if credited, would show either that one or more specific states exist in which it would be subject to suit or that its contacts with the United States are constitutionally insufficient. See generally Stephen B. Burbank, *The United States' Approach to International Civil Litigation: Recent Developments in Forum Selection*, 19 U. Pa. J. Int'l Econ. L. 1, 13 (1998) (suggesting a broad outline for a similar burden-shifting regime vis-à-vis the Rule 4(k)(2) negation requirement). Should the defendant default on its burden of production, the trier may infer that personal jurisdiction over the defendant is not available in any state court of general jurisdiction. If, however, the defendant satisfies its second-stage burden of production, then the aforementioned inference drops from the case.

What happens next depends on how the defendant satisfies its burden. If the defendant produces evidence indicating that it is subject to jurisdiction in a particular state, the plaintiff has three choices: he may move for a transfer to a district within that state, or he may discontinue his action (preliminary, perhaps, to the initiation of a suit in the courts of the identified state), or he may contest the defendant's proffer. If the plaintiff elects the last-mentioned course, the defendant will be deemed to have waived any claim that it is subject to personal jurisdiction in the courts of general jurisdiction of any state other than the state or states which it has identified, and the plaintiff, to fulfill the negation requirement, must prove that the defendant is not subject to suit in the identified forum(s).

Of course, the defendant may satisfy its burden of production by maintaining that it cannot constitutionally be subjected to jurisdiction in any state court. In that event, the defendant will be deemed to have conceded the negation issue, and the plaintiff, to succeed in his Rule 4(k)(2) initiative, need only prove that his claim arises under federal law and that the defendant has contacts with the United States as a whole sufficient to permit a federal court constitutionally to exercise personal jurisdiction over it.

We think that this schematic fairly balances the equities and comports with congressional intent, particularly since we envision the defendant's burden as a burden of production only. The plaintiff at all times retains the [burden] of persuasion on the ultimate issue. And while the burden-shifting framework puts defendants in an admittedly uncomfortable litigating position, that is to some degree the object of Rule 4(k)(2).

We return at this point to the proceedings below. Following the traditional rule, the trial court assigned the burden of proving negation to the plaintiff outright, and dismissed the complaint when the government failed to plead or proffer evidence anent the defendants' lack of jurisdictionally meaningful contacts throughout the fifty states[.] Given our holding that the Rule 4(k)(2) negation requirement evokes a modified burden-of-proof regime, that order of dismissal cannot stand unless dismissal is justified on some ground apart from negation.

In this posture of the case, we look first to the other two strands of Rule 4(k)(2). * * *

2. *"Arising Under" Federal Law.* [The appeals court concluded that the action brought by the United States, although not grounded in any congressionally created claim for relief but in federal common law (which might, in turn, adopt state law as the appropriate measure of federal common law), arose under federal law within the meaning of Rule 4(k)(2).]

3. *Adequacy of Contacts.* In addition to satisfying the negation and "arising under" requirements, the government must make one additional showing to gain access to Rule 4(k)(2): that the defendants have adequate contacts with the United States as a whole to support personal jurisdiction and that an assertion of jurisdiction over them would be reasonable. The government tried to make this showing below, but requested jurisdictional discovery to permit it to marshal the necessary proof. A timely and properly supported request for jurisdictional discovery merits solicitous attention. See Sunview Condo. Ass'n v. Flexel Int'l, Ltd., 116 F.3d 962, 964 (1st Cir. 1997) (explaining that "a diligent plaintiff who sues an out-of-state corporation and who makes out a colorable case for the existence of in personam jurisdiction may well be entitled to a modicum of jurisdictional discovery if the corporation interposes a jurisdictional defense")[.] The government claims that it fits within the *Sunview* rule. The defendants disagree. * * *

The district court denied the motion for limited discovery on the ground that the government had failed to negate state court jurisdiction. Our holding today, see supra Part II(C)(l), undermines the rationale for the district court's decision. We therefore vacate the denial of the government's motion for jurisdictional discovery. On remand, the court must reevaluate the government's request.

CONCLUSION

We need go no further. We agree with the district court that the government made an insufficient showing of personal jurisdiction over the defendants to engage the gears of the Massachusetts long-arm statute as incorporated by Rule 4(k)(1)(A), and to that extent we affirm the court's rulings. We disagree, however, with the court's approach to Rule 4(k)(2)'s negation requirement and view the question of whether Rule 4(k)(2) can be used here as open. Accordingly, we vacate the order of dismissal and remand for further proceedings consistent with this opinion. We also vacate the order denying jurisdictional discovery and remand for reconsideration of that matter. We intimate no view as to the eventual outcome of the resumed proceedings below.

NOTES AND QUESTIONS FOR DISCUSSION

1. What sort of showing on remand would suffice to establish the national contacts that *Swiss American* sees Rule 4(k)(2) as calling for? The opinion suggests that the U.S. should be treated as a single jurisdiction, and that the court should inquire whether the plaintiff has shown the requisite minimum contacts with the U.S. as a whole. If so, does it mean that a case such as *Swiss American* could constitutionally be brought in Hawaii, or anywhere else in the U.S.? In the Fourteenth Amendment context, fundamental fairness has to be considered in addition to minimum contacts with the forum. Should the analysis be similar under Fifth Amendment due process? If so, could Fifth Amendment due process ever limit the *particular* states in which suit could be brought, or is the only inquiry whether it is fair to be sued in the U.S.? Or should that task be left to nonconstitutional convenience mechanisms such as transfer of venue? See 28 U.S.C. § 1404. Again, consider the statement of the Advisory Commit-tee:

> * * * The Fifth Amendment requires that any defendant have affiliating contacts with the United States sufficient to justify the exercise of personal jurisdiction over that party. * * * There also may be a further Fifth Amendment constraint in that a plaintiff's forum selection might be so inconvenient to a defendant that it would be a denial of "fair play and substantial justice" required by the due process clause, even though the defendant had significant affiliating contacts with the U.S. * * *. See generally R. Lusardi, *Nationwide Service of Process: Due Process Limitations on the Power of the Sovereign*, 33 Vill. L. Rev. 1 (1988). * * *

> The district court should be especially scrupulous to protect aliens who reside in a foreign country from forum selections so onerous that injustice could result. "[G]reat care and reserve should be exercised when extending our notions of personal jurisdiction into the international field." [*Asahi.*]

> This narrow extension of the federal reach applies only if a claim is made against the defendant under federal law. It does not establish personal jurisdiction if the only claims are those arising under state law or the law of another country, even though there might be diversity or alienage subject matter jurisdiction as to such claims. If, however, personal jurisdiction is established under this paragraph with respect to a

federal claim, then 28 U.S.C. § 1367(a) provides supplemental jurisdiction over related claims against that defendant, subject to the court's discretion to decline exercise of that jurisdiction under 28 U.S.C. § 1367(c).

2. When suit has been brought under a federal statute that allows for a form of nationwide service of process, as under section 12 of the Clayton Act, 15 U.S.C. §§ 12 et seq., courts have also looked to a national-contacts standard for assessing minimum contacts, just as in *Swiss American*, where there was no such statute and service was available only under Rule 4(k)(2). See, e.g., Pinker v. Roche Holdings, Ltd., 292 F.3d 361 (3d Cir. 2002) (federal securities laws). Presumably, the same constitutional limits as those discussed above in the Rule 4(k)(2) context would also be applicable here, in the federal long-arm context. For a general discussion, see Jordon G. Lee, Note: *Section 12 of the Clayton Act: When Can Worldwide Service of Process Allow Suit in any District?*, 56 Fla. L. Rev 673 (2004).

3. Rule 4(k)(2) arguably contemplates the exercise of specific jurisdiction or general jurisdiction considering the U.S. as a whole. For example, if the claim in J. McIntyre Machinery v. Nicastro, 131 S.Ct. 2780 (2011) (see Section B, above), had been based on federal law, might there have been specific jurisdiction over J. McIntyre in the U.S., even if not in New Jersey (or any other state)? Of course, in connection with specific jurisdiction, the relevant events giving rise to the litigation will often be in a particular state or states, such that specific jurisdiction might already be available in that state, at least as a constitutional matter. Nevertheless, the state long arm statute could still come up short in a particular jurisdiction setting, and Rule 4(k)(2) will make up for the shortfall. Alternatively, if the theory under Rule 4(k)(2) is general jurisdiction in a given case, consider whether it is really possible that a foreign defendant will not have sufficient contacts with any one state for purposes of general jurisdiction in such state, but *will* have sufficeint contacts with the U.S. as a whole, so as to be "essentially at home" in the U.S., consistent with Goodyear Dunlop Tires Operations, S.A. v. Brown, 131 S.Ct. 2846 (2011). See Section C, above.

4. Rule 4(k) speaks to the jurisdictional reach of process for federal courts. It does not deal with the manner in which process must be served. Here, matters become more complicated, because the U.S. is a signatory to the Hague Convention on Service Abroad of Judicial and Extrajudicial Documents (the "Hague Convention"), reference to which is explicitly incorporated by Rule 4(f) and 4(h). We consider the in detail subject of manner of service on foreign defendants in Chapter 4.

F. LITIGATING PERSONAL JURISDICTION

Insurance Corp. of Ireland, Ltd. v. Compagnie des Bauxites de Guinée

Supreme Court of the United States, 1982.

456 U.S. 694.

JUSTICE WHITE delivered the opinion of the Court.

Rule 37(b), Federal Rules of Civil Procedure, provides that a district court may impose sanctions for failure to comply with discovery orders. Included among the available sanctions is:

> "An order that the matters regarding which the order was made or any other designated facts shall be taken to be established for the purposes of the action in accordance with the claim of the party obtaining the order." Rule 37(b)(2)(A)."[*]

The question presented by this case is whether this Rule is applicable to facts that form the basis for personal jurisdiction over a defendant. May a district court, as a sanction for failure to comply with a discovery order directed at establishing jurisdictional facts, proceed on the basis that personal jurisdiction over the recalcitrant party has been established? Petitioners urge that such an application of the Rule would violate due process: If a court does not have jurisdiction over a party, then it may not create that jurisdiction by judicial fiat. They contend also that until a court has jurisdiction over a party, that party need not comply with orders of the court; failure to comply, therefore, cannot provide the ground for a sanction. In our view, petitioners are attempting to create a logical conundrum out of a fairly straightforward matter.

I

Respondent Compagnie des Bauxites de Guinée (CBG) is a Delaware corporation, 49% of which is owned by the Republic of Guinea and 51% is owned by Halco (Mining) Inc. CBG's principal place of business is in the Republic of Guinea, where it operates bauxite mines and processing facilities. Halco, which operates in Pennsylvania, has contracted to perform certain administrative services for CBG. These include the procurement of insurance.

In 1973, Halco instructed an insurance broker, Marsh & McLennan, to obtain $20 million worth of business interruption insurance to cover CBG's operations in Guinea. The first half of this coverage was provided by the Insurance Company of North America (INA). The second half, or what is referred to as the "excess" insurance, was provided by a group of 21 foreign insurance companies, 14 of which are petitioners in this action (the excess insurers).

Marsh & McLennan requested Bland Payne to obtain the excess insurance in the London insurance market. Pursuant to normal business practice

---

[*] [Note that the Rule has since been slightly reworded, and can now be found at Rule 37(b)(2)(A)(i)—eds.]

"[i]n late January and in February, 1974, Bland Payne presented to the excess insurer [petitioners] a placing slip in the amount of $10,000,000, in excess of the first $10,000,000. [Petitioners] initialed said placing slip, effective February 12, 1974, indicating the part of said $10,000,000 each was willing to insure."

Once the offering was fully subscribed, Bland Payne issued a cover note indicating the amount of the coverage and specifying the percentage of the coverage that each excess insurer had agreed to insure. No separate policy was issued; the excess insurers adopted the INA policy "as far as applicable."

Sometime after February 12, CBG allegedly experienced mechanical problems in its Guinea operation, resulting in a business interruption loss in excess of $10 million. Contending that the loss was covered under its policies, CBG brought suit when the insurers refused to indemnify CBG for the loss. Whatever the mechanical problems experienced by CBG, they were perhaps minor compared to the legal difficulties encountered in the courts.

In December 1975, CBG filed a two-count suit in the Western District of Pennsylvania, asserting jurisdiction based on diversity of citizenship. The first count was against INA; the second against the excess insurers. INA did not challenge personal or subject-matter jurisdiction of the District Court. The answer of the excess insurers, however, raised a number of defenses, including lack of in personam jurisdiction. Subsequently, this alleged lack of personal jurisdiction became the basis of a motion for summary judgment filed by the excess insurers. The issue in this case requires an account of respondent's attempt to use discovery in order to demonstrate the court's personal jurisdiction over the excess insurers.

Respondent's first discovery request—asking for "[c]opies of all business interruption insurance policies issued by Defendant during the period from January 1, 1972 to December 31, 1975"—was served on each defendant in August 1976. In January 1977, the excess insurers objected, on grounds of burdensomeness, to producing such policies. Several months later, respondent filed a motion to compel petitioners to produce the requested documents. In June 1978, the court orally overruled petitioners' objections. This was followed by a second discovery request in which respondent narrowed the files it was seeking to policies which "were delivered in * * * Pennsylvania * * * or covered a risk located in * * * Pennsylvania." Petitioners now objected that these documents were not in their custody or control; rather, they were kept by the brokers in London. The court ordered petitioners to request the information from the brokers, limiting the request to policies covering the period from 1971 to date. That was in July 1978; petitioners were given 90 days to produce the information. On November 8, petitioners were given an additional 30 days to complete discovery. On November 24, petitioners filed an affidavit offering to make their records, allegedly some 4 million files, available at their offices in London for inspection by respondent. Respondent countered with a motion to compel production of the previously requested documents. On December 21, 1978, the court, noting that no conscientious effort had yet been made to produce the requested information and that no objection had been entered to the discovery order in July, gave petitioners 60 more days to produce the requested information. The District Judge also issued the following warning:

> "[I]f you don't get it to him in 60 days, I am going to enter an order saying that because you failed to give the information as requested, that I am going to assume, under Rule of Civil Procedure 37(b), subsection 2(A), that there is jurisdiction."

A few moments later he restated the warning as follows: "I will assume that jurisdiction is here with this court unless you produce statistics and other information in that regard that would indicate otherwise."

On April 19, 1979, the court, after concluding that the requested material had not been produced, imposed the threatened sanction, finding that "for the purpose of this litigation the Excess Insurers are subject to the in personam jurisdiction of this Court due to their business contacts with Pennsylvania." * * * [The insurers brought suit in England to rescind the insurance policies, but the district court enjoined them from pursuing of their lawsuit. There was an interlocutory appeal of the grant of injunctive relief.]

II

In McDonald v. Mabee, 243 U.S. 90 (1917), another case involving an alleged lack of personal jurisdiction, Justice Holmes wrote for the Court, "great caution should be used not to let fiction deny the fair play that can be secured only by a pretty close adhesion to fact." Petitioners' basic submission is that to apply Rule 37(b)(2) to jurisdictional facts is to allow fiction to get the better of fact and that it is impermissible to use a fiction to establish judicial power, where, as a matter of fact, it does not exist. In our view, this represents a fundamental misunderstanding of the nature of personal jurisdiction.

The validity of an order of a federal court depends upon that court's having jurisdiction over both the subject matter and the parties. Stoll v. Gottlieb, 305 U.S. 165, 171-172 (1938); Thompson v. Whitman, 18 Wall. 457, 465 (1874). The concepts of subject-matter and personal jurisdiction, however, serve different purposes, and these different purposes affect the legal character of the two requirements. Petitioners fail to recognize the distinction between the two concepts—speaking instead in general terms of "jurisdiction"—although their argument's strength comes from conceiving of jurisdiction only as subject-matter jurisdiction.

Federal courts are courts of limited jurisdiction. The character of the controversies over which federal judicial authority may extend are delineated in Art. III, 2, cl. 1. Jurisdiction of the lower federal courts is further limited to those subjects encompassed within a statutory grant of jurisdiction. * * *

Subject-matter jurisdiction, then, is an Art. III as well as a statutory requirement; it functions as a restriction on federal power, and contributes to the characterization of the federal sovereign. Certain legal consequences directly follow from this. For example, no action of the parties can confer subject-matter jurisdiction upon a federal court. Thus, the consent of the parties is irrelevant, California v. LaRue, 409 U.S. 109 (1972), principles of estoppel do not apply, American Fire & Casualty Co. v. Finn, 341 U.S. 6, 17-18 (1951), and a party does not waive the requirement by failing to challenge jurisdiction early in the proceedings. Similarly, a court, including an appellate court, will raise lack of subject-matter jurisdiction on its own motion. * * * Mansfield, C. & L.M.R. Co. v. Swan, 111 U.S. 379, 382 (1884).[9]

None of this is true with respect to personal jurisdiction. The requirement that a court have personal jurisdiction flows not from Art. III, but from the Due Process Clause. The personal jurisdiction requirement recognizes and protects an individual liberty interest. It represents a restriction on judicial power not as a matter of sovereignty, but as a matter of individual liberty.[10] Thus, the test for personal jurisdiction requires that "the maintenance of the suit * * * not offend 'traditional notions of fair play and substantial justice.'" International Shoe Co. v. Washington, 326 U.S. 310, 316 (1945), quoting Milliken v. Meyer, 311 U.S. 457, 463 (1940).

Because the requirement of personal jurisdiction represents first of all an individual right, it can, like other such rights, be waived. In *McDonald v. Mabee*, *supra*, the Court indicated that regardless of the power of the State to serve process, an individual may submit to the jurisdiction of the court by appearance. * * * Furthermore, the Court has upheld state procedures which find constructive consent to the personal jurisdiction of the state court in the voluntary use of certain state procedures. See Adam v. Saenger, 303 U.S. 59, 67-68 (1938) * * *. Finally, unlike subject-matter jurisdiction, which even an appellate court may review sua sponte, under Rule 12(h), Federal Rules of Civil Procedure, "[a] de-

---

[9] A party that has had an opportunity to litigate the question of subject-matter jurisdiction may not, however, reopen that question in a collateral attack upon an adverse judgment. It has long been the rule that principles of res judicata apply to jurisdictional determinations—both subject matter and personal. See Chicot County Drainage Dist. v. Baxter State Bank, 308 U.S. 371 (1940); Stoll v. Gottlieb, 305 U.S. 165 (1938).

[10] It is true that we have stated that the requirement of personal jurisdiction, as applied to state courts, reflects an element of federalism and the character of state sovereignty vis-à-vis other States. For example, in World-Wide Volkswagen Corp. v. Woodson, 444 U.S. 286, 291-292 (1980), we stated:

> "[A] state court may exercise personal jurisdiction over a nonresident defendant only so long as there exist 'minimum contacts' between the defendant and the forum State. The concept of minimum contacts, in turn, can be seen to perform two related, but distinguishable, functions. It protects the defendant against the burdens of litigating in a distant or inconvenient forum. And it acts to ensure that the States, through their courts, do not reach out beyond the limits imposed on them by their status as coequal sovereigns in a federal system." (Citation omitted.)

Contrary to the suggestion of JUSTICE POWELL, * * * our holding today does not alter the requirement that there be "minimum contacts" between the nonresident defendant and the forum State. Rather, our holding deals with how the facts needed to show those "minimum contacts" can be established when a defendant fails to comply with court-ordered discovery. The restriction on state sovereign power described in *World-Wide Volkswagen Corp.*, however, must be seen as ultimately a function of the individual liberty interest preserved by the Due Process Clause. That Clause is the only source of the personal jurisdiction requirement and the Clause itself makes no mention of federalism concerns. Furthermore, if the federalism concept operated as an independent restriction on the sovereign power of the court, it would not be possible to waive the personal jurisdiction requirement: Individual actions cannot change the powers of sovereignty, although the individual can subject himself to powers from which he may otherwise be protected.

fense of lack of jurisdiction over the person . . . is waived" if not timely raised in the answer or a responsive pleading.

In sum, the requirement of personal jurisdiction may be intentionally waived, or for various reasons a defendant may be estopped from raising the issue. These characteristics portray it for what it is—a legal right protecting the individual. The plaintiff's demonstration of certain historical facts may make clear to the court that it has personal jurisdiction over the defendant as a matter of law—i.e., certain factual showings will have legal consequences—but this is not the only way in which the personal jurisdiction of the court may arise. The actions of the defendant may amount to a legal submission to the jurisdiction of the court, whether voluntary or not.

The expression of legal rights is often subject to certain procedural rules: The failure to follow those rules may well result in a curtailment of the rights. Thus, the failure to enter a timely objection to personal jurisdiction constitutes, under Rule 12(h)(1), a waiver of the objection. A sanction under Rule 37(b)(2)(A) consisting of a finding of personal jurisdiction has precisely the same effect. As a general proposition, the Rule 37 sanction applied to a finding of personal jurisdiction creates no more of a due process problem than the Rule 12 waiver. Although "a court cannot conclude all persons interested by its mere assertion of its own power," *Chicago Life Ins. Co. v. Cherry, supra*, at 29, not all rules that establish legal consequences to a party's own behavior are "mere assertions" of power.

Rule 37(b)(2)(A) itself embodies the standard established in Hammond Packing Co. v. Arkansas, 212 U.S. 322 (1909), for the due process limits on such rules. There the Court held that it did not violate due process for a state court to strike the answer and render a default judgment against a defendant who failed to comply with a pretrial discovery order. Such a rule was permissible as an expression of

> "the undoubted right of the lawmaking power to create a presumption of fact as to the bad faith and untruth of an answer begotten from the suppression or failure to produce the proof ordered . . . . [T]he preservation of due process was secured by the presumption that the refusal to produce evidence material to the administration of due process was but an admission of the want of merit in the asserted defense." Id., at 350-351.

* * * Petitioners argue that a sanction consisting of a finding of personal jurisdiction differs from all other instances in which a sanction is imposed, including the default judgment in *Hammond Packing*, because a party need not obey the orders of a court until it is established that the court has personal jurisdiction over that party. If there is no obligation to obey a judicial order, a sanction cannot be applied for the failure to comply. Until the court has established personal jurisdiction, moreover, any assertion of judicial power over the party violates due process.

This argument again assumes that there is something unique about the requirement of personal jurisdiction, which prevents it from being established or waived like other rights. A defendant is always free to ignore the judicial proceedings, risk a default judgment, and then challenge that judgment on jurisdictional grounds in a collateral proceedings. See Baldwin v. Traveling Men's Assn., 283 U.S. 522, 525 (1931). By submitting to the jurisdiction of the court for the limited purpose of challenging jurisdiction, the defendant agrees to abide by that court's determination on the issue of jurisdiction: That decision will be res judicata on that issue in any further proceedings. Id., at 524; American Surety Co. v. Baldwin, 287 U.S. 156, 166 (1932). As demonstrated above, the manner in which the court determines whether it has personal jurisdiction may include a variety of legal rules and presumptions, as well as straightforward fact-finding. A particular rule may offend the due process standard of *Hammond Packing*, but the mere use of procedural rules does not in itself violate the defendant's due process rights.

[The Court went on to find that there was no abuse of discretion under Rule 37(b)(2) in the district court's imposition of its sanction.]

[The concurring opinion of JUSTICE POWELL is omitted.]

NOTES AND QUESTIONS FOR DISCUSSION

1. If a foreign defendant believes that personal jurisdiction is lacking in the forum in which it is sued, what should it do, if it does not wish to respond to discovery regarding personal jurisdiction? Within the U.S., it has always been available to a defendant not to make any appearance at all, and to suffer a default judgment. Doing so generally preserves the ability of the defendant to raise the lack of personal jurisdiction in an action brought later against the defendant to enforce the default judgment. The trade-off, however, is that the defendant ordinarily loses the ability to raise any issue on the merits of the litigation, even if it had a good substantive defense to the lawsuit. How often will defense counsel be so certain of the lack of personal jurisdiction (in the forum in which suit has been brought) that she will advise her client not to make any appearance at all?

2. Once a party has appeared, even by the limited mechanism of a motion to dismiss for lack of personal jurisdiction, the non-appearance option is lost. At that point, a party effectively submits to the personal jurisdiction of that court, at least for the purposes of that particular determination, i.e., of personal jurisdiction. Just as there is a kind of jurisdiction to determine jurisdiction in the context of subject matter jurisdiction, there seems to be a notion of personal jurisdiction to determine personal jurisdiction, although the power is triggered only by the appearance of the defendant who might be appearing only to contest personal jurisdiction.

3. Does the result in *Insurance Corp. of Ireland* mean that a plaintiff can undertake broad discovery on the personal jurisdiction question without any showing that such an argument is even colorable? Justice Powell concurred in the Court's judgment upholding the sanction only on the ground that the plaintiff had made out a prima facie case of personal jurisdiction.

> As recognized both by the District Court and the Court of Appeals, the respondent adduced substantial support for its jurisdictional assertions. By affidavit and other evidence, it made a prima facie showing of "minimum contacts." In the view of the District Court, the evidence ad-

duced actually was sufficient to sustain a finding of personal jurisdiction independently of the Rule 37 sanction.

> Where the plaintiff has made a prima facie showing of minimum contacts, I have little difficulty in holding that its showing was sufficient to warrant the District Court's entry of discovery orders. And where a defendant then fails to comply with those orders, I agree that the prima facie showing may be held adequate to sustain the court's finding that minimum contacts exist, either under Rule 37 or under a theory of "presumption" or "waiver."

456 U.S. at 716 (Powell, J., concurring in the judgment). Note that jurisdictional discovery in transnational litigation also has the potential to implicate the Hague Evidence Convention—a problem that we discuss in Chapter 6, Section D.

4. Federal appeals courts can ordinarily hear appeals from errors made by the trial court only after there has been a final judgment. 28 U.S.C. § 1291. Consequently, in the federal courts at least, appeals of denials of motions to dismiss based on personal jurisdiction grounds must ordinarily await the conclusion of trial, although no waiver is occasioned by litigation on the merits after denial of a timely motion to dismiss. Cf. Van Cauwenberghe v. Baird, 486 U.S. 517, 521 (1988) (holding that denial of a motion to dismiss based on immunity from service of process was not immediately appealable, and rejecting an argument that such denials came within the "collateral order doctrine" of Cohen v. Beneficial Indus. Loan Corp., 337 U.S. 541 (1949).) Matters can be different in state courts. Some systems follow the federal practice, but others either permit or require interlocutory relief from the denial of a motion to dismiss on personal jurisdiction grounds. And in some state jurisdictions, litigation on the merits after losing on a motion to dismiss on personal jurisdiction grounds operates as a waiver of the objection (unlike in the federal courts).

Does it make sense to have to wait on such matters, especially when the defendant is a foreign party who might have to go through the avoidable trial before being able to exercise its right to appeal? Or is that particular cost one of the inevitable trade-offs associated with a final judgment rule: The occasional costs of the possibly unneeded trial are outweighed by the certain costs of inevitable pre-trial appeals in most if not all cases? See also Section I, below (discussing the appealability of denials of motions to dismiss based on forum selection clauses). Note that other avenues of extraordinary review may be available— such as by having the district court, in its discretion, agree to certify the issue for appeal under 28 U.S.C. § 1292(b), and provided the court of appeals also agrees to hear it.

G. PERSONAL JURISDICTION IN EUROPE—THE BRUSSELS CONVENTION AND REGULATION

In this subsection we discuss the application of jurisdictional rules in cross-border litigation within the European Union. For over thirty years, these rules were embodied in the 1968 Convention on Jurisdiction and the Enforcement of Judgments in Civil and Commercial Matters (Brussels Convention). See Convention on Jurisdiction and the Enforcement of Judgments in Civil and Commercial Matters, Sept. 27, 1968, 1972 O.J. (L. 299) 32, reprinted in 8 I.L.M. 299 (1969), as amended by 1990 O.J. (C 189) 1, reprinted as amended in 29 I.L.M. 1413 (1990). It was only in 2002 that a so-called Council Regulation replaced the Convention. See Council Regulation 44/2001 on Jurisdiction and the Recognition of Judgments in Civil and Commercial Matters. O.J. (L 12) 1 (Jan. 16, 2001), reprinted in Appendix D. The Regulation did not introduce major changes, however, meaning that the existing case law under the Convention continues to provide important guidance in future disputes. We will therefore focus on this pre-existing case law to illustrate how European courts settle jurisdictional questions in trans-border litigation. (Note also that on December 6, 2012, the Council of the EU Justice Ministers adopted a recast version of the Brussels I Regulation. (Regulation (EU) 1215/2012 of the European Parliament and of the Council of 12 December 2012 on jurisdiction and the recognition and enforcement of judgments in civil and commercial matters (recast). Official Journal, OJ 20 December 2012, L 351/1)). This newest revision, however, will not be applicable until 2015.

In order better to understand the make up and operation of the Convention rules, one must first realize that the driving force behind the Convention was the desire to advance the goal of market integration in Europe. The European Economic Community (EEC) Treaty aimed at the creation of a common market and, for that purpose, contained explicit rules for the free movement of persons, goods, services and capital. Market integration requires more, however. Among other things, it requires the free movement of judgments—that is, the ability of market participants involved in commercial disputes to seek redress before the courts of one member state and to swiftly enforce the resultant judgment in another. Although the EEC Treaty did not contain directly applicable rules facilitating judgment recognition throughout the Community, the drafters recognized that need by calling on Member States to enter into negotiations with a view towards that end. See Article 220 (4) (now Article 293 (4)) (calling for negotiations with a view towards the "simplification of formalities governing the reciprocal recognition and enforcement of judgments of courts or tribunals and of arbitration awards.") In 1968, these negotiations resulted in the Brussels Convention, a body of law that not only established the rules for the recognition of judgments in civil or commercial litigation but also set out a limited number of circumstances in which courts may exercise personal jurisdiction over defendants domiciled in contracting states. Twenty years later, in 1988, the EC member states and the members of the European Free Trade Association (Austria, Finland, Iceland, Norway, Sweden Switzerland) entered into the so-called Lugano Convention which contains, for the most part, provisions that are identical with those of the Brussels Convention. See Convention on Jurisdiction and the Enforcement of Judgments in Civil and Commercial Matters, Sept. 16, 1988, 1988 O.J. (L 319) 9, reprinted in 28 I.L.M. 620 (1989).

The adoption of an exclusive set of jurisdictional rules proved crucial for the success of the Convention. The community-wide consensus over when the exercise of personal jurisdiction is appropriate effectively removed a major obstacle in international judgment recognition proceedings. Courts faced with a judgment rendered under these rules need not (and, in principle, must not) review the jurisdictional findings of the first tribunal.

The jurisdictional rules start from the principle that a defendant who is domiciled in a contracting state should generally be sued in the courts of that state. See Art. 2 of the Brussels Convention. Persons domiciled in a contracting state may be sued in the courts of another contracting state only if one of the special Convention rules so permits. See Art. 3. This "white list" of permissible jurisdictional bases provides, for example, that in matters relating to contract the plaintiff may sue at the place of performance (Art. 5.1). In matters of torts, the suit may be brought where the harmful event occurred (Art. 5.3), and with respect to disputes arising out of operation of a branch office or agency, the litigation may proceed in the courts in which the branch or agency is located. The exhaustive list of permissible jurisdictional bases also includes specific rules protecting systemically weaker parties, such as insurance policy holders (Arts. 7-12a) and consumers (Arts. 13-15), from having to litigate in foreign courts. These parties may sue and must be sued in the courts of the Contracting State in which they are domiciled.

For the most part, this white list provides a degree of certainty that does not come at the expense of procedural fairness. Courts that exercise jurisdiction under the rules of the Convention do not engage in any due process analysis that is so familiar to U.S. litigants. They do not inquire as to whether the defendant maintained minimum contacts with the forum. And they do not examine whether the defendant purposefully availed itself of the benefits and protections of the forum. Just as in purely domestic litigation, European courts limit themselves to applying the text of the Convention's rules to the facts. Unencumbered by a layer of constitutional inquiry that often results in lengthy and expensive pretrial litigation before U.S. courts, jurisdictional questions in Europe are quickly and, for the most part, predictably resolved.

Furthermore, jurisdiction based on unrelated assets, mandatory jurisdiction based on nationality, and other jurisdictional oddities still embedded in domestic laws of some member state countries, cannot threaten those domiciled in one of the Contracting States. These and other rules form a non-exhaustive black list of jurisdictional bases which are considered unacceptable by the group of the Contracting States as a whole. See id.

However, third country domiciliaries cannot avail themselves of this protection. In fact, the Convention is explicit in making these blacklisted exorbitant jurisdictional bases applicable to those parties who are not domiciled in a contracting state. See Art. 4 of the Brussels Convention. For example, as noted by Justice Ginsburg in her *Nicastro* dissent (footnote 5), Article 14 of the French Civil Code has been read to provide that a French national may sue a foreigner in French courts without regard to any connection between the cause of action and the French forum. Thus, Article 14 could be applied against a party domiciled in the U.S. For example, a U.S. citizen involved in a vehicular accident in the U.S. with a French national could be sued in France, consistent with Article 14. While the judgment would not likely be able to be enforced in the U.S., the exercise of such jurisdiction would not prevent the enforcement of the judgment in the courts of another Contracting State—in which the defendant might have assets—unless that state had entered into an agreement with the U.S. (or another third country) not to recognize such judgments. See Art. 59 of the Brussels Convention; see also Burbank & Palmer, *supra* (Section D), 48 Me. L. Rev. at 482-503 (discussing history and scope of Article 14). Note, however, that an effort is afoot that would have the current Regulation displace national rules of E.U. countries. See Silberman, *supra* (Section B), 63 S.C. L. Rev. at 607-11 (noting uncertain prospects of the proposal).

Although the jurisdictional rules of the Brussels Convention have, overall, produced the degree of legal certainty and outcomes that are considered fair for purposes of intra-community litigation, there have nevertheless been numerous cases in which the application of these rules to particular facts was not an easy exercise. In these instances, domestic courts, uncertain about the application of a Brussels Convention provision, stayed the proceedings before them and referred the question to the European Court of Justice. See Art. 234 of the EEC Treaty. The case law emanating from the European Court of Justice ("Court of Justice of the European Communities") (ECJ) has significantly improved the even-handed application of the Brussels Convention. We will take a closer look at some of these cases to illustrate how the ECJ has addressed such problems.

Johann Gruber v. Bay Wa AG

Court of Justice of the European Communities, 2005.

Case C-464/01, 2005 E.C.R. I-00439.

REFERENCE for a preliminary ruling under the Protocol of 3 June 1971 on the interpretation by the Court of Justice of the Convention of 27 September 1968 on Jurisdiction and the Enforcement of Judgments in Civil and Commercial Matters [.] * * *

Dispute in the main proceedings and the questions referred for a preliminary ruling

12. According to the documents in the main proceedings Mr. Gruber, a farmer, owns a farm building constructed around a square ('Vierkanthof'), situated in Upper Austria, close to the German border. He uses about a dozen rooms as a dwelling for himself and his family. In addition over 200 pigs are kept there, and there are fodder silos and a large machine room. Between 10% and 15% of the total fodder necessary for the farm is also stored there. The area of the farm building used for residential purposes is slightly more than 60% of the total floor area of the building.

13. Bay Wa operates a number of separately managed businesses in Germany. In Pocking (Germany), not far from the Austrian border, it has a building materials business and a DIY and garden centre. The latter published brochures which were also distributed in Austria.

14. Wishing to replace the roof tiles of his farm building, Mr. Gruber became aware of those advertising brochures, which were sent out with the Braunauer Rundschau, a local periodical distributed to households. The tiles offered for sale

by Bay Wa's building materials department in Pocking did not feature in those brochures.

15. Mr. Gruber made several telephone enquiries to an employee of Bay Wa concerning the different types of tiles and the prices, stating his name and address but not mentioning the fact that he was a farmer. The employee made him an offer by telephone but Mr. Gruber wished to inspect the tiles on site. On his visit to Bay Wa's premises, he was given by the employee a written quotation dated 23 July 1998. During that meeting Mr. Gruber told Bay Wa's employee that he had a farm and wished to tile the roof of the farm building. He stated that he also owned ancillary buildings that were used principally for the farm, but did not expressly state whether the building to be tiled was used mainly for business or for private purposes. The following day, Mr. Gruber called the employee, from Austria, to say that he accepted Bay Wa's quotation. Bay Wa then faxed a confirmation of the order to Mr. Gruber's bank in Austria.

16. Mr. Gruber considered that the tiles delivered by Bay Wa to tile the roof of his farm building showed significant variations in colour despite the warranty that the colour would be uniform. As a result the roof would have to be re-tiled. He therefore decided to bring proceedings on the basis of the warranty together with a claim for damages, seeking reimbursement of the cost of the tiles (ATS [pre-Euro, Austrian Schillings—eds.] 258,123) and of the expense of removing them and re-tiling the roof (ATS 141,877) and a declaration of liability for any future expenses.

17. For that purpose, Mr. Gruber commenced proceedings on 26 May 1999 before the Landesgericht Steyr (Austria), designated as the competent court in Austria by the Oberster Gerichtshof in accordance with Paragraph 28 of the Law of 1 August 1895 on the allocation of jurisdiction and the territorial jurisdiction of the ordinary courts in civil matters (Jurisdiktionsnorm, RGBl. 111).

18. By judgment of 29 November 2000, the Landesgericht (Regional Court) Steyr dismissed Bay Wa's objection of lack of jurisdiction and ruled that it was competent to hear the dispute.

19. According to the Landesgericht Steyr, the conditions for the application of Article 13 of the Brussels Convention are satisfied. Where a contract has a dual purpose, the predominant purpose, whether private or business, must be ascertained. Since the dividing line between private and business supplies is difficult to distinguish in the case of agricultural enterprises, the court found that the seller had had no way of ascertaining objectively whether one or other purpose predominated at the time when the contract was concluded so that, given the uncertainty, the contract was to be regarded as a consumer contract. Furthermore, in the context of Article 13(3)(a) of the Brussels Convention it mattered little whether the product ultimately bought by the consumer had itself been advertised. It was sufficient that there had been advertisements drawing attention to a particular undertaking. It was thanks to that advertising that Bay Wa was able to conclude a contract with Mr. Gruber, even though it came from a department other than the one which supplied the goods. Finally, the condition that there be a 'specific invitation' by the seller within the meaning of that

provision was satisfied in this case, since Mr. Gruber had received an offer by telephone. Whether that offer was accepted was irrelevant.

20. By judgment of 1 February 2001 the Oberlandesgericht (Higher Regional Court) Linz (Austria) upheld Bay Wa's appeal, however, and dismissed Mr. Gruber's claim on the ground that the Austrian courts do not have jurisdiction to hear the dispute.

21. According to the Oberlandesgericht Linz [Articles 13-15 were applicable only if Gruber "acted predominantly outside his trade or profession and if the other party . . . knew or should have been aware of the fact at the time."] * * *

23. Mr. Gruber then brought an appeal before the Oberster Gerichtshof (Supreme Court) against the judgment of 1 February 2001 of the Oberlandesgericht Linz.

24. In support of his appeal, Mr. Gruber claims that in order for him to be regarded as a consumer within the meaning of Article 13 of the Convention the private purpose of the supply must predominate. In this case, the private use of the farm building is greater than the business use thereof. The other party to the contract is under an obligation to make enquiries and to advise the client in that regard and bears the risk of any mistake. Mr. Gruber argues that in this case Bay Wa had sufficient reason to consider that the farm building was used essentially for private purposes, and in case of doubt it should have made enquiries of the purchaser about this. Furthermore, the sale of the tiles was preceded by an advertisement circulated in Austria by Bay Wa which led Mr. Gruber to deal with it, whereas before that advertisement he was unaware of that company. Finally, all the preparatory steps for the conclusion of the contract were taken by Mr. Gruber in Austria.

25. Bay Wa replies that in an agricultural enterprise the farm building is above all a place of work, and that in general supplies relating to it cannot be made on the basis of consumer contracts. In this case, the private use was in any event secondary and Bay Wa was unaware of such use. The consumer should clearly state in which capacity he is acting where, as in this case, it is possible to suppose, prima facie, that he is acting for a business purpose. The other party to the contract has no obligation to make enquiries in that respect. Where there is doubt as to whether a party is a consumer the Brussels Convention rules of jurisdiction on consumer contracts should not be applied. Furthermore, Bay Wa's building materials department, from which the tiles were ordered, did not benefit from the advertising by brochure, and its DIY and garden centres, for whose benefit the advertising was undertaken, do not sell roof tiles. In any event there was no advertising for the tiles. The steps necessary for the conclusion of the contract were not taken in Austria but in Germany, as, under German law, the statement of acceptance of the quotation by telephone constitutes evidence of intention requiring an acknowledgement, and the confirmation of the order by the seller was made by fax from Germany. Where offer and acceptance are not simultaneous, which is the case where the order is made by telephone on the basis of an earlier quotation, the contract is deemed to have been concluded in the place where the defendant is domiciled.

26. The Oberster Gerichtshof observes that whilst it follows from the case-law of the Court that the jurisdictional rules on consumer contracts in the Brussels Convention constitute a derogation from the principle that the courts of the Contracting State where the defendant is domiciled should have jurisdiction, so that the concept of consumer must be given a strict interpretation, the Court has not yet ruled on some of the conditions for the application of Article 13 of the Brussels Convention which are at issue in the case before it.

27. Taking the view that in those circumstances the resolution of the dispute before it depends on the interpretation of the Brussels Convention, the Oberster Gerichtshof decided to stay the proceedings and to refer the following questions to the Court of Justice for a preliminary ruling:

> 1. Where the purposes of a contract are partly private, does the status of consumer for the purposes of Article 13 of the Convention depend on which of the private and the trade or professional purposes is predominant, and what criteria are to be applied in determining which of the private and the trade or professional purposes predominates?

> 2. Does the determination of the purpose depend on the circumstances which could be objectively ascertained by the other party to the contract with the consumer?

> 3. In case of doubt, is a contract which may be attributed both to private and to trade or professional activity to be regarded as a consumer contract? * * *

The first three questions

28. By its first three questions, which it is appropriate to consider together, the national court asks, essentially, whether the rules of jurisdiction laid down by the Brussels Convention must be interpreted as meaning that a contract of the kind at issue in the main proceedings, which relates to activities which are partly business and partly private, must be regarded as having been concluded by a consumer for the purposes of the first paragraph of Article 13 of the Convention.

29. As is clear from the order for reference, the Oberster Gerichtshof wishes to know essentially whether, and if so in what circumstances, a contract which has a dual purpose, such as the contract that Mr. Gruber concluded with Bay Wa, is covered by the special rules of jurisdiction laid down in Articles 13 to 15 of the Brussels Convention. More specifically, the national court asks for clarification as to the circumstances of which it must take account in order to classify such a contract, the relevance of whether the contract was made predominantly for private or for business purposes, and the effect of knowledge of the party to the contract other than the party served by those purposes of either the purpose of the contract or the circumstances in which it was concluded.

30. As a preliminary point, it must be recalled that Title II, Section 4, of the Brussels Convention lays down the rules of jurisdiction for consumer contracts. The notion of a consumer contract is defined, as shown by the wording of the first paragraph of Article 13 of the Convention, 'as a contract concluded by a person for a purpose which can be regarded as being outside his trade or profession.'

31. According to settled case-law, the concepts used in the Brussels Convention—which include, in particular, that of 'consumer' for the purposes of Articles 13 to 15 of that Convention—must be interpreted independently, by reference principally to the scheme and purpose of the Convention, in order to ensure that it is uniformly applied in all the Contracting States * * *

32. First of all, within the scheme of the Brussels Convention, the jurisdiction of the courts of the Contracting State in which the defendant is domiciled constitutes the general principle enshrined in the first paragraph of Article 2, and it is only by way of derogation from that principle that the Convention provides for an exhaustive list of cases in which the defendant may or must be sued before the courts of another Contracting State. As a consequence, the rules of jurisdiction which derogate from that general principle are to be strictly interpreted, so that they cannot give rise to an interpretation going beyond the cases envisaged by the Convention. * * *

33. That interpretation must apply a fortiori with respect to a rule of jurisdiction, such as that contained in Article 14 of the Convention, which allows a consumer, within the meaning of the first paragraph of Article 13 of the Convention, to sue the defendant in the courts of the Contracting State in which the claimant is domiciled. Apart from the cases expressly provided for, the Convention does not appear to favour the attribution of jurisdiction to the courts of the claimant's domicile * * *

34. Second, the Court has repeatedly held that the special rules introduced by the provisions of Title II, Section 4, of the Brussels Convention, which derogate from the general rule laid down in the first paragraph of Article 2, and from the rules of special jurisdiction for contracts in general enshrined in Article 5(1) of the Convention, serve to ensure adequate protection for the consumer as the party deemed to be economically weaker and less experienced in legal matters than the other, commercial, party to the contract, who must not therefore be discouraged from suing by being compelled to bring his action before the courts in the Contracting State in which the other party to the contract is domiciled (see in particular Shearson Lehman Hutton, paragraph 18, and Gabriel, paragraph 39).

35. From the scheme of the rules of jurisdiction put in place by the Brussels Convention, as well as the rationale of the special rules introduced by the provisions of Title II, Section 4, the Court has concluded that those provisions only cover private final consumers, not engaged in trade or professional activities, as the benefit of those provisions must not be extended to persons for whom special protection is not justified. * * *

36. In paragraphs 16 to 18 of the judgment in *Benincasa* [Case C-269/95 [1997] ECR I-3767] the Court stated in that respect that the concept of 'consumer' for the purposes of the first paragraph of Article 13 and the first paragraph of Article 14 of the Brussels Convention must be strictly construed, reference being made to the position of the person concerned in a particular contract, having regard to the nature and aim of that contract and not to the subjective situation of the person concerned, since the same person may be regarded as a consumer in relation to certain supplies and as an economic operator in relation to others. The Court held that only contracts concluded

outside and independently of any trade or professional activity or purpose, solely for the purpose of satisfying an individual's own needs in terms of private consumption, are covered by the special rules laid down by the Convention to protect the consumer as the party deemed to be the weaker party. Such protection is unwarranted in the case of contracts for the purpose of a trade or professional activity.

37. It follows that the special rules of jurisdiction in Articles 13 to 15 of the Brussels Convention apply, in principle, only where the contract is concluded between the parties for the purpose of a use other than a trade or professional one of the relevant goods or services.

38. It is in the light of those principles that it is appropriate to examine whether and to what extent a contract such as that at issue in the main proceedings, which relates to activities of a partly professional and partly private nature, may be covered by the special rules of jurisdiction laid down in Articles 13 to 15.

39. In that regard, it is already clearly apparent from the purpose of Articles 13 to 15 of the Brussels Convention, namely to properly protect the person who is presumed to be in a weaker position than the other party to the contract, that the benefit of those provisions cannot, as a matter of principle, be relied on by a person who concludes a contract for a purpose which is partly concerned with his trade or profession and is therefore only partly outside it. It would be otherwise only if the link between the contract and the trade or profession of the person concerned was so slight as to be marginal and, therefore, had only a negligible role in the context of the supply in respect of which the contract was concluded, considered in its entirety.

40. As the Advocate General stated in paragraphs 40 and 41 of his Opinion, inasmuch as a contract is entered into for the person's trade or professional purposes, he must be deemed to be on an equal footing with the other party to the contract, so that the special protection reserved by the Brussels Convention for consumers is not justified in such a case.

41. That is in no way altered by the fact that the contract at issue also has a private purpose, and it remains relevant whatever the relationship between the private and professional use of the goods or service concerned, and even though the private use is predominant, as long as the proportion of the professional usage is not negligible.

42. Accordingly, where a contract has a dual purpose, it is not necessary that the purpose of the goods or services for professional purposes be predominant for Articles 13 to 15 of the Convention not to be applicable.

43. That interpretation is supported by the fact that the definition of the notion of consumer in the first paragraph of Article 13 of the Brussels Convention is worded in clearly restrictive terms, using a negative turn of phrase ('contract concluded . . . for a purpose . . . outside [the] trade or profession'). Moreover, the definition of a contract concluded by a consumer must be strictly interpreted as it constitutes a derogation from the basic rule of jurisdiction laid down in the first paragraph of Article 2, and confers exceptional jurisdiction on

the courts of the claimant's domicile (see paragraphs 32 and 33 of the present judgment).

44. That interpretation is also dictated by the fact that classification of the contract can only be based on an overall assessment of it, since the Court has held on many occasions that avoidance of multiplication of bases of jurisdiction as regards the same legal relationship is one of the main objectives of the Brussels Convention. * * *

45. An interpretation which denies the capacity of consumer, within the meaning of the first paragraph of Article 13 of the Brussels Convention, if the link between the purpose for which the goods or services are used and the trade or profession of the person concerned is not negligible is also that which is most consistent with the requirements of legal certainty and the requirement that a potential defendant should be able to know in advance the court before which he may be sued, which constitute the foundation of that Convention * * *

46. Having regard to the normal rules on the burden of proof, it is for the person wishing to rely on Articles 13 to 15 of the Brussels Convention to show that in a contract with a dual purpose the business use is only negligible, the opponent being entitled to adduce evidence to the contrary.

47. In the light of the evidence which has thus been submitted to it, it is therefore for the court seised to decide whether the contract was intended, to a non-negligible extent, to meet the needs of the trade or profession of the person concerned or whether, on the contrary, the business use was merely negligible. For that purpose, the national court should take into consideration not only the content, nature and purpose of the contract, but also the objective circumstances in which it was concluded.

48. Finally, as regards the national court's question as to whether it is necessary for the party to the contract other than the supposed consumer to have been aware of the purpose for which the contract was concluded and the circumstances in which it was concluded, it must be noted that, in order to facilitate as much as possible both the taking and the evaluation of the evidence, it is necessary for the court seised to base its decision mainly on the evidence which appears, de facto, in the file.

49. If that evidence is sufficient to enable the court to conclude that the contract served to a non-negligible extent the business needs of the person concerned, Articles 13 to 15 of the Brussels Convention cannot be applied in any event because of the status of those provisions as exceptions within the scheme introduced by the Convention. There is therefore no need to determine whether the other party to the contract could have been aware of the business purpose.

50. If, on the other hand, the objective evidence in the file is not sufficient to demonstrate that the supply in respect to which a contract with a dual purpose was concluded had a non-negligible business purpose, that contract should, in principle, be regarded as having been concluded by a consumer within the meaning of Articles 13 to 15, in order not to deprive those provisions of their effectiveness.

51. However, having regard to the fact that the protective scheme put in place by Articles 13 to 15 of the Brussels Convention represents a derogation, the court

seised must in that case also determine whether the other party to the contract could reasonably have been unaware of the private purpose of the supply because the supposed consumer had in fact, by his own conduct with respect to the other party, given the latter the impression that he was acting for business purposes.

52. That would be the case, for example, where an individual orders, without giving further information, items which could in fact be used for his business, or uses business stationery to do so, or has goods delivered to his business address, or mentions the possibility of recovering value added tax.

53. In such a case, the special rules of jurisdiction for matters relating to consumer contracts enshrined in Articles 13 to 15 of the Brussels Convention are not applicable even if the contract does not as such serve a non-negligible business purpose, and the individual must be regarded, in view of the impression he has given to the other party acting in good faith, as having renounced the protection afforded by those provisions.

54. In the light of all the foregoing considerations, the answer to the first three questions must be that the rules of jurisdiction laid down by the Brussels Convention are to be interpreted as follows:

> —a person who concludes a contract for goods intended for purposes which are in part within and in part outside his trade or profession may not rely on the special rules of jurisdiction laid down in Articles 13 to 15 of the Convention, unless the trade or professional purpose is so limited as to be negligible in the overall context of the supply, the fact that the private element is predominant being irrelevant in that respect;

> —it is for the court seised to decide whether the contract at issue was concluded in order to satisfy, to a non-negligible extent, needs of the business of the person concerned or whether, on the contrary, the trade or professional purpose was negligible;

> —to that end, that court must take account of all the relevant factual evidence objectively contained in the file. On the other hand, it must not take account of facts or circumstances of which the other party to the contract may have been aware when the contract was concluded, unless the person who claims the capacity of consumer behaved in such a way as to give the other party to the contract the legitimate impression that he was acting for the purposes of his business.

The last three questions

55. Since the last three questions were referred only if the capacity of consumer within the meaning of the first paragraph of Art. 13 of the Convention was established, and in view of the answer given in that respect to the first three questions, there is no longer any need to answer the last three questions, relating to the other conditions for the application of that provision.* * *

On those grounds, **THE COURT** (Second Chamber) rules as follows:

The rules of jurisdiction laid down by the Convention of 27 September 1968 on Jurisdiction and the Enforcement of Judgments in Civil and Commercial Matters, [as amended] must be interpreted as follows [Here, the Court reiterated the rules identified under paragraph 54, above.]

NOTES AND QUESTIONS FOR DISCUSSION

1.   In *Gruber*, the ECJ passes judgment on the applicability of Arts. 13-15 of the Brussels Convention (which became, slightly modified, Arts. 15-17 of the Brussels Regulation). These provisions contain special jurisdictional rules aimed at protecting consumers' procedural rights in certain types of transactions, such as installment credit sales contracts and loans to be repaid in installments. Article 13 (now 15) defines a consumer as a person concluding a contract "for a purpose which can be regarded outside his trade or profession." Article 14 (now 16) provides, among other things, that consumers may sue the other party at the consumer's domicile. According to Article 15 (now 17), parties to a consumer contract may derogate from the above provisions—i.e., they may agree on litigating in other forums, but only under narrowly defined circumstances. They may do so either after the dispute has arisen; or if the consumer is given additional choices as to where he may litigate; or if the agreement confers jurisdiction on the courts of a member state in which both parties were domiciled or habitually resident at the time they entered into the agreement. These rules clearly favor the consumer. Why do you think the Regulation is drafted in such a way? Is this type of consumer protection justified?

2.   According to the ECJ, a consumer cannot rely on Articles 13-15 if the professional purpose for concluding the contract with the defendant is not negligible (see paragraphs 39, 41 46), or if the other party was reasonably unaware of the private purpose underlying the contract (paragraph 51). Based on the decision in *Gruber*, who bears the burden of proof for these findings?

3.   In paragraph 50, the Court states:

> If, on the other hand, the objective evidence in the file is not sufficient to demonstrate that the supply in respect to which a contract with a dual purpose was concluded had a non-negligible business purpose, that contract should, in principle, be regarded as having been concluded by a consumer within the meaning of Articles 13 to 15, in order not to deprive those provisions of their effectiveness.

This language suggests that doubts based on the available "objective evidence" as to the purpose of the contract, will be resolved in favor of the consumer. However, in paragraphs 51-53, the Court appears to limit its holding: The consumer may be held to have "renounced the protection afforded by [Articles 13–15]" if he has given the other party the impression he was acting for business purposes. Is this qualification justified? See Art. 15 of the Brussels Convention (Note 1, above) and the limited grounds on which parties can derogate from the otherwise mandatory jurisdictional provisions in Articles 13 and 14 of the Convention.

4.   The ECJ leaves it to the domestic (Austrian) court to decide the case in accordance with the principles it just enunciated. Assume that that the Austrian court concludes that Articles 13-15 do not apply in the instant case. Where would the plaintiff then have to sue, and on the basis of which provision(s) of the Brussels Convention/Regulation?

Shevill v. Presse Alliance SA

Court of Justice of the European Communities, 1995.
Case C-68/93; 1995 E.C.R. I-415.

* * *

JUDGMENT: * * *

3. According to the documents before the Court, on 23 September 1989 Presse Alliance SA, which publishes the newspaper France-Soir, published an article about an operation which drug squad officers of the French police had carried out at one of the bureaux de change operated in Paris by Chequepoint SARL. That article, based on information provided by the agency France Presse, mentioned the company "Chequepoint" and "a young woman by the name of Fiona Shevill-Avril".

4. Chequepoint SARL, a company incorporated under French law whose registered office is in Paris, has operated bureaux de change in France since 1988. It is not alleged to carry on business in England or Wales.

5. Fiona Shevill was temporarily employed for three months in the summer of 1989 by Chequepoint SARL in Paris. She returned to England on 26 September 1989.

6. Ixora Trading Inc., which is not a company incorporated under the law of England and Wales, has since 1974 operated bureaux de change in England under the name "Chequepoint".

7. Chequepoint International Ltd, a holding company incorporated under Belgian law whose registered office is in Brussels, controls Chequepoint SARL and Ixora Trading Inc.

8. Miss Shevill, Chequepoint SARL, Ixora Trading Inc. and Chequepoint International Ltd considered that the abovementioned article was defamatory in that it suggested that they were part of a drug-trafficking network for which they had laundered money. On 17 October 1989 they issued a writ in the High Court of England and Wales claiming damages for libel from Presse Alliance SA in respect of the copies of France-Soir distributed in France and the other European countries including those sold in England and Wales. The plaintiffs subsequently amended their pleadings, deleting all references to the copies sold outside England and Wales. Since under English law there is a presumption of damage in libel cases, the plaintiffs did not have to adduce evidence of damage arising from the publication of the article in question.

9. It is common ground that France-Soir is mainly distributed in France and that the newspaper has a very small circulation in the United Kingdom, effected through independent distributors. It is estimated that more than 237,000 copies of the issue of France-Soir in question were sold in France and approximately 15,500 copies distributed in the other European countries, of which 230 were sold in England and Wales (5 in Yorkshire).

10. On 23 November 1989 France-Soir published an apology stating that it had not intended to allege that either the owners of Chequepoint bureaux de

change or Miss Shevill had been involved in drug trafficking or money launder-
ing.

11. On 7 December 1989 Presse Alliance SA issued a summons disputing
the jurisdiction of the High Court of England and Wales on the ground that no
harmful event within the meaning of Article 5(3) of the Convention had occurred in England.

12. That application * * * was dismissed by order of 10 April 1990. The appeal brought against that decision was dismissed by order of 14 May 1990.

13. On 12 March 1991 the Court of Appeal dismissed the appeal brought by
Presse Alliance SA against that decision and stayed the action brought by
Chequepoint International Limited.

14. Presse Alliance SA appealed against that decision to the House of Lords
pursuant to leave to appeal granted by the latter.

15. Presse Alliance SA argued essentially that under Article 2 of the Convention the French courts had jurisdiction in this dispute and that the English
courts did not have jurisdiction under Article 5(3) of the Convention since the
"place where the harmful event occurred" within the meaning of that provision
was in France and no harmful event had occurred in England.

16. Considering that the proceedings raised problems of interpretation of the
Convention, the House of Lords by order of 1 March 1993 decided to stay the
proceedings pending a preliminary ruling by the Court of Justice on the following questions:

"1. In a case of libel by a newspaper article, do the words 'the place where
the harmful event occurred' in Article 5(3) of the Convention mean:

(a) the place where the newspaper was printed and put into circulation;
or

(b) the place or places where the newspaper was read by particular individuals; or

(c) the place or places where the plaintiff has a significant reputation?

2. If and so far as the answer to the first question is (b), is 'the harmful
event' dependent upon there being a reader or readers who knew (or knew
of) the plaintiff and understood those words to refer to him?

3. If and in so far as harm is suffered in more than one country (because copies of the newspaper were distributed in at least one Member State other
than the Member State where it was printed and put into circulation), does a
separate harmful event or harmful events take place in each Member State
where the newspaper was distributed, in respect of which such Member
State has separate jurisdiction under Article 5(3), and if so, how harmful
must the event be, or what proportion of the total harm must it represent?
* * *

6. If, in a defamation case, the local court concludes that there has been an
actionable publication (or communication) of material, as a result of which
at least some damage to reputation would be presumed, is it relevant to the
acceptance of jurisdiction that other Member States might come to a differ-

ent conclusion in respect of similar material published within their respective jurisdictions? * * * "

The first, second, third and sixth questions

17. The national court's first, second, third and sixth questions, which should be considered together, essentially seek guidance from the Court as to the interpretation of the concept "the place where the harmful event occurred" used in Article 5(3) of the Convention, with a view to establishing which courts have jurisdiction to hear an action for damages for harm caused to the victim following distribution of a defamatory newspaper article in several Contracting States.

18. In order to answer those questions, reference should first be made to Article 5(3) of the Convention, which, by way of derogation from the general principle in the first paragraph of Article 2 of the Convention that the courts of the Contracting State of the defendant' s domicile have jurisdiction, provides:

> "A person domiciled in a Contracting State may, in another Contracting State, be sued: . . .

> (3) in matters relating to tort, delict or quasi-delict, in the courts for the place where the harmful event occurred; . . . "

19. It is settled case-law (see Case 21/76 Bier v. Mines de Potasse d'Alsace 1976 ECR 1735, paragraph 11, and Case C-220/88 Dumez France and Tracoba v. Hessische Landesbank (Helaba) and Others 1990 ECR I-49, paragraph 17) that that rule of special jurisdiction, the choice of which is a matter for the plaintiff, is based on the existence of a particularly close connecting factor between the dispute and courts other than those of the State of the defendant's domicile which justifies the attribution of jurisdiction to those courts for reasons relating to the sound administration of justice and the efficacious conduct of proceedings.

20. It must also be emphasized that in *Mines de Potasse d'Alsace* the Court held (at paragraphs 24 and 25) that, where the place of the happening of the event which may give rise to liability in tort, delict or quasi-delict and the place where that event results in damage are not identical, the expression "place where the harmful event occurred" in Article 5(3) of the Convention must be understood as being intended to cover both the place where the damage occurred and the place of the event giving rise to it, so that the defendant may be sued, at the option of the plaintiff, either in the courts for the place where the damage occurred or in the courts for the place of the event which gives rise to and is at the origin of that damage.

21. In that judgment, the Court stated (at paragraphs 15 and 17) that the place of the event giving rise to the damage no less than the place where the damage occurred could constitute a significant connecting factor from the point of view of jurisdiction, since each of them could, depending on the circumstances, be particularly helpful in relation to the evidence and the conduct of the proceedings.

22. The Court added (at paragraph 20) that to decide in favour only of the place of the event giving rise to the damage would, in an appreciable number of cases, cause confusion between the heads of jurisdiction laid down by Articles 2

and 5(3) of the Convention, so that the latter provision would, to that extent, lose its effectiveness.

23. Those observations, made in relation to physical or pecuniary loss or damage, must equally apply, for the same reasons, in the case of loss or damage other than physical or pecuniary, in particular injury to the reputation and good name of a natural or legal person due to a defamatory publication.

24. In the case of a libel by a newspaper article distributed in several Contracting States, the place of the event giving rise to the damage, within the meaning of those judgments, can only be the place where the publisher of the newspaper in question is established, since that is the place where the harmful event originated and from which the libel was issued and put into circulation.

25. The court of the place where the publisher of the defamatory publication is established must therefore have jurisdiction to hear the action for damages for all the harm caused by the unlawful act.

26. However, that forum will generally coincide with the head of jurisdiction set out in the first paragraph of Article 2 of the Convention.

27. As the Court held in *Mines de Potasse d'Alsace*, the plaintiff must consequently have the option to bring proceedings also in the place where the damage occurred, since otherwise Article 5(3) of the Convention would be rendered meaningless.

28. The place where the damage occurred is the place where the event giving rise to the damage, entailing tortious, delictual or quasi-delictual liability, produced its harmful effects upon the victim.

29. In the case of an international libel through the press, the injury caused by a defamatory publication to the honour, reputation and good name of a natural or legal person occurs in the places where the publication is distributed, when the victim is known in those places.

30. It follows that the courts of each Contracting State in which the defamatory publication was distributed and in which the victim claims to have suffered injury to his reputation have jurisdiction to rule on the injury caused in that State to the victim's reputation.

31. In accordance with the requirement of the sound administration of justice, the basis of the rule of special jurisdiction in Article 5(3), the courts of each Contracting State in which the defamatory publication was distributed and in which the victim claims to have suffered injury to his reputation are territorially the best placed to assess the libel committed in that State and to determine the extent of the corresponding damage.

32. Although there are admittedly disadvantages to having different courts ruling on various aspects of the same dispute, the plaintiff always has the option of bringing his entire claim before the courts either of the defendant's domicile or of the place where the publisher of the defamatory publication is established.

33. In light of the foregoing, the answer to the first, second, third and sixth questions referred by the House of Lords must be that, on a proper construction of the expression "place where the harmful event occurred" in Article 5(3) of the Convention, the victim of a libel by a newspaper article distributed in several

Contracting States may bring an action for damages against the publisher either before the courts of the Contracting State of the place where the publisher of the defamatory publication is established, which have jurisdiction to award damages for all the harm caused by the defamation, or before the courts of each Contracting State in which the publication was distributed and where the victim claims to have suffered injury to his reputation, which have jurisdiction to rule solely in respect of the harm caused in the State of the court seised. * * *

On those grounds, **THE COURT**, in answer to the questions referred to it by the House of Lords, by order of 1 March 1993, hereby rules:

1. On a proper construction of the expression "place where the harmful event occurred" in Article 5(3) of the Convention of 27 September 1968 on Jurisdiction and the Enforcement of Judgments in Civil and Commercial Matters, as amended by the Convention of 9 October 1978 on the accession of the Kingdom of Denmark, Ireland and the United Kingdom of Great Britain and Northern Ireland and by the Convention of 25 October 1982 on the accession of the Hellenic Republic, the victim of a libel by a newspaper article distributed in several Contracting States may bring an action for damages against the publisher either before the courts of the Contracting State of the place where the publisher of the defamatory publication is established, which have jurisdiction to award damages for all the harm caused by the defamation, or before the courts of each Contracting State in which the publication was distributed and where the victim claims to have suffered injury to his reputation, which have jurisdiction to rule solely in respect of the harm caused in the State of the court seised. * * *

NOTES AND QUESTIONS FOR DISCUSSION

1. According Article 5.3 of the Brussels Convention, a court adjudicating a tort claim has jurisdiction at "the place where the harmful event occurred." The ECJ interprets this language to refer to two places: the place where the event which gave rise to tort liability occurred; and the place where that event results in damage. Would there necessarily be "minimum contacts" in the U.S. sense between the defendant and the places referred to by the court? The question could be relevant in the event of judgment enforcement in the U.S. See Chapter 8. Do characterization problems such as "where the event occurred" present a less serious problem of jurisdictional uncertainty than U.S. constitutional questions?

2. Assume that Ms. Shevill's reputation has suffered damages to varying degrees in five different countries. Could she therefore sue for defamation in any one of them? If so, may she sue for damages that occurred in any or all of them? Consider whether it makes sense that the plaintiff might be able choose to bring multiple lawsuits over the same event.

3. American courts generally adhere to the so-called "single publication rule." See Keeton v. Hustler Magazine, Inc., 465 U.S. 770 (1984). Under this rule, plaintiffs are entitled to recover all damages to their reputation—those that occurred in the forum as well as those suffered elsewhere. Is this the better approach? Note, however, that there may be territorial limits on the ability of a state to award punitive damages based on activities outside the forum. See State Farm Mutual Automobile Ins. Co. v. Campbell, 538 U.S. 408 (2003).

4. Does *Shevill* apply beyond print media and to the Internet? In a pair of joined cases, which follow, the ECJ recently offered answers to such questions in the setting of internet infringement of publicity rights.

eDate Advertising GmbH v. X, *and*
Martinez v. MGN, Ltd.

Court of Justice of the European Communities, 2011.
Joined Cases C-509/09 and C-161/10; CELEX: 62009CJ0509.

[In the first case, the Plaintiff (X), a German national, sued eDate Advertising, an Austrian company that ran a dating website, over information that it made available through its website about the plaintiff in connection with a past criminal conviction of his which was still pending on appeal. (The website provided access to the report of the German case and did so in a way that disclosed the full name of X.) Suit was brought in a German court seeking to enjoin eDate from using his full name when reporting about him in connection with the crime. The main contention of eDate was that the German courts had no jurisdiction in the matter. Plaintiff was successful in the lower courts, and on appeal to the German high court (Bundesgerichtshof), the court stayed its proceedings and referred the jurisdictional (and other) questions to the ECJ.

In the second case, a French actor—Oliver Martinez—brought suit in France against the UK Sunday Mirror over interference with his private life when it stated on its website that "Kylie Minogue is back with Oliver Martinez," and added certain details of a meeting between them. The defendant, Mirror Group Newspapers (MGN) argued that the French court lacked jurisdiction.

The ECJ addressed the jurisdictional questions as follows:]

Interpretation of Article 5(3) of the Regulation

37. By the first two questions in Case C-509/09 and the single question in Case C-161/10, which it is appropriate to examine together, the national courts ask the Court, in essence, how the expression 'the place where the harmful event occurred or may occur', used in Article 5(3) of the Regulation, is to be interpreted in the case of an alleged infringement of personality rights by means of content placed online on an internet website.

38. In order to answer those questions, it should be borne in mind, first, that, according to settled case-law, the provisions of the Regulation must be interpreted independently, by reference to its scheme and purpose.

* * *

40. It is settled case-law that the rule of special jurisdiction laid down, by way of derogation from the principle of jurisdiction of the courts of the place of domicile of the defendant, in Article 5(3) of the Regulation is based on the existence of a particularly close connecting factor between the dispute and the courts of the place where the harmful event occurred, which justifies the attribution of jurisdiction to those courts for reasons relating to the sound administration of justice and the efficacious conduct of proceedings * * *.

41. It must also be borne in mind that the expression 'place where the harmful event occurred' is intended to cover both the place where the damage occurred and the place of the event giving rise to it. Those two places could constitute a significant connecting factor from the point of view of jurisdiction, since each of them could, depending on the circumstances, be particularly helpful in relation to the evidence and the conduct of the proceedings (see Case C-68/93 *Shevill and Others* [1995] ECR I-415, paragraphs 20 and 21).

42. In relation to the application of those two connecting criteria to actions seeking reparation for non-material damage allegedly caused by a defamatory publication, the Court has held that, in the case of defamation by means of a newspaper article distributed in several Contracting States, the victim may bring an action for damages against the publisher either before the courts of the Contracting State of the place where the publisher of the defamatory publication is established, which have jurisdiction to award damages for all of the harm caused by the defamation, or before the courts of each Contracting State in which the publication was distributed and where the victim claims to have suffered injury to his reputation, which have jurisdiction to rule solely in respect of the harm caused in the State of the court seised (*Shevill and Others*, paragraph 33).

43. In that regard, the Court has also stated that, while it is true that the limitation of the jurisdiction of the courts in the State of distribution solely to damage caused in that State presents disadvantages, the plaintiff always has the option of bringing his entire claim before the courts either of the defendant's domicile or of the place where the publisher of the defamatory publication is established (*Shevill and Others*, paragraph 32).

* * *

45. However, as has been submitted both by the referring courts and by the majority of the parties and interested parties which have submitted observations to the Court, the placing online of content on a website is to be distinguished from the regional distribution of media such as printed matter in that it is intended, in principle, to ensure the ubiquity of that content. That content may be consulted instantly by an unlimited number of internet users throughout the world, irrespective of any intention on the part of the person who placed it in regard to its consultation beyond that person's Member State of establishment and outside of that person's control.

46. It thus appears that the internet reduces the usefulness of the criterion relating to distribution, in so far as the scope of the distribution of content placed online is in principle universal. Moreover, it is not always possible, on a technical level, to quantify that distribution with certainty and accuracy in relation to a particular Member State or, therefore, to assess the damage caused exclusively within that Member State.

47. The difficulties in giving effect, within the context of the internet, to the criterion relating to the occurrence of damage which is derived from *Shevill and Others* contrasts, as the Advocate General noted at point 56 of his Opinion, with the serious nature of the harm which may be suffered by the holder of a personality right who establishes that information injurious to that right is available on a world-wide basis.

48. The connecting criteria referred to in paragraph 42 of the present judgment must therefore be adapted in such a way that a person who has suffered an infringement of a personality right by means of the internet may bring an action in one forum in respect of all of the damage caused, depending on the place in which the damage caused in the European Union by that infringement occurred. Given that the impact which material placed online is liable to have on an individual's personality rights might best be assessed by the court of the place where the alleged victim has his centre of interests, the attribution of jurisdiction to that court corresponds to the objective of the sound administration of justice, referred to in paragraph 40 above.

49. The place where a person has the centre of his interests corresponds in general to his habitual residence. However, a person may also have the centre of his interests in a Member State in which he does not habitually reside, in so far as other factors, such as the pursuit of a professional activity, may establish the existence of a particularly close link with that State.

50. The jurisdiction of the court of the place where the alleged victim has the centre of his interests is in accordance with the aim of predictability of the rules governing jurisdiction (see Case C-144/10 *BVG* [2011] ECR I-0000, paragraph 33) also with regard to the defendant, given that the publisher of harmful content is, at the time at which that content is placed online, in a position to know the centres of interests of the persons who are the subject of that content. The view must therefore be taken that the centre-of-interests criterion allows both the applicant easily to identify the court in which he may sue and the defendant reasonably to foresee before which court he may be sued.* * *

51. Moreover, instead of an action for liability in respect of all of the damage, the criterion of the place where the damage occurred, derived from *Shevill and Others*, confers jurisdiction on courts in each Member State in the territory of which content placed online is or has been accessible. Those courts have jurisdiction only in respect of the damage caused in the territory of the Member State of the court seised.

52. Consequently, the answer to the first two questions in Case C-509/09 and the single question in Case C-161/10 is that Article 5(3) of the Regulation must be interpreted as meaning that, in the event of an alleged infringement of personality rights by means of content placed online on an internet website, the person who considers that his rights have been infringed has the option of bringing an action for liability, in respect of all the damage caused, either before the courts of the Member State in which the publisher of that content is established or before the courts of the Member State in which the centre of his interests is based. That person may also, instead of an action for liability in respect of all the damage caused, bring his action before the courts of each Member State in the territory of which content placed online is or has been accessible. Those courts have jurisdiction only in respect of the damage caused in the territory of the Member State of the court seised. * * *

NOTES AND QUESTIONS FOR DISCUSSION

1. Consider in what respect(s) the court may have interpreted Article 5(3) differently than it did in *Shevill*. Given that many if not most print newspapers are also published as an online edition, would it be fair to say that, as a practical matter, the ECJ has overruled *Shevill* with this decision? The court, of course, did not seem to think that it was doing any such thing. Why not?

2. The scope of Internet jurisdiction within the U.S. is not fully settled. problem is associated with the difficulty of localizing Internet activities—a difficulty that makes it hard to know whether a defendant has purposely availed itself of the benefits and protections of a particular forum, or whether it has directed its activity towards that forum. Should the basic principles of minimum contacts and fairness apply in this setting just like any other? See A. Benjamin Spencer, *Jurisdiction and the Internet: Returning to Traditional Principles to Analyze Network-Mediated Contacts*, 2006 U. Ill. L. Rev. 71 (2006) (so arguing). Early decisions seemed to want to focus on the "level of interactivity and commercial nature" of the website. See, e.g., Zippo Mfg. Co. v. Zippo Dot Com, Inc., 952 F. Supp. 1119, 1124 (W.D. Pa. 1997). But more recent decisions have arguably reverted to more familiar, post-*International Shoe* approaches in which boundaries remain relevant, and in which the focus is on more traditional contacts, such as points of sale or product delivery. See generally Jack Goldsmith & Tim Wu, Who Controls the Internet?: Illusions of a Borderless World (2006). We consider a particularly aggressive example of Internet jurisdiction (and cross-border judgment enforcement) in Chapter 8 (discussing Yahoo!, Inc. v. La Ligue Contre Le Racisme et L'Antisemitisme, 169 F. Supp. 2d 1181 (N.D. Cal. 2001), reversed, 433 F.3d 1199 (9th Cir. 2006) (en banc)).

3. Consider one example of the application of traditional rules in the domestic setting. In Young v. New Haven Advocate, 315 F.3d 256 (4th Cir. 2002), the websites of the defendants, two Connecticut newspapers, contained articles that allegedly defamed the plaintiff in Virginia. The Fourth Circuit held that the Virginia courts had no personal jurisdiction over the defendants because they did not direct their website content to a Virginia audience. The decision was based on due process grounds. Does the analysis make sense? How else might courts (or legislatures) seek to limit the otherwise limitless reach of the Internet in a meaningful way for jurisdictional purposes?

H. Attachment and Global Assets

For many years, a traditional and readily available basis for the exercise of jurisdiction in American courts over a non-resident defendant was pre-trial attachment—i.e., the seizure of property of the defendant's in the forum in which suit was brought. Historically, this sort of jurisdiction could be acquired even if the seized property was unrelated to the subject of the lawsuit, and even though jurisdiction could not otherwise be established. Judgment in such a suit was ordinarily limited to the value of the property seized, however, in contrast to the occasional practice of some foreign jurisdictions that have allowed for personal judgments even above the amount of the property seized. In an era when personal jurisdiction was territorially limited (before *International Shoe* and state long-arm statutes), and when distances between states were once formidable, such "quasi-in-rem" jurisdiction often provided a home-forum safety-valve for resident plaintiffs harmed by a nonresident who was otherwise unreachable.

This sort of quasi-in-rem jurisdiction was challenged on due process grounds in Shaffer v. Heitner, 433 U.S. 186 (1977), where the Court concluded that "all assertions of state court jurisdiction must be evaluated according to the standards set forth in *International Shoe* and its progeny."[*] The plaintiff in *Shaffer* brought a shareholder derivative action against various individual officers and directors of a Delaware corporation for breach of their fiduciary duties. The plaintiff seized various shares of Delaware stock and stock options of the defendants pursuant to a Delaware statute allowing for the seizure of a nonresident's property as a means to secure jurisdiction even in litigation unrelated to that property. Because, the Supreme Court concluded that the presence of the defendants' shares of Delaware stock was unrelated to the litigation brought by the plaintiff, and because the Court found that the defendants otherwise lacked minimum contacts with Delaware, it concluded that the state's assertion of jurisdiction was unconstitutional.

Shaffer clearly meant that *jurisdiction* in a suit against a nonresident could not be premised merely on the presence of some item of the defendant's property in the forum that was unrelated to the subject matter of the lawsuit. But it hardly meant that the presence of property in a forum would no longer be relevant to litigation or even to the assertion of jurisdiction. For example, attachment of property in a second (judgment enforcing) jurisdiction would still be possible to allow the court to enforce a jurisdictionally valid judgment from another (judgment-rendering) jurisdiction. Indeed, the *Shaffer* Court itself acknowledged such a possibility even if the property in the judgment enforcing state was the judgment debtor's only contact with that state and was otherwise unrelated to the subject of the original litigation. See id. at 210 n.36.

In addition, nothing in *Shaffer* suggests that the presence of property could not serve as the basis for jurisdiction over a claim to determine ownership rights in the property itself. Nor did *Shaffer* foreclose the possibility that personal jurisdiction would exist over a nonresident where the nonresident's property was otherwise sufficiently related to the underlying subject matter of the litigation, as, for example, where the maintenance of the property in question is alleged to be the source of the plaintiff's injuries. Finally, *Shaffer* did not foreclose the possibility that property might be seized prior to litigation as a security device to guarantee the presence of property against which to enforce any eventual judgment.

---

[*] As noted immediately below, the *Shaffer* Court hedged a bit when it stated that it was not deciding whether the presence of the defendant's property in a state, without more, would be a sufficient basis for jurisdiction "when no other forum is available" in which the plaintiff could suit could bring suit. Id. at 211 n.37. But it is doubtful whether the Court meant to leave open the possibility of such quasi-in-rem jurisdiction simply because there was no other forum in the U.S. in which defendant could be sued (as opposed to no other forum in the world). See George A. Bermann, Transnational Litigation 52 (2003) (indicating that this is the view of "most courts").

In Carolina Power & Light Co. v. Uranex, 451 F. Supp. 1044 (N.D. Cal. 1977), for example, a California federal court upheld the garnishment of a French company's property that was located in California as pre-trial security in connection with a contract dispute that was then subject to proceedings brought against the defendant in New York. The Court acknowledged that minimum contacts over the French company (Uranex) would be lacking in California in a suit over the underlying claim, but upheld California's jurisdiction to order the attachment pending the filing of suit in a forum in which personal jurisdiction over Uranex could be had. At the pre-trial stage, and in the absence of a jurisdictionally valid judgment, should *Shaffer* be read to allow for such attachment?

In federal courts, the attachment rules of the state in which the federal court sits are ordinarily applicable, because they are expressly incorporated under Rule 69(a), Fed. R. Civ. P. For obtaining pre-trial attachment for security purposes, state practice would typically require a showing of some degree of likelihood of success on the merits, and that there is a real risk the defendant will dispose of the assets in the absence of attachment. Cf. Rule 65(b)(1)(A), Fed. R. Civ. P. (setting out prerequites for temporary injunctive relief). Attachment of assets of foreign sovereigns is governed by a more restrictive set of rules under the Foreign Sovereign Immunities Act (FSIA), which generally require that the assets are ones used for "commercial activity" in the U.S. and are being attached in order to satisfy a judgment already obtained or anticipated. See 28 U.S.C. § 1610. The FSIA is discussed in Chapter 3.

Finally, and more problematically, the *Shaffer* opinion did not resolve "whether the presence of a defendant's property in a State is a sufficient basis for jurisdiction when no other forum is available to the plaintiff," on some sort of theory of necessity.[*] *Shaffer*, 433 U.S. at 211 n.37. Can "necessity" explain why admiralty jurisdiction, which often relies on pre-judgment attachment to commence litigation, has been thought to escape many of the rigors of *Shaffer*? See, e.g., Amoco Overseas Oil Co. v. Compagnie Nationale Algerienne de Navigation, 605 F.2d 648, 655 (2d Cir. 1979) (stating that, *Shaffer* notwith-standing, attachment jurisdiction in admiralty is still viable because of the tradition of such seizure in admiralty, the "peripatetic" nature of maritime injury, and the existence of a separate constitutional grant over admiralty).

Of course, the fact that *Shaffer* itself may not have foreclosed certain of these possibilities does not mean that other principles might not operate to foreclose or limit them, as discussed in the following decision:

---

[*] It might also be possible to use attachment (if provided for by state statute), when minimum contacts otherwise exist over a nonresident defendant, but, for some reason or other, the state's long-arm statute does not reach to the full length of due process. Of course, the fact that the long-arm does not reach as far as the plaintiff would like might make it doubtful whether the state statute itself should be read as sanctioning the use of attachment jurisdiction as a gap filler.

Grupo Mexicano de Desarrollo, S.A. v. Alliance Bond Fund, Inc.

Supreme Court of the United States, 1999.

527 U.S. 308.

JUSTICE SCALIA delivered the opinion of the Court.

This case presents the question whether, in an action for money damages, a United States District Court has the power to issue a preliminary injunction preventing the defendant from transferring assets in which no lien or equitable interest is claimed.

[The respondents, including Alliance, were various investment funds that purchased unsecured 8.25% notes from Grupo Mexicano Desarrollo (GMD), a Mexican holding company. Four GMD subsidiaries guaranteed the notes. Because of a downturn in the Mexican economy, GMD suffered financial troubles and could not pay off the notes. Payment of the principal amount of the notes was then accelerated and Alliance and others filed suit against GMD and the guarantors in federal court for the amount due in a breach of contract action for over $80,000,000. Defendants did not object to personal jurisdiction. Alliance requested a preliminary injunction against GMD to restrain it from transferring certain of its assets in Mexico, alleging that GMD was at risk of insolvency and was preferring its Mexican creditors to others, and that these acts would frustrate any attempt by Alliance to enforce any eventual judgment. The lower court issued the injunction and ordered Alliance to post a security bond. The Second Circuit affirmed.]

III

We turn, then, to the merits question whether the District Court had the authority to issue the preliminary injunction in this case pursuant to Federal Rule of Civil Procedure 65.[3] The Judiciary Act of 1789 conferred on the federal courts jurisdiction over "all suits * * * in equity." 1 Stat. 78. We have long held that "[t]he 'jurisdiction' thus conferred * * * is an authority to administer in equity suits the principles of the system of judicial remedies which had been devised and was being administered by the English Court of Chancery at the time of the separation of the two countries." Atlas Life Ins. Co. v. W.I. Southern, Inc., 306 U.S. 563, 568 (1939). [Because the prerequisites for an injunction under Rule 65 depend on traditional equity principles] [w]e must ask * * * whether the relief respondents requested here was traditionally accorded by courts of equity.

---

[3] Although this is a diversity case, respondents' complaint sought the injunction pursuant to Rule 65, and the Second Circuit's decision was based on that rule and on federal equity principles. Petitioners [GMD] argue for the first time before this Court that under Erie R. Co. v. Tompkins, 304 U.S. 64 (1938), the availability of this injunction under Rule 65 should be determined by the law of the forum State (in this case New York). Because this argument was neither raised nor considered below, we decline to consider it.

A

Respondents do not even argue this point. The United States as amicus curiae, however, contends that the preliminary injunction issued in this case is analogous to the relief obtained in the equitable action known as a "creditor's bill." This remedy was used (among other purposes) to permit a judgment creditor to discover the debtor's assets, to reach equitable interests not subject to execution at law, and to set aside fraudulent conveyances. * * * It was well established, however, that, as a general rule, a creditor's bill could be brought only by a creditor who had already obtained a judgment establishing the debt. * * * The rule requiring a judgment was a product, not just of the procedural requirement that remedies at law had to be exhausted before equitable remedies could be pursued, but also of the substantive rule that a general creditor (one without a judgment) had no cognizable interest, either at law or in equity, in the property of his debtor, and therefore could not interfere with the debtor's use of that property. * * *

[The dissent] concedes that federal equity courts have traditionally rejected the type of provisional relief granted in this case. It invokes, however, "the grand aims of equity," and asserts a general power to grant relief whenever legal remedies are not "practical and efficient," unless there is a statute to the contrary. This expansive view of equity must be rejected. Joseph Story's famous treatise reflects what we consider the proper rule, both with regard to the general role of equity in our "government of law, not of men," and with regard to its application is the very case before us:

> "Mr. Justice Blackstone has taken considerable pains to refute this doctrine. 'It is said,' he remarks, 'that it is the business of a Court of Equity, in England, to abate the rigor of the common law. But no such power is contended for. Hard was the case of bond creditors, whose debtor devised away his real estate. * * * But a Court of Equity can give no relief * * * .' And illustrations of the same character may be found in every state of the Union. * * * In many [States], if not in all, a debtor may prefer one creditor to another, in discharging his debts, whose assets are wholly insufficient to pay all the debts." 1 Commentaries on Equity Jurisprudence § 12, pp. 14-15 (1836).

We do not question the proposition that equity is flexible; but in the federal system, at least, that flexibility is confined within the broad boundaries of traditional equitable relief. To accord a type of relief that has never been available before—and especially (as here) a type of relief that has been specifically disclaimed by longstanding judicial precedent—is to invoke a "default rule," not of flexibility but of omnipotence. When there are indeed new conditions that might call for a wrenching departure from past practice, Congress is in a much better position than we both to perceive them and to design the appropriate remedy. * * *

We note that none of the parties or amici specifically raised the applicability to this case of Federal Rule of Civil Procedure 18(b), which states:

> "Whenever a claim is one heretofore cognizable only after another claim has been prosecuted to a conclusion, the two claims may be joined

in a single action; but the court shall grant relief in that action only in accordance with the relative substantive rights of the parties. In particular, a plaintiff may state a claim for money and a claim to have set aside a conveyance fraudulent as to that plaintiff, without first having obtained a judgment establishing the claim for money."

Because the Rule was neither mentioned by the lower courts nor briefed by the parties, we decline to consider its application to the present case. We note, however, that it says nothing about preliminary relief, and specifically reserves substantive rights (as did the Rules Enabling Act, 28 U.S.C. § 2072(b)).[7] * * *

B

[The Court then distinguished an earlier decision, Deckert v. Independence Shares Corp., 311 U.S. 282 (1940), in which the plaintiffs sought equitable relief under federal securities laws, including the appointment of a receiver and an injunction restraining the transfer of defendant's assets. The Court concluded that "The preliminary relief available in a suit seeking equitable relief has nothing to do with the preliminary relief available in a creditor's bill seeking equitable assistance in the collection of a legal debt."]

In the second case relied on by respondents, United States v. First Nat. City Bank, 379 U.S. 378 (1965), the United States, in its suit to enforce a tax assessment and tax lien, requested a preliminary injunction preventing a third-party bank from transferring any of the taxpayer's assets which were held in a foreign branch office of the bank. Id. at 379-380. Relying on a statute giving district courts the power to grant injunctions "'necessary or appropriate for the enforcement of the internal revenue laws,'" id. at 380 (quoting former 26 U.S.C. § 7402(a) (1964 ed.)), we concluded that the temporary injunction was "appropriate to prevent further dissipation of assets," 379 U.S. at 385. We stated that if a district court could not issue such an injunction, foreign taxpayers could avoid their tax obligations.

First National is distinguishable from the present case on a number of grounds. First, of course, it involved not the Court's general equitable powers under the Judiciary Act of 1789, but its powers under the statute authorizing issuance of tax injunctions. Second, First National relied in part on the doctrine that courts of equity will "'go much farther both to give and withhold relief in furtherance of the public interest than they are accustomed to go when only private interests are involved,'" id. at 383 (quoting Virginia R. Co. v. Railway Employees, 300 U.S. 515, 552 (1937)). And finally, although the Court did not rely on this fact, the creditor (the Government) asserted an equitable lien on the property, see 379 U.S. at 379-380, which presents a different case from that of the unsecured general creditor.

---

[7] Several States have adopted the Uniform Fraudulent Conveyance Act (or its successor the Uniform Fraudulent Transfers Act), which has been interpreted as conferring on a nonjudgment creditor the right to bring a fraudulent conveyance claim. See generally P. Alces, Law of Fraudulent Transactions ¶5.04[3], p. 5-116 (1989). Insofar as Rule 18(b) applies to such an action, the state statute eliminating the need for a judgment may have altered the common-law rule that a general contract creditor has no interest in his debtor's property. Because this case does not involve a claim of fraudulent conveyance, we express no opinion on the point.

That *Deckert* and *First National* should not be read as establishing the principle relied on by respondents is strongly suggested by De Beers Consol. Mines, Ltd. v. United States, 325 U.S. 212 (1945). In that case the United States brought suit against several corporations seeking equitable relief against alleged antitrust violations. The United States also sought a preliminary injunction restraining the defendants from removing their assets from this country pending adjudication of the merits. We concluded that the injunction was beyond the power of the District Court. We stated that "[a] preliminary injunction is always appropriate to grant intermediate relief of the same character as that which may be granted finally," but that the injunction in that case dealt "with a matter lying wholly outside the issues in the suit." Id. at 220. We pointed out that "Federal and State courts appear consistently to have refused relief of the nature here sought[.]" * * *

C

As further support for the proposition that the relief accorded here was unknown to traditional equity practice, it is instructive that the English Court of Chancery, from which the First Congress borrowed in conferring equitable powers on the federal courts, did not provide an injunctive remedy such as this until 1975. In that year, the Court of Appeal decided Mareva Compania Naviera S.A. v. International Bulkcarriers S.A., 2 Lloyd's Rep. 509. *Mareva*, although acknowledging that the prior case of Lister & Co. v. Stubbs, [1890] 45 Ch. D. 1 (C.A.), said that a court has no power to protect a creditor before he gets judgment, relied on a statute giving courts the authority to grant an interlocutory injunction "'in all cases in which it shall appear to the court to be just or convenient,'" 2 Lloyd's Rep., at 510 (quoting Judicature Act of 1925, Law Reports 1925 (2), 15 & 16 Geo. V, ch. 49, § 45). It held (in the words of Lord Denning) that "if it appears that the debt is due and owing—and there is a danger that the debtor may dispose of his assets so as to defeat it before judgment—the Court has jurisdiction in a proper case to grant an interlocutory judgment so as to prevent him [sic] disposing of those assets." 2 Lloyd's Rep., at 510. The *Mareva* injunction has now been confirmed by statute. See Supreme Court Act of 1981, § 37, 11 Halsbury's Statutes 966, 1001 (4th ed. 1985).[9]

Commentators have emphasized that the adoption of *Mareva* injunctions was a dramatic departure from prior practice.

> "Before 1975 the courts would not grant an injunction to restrain a defendant from disposing of his assets pendente lite merely because the plaintiff feared that by the time he obtained judgment the defendant would have no assets against which execution could be levied. Applications for such injunctions were consistently refused in the English Commercial Court as elsewhere. They were thought to be so

---

[9] Apparently the first "Mareva" injunction was actually issued in Nippon Yusen Kaisha v. Karageorgis, [1975] 2 Lloyd's Rep. 137 (C.A.), in which Lord Denning recognized the prior practice of not granting such injunctions, but stated that "the time has come when we should revise our practice." Id. at 138; see also Hetherington, Introduction to the Mareva Injunction, in Mareva Injunctions 1, n.1 (M. Hetherington, ed. 1983). For whatever reason, *Mareva* has gotten the credit (or blame), and we follow the tradition of leaving *Nippon Yusen* in the shadows.

clearly beyond the powers of the court as to be 'wholly unarguable.'" Hetherington, supra n.9, at 3.

See also Wasserman, *Equity Renewed: Preliminary Injunctions to Secure Potential Money Judgments*, 67 Wash. L. Rev. 257, 337 (1992) (stating that *Mareva* "revolutionized English practice"). The *Mareva* injunction has been recognized as a powerful tool for general creditors; indeed, it has been called the "nuclear weapon of the law." R. Ough & W. Flenley, The Mareva Injunction and Anton Piller Order: Practice and Precedents xi (2d ed. 1993).

The parties debate whether *Mareva* was based on statutory authority or on inherent equitable power. Regardless of the answer to this question, it is indisputable that the English courts of equity did not actually exercise this power until 1975, and that federal courts in this country have traditionally applied the principle that courts of equity will not, as a general matter, interfere with the debtor's disposition of his property at the instance of a nonjudgment creditor. We think it incompatible with our traditionally cautious approach to equitable powers, which leaves any substantial expansion of past practice to Congress, to decree the elimination of this significant protection for debtors.

IV

The parties and amici discuss various arguments for and against creating the preliminary injunctive remedy at issue in this case. The United States suggests that the factors supporting such a remedy include

> "simplicity and uniformity of procedure; preservation of the court's ability to render a judgment that will prove enforceable; prevention of inequitable conduct on the part of defendants; avoiding disparities between defendants that have assets within the jurisdiction (which would be subject to pre-judgment attachment 'at law') and those that do not; avoiding the necessity for plaintiffs to locate a forum in which the defendant has substantial assets; and, in an age of easy global mobility of capital, preserving the attractiveness of the United States as a center for financial transactions."

But there are weighty considerations on the other side as well, the most significant of which is the historical principle that before judgment (or its equivalent) an unsecured creditor has no rights at law or in equity in the property of his debtor. As one treatise writer explained:

> "A rule of procedure which allowed any prowling creditor, before his claim was definitely established by judgment, and without reference to the character of his demand, to file a bill to discover assets, or to impeach transfers, or interfere with the business affairs of the alleged debtor, would manifestly be susceptible of the grossest abuse. A more powerful weapon of oppression could not be placed at the disposal of unscrupulous litigants." Wait, Fraudulent Conveyances, § 73, at 110-111.

The requirement that the creditor obtain a prior judgment is a fundamental protection in debtor-creditor law—rendered all the more important in our federal system by the debtor's right to a jury trial on the legal claim. There are other factors which likewise give us pause: The remedy sought here could render

Federal Rule of Civil Procedure 64, which authorizes use of state prejudgment remedies, a virtual irrelevance. Why go through the trouble of complying with local attachment and garnishment statutes when this all-purpose prejudgment injunction is available? More importantly, by adding, through judicial fiat, a new and powerful weapon to the creditor's arsenal, the new rule could radically alter the balance between debtor's and creditor's rights which has been developed over centuries through many laws—including those relating to bankruptcy, fraudulent conveyances, and preferences. Because any rational creditor would want to protect his investment, such a remedy might induce creditors to engage in a "race to the courthouse" in cases involving insolvent or near-insolvent debtors, which might prove financially fatal to the struggling debtor. (In this case, we might observe, the respondents did not represent all of the holders of the Notes; they were an active few who sought to benefit at the expense of the other noteholders as well as GMD's other creditors.) It is significant that, in England, use of the *Mareva* injunction has expanded rapidly. "Since 1975, the English courts have awarded *Mareva* injunctions to freeze assets in an ever-increasing set of circumstances both within and beyond the commercial setting to an ever-expanding number of plaintiffs." Wasserman, 67 Wash. L. Rev., at 339. As early as 1984, one observer stated that "there are now a steady flow of such applications to our Courts which have been estimated to exceed one thousand per month." Shenton, *Attachments and Other Interim Court Remedies in Support of Arbitration*, 1984 Int'l Bus. Law. 101, 104.

We do not decide which side has the better of these arguments. We set them forth only to demonstrate that resolving them in this forum is incompatible with the democratic and self-deprecating judgment we have long since made: that the equitable powers conferred by the Judiciary Act of 1789 did not include the power to create remedies previously unknown to equity jurisprudence. Even when sitting as a court in equity, we have no authority to craft a "nuclear weapon" of the law like the one advocated here. Joseph Story made the point many years ago:

> "If, indeed, a Court of Equity in England did possess the unbounded jurisdiction, which has been thus generally ascribed to it, of correcting, controlling, moderating, and even superceding the law, and of enforcing all the rights, as well as the charities, arising from natural law and justice, and of freeing itself from all regard to former rules and precedents, it would be the most gigantic in its sway, and the most formidable instrument of arbitrary power, that could well be devised. It would literally place the whole rights and property of the community under the arbitrary will of the Judge, acting, if you please, arbitrio boni judicis, and it may be, ex aequo et bono, according to his own notions and conscience; but still acting with a despotic and sovereign authority. A Court of Chancery might then well deserve the spirited rebuke of Seldon; 'For law we have a measure, and know what to trust to—Equity is according to the conscience of him, that is Chancellor; and as that is larger, or narrower, so is Equity. 'Tis all one, as if they should make the standard for the measure the Chancellor's foot. What an uncertain measure would this be? One Chancellor has a long foot; another a short

foot; a third an indifferent foot. It is the same thing with the Chancellor's conscience.'" 1 Commentaries on Equity Jurisprudence § 19, at 21.

The debate concerning this formidable power over debtors should be conducted and resolved where such issues belong in our democracy: in the Congress.

* * *

Because such a remedy was historically unavailable from a court of equity, we hold that the District Court had no authority to issue a preliminary injunction preventing petitioners from disposing of their assets pending adjudication of respondents' contract claim for money damages. We reverse the judgment of the Second Circuit and remand the case for further proceedings consistent with this opinion.

It is so ordered.

JUSTICE GINSBURG, with whom JUSTICE STEVENS, JUSTICE SOUTER, and JUSTICE BREYER join, dissenting.

I

Uncontested evidence presented to the District Court at the preliminary injunction hearing showed that petitioner Grupo Mexicano de Desarrollo, S. A. (GMD), had defaulted on its contractual obligations to respondents, a group of GMD noteholders (Alliance), that Alliance had satisfied all conditions precedent to its breach of contract claim, and that GMD had no plausible defense on the merits. Alliance also demonstrated that GMD had undertaken to treat Alliance's claims on the same footing as all other unsecured, unsubordinated debt, but that GMD was in fact satisfying Mexican creditors to the exclusion of Alliance. Furthermore, unchallenged evidence indicated that GMD was so rapidly disbursing its sole remaining asset that, absent provisional action by the District Court, Alliance would have been unable to collect on the money judgment for which it qualified.[1]

* * * [T]he judge employed a preliminary injunction "to preserve the relative positions of the parties until a trial on the merits [could] be held." University of Texas v. Camenisch, 451 U.S. 390, 395 (1981). The order enjoined GMD from distributing assets likely to be necessary to satisfy the judgment in the instant case, but gave Alliance no security interest in GMD's assets, nor any preference relative to GMD's other creditors. Moreover, the injunction expressly reserved to GMD the option of commencing proceedings under the bankruptcy laws of Mexico or the United States. In addition, the District Judge recorded his readiness to modify the interim order if necessary to keep GMD in business. The preliminary injunction thus constrained GMD only to the extent essential to the subsequent entry of an effective judgment.

---

[1] GMD did not seek Second Circuit review of the District Court's fact findings on irreparable harm or of that court's determination that Alliance almost certainly would prevail on the merits. Nor does GMD cast any doubt on those matters here. Instead, GMD forthrightly concedes that had the District Court declined to issue the preliminary injunction, GMD would have had no assets available to satisfy the money judgment that Alliance ultimately obtained.

The Court nevertheless disapproves the provisional relief ordered by the District Court, holding that a preliminary injunction freezing assets is beyond the equitable authority of the federal courts. I would not so disarm the district courts. As I comprehend the courts' authority, injunctions of this kind, entered in the circumstances presented here, are within federal equity jurisdiction. Satisfied that the injunction issued in this case meets the exacting standards for preliminary equitable relief, I would affirm the judgment of the Second Circuit.

II

* * * The District Court acted in this case in careful accord with [traditional equitable] prescriptions, issuing the preliminary injunction only upon well-supported findings that Alliance had "[no] adequate remedy at law," would be "frustrated" in its ability to recover a judgment absent interim injunctive relief, and was "almost certain" to prevail on the merits.[3]

The Court holds the District Court's preliminary freeze order impermissible principally because injunctions of this kind were not "traditionally accorded by courts of equity" at the time the Constitution was adopted. In my view, the Court relies on an unjustifiably static conception of equity jurisdiction. * * *

Compared to many contemporary adaptations of equitable remedies, the preliminary injunction Alliance sought in this case was a modest measure. In operation, moreover, the preliminary injunction to freeze assets pendente lite may be a less heavy-handed remedy than prejudgment attachment which deprives the defendant of possession and use of the seized property. See Wasserman, *Equity Renewed: Preliminary Injunctions to Secure Potential Money Judgments*, 67 Wash. L. Rev. 257, 281-282, 323-324 (1992). Taking account of the office of equity, the facts of this case, and the moderate, status quo preserving provisional remedy, I am persuaded that the District Court acted appropriately.

* * * [A]s the facts of this case so plainly show, for creditors situated as Alliance is, the remedy at law is worthless absent the provisional relief in equity's arsenal. Moreover, increasingly sophisticated foreign-haven judgment proofing strategies, coupled with technology that permits the nearly instantaneous transfer of assets abroad, suggests that defendants may succeed in avoiding meritorious claims in ways unimaginable before the merger of law and equity. See Lynn Lopucki, *The Death of Liability*, 106 Yale L. J. 1, 32-38 (1996). I am not ready to say a responsible Chancellor today would deny Alliance relief on the ground that prior case law is unsupportive.

The development of *Mareva* injunctions in England after 1975 supports the view of the lower courts in this case, a view to which I adhere. As the Court observes, * * * preliminary asset-freeze injunctions have been available in

---

[3] We have on three occasions considered the availability of a preliminary injunction to freeze assets pending litigation, see Deckert v. Independence Shares Corp., 311 U.S. 282 (1940); De Beers Consol. Mines, Ltd. v. United States, 325 U.S. 212 (1945); United States v. First Nat. City Bank, 379 U.S. 378 (1965). As the Court recognizes, these cases involved factual and legal circumstances markedly different from those presented in this case and thus do not rule out or in the provisional remedy at issue here.

English courts since the 1975 Court of Appeal decision in Mareva Compania Naviera S. A. v. International Bulkcarriers S. A., 2 Lloyd's Rep. 509. Although the cases reveal some uncertainty regarding *Mareva*'s jurisdictional basis, the better-reasoned and more recent decisions ground *Mareva* in equity's traditional power to remedy the "abuse" of legal process by defendants and the "injustice" that would result from defendants "making themselves judgment-proof" by disposing of their assets during the pendency of litigation. Iraqi Ministry of Defence v. Arcepey Shipping Co., 1 All E.R. 480, 484-487 (1979) (internal citations omitted)[.] * * *

III

A

The Court worries that permitting preliminary injunctions to freeze assets would allow creditors, "'on a mere statement of belief that the defendant can easily make away with or transport his money or goods, [to] impose an injunction on him, indefinite in duration, disabling him to use so much of his funds or property as the court deems necessary for security or compliance with its possible decree.'" (quoting De Beers Consol. Mines, Ltd. v. United States, 325 U.S. 212, 222 (1945)). Given the strong showings a creditor would be required to make to gain the provisional remedy, and the safeguards on which the debtor could insist, I agree with the Second Circuit "that this 'parade of horribles' [would] not come to pass." 143 F.3d 688, 696 (1998).

Under standards governing preliminary injunctive relief generally, a plaintiff must show a likelihood of success on the merits and irreparable injury in the absence of an injunction. Plaintiffs with questionable claims would not meet the likelihood of success criterion. See 11A Wright, Miller, & Kane, Federal Practice and Procedure § 2948.3, at p. 184-188. * * * The irreparable injury requirement would not be met by unsubstantiated allegations that a defendant may dissipate assets. See id. § 2948.1, at 153 ("Speculative injury is not sufficient."); see also Wasserman, supra, at 286-305 (discussing application of traditional preliminary injunction requirements to provisional asset-freeze requests). As the Court of Appeals recognized, provisional freeze orders would be appropriate in damages actions only upon a finding that, without the freeze, "the movant would be unable to collect [a money] judgment." 143 F.3d at 697. The preliminary asset-freeze order, in short, would rank and operate as an extraordinary remedy.

Federal Rule of Civil Procedure 65(c), moreover, requires a preliminary injunction applicant to post a bond "in such sum as the court deems proper, for the payment of such costs and damages as may be incurred or suffered by any party who is found to have been wrongfully enjoined." * * * The protections in place guard against any routine or arbitrary imposition of a preliminary freeze order designed to stop the dissipation of assets that would render a court's judgment worthless. The case we face should be paradigmatic. There was no question that GMD's debt to Alliance was due and owing. And the short span—less than four months—between preliminary injunction and summary judgment shows that the temporary restraint on GMD did not linger beyond the time necessary for a fair and final adjudication in a busy but efficiently operated court. Absent immediate judicial action, Alliance would have been left with a multimillion dollar judgment on which it could collect not a penny. In my view, the District Court properly invoked its equitable power to avoid that manifestly unjust result and to protect its ability to render an enforceable final judgment.

NOTES AND QUESTIONS FOR DISCUSSION

1. At the pre-trial stage, attachment of a foreign defendant's property might arise in a handful of settings. A court might be asked to attach the defendant's property within its jurisdiction for security purposes in a suit pending in that very court. Or, it might be asked to attach property within its jurisdiction in aid of a pending proceeding in another jurisdiction. In addition, a court might be asked to enjoin a party who is subject that that court's in personam jurisdiction to act or to refrain from acting in another jurisdiction with respect to property in that other jurisdiction. *Alliance Bond*, which addresses federal equitable powers, does nothing to prevent *state* courts from engaging in such practices. And, as noted below, *Alliance Bond* does not wholly foreclose federal courts from engaging in such practices.

2. In *Alliance Bond*, the assets whose transfer the plaintiff was trying to enjoin were in Mexico. Thus, unlike the decision in *Carolina Power & Light Co. v. Uranex, supra*, a federal court was not being asked to seize assets over which it otherwise had territorial control. Indeed, pursuant to Rule 64(a), Fed. R. Civ. P., pretrial attachment of assets *within* the a federal court's jurisdiction would appear to be governed by state law, in the absence of any relevant federal statute. The Rule provides that "every remedy is available that, under the law of the state where the court is located, provides for seizing a person or property to secure the satisfaction of the potential judgment." Id. If New York state law had allowed for it, would Rule 64(a) have permitted the federal district court in *Alliance Bond* to enjoin a party subject its personal jurisdiction to prevent its disposing of property outside the state? The *Alliance Bond* Court focused on Rule 65, but barely mentioned Rule 64. Was it right to do so?

3. The court in *Uranex*, as have some other federal courts, supposed that a security order could have extraterritorial effect in the proper case if issued against a party who is otherwise properly before the court, without regard to state law. See 451 F. Supp. at 1048 n.1. See also United States v. Thornton, 672 F.2d 101 (D.C. Cir. 1982). *Alliance Bond*, however, suggests that federal courts lack the power to enter such an order—not because of its possible extraterritorial effect, but because of inherent limitations on federal court equity powers, in the absence of a federal statute or rule. For an illustration of the pre-*Alliance Bond* approach to the problem of attachment, see *In re* Estate of Ferdinand Marcos, 25 F.3d 1467, 1476-90 (9th Cir. 1994). Are you persuaded by *Alliance Bond's* narrow (and somewhat static) construction of the federal courts' equity powers? For critical commentary on *Alliance Bond*, see David Capper, *The Need for Mareva Injunctions Reconsidered*, 73 Fordham L. Rev. 2161 (2005); Stephen B. Burbank, *The Bitter with the Sweet: Traditions, History, and Limitations on Federal Judicial Power—A Case Study*, 75 Notre Dame L. Rev. 1291 (2000).

4. As suggested in Note 2, if a defendant's assets are within the state in which the court sits, and if state law allows for it, a court (either state, or federal under

Rule 64) could—on the proper showing—order a pre-judgment seizure of those assets for security purposes. But after the decision in *Alliance Bond* (and barring resort to Rule 64 for an injunction against the foreign defendant with respect to the disposition of out-of-state property, if state law so allowed), what options will be available to a creditor who has sued a foreign defendant in a court in the U.S., who fears that assets may be squandered in the defendant's home country in the interim, and where the only assets to secure a judgment might be outside of the U.S.?

- Because *Alliance Bond* only speaks to the equitable powers of the federal courts, and does not ground its decision on any broader grounds implicating foreign assets or extraterritorial impact, a plaintiff could seek out a state court (or, perhaps, a foreign court) which—as discussed in footnote 7 of the opinion—has abandoned the traditional no-injunction rule. State courts are hardly bound by the equitable limitations outlined in *Alliance Bond*. Of course, absent a nondiverse defendant, such a lawsuit by a U.S. citizen against an alien would likely be removed to federal court. Would it then be open to the plaintiff to seek an injunction, in federal court, to prevent the defendant's transfer of assets based on the fact that state law would allow for such an injunction? The argument might be grounded in Rule 18(b), as Justice Scalia hints, if there were an equitable claim that an impending transfer would be fraudulent.

- Even absent such a possibility, an argument might be grounded in Erie Railroad Co. v. Tompkins, 304 U.S. 64 (1938), to the effect that the right to injunctive relief for security purposes in such settings is a substantive right. Cf. Cohen v. Beneficial Indus. Loan Corp., 337 U.S. 541 (1949) (holding that state class-action rules regarding pre-trial security must govern in federal court diversity class action based on state law). If so, and if state law should govern and should allow for the possibility, then the argument from general equitable powers of the federal courts is arguably beside the point. The *Alliance Bond* Court (in footnote 3) expressly did not address the applicability of *Erie*, because it was not raised by the parties below. Note that it was Grupo Mexicano who sought to raise the *Erie* question in the Supreme Court. Does that suggest that New York law operated *as a bar* to such pre-trial attachment? Cf. Alliance Bond Fund, Inc. v. Grupo Mexicano de Desarrollo, S.A., 143 F.3d 688, 692 (2d Cir. 1998) (indicating, in connection with Rule 64, that New York law would not permit such a preliminary injunction in a damages action unless the property is in-state).

- *Alliance Bond* held that a district court "has no authority to issue a preliminary injunction preventing [a party] from disposing of [its] assets pending adjudication of [a] contract claim." 527 U.S. at 333. The Court distinguished actions for money damages from an earlier case in which the relief being sought was equitable in nature and in which a preliminary injunction was proper. "The preliminary relief available in a suit seeking equitable relief has nothing to do with the preliminary relief available in a creditor's bill seeking equitable assistance in the collection of a legal debt." Id. at 324-26. Consequently, a preliminary injunction resembling the one sought in *Alliance Bond* could be issued in a suit in which equitable relief (perhaps in addition to legal relief) in relation to specific funds was being sought in the underlying lawsuit. See, e.g., Quantum Corp. Funding, Ltd. v. Assist You Home Servs. of Va., 144 F. Supp. 2d 241, 250 n.9 (S.D.N.Y. 2001); see also Gucci America, Inc. v. Weixing Li, 2011 U.S. Dist. LEXIS 97814 (S.D.N.Y. Aug. 23, 2011) (Lanham Act).

• Finally, Congress could take the cue and enact a statute giving federal courts the power to issue *Mareva*-style injunctions to prevent dissipation of a defendant's assets on foreign territory.

5. Property and Attachment: A Comparative Perspective. The Supreme Court in *Alliance Bond* declined to adopt the so-called "Mareva" injunctions that had been developed by English courts. See **Mareva Compania Naviera S.A. v. Int'l Bulkcarriers S.A., 2 Lloyd's Rep. 509 (1975).** As a matter of policy, are such injunctions a good idea? Their effect, of course, is to immobilize or freeze the assets that are attached, perhaps even on a world-wide basis. Analogously, under Article 24 of the Brussels Convention on Jurisdiction and Recognition of Judgments and its successor, the Brussels Regulation (Art. 31) (see Appendix D for the text of the Regulation), an E.U. member state court can entertain a request for provisional or interim relief in connection with a cause of action pending in another E.U. member state court. And it may do so whether or not it would otherwise have jurisdiction to decide the merits.

Nevertheless, as noted in Chapter 8, U.S. courts sometimes refuse to recognize or give comity to foreign decisions that run afoul of domestic "public policy" concerns. Could attachment proceedings in a foreign jurisdiction, for example, be so procedurally wanting that the order (or any judgment ultimately entered) ought to be given no respect here—for example, if a foreign court provisionally orders a U.S. defendant to act or refrain from acting in a particular way in the U.S., pending the foreign litigation? Cf. Finanz AG Zurich v. Banco Economico S.A., 192 F.3d 240, 246-49 (2d Cir. 1999) (upholding district court's decision, based on comity, to abstain in deference to Brazilian bankruptcy proceeding in which the same claim could be asserted, and finding no public policy or due process objection to Brazilian procedures). Is there any argument that such non-final interlocutory orders are deserving of less respect than a final judgment?

6. Property and Jurisdiction: A Comparative Perspective. Even as cases such as *Shaffer v. Heitner* show the U.S. has generally retreated from the use of property as a basis for jurisdiction on matters unrelated to that property, some European jurisdictions continue to allow for the practice. For example, under Section 23 of the German Code of Civil Procedure, a domiciliary may bring suit against a nondomiciliary in a German court where the nondomiciliary has assets, whether tangible or intangible. Moreover, the property need not be related in any respect to the underlying litigation, as would be called for by *Shaffer*. In addition, a judgment based on the presence of assets under Section 23 is not restricted to the value of those assets. Section 23, however, is not especially well received, even in the E.U. Under the Brussels Convention and the later Brussels Regulation, a judgment based on Section 23 will not be enforceable in other European Community member states against persons domiciled in those states. Nevertheless, they are enforceable in other member states if the judgment is against a person *not* domiciled in another member state (e.g., a U.S. citizen). In recent years, the German courts have themselves become reluctant to apply Section 23 in cases in which the dispute has no connection to Germany other than the presence of assets.

I. FORUM SELECTION CLAUSES

Given the vagaries of the law of personal jurisdiction, particularly in U.S. courts, parties seeking greater predictability might prefer to contractually agree in advance to a choice of forum in the event of a dispute. Such predictability may be especially important for international actors who are repeat players, and whose activities might otherwise open them up to successful invocation of personal jurisdiction in a variety of forums. Of course, such advance planning will not likely have occurred where the parties will not have had a chance to meet with one another prior to the events that give rise to the litigation. Personal injury and product liability cases often bring parties together for the first time, when it is too late to contractually agree on a choice of forum. But in the commercial and contract setting, such advance planning is certainly possible.

In this section, we address the problem of forum selection clauses in the setting of transnational civil litigation. As you approach these materials, consider whether courts should be hospitable to such agreements, and if so, under what circumstances. Should it matter that the choice of forum clause was actually bargained for? That one of the parties is a consumer or another has substantially greater bargaining power? That the chosen forum might apply law that is far less favorable to the plaintiff who may have filed suit elsewhere (in contravention of the agreement)? Or that the chosen forum turns out to be far less convenient than other possible forums? In addition, consider the fact that a choice of forum clause is itself a contractual agreement between the parties. Consequently, some law must apply to determine the validity of such an agreement. Whose law should that be? The case that follows is the classic modern decision by the Supreme Court on choice of law clauses.

The Bremen v. Zapata Off-Shore Co.

Supreme Court of the United States, 1972.

407 U.S. 1.

MR. CHIEF JUSTICE BURGER delivered the opinion of the Court.

We granted certiorari to review a judgment of the United States Court of Appeals for the Fifth Circuit declining to enforce a forum-selection clause governing disputes arising under an international towage contract between petitioners and respondent. The circuits have differed in their approach to such clauses. For the reasons stated hereafter, we vacate the judgment of the Court of Appeals.

In November 1967, respondent Zapata, a Houston-based American corporation, contracted with petitioner Unterweser, a German corporation, to tow Zapata's ocean-going, self-elevating drilling rig *Chaparral* from Louisiana to a point off Ravenna, Italy, in the Adriatic Sea, where Zapata had agreed to drill certain wells.

Zapata had solicited bids for the towage, and several companies including Unterweser had responded. Unterweser was the low bidder and Zapata requested it to submit a contract, which it did. The contract submitted by Unterweser contained the following provision, which is at issue in this case: "Any dispute arising must be treated before the London Court of Justice." In addition the contract contained two clauses purporting to exculpate Unterweser from liability for damages to the towed barge.

After reviewing the contract and making several changes, but without any alteration in the forum-selection or exculpatory clauses, a Zapata vice president executed the contract and forwarded it to Unterweser in Germany, where Unterweser accepted the changes, and the contract became effective.

On January 5, 1968, Unterweser's deep sea tug *Bremen* departed Venice, Louisiana, with the *Chaparral* in tow bound for Italy. On January 9, while the flotilla was in international waters in the middle of the Gulf of Mexico, a severe storm arose. The sharp roll of the *Chaparral* in Gulf waters caused its elevator legs, which had been raised for the voyage, to break off and fall into the sea, seriously damaging the *Chaparral*. In this emergency situation Zapata instructed the *Bremen* to tow its damaged rig to Tampa, Florida, the nearest port of refuge.

On January 12, Zapata, ignoring its contract promise to litigate "any dispute arising" in the English courts, commenced a suit in admiralty in the United States District Court at Tampa, seeking $ 3,500,000 damages against Unterweser *in personam* and the *Bremen in rem*, alleging negligent towage and breach of contract. Unterweser responded by invoking the forum clause of the towage contract, and moved to dismiss for lack of jurisdiction or on *forum non conveniens* grounds, or in the alternative to stay the action pending submission of the dispute to the "London Court of Justice." Shortly thereafter, in February, before the District Court had ruled on its motion to stay or dismiss the United States action, Unterweser commenced an action against Zapata seeking damages for breach of the towage contract in the High Court of Justice in London, as the contract provided. Zapata appeared in that court to contest jurisdiction, but its challenge was rejected, the English courts holding that the contractual forum provision conferred jurisdiction.[4]

---

[4] Zapata appeared specially and moved to set aside service of process outside the country. Justice Karminski of the High Court of Justice denied the motion on the ground the contractual choice-of-forum provision conferred jurisdiction and would be enforced, absent a factual showing it would not be "fair and right" to do so. He did not believe Zapata had made such a showing, and held that it should be required to "stick to [its] bargain." The Court of Appeal dismissed an appeal on the ground that Justice Karminski had properly applied the English rule. Lord Justice Willmer stated that rule as follows:

In the meantime, Unterweser was faced with a dilemma in the pending action in the United States court at Tampa. The six-month period for filing action to limit its liability to Zapata and other potential claimants was about to expire, but the United States District Court in Tampa had not yet ruled on Unterweser's motion to dismiss or stay Zapata's action. On July 2, 1968, confronted with difficult alternatives, Unterweser filed an action to limit its liability in the District Court in Tampa. That court entered the customary injunction against proceedings outside the limitation court, and Zapata refilled its initial claim in the limitation action.[6]

It was only at this juncture, on July 29, after the six-month period for filing the limitation action had run, that the District Court denied Unterweser's January motion to dismiss or stay Zapata's initial action. In denying the motion, that court relied on the prior decision of the Court of Appeals in Carbon Black Export, Inc. v. The Monrosa, 254 F.2d 297 (CA5 1958), cert. dismissed, 359 U.S. 180 (1959). In that case the Court of Appeals had held a forum-selection clause unenforceable, reiterating the traditional view of many American courts that "agreements in advance of controversy whose object is to oust the jurisdiction of the courts are contrary to public policy and will not be enforced." 254 F.2d, at 300-301. Apparently concluding that it was bound by the *Carbon Black* case, the District Court gave the forum-selection clause little, if any, weight. Instead, the court treated the motion to dismiss under normal *forum non conveniens* doctrine applicable in the absence of such a clause, citing *Gulf Oil Corp.* v. *Gilbert*, 330 U.S. 501 (1947). Under that doctrine "unless the balance is strongly in favor of the defendant, the plaintiff's choice of forum should rarely be disturbed." *Id.*, at 508. The District Court concluded: "The balance of conveniences here is not strongly in favor of [Unterweser] and [Zapata's] choice of forum should not be disturbed."

"The law on the subject, I think, is not open to doubt. . . . It is always open to parties to stipulate . . . that a particular Court shall have jurisdiction over any dispute arising out of their contract. Here the parties chose to stipulate that disputes were to be referred to the 'London Court,' which I take as meaning the High Court in this country. *Prima facie* it is the policy of the Court to hold parties to the bargain into which they have entered. . . . But that is not an inflexible rule, as was shown, for instance, by the case of *The Fehmarn*, [1957] 1 Lloyd's Rep. 511; (C.A.) [1957] 2 Lloyd's Rep. 55. . . .

"I approach the matter, therefore, in this way, that the Court has a discretion, but it is a discretion which, in the ordinary way and in the absence of strong reason to the contrary, will be exercised in favour of holding parties to their bargain. The question is whether sufficient circumstances have been shown to exist in this case to make it desirable, on the grounds of balance of convenience, that proceedings should not take place in this country . . . ." [1968] 2 Lloyd's Rep. 158, 162-163.

[6] In its limitation complaint, Unterweser stated it "reserve[d] all rights" under its previous motion to dismiss or stay Zapata's action, and reasserted that the High Court of Justice was the proper forum for determining the entire controversy, including its own right to limited liability, in accord with the contractual forum clause. Unterweser later counterclaimed, setting forth the same contractual cause of action as in its English action and a further cause of action for salvage arising out of the *Bremen*'s services following the casualty. In its counterclaim, Unterweser again asserted that the High Court of Justice in London was the proper forum for determining all aspects of the controversy, including its counterclaim.

Thereafter, on January 21, 1969, the District Court denied another motion by Unterweser to stay the limitation action pending determination of the controversy in the High Court of Justice in London and granted Zapata's motion to restrain Unterweser from litigating further in the London court. The District Judge ruled that, having taken jurisdiction in the limitation proceeding, he had jurisdiction to determine all matters relating to the controversy. He ruled that Unterweser should be required to "do equity" by refraining from also litigating the controversy in the London court, not only for the reasons he had previously stated for denying Unterweser's first motion to stay Zapata's action, but also because Unterweser had invoked the United States court's jurisdiction to obtain the benefit of the Limitation Act.

On appeal, a divided panel of the Court of Appeals affirmed, and on rehearing *en banc* the panel opinion was adopted, with six of the 14 *en banc* judges dissenting. As had the District Court, the majority rested on the *Carbon Black* decision, concluding that "'at the very least'" that case stood for the proposition that a forum-selection clause "'will not be enforced unless the selected state would provide a more convenient forum than the state in which suit is brought.'" From that premise the Court of Appeals proceeded to conclude that, apart from the forum-selection clause, the District Court did not abuse its discretion in refusing to decline jurisdiction on the basis of *forum non conveniens.* * * *

We hold, with the six dissenting members of the Court of Appeals, that far too little weight and effect were given to the forum clause in resolving this controversy. For at least two decades we have witnessed an expansion of overseas commercial activities by business enterprises based in the United States. The barrier of distance that once tended to confine a business concern to a modest territory no longer does so. Here we see an American company with special expertise contracting with a foreign company to tow a complex machine thousands of miles across seas and oceans. The expansion of American business and industry will hardly be encouraged if, notwithstanding solemn contracts, we insist on a parochial concept that all disputes must be resolved under our laws and in our courts. Absent a contract forum, the considerations relied on by the Court of Appeals would be persuasive reasons for holding an American forum convenient in the traditional sense, but in an era of expanding world trade and commerce, the absolute aspects of the doctrine of the *Carbon Black* case have little place and would be a heavy hand indeed on the future development of international commercial dealings by Americans. We cannot have trade and commerce in world markets and international waters exclusively on our terms, governed by our laws, and resolved in our courts.

Forum-selection clauses have historically not been favored by American courts. Many courts, federal and state, have declined to enforce such clauses on the ground that they were "contrary to public policy," or that their effect was to "oust the jurisdiction" of the court. Although this view apparently still has considerable acceptance, other courts are tending to adopt a more hospitable attitude toward forum-selection clauses. This view, advanced in the well-reasoned dissenting opinion in the instant case, is that such clauses are prima facie valid and should be enforced unless enforcement is shown by the resisting party to be "unreasonable" under the circumstances. We believe this is the correct doctrine to be followed by federal district courts sitting in admiralty. It is merely the other side of the proposition recognized by this Court in National Equipment Rental, Ltd. v. Szukhent, 375 U.S. 311 (1964), holding that in federal courts a party may validly consent to be sued in a jurisdiction where he cannot be found for service of process through contractual designation of an "agent" for receipt of process in that jurisdiction. In so holding, the Court stated:

> "It is settled * * * that parties to a contract may agree in advance to submit to the jurisdiction of a given court, to permit notice to be served by the opposing party, or even to waive notice altogether." Id., at 315-316.

This approach is substantially that followed in other common-law countries including England. It is the view advanced by noted scholars and that adopted by the Restatement of the Conflict of Laws.[13] It accords with ancient concepts of freedom of contract and reflects an appreciation of the expanding horizons of American contractors who seek business in all parts of the world. Not surprisingly, foreign businessmen prefer, as do we, to have disputes resolved in their own courts, but if that choice is not available, then in a neutral forum with expertise in the subject matter. Plainly, the courts of England meet the standards of neutrality and long experience in admiralty litigation. The choice of that forum was made in an arm's-length negotiation by experienced and sophisticated businessmen, and absent some compelling and countervailing reason it should be honored by the parties and enforced by the courts.

The argument that such clauses are improper because they tend to "oust" a court of jurisdiction is hardly more than a vestigial legal fiction. It appears to rest at core on historical judicial resistance to any attempt to reduce the power and business of a particular court and has little place in an era when all courts are overloaded and when businesses once essentially local now operate in world markets. It reflects something of a provincial attitude regarding the fairness of other tribunals. No one seriously contends in this case that the forum-selection clause "ousted" the District Court of jurisdiction over Zapata's action. The threshold question is whether that court should have exercised its jurisdiction to do more than give effect to the legitimate expectations of the parties, manifested in their freely negotiated agreement, by specifically enforcing the forum clause.

There are compelling reasons why a freely negotiated private international agreement, unaffected by fraud, undue influence, or overweening bargaining power, such as that involved here, should be given full effect. In this case, for example, we are concerned with a far from routine transaction between companies of two different nations contemplating the tow of an extremely costly piece of equipment from Louisiana across the Gulf of Mexico and the Atlantic Ocean, through the Mediterranean Sea to its final destination in the Adriatic Sea. In the course of its voyage, it was to traverse the waters of many jurisdictions. The *Chaparral* could have been damaged at any point along the route, and there were

---

[13] Restatement (Second) of the Conflict of Laws § 80 (1971); Reese, *The Contractual Forum: Situation in the United States*, 13 Am. J. Comp. Law 187 (1964); A. Ehrenzweig, Conflict of Laws § 41 (1962). See also Model Choice of Forum Act (National Conference of Commissioners on Uniform State Laws 1968).

countless possible ports of refuge. That the accident occurred in the Gulf of Mexico and the barge was towed to Tampa in an emergency were mere fortuities. It cannot be doubted for a moment that the parties sought to provide for a neutral forum for the resolution of any disputes arising during the tow. Manifestly much uncertainty and possibly great inconvenience to both parties could arise if a suit could be maintained in any jurisdiction in which an accident might occur or if jurisdiction were left to any place where the *Bremen* or Unterweser might happen to be found.[15] The elimination of all such uncertainties by agreeing in advance on a forum acceptable to both parties is an indispensable element in international trade, commerce, and contracting. There is strong evidence that the forum clause was a vital part of the agreement, and it would be unrealistic to think that the parties did not conduct their negotiations, including fixing the monetary terms, with the consequences of the forum clause figuring prominently in their calculations. Under these circumstances, as Justice Karminski reasoned in sustaining jurisdiction over Zapata in the High Court of Justice, "the force of an agreement for litigation in this country, freely entered into between two competent parties, seems to me to be very powerful."

Thus, in the light of present-day commercial realities and expanding international trade we conclude that the forum clause should control absent a strong showing that it should be set aside. Although their opinions are not altogether explicit, it seems reasonably clear that the District Court and the Court of Appeals placed the burden on Unterweser to show that London would be a more convenient forum than Tampa, although the contract expressly resolved that issue. The correct approach would have been to enforce the forum clause specifically unless Zapata could clearly show that enforcement would be unreasonable and unjust, or that the clause was invalid for such reasons as fraud or overreaching. Accordingly, the case must be remanded for reconsideration.

We note, however, that there is nothing in the record presently before us that would support a refusal to enforce the forum clause. The Court of Appeals suggested that enforcement would be contrary to the public policy of the forum under Bisso v. Inland Waterways Corp., 349 U.S. 85 (1955), because of the prospect that the English courts would enforce the clauses of the towage contract

---

[15] At the very least, the clause was an effort to eliminate all uncertainty as to the nature, location, and outlook of the forum in which these companies of differing nationalities might find themselves. Moreover, while the contract here did not specifically provide that the substantive law of England should be applied, it is the general rule in English courts that the parties are assumed, absent contrary indication, to have designated the forum with the view that it should apply its own law. * * * It is therefore reasonable to conclude that the forum clause was also an effort to obtain certainty as to the applicable substantive law.

The record contains an affidavit of a Managing Director of Unterweser stating that Unterweser considered the choice-of-forum provision to be of "overriding importance" to the transaction. He stated that Unterweser towage contracts ordinarily provide for exclusive German jurisdiction and application of German law, but that "in this instance, in an effort to meet [Zapata] half way, [Unterweser] proposed the London Court of Justice. Had this provision not been accepted by [Zapata], [Unterweser] would not have entered into the towage contract * * *." He also stated that the parties intended, by designating the London forum, that English law would be applied. A responsive affidavit by Hoyt Taylor, a vice president of Zapata, denied that there were any discussions between Zapata and Unterweser concerning the forum clause or the question of the applicable law.

purporting to exculpate Unterweser from liability for damages to the *Chaparral*. A contractual choice-of-forum clause should be held unenforceable if enforcement would contravene a strong public policy of the forum in which suit is brought, whether declared by statute or by judicial decision. See, *e. g.,* Boyd v. Grand Trunk W. R. Co., 338 U.S. 263 (1949). It is clear, however, that whatever the proper scope of the policy expressed in *Bisso*, it does not reach this case. *Bisso* rested on considerations with respect to the towage business strictly in American waters, and those considerations are not controlling in an international commercial agreement. Speaking for the dissenting judges in the Court of Appeals, Judge Wisdom pointed out:

> "We should be careful not to over-emphasize the strength of the [*Bisso*] policy. * * * Two concerns underlie the rejection of exculpatory agreements: that they may be produced by overweening bargaining power; and that they do not sufficiently discourage negligence. * * * Here the conduct in question is that of a foreign party occurring in international waters outside our jurisdiction. The evidence disputes any notion of overreaching in the contractual agreement. And for all we know, the uncertainties and dangers in the new field of transoceanic towage of oil rigs were so great that the tower was unwilling to take financial responsibility for the risks, and the parties thus allocated responsibility for the voyage to the tow. It is equally possible that the contract price took this factor into account. I conclude that we should not invalidate the forum-selection clause here unless we are firmly convinced that we would thereby significantly encourage negligent conduct within the boundaries of the United States." 428 F.2d, at 907-908. (Footnotes omitted.)

Courts have also suggested that a forum clause, even though it is freely bargained for and contravenes no important public policy of the forum, may nevertheless be "unreasonable" and unenforceable if the chosen forum is *seriously* inconvenient for the trial of the action. Of course, where it can be said with reasonable assurance that at the time they entered the contract, the parties to a freely negotiated private international commercial agreement contemplated the claimed inconvenience, it is difficult to see why any such claim of inconvenience should be heard to render the forum clause unenforceable. We are not here dealing with an agreement between two Americans to resolve their essentially local disputes in a remote alien forum. In such a case, the serious inconvenience of the contractual forum to one or both of the parties might carry greater weight in determining the reasonableness of the forum clause. The remoteness of the forum might suggest that the agreement was an adhesive one, or that the parties did not have the particular controversy in mind when they made their agreement; yet even there the party claiming should bear a heavy burden of proof. Similarly, selection of a remote forum to apply differing foreign law to an essentially American controversy might contravene an important public policy of the forum. For example, so long as *Bisso* governs American courts with respect to the towage business in American waters, it would quite arguably be improper to permit an American tower to avoid that policy by providing a foreign forum for resolution of his disputes with an American towee.

This case, however, involves a freely negotiated international commercial transaction between a German and an American corporation for towage of a vessel from the Gulf of Mexico to the Adriatic Sea. As noted, selection of a London forum was clearly a reasonable effort to bring vital certainty to this international transaction and to provide a neutral forum experienced and capable in the resolution of admiralty litigation. Whatever "inconvenience" Zapata would suffer by being forced to litigate in the contractual forum as it agreed to do was clearly foreseeable at the time of contracting. In such circumstances it should be incumbent on the party seeking to escape his contract to show that trial in the contractual forum will be so gravely difficult and inconvenient that he will for all practical purposes be deprived of his day in court. Absent that, there is no basis for concluding that it would be unfair, unjust, or unreasonable to hold that party to his bargain.

In the course of its ruling on Unterweser's second motion to stay the proceedings in Tampa, the District Court did make a conclusory finding that the balance of convenience was "strongly" in favor of litigation in Tampa. However, as previously noted, in making that finding the court erroneously placed the burden of proof on Unterweser to show that the balance of convenience was strongly in its favor. Moreover, the finding falls short of a conclusion that Zapata would be effectively deprived of its day in court should it be forced to litigate in London. Indeed, it cannot even be assumed that it would be placed to the expense of transporting its witnesses to London. It is not unusual for important issues in international admiralty cases to be dealt with by deposition. Both the District Court and the Court of Appeals majority appeared satisfied that Unterweser could receive a fair hearing in Tampa by using deposition testimony of its witnesses from distant places, and there is no reason to conclude that Zapata could not use deposition testimony to equal advantage if forced to litigate in London as it bound itself to do. Nevertheless, to allow Zapata opportunity to carry its heavy burden of showing not only that the balance of convenience is strongly in favor of trial in Tampa (that is, that it will be far more inconvenient for Zapata to litigate in London than it will be for Unterweser to litigate in Tampa), but also that a London trial will be so manifestly and gravely inconvenient to Zapata that it will be effectively deprived of a meaningful day in court, we remand for further proceedings. * * *

The judgment of the Court of Appeals is vacated and the case is remanded for further proceedings consistent with this opinion.

MR. JUSTICE WHITE, concurring [omitted].

MR. JUSTICE DOUGLAS, dissenting. * * *

Respondent is a citizen of this country. Moreover, if it were remitted to the English court, its substantive rights would be adversely affected. Exculpatory provisions in the towage contract provide (1) that petitioners, the masters and the crews "are not responsible for defaults and/or errors in the navigation of the tow" and (2) that "(d)amages suffered by the towed object are in any case for account of its Owners."

Under our decision in Dixilyn Drilling Corp v. Crescent Towing & Salvage Co., 372 U.S. 697, 698, "a contract which exempts the tower from liability for its own negligence" is not enforceable, though there is evidence in the present record that it is enforceable in England. That policy was first announced in Bisso v. Inland Waterways Corp., 349 U.S. 85; * * * Although the casualty occurred on the high seas, the *Bisso* doctrine is nonetheless applicable. * *

Moreover, the casualty occurred close to the District Court, a number of potential witnesses, including respondent's crewmen, reside in that area, and the inspection and repair work were done there. The testimony of the tower's crewmen, residing in Germany, is already available by way of depositions taken in the proceedings.

All in all, the District Court judge exercised his discretion wisely in enjoining petitioners from pursuing the litigation in England. I would affirm the judgment below.

NOTES AND QUESTIONS FOR DISCUSSION

1. Consider *The Bremen* in light of **CARNIVAL CRUISE LINES, INC. v. SHUTE, 499 U.S. 585 (1991)**, which involved a domestic (i.e., non-international) forum selection clause dictating where suit would have to be brought. Two passengers from the State of Washington sued Carnival Cruise Lines in a Washington federal court when the passengers sustained injuries on board a Carnival cruise in international waters off the Mexican coast. The passengers had boarded the ship in Los Angeles, California. The cruise ticket contained a forum selection clause designating Florida as the forum to resolve all disputes arising out of the Carnival tour. The lower courts held that the clause could not be enforced under *The Bremen,* because it was not "freely bargained for." The Supreme Court disagreed (id. at 593-94):

> In evaluating the reasonableness of the forum selection clause at issue in this case, we must refine the analysis of *The Bremen* to account for the realities of form passage contracts. As an initial matter we do not accept the Court of Appeals' determination that a nonnegotiated forum-selection clause in a form ticket contract is never enforceable simply because it is not the subject of bargaining. Including a reasonable forum clause in a form contract of this kind well may be permissible for several reasons: First, a cruise line has a special interest in limiting the fora in which it potentially could be subject to suit. Because a cruise ship typically carries passengers from many locales, it is not unlikely that a mishap on a cruise could subject the cruise line to litigation in several different fora * * *. Additionally, a clause establishing ex ante the forum for dispute resolution has the salutary effect of dispelling any confusion about where suits arising from the contract must be brought and defended, sparing litigants the time and expense of pretrial motions to determine the correct forum, and conserving judicial resources that otherwise would be devoted to deciding those motions. Finally, it stands to reason that passengers who purchase tickets containing a forum clause like that at issue in this case benefit in the form of reduced fares reflecting the savings that the cruise line enjoys by limiting the for a in which it may be sued.

The Court rejected the argument that plaintiffs had met their "heavy burden of proof" that litigating in Florida would be a serious inconvenience for them, or that it was a "remote alien forum" given the situs of the accident, and the greater remoteness of Washington courts from the accident. Although the Court indicated that "it bears emphasis that forum-selection clauses contained in form passage contracts are subject to judicial scrutiny for fundamental fairness," it concluded that there was no evidence of "bad faith motive" on Carnival Cruise's part to discourage litigation brought against it, nor was their evidence of "fraud" or "overreaching" in connection with the forum selection clause. Id. at 595. The Court also concluded that the clause did not violate a federal statute that forbade limiting "the right of any [ship passenger] to a trial by a court of competent jurisdiction on the question of liability for such loss or injury." 46 U.S.C. § 183(c). Florida courts, said the Court, clearly provided a competent jurisdiction.

2. Should *The Bremen* have controlled a domestic forum selection clause involving a species of a consumer transaction? Would *Carnival Cruise* apply if the forum selected had been a foreign forum? The Court in *Carnival Cruise* thinks that at some point convenience to the individual can become relevant to the question of enforcement. How inconvenient or unreasonable would a forum selection clause have to be before it is found to be unenforceable? Does *The Bremen* provide some answers?

3. *The Bremen* allows for the possibility that a forum selection clause may be unenforceable because it runs afoul of ordinary principles of contract law, such as fraud, or duress, or overreaching. *Carnival Cruise* seems to reinforce this idea, although it takes a relatively narrow view of what might constitute overreaching. Assuming such limits exist, consider whose law should apply to decide whether they have been exceeded by a particular forum selection clause. The law that would otherwise be applied to the contract as a whole, consistent with ordinary choice of law rules? Or should this sort of question regarding the interpretation of the forum selection clause be better viewed as a question of procedure, such that the forum could properly apply its own law?

4. *The Bremen* and *Carnival Cruise* involved choice of forum clauses. To be distinguished are choice-of-law clauses. Choice of law clauses do not change the forum in which litigation will go forward, but indicate the substantive law that the parties have agreed will apply to their case, regardless of the forum in which litigation is brought. We discuss choice of law clauses and choice of law more generally in Chapter 7. But note here that a choice-of-forum provision, as a practical matter, can have choice of law consequences, as *The Bremen* itself indicates in footnote 19. Another contractual means of avoiding jurisdictional disputes is an agreement to arbitrate. We consider that topic in Chapter 9.

5. As the Court in *The Bremen* points out, the traditional approach to forum selection clauses was one of hostility. Why do you suppose that was once true? Some states still adhere to the older approach and are reluctant to enforce forum selection clauses that would have the effect of ousting a state court possessed of good jurisdiction properly invoked, especially if jurisdiction has been invoked by an in-stater. See, e.g., Stewart Organization, Inc. v. Ricoh Corp., 487 U.S. 22 (1988) (discussing Alabama law). Apparently only two states adopted the Model Choice of Forum Act (1969), originally approved by the National Conference on

Uniform State Laws (but later withdrawn), and which provided for liberal recognition of forum selection clauses, subject to only a few exceptions. Note that both *The Bremen* and *Carnival Cruise* were admiralty cases, and the principle favoring enforcement of choice of forum clauses was developed uncontroversially as a matter of judge-made federal common-law of admiralty.

6. Should federal common law principles have any effect on the enforceability of international forum selection clauses in federal courts outside of admiralty litigation, or outside of litigation grounded in federal law? Should they have any impact on *state* courts outside such areas? For example, suppose a U.S. citizen and a foreign citizen enter into a contract overseas, but some aspects of performance are to occur in the U.S. and some overseas. The contract contains a forum selection clause designating the courts of the foreign national as the exclusive forum. When the foreign citizen fails to perform, suit is brought by the U.S. citizen in a federal court with good personal and subject matter jurisdiction. Is *The Bremen's* federal common law rule applicable in state court (or in federal court) simply because there is an "international agreement" that is at issue?

Under Erie Railroad Co. v. Tompkins, 304 U.S. 64 (1938), there may be some uncertainty whether, in a case *not* arising under federal law (or admiralty), and in the absence of a federal statute or rule, a federal court in a given state would be able to ignore the state's policy respecting the enforcement of such clauses, as least when the clause would require that litigation be brought in a foreign forum. To be sure, the Supreme Court has held that a state's anti-forum selection clause policy would not control in a motion to transfer venue from a federal court in one state to a federal court in another state. See *Stewart Organization, supra.* But that was said to be true because a federal statute—the transfer of venue statute, 28 U.S.C. § 1404—spoke to the question, and thus trumped state law. And even then, there was a powerful dissent from Justice Scalia based on *Erie*.

But the pro-forum-selection-clause principle of cases such as *The Bremen* and *Carnival Cruise* is not dictated by federal statute or rule, and there is no federal statute that mandates the enforceability of forum selection clauses in international contracts. (There is the Hague Convention on Choice of Courts (see Appendix C) that might someday cover some such actions—but as of March 1, 2013, it has not yet been ratified by the U.S.; see also below (briefly noting the Convention).) Congress might be able to enact such a law, either under its power to regulate commerce with foreign nations or incident to its necessary and proper powers to implement Article III. But there is still a question—given *Erie*, federalism concerns, as well as separation of powers concerns—whether federal *courts* could or should act to develop federal common law in this area when Congress has not spoken.

One possible argument for treating the enforceability of a choice of forum clause as a question of federal common law, is that it implicates a question of federal court procedure to which federal courts may freely speak, state law to the contrary notwithstanding. See, e.g., Wong v. PartyGaming Ltd., 589 F.3d 821, 827 (6th Cir 2009) (noting that six circuits have held that "the enforceability of a forum selection clause implicates federal procedure and should therefore be governed by federal law," and adopting that rule); cf. Royal Bed & Spring Co. v.

Famossul Industria e Commercia de Moveis Ltda., 906 F.2d 45, 52 (1st Cir. 1990) (approaching enforcement of choice of forum provision as an aspect of *forum non conveniens* and venue law); Lipcon v. Underwriters at Lloyd's of London, 148 F.3d 1285, 1290-91, 1295-96 (11th Cir. 1998) (viewing dismissal based on forum selection clause as implicating Rule 12(b)(3), Fed. R. Civ. P., governing venue). But see Abbott Labs. v. Takeda Pharm. Co., 476 F.3d 421, 423 (7th Cir. 2007) ("Simplicity argues for determining the validity . . . of a forum selection clause . . . by reference to the law of the jurisdiction whose law governs the rest of the contract.").

If the characterization of the enforceability of a forum selection clause as a question of *procedural* federal common law is correct, principles such as those in *The Bremen* will be applicable in federal courts in both diversity and federal question cases, but not in state courts. Consequently, in a state that adheres to different principles than those in *The Bremen*, there would be an incentive for plaintiffs not to file in federal court when facing a forum selection clause that the foreign defendant would likely raise. (Of course, the plaintiff might have to insure that the case could not be removed to federal court where the forum selection clause might more likely be enforced, but she can do so by the simple expedient of joining a non-diverse defendant on a nonfrivolous cause of action).

Alternatively, it might be argued that the enforcement of forum selection clauses is a question of *substantive* federal common law, in which case federal principles would be applicable in both federal courts *and* state courts. If so, what would be the authorization for creating judge-made federal law here? Is this an aspect of foreign affairs law? Would state law that is hostile to forum selection clauses somehow unduly burden commerce with foreign nations? Of course, if it is a question of substantive federal common law, the argument from separation of powers and federalism is perhaps at its strongest (and the argument for federal court (as opposed to congressional) lawmaking at its weakest).

7.   Suppose the parties to an international contract stipulate that a particular forum "may exercise jurisdiction" over any dispute arising out of the contract; or perhaps they stipulate that the courts of a particular country "shall have jurisdiction;" or that they "agree to be subject to the jurisdiction" of a particular country's courts. Does this sort of language mean that such disputes *must* be heard in the selected forum—or will jurisdiction be exclusive only if there is some clearer language to that effect? See IntraComm, Inc. v. Bajaj, 492 F.3d 285, 290 (4th Cir. 2007) ("A general maxim in interpreting forum selection clauses is that an agreement conferring jurisdiction in one forum will not be interpreted as excluding jurisdiction elsewhere unless it contains specific language of exclusion.") (internal quotation omitted). Would language stating that any such dispute "shall be brought" or "must be brought" in a particular forum do the trick? Note that the forum selection clause in *Zapata* used the language "must be treated before" a particular court, and it was therefore clearly exclusive (i.e., mandatory), as opposed to nonexclusive (i.e., permissive).

8.   Note also that unless language respecting *the scope* of the choice of forum clause in a contractual agreement also clearly provides that more than contract claims are covered, the clause may not be mandatory as to, for example, statutory claims or tort claims that grow out of the parties' agreement. See Smith, Valentino & Smith, Inc. v. Superior Court, 17 Cal.3d 491, 551 P.2d 1206 (1976) (indicating that language covering all disputes "arising under *or growing out of this agreement*" would be sufficient to extend a choice of forum provision to non-contractual claims) (emphasis in original). If there is a choice of law clause in a contract with a forum selection clause, should the court interpret the meaning of the latter based on the former? See See Yavuz v. 61 MM, Ltd., 465 F.3d 418, 431 (10th Cir. 2006) (so concluding); see also Albemarle Corp. v. Astra-Zenica U.K., Ltd., 628 F.3d 643 (4th Cir. 2010) (discussed in Chapter 7). Both choice of forum and choice of law clauses appear in the case that follows.

Richards v. Lloyd's of London

United States Court of Appeals, Ninth Circuit (en banc), 1998.

135 F.3d 1289.

GOODWIN, CIRCUIT JUDGE.

The primary question this case presents is whether the antiwaiver provisions of the Securities Act of 1933 and the Securities Exchange Act of 1934 void choice of law and choice of forum clauses in an international transaction. The district court found that they do not. [A three-judge panel of the Ninth Circuit reversed; but the en banc court affirmed the district court, rejecting the panel decision.]

Background

Appellants, all citizens or residents of the United States, are more than 600 "Names" who entered into underwriting agreements. The Names sued four defendants: the Corporation of Lloyd's, the Society of Lloyd's, the Council of Lloyd's, (collectively, "Lloyd's") and Lloyd's of London, (the "unincorporated association").

Lloyd's is a market in which more than three hundred Underwriting Agencies compete for underwriting business. Pursuant to the Lloyd's Act of 1871-1982, Lloyd's oversees and regulates the competition for underwriting business in the Lloyd's market. The market does not accept premiums or insure risks. Rather, Underwriting Agencies, or syndicates, compete for the insurance business. Each Underwriting Agency is controlled by a Managing Agent who is responsible for the financial status of its agency. The Managing Agent must attract not only underwriting business from brokers but also the capital with which to insure the risks underwritten.

The Names provide the underwriting capital. The Names become Members of the Society of Lloyd's through a series of agreements, proof of financial means, and the deposit of an irrevocable letter of credit in favor of Lloyd's. To become a Name, one must travel to England to acknowledge the attendant risks of participating in a syndicate and sign a General Undertaking. The General Undertaking is a two page document containing choice of forum and choice of law clauses (collectively the "choice clauses"), which form the basis for this dispute. The choice clauses read:

2.1 The rights and obligations of the parties arising out of or relating to the Member's membership of, and/or underwriting of insurance business at, Lloyd's and any other matter referred to in this Undertaking shall be governed by and construed in accordance with the laws of England.

2.2 Each party hereto irrevocably agrees that the courts of England shall have exclusive jurisdiction to settle any dispute and/or controversy of whatsoever nature arising out of or relating to the Member's membership of, and/or under writing of insurance business at, Lloyd's . . . .

By becoming a Member, the Names obtain the right to participate in the Lloyd's Underwriting Agencies. The Names, however, do not deal directly with Lloyd's or with the Managing Agents. Instead, the Names are represented by Members' Agents who, pursuant to agreement, stand in a fiduciary relationship with their Names. Upon becoming a Name, an individual selects the syndicates in which he wishes to participate. In making this decision, the individual must rely to a great extent on the advice of his Members' Agent. The Names generally join more than one underwriting agency in order to spread their risks across different types of insurance. When a Name undertakes an underwriting obligation, that Name is responsible only for his share of an agency's losses; however, his liability is unlimited for that share.

In this case, the risk of heavy losses has materialized and the Names now seek shelter under United States securities laws and the Racketeer Influenced and Corrupt Organizations Act ("RICO"), 18 U.S.C. § 1961 et seq. The Names claim that Lloyd's actively sought the investment of United States residents to fill an urgent need to build up capital. According to the Names, Lloyd's concealed information regarding the possible consequences of the risks undertaken and deliberately and disproportionately exposed the Names to massive liabilities for which sufficient underwriting capital or reinsurance was unavailable.

This appeal does not address the merits of the underlying claims. It addresses only the Names' contention that their disputes with Lloyd's should be litigated in the United States despite contract clauses binding the parties to proceed in England under English law. It also addresses whether default should have been entered against the unincorporated association.

Standard of Review

We review the district court's decision to enforce the choice clauses for abuse of discretion. Argueta v. Banco Mexicano, S.A., 87 F.3d 320, 323 (9th Cir. 1996). As we are reviewing a Rule 12(b)(3) motion decision, we need not accept the pleadings as true. Id. at 324. Whether the securities laws void the choice clauses is a question of law that we review de novo. Pinal Creek Group v. Newmont Mining Corp., 118 F.3d 1298, 1300 (9th Cir. 1997).

Discussion

The Names make three arguments for repudiating the choice clauses. They contend (1) that the antiwaiver provisions of the federal securities laws void such clauses, (2) that the choice clauses are invalid because they offend the strong public policy of preserving an investor's remedies under federal and state securities law and RICO and (3) that the choice clauses were obtained by fraud. We will address each of these in turn.

I

We analyze the validity of the choice clause under The Bremen v. Zapata Off-Shore Co., 407 U.S. 1 (1972), where the Supreme Court stated that courts should enforce choice of law and choice of forum clauses in cases of "freely negotiated private international agreement[s]." *Bremen*, 407 U.S. at 12-13.[1]

A

The Names dispute the application of *Bremen* to this case. They contend that *Bremen* does not apply to cases where Congress has spoken directly to the immediate issue—as they claim the antiwaiver provisions do here.

The Securities Act of 1933 (the " '33 Act") provides that:

> Any condition, stipulation, or provision binding any person acquiring any security to waive compliance with any provision of this subchapter or of the rules and regulations of the Commission shall be void.

15 U.S.C. § 77n. The 1934 Securities Exchange Act (the " '34 Act") contains a substantially similar provision. 15 U.S.C. § 78cc(a). The Names seize on these provisions and claim that they void the choice clauses in their agreement with Lloyd's.

Certainly the antiwaiver provisions are worded broadly enough to reach this case. They cover "any condition, stipulation, or provision binding any person acquiring any security to waive compliance with any provision of this subchapter . . . ." Indeed, this language is broad enough to reach any offer or sale of anything that could be alleged to be a security, no matter where the transaction occurs.

Nevertheless, this attempt to distinguish *Bremen* fails. In *Bremen* itself, the Supreme Court contemplated that a forum selection clause may conflict with relevant statutes. *Bremen*, 407 U.S. at 15 ("A contractual choice-of-forum clause should be held unenforceable if enforcement would contravene a strong public policy of the forum in which suit is brought, whether declared *by statute* or by judicial decision.") (emphasis added).

Moreover, in Scherk v. Alberto-Culver Co., 417 U.S. 506 (1974), the Supreme Court explicitly relied on *Bremen* in a case involving a securities transaction. Echoing the language of *Bremen*, the Court found that "[a] contractual provision specifying in advance the forum in which disputes shall be litigated and the law to be applied is . . . an almost indispensable precondition to achievement of the orderliness and predictability essential to any international business trans-

---

[1] While the contract in *Bremen* did not contain a choice of law clause, the Supreme Court explicitly recognized that the forum selection clause also acted as a choice of law clause. Id. at 13 n.15 ("[W]hile the contract here did not specifically provide that the substantive law of England should be applied, it is the general rule in English courts that the parties are assumed, absent a contrary indication, to have designated the forum with the view that it should apply its own law. . . . It is therefore reasonable to conclude that the forum clause was also an effort to obtain certainty as to the applicable substantive law.").

action." Id. at 516. See *Bremen*, 407 U.S. at 13-14 ("[A]greeing in advance on a forum acceptable to both parties is an indispensable element in international trade, commerce, and contracting."). This passage should leave little doubt as to the applicability of *Bremen* to the case at hand.

Indeed, were we to find that *Bremen* did not apply, the reach of United States securities laws would be unbounded. The Names simply prove too much when they assert that "*Bremen*'s judicially-created policy analysis under federal common law is not controlling when Congress has expressed its will in a statute." This assertion, if true, expands the reach of federal securities law to any and all such transactions, no matter how remote from the United States. We agree with the Fifth Circuit that "we must tread cautiously before expanding the operation of U.S. securities law in the international arena." Haynsworth v. The Corporation, 121 F.3d 956, 966 (5th Cir. 1997).

B

Having determined that *Bremen* governs international contracts specifying forum and applicable law, we turn to the question whether the contract between Lloyd's and the Names is international. Not surprisingly, the Names contend that these were purely domestic securities sales. They claim that Lloyd's solicited the Names in the United States and that the trip the Names made to England was a mere ritual without legal significance.

We disagree. The Names signed a contract with English entities to participate in an English insurance market and flew to England to consummate the transaction. That the Names received solicitations in the United States does not somehow erase these facts. Moreover, Lloyd's insistence that individuals travel to England to become a Name does not strike us as mere ritual. Lloyd's likely requires this precisely so that those who choose to be the Names understand that English law governs the transaction. Entering into the Lloyd's market in the manner described is plainly an international transaction.

II

We now apply *Bremen* to this case. *Bremen* emphasized that "in the light of present-day commercial realities and expanding international trade we conclude that the forum clause should control absent a strong showing that it should be set aside." *Bremen*, 407 U.S. at 15. The Court reasoned that "[t]he elimination of all [ ] uncertainties [regarding the forum] by agreeing in advance . . . is an indispensable element in international trade, commerce, and contracting." Id. at 13-14. Thus, "absent some compelling and countervailing reason [a forum selection clause] should be honored by the parties and enforced by the courts." Id. at 12. The party seeking to avoid the forum selection clause bears "a heavy burden of proof." Id. at 17.

The Supreme Court has identified three grounds for repudiating a forum selection clause: first, if the inclusion of the clause in the agreement was the product of fraud or overreaching; second, if the party wishing to repudiate the clause would effectively be deprived of his day in court were the clause enforced; and third, "if enforcement would contravene a strong public policy of the forum in which suit is brought." Id. at 12-13, 15, 18. The Names contend that the first and third grounds apply in this case.

A

The Names' strongest argument for escaping their agreement to litigate their claims in England is that the choice clauses contravene a strong public policy embodied in federal and state securities law and RICO. See Bonny v. Society of Lloyd's, 3 F.3d 156, 160-61 (7th Cir. 1993) (expressing "serious concerns" that the choice clauses offend public policy but ultimately ruling in Lloyd's favor), cert. denied, 510 U.S. 1113 (1994); Roby v. Corporation of Lloyd's, 996 F.2d 1353, 1364-66 (2nd Cir.) (substantially the same), cert. denied, 510 U.S. 945 (1993).

We follow our six sister circuits that have ruled to enforce the choice clauses. See *Haynsworth*, 121 F.3d 956; Allen v. Lloyd's of London, 94 F.3d 923 (4th Cir. 1996); Shell v. R.W. Sturge, Ltd., 55 F.3d 1227 (6th Cir. 1995); *Bonny*, 3 F.3d 156; *Roby*, 996 F.2d 1353; and Riley v. Kingsley Underwriting Agencies, Ltd., 969 F.2d 953 (10th Cir.), cert. denied, 506 U.S. 1021 (1992). We do so because we apply *Scherk* and because English law provides the Names with sufficient protection.

In *Scherk*, the Supreme Court was confronted with a contract that specified that all disputes would be resolved in arbitration before the International Chamber of Commerce in Paris, France. *Scherk*, 417 U.S. at 508. The arbitrator was to apply the law of the state of Illinois. Id. The Court enforced the forum selection clause despite then hostile precedent.[4] Id. at 520-21. See Wilko v. Swan, 346 U.S. 427 (1953), overruled by Rodriguez de Quijas v. Shearson/American Express, Inc., 490 U.S. 477, 485 (1989).

The Court's treatment of *Wilko* leaves little doubt that the choice clauses in this case are enforceable. In *Wilko*, the Supreme Court ruled that "the right to select the judicial forum is the kind of 'provision' that cannot be waived under § 14 of the Securities Act." *Wilko*, 346 U.S. at 435. In *Scherk*, the Court had before it a case where both the District Court and the Seventh Circuit found a forum selection clause invalid on the strength of *Wilko*. *Scherk*, 417 U.S. at 510.

In distinguishing *Wilko*, the Supreme Court stated that there were "significant and, we find, crucial differences between the agreement involved in *Wilko* and the one signed by the parties here." *Scherk*, 417 U.S. at 515. The first and primary difference that the Court relied upon was that "AlbertoCulver's contract . . . was a truly international agreement." Id. The Court reasoned that such a contract needs, as "an almost indispensable precondition," a "provision specifying in advance the forum in which disputes shall be litigated *and the law to be applied*." Id. at 516 (emphasis added).

Moreover, the Supreme Court has explained that, in the context of an international agreement, there is "no basis for a judgment that only United States laws and United States courts should determine this controversy in the face of a solemn agreement between the parties that such controversies be resolved elsewhere." Id. at 517 n.11. To require that "'American standards of fairness' must . . . govern the controversy demeans the standards of justice elsewhere in the

---

[4] The Court recognized that an agreement to arbitrate "is, in effect, a specialized kind of forum-selection clause." *Scherk*, 417 U.S. at 519.

world, and unnecessarily exalts the primacy of United States law over the laws of other countries." Id.

These passages from *Scherk*, we think, resolve the question whether public policy reasons allow the Names to escape their "solemn agreement" to adjudicate their claims in England under English law. *Scherk* involved a securities transaction. Id. at 514 n.8. The Court rejected *Wilko*'s holding that the antiwaiver provision of the '34 Act prohibited choice clauses. Id. at 515-16. It also recognized that enforcing the forum selection clause would, in some cases, have the same effect as choosing foreign law to apply. Id. at 516, 517 n.11. Yet the Court did not hesitate to enforce the forum selection clauses. It believed that to rule otherwise would "reflect a 'parochial concept that all disputes must be resolved under our laws and in our courts.'" Id. at 519 (quoting *Bremen,* 407 U.S. at 9). As the Supreme Court has explained, "'[w]e cannot have trade and commerce in world markets and international waters exclusively on our terms, governed by our laws, and resolved in our courts.'" Id. (quoting *Bremen*, 407 U.S. at 9).

Relying on Mitsubishi Motors Corp. v. Soler Chrysler-Plymouth, Inc., 473 U.S. 614, 634 (1985), the Names argue that federal and state securities laws are of "fundamental importance to American democratic capitalism." They claim that enforcement of the choice clauses will deprive them of important remedies provided by our securities laws. The Supreme Court disapproved of such an outcome, the Names contend, when it stated that "in the event the choice-of-forum and choice-of-law clauses operated in tandem as a prospective waiver of a party's right to pursue statutory remedies for antitrust violations, we would have little hesitation in condemning the agreement as against public policy." Id. at 637 n.19.

Without question this case would be easier to decide if this footnote in *Mitsubishi* had not been inserted. Nevertheless, we do not believe dictum in a footnote regarding antitrust law outweighs the extended discussion and holding in *Scherk* on the validity of clauses specifying the forum and applicable law. The Supreme Court repeatedly recognized in *Scherk* that parties to an international securities transaction may choose law other than that of the United States, *Scherk*, 417 at 516, 517 n.11, 519 n.13, yet it never suggested that this affected the validity of a forum selection clause. See also *Bremen*, 407 U.S. at 13 n.15 (recognizing that a forum selection clause also acts to select applicable law); Milanovich v. Costa Crociere, S.p.A., 954 F.2d 763, 767 n.7 (D.C. Cir. 1992) ("The *Bremen* involved a choice-of-forum clause, but the Supreme Court recognized that enforcing the provision would have the effect of subjecting the contract to foreign law.").

B

Of course, were English law so deficient that the Names would be deprived of any reasonable recourse, we would have to subject the choice clauses to another level of scrutiny. See Carnival Cruise Lines, Inc. v. Shute, 499 U.S. 585, 595 (1991) ("It bears emphasis that forum-selection clauses contained in form passage contracts are subject to judicial scrutiny for fundamental fairness."). In this case, however, there is no such danger. See *Haynsworth*, 121 F.3d at 969 ("English law provides a variety of protections for fraud and misrepresentations in securities transactions."). Cf. British Midland Airways Ltd. v. International

Travel, Inc., 497 F.2d 869, 871 (9th Cir. 1974) (This court is "hardly in a position to call the Queen's Bench a kangaroo court.").

We disagree with the dramatic assertion that "[t]he available English remedies are not adequate substitutes for the firm shields and finely honed swords provided by American securities law." Richards v. Lloyd's of London, 107 F.3d 1422, 1430 (9th Cir. 1997) [panel decision]. The Names have recourse against both the Member and Managing Agents for fraud, breach of fiduciary duty, or negligent misrepresentation. Indeed, English courts have already awarded substantial judgments to some of the other Names. See Arubuthnott v. Fagan and Feltrim Underwritings Ltd., 3 Re LR 145 (H.L. 1994); Deeny v. Gooda Walker Ltd., Queen's Bench Division (Commercial Court), The Times 7 October 1994.[6]

While it is true that the Lloyd's Act immunizes Lloyd's from many actions possible under our securities laws, Lloyd's is not immune from the consequences of actions committed in bad faith, including fraud. Lloyd's Act of 1982, Ch. 14(3)(e)(i). The Names contend that entities using the Lloyd's trade name willfully and fraudulently concealed massive long tail liabilities in order to induce them to join syndicates. If so, we have been cited to no authority that Lloyd's partial immunity would bar recovery.

C

The addition of RICO claims does not alter our conclusion. This court has already held that the loss of RICO claims does not suffice to bar dismissal for forum non conveniens. Lockman Found. v. Evangelical Alliance Mission, 930 F.2d 764, 768-79 (9th Cir. 1991). We agree with our sister circuit that has considered this issue and extend the logic of *Lockman* to this case. *Roby*, 996 F.2d at 1366.

D

The Names also argue that the choice clauses were the product of fraud. They claim that at the time of signing the General Undertaking, Lloyd's knew that the Names were effectively sacrificing valid claims under U.S. law by signing the choice clauses and concealed this fact from the Names. Had the Names known this fact, they contend, they never would have agreed to the choice clauses. The Names never allege, however, that Lloyd's misled them as to the legal effect of the choice clauses. Nor do they allege that Lloyd's fraudulently inserted the clauses without their knowledge. Accordingly, we view the allegations made by the Names as going only to the contract as a whole, with no allegations as to the inclusion of the choice clauses themselves.

Absent such allegations, these claims of fraud fail. The Supreme Court has noted that simply alleging that one was duped into signing the contract is not enough. *Scherk*, 417 U.S. at 519 n.14 (The fraud exception in *Bremen* "does not mean that any time a dispute arising out of a transaction is based upon an allegation of fraud . . . the clause is unenforceable."). For a party to escape a forum selection clause on the grounds of fraud, it must show that "the *inclusion of that clause in the contract* was the product of fraud or coercion." Id. (citing Prima

---

[6] The Names complain that the Member and Managing Agents are insolvent. If so, this is truly unfortunate. It does not, however, affect our analysis of the adequacy of English law.

Paint Corp. v. Flood & Conklin Mfg. Co., 388 U.S. 395 (1967)) (emphasis in original). See also *Prima Paint*, 388 U.S. at 404 ("[T]he statutory language [of the United States Arbitration Act] does not permit the federal court to consider claims of fraud in the inducement of the contract generally.").

E

The Names object that Moseley v. Electronic & Missile Facilities, Inc., 374 U.S. 167 (1963), requires the district court to adjudicate the claims of fraud before dismissal. In *Moseley*, the Supreme Court found that "it seems clear that the issue of fraud should first be adjudicated before the rights of the parties under the [contracts] can be determined." Id. at 171. Taken out of context, this statement would seem to support the Names' position.

When viewed in context, however, it becomes clear that this statement in fact provides no aid to the Names. The Supreme Court required an initial adjudication of the fraud claim after noting that "no request has been made here for the enforcement of the arbitration agreement included within the [contracts.]" Id. at 170. It was only "[w]ith the pleadings in this posture" that the Supreme Court required a trial on the fraud claims. Id. at 171. Here Lloyd's has clearly and vigorously called for the enforcement of the choice clauses. Accordingly, *Moseley* does not apply to the instant case and the Names are not entitled to a trial on their claims of fraud.

III

Because we decide that the district court correctly ruled to enforce the choice clauses, the request to enter default against the unincorporated association is moot. AFFIRMED.

THOMAS, CIRCUIT JUDGE, with whom JUDGE PREGERSON and JUDGE HAWKINS join, dissenting.

* * * The majority espouses a reasonable foreign policy, but one which emanates from the wrong branch of government. Congress has already explicitly resolved the question at hand. In the Securities Act of 1933 and the Securities Exchange Act of 1934 (the "Acts"), Congress expressly provided that investors cannot contractually agree to disregard United States securities law. Thus, in applying the "reasonableness" policy-weighing approach of M/S Bremen v. Zapata Off-Shore Co., 407 U.S. 1 (1972), the majority displaces Congress' specific statutory directive. Furthermore, even assuming that the *Bremen* analysis applies here, the circumstances surrounding this dispute compel the conclusion that enforcement of the choice clauses would be unreasonable. Accordingly, I respectfully dissent. * * *

NOTES AND QUESTIONS FOR DISCUSSION

1. As noted in Part II.A of the opinion, the decision in *Richards* was consistent with the majority of other circuit court decisions giving effect to (non-U.S.) forum selection clauses in settings in which the enforcement of federal statutory norms is at stake. But if a case such as *Richards* is one to which the federal securities laws would otherwise apply—apart from the choice of law clause—how can the express antiwaiver provisions of those federal laws be inapplicable? Was it right for the majority to substitute a "policy" favoring predictability in international commercial transactions in place of the (contrary) per se rule that Congress may have enacted?

2. The majority begins its analysis with *The Bremen*. Was that the right place to start in light of the existence of the federal securities statutes? As noted above, in Stewart Organization, Inc. v. Ricoh Corp., 487 U.S. 22 (1988), the Supreme Court stated, in a transfer of venue case in which there was also a choice of forum provision, "the first question [is] whether [28 U.S.C.] § 1404(a) [the transfer of venue statute] itself controls respondent's request to give effect to the parties' contractual choice of venue." 487 U.S. at 29. Lloyd's argument in *Richards* was to the effect that the federal securities laws were the proper place to begin the analysis—not *The Bremen*. The *Richards* majority responded: "[*Stewart*] however, involved a federal court sitting in diversity confronted with a purely domestic transaction. Thus it does not address this situation." 135 F.3d at 1293 n.3. Is that a fair response? Isn't the point that if a federal statute answers the question, then that may be the end of the judicial inquiry regarding enforcement of a choice of forum clause?

3. In Vimar Seguros y Reaseguros, S.A. v. M/V Sky Reefer, 515 U.S. 528, 529 (1995), the Supreme Court expressed concern that a forum selection clause combined with a choice of law clause might deprive a party of remedies under the Carriage of Goods by Sea Act ("COGSA"), 46 U.S.C. § 1300, et seq. Does *Vimar Seguros* suggest that the *Richards* court may have moved a bit too confidently in reaching its conclusion? In a footnote, *Richards* stated: "The Court's reasoning in *Vimar* . . . does not extend to the instant case, as *Vimar* involved COGSA, a statute designed to address international transactions. See [*Vimar Seguros*, 515 U.S.] at 537 ("COGSA is the culmination of a multilateral effort to establish uniform ocean bills of lading to govern the rights and liabilities of carriers and shippers inter se in international trade.") (internal quotations and citation omitted)." How, exactly, does this observation distinguish *Vimar Seguros* from *Richards*? We discuss *Vimar Seguros* at greater length in Chapter 3.

4. There continues to be disagreement in the federal courts over the proper procedural vehicle for enforcing a choice of forum clause, whether it be in the domestic or international setting. See supra Note 4 (after *The Bremen*). As noted above, *Stewart Organization* analyzed the effect of a forum selection clause under 28 U.S.C. § 1404 on defendant's motion to transfer venue. But there is disagreement as to how to proceed when § 1404 is not at issue or is unavailable (as when, for example, the forum selection clause designates a non-U.S. court). Some courts see the proper vehicle as a Rule 12(b)(3) motion to dismiss for improper venue. Lipcon v. Underwriters at Lloyd's of London, 148 F.3d 1285, 1290-91 (11th Cir. 1998). Others see the proper vehicle as a Rule 12(b)(6) motion to dismiss for failure to state a claim. LFC Lessors, Inc. v. Pacific Sewer Maintenance Corp., 739 F.2d 4 (1st Cir. 1984). Still others have employed a Rule 12(b)(1) motion to dismiss for lack of subject matter jurisdiction. AVC Nederland B.V. v. Inv. Partnership, 740 F.2d 148 (2d Cir. 1984). And finally, some courts have analyzed the problem in connection with motions to dismiss on *forum non conveniens* grounds. See, e.g., AAR Int'l, Inc. v. Nimelias Enters. S.A., 250 F.3d 510 (7th Cir. 2001). See generally Jonathan Corsico, Comment: *Forum Non Conveniens: A Vehicle for Federal Court Enforcement of Forum*

Selection Clauses That Name Non-Federal Forums as Proper, 97 Nw. U. L. Rev. 1853 (2003) (opting for *forum non conveniens* as the best of an imperfect lot).

5.   Appellate review and timing. Federal appeals courts can usually entertain appeals only after there has been a final judgment in the district court, such that all proceedings are over and done with. Appellate review of denials of personal jurisdiction objections, for example, must ordinarily await completion of the trial. Should a similar rule apply to denials of motions by foreign defendants to dismiss based on a forum selection clause? Obviously, if a motion to dismiss based on such a clause is granted, the case is over, and the ruling must be appealed. But what if the motion is denied? If an appeal is not immediately available, the defendant will be obliged to endure a trial in a forum other than that which the parties have agreed to, as a precondition to appealing the denial of the motion to dismiss. Is that the right result? Consider the following resolution of the issue:

In **LAURO LINES s.r.l. v. CHASSER, 490 U.S. 495 (1989)**, a wrongful death action was brought against Lauro Lines and others following the death of a passenger on the cruise ship Achille Lauro. The passenger, Ernst Klinghoffer, was killed by terrorists during a cruise in the Mediterranean. The contractual agreement on the ticket stated that any litigation arising out of the voyage would be litigated in a court in Naples, Italy. Suit was nevertheless brought by U.S. relatives of the deceased in a New York federal court. The motion to dismiss by Lauro Lines based on the forum selection clause was denied, and Lauro Lines immediately appealed. Justice Brennan wrote for the Court:

> Lauro Lines argues here that its contractual forum-selection clause provided it with a right to trial before a tribunal in Italy, and with a concomitant right not to be sued anywhere else. This "right not to be haled for trial before tribunals outside the agreed forum," petitioner claims, cannot effectively be vindicated by appeal after trial in an improper forum. * * * There is no obviously correct way to characterize the right embodied in petitioner's forum-selection provision: "all litigants who have a meritorious pretrial claim for dismissal can reasonably claim a right not to stand trial." * * * The right appears most like the right to be free from trial if it is characterized—as by petitioner—as a right not to be sued at all except in a Neapolitan forum. It appears less like a right not to be subjected to suit if characterized—as by the Court of Appeals—as "a right to have the binding adjudication of claims occur in a certain forum."

> * * * Even assuming that the former characterization is proper, however, petitioner is obviously not entitled under the forum-selection clause of its contract to avoid suit altogether, and an entitlement to avoid suit is different in kind from an entitlement to be sued only in a particular forum. Petitioner's claim that it may be sued only in Naples, while not perfectly secured by appeal after final judgment, is adequately vindicable at that stage—surely as effectively vindicable as a claim that the trial court lacked personal jurisdiction over the defendant—and hence does not fall within the third prong of the collateral order doctrine.

Petitioner argues that there is a strong federal policy favoring the enforcement of foreign forum-selection clauses, citing *The Bremen* * * * and that "the essential concomitant of this strong federal policy * * * is the right of immediate appellate review of district court orders denying their enforcement." * * * A policy favoring enforcement of forum-selection clauses, however, would go to the merits of petitioner's claim that its ticket agreement requires that any suit be filed in Italy and that the agreement should be enforced by the federal courts. Immediate appealability of a prejudgment order denying enforcement, insofar as it depends upon satisfaction of the third prong of the collateral order test, turns on the precise contours of the right asserted, and not upon the likelihood of eventual success on the merits. The Court of Appeals properly dismissed petitioner's appeal * * *.

490 U.S. at 500-01.

Justice Scalia concurred in the Court's opinion, but took a somewhat different approach.

The reason we say that the right not to be sued elsewhere than in Naples is "adequately vindicable," * * * by merely reversing any judgment obtained in violation of it is, quite simply, that the law does not deem the right *important enough* to be vindicated by, as it were, an injunction against its violation obtained through interlocutory appeal. The importance of the right asserted has always been a significant part of our collateral order doctrine. When first formulating that doctrine * * *, we said that it permits interlocutory appeal of final determinations of claims that are not only "separable from, and collateral to, rights asserted in the action," but also, we immediately added, "*too important* to be denied review." [Cohen v. Beneficial Indus. Loan Corp., 337 U.S. 541,] 546 (emphasis added). Our later cases have retained that significant requirement. For example, in Abney v. United States, 431 U.S. 651 (1977), we said that in order to qualify for immediate appeal the order must involve "an *important* right which would be 'lost, probably irreparably,' if review had to await final judgment." Id. at 568 (emphasis added). And in Coopers & Lybrand v. Livesay, 437 U.S. 463 (1978), we said that the order must "resolve an *important* issue completely separate from the merits of the action." Id. at 468 (emphasis added). * * *

While it is true, therefore, that the "right not to be sued elsewhere than in Naples" is not fully vindicated—indeed, to be utterly frank, is positively destroyed—by permitting the trial to occur [in New York] and reversing its outcome, that is vindication enough because the right is not sufficiently important to overcome the policies militating against interlocutory appeals. We have made that judgment when the right not to be tried in a particular court has been created through jurisdictional limitations established by Congress or by international treaty[.] The same judgment applies—if anything, *a fortiori*—when the right has been created by private agreement.

Id. at 502-03.

Is the outcome in *Lauro Lines* consistent with the decision in *Zapata*? Consistent with the observation in *Asahi* about the special burdens placed upon foreign defendants litigating in a foreign judicial system? For a critique of *Lauro Lines*, see Howard W. Schreiber, Note, *An Argument against "Canceling Out" The Bremen*, 57 Hofstra L. Rev. 463 (1988). Finally, note that a statutory exception (under 28 U.S.C. § 1292(b)) to the final judgment rule permits interlocutory review of certain decisions if the district court is able to certify that there is a controlling question of law; that there is a substantial ground for difference of opinion; and that an immediate appeal may advance the ultimate termination of the litigation. But under § 1292(b), not only must the district court make such findings, the court of appeals must also agree to permit the appeal in its discretion. Would denial of a motion to dismiss based on a forum selection clause fit within the parameters of § 1292(b)?

NOTE ON THE HAGUE CHOICE OF COURT CONVENTION

The Hague Convention of 30 June 2005 on Choice of Court Agreements is a proposal designed to promote the effectiveness of forum selection clauses between parties to international business transactions. We discuss the Convention in greater detail in Chapter 7. (For the text of the Convention, see Appendix C). It would apply to "exclusive choice of court agreements" (forum selection clauses) in "international cases" in "civil and commercial matters." Art. 1. The Convention limits its application primarily to choice of court agreements between businesses (Art. 2), and it expressly does *not* apply to agreements in a great number of matters, including personal injury, insolvency, employment, carriage of passengers and goods, antitrust, and most intellectual property litigation apart from copyright. Art. 2. The Convention is largely designed to ensure the enforcement of judgments in cases brought in chosen courts consistent with the Convention (Arts. 8-9) and to insure that the choice of forum clause will itself be enforceable.

If suit is filed in the chosen court and the chosen court concludes that the Convention applies to the choice of court agreement, the court is obligated to exercise jurisdiction over the case, and not dismiss, even "on the ground that the dispute should be decided in the court of another state." Art. 5. In addition, in the face of a choice of court agreement, other states "shall suspend or dismiss" actions brought before them (Art. 6), subject to a handful of exceptions. One exception is when the chosen court "has decided not to hear the case." Another is a public policy exception that is applicable when "giving effect to the agreement would lead to a manifest injustice or would be manifestly contrary to the public policy of the State of the court seised [i.e., the non-"chosen" court in which suit has been brought]."

Only Mexico has ratified the Convention as of March 1, 2013. And it takes two countries' ratifications for the Convention to enter into force. Nevertheless, the U.S. signed it on Jan. 19, 2009, the last day of President George W. Bush's tenure in office, as did the E.U. in April 2009. Both the U.S. and the E.U. have indicated their intention to ratify the treaty. Note that if the Convention should go into effect, its provisions would be binding on state court practice as well as on the federal courts.

NOTE ON FORUM SELECTION CLAUSES UNDER E.U. LAW

The validity and effect of forum selection clauses are governed by the so-called Brussels Regulation: Council Regulation (EC) No 44/2001 of 22 December 2000 on jurisdiction and the recognition and enforcement of judgments in civil and commercial matters, O.J. (L 12) 1 (Jan. 16, 2001), which contains binding European Union Law directly applicable in all European Union Member States except Denmark. (For the text of the Brussels Regulation see Appendix D.) This Regulation prescribes rules for the exercise of judicial jurisdiction and the enforcement of judgments in cross-border litigation within the European Union and beyond. As we noted earlier in Section G of this chapter, a recast version of the Regulation will go into effect in 2015.

Within their scope of application (see below), the Brussels Regulation rules displace domestic procedural law of the Member States. From an American perspective, the Brussels Regulation is thus akin to a system of Federal Rules of Civil Procedure. In contrast to American law, however, these Rules must be applied by (Member) State courts.

According to Article 1(1) of the Brussels Regulation, "the Regulation shall apply in civil and commercial matters whatever the nature of the court or tribunal." Article 23 governs the status (mandatory versus permissive) and validity of forum selection clauses. It provides in pertinent part:

Article 23

1. If the parties, one or more of whom is domiciled in a Member State, have agreed that a court or the courts of a Member State are to have jurisdiction to settle any disputes which have arisen or which may arise in connection with a particular legal relationship, that court or those courts shall have jurisdiction. Such jurisdiction shall be exclusive unless the parties have agreed otherwise. Such an agreement conferring jurisdiction shall be either:

(a) in writing or evidenced in writing; or

(b) in a form which accords with practices which the parties have established between themselves; or

(c) in international trade or commerce, in a form which accords with a usage of which the parties are or ought to have been aware and which in such trade or commerce is widely known to, and regularly observed by, parties to contracts of the type involved in the particular trade or commerce concerned.

2. Any communication by electronic means which provides a durable record of the agreement shall be equivalent to "writing".

3. Where such an agreement is concluded by parties, none of whom is domiciled in a Member State, the courts of other Member States shall

have no jurisdiction over their disputes unless the court or courts chosen have declined jurisdiction.

* * *

5. Agreements or provisions of a trust instrument conferring jurisdiction shall have no legal force if they are contrary to Articles 13, 17 or 21, or if the courts whose jurisdiction they purport to exclude have exclusive jurisdiction by virtue of Article 22.

To be valid under Article 23, forum selection clauses must meet a minimum threshold standard of specificity. Courts and commentators agree that forum selection clauses are sufficiently specific for purposes of Article 23 if they contain objective criteria which permit the determination of the place of jurisdiction. If such criteria exist, a clause need not even spell out any particular court at all. Thus, for example, if a forum selection clause reads "Jurisdiction is in Brussels," such clause would be sufficiently specific and therefore valid. Furthermore, and perhaps even more surprising to the American observer, is that such clause would be construed as a mandatory rather than permissive agreement. This is so because Brussels Regulation Article 23(1) provides that "[s]uch jurisdiction *shall be exclusive* unless the parties have agreed otherwise." (emphasis added). Compare Note 7, above (after *The Bremen*). Any doubt or ambiguity in the text of the choice of forum clause, "is to be understood as conferring exclusive jurisdiction on the chosen court even if the word 'exclusive' has not been used." (See Ulrich Magnus in: Brussels I Regulation (Ulrich Magnus & Peter Mankowsky, eds.) Article 23 Annot. 147 (2nd ed. 2012).) As a kind of corrective for this simple and yet far-reaching method of establishing mandatory forum selection agreements, Article 23(5) declares certain types of contracts, ineligible for such forum selection agreements. These rules are intended to protect the presumably/systemically weaker parties such as consumers and employees, from forum selection agreements that could be forced upon them due to their unequal bargaining power. Compare (and contrast) this approach with the one espoused by the U.S. Supreme Court in Carnival Cruise Lines, Inc. v. Shute, 499 U.S. 585 (1991), supra.

CHAPTER 2

Subject Matter Jurisdiction

A. INTRODUCTION

The national interests of the United States are arguably implicated in any transnational litigation brought in American courts, or in any case involving alien parties. It might therefore be supposed that federal courts, rather than state courts, would be the forums in which such litigation could always (or would usually) occur. But for a number of reasons, primarily based on our federal structure and separation of powers concerns, such a supposition would be inaccurate.

First of all, federal courts are courts of limited subject matter jurisdiction. As a constitutional matter, they can hear only those cases and controversies that are set out in Article III of the Constitution. Within Article III, a few categories seem to speak to transnational litigation including, most notably, suits between a citizen of a State and a citizen or subject of a foreign State (aka: alienage diversity jurisdiction) and cases arising under the Constitution, laws, and treaties of the U.S. (aka: federal question jurisdiction). There are also provisions conferring federal judicial power over suits affecting ambassadors, consuls, and ministers, as well as suits involving admiralty and maritime law, which may also implicate transnational issues. And while the applicable law in federal question and admiralty cases (for example) might be apparent from the jurisdictional grant itself, suits between a citizen of a state and an alien could include suits that arise under nonfederal law, such as state law or the law of a foreign country.

Furthermore, lower federal courts cannot hear cases, even though they appear on Article III's laundry list of cases to which the federal judicial power extends, unless Congress has enacted a jurisdictional provision enabling them to do so. And for better or worse, Congress has never conferred on the federal courts the entire jurisdiction that is provided for under Article III. For example, there has always been an amount-in-controversy requirement for suits between an alien and a citizen of one of the States (alienage diversity), just as for suits between citizens of different states (domestic diversity). Article III contains no such monetary requirement; only the diversity statute does. Failure to satisfy the amount-in-controversy requirement means that state courts, rather than federal courts will hear the suit, even though the parties are diverse from one another. In addition, as discussed below, cases presenting federal questions that only arise by way of defense to a state law (or foreign country law) claim will not arise under federal law within the meaning of the federal question statute, even though it is generally supposed that such cases arise under federal law for purposes of Article III of the Constitution,

In addition, the statutory grant of domestic diversity jurisdiction has been held to require "complete" diversity—i.e., no plaintiff can be a citizen of the same state as any defendant. Strawbridge v. Curtiss, 7 U.S. (3 Cranch) 267 (1806). Absent some basis for federal jurisdiction other than diversity, incomplete diversity suits must be heard in state court. As discussed below, to the extent that the complete diversity requirement attaches to alienage jurisdiction, many suits in which aliens are parties will be relegated to state courts.

As a final matter, it should be noted that even when federal jurisdiction attaches, it is ordinarily not exclusive. That is, the fact that Article III and federal statutes permit a case to be filed in federal court does not mean that it must be filed there, to the exclusion of filing in state court. As a rule of thumb, unless Congress has been explicit about ousting the state courts of jurisdiction in a case over which Congress has properly given the federal courts subject matter jurisdiction, the state courts can still exercise their own jurisdiction. The presumptive rule, therefore, typically permits plaintiffs to bring suit in state court in the first instance even when federal jurisdiction would be available, if they so choose. Nevertheless, Congress has also enacted various removal statutes that allow defendants in many (but not all) cases to veto the plaintiff's choice of a state forum, provided the suit is one that the plaintiff could have filed in federal court in the first instance but, for whatever reason, chose not to.

The jurisdictional allocations made by the Constitution, Congress, and the courts in interpreting these constitutional and statutory provisions raise a number of issues. These are of particular but not exclusive concern to foreign defendants who may find the unfamiliarity of the U.S. judicial system exacerbated still further by the fact that the lawsuit may be brought in a state court rather than a federal court. We will consider these issues in the context of three general, but related, questions in the next two sections of this chapter: (1) Who or what is an alien—a citizen or subject of a foreign country—for purposes of the alienage diversity jurisdiction of the federal courts? (2) How, if at all, does the requirement of complete diversity apply in the context of alienage jurisdiction? And (3) To what extent might matters implicating foreign law or international law be said to arise under federal law, thus providing an alternative basis for federal jurisdiction, apart from alienage diversity?

B. ALIENAGE AND DIVERSITY JURISDICTION

1. Citizens or Subjects of Foreign States

Article III of the Constitution provides that the federal judicial power shall extend to "Controversies . . . between a State, or the Citizens thereof, and Foreign States, Citizens or Subjects." In 1789, Congress provided for federal jurisdiction, concurrent with the state courts, over civil suits in law and equity, when the amount in controversy was in excess of $500, when "an alien is a party." (A constitutional question concerning the 1789 version of the statute is discussed below, along with the text of the current diversity statute.)

Consider the U.S. Supreme Court's assessment of the purposes of alienage diversity provisions—both constitutional and statutory—in **JPMORGAN CHASE BANK v. TRAFFIC STREAM (BVI) INFRASTRUCTURE LTD., 536 U.S. 88, 94-96 (2002)**:

> Both during and after the Revolution, state courts were notoriously frosty to British creditors trying to collect debts from American citizens, and state legislatures went so far as to hobble British debt collection by statute, despite the specific provision of the 1783 Treaty of Paris that creditors in the courts of either country would "meet with no lawful impediment" to debt collection. Definitive Treaty of Peace, United States-Great Britain, Art. IV, 8 Stat. 82. * * * Ultimately, the States' refusal to honor the treaty became serious enough to prompt protests by the British Secretary of State, particularly when irked by American demands for treaty compliance on the British side. * * *

> This penchant of the state courts to disrupt international relations and discourage foreign investment led directly to the alienage jurisdiction provided by Article III of the Constitution. See U.S. Const., Art. III, § 2 (federal jurisdiction "extends to . . . Controversies . . . between a State, or the Citizens thereof, and foreign States, Citizens or Subjects"). "The proponents of the Constitution . . . made it quite clear that the elimination or amelioration of difficulties with credit was the principal reason for having the alienage and diversity jurisdictions, and that it was one of the most important reasons for a federal judiciary." Holt, *"To Establish Justice": Politics, The Judiciary Act of 1789, and the Invention of the Federal Courts*, 1989 DUKE L.J. 1421, 1473. This is how James Wilson put it during the debates at the Pennsylvania ratification convention:

> > "Let us suppose the case, that a wicked law is made in some one of the states, enabling a debtor to pay his creditor with the fourth, fifth, or sixth part of the real value of the debt, and this creditor, a foreigner, complains to his prince . . . of the injustice that has been done him . . .. Bound by inclination, as well as duty, to redress the wrong his subject sustains . . . he must therefore apply to the United States; the United States must be accountable. 'My subject has received a flagrant injury: do me justice, or I will do myself justice.' If the United States are answerable for the injury, ought they not to possess the means of compelling the faulty state to repair it? They ought; and this is what is done here. For now, if complaint is made in consequence of such injustice, Congress can answer, 'Why did not your subject apply to the General Court . . . ?'" 2 Debates on the Federal Constitution 493 (J. Elliot ed. 1876).

Wilson emphasized that in order to "extend our manufactures and our commerce" there would need to be a "proper security . . . provided for the regular discharge of contracts. This security cannot be obtained, unless we give the power of deciding upon those contracts to the general government." *Id.*, at 492. His concerns were echoed by James Madison: "We well know, sir, that foreigners cannot get justice done them in these courts, and this has prevented many wealthy gentlemen from trading or residing among us." 3 *id.,* at 583. Madison also remarked that alienage jurisdiction was necessary to "avoid controversies with foreign powers" so that a single State's courts would not "drag the whole community into war." *Id.,* at 534; see also The Federalist No. 80, p. 536 (J. Cooke ed. 1961) (A. Hamilton) ("[A]n unjust sentence against a foreigner [may] be an aggression upon his sovereign" rendering alienage jurisdiction "essential to . . . the security of the public tranquility").

Thus, the First Congress granted federal courts the alienage jurisdiction authorized in the Constitution, even while general federal-question jurisdiction was withheld. See Judiciary Act of 1789, ch. 20, § 11, 1 Stat. 78 (providing for jurisdiction where "an alien is a party" and more than $ 500 in controversy). The language of the statute was amended in 1875 to track Article III by replacing the word "aliens" with "citizens, or subjects," Act of Mar. 3, 1875, 18 Stat. 470, the phrase that remains today. Although there is no need here to decide whether the current drafting provides jurisdiction up to the constitutional hilt, cf. *Tennessee* v. *Union & Planters' Bank*, 152 U.S. 454 (1894) (despite similar language, federal-question jurisdiction under 28 U.S.C. § 1331 does not extend as far as Article III), there is no doubt that the similarity of § 1332(a)(2) to Article III bespeaks a shared purpose.

The current diversity statute, in relevant part, provides as follows:

28 U.S.C. § 1332. Diversity of citizenship; amount in controversy; costs

(a) The district courts shall have original jurisdiction of all civil actions where the matter in controversy exceeds the sum or value of $75,000 * * * and is between —

(1) citizens of different States;

(2) citizens of a State and citizens or subjects of a foreign state, except that the district courts shall not have original jurisdiction under this subsection of any action between citizens of a State and citizens or subjects of a foreign state who are lawfully admitted for permanent residence in the United States and are domiciled in the same State;

(3) citizens of different States and in which citizens or subjects of a foreign state are additional parties; and

(4) a foreign state * * * as plaintiff and citizens of a State or of different States. * * *

The decision that follows addresses the question of who is an alien for purposes of the diversity statute. Note that at the time that the case was decided, § 1332 was worded somewhat differently and (among other things) had no provisions regarding permanent resident aliens as currently exists under § 1332(a)(2), set out above.

Sadat v. Mertes

Unites States Court of Appeals, Seventh Circuit, 1980.

615 F.2d 1176.

PER CURIAM.

[Sadat claimed to be a "citizen of the United States presently residing" in Egypt. He brought a negligence action in federal court against defendants alleged to be citizens of either Wisconsin or Connecticut arising out of an automobile accident. Defendants moved to dismiss for lack of subject matter jurisdiction. Sadat argued that diversity jurisdiction existed on two separate grounds: (1) he was a Pennsylvania domiciliary; (2) he was a citizen of Egypt as well as of the U.S. The district court dismissed, rejecting both arguments.]

II

THE PLAINTIFF'S TRAVELS AND TRAVAILS

An understanding of the jurisdictional dilemma facing the plaintiff requires a review of his wanderings over the last several decades. The plaintiff was born in Egypt, received his early schooling there, and apparently served in the Egyptian armed forces as a young man. He left his homeland during the 1950s and studied in Europe and worked in Kuwait before coming to the United States in 1963. While in the United States and prior to the events at issue here, he continued his education at several universities and at various times worked for several corporations. In 1973, he apparently was domiciled in Pittsburgh, Pennsylvania. He owned a home there; his wife worked for the University of Pittsburgh; and his children apparently attended the local schools there.

1973 was an eventful year for the plaintiff. With the permission of the government of Egypt he became a naturalized citizen of the United States. He also received an offer from Kohler International Ltd. to serve as the corporation's Area Manager for the Middle East. The job required the plaintiff, after a brief training period at the corporation's offices in Wisconsin, to relocate to Beirut, Lebanon. The plaintiff accepted the offer. His wife left her position with the university. He sold his house and began to move his family and personal property to Lebanon. On his way to O'Hare International Airport from Kohler's Wisconsin offices, the plaintiff was involved in the automobile accident giving rise to his complaint here. He nevertheless completed his move to Beirut and, once there, notified the U. S. Embassy that Beirut was his permanent overseas residence.

Mr. Sadat and his family stayed in Beirut for about two years. On April 15, 1975, apparently as a result of mutual dissatisfaction complicated by the political unrest in Lebanon, the plaintiff and his employer terminated their association with each other. * * * [Kohler agreed that it would pay to move Sadat's family "to the United States or other location specified by Mr. Sadat," but hostilities broke out in Lebanon, and the plaintiff took his family to Egypt.]

After the plaintiff's move to Egypt, he stayed in Cairo for several years. According to the plaintiff, Kohler refused to honor its commitment to pay for transportation for him and his family to the location of his choice. He claimed he was financially unable to transport himself or his family back to the United States. He also was unable to obtain employment in Egypt, and, in the interim, he and his family resided in a house in Cairo that his mother purchased for him and he registered with the U.S. Embassy as a permanent resident. Documents submitted by the plaintiff indicate that he was issued Egyptian driver's licenses, paid the real estate taxes on the home, and maintained a checking account in Cairo during this time. In 1978, the plaintiff returned to the States and is now residing in Milwaukee.

III

WAS THE PLAINTIFF A CITIZEN OF ANY OF THE UNITED STATES?

The plaintiff's travels over time have been many, but this court's inquiry must center on his status at the time of the commencement of this action. As the district court noted, that is the time at which the jurisdiction of the court is determined. Smith v. Sperling, 354 U.S. 91, 93 n.1 (1957). The plaintiff's status of June 7, 1976, therefore determines the capacity in which he brings this suit.

28 U.S.C. § 1332(a)(1) creates the federal courts' jurisdiction over actions between "citizens of different States." For a natural person to fall within the provision he must be both (1) a citizen of the United States and (2) a citizen of a particular state. See Scott v. Sandford, 60 U.S. (19 How.) 393, 405-06 (1857). * * * It is not disputed here that the plaintiff having been naturalized in 1973 is a citizen of the United States. What is contested is whether in 1976 when his complaint was filed he was a citizen of one of the United States. The issue is crucial to the plaintiffs claim of jurisdiction under 28 U.S.C. § 1332(a)(1) because settled precedent establishes that a citizen of the United States who is not also a citizen of one of the United States may not maintain suit under that section. Meyers v. Smith, 460 F. Supp. 621 (D.D.C.1978); * * *. Although this doctrine excluding Americans domiciled abroad from the federal courts has been questioned, the plaintiff does not directly attack it here and we see no reason for upsetting settled law now.

State citizenship for the purpose of the state diversity provision is equated with domicile. The standards for determining domicile in this context are found by resort to federal common law. * * * To establish a domicile of choice a person generally must be physically present at the location and intend to make that place his home for the time at least. See Restatement (Second) of Conflict of

Laws §§ 15, 16, 18 (1971). Applying these standards, the district court found
that the plaintiff was domiciled in Egypt in 1976. The plaintiff, however, contends that he should be considered a domiciliary of the State of Pennsylvania.
He apparently bases his claim upon his previous domicile there in 1973 and his
alleged intention to return there upon leaving Lebanon in 1975. "Unfortunately," the plaintiffs brief opines, "the successive events required [him] to move
from Beirut, Lebanon to Cairo, Egypt and to take up residence there until he
was able to return to the United States in 1978."

   The plaintiff's deposition testimony makes clear that his move from Pennsylvania to Lebanon in 1973 effected a change in his domicile. He moved his
belongings, his family, and his business to Lebanon. Then, in 1975 he moved
again to Egypt where he and his family stayed through 1976, the year of the filing of his complaint. The plaintiffs affidavit in opposition to the defendants'
motion to dismiss states that he "owns his home in Cairo, Egypt and considers
himself a resident of Egypt where he was born and raised [and] that he maintains said home in Cairo, Egypt, which home contains his furniture, books, records and valuables." He also sent his children to school there and secured Egyptian driver's licenses there. This evidence was sufficient to permit the district
court to find that the plaintiff was domiciled in Egypt notwithstanding his assertion that he never intended to make Egypt his home.[5] Although the plaintiff disclaimed any intention of settling in Cairo, "[i]ntent is a state of mind which must
be evaluated through the circumstantial evidence of a person's manifested conduct," * * * and "statements of intent are entitled to little weight when in conflict with the facts". * * *

   But even if the district court's conclusion that the plaintiff intended to make
Egypt his home was erroneous, cf. Restatement (Second) of Conflict of Laws §
17, comment *f* (1971), that does not establish that Pennsylvania was the plaintiffs domicile. It only leads to the conclusion that Lebanon was. "A domicil
once established continues until it is superseded by a new domicil." Id. at § 19.
The plaintiff never returned to Pennsylvania after leaving for Lebanon in 1973
and thus never established the physical presence necessary to reestablish his
domicile there. Moreover, his claimed intention to return to that state, assuming
arguendo that in these circumstances intention alone would be sufficient to establish a new domicile, is refuted by the facts. First, the contract providing for
Kohler to pay his moving expenses, contrary to his assertion in his brief, did not
specify Pittsburgh as his destination. It gave the plaintiff his choice of destina-
tions and provided that reimbursement would not exceed the cost of relocating
the plaintiff to Pittsburgh. Second, the plaintiff's own deposition testimony indicates that his intention to return to Pennsylvania was less than firm. The compulsion which kept the plaintiff in Egypt was a financial one. Arguably, it may
have prevented him from forming the intent to make Egypt his home, but it did

---

[5] The plaintiff apparently did vote in the 1976 presidential elections by an absentee ballot sent to
him from Pa. A party's voting practice, however, is only one of the factors considered in determining that person's domicile. No single factor is conclusive. 15 C. Wright, A. Miller, & E.
Cooper, Federal Practice and Procedure § 3612 at 717 (1975).

not establish that his domicile was in one of the United States. Because the plaintiff, an American citizen, was domiciled abroad in 1976, he was not a citizen of a state within the meaning of 28 U.S.C. § 1332(a)(1). The jurisdiction of the district court, if it exists, must be found under 28 U.S.C. § 1332(a)(2).

IV
IS THE PLAINTIFF A CITIZEN OR SUBJECT OF A FOREIGN STATE?

The plaintiff's second argument is that if he is not a citizen of one of the United States, then he is by virtue of his dual American-Egyptian citizenship a citizen of a foreign state and jurisdiction therefore exists under 28 U.S.C. § 1332(a)(2). * * *

28 U.S.C. § 1332(a)(2) vests the district courts with jurisdiction over civil actions between state citizens and citizens of foreign states. This power is sometimes referred to as alienage jurisdiction. Although the basis for alienage jurisdiction is similar to that over controversies between state citizens, it is founded on more concrete concerns than the arguably unfounded fears of bias or prejudice by forums in one of the United States against litigants from another of the United States.

The dominant considerations which prompted the provision for such jurisdiction appear to have been:

> (1) Failure on the part of the individual states to give protection to foreigners under treaties; Farrand, "The Framing of the Constitution" 46 (1913); Nevins, "The American State During and After the Revolution" 644—656 (1924); Friendly, 41 Harvard Law Review 483, 484.

> (2) Apprehension of entanglements with other sovereigns that might ensue from failure to treat the legal controversies of aliens on a national level. Hamilton, "The Federalist" No. 80.

Blair Holdings Corp. v. Rubinstein, 133 F. Supp. 496, 500 (S.D.N.Y. 1955). Thus, alienage jurisdiction was intended to provide the federal courts with a form of protective jurisdiction over matters implicating international relations where the national interest was paramount. See The Federalist No. 80 (A. Hamilton) ("[T]he peace of the WHOLE ought not to be left at the disposal of a PART. The Union will undoubtedly be answerable to foreign powers for the conduct of its members. And the responsibility for an injury ought ever to be accompanied with the faculty for preventing it.")[7] Recognizing this obvious national interest in such controversies, not even the proponents of the abolition of diversity jurisdiction over suits between citizens of the several United States have advocated elimination of alienage jurisdiction. See, e.g., H. Friendly, *Fed-*

---

[7] See also *American Law Institute, Study of the Division of Jurisdiction Between State and Federal Courts* 105 (1969):

> It is important in the relations of this country with other nations that any possible appearance of injustice or tenable ground for resentment be avoided. This objective can best be achieved by giving the foreigner the assurance that he can have his cases tried in a court with the best procedures the federal government can supply and with the dignity and prestige of the United States behind it.

eral Jurisdiction: A General View 149-50 (1973); Rowe, *Abolishing Diversity Jurisdiction: Positive Side Effects and Potential for Further Reforms*, 92 Harv. L. Rev. 963, 966-68 (1979). * * *

The generally accepted test for determining whether a person is a foreign citizen for purposes of 28 U.S.C. § 1332(a)(2) is whether the country in which citizenship is claimed would so recognize him. This is in accord with the principle of international law that "it is the inherent right of every independent nation to determine for itself, and according to its own constitution and laws, what classes of persons shall be entitled to its citizenship." United States v. Wong Kim Ark, 169 U.S. 649, 668 (1898). * * *

Relying on this principle, the plaintiff maintains that notwithstanding his U.S. naturalization, Egypt still regards him as an Egyptian citizen. The evidence in the record tends to sustain his contention. * * * A letter from the Egyptian Minister of Exterior to the plaintiff states:

> Greetings, we have the honor to inform you that it has been agreed to permit you to be naturalized with United States Citizenship but retaining your Egyptian citizenship. * * *

This evidence is sufficient to establish that, despite his naturalization in the United States, the plaintiff is an Egyptian under that country's laws. Consequently, under the ordinary choice of law rule for determining nationality under 28 U.S.C. § 1332(a)(2) he would be so regarded for the purpose of determining the district court's jurisdiction over the subject matter. Thus, the issue squarely presented to this court is whether a person possessing dual nationality, one of which is United States citizenship, is "a citizen or subject of a foreign state" under 28 U.S.C. § 1332(a)(2). * * *

Whether a person possessing dual nationality should be considered a citizen or subject of a foreign state within the meaning of 28 U.S.C. § 1332(a)(2) is a question of first impression in the courts of appeals. The two district courts other than the district court below which have addressed the question have reached seemingly different conclusions. In Aguirre v. Nagel, 270 F. Supp. 535 (E.D. Mich.1967), the plaintiff, a citizen of the United States and the State of Michigan, sued a Michigan citizen for injuries sustained when she was hit by the defendant's car. The court * * * [found] jurisdiction under 28 U.S.C. § 1332(a)(2) because the plaintiff's parents were citizens of Mexico and Mexico regarded her as a Mexican citizen by virtue of her parentage. The *Aguirre* court's opinion did no more than determine that the cause fell within the literal language of the statute without regard to the policies underlying alienage jurisdiction. As a result, it has been questioned by the commentators, see 1 Moore's Federal Practice ¶¶ 0.75[1.-1] at 709.4-.5 (2d ed. 1979); 13 C. Wright, A. Miller, & E. Cooper, Federal Practice and Procedure § 3621 at 759-60 (1975), and rejected by one other district court in addition to the court below. See Raphael v. Hertzberg, 470 F. Supp. 984 (C.D. Cal.1979). * * *

In rejecting the authority of *Aguirre,* the court [in *Raphael*] noted several possible objections to permitting naturalized Americans to assert their foreign citizenship:

To begin with, the holding in *Aguirre* violates the requirement of complete diversity (Strawbridge v. Curtiss, 7 U.S. (3 Cranch) 267 (1806)) since *Aguirre,* like the present case, involved opposing parties who were both American citizens and who resided in the same state. Moreover, where both parties are residents of the state in which the action is brought, there is no reason to expect bias from the state courts. Finally, so long as the party asserting diversity jurisdiction is an American citizen, there is little reason to fear that a foreign government may be affronted by a decision adverse to that citizen, even if the American citizen also purports to be a citizen of that foreign nation.

The rule proposed by the plaintiff would give naturalized citizens nearly unlimited access to the federal courts, access which has been denied to native-born citizens. Such favored treatment is unsupported by the policies underlying 28 U.S.C. § 1332(a)(2). Finally, a new rule that would extend the scope of § 1332 is particularly undesirable in light of the ever-rising level of criticism of the very concept of diversity jurisdiction.

Although the issue facing the courts in *Aguirre* and *Raphael* is the same as the one presented here, the facts in this case are somewhat different. All commentators addressing the issue have noted the anomaly of permitting an American citizen claiming dual citizenship to obtain access to the federal court under 28 U.S.C. § 1332(a)(2) when suing a citizen domiciled in the same state. *See* 1 Moore's Federal Practice ¶ 0.75[1-1] at 709.5 (2d ed. 1979):

> This result is inconsistent with the complete diversity rule of *Strawbridge v. Curtiss,* . . . including the analogous situation of a suit between a citizen of State A and a corporation chartered in State B with its principal place of business in State A. Both state citizenships of the corporation must be considered and diversity is thus found lacking.[12]

In the present case, however, the plaintiff was domiciled abroad when he initiated this action and therefore was not a citizen of any state. Thus, permitting suit under alienage jurisdiction would not run counter to the complete diversity considerations which arguably should have controlled the decisions in *Aguirre* and *Raphael*.[13]

---

[12] The requirement of complete diversity has been held to preclude jurisdiction over actions which otherwise could have been maintained under 28 U.S.C. § 1332(a)(2). See Ed & Fred, Inc. v. Puritan Marine Ins. Underwriters Corp., 506 F.2d 757 (5th Cir. 1975).

[13] Moreover, because in this case unlike *Aguirre* and *Raphael* the plaintiff is domiciled abroad, there might be some reason to fear bias if the suit were brought in the state courts. The fear of bias against out-of-state litigants, while a traditional basis for positing jurisdiction, has of recent years been subject to questioning as being too remote and speculative a basis. And, because the plaintiff is an American citizen as well as an Egyptian, the risk of bias in a state forum against the litigant because he is also a foreign national would appear less substantial. The plaintiff's position, therefore, is little different than that of any other American national domiciled abroad. Such people, of course, cannot obtain access to the federal courts under the diversity or alienage jurisdiction provisions.

The plaintiff seizing upon this factual difference would apparently have this court recognize his dual nationality for purposes of 28 U.S.C. § 1332 in much the same way corporations are regarded as having dual citizenship pursuant to 28 U.S.C. § 1332(c). Because in this case, even applying the corporate citizenship analogy, the complete diversity requirement is satisfied, the plaintiff argues that jurisdiction under 28 U.S.C. § 1332(a)(2) attaches. Such an approach, however, may be both too broad and too narrow and it ignores the paramount purpose of the alienage jurisdiction provision to avoid offense to foreign nations because of the possible appearance of injustice to their citizens. Imagine, for example, a native-born American, born of Japanese parents, domiciled in the State of California, and now engaged in international trade. A dispute could arise in which an Australian customer seeks to sue the American for, say, breach of contract in a federal court in California. The native-born American possibly could claim Japanese citizenship by virtue of his parentage * * * as well as his status as a citizen of California and defeat the jurisdiction of the federal courts because of the absence of complete diversity. Arguably, cases such as this are precisely those in which a federal forum should be afforded the foreign litigant in the interest of preventing international friction.

This hypothetical suggests that the analogy to the dual citizenship of corporations should not be controlling. Instead, the paramount consideration should be whether the purpose of alienage jurisdiction to avoid international discord would be served by recognizing the foreign citizenship of the dual national. Because of the wide variety of situations in which dual nationality can arise, * * * perhaps no single rule can be controlling. Principles establishing the responsibility of nations under international law with respect to actions affecting dual nationals, however, suggest by analogy that ordinarily, as the district court held, only the American nationality of the dual citizen should be recognized under 28 U.S.C. § 1332(a).

Under international law, a country is responsible for official conduct harming aliens, for example, the expropriation of property without compensation. See Restatement (Second) of the Foreign Relations Law of the United States §§ 164-214 (1965). It is often said, however, that a state is not responsible for conduct which would otherwise be regarded as wrongful if the injured person, although a citizen of a foreign state, is also a national of the state taking the questioned action. See id. at §171, comm. b & c. This rule recognizes that in the usual case a foreign country cannot complain about the treatment received by one of its citizens by a country which also regards that person as a national. * * *

Despite the general rule of nonresponsibility under international law for conduct affecting dual nationals, there are recognized exceptions. One is the concept of effective or dominant nationality. As qualified by the Restatement, this exception provides that a country (respondent state) will be responsible for wrongful conduct against one of its citizens whose dominant nationality is that of a foreign state, that is,

> (i) his dominant nationality, by reason of residence or other association subject to his control (or the control of a member of his family whose nationality determines his nationality) is that of the other state and (ii)

he (or such member of his family) has manifested an intention to be a national of the other state and has taken all reasonably practicable steps to avoid or terminate his status as a national of the respondent state.

* * *

Although at the time of the filing of his complaint in 1976 the plaintiff resided in Egypt, his voluntary naturalization in the United States in 1973 indicates that his dominant nationality is not Egyptian. As part of the naturalization process he swore allegiance to the United States and renounced any to foreign states. His actions subsequent to his naturalization evince his resolve to remain a U.S. citizen despite his extended stay abroad. * * * Certainly neither he nor the government of Egypt can complain if he is not afforded a federal forum when the same would be denied a similarly situated native-born American. [Affirmed.]

NOTES AND QUESTIONS FOR DISCUSSION

1. At its core, diversity jurisdiction in the federal courts is thought to provide non-residents of a state (outsiders) a more hospitable forum than would a state court in resolving a dispute with an in-stater. It is not that the federal courts today will apply a different substantive law to the dispute than would a state court. Rather, the protections associated with diversity jurisdiction may be thought to arise from the political insulation of life-tenured federal judges, from their greater procedural controls over juries, from the availability of uniform federal procedures, and perhaps from an institutional mind-set that may be less parochial and more national in its orientation. Whether this is true in every case may be uncertain. But it may be true overall, and from the perception of out-of-state defendants federal courts may seem like a safer haven.

2. Alienage jurisdiction serves a similar purpose insofar as aliens are the ultimate outsiders. Indeed, as noted in *JPMorgan Chase Bank, supra*, at the time of the framing of the Constitution, the need for a diversity provision in suits in which aliens were adverse to a citizen of a state was perceived even more acutely than in suits between citizens of different states. See Wythe Holt, *"To Establish Justice": Politics, The Judiciary Act of 1789, and the Invention of the Federal Courts*, 1989 Duke L.J. 1421 (arguing that, at the time of the Constitution's framing and the passage of the first judiciary statute, alienage jurisdiction was understood as the most critical of the Article III grants of power). Of course, at the time, it may also have been supposed that the federal courts might apply different substantive principles than those that a state court would have applied to the same controversy. Does the fact that federal courts would now (under Erie Railroad Co. v. Tompkins, 304 U.S. 64 (1938)) be obliged to apply the substantive law that a state court would apply lessen the need for alienage diversity? Cf. Kevin M. Clermont & Theodore Eisenberg, *Xenophilia or Xenophobia in U.S. Courts? Before and After 9/11*, 4 J. of Empirical Legal Stud. 441 (2007) (indicating that data suggest foreign parties in federal courts actually fare better than their domestic counterparts, but noting a countertrend since 9/11).

3. Today, there is "an emerging consensus" that, for a dual national citizen, only the American citizenship is relevant for purposes of diversity. Coury v. Prot, 85 F.3d 244, 250 (5th Cir. 1996); see also Molinos Valle del Cibao, C. por A. v. Lama, 633 F.3d 1330, 1341 (11th Cir. 2011) ("The courts of appeals deciding this issue have uniformly held that . . . an individual who is a dual citizen of the United States and another nation is only a citizen of the United States for purposes of diversity jurisdiction[.]"). Consequently, as a U.S. citizen who was not domiciled in any state at the time the lawsuit was filed, Sadat could not have been diverse from any U.S. citizen. He was not an alien (since only the U.S. citizenship counts); and he was not a citizen of any state. And as the Supreme Court has said, U.S. citizens domiciled abroad are neither a "citizens of a State" under § 1332(a) nor "citizens or subjects of a foreign state" and therefore are not proper parties to a diversity action in federal court. See Newman-Green, Inc. v. Alfonzo-Larrain, 490 U.S. 826, 828-29 (1989). Does a party in Sadat's position really have any less need for the protection a federal court supposedly provides than an alien without dual citizenship?

4. Is the court persuasive in its conclusion that Sadat's move to Lebanon effected a change in domicile—i.e., that he "lost" his Pennsylvania domicile? The court says that to acquire a new domicile one needs physical presence and an intent to make that place his home "for the time at least." Often the state of mind requirement is phrased more stringently as "an intention to remain there indefinitely; or, as some courts articulate it, the absence of any intention to go elsewhere." Coury, 85 F.3d at 250. Did the evidence satisfy that standard? Finally, note that whether a party is an alien turns not on the question of domicile, but on the question of nationality. A non-dual national alien (i.e., unlike Sadat) is still an alien, even if he is domiciled in one of the U.S. states. As noted below, however, there will be no diversity between a citizen of a state and an alien admitted to permanent resident alien status who is domiciled in that same state.

5. It has long been the case in federal courts that all plaintiffs must be diverse from all defendants, as matter of the diversity statute. Strawbridge v. Curtiss, 7 U.S. (3 Cranch) 267 (1806). In most cases alienage diversity jurisdiction is treated no differently. See, e.g., Eze v. Yellow Cab Co., 782 F.2d 1064, 1065 (D.C. Cir. 1986). Thus, even though an alien is a party in a case (for example, as a defendant), complete diversity will be lacking if the U.S. plaintiff also sues a U.S. defendant who is a citizen of the same state as the plaintiff. Obviously, this gives U.S. plaintiffs a way to avoid having to file a case against an alien in federal court, if that is their preference. And it also prevents removal of such a case when it is filed in a state court—as discussed below. It is important to note, however, that it is generally supposed that the complete diversity rule is not constitutionally compelled. In other words, Article III is satisfied so long as there is "minimal diversity"—i.e., so long as any two adverse parties are diverse from one another. State Farm Fire & Cas. Co. v. Tashire, 386 U.S. 523, 530-31 (1967). Consequently, if Congress wanted to abolish the complete diversity rule for suits involving aliens (or U.S. citizens), it could do so. Indeed, as discussed in the Notes that follow the next case, Congress has made a limited exception to the complete diversity rule in at least some cases involving aliens as parties.

While it might be supposed that any case in which an alien is a party would be susceptible to federal court jurisdiction, the precise language of Article III, section 2 is not supportive of such a conclusion. Consider the Supreme Court's early encounter with a jurisdictional statute that seemed to go beyond the limits of Article III, by seeming to provide jurisdiction whenever an alien was a party.

Hodgson v. Bowerbank

Supreme Court of the United States, 1809.

9 U.S. (5 Cranch) 303.

ERROR to the Circuit Court for the District of Maryland.

[Jurisdiction over the case was asserted based on section 11 of the Judiciary Act of 1789, purporting to confer on the circuit court's jurisdiction over cases in which an alien is a party: "The circuit courts shall have original cognizance, concurrent with the courts of the several States, of all suits of a civil nature at common law or in equity, where the matter in dispute exceeds [$500], and the United States are plaintiffs, or petitioners; or an alien is a party, or the suit is between a citizen of the State where the suit is brought, and a citizen of another State."]

The defendants below were described in the record as "late of the district of Maryland, merchants," but were not stated to be citizens of the State of Maryland. The plaintiffs were described as "aliens and subjects of the king of the United Kingdom of Great Britain and Ireland."

MARSHALL, CHIEF JUSTICE.

Turn to the article of the constitution of the United States, for the statute cannot extend the jurisdiction beyond the limits of the constitution. (The words of the constitution were found to be "between a state, or the citizens thereof, and foreign states, citizens, or subjects.")

The Court said the objection was fatal. * * *

NOTES AND QUESTIONS FOR DISCUSSSION

1. Because the plaintiff did not sufficiently allege that the defendants were citizens of the U.S. or of any state, they could not be diverse from an alien as a matter of Article III. Although it is not clear from the facts of the case that the defendants were aliens, *Hodgson* is generally read as saying that aliens will not be considered diverse from one another. Rather, such suits will have to be heard in a state court (unless, of course, an alternative jurisdictional hook may be found, such as federal question or admiralty). But isn't a suit between two aliens (if that is what *Hodgson* was) a suit that federal courts *ought* to be able to hear? Or should it be supposed that because aliens are on both sides of the litigation, the kind of state court bias that alienage jurisdiction was designed to police—hostility to foreign nationals—would effectively be canceled out?

2. The Court's reported opinion in *Hodgson* is not a model of clarity. Did Chief Justice Marshall hold section 11 of the Judiciary Act of 1789 unconstitutional, or did he construe the statute to require that a citizen of a U.S. state be a party to the suit brought by an alien? See Dennis J. Mahoney, *A Historical Note on* Hodgson v. Bowerbank, 49 U. Chi. L. Rev. 725 (1982) (suggesting, contrary to common assumption, that *Hodgson* narrowly construed section 11 to avoid a constitutional question).

3. Whether or not *Hodgson* was a holding of constitutional dimension, consider the constitutional problems that would be posed if Congress granted lower federal courts jurisdiction over cases involving only aliens. Does the current diversity jurisdiction statute manage to avoid these problems? Why did the first Congress, many of whose members had been involved in the drafting and ratification of the Constitution, say that federal courts were to have jurisdiction whenever "an alien is a party"?

4. Note that § 1332(a)(3) currently provides for jurisdiction in suits between "citizens of different States and in which citizens or subjects of a foreign state are additional parties." To provide a simple example: A (NY) could sue B (VA) and C (Italy), consistent with this provision of the diversity statute. Such a configuration would also comply with the principles of the complete diversity rule. But § 1332(a)(3) would also allow for federal jurisdiction if, in addition to A (NY), D (France) was also a plaintiff: A (NY) + D (France) vs. B (VA) + C (Italy). The suit is one between citizens of different states (A and B), and aliens are additional parties. To be sure, this action pits one alien against another, and after *Hodgson*, aliens are not diverse from other aliens. But if the complete diversity rule is not constitutionally compelled, then Article III is satisfied, because there is minimal diversity in such a case.

2. Permanent Resident Aliens and Alienage Jurisdiction

In the latest version of 28 U.S.C. § 1332, Congress has provided that permanent resident aliens are treated as aliens for diversity purposes, "except that" diversity jurisdiction will not extend to suits in which a permanent resident alien is adverse to a U.S. citizen domiciled in the same state as the permanent resident alien. What do you suppose was the purpose of such a provision? Note that the provision built on (and partially undid) an earlier change to § 1332 made in 1988 as part of a package of amendments—including a drastic, five-fold increase in the jurisdictional amount—which was designed, at least in the aggregate, to cut back on the diversity jurisdiction caseload of the federal courts. When involved in a dispute with a co-domicilary U.S. citizen, does the permanent resident alien have less reason to fear being treated as an outsider than a nonresident alien?

Antonier v. Miller

Unites States District Court, Middle District of Florida, 2012.

2012 U.S. Dist. LEXIS 22578.

SUSAN C. BUCKLEW, DISTRICT JUDGE.

This cause comes before the Court on Defendant Robert Miller's Motion to Dismiss. * * * As explained below, the motion to dismiss is granted to the extent that the Court finds that it lacks subject matter jurisdiction over this case.

I. *Background*

On May 20, 2011, Plaintiff Margaret Antonier filed suit against her former husband, Defendant Robert Miller, and her two sons, Defendants Rodney Miller and Frederick Miller, with regard to their alleged role as Trustees of the Robert Miller Spousal Trust ("Trust"). Specifically, Plaintiff alleges that despite the fact that she is the sole income beneficiary of the Trust, which was created in 2005, she has never received any of the income from the Trust. As a result, Plaintiff asserts a claim against Defendants for an accounting.

II. *Subject Matter Jurisdiction*

Plaintiff alleges that this Court has diversity subject matter jurisdiction over this case. Plaintiff is a Canadian citizen, but she resides in Florida because the United States has awarded her "treaty investor status" under the E-2 visa program.[2] Plaintiff contends that her "treaty investor status" is similar to permanent resident status. See Hall v. McLaughlin, 864 F.2d 868, 870-71 (D.C. Cir. 1989).

Defendants Robert Miller, Rodney Miller, and Frederick Miller are Canadian citizens that reside in Canada. Because Plaintiff and Defendants are all Canadian citizens, Defendant Robert Miller filed the instant motion to dismiss for lack of subject matter jurisdiction. Specifically, he argues that this Court does not have diversity jurisdiction over a case solely involving alien parties.

Plaintiff responds that this Court has diversity jurisdiction due to the final sentence of 28 U.S.C. § 1332(a), which at the time that this lawsuit was filed,[4] provided that certain aliens were deemed citizens of the state in which they were domiciled. Specifically, at the time that this lawsuit was filed, § 1332(a) provided that this Court has original jurisdiction over all civil actions in which the matter in controversy exceeds $75,000.00 in value and is between:

> (1) citizens of different States;
>
> (2) citizens of a State and citizens or subjects of a foreign state;

---

[2] "[A]n E-2 visa . . . is a form of nonimmigrant visa that permits an alien to come to the United States to develop and direct the operations of a business enterprise in which he has invested a substantial amount of capital." See Hall v. McLaughlin, 864 F.2d 868, 870 (D.C. Cir. 1989) (citing 8 U.S.C. § 1101(a)(15)(E)(ii)). Treaty investor status is further explained in 22 C.F.R. § 41.51(b).

[4] This statute was recently amended, effective January 5, 2012. See 2011 Acts. Pub.L. 112-63, Title I, § 105, Dec. 7, 2011, 125 Stat. 762.

(3) citizens of different States and in which citizens or subjects of a foreign state are additional parties; and

(4) a foreign state . . . as plaintiff and citizens of a State or of different States.

The final sentence of [old] § 1332(a) (which courts have referred to as "the deeming clause") contained the following statement: "For purposes of this section . . . an alien admitted to the United States for permanent residence shall be deemed a citizen of the State in which such alien is domiciled." Plaintiff argues that due to the deeming clause of § 1332(a), she is deemed to be a citizen of Florida. As such, Plaintiff argues that this Court has diversity jurisdiction over this case, pursuant to § 1332(a)(2), because it is a civil action between a "deemed" citizen of Florida and citizens of Canada. This argument, however, is flawed.

Several courts addressing the deeming clause of § 1332(a) have found that the clause was added to § 1332(a) in 1988 for the purpose of reducing diversity jurisdiction. See, e.g., Saadeh v. Farouki, 107 F.3d 52 (D.C. Cir. 1997); Banci v. Wright, 44 F. Supp.2d 1272, 1275 (S.D. Fla. 1999); * * *. Specifically, such courts noted that the legislative history revealed that the deeming clause was added in order to divest federal courts of jurisdiction over cases between a citizen of state A and a permanent resident alien domiciled in state A. See id. Thus, in cases between a citizen of state A and a permanent resident alien domiciled in state A, there would be no diversity jurisdiction because both parties would be deemed to be citizens of state A.

Furthermore, courts have noted the potential constitutional problem that arises if diversity jurisdiction was found to exist in a case between a permanent resident alien and a non-resident alien based on the deeming clause. See * * * Singh v. Daimler-Benz AG, 9 F.3d 303, 311-12 (3d Cir. 1993); Saadeh, 107 F.3d at 58; Banci, 44 F. Supp.2d at 1275. Specifically, as explained by one court:

> Article III . . . does not permit actions between aliens. In [Hodgson v. Bowerbank, 9 U.S. 303 (1809)], the Supreme Court held that if the Judiciary Act of 1789 were interpreted to allow suits solely between aliens in federal courts, the statutory provisions would be unconstitutional.

Gardiner v. Kelowna Flightcraft, Ltd., 2011 WL 3904997, at *3 (S.D. Ohio 2011); see also Banci, 44 F. Supp.2d at 1275 (stating that it is clear that Article III does not give Congress the power to grant jurisdiction over an action between two aliens); * * *

Based on the above, it is clear that diversity subject matter jurisdiction does not exist in this case. Furthermore, it appears that Congress has recently amended § 1332(a) to eliminate the confusion caused by the deeming clause. The current version of § 1332(a), which became effective in January of 2012, eliminates the deeming clause at the end of § 1332(a) and amends § 1332(a)(2) to apply to civil actions between "citizens of a State and citizens or subjects of a foreign state, except that the district courts shall not have original jurisdiction under this subsection of an action between citizens of a State and citizens or subjects of a foreign state who are lawfully admitted for permanent residence in the United States and are domiciled in the same State." Thus, the newly amended version of § 1332(a) makes it clear that: (1) diversity jurisdiction does not exist over cases between a citizen of state A and a permanent resident alien domiciled in state A; and (2) diversity jurisdiction does not exist over cases involving only aliens.

III. *Conclusion*

Accordingly, it is ORDERED AND ADJUDGED that Defendant Robert Miller's Motion to Dismiss is GRANTED TO THE EXTENT that the Court finds that it lacks subject matter jurisdiction over this case.

NOTES AND QUESTIONS FOR DISCUSSION

1. Insofar as the diversity *statute* is concerned, there is now no basis for alien A to bring suit in federal court against alien B, no matter what foreign country or countries the parties are citizens of. And, after *Hodgson v. Bowerbank*, it would likely be unconstitutional if Congress were to allow an alien "lawfully admitted for permanent residence" (i.e., a permanent resident alien (PRA)) to sue an alien on a nonfederal claim for relief in federal court. Although such a statute might consider the PRA to be, for example, a citizen of the state in which he was domiciled, Article III would likely still view him as an alien.

2. Nevertheless, the prior version of the diversity statute quoted by the court in *Antonier* arguably allowed for such a possibility, to the extent that it deemed a PRA to be a citizen of the state in which he permanently resided. As the *Antonier* court notes, the current version of the statute eliminates this possibility. A permanent resident alien is treated as an alien for diversity purposes, "except that" when he is adverse to a U.S. citizen who is domiciled in the same state, there is no diversity. So, X (a PRA from France domiciled in New York) would not be diverse from Y (a German citizen), nor from Z (a U.S. citizen domiciled in New York); but X *would* be diverse (as an alien) from a U.S. citizen domiciled in any other state than New York.

3. Under old § 1332(a)(3), as under the current version (as noted above), diversity existed when there was a suit between "citizens of different states" and in which aliens were "additional parties." In Singh v. Daimler-Benz AG, 9 F.3d 303 (3d Cir. 1993)—cited in *Antonier* and brought under the prior version of the diversity statute that treated PRAs as citizens of their state of permanent residence in all cases—a PRA domiciled in Virginia sued a German corporation and a Delaware/New Jersey corporation. Thus, the configuration was PRA (VA) vs. (Ger) + (DE/NJ). The court read § 1332(a)(3) as allowing for jurisdiction on the understanding that—from the statute's perspective—this was a suit between "citizens of different states" and in which an alien was an additional party. It also concluded that such a configuration did *not* present a constitutional problem. The argument was that—from Article III's perspective—the suit was one between an alien (the PRA) and a U.S. citizen (the Delaware/New Jersey corporation), which was constitutionally unproblematic. In addition, there was constitutionally permissible supplemental jurisdiction over the PRA's claim against the alien (the German corporation)—even though the supplemental clam was "alien vs. alien." Other courts came to a different conclusion, however, and did not read the statute as allowing jurisdiction when a resident alien sued a nonresident alien along with a citizen of another state. See, e.g., Saadeh v. Farouki, 107 F.3d 52 (D.C. Cir. 1997) (finding that a literal reading of § 1332(a)(3) would present a "potentially unconstitutional result" if applied to a suit brought by a nonresident alien against an alien permanently residing in D.C. and a D.C. corporation). See also Intec USA, LLC v. Engle, 467 F.3d 1038 (7th Cir. 2006) (concluding that *Singh* was wrong but raising doubts whether *Saadeh* was right). Is there a constitutional problem with the configuration in *Singh,* or with the one described in *Saadeh*?

4. Under the current diversity statute, would there be a basis for jurisdiction over a suit such as that in *Singh* (or *Saadeh*)? Section 1332(a)(3) still allows for supplemental jurisdiction over aliens who are "additional parties" in suits between "citizens of different States." See Note 3, following *Hodgson v. Bowerbank, supra.* But would a suit between a PRA of one state and a U.S. citizen of another state even be capable any longer of being considered a suit "between . . . citizens of different states" (as it was in *Singh*) in which supplemental jurisdiction could attach to the claim by the PRA against a nonresident alien defendant?

5. Does the language in 28 U.S.C. § 1332(a)(2) that treats PRAs as aliens for diversity purposes—"except that the district courts shall not have original jurisdiction *under this subsection*" of actions between citizens of a state and a PRA from the same state—also apply to § 1332(a)(3)? In other words, does the exception stated in (a)(2) take away jurisdiction that (a)(3) would otherwise confer, or is it just an exception to (a)(2)? Consider the following configuration: A (a Virginia citizen) sues B (a New York citizen) and C (a permanent resident alien domiciled in Virginia). This is a suit between citizens of different states, in which an alien is an additional party; but does the limitation in (a)(2) prevent jurisdiction from attaching that would otherwise exist under (a)(3)?

6. Finally, suppose that A (a French citizen) sues B (a U.S. citizen domiciled in New York), and C (a German citizen). Is there a statutory basis for such a suit under § 1332(a)? In other words, is this a suit between "citizens of a State and citizens or subjects of a foreign state"? The configuration implicates the complete diversity rule and whether it should apply in alienage cases to the same extent that it does in suits between "citizens of different states." As noted above, the complete diversity rule is not thought to be of constitutional, but merely of statutory dimension, and therefore subject to congressional alteration. Yet the Supreme Court appears to have concluded, albeit in dicta, that the complete diversity rule still applies in the context of alienage jurisdiction. See Ruhrgas AG v. Marathon Oil Co., 526 U.S. 574, 578-80 nn.1-2 (1999) (indicating that diversity jurisdiction would not attach in a suit brought by a Norwegian corporation and a U.S. corporation against a German corporation). But as also noted above, the current version of the diversity statute expressly allows for lifting of the complete diversity rule in one particular context—i.e., when the suit is between diverse citizens, and aliens are additional parties. See § 1332(a)(3).

3. Foreign Corporations and Diversity

There is a separate provision in the diversity statute for jurisdiction respecting domestic and foreign corporations:

28 U.S.C. § 1332. * * *

(c) For the purposes of this section and section 1441 of this title—

(1) a corporation shall be deemed to be a citizen of every State and foreign state by which it has been incorporated and of the State or foreign state where it has its principal place of business, * * *.

Since 1958, a domestic (U.S.) corporation's citizenship has consisted of its state(s) of incorporation as well as its principal place of business. While the typical corporation is incorporated in a single state, the statute contemplates that a corporation could have more than one state of incorporation. If so, the corporation would be a citizen of each of those states of incorporation. However, the statute appears to contemplate only a single state in which the principal place of business may be found. And the Supreme Court has held that courts should generally look to the corporate headquarters or "nerve center" when ascertaining a corporation's principal place of business. See Hertz Corp. v. Friend, 559 U.S. 77 (2010). To be diverse from a U.S. corporation, therefore, the opposing party would have to be diverse from the state or states of incorporation *as well as* the principal place of business of the corporation. Thus, for example, if a defendant corporation is incorporated in Delaware and has its principal place of business in Texas, it is a citizen of both of those states, and diversity will be lacking if the plaintiff is a citizen of either Delaware of Texas. But the corporation would be diverse from an alien.

Until the revision of the diversity statute in late 2011 (as noted in *Antonier*), there had been no special provisions in the diversity statute for foreign-chartered corporations. Often, they were simply considered to be covered by the more general alienage provisions of § 1332. See, e.g., Nat'l Steam-Ship Co. v. Tugman, 106 U.S. 118 (1882) (concluding that a foreign corporation was a citizen or subject of the country by which it was incorporated); cf. JPMorgan Chase Bank v. Traffic Stream (BVI) Infrastructure Ltd., 536 U.S. 88 (2002) (finding British Virgin Island corporation was citizen or subject of United Kingdom). But for over a half century—i.e., since the 1958 reforms that made a corporation a citizen of its state of incorporation *and* its state of principal place of business—it was uncertain whether an alien-chartered corporation would be considered a citizen of a (U.S.) state if the corporation had its principal place of business in one of the states. That is because the diversity statute, as it then stood, stated that "a corporation shall be deemed to be a citizen of any State by which it has been incorporated and of the state of its principal place of business;" it made no reference to foreign corporations or foreign principal places of business. See, e.g., Jerguson v. Blue Dot Inv., Inc., 659 F.2d 31, 33-35 (5th Cir. 1981) (holding alien corporation was a citizen of the U.S. state in which it had its principal place of business, but noting division among courts); see also Rory Ryan, *Consistent "Deeming": A Cohesive Construction of 28 U.S.C. § 1332 in Cases Involving International Corporations and Permanent-Resident Aliens*, 3

Seton Hall Cir. Rev. 73 (2006); Note, *Alien Corporations and Federal Diversity Jurisdiction*, 84 Colum. L. Rev. 177 (1984). And it was similarly uncertain how a corporation chartered in a U.S. state should be treated if its principal place of business was in a foreign country.

Under the most recent version of the diversity statute, however, a corporation chartered in a foreign country will be considered an alien under § 1332(c). And if it has its principal place of business in one of the states, it will *also* be considered a citizen of that state as well. Consequently, an alien corporation with its principal place of business in one of the states of the U.S. will be non-diverse from a citizen of that same state (and under the complete diversity rule, all citizenships of the corporation would have to be diverse from any party adverse to it). The current version of the diversity statute thus solved the problem that had been judicially answered in cases such as *Jerguson, supra.* Does the statute reach the right result? Do you think that alien corporations might face dangers of possible local prejudice that an out-of-state (U.S.) corporation would not face, even if it had its principal place of business in the state of the party adverse to it?

The latest version of the diversity statute also solved the reverse problem—the problem of a U.S. corporation that was chartered in one of the states but that had its principal place of business in a foreign country. Under the earlier version of the statute—which made no reference to foreign corporations or foreign principal places of business (see above)—some courts concluded that "for diversity purposes a corporation incorporated in the United States with its principal place of business abroad is . . . solely a citizen only of its 'State' of incorporation," not a citizen of the foreign country in which it had its principal place of business. Torres v. Southern Peru Copper Corp., 113 F.3d 540, 544 (5th Cir. 1997). See also MAS Capital, Inc. v. Biodelivery Sciences Int'l, Inc., 524 F.3d 831 (7th Cir. 2008) (holding that foreign principal place of business of a U.S. chartered corporation should be ignored in assessing citizenship). It was therefore possible, for example, for A (Argentina) to sue B (Texas) and C (a New York corporation with its principal place of business in Brazil) in a federal court under the rubric of diversity. 28 U.S.C. § 1332(a)(2). Now, the statute expressly makes corporation C a citizen of Brazil as well as New York, thus destroying complete diversity in the example just noted. Which result makes more sense: *Torres* and *MAS Capital*? Or the 2011 revisions to § 1332(c)?

NOTE ON REMOVAL TO FEDERAL COURT

The basic removal statute provides that suits which could have been filed in federal court—consistent with federal jurisdictional requirements—but which the plaintiff filed instead in state court, can be ordinarily removed by the defendant to the federal district court in the district that geographically encompasses the state court. See generally 28 U.S.C. § 1441(a)-(b). Because of the complete diversity rule, this means that a U.S. plaintiff wishing to keep the litigation in a state court and to prevent the alien defendant from removing may succeed in doing so by adding a nonfrivolous claim against a citizen of the same state as the plaintiff. There is no "partial" removal for diversity claims (or for alienage diversity claims) under the basic removal statute; and if the entire case could not have been filed as an original matter in federal court because of incomplete diversity, it cannot be removed from state court if filed there instead. There is also an exception in the removal statutes that bars removal in nonfederal question cases if any of the defendants is a citizen of the state in which the suit has been brought. Id. at § 1441(b)(2). This gives U.S. plaintiffs yet another way to keep litigation against an alien defendant in a state court, by adding a U.S. defendant who is a citizen of the state in which suit is brought, even if the U.S. defendant is diverse from the plaintiff, and the case otherwise could have been filed in federal court in the first instance. Various other requirements, including the time within which removal must be taken, are spelled out in the provisions of 28 U.S.C. §§ 1446-1447.

Of course, if a foreign defendant is sued in a state court and removal is not possible on diversity grounds, it might be possible for the defendant to remove on some other jurisdictional basis—for example, federal question jurisdiction. If the plaintiff's cause of action arises under federal law (consistent with the "well-pleaded complaint" rule), removal would be unproblematic under 28 U.S.C. § 1441(a)-(b). (We discuss federal question jurisdiction in Section C, below.) A foreign defendant may prefer the litigation to go forward in a federal court not simply because of the perception that the federal court may be less hostile to aliens; it may also be because, once in federal court, dismissal in favor of a foreign forum may be appropriate under current doctrines of *forum non conveniens* (discussed in Chapter 5) that are applied in the federal courts.

C. CASES ARISING UNDER FEDERAL LAW

As just noted, alienage diversity is not the only way for international civil litigation to make its way into federal court. For example, admiralty cases frequently implicate foreign parties and/or foreign events, and are covered by a statute that has long conferred jurisdiction on the lower federal courts: 28 U.S.C. § 1333. In addition, foreign plaintiffs may sue or may be sued under various federal statutes such as antitrust laws, securities laws, and anti-racketeering laws. Many of these disputes implicate the extraterritorial effect of such laws—an issue we take up in detail in Chapter 7. But extraterritoriality concerns to aside, such federal statutory claims unproblematically arise under federal law and may come into federal court under Article III and the general federal question statute, 28 U.S.C. § 1331. Article III provides that the federal judicial power shall extend to "all Cases, in Law and Equity, arising under this Constitution, the Laws of the United States, and Treaties made, or which shall be made, under their Authority." And the federal question statute provides:

28 U.S.C. § 1331. Federal Question

The district courts shall have original jurisdiction of all civil actions arising under the Constitution, laws, or treaties of the United States.

The only serious limitation on jurisdiction under the general federal question statute is that jurisdiction must be apparent on the face of the plaintiff's well-pleaded complaint. See Franchise Tax Bd. v. Constr. Laborers Vacation Trust, 463 U.S. 1, 9-11 (1983). Generally, this means that the plaintiff's cause of action must be created by federal law (or, more unusually, it might be a state law claim that requires the plaintiff to plead and prove a substantial proposition of federal law in order to prevail on her state law claim). It is not sufficient if the federal issues arise solely by way of defense to a claim under non-federal law.

Of course, some federal statutes have their own jurisdictional provisions, independent of the general federal question statute. If claims under these statutes can satisfy Article III's provisions (i.e., they arise under federal law within the meaning of the Constitution), they may be maintained in federal court. Thus, for example, if the claim was one alleging patent infringement, it would not matter that complete diversity was missing. See 28 U.S.C. § 1338. And if the suit fell under the Alien Tort Statute, 28 U.S.C. § 1350, or under the Torture Victim Protection Act of 1991, id. (Note), or under the Foreign Sovereign Immunities Act, 28 U.S.C. §§ 1330, 1605-07, jurisdiction may be had in a federal court. Indeed, if a case properly arises under federal law within the meaning of Article III, and assuming a statutory basis, one alien may sue another alien without regard to the limits under diversity jurisdiction because Article III's bases of jurisdiction are alternative to one another. See, e.g., Verlinden B.V. v. Central Bank of Nigeria, 461 U.S. 480 (1983) (upholding federal jurisdiction in suit between a Dutch corporation and a Nigerian defendant when premised on Foreign Sovereign Immunities Act, as a case arising under federal law within the meaning of Article III). Similarly, cases arising under U.S. treaties would fit within the general federal question statute, although such cases often present difficult issues respecting the judicial enforceability of treaties, as discussed in Section C, subpart 6, below.

In the materials that follow, we provide illustrations of cases that might arise under federal law, focusing on human rights litigation under the Alien Tort Statute (ATS) and the Torture Victim Protection Act (TVPA). Human rights litigation in the federal courts has mushroomed in recent years, and litigation under both of these provisions remains in considerable flux. We also include examples of cases raising U.S. foreign policy concerns and cases arising under treaties. Suits against foreign sovereigns are treated separately in Chapter 3. In addition, suits under other federal statutes, such as antitrust and securities laws, are treated in Chapter 7 insofar as they might bear on the question of extraterritorial application of U.S. law.

1. Human Rights Litigation under the Alien Tort Statute

The Alien Tort Statute (or as it is sometimes called, "the Alien Tort Claims Act" or "Alien Tort Act") had a modest beginning. It was simply one of many jurisdictional provisions that made up part of the first Judiciary Act. Act of Sept. 24, 1789, ch. 20, § 9, 1 Stat. 73, 77. As currently codified, it provides (in language only slightly modified from its original version):

28 U.S.C. § 1350. Alien's Action for Tort.

> The district courts shall have original jurisdiction of any civil action by an alien for a tort only, committed in violation of the law of nations or a treaty of the United States.

It has been said that the origins of the provision are less than clear—and in the words of Judge Henry Friendly, it was a kind of "legal Lohengrin." IIT v. Vencap, Ltd., 519 F.2d 1001, 1015 (2d Cir. 1975) ("[N]o one seems to know from whence it came."). But many of the concerns regarding international relations that lay behind the general grant of alienage jurisdiction, as well as other grants of jurisdiction, may have prompted this provision as well.

For a great many years the statute was effectively dormant, until the Second Circuit's path-breaking decision in **FILARTIGA v. PENA-IRALA, 630 F.2d 876 (2d Cir. 1980).** *Filartiga* concluded that under § 1350, a federal court could hear a suit brought by two Paraguayan citizens against a Paraguayan official over an act of political torture that took place in Paraguay. Although § 1350 may have provided for statutory jurisdiction in the federal courts, there was a difficult constitutional question whether the suit was one within the ambit of Article III. There was no diversity of citizenship—not even minimal diversity. But the court of appeals found that the exercise of jurisdiction under § 1350 was consistent with Article III on the ground that the case "arose under" federal law. Personal jurisdiction was secured by "tagging" the defendant—that is, personally serving him while he was physically present in the U.S. (having overstayed his visa, residing here for over nine months).

With respect to the Article III question, the court reasoned (1) that § 1350 allowed a cause of action for "a tort only in violation of the law of nations"; (2) that the law of nations proscribes certain egregious violations of human rights, including official torture; (3) that the law of nations, like many other aspects of international law, is a species of federal common law; and therefore (4) that an alien's tort suit alleging a gross violation of fundamental human rights "arises under" federal law within the meaning of Article III of the Constitution (thus making the alien status of the defendant jurisdictionally irrelevant).

Filartiga's key move, of course, was its contestable assumption that a violation of the law of nations would be a violation of federal law, thus bringing the suit between alien parties within the limits of Article III. But the court did not linger long over the issue. It observed that in cases such as The Paquete Habana, 175 U.S. 677 (1900), the Supreme Court had said long ago that "[i]nternational law is part of our law" and it was law that federal courts and state courts alike would apply.

> Appellee submits that even if the tort alleged is a violation of modern international law, federal jurisdiction may not be exercised consistent with the dictates of Article III of the Constitution. The claim is without merit. Common law courts of general jurisdiction regularly adjudicate transitory tort claims between individuals over whom they exercise personal jurisdiction, wherever the tort occurred. Moreover, as part of an articulated scheme of federal control over external affairs, Congress

provided, in the first Judiciary Act, § 9(b), 1 Stat. 73, 77 (1789), for federal jurisdiction over suits by aliens where principles of international law are in issue. The constitutional basis for the Alien Tort Statute is the law of nations, which has always been part of the federal common law.

Filartiga, 630 F.2d at 885. The appeals court went on to conclude that state-sanctioned torture was prohibited under the contemporary law of nations, as evidenced in U.N. Declarations such as the Universal Declaration on Human Rights, various multilateral treaties, and the domestic law of many nations.

Filartiga's position that international law is federal law is what scholars call the "modern position." See A.J. Bellia & Bradford R. Clark, *The Federal Common Law of Nations*, 109 Colum. L. Rev. 1 (2009) (describing the modern position). Indeed, the Restatement (Third) of Foreign Relations Law of the United States (1987), states that "[i]nternational law . . .[is] law of the United States," which federal and state courts are "bound" to honor. Id. at § 111(1), (3). But there is also a "revisionist" position that has grown up in the wake of *Filartiga*, and revisionist scholars argue that international law should not be considered federal law until operationalized as such by the political branches. See, e.g., Curtis A. Bradley & Jack L. Goldsmith, *Customary International Law as Federal Common Law: A Critique of the Modern Position*, 110 Harv. L. Rev. 815 (1997). Revisionists maintain that the modern position, which treats customary international law as federal law, fails to comport with principles of federalism (because it displaces otherwise applicable state law); with separation of powers (because the judiciary positions itself at the forefront of law-shaping and law-articulation); and with democratic legitimacy (to the extent that customary international law is not necessarily made through ordinary lawmaking—or treaty-ratifying procedures. Revisionists believe that the many older references to the law of nations as being a part of "our law" were likely references to a body of "general" but nonfederal international law that all U.S. courts would ordinarily apply, but only if they otherwise had subject matter jurisdiction.

In *The Paquete Habana*, for example, the turn of the century decision invoked by *Filartiga*, the federal courts had jurisdiction of the case—a suit to condemn two Cuban vessels off the coast of Cuba while the U.S. was enforcing a blockade of Cuba during the Spanish American War—under the federal courts' admiralty and prize jurisdiction. Thus, the determination of questions of international law was possible, not because the case arose under federal law within the meaning of the federal question statute, but because it was a case of admiralty and prize jurisdiction. Given the decision in Erie Railroad Co. v. Tompkins, 304 U.S. 64 (1938), which concluded that there was no "federal general common law," revisionist scholars argue that such general law principles should now be considered state law in the absence of action by the federal political branches respecting such law. In addition, there is doubt whether the framers of Article III would have understood "federal law" to encompass all features of the law of nations, but scholars are divided. Compare Curtis A. Bradley, *The Alien Tort Statute and Article III*, 42 Va. J. Int'l L. 587 (2002) (expressing serious doubt), with William S. Dodge, *The Constitutionality of the Alien Tort Statute*, 42 Va. J. Int'l L. 687 (2002) (expressing little doubt).

Of course, if the law of nations is not federal law, does that really mean it is state law, and if so, does that make sense? See Harold Koh, *Is International Law Really State Law?*, 111 Harv. L. Rev. 1824 (1998) (responding to Bradley and Goldsmith, *supra*). Or could there be an intermediate position? See Ernest A. Young, *Sorting Out the Debate Over Customary International Law*, 42 Va. J. Int'l L. 365, 369-70 (2002) (proposing that much of customary international law should continue to be viewed as non-supreme "general" law, as it was prior to *Erie*); see also A.J. Bellia & Bradford R. Clark, *The Alien Tort Statute and the Law of Nations*, 78 U. Chi. L. Rev. 445, 528 (2011) (suggesting that some but not all aspects of customary international law may be federal).

In any event, by making the formerly non-federal "general" law of nations a species of federal law, *Filartiga* promised that federal courts would be in a position to enter awards of damages against those who had violated certain norms of international law, even in actions arising abroad between co-domiciliary aliens, as in *Filartiga* itself. In many respects, the decision reflected the journey of the law of nations itself, from an early focus on nation-to-nation concerns to a post-World War II focus on individual rights—many of them articulated in U.N. declarations, international agreements, and treaties.

To be sure, *Filartiga* purported to limit the sorts of wrongs that the ATS could reach. It stated that "[t]he requirement that a rule command the 'general assent of civilized nations' to become binding upon them all is a stringent one. Were this not so, the courts of one nation might feel free to impose idiosyncratic rules upon others, in the name of applying international law." 630 F.2d at 881. Elsewhere the court spoke of limiting the reach of the ATS to "well-established, universally recognized norms of international law." Id. at 888. And not all (or even most) human rights norms found in the Universal Declaration of Human Rights or treaties have ripened into customary international law enforceable in domestic courts. After *Filartiga*, therefore, it was unclear what other arguable violations of international law would be included under this standard, or how specific they would have to be, or how "general assent" was to be determined.

There was a brief flicker of dissent to some of the conclusions of *Filartiga* in the various opinions in **Tel-Oren v. Libyan Arab Republic, 726 F.2d 774 (D.C. Cir. 1984)** (per curiam), cert. denied, 470 U.S. 1003 (1985). There, the court unanimously dismissed an ATS action against the Palestine Liberation Organization for a terrorist killing done in Israel. (Libya was also a defendant, but as a foreign sovereign it was immune under the Foreign Sovereign Immunities Act, as noted below and in Chapter 3.) But there was no single opinion in *Tel-Oren*. Judge Edwards, who otherwise "endorse[d] the legal principles set forth in *Filartiga*," indicated that the law of nations could not ordinarily be violated by a non-state actor, and the PLO was not a recognized state nor were its members state actors. *Filartiga* had found that "official torture" was a violation of the law of nations, but according to Judge Edwards, the plaintiffs in *Tel-Oren* "[did] not allege facts to show that official or state-initiated torture is implicated in this action." Id. at 791.

Judge Bork concurred in the judgment of dismissal, but he posited that § 1350 merely provided jurisdiction, and did itself not provide a cause of action. For him, a cause of action would not exist until Congress affirmatively created one. See id. at 820 (concurring opinion). Judge Bork was particularly concerned that if the ATS created not only jurisdiction but also a federal cause of action—which is what he read *Filartiga* to have done—then, because the ATS also spoke of torts "in violation of . . . a treaty," it would effectively make all treaties self-executing once they were ratified. As discussed later in this chapter, most treaties are not self-executing in the sense that a violation of a treaty could itself give rise to a cause of action. In other words, they usually need affirmative implementation by Congress before their violation will become judicially actionable. As a result, Judge Bork concluded that such a reading of the ATS would "stand[] in flat opposition to almost two hundred years of our jurisprudence, and it is simply too late to discover such a revolutionary effect in this little-noticed statute." Id.

Finally, Judge Robb doubted whether the U.S. courts were institutionally capable of effectively resolving such disputes, in part because of the difficulties of ascertaining the command of the law of nations, and in part because there would be a "frustration of the trial process as we know it" since the defendants would likely not be in attendance nor "engage in a meaningful judicial process." Id. at 824 (concurring opinion).

Tel-Oren's skepticism notwithstanding, lower federal courts and human rights litigants made considerable use of the ATS. In addition to actions alleging state-sponsored torture, ATS suits have been brought alleging state-sponsored kidnapping, environmental harms, forced labor, and the aiding and abetting various human rights violation. Many of these suits were brought against corporate defendants, although the issue of corporate liability under the ATS remains (as of this writing) undecided. The Supreme Court weighed in on the ATS almost a quarter century after the decision in *Filartiga*, in the following decision.

Sosa v. Alvarez-Machain

Supreme Court of the United States, 2004.

542 U.S. 692.

Justice Souter delivered the opinion of the Court.

The two issues are whether respondent Alvarez-Machain's allegation that the Drug Enforcement Administration [DEA] instigated his abduction from Mexico for criminal trial in the United States supports a claim against the Government under the Federal Tort Claims Act (FTCA or Act), 28 U.S.C. § 1346(b)(1), §§ 2671-2680, and whether he may recover under the Alien Tort Statute (ATS), 28 U.S.C. § 1350. We hold that he is not entitled to a remedy under either statute.

[I-II]

[Humberto Alvarez-Machain was a Mexican physician whom U.S. Drug Enforcement Agency Officials believed assisted in the interrogation and torture of a DEA agent in Mexico. A U.S. criminal indictment was issued against Alvarez. When negotiations with the Mexican government broke down to have Alvarez arrested, the DEA hired some Mexican nationals, including Jose Francisco Sosa to abduct Alvarez and bring him to the U.S. Alvarez was eventually tried and acquitted. After returning to Mexico, he filed a civil action in the U.S. against Sosa and others under the ATS. He also sued the U.S. under the FTCA, which gives a right of action against the U.S. for certain torts committed by federal officials. The trial court dismissed the FTCA claim but upheld an award under the ATS. The Ninth Circuit affirmed the ATS claim, but it also concluded that the FTCA claim should not have been dismissed. The Supreme Court took certiorari. It first reversed the Ninth Circuit's FTCA ruling, finding that the FTCA did not waive the sovereign immunity of the U.S. in connection with claims "arising in a foreign country." 28 U.S.C. § 2680(k). It then turned to Alvarez's ATS claim.]

III

[Sosa] argues (as does the United States supporting him) that there is no relief under the ATS because the statute does no more than vest federal courts with jurisdiction, neither creating nor authorizing the courts to recognize any particular right of action without further congressional action. Although we agree the statute is in terms only jurisdictional, we think that at the time of enactment the jurisdiction enabled federal courts to hear claims in a very limited category defined by the law of nations and recognized at common law. We do not believe, however, that the limited, implicit sanction to entertain the handful of international law cum common law claims understood in 1789 should be taken as authority to recognize the right of action asserted by Alvarez here. * * *

The parties and amici here advance radically different historical interpretations of this terse provision. Alvarez says that the ATS was intended not simply as a jurisdictional grant, but as authority for the creation of a new cause of action for torts in violation of international law. We think that reading is implausible. As enacted in 1789, the ATS gave the district courts "cognizance" of certain causes of action, and the term bespoke a grant of jurisdiction, not power to mold substantive law. The fact that the ATS was placed in § 9 of the Judiciary Act, a statute otherwise exclusively concerned with federal-court jurisdiction, is itself support for its strictly jurisdictional nature. * * * It is unsurprising, then, that an authority on the historical origins of the ATS has written that "section 1350 clearly does not create a statutory cause of action," and that the contrary suggestion is "simply frivolous." William Casto, *The Federal Courts' Protective Jurisdiction Over Torts Committed in Violation of the Law of Nations*, 18 Conn. L. Rev. 467, 479, 480 (1986) (hereinafter Casto, Law of Nations); cf. William S. Dodge, *The Constitutionality of the Alien Tort Statute: Some Observations on Text and Context*, 42 Va. J. Intl L. 687, 689 (2002). In sum, we think the statute was intended as jurisdictional in the sense of addressing the power of the courts to entertain cases concerned with a certain subject.

But holding the ATS jurisdictional raises a new question, this one about the interaction between the ATS at the time of its enactment and the ambient law of the era. Sosa would have it that the ATS was stillborn because there could be no claim for relief without a further statute expressly authorizing adoption of causes of action. Amici professors of federal jurisdiction and legal history take a different tack, that federal courts could entertain claims once the jurisdictional grant was on the books, because torts in violation of the law of nations would have been recognized within the common law of the time. Brief for Vikram Amar et al. as Amici Curiae. We think history and practice give the edge to this latter position.

1

"When the United States declared their independence, they were bound to receive the law of nations, in its modern state of purity and refinement." *Ware v. Hylton*, 3 U.S. (3 Dall.) 199, 281 (1796) (Wilson, J.). In the years of the early Republic, this law of nations comprised two principal elements, the first covering the general norms governing the behavior of national states with each other. * * * This aspect of the law of nations thus occupied the executive and legislative domains, not the judicial. W. Blackstone, Commentaries on the Laws of England 68 (1769) (hereinafter Commentaries) ("Offenses against" the law of nations are "principally incident to whole states or nations").

The law of nations included a second, more pedestrian element, however, that did fall within the judicial sphere, as a body of judge-made law regulating the conduct of individuals situated outside domestic boundaries and consequently carrying an international savor. To Blackstone, the law of nations in this sense was implicated "in mercantile questions, such as bills of exchange and the like; in all marine causes, relating to freight, average demurrage, insurances, bottomry . . . ; [and] in all disputes relating to prizes, to shipwrecks, to hostages, and ransom bills." Id., at 67. The law merchant [that] emerged from the customary practices of international traders and admiralty required its own transnational regulation. And it was the law of nations in this sense that our precursors spoke about when the Court explained the status of coast fishing vessels in wartime grew from "ancient usage among civilized nations, beginning centuries ago, and gradually ripening into a rule of international law. . . ." The Paquete Habana, 175 U.S. 677, 686 (1900).

There was, finally, a sphere in which these rules binding individuals for the benefit of other individuals overlapped with the norms of state relationships. Blackstone referred to it when he mentioned three specific offenses against the law of nations addressed by the criminal law of England: violation of safe conducts, infringement of the rights of ambassadors, and piracy. 4 Commentaries 68. An assault against an ambassador, for example, impinged upon the sovereignty of the foreign nation and if not adequately redressed could rise to an issue of war. It was this narrow set of violations of the law of nations, admitting of a judicial remedy and at the same time threatening serious consequences in international affairs, that was probably on minds of the men who drafted the ATS with its reference to tort.

2

Before there was any ATS, a distinctly American preoccupation with these hybrid international norms had taken shape owing to the distribution of political power from independence through the period of confederation. The Continental Congress was hamstrung by its inability to "cause infractions of treaties, or of the law of nations to be punished," J. Madison, Journal of the Constitutional Convention 60 (E. Scott ed. 1893), and in 1781 the Congress implored the States to vindicate rights under the law of nations. In words that echo Blackstone, the congressional resolution called upon state legislatures to "provide expedition, exemplary, and adequate punishment" for "the violation of safe conducts or passports, . . . of hostility against such as are in amity, . . . with the U.S, . . . infractions of the immunities of ambassadors and other public ministers . . . [and] infractions of treaties and conventions to which the U.S. are a party." 21 Journals of the Continental Congress 1136-37 (G. Hunt ed. 1912). The resolution recommended that the States "authorize suits . . . for damages by the party injured, and for compensation to the United States for damage sustained by them from an injury done to a foreign power by a citizen." Id. at 1137. * * * Apparently only one State acted upon the recommendation[.] * * *

Appreciation of the Continental Congress's incapacity to deal with this class of cases was intensified by the so-called Marbois incident of May 1784, in which a French adventurer, Longchamps, verbally and physically assaulted the Secretary of the French Legion in Philadelphia. See *Republica v. De Longchamps,* 1 Dall. 111 (O.T. Phila. 1784). Congress called again for state legislation addressing such matters, and concern over the inadequate vindication of the law of nations persisted through the time of the constitutional convention. See 1 Records of the Federal Convention of 1787, p. 25 (M. Farrand ed. 1911) (speech of J. Randolph). During the Convention itself, in fact, a New York City constable produced a reprise of the Marbois affair and Secretary Jay reported to Congress on the Dutch Ambassador's protest, with the explanation that "the federal government does not appear . . . to be vested with any judicial Powers competent to the Cognizance and Judgment of such Cases." Casto, *Law of Nations* 494, and n.152.

The Framers responded by vesting the Supreme Court with original jurisdiction over "all Cases affecting Ambassadors, other public ministers and Consuls," U.S. Const., Art. III, § 2, and the First Congress followed through. The Judiciary Act reinforced this Court's original jurisdiction over suits brought by diplomats, see § 13, created alienage jurisdiction, § 11 and, of course, included the ATS, § 9. * * *

3

Although Congress modified the draft of what became the Judiciary Act, it made hardly any changes to the provisions on aliens, including what became the ATS, see Casto, *Law of Nations* 498. There is no record of congressional discussion about private actions that might be subject to the jurisdictional provision, or about any need for further legislation to create private remedies; there is no record even of debate on the section. * * * But despite considerable scholarly attention, it is fair to say that a consensus understanding of what Congress intended has proven elusive.

Still, the history does tend to support two propositions. First, there is every reason to suppose that the First Congress did not pass the ATS as a jurisdictional convenience to be placed on the shelf for use by a future Congress or state legislature that might, some day, authorize the creation of causes of action or itself decide to make some element of the law of nations actionable for the benefit of foreigners. The anxieties of the preconstitutional period cannot be ignored easily enough to think that the statute was not meant to have a practical effect. * * *

The second inference to be drawn from the history is that Congress intended the ATS to furnish jurisdiction for a relatively modest set of actions alleging violations of the law of nations. Uppermost in the legislative mind appears to have been offenses against ambassadors, violations of safe conduct were probably understood to be actionable, and individual actions arising out of prize captures and piracy may well have also been contemplated. But the common law appears to have understood only those three of the hybrid variety as definite and actionable, or at any rate, to have assumed only a very limited set of claims. As Blackstone had put it, "offences against this law [of nations] are principally incident to whole states or nations," and not individuals seeking relief in court. 4 Commentaries 68. * * *

In sum, although the ATS is a jurisdictional statute creating no new causes of action, the reasonable inference from the historical materials is that the statute was intended to have practical effect the moment it became law. The jurisdictional grant is best read as having been enacted on the understanding that the common law would provide a cause of action for the modest number of international law violations with a potential for personal liability at the time.

IV

We think it is correct, then, to assume that the First Congress understood that the district courts would recognize private causes of action for certain torts in violation of the law of nations, though we have found no basis to suspect Congress had any examples in mind beyond those torts corresponding to Blackstone's three primary offenses: violation of safe conducts, infringement of the rights of ambassadors, and piracy. We assume, too, that no development in the two centuries from the enactment of § 1350 to the birth of the modern line of cases beginning with *Filartiga v. Pena-Irala,* 630 F.2d 876 (2d Cir. 1980), has categorically precluded federal courts from recognizing a claim under the law of nations as an element of common law; Congress has not in any relevant way amended § 1350 or limited civil common law power by another statute. Still, there are good reasons for a restrained conception of the discretion a federal court should exercise in considering a new cause of action of this kind. Accordingly, we think courts should require any claim based on the present-day law of nations to rest on a norm of international character accepted by the civilized world and defined with a specificity comparable to the features of the 18th-century paradigms we have recognized. This requirement is fatal to Alvarez's claim.

A

A series of reasons argue for judicial caution when considering the kinds of individual claims that might implement the jurisdiction conferred by the early statute. First, the prevailing conception of the common law has changed since 1789 in a way that counsels restraint in judicially applying internationally generated norms. When § 1350 was enacted, the accepted conception was of the common law as "a transcendental body of law outside of any particular State but obligatory within it unless and until changed by statute." *Black and White Taxicab & Transfer Co. v. Brown and Yellow Taxicab & Transfer Co.*, 276 U.S. 518, 533 (1928) (Holmes, J., dissenting). Now, however, in most cases where a court is asked to state or formulate a common law principle in a new context, there is a general understanding that the law is not so much found or discovered as it is either made or created. * * * [A] judge deciding in reliance on an international norm will find a substantial element of discretionary judgment in the decision.

Second, along with, and in part driven by, that conceptual development in understanding common law has come an equally significant rethinking of the role of the federal courts in making it. *Erie R. Co. v. Tompkins*, 304 U.S. 64 (1938), was the watershed in which we denied the existence of any federal "general" common law, which largely withdrew to havens of specialty, some of them defined by express congressional authorization to devise a body of law directly, *e.g., Textile Workers v. Lincoln Mills of Ala.*, 353 U.S. 448 (1957) (interpretation of collective-bargaining agreements). Elsewhere, this Court has thought it was in order to create federal common law rules in interstitial areas of particular federal interest. And although we have even assumed competence to make judicial rules of decision of particular importance to foreign relations, such as the act of state doctrine, see *Banco Nacional de Cuba v. Sabbatino*, 376 U.S. 398, 427 (1964), the general practice has been to look for legislative guidance before exercising innovative authority over substantive law. It would be remarkable to take a more aggressive role in exercising a jurisdiction that remained largely in shadow for much of the prior two centuries.

Third, this Court has recently and repeatedly said that a decision to create a private right of action is one better left to legislative judgment in the great majority of cases. * * * The creation of a private right of action raises issues beyond the mere consideration whether underlying primary conduct should be allowed or not, entailing, for example, a decision to permit enforcement without the check imposed by prosecutorial discretion. Accordingly, even when Congress has made it clear by statute that a rule applies to purely domestic conduct, we are reluctant to infer intent to provide a private cause of action where the statute does not supply one expressly. While the absence of congressional action addressing private rights of action under an international norm is more equivocal than its failure to provide such a right when it creates a statute, the possible collateral consequences of making international rules privately actionable argue for judicial caution.

Fourth, the subject of those collateral consequences is itself a reason for a high bar to new private causes of action for violating international law, for the potential implications for the foreign relations of the United States of recognizing such causes should make courts particularly wary of impinging on the discretion of the Legislative and Executive Branches in managing foreign affairs. It is one thing for American courts to enforce constitutional limits on our own State and Federal Governments' power, but quite another to consider suits under rules that would go so far as to claim a limit on the power of foreign governments over their own citizens, and to hold that a foreign government or its agent has transgressed those limits. Yet modern international law is very much concerned with just such questions, and apt to stimulate calls for vindicating private interests in § 1350 cases. Since many attempts by federal courts to craft remedies for the violation of new norms of international law would raise risks of adverse foreign policy consequences, they should be undertaken, if at all, with great caution. * * *

The fifth reason is particularly important in light of the first four. We have no congressional mandate to seek out and define new and debatable violations of the law of nations, and modern indications of congressional understanding of the judicial role in the field have not affirmatively encouraged greater judicial creativity. It is true that a clear mandate appears in the Torture Victim Protection Act of 1991, providing authority that "establishes an unambiguous and modern basis for" federal claims of torture and extrajudicial killing, H. R. Rep. No. 102-367, pt. 1, p.3 (1991). But that affirmative authority is confined to specific subject matter, and although the legislative history includes the remark that § 1350 should "remain intact to permit suits based on other norms that already exist or may ripen in the future into rules of customary international law," Congress as a body has done nothing to promote such suits. Several times, indeed, the Senate has expressly declined to give the federal courts the task of interpreting and applying international human rights law, as when its ratification of the International Covenant on Civil and Political Rights declared that the substantive provisions of the document were not self-executing. * * *

                                            B

These reasons argue for great caution in adapting the law of nations to private rights. JUSTICE SCALIA concludes that caution is too hospitable, and a word is in order to summarize where we have come so far and to focus our difference with him on whether some norms of today's law of nations may ever be recognized legitimately by federal courts in the absence of congressional action beyond § 1350. All Members of the Court agree that § 1350 is only jurisdictional. We also agree, or at least JUSTICE SCALIA does not dispute, that the jurisdiction was originally understood to be available to enforce a small number of international norms that a federal court could properly recognize as within the common law enforceable without further statutory authority. JUSTICE SCALIA concludes, however, that two subsequent developments should be understood to preclude federal courts from recognizing any further international norms as judicially enforceable today, absent further congressional action. As described before, we now tend to understand common law not as a discoverable reflection of universal reason but, in a positivistic way, as a product of human choice. And we now adhere to a conception of limited judicial power first expressed in reorienting federal diversity jurisdiction, see *Erie R. Co. v. Tompkins*, that federal courts have no authority to derive "general" common law.

Whereas JUSTICE SCALIA sees these developments as sufficient to close the door to further independent judicial recognition of actionable international norms, other considerations persuade us that the judicial power should be exercised on the understanding that the door is still ajar subject to vigilant doorkeeping, and thus open to a narrow class of international norms today. *Erie* did not in terms bar any judicial recognition of new substantive rules, no matter what the circumstances, and post-*Erie* under-standing has identified limited enclaves in which federal courts may derive some substantive law in a common law way. For two centuries we have affirmed that the domestic law of the United States recognizes the law of nations. See, e.g., *Sabbatino*, at 423 ("It is, of course, true that United States courts apply international law as a part of our own in appropriate circumstances"); *The Paquete Habana*, 175 U.S. 677, 700 (1900) ("International law is part of our law, and must be ascertained and administered by the courts of justice of appropriate jurisdiction, as often as questions of right depending upon it are duly presented for their determination"). It would take some explaining to say now that federal courts must avert their gaze entirely from any international norm intended to protect individuals.

We think an attempt to justify such a position would be particularly unconvincing in light of what we know about congressional understanding bearing on this issue lying at the intersection of the judicial and legislative powers. The First Congress, which reflected the understanding of the framing generation and included some of the Framers, assumed that federal courts could properly identify some international norms as enforceable in the exercise of § 1350 jurisdiction. We think it would be unreasonable to assume that the First Congress would have expected federal courts to lose all capacity to recognize enforceable international norms simply because the common law might lose some metaphysical cachet on the road to modern realism. Later Congresses seem to have shared our view. The position we take today has been assumed by some federal courts for 24 years, ever since the Second Circuit decided *Filartiga* * * * . Congress, however, has not only expressed no disagreement with our view of the proper exercise of the judicial power, but has responded to its most notable instance by enacting legislation supplementing the judicial determination in some detail. See supra (discussing the TVPA).

While we agree with JUSTICE SCALIA to the point that we would welcome any congressional guidance in exercising jurisdiction with such obvious potential to affect foreign relations, nothing Congress has done is a reason for us to shut the door to the law of nations entirely. It is enough to say that Congress may do that at any time (explicitly, or implicitly by treaties or statutes that occupy the field) just as it may modify or cancel any judicial decision so far as it rests on recognizing an international norm as such.[19]

C

We must still, however, derive a standard or set of standards for assessing the particular claim Alvarez raises, and for this case it suffices to look to the historical antecedents. Whatever the ultimate criteria for accepting a cause of action subject to jurisdiction under § 1350, we are persuaded that federal courts should not recognize private claims under federal common law for violations of any international law norm with less definite content and acceptance among civilized nations than the historical paradigms familiar when § 1350 was enacted. This limit upon judicial recognition is generally consistent with the reasoning of many of the courts and judges who faced the issue before it reached this Court. See *Filartiga*, 630 F.2d, at 890 ("For purposes of civil liability, the torturer has become—like the pirate and slave trader before him—*hostis humani generis*, an enemy of all mankind"). And the determination whether a norm is sufficiently definite to support a cause of action[20] should (and, indeed, inevitably must) involve an element of judgment about the practical consequences of making that cause available to litigants in the federal courts.[21]

---

[19] Our position does not, as JUSTICE SCALIA suggests, imply that every grant of jurisdiction to a federal court carries with it an opportunity to develop common law (so that the grant of federal-question jurisdiction would be equally as good for our purposes as §1350). Section 1350 was enacted on the congressional understanding that courts would exercise jurisdiction by entertaining some common law claims derived from the law of nations; and we know of no reason to think that federal-question jurisdiction was extended subject to any comparable congressional assumption. Further, our holding today is consistent with the division of responsibilities between federal and state courts after *Erie*, as a more expansive common law power related to 28 U.S.C. § 1331 might not be.

[20] A related consideration is whether international law extends the scope of liability for a violation of a given norm to the perpetrator being sued, if the defendant is a private actor such as a corporation or individual.* * *

[21] This requirement of clear definition is not meant to be the only principle limiting the availability of relief in the federal courts for violations of customary international law, though it disposes of this case. For example, the European Commission argues as amicus curiae that basic principles of international law require that before asserting a claim in a foreign forum, the claimant must have exhausted any remedies available in the domestic legal system, and perhaps in other fora such as international claims tribunals. Cf. Torture Victim Protection Act of 1991, § 2(b) (exhaustion requirement). We would certainly consider this requirement in an appropriate case.

Another possible limitation that we need not apply here is a policy of case-specific deference to the political branches. For example, there are now pending in federal district court several class actions seeking damages from various corporations alleged to have participated in, or abetted, the regime of apartheid that formerly controlled South Africa. See *In re South African Apartheid Litigation*, 238 F. Supp. 2d 1379 (JPML 2002) (granting a motion to transfer the cases to the Southern District of New York). The Government of South Africa has said that these cases interfere with the policy embodied by its Truth and Reconciliation Commission, which "deliberately avoided a 'victors' justice' approach to the crimes of apartheid and chose instead one based on confession and absolution, informed by the principles of reconciliation, reconstruction, reparation and goodwill." * * * The United States has agreed. * * * In such cases, there is a strong argument that federal

Thus, Alvarez's detention claim must be gauged against the current state of international law, looking to those sources we have long, albeit cautiously, recognized.

> Where there is no treaty, and no controlling executive or legislative act or judicial decision, resort must be had to the customs and usages of civilized nations; and, as evidence of these, to the works of jurists and commentators, who by years of labor, research and experience, have made themselves peculiarly well acquainted with the subjects of which they treat. Such works are resorted to by judicial tribunals, not for the speculations of their authors concerning what the law ought to be, but for trustworthy evidence of what the law really is. *The Paquete Habana*, 175 U.S. at 700.

To begin with, Alvarez cites two well-known international agreements that, despite their moral authority, have little utility under the standard set out in this opinion. He says that his abduction by Sosa was an "arbitrary arrest" within the meaning of the Universal Declaration of Human Rights (Declaration), G.A. Res. 217A (III), U.N. Doc. A/810 (1948). And he traces the rule against arbitrary arrest not only to the Declaration, but also to article nine of the International Covenant on Civil and Political Rights (Covenant), Dec. 19, 1996, 999 U.N.T.S. 171, to which the United States is a party, and to various other conventions to which it is not. But the Declaration does not of its own force impose obligations as a matter of international law. * * * And, although the Covenant does bind the United States as a matter of international law, the United States ratified the Covenant on the express understanding that it was not self-executing and so did not itself create obligations enforceable in the federal courts. Accordingly, Alvarez cannot say that the Declaration and Covenant themselves establish the relevant and applicable rule of international law. He instead attempts to show that prohibition of arbitrary arrest has attained the status of binding customary international law.

Here, it is useful to examine Alvarez's complaint in greater detail. As he presently argues it, the claim does not rest on the cross-border feature of his abduction. Although the District Court granted relief in part on finding a violation of international law in taking Alvarez across the border from Mexico to the United States, the Court of Appeals rejected that ground of liability for failure to identify a norm of requisite force prohibiting a forcible abduction across a border. Instead, it relied on the conclusion that the law of the United States did not authorize Alvarez's arrest, because the DEA lacked extraterritorial authority under 21 U.S.C. § 878, and because Federal Rule of Criminal Procedure 4(d)(2) [as then worded] limited the warrant for Alvarez's arrest to "the jurisdiction of the United States." It is this position that Alvarez takes now: that his arrest was arbitrary and as such forbidden by international law not because it infringed the prerogatives of Mexico, but because no applicable law authorized it.

---

courts should give serious weight to the Executive Branch's view of the case's impact on foreign policy. * * *

Alvarez thus invokes a general prohibition of "arbitrary" detention defined as officially sanctioned action exceeding positive authorization to detain under the domestic law of some government, regardless of the circumstances. Whether or not this is an accurate reading of the Covenant, Alvarez cites little authority that a rule so broad has the status of a binding customary norm today. He certainly cites nothing to justify the federal courts in taking his broad rule as the predicate for a federal lawsuit, for its implications would be breathtaking. His rule would support a cause of action in federal court for any arrest, anywhere in the world, unauthorized by the law of the jurisdiction in which it took place, and would create a cause of action for any seizure of an alien in violation of the Fourth Amendment, supplanting the actions under 42 U.S.C. § 1983 and *Bivens v. Six Unknown Fed. Narcotics Agents,* 403 U.S. 388 (1971), that now provide damages remedies for such violations. It would create an action in federal court for arrests by state officers who simply exceed their authority; and for the violation of any limit that the law of any country might place on the authority of its own officers to arrest. And all of this assumes that Alvarez could establish that Sosa was acting on behalf of a government when he made the arrest, for otherwise he would need a rule broader still.

Alvarez's failure to marshal support for his proposed rule is underscored by the Restatement (Third) of Foreign Relations Law of the United States § 702 (1987), which says in its discussion of customary international human rights law that a "state violates international law if, as a matter of state policy, it practices, encourages, or condones . . . prolonged arbitrary detention." Although the Restatement does not explain its requirements of a "state policy" and of "prolonged" detention, the implication is clear. Any credible invocation of a principle against arbitrary detention that the civilized world accepts as binding customary international law requires a factual basis beyond relatively brief detention in excess of positive authority. * * *

Whatever may be said for the broad principle Alvarez advances, in the present, imperfect world, it expresses an aspiration that exceeds any binding customary rule having the specificity we require. Creating a private cause of action to further that aspiration would go beyond any residual common law discretion we think it appropriate to exercise. It is enough to hold that a single illegal detention of less than a day, followed by the transfer of custody to lawful authorities and a prompt arraignment, violates no norm of customary international law so well defined as to support the creation of a federal remedy.

The judgment of the Court of Appeals is *reversed.*

JUSTICE SCALIA, with whom THE CHIEF JUSTICE and JUSTICE THOMAS join concurring in part and concurring in the judgment.

There is not much that I would add to the Court's detailed opinion, and only one thing that I would subtract: its reservation of a discretionary power in the Federal Judiciary to create causes of action for the enforcement of international-law-based norms. * * *

I

* * * At the time of its enactment, the ATS provided a federal forum in which aliens could bring suit to recover for torts committed in "violation of the law of nations." The law of nations that would have been applied in this federal forum was at the time part of the so-called general common law. * * *

General common law was not federal law under the Supremacy Clause, which gave that effect only to the Constitution, the laws of the United States, and treaties. Federal and state courts adjudicating questions of general common law were not adjudicating questions of federal or state law, respectively—the general common law was neither. * * *

This Court's decision in *Erie R. Co. v. Tompkins*, 304 U.S. 64 (1938), signaled the end of federal-court elaboration and application of the general common law. *Erie* repudiated the holding of *Swift v. Tyson*, 41 U.S. 1 (1842), that federal courts were free to "express our own opinion" upon "the principles established in the general commercial law." After canvassing the many problems resulting from "the broad province accorded to the so-called 'general law' as to which federal courts exercised an independent judgment," the *Erie* Court extirpated that law with its famous declaration that "there is no federal general common law." *Erie* affected the status of the law of nations in federal courts not merely by the implication of its holding but quite directly, since the question decided in *Swift* turned on the "law merchant," then a subset of the law of nations.

After the death of the old general common law in *Erie* came the birth of a new and different common law pronounced by federal courts. * * * Unlike the general common law that preceded it, however, federal common law was self-consciously "made" rather than "discovered," by judges. * * *

Because post-*Erie* federal common law is made, not discovered, federal courts must possess some federal-common-law-making authority before undertaking to craft it. * * *

The general rule as formulated in *Texas Industries, Inc. v. Radcliff Materials, Inc.,* 451 U.S. 630, 640-41 (1981), is that "the vesting of jurisdiction in the federal courts does not in and of itself give rise to authority to formulate federal common law." * * *

The rule against finding a delegation of substantive lawmaking power in a grant of jurisdiction is subject to exceptions, some better established than others. The most firmly entrenched is admiralty law, derived from the grant of admiralty jurisdiction in Article III, § 2, cl. 3, of the Constitution. In the exercise of that jurisdiction federal courts develop and apply a body of general maritime law, "the well-known and well-developed venerable law of the sea which arose from the custom among seafaring men." *R.M.S. Titanic, Inc. v. Haver*, 171 F.3d 943, 960 (4th Cir. 1999) (Niemeyer, J.) At the other extreme is *Bivens v. Six Unknown Fed. Narcotics Agents*, 403 U.S. 388 (1971), which created a private damages cause of action against federal officials for violation of the Fourth Amendment. We have said that the authority to create this cause of action was derived from "our general jurisdiction to decide all cases 'arising under the

Constitution, laws, or treaties of the United States.'" *Correctional Services Corp. v. Malesko,* 534 U.S. 61, 66 (2001) (quoting 28 U.S.C. § 1331). While *Bivens* stands, the ground supporting it has eroded. For the past 25 years, "we have consistently refused to extend *Bivens* liability to any new context." *Correctional Services Corp.,* at 68. *Bivens* is "a relic of the heady days in which this Court assumed common-law powers to create causes of action." 534 U.S. at 75 (SCALIA, J., concurring).

II

With these general principles in mind, I turn to the question presented. The Court's detailed exegesis of the ATS conclusively establishes that it is "a jurisdictional statute creating no new causes of action." The Court provides a persuasive explanation of why respondent's contrary interpretation, that "the ATS was intended not simply as a jurisdictional grant, but as authority for the creation of a new cause of action for torts in violation of international law," is wrong. Indeed, the Court properly endorses the views of one scholar that this interpretation is "'simply frivolous.'" * * *

These conclusions are alone enough to dispose of the present case in favor of petitioner Sosa. None of the exceptions to the general rule against finding substantive lawmaking power in a jurisdictional grant apply. *Bivens* provides perhaps the closest analogy. That is shaky authority at best, but at least it can be said that *Bivens* sought to enforce a command of our *own* law—the *United States Constitution.* In modern international human rights litigation of the sort that has proliferated since *Filartiga v. Pena-Irala,* 630 F.2d 876 (2d Cir. 1980), a federal court must first *create* the underlying federal command. But "the fact that a rule has been recognized as [customary international law], by itself, is not an adequate basis for viewing that rule as part of federal common law." Daniel J. Meltzer, *Customary International Law, Foreign Affairs, and Federal Common Law,* 42 Va. J. Int'l L. 513, 519 (2002). In Benthamite terms, creating a federal command (federal common law) out of "international norms," and then constructing a cause of action to enforce that command through the purely jurisdictional grant of the ATS, is nonsense upon stilts.

III

The analysis in the Court's opinion departs from my own in this respect: After concluding in Part III that "the ATS is a jurisdictional statute creating no new causes of action," the Court addresses at length in Part IV the "good reasons for a restrained conception of the *discretion* a federal court should exercise in considering a new cause of action" under the ATS (emphasis added). By framing the issue as one of "discretion," the Court skips over the antecedent question of authority. This neglects the "lesson of *Erie,*" that "grants of jurisdiction alone" (which the Court has acknowledged the ATS to be) "are not themselves grants of law-making authority." Meltzer, *supra* at 541. On this point, the Court observes only that no development between the enactment of the ATS (in 1789) and the birth of modern international human rights litigation under that statute (in 1980) "has categorically *precluded* federal courts from recognizing a claim under the law of nations as an element of common law" (emphasis added). This turns our jurisprudence regarding federal common law on its head. The question is not what case or congressional action *prevents* federal courts from applying the law of nations as part of the general common law; it is what *authorizes* that peculiar exception from *Erie's* fundamental holding that a general common law *does not exist*.

The Court would apparently find authorization in the understanding of the Congress that enacted the ATS, that "district courts would recognize private causes of action for certain torts in violation of the law of nations." But as discussed above, that understanding rested upon a notion of general common law that has been repudiated by *Erie*. * * *

Because today's federal common law is not our Framers' general common law, the question presented by the suggestion of discretionary authority to enforce the law of nations is not whether to extend old-school general-common-law adjudication. Rather, it is whether to create new federal common law. The Court masks the novelty of its approach when it suggests that the difference between us is that we would "close the door to further independent judicial recognition of actionable international norms," whereas the Court would permit the exercise of judicial power "on the understanding that the door is still ajar subject to vigilant doorkeeping." The general common law was the old door. We do not close that door today, for the deed was done in *Erie*. Federal common law is a *new* door. The question is not whether that door will be left ajar, but whether this Court will open it. * * *

We Americans have a method for making the laws that are over us. We elect representatives to two Houses of Congress, each of which must enact the new law and present it for the approval of a President, whom we also elect. For over two decades now, unelected federal judges have been usurping this lawmaking power by converting what they regard as norms of international law into American law. Today's opinion approves that process in principle, though urging the lower courts to be more restrained.

This Court seems incapable of admitting that some matters—*any* matters—are none of its business. In today's latest victory for its Never Say Never Jurisprudence, the Court ignores its own conclusion that the ATS provides only jurisdiction, wags a finger at the lower courts for going too far, and then—repeating the same formula the ambitious lower courts *themselves* have used—invites them to try again. * * *

JUSTICE GINSBURG, joined by JUSTICE BREYER, concurring in part and concurring in the judgment [omitted.]

JUSTICE BREYER, concurring in part and concurring in the judgment [omitted.]

NOTES AND QUESTIONS FOR DISCUSSION

1.   After all the dust settles on the historical debate, do you suppose that the framers of the ATS considered the "law of nations" to be one of the "Laws of the United States" within the meaning of Article III? Note that the ATS was contained in the Judiciary Act of 1789, which also contained the provision that

was involved in *Hodgson v. Bowerbank, supra*, and that purported to provide Circuit Court jurisdiction whenever "an alien is a party." Might these two provisions suggest that the First Congress thought it had a broader authority to confer alienage jurisdiction on the federal courts than *Hodgson* will sustain? Or does the ATS only contemplate cases in which a U.S. citizen is also a party? See Curtis A. Bradley, *The Alien Tort Statute and Article III*, 42 Va. J. Int'l L. 587 (2002) (taking such a view).

2. The *Sosa* Court seems willing to allow for at least some limited development of claims for relief under the law of nations that could be maintained under § 1350, beyond the sorts of international law violations described by Blackstone. Those violations, which included piracy, safe passage, and ambassadorial protection were likely to give a cause for war if they went unremedied. Is the *Sosa* dissent right that the ATS should have been read to have gone thus far and no further? Were the events in *Filartiga* the sorts of things that would give rise to international reprisal against the U.S. if a U.S. court did not remedy them? What about the events at issue in *Sosa*?

3. As the *Sosa* Court notes, statements such as those in *The Paquete Habana* to the effect that the law of nations was part of "our law" were made during the era when the federal courts enforced the general law—law that was neither federal nor state. Once the Supreme Court decided *Erie*, why did the law of nations become federalized? Does the *Sosa* Court even attempt to provide an explanation? Is it because such suits relate to the foreign affairs powers thought to reside in the political branches? Note also that Article I of the Constitution specifically gives to Congress the power to prescribe criminal penalties for the violation of the law of nations. Does this help the inquiry, and if so, does it tend to support or undermine the result in *Sosa*?

4. Post-*Sosa*, what sorts of violations of international law will the ATS reach? The Court rejects Alvarez's argument based on the Universal Declaration of Human Rights on the grounds that it does not create enforceable obligations, and the Court rejects his argument from the International Covenant on Civil and Political Rights on the grounds that it was not self-enforcing. Could the ATS itself be thought of as a congressional implementation of such international agreements and conventions? Even if the U.S. was a party to them? The *Sosa* Court also looked to customary international law, but it concluded that there was no "binding customary norm" against arbitrary arrests like the one suffered by Sosa. *Sosa* also attempts to limit the rights violations that the ATS can embrace by excluding those "with less definite content and acceptance among civilized nations than the historical paradigms familiar when § 1350 was enacted." 542 U.S. at 732. After *Sosa*, is there any way to predict what sort of "definite content" and "acceptance" will be enough in future cases (even if it was lacking in *Sosa* itself)? Some of these questions are addressed in Kadic v. Karadzic, 70 F.3d 232 (2d Cir. 1995), a pre-*Sosa* decision that is excerpted below.

5. As discussed further in Chapter 3, the Supreme Court in Argentine Republic v. Amerada Hess Shipping Corporation, 488 U.S. 428 (1989), limited the scope of the ATS by holding that the Foreign Sovereign Immunities Act, 28 U.S.C. §§ 1330, 1602-1611 (FSIA), constituted the exclusive basis for obtaining relief against a foreign state in U.S. courts. The case involved a suit by the owners of a Liberian crude oil tanker that was severely damaged when attacked on the high seas by Argentinian aircraft during the Falkland Islands war. The plaintiffs attempted to invoke federal court jurisdiction under the ATS, claiming that such an attack on neutral shipping represented a violation of international law. Because the plaintiffs sued Argentina, a unanimous Court held that the suit could only be maintained if authorized by the FSIA, which a majority held it was not. 488 U.S. at 436 ("[Under the FSIA] immunity is granted in those cases involving alleged violations of international law that do not come within one of the FSIA's exceptions"). Thus, *Amerada Hess* largely limits cases brought under the ATS to cases brought against non-sovereign defendants for torts in violation of international law.

6.   For a brief sampling of the voluminous scholarship on the federal nature (or not) of the law of nations, in addition to the articles cited in *Sosa* and in prior notes in this chapter, see Thomas H. Lee, *The Safe-Conduct Theory of the Alien Tort Statute*, 106 Colum. L. Rev. 830 (2006); Eugene Kontorovich, *Implementing* Sosa v. Alvarez-Machain: *What Piracy Reveals Abut the Limits of the Alien Tort Statute*, 80 Notre Dame L. Rev. 111 (2004); Michael G. Collins, *The Diversity Theory of the Alien Tort Statute*, 42 Va. J. Int'l L. 649 (2002). Helpful older works include Arthur M. Weisburd, *State Courts, Federal Courts, and International Cases*, 20 Yale J. Int'l L. 1 (1995); Kenneth Randall, Federal Courts and the International Human Rights Paradigm 37-57 (1990); Stewart Jay, *The Status of the Law of Nations in Early American Law*, 42 Vand. L. Rev. 819 (1989); Phillip R. Trimble, *A Revisionist View of Customary International Law*, 33 UCLA L. Rev. 665 (1986).

2. *Claims under the Torture Victim Protection Act*

The Torture Victim Protection Act of 1991, Pub. L. No. 102-256, § 2, 106 Stat. 73 (codified at 28 U.S.C. § 1350, Note) provides a federal clause of action against an individual for certain acts of torture and extrajudicial killing.

> **(a) Liability.** An individual who, under any actual or apparent authority, or color of law, of any foreign nation—
>
> > (1) subjects an individual to torture shall, in a civil action, be liable for damages to that individual; or
> >
> > (2) subjects an individual to extrajudicial killing shall, in a civil action, be liable for damages to the individual's legal representative, or to any person who may be a claimant in an action for wrongful death.
>
> **(b) Exhaustion of Remedies.** A court shall decline to hear a claim under this section if the claimant has not exhausted adequate and available remedies in the place in which the conduct giving rise to the claim occurred.
>
> **(c) Statute of Limitations.** No action shall be maintained under this section unless it is commenced within 10 years after the cause of action arose.

The TVPA elsewhere defines "extrajudicial killing" and "torture" (§ 3(a)-(b)), but it does not define who an "individual" is who would be capable of violating the Act.   As just noted, foreign states are not suable "individuals" under the TVPA because its language does not create an exception to the FSIA. *Amerada Hess, supra.*

Note that the TVPA effectively codifies the sort of claim alleged in *Filartiga* (in which the claims of official torture would have satisfied the TVPA's "color of law" requirement). But the TVPA goes further insofar as it would give such a cause of action to a citizen of the U.S. In addition, the TVPA provides the sort of affirmative congressional action that Judge Bork insisted on in his *Tel-Oren* opinion as a precondition to allowing suit under the ATS. At the same time, the legislative history of the TVPA indicates that it did not seek to displace the ATS because "Claims based on torture or summary executions do not exhaust the list of actions that may appropriately be covered [by the ATS]. That statute should remain intact to permit suits based on other norms that already exist or may ripen in the future into rules of customary international law." H.R. Rep. No. 102-367(I), at 4 (1991), reprinted in 1992 U.S.C.C.A.N. 84, 86; see also *Sosa*, 542 U.S. at 728.

In **Mohamad v. Palestinian Authority, 132 S.Ct. 1702 (2012),** the Supreme Court was faced with the question whether the term "individual" in section (a) of the TVPA included acts by *non*sovereign organizations. *Mohamad* was brought under the TVPA by the relatives of Azzam Rahim, a naturalized U.S. citizen who was imprisoned by Palestinian Authority intelligence officers, tortured, and then killed. The defendants were the Palestinian Authority and the Palestine Liberation Organization. Relying largely on what it considered to be the plain meaning of the word "individual," the Court held that the TVPA applied only to acts of "natural persons."

> We * * * decline petitioners' suggestion to construe the TVPA's scope of liability to conform with other federal statutes that petitioners contend provide civil remedies to victims of torture or extrajudicial killing. None of the three statutes petitioners identify employs the term "individual" to describe the covered defendant, and so none assists in the interpretive task we face today. See 42 U.S.C. §1983 [the 1871 Civil Rights Act which refers to the liability of "persons"]; 28 U.S.C. §§1603(a), 1605A(c) (2006 ed., Supp. IV) [the FSIA]; 18 U.S.C. §§2333, 2334(a)–(b), 2337 [The Anti-Terrorism Act of 1990 that references liability of "persons"]. The same is true of the Alien Tort Statute, 28 U.S.C. §1350, so it offers no comparative value here regardless of whether corporate entities can be held liable in a federal common-law action brought under that statute. Compare Doe v. Exxon Mobil Corp., 654 F.3d 11 (CADC 2011), with Kiobel v. Royal Dutch Petroleum Co., 621 F.3d 111 (CA2 2010), cert. granted, 565 U.S. ___ (2011). Finally, although petitioners rightly note that the TVPA contemplates liability against officers who do not personally execute the torture or extrajudicial killing, see, e.g., Chavez v. Carranza, 559 F.3d 486 (CA6 2009), it does not follow (as petitioners argue) that the Act embraces liability against nonsovereign organizations. An officer who gives an order to

torture or kill is an "individual" in that word's ordinary usage; an organization is not.

132 S.Ct. at 1709. Whether corporations may be sued under the ATS is, for the moment, an open question, as noted below.

3. Claims under the Anti-Terrorism Act of 1990

In addition, some plaintiffs may be able to seek relief under the Anti-Terrorism Act of 1990, 18 U.S.C. §§ 2333-2334(a)-(b), 2337. Much of the Act is devoted to criminalizing various acts of terrorism. But within its provisions is a civil remedy. In relevant part it provides:

> **Section 2333—Civil Remedies**
>
> **(a) Action and jurisdiction.** Any national of the United States injured in his or her person, property, or business by reason of an act of international terrorism, or his or her estate, survivors, or heirs, may sue therefor in any appropriate district court of the United States and shall recover threefold the damages he or she sustains and the cost of the suit, including attorney's fees. * * *

Elsewhere, the Act refers to the civil remedy under § 2333 as addressing the liability of "any person." 28 U.S.C. § 2334(b). Importantly, however, the Act declares that civil actions under § 2333 cannot be maintained against governments, governmental agencies, or their officers and employees when acting under color of authority, including both the U.S. and foreign governments. 28 U.S.C. § 2337.

The 1990 Act also provides that a district court shall not dismiss an action on *forum non conveniens* grounds unless the foreign court would have subject matter and personal jurisdiction over all defendants, the foreign court "is significantly more convenient and appropriate," and the foreign court "offers a remedy which is substantially the same as the one available in the courts of the United States." 28 U.S.C. § 2334(d).

4. Suability of Private Actors and Related Matters

Under the TVPA, there is a kind of state-action requirement for individual liability. The defendant individual must have acted "under any actual or apparent authority, or color of law, of any foreign nation." Under the Anti-Terrorism Act of 1990, however, the defendant must *not* have acted under color of law. Is there any kind of state-action requirement under the ATS similar to that under the TVPA? Another way of phrasing the question is: Can private actors (those not acting under color of foreign-state law) violate customary international law or commit torts in violation of the law of nations? If not, why not? But if so, to what extent? The opinion that follows was decided prior to *Sosa v. Alvarez-Machain*. However, it deals with a number of matters that *Sosa* did not address, including liability of non-state actors for claims under the ATS, subject matter jurisdiction for TVPA claims, personal jurisdiction, *forum non conveniens*, and concerns about "justiciability." Recall that in *Sosa* itself (at footnote 21), the Court indicated that a federal court might defer to the expressed wishes of the political branches not to interfere with foreign country interests in a proper case by dismissing an ATS claim.

Kadic v. Karadzic

United States Court of Appeals, Second Circuit, 1995.
70 F.3d 232.

JON O. NEWMAN, CHIEF JUDGE.

Most Americans would probably be surprised to learn that victims of atrocities committed in Bosnia are suing the leader of the insurgent Bosnian-Serb forces in a United States District Court in Manhattan. * * * The pending appeals pose additional significant issues as to the scope of the Alien Tort Act: whether some violations of the law of nations may be remedied when committed by those not acting under the authority of a state; if so, whether genocide, war crimes, and crimes against humanity are among the violations that do not require state action; and whether a person, otherwise liable for a violation of the law of nations, is immune from service of process because he is present in the United States as an invitee of the United Nations.

* * * For the reasons set forth below, we hold that subject-matter jurisdiction exists, that Karadzic may be found liable for genocide, war crimes, and crimes against humanity in his private capacity and for other violations in his capacity as a state actor, and that he is not immune from service of process. We therefore reverse and remand.

BACKGROUND

The plaintiffs-appellants are Croat and Muslim citizens of the internationally recognized nation of Bosnia-Herzegovina, formerly a republic of Yugoslavia. Their complaints, which we accept as true for purposes of this appeal, allege that they are victims, and representatives of victims, of various atrocities, including brutal acts of rape, forced prostitution, forced impregnation, torture, and summary execution, carried out by Bosnian-Serb military forces as part of a genocidal campaign conducted in the course of the Bosnian civil war. Karadzic, formerly a citizen of Yugoslavia and now a citizen of Bosnia-Herzegovina, is the President of a three-man presidency of the self-proclaimed Bosnian-Serb republic within Bosnia-Herzegovina, sometimes referred to as "Srpska," which claims to exercise lawful authority, and does in fact exercise actual control, over large parts of the territory of Bosnia-Herzegovina. In his capacity as President, Karadzic possesses ultimate command authority over the Bosnian-Serb military forces, and the injuries perpetrated upon plaintiffs were committed as part of a pattern of systematic human rights violations that was directed by Karadzic and carried out by the military forces under his command. The complaints allege that Karadzic acted in an official capacity either as the titular head of Srpska or in collaboration with the government of the recognized nation of the former Yugoslavia and its dominant constituent republic, Serbia.

[Plaintiffs] asserted causes of action for genocide, rape, forced prostitution and impregnation, torture and other cruel, inhuman, and degrading treatment, assault and battery, sex and ethnic inequality, summary execution, and wrongful death. They sought compensatory and punitive damages, attorney's fees, and, in one of the cases, injunctive relief. Plaintiffs grounded subject-matter jurisdiction in the Alien Tort Act, the Torture Victim Protection Act of 1991 ("Torture Victim Act"), Pub.L. No. 102-256, 106 Stat. 73 (1992), codified at 28 U.S.C. § 1350 note (Supp. V 1993), the general federal-question jurisdictional statute, 28 U.S.C. § 1331 (1988), and principles of supplemental jurisdiction, 28 U.S.C. § 1367 (Supp. V 1993).

In early 1993, Karadzic was admitted to the United States on three separate occasions as an invitee of the United Nations. According to affidavits submitted by the plaintiffs, Karadzic was personally served with the summons and complaint in each action during two of these visits while he was physically present in Manhattan. * * *

In the District Court, Karadzic moved for dismissal of both actions on the grounds of insufficient service of process, lack of personal jurisdiction, lack of subject-matter jurisdiction, and nonjusticiability of plaintiffs' claims. [The District Court dismissed both actions on grounds of subject matter jurisdiction.]

DISCUSSION

Though the District Court dismissed for lack of subject-matter jurisdiction, the parties have briefed not only that issue but also the threshold issues of personal jurisdiction and justiciability under the political question doctrine. Karadzic urges us to affirm on any one of these three grounds. We consider each in turn.

I

SUBJECT-MATTER JURISDICTION

Appellants allege three statutory bases for the subject-matter jurisdiction of the District Court—the Alien Tort Act, the Torture Victim Act, and the general federal-question jurisdictional statute.

A. The Alien Tort Act

    1. General Application to Appellants' Claims

* * * [The] only disputed issue [under § 1350] is whether plaintiffs have pleaded violations of international law. * * * There is no federal subject-matter jurisdiction under the Alien Tort Act unless the complaint adequately pleads a violation of the law of nations (or treaty of the United States). * * *

Karadzic contends that appellants have not alleged violations of the norms of international law because such norms bind only states and persons acting under color of a state's law, not private individuals. In making this contention, Karadzic advances the contradictory positions that he is not a state actor, even as he asserts that he is the President of the self-proclaimed Republic of Srpska[.]
    * * *

We do not agree that the law of nations, as understood in the modern era, confines its reach to state action. Instead, we hold that certain forms of conduct violate the law of nations whether undertaken by those acting under the auspices of a state or only as private individuals. An early example of the application of the law of nations to the acts of private individuals is the prohibition against piracy. See United States v. Smith, 18 U.S. (5 Wheat.) 153, 161 (1820); United States v. Furlong, 18 U.S. (5 Wheat.) 184, 196-97 (1820). * * * Later examples are prohibitions against the slave trade and certain war crimes. * * *

The liability of private persons for certain violations of customary international law and the availability of the Alien Tort Act to remedy such violations was early recognized by the Executive Branch in an opinion of Attorney General Bradford in reference to acts of American citizens aiding the French fleet to plunder British property off the coast of Sierra Leone in 1795. See Breach of Neutrality, 1 Op. Att'y Gen. 57, 59 (1795). The Executive Branch has emphatically restated in this litigation its position that private persons may be found liable under the Alien Tort Act for acts of genocide, war crimes, and other violations of international humanitarian law. * * *

The Restatement (Third) of the Foreign Relations Law of the United States (1986) ("*Restatement (Third)*") proclaims: "Individuals may be held liable for offenses against international law, such as piracy, war crimes, and genocide." Restatement (Third) pt. II, introductory note. The Restatement is careful to identify those violations that are actionable when committed by a state, *Restatement (Third)* § 702,[3] and a more limited category of violations of "universal concern," id. § 404,[4] partially overlapping with those listed in section 702. Though the immediate focus of section 404 is to identify those offenses for which a state has jurisdiction to punish without regard to territoriality or the nationality of the offenders, cf. id. § 402(1)(a), (2), the inclusion of piracy and slave trade from an earlier era and aircraft hijacking from the modern era demonstrates that the offenses of "universal concern" include those capable of being committed by non-state actors. Although the jurisdiction authorized by section 404 is usually exercised by application of criminal law, international law also permits states to establish appropriate civil remedies, id. § 404 cmt. b, such as the tort actions authorized by the Alien Tort Act. Indeed, the two cases invoking the Alien Tort Act prior to *Filartiga* both applied the civil remedy to private action. See Adra v. Clift, 195 F.Supp. 857 (D. Md. 1961); Bolchos v. Darrel, 3 F.Cas. 810 (D.S.C.1795) (No. 1,607).

Karadzic disputes the application of the law of nations to any violations committed by private individuals, relying on *Filartiga* and the concurring opinion of Judge Edwards in Tel-Oren v. Libyan Arab Republic, 726 F.2d 774, 775

---

[3] Section 702 provides: A state violates international law if, as a matter of state policy, it practices, encourages, or condones: (a) genocide, (b) slavery or slave trade, (c) the murder or causing the disappearance of individuals, (d) torture or other cruel, inhuman, or degrading treatment or punishment, (e) prolonged arbitrary detention, (f) systematic racial discrimination, or (g) a consistent pattern of gross violations of internationally recognized human rights.

[4] Section 404 provides: A state has jurisdiction to define and prescribe punishment for certain offenses recognized by the community of nations as of universal concern, such as piracy, slave trade, attacks on or hijacking of aircraft, genocide, war crimes, and perhaps certain acts of terrorism, even where [no other basis of jurisdiction] is present.

(D.C.Cir.1984), cert. denied, 470 U.S. 1003 (1985). *Filartiga* involved an allegation of torture committed by a state official. Relying on the United Nations' Declaration on the Protection of All Persons from Being Subjected to Torture, G.A.Res. 3452, U.N. GAOR, U.N. Doc. A/1034 (1975) (hereinafter "Declaration on Torture"), as a definitive statement of norms of customary international law prohibiting states from permitting torture, we ruled that "*official* torture is now prohibited by the law of nations." *Filartiga*, 630 F.2d at 884 (emphasis added). We had no occasion to consider whether international law violations other than torture are actionable against private individuals, and nothing in *Filartiga* purports to preclude such a result.

Nor did Judge Edwards in his scholarly opinion in *Tel-Oren* reject the application of international law to any private action. On the contrary, citing piracy and slave-trading as early examples, he observed that there exists a "handful of crimes to which the law of nations attributes individual responsibility," 726 F.2d at 795. Reviewing authorities similar to those consulted in *Filartiga*, he merely concluded that torture—the specific violation alleged in *Tel-Oren*—was not within the limited category of violations that do not require state action.

Karadzic also contends that Congress intended the state-action requirement of the Torture Victim Act to apply to actions under the Alien Tort Act. We disagree. Congress enacted the Torture Victim Act to codify the cause of action recognized by this Circuit in *Filartiga*, and to further extend that cause of action to plaintiffs who are U.S. citizens. See H.R.Rep. No. 367, 102d Cong., 2d Sess., at 4 (1991), reprinted in 1992 U.S.C.C.A.N. 84, 86 (explaining that codification of *Filartiga* was necessary in light of skepticism expressed by judge Bork's concurring opinion in *Tel-Oren*). At the same time, Congress indicated that the Alien Tort Act "has other important uses and should not be replaced," because

> Claims based on torture and summary executions do not exhaust the list of actions that may appropriately be covered [by the Alien Tort Act]. That statute should remain intact to permit suits based on other norms that already exist or may ripen in the future into rules of customary international law.

Id. The scope of the Alien Tort Act remains undiminished by enactment of the Torture Victim Act.

2. Specific Application of Alien Tort Act to Appellants' Claims

In order to determine whether the offenses alleged by the appellants in this litigation are violations of the law of nations that may be the subject of Alien Tort Act claims against a private individual, we must make a particularized examination of these offenses, mindful of the important precept that "evolving standards of international law govern who is within the [Alien Tort Act's] jurisdictional grant." *Amerada Hess*, 830 F.2d at 425. In making that inquiry, it will be helpful to group the appellants' claims into three categories: (a) genocide, (b) war crimes, and (c) other instances of inflicting death, torture, and degrading treatment.

(a) Genocide. In the aftermath of the atrocities committed during the Second World War, the condemnation of genocide as contrary to international law

quickly achieved broad acceptance by the community of nations. In 1946, the General Assembly of the United Nations declared that genocide is a crime under international law that is condemned by the civilized world, whether the perpetrators are "private individuals, public officials or statesmen." G.A.Res. 96(I), 1 U.N.GAOR, U.N. Doc. A/64/Add.1, at 188-89 (1946). The General Assembly also affirmed the principles of Article 6 of the Agreement and Charter Establishing the Nuremberg War Crimes Tribunal for punishing "'persecutions on political, racial, or religious grounds,'" regardless of whether the offenders acted "'as individuals or as members of organizations.'" *In re* Extradition of Demjanjuk, 612 F. Supp. 544, 555 n. 11 (N.D.Ohio 1985) (quoting Article 6). See G.A.Res. 95(I), 1 U.N.GAOR, U.N.Doc. A/64/Add.1, at 188 (1946).

The Convention on the Prevention and Punishment of the Crime of Genocide, 78 U.N.T.S. 277, entered into force Jan. 12, 1951, for the United States Feb. 23, 1989 (hereinafter "Convention on Genocide"), provides a more specific articulation of the prohibition of genocide in international law. The Convention, which has been ratified by more than 120 nations, including the United States, see U.S. Dept. of State, Treaties in Force 345 (1994), defines "genocide" to mean:

> any of the following acts committed with intent to destroy, in whole or in part, a national, ethnical, racial or religious group, as such:
>
> (a) Killing members of the group;
>
> (b) Causing serious bodily or mental harm to members of the group;
>
> (c) Deliberately inflicting on the group conditions of life calculated to bring about its physical destruction in whole or in part;
>
> (d) Imposing measures intended to prevent births with the group;
>
> (e) Forcibly transferring children of the group to another group.

Convention on Genocide art. II. Especially pertinent to the pending appeal, the Convention makes clear that "[p]ersons committing genocide . . . shall be punished, *whether they are constitutionally responsible rulers, public officials or private individuals.*" Id. art. IV (emphasis added). These authorities unambiguously reflect that, from its incorporation into international law, the proscription of genocide has applied equally to state and non-state actors.

The applicability of this norm to private individuals is also confirmed by the Genocide Convention Implementation Act of 1987, 18 U.S.C. § 1091 (1988), which criminalizes acts of genocide without regard to whether the offender is acting under color of law, see id. § 1091(a) ("[w]hoever" commits genocide shall be punished), if the crime is committed within the United States or by a U.S. national, id. § 1091(d). Though Congress provided that the Genocide Convention Implementation Act shall not "be construed as creating any substantive or procedural right enforceable by law by any party in any proceeding," id. § 1092, the legislative decision not to create a new private remedy does not imply that a private remedy is not already available under the Alien Tort Act. Nothing in the Genocide Convention Implementation Act or its legislative history reveals an intent by Congress to repeal the Alien Tort Act insofar as it applies to genocide, and the two statutes are surely not repugnant to each other. Under these circumstances, it would be improper to construe the Genocide Convention Implementation Act as repealing the Alien Tort Act by implication. * * *

Appellants' allegations that Karadzic personally planned and ordered a campaign of murder, rape, forced impregnation, and other forms of torture designed to destroy the religious and ethnic groups of Bosnian Muslims and Bosnian Croats clearly state a violation of the international law norm proscribing genocide, regardless of whether Karadzic acted under color of law or as a private individual. The District Court has subject-matter jurisdiction over these claims pursuant to the Alien Tort Act.

(b) War crimes. Plaintiffs also contend that the acts of murder, rape, torture, and arbitrary detention of civilians, committed in the course of hostilities, violate the law of war. Atrocities of the types alleged here have long been recognized in international law as violations of the law of war. See *In re* Yamashita, 327 U.S. 1, 14 (1946). Moreover, international law imposes an affirmative duty on military commanders to take appropriate measures within their power to control troops under their command for the prevention of such atrocities. Id. at 15-16.

After the Second World War, the law of war was codified in the four Geneva Conventions, which have been ratified by more than 180 nations, including the United States, see Treaties in Force, *supra*, at 398-99. Common article 3, which is substantially identical in each of the four Conventions, applies to "armed conflict[s] not of an international character" and binds "each Party to the conflict . . . to apply, as a minimum, the following provisions":

> Persons taking no active part in the hostilities . . . shall in all circumstances be treated humanely, without any adverse distinction founded on race, colour, religion or faith, sex, birth or wealth, or any other similar criteria.
>
> To this end, the following acts are and shall remain prohibited at any time and in any place whatsoever with respect to the above-mentioned persons:
>
> > (a) violence to life and person, in particular murder of all kinds, mutilation, cruel treatment   and torture;
> >
> > (b) taking of hostages;
> >
> > (c) outrages upon personal dignity, in particular humiliating and degrading treatment;
> >
> > (d) the passing of sentences and carrying out of executions without previous judgment   pronounced by a regularly constituted court. . . .

Geneva Convention I art. 3(1). Thus, under the law of war as codified in the Geneva Conventions, all "parties" to a conflict—which includes insurgent military groups—are obliged to adhere to these most fundamental requirements of the law of war.

The offenses alleged by the appellants, if proved, would violate the most fundamental norms of the law of war embodied in common article 3, which binds parties to internal conflicts regardless of whether they are recognized nations or roving hordes of insurgents. The liability of private individuals for committing war crimes has been recognized since World War I and was confirmed at Nuremberg after World War II, * * * and remains today an important aspect of international law. The District Court has jurisdiction pursuant to the Alien Tort Act over appellants' claims of war crimes and other violations of international humanitarian law.

(c) Torture and summary execution. In *Filartiga*, we held that official torture is prohibited by universally accepted norms of international law, see 630 F.2d at 885, and the Torture Victim Act confirms this holding and extends it to cover summary execution. Torture Victim Act §§ 2(a), 3(a). However, torture and summary execution—when not perpetrated in the course of genocide or war crimes—are proscribed by international law only when committed by state officials or under color of law. See Declaration on Torture art. 1 (defining torture as being "inflicted by or at the instigation of a public official"); Convention Against Torture and Other Cruel, Inhuman, or Degrading Treatment or Punishment pt. I, art. 1, 23 I.L.M. 1027 (1984), as modified, 24 I.L.M. 535 (1985), entered into force June 26, 1987, ratified by United States Oct. 21, 1994, 34 I.L.M. 590, 591 (1995) (defining torture as "inflicted by or at the instigation of or with the consent or acquiescence of a public official or other person acting in an official capacity"); Torture Victim Act § 2(a) (imposing liability on individuals acting "under actual or apparent authority, or color of law, of any foreign nation").

In the present case, appellants allege that acts of rape, torture, and summary execution were committed during hostilies by troops under Karadzic's command and with the specific intent of destroying appellants' ethnic-religious groups. Thus, many of the alleged atrocities are already encompassed within the appellants' claims of genocide and war crimes. Of course, at this threshold stage in the proceedings it cannot be known whether appellants will be able to prove the specific intent that is an element of genocide, or prove that each of the alleged torts were committed in the course of an armed conflict, as required to establish war crimes. It suffices to hold at this stage that the alleged atrocities are actionable under the Alien Tort Act, without regard to state action, to the extent that they were committed in pursuit of genocide or war crimes, and otherwise may be pursued against Karadzic to the extent that he is shown to be a state actor. Since the meaning of the state action requirement for purposes of international law violations will likely arise on remand and has already been considered by the District Court, we turn next to that requirement.

3.   The State Action Requirement for International Law Violations

In dismissing plaintiffs' complaints for lack of subject-matter jurisdiction, the District Court concluded that the alleged violations required state action and that the "Bosnian-Serb entity" headed by Karadzic does not meet the definition of a state. Appellants contend that they are entitled to prove that Srpska satisfies the definition of a state for purposes of international law violations and, alternatively, that Karadzic acted in concert with the recognized state of the former Yugoslavia and its constituent republic, Serbia.

(a) Definition of a state in international law. The definition of a state is well established in international law: "Under international law, a state is an entity that has a defined territory and a permanent population, under the control of its own government, and that engages in, or has the capacity to engage in, formal relations with other such entities." *Restatement (Third)* § 201; * * *.

Although the Restatement's definition of statehood requires the capacity to engage in formal relations with other states, it does not require recognition by other states. See *Restatement (Third)* § 202 cmt. B. Recognized states enjoy certain privileges and immunities relevant to judicial proceedings, see, e.g., Pfizer Inc. v. India, 434 U.S. 308, 318-20 (1978) (diversity jurisdiction); Banco Nacional de Cuba v. Sabbatino, 376 U.S. 398, 408-12 (1964) (access to U.S. courts); *Lafontant*, 844 F.Supp. at 131 (head-of-state immunity), but an unrecognized state is not a juridical nullity. Our courts have regularly given effect to the "state" action of unrecognized states. * * *

The customary international law of human rights, such as the proscription of official torture, applies to states without distinction between recognized and unrecognized states. See *Restatement (Third)* § 207, 702. It would be anomalous indeed if non-recognition by the United States, which typically reflects disfavor with a foreign regime—sometimes due to human rights abuses—had the perverse effect of shielding officials of the unrecognized regime from liability for those violations of international law norms that apply only to state actors.

Appellants' allegations entitle them to prove that Karadzic's regime satisfies the criteria for a state, for purposes of those international law violations requiring state action. Srpska is alleged to control defined territory, control populations within its power, and to have entered into agreements with other governments. It has a president, a legislature, and its own currency. These circumstances readily appear to satisfy the criteria for a state in all aspects of international law. Moreover, it is likely that the state action concept, where applicable for some violations like "official" torture, requires merely the semblance of official authority. The inquiry, after all, is whether a person purporting to wield official power has exceeded internationally recognized standards of civilized conduct, not whether statehood in all its formal aspects exists.

(b) Acting in concert with a foreign state. Appellants also sufficiently alleged that Karadzic acted under color of law insofar as they claimed that he acted in concert with the former Yugoslavia, the statehood of which is not disputed. The "color of law" jurisprudence of 42 U.S.C. § 1983 is a relevant guide to whether a defendant has engaged in official action for purposes of jurisdiction under the Alien Tort Act. See Forti v. Suarez-Mason, 672 F. Supp. 1531, 1546 (N.D.Cal.1987), reconsideration granted in part on other grounds, 694 F. Supp. 707 (N.D.Cal.1988). A private individual acts under color of law within the meaning of section 1983 when he acts together with state officials or with significant state aid. See Lugar v. Edmondson Oil Co., 457 U.S. 922, 937 (1982). The appellants are entitled to prove their allegations that Karadzic acted under color of law of Yugoslavia by acting in concert with Yugoslav officials or with significant Yugoslavian aid.

B. The Torture Victim Protection Act

The Torture Victim Act, enacted in 1992, provides a cause of action for official torture and extrajudicial killing * * *

By its plain language, the Torture Victim Act renders liable only those individuals who have committed torture or extrajudicial killing "under actual or apparent authority, or color of law, of any foreign nation." Legislative history confirms that this language was intended to "make[] clear that the plaintiff must establish some governmental involvement in the torture or killing to prove a claim," and that the statute "does not attempt to deal with torture or killing by purely private groups." H.R.Rep. No. 367, 102d Cong., 2d Sess., at 5 (1991), reprinted in 1992 U.S.C.C.A.N. 84, 87. In construing the terms "actual or apparent authority" and "color of law" courts are instructed to look to principles of agency law and to jurisprudence under 42 U.S.C. § 1983, respectively. Id.

Though the Torture Victim Act creates a cause of action for official torture, this statute, unlike the Alien Tort Act, is not itself a jurisdictional statute. The Torture Victim Act permits the appellants to pursue their claims of official torture under the jurisdiction conferred by the Alien Tort Act and also under the general federal question jurisdiction of [28 U.S.C.] section 1331, * * * .

II

SERVICE OF PROCESS AND PERSONAL JURISDICTION

Appellants aver that Karadzic was personally served with process while he was physically present in the Southern District of New York. * * *

Fed.R.Civ.P. 4(e)(2) specifically authorizes personal service of a summons and complaint upon an individual physically present within a judicial district of the United States, and such personal service comports with the requirements of due process for the assertion of personal jurisdiction. See Burnham v. Superior Court of California, 495 U.S. 604 (1990).

Nevertheless, Karadzic maintains that his status as an invitee of the United Nations during his visits to the United States rendered him immune from service of process. He relies on both the Agreement Between the United Nations and the United States of America Regarding the Headquarters of the United Nations, reprinted at 22 U.S.C. § 287 note (1988) ("Headquarters Agreement"), and a claimed federal common law immunity. We reject both bases for immunity from service. [The court ruled that if appellants personally served Karadzic with the summons and complaint while he was in New York but outside of the U.N. headquarters district, as they were prepared to prove, he is subject to the personal jurisdiction of the District Court.]

III

JUSTICIABILITY

We recognize that cases of this nature might pose special questions concerning the judiciary's proper role when adjudication might have implications in the conduct of this nation's foreign relations. * * *

Two nonjurisdictional, prudential doctrines reflect the judiciary's concerns regarding separation of powers: the political question doctrine and the act of state doctrine. It is the "'constitutional' underpinnings" of these doctrines that influenced the concurring opinions of Judge Robb and Judge Bork in *Tel-Oren*. Although we too recognize the potentially detrimental effects of judicial action in cases of this nature, we do not embrace the rather categorical views as to the inappropriateness of judicial action urged by Judges Robb and Bork. Not every case "touching foreign relations" is nonjusticiable, see Baker v. Carr, 369 U.S. 186, 211 (1962); Lamont v. Woods, 948 F.2d 825, 831-32 (2d Cir.1991), and judges should not reflexively invoke these doctrines to avoid difficult and somewhat sensitive decisions in the context of human rights. We believe a preferable approach is to weigh carefully the relevant considerations on a case-by-case basis. This will permit the judiciary to act where appropriate in light of the express legislative mandate of the Congress in section 1350, without compromising the primacy of the political branches in foreign affairs.

[The court first rejected the suggestion that ATS cases implicated the political question doctrine—a doctrine that would reject jurisdiction over issues for which there are no discernable legal standards or that are textually committed by the Constitution to either the legislative or executive branch.]

The act of state doctrine, under which courts generally refrain from judging the acts of a foreign state within its territory, *see Sabbatino*, 376 U.S. at 428, might be implicated in some cases arising under section 1350. However, * * * we doubt that the acts of even a state official, taken in violation of a nation's fundamental law and wholly unratified by that nation's government, could properly be characterized as an act of state. * * *

[But] the appellee has not had the temerity to assert in this Court that the acts he allegedly committed are the officially approved policy of a state. Finally, as noted, we think it would be a rare case in which the act of state doctrine precluded suit under section 1350. * * *

Finally, we note that at this stage of the litigation no party has identified a more suitable forum, and we are aware of none. Though the Statement of the United States suggests the general importance of considering the doctrine of *forum non conveniens*, it seems evident that the courts of the former Yugoslavia, either in Serbia or war-torn Bosnia, are not now available to entertain plaintiffs' claims, even if circumstances concerning the location of witnesses and documents were presented that were sufficient to overcome the plaintiffs' preference for a United States forum.

CONCLUSION

The judgment of the District Court dismissing appellants' complaints for lack of subject-matter jurisdiction is reversed, and the cases are remanded for further proceedings in accordance with this opinion.

NOTES AND QUESTIONS FOR DISCUSSION

1. The court in *Kadic* agreed that customary international law could usually only be violated by governmental actors, but it found that private individuals could be liable for some violations of international law such as war crimes and genocide. In doing so, the court focused heavily on the fact that international law recognized criminal liability for violations of international law, such as piracy. Does the availability of criminal liability for such behavior as a matter of international law translate to civil liability as a matter of international law (or U.S. law)? In that same effort, *Kadic* also relied on a number of conventions and agreements without considering whether they were ones to which the U.S. was a party or whether they created judicially enforceable rights. Was that consistent with the Supreme Court's later analysis in *Sosa*?

2. Professors Bradley and Goldsmith note that prior to *Kadic*, there had been very little litigation under the ATS against corporations (and after Mohamad v. Palestinian Authority, 132 S.Ct. 1702 (2012)—discussed above—suits against corporations are no longer possible under the TVPA). But by *Kadic*'s opening up the possibility that non-state actors could be liable for some violations of international law, there was a realistic possibility of corporate liability for their own human rights violations under the ATS. See Curtis Bradley & Jack Goldsmith, Foreign Relations Law 679-83 (4th ed. 2011). Obviously, the presence of a corporate defendant in an ATS suit presents a far greater likelihood that a damages judgment would get paid than would a suit against a state actor or other individual, such as the multimillion dollar judgment ultimately entered against Karadzic himself. In addition, after *Kadic*, there was the possibility that corporations might be liable for violations of international law for which only governmental actors could be liable, if it could be shown that they acted sufficiently in concert with governmental actors to be found to have acted under color of law.

3. In the wake of *Kadic*, corporations have been sued under the ATS (not always successfully) for such things as aiding and abetting murder, torture, sexual assault, and false imprisonment through employment of local military as a security force (Doe v. Exxon Mobil Corp., 654 F.3d 11 (D.C. Cir. 2011) (reversing pre-trial dismissal of ATS claims)); for collaborating with foreign government military forces in intimidating, kidnapping, detaining, and torturing trade unionists (Sinaltrainal v. Coca-Cola Co., 578 F.3d 1252 (11th Cir. 2009) (dismissing suit on pleading grounds)); for aiding and abetting state-sponsored genocide, torture, and crimes against humanity (Presbyterian Church of Sudan v. Talisman Energy, Inc., 582 F.3d 244 (2d Cir. 2009) (dismissing claims), cert. denied, 131 S.Ct. 79 (2010)); for supporting South Africa's apartheid regime (*In re* South African Apartheid Litigation, 346 F. Supp. 2d 538, 554 (S.D.N.Y. 2004) (finding that "doing business in apartheid South Africa is not a violation of international law that would support [an ATS claim]")); for using forced labor in the construction of a state-owned pipeline (Doe I v. Unocal Corp., 395 F.3d 932 (9th Cir. 2002) (finding case proper for jury resolution, prior to decision being vacated for en banc rehearing, which the parties' settlement rendered moot); and for "intranational" environmental pollution and "rights to life and health" (Flores v. Southern Peru Copper Corp., 343 F.3d 140 (2d Cir. 2003) (dismissing claims)).

4. Suits against corporations raised fundamental questions whether corporations—as opposed to individuals—could, in fact, be directly liable for their own human rights violations as a matter of international law (or U.S. law), or whether they could be indirectly liable for aiding and abetting such harms (and if so, what that standard might be). Compare, e.g., *Talisman Energy*, 583 F.3d at 247 (holding, in an ATS suit, that "under international law, a claimant must show that the [corporate] defendant provided substantial assistance with the purpose of facilitating the alleged offense") with *Unocal*, 395 F.3d at 951 (requiring "knowing practical assistance or encouragement that has a substantial effect on the perpetration of [human rights abuses by the military]"). Should any such aiding and abetting liability be imposed under the ATS without legislative authorization? Or is it wholly a question of international law?

5. In **Kiobel v. Royal Dutch Petroleum Co., 621 F.3d 111 (2d Cir. 2010),** cert. granted, 132 S.Ct. 472 (2011), a divided court of appeals concluded that corporations could not be sued under the ATS, because it was not settled as a matter of international law whether corporations could be sued for human rights violations. The question had been specifically left open in *Sosa*—see footnote 20. And the Court's decision in *Mohamad v. Palestinian Authority, supra*—a case decided after the Second Circuit's decision in *Kiobel* and in which the Court concluded that the word "individual" in the TVPA did not include corporations—specifically noted that the word "individual" was missing from the ATS.

The plaintiff in *Kiobel* (a Nigerian) alleged that three multinational oil companies arranged with the Nigerian government to have it use military force to suppress resistance to their drilling in a particular region of Nigeria. On appeal to the Supreme Court, the argument centered on the question whether international law should supply the rule of decision respecting corporate liability, or whether U.S. law (or perhaps the ATS itself) could be looked to instead. After oral argument, however, the Court ordered the case reargued and called for briefing on whether the ATS allowed a federal court to hear suits for violations of international law that took place wholly outside U.S. territory, and if so, in what circumstances. Unlike the question of corporate liability, the extraterritoriality question bears directly on jurisdictional questions. A negative decision on the question of the reach of the ATS would have the obvious potential to undermine ATS decisions such as *Filartiga* and the many cases based on it. And the Court will presumably render a decision on the question of corporate liability only in the event that it concludes that the ATS is available for a claim such as that raised in *Kiobel* itself. The case was reargued on October 2, 2012 and is expected to be decided before the end of the Court's 2012-13 Term.

5. Cases Implicating Foreign Policy Concerns

More problematic for purposes of federal question jurisdiction are non-ATS and non-TVPA cases that implicate U.S. foreign policy concerns. For example, some parties have persuaded courts that, because of the potential impact that a judgment against a foreign corporation might have on the sovereignty interests of its home country and U.S. foreign relations with that country, "federal" questions were sufficiently implicated to make the case one arising under federal law for purposes of § 1331. See, e.g., Torres v. Southern Peru Copper Corp., 113 F.3d 540 (5th Cir. 1997) (upholding federal question jurisdiction when plaintiffs' lawsuit against large (nominally private) Peruvian mining company implicated "vital economic interests" of Peru and "Peru's sovereign interests"). *Torres* and cases like it rest on the Supreme Court's admonition in Banco Nacional de Cuba v. Sabbatino, 376 U.S. 398, 425 (1964), that "our relationships with other members of the international community must be treated exclusively as an aspect of federal law." See also, e.g., Republic of the Philippines v. Marcos, 806 F.2d 344 (2d Cir. 1986) (finding that foreign country's lawsuit brought in state court for conversion and for imposition of a constructive trust on assets of former head of state arose under federal law).

However, *Sabbatino* (discussed in Chapter 3) involved only one particular aspect of international relations law: the Act of State doctrine. That doctrine basically requires U.S. courts not to second guess the validity of certain acts of foreign governments taken on their own soil. Consequently, there is an issue whether *Sabbatino* stands for the broader proposition that any case that might have some impact on the sovereignty interests of foreign countries or on U.S. foreign relations with them, ought to be treated as a case arising under federal law. In addition, in *Torres*, federal law did not appear to create the plaintiffs' cause of action. To be sure, a case can arise under federal law if the relevant federal law is federal common law rather than a federal statute. See Illinois v. City of Milwaukee, 406 U.S. 91, 100 (1972) ("Section 1331 jurisdiction will support claims founded upon federal common law as well as those of a statutory origin"). But to the extent that questions of international law, or foreign relations law, or act of state doctrines might arise in a case—and even assuming that all such questions may properly be treated as a species of federal common law— they might be questions that arise only by way of defense to a state law (or other nonfederal) claim, in violation of the well-pleaded complaint rule. Consider the following opinion's treatment of some of these issues.

Patrickson v. Dole Food Co.

United States Court of Appeals, Ninth Circuit, 2001.[*]
251 F.3d 795.

Kozinski, Circuit Judge.

We consider whether the federal courts have jurisdiction over a class action brought by Latin American banana workers against multinational fruit and chemical companies alleged to have exposed the workers to a toxic pesticide.

I

Dibromochloropropane (DBCP) is a powerful pesticide. Tough on pests, it's no friend to humans either. Absorbed by the skin or inhaled, it's alleged to cause sterility, testicular atrophy, miscarriages, liver damage, cancer and other ail-

---

[*] A writ of certiorari was later dismissed by the Supreme Court on the federal common law issues raised by this case. See Dole Food Co. v. Patrickson, 580 U.S. 468 (2003). Nevertheless, the Court granted certiorari and affirmed as to another issue raised in the case involving the Foreign Sovereign Immunities Act. See Chapter 3, Section A (excerpting the Court's opinion in *Dole Food*).

ments that you wouldn't wish on anyone. Originally manufactured by Dow Chemical and Shell Oil, the pesticide was banned from general use in the United States by the Environmental Protection Agency in 1979. But the chemical companies continued to distribute it to fruit companies in developing nations.

In our case, banana workers from Costa Rica, Ecuador, Guatemala and Panama brought a class action against Dole Food Company, other major fruit companies and chemical companies (hereinafter "Dole") for injuries allegedly sustained from exposure to DBCP in their home countries. This case represents one front in a broad litigation war between these plaintiffs' lawyers and these defendants. In some of the cases, plaintiffs have reportedly won multimillion dollar settlements. * * * In others, defendants have managed to have the cases dismissed for forum non conveniens. * * *

The merits are not before us. Instead, we must decide whether the case is properly in federal court. The workers brought suit in Hawaii state court. * * * Dole likewise removed * * * based on federal-question jurisdiction, 28 U.S.C. § 1331. The district court denied plaintiffs' remand motion and then dismissed the case for forum non conveniens.

II

Dole was entitled to remove the case to federal court if plaintiffs could have brought it there to begin with. *See* 28 U.S.C. § 1441(a). We must therefore consider whether plaintiffs could have brought the case in district court under federal-question jurisdiction * * * [*See id.* at § 1441(b). Dole was a citizen of Hawaii and therefore could not remove on the basis of diversity jurisdiction.—eds.]

A. Federal-Question Jurisdiction

We are courts of limited jurisdiction. This means we hear only those cases that Congress directs and the Constitution permits us to hear. Under Article III, federal courts may assert jurisdiction over federal questions, extending to all cases "arising under this Constitution, the Laws of the United States, and Treaties made, or which shall be made, under their Authority." U.S. Const. art. III, § 2. Although any federal ingredient may be sufficient to satisfy Article III, the statutory grant of jurisdiction under 28 U.S.C. § 1331 requires more. *See* Verlinden B.V. v. Central Bank of Nigeria, 461 U.S. 480, 495 (1983) ("Article III 'arising under' jurisdiction is broader than federal-question jurisdiction under § 1331 . . . .").

Even if the case turns entirely on the validity of a federal defense, federal courts may not assert jurisdiction unless a federal right or immunity is "an element, and an essential one, of the plaintiff's cause of action." Franchise Tax Bd. v. Construction Laborers Vacation Trust, 463 U.S. 1, 11 (1983) * * * . This venerable "well-pleaded complaint" rule keeps us from becoming entangled in state law controversies on the conjecture that federal law may come into play at some point during the litigation; it also ensures that Congress retains control over the size of federal court dockets.

Under conventional principles, the class action here unquestionably arises under state law. Plaintiffs seek relief under the common law of Hawaii for negligence, conspiracy, strict liability, intentional torts and breach of implied warranty. None of the claims has an element premised on a right created by Congress or the Constitution. Dole nonetheless argues that we have federal-question jurisdiction because the case calls for an application of the federal common law of foreign relations.

Although there is no general federal common law, "there are enclaves of federal judge-made law which bind the States." Banco Nacional de Cuba v. Sabbatino, 376 U.S. 398, 426 (1964). In *Sabbatino*, the Court held that one of those enclaves concerns the legal principles governing the nation's relationship with other members of the international community. The case considered whether the "act of state doctrine" requires U.S. courts to recognize the validity of the Cuban government's expropriation of private property. A long-standing common law principle, the act of state doctrine precludes courts from questioning the legality of actions that a foreign government has taken within its own borders. *See* Underhill v. Hernandez, 168 U.S. 250, 252 (1897). *Sabbatino* considered whether the doctrine was a matter of state or federal law.

Because the Constitution gives the federal government exclusive authority to manage the nation's foreign affairs, the Court concluded that "rules of international law should not be left to divergent and perhaps parochial state interpretations." *Sabbatino,* 376 U.S. at 425. Whether a foreign state's act is given legal force in the courts of the United States is a "uniquely federal" question directly implicating our nation's foreign affairs. Therefore, it was appropriate to fashion a single federal standard to govern such cases, rather than rely on a patchwork of separate state standards. Equally important, the Supreme Court in *Sabbatino* reserved to itself ultimate review of all cases raising the act of state doctrine, rather than leaving them to the various state supreme courts. *See* Republic of Iraq v. First Nat'l City Bank, 353 F.2d 47, 51 (2d Cir. 1965) (Friendly, J.) *(Sabbatino* held that "all questions relating to an act of state are questions of federal law, to be determined ultimately, if need be, by the Supreme Court of the United States.").

Federal-question jurisdiction was not an issue in *Sabbatino*; the district court already had jurisdiction because of diversity of citizenship. The question presented was what substantive law would apply—state law pursuant to Erie R.R. Co. v. Tompkins, 304 U.S. 64 (1938), or federal law. *Sabbatino* held that the common law of foreign relations falls outside *Erie's* general rule and so federal law applies. Federal common law is, of course, federal law; so if a plaintiff's claim arises under the federal common law recognized by *Sabbatino*, the federal courts will have jurisdiction under 28 U.S.C. § 1331.

This is as far as *Sabbatino* goes, and it's not far enough, because nothing in plaintiffs' complaint turns on the validity or invalidity of any act of a foreign state. Plaintiffs seek compensation for injuries sustained from the defendants' manufacture, sale and use of DBCP. Plaintiffs don't claim that any foreign government participated in such activities or that the defendants acted under the color of foreign law. The case—at least as framed by plaintiffs—does not require us to evaluate any act of state or apply any principle of international law. The common law of foreign relations will become an issue only when—and if—it is raised as a defense.

Dole nonetheless argues that we must assert federal-question jurisdiction because the case concerns a vital sector of the economies of foreign countries and so has implications for our nation's relations with those countries. Plaintiffs represent a class of perhaps thousands of foreign nationals who allege that large multinational corporations harmed them in their home countries. Dole argues that, by granting relief, American courts would damage the banana industry—one of the most important sectors of those countries' economies—and cast doubt on the balance those governments have struck between agricultural development and labor safety. Although plaintiffs allege only state law claims, Dole argues, this case implicates the "uniquely federal" interest in foreign relations, and so must be heard in a federal forum. In essence, Dole interprets *Sabbatino* as creating an exception not only to *Erie*, but to the well-pleaded complaint rule as well.

Dole's position is not without support. In Torres v. Southern Peru Copper Corp., 113 F.3d 540, 543 (5th Cir. 1997), the Fifth Circuit asserted federal-question jurisdiction over a state tort action brought by hundreds of Peruvian citizens against an American company because of injuries they had allegedly suffered from exposure to toxic gases during copper smelting and refining operations in Peru. The court concluded that, although the Peruvian government was not a party, it had "participated substantially" in the mining project through ownership of the land and minerals on which the mining operation was located. *See id.* The court also noted that the mining industry made up a significant part of Peru's gross national product, and the Peruvian government had vigorously protested to our State Department that the case threatened Peru's sovereign interests. As a consequence, the Fifth Circuit held that the "plaintiffs' complaint raises substantial questions of federal common law by implicating important foreign policy concerns." *Id.* While reaching the opposite result on the facts before it, the Eleventh Circuit seems to have adopted the Fifth Circuit's theory in *Torres. See* Pacheco de Perez v. AT&T Co., 139 F.3d 1368, 1377 (11th Cir. 1998) (noting that, "where a state law action has as a substantial element an issue involving foreign relations or foreign policy matters, federal jurisdiction is present" but concluding that a suit brought by Venezuelan citizens injured in a pipeline explosion did not affect American foreign policy).

Torres and *Pacheco de Perez* relied principally on Republic of Philippines v. Marcos, 806 F.2d 344, 353 (2d Cir. 1986), which seems to have been the first case to conclude that "there is federal question jurisdiction over actions having important foreign policy implications."[4] In *Marcos*, the Republic of the Philippines sued its former dictator to enjoin him from disposing of property allegedly looted from the government and claimed as state property under an executive

---

[4] * * * *Torres* * * * distinguished Aquafaith Shipping, Ltd. v. Jarillas, 963 F.2d 806, 808 (5th Cir. 1992), which had held that the well-pleaded complaint rule applies with full force to cases arising under the federal common law of foreign relations. In *Aquafaith*, the defendants alleged that a maritime suit arose under federal law because the Philippine government had involved itself with the plaintiff's claims. *Aquafaith* rejected the claim on the ground that the foreign government's involvement didn't appear anywhere in the plaintiff's complaint. *Id.* at 809. *Torres* concluded that the plaintiff's claims in *Aquafaith* had not "necessarily implicated vital economic and sovereign interests" of a foreign power, as they did in *Torres*. 113 F.3d at 542 n.8.

order of the Philippine government. *See id.* at 347. Because the Republic's claims rested on the Philippine executive order, *Marcos* could be read as an act of state case, and the Second Circuit may well have grounded federal jurisdiction entirely on that basis. *See id.* at 354 ("Federal jurisdiction is present in any event because the claim raises, as a necessary element, the question whether . . . the American courts should enforce the foreign government's directives to freeze property . . . .").

However, *Marcos* clearly *said* more, broadly suggesting that federal-question jurisdiction could "probably" be premised on the fact that a case may affect our nation's foreign relations, whether or not federal law is raised by the plaintiff's complaint: "An action brought by a foreign government against its former head of state arises under federal common law because of the necessary implications of such an action for United States foreign relations." *Id.* This reads far too much into *Sabbatino.* As noted, *Sabbatino* was about choice of law, not jurisdiction. The Court left no doubt that the substantive law of foreign relations must be federal, and it stressed the need for national uniformity. But *Sabbatino* does not say that federal courts alone are competent to develop this body of law. To the contrary, *Sabbatino* notes that the law of foreign relations is like other "enclaves of federal judge-made law which bind the States," such as the rules filling the interstices of federal statutes and the laws regulating interstate boundary issues. *Sabbatino,* 376 U.S. at 426. The Court's reference to binding the states makes sense only if one assumes that state courts will be called upon to apply the law of foreign relations. *Sabbatino* says as much: "The act of state doctrine is a principle of decision binding on federal and state courts alike . . . ." *Id.* at 427; *see also* Henry Friendly, *In Praise of Erie—and of the New Federal Common Law,* 39 N.Y.U.L. Rev. 383, 405 (1964) ("*Erie* led to the emergence of a federal decisional law in areas of national concern that is truly uniform because, under the *supremacy clause,* it is binding in every forum . . . .").

State courts apply federal law in a wide variety of cases and, by doing so, they necessarily develop it. This does not undermine the nationwide uniformity of federal law much more than having somewhat different applications of federal law in the various federal circuits. Ultimately, the Supreme Court has the final say on any question of federal law, whether it arises in federal or state court, and this is thought sufficient to ensure nationwide uniformity in areas as diverse as criminal procedure, patent law and labor law.

We see no reason to treat the federal common law of foreign relations any differently than other areas of federal law. Certainly, federal courts have preeminence in developing all areas of federal law by virtue of the fact that almost all cases premised on federal law may be brought in or removed to federal court. In addition, Congress has provided federal jurisdiction in certain cases implicating our foreign relations, regardless of the nature of the claim. *See, e.g.,* 28 U.S.C. § 1251(b)(1) (suits where ambassadors or other foreign government officials are parties); *id.* § 1351 (suits against foreign consuls or other diplomatic personnel); *id.* § 1330 (suits against a foreign state); *see also id.* § 1350 (suits brought by an alien for a tort committed in violation of international law). What Congress has not done is to extend federal-question jurisdiction to all suits where the federal common law of foreign relations might arise as an issue. We interpret congressional silence outside these specific grants of jurisdiction as an endorsement of the well-pleaded complaint rule.

We therefore decline to follow *Marcos*, *Torres* and *Pacheco de Perez* insofar as they stand for the proposition that the federal courts may assert jurisdiction over a case simply because a foreign government has expressed a special interest in its outcome. *Accord In re* Tobacco/Governmental Health Care Costs Litig., 100 F. Supp. 2d 31, 36-38 (D.D.C. 2000). It may well be that our foreign relations will be implicated by the pendency of a lawsuit on a subject that affects that government's sovereign interests; the courts in *Marcos* and *Torres* certainly believed this to be the case. But we see no logical connection between such an effect and the assertion of federal-question jurisdiction. That the case is litigated in federal court, rather than state court, will not reduce the impact of the case on the foreign government. Federal judges cannot dismiss a case because a foreign government finds it irksome, nor can they tailor their rulings to accommodate a non-party. Federal judges, like state judges, are bound to decide cases before them according to the rule of law. If a foreign government finds the litigation offensive, it may lodge a protest with our government; our political branches can then respond in whatever way they deem appropriate—up to and including passing legislation. Our government may, of course, communicate its own views as to the conduct of the litigation, and the court—whether state or federal—can take those views into account. [7] But it is quite a different matter to suggest that courts—state or federal—will tailor their rulings to accommodate the expressed interests of a foreign nation that is not even a party.

Nor do we understand how a court can go about evaluating the foreign policy implications of another government's expression of interest. Assuming that foreign relations are an appropriate consideration at all, the relevant question is not whether the foreign government is pleased or displeased by the litigation, but how the case affects the interests of the United States. That is an inherently political judgment, one that courts—whether state or federal—are not competent to make. *See* Container Corp. of Am. v. Franchise Tax Bd., 463 U.S. 159, 194 (1983) ("This Court has little competence in determining precisely when foreign nations will be offended by particular acts . . . ."); Chicago & S. Air Lines, Inc. v. Waterman S.S. Corp., 333 U.S. 103, 111 (1948) ("The very nature of executive decisions as to foreign policy is political, not judicial."); *In re* Tobacco Litig., 100 F. Supp. 2d at 38 ("The federal courts have little context or expertise by which to analyze and address the potential implications of a lawsuit on foreign relations."). If courts were to take the interests of the foreign government into account, they would be conducting foreign policy by deciding whether it serves our national interests to continue with the litigation, dismiss it on some ground such as forum non conveniens, or deal with it in some other way. *See* Jack L. Goldsmith, *Federal Courts, Foreign Affairs, and Federalism*, 83 Va. L. Rev. 1617, 1667 (1997). Because such political judgments are not within the competence of either state or federal courts, we can see no support for the proposition that federal courts are better equipped than state courts to deal with cases raising such concerns.

As Justice Frankfurter noted in Romero v. International Terminal Operating Co., 358 U.S. 354, 379 (1959), federal courts must be hesitant "to expand the jurisdiction of the federal courts through a broad reading of jurisdictional statutes." If federal courts are so much better suited than state courts for handling cases that might raise foreign policy concerns, Congress will surely pass a statute giving us that jurisdiction. Because we see no evidence that Congress meant for the federal courts to assert jurisdiction over cases simply because foreign governments have an interest in them, we must part company with our sister circuits. * * *

III

The federal courts do not have jurisdiction over this case * * * [W]e REVERSE the judgment of the district court and REMAND with instructions that the district court remand the case to Hawaii state court.

NOTES AND QUESTIONS FOR DISCUSSION

1. As *Dole* points out, there is a split among lower courts in connection with the question of when, if ever, a case that touches on foreign relations issues will be treated as one that arises under federal law. *Dole* probably expresses what might be called the strict view. *Torres*, *Marcos,* and other cases noted by *Dole* take a more relaxed view. Note that two sets of issues are involved in such cases: (1) To what extent do the international law or foreign relations law issues presented by a case operate as genuinely federal law?, and (2) Assuming the case presents genuinely federal issues, are they ones that arise on the face of the plaintiff's well-pleaded complaint—i.e., are they issues that the plaintiffs bear the burden of pleading and proving in order to prevail on their nonfederal claim? *Dole*'s "strict view" seems to focus primarily on the second of these concerns.

2. Note also in connection with inquiry (2), that—subsequent to *Dole*—the Supreme Court has narrowed the circumstances in which a case premised on a state law (or nonfederal law) cause of action will be found to arise under federal law, simply because federal law forms some element of the plaintiff's claim. See Empire Healthchoice Assur., Inc. v. McVeigh, 547 U.S. 677, 701 (2006) (noting that such cases constitute a "slim category" and that "it takes more than a federal element to open the arising under door"); Grable & Sons Metal Prods., Inc. v. Darue Engineering & Mfg., 545 U.S. 308, 313 (2005) (noting that an important consideration in such cases is whether the sort of claim is one that will have only a slight impact on federal court dockets). How should these more recent developments impact cases such as *Torres* and *Marcos*?

3. Of course, even if the plaintiff's claim purports to be premised on nonfederal law alone, it is possible that her claim is nevertheless federal. Under Metropolitan Life Ins. Co. v. Taylor, 481 U.S. 58 (1987), federal law may sometimes "completely pre-empt" the plaintiff's attempted nonfederal claim, effectively converting it into a federal claim. In such settings, the focus is typically on congressional intent to displace the pre-existing state law claim and substitute a federal claim in its place. See id. at 66-67. See also Beneficial Nat'l Bank v. Anderson, 539 U.S. 1 (2003). Note, however, that such pre-emption may be harder to argue if the plaintiff's claims are ones that only implicate federal common law, because it may be harder to argue that there is a federal common law claim that has substituted itself for the pre-existing state claim. Alternatively, it is possible that the relief sought by the plaintiff under state law could be constitutionally pre-empted in a different sense—for example, by principles of foreign relations law. But if so, that would likely present a more ordinary type of preemption question (as opposed to "complete" pre-emption), in which case the pre-emption questions would only be a defense to relief on the nonfederal claim. As such, the case could not be brought in federal court in the first instance as one arising under federal law nor could it be removed from state court on that basis.

4.   Sometimes, the affected foreign country may raise a protest to the suit, even though it is not a party. In *Torres*, for example, the Peruvian government filed a letter with the State Department and an amicus brief with the federal courts. Although the *Torres* court noted that these actions "standing alone" do not "create a question of federal law," they nevertheless "alerted [the court] to the foreign policy issues implicated by this case." 113 F.3d at 542-43. Indeed, outcomes may turn on the presence or absence of such foreign country protest. With *Torres*, compare, e.g., Pacheco de Perez v. AT&T Co., 139 F.3d 1368 (11th Cir. 1998) (finding it "significant" for federal jurisdiction purposes that the Venezuelan government took no position on whether the suit should proceed in the U.S. or in Venezuela), and O'Neill v. St. Jude Medical, Inc., Civ. No. 2004 U.S. Dist. LEXIS 15203 (D. Minn. Aug. 5, 2004) (noting absence of foreign governmental involvement as relevant factor in determining federal question jurisdiction).

5.   As noted earlier in this chapter, alien parties often seek out federal courts for their perceived greater hospitality as compared to state courts. Yet it was the U.S. defendant that was arguing for federal court jurisdiction in *Dole*, while the foreign plaintiffs were arguing that the case should be heard in state court. That was also true in *Torres* and *Pacheco de Perez*, both discussed in *Dole*. In all three of these cases, one of the primary reasons for the defendant's seeking out federal jurisdiction on removal was the possibility that the U.S. defendant could then attempt to have the case dismissed on *forum non conveniens* grounds, thus forcing the plaintiffs to refile in a foreign country. Thus, Dole's argument in favor of federal court jurisdiction in these cases was so that federal jurisdiction would ultimately go unexercised.

NOTE ON "UNIVERSAL JURISDICTION"

International law recognizes that some violations of international law are capable of being subject to "universal jurisdiction." In other words, the courts of a country may hear lawsuits over certain kinds of wrongs even if the forum otherwise has no connection with the wrong committed or with the parties involved. The Restatement (Third) of Foreign Relations of the United States § 404 (1987), for example, would authorize universal jurisdiction over offenses "recognized by the community of nations as of universal concern, such as piracy, slave trade, attacks on or hijacking of aircraft, genocide, war crimes, and perhaps certain acts of terrorism."

Even if such universal jurisdiction were to be embraced in the U.S. as a matter of principle, there would still be hurdles to its implementation. Congress has the power to define and punish violations of the Law of Nations, and it has become a basic principle of U.S. law that the federal government may not prosecute for a crime that has not been statutorily prescribed. As for possible civil actions based on such a principle, there would have to be good subject matter jurisdiction over the claim if suit were to be brought in a federal court, in addition to personal jurisdiction. International piracy, for example, might fall under the rubric of admiralty jurisdiction under Article III.

Absent resort to a jurisdictional hook such as admiralty, and absent diversity, the claim itself would have to arise under federal law. If a federal statute created the plaintiff's cause of action, there might be problems surrounding the question whether Congress intended for the statute to have "universal" territorial application, given the limits on extraterritoriality usually associated with federal legislation. See Chapter 8. Absent a congressional statute clearly meant to apply extraterritorially (or universally), perhaps the claim could be said to arise under the law of some foreign nation. But if so, that would mean that the case did not arise under federal law. On the other hand, if the claim were a violation of rights under international law, then the federal court would have to face the question noted above—namely whether any or all claims arising under international law necessarily arise under federal law, within the meaning of Article III (and, apart from claims under the ATS, within the meaning of the general federal question statute). Some claims under the ATS, such as those in *Filartiga*, appear to reflect the exercise of a kind of universal jurisdiction. But as noted above, even in the ATS setting there may be some question whether it applies universally, as a matter of congressional intent, and even if it does so apply, then in what settings.

6. Cases Arising Under Treaties

It may also be possible for parties to bring suit to enforce violations of rights under treaties, and thereby secure federal jurisdiction. Indeed, the Alien Tort Statute itself speaks of an alien's suit for a "tort only, in violation of . . . a treaty"—not just "in violation of the law of nations." And, unlike with the law of nations, no similar doubts whether a treaty is genuinely federal law would arise in such cases under the ATS. But treaty claims might also be brought without reference to the ATS, as cases arising under federal law under the general federal question statute, 28 U.S.C. § 1331—a statute that was not in place at the time of the enactment of the ATS. Under the Constitution's Supremacy Clause, moreover, treaties into which the U.S. has entered are the supreme law of the land, binding on the federal and state courts alike. U.S. Const. art. VI, cl. 2. And unlike under the ATS, U.S. citizens could conceivably maintain actions against treaty violators, assuming that they can properly assert rights under the treaty and assuming that they have standing to sue.

A primary problem with treaty enforcement, however, is that many (if not most) treaties—particularly multilateral treaties—are not considered to be "self-enforcing." That is, it usually takes congressional implementation before a civil cause of action will be available to enforce a violation of a treaty. Of course, it might be possible for a treaty to be invoked defensively in litigation (even if the treaty is not otherwise self-enforcing) to avoid liability. But even that possibility is not one on which scholars agree. See Ann Woolhandler, *Treaties, Self-Execution, and the Public Law Litigation Model*, 42 Va. J. Int'l L. 757, 767 & n.51 (2002) (noting debate over availability of defensive invocation of non-self-enforcing treaties). And if the treaty question arises by way of defense only, the case will not be able to be filed originally in a federal court or removed there if filed in state court.

Note also that the preliminary question whether a treaty is self-enforcing is a matter of interpretation of the treaty, although there is disagreement as to how that determination ought to be made. For many courts, the relevant intent is that of the "signatory parties as manifested by the language of the instrument, and, if the instrument is uncertain, recourse must be had to the circumstances surrounding its execution." Diggs v. Richardson, 555 F.2d 848, 851 (D.C. Cir. 1976). On the other hand, The Restatement (Third) of Foreign Relations of the United States § 111 comment. (h), states that because "it is ordinarily for the U.S. to decide how it will carry out its international obligations," it is "the intention of the U.S. [that] determines whether an agreement is to be self-executing in the U.S. or should await implementation" by the political branches. Does one approach make more sense than the other?

In the cases that follow, we offer two examples of parties seeking to vindicate rights in connection with the Warsaw Convention of 1929 (which covers international transportation by air) and its successor, the Montreal Convention of 1999. We chose these cases in part because they illustrate how courts go about solving the question of when, if ever, a federal cause of action should be available for enforcing a treaty violation, and what role (if any) might remain for recovery under state law.

Benjamins v. British European Airways

Unites States Court of Appeals, Second Circuit, 1978.
572 F.2d 913.

LUMBARD, CIRCUIT JUDGE.

This appeal, arising out of the death of Hilde Benjamins in the air crash disaster at Staines, England, on June 18, 1972, once again presents us with the much-discussed question whether the Warsaw Convention [Convention for the Unification of Certain Rules Relating to International Transportation by Air, 49 Stat. 3000, T.S. No. 876 (concluded Oct. 12, 1929; adhered to by United States June 27, 1934)] creates a cause of action. The District Court for the Eastern District dismissed the complaint herein, believing itself bound by our prior decisions to answer that question in the negative. We reverse.

I

On June 18, 1972, a Trident 1 Jet Aircraft—designed and manufactured by Hawker Siddeley Aviation, Ltd. ["HSA"], and owned and operated by British

European Airways ["BEA"]—took off for Brussels from London's Heathrow Airport. Soon thereafter, the plane stalled and crashed into a field, killing all 112 passengers, including Hilde Benjamins. Hilde Benjamins was survived by her husband Abraham; both were Dutch citizens permanently residing in California. BEA and HSA are British corporations with their principal places of business in the United Kingdom. The ticket on which Hilde Benjamins was travelling had been purchased in Los Angeles, and clearly provided "international transportation" within the meaning of Article 1 of the Convention. Therefore, since the United States and the United Kingdom are both High Contracting Parties, the Convention is applicable to this proceeding.

This suit for wrongful death and baggage loss was brought in April of 1974 in the Eastern District of New York by Abraham Benjamins, as representative of his widow's estate, on behalf of himself and the children of the marriage. * * * The major allegations in the complaint invoked Articles 17 and 18 of the Convention. These read, in relevant part, as follows:

> *Article 17.* The carrier shall be liable for damage sustained in the event of the death or wounding of a passenger or any other bodily injury suffered by a passenger, if the accident which caused the damage so sustained took place on board the aircraft or in the course of any of the operations of embarking or disembarking.

> *Article 18(1).* The carrier shall be liable for damage sustained in the event of the destruction or loss of, or of damage to, any checked baggage or any goods, if the occurrence which caused the damage so sustained took place during the transportation by air.

Dismissed once for lack of subject matter jurisdiction—only diversity was originally alleged—the complaint was amended to invoke 28 U.S.C. §§ 1331 * * *. After both sides had submitted briefs, Judge Weinstein ruled that this suit did not "arise" under a treaty of the United States, as § 1331 requires; he relied on Second Circuit precedent indicating that the Convention does not create a cause of action, but only establishes conditions for a cause of action created by domestic law. This appeal followed. [There was no objection to personal jurisdiction respecting the two defendant. Subject matter jurisdiction over HSA's claim was premised on pendent jurisdiction—eds.]

II

The first question we address is whether any court in this country has jurisdiction in the "international or treaty sense." Only then may we consider "the power of a particular United States court, under federal statutes and practice, to hear a Warsaw Convention case—jurisdiction in the domestic law sense." *Id.*

Jurisdiction in the treaty sense is determined by Article 28(1) of the Convention, which provides that

> an action for damages must be brought, at the option of the plaintiff, in the territory of one of the high contracting parties, either [1] before the court of the domicile of the carrier or [2] of his principal place of business, or [3] where he has a place of business through which the contract has been made, or [4] before the court at the place of destination.

The third alternative of Article 28(1) is satisfied in this case: the ticket which constituted the contract of carriage was purchased in Los Angeles, through BEA. The fourth alternative appears also to fit, as decedent's round-trip ticket provided for an ultimate destination in the United States.

Nonetheless, courts in the United States, and particularly the federal courts, are not the only possible forum for Abraham Benjamins. The courts of England are open to his suit—permitted by the first and second alternatives of Article 28(1)—as are the state courts of California. Plaintiff's burden is not met by a showing that Article 28(1) permits some court of this country to hear his complaint; he must further show that some jurisdictional statute permits a federal court to do so.

* * *

IV

Accordingly, we must determine whether any of the causes of action pleaded by Benjamins "arise under" the Warsaw Convention. It is true that in the past we have said that the Warsaw Convention does not create a cause of action. We believe, however, that a re-examination of the question requires a different answer.

A

At the time the United States adhered to the Convention, it seemed obvious to all that the Convention created causes of action for wrongful death or personal injury (Article 17), and for damage to baggage (Article 18). One court went so far as to say, "If the Convention did not create a cause of action in Art. 17, it is difficult to understand just what Art. 17 did do." Salamon v. Koninklijke Luchtvaart Maatschappij, N.V., 107 N.Y.S.2d 768, 773 (Sup. Ct. 1951), *aff'd mem.*, 281 App. Div. 965, 120 N.Y.S.2d 917 (1st Dept. 1953).

The view that the Convention does not create a cause of action is, in large part, attributable to two cases we decided in the 1950s, Komlos v. Compagnie Nationale Air France, 209 F.2d 436 (2d Cir. 1953), *rev'g on other grounds*, 111 F. Supp. 393 (S.D.N.Y. 1952), *cert. denied*, 348 U.S. 820 (1954), and Noel v. Linea Aeropostal Venezolana, 247 F.2d 677 (2d Cir.), *cert. denied*, 355 U.S. 907 (1957) * * *.

The analysis on which this structure of holding rests is to be found in Judge Leibell's opinion for the district court in *Komlos*. In determining whether a cause of action had been assigned to an insurer or remained the property of an estate, Judge Leibell held that the action envisioned by Article 17 was one created by domestic law, except in cases where the forum provided no analogous action.

Judge Leibell relied heavily on a letter sent by Secretary of State Cordell Hull to President Roosevelt on March 31, 1934, recommending adherence to the Convention. In the course of a lengthy discussion of the benefits of adherence, Hull wrote: "The effect of article 17 (ch. III) of the Convention is to create a presumption of liability against the aerial carrier on the mere happening of an accident occasioning injury or death of a passenger subject to certain defenses allowed under the Convention to the aerial carrier." [1934] U.S. Av. Rep. 240,

243. This was seen by Judge Leibell as clear evidence that the Convention created only presumptions, not new causes of action.

In reversing Judge Leibell on another issue, we did not refer to the portion of his opinion discussed above, or, indeed, even mention the Warsaw Convention. Nonetheless, in *Noel*, we followed our opinion in *Komlos*, which, we said, had "impliedly agreed" with Judge Leibell. Though most of our opinion in *Noel* was devoted to disapproving Judge Leibell's suggestion that Article 17 might create a cause of action for wrongful death where domestic law did not, it is apparent that—however founded—*Noel*, as the law of this circuit, stands for the proposition that the Convention does not create a cause of action.

Recently, an inconsistency has developed between this rule and another line of Warsaw cases we have decided. For example, in Reed v. Wiser, 555 F.2d 1079 (2d Cir.), *cert. denied*, 434 U.S. 922 (1977), we indicated—without addressing the question in the instant case—that "the Convention was intended to act as an international uniform law," *id.* at 1083, and that the substantive law of the Convention was binding on the forum, *id.* at 1092. The time has come to examine the question whether our view of the Convention as an internationally binding body of uniform air law permits us any longer to deny that a cause of action may be founded on the Convention itself, rather than on any domestic law.

B

1. The minutes and documents of the meetings, held in 1925 and 1929, which led to the adoption of the Convention do not specifically indicate whether the parties contemplated that an action for damages under the Convention would arise under the terms of the treaty or those of domestic law. What is made quite clear is the extent to which the delegates were concerned with creating a uniform law to govern air crashes, with absolutely no reference to any national law (except for the questions of standing to sue for wrongful death, effects of contributory negligence and procedural matters; *see* Articles 21, 24(2), 28(2)).

The delegates were concerned lest major air crash cases be brought before courts of nations whose courts were not (according to current Western standards) well organized, nor whose substantive law (according to the same standards) progressive. To avoid the "prospect of a junglelike chaos," *Reed v. Wiser, supra*, 555 F.2d at 1092, the Convention laid down rules that were to be universally applicable. While it is not literally inconsistent with this universal applicability to insist that a would-be plaintiff first find an appropriate cause of action in the domestic law of a signatory authorized by Article 28 to hear his claim, it is inconsistent with its spirit. This inconsistency is an argument against the rule of *Noel* and *Komlos*, for the Convention is to be so construed as to further its purposes to the greatest extent possible, even if that entails rejecting a literal reading.

2. Other articles of the Convention throw some light on the question whether Articles 17 and 18 create causes of action. Article 30(3) provides that in the case of transportation by several carriers constituting one undivided transportation,

as regards baggage or goods, the passenger or consignor shall have a right of action against the first carrier, and the passenger or consignee who is entitled to delivery shall have a right of action against the last carrier, and further, each may take action against the carrier who performed the transportation during which the destruction, loss, damage, or delay took place. . . .

The most reasonable interpretation of this section is that Articles 18 and 30(3) create a cause of action against the appropriate carrier when more than one carrier is involved. See Seth v. British Overseas Airways Corp., 329 F.2d 302, 305 (1st Cir.), *cert. denied*, 379 U.S. 858 (1964): "Thus, the Convention not only imposes liability on an air carrier for the loss of checked baggage but also gives a passenger whose baggage is lost a right of action to enforce that liability. Seth's action, therefore, seems clearly to be one arising under a treaty of the United States." There is no reason to believe that the Convention's effect is any different when only one carrier is involved.

Article 24 been cited by proponents of both views of the Convention. * * * The unofficial translation reads:

(1) In the cases covered by articles 18 and 19 any action for damages, however founded, can only be brought subject to the conditions and limits set out in this convention. (2) In the cases covered by article 17 the provisions of the preceding paragraph shall also apply. . . .

The crucial phrases, of course, are "however founded" ("a quelque titre que ce soit"), and "conditions" ("conditions"). There is no internal evidence to indicate whether "however founded" was intended to refer to a number of possible domestic law sources or to a number of possible factual bases for the envisioned action.

As to "conditions," that term in English does imply that the source of the action must be sought elsewhere than the Convention, which supplies only conditions and limits. Nonetheless, there is some evidence for the view that the French has not been so translated here as to provide the best interpretation of the delegates' meaning, and that "basis" or "terms" would be a closer translation in this context of "conditions." * * * The arguments as to Article 24 are not conclusive either way.

3. More compelling is the evidence of how other signatories of the Convention have interpreted its provisions. The clearest picture is found in other common-law jurisdictions. In the statute enacting the original 1929 Convention in the United Kingdom, it was provided that "any liability imposed by Article seventeen of the said [Warsaw Convention] on a carrier in respect of the death of a passenger shall be in substitution for any liability of the carrier in respect of the death of that passenger either under any statute or at common law. . . ." Carriage by Air Act, 1932, 22 & 23 Geo. 5, c. 36, § 1(4). When the Convention was reenacted as amended at the Hague in 1955, Carriage by Air Act, 1962, 9 & 10 Eliz. 2, c. 27, this language was omitted, but there is no indication that any change of substantive law was intended. No case law since 1962 has demonstrated that the

source of carrier liability lies anywhere but in the Convention. *See also* Carriage by Air Act, 1939, 3 Geo. 6, c. 12 (Canada).

V

The fact that a proposition of law has been accepted for some twenty years is evidently a sign that circumspection is needed in seeking to overturn that proposition. We recognize that our holdings in *Komlos* and *Noel* have become the rule not of this circuit alone, but of others as well. *See, e.g.,* Maugnie v. Compagnie Nationale Air France, 549 F.2d 1256, 1258 (9th Cir.), *cert. denied*, 431 U.S. 974 (1977). Nonetheless, we are convinced that—in light of both the paucity of analysis that accompanied the creation of the rule and the strong arguments in favor of the opposite rule—the *Komlos/Noel* rule ought no longer to be followed.

We do not believe that the passing remark of Secretary Hull in a lengthy letter was intended to state the total of what Article 17 might provide; we do not see what there was about our decision in *Komlos* that constituted implicit agreement with Judge Leibell, and compelled the result in *Noel*; we do not find technical and disputable interpretations of the language of other articles of the Convention conclusive in determining this important question of policy.

We do, on the other hand, believe that the desirability of uniformity in international air law can best be recognized by holding that the Convention, otherwise universally applicable, is also the universal source of a right of action. We do see that uniformity of development can better be achieved by making federal as well as state courts accessible to Convention litigation. We do find the opinions of our sister signatories to be entitled to considerable weight.

One factor which makes federal jurisdiction peculiarly appropriate in large air crash cases was not present at the time *Komlos* and *Noel* were decided. Section 1407 of 28 U.S.C., enacted by Pub. L. No. 90-296, 90th Cong., 2d Sess., 82 Stat. 109 (April 29, 1968), created the Judicial Panel on Multidistrict Litigation, and authorized the creation of the procedures found in the *Manual for Complex Litigation*. These procedures, such as consolidation and assignment to one expert judge, can—by reducing expenses and expediting dispositions—benefit all parties to air disaster actions, in which the plaintiff/victims may come from many different parts of the country. Obviously, these procedures are unavailable among the courts of the several states.

Finally, we do not anticipate any large increase in the volume of federal litigation as a result of our holding. Most cases will fall under 28 U.S.C. § 1332, as they do today; only when plaintiffs and defendants are all aliens, but the United States is a nation with treaty jurisdiction, will it be necessary to invoke 28 U.S.C. § 1331.

VI

Accordingly, we reverse Judge Weinstein's order of dismissal. We leave it to his discretion to determine, in a manner consistent with our opinion, which of Benjamins' causes of action he may decide and which, if any, he may not; in particular, we leave to him the question whether to take pendent jurisdiction over the claims against HSA.

Reversed and remanded for further proceedings consistent with our opinion.

VAN GRAAFEILAND, CIRCUIT JUDGE, dissenting:

* * *

In 1934, when Secretary of State Cordell Hull sent the Warsaw Convention to President Roosevelt for transmission to the Senate, he wrote that the effect of Article 17 was to "create a presumption of liability." We may assume, I believe, that the Senate relied upon the Secretary of State's assurances. Without question, the courts have done so. *See Noel v. Linea Aeropostal Venezolana*, 247 F.2d 677 (2d Cir.), *cert. denied*, 355 U.S. 907 (1957) * * *. In *Noel* we said:

> Secretary of State Hull's letter to President Roosevelt, dated March 31, 1934, indicated that the effect of Article 17 on which plaintiffs rely for their argument was only to create a presumption of liability, leaving it for local law to grant the right of action. As one authority has stated, the purpose of the Convention was only "to effect a uniformity of procedure and remedies." Orr, *The Warsaw Convention*, 31 Va. L. Rev. 423 (1945);
> * * *

Completely reversing our field, we now hold that Article 17 creates a cause of action for wrongful death. * * * A court should proceed cautiously when asked to overturn a well-settled doctrine of law. This is especially true in this case because a sensitive question concerning the scope of federal jurisdiction is involved. But even more importantly, circumspection is required here because amendments to the Warsaw Convention that may end this entire controversy are currently pending [in the political branches].

* * *

Even if I were persuaded that a re-examination of *Noel* was appropriate at this time, I would not be convinced that it was incorrectly decided. Article 17 states that "the carrier shall be liable for damage sustained in the event of the death or wounding of a passenger . . ." and the plain language of this article is the majority's strongest argument that the Convention created a right to sue. However, a close analysis of this section reveals that its meaning is not as clear as might appear on its face.

At the time the Convention was drafted it was generally accepted in this country that a cause of action for wrongful death could not be maintained in the absence of a specific statute authorizing such suit. * * * All American states have such statutes, but the statutes differ widely with respect to "the persons for whose benefit a death action may be maintained, and the measure, elements and distribution of damages recoverable." 1 S. Speiser, *Recovery for Wrongful Death* § 1.9 at 29 (2d ed. 1975) (footnotes omitted). Although the statutes take different approaches, they are alike in the fact that they all expressly deal with these crucial questions. Article 17 of the Convention, on the other hand, does not specify who are the beneficiaries of the action, nor what types of damages may be recovered. Indeed, the Convention provides that an action for a passenger's death is brought "without prejudice to the questions as to who are the persons who have the right to bring suit and what are their respective rights." Article

24(2). Thus, Article 17 at best goes only half way towards creating a cause of action for wrongful death. I am not persuaded that this legislatively created "liability," which designates neither the beneficiaries of the right of recovery nor the measure of their damages creates a cause of action. The phrase "the carrier shall be liable" had a different purpose, as becomes apparent when Article 17 is examined in the context of the entire Convention.

The purpose of Warsaw was "to effect a uniformity of procedure and remedies." *Noel*, 247 F.2d at 679 (quoting Orr, *The Warsaw Convention*, 31 Va. L. Rev. 423 (1945)). To accomplish this goal, the drafters could have created a single cause of action to be asserted wherever suit was brought for wrongful death in international air travel. Alternatively, the drafters could have created a set of conditions and limitations uniformly applicable to all the various causes of action created by local law of the countries around the world. The drafters' choice of the latter alternative is evidenced by Article 24, which provides that any action "however founded" may only be brought "subject to" the "conditions and limits set out in [the] convention." Husserl v. Swiss Air Transport Co., 388 F. Supp. 1238, 1251-52 (S.D.N.Y. 1975). Thus, no matter whether the action is founded in tort or contract, whether in domestic or foreign law, the limitations and conditions of the Convention will apply. See *Reed v. Wiser*, 555 F.2d at 1092.

Within this structure, Article 17 plays an important role. The basic trade-off under Warsaw was that the carrier was given a limitation on liability while the claimant gained a simplified recovery procedure. * * * The claimant's task was simplified by shifting the burden of proof to the defendant. The manner in which the drafters shifted the burden is important. By stating that "the carrier shall be liable" in Article 17, the drafters created a presumption of liability which could then be rebutted under Article 20(1) by the carrier's proof that it was free from negligence. A. Lowenfeld & A. Mendelsohn, *The United States and the Warsaw Convention*, 80 Harv. L. Rev. 497, 519-22 (1967). The new burden of proof, like the limitation on liability, is applicable to any action "however founded." Viewed in this light, I think it entirely reasonable to conclude, as we did in *Noel*, that the phrase "the carrier shall be liable" does not itself create a right to sue, but merely conditions the cause of action generated by the underlying substantive law.

The majority finds a right of action in the language of Article 17 mainly because it believes that "the desirability of uniformity in international air law can best be recognized" in this way. Even were I to agree with this approach, I should not be sure that the majority opinion promotes uniformity. There is no reason to believe that the new right of action is exclusive. State and federal rights of action will co-exist and may be pleaded in the same case. Moreover, federal courts will be required to supply the elements missing in the Convention's "cause of action". Unless the federal courts develop a body of federal common law, they must look to other sources of law for these elements. They must look to local law to determine whether a plaintiff was guilty of contributory negligence, Article 21, whether his damage was caused by the carrier's wilful misconduct, Article 25, whether he has a right of recovery for wrongful death, and the measure of his damages, Article 24(2). There can be no uniformity here.

I fear that when my brothers discuss uniformity, they are really talking about federal jurisdiction. State courts handle Warsaw Convention matters as wisely and fairly as do federal courts and with greater knowledge of the state law that must be applied. I see no reason to upset a long-standing rule of law simply to give the plaintiff access to the federal courts.

For the foregoing reasons, I respectfully dissent.

Narkiewicz-Laine v. Scandanavian Airlines Systems

Unites States District Court, Northern District of Illinois, 2008.

587 F. Supp. 2d 888.

PHILIP G. REINHARD, DISTRICT JUDGE.

Plaintiff, Christian K. Narkiewicz-Laine, filed this action claiming breach of contract against defendant, Scandinavian Airlines Systems, in state court, the 15th Judicial Circuit Court, Jo Daviess County, Illinois. Defendant removed under 28 U.S.C. § 1441 claiming this court has subject matter jurisdiction under 28 U.S.C. § 1331 because the action arises under a treaty of the United States, the Convention for the Unification of Certain Rules for International Carriage by Air Concluded at Montreal, Canada, May 28, 1999 ("Montreal Convention"). Defendant argues this treaty preempts plaintiff's state-law claims. Plaintiff moves to remand and defendant moves to transfer venue to the Eastern Division of the Northern District of Illinois.

Plaintiff's complaint alleges two claims: (1) defendant's flight, on which plaintiff was a scheduled passenger, from Dublin to Copenhagen on March 6, 2008, was delayed causing him to miss his connection to Helsinki and the flight he was rescheduled on arrived 1½ hours later in Helsinki than his originally scheduled flight; (2) defendant did not refund or re-book another ticket plaintiff purchased to fly from Dublin to Oslo on June 21, 2006, even though plaintiff had called defendant on the scheduled day of departure and advised defendant he was sick and unable to travel.

Plaintiff seeks to remand arguing "a refund of a ticket has nothing to do whatsoever with the Montreal Convention or a Treaty with the United States . . . . This was a simple credit card transaction that resulted in a broken contract." Plaintiff further asserts that his claim for refusal to re-book his Oslo flight due to illness is not governed by the Montreal Convention nor any other treaty. Defendant agrees that the claim for the Oslo flight is not covered by the Montreal Convention but asserts supplemental jurisdiction under 28 U.S.C. § 1367 over this claim.

Ordinarily, when a case is removed, the court looks only to plaintiff's statement of his own claim in his well-pleaded complaint to see if it is one arising under "the Constitution or a law or treaty of the United States" so as to confer federal-question jurisdiction. * * * Generally, federal preemption is a defense to a state law claim and does not provide grounds for removal because a *defense* based on federal law is not a *claim* arising under federal law. See Metro Life Ins. Co. v. Taylor, 481 U.S. 58, 63 (1987). Complete preemption is the exception to this rule. "Complete preemption, really a jurisdictional rather than a preemption doctrine, confers * * * federal jurisdiction in certain instances where Congress intended the scope of a federal law to be so broad as to entirely replace any state-law claim." Franciscan Skemp Healthcare, Inc. v. Central States Joint Bd. Health & Welfare Trust Fund, 538 F.3d 594 (7th Cir. 2008). The question is whether the Montreal Convention completely preempts any state-law claims so that this action is in reality based on the treaty. *See id.*

The Montreal Convention entered into force on September 5, 2003, after its ratification by the United States Senate. *See* Sompo Japan Ins., Inc. v. Nippon Cargo Airlines Co., Ltd., 522 F.3d 776, 781 (7th Cir. 2008). The Montreal Convention replaced the Warsaw Convention and its supplementary amendments added over the years. *Id.* at 780-81. The Montreal Convention, according to its terms, "applies to all international carriage of persons, baggage or cargo performed by aircraft for reward." Article 1. Article 19 provides "[t]he carrier is liable for damage occasioned by delay in the carriage by air of passengers, baggage or cargo." Article 29 states "[i]n the carriage of passengers, baggage and cargo, any action for damages, however founded, whether under this Convention or in contract or in tort or otherwise, can only be brought subject to the conditions and such limits of liability as are set out in this Convention without prejudice to the question as to who are the persons who have the right to bring suit and what are their respective rights. In any such action, punitive, exemplary or any other non-compensatory damages shall not be recoverable."

The language of Article 29 is very similar to the language of Article 24, paragraph 2 of the Warsaw Convention, as amended by Montreal Protocol No. 4. This amendment went into effect in the United States on March 4, 1999. Paragraph 2 of amended Article 24 provides "[i]n the carriage of cargo, any action for damages, however founded, whether under this Convention, or in contract or in tort or otherwise, can only be brought subject to the conditions and limits of liability set out in this Convention." El Al Israel Airlines, Ltd. v. Tsui Yuan Tseng, 525 U.S. 155, 175 n.15 (1999) (quoting Article 24, as amended by Montreal Protocol No. 4). Article 29 of the Montreal Convention uses nearly identical language but applies it to the carriage of passengers and baggage, as well as cargo.

The Seventh Circuit recently considered the language of Article 24 of the amended Warsaw Convention and stated "Article 24 expressly contemplates that an action may be brought in contract or in tort. The liability limitation provisions of the Warsaw Convention simply operate as an affirmative defense." *Sompo,* 522 F.3d at 785. This reasoning logically extends to the strikingly similar language of Article 29 of the Montreal Convention. Accordingly, claims may be brought under the Convention or they may be brought "in contract or in tort or otherwise" but such claims are subject to an affirmative defense based on the conditions and limits of liability set out in the Montreal Convention. Plaintiff brought state-law breach of contract claims. Because the conditions and limits of the Montreal Convention are defenses to the state-law claims raised by plaintiff, they do not provide a basis for federal-question subject matter jurisdiction. * * * Plaintiff's claims do not arise under the Constitution or a law or treaty of the United States. The complete preemption doctrine does not apply. This case is remanded to the 15th Judicial Circuit Court, Jo Daviess County, Illinois for lack of subject matter jurisdiction. * * *

NOTES AND QUESTIONS FOR DISCUSSION

1. The *Benjamins* court distinguished between the rules of decision that a treaty might create which would be binding on state and federal courts, and whether the treaty itself supplies a private right of action. Both could be aspects of self-executing treaties. In other words, a treaty might not supply a cause of action, but it might nevertheless be binding on the court that entertains a state law claim in which the treaty is relevant. (And as noted above, some argue that even non self-executing treaties might be able to supply rules of decision.) That dichotomy is illustrated by pre-*Benjamins* practice in the Second Circuit when the Warsaw Convention was *not* thought to supply a cause of action, but treaty provisions were nevertheless applicable to the state law cause of action that parties might bring against international carriers. Note in this regard that *Benjamins* is an unusual case. That is because courts will not routinely read a treaty to have itself created a private right of action—i.e., without congressional implementing action. See generally Curtis Bradley & Jack Goldsmith, Foreign Relations Law 482-97 (4th ed. 2011).

2. Zicherman v. Korean Air Lines Co., Ltd., 516 U.S. 217 (1996), involved litigation arising from the (then) Soviet Union's downing of Korean Airlines Flight KE007 over the Sea of Japan after it strayed into Soviet air space. The Supreme Court was faced with the question of what damages were recoverable when an airplane flight covered by the Warsaw Convention resulted in a death on the high seas. As noted in *Benjamins*, Article 17 of the Convention provides that "[t]he carrier shall be liable for damage sustained in the event of the death . . . of a passenger . . . on board the aircraft." Writing for a unanimous Court, Justice Scalia concluded that the term "damage" meant damage legally compensable under relevant domestic law. The Court then concluded that the appropriate measure of domestic law was not the "general maritime law" as applied by courts of the U.S. (and which would have provided that survivors economically dependent on a decedent could recover for their non-pecuniary losses). Rather, the Court held that the appropriate domestic law was the Death on the High Seas Act (DOHSA), 46 U.S.C. §§ 30301-08, which applied (as then worded) "[w]henever the death of a person shall be caused by wrongful act . . . on the high seas beyond a marine league from the shore of any State . . . or the Territories or dependencies of the United States." At the time, however, DOHSA, did not provide for the recovery of any non-pecuniary damages by any survivor, and thus plaintiffs could not recover such damages. The Court was unpersuaded that its result would lead to various nonuniform rules of damages for international flights depending on whether or not the crash occurred over the high seas.

Does *Zicherman's* conclusion that plaintiffs must look to the remedies available under domestic law undermine the majority's conclusion in *Benjamins* that the Warsaw Convention itself provided a private right of action for wrongful death? Note that DOHSA was subsequently amended specifically to cover commercial aviation accidents beyond 12 nautical miles from U.S. shores, and to allow compensation for "nonpecuniary damages" including "loss of care, comfort, and companionship." Punitive damages were excluded. Note also that the current Montreal Convention (as referenced in *Narkiewicz-Laine*) more clearly indicates that a damages action may be founded directly under the Convention, insofar as it refers to "any action for damages, however founded, whether under this Convention, or in contract or tort or otherwise." The original Warsaw Convention lacked the explanatory phrase after "however founded,"— the language that had divided the judges in *Benjamins*.

3. Although the *Benjamins* court was focused on problems of uniformity in the interpretation and implementation of a treaty, it did not conclude that the cause of action created by the Warsaw Convention was within the federal courts' exclusive jurisdiction. The usual practice is to presume that state courts have concurrent jurisdiction over claims arising under federal law absent some express indication to the contrary. Tafflin v. Levitt, 493 U.S. 455 (1990) (requiring a clear statement, unmistakable legislative history, or "clear incompatibility" before presumption of concurrency will be overcome). Consequently, state courts could hear such actions as well, although they would be removable at the defendant's option if filed in state court. Is this a problem for "uniformity"? Or is it sufficient that the U.S. Supreme Court can review the state court's decision, and that either party can effectively exercise a veto on the case going forward in state court?

4. Article 30(3) of the Warsaw Convention, referred to in *Benjamins*, expressly states that with respect to certain baggage claims involving multiple carriers, a party shall have a "right of action" against appropriate carriers, as defined therein. The court uses this language to suggest that the Convention could not be understood as treating claims *not* involving multiple carriers differently. But couldn't the express reference to a "right of action" in some settings be an indication that the parties to the Convention knew how to provide clearly for a right of action when they wanted to? Alternatively, could it be that the "right of action" referred to was the right of action created by domestic law, and that Article 30(3) was simply indicating the carriers who would be liable on such a claim?

5. *Narkiewicz-Laine* addresses a common issue in litigation respecting treaties: the extent to which the treaty might be supposed to have pre-empted state law causes of action. Note that such preemption can arise whether or not the treaty itself provides for a right of action. Note also that unlike the plaintiff's action in *Narkiewicz-Laine* which the court found not to be pre-empted, tort suits by passengers against international carriers for in-flight injuries are thought to be preempted, because the scope of the Convention clearly reaches such matters. See, e.g., El Al Israel Airlines, Ltd. v. Tsui Yuan Tseng, 525 U.S. 155, 161 (1999) ("Recovery for personal injury suffered on board an aircraft or in the course of any of the operations of embarking or disembarking . . . if not allowed under the [1929 Warsaw] Convention, is not available at all."). A treaty may also preempt a pre-existing federal statute. Mikerina v. Delta Air Lines, Inc., 834 F. Supp. 2d 54 (D. Mass. 2011) (finding that passenger mistreatment and discrimination claims under federal statutes were preempted). Nevertheless, the traditional rule is that a post-treaty legislative enactment can itself trump a treaty as a matter of domestic law. See, e.g., Whitney v. Robertson, 124 U.S. 190 (1888) (holding that courts must focus on "the latest expression of the sovereign will").

D. VENUE AND ALIEN DEFENDANTS

Even when a court can properly exercise personal and subject matter jurisdiction, other doctrines may come into play that further limit the plaintiff's choice of forum. In the federal courts, for example, the general venue provisions of 28 U.S.C. § 1391(b), as amended in late 2011, spell out the federal district(s) in which the suit may be brought. By way of summary, venue is proper (1) in a district where "any" defendant resides, provided all defendants reside in the same state in which the district is located; (2) in a district in which "a substantial part of the events" giving rise to the claim occurred; or (3) if there is no district as defined in (1) or (2), then in a judicial district in which "any defendant" is subject to the court's personal jurisdiction. State courts have venue provisions of their own, but often they bear a rough similarity to the basic federal venue provisions, although they tend to lack the detail regarding aliens and alien corporations, as noted below.

1. Venue in Suits Against Aliens

With respect to alien defendants, two provisions are relevant. Under § 1391(c)(3), "a defendant not resident in the United States may be sued in any judicial district." And under § 1391(c)(1), an alien lawfully admitted to permanent resident status—like any "natural person"—is "deemed to reside in the judicial district in which that person is domiciled." Do not be misled by the language of § 1391(c)(3), however. Non-resident aliens, in fact, may *not* be sued in "any" judicial district of the plaintiff's choosing. Personal jurisdiction must always be established, quite apart from venue (not to mention subject matter jurisdiction). Thus, a non-resident alien may be sued in any federal district in a state in which personal jurisdiction exists and when federal subject matter jurisdiction is present. Of course, personal jurisdiction and venue might be available against an alien in any district in which the alien is able to be "tagged"—i.e., subjected to transient jurisdiction. But in such event, although venue may be good, there may still be an argument for transfer of venue to a substantially more convenient forum. See Note 4, below. And foreign courts might refuse to enforce a U.S. judgment that is premised on tag jurisdiction. See Chapter I, Section D; see generally Chapter 8. Is it clear whether aliens who are *not* lawfully admitted to permanent residence, but who are arguably domiciled in a state in the U.S., fit under the current statute?

Note that a foreign (alien) corporation whose principal place of business is outside the U.S. could arguably be treated as a non-resident alien for venue purposes and thus suable in any district. See § 1391(c)(3). But § 1391(c)(2) provides a more specific rule for corporations and other business entities that deems them resident in any district in which they would be subject to personal jurisdiction. See also § 1391(d) (indicating that in states with multiple districts, each district should be treated as a separate state in conducting the personal jurisdiction analysis for corporations). Whichever provision is proper, results should not vary greatly, although the first option would allow such a corporation to be sued in a district in a state in which there was personal jurisdiction, but perhaps not in the particular district.

2. Venue in Suits against Alien and Non-Alien Defendants

Suppose there are multiple defendants, one of whom is a non-resident alien. Under the venue statute, such a party "shall be disregarded in determining where the action may be brought." 28 U.S.C. § 1391(c)(3). Thus, for example, a plaintiff would have the option of suing in a district in which any one of the *non-alien* defendants resided, if all of the non-alien defendants resided in the same state in which the district is located. If no such district existed (because, for example, there was more than one non-alien defendant and they did not all reside in the same state), the plaintiff could lay venue in any district in which substantial events giving rise to the litigation occurred—assuming, of course, that such events did indeed occur in a U.S. federal judicial district. 28 U.S.C. § 1391(b)(2).

3. Fallback Venue

As noted above, a fallback provision, § 1391(b)(3), allows for venue to be laid wherever any defendant may be "subject to the court's personal jurisdiction." This provision can be triggered, however, only when there is "*no district*" in the U.S. in which suit may otherwise be brought. Id. (emphasis added). Consequently, the fallback provision will generally *not* be triggered unless both of the following are true: (1) no substantial part of the events giving rise to the lawsuit occurred in any district within the U.S. (i.e., the claim arose in a foreign country), *and* (2) there are multiple non-alien defendants in the case who do not reside in the same state. Of course, here too the venue statute can be misleading. Suppose there is more than one non-alien defendant. Venue will be good in any district in which any defendant is subject to personal jurisdiction. But personal jurisdiction must be had over all defendants, and not every district in which one defendant is subject to personal jurisdiction will be a district in which all defendants will be subject to personal jurisdiction. In short, under the fallback venue statute, venue and personal jurisdiction will be good as against all defendants only in a district in which all defendants are subject to personal jurisdiction.

4. Transfer of Venue

Even if personal jurisdiction, subject matter jurisdiction, and venue are all met, discretionary doctrines may permit a federal court to decline to exercise jurisdiction in favor of having the litigation go forward in some other federal district court that is more convenient. For example, a party sued in a federal court in one district may move to have the case transferred "[f]or the convenience of the parties and witnesses, in the interest of justice" pursuant to 28 U.S.C. § 1404(a), to another federal court in another district in which the action might have been brought. Prior to the 1948 enactment of § 1404 and its relatively simple mechanism of transfer, federal courts had developed their own set of judge-made principles for dismissing a case on *forum non conveniens* grounds in favor of having it go forward in another federal district. Under Gulf Oil Corp. v. Gilbert, 330 U.S. 501 (1947), federal courts were to consider an amalgam of public and private considerations. The "private" factors included the "relative ease of access to sources of proof; availability of compulsory process for attendance of unwilling, and the cost of obtaining attendance of willing, witnesses; possibility of view of premises, if view would be appropriate to the action; and all other practical problems that make trial of a case easy, expeditious and inexpensive." Id. at 508. "Public factors" might include the local interest in having localized controversies decided at home, the interest in having the trial of a diversity case in a forum that is at home with the law that must govern the action; the avoidance of unnecessary problems in conflict of laws; and the unfairness of burdening citizens in an unrelated forum with jury duty. See id. at 508-09.

5. *Transfer of Venue versus Forum Non Conveniens*

Even though transfer of venue as between federal courts is now governed by statute (and are largely informed by the *Gilbert* standards), those same judge-made *Gilbert* standards remain the exclusive point of reference for dismissals from federal court on *forum non conveniens* grounds. (We treat international *forum non conveniens* in Chapter 5). Such a motion argues, in effect, that litigation should go forward, not in some other federal district (via transfer) but that it should go forward outside of the U.S. altogether. Thus, a *forum non conveniens* motion made to a federal district court necessarily asks that the litigation not proceed in the U.S. (but to proceed, if at all, in a foreign jurisdiction). By contrast, a *forum non conveniens* motion directed to a *state* court in which suit has been filed seeks to have the case dismissed in favor either of another state's courts or a foreign (non U.S.) court. States, moreover, may employ *forum non conveniens* rules that are quite unlike those applied in the federal courts, thus setting up a real risk of forum shopping between state and federal courts within a given state.

Although there are some rough similarities in the methodology by which *forum non conveniens* motions and transfer of venue motions are decided, the consequences can be dramatically different. As just noted, transfer of venue keeps the litigation within the U.S., whereas a federal court's *forum non conveniens* dismissal does not. In addition, transfer of venue under § 1404 does not result in a change in the law that would have been applied in the district court in which the case was originally filed. See Van Dusen v. Barrack, 376 U.S. 612 (1964) (involving transfer of a diversity case). But in *forum non conveniens* dismissals, there is no similar transfer of the law along with the case.

*NOTE ON THE SEQUENCING OF JURISDICTIONAL AND
RELATED OBJECTIONS*

A defendant might have personal jurisdiction, subject matter jurisdiction, and even *forum non conveniens* objections to having the suit proceed in the forum in which it has been brought. Should a court have the freedom to dismiss on one of the *non* subject matter jurisdiction grounds, if such grounds are available, or must subject matter jurisdiction always be addressed first? The Supreme Court has insisted that, ordinarily, questions of subject matter jurisdiction are antecedent to the merits, on the theory that a court that lacks jurisdiction has no power to do anything but to note its absence and dismiss. See Steel Co. v. Citizens for a Better Environment, 523 U.S. 83 (1998). Nevertheless, in Ruhrgas AG v. Marathon Oil Co., 526 U.S. 574 (1999), the Supreme Court reversed a decision of the Fifth Circuit which had concluded, based on *Steel Co.*, that the question of subject matter jurisdiction must always be decided before resolving any question of personal jurisdiction. The Court rejected the suggestion that there is an unyielding jurisdictional hierarchy requiring subject matter jurisdiction always to be resolved ahead of challenges to personal jurisdiction. This was true, even though a decision on the latter question might disable a state court from adjudicating a dispute, whereas a decision finding a lack of federal subject matter jurisdiction would not. Instead, the *Ruhrgas* Court held that when the question of personal jurisdiction appears dispositive and uncomplicated, and when the question of subject matter jurisdiction appears difficult, a federal court has the "discretion" to decide the personal jurisdiction question first. *Steel Co.* was distinguished as having concluded only that jurisdictional questions must be resolved before the merits..

The supposedly difficult subject matter jurisdiction question in *Ruhrgas* seemed to implicate the limits of federal question jurisdiction, insofar as the Court had assumed that complete diversity would be lacking. The case involved a U.S. corporation (Marathon) and a Norwegian corporation (Norge), both of whom sued a German corporation (Ruhrgas) on various state law claims arising from a deal to produce gas from a field in the North Sea. Ruhrgas, who removed the case from state to federal court, argued that because lurking questions of "foreign and international relations" were implicated in the underlying contractual agreement, the suit arose under federal law and was therefore properly removable, despite the lack of complete diversity. Apparently this was the difficult question of subject matter jurisdiction that could take a back seat to dismissal on personal jurisdiction grounds, if the district court so chose. Cf. *Patrickson v. Dole Foods, supra*.

Should a rule similar to that in *Ruhrgas* be applied in the *forum non conveniens* setting to allow for dismissal even without reaching the jurisdictional objections? In Sinochem Int'l Co. Ltd. v. Malaysia Int'l Shipping Corp., 549 U.S. 422 (2007), the Supreme Court upheld dismissal on *forum non conveniens* grounds, concluding that federal courts did not have to resolve the subject matter jurisdiction question first.

CHAPTER 3

Suits Against Foreign Sovereigns

SECTION A. THE FOREIGN SOVEREIGN IMMUNITIES ACT

1. Origins and Structure

American law recognized the sovereign immunity of foreign governments early in the nation's history, at nearly the same time that the sovereign immunity of the states and the federal government became accepted legal doctrine. The seminal decision is The Schooner Exchange v. McFadden, 11 U.S. (7 Cranch) 116 (1812), which involved the seizure of a French warship by a federal court in Philadelphia under a claim that the vessel had been unlawfully taken from the plaintiffs on the high seas. The Supreme Court ordered the vessel to be released. As Chief Justice Marshall framed the question presented, it was "whether an American citizen can assert, in an American court, a title to an armed national vessel found within the waters of the United States." Id. at 136. The case accordingly was decided on equally narrow grounds: that "national ships of war, entering the port of a friendly power open for their reception, are to be considered as exempted by the consent of that power from its jurisdiction." Id. at 145-46. That consent could be withdrawn by the political branches of government, but "until such power be exerted in a manner not to be misunderstood, the sovereign cannot be considered as having imparted to the ordinary tribunals a jurisdiction, which it would be a breach of faith to exercise." Id. at 146.

Having gained this narrow foothold in American law, foreign sovereign immunity expanded along with the modern state, involving increased regulation and participation in the economy, and in some socialist countries, nearly a complete takeover of basic economic functions. Coupled with the natural tendency of plaintiffs to seek recovery from any solvent defendant, litigation turned increasingly to entities owned or controlled by the state, giving rise to increased assertions of sovereign immunity. These tendencies resulted initially in expansion of sovereign immunity to cover any action of a foreign state, whether or not it was in the exercise of its sovereign powers or as a participant in ordinary commercial activity. See, e.g., Berizzi Bros. Co. v. S.S. Pesaro, 271 U.S. 562 (1926). Based on an expansive interpretation of *The Schooner Exchange*, such decisions look to the sovereign as the author of the activity to grant the immunity, rather than to the nature of the activity itself.

From this high water mark in the early twentieth century, the immunity has been in retreat ever since. The State Department issued "suggestions of immunity" at the request of any friendly government that sought such relief. This practice, too, followed the precedent set in *The Schooner Exchange*, in which the U.S. filed such a suggestion in order to preserve "a state of peace and amity" with France. That practice came up against a growing trend in other nations to adopt the "restrictive theory" of sovereign immunity, in which it did not apply to the commercial activity or other private acts of a foreign state. In the "Tate Letter" of 1952, the State Department adopted this theory, indicating that it would suggest immunity only if the claim against the foreign state did not arise out of private acts, as opposed to sovereign acts, of a foreign nation. If a foreign nation requested a "Suggestion of Immunity," the decision of the State Department on whether to grant one was taken to be binding in subsequent litigation. If no such request were made, then the court had to decide the issue of immunity in the first instance. This regime led to judicial decisions inconsistent with those of the State Department on similar facts, and to broader concerns that the State Department was essentially taking over a judicial function when the courts deferred to its determinations.

More than two decades of experience with such problems led Congress to pass the Foreign Sovereign Immunities Act of 1976 (FSIA). (The Act is set out in full in Appendix F.) It codified the restrictive theory of sovereign immunity, and in doing so, removed any formal binding effect of suggestions of immunity by the State Department. (The department could still appear in the role of amicus curiae, whether by invitation of the court or on its own motion.) The essence of the FSIA consisted of two provisions: a general grant of immunity to foreign sovereigns from the jurisdiction of any court in the U.S., state or federal, 28 U.S.C. § 1604, and a limited but complex series of exceptions to this immunity, of which the most important was for claims based upon "commercial activity," 28 U.S.C. § 1605. Other provisions of the act, themselves quite complicated, elaborated upon the basic principle of limited immunity.

The first case in this chapter took up the question whether this statutory scheme was constitutional. That question arose because sovereign immunity was framed from its inception as a matter of jurisdiction: when the immunity attached, the foreign sovereign was immune from both the subject-matter and the personal jurisdiction of national courts. When immunity did not attach, the FSIA provided that any suit against a foreign sovereign could be brought in federal court, either as an initial matter under 28 U.S.C. § 1330, or by removal from state court under 28 U.S.C. § 1441(d). In order to assure an expert and sympathetic application of the federal statute and its standards for immunity, the FSIA provided that federal courts would always be available to hear cases under the Act. To be sure, the federal court might dismiss the case for lack of subject-matter and personal jurisdiction, but it would make that determination with full recognition of the federal interests in protecting the immunity of foreign nations. Even in cases removed from state court, the removal to federal court would be accomplished before any ruling on immunity. This comprehensive scheme of federal jurisdiction was a key feature of the FSIA and its very comprehensiveness led to the challenge to its constitutionality.

2. *Constitutionality*

Verlinden B.V. v. Central Bank of Nigeria

Supreme Court of the United States, 1983.
461 U.S. 480.

CHIEF JUSTICE BURGER delivered the opinion of the Court.

We granted certiorari to consider whether the Foreign Sovereign Immunities Act of 1976, by authorizing a foreign plaintiff to sue a foreign state in a United States District Court on a non-federal cause of action, violates Article III of the Constitution.

I

On April 21, 1975, the Federal Republic of Nigeria and petitioner Verlinden B.V., a Dutch corporation with its principal offices in Amsterdam, The Netherlands, entered into a contract providing for the purchase of 240,000 metric tons of cement by Nigeria. The parties agreed that the contract would be governed by the laws of the Netherlands and that disputes would be resolved by arbitration before the International Chamber of Commerce, Paris, France.

The contract provided that the Nigerian government was to establish an irrevocable, confirmed letter of credit for the total purchase price through Slavenburg's Bank in Amsterdam. According to petitioner's amended complaint, however, respondent Central Bank of Nigeria, an instrumentality of Nigeria, improperly established an unconfirmed letter of credit payable through Morgan Guaranty Trust Company in New York.

In August 1975, Verlinden subcontracted with a Liechtenstein corporation, Interbuco, to purchase the cement needed to fulfill the contract. Meanwhile, the ports of Nigeria had become clogged with hundreds of ships carrying cement, sent by numerous other cement suppliers with whom Nigeria also had entered contracts. In mid-September, Central Bank unilaterally directed its correspondent banks, including Morgan Guaranty, to adopt a series of amendments to all letters of credit issued in connection with the cement contracts. Central Bank also directly notified the suppliers that payment would be made only for those shipments approved by Central Bank two months before their arrival in Nigerian waters.

Verlinden then sued Central Bank in United States District Court for the Southern District of New York, alleging that Central Bank's actions constituted an anticipatory breach of the letter of credit. Verlinden alleged jurisdiction under § 2 of the Foreign Sovereign Immunities Act, 28 U.S.C. § 1330.[4] Respondent

---

[4]   Section 2, 28 U.S.C. § 1330, provides:

> "(a) The district courts shall have original jurisdiction without regard to amount in controversy of any nonjury civil action against a foreign state as defined in section 1603(a) of this title as to any claim for relief in personam with respect to which the foreign state is not entitled to immunity either under sections 1605-1607 of this title or under any applicable international agreement.

moved to dismiss for, among other reasons, lack of subject matter and personal jurisdiction.

The District Court first held that a federal court may exercise subject matter jurisdiction over a suit brought by a foreign corporation against a foreign sovereign. [It then went on, however, to find no applicable exception under the FSIA allowing suit in this case. The court of appeals affirmed, but on the ground that a federal court could not exercise jurisdiction under the Constitution.]

We granted certiorari, 454 U.S. 1140 (1982), and we reverse and remand.

II

For more than a century and a half, the United States generally granted foreign sovereigns complete immunity from suit in the courts of this country. In The Schooner Exchange v. M'Faddon, 7 Cranch 116, 3 L.Ed. 287 (1812), Chief Justice Marshall concluded that, while the jurisdiction of a nation within its own territory "is susceptible of no limitation not imposed by itself," id., at 136, the United States had impliedly waived jurisdiction over certain activities of foreign sovereigns. Although the narrow holding of *The Schooner Exchange* was only that the courts of the United States lack jurisdiction over an armed ship of a foreign state found in our port, that opinion came to be regarded as extending virtually absolute immunity to foreign sovereigns. See, e.g., Berizzi Brothers Co. v. S.S. Pesaro, 271 U.S. 562 (1926); von Mehren, The Foreign Sovereign Immunities Act of 1976, 17 Colum. J. Transnat'l L. 33, 39-40 (1978).

As *The Schooner Exchange* made clear, however, foreign sovereign immunity is a matter of grace and comity on the part of the United States, and not a restriction imposed by the Constitution. Accordingly, this Court consistently has deferred to the decisions of the political branches-in particular, those of the Executive Branch-on whether to take jurisdiction over actions against foreign sovereigns and their instrumentalities. See, e.g., Ex parte Peru, 318 U.S. 578, 586-590 (1943); Mexico v. Hoffman, 324 U.S. 30, 33-36 (1945).

Until 1952, the State Department ordinarily requested immunity in all actions against friendly foreign sovereigns. But in the so-called Tate Letter, the State Department announced its adoption of the "restrictive" theory of foreign sovereign immunity. Under this theory, immunity is confined to suits involving the foreign sovereign's public acts, and does not extend to cases arising out of a foreign state's strictly commercial acts.

The restrictive theory was not initially enacted into law, however, and its application proved troublesome. As in the past, initial responsibility for deciding questions of sovereign immunity fell primarily upon the Executive acting through the State Department, and the courts abided by "suggestions of immunity" from the State Department. As a consequence, foreign nations often placed diplomatic pressure on the State Department in seeking immunity. On occasion, political considerations led to suggestions of immunity in cases where immunity would not have been available under the restrictive theory.

"(b) Personal jurisdiction over a foreign state shall exist as to every claim for relief over which the district courts have jurisdiction under subsection (a) where service has been made under section 1608 of this title."

An additional complication was posed by the fact that foreign nations did not always make requests to the State Department. In such cases, the responsibility fell to the courts to determine whether sovereign immunity existed, generally by reference to prior State Department decisions. See generally Lowenfeld, Claims against Foreign States—A Proposal for Reform of United States Law, 44 N.Y.U.L.Rev. 901, 909-912 (1969). Thus, sovereign immunity determinations were made in two different branches, subject to a variety of factors, sometimes including diplomatic considerations. Not surprisingly, the governing standards were neither clear nor uniformly applied. See, e.g., id., at 906-909; Weber, The Foreign Sovereign Immunities Act of 1976: Its Origin, Meaning and Effect, 3 Yale Stud. in World Pub. Order 1, 11-13, 15-17 (1976).

In 1976, Congress passed the Foreign Sovereign Immunities Act in order to free the Government from the case-by-case diplomatic pressures, to clarify the governing standards, and to "assur[e] litigants that . . . decisions are made on purely legal grounds and under procedures that insure due process," H.R.Rep. No. 94-1487, p. 7 (1976), reprinted in [1976] U.S.Code Cong. & Ad.News 6604. To accomplish these objectives, the Act contains a comprehensive set of legal standards governing claims of immunity in every civil action against a foreign state or its political subdivisions, agencies or instrumentalities.

For the most part, the Act codifies, as a matter of federal law, the restrictive theory of sovereign immunity. A foreign state is normally immune from the jurisdiction of federal and state courts, 28 U.S.C. § 1604, subject to a set of exceptions specified in §§ 1605 and 1607. Those exceptions include actions in which the foreign state has explicitly or impliedly waived its immunity, § 1605(a)(1), and actions based upon commercial activities of the foreign sovereign carried on in the United States or causing a direct effect in the United States, § 1605(a)(2). When one of these or the other specified exceptions applies, "the foreign state shall be liable in the same manner and to the same extent as a private individual under like circumstances," 28 U.S.C. § 1606.

The Act expressly provides that its standards control in "the courts of the United States and of the States," id. § 1604, and thus clearly contemplates that such suits may be brought in either federal or state courts. However, "[i]n view of the potential sensitivity of actions against foreign states and the importance of developing a uniform body of law in this area," H.R.Rep. No. 94-1487, at 32, the Act guarantees foreign states the right to remove any civil action from a state court to a federal court, id. § 1441(d). The Act also provides that any claim permitted under the Act may be brought from the outset in federal court, id. § 1330(a). If one of the specified exceptions to sovereign immunity applies, a federal district court may exercise subject matter jurisdiction under § 1330(a); but if the claim does not fall within one of the exceptions, federal courts lack subject matter jurisdiction. In such a case, the foreign state is also ensured immunity from the jurisdiction of state courts by § 1604.

III

The District Court and the Court of Appeals both held that the Foreign Sovereign Immunities Act purports to allow a foreign plaintiff to sue a foreign sovereign in the courts of the United States, provided the substantive requirements of the Act are satisfied. We agree.

On its face, the language of the statute is unambiguous. The statute grants jurisdiction over "any non-jury civil action against a foreign state . . . with respect to which the foreign state is not entitled to immunity," 28 U.S.C. § 1330(a). The Act contains no indication of any limitation based on the citizenship of the plaintiff.

The legislative history is less clear in this regard. [But the Court interpreted it to support the same conclusion.]

IV

We now turn to the core question presented by this case: whether Congress exceeded the scope of Article III of the Constitution by granting federal courts subject matter jurisdiction over certain civil actions by foreign plaintiffs against foreign sovereigns where the rule of decision may be provided by state law.

This Court's cases firmly establish that Congress may not expand the jurisdiction of the federal courts beyond the bounds established by the Constitution. See, e.g., Hodgson v. Bowerbank, 5 Cranch 303, 3 L.Ed. 108 (1809); Kline v. Burke Constr. Co., 260 U.S. 226, 234, (1923). Within Article III of the Constitution, we find two sources authorizing the grant of jurisdiction in the Foreign Sovereign Immunities Act: the diversity clause and the "arising under" clause.[17] The diversity clause, which provides that the judicial power extends to controversies between "a State, or the Citizens thereof, and foreign States," covers actions by citizens of states. Yet diversity jurisdiction is not sufficiently broad to support a grant of jurisdiction over actions by foreign plaintiffs, since a foreign plaintiff is not "a State, or [a] Citize[n] thereof." See Mossman v. Higginson, 4 Dall. 12, 1 L.Ed. 720 (1800).[18] We conclude, however, that the "arising under" clause of Article III provides an appropriate basis for the statutory grant of subject matter jurisdiction to actions by foreign plaintiffs under the Act.

The controlling decision on the scope of Article III "arising under" jurisdiction is Chief Justice Marshall's opinion for the Court in Osborn v. Bank of the United States, 9 Wheat. 738, 6 L.Ed. 204 (1824). In *Osborn*, the Court upheld the constitutionality of a statute that granted the Bank of the United States the right to sue in federal court on causes of action based upon state law. There, the Court concluded that the "judicial department may receive . . . the power of construing every . . . law" that "the Legislature may constitutionally make," id., at 818. The rule was laid down that:

> "[I]t is a sufficient foundation for jurisdiction, that the title or right set up by the party, may be defeated by one construction of the constitution or

---

[17] In view of our conclusion that proper actions by foreign plaintiffs under the Foreign Sovereign Immunities Act are within Article III "arising under" jurisdiction, we need not consider petitioner's alternative argument that the Act is constitutional as an aspect of so-called "protective jurisdiction." See generally Note, The Theory of Protective Jurisdiction, 57 N.Y.U.L.Rev. 933 (1982).

[18] Since Article III requires only "minimal diversity," see State Farm Fire & Casualty Co. v. Tashire, 386 U.S. 523, 530 (1967), diversity jurisdiction would be a sufficient basis for jurisdiction where at least one of the plaintiffs is a citizen of a State.

laws of the United States, and sustained by the opposite construction." Id., at 822.

Osborn thus reflects a broad conception of "arising under" jurisdiction, according to which Congress may confer on the federal courts jurisdiction over any case or controversy that might call for the application of federal law. The breadth of that conclusion has been questioned. It has been observed that, taken at its broadest, *Osborn* might be read as permitting "assertion of original federal jurisdiction on the remote possibility of presentation of a federal question." Textile Workers Union v. Lincoln Mills, 353 U.S. 448, 482 (1957) (Frankfurter, J., dissenting). See, e.g., P. Bator, P. Mishkin, D. Shapiro & H. Wechsler, Hart & Wechsler's The Federal Courts and the Federal System 866-867 (2d ed. 1973). We need not now resolve that issue or decide the precise boundaries of Article III jurisdiction, however, since the present case does not involve a mere speculative possibility that a federal question may arise at some point in the proceeding. Rather, a suit against a foreign state under this Act necessarily raises questions of substantive federal law at the very outset, and hence clearly "arises under" federal law, as that term is used in Article III.

By reason of its authority over foreign commerce and foreign relations, Congress has the undisputed power to decide, as a matter of federal law, whether and under what circumstances foreign nations should be amenable to suit in the United States. Actions against foreign sovereigns in our courts raise sensitive issues concerning the foreign relations of the United States, and the primacy of federal concerns is evident. See, e.g., Banco Nacional de Cuba v. Sabbatino, 376 U.S. 398, 423-425 (1964); Zschernig v. Miller, 389 U.S. 429, 440-441 (1968).

To promote these federal interests, Congress exercised its Article I powers by enacting a statute comprehensively regulating the amenability of foreign nations to suit in the United States. The statute must be applied by the District Courts in every action against a foreign sovereign, since subject matter jurisdiction in any such action depends on the existence of one of the specified exceptions to foreign sovereign immunity, 28 U.S.C. § 1330(a). At the threshold of every action in a District Court against a foreign state, therefore, the court must satisfy itself that one of the exceptions applies-and in doing so it must apply the detailed federal law standards set forth in the Act. Accordingly, an action against a foreign sovereign arises under federal law, for purposes of Article III jurisdiction.

In reaching a contrary conclusion, the Court of Appeals relied heavily upon decisions construing 28 U.S.C. § 1331, the statute which grants district courts general federal question jurisdiction over any case that "arises under" the laws of the United States. The court placed particular emphasis on the so-called "well-pleaded complaint" rule, which provides, for purposes of statutory "arising under" jurisdiction, that the federal question must appear on the face of a well-pleaded complaint and may not enter in anticipation of a defense. See, e.g., Louisville & Nashville R. Co. v. Mottley, 211 U.S. 149 (1908); Gully v. First National Bank, 299 U.S. 109 (1936); 13 C. Wright, A. Miller & E. Cooper, Federal Practice and Procedure § 3562 (1975) (hereinafter Wright, Miller & Cooper). In the view of the Court of Appeals, the question of foreign sovereign immunity in this case arose solely as a defense, and not on the face of Verlinden's well-pleaded complaint.

Although the language of § 1331 parallels that of the "arising under" clause of Article III, this Court never has held that statutory "arising under" jurisdiction is identical to Article III "arising under" jurisdiction. Quite the contrary is true. Section 1331, the general federal question statute, although broadly phrased,

> "has been continuously construed and limited in the light of the history that produced it, the demands of reason and coherence, and the dictates of sound judicial policy which have emerged from the [statute's] function as a provision in the mosaic of federal judiciary legislation. *It is a statute, not a Constitution, we are expounding.*" Romero v. International Terminal Operating Co., 358 U.S. 354, 379 (1959) (emphasis added).

In an accompanying footnote, the Court further observed, "Of course the many limitations which have been placed on jurisdiction under § 1331 are not limitations on the constitutional power of Congress to confer jurisdiction on the federal courts." Id., at 379 n. 51. We reiterated that conclusion in Powell v. McCormack, 395 U.S. 486, 515 (1969). As these decisions make clear, Article III "arising under" jurisdiction is broader than federal question jurisdiction under § 1331, and the Court of Appeals' heavy reliance on decisions construing that statute was misplaced.

In rejecting "arising under" jurisdiction, the Court of Appeals also noted that § 2 of the Foreign Sovereign Immunities Act, 28 U.S.C. § 1330, is a jurisdictional provision.[22] Because of this, the court felt its conclusion compelled by prior cases in which this Court has rejected Congressional attempts to confer jurisdiction on federal courts simply by enacting jurisdictional statutes. In Mossman v. Higginson, 4 Dall. 12, 1 L.Ed. 720 (1800), for example, this Court found that a statute purporting to confer jurisdiction over actions "where an alien is a party" would exceed the scope of Article III if construed to allow an action solely between two aliens. And in The Propeller Genesee Chief v. Fitzhugh, 12 How. 443, 451-453, 13 L.Ed. 1058 (1852), the Court, while upholding a statute granting jurisdiction over vessels on the Great Lakes as an exercise of maritime jurisdiction, rejected the view that the jurisdictional statute itself constituted a federal regulation of commerce upon which "arising under" jurisdiction could be based.

From these cases, the Court of Appeals apparently concluded that a jurisdictional statute can never constitute the federal law under which the action arises, for Article III purposes. Yet the statutes at issue in these prior cases sought to do

---

[22] Although a major function of the Act as a whole is to regulate jurisdiction of federal courts over cases involving foreign states, the Act's purpose is to set forth "comprehensive rules governing sovereign immunity." H.R.Rep. No. 94-1487, at 12. The Act also prescribes procedures for commencing lawsuits against foreign states in federal and state courts and specifies the circumstances under which attachment and execution may be obtained against the property of foreign states. Ibid. In addition, the Act defines "Extent of Liability," setting out a general rule that the foreign sovereign is "liable in the same manner and to the same extent as a private individual," subject to certain specified exceptions, 28 U.S.C. § 1606. In view of our resolution of this case, we need not consider petitioner's claim that § 1606 itself renders every claim against a foreign sovereign a federal cause of action. See generally 13 Wright, Miller & Cooper § 3563, at 418-419.

nothing more than grant jurisdiction over a particular class of cases. As the Court stated in *The Propeller Genesee Chief,* "The law . . . contains no regulations of commerce . . . . *It merely confers a new jurisdiction on the district courts; and this is its only object and purpose.* . . . It is evident . . . that Congress, in passing [the law], did not intend to exercise their power to regulate commerce . . . ." 12 How., at 451 (emphasis added).

In contrast, in enacting the Foreign Sovereign Immunities Act, Congress expressly exercised its power to regulate foreign commerce, along with other specified Article I powers. As the House Report clearly indicates, the primary purpose of the Act was to "se[t] forth comprehensive rules governing sovereign immunity," H.R. Rep. No. 94-1487, at p. 12; the jurisdictional provisions of the Act are simply one part of this comprehensive scheme. The Act thus does not merely concern access to the federal courts. Rather, it governs the types of actions for which foreign sovereigns may be held liable in a court in the United States, federal or state. The Act codifies the standards governing foreign sovereign immunity as an aspect of substantive federal law, see *Ex parte Peru, supra,* 318 U.S. [578,] 588 [(1943)]; *Mexico v. Hoffman, supra,* 324 U.S. [30,] 36 [(1945)]; and applying those standards will generally require interpretation of numerous points of federal law. Finally, if a court determines that none of the exceptions to sovereign immunity applies, the plaintiff will be barred from raising his claim in any court in the United States—manifestly, "the title or right set up by the party, may be defeated by one construction of the . . . laws of the United States, and sustained by the opposite construction." *Osborn v. Bank of the United States, supra,* 9 Wheat., at 822. That the inquiry into foreign sovereign immunity is labeled under the Act as a matter of jurisdiction does not affect the constitutionality of Congress' action in granting federal courts jurisdiction over cases calling for application of this comprehensive regulatory statute.

Congress, pursuant to its unquestioned Article I powers, has enacted a broad statutory framework governing assertions of foreign sovereign immunity. In so doing, Congress deliberately sought to channel cases against foreign sovereigns away from the state courts and into federal courts, thereby reducing the potential for a multiplicity of conflicting results among the courts of the 50 states. The resulting jurisdictional grant is within the bounds of Article III, since every action against a foreign sovereign necessarily involves application of a body of substantive federal law, and accordingly "arises under" federal law, within the meaning of Article III. * * *

NOTES AND QUESTIONS FOR DISCUSSION

1. The terms of the FSIA precluded any reliance upon the standard grounds for finding federal jurisdiction under the Constitution. The breadth of the statute extended it to suits by aliens against foreign sovereigns, preventing reliance upon diversity of citizenship as a constitutional ground of jurisdiction. Even minimal diversity did not extend so far, since it required at least one party to be a state citizen. Paradoxically, the framing of the immunity in terms of jurisdiction complicated any straightforward application of federal question jurisdiction. Federal question jurisdiction under Article III cannot itself be premised solely on the question whether federal jurisdiction exists, since that would erase all limits on federal judicial power. In other words, on such a view, whenever the jurisdiction of the federal courts was itself in question, that alone would be sufficient to confer federal question jurisdiction. The Supreme Court avoids such a conceptual dilemma in *Verlinden* by finding that the FSIA also determines the merits of claims against foreign sovereigns.

That shift allows the Court to invoke the general principle, dating back to Osborn v. Bank of the United States, 22 U.S. (9 Wheat.) 738, 822 (1824), that federal question jurisdiction may be conferred over any case in which "the title or right set up by the party, may be defeated by one construction of the . . . law of the United States, and sustained by the opposite construction." Any federal issue crucial to a claim or defense may be sufficient for federal question jurisdiction under Article III. Does that principle accurately fit the jurisdictional immunity conferred by the FSIA? Recent scholarship has challenged the broad view of *Osborn*, limiting it to the form of the particular claim at issue in that case, which required the plaintiff to plead the federal issue that the Bank of the United States was a properly constituted legal person under federal law. See Anthony J. Bellia, *The Origins of Article III "Arising Under" Jurisdiction*, 57 Duke L.J. 263 (2007); Anthony J. Bellia, *Article III and the Cause of Action*, 89 Iowa L. Rev. 777 (2004). On this view of *Osborn*, sovereign immunity would not be sufficient because of its status as a defense. Is it sufficient to address this problem, as the Court does, by stating that the court should raise the issue of sovereign immunity on its own because it goes to an issue of subject-matter jurisdiction? Or does this response just return to the conundrum that a federal question regarding subject-matter jurisdiction is not itself enough to confer jurisdiction?

Of course, a federal defense would be sufficient to confer jurisdiction under Article III. Although it is not sufficient to do so under the general federal question statute, 28 U.S.C. § 1331, the FSIA contains its own specialized statutory provisions for jurisdiction. Federal defense removal has been upheld by the Supreme Court, for instance, in claims against federal employees. E.g., Mesa v. California, 489 U.S. 121 (1989). Yet those decisions depend upon the fact that the defense has actually been raised. The FSIA contains no such requirement and the Court in *Verlinden* simply assumes that some such defense will be raised "since every action against a foreign sovereign necessarily involves application of a body of substantive federal law." *Verlinden*, 461 U.S. at 497. What if the foreign sovereign simply consents to suit, as it is allowed to do under 28 U.S.C. § 1605(a)(1)?

2.   An alternative argument for jurisdiction, which the Court disclaims any reliance upon, is "protective jurisdiction." As originally formulated, it applies where Congress has "an articulated and active federal policy regulating a field," and it "permits the conferring of jurisdiction on the national courts of all cases in the area—including those substantively governed by state law." Paul J. Mishkin, *The Federal "Question" in the District Courts*, 53 Colum. L. Rev. 157, 192 (1953). Does this basis for jurisdiction accurately describe the situation in *Verlinden*? The plaintiff's claim might not be governed by federal law. Indeed, the claim is not supplied by the FSIA, which addresses only the issue of immunity. Yet Congress has created a statutory scheme designed to achieve fair and balanced adjudication of claims against foreign sovereigns. Is the protective jurisdiction rationale more persuasive than the Court's attempt to find a federal issue in every case within the jurisdictional provisions of the FSIA?

How farfetched is the Court's own attempt? From its origins in *The Schooner Exchange*, foreign sovereign immunity has been a federal issue, derived from the nearly exclusive control that the federal government exercises over foreign relations under the Constitution. Against that background, the assumption that a federal issue would arise in nearly every lawsuit against a foreign sovereign appears to be well-founded. If so, the cases in which no federal issue arose would be few and far between, even more so than cases like *Verlinden* in which aliens were suing aliens without any basis for diversity jurisdiction. Given the rarity of cases without any federal issues, should the whole statutory scheme in the FSIA have been struck down because it extended to a few anomalous cases? Or does this line of reasoning just lead back to the argument for protective jurisdiction in the absence of an actual federal issue?

At this level of abstraction, the vindication of the FSIA might be regarded as a foregone conclusion. Even if *Verlinden* had been decided differently, the FSIA would have been upheld in some form, with the exercise of jurisdiction trimmed by interpretation or by amendment to conform to the precise requirements of Article III. If so, only a few cases would have been excluded from federal jurisdiction: those involving aliens alone, without any citizen present to create minimal diversity jurisdiction, and without any actual federal issue to create federal question jurisdiction. Was it worthwhile for the Court to exclude these cases from federal jurisdiction, at the risk of forcing Congress to go back and re-enact the FSIA after it had already waited several decades to resolve this matter involving the foreign relations of the U.S.? Did the practicalities of establishing a workable regime of adjudicating foreign sovereign immunity overwhelm arguments based only on constitutional doctrine?

3. The foreign relations context of *Verlinden* suggests that its implications for other attempts to expand federal jurisdiction remain limited at best. The ultimate persuasiveness of the opinion rests upon the national interest in uniform adjudication of issues involving foreign sovereigns. Nevertheless, within that sphere, the decision has had an enormous impact. It has placed federal courts at the center of disputes over the scope and implications of the immunity, one that leaves them, in the first instance, to resolve the many issues left open by the statute. These issues could be characterized simply as matters of statutory interpretation, but given the history of the immunity as a doctrine adopted from international law, it takes on larger implications. These have several dimensions.

From one perspective, the FSIA represents congressional ratification of the role of federal courts in bringing American law into conformity with international law. Chief Justice Marshall relied on international law and international practice in first recognizing foreign sovereign immunity in *The Schooner Exchange*. That principle goes back to an even earlier opinion by Chief Justice Marshall, Murray v. The Schooner Charming Betsy, 6 U.S. (2 Cranch) 64, 118 (1804): "an act of Congress ought never to be construed to violate the law of nations if any other possible construction remains." *The Charming Betsy* canon, as it is called, has proved to be controversial when international law alone supports the result reached by the courts. But in international civil litigation, it has been accepted without dispute when it accords generally with statutes, treaties, and the foreign policy of the U.S. The FSIA stands in a long line of enactments that recognize case law first based on international law.

That said, from another perspective, the FSIA reasserts the dominance of the political branches in the law of foreign affairs. After the act was upheld in *Verlinden*, it became the foundation for determinations of foreign sovereign immunity. The main contours of the immunity, the terms in which it was to be analyzed, and the procedures for doing so, all are set forth in the Act. The courts have to make decisions and offer interpretations within this structure. They cannot, for instance, revert to the absolute version of the immunity or the regime of deference to the State Department in the Tate Letter. Both Congress in passing the FSIA, and the President in signing it, committed the political branches to a different scheme. Given their dominant role in making foreign policy, the political branches exercise a similar decisive influence over the form and structure of litigation against foreign sovereigns.

That influence, however, has not proved to be exclusive of the courts, but inclusive of their role in interpretation and implementation. It yields a form of federal common law, made by judges, based on federal statutes and constitutional principles allocating power between the states and the federal government, and subject to revision by Congress. Federal common law in this sense is binding upon the states, whose courts must allow removal of claims under the FSIA to federal court, and it sets the baseline for future federal legislation. It determines the background against which Congress must act to revise the status quo created by interpretation of existing federal law. As the following cases in this chapter reveal, decisions under the FSIA embrace a number of controversial issues, from human rights to expropriation of private property. The resolution of these issues by the federal courts remains in place, until the inertia inherent in the federal legislative process can be overcome and a revising federal statute enacted. If Congress sets the terms in which these issues must be addressed, the federal courts determine how, in the first instance, and often long thereafter, they are resolved.

4.   For general discussions of the concept of protective jurisdiction, see James E. Pfander, *Protective Jurisdiction, Aggregate Litigation, and the Limits of Article III*, 95 Calif. L. Rev. 1423 (2007); Carole E. Goldberg-Ambrose, *The Protective Jurisdiction of the Federal Courts*, 30 UCLA L. Rev. 542 (1983). For specific application of the concept to litigation against foreign sovereigns, see Carlos M. Vazquez, *The Federal "Claim" in the District Courts: Osborn, Verlinden, and Protective Jurisdiction*, 95 Calif. L. Rev. 1731 (2007); Ernest A. Young, *Stalking the Yeti: Protective Jurisdiction, Foreign Affairs Removal, and Complete Preemption*, 95 Calif. L. Rev. 1775 (2007).

3. *Scope*

Argentine Republic v. Amerada Hess Shipping Corp.

Supreme Court of the United States, 1989.

488 U.S. 428.

CHIEF JUSTICE REHNQUIST delivered the opinion of the Court.

Two Liberian corporations sued the Argentine Republic in a United States District Court to recover damages for a tort allegedly committed by its armed forces on the high seas in violation of international law. We hold that the District Court correctly dismissed the action, because the Foreign Sovereign Immunities Act of 1976 (FSIA), 28 U.S.C. § 1330 et seq., does not authorize jurisdiction over a foreign state in this situation.

Respondents alleged the following facts in their complaints. Respondent United Carriers, Inc., a Liberian corporation, chartered one of its oil tankers, the Hercules, to respondent Amerada Hess Shipping Corporation, also a Liberian corporation. The contract was executed in New York City. Amerada Hess used the Hercules to transport crude oil from the southern terminus of the Trans-Alaska Pipeline in Valdez, Alaska, around Cape Horn in South America, to the Hess refinery in the United States Virgin Islands. On May 25, 1982, the Hercules began a return voyage, without cargo but fully fueled, from the Virgin Islands to Alaska. At that time, Great Britain and petitioner Argentine Republic were at war over an archipelago of some 200 islands—the Falkland Islands to the British, and the Islas Malvinas to the Argentineans—in the South Atlantic off the Argentine coast. On June 3, United States officials informed the two belligerents of the location of United States vessels and Liberian tankers owned by United States interests then traversing the South Atlantic, including the Hercules, to avoid any attacks on neutral shipping.

By June 8, 1982, after a stop in Brazil, the Hercules was in international waters about 600 nautical miles from Argentina and 500 miles from the Falklands; she was outside the "war zones" designated by Britain and Argentina. At 12:15 Greenwich mean time, the ship's master made a routine report by radio to Argentine officials, providing the ship's name, international call sign, registry, position, course, speed, and voyage description. About 45 minutes later, an Argentine military aircraft began to circle the Hercules. The ship's master repeated his earlier message by radio to Argentine officials, who acknowledged receiving it. Six minutes later, without provocation, another Argentine military plane began to bomb the Hercules; the master immediately hoisted a white flag. A second bombing soon followed, and a third attack came about two hours later, when an Argentine jet struck the ship with an air-to-surface rocket. Disabled but not destroyed, the Hercules reversed course and sailed to Rio de Janeiro, the nearest safe port. At Rio de Janeiro, respondent United Carriers determined that the ship had suffered extensive deck and hull damage, and that an undetonated bomb remained lodged in her No. 2 tank. After an investigation by the Brazilian Navy, United Carriers decided that it would be too hazardous to remove the undetonated bomb, and on July 20, 1982, the Hercules was scuttled 250 miles off the Brazilian coast.

Following unsuccessful attempts to obtain relief in Argentina, respondents commenced this action in the United States District Court for the Southern District of New York for the damage that they sustained from the attack. United Carriers sought $10 million in damages for the loss of the ship; Amerada Hess sought $1.9 million in damages for the fuel that went down with the ship. Respondents alleged that petitioner's attack on the neutral Hercules violated international law. They invoked the District Court's jurisdiction under the Alien Tort Statute, 28 U.S.C. § 1350, which provides that "[t]he district courts shall have original jurisdiction of any civil action by an alien for a tort only, committed in violation of the law of nations or a treaty of the United States." Amerada Hess also brought suit under the general admiralty and maritime jurisdiction, 28 U.S.C. § 1333, and "the principle of universal jurisdiction, recognized in customary international law." Complaint of Amerada Hess p. 5. The District Court dismissed both complaints for lack of subject-matter jurisdiction, 638 F. Supp. 73 (1986), ruling that respondents' suits were barred by the FSIA.

A divided panel of the United States Court of Appeals for the Second Circuit reversed. The Court of Appeals held that the District Court had jurisdiction under the Alien Tort Statute, because respondents' consolidated action was brought by Liberian corporations, it sounded in tort ("the bombing of a ship without justification"), and it asserted a violation of international law ("attacking a neutral ship in international waters, without proper cause for suspicion or investigation"). Viewing the Alien Tort Statute as "no more than a jurisdictional grant based on international law," the Court of Appeals said that "who is within" the scope of that grant is governed by "evolving standards of international law" (citing Filartiga v. Pena-Irala, 630 F.2d 876, 880 (CA2 1980)). The Court of Appeals reasoned that Congress' enactment of the FSIA was not meant to eliminate "existing remedies in United States courts for violations of international law" by foreign states under the Alien Tort Statute. The dissenting judge took the view that the FSIA precluded respondents' action. We granted certiorari, and now reverse.

We start from the settled proposition that the subject-matter jurisdiction of the lower federal courts is determined by Congress "in the exact degrees and character which to Congress may seem proper for the public good." Cary v. Curtis, 44 U.S. (3 How.) 236, 245 576 (1845). In the FSIA, Congress added a new chapter 97 to Title 28 of the United States Code, 28 U.S.C. §§ 1602-1611, which is entitled "Jurisdictional Immunities of Foreign States." Section 1604 provides that "[s]ubject to existing international agreements to which the United States [was] a party at the time of the enactment of this Act[,] a foreign state shall be immune from the jurisdiction of the courts of the United States and of the States except as provided in sections 1605 to 1607 of this chapter." The FSIA also added § 1330(a) to Title 28; it provides that "[t]he district courts shall have original jurisdiction without regard to amount in controversy of any nonjury civil action against a foreign state . . . as to any claim for relief in personam with respect to which the foreign state is not entitled to immunity under sections 1605-1607 of this title or under any applicable international agreement." § 1330(a).

We think that the text and structure of the FSIA demonstrate Congress' intention that the FSIA be the sole basis for obtaining jurisdiction over a foreign state in our courts. Sections 1604 and 1330(a) work in tandem: § 1604 bars federal and state courts from exercising jurisdiction when a foreign state is entitled to immunity, and § 1330(a) confers jurisdiction on district courts to hear suits brought by United States citizens and by aliens when a foreign state is not entitled to immunity. As we said in *Verlinden*, the FSIA "must be applied by the district courts in every action against a foreign sovereign, since subject-matter jurisdiction in any such action depends on the existence of one of the specified exceptions to foreign sovereign immunity." Verlinden B.V. v. Central Bank of Nigeria, 461 U.S. 480, 493 (1983).[3]

The Court of Appeals acknowledged that the FSIA's language and legislative history support the "general rule" that the Act governs the immunity of foreign states in federal court. * * * The Court of Appeals, however, thought that the FSIA's "focus on commercial concerns" and Congress' failure to "repeal" the Alien Tort Statute indicated Congress' intention that federal courts continue to exercise jurisdiction over foreign states in suits alleging violations of international law outside the confines of the FSIA. The Court of Appeals also believed that to construe the FSIA to bar the instant suit would "fly in the face" of Congress' intention that the FSIA be interpreted pursuant to "'standards recognized under international law.'" (quoting H.R. Rep., at 14, U.S. Code Cong. & Admin. News 1976, p. 6613.)

Taking the last of these points first, Congress had violations of international law by foreign states in mind when it enacted the FSIA. For example, the FSIA specifically denies foreign states immunity in suits "in which rights in property taken in violation of international law are in issue." 28 U.S.C. § 1605(a)(3). Congress also rested the FSIA in part on its power under Art. I, § 8, cl. 10, of the Constitution "[t]o define and punish Piracies and Felonies committed on the high Seas, and Offenses against the Law of Nations." See H.R. Rep., at 12; S. Rep., at 12, U.S. Code Cong. & Admin. News 1976, p. 6611. From Congress' decision to deny immunity to foreign states in the class of cases just mentioned, we draw the plain implication that immunity is granted in those cases involving alleged violations of international law that do not come within one of the FSIA's exceptions.

---

[3] Subsection (b) of 28 U.S.C. § 1330 provides that "[p]ersonal jurisdiction over a foreign state shall exist as to every claim for relief over which the district courts have [subject-matter] jurisdiction under subsection (a) where service has been made under [28 U.S.C. § 1608]." Thus, personal jurisdiction, like subject-matter jurisdiction, exists only when one of the exceptions to foreign sovereign immunity in §§ 1605-1607 applies. *Verlinden, supra*, at 485, 489, and n. 14. Congress' intention to enact a comprehensive statutory scheme is also supported by the inclusion in the FSIA of provisions for venue, 28 U.S.C. § 1391(f), removal, § 1441(d), and attachment and execution, §§ 1609-1611. Our conclusion here is supported by the FSIA's legislative history. See, e.g., H.R. Rep. No. 94-1487, p. 12 (1976) (H.R. Rep.); S. Rep. No. 94-1310, pp. 11-12 (1976) (S. Rep.), U.S. Code Cong. & Admin. News 1976, pp. 6604, 6610 (FSIA "sets forth the sole and exclusive standards to be used in resolving questions of sovereign immunity raised by sovereign states before Federal and State courts in the United States," and "prescribes . . . the jurisdiction of U.S. district courts in cases involving foreign states").

As to the other point made by the Court of Appeals, Congress' failure to enact a pro tanto repealer of the Alien Tort Statute when it passed the FSIA in 1976 may be explained at least in part by the lack of certainty as to whether the Alien Tort Statute conferred jurisdiction in suits against foreign states. Enacted by the First Congress in 1789, the Alien Tort Statute provides that "[t]he district courts shall have original jurisdiction of any civil action by an alien for a tort only, committed in violation of the law of nations or a treaty of the United States." 28 U.S.C. § 1350. The Court of Appeals did not cite any decision in which a United States court exercised jurisdiction over a foreign state under the Alien Tort Statute, and only one such case has come to our attention—one which was decided after the enactment of the FSIA.

In this Court, respondents argue that cases were brought under the Alien Tort Statute against foreign states for the unlawful taking of a prize during wartime. The Alien Tort Statute makes no mention of prize jurisdiction, and § 1333(2) now grants federal district courts exclusive jurisdiction over "all proceedings for the condemnation of property taken as a prize." In The Santissima Trinidad, 20 U.S. (7 Wheat.) 283, 353-354 (1822), we held that foreign states were not immune from the jurisdiction of United States courts in prize proceedings. That case, however, was not brought under the Alien Tort Statute but rather as a libel in admiralty. Thus there is a distinctly hypothetical cast to the Court of Appeals' reliance on Congress' failure to repeal the Alien Tort Statute, and respondents' arguments in this Court based on the principle of statutory construction that repeals by implication are disfavored.

We think that Congress' failure in the FSIA to enact an express pro tanto repealer of the Alien Tort Statute speaks only faintly, if at all, to the issue involved in this case. In light of the comprehensiveness of the statutory scheme in the FSIA, we doubt that even the most meticulous draftsman would have concluded that Congress also needed to amend pro tanto the Alien Tort Statute and presumably such other grants of subject-matter jurisdiction in Title 28 as § 1331 (federal question), § 1333 (admiralty), § 1335 (interpleader), § 1337 (commerce and antitrust), and § 1338 (patents, copyrights, and trademarks).[5] Congress provided in the FSIA that "[c]laims of foreign states to immunity should *henceforth* be decided by courts of the United States in conformity with the principles set forth in this chapter," and very likely it thought that should be sufficient. § 1602 (emphasis added); see also H.R. Rep., at 12; S. Rep., at 11, U.S. Code Cong. & Admin. News 1976, p. 6610 (FSIA "intended to preempt any other State and

---

[5]   The FSIA amended the diversity statute to delete references to suits in which a "foreign stat[e]" is a party either as plaintiff or defendant, see 28 U.S.C. §§ 1332(a)(2) and (3) (1970 ed.), and added a new paragraph (4) that preserves diversity jurisdiction over suits in which foreign states are plaintiffs. As the legislative history explained, "[s]ince jurisdiction in actions against foreign states is comprehensively treated by the new section 1330, a similar jurisdictional basis under section 1332 becomes superfluous." H.R. Rep., at 14; S. Rep., at 13, U.S. Code Cong. & Admin. News 1976, p. 6613. Unlike the diversity statute, however, the Alien Tort Statute and the other statutes conferring jurisdiction in general terms on district courts cited in the text did not in 1976 (or today) expressly provide for suits against foreign states.

Federal law (excluding applicable international agreements) for according immunity to foreign sovereigns").

For similar reasons we are not persuaded by respondents' arguments based upon the rule of statutory construction under which repeals by implication are disfavored. This case does not involve two statutes that readily could be seen as supplementing one another, see Wood v. United States, 41 U.S. (16 Pet.) 342, 363 (1842), nor is it a case where a more general statute is claimed to have repealed by implication an earlier statute dealing with a narrower subject. See Morton v. Mancari, 417 U.S. 535, 549-551 (1974). We think that Congress' decision to deal comprehensively with the subject of foreign sovereign immunity in the FSIA, and the express provision in § 1604 that "a foreign state shall be immune from the jurisdiction of the courts of the United States and of the States except as provided in sections 1605-1607," preclude a construction of the Alien Tort Statute that permits the instant suit. See Red Rock v. Henry, 106 U.S. 596, 601-602 (1883); United States v. Tynen, 78 U.S. (11 Wall.) 88, 92 (1871). The Alien Tort Statute by its terms does not distinguish among classes of defendants, and it of course has the same effect after the passage of the FSIA as before with respect to defendants other than foreign states.

Respondents also argue that the general admiralty and maritime jurisdiction, § 1333(1), provides a basis for obtaining jurisdiction over petitioner for violations of international law, notwithstanding the FSIA. But Congress dealt with the admiralty jurisdiction of the federal courts when it enacted the FSIA. Section 1605(b) expressly permits an in personam suit in admiralty to enforce a maritime lien against a vessel or cargo of a foreign state. Unless the present case is within § 1605(b) or another exception to the FSIA, the statute conferring general admiralty and maritime jurisdiction on the federal courts does not authorize the bringing of this action against petitioner.

Having determined that the FSIA provides the sole basis for obtaining jurisdiction over a foreign state in federal court, we turn to whether any of the exceptions enumerated in the Act apply here. These exceptions include cases involving the waiver of immunity, § 1605(a)(1), commercial activities occurring in the United States or causing a direct effect in this country, § 1605(a)(2), property expropriated in violation of international law, § 1605(a)(3), inherited, gift, or immovable property located in the United States, § 1605(a)(4), non-commercial torts occurring in the United States, § 1605(a)(5), and maritime liens, § 1605(b). We agree with the District Court that none of the FSIA's exceptions applies on these facts. See 638 F. Supp., at 75-77.

Respondents assert that the FSIA exception for noncommercial torts, § 1605(a)(5), is most in point. This provision denies immunity in a case

> "in which money damages are sought against a foreign state for personal injury or death, or damage to or loss of property, occurring in the United States and caused by the tortious act or omission of that foreign state or of any official or employee of that foreign state while acting within the scope of his office or employment." 28 U.S.C. § 1605(a)(5).

Section 1605(a)(5) is limited by its terms, however, to those cases in which the damage to or loss of property occurs in the United States. Congress' primary purpose in enacting § 1605(a)(5) was to eliminate a foreign state's immunity for traffic accidents and other torts committed in the United States, for which liability is imposed under domestic tort law. See H.R. Rep., at 14, 20-21; S. Rep., at 14, 20-21.

In this case, the injury to respondents' ship occurred on the high seas some 5,000 miles off the nearest shores of the United States. Despite these telling facts, respondents nonetheless claim that the tortious attack on the Hercules occurred "in the United States." They point out that the FSIA defines "United States" as including all "territory and waters, continental and insular, subject to the jurisdiction of the United States," § 1603(c), and that their injury occurred on the high seas, which is within the admiralty jurisdiction of the United States, see The Plymouth, 70 U.S. (3 Wall.) 20, 36 (1866). They reason, therefore, that "by statutory definition" petitioner's attack occurred in the United States.

We find this logic unpersuasive. We construe the modifying phrase "continental and insular" to restrict the definition of United States to the continental United States and those islands that are part of the United States or its possessions; any other reading would render this phrase nugatory. Likewise, the term "waters" in § 1603(c) cannot reasonably be read to cover all waters over which United States courts might exercise jurisdiction. When it desires to do so, Congress knows how to place the high seas within the jurisdictional reach of a statute.[7] We thus apply "[t]he canon of construction which teaches that legislation of Congress, unless contrary intent appears, is meant to apply only within the territorial jurisdiction of the United States." Foley Brothers v. Filardo, 336 U.S. 281, 285 (1949); see also Weinberger v. Rossi, 456 U.S. 25, 32 (1982). Because respondents' injury unquestionably occurred well outside the 3-mile limit then in effect for the territorial waters of the United States, the exception for noncommercial torts cannot apply.

The result in this case is not altered by the fact that petitioner's alleged tort may have had effects in the United States. Respondents state, for example, that the Hercules was transporting oil intended for use in this country and that the loss of the ship disrupted contractual payments due in New York. Under the commercial activity exception to the FSIA, § 1605(a)(2), a foreign state may be liable for its commercial activities "outside the territory of the United States" having a "direct effect" inside the United States. But the noncommercial tort exception, § 1605(a)(5), upon which respondents rely, makes no mention of "territory outside the United States" or of "direct effects" in the United States. Congress' decision to use explicit language in § 1605(a)(2), and not to do so in § 1605(a)(5), indicates that the exception in § 1605(a)(5) covers only torts occur-

---

[7] See, e.g., 14 U.S.C. § 89(a) (empowering Coast Guard to search and seize vessels "upon the high seas and waters over which the United States has jurisdiction" for "prevention, detection, and suppression of violations of laws of the United States"); 18 U.S.C. § 7 ("special maritime and territorial jurisdiction of the United States" in Federal Criminal Code extends to United States vessels on "[t]he high seas, any other waters within the admiralty and maritime jurisdiction of the United States, and out of the jurisdiction of any particular State"); 19 U.S.C. § 1701 (permitting President to declare portions of "high seas" as customs-enforcement areas).

ring within the territorial jurisdiction of the United States. Respondents do not claim that § 1605(a)(2) covers these facts.

We also disagree with respondents' claim that certain international agreements entered into by petitioner and by the United States create an exception to the FSIA here. As noted, the FSIA was adopted "[s]ubject to international agreements to which the United States [was] a party at the time of [its] enactment." § 1604. This exception applies when international agreements "expressly conflic[t]" with the immunity provisions of the FSIA, H.R. Rep., at 17; S. Rep., at 17, U.S. Code Cong. & Admin. News 1976, p. 6616, hardly the circumstances in this case. Respondents point to the Geneva Convention on the High Seas, Apr. 29, 1958, [1962] 13 U.S.T. 2312, T.I.A.S. No. 5200, and the Pan American Maritime Neutrality Convention, Feb. 20, 1928, 47 Stat.1989, 1990-1991, T.S. No. 845. These conventions, however, only set forth substantive rules of conduct and state that compensation shall be paid for certain wrongs. They do not create private rights of action for foreign corporations to recover compensation from foreign states in United States courts. Cf. Head Money Cases, 112 U.S. 580, 598-599 (1884); Foster v. Neilson, 27 U.S. (2 Pet.) 253, 314 (1829). Nor do we see how a foreign state can waive its immunity under § 1605(a)(1) by signing an international agreement that contains no mention of a waiver of immunity to suit in United States courts or even the availability of a cause of action in the United States. We find similarly unpersuasive the argument of respondents and Amicus Curiae Republic of Liberia that the Treaty of Friendship, Commerce and Navigation, Aug. 8, 1938, United States-Liberia, 54 Stat. 1739, T.S. No. 956, carves out an exception to the FSIA. Article I of this Treaty provides, in pertinent part, that the nationals of the United States and Liberia "shall enjoy freedom of access to the courts of justice of the other on conforming to the local laws." The FSIA is clearly one of the "local laws" to which respondents must "conform" before bringing suit in United States courts.

We hold that the FSIA provides the sole basis for obtaining jurisdiction over a foreign state in the courts of this country, and that none of the enumerated exceptions to the Act apply to the facts of this case. The judgment of the Court of Appeals is therefore

Reversed.

JUSTICE BLACKMUN, with whom JUSTICE MARSHALL joins, concurring in part.

I join the Court's opinion insofar as it holds that the FSIA provides the sole basis for obtaining jurisdiction over a foreign state in federal court.

I, however, do not join the latter part of the Court's opinion to the effect that none of the FSIA's exceptions to foreign sovereign immunity apply in this case. As the majority notes, the Court of Appeals did not decide this question, and, indeed, specifically reserved it. 830 F.2d 421, 429, n.3 (CA2 1987). Moreover, the question was not among those presented to this Court in the petition for certiorari, did not receive full briefing, and is not necessary to the disposition of the case. Accordingly, I believe it inappropriate to decide here, in the first instance, whether any exceptions to the FSIA apply in this case. See this Court's Rule 21.1(a) (Court will consider only questions presented in petition); Youakim v.

Miller, 425 U.S. 231, 234 (1976) (Court ordinarily will not decide questions not passed on below). I would remand the case to the Court of Appeals on this issue.

NOTES AND QUESTIONS FOR DISCUSSION

1. Did the Supreme Court have any real choice in deciding "that the FSIA provides the sole basis for obtaining jurisdiction over a foreign state in the courts of this country"? How else could the Court make sense out of the command in § 1604 that foreign states "shall be immune" except as provided by §§ 1605-07 of the FSIA? The statute itself dictates that the exceptions to immunity that it allows shall be exclusive.

The plaintiffs sought a different result by implying an exception based on the Statute, 28 U.S.C. § 1350, which confers jurisdiction on the federal courts of claims "by an alien for a tort only, committed in violation of the law of nations or a treaty of the United States." See Chapter 2, Section C. It has frequently been invoked in human rights cases, both as discussed in Chapter 2 and as we shall see later in this chapter, despite obscure origins that date back to the Judiciary Act of 1789. The plaintiffs argued that such a venerable statute could not have been impliedly repealed by the FSIA. But doesn't its age suggest that it was precisely the kind of statute that the FSIA was meant to qualify? What is the point of a statute granting an immunity if it fails to do so against longstanding claims of liability that might be asserted against a foreign sovereign?

The proclaimed exclusivity of the FSIA could be modified by subsequently enacted legislation, and on several occasions, Congress has removed the immunity of foreign states, particularly with respect to human rights violations. Nevertheless, such legislation has invariably appeared as amendments to the FSIA and has been framed in highly detailed provisions, as in § 1605(a)(7) on acts of state-sponsored terrorism. These exceptions were enacted after *Amerada Hess*, but doesn't the possibility that Congress could take such action to create express exceptions fatally undermine the plaintiffs' argument for an implied exception?

2. The Court also holds that none of the exceptions under the FSIA apply to the claim in this case, and in particular, that the exception for noncommercial torts in § 1605(a)(5) does not apply because the territorial restriction on that exception has not been met. It requires that the plaintiff's claim must be for loss "occurring in the United States." The territory of the United States, in turn, is defined to include the "territory and waters, continental or insular, subject to the jurisdiction of the United States." § 1603(c). Since the plaintiff's loss occurred on the "high seas," well beyond the boundary of the territorial seas of the U.S. (at the time three miles and now twelve miles), this exception did not, by its literal terms, apply to this case.

The plaintiffs, instead, turned to admiralty jurisdiction for an analogy. Since admiralty courts regularly hear cases arising on the high seas, they argued, "the jurisdiction of the United States" also could be construed to reach so far. Does this analogy just depend upon the ambiguities in the term "jurisdiction"? It could mean "adjudicatory jurisdiction"—i.e., subject-matter and personal jurisdiction of the courts, which is the immediate subject of the FSIA. Or it could mean "legislative jurisdiction": the power of a state to prescribe what the law is. The definition of territorial boundaries in § 1603 plainly seems to refer to this last sense since a state's lawmaking authority primarily applies to territory under its control. Moreover, reliance on the first of the two senses would make the limited exceptions to immunity under the FSIA circular, allowing personal and subject-matter jurisdiction in cases in which such jurisdiction already existed.

Nevertheless, if admiralty jurisdiction existed, why didn't the plaintiffs rely upon it as the basis for an implied exception to the FSIA? Going back to *The Schooner Exchange*, admiralty cases have been a fertile source of cases on sovereign immunity, and indeed, the plaintiffs relied upon an old "prize" case, *The Santissima Trinidad*, 20 U.S. (7 Wheat.) 283 (1822), for jurisdiction over foreign sovereigns. Prize cases involve the seizure of a vessel operating under the flag of a hostile state. Yet prize cases, particularly those involving seizure by a private party, have been virtually eliminated as a heading of admiralty jurisdiction, as Congress has restricted seizure to actions of the military and other public officials. A further problem with the plaintiffs' argument has to do with the exception to sovereign immunity in admiralty cases, in § 1605(b), which also is subject to restrictions, chiefly that it is "based upon a commercial activity." Could Congress have allowed an implied exception for admiralty claims like the one in this case, arising from the hostile act of a foreign nation in the course of a war with another country, when it expressly limited the scope of the express exception for admiralty cases?

3. On examination, all of the plaintiffs' arguments for an implied exception to the FSIA seem unconvincing, so much so that the Supreme Court was unanimous in rejecting them. The separate opinion by Justice Blackmun simply would have reserved the question of the application of an express exception. Why did the plaintiffs feel compelled to advance an argument that went so much against the grain of the FSIA? Did they depend upon the moral force of the argument that a neutral vessel far from the zone of conflict should not be subject to hostile attacks, especially when it made its neutrality plain to the attacking nation? Or did they simply have no other remedy available to them? After this decision, the courts of the U.S. were closed to them, although they might have sought relief in the courts of another country. Was one likely to be open to them? Could they have turned outside the judicial system entirely to seek relief through diplomatic channels? How much leverage would Liberia have, where the plaintiff corporations were incorporated, or would the the U.S., where Amerada Hess Corp., the parent of the plaintiff companies, has its headquarters? Note that the U.S. eventually sided with the United Kingdom and against Argentina in the conflict.

4. The Supreme Court confirmed the broad scope of the FSIA in **Republic of Austria v. Altmann, 541 U.S. 677 (2004)**. That decision arose from the expropriation of paintings by the Nazi regime in Austria and subsequent transfer of the paintings to the Austrian Gallery. When the details of the expropriation became public in 1998, Austria enacted a law providing for restitution, but the plaintiff in this case—a descendant of the Jewish owner of the paintings that were seized—could not sue in the Austrian courts. That is because Austria required the plaintiff to post bond for a percentage of the value of the property in dispute, which in this case was approximately $200 million. The plaintiff decided to sue instead in the United States.

Without reaching the question whether the plaintiff could take advantage of any exception in the FSIA, the Supreme Court held that the statute applied retroactively to determine the scope of the immunity—in this case to a seizure that occurred nearly three decades before its enactment. The Court relied on three reasons to depart from the usual presumption against retroactive application of a statute to claims arising from events before it was enacted. First, jurisdiction under the FSIA depends upon events at the time the case was filed, an issue explored more fully in the next principal case. Second, the FSIA represents the most recent statement by the political branches of the policy of the U.S. with respect to foreign sovereign immunity. And third, the FSIA was intended to restate and clarify the restrictive version of sovereign immunity, dating back to the Tate Letter of 1952, which itself had been applied retroactively. Relying directly upon *Amerada Hess*, the Court concluded that "Congress' purposes in enacting such a comprehensive jurisdictional scheme would be frustrated if, in postenactment cases concerning preenactment conduct, courts were to continue to follow the same ambiguous and politically charged 'standards' that the FSIA replaced." *Altmann*, 541 U.S. at 699. Of course, an added reason, not far below the surface of the case, concerned the Nazi policies of anti-Semitism and genocide that gave rise to the plaintiff's claim. Could the Court realistically have excluded confiscations of Jewish property from application of the FSIA?

Does that make this case easier or harder than *Amerada Hess*? This decision left open the possibility, subsequently exploited on remand, that confiscation of the plaintiff's property fell within the exception for expropriation of property under § 1605(a)(3). On remand, the Austria agreed to arbitration of the plaintiff's claim, which resulted in the award of the paintings to her. In *Amerada Hess*, by contrast, finding coverage under the FSIA led to the conclusion that the defendant was immune from liability. Does finding coverage under the FSIA make so much difference when it can lead to such inconsistent results? Or does the coverage of the statute sort out claims according to the plaintiff's ability to establish that one of the exceptions to immunity applies? Is that the right result as a matter of congressional policy? As a matter of the moral appeal of the plaintiff's claim? Or was the result in *Altmann* driven by the high value of the property at stake?

5. For scholarship on the history and scope of the FSIA, see Working Group of the American Bar Association, *Reforming the Foreign Sovereign Immunities Act*, 40 Colum. J. Transnat'l L. 489 (2002); Joseph W. Dellapenna, *Refining the Foreign Sovereign Immunities Act*, 9 Willamette J. Int'l L. & Disp. Resol. 57 (2001); Mark B. Feldman, *The United States Foreign Sovereign Immunities Act of 1976 in Perspective: A Founder's View*, 35 Int'l & Comp. L.Q. 302 (1986); Robert B. von Mehren, *The Foreign Sovereign Immunities Act of 1976*, 17 Colum. J. Transnat'l L.J. 33 (1978). For articles on the issues raised by *Altmann*, see Alicia M. Hilton, *Terror Victims at the Museum Gates: Testing the Commercial Activity Exception Under the Foreign Sovereign Immunities Act*, 53 Vill. L. Rev. 479 (2008); Lauren Redman, *The Foreign Sovereign Immunities Act: Using a "Shield" Statute as a "Sword" for Obtaining Federal Jurisdiction in Art and Antiquities Cases*, 31 Fordham Int'l L.J. 781 (2008); Yonaton Lupu & Clay Risen, *Retroactive Application of the Foreign Sovereign Immunities Act:* Landgraf *Analysis and the Political Question Doctrine*, 8 UCLA J. Int'l L. & Foreign Aff.

239 (2003); Karen Halverson, *Is a Foreign State a "Person"? Does it Matter?: Personal Jurisdiction, Due Process, and the Foreign Sovereign Immunities Act*, 34 N.Y.U. J. Int'l L. & Pol. 115 (2001).

Dole Food Co. v. Patrickson

Supreme Court of the United States, 2003.

538 U.S. 468.

JUSTICE KENNEDY delivered the opinion of the Court.

Foreign states may invoke certain rights and immunities in litigation under the Foreign Sovereign Immunities Act of 1976 (FSIA or Act), Pub. L. 94-583, 90 Stat. 2891. Some of the Act's provisions also may be invoked by a corporate entity that is an "instrumentality" of a foreign state as defined by the Act. Republic of Argentina v. Weltover, Inc., 504 U.S. 607, 611 (1992); Verlinden B.V. v. Central Bank of Nigeria, 461 U.S. 480, 488 (1983). The corporate entities in this action claim instrumentality status to invoke the Act's provisions allowing removal of state-court actions to federal court. As the action comes to us, it presents two questions. The first is whether a corporate subsidiary can claim instrumentality status where the foreign state does not own a majority of its shares but does own a majority of the shares of a corporate parent one or more tiers above the subsidiary. The second question is whether a corporation's instrumentality status is defined as of the time an alleged tort or other actionable wrong occurred or, on the other hand, at the time suit is filed. We granted certiorari, 536 U.S. 956 (2002).

I

The underlying action was filed in a state court in Hawaii in 1997 against Dole Food Company and other companies (Dole petitioners). Plaintiffs in the action were a group of farm workers from Costa Rica, Ecuador, Guatemala, and Panama who alleged injury from exposure to dibromochloropropane, a chemical used as an agricultural pesticide in their home countries. The Dole petitioners impleaded petitioners Dead Sea Bromine Co., Ltd., and Bromine Compounds, Ltd. (collectively, the Dead Sea Companies). The merits of the suit are not before us.

[The Dead Sea Companies removed under the theory that they were instrumentalities of a foreign state as defined by the FSIA, entitling them to removal under § 1441(d). The district court and the court of appeals both denied removal on this ground.]

In order to prevail here, the Dead Sea Companies must show both that instrumentality status is determined as of the time the alleged tort occurred and that they can claim instrumentality status even though they were but subsidiaries of a parent owned by the State of Israel. We address each question in turn. In No. 01-594, the case in which the Dead Sea Companies are petitioners, we now affirm.

II

A

Title 28 U.S.C. § 1441(d) governs removal of actions against foreign states. It provides that "[a]ny civil action brought in a State court against a foreign state as defined in [28 U.S.C. § 1603(a)] may be removed by the foreign state to the district court of the United States for the district and division embracing the place where such action is pending." See also § 1330 (governing original jurisdiction). Section 1603(a), part of the FSIA, defines "foreign state" to include an "agency or instrumentality of a foreign state." "[A]gency or instrumentality of a foreign state" is defined, in turn, as:

"[A]ny entity—

"(1) which is a separate legal person, corporate or otherwise, and

"(2) which is an organ of a foreign state or political subdivision thereof, or a majority of whose shares or other ownership interest is owned by a foreign state or political subdivision thereof, and

"(3) which is neither a citizen of a State of the United States . . . nor created under the laws of any third country." § 1603(b).

B

The Court of Appeals resolved the question of the FSIA's applicability by holding that a subsidiary of an instrumentality is not itself entitled to instrumentality status. Its holding was correct.

The State of Israel did not have direct ownership of shares in either of the Dead Sea Companies at any time pertinent to this suit. Rather, these companies were, at various times, separated from the State of Israel by one or more intermediate corporate tiers. For example, from 1984-1985, Israel wholly owned a company called Israeli Chemicals, Ltd. which owned a majority of shares in another company called Dead Sea Works, Ltd.; which owned a majority of shares in Dead Sea Bromine Co., Ltd.; which owned a majority of shares in Bromine Compounds, Ltd.

The Dead Sea Companies, as indirect subsidiaries of the State of Israel, were not instrumentalities of Israel under the FSIA at any time. Those companies cannot come within the statutory language which grants status as an instrumentality of a foreign state to an entity a "majority of whose shares or other ownership interest is owned by a foreign state or political subdivision thereof." § 1603(b)(2). We hold that only direct ownership of a majority of shares by the foreign state satisfies the statutory requirement.

Section 1603(b)(2) speaks of ownership. The Dead Sea Companies urge us to ignore corporate formalities and use the colloquial sense of that term. They ask whether, in common parlance, Israel would be said to own the Dead Sea Companies. We reject this analysis. In issues of corporate law structure often matters. It is evident from the Act's text that Congress was aware of settled principles of corporate law and legislated within that context. The language of § 1603(b)(2) refers to ownership of "shares," showing that Congress intended statutory coverage to turn on formal corporate ownership. Likewise, § 1603(b)(1), another component of the definition of instrumentality, refers to a "separate legal person, corporate or otherwise." In light of these indicia that Congress had corporate formalities in mind, we assess whether Israel owned shares in the Dead Sea Companies as a matter of corporate law, irrespective of whether Israel could be said to have owned the Dead Sea Companies in everyday parlance.

A basic tenet of American corporate law is that the corporation and its shareholders are distinct entities. See, e.g., First Nat. City Bank v. Banco Para El Comercio Exterior de Cuba, 462 U.S. 611, 625 (1983) ("Separate legal personality has been described as 'an almost indispensable aspect of the public corporation'"); Burnet v. Clark, 287 U.S. 410, 415 (1932) ("A corporation and its stockholders are generally to be treated as separate entities"). An individual shareholder, by virtue of his ownership of shares, does not own the corporation's assets and, as a result, does not own subsidiary corporations in which the corporation holds an interest. See 1 W. Fletcher, Cyclopedia of the Law of Private Corporations § 31 (rev. ed. 1999). A corporate parent which owns the shares of a subsidiary does not, for that reason alone, own or have legal title to the assets of the subsidiary; and, it follows with even greater force, the parent does not own or have legal title to the subsidiaries of the subsidiary. See id., § 31, at 514 ("The properties of two corporations are distinct, though the same shareholders own or control both. A holding corporation does not own the subsidiary's property"). The fact that the shareholder is a foreign state does not change the analysis. See *First Nat. City Bank, supra*, at 626-627 ("[G]overnment instrumentalities established as juridical entities distinct and independent from their sovereign should normally be treated as such").

Applying these principles, it follows that Israel did not own a majority of shares in the Dead Sea Companies. The State of Israel owned a majority of shares, at various times, in companies one or more corporate tiers above the Dead Sea Companies, but at no time did Israel own a majority of shares in the Dead Sea Companies. Those companies were subsidiaries of other corporations.

The veil separating corporations and their shareholders may be pierced in some circumstances, and the Dead Sea Companies essentially urge us to interpret the FSIA as piercing the veil in all cases. The doctrine of piercing the corporate veil, however, is the rare exception, applied in the case of fraud or certain other exceptional circumstances, see, e.g., *Burnet, supra*, at 415; Fletcher, *supra*, §§ 41 to 41.20, and usually determined on a case-by-case basis. The Dead Sea Companies have referred us to no authority for extending the doctrine so far that, as a categorical matter, all subsidiaries are deemed to be the same as the parent corporation. The text of the FSIA gives no indication that Congress intended us to depart from the general rules regarding corporate formalities.

Where Congress intends to refer to ownership in other than the formal sense, it knows how to do so. Various federal statutes refer to "direct and indirect ownership." See, e.g., 5 U.S.C. § 8477(a)(4)(G)(iii) (referring to an interest "owned directly or indirectly"); 12 U.S.C. § 84(c)(5) (referring to "any corporation wholly owned directly or indirectly by the United States"); 15 U.S.C. § 79b(a)(8)(A) (referring to securities "which are directly or indirectly owned, controlled, or held with power to vote"); § 1802(3) ("The term 'newspaper owner' means any person who owns or controls directly, or indirectly through separate or subsidiary corporations, one or more newspaper publications"). The absence of this language in 28 U.S.C. § 1603(b) instructs us that Congress did not intend to disregard structural ownership rules.

The FSIA's definition of instrumentality refers to a foreign state's majority ownership of "shares or other ownership interest." § 1603(b)(2). The Dead Sea Companies would have us read "other ownership interest" to include a state's "interest" in its instrumentality's subsidiary. The better reading of the text, in our view, does not support this argument. The words "other ownership interest," when following the word "shares," should be interpreted to refer to a type of interest other than ownership of stock. The statute had to be written for the contingency of ownership forms in other countries, or even in this country, that depart from conventional corporate structures. The statutory phrase "other ownership interest" is best understood to accomplish this objective. Reading the term to refer to a state's interest in entities lower on the corporate ladder would make the specific reference to "shares" redundant. Absent a statutory text or structure that requires us to depart from normal rules of construction, we should not construe the statute in a manner that is strained and, at the same time, would render a statutory term superfluous. See Mertens v. Hewitt Associates, 508 U.S. 248, 258 (1993) ("We will not read the statute to render the modifier superfluous"); United States v. Nordic Village, Inc., 503 U.S. 30, 36 (1992) (declining to adopt a construction that would violate the "settled rule that a statute must, if possible, be construed in such fashion that every word has some operative effect").

The Dead Sea Companies say that the State of Israel exercised considerable control over their operations, notwithstanding Israel's indirect relationship to those companies. They appear to think that, in determining instrumentality status under the Act, control may be substituted for an ownership interest. Control and ownership, however, are distinct concepts. See, e.g., United States v. Bestfoods, 524 U.S. 51, 64-65 (1998) (distinguishing between "operation" and "ownership" of a subsidiary's assets for purposes of Comprehensive Environmental Response, Compensation, and Liability Act of 1980 liability). The terms of § 1603(b)(2) are explicit and straightforward. Majority ownership by a foreign state, not control, is the benchmark of instrumentality status. We need not delve into Israeli law or examine the extent of Israel's involvement in the Dead Sea Companies' operations. Even if Israel exerted the control the Dead Sea Companies describe, that would not give Israel a "majority of [the companies'] shares or other ownership interest." The statutory language will not support a control test that mandates inquiry in every case into the past details of a foreign nation's relation to a corporate entity in which it does not own a majority of the shares.

The better rule is the one supported by the statutory text and elementary principles of corporate law. A corporation is an instrumentality of a foreign state under the FSIA only if the foreign state itself owns a majority of the corporation's shares.

We now turn to the second question before us, which provides an alternative reason for affirming the Court of Appeals. See Woods v. Interstate Realty Co., 337 U.S. 535, 537 (1949).

C

To be entitled to removal under § 1441(d), the Dead Sea Companies must show that they are entities "a majority of whose shares or other ownership interest is owned by a foreign state." § 1603(b)(2). We think the plain text of this provision, because it is expressed in the present tense, requires that instrumentality status be determined at the time suit is filed.

Construing § 1603(b) so that the present tense has real significance is consistent with the "longstanding principle that 'the jurisdiction of the Court depends upon the state of things at the time of the action brought.'" Keene Corp. v. United States, 508 U.S. 200, 207 (1993) (quoting Mollan v. Torrance, 9 Wheat. 537, 539, 6 L.Ed. 154 (1824)). It is well settled, for example, that federal-diversity jurisdiction depends on the citizenship of the parties at the time suit is filed. See, e.g., Anderson v. Watt, 138 U.S. 694, 702-703 (1891) ("And the [jurisdictional] inquiry is determined by the condition of the parties at the commencement of the suit"); see also Minneapolis & St. Louis R. Co. v. Peoria & Pekin Union R. Co., 270 U.S. 580, 586 (1926) ("The jurisdiction of the lower court depends upon the state of things existing at the time the suit was brought"). The Dead Sea Companies do not dispute that the time suit is filed is determinative under § 1332(a)(4), which provides for suits between "a foreign state, defined in section 1603(a) . . . , as plaintiff and citizens of a State or of different States." It would be anomalous to read § 1441(d)'s words, "foreign state as defined in section 1603(a)," differently.

The Dead Sea Companies urge us to administer the FSIA like other status-based immunities, such as the qualified immunity accorded a state actor, that are based on the status of an officer at the time of the conduct giving rise to the suit. We think its comparison is inapt. * * *

The reason for the official immunities in those cases does not apply here. The immunities for government officers prevent the threat of suit from "crippl[ing] the proper and effective administration of public affairs." *Spalding v. Vilas, supra,* [161 U.S. 483,] 498 [(1896)] (discussing immunity for executive officers); see also Pierson v. Ray, 386 U.S. 547, 554 (1967) (judicial immunity serves the public interest in judges who are "at liberty to exercise their functions with independence and without fear of consequences" (internal quotation marks omitted)). Foreign sovereign immunity, by contrast, is not meant to avoid chilling foreign states or their instrumentalities in the conduct of their business but to give foreign states and their instrumentalities some protection from the inconvenience of suit as a gesture of comity between the United States and other sovereigns. *Verlinden,* 461 U.S., at 486. * * *

Any relationship recognized under the FSIA between the Dead Sea Companies and Israel had been severed before suit was commenced. As a result, the Dead Sea Companies would not be entitled to instrumentality status even if their theory that instrumentality status could be conferred on a subsidiary were accepted. * * *

JUSTICE BREYER, with whom JUSTICE O'CONNOR joins, concurring in part and dissenting in part.

I join Parts I, II-A, and II-C, and dissent only from Part II-B, of the Court's opinion. Unlike the majority, I believe that the statutory phrase "other ownership interest . . . owned by a foreign state," 28 U.S.C. § 1603(b)(2), covers a Foreign Nation's legal interest in a Corporate Subsidiary, where that interest consists of the Foreign Nation's ownership of a Corporate Parent that owns the shares of the Subsidiary. * * *

Statutory interpretation is not a game of blind man's bluff. Judges are free to consider statutory language in light of a statute's basic purposes. And here * * * an examination of those purposes sheds considerable light. The statute itself makes clear that it seeks: (1) to provide a foreign-state defendant in a legal action the right to have its claim of a sovereign immunity bar decided by the "courts of the United States," i.e., the federal courts, 28 U.S.C. § 1604; see § 1441(d); and (2) to make certain that the merits of unbarred claims against foreign states, say, states engaging in commercial activities, see § 1605(a)(2), will be decided "in the same manner" as similar claims against "a private individual," § 1606; but (3) to guarantee a foreign state defending an unbarred claim certain protections, including a prohibition of punitive damages, the right to removal to federal court, a trial before a judge, and other procedural rights (related to service of process, venue, attachment, and execution of judgments). §§ 1330, 1391(f), 1441(d), 1606, 1608-1611.

Most important for present purposes, the statute seeks to guarantee these protections to the foreign nation not only when it acts directly in its own name but also when it acts through separate legal entities, including corporations and other "organ[s]." 28 U.S.C. § 1603(b).

Given these purposes, what might lead Congress to grant protection to a Foreign Nation acting through a Corporate Parent but deny the same protection to the Foreign Nation acting through, for example, a wholly owned Corporate Subsidiary? The answer to this question is: In terms of the statute's purposes, nothing at all would lead Congress to make such a distinction.

As far as this statute is concerned, decisions about how to incorporate, how to structure corporate entities, or whether to act through a single corporate layer or through several corporate layers are matters purely of form, not of substance. Cf. H.R. Rep. No. 94-1487, at 15, U.S. Code Cong. & Admin. News 1976, at pp. 6604, 6614 (agencies or instrumentalities "could assume a variety of forms"); First Nat. City Bank v. Banco Para El Comercio Exterior de Cuba, 462 U.S. 611, 625 (1983) (noting that "developing countries" often "establish separate juridical entities . . . to make large-scale national investments"). The need for federal-court determination of a sovereign immunity claim is no less important where subsidiaries are involved. The need for procedural protections is no less compelling. The risk of adverse foreign policy consequences is no less great.

That is why I doubt the majority's claim that its reading of the text of the FSIA is "[t]he better reading," leading to "[t]he better rule." The majority's rule is not better for a foreign nation, say, Mexico or Honduras, which may use "a tiered corporate structure to manage and control important areas of national interest, such as natural resources," ABA Working Group 523, and, as a result, will find its ability to use the federal courts to adjudicate matters of national importance and "potential sensitivity" restricted, H.R. Rep. No. 94-1487, at 32, U.S. Code Cong. & Admin. News 1976, at pp. 6604, 6631. Congress is most unlikely to characterize as "better" a rule tied to legal formalities that undercuts its basic jurisdictional objectives. And working lawyers will now have to factor into complex corporate restructuring equations (determining, say, whether to use an intermediate holding company when merging or disaggregating even wholly owned government corporations) a risk that the government might lose its previously available access to federal court.

Given these consequences, from what perspective can the Court's unnecessarily technical reading of this part of the statute produce a "better rule"? To hold, as the Court does today, that for purposes of the FSIA "other ownership interest" does not include the interest that a Foreign Nation has in a tiered Corporate Subsidiary "would be not merely to depart from the primary rule that words are to be taken in their ordinary sense, but to narrow the operation of the statute to an extent that would seriously imperil the accomplishment of its purpose." Danciger v. Cooley, 248 U.S. 319, 326. * * *

NOTES AND QUESTIONS FOR DISCUSSION

1. In *Dole Foods*, the Supreme Court adopts a highly formalistic test for determining whether a corporation is an "instrumentality of a foreign state" and therefore covered by the FSIA. To what degree does this holding simply follow from the literal terms of the statute, making a legal person into an instrumentality if "a majority of whose shares" are owned by a foreign state? The dissent relies on the following clause, "or other ownership interest." § 1603(b)(2). If these clauses are not enough to resolve the issue, do the functional considerations identified by the dissent require a different result?

The dissent identifies the dominant statutory purpose to be that of protecting foreign sovereigns with immunity when they act through institutions that they control. Is that the only purpose plausibly served by the FSIA? Recall that it was enacted to codify the restrictive theory of sovereign immunity. Is that theory better served by a broad or a narrow interpretation of corporations subject to the control of foreign sovereigns? The formal interpretation adopted by the Court, like any formal interpretation, simplifies the process of judicial decisionmaking. On the facts of *Dole Foods*, the Court avoided any need to inquire whether the State of Israel exercised actual control over the defendant corporations through a web of other corporations and their subsidiaries. How easy or difficult would that inquiry have been? Even if a court could manage it, after the fact, in litigation, how easy would it be for a party dealing with a nominally private corporation to ascertain its position in a hierarchy of ownership by a foreign state? Should doubts be resolved in favor of the commercial or the sovereign status of corporations whose shares are not subject to majority ownership by a foreign state?

The majority confines the phrase "other ownership interest" to entities not structured in the corporate form, while the dissent would extend it to means of control of corporations other than majority ownership of shares, leaving discretion to foreign states to structure their corporate holdings as they see fit. How much flexibility does the majority allow to foreign states? They can always choose not to use the corporate form at all, with majority control then determined by "other ownership interest." The dissent reads the FSIA to make decisions about corporate structure "matters purely of form, not of substance," but if the foreign state chooses the corporate form, why shouldn't instrumentality status be determined by majority ownership of shares?

2. One holding in *Dole Foods* concerns the time at which instrumentality status is determined. Following the prevailing rule that jurisdiction is determined at the time suit is filed, the Court examines the majority interest of a foreign state in a corporation at that time. No justice dissents from this part of the opinion. But isn't it, too, driven by concerns of form over substance? This rule eases the determination of instrumentality status by tying it to the moment suit is filed, rather than the period, possibly extended, over which the plaintiff's claim arose.

The Court also contrasts immunity under the FSIA with immunity under other statutes, such as the federal civil rights statutes. Immunity in that context applies to individual officers, who might otherwise be deterred from vigorously enforcing the law by the prospect of liability for civil rights violations. The Court finds no such purpose behind the grant of foreign sovereign immunity, which it attributes solely to protecting foreign states "from the inconvenience of suit as a gesture of comity between the United States and other sovereigns." Consider whether such a purely prospective view oversimplifies the aims of immunity and its consequences. Doesn't the grant or denial of immunity also affect how a foreign state and its instrumentalities act in light of possible liability under American law?

3. The distinction between individual immunity and the immunity of instrumentalities came up more sharply in the more recent decision in Samantar v. Yousuf, 130 S.Ct. 2278 (2010). The plaintiffs there alleged human rights violations by high officials in the Somali government. They did not sue the government or its instrumentalities, but only individual officials and only in their personal capacity. The Supreme Court held that the FSIA did not cover such claims because the definition of "agency or instrumentality of a foreign state" in § 1603(a) extended only to entities, not to natural persons. Individual officials did not fit within the phrase "separate legal person, corporate or otherwise" used in the statutory definition, which most commonly refers to artificial persons. Nor do they fit within the phrase "organ of a foreign state or political subdivision thereof," also used in the definition, which refers only to institutions controlled by the state. These observations about usage might not be absolutely conclusive, because a natural individual literally is a "separate legal person" and could be construed as an "organ of a foreign state," but they reveal a glaring omission in the statutory definition, which is its failure to mention individuals at all. Most likely, this omission derived from the relative scarcity lawsuits against foreign officials who invoked the defense of sovereign immunity before the enactment of the FSIA. For the relevant history, see Curtis A. Bradley & Laurence R. Helfer, *International Law and the U.S. Common Law of Foreign Official Immunity*, 2010 Sup. Ct. Rev. 213, 232-33. As the Supreme Court unanimously recognized, the text of the FSIA simply neglected immunity of foreign officials.

That raises the question of what inference to draw from congressional silence. The Court chose to find no immunity under the FSIA, but to remand for consideration of immunity as a matter of federal common law. Does reframing the issue in these terms simply muddy the waters that the FSIA sought to clarify? Any litigant faced with possible immunity under the FSIA can now simply sue foreign officials as an alternative. The courts then must decide the officials' immunity as a matter of federal common law, presumably influenced by the FSIA but not bound by its terms.

The commingling of statutory and common law issues is further complicated by the different distinctions deployed in the domestic law governing suits against government officials and the distinction deployed in international law governing suits against foreign officials. In domestic law, a suit against government officials in their "official capacity" is just another term for suing the government itself. *Hafer v. Melo*, 502 U.S. 21 (1991). In such cases, the officials ordinarily have immunity to the extent that the government has immunity. If such a suit properly results in a judgment for the plaintiff, it can be collected from the government. In *Samantar*, the Court decided only that suits against foreign officials in their "personal capacity" were not covered by the FSIA, leaving open the question whether suits against them in their official capacity were suits against the foreign state, and so, by implication, covered by the FSIA. As the Court said, "it may be the case that some actions against an official in his official capacity should be treated as actions against the foreign state itself, as the state is the real party in interest." *Samantar*, 130 S.Ct. at 2292.

Under domestic law, however, suits against government officials in their personal capacity, result in a judgment that can only be collected from their personal assets. If the suit results in an injunction, requiring officials to conform their action to law, it still runs against them in their personal capacity, on the ground that they have no authority to act contrary to law. To dispel any confusion resulting from this distinction, plaintiffs usually allege claims against domestic officials in both their official and their personal capacities. In the former, they are subject to liability under any waiver or abrogation of sovereign immunity of their government; and in the latter, they are subject to liability as individuals. Even in their personal capacity, however, domestic officials have various kinds of immunity, either absolute or qualified, that prevents the entry of a judgment against them for damages. Moreover, even if these immunities are overcome and they are held liable, they almost always are reimbursed by the government for any judgment against them.

If this conceptual scheme were transplanted to the international context, foreign officials could be held liable in their official capacity only if the foreign government could itself be held liable under an exception in the FSIA. Foreign officials also could be held liable in their personal capacity for injunctive relief to conform their conduct to superior law, and most significantly, for damages recoverable from their own assets. As a practical matter, any such relief could be obtained against foreign officials only outside their own country. Personal jurisdiction would then depend upon the extent of their actions abroad and execution of any judgment would depend upon the assets they hold abroad. Does it make sense to import wholesale the rules governing immunity under domestic law to cases with an international dimension?

4. One reason for caution has to do with the different distinctions applied to questions of individual immunity under international law: chiefly, between the immunity of foreign officials based on their position alone, and their immunity based also on their performance of official functions. Longstanding treaties, statutes, and customary international law govern the immunity of diplomats and of foreign heads of state, dividing the immunity into two kinds: status immunity (immunity "ratione personae"), which confers a blanket exemption on diplomats and heads of state from the jurisdiction of national courts, and conduct immunity (immunity "ratione materiae"), which exempts other foreign officials only for their official acts. The distinction between these two kinds of immunity does not track either the exceptions to sovereign immunity under the FSIA or the immunities under domestic civil rights laws. The crucial difference concerns the status immunity of high foreign officials, whose actions and interests might be contrary to those of the host government and could be questioned in its courts only at the risk of damaging international relations. A foreign president could not be arrested and tried on a visit to this country without effectively severing relations with his or her country.

The second kind of immunity has its basis in American law in Underhill v. Hernandez, 168 U.S. 250 (1897), a case brought by an American citizen for assault and detention in Venezuela by a military commander there. The commander was part of a revolutionary movement that subsequently gained power and was recognized by the U.S. The Supreme Court held these facts sufficient to confer immunity upon him because "the acts of the defendant were the acts of the government of Venezuela." Id. at 254. This basis for immunity extends beyond high officials to the actions of any foreign official in performance of official duties.

Both status and conduct immunity, if applicable, protect foreign officials from liability in any capacity, official as well personal as those terms are used in domestic law. Those terms come into play only when immunity under international law is translated into domestic law, as well it might be after *Samantar*. The Supreme Court left the immunity of foreign officials to be determined by federal common law, most of which has developed in the context of civil rights claims against state and federal officials. That invites the inference that the immunity of foreign officials in their official capacity is equivalent to the immunity of their government under the FSIA. If it is, however, then the reference to the federal common law takes the analysis of official immunity right back to the FSIA. If it isn't, then the reference to federal common law carries the risk of seemingly inconsistent results, particularly if the immunity of a foreign official in his official capacity is narrower than sovereign immunity under the FSIA.

Human rights cases, like *Samantar*, raise distinctive issues addressed later in this chapter. A preview of these problems appears in a simple variant in Saudi Arabia v. Nelson, 507 U.S. 349 (1993), which appears below as a principal case. The Supreme Court held that the Saudi government was immune to liability for tort claims arising mainly in Saudi Arabia. Suppose, however, that the plaintiffs also sued a Saudi government official. Could he be denied official immunity or, for that matter, personal immunity, without undermining the immunity that the government received under the FSIA? Conversely, if the government was not immune, would it follow that the official wasn't immune either? The hardest cases arise when one defendant is subject to personal jurisdiction and has assets from which a judgment might be satisfied, but another defendant does not. The plaintiff, of course, will always go after the more vulnerable defendant, and if there is any doubt, sue both institutional and individual defendants. That makes the individual's immunity under federal common law a pressing issue in a wide range of cases—not necessarily ones involving human rights, but any action by a foreign official. Even if the FSIA doesn't directly address questions of individual immunity, what role should it have in resolving them?

5. For articles on the issues raised by *Nelson*, see Michael A. Granne, *Defining "Organ of a Foreign State" Under the Foreign Sovereign Immunities Act of 1976*, 42 U.C. Davis L. Rev. 1 (2008); Clinton L. Narver, *Putting the "Sovereign" Back in the Foreign Sovereign Immunities Act: The Case for a Time of Filing Test for Agency or Instrumentality Status*, 19 B.U. Int'l L.J. 163 (2001). For articles on *Samantar*, and more generally, on individual immunity of foreign officials, see Ingrid Wuerth, *Foreign Official Immunity Determinations in U.S. Courts: The Case Against the State Department,"* 51 Va. J. Int'l L. 915 (2011); Symposium, *Foreign Official Immunity After* Samantar v. Yousuf, 15 Lewis & Clark L. Rev. 555 (2011); Curtis Bradley & Jack Goldsmith, *Foreign Sovereign Immunity and Domestic Officer Suits*, 13 Green Bag 2d 137 (2010).

4. Exceptions to Sovereign Immunity

Republic of Argentina v. Weltover, Inc.

Supreme Court of the United States, 1992.

504 U.S. 607.

JUSTICE SCALIA delivered the opinion of the Court.

This case requires us to decide whether the Republic of Argentina's default on certain bonds issued as part of a plan to stabilize its currency was an act taken "in connection with a commercial activity" that had a "direct effect in the United States" so as to subject Argentina to suit in an American court under the Foreign Sovereign Immunities Act of 1976, 28 U.S.C. § 1602 et seq.

I

Since Argentina's currency is not one of the mediums of exchange accepted on the international market, Argentine businesses engaging in foreign transactions must pay in United States dollars or some other internationally accepted currency. In the recent past, it was difficult for Argentine borrowers to obtain such funds, principally because of the instability of the Argentine currency. To address these problems, petitioners, the Republic of Argentina and its central bank, Banco Central (collectively Argentina), in 1981 instituted a foreign exchange insurance contract program (FEIC), under which Argentina effectively agreed to assume the risk of currency depreciation in cross-border transactions involving Argentine borrowers. This was accomplished by Argentina's agreeing to sell to domestic borrowers, in exchange for a contractually predetermined amount of local currency, the necessary United States dollars to repay their foreign debts when they matured, irrespective of intervening devaluations.

Unfortunately, Argentina did not possess sufficient reserves of United States dollars to cover the FEIC contracts as they became due in 1982. The Argentine Government thereupon adopted certain emergency measures, including refinancing of the FEIC-backed debts by issuing to the creditors government bonds. These bonds, called "Bonods," provide for payment of interest and principal in United States dollars; payment may be made through transfer on the London, Frankfurt, Zurich, or New York market, at the election of the creditor. Under this refinancing program, the foreign creditor had the option of either accepting the Bonods in satisfaction of the initial debt, thereby substituting the Argentine Government for the private debtor, or maintaining the debtor/creditor relationship with the private borrower and accepting the Argentine Government as guarantor.

When the Bonods began to mature in May 1986, Argentina concluded that it lacked sufficient foreign exchange to retire them. Pursuant to a Presidential Decree, Argentina unilaterally extended the time for payment and offered bondholders substitute instruments as a means of rescheduling the debts. Respondents, two Panamanian corporations and a Swiss bank who hold, collectively, $1.3 million of Bonods, refused to accept the rescheduling and insisted on full payment, specifying New York as the place where payment should be made. Argentina did not pay, and respondents then brought this breach-of-contract action in the United States District Court for the Southern District of New York, relying on the Foreign Sovereign Immunities Act of 1976 as the basis for jurisdiction. Petitioners moved to dismiss for lack of subject-matter jurisdiction, lack of personal jurisdiction, and forum non conveniens. The District Court denied these motions, 753 F. Supp. 1201 (S.D.N.Y. 1991), and the Court of Appeals affirmed, 941 F.2d 145 (CA2 1991). We granted Argentina's petition for certiorari, which challenged the Court of Appeals' determination that, under the Act, Argentina was not immune from the jurisdiction of the federal courts in this case. 502 U.S. 1024 (1992).

II

The Foreign Sovereign Immunities Act of 1976 (FSIA), 28 U.S.C. § 1602 et seq., establishes a comprehensive framework for determining whether a court in this country, state or federal, may exercise jurisdiction over a foreign state. Under the Act, a "foreign state *shall* be immune from the jurisdiction of the courts of the United States and of the States" unless one of several statutorily defined exceptions applies. § 1604 (emphasis added). The FSIA thus provides the "sole basis" for obtaining jurisdiction over a foreign sovereign in the United States. See Argentine Republic v. Amerada Hess Shipping Corp., 488 U.S. 428, 434-439 (1989). The most significant of the FSIA's exceptions—and the one at issue in this case—is the "commercial" exception of § 1605(a)(2), which provides that a foreign state is not immune from suit in any case

> "in which the action is based upon a commercial activity carried on in the United States by the foreign state; or upon an act performed in the

United States in connection with a commercial activity of the foreign state elsewhere; or upon an act outside the territory of the United States in connection with a commercial activity of the foreign state elsewhere and that act causes a direct effect in the United States." § 1605(a)(2).

In the proceedings below, respondents relied only on the third clause of § 1605(a)(2) to establish jurisdiction, and our analysis is therefore limited to considering whether this lawsuit is (1) "based . . . upon an act outside the territory of the United States"; (2) that was taken "in connection with a commercial activity" of Argentina outside this country; and (3) that "cause[d] a direct effect in the United States." The complaint in this case alleges only one cause of action on behalf of each of the respondents, viz., a breach-of-contract claim based on Argentina's attempt to refinance the Bonods rather than to pay them according to their terms. The fact that the cause of action is in compliance with the first of the three requirements—that it is "based upon an act outside the territory of the United States" (presumably Argentina's unilateral extension)—is uncontested. The dispute pertains to whether the unilateral refinancing of the Bonods was taken "in connection with a commercial activity" of Argentina, and whether it had a "direct effect in the United States." We address these issues in turn.

A

Respondents and their amicus, the United States, contend that Argentina's issuance of, and continued liability under, the Bonods constitute a "commercial activity" and that the extension of the payment schedules was taken "in connection with" that activity. The latter point is obvious enough, and Argentina does not contest it; the key question is whether the activity is "commercial" under the FSIA.

The FSIA defines "commercial activity" to mean:

> "[E]ither a regular course of commercial conduct or a particular commercial transaction or act. The commercial character of an activity shall be determined by reference to the nature of the course of conduct or particular transaction or act, rather than by reference to its purpose." 28 U.S.C. § 1603(d).

This definition, however, leaves the critical term "commercial" largely undefined: The first sentence simply establishes that the commercial nature of an activity does not depend upon whether it is a single act or a regular course of conduct; and the second sentence merely specifies what element of the conduct determines commerciality (i.e., nature rather than purpose), but still without saying what "commercial" means. Fortunately, however, the FSIA was not written on a clean slate. As we have noted, see Verlinden B.V. v. Central Bank of Nigeria, 461 U.S. 480, 486-489 (1983), the Act (and the commercial exception in particular) largely codifies the so-called "restrictive" theory of foreign sovereign immunity first endorsed by the State Department in 1952. The meaning of "commercial" is the meaning generally attached to that term under the restrictive theory at the time the statute was enacted. See McDermott Int'l, Inc. v. Wilander, 498 U.S. 337, 342 (1991) ("[W]e assume that when a statute uses [a term of art], Congress intended it to have its established meaning"); NLRB v. Amax Coal

Co., 453 U.S. 322, 329 (1981); Morissette v. United States, 342 U.S. 246, 263 (1952).

This Court did not have occasion to discuss the scope or validity of the restrictive theory of sovereign immunity until our 1976 decision in Alfred Dunhill of London, Inc. v. Republic of Cuba, 425 U.S. 682. Although the Court there was evenly divided on the question whether the "commercial" exception that applied in the foreign-sovereign-immunity context also limited the availability of an act-of-state defense, compare id., at 695-706 (plurality opinion), with id., at (Marshall, J., dissenting), there was little disagreement over the general scope of the exception. The plurality noted that, after the State Department endorsed the restrictive theory of foreign sovereign immunity in 1952, the lower courts consistently held that foreign sovereigns were not immune from the jurisdiction of American courts in cases "arising out of purely commercial transactions," id., at 703. The plurality further recognized that the distinction between state sovereign acts, on the one hand, and state commercial and private acts, on the other, was not entirely novel to American law. See 425 U.S., at 695-696. The plurality stated that the restrictive theory of foreign sovereign immunity would not bar a suit based upon a foreign state's participation in the marketplace in the manner of a private citizen or corporation. 425 U.S., at 698-705. A foreign state engaging in "commercial" activities "do[es] not exercise powers peculiar to sovereigns"; rather, it "exercise[s] only those powers that can also be exercised by private citizens." Id., at 704. The dissenters did not disagree with this general description. See id., at 725. Given that the FSIA was enacted less than six months after our decision in *Alfred Dunhill* was announced, we think the plurality's contemporaneous description of the then-prevailing restrictive theory of sovereign immunity is of significant assistance in construing the scope of the Act.

In accord with that description, we conclude that when a foreign government acts, not as regulator of a market, but in the manner of a private player within it, the foreign sovereign's actions are "commercial" within the meaning of the FSIA. Moreover, because the Act provides that the commercial character of an act is to be determined by reference to its "nature" rather than its "purpose," 28 U.S.C. § 1603(d), the question is not whether the foreign government is acting with a profit motive or instead with the aim of fulfilling uniquely sovereign objectives. Rather, the issue is whether the particular actions that the foreign state performs (whatever the motive behind them) are the type of actions by which a private party engages in "trade and traffic or commerce," Black's Law Dictionary 270 (6th ed. 1990). Thus, a foreign government's issuance of regulations limiting foreign currency exchange is a sovereign activity, because such authoritative control of commerce cannot be exercised by a private party; whereas a contract to buy army boots or even bullets is a "commercial" activity, because private companies can similarly use sales contracts to acquire goods, see, e.g., Stato di Rumania v. Trutta, [1926] Foro It. I 584, 585-586, 589 (Corte di Cass. del Regno, Italy), translated and reprinted in part in 26 Am. J. Int'l L. 626-629 (Supp. 1932).

The commercial character of the Bonods is confirmed by the fact that they are in almost all respects garden-variety debt instruments: They may be held by private parties; they are negotiable and may be traded on the international market (except in Argentina); and they promise a future stream of cash income. We recognize that, prior to the enactment of the FSIA, there was authority suggesting that the issuance of public debt instruments did not constitute a commercial activity. *Victory Transport*, 336 F.2d, at 360 (dicta). There is, however, nothing distinctive about the state's assumption of debt (other than perhaps its purpose) that would cause it always to be classified as jure imperii, and in this regard it is significant that *Victory Transport* expressed confusion as to whether the "nature" or the "purpose" of a transaction was controlling in determining commerciality, id., at 359-360. Because the FSIA has now clearly established that the "nature" governs, we perceive no basis for concluding that the issuance of debt should be treated as categorically different from other activities of foreign states.

Argentina contends that, although the FSIA bars consideration of "purpose," a court must nonetheless fully consider the context of a transaction in order to determine whether it is "commercial." Accordingly, Argentina claims that the Court of Appeals erred by defining the relevant conduct in what Argentina considers an overly generalized, acontextual manner and by essentially adopting a per se rule that all "issuance of debt instruments" is "commercial." * * * We have no occasion to consider such a per se rule, because it seems to us that even in full context, there is nothing about the issuance of these Bonods (except perhaps its purpose) that is not analogous to a private commercial transaction.

Argentina points to the fact that the transactions in which the Bonods were issued did not have the ordinary commercial consequence of raising capital or financing acquisitions. Assuming for the sake of argument that this is not an example of judging the commerciality of a transaction by its purpose, the ready answer is that private parties regularly issue bonds, not just to raise capital or to finance purchases, but also to refinance debt. That is what Argentina did here: By virtue of the earlier FEIC contracts, Argentina was already obligated to supply the United States dollars needed to retire the FEIC-insured debts; the Bonods simply allowed Argentina to restructure its existing obligations. Argentina further asserts (without proof or even elaboration) that it "received consideration [for the Bonods] in no way commensurate with [their] value," Brief for Petitioners 22. Assuming that to be true, it makes no difference. Engaging in a commercial act does not require the receipt of fair value, or even compliance with the common-law requirements of consideration.

Argentina argues that the Bonods differ from ordinary debt instruments in that they "were created by the Argentine Government to fulfill its obligations under a foreign exchange program designed to address a domestic credit crisis, and as a component of a program designed to control that nation's critical shortage of foreign exchange." Id., at 23-24. In this regard, Argentina relies heavily on De Sanchez v. Banco Central de Nicaragua, 770 F.2d 1385 (1985), in which the Fifth Circuit took the view that "[o]ften, the essence of an act is defined by its purpose"; that unless "we can inquire into the purposes of such acts, we cannot determine their nature"; and that, in light of its purpose to control its reserves of foreign currency, Nicaragua's refusal to honor a check it had issued to cover a private bank debt was a sovereign act entitled to immunity. Id., at 1393. Indeed, Argentina asserts that the line between "nature" and "purpose" rests upon a "formalistic distinction [that] simply is neither useful nor warranted." We think this line of argument is squarely foreclosed by the language of the FSIA. However difficult it may be in some cases to separate "purpose" (i.e., the reason why the foreign state engages in the activity) from "nature" (i.e., the outward form of the conduct that the foreign state performs or agrees to perform), see *De Sanchez, supra,* at 1393, the statute unmistakably commands that to be done, 28 U.S.C. § 1603(d). We agree with the Court of Appeals that it is irrelevant why Argentina participated in the bond market in the manner of a private actor; it matters only that it did so. We conclude that Argentina's issuance of the Bonods was a "commercial activity" under the FSIA.

B

The remaining question is whether Argentina's unilateral rescheduling of the Bonods had a "direct effect" in the United States, 28 U.S.C. § 1605(a)(2). In addressing this issue, the Court of Appeals rejected the suggestion in the legislative history of the FSIA that an effect is not "direct" unless it is both "substantial" and "foreseeable." That suggestion is found in the House Report, which states that conduct covered by the third clause of § 1605(a)(2) would be subject to the jurisdiction of American courts "consistent with principles set forth in section 18, Restatement of the Law, Second, Foreign Relations Law of the United States (1965)." H. R. Rep. No. 94-1487, pp. 1, 19, U.S. Code Cong. & Admin. News 1976, pp. 6604, 6618 (1976). Section 18 states that American laws are not given extraterritorial application except with respect to conduct that has, as a "direct and foreseeable result," a "substantial" effect within the United States. Since this obviously deals with jurisdiction to legislate rather than jurisdiction to adjudicate, this passage of the House Report has been charitably described as "a bit of a non sequitur," Texas Trading & Milling Corp. v. Federal Republic of Nigeria, 647 F.2d 300, 311 (CA2 1981), cert. denied, 454 U.S. 1148 (1982). Of course the generally applicable principle *de minimis non curat lex* ensures that jurisdiction may not be predicated on purely trivial effects in the United States. But we reject the suggestion that § 1605(a)(2) contains any unexpressed requirement of "substantiality" or "foreseeability." As the Court of Appeals recognized, an effect is "direct" if it follows "as an immediate consequence of the defendant's . . . activity."

The Court of Appeals concluded that the rescheduling of the maturity dates obviously had a "direct effect" on respondents. It further concluded that that effect was sufficiently "in the United States" for purposes of the FSIA, in part because "Congress would have wanted an American court to entertain this action" in order to preserve New York City's status as "a preeminent commercial center." The question, however, is not what Congress "would have wanted" but what Congress enacted in the FSIA. Although we are happy to endorse the Second Circuit's recognition of "New York's status as a world financial leader," the effect of Argentina's rescheduling in diminishing that status (assuming it is not too speculative to be considered an effect at all) is too remote and attenuated to satisfy the "direct effect" requirement of the FSIA.

We nonetheless have little difficulty concluding that Argentina's unilateral rescheduling of the maturity dates on the Bonods had a "direct effect" in the United States. Respondents had designated their accounts in New York as the place of payment, and Argentina made some interest payments into those accounts before announcing that it was rescheduling the payments. Because New York was thus the place of performance for Argentina's ultimate contractual obligations, the rescheduling of those obligations necessarily had a "direct effect" in the United States: Money that was supposed to have been delivered to a New York bank for deposit was not forthcoming. We reject Argentina's suggestion that the "direct effect" requirement cannot be satisfied where the plaintiffs are all foreign corporations with no other connections to the United States. We expressly stated in *Verlinden* that the FSIA permits "a foreign plaintiff to sue a foreign sovereign in the courts of the United States, provided the substantive requirements of the Act are satisfied," 461 U.S., at 489.

Finally, Argentina argues that a finding of jurisdiction in this case would violate the Due Process Clause of the Fifth Amendment, and that, in order to avoid this difficulty, we must construe the "direct effect" requirement as embodying the "minimum contacts" test of International Shoe Co. v. Washington, 326 U.S. 310, 316 (1945). Assuming, without deciding, that a foreign state is a "person" for purposes of the Due Process Clause, cf. South Carolina v. Katzenbach, 383 U.S. 301, 323-324 (1966) (States of the Union are not "persons" for purposes of the Due Process Clause), we find that Argentina possessed "minimum contacts" that would satisfy the constitutional test. By issuing negotiable debt instruments denominated in United States dollars and payable in New York and by appointing a financial agent in that city, Argentina "'purposefully avail[ed] itself of the privilege of conducting activities within the [United States].'" Burger King Corp. v. Rudzewicz, 471 U.S. 462, 475 (1985), quoting Hanson v. Denckla, 357 U.S. 235, 253 (1958).

* * *

We conclude that Argentina's issuance of the Bonods was a "commercial activity" under the FSIA; that its rescheduling of the maturity dates on those instruments was taken in connection with that commercial activity and had a "direct effect" in the United States; and that the District Court therefore properly asserted jurisdiction, under the FSIA, over the breach-of-contract claim based on that rescheduling. Accordingly, the judgment of the Court of Appeals is

Affirmed.

NOTES AND QUESTIONS FOR DISCUSSION

1. The definition of "commercial activity" stands at the center of the restrictive theory of sovereign immunity and therefore at the heart of the FSIA. As the Court points out, the importance of the definition is matched only by its circularity. Section 1603(d) defines the term as "a regular course of commercial conduct or a particular commercial transaction or act." This provision limits the definition only by requiring that the commercial character of an activity "shall be determined by reference to the nature of the course of conduct or particular transaction or act, rather than by reference to its purpose." As it appears in the exceptions to sovereign immunity, in § 1605(a)(2), commercial activity must be accompanied by sufficient contacts with the U.S. The Court addresses both limiting features of the exception in *Weltover*.

The excluded "purpose" of the activity, in the Court's view, concerns a form of specific intent rather than general intent—specific in that it refers to goals beyond the commercial activity itself, not the general intent that accompanies any commercial activity. Parties invariably engage in commercial activity with the general intent to do so, rather than by stumbling into commercial activity by accident. In this general sense, intent goes to the "nature" of the activity rather its further "purpose." As the Court says, "the question is not whether the foreign government is acting with a profit motive or instead with the aim of fulfilling uniquely sovereign objectives." Argentina intentionally engaged in commercial activity in not paying off the bonds that it had issued according to their original schedule. That intent determined the nature of its activity. Its further purpose in protecting Argentina's foreign exchange reserves and alleviating a credit crisis, although a matter of government regulation of the economy, did not affect the commercial nature of the underlying activity.

Commercial activity, according to the Court, depended upon whether it could have been engaged in by a private party: "when a foreign government acts, not as regulator of a market, but in the manner of a private player within it, the foreign sovereign's actions are 'commercial' with the meaning of the FSIA." *Weltover*, 504 U.S. at 614. Since a private institution could have issued bonds, Argentina engaged in commercial activity when it did so. The Court acknowledged that Argentina would have acted in its sovereign capacity if it had imposed exchange controls that would have prevented the government from repaying the bonds. How is that different from what Argentina did do? Does the "nature" of the activity depend upon how generally applicable it is?

Another provision in the FSIA specifically protects foreign exchanges reserves that constitute property "of a foreign central bank or monetary authority held for its own account." Section 1611(b)(1) exempts such property from any attempt to attach it or to execute upon it in satisfaction of a judgment. Does this provision support an argument that an attempt to protect foreign exchange reserves should be treated as sovereign action? Or does its limited scope indicate that market activity with this purpose should be treated as ordinary commercial activity?

2. The further holding in *Weltover* concerned the contacts of Argentina's commercial activity with the U.S. Since the bonds were to be repaid in New York, the Court held that Argentina's unilateral rescheduling of repayment had a "direct effect" in the U.S. under the third clause of § 1605(a)(2). It involved "an act outside the territory of the United States in connection with a commercial activity of the foreign state elsewhere and that act causes a direct effect in the United States." 504 U.S. at 611. What if the bonds had provided for repayment outside the U.S.? Would the effect on American investors of delayed payment still count as "direct"? If so, does this holding transform a seemingly minor term in the contracts involved in the bonds into a crucial provision concerning recourse against the Argentine government?

How does the issue of contacts with the U.S. interact with the issue of whether the activity in question is commercial? Is a foreign sovereign's activity with effects outside its borders more or less likely to be commercial than activity with effects only within its borders? Claims against foreign sovereigns are most likely to be brought in U.S. courts when the underlying activity has some effect in this country. Otherwise the plaintiff would probably (although not certainly) have chosen a foreign court in which to litigate. Does that make the scope of the commercial exception, at least under its third clause, depend mainly upon what constitutes a "direct effect"? Economic effects are conspicuously systemic and widespread, especially in today's globally interconnected economy. Does that mean that the distinction between direct and indirect effects of economic activity will be more a matter of degree than of kind? Or can the parties manipulate the distinction by formal means, such as the terms for repayment of the bonds in *Weltover*?

3. The definition of "commercial activity" in *Weltover* also lends itself to manipulation: in initially describing the underlying transaction, in characterizing it during litigation, and by the courts in deciding what the correct characterization is. Activities that are arguably commercial can be described at many different levels of generality and in many different ways. The Court identifies the purchase of "army boots or even bullets" as a commercial transaction because private parties could engage in them. The same activity, characterized as supplying an army, however, cannot be assimilated to private commerce. To pursue the Court's example, would the purchase of a tank, a naval vessel, or fighter aircraft also be commercial? The same set of questions could be asked about the contacts of such contracts with the United States. If delivery of the arms and payment occurred in a foreign country, would that have a "direct effect" in the U.S.? The next case, as we shall see, raises exactly these questions about a contract for employment of a U.S. citizen in a foreign country by the instrumentality of a foreign government.

Regardless of how these questions are resolved, how much has Congress contributed to resolving them? Much of the work appears to be left to the courts in interpreting the crucial terms of the statute. Having defined "commercial activity" in terms of conduct, transactions, or acts that are "commercial," and having left terms like "direct effect" entirely undefined, has Congress delegated to the courts the task of delineating the contours of the restrictive theory of sovereign immunity? Is this a matter simply of statutory interpretation or does it constitute a form of federal common law? Does it make any difference so long as the source of any judicial decision remains consistent with the basic policy judgments embodied in the FSIA?

4. For articles on the commercial exception to the FSIA, see Joseph F. Morrissey, *Simplifying the Foreign Sovereign Immunities Act: If a Sovereign Acts Like a Private Party, Treat it Like One*, 5 Chi. J. Int'l L. 675 (2005); M. Mofidi, *The Foreign Sovereign Immunities Act and the "Commercial Activity" Exception: The Gulf Between Theory and Practice*, 5 J. Int'l Leg. Stud. 95 (1999); Mark B. Baker, *Whither* Weltover: *Has the U.S. Supreme Court Clarified or Confused the Exceptions Enumerated in the Foreign Sovereign Immunities Act?* 9 Temp. Int'l & Comp. L.J. 1 (1995); Joan E. Donoghue, *Taking the "Sovereign Out of the Foreign Sovereign Immunities Act: A Functional Approach to the Commercial Activity Exception*, 17 Yale J. Int'l L. 489 (1992).

Saudi Arabia v. Nelson

Supreme Court of the United States, 1993.
507 U.S. 349.

JUSTICE SOUTER delivered the opinion of the Court.

The Foreign Sovereign Immunities Act of 1976 entitles foreign states to immunity from the jurisdiction of courts in the United States, 28 U.S.C. § 1604, subject to certain enumerated exceptions. § 1605. One is that a foreign state shall not be immune in any case "in which the action is based upon a commercial activity carried on in the United States by the foreign state." § 1605(a)(2). We hold that respondents' action alleging personal injury resulting from unlawful detention and torture by the Saudi Government is not "based upon a commercial activity" within the meaning of the Act, which consequently confers no jurisdiction over respondents' suit.

I

Because this case comes to us on a motion to dismiss the complaint, we assume that we have truthful factual allegations before us, see United States v. Gaubert, 499 U.S. 315, 327 (1991), though many of those allegations are subject to dispute, Petitioner Kingdom of Saudi Arabia owns and operates petitioner King Faisal Specialist Hospital in Riyadh, as well as petitioner Royspec Purchasing Services, the hospital's corporate purchasing agent in the United States. The Hospital Corporation of America, Ltd. (HCA), an independent corporation existing under the laws of the Cayman Islands, recruits Americans for employment at the hospital under an agreement signed with Saudi Arabia in 1973.

In its recruitment effort, HCA placed an advertisement in a trade periodical seeking applications for a position as a monitoring systems engineer at the hospital. The advertisement drew the attention of respondent Scott Nelson in September 1983, while Nelson was in the United States. After interviewing for the position in Saudi Arabia, Nelson returned to the United States, where he signed an employment contract with the hospital, satisfied personnel processing requirements, and attended an orientation session that HCA conducted for hospital employees. In the course of that program, HCA identified Royspec as the point of contact in the United States for family members who might wish to reach Nelson in an emergency.

In December 1983, Nelson went to Saudi Arabia and began work at the hospital, monitoring all "facilities, equipment, utilities and maintenance systems to insure the safety of patients, hospital staff, and others." He did his job without significant incident until March 1984, when he discovered safety defects in the hospital's oxygen and nitrous oxide lines that posed fire hazards and otherwise endangered patients' lives. Over a period of several months, Nelson repeatedly advised hospital officials of the safety defects and reported the defects to a Saudi Government commission as well. Hospital officials instructed Nelson to ignore the problems.

The hospital's response to Nelson's reports changed, however, on September 27, 1984, when certain hospital employees summoned him to the hospital's security office where agents of the Saudi Government arrested him. The agents transported Nelson to a jail cell, in which they "shackled, tortured and bea[t]" him, and kept him four days without food. Although Nelson did not understand Arabic, government agents forced him to sign a statement written in that language, the content of which he did not know; a hospital employee who was supposed to act as Nelson's interpreter advised him to sign "anything" the agents gave him to avoid further beatings. Two days later, government agents transferred Nelson to the Al Sijan Prison "to await trial on unknown charges."

At the prison, Nelson was confined in an overcrowded cell area infested with rats, where he had to fight other prisoners for food and from which he was taken only once a week for fresh air and exercise. Although police interrogators repeatedly questioned him in Arabic, Nelson did not learn the nature of the charges, if any, against him. For several days, the Saudi Government failed to advise Nelson's family of his whereabouts, though a Saudi official eventually told Nelson's wife, respondent Vivian Nelson, that he could arrange for her husband's release if she provided sexual favors.

Although officials from the United States Embassy visited Nelson twice during his detention, they concluded that his allegations of Saudi mistreatment were "not credible" and made no protest to Saudi authorities. It was only at the personal request of a United States Senator that the Saudi Government released Nelson, 39 days after his arrest, on November 5, 1984. Seven days later, after failing to convince him to return to work at the hospital, the Saudi Government allowed Nelson to leave the country.

In 1988, Nelson and his wife filed this action against petitioners in the United States District Court for the Southern District of Florida seeking damages for personal injury. The Nelsons' complaint sets out 16 causes of action, which fall into three categories. Counts II through VII and counts X, XI, XIV, and XV allege that petitioners committed various intentional torts, including battery, unlawful detainment, wrongful arrest and imprisonment, false imprisonment, inhuman torture, disruption of normal family life, and infliction of mental anguish. Counts I, IX, and XIII charge petitioners with negligently failing to warn Nelson of otherwise undisclosed dangers of his employment, namely, that if he attempted to report safety hazards the hospital would likely retaliate against him and the Saudi Government might detain and physically abuse him without legal cause. Finally, counts VIII, XII, and XVI allege that Vivian Nelson sustained derivative injury resulting from petitioners' actions. Presumably because the employment contract provided that Saudi courts would have exclusive jurisdiction over claims for breach of contract, the Nelsons raised no such matters.

[The District Court dismissed for lack of subject-matter jurisdiction under the FSIA.] The Court of Appeals reversed. It concluded that Nelson's recruitment and hiring were commercial activities of Saudi Arabia and the hospital, carried on in the United States for purposes of the Act, and that the Nelsons' action was "based upon" these activities within the meaning of the statute. There was, the court reasoned, a sufficient nexus between those commercial activities and the wrongful acts that had allegedly injured the Nelsons: "the detention and torture of Nelson are so intertwined with his employment at the Hospital," the court explained, "that they are 'based upon' his recruitment and hiring" in the United States. * * * We now reverse.

II

The Foreign Sovereign Immunities Act "provides the sole basis for obtaining jurisdiction over a foreign state in the courts of this country." Argentine Republic v. Amerada Hess Shipping Corp., 488 U.S. 428, 443 (1989). Under the Act, a foreign state is presumptively immune from the jurisdiction of United States courts; unless a specified exception applies, a federal court lacks subject-matter jurisdiction over a claim against a foreign state. Verlinden B.V. v. Central Bank of Nigeria, 461 U.S. 480, 488-489 (1983); see 28 U.S.C. § 1604; J. Dellapenna, *Suing Foreign Governments and Their Corporations* 11, and n. 64 (1988).

Only one such exception is said to apply here. The first clause of § 1605(a)(2) of the Act provides that a foreign state shall not be immune from the jurisdiction of United States courts in any case "in which the action is based upon a commercial activity carried on in the United States by the foreign state." The Act defines such activity as "commercial activity carried on by such state and having substantial contact with the United States," § 1603(e), and provides that a commercial activity may be "either a regular course of commercial conduct or a particular commercial transaction or act," the "commercial character of [which] shall be determined by reference to" its "nature," rather than its "purpose," § 1603(d).

There is no dispute here that Saudi Arabia, the hospital, and Royspec all qualify as "foreign state[s]" within the meaning of the Act. See 28 U.S.C. §§ 1603(a), (b) (term "'foreign state'" includes "'an agency or instrumentality of a foreign state'"). For there to be jurisdiction in this case, therefore, the Nelsons' action must be "based upon" some "commercial activity" by petitioners that had "substantial contact" with the United States within the meaning of the Act. Because we conclude that the suit is not based upon any commercial activity by petitioners, we need not reach the issue of substantial contact with the United States.

We begin our analysis by identifying the particular conduct on which the Nelsons' action is "based" for purposes of the Act. Although the Act contains no definition of the phrase "based upon," and the relatively sparse legislative history offers no assistance, guidance is hardly necessary. In denoting conduct that forms the "basis," or "foundation," for a claim, the phrase is read most naturally to mean those elements of a claim that, if proven, would entitle a plaintiff to relief under his theory of the case. See Callejo v. Bancomer, S.A., 764 F.2d 1101, 1109 (CA5 1985) (focus should be on the "gravamen of the complaint"); accord, Santos v. Compagnie Nationale Air France, 934 F.2d 890, 893 (CA7 1991) ("An action is based upon the elements that prove the claim, no more and no less"); Millen Industries, Inc. v. Coordination Council for North American Affairs, 855 F.2d 879, 885 (1988).

What the natural meaning of the phrase "based upon" suggests, the context confirms. Earlier, we noted that § 1605(a)(2) contains two clauses following the one at issue here. The second allows for jurisdiction where a suit "is based . . . upon an act performed in the United States in connection with a commercial activity of the foreign state elsewhere," and the third speaks in like terms, allowing for jurisdiction where an action "is based . . . upon an act outside the territory of the United States in connection with a commercial activity of the foreign state elsewhere and that act causes a direct effect in the United States. "Distinctions among descriptions juxtaposed against each other are naturally understood to be significant, see Melkonyan v. Sullivan, 501 U.S. 89, 94-95 (1991), and Congress manifestly understood there to be a difference between a suit "based upon" commercial activity and one "based upon" acts performed "in connection with" such activity. The only reasonable reading of the former term calls for something more than a mere connection with, or relation to, commercial activity.[4]

In this case, the Nelsons have alleged that petitioners recruited Scott Nelson for work at the hospital, signed an employment contract with him, and subsequently employed him. While these activities led to the conduct that eventually injured the Nelsons, they are not the basis for the Nelsons' suit. Even taking each of the Nelsons' allegations about Scott Nelson's recruitment and employment as true, those facts alone entitle the Nelsons to nothing under their theory of the case. The Nelsons have not, after all, alleged breach of contract, but personal injuries caused by petitioners' intentional wrongs and by petitioners' negligent failure to warn Scott Nelson that they might commit those wrongs. Those torts, and not the arguably commercial activities that preceded their commission, form the basis for the Nelsons' suit.

Petitioners' tortious conduct itself fails to qualify as "commercial activity" within the meaning of the Act, although the Act is too "obtuse" to be of much help in reaching that conclusion. *Callejo, supra*, at 1107 (citation omitted). We have seen already that the Act defines "commercial activity" as "either a regular course of commercial conduct or a particular commercial transaction or act," and provides that "[t]he commercial character of an activity shall be determined by reference to the nature of the course of conduct or particular transaction or act, rather than by reference to its purpose." 28 U.S.C. § 1603(d). If this is a definition, it is one distinguished only by its diffidence; as we observed in our most recent case on the subject, it "leaves the critical term 'commercial' largely undefined." Republic of Argentina v. Weltover, Inc., 504 U.S. 607, 612 (1992). We do not, however, have the option to throw up our hands. The term has to be given some interpretation, and congressional diffidence necessarily results in judicial responsibility to determine what a "commercial activity" is for purposes of the Act. * * *

Under the restrictive, as opposed to the "absolute," theory of foreign sovereign immunity, a state is immune from the jurisdiction of foreign courts as to its sovereign or public acts (jure imperii), but not as to those that are private or commercial in character (jure gestionis). *Verlinden B.V. v. Central Bank of Ni-*

---

[4] We do not mean to suggest that the first clause of § 1605(a)(2) necessarily requires that each and every element of a claim be commercial activity by a foreign state, and we do not address the case where a claim consists of both commercial and sovereign elements. We do conclude, however, that where a claim rests entirely upon activities sovereign in character, as here, jurisdiction will not exist under that clause regardless of any connection the sovereign acts may have with commercial activity.

geria, 461 U.S., at 487, that a state engages in commercial activity under the restrictive theory where it exercises "'only those powers that can also be exercised by private citizens,'" as distinct from those "'powers peculiar to sovereigns.'" Put differently, a foreign state engages in commercial activity for purposes of the restrictive theory only where it acts "in the manner of a private player within" the market. *Weltover*, 504 U.S., at 614; see Restatement (Third) of the Foreign Relations Law of the United States § 451 (1987) ("Under international law, a state or state instrumentality is immune from the jurisdiction of the courts of another state, except with respect to claims arising out of activities of the kind that may be carried on by private persons").

We emphasized in *Weltover* that whether a state acts "in the manner of" a private party is a question of behavior, not motivation. * * * We did not ignore the difficulty of distinguishing "'purpose' (i.e., the *reason* why the foreign state engages in the activity) from 'nature' (i.e., the outward form of the conduct that the foreign state performs or agrees to perform)," but recognized that the Act "unmistakably commands" us to observe the distinction. 504 U.S., at 617 (emphasis in original). Because Argentina had merely dealt in the bond market in the manner of a private player, we held, its refinancing of the bonds qualified as a commercial activity for purposes of the Act despite the apparent governmental motivation. Ibid.

Unlike Argentina's activities that we considered in *Weltover*, the intentional conduct alleged here (the Saudi Government's wrongful arrest, imprisonment, and torture of Nelson) could not qualify as commercial under the restrictive theory. The conduct boils down to abuse of the power of its police by the Saudi Government, and however monstrous such abuse undoubtedly may be, a foreign state's exercise of the power of its police has long been understood for purposes of the restrictive theory as peculiarly sovereign in nature. See Arango v. Guzman Travel Advisors Corp., 621 F.2d 1371, 1379 (CA5 1980); Victory Transport Inc. v. Comisaria General de Abastecimientos y Transportes, 336 F.2d 354, 360 (CA2 1964) (restrictive theory does extend immunity to a foreign state's "internal administrative acts"), cert. denied, 381 U.S. 934 (1965).

The Nelsons and their amici urge us to give significance to their assertion that the Saudi Government subjected Nelson to the abuse alleged as retaliation for his persistence in reporting hospital safety violations, and argue that the character of the mistreatment was consequently commercial. One amicus, indeed, goes so far as to suggest that the Saudi Government "often uses detention and torture to resolve commercial disputes." Brief for Human Rights Watch as Amicus Curiae 6. But this argument does not alter the fact that the powers allegedly abused were those of police and penal officers. In any event, the argument is off the point, for it goes to purpose, the very fact the Act renders irrelevant to the question of an activity's commercial character. Whatever may have been the Saudi Government's motivation for its allegedly abusive treatment of Nelson, it remains the case that the Nelsons' action is based upon a sovereign activity immune from the subject-matter jurisdiction of United States courts under the Act.

In addition to the intentionally tortious conduct, the Nelsons claim a separate basis for recovery in petitioners' failure to warn Scott Nelson of the hidden dangers associated with his employment. The Nelsons allege that, at the time petitioners recruited Scott Nelson and thereafter, they failed to warn him of the possibility of severe retaliatory action if he attempted to disclose any safety hazards he might discover on the job. In other words, petitioners bore a duty to warn of their own propensity for tortious conduct. But this is merely a semantic ploy. For aught we can see, a plaintiff could recast virtually any claim of intentional tort committed by sovereign act as a claim of failure to warn, simply by charging the defendant with an obligation to announce its own tortious propensity before indulging it. To give jurisdictional significance to this feint of language would effectively thwart the Act's manifest purpose to codify the restrictive theory of foreign sovereign immunity. * * *

JUSTICE WHITE, with whom JUSTICE BLACKMUN joins, concurring in the judgment.

According to respondents' complaint, Scott Nelson's employer retaliated against him for reporting safety problems by "summon[ing him] . . . to the hospital's security office from which he was transported to a jail cell." Once there, he allegedly was "shackled, tortured and beaten by persons acting at the direction, instigation, provocation, instruction or request of" petitioners-Saudi Arabia, King Faisal Specialist Hospital, and Royspec. The majority concludes that petitioners enjoy sovereign immunity because respondents' action is not "based upon a commercial activity." I disagree. I nonetheless concur in the judgment because in my view the commercial conduct upon which respondents base their complaint was not "carried on in the United States."

I

* * *

B

To run and operate a hospital, even a public hospital, is to engage in a commercial enterprise. The majority never concedes this point, but it does not deny it either, and to my mind the matter is self-evident. By the same token, warning an employee when he blows the whistle and taking retaliatory action, such as harassment, involuntary transfer, discharge, or other tortious behavior, although not prototypical commercial acts, are certainly well within the bounds of commercial activity. The House and Senate Reports accompanying the legislation virtually compel this conclusion, explaining as they do that "a foreign government's . . . employment or engagement of laborers, clerical staff or marketing agents . . . would be among those included within" the definition of commercial activity. H.R. Rep. No. 94-1487, p. 16 (1976) (House Report); S. Rep. No. 94-1482 1310, p. 16 (1976) (Senate Report), U.S.Code Cong. & Admin. News 1976, pp. 6604, 6615. Nelson alleges that petitioners harmed him in the course of engaging in their commercial enterprise, as a direct result of their commercial acts. His claim, in other words, is "based upon commercial activity."

Indeed, I am somewhat at a loss as to what exactly the majority believes petitioners have done that a private employer could not. As countless cases attest, retaliation for whistle-blowing is not a practice foreign to the marketplace. * * *

Therefore, had the hospital retaliated against Nelson by hiring thugs to do the job, I assume the majority—no longer able to describe this conduct as "a foreign state's exercise of the power of its police,"—would consent to calling it "commercial." For, in such circumstances, the state-run hospital would be operating as any private participant in the marketplace and respondents' action would be based on the operation by Saudi Arabia's agents of a commercial business.

At the heart of the majority's conclusion, in other words, is the fact that the hospital in this case chose to call in government security forces. I find this fixation on the intervention of police officers, and the ensuing characterization of the conduct as "peculiarly sovereign in nature," to be misguided. To begin, it fails to capture respondents' complaint in full. Far from being directed solely at the activities of the Saudi police, it alleges that agents of the hospital summoned Nelson to its security office because he reported safety concerns and that the hospital played a part in the subsequent beating and imprisonment. Without more, that type of behavior hardly qualifies as sovereign. Thus, even assuming for the sake of argument that the role of the official police somehow affected the nature of petitioners' conduct, the claim cannot be said to "res[t] entirely upon activities sovereign in character." At the very least it "consists of both commercial and sovereign elements," thereby presenting the specific question the majority chooses to elude. The majority's single-minded focus on the exercise of police power, while certainly simplifying the case, thus hardly does it justice. * * *

II

Nevertheless, I reach the same conclusion as the majority because petitioners' commercial activity was not "carried on in the United States." The Act defines such conduct as "commercial activity . . . having substantial contact with the United States." 28 U.S.C. § 1603(e). Respondents point to the hospital's recruitment efforts in the United States, including advertising in the American media, and the signing of the employment contract in Miami. As I earlier noted, while these may very well qualify as commercial activity in the United States, they do not constitute the commercial activity upon which respondents' action is based. Conversely, petitioners' commercial conduct in Saudi Arabia, though constituting the basis of the Nelsons' suit, lacks a sufficient nexus to the United States. Neither the hospital's employment practices, nor its disciplinary procedures, has any apparent connection to this country. On that basis, I agree that the Act does not grant the Nelsons access to our courts.

JUSTICE KENNEDY, with whom JUSTICE BLACKMUN and JUSTICE STEVENS join as to Parts I-B and II, concurring in part and dissenting in part.

I join all of the Court's opinion except the last paragraph of Part II, where, with almost no explanation, the Court rules that, like the intentional tort claim, the claims based on negligent failure to warn are outside the subject-matter jurisdiction of the federal courts. These claims stand on a much different footing from the intentional tort claims for purposes of the Foreign Sovereign Immunities Act (FSIA). In my view, they ought to be remanded to the District Court for further consideration.

I

* * *

B

By the same token, however, the Nelsons' claims alleging that the hospital, the Kingdom, and Royspec were negligent in failing during their recruitment of Nelson to warn him of foreseeable dangers are based upon commercial activity having substantial contact with the United States. As such, they are within the commercial activity exception and the jurisdiction of the federal courts. Unlike the intentional tort counts of the complaint, the failure to warn counts do not complain of a police beating in Saudi Arabia; rather, they complain of a negligent omission made during the recruiting of a hospital employee in the United States. To obtain relief, the Nelsons would be obliged to prove that the hospital's recruiting agent did not tell Nelson about the foreseeable hazards of his prospective employment in Saudi Arabia. Under the Court's test, this omission is what the negligence counts are "based upon."

Omission of important information during employee recruiting is commercial activity as we have described it. See Republic of Argentina v. Weltover, Inc., 504 U.S. 607 (1992). It seems plain that recruiting employees is an activity undertaken by private hospitals in the normal course of business. Locating and hiring employees implicates no power unique to the sovereign. In explaining the terms and conditions of employment, including the risks and rewards of a particular job, a governmental entity acts in "the manner of a private player within" the commercial marketplace. Id., at 614. Under the FSIA, as a result, it must satisfy the same general duties of care that apply to private actors under state law. If a private company with operations in Saudi Arabia would be obliged in the course of its recruiting activities subject to state law to tell a prospective employee about the risk of arbitrary arrest and torture by Saudi authorities, then so would King Faisal Specialist Hospital.

The recruiting activity alleged in the failure to warn counts of the complaint also satisfies the final requirement for invoking the commercial activity exception: that the claims be based upon commercial activity "having substantial contact with the United States." 28 U.S.C. § 1603(e). Nelson's recruitment was performed by Hospital Corporation of America, Ltd. (HCA), a wholly owned subsidiary of a United States corporation, which, for a period of at least 16 years beginning in 1973, acted as the Kingdom of Saudi Arabia's exclusive agent for recruiting employees for the hospital. HCA in the regular course of its business seeks employees for the hospital in the American labor market. HCA advertised in an American magazine, seeking applicants for the position Nelson later filled. Nelson saw the ad in the United States and contacted HCA in Tennessee. After an interview in Saudi Arabia, Nelson returned to Florida, where he signed an employment contract and underwent personnel processing and application procedures. Before leaving to take his job at the hospital, Nelson attended an orientation session conducted by HCA in Tennessee for new employees. These activities have more than substantial contact with the United States; most of them were "carried on in the United States." 28 U.S.C. § 1605(a)(2). In alleging that the petitioners neglected during these activities to tell him what they were bound to under state law, Nelson meets all of the statutory requirements for invoking federal jurisdiction under the commercial activity exception. * * *

JUSTICE BLACKMUN, concurring in the judgment in part and dissenting in part.

I join JUSTICE WHITE's opinion because it finds that respondents' intentional tort claims are "based upon a commercial activity" and that the commercial activity at issue in those claims was not "carried on in the United States." I join JUSTICE KENNEDY's opinion insofar as it concludes that the "failure to warn" claims should be remanded.

JUSTICE STEVENS, dissenting.

Under the Foreign Sovereign Immunities Act of 1976 (FSIA), a foreign state is subject to the jurisdiction of American courts if two conditions are met: The action must be "based upon a commercial activity" and that activity must have a "substantial contact with the United States." These two conditions should be separately analyzed because they serve two different purposes. The former excludes commercial activity from the scope of the foreign sovereign's immunity from suit; the second identifies the contacts with the United States that support the assertion of jurisdiction over the defendant.

In this case, as JUSTICE WHITE has demonstrated, petitioner Kingdom of Saudi Arabia's operation of the hospital and its employment practices and disciplinary procedures are "commercial activities" within the meaning of the statute, and respondent Scott Nelson's claim that he was punished for acts performed in the course of his employment was unquestionably "based upon" those activities. Thus, the first statutory condition is satisfied; petitioner is not entitled to immunity from the claims asserted by respondent.

Unlike JUSTICE WHITE, however, I am also convinced that petitioner's commercial activities—whether defined as the regular course of conduct of operating a hospital or, more specifically, as the commercial transaction of engaging respondent "as an employee with specific responsibilities in that enterprise,"—have sufficient contact with the United States to justify the exercise of federal jurisdiction. Petitioner Royspec maintains an office in Maryland and purchases hospital supplies and equipment in this country. For nearly two decades the hospital's American agent has maintained an office in the United States and regularly engaged in the recruitment of personnel in this country. Respondent himself was recruited in the United States and entered into his employment contract with the hospital in the United States. Before traveling to Saudi Arabia to assume his position at the hospital, respondent attended an orientation program in Tennessee. The position for which respondent was recruited and ultimately hired was that of a monitoring systems manager, a troubleshooter, and, taking respondent's allegations as true, it was precisely respondent's performance of those responsibilities that led to the hospital's retaliatory actions against him.

Whether the first clause of § 1605(a)(2) broadly authorizes "general" jurisdiction over foreign entities that engage in substantial commercial activity in this country, or, more narrowly, authorizes only "specific" jurisdiction over particular commercial claims that have a substantial contact with the United States, petitioners' contacts with the United States in this case are, in my view, plainly sufficient to subject petitioners to suit in this country on a claim arising out of their nonimmune commercial activity relating to respondent. If the same activities had been performed by a private business, I have no doubt jurisdiction would be upheld. And that, of course, should be a touchstone of our inquiry; for as Justice WHITE explains, when a foreign nation sheds its uniquely sovereign status and seeks out the benefits of the private marketplace, it must, like any private party, bear the burdens and responsibilities imposed by that marketplace. I would therefore affirm the judgment of the Court of Appeals.[4]

NOTES AND QUESTIONS FOR DISCUSSION

1. *Saudi Arabia v. Nelson* elicited a variety of separate opinions, only one of which, by Justice Stevens, entirely dissents from the majority's conclusion that the defendants were entitled to immunity. Speaking for the Court, Justice Souter found no "commercial activity" either in the retaliation against Nelson in Saudi Arabia or in the failure to warn him of the risk of such retaliation before he was hired. Justice White disagreed with the conclusion that these acts were not commercial but concluded that they were not "carried on in the United States." Justice Kennedy agreed with the majority on the retaliation claim, but not on the failure to warn claim, which he would have remanded for consideration on the merits. Justice Stevens filed the only opinion disagreeing with the majority on both the retaliation and the failure to warn claims.

As in *Weltover*, these different positions depended upon characterization along the two dimensions of the commercial exception: the nature of the defendants' activities and their contacts with the U.S. These activities stretched over the period from Nelson's recruitment in the U.S., through his employment at the hospital in Saudi Arabia, and his subsequent detention and alleged torture by the Saudi Government. Different slices of this whole course of conduct could be characterized in different ways, as the various opinions in *Nelson* make clear. Recruitment and employment by a hospital, even on the majority's view, would constitute commercial activity, because it met the test in *Weltover* that it could have been done by a private party. The majority gives no hint, however, about whether this activity would have had a sufficient connection to the U.S. The majority emphasizes that the claim of retaliation involved the abuse of Saudi Arabia's police power, an indisputably sovereign function of the Saudi government. How can this abuse be divorced from Nelson's whistleblowing and the conditions at the hospital that gave rise to it?

2. The majority's conclusion that the gravamen of the plaintiffs' claims did not involve commercial activity has the unsettling consequence that the worse the alleged abuse, the more likely it is to result in immunity. The plaintiffs' tort claims could easily be reconstrued as human rights claims, although founded for the most part upon state law. The decision therefore implies that the commercial exception to sovereign immunity does not generally extend to human rights claims. Along the dimension of moral outrage, this interpretation of the restric-

---

[4] My affirmance would extend to respondents' failure to warn claims. I am therefore in agreement with JUSTICE KENNEDY's analysis of that aspect of the case.

tive theory of sovereign immunity appears to get priorities exactly backwards: torture claims remain subject to immunity while ordinary commercial transactions do not. Is this an undesirable side effect of the restrictive theory or a necessary feature of it? Does the theory need to be expanded by exceptions specifically addressed to human rights claims? Section 1605(a)(5), for tort claims for losses in in the U.S., and § 1605(a)(7), on a very limited range of human rights claims, make a start in this direction.

Saudi Arabia v. Nelson takes a step in the opposite direction, relying heavily on the police power as an essential function of government. That allows the Court to minimize the significance of the activity that occurred at the hospital and in the U.S. Suppose the plaintiffs alleged retaliation in a less central function of government, for instance, in denying Nelson government benefits such as subsidized housing? The initial issue raised by such a hypothetical is whether this activity itself could be characterized as sovereign rather than commercial. It might not, on the ground that private individuals and firms could also provide subsidies; but supposing that it is characterized as a sovereign activity, would it also cancel out the commercial aspects of the hospital's operations? How about the commercial aspects of offering Nelson employment in the U.S.? Would it make a difference if the hospital had emphasized these benefits as an inducement to agree to employment in Saudi Arabia?

Following up on Justice White's criticism of the majority opinion, what if the hospital had used its own security guards to detain and torture Nelson and the Saudi Arabian government had refused to do anything to stop it or to provide a remedy to Nelson? Would the decision then be that the actions of the hospital fall within the commercial exception, despite the fact that it was an instrumentality of the Saudi government, and the actions of the Saudi government fall outside the exception, because protecting individuals from crime is another essential function of government? Suppose the Saudi government had expressly delegated the police function to the hospital and its security personnel again had detained and tortured Nelson. Would the hospital's actions then fall outside the commercial exception because its security personnel would be performing a sovereign function of government? To paraphrase a famous saying from the law of obscenity, did the majority just insist that "we know commercial action when we see it, and this isn't it"?

3. The majority also rejects the claims based on recruiting in the U.S., dismissing the argument that the defendants "bore a duty to warn of their own propensity for tortious conduct" as "merely a semantic ploy." Such a claim would fall within the commercial exception, however, only if it had sufficient contacts with the U.S. under the three headings specified in § 1605(a): The plaintiff's claim must be "based upon a commercial activity carried on in the United States by the foreign state; or upon an act performed in the United States in connection with a commercial activity of the foreign state elsewhere; or upon an act outside the territory of the United States in connection with a commercial activity of the foreign state elsewhere and that act causes a direct effect in the United States." The last of these clauses figured in the decision in *Weltover* and the first figured in the separate opinions in *Saudi Arabia v. Nelson*. Justice White held that it was not satisfied, while Justice Kennedy held that it was. (Although no Justice discussed the second clause, their reasoning about the first indicated that they would take a similar position on the second. Justice White would have found that it was not satisfied and Justice Kennedy that it was.)

The first clause itself is defined in the statute, just like "commercial activity," in a manner that is not altogether helpful. Under § 1603(e), "commercial activity carried on in the United States" must have "substantial contact with the United States." Justice White does not doubt that this definition is satisfied by the hospital's recruitment efforts in the U.S., but he concludes that the plaintiffs' claims were not "based upon" these efforts as required by § 1605(a)(2). Like the majority, he locates the gravamen of the plaintiffs' claims in tortious conduct in Saudi Arabia, not in a failure to warn of such conduct in the U.S. Justice Kennedy reaches the opposite conclusion about the basis for the plaintiffs' claims, finding it sufficient that they alleged that the defendants "neglected during these activities [in the U.S.] to tell him what they were bound to under state law."

All of the opinions are notable for the cursory treatment that they give to the claims of failure to warn in the U.S. The majority finds it to be an evasion. Justice White finds it to be beyond the scope of the plaintiffs' claims, while Justice Kennedy finds it well within those claims as defined by state law. Is it more accurate to say that the justices who deny an exception on this ground impose impermeable limits on its scope? The dissenters on this issue, by contrast, open the exception to liability for conduct, as alleged in this case, which is particularly egregious. Do the dissenters end up expanding the commercial exception to accommodate human rights claims? Is this consistent with the restrictive theory of sovereign immunity, which arose in an era before human rights claims generally were recognized either in international or in national law?

4. As noted earlier, the FSIA contains straightforward exceptions applicable to egregious misconduct in § 1605(a)(5), for tort claims, in § 1605(a)(7), for human rights claims. The restrictive conditions for applying these exceptions were not met in *Saudi Arabia v. Nelson* because the plaintiffs did not suffer "personal injury or death, or damage to or loss of property, occurring in the United States," under the tort exception, and because Saudi Arabia was not "designated as a state sponsor of terrorism" under the human rights exception. Did these provisions effectively sound the death knell for the plaintiffs' claims, which were all denominated as tort claims?

Nelson had agreed in his contract of employment that any contract claims would be governed by Saudi law. The plaintiffs were therefore limited to asserting tort claims, which most naturally would have been analyzed under § 1605(a)(5) or § 1605(a)(7). Having failed to meet the restrictions in those sections, were the plaintiffs compromised in using the commercial exception as an alternative? To be sure, they could invoke any exception to sovereign immunity so long as it applied in its own terms. But having characterized their claims as sounding in tort to avoid the restriction in the contract, did it look like they then characterized them differently to avoid the restrictions in the FSIA? They were faced in any event with three different issues of characterization: tort or contract, commercial or sovereign, within the U.S. or outside it. Do these different levels of characterization give the courts the discretion to implement the compromise struck by Congress in the FSIA? Or the freedom to reach any result that they believe to be desirable?

5. For articles on *Nelson*, see Dean Brockbank, *The Sovereign Immunity Circle: An Economic Analysis of* Nelson v. Saudi Arabia *and the Foreign Sovereign Immunities Act*, 2 Geo. Mason L. Rev. 1 (1994); Everett C. Johnson, Saudi Arabia v. Nelson: *The Foreign Sovereign Immunities Act in Perspective,* 16 Hous. J. Int'l L. 291 (1993); Alexander J. Mueller, Nelson v. Saudi Arabia *and the Need for a Human Rights Exception to the Foreign Sovereign Immunities Act*, 13 N.Y. Int'l L. Rev. 87 (2000).

Cicippio-Puleo v. Islamic Republic of Iran

United States Court of Appeals, D.C. Circuit, 2004.

353 F.3d 1024.

HARRY T. EDWARDS, CIRCUIT JUDGE.

This case involves a lawsuit brought against the Islamic Republic of Iran ("Iran") under the terrorism exception, 28 U.S.C. § 1605 (a)(7), to the Foreign Sovereign Immunities Act ("FSIA"), 28 U.S.C. §§ 1330, 1602-11 (2000). The plaintiffs in the suit are the adult children and siblings of Joseph J. Cicippio, a victim of terrorist hostage-taking. Joseph Cicippio was abducted in 1986 by Hezbollah, an Islamic terrorist organization that receives material support from Iran. He was held hostage until 1991, confined in inhumane conditions and frequently beaten. In 1996, Joseph Cicippio and his wife sued Iran for the tortious injuries they sustained as a result of Mr. Cicippio's kidnaping, imprisonment, and torture. Iran failed to respond to the complaint and default was entered on November 13, 1997. The case was tried ex parte and, on August 27, 1998, the District Court entered judgment against Iran in favor of Mr. and Mrs. Cicippio in the amount of $30 million. No appeal was taken.

In 2001, Joseph Cicippio's children and siblings sued Iran for the intentional infliction of emotional distress and loss of solatium they suffered as a result of Mr. Cicippio's ordeal. The Iranian defendants failed to respond to the complaint and the District Court entered default on January 2, 2002. The Cicippios filed a motion for summary judgment on January 10, 2002. Subsequently, on January 24, 2002, plaintiffs moved to consolidate their suit with Mr. and Mrs. Cicippio's case, which by then had been closed. On June 21, 2002, the District Court denied the motions for summary judgment and consolidation. The court also sua sponte dismissed the Cicippios' complaint under Federal Rules of Civil Procedure 12(b)(6) and 12(h)(3), holding that "the FSIA, as amended, does not confer subject matter jurisdiction upon it to entertain claims for emotional distress and solatium brought by claimants situated as are these plaintiffs upon the allegations of their complaint." Cicippio-Puleo v. Islamic Republic of Iran, Civ. No. 01-1496, slip op. at 2, (D.D.C. June 21, 2002). Joseph Cicippio's children and siblings now appeal. Responding to our request, the Justice Department has filed a brief as amicus curiae stating the position of the United States. The Government's position is that neither section 1605(a)(7) of the FSIA nor the Flatow Amendment,

28 U.S.C. § 1605 note, creates a private cause of action against foreign governments for acts of hostage taking or torture.

We affirm the judgment of the District Court. Section 1605(a)(7) of the FSIA abrogates foreign sovereign immunity and provides jurisdiction in specified circumstances, but it does not create a private cause of action. By its clear terms, the Flatow Amendment provides a private right of action only against individual officials, employees, and agents of a foreign state, but not against a foreign state itself. Plainly, neither section 1605(a)(7) nor the Flatow Amendment, separately or together, establishes a cause of action against foreign state sponsors of terrorism. Therefore, the Cicippios' suit cannot proceed on these grounds. However, because the Cicippios' suit was filed in the wake of judgments in favor of Mr. and Mrs. Cicippio and other hostage victims, they may have been misled in assuming that the Flatow Amendment afforded a cause of action against foreign state sponsors of terrorism. We therefore affirm the judgment of the District Court, but remand the case to allow plaintiffs an opportunity to amend their complaint to state a cause of action under some other source of law. We reserve judgment, however, on whether the Cicippios have any viable basis for an action against Iran, leaving that issue to the District Court in the first instance.

I. BACKGROUND

A. Facts

On the morning of September 12, 1986, Joseph. J. Cicippio was kidnaped in Beirut, Lebanon, by the terrorist group Hezbollah, an agent of Iran's Ministry of Information and Security ("MOIS"). At the time of his abduction, Mr. Cicippio was comptroller of the American University of Beirut. Hezbollah held him hostage for 1,908 days. During that time, he was randomly beaten, confined in rodent- and scorpion-infested cells, and bound by chains. He suffered from numerous medical problems emanating from the inhumane treatment that he experienced during his captivity. At some point after Mr. Cicippio was taken hostage, he was forced to undergo major surgery for an unidentified abdominal condition that has left a ten-inch scar on his abdomen.

In 1996, Joseph Cicippio filed suit against Iran under the "terrorism exception" to the FSIA, 28 U.S.C. § 1605(a)(7), and the Flatow Amendment, 28 U.S.C. § 1605 note. His lawsuit was joined by his wife, Elham Cicippio, two other hostage victims, and the wife of one of the other victims. The Iranian defendants did not respond to the complaint and were found in default. The case was tried ex parte and, on August 27, 1998, the District Court rendered a judgment for Joseph Cicippio in the amount of $20 million in damages for lost wages and opportunities and compensatory damages for pain and suffering and mental anguish, and $10 million for Mrs. Cicippio in damages for loss of her husband's society and companionship and mental anguish. Iran never entered an appearance in the case and no appeal was taken from the judgment of the District Court.

The instant case arises from a lawsuit brought in 2001 by Joseph Cicippio's seven adult children and seven siblings against Iran and MOIS for the intentional infliction of emotional distress and loss of solatium they sustained as a result of Mr. Cicippio's ordeal. The suit was based on claims purporting to arise under section 1605(a)(7) and the Flatow Amendment. On January 2, 2002, after Iran failed to respond to the complaint, the District Court entered a default judgment for the Cicippio children and siblings. On January 10, 2002, the Cicippios filed a motion for summary judgment. They subsequently filed a motion to consolidate their case with Mr. and Mrs. Cicippio's lawsuit against Iran, which by then had been closed. The motion for summary judgment included affidavits from the children and siblings establishing that Mr. Cicippio's captivity caused them to suffer from emotional distress by virtue of the harm done to him.

B. The Statutory Framework

* * * In 1996, as part of the comprehensive Antiterrorism and Effective Death Penalty Act ("AEDPA"), Congress enacted the "terrorism exception" to the FSIA, waiving the immunity of foreign states and their agents in any case

> in which money damages are sought against a foreign state for personal injury or death that was caused by an act of torture, extrajudicial killing, aircraft sabotage, hostage taking, or the provision of material support or resources (as defined in section 2339A of title 18) for such an act if such act or provision of material support is engaged in by an official, employee, or agent of such foreign state while acting within the scope of his or her office, employment, or agency * * * .

28 U.S.C. § 1605(a)(7). This provision only waives the immunity of a foreign state defendant that has been specifically designated by the State Department as a "state sponsor of terrorism," 28 U.S.C. § 1605(a)(7)(A), and does not apply if

> (i) the act occurred in the foreign state against which the claim has been brought and the claimant has not afforded the foreign state a reasonable opportunity to arbitrate the claim in accordance with accepted international rules of arbitration; or

> (ii) neither the claimant nor the victim was a national of the United States (as that term is defined in section 101(a)(22) of the Immigration and Nationality Act) when the act upon which the claim is based occurred.

28 U.S.C. § 1605(a)(7)(B).

Five months after the passage of AEDPA, Congress enacted a separate provision, titled Civil Liability for Acts of State Sponsored Terrorism, which created a private right of action against officials, employees, and agents of foreign states for the conduct described in § 1605(a)(7). See Omnibus Consolidated Appropriations Act of 1997, Pub.L. No. 104-208, Div. A, Title I, § 101(c) [Title V, § 589], 110 Stat. 3009-172 (codified at 28 U.S.C. § 1605 note). This provision is known as the "Flatow Amendment," in recognition of the family of Alisa Flatow, a woman who died as the result of a terrorist bombing in Israel. See Flatow v. Islamic Republic of Iran, 999 F.Supp. 1, 12 (D.D.C.1998). The Flatow Amendment provides:

> (a) An official, employee, or agent of a foreign state designated as a state sponsor of terrorism designated under section 6(j) of the Export Administration Act of 1979 [section 2405(j) of the Appendix to Title 50, War and National Defense] while acting within the scope of his or her office, employment, or agency shall be liable to a United States national

or the national's legal representative for personal injury or death caused by acts of that official, employee, or agent for which the courts of the United States may maintain jurisdiction under section 1605(a)(7) of title 28, United States Code [subsec. (a)(7) of this section] for money damages which may include economic damages, solatium, pain, and suffering, and punitive damages if the acts were among those described in section 1605(a)(7) [subsec. (a)(7) of this section].

28 U.S.C. § 1605 note.

It is undisputed that the Flatow Amendment permits U.S. nationals to pursue a private right of action for terrorism against officials, employees, and agents of designated foreign states acting in their personal capacities. At issue here is whether section 1605(a)(7) and the Flatow Amendment similarly provide a cause of action against a foreign state. * * *

After receiving a two-day extension of time in which to submit its position, the United States filed a brief as amicus curiae on December 3, 2003, stating the firm view that the Flatow Amendment does not provide a private right of action against a foreign state:

> Neither Section 1605(a)(7) nor the Flatow Amendment, nor the two considered in tandem, offers any indication that Congress intended to take the more provocative step of creating a private right of action against foreign governments themselves. Such a move could have serious adverse consequences for the conduct of foreign relations by the Executive Branch, and therefore an intent to do so should not be inferred - it should be recognized only if Congress has acted clearly in that direction.

II. ANALYSIS

* * *

B. The Limited Cause of Action under the Flatow Amendment

* * * This court, however, has never affirmed a judgment that the Flatow Amendment, either alone or in conjunction with section 1605(a)(7), provides a cause of action against a foreign state. The issue was raised in Bettis v. Islamic Republic of Iran, 315 F.3d 325, 333 (D.C.Cir. 2003), but the appeal was resolved on other grounds. In Roeder v. Islamic Republic of Iran, 333 F.3d 228 (D.C.Cir. 2003), the court noted that, "[i]n view of the Flatow amendment's failure to mention the liability of foreign states, it is 'far from clear' that a plaintiff has a substantive claim against a foreign state under the Foreign Sovereign Immunities Act," id. at 234 n. 3, but that appeal was also decided on other grounds.

We now hold that neither 28 U.S.C. § 1605(a)(7) nor the Flatow Amendment, nor the two considered in tandem, creates a private right of action against a foreign government. Section 1605(a)(7) merely waives the immunity of a foreign state without creating a cause of action against it, and the Flatow Amendment only provides a private right of action against officials, employees, and agents of a foreign state, not against the foreign state itself. Because we hold that there is no statutory cause of action against Iran under these provisions, we affirm the District Court's judgment without deciding whether the evidence presented by the plaintiffs is sufficient to recover for intentional infliction of emotional distress or loss of solatium.

****

There is a clearly settled distinction in federal law between statutory provisions that waive sovereign immunity and those that create a cause of action. It cannot be assumed that a claimant has a cause of action for damages against a government agency merely because there has been a waiver of sovereign immunity. See FDIC v. Meyer, 510 U.S. 471, 483-84. * * *

The Supreme Court has also made it clear that the federal courts should be loathe to "imply" a cause of action from a jurisdictional provision that "creates no cause of action of its own force and effect . . . [and] imposes no liabilities." See Touche Ross & Co. v. Redington, 442 U.S. 560, 577 (1979). "The ultimate question is one of congressional intent, not one of whether this Court thinks that it can improve upon the statutory scheme that Congress enacted into law." Id. at 578. In adhering to this view, the Supreme Court has declined to construe statutes to imply a cause of action where Congress has not expressly provided one. See, e.g., Correctional Servs. Corp. v. Malesko, 534 U.S. 61, 67 n. 3 (2001) (recognizing the Court's retreat from its previous willingness to imply a cause of action where Congress has not provided one); Alexander v. Sandoval, 532 U.S. 275, 286 (2001) ("Like substantive federal law itself, private rights of action to enforce federal law must be created by Congress."). * * *

The language of section 1605(a)(7) and the Flatow Amendment—the only provisions upon which plaintiffs rely—is clear. In declaring that "[a] foreign state shall not be immune from the jurisdiction of courts of the United States or of the States . . .," 28 U.S.C. § 1605(a)(7) merely abrogates the immunity of foreign states from the jurisdiction of the courts in lawsuits for damages for certain enumerated acts of terrorism. It does not impose liability or mention a cause of action. The statute thus confers subject matter jurisdiction on federal courts over such lawsuits, but does not create a private right of action.

As noted above, the Flatow Amendment imposes liability and creates a cause of action. But the liability imposed by the provision is precisely limited to "an official, employee, or agent of a foreign state designated as a state sponsor of terrorism." "Foreign states" are not within the compass of the cause of action created by the Flatow Amendment. In short, there is absolutely nothing in section 1605(a)(7) or the Flatow Amendment that creates a cause of action against foreign states for the enumerated acts of terrorism.

We also agree with the United States that, insofar as the Flatow Amendment creates a private right of action against officials, employees, and agents of foreign states, the cause of action is limited to claims against those officials in their individual, as opposed to their official, capacities:

> As the Supreme Court repeatedly has explained, an official-capacity claim against a government official is in substance a claim against the government itself. See, e.g., Kentucky v. Graham, 473 U.S. 159, 165 (1985). . . . By definition, a damages judgment in an official-capacity suit is enforceable against the state itself (and only against the state). See Graham, 473 U.S. at 166 . . . ; see also Fed.R.Civ.P. 25(d). . . . Thus, to

construe the Flatow Amendment as permitting official-capacity claims would eviscerate the recognized distinction between suits against governments and suits against individual government officials. . . . [T]he text of the Flatow Amendment and Section 1605(a)(7), as well as all relevant background interpretive principles . . . foreclose any such construction.

Br. for the United States as Amicus Curiae at 17.

****

The plaintiffs and amicus curiae dispute both the meaning and relevance of the legislative history of the FSIA or the Flatow Amendment in support of their competing arguments to the court. The legislative history is largely irrelevant, however, because the statutory language is clear—nothing in § 1605(a)(7) or the Flatow Amendment establishes a cause of action against foreign states. * * *

There is nothing anomalous in Congress's approach in enacting the Flatow Amendment. The passage of § 1605(a)(7) involved a delicate legislative compromise. While Congress sought to create a judicial forum for the compensation of victims and the punishment of terrorist states, it proceeded with caution, in part due to executive branch officials' concern that other nations would respond by subjecting the American government to suits in foreign countries.

The plaintiffs suggest that our construction of the Flatow Amendment "w[ill] mean that what Congress gave with one hand in section 1605(a)(7) it immediately took away with the other in the Flatow Amendment." We disagree. Section 1605(a)(7) does not purport to grant victims of terrorism a cause of action against foreign states, or against officials, employees, or agents of those states acting in either their official or personal capacities. Therefore, the Flatow Amendment's authorization of a limited cause of action against officials, employees, and agents acting in their personal capacities takes nothing away from § 1605 (a)(7). What § 1605(a)(7) does is to make it clear that designated foreign state sponsors of terrorism will be amenable to suits in United States courts for acts of terrorism in cases in which there is a viable cause of action.

Clearly, Congress's authorization of a cause of action against officials, employees, and agents of a foreign state was a significant step toward providing a judicial forum for the compensation of terrorism victims. Recognizing a federal cause of action against foreign states undoubtedly would be an even greater step toward that end, but it is a step that Congress has yet to take. And it is for Congress, not the courts, to decide whether a cause of action should lie against foreign states. Therefore, we decline to imply a cause of action against foreign states when Congress has not expressly recognized one in the language of section 1605(a)(7) or the Flatow Amendment. [The court nevertheless remanded for consideration of possible claims under sources of law other than the Flatow Amendment, such as state law.]

NOTES AND QUESTIONS FOR DISCUSSION

1. The opinion in *Cicippio-Puleo* begins from the obvious, if neglected, premise that the FSIA creates no cause of action. It only establishes exceptions to immunity, which come into play once the plaintiff has asserted a claim grounded in some other source of law. The Flatow Amendment seemed to provide that source of law to the plaintiffs, but it imposes liability only upon "an official, employee, or agent of" a foreign state identified. The D.C. Circuit interprets this clause to refer only to actions against such individuals in their personal capacity rather than their official capacity. In this respect, the decision follows reasoning similar to Samantar v. Yousef, 130 S. Ct. 2278 (2010), discussed in the notes after *Dole Foods*. Under *Samantar*, foreign officials have no immunity in their personal capacity under the FSIA because they are not "an agency or instrumentality of a foreign state." Under *Cicippio-Puleo*, they have no liability under the Flatow Amendment in their official capacity, because that would, in the D.C. Circuit's view, be equivalent to subjecting the foreign government to liability. The combined effect of both decisions is to leave foreign officials subject to liability in their personal capacity with immunity determined under federal common law.

That analysis, as far as it goes, gives some hope to the plaintiffs that they might succeed in bringing a claim against Iranian officials under the Flatow Amendment. They would still, however, have to establish personal jurisdiction over the individual defendants and find assets of the defendants from which any judgment could be collected. In addition, the established international law of individual immunity might bar liability either because of the status of the defendants as high officials or because of their conduct in performing their official duties. In short, the prospects for trying, winning, and collecting on any claim against individual officials remain daunting.

2. Instead of relying upon this alternative, the plaintiffs (and other human rights advocates) went back to Congress and obtained an amendment to the Flatow Amendment, now codified in § 1605A. This provision goes beyond an exception to sovereign immunity to create a claim under federal law directly against the foreign government. Like its predecessor, § 1605(a)(7), its application is conditioned upon a designation by the President that the foreign government is a "state sponsor of terrorism." This condition gives the executive branch control over the defendants subject to liability in private actions, preserving a degree of uniformity in American relations with foreign government. Private plaintiffs cannot sue just any government whose actions they believe to be in violation of recognized human rights.

The plaintiffs' control over their claims remains limited in another way as well. The lesson from cases like *Cicippio-Puleo* is that plaintiffs must succeed on three separate steps in order to recover from a foreign government: they must have a claim; they must be within an exception to foreign sovereign immunity; and they must be able to collect on any resulting judgment. Litigation, by itself, might succeed in calling attention to human rights abuses, but unless it is successful, it does little to deter such abuses or to remedy them. In fact, a purely symbolic victory might only succeed in convincing human rights violators that they can act with impunity. Section 1605A addresses the first two steps, liability and immunity. The third, collection, is addressed by § 1610.

The FSIA generally confers immunity on the assets of a foreign state, subject to a complex set of exceptions for assets used in commercial activity. The exceptions in § 1610 have been augmented by exceptions tailored to specific human rights claims, often focused upon particular assets of a particular foreign state. Because of its longstanding hostility to the U.S., Iran has been a favorite target of such legislation. The oil wealth accumulated by Iran and its extensive dealings with the U.S. before the revolution against the Shah have left substantial assets in this country vulnerable to collection efforts. These assets, however, received a degree of protection in the legislation establishing the Iran-United States Claims Tribunal. As a result, a complicated web of interconnected statutes governs collection efforts directed against Iran, which are analyzed in detail in Ministry of Defense and Support v. Elahi, 556 U.S. 366 (2009). The Supreme Court refused to allow execution against Iranian assets in that case because the plaintiffs had accepted compensation directly from the federal government in lieu of pursuing further claims against Iran. The decision reveals the contrast between victims of terrorism, who receive a sympathetic hearing in Congress; the claims to immunity by a hostile government, which currently has no constituency in this country but formerly was an ally; and the efforts of the State Department to maintain control over relations with foreign governments. For a similarly complicated claim against Iraq, in which the Supreme Court also upheld immunity, see Republic of Iraq v. Beaty, 556 U.S. 848 (2009). Is there any reason to expect a simple principle to emerge in cases governed by all these competing considerations?

3. Human rights plaintiffs have succeeded most visibly at the federal level in obtaining legislation like § 1605A. They have also succeeded in gaining an expanded interpretation of the Alien Tort Statute, 28 U.S.C. § 1350, and passage of new laws like the Torture Victim Protection Act, Pub. L. No. 102-256, 106 Stat. 73 (1992). (The ATS and the TVPA are discussed in Chapter 2.) This patchwork of federal laws makes the plaintiff's claim dependent upon the identity of parties and the wrongful action alleged. The ATS only supports claims by aliens; § 1605A, as we have seen, supports claims only against designated state sponsors of terrorism; and the TVPA creates claims only for torture and extrajudicial killing. These federal laws hardly cover the field of possible human rights claims.

In *Cicippio-Puleo*, the D.C. Circuit also held out the alternative possibility of applying state tort law. Recall that the plaintiffs in *Saudi Arabia v. Nelson* asserted claims on this basis. The interjection of state law into issues of human rights and foreign relations strikes a discordant note, not present in the typical commercial case under the restrictive theory of sovereign immunity. In those cases, state law plays its ordinary role of governing market transactions not subject to federal law. Human rights claims arising in Lebanon do not fit this mold. State law, if it applies at all, does so by default, in the absence of federal law or foreign law applicable under ordinary choice of law principles. Those principles traditionally gave priority to the law of the state where the tort occurred (aka, the "lex loci delicti"). Hence the tort exception to foreign sovereign immunity in § 1605(a)(5) applies only to cases in which the loss occurred in the U.S. Similar limitations based on location of property or commercial activity restrict the exceptions for expropriation claims in § 1605(a)(3) and (4), as discussed in the next principal case. These provisions reflect an assumption that the liability of foreign sovereigns, when it extends outside of purely commercial transactions, depends upon a strong connection to the U.S.

Human rights claims aspire to universal scope and extraterritorial application, inconsistent with the traditional limits imposed by choice-of-law rules. These rules were relaxed in the second half of the 20th century, usually through a case-by-case analysis of a state's interest in applying its own law to a controversy because, for instance, its own citizens were involved. That approach departed from hard-and-fast rules such as lex loci delicti and opened the way to application of the forum state's law to claims arising outside its borders. Usually, these claims arose in another state, but the logic of interest analysis extended also to claims arising in foreign countries. Constitutional limits on state choice of law also were relaxed, leaving each state considerable latitude to decide whether to apply its own law extraterritorially.

The restraint on application of state law has to be found elsewhere, most likely in preemption by federal law, based ultimately on the power of the federal government over foreign relations. Preemption could be accomplished by an explicit statement of Congress, the implication from the detailed provisions of a federal statute, or perhaps by the force of federal common law. Human rights plaintiffs seldom want to make such arguments, since they would like to preserve the ability to resort to state law if they cannot find a basis for their claims in federal law. Yet statutes like § 1605A do not easily coexist with state claims. If the President limits claims against a foreign government by failing to designate it as a state sponsor of terror, or if any of the other detailed requirements of § 1605A are not met, applying state tort law threatens the compromise inherent in the statute: recognizing a claim but restricting its scope.

To the extent that federal law recognizes a claim, it tends naturally to displace state law. If the plaintiffs in *Cicippio-Puleo* can now assert a claim under § 1605A, they have no need to search for one under state law. The developing federal law of human rights law might give them everything they need. When it does not, however, they might well turn to state law to support claims not yet established as a matter of federal law. Whether the role of state law is transitory or permanent, it constitutes one source for arguments to recognize new human rights claims. Is there any reason to cut off this source simply because it concerns human rights and international relations, as opposed to wholly domestic law? Does the answer depend upon how state law fits with existing federal law, either in filling in the gaps that it has left open or in covering much the same ground? Should the preemptive effect of federal law be any more extensive in international civil litigation than it is in any other?

4. For discussion of the consequences of *Cicippio-Puleo*, see Aron Ketchel, Note, *Deriving Lessons for the Alien Tort Claims Act from the Foreign Sovereign Immunities Act*, 32 Yale J. Int'l L. 191 (2007); Ruthanne M. Deutsch, *Suing State-Sponsors of Terrorism Under the Foreign Sovereign Immunities Act: Giving Life to the Jurisdictional Grant After* Cicippio-Puleo, 38 Int'l Law. 891 (2004). For articles on background to the decision, see Lee M. Caplan, *The Constitution and Jurisdiction Over Foreign States: The 1996 Amendment to the Foreign Sovereign Immunities Act in Perspective*, 41 Va. J. Int'l L. 369 (2001); Joseph W. Glannon and Jeffery Atik, *Politics and Personal Jurisdiction: Suing State Sponsors of Terrorism Under the 1996 Amendments to the Foreign Sovereign Immunities Act*, 87 Geo. L.J. 675 (1999); Monroe Leigh, *1996 Amendments* *to the Foreign Sovereign Immunities Act with Respect to Terrorist Activities*, 91 Am. J. Int'l L. 187 (1997).

Zappia Middle East Constr. Co. Ltd. v. Emirate of Abu Dhabi

United States Court of Appeals, Second Circuit, 2000.
215 F.3d 247.

PAULEY, DISTRICT JUDGE.[*]

Plaintiff-appellant Zappia Middle East Construction Company Limited ("ZMEC") appeals from an order of the United States District Court for the Southern District of New York (Wood, J.) dismissing its complaint for lack of subject matter jurisdiction. The district court held that the plaintiff failed to establish facts sufficient to bring the action within the purview of the expropriation exception of the Foreign Sovereign Immunities Act ("FSIA"), 28 U.S.C. § 1605(a)(3) (1994). We affirm.

BACKGROUND

* * *

ZMEC is a construction company incorporated in the British Virgin Islands with a place of business in Canada. ZMEC is owned by Joseph Zappia. Mr. Zappia is a citizen of Italy and Canada and a resident of Rome, though at all times relevant to this action he resided in the Emirate of Abu Dhabi. Defendant-appellee Abu Dhabi Investment Authority ("ADIA") is an investment institution wholly owned by Abu Dhabi. ADIA owns a majority of the shares of defendant-appellee Abu Dhabi Commercial Bank ("ADCB").

From 1979 to 1982, ZMEC entered into a series of eight construction contracts in Abu Dhabi to build public works facilities in the Emirate. The contracts called for the Emirate to make periodic progress payments to ZMEC. In mid-1982, the Emirate delayed making payments, and in some instances refused to pay ZMEC the monies due under the contracts. The Emirate also allegedly forced ZMEC to perform work beyond that specified in the contracts. To remain solvent, ZMEC borrowed funds from Emirates Commercial Bank ("ECB") on unfavorable terms.

In January 1983, ZMEC reached the limit of its credit with ECB. On January 10, 1983, ZMEC entered into an agreement with ECB (the "1983 Agreement") pursuant to which day-to-day management of ZMEC was turned over to another construction contractor, Bovis International Limited ("Bovis"), and supervision of ZMEC was turned over to a management committee comprised of three representatives of ECB, one representative of Bovis, and Mr. Zappia or alternatively his assistant. The 1983 Agreement also prevented ZMEC from incurring any further debts or liabilities without the written consent of ECB.

---

[*] The Honorable William H. Pauley III, of the United States District Court for the Southern District of New York, sitting by designation.

ZMEC alleges that Mr. Zappia signed the 1983 Agreement under threat of imprisonment. At the January 10, 1983 meeting, ECB also forced Mr. Zappia to surrender his passport. Thereafter, Mr. Zappia's passport was withheld until the Emirate's acting Interior Minister returned it months later.

Ten days after the 1983 Agreement was executed, ECB wrote to Sheikh Kalifa Bin Zayed Al Nahyan ("Sheikh Kalifa"), the Crown Prince of Abu Dhabi and the Chairman of Abu Dhabi's executive council, petitioning him to direct the various government departments to extend the duration of ZMEC's projects so that Bovis could complete them.

In July 1985, more than two years after the execution of the 1983 Agreement, ECB and two other banks were recapitalized by the Emirate and merged into the newly formed ADCB. By then, several of the construction projects had been completed and Bovis was liquidating ZMEC's construction equipment and preparing claims for compensation on ZMEC's behalf. After the merger, Bovis completed the remaining projects and sold the rest of ZMEC's construction equipment. No proceeds from the sales of equipment were paid to the Emirate or ADIA, and none of the equipment or the proceeds of the sales are present in the United States.

In 1994, ZMEC instituted this suit seeking payments under the original construction contracts. ZMEC alleged that the defendants had taken its property in violation of international law and asserted jurisdiction based upon the expropriation exception to the FSIA, 28 U.S.C. § 1605(a)(3). The case was referred to a magistrate judge for pretrial management and a report and recommendation on dispositive motions. The defendants promptly moved to dismiss the complaint for lack of subject matter jurisdiction. The parties subsequently conducted two years of discovery solely on the jurisdictional issue.

Based on the documentary evidence amassed by the parties, the magistrate judge concluded in a thorough report and recommendation that there was no evidence that ECB was controlled by the Emirate or the royal family. Consequently, the magistrate judge determined that no expropriation by the sovereign had taken place. Adopting the report and recommendation, the district judge also concluded that the evidence did not support ZMEC's assertions that the Emirate expropriated ZMEC's property and dismissed the complaint.

ZMEC appeals the district court's finding that rights in intangible property are not "rights in property" under the FSIA, and that there was no expropriation by Abu Dhabi and ADIA. ZMEC also asserts that the district court abused its discretion in failing to hold an evidentiary hearing on the jurisdictional issues.

DISCUSSION

I. The Expropriation Exception

It is undisputed that the defendants-appellees are either foreign sovereigns or instrumentalities of a foreign sovereign. * * *

Although this action involves a commercial contract dispute, the FSIA "commercial activities" exception, 28 U.S.C. § 1605(a)(2)(1994), does not apply because no commercial acts or their effects were felt in the United States. However, ZMEC contends that the FSIA expropriation exception applies.

The expropriation exception provides that a foreign sovereign is not immune from suit in any case

> in which rights in property taken in violation of international law are in issue and that property or any property exchanged for such property is present in the United States in connection with a commercial activity carried on in the United States by the foreign state; or that property or any property exchanged for such property is owned or operated by an agency or instrumentality of the foreign state and that agency or instrumentality is engaged in a commercial activity in the United States.

28 U.S.C. § 1605(a)(3). Thus, in order to establish jurisdiction pursuant to the FSIA expropriation exception, a plaintiff must show that: (1) rights in property are in issue; (2) that the property was "taken"; (3) that the taking was in violation of international law; and (4) that one of the two nexus requirements is satisfied. The district court found that ZMEC failed to satisfy the first two criteria because intangible contract rights are not rights in property and there was no governmental taking. We need not determine whether intangible contract rights are property under the statute, however, because defendants-appellees' actions did not constitute a taking within the meaning of the FSIA.

The FSIA does not define the term "taken." However, the legislative history makes clear that the phrase "taken in violation of international law" refers to "the nationalization or expropriation of property without payment of the prompt adequate and effective compensation required by international law," including "takings which are arbitrary or discriminatory in nature." H.R. Rep. No. 94-1487, at 19 (1976), reprinted in 1976 U.S.C.C.A.N. 6604, 6618. The term "taken" thus clearly refers to acts of a sovereign, not a private enterprise, that deprive a plaintiff of property without adequate compensation. Accord Alfred Dunhill of London, Inc. v. Republic of Cuba, 425 U.S. 682, 685 (1976).

ZMEC argues that ECB and ADCB were alter egos of the Emirate, which surreptitiously expropriated ZMEC's property under the 1983 Agreement. However, government instrumentalities are presumed to be distinct and independent from their sovereign and normally are treated as such. See First Nat'l City Bank v. Banco Para El Comercio Exterior de Cuba, 462 U.S. 611, 626-27 (1983). As the Supreme Court has explained,

> [f]reely ignoring the separate status of government instrumentalities would result in substantial uncertainty over whether an instrumentality's assets would be diverted to satisfy a claim against the sovereign, and might thereby cause third parties to hesitate before extending credit to a government instrumentality. As a result, the efforts of sovereign nations to structure their governmental activities in a manner deemed necessary to promote economic development and efficient administration would surely be frustrated.

Id. at 626.

While the presumption of separateness is a strong one, it may be overcome if a corporate entity is so extensively controlled by the sovereign that the latter is effectively the agent of the former, or if recognizing the corporate entity as independent would work a fraud or injustice. See id. at 629-630; De Letelier v. Republic of Chile, 748 F.2d 790, 794-95 (2d Cir. 1984).

ZMEC bears the burden of proving that the corporate entity should not be presumed distinct from a sovereign or sovereign entity. See id. at 795. ZMEC challenges ECB's and ADCB's status as separate corporate entities on the following evidence: the Emirate forced ZMEC into debt by withholding required contract payments, which in turn lead ZMEC to take out a loan from ECB; ECB officials threatened to disavow ZMEC's checks, which could have led to Mr. Zappia's imprisonment; ECB seized Mr. Zappia's passport and submitted it to a government official who withheld it for months; the 1983 Agreement included a provision that prevented ZMEC from incurring additional debt which effectively acted as an "embargo"; after the 1983 Agreement was executed, ECB sought Sheikh Khalifa's approval of an extension of time in which to complete the construction of government buildings; and after entering into the 1983 Agreement, ECB rushed to complete the construction projects increasing ZMEC's debt exposure.

This evidence does not demonstrate a sufficient intermingling of the private bank with the sovereign to overcome the presumption of separateness. There is no evidence that Abu Dhabi or ADIA ignored ECB's separate status, or that the sovereign so abused the corporate form that considerations of fair dealing require that we disregard the presumption of separateness. The facts merely show that the government, acting as a commercial entity, reneged on its contractual obligations. ZMEC then turned to a private commercial bank, ECB, for a loan. When it could not meet its loan obligations, ECB levied on the only available security interest—ZMEC. After ECB merged into ADCB in 1985, ADCB merely acted pursuant to the agreement its predecessor had negotiated. The acts of a private commercial entity, even one that supports a government, cannot be attributed to a government that has not authorized the private entity to act on its behalf. Accord Short v. Islamic Republic of Iran, 16 Iran-U.S. Cl. Trib. Rep. 76, 84-85 (1987). The strong presumption of separateness cannot be overcome on the facts of this case.

ZMEC also asserts that the acts of Abu Dhabi and ADIA alone are sufficient to serve as a basis for jurisdiction under the FSIA expropriation exception. Specifically, ZMEC relies on Abu Dhabi's refusal to pay ZMEC under the construction contracts and ADIA chairman Sheikh Khalifa's ex post facto approval of the 1983 Agreement as a basis for subject matter jurisdiction. Tellingly, ZMEC does not cite any law in support of that proposition. Abu Dhabi's alleged refusal to pay ZMEC under the construction contracts no doubt supports a commercial breach of contract claim. However, breach of a commercial contract alone does not constitute a taking pursuant to international law. See First Fidelity Bank, N.A. v. Government of Antigua & Barbuda-Permanent Mission, 877 F.2d 189, 193 (2d Cir. 1989). Moreover, the government did not seize control of ZMEC. ECB transferred the management of ZMEC to a management team that consisted solely of private actors and included Mr. Zappia. As for ADIA, it was not even a party to any of the contracts at issue in this action. Although Sheikh Khalifa was the chairman of ADIA, his ex post facto approval of the 1983 Agreement alone is not sufficient to establish jurisdiction over ADIA.

Accordingly, the district court did not err in dismissing the complaint for lack of jurisdiction. * * *

NOTES AND QUESTIONS FOR DISCUSSION

1. The expropriation alleged in *Zappia* was of the assets and operations of the ZMEC Corporation. Through a series of contracts, the owner of ZMEC gave control of its assets and operations to the Emirates Commercial Bank (ECB), which was later merged into the Abu Dhabi Commercial Bank (ADCB). The banks, ECB and ADCB, argued that they had seized control because ZMEC's assets and operations had been pledged as security for loans that they had extended to the corporation. ZMEC argued that the seizure constituted a taking by the government of Abu Dhabi, effected through the actions of ECB and ADCB, as part of a continuing contract dispute between the government and the corporation. The case essentially arose from this commercial contract.

If so, why didn't ZMEC invoke the commercial exception in § 1605(a)(2)? The apparent answer lies in the failure of Abu Dhabi's commercial activity to have the necessary connection to the U.S. No commercial activity, or act in connection with such activity, or direct effect of such activity occurred in the U.S. If that is true, why should ZMEC be allowed to invoke the takings exception in § 1605(a)(3)? Note also that the additional taking exception in § 1605(a)(4) does not apply because no rights by succession or gift or rights in "immoveable property situated in the United States" were in issue. Do these considerations lead the Second Circuit to adopt a narrow the interpretation of § 1605(a)(3) to avoid the limitations inherent in these other exceptions?

2. As the Second Circuit analyzes the case, it falls within the expropriation exception in § 1605(a)(3) only if four conditions are met: "(1) rights in property are in issue; (2) that the property was 'taken'; (3) that the taking was in violation of international law; and (4) that one of the two nexus requirements is satisfied." *Zappia*, 215 F.3d at 251. The court holds that the claim with respect to corporate assets fails to meet the second requirement and the claim with respect to contract rights fails to meet the first requirement. The third requirement goes to the merits of both claims, which the court does not address. The fourth requirement goes to the connection with the U.S., which could be met only if ECB and ADCB were instrumentalities of Abu Dhabi and they had commercial operations in the U.S.

Turning for a moment to this last requirement, note that Abu Dhabi did not directly own a majority of shares in either corporation, so they would not now be instrumentalities of Abu Dhabi under *Dole Food*. The Supreme Court decided *Dole Food* a few years after the Second Circuit decided *Zappia*, so the law on instrumentalities was not as clear as it is now. Would this case simply fall under *Dole Food* now? ECB and ADCB might well do banking business in the U.S., but since they were not instrumentalities of Abu Dhabi, they could not satisfy this version of the nexus requirement. The only nexus with the U.S. available would have to be through the transfer of the property, or some property exchanged for it, to an entity that is an instrumentality of Abu Dhabi and that engages in commercial activity in the U.S. Is this likely? How could it be established?

Of course, if ECB and ADCB were not considered state instrumentalities, they could not invoke sovereign immunity at all. ZMEC could have sued them directly and tried to collect any resulting judgment from their assets in the U.S. Suppose, however, that ECB and ADCB were instrumentalities of Abu Dhabi and that they did engage in commercial activity inside the U.S. That would bring them within the FSIA and it would also satisfy the nexus requirement in § 1605(a)(3). Would it change the Second Circuit's analysis in any other respect?

3. The first requirement, that the seizure involve property, would not appear to be affected. As an initial matter, "rights in property" obviously extends to intangible property, which describes many financial assets, such as stock and bonds, as well as the rights in the corporation in this case. To exclude all such rights from the expropriation exception would drastically narrow its scope. Note that the intangible nature of property makes it more difficult to trace and more difficult to identify property exchanged for it.

The Second Circuit held that the rights that ZMEC held under its contracts with Abu Dhabi do not constitute property because they were rights only to payment under the contracts, not rights to property already owned or in possession of ZMEC. In terms of remedies, ZMEC could only obtain damages from Abu Dhabi for breach of the contracts, not some form of injunctive relief that extended beyond the required payments.

Do the rights to control the assets and operations of ZMEC, ceded to ECB and ADCB by agreement, also constitute only contract rights? The rights to the assets of the corporation certainly go beyond contract rights. They are rights to whatever real and personal property the corporation owns and they are not deprived of their status as property rights because they were also subject to a contract. For example, the right to own a house does not become simply a contract right because the house is subject to a contract of sale. Rights to operate the corporation appear to be more problematic, because they are less closely connected to particular pieces of property, but they, too, might be treated as analogous to the right to a majority of shares in the corporation. Although that was not the form that the seizure took in this case, because the owner of ZMEC retained his shares in the corporation, but he lost his right to any interest in the corporation when control over its assets and operations were ceded to ECB and ADCB. Would that be enough to constitute a seizure of property?

4. The Second Circuit devotes most of its attention to the second requirement: that the seizure be by the government. The court follows the corporate form, recognizing ECB as an entity separate from Abu Dhabi, and therefore its actions as separate from the government's. As the court observes: "There is no evidence that Abu Dhabi or ADIA [its wholly owned investment bank] ignored ECB's separate status, or that the sovereign so abused the corporate form that considerations of fair dealing require that we disregard the presumption of separateness." *Zappia*, 215 F.3d at 252. How is this reasoning affected by ECB's status, after *Dole Food*, as something other than an instrumentality of Abu Dhabi? Does this status make the inference still stronger that ECB did not act on Abu Dhabi's behalf?

Could a non-instrumentality ever engage in a taking? Consider an explicit authorization granted by Abu Dhabi to ECB to take ADIA's property without compensation. Would that be sufficient to make the taking one by the government? If so, why is the Second Circuit so confident that simple observance of the corporate form relieves Abu Dhabi of any responsibility for the seizure? Conversely, suppose that ECB were an instrumentality of Abu Dhabi. Would that automatically make the seizure a taking attributable to the government? Should the question of instrumentality status, whatever its other implications, serve just as one factor that determines whether a seizure is a taking by the government?

Whatever the resolution of these questions, § 1605(a)(3) also requires that the taking be in violation of international law. The Second Circuit does not address this question, but it, too, might be affected by attribution of ECB's actions to Abu Dhabi. Most of international law applies only to states and their instrumentalities, not to individuals acting in their private capacity. Absent some form of state responsibility for the seizure, no violation of international law might have occurred. As we shall see in the next section, even a violation of international law might not be enough to subject a foreign state to liability, even in an expropriation.

Section B. The Act of State Doctrine

Banco Nacional de Cuba v. Sabbatino

Supreme Court of the United States, 1964.
376 U.S. 398.

Mr. Justice Harlan delivered the opinion of the Court.

The question which brought this case here, and is now found to be the dispositive issue, is whether the so-called act of state doctrine serves to sustain petitioner's claims in this litigation. Such claims are ultimately founded on a decree of the Government of Cuba expropriating certain property, the right to the proceeds of which is here in controversy. The act of state doctrine in its traditional formulation precludes the courts of this country from inquiring into the validity of the public acts a recognized foreign sovereign power committed within its own territory.

I.

In February and July of 1960, respondent Farr, Whitlock & Co., an American commodity broker, contracted to purchase Cuban sugar, free alongside the steamer, from a wholly owned subsidiary of Compania Azucarera Vertientes-Camaguey de Cuba (C.A.V.), a corporation organized under Cuban law whose capital stock was owned principally by United States residents. Farr, Whitlock agreed to pay for the sugar in New York upon presentation of the shipping documents and a sight draft.

On July 6, 1960, the Congress of the United States amended the Sugar Act of 1948 to permit a presidentially directed reduction of the sugar quota for Cuba.

On the same day President Eisenhower exercised the granted power. The day of the congressional enactment, the Cuban Council of Ministers adopted "Law No. 851," which characterized this reduction in the Cuban sugar quota as an act of "aggression, for political purposes" on the part of the United States, justifying the taking of countermeasures by Cuba. The law gave the Cuban President and Prime Minister discretionary power to nationalize by forced expropriation property or enterprises in which American nationals had an interest. Although a system of compensation was formally provided, the possibility of payment under it may well be deemed illusory. Our State Department has described the Cuban law as "manifestly in violation of those principles of international law which have long been accepted by the free countries of the West. It is in its essence discriminatory, arbitrary and confiscatory."

Between August 6 and August 9, 1960, the sugar covered by the contract between Farr, Whitlock and C.A.V. was loaded, destined for Morocco, onto the S.S. Hornfels, which was standing offshore at the Cuban port of Jucaro (Santa Maria). On the day loading commenced, the Cuban President and Prime Minister, acting pursuant to Law No. 851, issued Executive Power Resolution No. 1. It provided for the compulsory expropriation of all property and enterprises, and of rights and interests arising therefrom, of certain listed companies, including C.A.V., wholly or principally owned by American nationals. The preamble reiterated the alleged injustice of the American reduction of the Cuban sugar quota and emphasized the importance of Cuba's serving as an example for other countries to follow "in their struggle to free themselves from the brutal claws of Imperialism." In consequence of the resolution, the consent of the Cuban Government was necessary before a ship carrying sugar of a named company could leave Cuban waters. In order to obtain this consent, Farr, Whitlock, on August 11, entered into contracts, identical to those it had made with C.A.V., with the Banco Para el Comercio Exterior de Cuba, an instrumentality of the Cuban Government. The S.S. Hornfels sailed for Morocco on August 12.

Banco Exterior assigned the bills of lading to petitioner, also an instrumentality of the Cuban Government, which instructed its agent in New York, Societe Generale, to deliver the bills and a sight draft in the sum of $175,250.69 to Farr, Whitlock in return for payment. Societe Generale's initial tender of the documents was refused by Farr, Whitlock, which on the same day was notified of C.A.V.'s claim that as rightful owner of the sugar it was entitled to the proceeds. In return for a promise not to turn the funds over to petitioner or its agent, C.A.V. agreed to indemnify Farr, Whitlock for any loss. Farr, Whitlock subsequently accepted the shipping documents, negotiated the bills of lading to its customer, and received payment for the sugar. It refused, however, to hand over the proceeds to Societe Generale. Shortly thereafter, Farr, Whitlock was served with an order of the New York Supreme Court, which had appointed Sabbatino as Temporary Receiver of C.A.V.'s New York assets, enjoining it from taking any action in regard to the money claimed by C.A.V. that might result in its removal from the State. Following this, Farr, Whitlock, pursuant to court order, transferred the funds to Sabbatino, to abide the event of a judicial determination as to their ownership.

Petitioner then instituted this action in the Federal District Court for the Southern District of New York. Alleging conversion of the bills of lading it sought to recover the proceeds thereof from Farr, Whitlock and to enjoin the receiver from exercising any dominion over such proceeds. * * * Proceeding on the basis that a taking invalid under international law does not convey good title, the District Court found the Cuban expropriation decree to violate such law in three separate respects: it was motivated by a retaliatory and not a public purpose; it discriminated against American nationals; and it failed to provide adequate compensation. Summary judgment against petitioner was accordingly granted.

The Court of Appeals affirming the decision on similar grounds, relied on two letters (not before the District Court) written by State Department officers which it took as evidence that the Executive Branch had no objection to a judicial testing of the Cuban decree's validity. * * *

III.

Respondents claimed in the lower courts that Cuba had expropriated merely contractual rights the situs of which was in New York, and that the propriety of the taking was, therefore, governed by New York law. The District Court rejected this contention on the basis of the right of ownership possessed by C.A.V. against Farr, Whitlock prior to payment for the sugar. That the sugar itself was expropriated rather than a contractual claim is further supported by Cuba's refusal to let the S.S. Hornfels sail until a new contract had been signed. Had the Cuban decree represented only an attempt to expropriate a contractual right of C.A.V., the forced delay of shipment and Farr, Whitlock's subsequent contract with petitioner's assignor would have been meaningless. Neither the District Court's finding concerning the location of the S.S. Hornfels nor its conclusion that Cuba had territorial jurisdiction to expropriate the sugar, acquiesced in by the Court of Appeals, is seriously challenged here. Respondents' limited view of the expropriation must be rejected.

Respondents further contend that if the expropriation was of the sugar itself, this suit then becomes one to enforce the public law of a foreign state and as such is not cognizable in the courts of this country. They rely on the principle enunciated in federal and state cases that a court need not give effect to the penal or revenue laws of foreign countries or sister states. * * *.[15]

The extent to which this doctrine may apply to other kinds of public laws, though perhaps still an open question, need not be decided in this case. For we have been referred to no authority which suggests that the doctrine reaches a public law which, as here, has been fully executed within the foreign state. Cuba's restraint of the S.S. Hornfels must be regarded for these purposes to have constituted an effective taking of the sugar, vesting in Cuba C.A.V.'s property right in it. Farr, Whitlock's contract with the Cuban bank, however compelled to sign Farr, Whitlock may have felt, represented indeed a recognition of Cuba's dominion over the property. * * *

---

[15] As appears from the cases cited, a penal law for the purposes of this doctrine is one which seeks to redress a public rather than a private wrong.

IV.

The classic American statement of the act of state doctrine, which appears to have taken root in England as early as 1674, and began to emerge in the jurisprudence of this country in the late eighteenth and early nineteenth centuries, is found in Underhill v. Hernandez, 168 U.S. 250, p. 252, where Chief Justice Fuller said for a unanimous Court:

> "Every sovereign state is bound to respect the independence of every other sovereign state, and the courts of one country will not sit in judgment on the acts of the government of another, done within its own territory. Redress of grievances by reason of such acts must be obtained through the means open to be availed of by sovereign powers as between themselves."

Following this precept the Court in that case refused to inquire into acts of Hernandez, a revolutionary Venezuelan military commander whose government had been later recognized by the United States, which were made the basis of a damage action in this country by Underhill, an American citizen, who claimed that he had had unlawfully assaulted, coerced, and detained in Venezuela by Hernandez. * * *

In deciding the present case the Court of Appeals relied in part upon an exception to the unqualified teachings of *Underhill*, [and cases following it]. In Bernstein v. Van Heyghen Freres Societe Anonyme, 2 Cir., 163 F.2d 246, suit was brought to recover from an assignee property allegedly taken, in effect, by the Nazi Government because plaintiff was Jewish. Recognizing the odious nature of this act of state, the court, through Judge Learned Hand, nonetheless refused to consider it invalid on that ground. Rather, it looked to see if the Executive had acted in any manner that would indicate that United States Courts should refuse to give effect to such a foreign decree. Finding no such evidence, the court sustained dismissal of the complaint. In a later case involving similar facts the same court again assumed examination of the German acts improper, Bernstein v. N.V. Nederlandsche-Amerikaansche Stoomvaart-Maatschappij, 2 Cir., 173 F.2d 71, but, quite evidently following the implications of Judge Hand's opinion in the earlier case, amended its mandate to permit evidence of alleged invalidity, 2 Cir., 210 F.2d 375, subsequent to receipt by plaintiff's attorney of a letter from the Acting Legal Adviser to the State Department written for the purpose of relieving the court from any constraint upon the exercise of its jurisdiction to pass on that question.

This Court has never had occasion to pass upon the so-called *Bernstein* exception, nor need it do so now. For whatever ambiguity may be thought to exist in the two letters from State Department officials on which the Court of Appeals relied, is now removed by the position which the Executive has taken in this Court on the act of state claim; respondents do not indeed contest the view that these letters were intended to reflect no more than the Department's then wish not to make any statement bearing on this litigation.

The outcome of this case, therefore, turns upon whether any of the contentions urged by respondents against the application of the act of state doctrine in the premises is acceptable: (1) that the doctrine does not apply to acts of state which violate international law, as is claimed to be the case here; (2) that the doctrine is inapplicable unless the Executive specifically interposes it in a particular case; and (3) that, in any event, the doctrine may not be invoked by a foreign government plaintiff in our courts.

V.

Preliminarily, we discuss the foundations on which we deem the act of state doctrine to rest, and more particularly the question of whether state or federal law governs its application in a federal diversity case.

We do not believe that this doctrine is compelled either by the inherent nature of sovereign authority, as some of the earlier decision seem to imply, see *Underhill, supra*; * * *, or by some principle of international law. If a transaction takes place in one jurisdiction and the forum is in another, the forum does not by dismissing an action or by applying its own law purport to divest the first jurisdiction of its territorial sovereignty; it merely declines to adjudicate or makes applicable its own law to parties or property before it. The refusal of one country to enforce the penal laws of another is a typical example of an instance when a court will not entertain a cause of action arising in another jurisdiction. While historic notions of sovereign authority do bear upon the wisdom or employing the act of state doctrine, they do not dictate its existence. * * *

The act of state doctrine does, however, have "constitutional" underpinnings. It arises out of the basic relationships between branches of government in a system of separation of powers. It concerns the competency of dissimilar institutions to make and implement particular kinds of decisions in the area of international relations. The doctrine as formulated in past decisions expresses the strong sense of the Judicial Branch that its engagement in the task of passing on the validity of foreign acts of state may hinder rather than further this country's pursuit of goals both for itself and for the community of nations as a whole in the international sphere. Many commentators disagree with this view; they have striven by means of distinguishing and limiting past decisions and by advancing various considerations of policy to stimulate a narrowing of the apparent scope of the rule. Whatever considerations are thought to predominate, it is plain that the problems involved are uniquely federal in nature. If federal authority, in this instance this Court, orders the field of judicial competence in this area for the federal courts, and the state courts are left free to formulate their own rules, the purposes behind the doctrine could be as effectively undermined as if there had been no federal pronouncement on the subject. * * *

However, we are constrained to make it clear that an issue concerned with a basic choice regarding the competence and function of the Judiciary and the National Executive in ordering our relationships with other members of the international community must be treated exclusively as an aspect of federal law. It seems fair to assume that the Court did not have rules like the act of state doctrine in mind when it decided *Erie R. Co. v. Tompkins* [304 U.S 64 (1938)]. Soon thereafter, Professor Philip C. Jessup, now a judge of the International Court of Justice, recognized the potential dangers were *Erie* extended to legal problems affecting international relations.[24] He cautioned that rules of international law should not be left to divergent and perhaps parochial state interpretations. His basic rationale is equally applicable to the act of state doctrine. * * *

VI.

If the act of state doctrine is a principle of decision binding on federal and state courts alike but compelled by neither international law nor the Constitution, its continuing vitality depends on its capacity to reflect the proper distribution of functions between the judicial and political branches of the Government on matters bearing upon foreign affairs. It should be apparent that the greater the degree of codification or consensus concerning a particular area of international law, the more appropriate it is for the judiciary to render decisions regarding it, since the courts can then focus on the application of an agreed principle to circumstances of fact rather than on the sensitive task of establishing a principle not inconsistent with the national interest or with international justice. It is also evident that some aspects of international law touch much more sharply on national nerves than do others; the less important the implications of an issue are for our foreign relations, the weaker the justification for exclusivity in the political branches. The balance of relevant considerations may also be shifted if the government which perpetrated the challenged act of state is no longer in existence, as in the *Bernstein* case, for the political interest of this country may, as a result, be measurably altered. Therefore, rather than laying down or reaffirming an inflexible and all-encompassing rule in this case, we decide only that the Judicial Branch will not examine the validity of a taking of property within its own territory by a foreign sovereign government, extant and recognized by this country at the time of suit, in the absence of a treaty or other unambiguous agreement regarding controlling legal principles, even if the complaint alleges that the taking violates customary international law.

There are few if any issues in international law today on which opinion seems to be so divided as the limitations on a state's power to expropriate the property of aliens. * * *

The disagreement as to relevant international law standards reflects an even more basic divergence between the national interests of capital importing and capital exporting nations and between the social ideologies of those countries that favor state control of a considerable portion of the means of production and those that adhere to a free enterprise system. It is difficult to imagine the courts of this country embarking on adjudication in an area which touches more sensitively the practical and ideological goals of the various members of the community of nations. * * *

The possible adverse consequences of a conclusion to the contrary of that implicit in these cases in highlighted by contrasting the practices of the political branch with the limitations of the judicial process in matters of this kind. Following an expropriation of any significance, the Executive engages in diplomacy aimed to assure that United States citizens who are harmed are compensated

---

[24] The Doctrine of Erie Railroad v. Tompkins Applied to International Law, 33 Am.J.Int'l L. 740 (1939).

fairly. Representing all claimants of this country, it will often be able, either by bilateral or multilateral talks, by submission to the United Nations, or by the employment of economic and political sanctions, to achieve some degree of general redress. Judicial determinations of invalidity of title can, on the other hand, have only an occasional impact, since they depend on the fortuitous circumstance of the property in question being brought into this country. Such decisions would, if the acts involved were declared invalid, often be likely to give offense to the expropriating country; since the concept of territorial sovereignty is so deep seated, any state may resent the refusal of the courts of another sovereign to accord validity to acts within its territorial borders. Piecemeal dispositions of this sort involving the probability of affront to another state could seriously interfere with negotiations being carried on by the Executive Branch and might prevent or render less favorable the terms of an agreement that could otherwise be reached. Relations with third countries which have engaged in similar expropriations would not be immune from effect.

The dangers of such adjudication are present regardless of whether the State Department has, as it did in this case, asserted that the relevant act violated international law. If the Executive Branch has undertaken negotiations with an expropriating country, but has refrained from claims of violation of the law of nations, a determination to that effect by a court might be regarded as a serious insult, while a finding of compliance with international law would greatly strengthen the bargaining hand of the other state with consequent detriment to American interests.

Even if the State Department has proclaimed the impropriety of the expropriation, the stamp of approval of its view by a judicial tribunal, however, impartial, might increase any affront and the judicial decision might occur at a time, almost always well after the taking, when such an impact would be contrary to our national interest. Considerably more serious and far-reaching consequences would flow from a judicial finding that international law standards had been met if that determination flew in the face of a State Department proclamation to the contrary. When articulating principles of international law in its relations with other states, the Executive Branch speaks not only as an interpreter of generally accepted and traditional rules, as would the courts, but also as an advocate of standards it believes desirable for the community of nations and protective of national concerns. In short, whatever way the matter is cut, the possibility of conflict between the Judicial and Executive Branches could hardly be avoided.

Respondents contend that, even if there is not agreement regarding general standards for determining the validity of expropriations, the alleged combination of retaliation, discrimination, and inadequate compensation makes it patently clear that this particular expropriation was in violation of international law. If this view is accurate, it would still be unwise for the courts so to determine. Such a decision now would require the drawing of more difficult lines in subsequent cases and these would involve the possibility of conflict with the Executive view. Even if the courts avoided this course, either by presuming the validity of an act of state whenever the international law standard was thought unclear or by following the State Department declaration in such a situation, the very expression of judicial uncertainty might provide embarrassment to the Executive Branch.

Another serious consequence of the exception pressed by respondents would be to render uncertain titles in foreign commerce, with the possible consequence of altering the flow of international trade. If the attitude of the United States courts were unclear, one buying expropriated goods would not know if he could safely import them into this country. Even were takings known to be invalid, one would have difficulty determining after goods had changed hands several times whether the particular articles in question were the product of an ineffective state act. * * *

It is suggested that if the act of state doctrine is applicable to violations of international law, it should only be so when the Executive Branch expressly stipulates that it does not wish the courts to pass on the question of validity. See Association of the Bar of the City of New York, Committee on International Law, A Reconsideration of the Act of State Doctrine in United States Courts (1959). We should be slow to reject the representations of the Government that such a reversal of the *Bernstein* principle would work serious inroads on the maximum effectiveness of United States diplomacy. Often the State Department will wish to refrain from taking an official position, particularly at a moment that would be dictated by the development of private litigation but might be inopportune diplomatically. Adverse domestic consequences might flow from an official stand which could be assuaged, if at all, only by revealing matters best kept secret. Of course, a relevant consideration for the State Department would be the position contemplated in the court to hear the case. It is highly questionable whether the examination of validity by the judiciary should depend on an educated guess by the Executive as to probable result and, at any rate, should a prediction be wrong, the Executive might be embarrassed in its dealings with other countries. We do not now pass on the *Bernstein* exception, but even if it were deemed valid, its suggested extension is unwarranted.

However offensive to the public policy of this country and its constituent States an expropriation of this kind may be, we conclude that both the national interest and progress toward the goal of establishing the rule of law among nations are best served by maintaining intact the act of state doctrine in this realm of its application.

VII.

Finally, we must determine whether Cuba's status as a plaintiff in this case dictates a result at variance with the conclusions reached above. If the Court were to distinguish between suits brought by sovereign states and those of assignees, the rule would have little effect unless a careful examination were made in each case to determine if the private party suing had taken property in good faith. Such an inquiry would be exceptionally difficult, since the relevant transaction would almost invariably have occurred outside our borders. If such an investigation were deemed irrelevant, a state could always assign its claim. * * *

Mr. Justice White, dissenting.

I am dismayed that the Court has, with one broad stroke, declared the ascertainment and application of international law beyond the competence of the courts of the United States in a large and important category of cases. I am also disappointed in the Court's declaration that the acts of a sovereign state with regard to the property of aliens within its borders are beyond the reach of international law in the courts of this country. However clearly established that law may be, a sovereign may violate it with impunity, except insofar as the political branches of the government may provide a remedy. This backward-looking doctrine, never before declared in this Court, is carried a disconcerting step further: not only are the courts powerless to question acts of state proscribed by international law but they are likewise powerless to refuse to adjudicate the claim founded upon a foreign law; they must render judgment and thereby validate the lawless act. Since the Court expressly extends its ruling to all acts of state expropriating property, however clearly inconsistent with the international community, all discriminatory expropriations of the property of aliens, as for example the taking of properties of persons belonging to certain races, religions or nationalities, are entitled to automatic validation in the courts of the United States. No other civilized country has found such a rigid rule necessary for the survival of the executive branch of its government; the executive of no other government seems to require such insulation from international law adjudications in its courts; and no other judiciary is apparently so incompetent to ascertain and apply international law.

I do not believe that the act of state doctrine, as judicially fashioned in this Court, and the reasons underlying it, require American courts to decide cases in disregard of international law and of the rights of litigants to a full determination on the merits. * * *

IV.

The reasons for nonreview, based as they are on traditional concepts of territorial sovereignty, lose much of their force when the foreign act of state is shown to be a violation of international law. All legitimate exercises of sovereign power, whether territorial or otherwise, should be exercised consistently with rules of international law, including those rules which mark the bounds of lawful state action against aliens or their property located within the territorial confines of the foreign state. Although a state may reasonably expect that the validity of its laws operating on property within its jurisdiction will not be defined by local notions of public policy of numerous other states (although a different situation may well be presented when courts of another state are asked to lend their enforcement machinery to effectuate the foreign act), it cannot with impunity ignore the rules governing the conduct of all nations and expect that other nations and tribunals will view its acts as within the permissible scope of territorial sovereignty. Contrariwise, to refuse inquiry into the question of whether norms of the international community have been contravened by the act of state under review would seem to deny the existence or purport of such norms, a view that seems inconsistent with the role of international law in ordering the relations between nations. Finally, the impartial application of international law would not only be an affirmation of the existence and binding effect of order, but also a refutation of the notion that this body of law consists of no more than the divergent and parochial views of the capital importing and exporting nations, the socialist and free-enterprise nations.

The Court puts these considerations to rest with the assumption that the decisions of the courts "of the world's major capital exporting country and principal exponent of the free enterprise system" would hardly be accepted as impartial expressions of sound legal principle. The assumption, if sound, would apply to any other problem arising from transactions that cross state lines and is tantamount to a declaration excusing this Court from any future consequential role in the clarification and application of international law. See National City Bank of New York v. Republic of China, 348 U.S. 356, 363. This declaration ignores the historic role which this Court and other American courts have played in applying and maintaining principles of international law. * * *

V.

There remains for consideration the relationship between the act of state doctrine and the power of the executive over matters touching upon the foreign affairs of the Nation. It is urged that the act of state doctrine is a necessary corollary of the executive's authority to direct the foreign relations of the United States and accordingly any exception in the doctrine, even if limited to clear violations of international law, would impede or embarrass the executive in discharging his constitutional responsibilities. Thus, according to the Court, even if principles of comity do not preclude inquiry into the validity of a foreign act under international law, due regard for the executive function forbids such examination in the courts.

Without doubt political matters in the realm of foreign affairs are within the exclusive domain of the Executive Branch, as, for example, issues for which there are no available standards or which are textually committed by the Constitution to the executive. But this is far from saying that the Constitution vests in the executive exclusive absolute control of foreign affairs or that the validity of a foreign act of state is necessarily a political question. International law, as well as a treaty or executive agreement, see United States v. Pink, 315 U.S. 203, provides an ascertainable standard for adjudicating the validity of some foreign acts, and courts are competent to apply this body of law, notwithstanding that there may be some cases where comity dictates giving effect to the foreign act because it is not clearly condemned under generally accepted principles of international law. And it cannot be contended that the Constitution allocates this area to the exclusive jurisdiction of the executive, for the judicial power is expressly extended by that document to controversies between aliens and citizens or States, aliens and aliens, and foreign states and American citizens or States.

A valid statute, treaty or executive agreement could, I assume, confine the power of federal courts to review or award relief in respect of foreign acts or otherwise displace international law as the rule of decision. I would not disregard a declaration by the Secretary of State or the President that an adjudication in the courts of the validity of a foreign expropriation would impede relations between the United States and the foreign government or the settlement of the controversy through diplomatic channels. But I reject the presumption that these undesirable consequences would follow from adjudication in every case, regardless of the circumstances. Certainly the presumption is inappropriate here. * * *

VI.

Obviously there are cases where an examination of the foreign act and declaration of invalidity or validity might undermine the foreign policy of the Executive Branch and its attempts at negotiating a settlement for a nationalization of the property of Americans. The respect ordinarily due to a foreign state, as reflected in the decisions of this Court, rests upon a desire not to disturb the relations between countries and on a view that other means, more effective than piecemeal adjudications of claims arising out of a large-scale nationalization program of settling the dispute, may be available. Precisely because these considerations are more or less present, or absent, in any given situation and because the Department of our Government primarily responsible for the formulation of foreign policy and settling these matters on a state-to-state basis is more competent than courts to determine the extent to which they are involved, a blanket presumption of nonreview in each case is inappropriate and a requirement that the State Department render a determination after reasonable notice, in each case, is necessary. Such an examination would permit the Department to evaluate whether adjudication would "vex the peace of nations," whether a friendly foreign sovereign is involved, and whether settlement through diplomacy or through an international tribunal or arbitration is impending. Based upon such an evaluation, the Department may recommend to the court that adjudication should not proceed at the present time. Such a request I would accord considerable deference and I would not require a full statement of reasons underlying it. But I reject the contention that the recommendation itself would somehow impede the foreign relations of the United States or unduly burden the Department. * * *

NOTES AND QUESTIONS FOR DISCUSSION

1.   In *Sabbatino*, the Supreme Court announced a version of the act of state doctrine hedged with several qualifications: "that the (Judicial Branch) will not examine the validity of a taking of property within its own territory by a foreign sovereign government, extant and recognized by this country at the time of suit, in the absence of a treaty or other unambiguous agreement regarding controlling legal principles, even if the complaint alleges that the taking violates customary international law." 376 U.S. at 428. Among the several limitations in this holding, it applies only to the taking of property, only within the territory of a foreign government, and only in the absence of other "controlling legal principles." The last excludes customary international law, apart from the act of state doctrine itself, but includes "a treaty or other unambiguous agreement." These limitations on the act of state doctrine have come to dominate its interpretation, but the role that the Court assigns to federal common law remains the most important legacy of the decision.

In a magisterial opinion that surveys the entire landscape of legal sources that might bear upon the question, Justice Harlan concludes that state law has no role to play in defining the scope and content of the act of state doctrine. This conclusion might appear to be foreordained, given the predominant role that the Constitution assigns to the federal government in the conduct of foreign relations. Yet it runs directly counter to the *Erie* doctrine which, in its most general form, preserves the role of state law as the residual source of law in the absence of federal statutes, treaties, or the Constitution. The Court in *Sabbatino* takes over that role for itself, explicitly with respect to the act of state doctrine and implicitly with respect to other features of international litigation that might impair the foreign relations of the country.

The Court frames the act of state doctrine as one disclaiming power by the courts, but as subsequent cases have made clear, it furnishes a rule of decision in favor of the party who benefitted from the foreign act of state. Applied to the facts of *Sabbatino*, it dictates that the Banco Nacional de Cuba, which gained title to the sugar through the seizure by the Cuban government, gets to keep it and any proceeds from its sale. Unlike foreign sovereign immunity, the doctrine also can work to the benefit of private parties: whoever received the sugar or the proceeds from its sale would own them, whether or not they were an agency or instrumentality of Cuba. Whatever the other limits on the act of state doctrine, it constituted a strong assertion by the Supreme Court of its power to make federal common law. That assertion did not go unchallenged.

2.   Soon after *Sabbatino* was handed down, Congress effectively overruled it on its facts. It passed the "Second Hickenlooper Amendment," 22 U.S.C. § 2370(e)(2):

> Notwithstanding any other provision of law, no court in the United States shall decline on the ground of the federal act of state doctrine to make a determination on the merits giving effect to the principles of international law in a case in which a claim of title or other right to property is asserted by any party including a foreign state (or a party claiming through such state) based upon (or traced through) a confiscation or other taking after January 1, 1959, by an act of that state in violation of the principles of international law, including the principles of compensation and the other standards set out in this subsection: *Provided,* That this subparagraph shall not be applicable (1) in any case in which an act of a foreign state is not contrary to international law or with respect to a claim of title or other right to property acquired pursuant to an irrevocable letter of credit of not more than 180 days duration issued in good faith prior to the time of the confiscation or other taking, or (2) in any case with respect to which the President determines that application of the act of state doctrine is required in that particular case by the foreign policy interests of the United States and a suggestion to this effect is filed on his behalf in that case with the court.

This statute was applied to *Sabbatino* itself to reverse the outcome of the Supreme Court's decision, resulting in a judgment for the parties whose title derived from the original property owners. Banco Nacional de Cuba v. Farr, 383 F.2d 166 (2d Cir. 1967), cert. denied, 390 U.S. 956 (1968).

Some might view the congressional reaction to *Sabbatino* as a rebuke to the Supreme Court; others might see it as vindicating the act of state doctrine insofar as the decision prompted a reaction from the political branches of government. On either interpretation, it reflected the dependence of federal common law in its modern form on actions endorsed by the ordinary processes of federal lawmaking. Judge-made federal law must find some basis in the Constitution, statutes, or treaties of the U.S. To the extent it becomes inconsistent with those sources of law, it must yield to what they require.

The Second Hickenlooper Amendment has sometimes received a narrow construction, confining it only to the expropriation of property that made its way eventually, or through its proceeds, to the U.S. Compania de Gas de Nuevo Laredo, S.A. v. Entex, Inc., 686 F.2d 322 (5th Cir. 1982). That restriction, however, has no basis in the text of the amendment, and whatever the scope of the amendment, the federal courts have nevertheless absorbed its basic lesson that the act of state doctrine should be narrowly construed. A variety of devices have been used to do so. Congress itself has adopted similar provisions in other legislation, specifically targeted on particular claims. 22 U.S.C. § 6082(a)(6) (claims for trafficking in property confiscated from U.S. citizens by Cuba); 9 U.S.C. § 15 (actions to enforce arbitration clauses and arbitration awards).

3. The Second Hickenlooper Amendment revived the practice of judicial deference to "Bernstein letters" issued by the State Department, but with a reversal of the presumption existing in the absence of the letter. In the original *Bernstein* case, the federal courts followed the act of state doctrine unless the State Department issued a letter recommending to the contrary. Under the Second Hickenlooper Amendment, the federal courts do not apply the doctrine in the absence of a letter. Because the scope of the amendment has been limited, so has the issuance of letters under its provisions. Litigants nevertheless persisted in seeking the support of the State Department to avoid the act of state doctrine.

Just as the regime for determining sovereign immunity under the Tate letter led to doubts that the executive branch was taking over a judicial function, the continued issuance of Bernstein letters led to the same suspicions. These came before the Supreme Court in First National City Bank v. Banco Nacional de Cuba, 406 U.S. 759 (1972), where they were intertwined with a set-off asserted to a claim by the foreign sovereign. The Cuban government had seized all the branches of First National City Bank in Cuba, and in retaliation, the bank sold collateral posted as security for loans that it had extended to the government. The proceeds of the sale exceeded the balance owed on the loans and Cuba, through the Banco Nacional, sued to recover the excess. Against this liability, First National City Bank sought to set off the loss resulting from the seizure of its branches in Cuba. Banco Nacional, in turn, invoked the act of state doctrine. A plurality of three Justices found the doctrine inapplicable because the State Department had issued a Bernstein letter in support of the set-off by First National City Bank. Id. at 769-70 (opinion of Rehnquist, J.). Two other Justices rejected assertion of the act of state doctrine, either because it did not apply to set-offs, id. at 772-73 (Douglas, J., concurring in the result), or because it had been framed too broadly in *Sabbatino*, id. at 775-76 (Powell, J., concurring in the judgment). Four Justices would have applied the act of state doctrine despite the Bernstein letter. Id. at 776-77 (Brennan, J., dissenting).

In his separate opinion, Justice Douglas memorably rejected the *Bernstein* exception because it makes the Court "a mere errand boy for the Executive Branch which may choose to pick some people's chestnuts from the fire, but not others." Id. at 773. Even on his view, the influence of the State Department could still be felt through the positions taken by the Solicitor General as an amicus curiae in litigation. Of course, in that procedural posture, the views of the executive branch need not receive any deference from the courts, which can treat them the same as the views of any other party with an interest in a case. Should the courts nevertheless take the views expressed by the State Department especially seriously? Who else is in a position to call attention to the impact of a case on foreign relations?

4. All of the cases discussed in the preceding notes were, like *Sabbatino* itself, concerned with expropriation of property, not with human rights violations that involve other deprivations. What implications can be drawn for the narrow scope of the doctrine as applied to deprivation of property? Does it imply that deprivations of life and liberty, generally considered to be more serious, are more deserving of remedies and therefore even more likely to lie beyond the scope of the state action doctrine? Or does it imply the opposite: that property claims actually brought against foreign governments involve a narrow category of cases in which courts can evaluate the conformity with international law without seriously disrupting foreign relations?

Partly out of concern for its implications in human rights cases, and more generally for the impediments it imposes to the development of international law in American courts, the act of state doctrine has been subject to criticism since its inception. Michael J. Bazyler, *Abolishing the Act of State Doctrine*, 134 U. Pa. L. Rev. 325 (1986); Louis Henkin, *The Foreign Affairs Power of the Federal Courts:* Sabbatino, 64 Colum. L. Rev. 805 (1964); Harold Hongju Koh, *Transnational Public Law Litigation*, 100 Yale L.J. 2347 (1991). For a response to the critics, see Andrew D. Patterson, *The Act of State Doctrine is Alive and Well: Why Critics of the Doctrine are Wrong*, 15 U.C. Davis J. Int'l L. & Pol'y 111 (2008). For general accounts of the doctrine, see Anne-Marie Burley, *Law Among Liberal States: Liberal Internationalism and the Act of State Doctrine*, 92 Colum. L. Rev. 1907 (1992); Joseph W. Dellapenna, *Deciphering the Act of State Doctrine*, 35 Vill. L. Rev. 1 (1990).

Alfred Dunhill of London, Inc. v. Republic of Cuba

Supreme Court of the United States, 1976.

425 U.S. 682.

MR. JUSTICE WHITE delivered the opinion of the Court.[*]

The issue in this case is whether the failure of respondents to return to petitioner Alfred Dunhill of London, Inc. (Dunhill), funds mistakenly paid by Dunhill for cigars that had been sold to Dunhill by certain expropriated Cuban cigar businesses was an "act of state" by Cuba precluding an affirmative judgment against respondents.

---

[*] Part III of this opinion is joined only by THE CHIEF JUSTICE, MR. JUSTICE POWELL, and MR. JUSTICE REHNQUIST.

I

* * * In 1960, the Cuban Government confiscated the business and assets of the five leading manufacturers of Havana cigars. These companies, three corporations and two partnerships, were organized under Cuban law. Virtually all of their owners were Cuban nationals. None were American. These companies sold large quantities of cigars to customers in other countries, including the United States, where the three principal importers were Dunhill, Saks & Co. (Saks), and Faber, Coe & Gregg, Inc. (Faber). The Cuban Government named "interventors" to take possession of and operate the business of the seized Cuban concerns. Interventors continued to ship cigars to foreign purchasers, including the United States importers.

This litigation began when the former owners of the Cuban companies, most of whom had fled to the United States, brought various actions against the three American importers for trademark infringement and for the purchase price of any cigars that had been shipped to importers from the seized Cuban plants and that bore United States trademarks claimed by the former owners to be their property. [Following the conclusion of related litigation, the Cuban interventors and the Republic of Cuba were allowed to intervene in these actions. The former owners and the interventors each asserted rights due from the importers for postintervention shipments and rights to preintervention payments made by the importers to the interventors. Applying the act of state doctrine, the district court held that the interventors were entitled to collect from the importers all amounts due and unpaid with respect to shipments made after the date of intervention. The district court concluded, however, that the former owners were entitled to accounts owing at the time of intervention because the situs of those accounts was with the importers in the United States. The court of appeals applied the act of state doctrine to both sets of rights and awarded them to the interventors. (In reaching this conclusion, court of appeals rejected the importers' contention that the Hickenlooper Amendment precluded interventors from invoking the act of state doctrine, a ruling that was not reviewed by the Supreme Court.)

II

The District Court and the Court of Appeals held that for purposes of this litigation interventors were not entitled to the preintervention accounts receivable by virtue of the 1960 confiscation and that, despite other arguments to the contrary, nothing based on their claim to those accounts entitled interventors to retain monies mistakenly paid on those accounts by importers. We do not disturb these conclusions. The Court of Appeals nevertheless observed that interventors had "ignored" demands for the return of the monies and had "fail(ed) to honor the importers' demand (which was confirmed by the Cuban government's counsel at trial)." This conduct was considered to be the Cuban government's repudiation of its obligation to return the funds" and to constitute an act of state not subject to question in our courts. We cannot agree.

If interventors, having had their liability adjudicated and various defenses rejected, including the claimed act of state, with respect to preintervention accounts, represented by the Cuban confiscation in 1960, were nevertheless to escape repayment by claiming a second and later act of state involving the funds mistakenly paid them, it was their burden to prove that act. Concededly, they declined to pay over the funds; but refusal to repay does not necessarily assert anything more than what interventors had claimed from the outset and what they have continued to claim in this Court that the preintervention accounts receivable were theirs and that they had no obligation to return payments on those accounts. Neither does it demonstrate that in addition to authority to operate commercial businesses, to pay their bills and to collect their accounts receivable, interventors had been invested with sovereign authority to repudiate all or any part of the debts incurred by those businesses. Indeed, it is difficult to believe that they had the power selectively to refuse payment of legitimate debts arising from the operation of those commercial enterprises.

[After discussing prior decisions, the Court concluded that the interventors had to prove an act of state and that they failed to do so. They could not rely simply upon their retention of payments made to them for preintervention accounts receivable.] No statute, decree, order, or resolution of the Cuban Government itself was offered in evidence indicating that Cuba had repudiated its obligations in general or any class thereof or that it had as a sovereign matter determined to confiscate the amounts due three foreign importers.

III

If we assume with the Court of Appeals that the Cuban Government itself had purported to exercise sovereign power to confiscate the mistaken payments belonging to three foreign creditors and to repudiate interventors' adjudicated obligation to return those funds, we are nevertheless persuaded by the arguments of petitioner and by those of the United States that the concept of an act of state should not be extended to include the repudiation of a purely commercial obligation owed by a foreign sovereign or by one of its commercial instrumentalities. Our cases have not yet gone so far, and we decline to expand their reach to the extent necessary to affirm the Court of Appeals.

Distinguishing between the public and governmental acts of sovereign states on the one hand and their private and commercial acts on the other is not a novel approach. As the Court stated through Mr. Chief Justice Marshall long ago in Bank of the United States v. Planters' Bank of Georgia, 9 Wheat. 904, 907, (1824):

> "It is, we think, a sound principle, that when a government becomes a partner in any trading company, it divests itself, so far as concerns the transactions of that company, of its sovereign character, and takes that of a private citizen. Instead of communicating to the company its privileges and its prerogatives, it descends to a level with those with whom it associates itself, and takes the character which belongs to its associates, and to the business which is to be transacted."

* * *

It is the position of the United States, stated in an Amicus brief filed by the Solicitor General, that such a line should be drawn in defining the outer limits of the act of state concept and that repudiations by a foreign sovereign of its commercial debts should not be considered to be acts of state beyond legal question in our courts. [T]he Department of State, speaking through its Legal Adviser agrees with the brief filed by the Solicitor General and, more specifically, declares that "we do not believe that the Dunhill case raises an act of state question because the case involves an act which is commercial, and not public, in nature."

The major underpinning of the act of state doctrine is the policy of foreclosing court adjudications involving the legality of acts of foreign states on their own soil that might embarrass the Executive Branch of our Government in the conduct of our foreign relations. *Banco Nacional de Cuba v. Sabbatino*, 376 U.S., at 427-428, 431-433. But based on the presently expressed views of those who conduct our relations with foreign countries, we are in no sense compelled to recognize as an act of state the purely commercial conduct of foreign governments in order to avoid embarrassing conflicts with the Executive Branch. On the contrary, for the reasons to which we now turn, we fear that embarrassment and conflict would me likely ensue if we were to require that the repudiation of a foreign government's debts arising from its operation of a purely commercial business be recognized as an act of state and immunized from question in our courts.

[The Court then recounted the development of the restrictive theory of sovereign immunity, although it stopped short of any discussion of the Foreign Sovereign Immunities Act because it was then under consideration by Congress and was not passed until several months after this case was decided.]

Of course, sovereign immunity has not been pleaded in this case; but it is beyond cavil that part of the foreign relations law recognized by the United States is that the commercial obligations of a foreign government may be adjudicated in those courts otherwise having jurisdiction to enter such judgments. Nothing in our national policy calls on us to recognize as an act of state a repudiation by Cuba of an obligation adjudicated in our courts and arising out of the operation of a commercial business by one of its instrumentalities. For all the reasons which led the Executive Branch to adopt the restrictive theory of sovereign immunity, we hold that the mere assertion of sovereignty as a defense to a claim arising out of purely commercial acts by a foreign sovereign is no more effective if given the label "Act of State" than if it is given the label "sovereign immunity." In describing the act of state doctrine in the past we have said that it "precludes the courts of this country from inquiring into the validity of the *public* acts a recognized foreign sovereign power committed within its own territory." *Banco Nacional de Cuba v. Sabbatino, supra*, 376 U.S., at 401 (emphasis added), and that it applies to "acts done within their own States, in the exercise of *governmental* authority." *Underhill v. Hernandez*, 168 U.S., at 252 (emphasis added). We decline to extend the act of state doctrine to acts committed by foreign sovereigns in the course of their purely commercial operations. Because the act relied on by respondents in this case was an act arising out of the conduct by Cuba's agents in the operation of cigar businesses for profit, the act was not an act of state. *Reversed.*

Mr. JUSTICE POWELL, concurring.

I join the opinion of the Court. Since the line between commercial and political acts of a foreign state often will be difficult to delineate, I write to reaffirm my view that even in cases deemed to involve purely political acts, it is the duty of the judiciary to decide for itself whether deference to the political branches of Government requires abstention. As I stated in First Nat. City Bank v. Banco Nacional de Cuba, 406 U.S. 759, 775-776, 1817 (1972) (concurring in judgment):

> "Unless it appears that an exercise of jurisdiction would interfere with delicate foreign relations conducted by the political branches, I conclude that federal courts have an obligation to hear cases such as this."

Just as I saw no circumstances requiring judicial abstention in that case, I see none here. Nor can I foresee any in cases involving only the commercial acts of a foreign state.

Mr. Justice Stevens, concurring.

For reasons stated in Parts I and II of the Court's opinion, I agree that the act of state doctrine does not bar the entry of the judgment in favor of Dunhill.

Mr. Justice Marshall, with whom Mr. Justice Brennan, Mr. Justice Stewart, and Mr. Justice Blackmun join, dissenting.

The act of state doctrine commits the courts of this country not to sit in judgment on the acts of a foreign government performed within its own territory. Under any realistic view of the facts of this case, the interventors' retention of and refusal to return funds paid to them by Dunhill constitute an act of state, and no affirmative recovery by Dunhill can rest on the invalidity of that conduct. The Court of Appeals so concluded, and I would affirm its judgment.

I

* * *

Since the date of intervention, the interventors have taken the position that they were also entitled to receive the amounts due to the intervened firms for preintervention shipments in the case of Dunhill, $148,600. And throughout this litigation, respondents, the interventors and the Republic of Cuba, have insisted that the act of state doctrine requires our courts to give full legal effect to the intervention decree insofar as it purported to nationalize the accounts receivable of the intervened firms. * * *

[After a discussion of precedent, Justice Marshall concluded:] That a foreign sovereign has issued no formal decree and performed no "affirmative" act is not fatal, then, to an act of state claim. If the foreign state has exercised a sovereign power either to act or to refrain from acting there is an act of state. In a case very similar to this one, the New York Court of Appeals held that the Cuban bank's dishonoring of tax exemption certificates, the redemption of which had been suspended by a decision of the Cuban Currency Stabilization Fund, was an act of state. French v. Banco Nacional de Cuba, 23 N.Y.2d 46, 295 N.Y.S.2d 433, 452, 242 N.E.2d 704, 717 (1968). The act of state, the court wrote, "was the defendant's refusal to perform; the currency regulations, though equally the product of an act of state, were simply the justification for the refusal." The quoted statement appears in the concurring opinion of Judge Hopkins, 23 N.Y.2d, at 66, 242 N.E.2d, at 717, which was joined by the same majority that subscribed to the opinion of Chief Judge Fuld, in which the court held:

"(T)he breach of contract, of which the plaintiff complains, resulted from, and, indeed, itself constitutes, an act of state." Id., at 53, 242 N.E.2d, at 709.

The Court, I take it, does not dispute that a refusal to act constitutes an act of state when shown to reflect the exercise of sovereign power. Rather, the Court finds no exercise of sovereign power to retain the funds at issue after they arrived in Cuba. Refusal to repay, the Court suggests, does not necessarily reflect anything more than the interventors' initial contention, rejected by the District Court and the Court of Appeals, that the September 15, 1960, intervention decree operated to seize the accounts receivable of the intervened firms. And the Court is unwilling "to infer from the fact that Cuba seized the assets of the cigar business from Cuban nationals that they must necessarily . . . have made a later discriminatory and confiscatory seizure of money belonging to the United States companies." Ante, at n. 8.

As I have already indicated, however, the respondents' position has not been, and need not be, limited to the contention that the September 15 decree operated to seize the preintervention accounts receivable. Counsel for the interventors and the Republic of Cuba stated at trial, in his brief to this Court, and again in his oral argument in this Court. * * *

II

Mr. JUSTICE WHITE advances a contention, not adopted by the Court, that even if the Cuban Government "had purported to exercise sovereign power to confiscate" the monies at issue, the act of state doctrine is inapplicable because of the "purely commercial" nature of the confiscation. While I am prompted to make several observations on the suggested rationale for a broad "commercial act" exception to the act of state doctrine, ultimately there is no need to consider whether, and under what circumstances, an exception for commercial acts might be appropriate. It will suffice to say that no such exception is appropriate in this case. * * *

Cuba's retention of and refusal to repay the funds at issue in this case took place against the background of the intervention, or nationalization, of the businesses and assets of five cigar manufacturers. As I have already indicated, the seizure and retention of the Dunhill funds were pursuant to the initial intervention decree. For all practical purposes, the seizure of the funds once they arrived in Cuba is indistinguishable from the seizure of the remainder of the cigar manufacturers' businesses. The seizure of the funds, like the initial seizures on September 15, reflected a purpose to exert sovereign power to its territorial limits in order to effectuate the intervention of ongoing cigar manufacturing businesses. It matters not that the funds have been determined by a United States court in this case to have belonged to Dunhill rather than the cigar manufacturers. What does matter is that Cuba retained the money in the course of its program of expropriating what it viewed as part and parcel of the businesses.

The applicability of the act of state doctrine in these circumstances is controlled by *Sabbatino* itself. As the Court there noted: "There are few if any issues in international law today on which opinion seems to be so divided as the limitation on a state's power to expropriate the property of aliens." 376 U.S., at 428. Indeed, the absence of any suggestion that Cuba's intervention program was discriminatory against United States citizens renders the lack of consensus as to applicable principles of law even more apparent here than in *Sabbatino*. And unless one takes the position that the amount of money or the value of property seized materially affects the sensitivity of the issues, we are guided in this case by the following observation in *Sabbatino*:

> "It is difficult to imagine the courts of this country embarking on adjudication in an area which touches more sensitively the practical and ideological goals of the various members of the community of nations." 376 U.S., at 430 (footnote omitted).

Regardless, then, of whether the presence of consensus as to controlling legal principles, or any other circumstances, would render the act of state doctrine inapplicable to some, or even most, acts that could be characterized as "purely commercial," the doctrine is fully applicable in this case. * * *

NOTES AND QUESTIONS FOR DISCUSSION

1. Only four justices in *Dunhill* would have recognized a commercial exception to the act of state doctrine. These four, represented by Justice White's plurality opinion, included Justice Powell, although he would have abandoned the act of state doctrine entirely. Justice Stevens provided the crucial fifth vote, but only on the narrower ground adopted by the plurality: that the refusal of the interventors to repay proceeds from the sale of cigars and the statement of their counsel that the government of Cuba also took this position. Four dissenters, represented by Justice Marshall's opinion, would have applied the act of state doctrine and decided the case in favor of the interventors. In the end, therefore, six justices refused to adopt a commercial exception to the act of state doctrine.

To what extent was that refusal based on the absence of a statutory basis for the commercial exception? The FSIA had not yet been adopted, so that the restrictive theory of sovereign immunity rested only on the practice of the Executive Branch and the judicial decisions accepting it as a basis for jurisdiction over foreign sovereigns. Recall that the act of state doctrine goes to the merits, not to jurisdiction, and so can be invoked in litigation between wholly private parties. There would have been, for instance, no need to inquire that the interventors in *Dunhill* were instrumentalities of the Cuban government. Are the differences between finding jurisdiction and a decision on the merits sufficient to distinguish the commercial exception to sovereign immunity from an exception to the act of state doctrine? Wouldn't both exceptions serve the same purpose: to hold foreign sovereigns to the same standards as other participants in market transactions?

Even after passage of the FSIA, a commercial exception to the act of state doctrine has failed to take hold. See, e.g., Glen v. Club Mediterranee, S.A., 450 F.3d 1251, 1254 n.2 (11th Cir. 2006). Partly, this results from the disclaimer in the legislative history of the FSIA, that it had no effect on the act of state doctrine. H.R. Rep. No. 94-1487, 94th Cong., 2d Sess. 20 (1976). But partly it also results from the actual holding in *Dunhill*: that a purely commercial act does not, by itself, constitute a formal act of state sufficient to invoke operation of the doctrine. Refusing to repay the proceeds from the sale of cigars did not receive a sufficiently formal endorsement from the Cuban government to constitute an act of state. Foreign states, in order to take advantage of the doctrine, must publicize their formal rejection of ordinary commercial law. What effect does this have on their prospects for engaging in commercial transactions in the future?

2. A further reason why a commercial exception has not proved to be necessary arises from another limitation on the act of state doctrine: that it applies only to acts within the boundaries of the foreign state. On the facts of *Dunhill*, for instance, the proceeds from the sale of cigars that had not been repaid to the interventors remained in the U.S., and because of their situs there, remained outside the scope of the act of state doctrine. This aspect of the case depended upon the principle that the situs of a debt follows the situs of the debtor. With respect to intangible obligations, which constitute much of international trade, the debtor often remains beyond the boundaries of the foreign state. Moreover, the transaction often can be structured to minimize the presence of debtors, or more generally the exposure of moveable assets, to the acts of state of a potentially hostile sovereign. To the extent these maneuvers succeed, they furnish a party both with a basis of personal jurisdiction over some defendant and assets from which any judgment might be recovered.

A variation upon the facts of *Sabbatino* furnishes an apt example of how these principles operate. If the seizure in that case had not been of the sugar, which was still in Cuba at the time, but of the rights under a bill of lading for the shipment, then the act of state doctrine could only have applied if the bill of lading remained in Cuba when the seizure was effected. The moment it went outside Cuban territory, which might well have preceded the progress of the shipment into international waters, the situs of the rights and obligations it created also escaped.

Modern concepts of personal jurisdiction would not impede litigation based on the situs of property when it concerns claims to the property itself, as it does in expropriation cases. The leading decision, Shaffer v. Heitner, 433 U.S. 186 (1977), discussed in Chapter 1, allowed jurisdiction in most cases based on the location of property "when claims to the property itself are the source of the underlying controversy between the plaintiff and the defendant." Id. at 207 (footnote omitted). The more problematic step, both under the act of state doctrine and for personal jurisdiction, involves assigning a situs to intangible obligations. The traditional rule assigns it to the location of the debtor, on the ground that any attempt to require payment of obligation must be limited to locations in which the debtor can be subject to suit.

The location of a debt nevertheless involves nuances of the obligation itself. Courts have engaged in an analysis similar to that in *Republic of Argentina v. Weltover*, where the Supreme Court found obligations payable in New York to have a sufficient connection to the U.S. to trigger the commercial exception under the FSIA. Thus, in a close case, the Second Circuit found that bank deposits made at the branch of an American bank in Cuba nevertheless were located in the U.S. because they could be withdrawn at branches here. Garcia v. Chase Manhattan Bank, N.A., 735 F.2d 645 (2d Cir. 1984). The expropriation of the bank's branches in Cuba did not constitute a seizure of the underlying obligation to pay the deposit. The similarity of this reasoning to the analysis in *Weltover* under the FSIA reveals how much influence the restrictive theory of sovereign immunity has on the act of state doctrine, even if it does not generate an explicit exception for commercial activity.

3.   The various constraints on the act of state doctrine signal its continued retreat, although they leave the core of its application in *Sabbatino* untouched: sovereign acts of a foreign state within its own territory without immediate effect outside its borders. Even the Second Hickenlooper Amendment creates an exception only in the rare circumstance when the expropriated property arrives in the U.S. As the scope of the act of state doctrine has diminished, the need to identify its rationale has become more urgent. Without some persuasive justification, the doctrine might otherwise disappear entirely. The rationales usually put forward involve some mixture of respect for the actions of foreign sovereigns within their own territory and reluctance to entangle the judiciary in the conduct of foreign relations by the political branches. The first rationale requires a formal act by the sovereign after *Dunhill*. Repudiation of a commercial contract does not suffice. The second rationale requires some indication from the Executive Branch or from Congress that adjudication on the merits would interfere with foreign relations. In *Dunhill*, however, the Executive Branch supported a commercial exception to the act of state doctrine. The later enactment of the FSIA, although it did not formally adopt the commercial exception, ratified it as an exception to foreign sovereign immunity. Neither rationale for the act of state doctrine came into play within any force in *Dunhill*.

The question remains whether these rationales can come into play in a significant range of cases. The next case narrows that range of cases even further. Some might conclude that the doctrine is gradually diminishing to the vanishing point, covering fewer and fewer cases with less and less force. Others see the doctrine returning to its historic role with its effect concentrated on the cases to which it has traditionally applied. On this view, the territorial allocation of power among sovereign nations requires some degree of deference to the acts that each undertakes within its boundaries. If a nation commits itself to the official character of acts within those boundaries, other nations must respect what it has done. Alternative principles, such as sovereign immunity, can accomplish the same goal, but since they extend only to suits against the sovereign, they do not account for all the situations in which acts of a foreign nation must be given the force of law. Does the act of state doctrine continue to have a limited but forceful role to play for this reason?

4.   For articles discussing the act of state doctrine and the FSIA, see Michael D. Ramsey, *Acts of State and Foreign Sovereign Obligations*, 39 Harv. Int'l L.J. 1 (1998); Marianne Short & Charles Brower, II, *The Taming of the Shrew: May the Act of State Doctrine and Foreign Sovereign Immunity Eat and Drink as Friends?* 20 Hamline L. Rev. 723 (1997). For discussion of other issues raised by *Dunhill*, see Ariel Oscar Diaz, Comment, *The Territoriality Inquiry Under the Act of State Doctrine: Continuing the Search for an Appropriate Application of Situs of Debt Rules in International Debt Disputes*, 10 I.L.S.A. J. Int'l & Comp. L. 525 (2004); Jake S. Tyshow, Note, *Informal Foreign Affairs Formalism: The Act of State Doctrine and the Reinterpretation of International Comity*,

43 Va. J. Int'l L. 275 (2002); Lynn Parseghian, Comment, *Defining the "Public Act" Requirement in the Act of State Doctrine,* 58 U. Chi. L. Rev. 1151 (1991).

W.S. Kirkpatrick & Co., Inc. v. Environmental Tectonics Corp., Int'l

Supreme Court of the United States, 1990.

493 U.S. 400.

JUSTICE SCALIA delivered the opinion of the Court.

In this case we must decide whether the act of state doctrine bars a court in the United States from entertaining a cause of action that does not rest upon the asserted invalidity of an official act of a foreign sovereign, but that does require imputing to foreign officials an unlawful motivation (the obtaining of bribes) in the performance of such an official act.

I

The facts as alleged in respondent's complaint are as follows: In 1981, Harry Carpenter, who was then chairman of the board and chief executive officer of petitioner W.S. Kirkpatrick & Co., Inc. (Kirkpatrick), learned that the Republic of Nigeria was interested in contracting for the construction and equipment of an aeromedical center at Kaduna Air Force Base in Nigeria. He made arrangements with Benson "Tunde" Akindele, a Nigerian citizen, whereby Akindele would endeavor to secure the contract for Kirkpatrick. It was agreed that, in the event the contract was awarded to Kirkpatrick, Kirkpatrick would pay to two Panamanian entities controlled by Akindele a "commission" equal to 20% of the contract price, which would in turn be given as a bribe to officials of the Nigerian Government. In accordance with this plan, the contract was awarded to petitioner W.S. Kirkpatrick & Co., International (Kirkpatrick International), a wholly owned subsidiary of Kirkpatrick; Kirkpatrick paid the promised "commission" to the appointed Panamanian entities; and those funds were disbursed as bribes. All parties agree that Nigerian law prohibits both the payment and the receipt of bribes in connection with the award of a government contract.

FCPA violation

Respondent Environmental Tectonics Corporation, International, an unsuccessful bidder for the Kaduna contract, learned of the 20% "commission" and brought the matter to the attention of the Nigerian Air Force and the United States Embassy in Lagos. Following an investigation by the Federal Bureau of Investigation, the United States Attorney for the District of New Jersey brought charges against both Kirkpatrick and Carpenter for violations of the Foreign Corrupt Practices Act of 1977, as amended, 15 U.S.C. § 78dd-1 et seq., and both pleaded guilty.

Respondent then brought this civil action in the United States District Court for the District of New Jersey against Carpenter, Akindele, petitioners, and others, seeking damages under the Racketeer Influenced and Corrupt Organizations Act, 18 U.S.C. § 1961 et seq. [and other statutes].

[The District Court granted summary judgment to defendants based on the act of state doctrine, but the Court of Appeals reversed]. Although agreeing with the District Court that "the award of a military procurement contract can be, in certain circumstances, a sufficiently formal expression of a government's public interests to trigger application" of the act of state doctrine, it found application of the doctrine unwarranted on the facts of this case. The Court of Appeals found particularly persuasive the letter to the District Court from the legal adviser to the Department of State, which had stated that in the opinion of the Department judicial inquiry into the purpose behind the act of a foreign sovereign would not produce the "unique embarrassment, and the particular interference with the conduct of foreign affairs, that may result from the judicial determination that a foreign sovereign's acts are invalid." The Court of Appeals acknowledged that "the Department's legal conclusions as to the reach of the act of state doctrine are not controlling on the courts," but concluded that "the Department's factual assessment of whether fulfillment of its responsibilities will be prejudiced by the course of civil litigation is entitled to substantial respect." In light of the Department's view that the interests of the Executive Branch would not be harmed by prosecution of the action, the Court of Appeals held that Kirkpatrick had not met its burden of showing that the case should not go forward * * *.

II

* * *

In every case in which we have held the act of state doctrine applicable, the relief sought or the defense interposed would have required a court in the United States to declare invalid the official act of a foreign sovereign performed within its own territory. In Underhill v. Hernandez, 168 U.S. 250, 254 (1897), holding the defendant's detention of the plaintiff to be tortious would have required denying legal effect to "acts of a military commander representing the authority of the revolutionary party as government, which afterwards succeeded and was recognized by the United States." In *Oetjen v. Central Leather Co., supra,* [246 U.S. 297 (1918)] and in *Ricaud v. American Metal Co., supra,* [246 U.S. 304 (118)] denying title to the party who claimed through purchase from Mexico would have required declaring that government's prior seizure of the property, within its own territory, legally ineffective. In *Sabbatino,* upholding the defendant's claim to the funds would have required a holding that Cuba's expropriation of goods located in Havana was null and void. In the present case, by contrast, neither the claim nor any asserted defense requires a determination that Nigeria's contract with Kirkpatrick International was, or was not, effective.

Petitioners point out, however, that the facts necessary to establish respondent's claim will also establish that the contract was unlawful. Specifically, they note that in order to prevail respondent must prove that petitioner Kirkpatrick made, and Nigerian officials received, payments that violate Nigerian law, which would, they assert, support a finding that the contract is invalid under Nigerian law. Assuming that to be true, it still does not suffice. The act of state doctrine is not some vague doctrine of abstention but a *"principle of decision* binding on federal and state courts alike." *Sabbatino, supra,* 376 U.S., at 427 (emphasis added). As we said in *Ricaud,* "the act within its own boundaries of one sovereign State . . . becomes . . . a rule of decision for the courts of this country." 246 U.S., at 310. Act of state issues only arise when a court must decide—that is, when the outcome of the case turns upon-the effect of official action by a foreign sovereign. When that question is not in the case, neither is the act of state doctrine. That is the situation here. Regardless of what the court's factual findings may suggest as to the legality of the Nigerian contract, its legality is simply not a question to be decided in the present suit, and there is thus no occasion to apply the rule of decision that the act of state doctrine requires.

     * * *

Petitioners insist, however, that the policies underlying our act of state cases—international comity, respect for the sovereignty of foreign nations on their own territory, and the avoidance of embarrassment to the Executive Branch in its conduct of foreign relations—are implicated in the present case because, as the District Court found, a determination that Nigerian officials demanded and accepted a bribe "would impugn or question the nobility of a foreign nation's motivations," and would "result in embarrassment to the sovereign or constitute interference in the conduct of foreign policy of the United States." The United States, as amicus curiae, favors the same approach to the act of state doctrine, though disagreeing with petitioners as to the outcome it produces in the present case. We should not, the United States urges, "attach dispositive significance to the fact that this suit involves only the 'motivation' for, rather than the 'validity' of, a foreign sovereign act," and should eschew "any rigid formula for the resolution of act of state cases generally." In some future case, perhaps, "litigation . . . based on alleged corruption in the award of contracts or other commercially oriented activities of foreign governments could sufficiently touch on 'national nerves' that the act of state doctrine or related principles of abstention would appropriately be found to bar the suit," (quoting *Sabbatino*, 376 U.S., at 428), and we should therefore resolve this case on the narrowest possible ground, viz., that the letter from the legal adviser to the District Court gives sufficient indication that, "in the setting of this case," the act of state doctrine poses no bar to adjudication.

These urgings are deceptively similar to what we said in *Sabbatino*, where we observed that sometimes, even though the validity of the act of a foreign sovereign within its own territory is called into question, the policies underlying the act of state doctrine may not justify its application. We suggested that a sort of balancing approach could be applied—the balance shifting against application of the doctrine, for example, if the government that committed the "challenged act of state" is no longer in existence. 376 U.S., at 428. But what is appropriate in order to avoid unquestioning judicial acceptance of the acts of foreign sovereigns is not similarly appropriate for the quite opposite purpose of expanding judicial incapacities where such acts are not directly (or even indirectly) involved. It is one thing to suggest, as we have, that the policies underlying the act of state doctrine should be considered in deciding whether, despite the doctrine's technical availability, it should nonetheless not be invoked; it is something quite different to suggest that those underlying policies are a doctrine unto themselves, justifying expansion of the act of state doctrine (or, as the United States puts it, unspecified "related principles of abstention") into new and uncharted fields.

The short of the matter is this: Courts in the United States have the power, and ordinarily the obligation, to decide cases and controversies properly presented to them. The act of state doctrine does not establish an exception for cases and controversies that may embarrass foreign governments, but merely requires that, in the process of deciding, the acts of foreign sovereigns taken within their own jurisdictions shall be deemed valid. That doctrine has no application to the present case because the validity of no foreign sovereign act is at issue.

The judgment of the Court of Appeals for the Third Circuit is affirmed.

NOTES AND QUESTIONS FOR DISCUSSION

1. The opinion in *Kirkpatrick* reformulates the act of state doctrine almost as a principle of choice of law or recognition of judgments: that American courts are bound by a foreign sovereign's assertion of the validity of its own acts within its own territory. That assertion must be made before litigation, not afterwards, with the requisite degree of formality, and it must concern an act within the boundaries of the foreign state. Both *Kirkpatrick* and *Dunhill* insist on the requirement of formality. An expedient assertion of a sovereign nature of a disputed act does not trigger application of the doctrine. The territorial limitation of the doctrine returns to traditional principles of choice of law, under which the location of an act determines its legal validity. The immediate effect of an act of state cannot extend beyond the foreign nation's boundaries. Like most principles of choice of law, these limitations can be extended or overridden by a federal statute or treaty. The act of state doctrine remains a creature of federal common law.

The formality and territoriality of asserted acts of state fit the original context in which it arose, mainly from expropriation by the government of Cuba. A valid taking of property usually requires a formal act of the government and property can usually be assigned a determinate situs, with some questions about certain forms of intangible property. Moreover, the hostile relations between the U.S. and Cuba assured that the political branches would respond to any such action. The general disapproval that such acts received created a climate inviting further restrictions on the scope and effect of the doctrine. The formal and territorial prerequisites for finding an act of state became the basis for imposing obstacles to its invocation and narrowing its scope. The attempts in both *Kirkpatrick* and *Dunhill* to take the doctrine to issues other than expropriation failed. Nevertheless, the doctrine as formulated in these cases still applies beyond expropriation.

The absence of decisions upholding the doctrine in such cases might result from either of two competing causes: either its obvious failure to apply, leading no party to attempt to take advantage of it (or the courts summarily to reject it); or its obvious application, leading no party to challenge it (or the courts simply to accept it). Clear limits on the doctrine could enhance both effects, deterring parties from needless litigation over an issue with a foregone conclusion. The same dynamics might affect the actions of foreign states. To the extent that they take the doctrine into account, they undertake the requisite formalities within their own borders, but when the cost of invoking the doctrine becomes too high, they forego whatever benefits the doctrine might bring to them. Few countries would endorse the bribery alleged in *Kirkpatrick* as official policy, despite the fact that they might tolerate it as an entrenched feature of local government. Does the paucity of cases applying the doctrine indicate that it has achieved its purpose or that it has failed to do so? Or is it risky to draw any firm conclusion from the evidence of things unseen: cases not filed, decisions not made, and opinions not published?

2. The alleged bribe in *Kirkpatrick* did not constitute an act of state and no official act of the Nigerian government legitimized this practice. What further official act would have brought the act of state doctrine into play? If Nigeria had recharacterized the alleged bribe as a tax, which then had been misappropriated by the official in question, would that have satisfied the formality required of an act of state? Of course, in that situation, the exaction of the fee would not have left any of the bidders for the contract at a competitive disadvantage, since a publicized tax would have been imposed on all of them equally. A formally official act would have changed the complexion of the case entirely and might well have prevented it from arising in the first place.

These consequences can be generalized. Formally adopting the disputed conduct as an act of state puts the foreign sovereign to a choice: either to establish some rule that is less controversial—transforming a bribe into a tax in the hypothetical—or avowing conduct that alienates other nations or trading parties—authorizing bribes to be taken by government officials. The former alternative removes the underlying controversy, which preempts the need to apply the act of state doctrine, while the latter intensifies the controversy, so much so that it might lead to American legislation creating an exception to the act of state doctrine, such as the Second Hickenlooper Amendment. Either way, the formality requirement operates as a powerful restraint on the number of occasions in which the doctrine can successfully operate. For a discussion of this issue, see Paul B. Stephan III, *International Law in the Supreme Court,* 1990 Sup. Ct. Rev. 133.

3. Human rights claims might provide a fertile ground for renewed examination of the act of state doctrine. Consider a variation on the facts of Saudi Arabia v. Nelson, 507 U.S. 349 (1993), discussed above. Recall that the Supreme Court found no basis for the commercial exception to the FSIA in that case because the gravamen of the complaint involved mistreatment by the Saudi government rather than mistreatment by Nelson's employer. As the Court characterized the conduct at issue: it "boils down to abuse of the power of its police by the Saudi Government, and however monstrous such abuse undoubtedly may be, a foreign state's exercise of the power of its police has long been understood for purposes of the restrictive theory as peculiarly sovereign in nature." Id. at 361. This characterization goes far toward applying the act of state doctrine. Of course, the defendants did not need to invoke the act of state doctrine because they had jurisdictional immunity under the FSIA. Suppose, however, that immunity had been subject to an exception, either through a commercial act of the defendants in the U.S., or more plausibly, through an amendment to the FSIA like § 1605A. Would such an exception prove to be futile because it would only transform a dismissal for lack of jurisdiction—the result in *Nelson*—into dismissal on the merits—the result under the act of state doctrine?

Under the plurality opinion in *Dunhill,* an exception to the FSIA can be used to imply an exception to the act of state doctrine. But the plurality consisted of only four justices, only three of whom firmly accepted that line of reasoning. A majority of justices did not. An alteration of the facts in *Nelson* that supported the commercial exception to the FSIA would not generate a corresponding exception to the act of state doctrine. The unequivocal holding in *Dunhill* and then in *Kirkpatrick* does require a formal act of the Saudi government, which apparently was missing on the facts of *Nelson*. The unilateral act of Saudi officials in abusing their power to throw the plaintiff in jail and torture him does not, by itself, amount to an act of state.

Suppose, however, that the facts of *Nelson* were changed further and that the plaintiff was imprisoned and tortured pursuant to a decree of the Saudi government or the judgment of a Saudi court. Those would appear to be sovereign acts. Suppose further that the plaintiff had a claim and an exception to sovereign immunity under a revised and expanded version of § 1605A. Would the act of state doctrine defeat the plaintiff's claim on the merits? Or would the plaintiff prevail on the ground that Congress, in passing the new § 1605A, has impliedly limited the act of state of doctrine? Of course, everything depends upon how the new statute was framed and, in particular, whether Congress addressed its effect on the act of state doctrine. Suppose, however, that the new statute, like the existing § 1605A, said nothing about the act of state doctrine. Would it have no effect upon the doctrine's application, as the majority of justices reasoned in *Dunhill*? Or is this reading too much into the position of justices, none of whom is now on the Supreme Court, who could not coalesce around a majority opinion?

For a discussion of the role of the act of state doctrine in human rights cases, see Gergana Halpern, Note *Punishing Aggressors in U.S. Courts: Will the Act of State Doctrine Bar National Prosecution of the Crime of Aggression?*, 7 Cardozo Pub. L. Pol'y & Ethics J. 239 (2008); Michael J. O'Donnell, Note, *A Turn For The Worse: Foreign Relations, Corporate Human Rights Abuse, and the Courts*, 24 B.C. Third World L.J. 223, 224-25 (2004); Rosica Popova, Sarei v. Rio Tinto *and the Exhaustion of Local Remedies Rule in the Context of the Alien Tort Claims Act: Short-Term Justice, But at What Cost?*, 28 Hamline J. Pub. L. & Pol'y 517, 554 (2007).

4. As noted earlier, domestic civil rights cases offer a tempting analogy to international human rights cases. Claims for denial of federal rights under color of state law, under 42 U.S.C. § 1983, have resulted in an elaborate body of law on the existence of a cause of action; the liability of state agencies, subdivisions, and officials; various forms of sovereign and individual immunity; and other restrictions on liability and remedies. All attempts to draw such an analogy founder on the different choice of law principles that apply in the domestic and the international situation. Federal law preempts state law under the Supremacy Clause in domestic cases, so that denial of federal rights under color of state law wholly displaces any authority conferred by the state. Domestic civil rights law recognizes no analogue to the act of state doctrine. In international cases, the effect of the foreign act of state depends upon the authority conferred upon it by foreign law. That law might be displaced by American law, but not because American law is supreme over foreign.

For that matter, arguments that particularly egregious acts of state have no authority because they contravene basic principles of international law suffer from a similar defect. Such arguments presuppose that international law assumes priority over foreign law. Yet that presupposition has to be supported by principles of choice of law that recognize the generally equal status of sovereign nations. No supremacy clause in international law dictates its superiority to the law of any particular nation. Thus in *Sabbatino*, the act of state doctrine required dismissal of the plaintiff's claim *despite* the contention that the seizure in question violated international law. The latter could not, by its own force, deprive the act of the Cuban government within its own territory, of authoritative force.

Seen from this perspective, the act of state doctrine becomes purely an issue of comity: whether American courts will defer to a foreign act of state, as a matter of American choice of law. For an analysis along these lines, see Gregory H. Fox, *Reexamining the Act of State Doctrine: An Integrated Conflicts Analysis*, 33 Harv. Int'l L.J. 521 (1992). It is not a principle of international law that either does or does not require recognition of the acts of a foreign government. Some scholars have argued to the contrary, but even they have recognized that, regardless of its roots in international law, the act of state doctrine requires adoption by American courts as a feature of American law. Restatement (Third) of Foreign Relations Law of the United States § 111 (1987), Reporters' Notes 1 and 3. The scope and effect of the doctrine therefore become matters of deference to other nations, rather than enforcing the supervening requirements of international law. State law receives no such deference in domestic civil rights cases. Accordingly, what constitutes action under color of state law, or what acts receive various forms of immunity, do not translate directly to international cases.

CHAPTER 4

Service of Process

Personal Jurisdiction and Subject Matter Jursidiction are prerequisites to the exercise of jurisdiction, but they are not the only prerequisites. The plaintiff must also be able to secure good service of process on the defendant. And in the context of foreign defendants—whether individuals or corporations—service can become very complex very quickly, particularly as it relates to service abroad. In addition, service of process issues involve the direct interaction of the judicial systems of different countries. And in some foreign jurisdictions—particularly civil law jurisdictions—certain methods of service that might be common in the U.S. are impermissible, largely because process serving on foreign soil is considered to be an official function, to be performed by officers and agents of the country in which process is served. What is more, service abroad is regulated in substantial part by various internationally agreed means, such as the Hague Convention on the Service Abroad of Judicial and Extrajudicial Documents (Hague Service Convention). Yet service on foreign parties in federal court is also regulated by Rule 4 of the Federal Rules of Civil Procedure (as well as by state law in state courts). Consequently, there can be a number of difficult issues involving the relationship and coordination between the Rules and international agreements. We consider some of these issues in this chapter.

A. Service on Foreign Defendants under the Federal Rules

American students of Civil Procedure are generally familiar with the concept of service of process. Process itself generally consists of a copy of the plaintiff's complaint and the summons, compelling the defendant to respond to the lawsuit on penalty of default. It simultaneously provides the mechanism for enforcing a court's judicial jurisdiction and for providing notice to the defendant of the pendency of proceedings, thus providing the defendant with an opportunity to respond. Perhaps surprisingly, many of the features of service of process for domestic defendants and foreign defendants are the same, at least as far as the Federal Rules are concerned. There are, however, important differences as well.

1. Waiver of Service

An important feature of the Federal Rules of Civil Procedure (and of state courts that have borrowed this feature from the Federal Rules) is what is known as a "waiver of service" provision. The waiver provisions of the Federal Rules are applicable to individuals, corporations, partnerships, and unincorporated associations, foreign or domestic. And they expressly apply not just to domestic defendants but to foreign individuls and entities as well. Under Rule 4(d), any such defendant "has a duty to avoid unnecessary expenses of serving the summons," and consequently, the plaintiff may request a waiver of service from the defendant, pursuant to the procedures articulated in Rule 4(d)(1). In short, the plaintiff may send the defendant the request in writing, accompanied by a copy of the complaint, "by first class mail or other reliable means." Among other things, the request must inform the defendant of the court in which he has been sued and—for defendants served in the U.S.—of the conseqences of not waiving service (i.e., having to pay the expenses of service).

Of course, a foreign defendant might not be located within a federal judicial district—for example, if they are outside the U.S. Nevertheless, the general waiver of service provisions are still applicable, although such a defendant is entitled to a longer time within which to respond to the waiver request (60 days from the time the waiver request was sent, instead of 30). In addition, such a defendant is not subject to the sanctions for failure to waive service. If the defendant (foreign or domestic) signs and timely returns the waiver, it is as if the summons and complaint had been served at the time the plaintiff files the defendant's waiver with the court. Otherwise, service in federal court must be made in one of the modes elsewhere provided by Rule 4. Note that a waiver of service of the summons "does not waive any objection to personal jursidiction or to venue." In addition, if a defendant is prepared to accept service voluntarily, there may be a practical incentive to proceed under the waiver of service provisions of the Rules and thereby avoid the costs associated with service under the Convention.

2. Absent a Waiver of Service

(a) Serving foreign defendants within a U.S. federal judicial district

A foreign defendant from whom a waiver of service is *not* forthcoming could sometimes be located within a federal judicial district, and thus be subject to the rules for service on individuals or corporations, respectively. For individuals located within a judicial district who have not waived service, the plaintiff in a federal court has a number of options under Rule 4(e). For example, she could resort to state law methods for serving a summons in the courts of the state in which the federal court is situated. Rule 4(e)(1). Alternatively, she could have someone prsonally serve the defendant with a copy of the summons and complaint; or leave a copy of the summons and complaint at the defendant's "dwelling or usual place of abode"; or she could have them deliver "a copy of each to an agent authorized by appointment or by law" to receive service. Rule 4(e)(2)(A)-(C). For foreign corporations, partnerships, or associations that are located within a federal judicial district in the U.S.—as with similar domestic entities—the plaintiff may resort to state law methods of service as described under Rule 4(e)(1). See Rule 4(h)(1)(A). Alternatively, the plaintiff may arrange to serve "an officer, a managing or general agent, or any other agent authorized by appointment or by law" to receive service. Rule 4(h)(1)(B). Of course, such service has the potential to conflict with internationally agreed means of service in the Hague Service Convention—an issue we discuss below in our treatment of Volkswagenwerk Aktiengesellschaft v. Schlunk, 486 U.S. 694 (1988), later in this chapter.

(b) Serving foreign defendants in a foreign country

In most cases, however, a foreign defendant from whom a waiver of service is not forthcoming will likely not be subject to service within a U.S. judicial district. The provisions for service on such defendants are quite detailed. We set them out here:

Rule 4(f), Fed. R. Civ. P.

Serving an Individual in a Foreign Country. Unless federal law provides otherwise, an individual—other than a minor, an incompetent person, or a person whose waiver has been filed—may be served at a place not within any judicial district of the United States:

> (1) by any internationally agreed means of service that is reasonably calculated to give notice, such as those authorized by the Hague Convention on the Service Abroad of Judicial and Extrajudicial Documents;
>
> (2) if there is no internationally agreed means, or if an international agreement allows but does not specify other means, by a method that is reasonably calculated to give notice:
>
>> (A) as prescribed by the foreign country's law for service in that country in an action in its courts of general jurisdiction;
>>
>> (B) as the foreign authority directs in response to a letter rogatory or letter of request; or
>>
>> (C) unless prohibited by the foreign country's law, by:
>>
>>> (i) delivering a copy of the summons and of the complaint to the individual personally; or
>>>
>>> (ii) using any form of mail that the clerk addresses and sends to the individual and that requires a signed receipt; or
>
> (3) by other means not prohibited by international agreement, as the court orders.

Note that Rule 4(f)(1) is designed to incorporate treaties and other international agreements to which the U.S. may be a party as permissible modes of service. One such agreement—the Hague Service Convention—is discussed in the materials that follow. Note further that the various means of service described in Rule 4(f)(2) will have to be nonviolative of foreign country law (i.e., the law of the country in which service is to take place), even if there is no internationally agreed means of service or if such agreement would allow for other (but unspecified) means of service. That is because Rule 4(f)(2)(A) and (C) specifically reference adherence to foreign law, and Rule 4(f)(2)(B) references a mode of service that is necessarily pursuant to foreign country procedure. (A "letter rogatory," referenced in Rule 4(f)(2)(B), is basically a formal request made by one court to a foreign court for judicial assistance, such as with service of process or the production of evidence abroad.) Rule 4(f)(3) is a kind of catch-all provision, but by its terms, it only requires non-violation of any international agreement; it does not expressly require compliance with foreign country law.

Note also that Rule 4(f) is the procedure to be followed when serving *an individual* abroad—i.e., at a place not within any federal judicial district. A separate provision provides for service upon a "Corporation, Partnership, or Association," including foreign entities not subject to service within a judicial district. See Rule 4(h). The latter Rule allows for service on such foreign entities in the same manner prescribed for individuals in Rule 4(f), above, *but excluding* 4(f)'s provision for personal service under Rule 4(f)(2)(C)(i). See Rule 4(h)(2).

B. SERVICE UNDER THE HAGUE CONVENTION

The Hague Service Convention is a multilateral treaty formulated by the 10th Session of the Hague Conference of Private International Law, and was concluded on November 15, 1965. The Convention revised parts of the Hague Conventions on Civil Procedure of 1905 and 1954. The revision was intended to provide a simpler way to serve process abroad, as well as to assure that defendants sued in foreign jurisdictions would receive actual and timely notice of suit. In 1969, the Convention entered into force in the United States. Currently, over 70 nations have ratified the Convention, including Russia, China and the vast majority of western European countries. It is probably the most frequently used mechanism for service abroad. We offer a brief outline of the Convention here, and we provide a more complete version at Appendix A.

Article 1 of the Convention defines the Convention's scope: "The present Convention shall apply in all cases, in civil or commercial matters, where there is occasion to transmit a judicial or extrajudicial document for service abroad." Article 2 of the Convention requires each state to "designate a Central Authority . . . to receive requests for service" of documents from other countries that are parties to the Convention. The Central Authority must receive a formal request in the appropriate form (see Arts. 3-4).[*] Once the Central Authority receives a proper request, it must then serve the documents by a method prescribed "(a) . . . by its internal law for the service of documents in domestic actions upon persons who are within its territory, or (b) by a particular method requested by the applicant, unless such a method is incompatible with the law of the State addressed." Art. 5. (If the request for service complies with the Convention, the addressed state may not refuse to comply unless it concludes that service will "infringe its sovereignty or security." Art. 13. Upon service, the central authority must then provide a certificate of proof of service that conforms to a specified model that is annexed to the Convention. Art. 6. In addition, a state also may consent to methods of service within its boundaries other than through a request to its cen-

---

[*] In connection with lawsuits brought in a U.S. court, the proper form (USM-94 "Request for Service Abroad of Judicial or Extrajudicial Documents") may be obtained from the U.S. Marshall's office. See http://www.usmarshals.gov/forms/usm94.pdf.

tral authority. Arts. 8-11, 19. (U.S. practice, however, is—in most cases—not to allow U.S. litigants to serve process abroad through U.S. consular channels, which the Convention would otherwise allow for. 22 C.F.R. § 92.85. Other provisions of the Convention limit the circumstances in which a default judgment may be entered against a defendant who had to be served abroad and did not appear, and also provide some means for relief from such a judgment. See Arts. 15, 16. More specifically, Article 15 states that a default judgment may not be entered absent a showing that either (1) service of process was effected in accordance with the local law of the country in which service was made; or (2) that service of process was actually delivered to the defendant or his usual place of abode by means allowed by the Convention. Article 15 also requires that service be effected "in sufficient time to enable the defendant to defend." Under Article 21 of the Convention, each signatory nation may object to provisions or ratify its provisions subject to conditions, and a number of nations have made objections or reservations with respect to certain parts of the Convention.

A particularly important provision that has given rise to much litigation, and which is the subject of the two following cases, is Article 10 of the Convention. In relevant part, it states:

> **Art. 10.** Provided the State of destination does not object, the present Convention shall not interfere with (a) the freedom to send judicial documents, by postal channels, directly to persons abroad, * * *

Consider whether this provision—which allows for the "send[ing]" of documents by "postal channels" allows for the "service" of process by means such as first class or registered mail, or by international express. If so, is such service possible only if those means are *otherwise* authorized by the law of the forum, such as by Rule 4 if suit is brought in a federal court (or, if suit is brought in state court, by a relevant provision under state law)?

C. COORDINATING THE HAGUE CONVENTION AND THE FEDERAL RULES

The major difficulty surrounding Rule 4(f) is its approval of "internationally agreed means of service" on persons outside the U.S., "such as those authorized by the Hague Convention." But if such internationally agreed means of service exist and are applicable, will they be exclusive of other means of service allowed under Rule 4? Rule 4 seems to assume that the Rules may be resorted to even if an international agreement is applicable, and Rule 4(f)(3) expressly provides that other methods may be used when "not prohibited by international agreement." But is an international agreement such as the Hague Service Convention prohibitive of means other than those mentioned in the agreement? Does Article 10(a) suggest that the mails may be resorted to if otherwise authorized by the Federal Rules (or, in state courts, by state law)? Considerable controversy surrounds the question.

Bankston v. Toyota Motor Corp.

Unites States Court of Appeals, Eighth Circuit, 1989.

889 F.2d 172.

ROSS, SENIOR CIRCUIT JUDGE.

Appellants Charles Bankston, Sr. and Regina Dixon filed suit in the United States District Court for the Western District of Arkansas against Toyota Motor Corporation, a Japanese corporation, seeking damages resulting from an accident involving a Toyota truck. The appellants first attempted service of process upon Toyota by serving an affiliated United States corporation in Torrance, California, as Toyota's purported agent. Toyota filed a motion to dismiss for improper service of process. The district court denied Toyota's motion but granted the appellants 45 days in which to serve Toyota in accordance with the Hague Convention.

The appellants next attempted to serve process upon Toyota by sending a summons and complaint by registered mail, return receipt requested, to Tokyo, Japan. The documents were in English and did not include a translation into Japanese. The receipt of service was signed and returned to appellants. Toyota renewed its motion to dismiss, arguing that the appellants' proposed method of service still did not comply with the Hague Convention.

The district court concluded that Article 10(a) of the Hague Convention does not permit service of process upon a Japanese corporation by registered mail. In an order dated January 4, 1989, the district court gave the appellants an additional sixty days in which to effect service in compliance with the Hague Convention.

On January 13, 1989, the district court granted the appellants' motion to amend the order * * * and certified the issue for interlocutory appeal to this court. On February 9, 1989, this court entered an order granting appellants leave to take an interlocutory appeal pursuant to 28 U.S.C. § 1292(b).

The Hague Convention is a multinational treaty, formed in 1965 for the purpose of creating an "appropriate means to ensure that judicial and extrajudicial documents to be served abroad shall be brought to the notice of the addressee in sufficient time." Hague Convention preamble, 20 U.S.T 361, 362, T.I.A.S. No. 6638, *reprinted in* 28 U.S.C.A. Fed.R.Civ.P. 4, at 130 (West Supp. 1989). The Convention sets out specific procedures to be followed in accomplishing service of process. Articles 2 through 6 provide for service through a central authority in each country. Article 8 allows service by way of diplomatic channels. Article 19 allows service by any method of service permitted by the internal law of the country in which service is made. Under Article 21 of the Convention, each signatory nation may ratify its provisions subject to conditions or objections.

The crucial article for this discussion is Article 10, under which appellants herein purportedly attempted to serve process upon Toyota by registered mail. Article 10 provides in relevant part:

Provided the State of destination does not object, the present Convention shall not interfere with—

(a) the freedom to send judicial documents, by postal channels, directly to persons abroad,

(b) the freedom of judicial officers, officials or other competent persons of the State of origin to effect service of judicial documents directly through the judicial officers, officials or other competent persons of the State of destination,

(c) the freedom of any person interested in a judicial proceeding to effect service of judicial documents directly through the judicial officers, officials or other competent persons of the State of destination.

Japan has objected to subparagraphs (b) and (c), but not to subparagraph (a). The issue before this court is whether subparagraph (a) permits service on a Japanese defendant by direct mail.

In recent years, two distinct lines of Article 10(a) interpretation have arisen. Some courts have ruled that Article 10(a) permits service of process by mail directly to the defendant without the necessity of resorting to the central authority, and without the necessity of translating the documents into the official language of the nation where the documents are to be served.

In general, these courts reason that since the purported purpose of the Hague Convention is to facilitate service abroad, the reference to "'the freedom to send judicial documents by postal channels, directly to persons abroad' would be superfluous unless it was related to the sending of such documents for the purpose of service." Ackermann v. Levine, 788 F.2d 830, 839 (2d Cir. 1986). See also Smith v. Dainichi Kinzoku Kogyo Co., 680 F. Supp. 847, 850 (W.D.Tex. 1988); Newport Components, Inc. v. NEC Home Electronics, Inc., 671 F. Supp. 1525, 1541 (C.D.Cal. 1987). These courts have further found that the use of the "send" rather than "service" in Article 10 (a) "must be attributed to careless drafting." *Ackermann v. Levine, supra*, 788 F.2d at 839.

The second line of interpretation, advocated by Toyota, is that the word "send" in Article 10(a) is not the equivalent of "service of process." The word "service" is specifically used in other sections of the Convention, including subsections (b) and (c) of Article 10. If the drafters of the Convention had meant for subparagraph (a) to provide an additional manner of service of judicial documents, they would have used the word "service." Subscribers to this interpretation maintain that Article 10(a) merely provides a method for sending subsequent documents after service of process has been obtained by means of the central authority. See, e.g., Hantover, Inc. v. Omet, 688 F. Supp. 1377, 1385 (W.D.Mo. 1988); Prost v. Honda Motor Co., 122 F.R.D. 215, 216 (E.D.Mo. 1987); Pochop v. Toyota Motor Co., 111 F.R.D. 464, 466 (S.D.Miss. 1986); Mommsen v. Toro Co., 108 F.R.D. 444, 446 (S.D.Iowa 1985); Suzuki Motor Co. v. Superior Court, 200 Cal. App. 3d 1476, 249 Cal. Rptr. 376 (1988).

We find this second line of authority to be more persuasive. It is a "familiar canon of statutory construction that the starting point for interpreting a statute is the language of the statute itself. Absent a clearly expressed legislative intention to the contrary, that language must ordinarily be regarded as conclusive." Consumer Prod. Safety Comm. v. GTE Sylvania, 447 U.S. 102, 108 (1980). In addition, where a legislative body "includes particular language in one section of a statute but omits it in another section of the same Act, it is generally presumed that [the legislative body] acts intentionally and purposely in the disparate inclusion or exclusion." Russello v. United States, 464 U.S. 16, 23 (1983). In *Suzuki*, 249 Cal.Rptr. at 379, the court found that because service of process by registered mail was not permitted under Japanese law, it was "extremely unlikely" that Japan's failure to object to Article 10(a) was intended to authorize the use of registered mail as an effective mode of service of process, particularly in light of the fact that Japan had specifically objected to the much more formal modes of service by Japanese officials which were available in Article 10(b) and (c).

We conclude that sending a copy of a summons and complaint by registered mail to a defendant in a foreign country is not a method of service of process permitted by the Hague Convention. We affirm the judgment of the district court and remand this case with directions that appellants be given a reasonable time from the date of this Order in which to effectuate service of process over appellee * * * in compliance with the terms of the Hague Convention.

JOHN R. GIBSON CIRCUIT JUDGE, concurring.

I concur in the court's opinion today in every respect. The court correctly interprets the Hague Convention. I write separately only to express nagging concerns I have about the practical effect of our opinion. Automobiles are subject to a plethora of regulations requiring particular equipment and detailed warnings. Should an automobile manufactured in Japan carry a disclosure that, if litigation ensues from its purchase and use, service of process on the Japanese manufacturer can only be obtained under the Hague Convention? Should the purchaser also be informed that this special service of process will cost $800 to $900, as we are told, and must include a translation of the suit papers in Japanese? These decisions we must leave to others. I write only to express my discomfort with the practical effect of Toyota's insistence on strict compliance with the letter of the Hague Convention.

Brockmeyer v. May

United States Court of Appeals, Ninth Circuit, 2004.

383 F.3d 798.

WILLIAM FLETCHER, CIRCUIT JUDGE.

Plaintiffs in this case attempted to serve process on an English defendant by using ordinary first class mail to send a summons and complaint from the United States to England. We join the Second Circuit in concluding that the Convention on the Service Abroad of Judicial and Extrajudicial Documents ("Hague Convention," or the "Convention") does not prohibit—or, in the words of the Convention, does not "interfere with"—service of process by international mail. But this conclusion tells us only that the Hague Convention does not prohibit such service. For service by international mail to be effective in federal court, it must also be affirmatively authorized by some provision in federal law.

Federal Rule of Civil Procedure 4 governs service of process in federal district court. In this case, after determining that the Hague Convention does not prohibit service by international mail, the necessary next step is to analyze Rule 4(f) to determine whether it affirmatively authorizes such service. The plaintiffs' attempted service fails because they failed to follow the requirements of that rule. We therefore reverse and remand to the district court with instructions to vacate the judgment.

I. BACKGROUND: PLAINTIFFS' ATTEMPTS TO SERVE PROCESS

Ronald B. Brockmeyer is the owner of the trademark <<O>> under which he publishes and distributes adult entertainment media and novelties. On August 3, 1998, Brockmeyer and his company, Eromedia, filed suit against Marquis Publications, Ltd. ("Marquis") and several other defendants in federal district court in the Southern District of New York, alleging trademark infringement and various state-law causes of action. Marquis is a company registered under British law. Plaintiffs' counsel made two attempts at service on Marquis.

Plaintiffs' counsel made his first attempt on October 7, 1998. He sent the summons and complaint, together with a request for waiver of service, by ordinary first class mail to a post office box in England. Marquis did not respond.

On April 5, 1999, the district court in New York transferred the suit to the Central District of California. On October 6, 1999, the district court in California entered an order to show cause ("OSC") why the suit should not be dismissed for lack of prosecution. Plaintiffs were required to respond to the OSC by October 25, 1999.

Plaintiffs' counsel made his second attempt at service four days before the OSC deadline, on October 21, 1999. This time, instead of sending the summons and complaint together with a request for waiver of service, he sent only the summons and complaint. He sent them by first class mail to the same post office box in England to which he had previously sent the request for waiver. Marquis still did not respond.

Default was entered by the court clerk against several defendants (not including Marquis) on November 24, 1999. Default was entered against Marquis a year later, on November 8, 2000. On February 22, 2002, the district court entered a default judgment of $ 410,806.12, plus attorneys' fees and costs, against Marquis and two German defendants.

The German defendants moved to set aside the default judgment against them. On June 6, 2002, the district court granted the motion on the ground that they had not been properly served under the Hague Convention and German law. The court ordered plaintiffs to serve the German defendants properly within 90 days or face dismissal. The district court subsequently gave plaintiffs a two-month extension until November 4, 2002. Seven days before the expiration of the extended deadline, plaintiffs' counsel finally submitted documents to the German Central Authority for service. The Central Authority rejected the documents the same day for failure to comply with German law. Almost two months later, plaintiffs' counsel resubmitted documents to the German Central Authority. Nothing in the record indicates whether these resubmitted documents complied with German law. On January 2, 2003, the district court dismissed the suit against the German defendants for failure to serve process within the time allowed under the extended deadline. Plaintiffs have not appealed that dismissal.

Marquis moved independently to set aside the default judgment against it. Among other things, Marquis contended that international mail service must be made by certified or registered mail. On June 26, 2002, the district court denied Marquis's motion, holding that plaintiffs' second attempt at service had been successful. It ruled that mail service is not forbidden by the Hague Convention, and that service by ordinary international first class mail is proper.

Marquis appeals the district court's denial of its motion to set aside plaintiffs' default judgment. * * * Once service is challenged, plaintiffs bear the burden of establishing that service was valid under Rule 4. * * *

II. DISCUSSION

A. The Hague Convention

The resolution of this appeal depends on whether Marquis was properly served. Because service of process was attempted abroad, the validity of that service is controlled by the Hague Convention, to the extent that the Convention applies. Volkswagenwerk Aktiengesellschaft v. Schlunk, 486 U.S. 694, 705 (1988) ("Compliance with the Convention is mandatory in all cases to which it applies.").

The Hague Convention, * * * regularized and liberalized service of process in international civil suits. The primary means by which service is accomplished under the Convention is through a receiving country's "Central Authority." The Convention affirmatively requires each member country to designate a Central Authority to receive documents from another member country. See Hague Convention, art. 2. The receiving country can impose certain requirements with respect to those documents (for example, that they be translated into the language of that country). See id., art. 5. If the documents comply with applicable requirements, the Convention affirmatively requires the Central Authority to effect service in its country. See id., arts. 4 & 5.

The Convention also provides that it does not "interfere with" other methods of serving documents. Article 10(a) of the Convention recites: "Provided the State of destination does not object, the present Convention shall *not interfere with*—(a) the freedom to *send* judicial documents, by postal channels, directly to persons abroad." (Emphasis added.) American courts have disagreed about whether the phrase "the freedom to *send* judicial documents" in Article 10(a) includes within its meaning the freedom to *serve* judicial documents.

One line of cases follows Bankston v. Toyota Motor Corp., 889 F.2d 172, 173-74 (8th Cir. 1989). In *Bankston*, the Eighth Circuit held that the meaning of the word "send" in Article 10(a) does not include "serve"; that is, it held that "send" permitted the sending of judicial documents by mail, but only after service of process was accomplished by some other means. In Nuovo Pignone v.

Storman Asia M/V, 310 F.3d 374, 384 (5th Cir. 2002), the Fifth Circuit similarly held that a strict reading of the Hague Convention did not permit an Italian plaintiff who filed suit in the United States to serve an Italian defendant in Italy by Federal Express.

A second line of cases follows Ackermann v. Levine, 788 F.2d 830, 838 (2d Cir. 1986), in which the Second Circuit approved a German plaintiff's service of process by mail, when the plaintiff filed suit in Germany and served by registered mail a defendant in the United States. *Ackermann* relied primarily on the purpose and history of the convention to interpret the word "send" in Article 10(a) to include the meaning "serve." *See id.*

Whether service by mail is permitted under the Hague Convention is an open question in our circuit. We briefly discussed Article 10(a) in Lidas, Inc. v. United States, 238 F.3d 1076, 1084 (9th Cir. 2001), but we did not confront the question whether Article 10(a) allows service by mail. District courts within our circuit are split. * * *

Today we join the Second Circuit in holding that the meaning of "send" in Article 10(a) includes "serve." *See Ackermann,* 788 F.2d at 838. In so doing, we also join the essentially unanimous view of other member countries of the Hague Convention. *See, e.g.,* Case C-412/97, E.D. Srl. v. Italo Fenocchio, 1999 E.C.R. I-3845, [2000] C.M.L.R. 855 (Court of Justice of the European Communities) ("Article 10(a) of [the Hague Convention] allows service by post."); Integral Energy & Envtl. Eng'g Ltd. v. Schenker of Canada Ltd., (2001) 2001 A.R. LEXIS 896, 295 A.R. 233, 2001 WL 454163 (Alberta Queens Bench) ("Article 10(a) of the Hague Convention provides that if the state of destination does not object, judicial documents may be served by postal channels"), *rev'd on other grounds,* (2001) 2001 A.R. LEXIS 914, 293 A.R. 327; R. v. Re Recognition of an Italian Judgment, [2002] I.L.Pr. 15, 2000 WL 33541696 (Thessaloniki Court of Appeal, Greece) ("It should be noted that the possibility of serving judicial documents in civil and commercial cases through postal channels . . . is envisaged in Article 10(a) of the Hague Convention.").

We agree with the Second Circuit that this holding is consistent with the purpose of the Convention to facilitate international service of judicial documents. *See* Hague Convention, art.1 ("[T]he present Convention shall apply in all cases, in civil or commercial matters, where there is occasion to transmit a judicial or extrajudicial document for *service* abroad.") (emphasis added); *see also* 1 Moore's Federal Practice § 4.52[2][d] (stating that "it comports with the broad purpose of the Hague Convention" to construe "send" to mean "serve").

Commentaries on the history of negotiations leading to the Hague Convention further indicate that service by mail is permitted under Article 10(a). According to the official Rapporteur's report, the first paragraph of Article 10 of the draft Convention, which "except for minor editorial changes" is identical to Article 10 of the final Convention, was intended to permit service by mail. *See* 1 Bruno A. Ristau, *International Judicial Assistance* § 4-3-5, at 204-05 (2000) (quoting the Service Convention Negotiating Document) (translated from French by Ristau). A "Handbook" published by the Permanent Bureau of the Hague Convention, which summarizes meetings of a "Special Commission of Experts," states that to interpret Article 10(a) not to permit service by mail would "contradict what seems to have been the implicit understanding of the delegates at the 1977 Special Commission meeting, and indeed of the legal literature on the Convention and its predecessor treaties." Permanent Bureau of the Hague Convention, *Practical Handbook on the Operation of the Hague Convention of 15 November 1965 on the Service Abroad of Judicial and Extrajudicial Documents in Civil or Commercial Matters* 44 (1992). As further evidence of the understanding of the parties at the time the Hague Convention was signed, the United States delegate to the Hague Convention reported to Congress that Article 10(a) permitted service by mail. *See* S. Exec. R. No. 6, at 13 (1967) (statement by Philip W. Amram).

The United States government, through the State Department, has specifically disapproved the Eighth Circuit's holding in *Bankston*. On March 14, 1991, the Deputy Legal Advisor of the State Department wrote a letter to the Administrative Office of the United States Courts. After discussing Article 10(a) and noting that Japan did not object to the use of postal channels under Article 10(a), the letter concluded[:] "We therefore believe that the decision of the Court of Appeals in *Bankston* is incorrect to the extent that it suggests that the Hague Convention does not permit as a method of service of process the sending of a copy of a summons and complaint by registered mail to a defendant in a foreign country." The letter also emphasized that, "while courts in the United States have final authority to interpret international treaties for the purposes of their application as law of the United States, they give great weight to treaty interpretations made by the Executive Branch." * * *

State Department circulars also indicate that service by mail is permitted in international civil litigation. * * *

The purpose and history of the Hague Convention, as well as the position of the U.S. State Department, convince us that "send" in Article 10(a) includes "serve." We therefore hold that the Convention permits—or, in the words of the Convention, does not "interfere with"—service of process by international mail, so long as the receiving country does not object.

B. Rule 4(f): "Service Upon Individuals in a Foreign Country"

Article 10(a) does not itself affirmatively authorize international mail service. It merely provides that the Convention "shall not interfere with" the "freedom" to use postal channels if the "State of destination" does not object to their use. As the Rapporteur for the Convention wrote in explaining Article 10(a), "It should be stressed that in permitting the utilization of postal channels, . . . the draft convention did not intend to pass on the validity of this mode of transmission under the law of the forum state: *in order for the postal channel to be utilized, it is necessary that it be authorized by the law of the forum state.*" 1 Ristau § 4-3-5, at 205 (emphasis added) (quoting Service Convention Negotiating Document); * * *.

In other words, we must look outside the Hague Convention for affirmative authorization of the international mail service that is merely not forbidden by Article 10(a). * * *

Federal Rule of Civil Procedure 4(h)(2) directs that service on a foreign corporation, if done outside of the United States, shall be effected "in any manner prescribed for individuals by subdivision (4)(f) except personal delivery as provided in paragraph (2)(C)(i) thereof," unless a waiver of service has been obtained and filed. No waiver of service under Rule 4(d) was obtained in this case. To determine whether service of process was proper, we therefore look to Federal Rule of Civil Procedure 4(f). As will be seen, no part of Rule 4(f) authorizes service by ordinary international first class mail.

1. Rule 4(f)(1)

Rule 4(f)(1) authorizes service by those methods of service authorized by international agreements, including the Hague Convention. * * *

* * * [However,] it is undisputed that Brockmeyer did not use either the Central Authority under the Hague Convention, or any other internationally agreed means, for accomplishing service. Rule 4(f)(1), therefore, does not provide a basis for service in this case.

2. Rule 4(f)(2)(C)(ii)

Explicit, affirmative authorization for service by international mail is found only in Rule 4(f)(2)(C)(ii). This rule authorizes service abroad by mail for which a signed receipt is required, when such mail is addressed and mailed by the clerk of the federal district court in which the suit is filed. * * *

It is undisputed that the plaintiffs in this case did not comply with the requirements of Rule 4(f)(2)(C)(ii), as notice was not sent by the clerk of the district court, nor by a form of mail requiring a signed receipt. Rule 4(f)(2)(C)(ii) therefore does not provide a basis for service in this case.

3. Rule 4(f)(3)

Rule 4(f)(3) affirmatively authorizes the federal district court to direct any form of service that is not prohibited by an international agreement. It provides:

> (f) Service . . . may be effected in a place not within any judicial district of the United States:
>
> * * * *(3) by other means not prohibited by inter-national agreement as may be directed by the court.* (Emphasis added.)

The decision whether to allow alternative methods of serving process under Rule 4(f)(3) is committed to the "sound discretion of the district court." Rio Props., Inc. v. Rio Int'l Interlink, 284 F.3d 1007, 1016 (9th Cir. 2002) (permitting service on a foreign corporation by regular mail and by e-mail, when authorized by the district court). The classic case is Levin v. Ruby Trading Co., 248 F. Supp. 537 (S.D.N.Y. 1965), in which the court authorized service abroad by ordinary mail under previous Rule 4(i)(1)(E), which was identical to current Rule 4(f)(3). * * *

Courts have authorized a variety of alternative methods of service abroad under current Rule 4(f)(3) and former Rule 4(i)(1)(E), including not only ordinary mail and e-mail but also publication and telex. * * * However, in *Rio* (and in all the cases it cites as applying Rule 4(f)(3)), plaintiffs are required to take a step that the plaintiffs in this case failed to take: They must obtain prior court approval for the alternative method of serving process. Rule 4(f)(3) thus is of no use to plaintiffs in this case.

4. Rule 4(f)(2)(A)

Because it is undisputed in this case that the plaintiffs neither effected service under the Hague Convention or other international agreement in accordance with Rule 4(f)(1), nor effected service by registered mail by the clerk of the court in accordance with the requirements of Rule 4(f)(2)(C)(ii), nor obtained a court order in accordance with Rule 4(f)(3), the only remaining section on which plaintiffs can conceivably rely is Rule 4(f)(2)(A). Rule 4(f)(2)(A) affirmatively authorizes service by means used in the receiving country for service in an action in its courts of general jurisdiction. As we read Rule 4(f)(2)(A), such means do not include service by international mail. * * *

The district court held that service was proper because the United Kingdom allows service for domestic suits in that country by both ordinary and registered post. A number of factors counsel against reading Rule 4(f)(2)(A) to authorize service by international mail, however.

First, the common understanding of Rule 4(f)(2)(A) is that it is limited to personal service. A well-known example of service under Rule 4(f)(2)(A) is "substituted service in Italy by delivery to the concierge of the building where the person to be served lives, as long as the method of service is likely to give the actual notice required by United States due process concepts." Gary N. Horlick, *A Practical Guide to Service of United States Process Abroad*, 14 Int'l Law. 637, 640 (1980) (interpreting previous Rule 4(i)(1)(A) (1963)). Consistent with this example, courts have applied Rule 4(f)(2)(A) to approve personal service carried out in accordance with foreign law. * * *

Another reason to read Rule 4(f)(2)(A) not to authorize service by international mail is the explicit mention of international registered mail in Rule 4(f)(2)(C)(ii), considered above, and the absence of any such mention in Rule 4(f)(2)(A). Indeed, the Advisory Committee Note to Rule 4(i)(1)(D), Rule 4(f)(2)(C)(ii)'s nearly identical predecessor, stated that "service by mail is proper only when it is addressed to the party to be served and a form of mail requiring a signed receipt is used." Fed. R. Civ. P. 4(i)(1)(D) (1963) Advisory Committee Note.

A further reason to read Rule 4(f)(2)(A) not to authorize service on foreign defendants by international mail to England—and, in particular, by ordinary international first class mail—is found in an exchange between the British government and the United States Department of State in 1991, in which the British objected to a then-proposed revision to Federal Rule of Civil Procedure 4. See 127 F.R.D. 266-84 (1989); 146 F.R.D. 515-16 (1992). As amended, this proposal eventually became what is now Rule 4(d), authorizing a plaintiff to request a waiver of service.

Current Rule 4(d) allows a plaintiff to send a summons and complaint by ordinary first class mail, with a request for waiver of service. If the defendant agrees to waive service, the defendant's waiver has the same effect as actual service. Waiver of service under Rule 4(d) is valid for both domestic and foreign defendants. As originally proposed in 1989, Rule 4(d) would have assessed costs incurred in effecting service against all defendants who failed to waive service, including defendants outside the United States. *See* 127 F.R.D. 271-72. The British government strongly objected to assessment of costs against non-waiving defendants living in the United Kingdom. * * *

* * * In response, the Advisory Committee revised the proposed rule to eliminate the provision assessing costs of service against foreign defendants that decline to waive service. * * * The Committee specifically explained that its revision addressed concerns raised by the British government. *See* 146 F.R.D. 521 (Attachment B to letter to Hon. Robert E. Keeton, Chairman, May 1, 1992).

The objection of the British government to the proposed rule makes sense only if the British government understood Rule 4(f) not to permit service by ordinary, international first class mail against a defendant in England. This is so because if Rule 4(f)(2)(A) had authorized service by international first class mail, a plaintiff would never need to send a request for waiver of service by international first class mail. The plaintiff would simply *effect service* by international first class mail.

The purpose of Rule 4(f)(2)(A) supports our interpretation of the exchange between the British Embassy and the State Department and our conclusion that the rule does not authorize ordinary international mail service to England. According to the 1963 Committee Notes accompanying Rule 4(i)(1)(A), the predecessor to Rule 4(f)(2)(A), the purpose of the Rule is to provide an alternative method of service "that is likely to create least objection in the place of service." *See also* Ronan E. Degnan and Mary Kay Kane, *The Exercise of Jurisdiction Over and Enforcement of Judgments Against Alien Defendants,* 39 Hastings L.J. 799, 840 (1988) ("The approach [of Rule 4(i)(1)(A)] assures that the receiving state can have no objection to the means of transmitting notice."). From the exchange, it is clear that an interpretation of Rule 4(f)(2)(A) permitting service of process on an English defendant by ordinary first class mail sent from the United States is not "likely to create least objection in the place of service." Rather, this exchange shows us that such an interpretation is likely to create a substantial objection.

Finally, we have found no cases upholding service of process by international mail under Rule 4(f)(2)(A). Rather, there are a number of cases rejecting service of process by international mail under that rule. See, e.g., Prewitt Enters. v. OPEC, 353 F.3d 916, 925 (11th Cir. 2003) (rejecting plaintiff's argument that Rule 4(f)(2)(A) authorized service of process on OPEC by international registered mail sent to Austria); Res. Ventures, Inc. v. Res. Mgmt. Int'l, 42 F. Supp. 2d 423, 430 (D. Del. 1999) (holding that service of process by international registered mail to Indonesia was not an appropriate method of service under Rule 4(f)(2)(A)); Dee-K Enters. v. Heveafil Sdn. Bhd., 174 F.R.D. 376, 378-79 (E.D. Va. 1997) (holding that rule 4(f)(2)(A) was inapplicable to authorize service of process by international mail to Indonesia or Malaysia).

We therefore conclude, along with the other courts that have considered the question, that Rule 4(f)(2)(A) does not authorize service of process by ordinary first class international mail.

CONCLUSION

Today we join the Second Circuit in holding that the Hague Convention allows service of process by international mail. At the same time, however, we hold that any service by mail in this case was required to be performed in accordance with the requirements of Rule 4(f). * * * attempted service was therefore ineffective, and the default judgment against Marquis cannot stand.

REVERSED and REMANDED, with instructions to VACATE the judgment.

NOTES AND QUESTIONS FOR DISCUSSION

1. The issue surrounding article 10(a) of the Hague Service Convention continues to be one that is, as yet, not definitively resolved. As between the competing approaches of *Bankston* and *Brockmeyer,* is there a clear winner? Given the uncertainly that continues to linger in the U.S., parties will be compelled to consult the rule of their own circuit (or state law, if suit is filed in state court) in determining whether they will be able to affect service by mail.

2. Much of the debate between the two decisions turns on the so-called plain meaning of Article 10(a) as actually permitting service of process by mail. Does the word "send" plainly include "service"? The *Brockmeyer* court suggests that the final text of the treaty may have been the result of a drafting error. But isn't this argument inconsistent with a "plain meaning" argument? When delegates voted on the final text, shouldn't they be assumed to have enacted only the final text, rather than a prior draft? In addition, the Convention went to great lengths to create an elaborate set of procedures for the service of process, including the creation of a central authority. Given that effort, how likely is it that the Convention would permit litigants basically to circumvent those procedures simply by sending something through the mail? And given that the U.K. objected to the adequacy of the more vigorous measures of Articles 10(b) and 10(c), is it credible to argue that the U.K. would have consented to such a relaxed method of service by mail under Article 10(a)? Not all countries have consented to 10(a), including Germany and China.

3. Although the approach taken by *Brockmeyer* has substantial scholarly support (as the opinion notes), it is not as though the *Bankston* position is wanting in such support. See, e.g., L. Andrew Cooper, Note, *International Service of Process By Mail Under the Hague Service Convention*, 13 Mich. J. Int'l L. 698 (1992); Michael H. Altman, Comment, *Mailing Service to Japan: Does Article 10(a) of the Hague Convention Authorize A Separate Method?,* 69 Wash. U.L.Q. 635 (1991); Peter D. Trooboff, *Hague Service Convention—Scope and Application—Role of Internal Law*, 82 Am. J. Int'l L. 816 (1988).

4. As discussed further below in connection with Volkswagenwerk Aktiengesellschaft v. Schlunk, 486 U.S. 694 (1988), *Brockmeyer* notes that the Hague Convention is the exclusive means of service of process in cases to which it applies. Yet by reading Article 10(a) to include service by mail provided such service is allowed by the forum country, as *Brockmeyer* does, Article 10(a) turns out not to be exclusive of the Federal Rules to the extent the Rules (or, in state courts, state rules) would allow service by mail.

5. Was *Brockmeyer* right in *not* reading Article 10(a) as a free-standing authorization of power to serve process through the mails per the Convention (to which federal courts could resort under Rule 4(f)(1)), rather than as a mere allowance of such practice only if forum law provided for it (under (f)(2) or (f)(3))? If service is made in accordance with one of the procedures elsewhere in the Convention (i.e., outside of Article 10(a)), should it matter that no similar means of service is provided for under the Federal Rules (or, in state courts, under state law)?

6. Even though some Circuits read Article 10(a) as allowing for various forms of mailed service otherwise allowed under the Federal Rules, foreign recognition and enforcement of the U.S. judgment obtained may prove difficult if the mode of service is problematic to the foreign courts. Of course, some of the provisions under Rule 4(f) specially condition their use on their not being "prohibited by the foreign country's law." But under Rule 4(f)(3), a federal court may theoretically order service that foreign law does indeed prohibit (provided it is not "prohibited by international agreement"). In addition, many countries look with disapproval on such practices as "tag" jurisdiction when made upon a foreign individual while temporarily in the U.S. (even though, in such cases, the Convention would not be triggered because it does not amount to "service abroad"). See Chapter 1, Section D. Consequently, where time and cost is not an issue, the safest route may be to proceed under the Convention and to have service made through the relevant designated Central Authority.

7. There is a split of authority regarding whether documents forwarded pursuant to mail under Article 10(a) are required to be translated into the language of the destination country. Such translation is required when service is sought through a foreign central authority, potentially adding to the cost of that more formal mode of service. See Lobo v. Celebrity Cruises, Inc., 667 F. Supp. 2d 1324, 1338-39 (S.D. Fla. 2009) (noting split).

8. Note also that in 2006, the Permanent Bureau of the Hague Conference on Private International Law (Permanent Bureau), declared that the sending of documents via postal channels can include transmission by modern commercial and technological means, provided that transmission through these alternative means constitutes the "functional equivalent" of a postal channel. Is this likely to clarify matters? See Richard J. Hawkins, Comment, *Dysfunctional Equivalence: The New Approach to Defining "Postal Channels" Under the Hague Service Convention*, 55 UCLA L. Rev. 205 (2007) (offering a skeptical assessment).

D. DETERMINING THE APPLICABILITY OF THE HAGUE CONVENTION

There was no doubt that the Hague Service Convention was applicable in *Bankston* and *Brockmeyer*. The only question in those cases was whether the Convention allowed for the use of postal channels to effect service of process.

Bankston holds that it does not; *Brockmeyer* holds that it does, provided that the law of the forum in which suit was brought otherwise allows for such service. But how can one be sure when the Convention's provisions will be triggered at all? Recall Article I of the Convention: "The present Convention shall apply in all cases, in civil or commercial matters, where there is occasion to transmit a judicial or extrajudicial document for service abroad." If it is possible to serve a foreign defendant domestically—for example, through an appropriate agent in the U.S.—does the Convention even apply? And whose law determines whether there is "occasion to transmit a judicial . . . document for service abroad"? If the Convention does not apply, consider how a court should proceed, whether under Rule 4, or under state law. The Supreme Court provided responses to some of these questions in the following decision.

Volkswagenwerk Aktiengesellschaft v. Schlunk

Supreme Court of the United States, 1988.

486 U.S. 694.

JUSTICE O'CONNOR delivered the opinion of the Court.

This case involves an attempt to serve process on a foreign corporation by serving its domestic subsidiary which, under state law, is the foreign corporation's involuntary agent for service of process. We must decide whether such service is compatible with the Convention on Service Abroad of Judicial and Extrajudicial Documents in Civil and Commercial Matters, Nov. 15, 1965 (Hague Service Convention), 1969. 20 U.S.T. 361, T.I.A.S. No. 6638.

I

The parents of respondent Herwig Schlunk were killed in an automobile accident in 1983. Schlunk filed a wrongful death action on their behalf in the [state] Circuit Court of Cook County, Illinois. Schlunk alleged that Volkswagen of America, Inc. (VWoA), had designed and sold the automobile that his parents were driving, and that defects in the automobile caused or contributed to their deaths. Schlunk also alleged that the driver of the other automobile involved in the collision was negligent; Schlunk has since obtained a default judgment against that person, who is no longer a party to this lawsuit. Schlunk successfully served his complaint on VWoA, and VWoA filed an answer denying that it had designed or assembled the automobile in question. Schlunk then amended the complaint to add as a defendant Volkswagen Aktiengesellschaft (VWAG), which is the petitioner here. VWAG, a corporation established under the laws of the Federal Republic of Germany, has its place of business in that country. VWoA is a wholly owned subsidiary of VWAG. Schlunk attempted to serve his amended complaint on VWAG by serving VWoA as VWAG's agent.

VWAG filed a special and limited appearance for the purpose of quashing service. VWAG asserted that it could be served only in accordance with the Hague Service Convention, and that Schlunk had not complied with the Convention's requirements. The Circuit Court denied VWAG's motion. It first observed that VWoA is registered to do business in Illinois and has a registered agent for receipt of process in Illinois. The court then reasoned that VWoA and VWAG are so closely related that VWoA is VWAG's agent for service of process as a matter of law, notwithstanding VWAG's failure or refusal to appoint VWoA formally as an agent. The court relied on the facts that VWoA is a wholly owned subsidiary of VWAG, that a majority of the members of the board of directors of VWoA are members of the board of VWAG, and that VWoA is by contract the exclusive importer and distributor of VWAG products sold in the United States. The court concluded that, because service was accomplished within the United States, the Hague Service Convention did not apply.

The [Illinois state] Circuit Court certified two questions to the Appellate Court of Illinois. For reasons similar to those given by the Circuit Court, the Appellate Court determined that VWoA is VWAG's agent for service of process under Illinois law, and that the service of process in this case did not violate the Hague Service Convention. 145 Ill. App. 3d 594, 503 N.E.2d 1045 (1986). After the Supreme Court of Illinois denied VWAG leave to appeal, * * * VWAG petitioned this Court for a writ of certiorari to review the Appellate Court's interpretation of the Hague Service Convention. We granted certiorari to address this issue, which has given rise to disagreement among the lower courts. * * *

II

* * * By virtue of the Supremacy Clause, U.S. Const. Art. VI, the Convention pre-empts inconsistent methods of service prescribed by state law in all cases to which it applies. Schlunk does not purport to have served his complaint on VWAG in accordance with the Convention. Therefore, if service of process in this case falls within Article 1 of the Convention, the trial court should have granted VWAG's motion to quash.

When interpreting a treaty, we "begin 'with the text of the treaty and the context in which the written words are used.'" Société Nationale Industrielle Aérospatiale v. U.S. District Court, 482 U.S. 522, 534 (1987) (quoting Air France v. Saks, 470 U.S. 392, 397 (1985)). Other general rules of construction may be brought to bear on difficult or ambiguous passages. "'Treaties are construed more liberally than private agreements, and to ascertain their meaning we may look beyond the written words to the history of the treaty, the negotiations, and the practical construction adopted by the parties.'" Air France v. Saks, supra, at 396 (quoting Choctaw Nation of Indians v. United States, 318 U.S. 423, 431-432 (1943)).

The Convention does not specify the circumstances in which there is "occasion to transmit" a complaint "for service abroad." But at least the term "service of process" has a well-established technical meaning. Service of process refers to a formal delivery of documents that is legally sufficient to charge the defendant with notice of a pending action. 1 Ristau 4-5(2), p. 123 (interpreting the Convention); Black's Law Dictionary 1227 (5th ed. 1979); see 4 C. Wright & A. Miller, Federal Practice and Procedure § 1063, p. 225 (2d ed. 1987). The legal sufficiency of a formal delivery of documents must be measured against some standard. The Convention does not prescribe a standard, so we almost necessarily must refer to the internal law of the forum state. If the internal law of the forum state defines the applicable method of serving process as requiring the transmittal of documents abroad, then the Hague Service Convention applies.

The negotiating history supports our view that Article 1 refers to service of process in the technical sense. The committee that prepared the preliminary draft deliberately used a form of the term "notification" (formal notice), instead of the more neutral term "remise" (delivery), when it drafted Article 1. 3 Actes et Documents, at 78-79. Then, in the course of the debates, the negotiators made the language even more exact. The preliminary draft of Article 1 said that the present Convention shall apply in all cases in which there are grounds to transmit or to give formal notice of a judicial or extrajudicial document in a civil or commercial matter to a person staying abroad. Id., at 65. * * * To be more precise, the delegates decided to add a form of the juridical term "signification" (service), which has a narrower meaning than "notification" in some countries, such as France, and the identical meaning in others, such as the United States. Id., at 152-153, 155, 159, 366. The delegates also criticized the language of the preliminary draft because it suggested that the Convention could apply to transmissions abroad that do not culminate in service. Id., at 165-167. The final text of Article 1, supra, eliminates this possibility and applies only to documents transmitted for service abroad. The final report (Rapport Explicatif) confirms that the Convention does not use more general terms, such as delivery or transmission, to define its scope because it applies only when there is both transmission of a document from the requesting state to the receiving state, and service upon the person for whom it is intended. Id., at 366.

The negotiating history of the Convention also indicates that whether there is service abroad must be determined by reference to the law of the forum state. The preliminary draft said that the Convention would apply "where there are grounds" to transmit a judicial document to a person staying abroad. The committee that prepared the preliminary draft realized that this implied that the forum's internal law would govern whether service implicated the Convention. Id., at 80-81. The reporter expressed regret about this solution because it would decrease the obligatory force of the Convention. Id., at 81. Nevertheless, the delegates did not change the meaning of Article 1 in this respect.

The Yugoslavian delegate offered a proposal to amend Article 1 to make explicit that service abroad is defined according to the law of the state that is requesting service of process. Id., at 167. The delegate from the Netherlands supported him. Ibid. The German delegate approved of the proposal in principle, although he thought it would require a corresponding reference to the significance of the law of the state receiving the service of process, and that this full explanation would be too complicated. Id., at 168. The President opined that there was a choice to be made between the phrase used by the preliminary draft, "where grounds exist," and the Yugoslavian proposal to modify it with the phrase, "according to the law of the requesting state." Ibid. This prompted the Yugoslavian delegate to declare that the difference was immaterial, because the phrase "where grounds exist" necessarily refers to the law of the forum. Ibid. The French delegate added that, in his view, the law of the forum in turn is equivalent to the law of the requesting state. Id., at 169. At that point, the President recommended entrusting the problem to the drafting committee.

The drafting committee then composed the version of Article 1 that ultimately was adopted, which says that the Convention applies "where there is occasion" to transmit a judicial document for service abroad. Id., at 211. After this revision, the reporter again explained that one must leave to the requesting state the task of defining when a document must be served abroad; that this solution was a consequence of the unavailability of an objective test; and that while it decreases the obligatory force of the Convention, it does provide clarity. Id., at 254. The inference we draw from this history is that the Yugoslavian proposal was rejected because it was superfluous, not because it was inaccurate, and that "service abroad" has the same meaning in the final version of the Convention as it had in the preliminary draft.

VWAG protests that it is inconsistent with the purpose of the Convention to interpret it as applying only when the internal law of the forum requires service abroad. One of the two stated objectives of the Convention is "to create appropriate means to ensure that judicial and extrajudicial documents to be served abroad shall be brought to the notice of the addressee in sufficient time." 20 U.S.T., at 362. The Convention cannot assure adequate notice, VWAG argues, if the forum's internal law determines whether [the Convention] applies. VWAG warns that countries could circumvent the Convention by defining methods of service of process that do not require transmission of documents abroad. Indeed, VWAG contends that one such method of service already exists and that it troubled the Conference: *notification au parquet.*

Notification au parquet permits service of process on a foreign defendant by the deposit of documents with a designated local official. Although the official generally is supposed to transmit the documents abroad to the defendant, the statute of limitations begins to run from the time that the official receives the documents, and there allegedly is no sanction for failure to transmit them. * * * At the time of the 10th Conference, France, the Netherlands, Greece, Belgium, and Italy utilized some type of *notification au parquet.* 3 Actes et Documents, at 75.

There is no question but that the Conference wanted to eliminate *notification au parquet.* Id., at 75-77. It included in the Convention two provisions that address the problem. Article 15 says that a judgment may not be entered unless a foreign defendant received adequate and timely notice of the lawsuit. Article 16 provides means whereby a defendant who did not receive such notice may seek relief from a judgment that has become final. 20 U.S.T., at 364-365. Like Article 1, however, Articles 15 and 16 apply only when documents must be transmitted abroad for the purpose of service. 3 Actes et Documents, at 168-169. VWAG argues that, if this determination is made according to the internal law of the forum state, the Convention will fail to eliminate variants of *notification au parquet* that do not expressly require transmittal of documents to foreign defendants. Yet such methods of service of process are the least likely to provide a defendant with actual notice.

The parties make conflicting representations about whether foreign laws authorizing *notification au parquet* command the transmittal of documents for service abroad within the meaning of the Convention. The final report is itself somewhat equivocal. It says that, although the strict language of Article 1 might raise a question as to whether the Convention regulates *notification au parquet*, the understanding of the drafting Commission, based on the debates, is that the Convention would apply. Id., at 367. Although this statement might affect our decision as to whether the Convention applies to *notification au parquet*, an issue we do not resolve today, there is no comparable evidence in the negotiating history that the Convention was meant to apply to substituted service on a subsidiary like VWoA, which clearly does not require service abroad under the forum's internal law. Hence neither the language of the Convention nor the negotiating history contradicts our interpretation of the Convention, according to which the internal law of the forum is presumed to determine whether there is occasion for service abroad.

Nor are we persuaded that the general purposes of the Convention require a different conclusion. One important objective of the Convention is to provide means to facilitate service of process abroad. Thus the first stated purpose of the Convention is "to create" appropriate means for service abroad, and the second stated purpose is "to improve the organisation of mutual judicial assistance for that purpose by simplifying and expediting the procedure." 20 U.S.T., at 362. By requiring each state to establish a central authority to assist in the service of process, the Convention implements this enabling function. Nothing in our decision today interferes with this requirement.

VWAG correctly maintains that the Convention also aims to ensure that there will be adequate notice in cases in which there is occasion to serve process abroad. Thus compliance with the Convention is mandatory in all cases to which it applies, see supra, and Articles 15 and 16 provide an indirect sanction against those who ignore it, see 3 Actes et Documents, at 92, 363. Our interpretation of the Convention does not necessarily advance this particular objective, inasmuch as it makes recourse to the Convention's means of service dependent on the forum's internal law. But we do not think that this country, or any other country, will draft its internal laws deliberately so as to circumvent the Convention in cases in which it would be appropriate to transmit judicial documents for service abroad. For example, there has been no question in this country of excepting foreign nationals from the protection of our Due Process Clause. Under that Clause, foreign nationals are assured of either personal service, which typically will require service abroad and trigger the Convention, or substituted service that provides "notice reasonably calculated, under all the circumstances, to apprise interested parties of the pendency of the action and afford them an opportunity to present their objections." Mullane v. Central Hanover Bank & Trust Co., 339 U.S. 306, 314 (1950).

Furthermore, nothing that we say today prevents compliance with the Convention even when the internal law of the forum does not so require. The Convention provides simple and certain means by which to serve process on a foreign national. Those who eschew its procedures risk discovering that the forum's internal law required transmittal of documents for service abroad, and that the Convention therefore provided the exclusive means of valid service. In addition, parties that comply with the Convention ultimately may find it easier to enforce their judgments abroad. See Westin, *Enforcing Foreign Commercial Judgments and Arbitral Awards in the United States, West Germany, and England*, Law & Policy Int'l Bus. 325, 340-341 (1987). For these reasons, we anticipate that parties may resort to the Convention voluntarily, even in cases that fall outside the scope of its mandatory application.

III

In this case, the Illinois long-arm statute authorized Schlunk to serve VWAG by substituted service on VWoA, without sending documents to Germany. See Ill. Rev. Stat., ch. 110, § 2-209(a)(1) (1985). VWAG has not petitioned for review of the Illinois Appellate Court's holding that service was proper as a matter of Illinois law. VWAG contends, however, that service on VWAG was not complete until VWoA transmitted the complaint to VWAG in Germany. According to VWAG, this transmission constituted service abroad under the Hague Service Convention.

VWAG explains that, as a practical matter, VWoA was certain to transmit the complaint to Germany to notify VWAG of the litigation. Indeed, as a legal matter, the Due Process Clause requires every method of service to provide "notice reasonably calculated, under all the circumstances, to apprise interested parties of the pendency of the action and afford them an opportunity to present their objections." *Mullane, supra*, at 314. VWAG argues that, because of this notice requirement, every case involving service on a foreign national will present an "occasion to transmit a judicial . . . document for service abroad" within the meaning of Article 1. VWAG emphasizes that in this case, the Appellate Court upheld service only after determining that "the relationship between VWAG and VWoA is so close that it is certain that VWAG 'was fully apprised of the pendency of the action' by delivery of the summons to VWoA." 145 Ill. App. 3d, at 606, 503 N.E.2d, at 1053 (quoting Maunder v. DeHavilland Aircraft of Canada, Ltd., 102 Ill.2d 342, 353, 466 N.E.2d 217, 223, cert. denied, 469 U.S. 1036 (1984)).

We reject this argument. Where service on a domestic agent is valid and complete under both state law and the Due Process Clause, our inquiry ends and the Convention has no further implications. Whatever internal, private communications take place between the agent and a foreign principal are beyond the concerns of this case. The only transmittal to which the Convention applies is a transmittal abroad that is required as a necessary part of service. And, contrary to VWAG's assertion, the Due Process Clause does not require an official transmittal of documents abroad every time there is service on a foreign national. Applying this analysis, we conclude that this case does not present an occasion to transmit a judicial document for service abroad within the meaning of Article 1. Therefore the Hague Service Convention does not apply, and service was proper. The judgment of the Appellate Court is

Affirmed.

JUSTICE BRENNAN, with whom JUSTICE MARSHALL and JUSTICE BLACKMUN join, concurring in the judgment.

We acknowledged last Term, and the Court reiterates today, that the terms of the Convention on Service Abroad * * * are "mandatory," not "optional" with respect to any transmission that Article 1 covers. Société Nationale Industrielle Aérospatiale v. United States District Court, 482 U.S. 522, 534, and n.15 (1987). Even so, the Court holds, and I agree, that a litigant may, consistent with the Convention, serve process on a foreign corporation by serving its wholly owned domestic subsidiary, because such process is not "service abroad" within the meaning of Article 1. The Court reaches that conclusion, however, by depriving the Convention of any mandatory effect, for in the Court's view the "forum's internal law" defines conclusively whether a particular process is "service abroad," which is covered by the Convention, or domestic service, which is not. I do not join the Court's opinion because I find it implausible that the Convention's framers intended to leave each contracting nation, and each of the 50 States within our Nation, free to decide for itself under what circumstances, if any, the Convention would control. Rather, in my view, the words "service abroad," read in light of the negotiating history, embody a substantive standard that limits a forum's latitude to deem service complete domestically.

The first of two objectives enumerated in the Convention's preamble is "to create appropriate means to ensure that judicial . . . documents to be served abroad shall be brought to the notice of the addressee in sufficient time . . . ." * * * Until the Convention was implemented, the contracting nations followed widely divergent practices for serving judicial documents across international borders, some of which did not ensure any notice, much less timely notice, and therefore often produced unfair default judgments. * * * Particularly controversial was a procedure, common among civil-law countries, called *"notification au parquet,"* which permitted delivery of process to a local official who was then ordinarily supposed to transmit the document abroad through diplomatic or other channels. * * * Typically, service was deemed complete upon delivery of the document to the official whether or not the official succeeded in transmitting it to the defendant and whether or not the defendant otherwise received notice of the pending lawsuit.

The United States delegation to the Convention objected to *notification au parquet* as inconsistent with "the requirements of 'due process of law' under the Federal Constitution." * * * The head of the delegation has derided its "'[i]njustice, extravagance, [and] absurdity . . . .'" Amram 651 (citation omitted). In its classic formulation, he observed, *notification au parquet* "'totally sacrificed all rights of the defense in favor of the plaintiff.'" * * * The Convention's official reporter noted similar "'spirited criticisms of the system' . . . which we wish to see eliminated." * * *

In response to this and other concerns, the Convention prescribes the exclusive means for service of process emanating from one contracting nation and culminating in another. As the Court observes, the Convention applies only when the document is to be "transmit[ted] . . . for service abroad"; it covers not every transmission of judicial documents abroad, but only those transmissions abroad that constitute formal "service." It is common ground that the Convention governs when the procedure prescribed by the internal law of the forum nation or state provides that service is not complete until the document is transmitted abroad. That is not to say, however, as does the Court, that the forum nation may designate any type of service "domestic" and thereby avoid application of the Convention.

Admittedly, as the Court points out, the Convention's language does not prescribe a precise standard to distinguish between "domestic" service and "service abroad." But the Court's solution leaves contracting nations free to ignore its terms entirely, converting its command into exhortation. Under the Court's analysis, for example, a forum nation could prescribe direct mail service to any foreigner and deem service effective upon deposit in the mailbox, or could arbitrarily designate a domestic agent for any foreign defendant and deem service complete upon receipt domestically by the agent even though there is little likelihood that service would ever reach the defendant. In fact, so far as I can tell, the Court's interpretation permits any contracting nation to revive *notification au parquet* so long as the nation's internal law deems service complete domestically, even though, as the Court concedes, "such methods of service are the least likely to provide a defendant with actual notice," and even though "[t]here is no question but that the Conference wanted to eliminate *notification au parquet*," (citation omitted).

The Court adheres to this interpretation, which (in the Court's words) "does not necessarily advance" the primary purpose that the Convention itself announces, notwithstanding its duty to read the Convention "with a view to effecting the objects and purposes of the States thereby contracting." Rocca v. Thompson, 223 U.S. 317, 331-332 (1912). * * * Even assuming any quantum of evidence from the negotiating history would suffice to support an interpretation so fundamentally at odds with the Convention's primary purpose, the evidence the Court amasses in support of its reading—two interim comments by the reporter on initial drafts of the Convention suggesting that the forum's internal law would dictate whether a particular form of service implicates the Convention—falls far short.

In the first place, the reporter's comments were by no means uncontroversial. One participant, for example, directly challenged the "report['s] allusion . . . to the danger that the court hearing the proceeding could decide that there were no grounds for service," and observed that "[n]ow, the preamble of [the] draft specifies the objective of the convention, which is to ensure the service of writs to persons in foreign countries in order *to guarantee that these persons will have knowledge of them*." 3 Actes et Documents 165 (United Kingdom delegate) (emphasis added). In fact, the delegates considered a version of Article 1 explicitly prescribing that the Convention's scope would be defined "'according to the law of the petitioning state,'" id., at 167 (quoting proposal of Yugoslavian delegate), but rejected the proposal at least in part "because it would allow [domestic] law to determine the cases in which transmission is not obligatory." Ibid. (Italian delegate).

If the delegates did not resolve their differences upon tabling the proposal, they apparently did by the time the official reporter issued his Rapport Explicatif. This final report, which presumably supersedes all interim comments, stresses "the opinion of the Third Commission [that] the Convention was 'obligatory,'" making no reference to internal law. 3 Actes et Documents 366. By way of example, the Rapport acknowledges that a literal reading of the Convention might raise doubts as to the Convention's coverage of *notification au parquet*, yet announces the understanding of the drafting commission that the Convention would prohibit such service. Thus, reading Article 1 "'in the liberal spirit in which it is intended[,] to address "'the hardship and injustice, which [the Convention] seeks to relieve,'" id., at 367, the Rapport interprets the Convention to impose a substantive standard proscribing *notification au parquet* whether the forum nation deems the service "domestic" or "abroad." That substantive standard is captured in the Rapport's admonition that

> "'[a]ll of the transmission channels (prescribed by the convention) *must have as a consequence the fact that the act reach the addressee in due time*. That is a requirement of justice, which assumes its full importance when the act to be transmitted is an act instituting proceedings.'" Ibid. (translation) (footnote omitted; emphasis added).

The Court belittles the Rapport's significance by presuming that the reporter assumed, as a matter of the internal law of the various nations then permitting *notification au parquet*, that such service always required transmission abroad, and therefore would always have been deemed "service abroad." But the above-cited passage purports to interpret the Convention, not to survey the various forms of *notification au parquet* then prevalent, and does not so much as hint at the possibility that *notification au parquet* might continue if the domestic law of a forum nation were to deem it "domestic." Moreover, the assumption that the Court imputes to the Rapport is inaccurate; as noted above, *notification au parquet* was typically deemed complete upon delivery to the local official. Any requirement of transmission abroad was no more essential to formal service than is the informal arrangement by which a domestic subsidiary might transmit documents served on it as an agent for its foreign parent. See, e.g., 3 Actes et Documents 169. Thus, if the Court entertains the possibility that the Convention bans *notification au parquet* under all circumstances, it can only be because (notwithstanding the Court's stated analysis) the Convention, read in light of its negotiating history, sets some substantive limit on the forum state's latitude to deem such service "domestic."

Significantly, our own negotiating delegation, whose contemporaneous views are "entitled to great weight," *Société Nationale*, 482 U.S., at 536, n.19, took seriously the Rapport's conclusion that the Convention is more than just precatory. The delegation's report applauded the Convention as "mak[ing] substantial changes in the practices of many of the civil law countries, moving their practices in the direction of the U.S. approach to international judicial assistance *and* our concepts of due process in the service of process." S. Exec. Doc. C, at 20 (emphasis added). The delegation's chief negotiator emphasized that "the convention sets up the minimum standards of international judicial assistance which each country which ratifies the convention *must* offer to all others who ratify." S. Exec. Rep. No. 6, at 13 (statement by Philip W. Amram) (emphasis in original). Then-Secretary of State Rusk reiterated the same point, as did the State Department's Deputy Legal Advisor, and President Johnson. The repeated references to "due process" were not, of course, intended to suggest that every contracting nation submitted itself to the intricacies of our constitutional jurisprudence. Rather, they were shorthand formulations of the requirement, common to both due process and the Convention, that process directed on a party abroad should be designed so that the documents "reach the addressee in due time," 3 Actes et Documents 367.

The negotiating history and the uniform interpretation announced by our own negotiators confirm that the Convention limits a forum's ability to deem service "domestic," thereby avoiding the Convention's terms. Admittedly, the Convention does not precisely define the contours. But that imprecision does not absolve us of our responsibility to apply the Convention mandatorily, any more than imprecision permits us to discard the words "due process of law," U.S. Const. Amdt. 14, 1. And however difficult it might be in some circumstances to discern the Convention's precise limits, it is remarkably easy to conclude that the Convention does not prohibit the type of service at issue here. Service on a wholly owned, closely controlled subsidiary is reasonably calculated to reach the parent "in due time" as the Convention requires. * * * That is, in fact, what our own Due Process Clause requires, see Mullane v. Central Hanover Bank & Trust Co., 339 U.S. 306, 314-315 (1950), and since long before the Convention's implementation our law has permitted such service, see, e. g., Perkins v. Benguet Consolidated Mining Co., 342 U.S. 437, 444-445 (1952); Latimer v. S/A Industrias Reunidas F. Matarazzo, 175 F.2d 184, 185 (CA2 1949) (L. Hand, J.). This is significant because our own negotiators made clear to the Senate their understanding that the Convention would require no major changes in federal or state service-of-process rules. Thus, it is unsurprising that nothing in the negotiating history suggests that the contracting nations were dissatisfied with the practice at issue here, of which they were surely aware, much less that they intended to abolish it like they intended to abolish *notification au parquet*. And since notice served on a wholly owned domestic subsidiary is infinitely more likely to reach the foreign parent's attention than was notice served *au parquet* (or by any other procedure that the negotiators singled out for criticism) there is no reason to interpret the Convention to bar it.

My difference with the Court does not affect the outcome of this case, and, given that any process emanating from our courts must comply with due process, it may have little practical consequence in future cases that come before us. But cf. S. Exec. Rep. No. 6, at 15 (statement by Philip W. Amram suggesting that Convention may require "a minor change in the practice of some of our States in long-arm and automobile accident cases" where "service on the appropriate official need be accompanied only by a minimum effort to notify the defendant"). Our Constitution does not, however, bind other nations haling our citizens into their courts. Our citizens rely instead primarily on the forum nation's compliance with the Convention, which the Senate believed would "provide increased protection (due process) for American Citizens who are involved in litigation abroad." Id., at 3. And while other nations are not bound by the Court's pronouncement that the Convention lacks obligatory force, after today's decision their courts will surely sympathize little with any United States national pleading that a judgment violates the Convention because (notwithstanding any local characterization) service was "abroad."

It is perhaps heartening to "think that [no] countr[y] will draft its internal laws deliberately so as to circumvent the Convention in cases in which it would be appropriate to transmit judicial documents for service abroad," although from the defendant's perspective "circumvention" (which, according to the Court, entails no more than exercising a prerogative not to be bound) is equally painful whether deliberate or not. The fact remains, however, that had we been content to rely on foreign notions of fair play and substantial justice, we would have found it unnecessary, in the first place, to participate in a Convention "to ensure that judicial . . . documents to be served abroad [would] be brought to the notice of the addressee in sufficient time," 20 U.S.T., at 362.

NOTES AND QUESTIONS FOR DISCUSSION

1. Should the applicability of a treaty (like the Convention) be premised on domestic (U.S.) notions of when "service abroad" is called for? *Schlunk* states that some standard must govern, that the treaty itself does not provide one, and therefore forum law must apply. Is the Court persuasive in rejecting the suggestion of the concurrence that the standard should be one that the courts ought to develop as part of their effort to construe the Convention? Does the Convention provide no limits on local creativity to provide for service on the foreign defendant locally rather than abroad? What about notions of comity among nations? Cf. Société Nationale Industrielle Aérospatiale v. U.S. District Court, 482 U.S. 522 (1987) (noting role of international comity in application of Hague Evidence Convention) (*Aérospatiale* is discussed in Chapter 6).

2. Note that even if the Convention, or comity, or notions of federal common law, all fail to impose limits on a forum's ability to determine whether "service abroad" is called for (thus triggering the Convention), due process is also a limit. Is it odd that U.S. due process might impose a limit on whether service abroad is implicated under the Hague Convention, but the Convention itself might not?

3. As previously noted in both *Bankston* and *Brockmeyer*, the Supreme Court in *Schlunk* concludes that the Hague Service Convention provides the exclusive means of service when the Convention is applicable (which it was not, in *Schlunk* itself). Is that a necessary reading of the Convention? Because the Convention is a treaty, it is supreme law applicable to the state courts, not just the federal courts, and because it is exclusive when applicable, it is preemptive of state law, not just contrary federal law. As noted in the preceding section, however, to the extent that Article 10(a) of the Convention is read to allow for service of process by mail, domestic methods of service are in fact *not* preempted even when the Convention applies.

4. *Schlunk* involved a state law that allowed for service on a foreign corporation by through service on its domestic subsidiary as its "involuntary agent" for service of process. Different states will have different laws regarding when service on a subsidiary, or alter ego, or agent of a corporation is appropriate. And *Schlunk* seems to allow states a lot of flexibility in achieving domestic service, thereby enabling them to avoid the Convention. In addition, a plaintiff in a federal court can take advantage of state law methods of service so long as the method does not require service abroad as a matter of state law (and assuming such service is consistent with due process). See Rule 4(e)(1) (incorporating state service rules as a permissible option in suits against individuals); Rule 4(h)(1)(A) (incorporating Rule 4(e)(1) in suits against business entities, including corporations).

5. When it comes to corporations that are doing business in a state, states often make a particular state official the agent for service of process in suits arising out of that conduct. And just as often, the state official will forward a copy of the summons and complaint to the foreign defendant. Does such service avoid the "service abroad" requirement for the Convention to apply? Does it matter whether, under state law, such service is considered to be complete at the time it reaches the official as opposed to being complete only upon the sending of the documents abroad? See Fleming v. Yamaha Motor Corp., USA, 774 F. Supp. 992 (W.D. Va. 1991) (concluding that because "under Virginia law" substituted service on state officer was not "completed" until documents were forwarded abroad directly to the foreign corporation, the Convention was applicable). Even if it is supposed that the Convention is implicated in such circumstances, is there an argument that Article 10(a) would allow such service anyway? See Conax Florida Corp. v. Astrium, Ltd., 499 F. Supp. 2d 1287, 1292-93 (M.D. Fla. 2007) (so indicating). What about Rule 4(h)(2)?

6. By indicating what sort of process may be permissible when the Hague Convention does not apply, *Schlunk* sheds light on what will happen if service is sought in a country that is not a party to the Convention (or to any other convention to which the U.S. is a party). In cases filed in state courts, service may be made by any constitutional means available in the forum state. And for cases filed in federal court against foreign individuals, it means that Rule 4(f)(2) (or, for foreign corporations, Rule 4(h)(2), which largely incorporates (f)(2)'s service provisions for foreign individuals) is triggered, as an independent set of service rules when no international agreement is applicable. And Rule 4(f)(3)—a court-ordered method of service—is available whether or not there is an international agreement, although the Rule is qualified by the proviso that such service cannot be a method "prohibited by international agreement."

7. Another internationally agreed means of service that American and international lawyers may encounter is the Inter-American Service Convention on Letter Rogatory, to which the U.S. is a party. (For text of the Convention, see http://www.oas.org/juridico/english/treaties/b-36.html.) Its members include a number of members from the Organization of American States, including various Central and South American countries. These countries are, for the most part, not signatories to the Hague Service Convention. Its goals, however, are similar to those of the Hague Service Convention insofar as it creates a uniform set of procedures for service. And like the Hague Convention, it is limited to civil litigation and commercial matters. In addition, the Convention provides that each member state set up a central authority to which requests for service can be made. Unlike the Hague Convention, however, courts have suggested that the Inter-American Service Convention (IASC) is not the exclusive mechanism for service as between signatory countries. See, e.g., Russell Brands, LLC v. GVD Int'l Trading, S.A., 282 F.R.D. 21 (D. Mass. 2012) (noting authority). There are also other formalities applicable to the IASC that are not required under the Hague Convention. And it is unclear whether service may be made by mail under the IASC , which fails to make provision for such service.

NOTE ON SERVICE OF PROCESS WITHIN THE E.U.

Effecting service of process in transnational litigation within the European Union is governed by a Regulation that is binding on all EU Member States, except Denmark. Regulation (EC) No 1393/2007 of the European Parliament and of the Council of 13 November 2007 on the service in the Member States of judicial and extrajudicial documents in civil or commercial matters (service of documents), and repealing Council Regulation (EC) No 1348/2000 (*Official Journal L 324, 10/12/2007 P. 0079-0120*).

Compared with the Hague Service Convention, there are several differences. For example, Article 14 of the Regulation, provides that "[e]ach Member State shall be free to effect service of judicial documents directly by postal services on persons residing in another Member State by registered letter with acknowledgement of receipt or equivalent." Unlike the Hague Service Convention which permits its members to object to this type of service (according to Art. 10(a) of the Convention), the EU-Regulation does not provide a right to object. What could be the reason(s) for unqualifiedly permitting service by mail within Europe? Furthermore, the documents to be served need not be translated under the Regulation. The recipient, however, has the right to refuse acceptance of untranslated documents, under Article 8 of the Regulation. Also in contrast to Article 13 of the Hague Service Convention which entitles member states to refuse judicial assistance on grounds of public policy (see discussion below), the Regulation contains no such public policy exception in favor of the states where service is to be completed.

E. SERVICE IN VIOLATION OF FOREIGN LAW

1. *Introduction*

As noted above, it is possible that service abroad on a foreign defendant may be consistent with federal or state law and yet violate foreign law. Under the Hague Convention, of course, service through a foreign country's central authority will typically not raise such problems, because service is accomplished either pursuant to, or in a means not inconsistent with, that country's law. But even if the Convention is applicable such conflict may still arise—for example, in seeking to accomplish service by mail under Article 10(a) in a country that has not objected to 10(a), but which nevertheless rejects certain forms of service that

10(a) might allow. And, under Article 13, even if a request for service complies with the Convention, the addressed state may refuse to comply if it concludes that service will "infringe its sovereignty or security."

In addition to creating friction between countries, service in violation of foreign law can produce various sorts of adverse fallout. As discussed further below, many countries—particularly civil law countries—consider service of process to involve a governmental act, which generally can only be accomplished by officials from that country. Attempts at service in violation of foreign country law might therefore trigger diplomatic protests. Some countries allow for a means by which service can be quashed in their own courts, and others have criminalized private service of process taking place on their soil. See Swiss Penal Code, Art. 271. In addition, while a domestic (U.S.) judgment may be unassailable domestically because of compliance with American service provisions, there may be problems down the road if recognition and enforcement of a U.S. judgment is sought in the country whose service laws have been violated. The Restatement (Third) of Foreign Relations Law of the United States § 471(1) (1987) captures this notion: "Under international law, a state may determine the conditions for service of process in its territory in aid of litigation in another state, but the state where the litigation is pending may determine the effect of such service."

Since the time of revisions to Rule 4 made in 1993, much (but not all) of federal court practice builds-in a requirement that service abroad not run afoul of foreign country law. Compare Umbenhauer v. Woog, 969 F.2d 25, 32-33 (3d Cir. 1992) (stating that service of process under Rule 4—prior to its 1993 amendments—was valid, even when it violated Swiss law). Look again at Rule 4(f), above. Section (f)(1) states that service may be made pursuant to international agreement if such agreement exists. Section (f)(2) provides various modes of service when there is no such agreement, but only if those modes of service do not violate foreign law—the law of the country in which service is made. However, section (f)(3) allows for service "by other means not prohibited by international agreement, as the court orders." Rule 4(f)(3) thus provides a wide-ranging discretionary mechanism by which the district judge may order service in various ways not mentioned elsewhere in Rule 4. As noted in *Brockmeyer*, courts have made creative use of the Rule, authorizing service by fax, by email, by ordinary mail, and by publication. There appears to be no qualification under (f)(3) that service must not be in violation of foreign law; only a requirement that it not be in violation of an international agreement (nor, presumably, the U.S. Constitution or federal law). Thus, it is theoretically possible that service authorized under the federal rules may violate foreign country law. Rio Properties, Inc. v. Rio International Interlink, 284 F.3d 1007, 1014 (9th Cir. 2002) (so noting). Indeed, most (but not all) courts have concluded that Rule 4(f)(3) is not a rule of "last resort," available only when other means have failed. Id. at 1015 ("By all indications, court-directed service under Rule 4(f)(3) is as favored as service available under Rule 4(f)(1) or Rule 4(f)(2)."). In addition, state courts may have service rules of their own that are not constrained by non-violation of foreign law.

To be sure, and as discussed further below, there are canons of statutory construction that aim to interpret ambiguous statutes in such a way as not to run afoul of customary international law. See, e.g., Murray v. The Schooner Charming Betsy, 6 U.S. (2 Cranch) 64 (1806). But it may not be very easy to read into Rule 4(f)(3) an implied requirement of non-violation of foreign law, because the Rule was elsewhere very clear about when it wanted service not to be violative of foreign law. But see Prewitt Enters., Inc. v. OPEC, 353 F.3d 916, 928 (11th Cir. 2003) (construing Rule 4(f)(3) so as to "minimize offense to foreign law"). Of course, as a practical matter, it might be hard to get a federal court to rely on Rule 4(f)(3) if other means seem readily available, especially if the means at issue would be violative of foreign law. And the Advisory Committee Note to Fed. R. Civ. P. 4(f)(2) (which, unlike (f)(3), *does* have an express requirement that service under its provisions not violate foreign law) states generally that "service by methods that would violate foreign law is not generally authorized." Moreover, American courts will not be eager to provide for service through a means that will inevitably put any judgment in doubt, thus wasting their time and effort.

2. *Article 13 of the Hague Service Convention*

As indicated above, Article 13 of the Hague Service Convention provides, among other things, that "[w]here a request for service complies with the terms of the present Convention, the State addressed may refuse to comply therewith only if it deems that compliance would infringe its sovereignty or security." While it is undisputed that the limits of "sovereignty" and "security" may only be invoked as last resort in extreme cases which threaten these values, it is unclear exactly under which circumstance service of process actually poses such a threat. On several occasions, the German Federal Constitutional Court has been called upon to decide whether the service of process of U.S. complaints containing claims for punitive damages would constitute a violation of Article 13. Consider the decision by the 1st Senate of that Court below. Although this decision does not involve service of process in a manner that is violative of foreign law, it still implicates a potential ground for illegality of service within the meaning of Article 13.

Proceedings Concerning the Constitutional Complaint of L. . . . GmbH [sic]

German Federal Constitutional Court, 1994.

34 I.L.M. 986.

The Constitutional Complaint is dismissed. *Grounds:*

A:

The constitutional complaint concerns the question of whether a complaint may be served by way of judicial assistance, in accordance with which a claim is to be made against a legal person under German law in a court of the United States of America for, *inter alia,* punitive or exemplary damages.

I

1. The Petitioner, a limited liability company with its seat in Berlin, has a subsidiary company in the United States of America which is incorporated under American law. This subsidiary concluded a distribution agreement for pharmaceutical products with Traditional Medicinals Inc. The latter initiated proceedings before a court in Pittsburgh, Pennsylvania, against both the American subsidiary of the Petitioner and the Petitioner itself regarding differences arising out of the distribution relationship. The action seeks not only compensation for material damages of at least US $2 million, but also the awarding of "punitive and exemplary damages".

The action has been served on the subsidiary; service on the Petitioner in the United States was unsuccessful. The American counsel of Traditional Medicinals Inc. then sent its complaint to the Governmental Administration for Justice [Senatsverwaltung für Justiz] in Berlin and requested that it serve the action on the Petitioner under the terms of the Hague Convention of 15 November 1965 on Service Abroad of Judicial and Extrajudicial Documents in Civil or Commercial Matters.

The Governmental Administration for Justice approved the requested judicial assistance and forwarded the Complaint to the * * * Local Court for further action.

2. The Petitioner applied * * * to the Berlin Court of Appeal for the order of the Governmental Administration to be lifted. The Berlin Court of Appeal rejected this application by the order which has been challenged by the constitutional complaint, for the following reasons:

> The Hague Convention is applicable. An action by which, *inter alia,* "punitive damages" are being claimed has as its object a claim to payment under civil law. There are no grounds for refusal under Article 13(1) of the Hague Convention. Even if in the view of the Court, a judgment awarding "punitive damages" could normally not be recognized and declared enforceable in accordance with the jurisprudence of the Federal Supreme Court, it does not follow that German authorities may not even assist in the service of such actions. In case of defeat, enforcement may indeed be effected against the assets of the German defendant located in the United States of America. Seizure of the German defendant's assets in Germany may, however, still be prevented at a later stage if it is established whether, in what amount, and on what legal basis damages have been awarded against the defendant. Anyone becoming active in international business must accept the risk that enforcement may be had against its assets located within the area of territorial application of a foreign legal system by such foreign legal system. A comprehensive and lengthy study of the legal arguments in the document to be served contradicts, in the view of the Court, the sense and purpose of the Hague Convention, which are to simplify and accelerate

the process of mutual judicial assistance. Furthermore, the amount of punitive damages is, as a rule, not quantified in a complaint. Mere assumptions about a possible future decision of the foreign court should not, however, cause service to be refused. This is, in the view of the Court, also foreign to German legal concepts. The service of a complaint is not dependent upon investigations into the background, reason, or justification of the action.

II

1.(a). By its constitutional complaint the Petitioner challenges a violation of its civil rights under Article 2(1) of the German Basic Law [Grundgesetz] in connection with the principle of the rule of law.

The grounds for refusal under Article 13(1) of the Hague Convention represent, in the view of the Petitioner, a special form of public policy. Actions may not be served which violate important principles of freedom and democracy in a State under the rule of law within the meaning of the Basic Law. The Berlin Court of Appeal did not, in the view of the Petitioner, deal with the fact that the legal institution of "punitive damages" fundamentally violates federal German legal conceptions of the rule of law as expressed in the principle of proportionality and the State's monopoly on punishment. The German authorities may not assist in a sovereign proceeding, the declared intention of which is a judgment that fundamentally contradicts the German principle of the rule of law. They should not even grant judicial assistance in respect to initiation of the action. In the absence of service of the complaint, the proceedings in the United States of America cannot begin.

2. The Federal Ministry of Justice, which has commented on behalf of the Federal Government, considers the Constitutional Complaint to be unfounded.

It argues that the intended service of documents is within the bounds of the constitutional order. An action in which punitive damages are sought has as its object a claim for payment under civil law. The amount of the sum sued for is not important in respect of the question of carrying out the service. Sovereign rights or the security of the Federal Republic of Germany would not be endangered by the service of such a complaint. Service may not, in the view of the Ministry of Justice, be refused based on the public policy [ordre public] of the State executing the service, which principle is also in line with the principle of proportionality [Verhältnismäßigkeitsgrundsatz].

A general refusal to serve actions for punitive damages would endanger the consensus existing within the USA regarding the exclusivity of the Hague Convention on the Service Abroad of Documents. The German Federal Government has, argues the Ministry of Justice, repeatedly insisted on this exclusivity, not least because of the provisions set out in the Convention for the protection of those upon whom documents are served in Germany. * * *

B:

The Constitutional Complaint is admissible, but unfounded. The Petitioner's civil right under Article 2(1) of the Basic Law in connection with the principle of the rule of law are not violated by the order under appeal, which holds the approval of judicial assistance (service of the Complaint) by the Governmental Administration to be lawful. * * *

II

1. There is no need for us to decide whether service of process intrudes on the area protected by Article 2(1) of the Basic Law or is to be measured only against the requirements derived from the State's duty of protection, because the constitutional requirements for intrusion are satisfied here, and in any case no stricter standards follow from the duty of protection.

Service is a sovereign act of the State by which foreign court proceedings are assisted. The recipient of the service is neither required to cease a certain action nor prohibited from certain conduct. It must, however, submit to the foreign proceedings if it does not wish to suffer legal disadvantages which it could possibly avoid by active participation in the proceedings. It is also exposed to the risk of a judgment, which can lead to enforcement against its assets located abroad without the German authorities being able to protect it against this.

2. Even if this is seen as an intrusion, it is, however, compatible with Article 2(1) of the Basic Law.

(a) The legal basis for service is the Convention of 15 November 1965 on the Service Abroad of Judicial and Extrajudicial Documents in Civil or Commercial Matters * * *, hereinafter the Hague Convention. There are no objections to the Convention's constitutionality, insofar as this is relevant to the issues in this case. The Convention is intended, according to its Preamble, to ensure that judicial and extrajudicial documents to be served abroad are brought to the attention of their recipients in a timely fashion. It is also intended to improve mutual judicial assistance among the signatory countries by simplifying and accelerating the technicalities of service. The Convention thereby serves important interests of the common good which justify intrusion into general freedom of action.

The statutory provision also does not violate the principle of proportionality, since service may not in principle be refused simply because of the incompatibility of the plaintiffs claim with the internal public policy of the State, but only if the State requested to carry out the service considers that such service would endanger its sovereignty or security (cf. Article 13 of the Hague Convention). This restriction on the authority to examine the action to be served is justified because of the goal of the Convention. If the principles of the internal legal order were set as the standard for service, then the flow of international judicial assistance would be significantly hindered. Examination of complaints for their compatibility with internal public policy would on the one hand lead to long delays in carrying out service, and on the other hand would amount to the extension of domestic legal concepts to other countries and run contrary to the goal of facilitating proceedings abroad by a foreign plaintiff against a domestic defendant. Such a restriction on the flow of judicial assistance is fundamentally all the less necessary insofar as the outcome of the proceedings is, at the time of service, still completely open.

In addition, it must be considered that the Hague Convention decidedly improves the legal position of parties with a registered office or domicile in Germany who are involved in a civil dispute in one of the other signatory countries, by ensuring that these parties cannot become involved in civil proceedings abroad of which they have no knowledge.

In connection with the signing of the Convention, it was expected that the signatory countries would withdraw any methods of domestic service on foreigners still existing under their national law and not excluded by the Convention, for example, the possibility of "public service", the admissibility of which is dependent solely on the circumstance that the party to be served has its registered office or domicile abroad. Insofar as service abroad upon foreigners is necessary under national law, the Convention ensures that the foreign party is served with the complaint in such a way as to guarantee its being given a fair hearing. As understood by all signatories, at any rate by the Federal Republic of Germany and the USA, the Convention excludes the possibility of forms of service abroad other than those envisaged therein being effective, such as the sending of a complaint by registered mail, which is permissible under American law. The Federal Republic of Germany was previously unable to prevent US courts from treating as effective service made in this way on parties in Germany, with the consequence that a judgment could be rendered against them.

Conversely, service in accordance with the Hague Convention offers a better guarantee that a German party can defend itself effectively against the action. Service must generally be effected in a form stipulated under the law of the requested State for service of documents drawn up in its sovereign territory upon persons who are within its territory (Article 5(1) a of the Hague Convention); accordingly, a foreign complaint must be served in the Federal Republic of Germany in accordance with the provisions of the Code of Civil Procedure [Zivilprozeflordrning or ZPO] with regard to service to be effected *ex officio* (§ 208 ZPO). If the document has to be served formally, it must be written in German or translated into German (Article 5(3) of the Hague Convention in connection with § 3 of the Implementation Law [Ausführungsgesetz]. * * *

(b) Whether service of an action would even then be compatible with Article 2(1) of the Basic Law in association with the principle of the rule of law, if the aim of a complaint would clearly violate non-derogable principles of a free, democratic State under the rule of law, for instance as incorporated in international human rights conventions, does not require any basic clarification here. The service of an action by means of which, *inter alia,* punitive or exemplary damages are sought under the law of the United States of America is in any case not unreasonable [unzumutbar].

(aa) Punitive damages under American law are, it is true, foreign to the German system of civil law sanctions. They are awarded if the defendant not only fulfills the requirements of general liability, but has in addition demonstrated intentional, malicious, or reckless misconduct * * *.

The awarding of punitive damages pursues various aims. The main aim is punishment and deterrence; the party liable is punished for reckless conduct, partly so that acts of revenge by the victim are avoided. Punitive damages are also supposed to deter from future anti-social behaviour, insofar as the duty to compensate the damage or loss actually suffered is not deemed sufficient to guide behaviour. The injured party is also supposed to be rewarded for upholding the legal order by its efforts, which reinforces the rule of law in general. In addition, the victim is supposed to receive a supplement to compensation for damages which would otherwise be inadequate. A lack of social protection for the injured party also plays a role here. It is further taken into consideration in this connection whether the injuring party has refused to cooperate in compensating the damage or loss and therefore additional compensation is to be awarded to the injured party * * *. Finally, the fact that American law governing litigation costs awards costs even to the prevailing party only in exceptional cases may be taken into consideration in awarding punitive damages. With the aid of punitive damages, the costs of an injured party who prevails can also be shifted to the injuring party.

(bb) Whether the opinion of the Federal Supreme Court that punitive damages are a sanction which falls within the State's monopoly on punishment * * * is binding as a matter of constitutional law need not be decided here. Even the Federal Supreme Court acknowledges that punitive damages can partly serve ends which are compatible with the legal order of the Federal Republic of Germany. Non-derogable principles of the free State under the rule of law are, in any case, not violated by the mere possibility that punitive damages may be awarded. It also cannot be ignored in this connection that intangible damages can be compensated by means of punitive damages, a concept which is not alien to the German law of damages, and that compensation for litigation costs likewise does not in itself violate German public policy * * *.

Moreover, service has the effect at most of threatening the financial interests of the defendant. Although it becomes a party to the proceedings, whether it will actually be ordered to pay punitive damages emerges only at the end of the proceedings when the judgment is handed down. A German defendant can in these proceedings seek to have the complaint dismissed. Involvement in foreign proceedings by virtue of the service of documents can all the more reasonably be expected of it, as it can prevent seizure of its domestic assets by a foreign creditor under the conditions set forth in § 328(1) No. 4 ZPO * * *.

In addition, even a refusal of service would not guarantee an improvement in the legal position of a German defendant, since a domestic defendant would not be protected against being made a party to the action anyway by an American plaintiff. As already mentioned, foreign proceedings can be carried on according to Article 15(2) of the Hague Convention even without proof of service. Also, the opinion is held under American law that service upon an American subsidiary of a German parent company can be made simultaneously upon the latter (Volkswagen AG vs. Schlunk). The Hague Convention does not in any case exclude the possibility of serving in Germany by way of judicial assistance an action in which only compensatory damages are claimed initially, and, if the German defendant uses an attorney in the USA to defend itself against this action, an amended complaint for punitive damages is then validly served upon this attorney. * * *

Finally, it must be taken into consideration that the possibilities for the Federal Republic of Germany to guarantee domestic parties a form of service in relation to the United States of America which ensures their chances of effective participation would be seriously impaired if the service of such actions were to be refused.

NOTES AND QUESTIONS FOR DISCUSSION

1. The 1st Senate of the German Constitutional Court (Bundesverfassungsgericht) acknowledged that American punitive damages awards may violate German constitutional principles and may thus not be enforceable in Germany if recognition and enforcement of an American verdict is sought in Germany. (See Chapter 8.) However, the court distinguished between judicial assistance aimed at effecting service of process—which it held to be acceptable even if the foreign claim was for punitive damages—and the recognition and enforcement of a final decision through German courts. What explains the distinction?

2. Prior to the decision excerpted above, the petitioner had applied for and the Federal Constitutional Court had granted an ex parte temporary order pursuant to which service of process of the American complaint was halted on grounds of Article 13 of the Convention. Among other things, the Court stated that: "If the temporary order is not granted, and the granting of judicial assistance in the main proceedings proves conversely to be unconstitutional, then the Federal Constitutional Court must, as far as is known at present, assume that the Petitioner has effectively become a party in the action before the American court." (34 I.L.M. 980, 985 (1995)). It was only in the main proceedings on the merits (excerpted above) that the court held service of the punitive damages complaint to be permissible under the Hague Convention.

3. In 2003, the German Federal Constitutional Court again issued a temporary order (Order of the German Federal Constitutional Court of 25 July 2003, 2 BVR 1198/03), denying service of process of a complaint in a U.S. class action lawsuit against the German media publisher Bertelsmann AG in Germany for having provided financial backing to Napster when it operated as an illegal file-sharing service. The Court rested its temporary order on the (constitutional) argument that the U.S. class action claims of up to $17 billion in punitive damages could conceivably imperil Bertelsmann's rights under the German constitution. See Bettina Friedrich, *Federal Constitutional Court Grants Interim Protection Against Service of a Writ of Punitive Damages Suit*, 4 German L.J. 1233 (2003). The Court never finally decided on the merits whether to lift or confirm this order because the parties eventually settled the lawsuit.

4. For many years, a considerable risk for U.S. parties has been service of process in violation of Swiss law. Swiss Penal Code Art. 271 currently provides:

> Whoever, without being authorized, performs acts for a foreign state on Swiss territory that are reserved to an authority or an official, whoever performs for a foreign party or another foreign organization, whoever aids and abets such acts, shall be punished with imprisonment for up to

three years or a monetary penalty, in serious cases with imprisonment for not less than one year. [Translation.]

The Swiss apparently consider a summons from a U.S. court to be an act attributable to a governmental authority, and execution of that act (i.e., service of the summons) implicates Art. 271. The statute expresses the sentiment that service of process is an official act in the country in which service is made, to be performed by officials of that country alone. Perhaps the thinking is purely territorialist: Governmental actors and agents of one jurisdiction ordinarily lack power in another. And just as the sheriff of one county cannot serve process in another, only the officials of the state in which service is to be made may serve process. In addition, perhaps service by local officials is more likely to be done in a manner that does not otherwise run afoul of local policy. Other countries, such as France and Germany have similar sorts of objections to international service on their soil by private actors, albeit without the sanctions of the Swiss. All of this is seems to be consistent with the Restatement (Third) of Foreign Relations Law of the United States (1987) (see Introductory Note to Part IV, Chapter 7, Section A): "[A] state may not conduct official activities in the territory of another state without that state's consent, express or implied. That principle is generally applied as well to the service of judicial documents."

5. Despite these attempts at explanation, are the concerns expressed by provisions such as Article 271 convincing ones? Is service of process, for example by an international courier such as FedEx or DHL, a governmental act? In federal courts in the U.S., service of process has been greatly privatized and has all but lost its formal connection to the court under Rules that rarely require service by governmental officials or service pursuant to court order. For a classic critique of such ideas such as those embodied in Article 271, see Hans Smit, *International Co-operation in Civil Litigation*, 9 Netherlands Int'l L. Rev. 137 (1963).

6. Interestingly, the Swiss statute does not seem to have posed much of a problem lately for U.S. parties and their counsel. Perhaps it is because there are relatively few opportunities to serve in violation of foreign law under provisions such as Rule 4. And perhaps it is also because effective January 1, 1995, Switzerland joined the Hague Convention, and U.S. plaintiffs and their counsel are probably aware of what that means and requires in terms of service.

3. Statutory Construction and U.S. Service Provisions

As noted above, Rule 4(f)(3) seems to allow for service of process in a manner that might violate foreign law, so long as the manner of service does not run afoul of an international agreement to which the U.S. is a party, such as the Hague Service Convention. In addition, it is also possible that federal statutes might expressly allow for a particular form of service that runs afoul of foreign law (even if it does not run afoul of any international agreement).

The issue seems to have come up largely in connection with efforts of U.S. agencies to serve investigative subpoenas on foreign parties by means that would be clearly allowed domestically. As a general matter, "[f]ederal courts must give effect to a valid, unambiguous congressional mandate, even if such effect would conflict with another nation's law or violate international law." Commodity Futures Trading Comm'n v. Nahas, 738 F.2d 487, 494 (D.C. Cir. 1984). But the fact that Congress (or the Rules' drafters) may have the power to provide for service in violation of foreign law does not mean that courts will construe less than clear statutes to allow for such service. Consider the general statement of the problem as noted in **F.T.C. v. Compagnie de Saint-Gobain-Pont-à-Mousson, 636 F.2d 1300 (D.C. Cir. 1980):**

> This case addresses a narrow issue of broad international consequence: did Congress expressly or impliedly authorize the Federal Trade Commission (FTC or Commission) to serve its investigatory subpoenas directly upon citizens of other countries by means of registered mail? Although on the surface this question appears to rest solely upon statutory interpretation, our answer to it is primarily guided by our recognition of established and fundamental principles of international law.

> Federal courts have long acknowledged that the investigatory and regulatory reach of domestic agencies may, and often must, extend across national boundaries. This court has previously recognized that those agencies may under certain circumstances compel production of documents located abroad. We cannot, however, simply assume from these precedents that Congress intended to authorize regulatory agencies in general and the FTC in particular to employ any and all methods to serve compulsory process when conducting their investigations. When an American regulatory agency directly serves its compulsory process upon a citizen of a foreign country, the act of service itself constitutes an exercise of American sovereign power within the area of the foreign country's territorial sovereignty. Though some techniques of service may prove less obnoxious than others to foreign sensibilities, our recognition of those sensibilities must affect our willingness to infer congressional authorization for a particular mode of service from an otherwise silent statute. In the face of the foreign country's direct protest to the mode of service employed here, and in the absence of clear congressional intent at the time this subpoena was served to authorize that manner of exercise of American sovereign power, we decline to infer the necessary statutory authority for the FTC's chosen mode of subpoena service.

Id. at 1304.

How deferential to foreign law or international law should federal courts be in construing a federal statute to allow for service in violation of such law? Don't cases such as *Compagnie de Saint-Gobain* effectively impose a "clear statement" requirement before such service will be found to be authorized by a federal statute? In *Nahas, supra,* service by the Federal Trade Commission on a Brazilian citizen by "substituted service in Sao Palo, Brazil" was met with a diplomatic protest. (Apparently the FTC sent the subpoena to a Brazilian attorney whom the State Department had concluded could act as an agent for the FTC, who then delivered the subpoena to the defendant's office.) Brazilian law required that service from foreign countries be "made pursuant to letters rogatory or a letter of request transmitted through diplomatic channels." The *Nahas* court considered the protest to be strong evidence of the intrusiveness of the service on Brazilian sovereignty, which it felt ought to be minimized, absent a clearer expression of intent by Congress to allow for such service internationally.

F. SERVICE ON FOREIGN STATES, AGENCIES, AND INSTRUMENTALITIES

The substance of the Foreign Sovereign Immunities Act (FSIA) is discussed at length in Chapter 3. See also Appendix F. Service of process on foreign states, political subdivisions, agents and instrumentalities is also governed by the FSIA. See Fed. R. Civ. P., Rule 4(j)(1). The service provisions under the FSIA are applicable not only to federal courts but to state courts as well. And they are the exclusive means for service on such defendants. There are two main sets of service provisions in the FSIA. They address: (1) service on a "foreign state or political subdivisions," and (2) service on "an agency or instrumentality of a foreign state."

(1) Under 28 U.S.C. § 1608(a)(1)-(4), service of process on a foreign state or a political subdivision of a foreign state can be made (1) "in accordance with any special arrangement for service between the plaintiff and the foreign state or subdivision"; or (2) if no special arrangement exists, then "in accordance with an applicable international convention" (such as the Hague Convention). However, if service is not possible under either (1) or (2), then service may be made (3) through "any form of mail requiring a signed receipt" sent from the court clerk to the head of the ministry of foreign affairs of the foreign state; and (4) if service cannot be made within 30 days under (3), service may be made through diplomatic channels.

(2) Under 28 U.S.C. § 1608(b)(1)-(3), service on an agency or instrumentality of a foreign state can be made in a manner similar to (1) and (2), above. And when such service cannot be made, then (3): "if reasonably calculated to give actual notice," service may be made by delivering a copy of the summons and complaint, together with a translation, (A) as directed by a foreign authority in response to a letter rogatory or request; or (B) by any form of mail requiring a signed receipt, sent from the court clerk "to the agency or instrumentality to be served"; or (C) as directed by the court, consistent with the law of the place where service is to be made.

Transaero, Inc. v. La Fuerza Aerea Boliviana

United States Court of Appeals, D.C. Circuit, 1994.
30 F.3d 148.

SENTELLE, CIRCUIT JUDGE.

Transaero, Inc., a New York corporation, obtained a default judgment against La Fuerza Aerea Boliviana ("the Bolivian Air Force") in the Eastern District of

New York and registered the judgment in the district court for the District of Columbia. The Bolivian Air Force moved for summary judgment, claiming that the district court in New York lacked personal jurisdiction because the default judgment had been obtained without the service of process required by the Foreign Sovereign Immunities Act, 28 U.S.C. §§ 1330, 1602-1611 (1988) ("the Act"). The Bolivian Air Force contended that because it is a "foreign state or political subdivision of a foreign state" within the meaning of section 1608 of the Act, Transaero had served it improperly. The district court held instead that the Bolivian Air Force is an "agency or instrumentality" of Bolivia under the service provisions of section 1608, so that Transaero's method of service gave the New York court jurisdiction. The Bolivian Air Force has taken an interlocutory appeal from the order. See Foremost-McKesson, Inc. v. Islamic Republic of Iran, 284 U.S. App. D.C. 333, 905 F.2d 438, 443 (D.C. Cir. 1990) (denial of a claim of sovereign immunity is an immediately appealable collateral order).

We hold that the Bolivian Air Force is a "foreign state or political subdivision" within the meaning of section 1608 and that Transaero's method of service was defective. We therefore reverse and remand with directions to dismiss.

I.

Transaero sold aviation parts to the Bolivian Air Force throughout the early 1980s. In 1988, Transaero filed a complaint in the Eastern District of New York that alleged breach of contract and sought $ 983,696.60 in damages. On September 15, 1988, the Clerk of Court dispatched translations of the summons and complaint to the Bolivian Air Force in La Paz, Bolivia by registered mail with a return receipt requested. The Bolivian Air Force received the summons and complaint and sent a return receipt to the Clerk on September 23, 1988. The Bolivian Air Force made no appearance, and Judge Mishler scheduled a hearing on Transaero's motion for default judgment for March 30, 1989. Transaero sent notice of the hearing to the Bolivian Air Force, to the Bolivian First Minister in La Paz, Bolivia, and to the Bolivian Ambassador and Consul General in Washington. When the Bolivian Air Force failed to appear at the hearing, Judge Mishler granted the motion for default judgment. The court found that service had been properly effected under section 1608(b), but made no findings on the adequacy of service under 1608(a). The court also held that it had subject matter jurisdiction over the contract claim under section 1605(a)(2) of the Act, which creates an exception to the general rule of sovereign immunity for claims arising from "commercial activities" conducted by foreign states.

In 1991, Transaero registered the default judgment in the district court for the District of Columbia under 28 U.S.C. § 1963 (Supp. IV 1992) and served a set of interrogatories under Federal Rule of Civil Procedure 69. The Bolivian Air Force entered an appearance and moved to quash the interrogatories and dismiss the proceedings, arguing that the District Court for the Eastern District of New York lacked jurisdiction because the Bolivian Air Force had not been served in compliance with section 1608(a) of the Act. In an order dated September 25, 1992, the District Court for the District of Columbia denied the motion. The court found that Transaero had originally served the Bolivian Air Force under section 1608(b); that the Bolivian Air Force received actual notice of Transaero's lawsuit; and that the Bolivian Air Force was notified by mail of the hearing on Transaero's motion for default judgment. The court then ruled that, as a matter of law, the Bolivian Air Force is an "agency or instrumentality" of Bolivia and that service under section 1608(b) was proper. * * *

II.

A.

Under the Act, "subject matter jurisdiction plus service of process equals personal jurisdiction." Texas Trading & Milling Corp. v. Federal Republic of Nigeria, 647 F.2d 300, 308 (2d Cir. 1981), cert. denied, 454 U.S. 1148 (1982). The Bolivian Air Force admits that the New York court had subject matter jurisdiction under the "commercial activities" provision of section 1605(a)(2). It claims only that Transaero's service failed to comply with sections 1603 and 1608 of the Act. Section 1603 provides:

> (a) A "foreign state", *except as used in section 1608 of this title*, includes a political subdivision of a foreign state or an agency or instrumentality of a foreign state as defined in subsection (b).

> (b) An "agency or instrumentality of a foreign state" means any entity—

>> (1) which is a separate legal person, corporate or otherwise, and

>> (2) which is an organ of a foreign state or political subdivision thereof, or a majority of whose shares or other ownership interest is owned by a foreign state or political subdivision thereof, and

>> (3) which is neither a citizen of a State of the United States . . . , nor created under the laws of any third country.

28 U.S.C. § 1603 (emphasis added). Section 1608 does not further define either term. Section 1608(a) establishes certain requirements for service on "a foreign state or political subdivision of a foreign state," while section 1608(b) establishes different requirements for service on "agencies or instrumentalities" of foreign states.

B.

The nub of the dispute is whether the Bolivian Air Force counts as a "foreign state" or rather as an "agency or instrumentality" under section 1608. That in turn depends upon whether the Bolivian Air Force is a "separate legal person, corporate or otherwise" under section 1603(b)(1).[2] The words in themselves are opaque. Some district courts have sought to illuminate them by balancing three "characteristics" of separate legal status: whether, under the law of the foreign state where it was created, the entity can sue and be sued in its own name, contract in its own name, or hold property in its own name. Bowers v. Transportes Navieros Ecuadorianos, 719 F. Supp. 166, 170 (S.D.N.Y. 1989); see also Unidyne Corp. v. Aerolineas Argentinas, 590 F. Supp. 398, 400 (E.D. Va. 1984). But other courts have thought the distinction is instead a categorical one, and depends

---

[2] Both parties agree that the Air Force falls within the other components of the definition in §§ 1603(b)(2) and (b)(3).

on whether the defendant is the type of entity "that is an integral part of a foreign state's political structure, [or rather] an entity whose structure and function is predominantly commercial." Segni v. Commercial Office of Spain, 650 F. Supp. 1040, 1041-42 (N.D. Ill. 1988). The amicus curiae brief of the United States in this case proposes a similar test that looks to the "core function" of the foreign governmental body at issue.

We think that the categorical approach adopted in *Segni* and urged, in a somewhat different form, by the United States—whether the core functions of the foreign entity are predominantly governmental or commercial—best captures the statutory meaning. Congress spoke against a rich background of federal and international law that colors the statutory terms and fills them out. The Supreme Court has held that the Act largely codifies the "restrictive" theory of sovereign immunity, under which "immunity is confined to suits involving the foreign sovereign's public acts, and does not extend to cases arising out of a foreign state's strictly commercial acts." Verlinden B.V. v. Central Bank of Nigeria, 461 U.S. 480, 487 (1983). See also Republic of Argentina v. Weltover, Inc., 504 U.S. 607 (1992). Thus the Act repealed foreign immunity for "commercial activities," § 1605(a)(2), but preserved it for inherently sovereign or public acts. See Saudi Arabia v. Nelson, 507 U.S. 349 (1993); *Weltover*, 504 U.S. at 614. The distinction between foreign states and their instrumentalities establishes two categories of actors that correspond to the restrictive theory's two categories of acts.

Besides section 1608, the distinction appears in the venue provisions of 28 U.S.C. § 1391 (1988). Section 1391(f) makes the federal district court for the District of Columbia the venue for civil actions against foreign states and their subdivisions; but it allows venue in suits against an agency or instrumentality of a foreign state "in any judicial district in which the agency or instrumentality is licensed to do business or is doing business," § 1391(f)(3), a provision of doubtful coherence if extended beyond the category of commercial enterprises. Moreover the phrase "agency or instrumentality," or some close variant, is commonplace in the enabling charters of government corporations, both in the United States and abroad. The statute that created the Panama Railroad Company labelled it an "agency and instrumentality of the United States." See Panama Railroad Company Act, ch. 706, 62 Stat. 1076 (1948), at § 245. See also United States ex rel. Skinner & Eddy Corp. v. McCarl, 275 U.S. 1, 5, 6, 8 (1927) (referring to the United States Shipping Board Emergency Fleet Corporation as "an instrumentality of the Government," an "incorporated agency," and a "government-owned private corporation[]").

The courts that have construed "agency or instrumentality" to reference the defendant's powers under foreign law have relied principally on the House Report on the Act, which said:

> [The] criterion, that the entity be a separate legal person, is intended to include a corporation, association, foundation, or any other entity which, under the law of the foreign state where it was created, can sue or be sued in its own name, contract in its own name or hold property in its own name. . . . As a general matter, entities which meet the definition of an "agency or instrumentality of a foreign state" could assume a variety

of forms, including a state trading corporation, a mining enterprise, a transport organization such as a shipping line or airline, a steel company, a central bank, an export association, a governmental procurement agency or a department or ministry which acts and is suable in its own name.

H.R. Rep. No. 1487, 94th Cong., 2d Sess. 15-16 (1976), reprinted in 1976 U.S.C.C.A.N. 6604, 6614.

Without debating the legitimacy of reliance upon legislative history in other circumstances, we note that this Report is at odds with itself. All the specific examples recited fall into the category of public commercial enterprises; but the Report also states a general test that might bar those very examples and might also sweep well beyond them. The United States points out that any nation may well find it convenient (as does ours) to give powers of contract and litigation to entities that on any reasonable view must count as part of the state itself. See Br. of United States, at 7-8 (noting that under the House Report test the Departments of State and of Defense would count as "instrumentalities" of the United States). We adopt today an analysis designed to winnow the applications Congress desired from the ones it meant to exclude.

A final reason to favor the categorical approach is ease of administration in the district courts. Service of process should be the prologue to the suit rather than the central drama. When the adequacy of service is made to turn on a complex inquiry carried out long after the litigation has begun, and in which the court must apply foreign law to foreign facts, the service provisions may derail cases rather than ensuring their prompt and orderly commencement. The case before us paints the dangers of section 1608 in somber tones. Today we must face the possibility that an attempt at service made six years ago was defective—a result we seek to forestall in future cases by tying service to the obvious functions, rather than the uncertain powers, of the foreign defendant. The district courts have perforce acquired expertise in delineating the categories of "governmental" and "commercial" under the immunity provisions of the Act, and if section 1608 is construed to turn on a similar distinction that expertise will benefit all concerned.

C.

The question, then, is whether the core functions of the armed forces of a foreign sovereign are governmental or commercial. We hold that armed forces are as a rule so closely bound up with the structure of the state that they must in all cases be considered as the "foreign state" itself, rather than a separate "agency or instrumentality" of the state. The "powers to declare and wage war" are among the "necessary concomitants" of sovereignty. United States v. Curtiss-Wright Export Corp., 299 U.S. 304, 318 (1936). Since the passage of the Foreign Sovereign Immunities Act, the two federal cases to squarely consider the question have held that a foreign military force is a "foreign state" rather than an "agency or instrumentality of a foreign state." See Marlowe v. Argentine Naval Comm'n, 604 F. Supp. 703, 707 (D.D.C. 1985); *Unidyne*, 590 F. Supp. at 400. Apart from authority it is hard to see what would count as the "foreign state" if its armed forces do not. Any government of reasonable complexity must act through men organized into offices and departments. If a separate name and some power to conduct its own affairs suffices to make a foreign department an "agency" rather than a part of the state itself, the structure of section 1608 will list too far to one side. We hold that the armed forces of a foreign sovereign are the "foreign state" and must be served under section 1608(a).

III.

As relevant here, section 1608(a) requires that service on foreign states be made:

> (3) . . . by sending a copy of the summons and complaint and a notice of suit, together with a translation of each into the official language of the foreign state, by any form of mail requiring a signed receipt, to be addressed and dispatched by the clerk of the court to the head of the ministry of foreign affairs of the foreign state concerned, or

> (4) . . . by sending two copies of the summons and complaint and a notice of suit, together with a translation of each into the official language of the foreign state, by any form of mail requiring a signed receipt, to be addressed and dispatched by the clerk of the court to the Secretary of State in Washington. . . .

Both district courts to hear the case found that Transaero effected service under section 1608(b). The record reveals that Transaero never attempted the methods of service prescribed in sections 1608(a)(3) and (a)(4), electing instead to serve the Bolivian Ambassador and Consul General in Washington, and the Bolivian First Minister and the Bolivian Air Force in La Paz—but never the Ministry of Foreign Affairs or the Secretary of State. Before this court, Transaero does not claim that it strictly complied with section 1608(a), but rather asks that we pronounce the attempted service sufficient because the Bolivian government received actual notice of the suit.

The authorities generally hold that section 1608(b) may be satisfied by technically faulty service that gives adequate notice to the foreign state. See Sherer v. Construcciones Aeronauticas, S.A., 987 F.2d 1246, 1250 (6th Cir.), cert. denied, 510 U.S. 818 (1993); Velidor v. L/P/G Benghazi, 653 F.2d 812, 821-22 (3d Cir. 1981), cert. dismissed, 455 U.S. 929 (1982); Harris Corp. v. National Iranian Radio and Television, 691 F.2d 1344, 1352 (11th Cir. 1982). In cases under section 1608(a), however, the decisions have rarely excused defective service. See Gerritsen v. Consulado General de Mexico, 989 F.2d 340, 345 (9th Cir.), cert. denied, 510 U.S. 828 (1993) (service inadequate for failure to include translation of complaint); Alberti v. Empresa Nicaraguense De La Carne, 705 F.2d 250, 253 (7th Cir. 1983) (holding that service on Ambassador did not satisfy § 1608(a) requirement of service on "head of the ministry of foreign affairs"). But see *Marlowe*, 604 F. Supp. at 708 (using "substantial compliance" test under 1608(a)).

Leniency in this case would disorder the statutory scheme. The Committee Report states that section 1608(a) "sets forth the exclusive procedures for service on a foreign state," but contains no such admonition for section 1608(b). See H.R. Rep. No. 1487 at 24, reprinted in 1976 U.S.C.C.A.N. at 6623. Section 1608(b)(3) allows simple delivery "if reasonably calculated to give actual notice," showing that Congress was there concerned with substance rather than form; but the analogous subsection of section 1608(a) says nothing about actual notice. The distinction is neatly tailored to the differences between "foreign states" and "agencies or instrumentalities." The latter, typically international commercial enterprises, often possess a sophisticated knowledge of the United States legal system that other organs of foreign governments may lack. Cf. Practical Concepts, Inc. v. Republic of Bolivia, 811 F.2d 1543, 1546 (D.C. Cir. 1987) (in suit against foreign state, the rule that objections to personal jurisdiction are waived by an appearance should be sparingly applied because of foreign unfamiliarity with legal process). Thus section 1608(a) mandates service of the Ministry of Foreign Affairs, the department most likely to understand American procedure. We hold that strict adherence to the terms of 1608(a) is required. As Transaero failed to do so, the Bolivian Air Force was not properly served.

IV.

The Eastern District of New York lacked personal jurisdiction, and the default judgment registered in the District of Columbia was therefore void and unenforceable. We reverse and remand with directions to dismiss the proceedings.

It is so ordered.

MIKVA CHIEF JUDGE, dissenting.

The majority's standard for differentiating between those entities that are "foreign states" and those that are "agencies or instrumentalities" of foreign states under the Foreign Sovereign Immunities Act ("FSIA"), 28 U.S.C. §§ 1330, 1602-11, is attractive on administrability grounds. But I fear that in formulating their interpretation my colleagues have placed efficiency concerns—and perhaps their international policy preferences—above the apparent meaning of the statute. Because this case requires us to interpret Congress's enactment, and not to devise common-law rules, I think the majority's approach is insufficiently deferential to the legislature. I therefore—reluctantly—dissent. * * *

* * * Despite the majority's able argument, the FSIA and its legislative history suggest no conclusive presumption that a military entity is "a foreign state" and not "an agency or instrumentality" thereof. Instead, the statute lists three factors that define "agency or instrumentality." 28 U.S.C. § 1603(b). The only disputed factor in this case is that the entity must be "a separate legal person." Id. § 1603(b)(1). The House Report amplifies the meaning of this phrase: an agency or instrumentality may be "a department or ministry which acts and is suable in its own name." H.R. Rep. No. 94-1487, 94th Cong., 2d Sess. 15-16 (1976) * * *. This suggests to me that any presumption—let alone the conclusive presumption the majority adopts—is disfavored. Instead, every foreign entity starts out on the same footing, and a court must decide whether the particular entity is a separate legal person—that is, whether it "acts and is suable in its own name." I suspect the majority is right that most foreign military entities are not legally separate from their sovereign states, but I think it is contrary to the statute to cast this suspicion in terms of a rule.

Nothing in the language of the statute or in the remainder of its legislative history casts doubt upon the House Report's definition of "separate legal person." But the majority sweeps aside this definition with its speculation that an agency or instrumentality must be a commercial, as opposed to a public, enterprise. This distinction is nowhere to be found in the statute or legislative history. Indeed, the distinction seems inapt, because the FSIA explicitly creates an exception to the general sovereign immunity of foreign states and their agencies and instrumentalities for "commercial activity," 28 U.S.C. § 1605(a)(2), but the statute in no way indicates that a similar test determines "agency" status. The FSIA waives immunity depending on the nature of the activity on which the lawsuit is based, not the nature of the government entity against which the suit is brought. In contrast, for secondary matters (service of process, venue, attachment of property, and punitive damages) the FSIA does distinguish based on the identity of the defendant—it distinguishes between a foreign state and its agencies and instrumentalities. See 28 U.S.C. §§ 1391, 1606, 1608, 1610. These are separate distinctions, with different consequences. Yet the majority assumes that the "two categories of actors . . . correspond to the . . . two categories of acts." Absent some concrete evidence of statutory intent, I think this is a dangerous assumption.

As its statutory evidence, the majority points to one of the venue provisions of 28 U.S.C. § 1391(f), permitting suits against an agency or instrumentality "in any judicial district in which the agency or instrumentality is licensed to do business or is doing business," 28 U.S.C. § 1391(f)(3), but permitting suits against a foreign state in the United States District Court for the District of Columbia. 28 U.S.C. § 1391(f)(4). What the majority neglects to mention is that § 1391(f)(3) is not exclusive. If the agency or instrumentality is not "doing business," it may be sued "in any judicial district in which a substantial part of the events or omissions giving rise to the claim occurred, or a substantial part of property that is the subject of the action is situated." 28 U.S.C. § 1391(f)(1). The venue provision simply recognizes that many agencies and instrumentalities are commercial enterprises that may conveniently defend suits where they do business. It in no way establishes that an "agency or instrumentality" must always be a commercial enterprise.

The same response applies to the majority's assertion that the House Report "is at odds with itself," because its examples of agencies and instrumentalities tend to be commercial enterprises, while at the same time it seems to adopt a broader general definition of "agency or instrumentality." Again, that many, even most, agencies and instrumentalities may be primarily commercial in nature does not prove that all must be. If Congress meant for commerciality to be a defining characteristic, it could have said so. Instead, Congress said "separate legal person." 28 U.S.C. § 1603(b)(1). In sum, I see no good reason to focus on a distinction between commercial and non-commercial activities as the touchstone of juridical separateness.

Then what does it mean to be legally separate? The House Report gives us a sketchy definition: an entity that "acts and is suable in its own name." In keeping with several district court precedents, the court below looked at contracts executed by La Fuerza, apparently in its own name, and at previous lawsuits in which La Fuerza was mentioned by name (admittedly, an ambiguous indicator), to find that La Fuerza is a separate legal person. * * * Although I would prefer more extensive factfinding with regard to La Fuerza's activities—e.g., property ownership, previous contracting history—I think the district court was on the right track.

I think the language, policy, and legislative history of the FSIA suggest that commercial activity is not the ultimate touchstone for FSIA analysis. It makes more sense to engage in a wider factual inquiry into the actions of the entity to determine whether it is a separate legal person. Because I think the district court was basically correct, and because I would prefer to avoid incongruity with the law of this case in the Second Circuit, I respectfully dissent from the majority opinion.

NOTES AND QUESTIONS FOR DISCUSSION

1. Is the majority's governmental/commercial dichotomy a fair reading of the text of the service provisions in the FSIA? See Appendix F. Note that for purposes of the substantive immunity provisions of the FSIA, agencies and instrumentalities of a foreign state are considered to be the foreign state. See generally Chapter 3. In other words, there is no distinction between a state and its agencies or instrumentalities for purposes of immunities under the Act. But there is such a distinction in the service of process provision (and in other areas such as enforcement of judgments). Why do the service provisions make a distinction that the immunity provisions do not? As discussed in Chapter 3, the governmental/commercial dichotomy is relevant to whether acts of a foreign state, including those of its agencies or instrumentalities, will give rise to liability. Why should that same dichotomy be relevant under the service provisions of the FSIA?

2. Note that if a suit under the FSIA is proceeding in state court, lower federal court precedent as to the meaning of the FSIA's service requirements will be persuasive at best. That is because lower federal courts cannot generate binding precedent on state courts, even as to federal law. While state courts are bound by the FSIA, they are presumably capable of giving it their own best-informed interpretation. Does the potential for such diversity of opinion in connection with service in such sensitive cases present problems for foreign relations? Or is it a sufficient safeguard that the U.S. Supreme Court can superintend the lower federal courts as well as the state courts, should it be so motivated?

3. Suppose a plaintiff is unsure whether the entity she is suing is a foreign state, or an agency or instrumentality of that state. Is there any way for the plaintiff to play it safe without having to resolve the question? Note that some of the forms of service on foreign states are the same as that for agencies and instrumentalities.

4. *Transaero* involved a default judgment. The FSIA provides that a foreign state, political subdivision, or agency or instrumentality has 60 days within which to respond to a complaint, and that no default shall be entered "unless the claimant establishes his claim or right to relief by evidence satisfactory to the court." 28 U.S.C. § 1608(d)-(e). Section 1609 of the FSIA provides that property of a foreign state in the U.S. "shall be immune from attachment, arrest and execution" subject, however, to any international agreements to which the U.S. is a party, and subject to a rather intricate and lengthy set of provisions in §§

1610-1611 of the Act that provide various exemptions to immunity from attachment and enforcement.

5.   After having its motion to dismiss denied by the D.C. district court judge, but before appealing to the D.C. Circuit, the Bolivian Air Force (BAF) made a motion in the N.Y. district court (which had initially entered the default), arguing that the default should be vacated because Transaero had procured the judgment by fraudulent representations. BAF lost that motion, and the Second Circuit affirmed. Indeed, the Second Circuit noted that both the New York district court and the D.C. district court had concluded that service on BAF was proper. Should that decision have operated to estop BAF from arguing to the D.C. Circuit that it had been improperly served?

CHAPTER 5

Parallel Litigation

Even when a litigant has obtained good personal and subject matter jurisdiction, and has effected proper service on a defendant, there is no guarantee litigation will go forward in the litigant's chosen forum. It may still be possible for the defendant to have the litigation go forward in a forum of the defendant's choosing. For example, a foreign defendant sued in a U.S. court might prefer the litigation to proceed closer to home, outside of the U.S. An amalgam of related doctrines and strategies may be implicated in such settings. By means of a motion to dismiss based on *forum non conveniens*, the defendant may be able to convince the judge in the plaintiff's chosen (U.S.) forum that litigation ought to go forward elsewhere, in a substantially more convenient locale abroad. In addition, a defendant might choose to file its own suit in its preferred forum, by bringing an action against the plaintiff on the very same transaction that is the subject of the plaintiff's claim, only now the former plaintiff is a defendant and the former defendant a plaintiff. In the event of such parallel litigation, either of the court systems (U.S. or foreign) might choose, for various possible reasons, to stay its own proceedings in deference to the other. Or, the plaintiff in one of the two suits might seek to have the other suit enjoined. In all of these scenarios, domestic and foreign courts must decide which forum is to be preferred, or whether to allow the litigation to go forward on perhaps multiple fronts.

In this chapter, we consider each of these interrelated possibilities: (1) *forum non conveniens* dismissals; (2) stays of proceedings of one court in deference to another; and (3) injunctions by one court that seek to bring a halt to proceedings in another court. Common to all of these possibilities is a fundamental question of how or why litigation in one chosen forum should be privileged over litigation in the chosen forum of the opposing party, and the source of judicial power to make that decision. The problem has been aptly characterized as one of "jurisdictional equilibriation." Steven B. Burbank, *Jurisdictional Equilibriation, the Proposed Hague Convention and Progress in National Law*, 49 Am. J. Comp. L. 203 (2001).

A. INTERNATIONAL *FORUM NON CONVENIENS*

The doctrine of *forum non conveniens* was devised to respond to those limited instances in which the plaintiff's chosen forum was highly inconvenient, either from the perspective of the defendant or the chosen forum. Since 1948—and as discussed in Chapter 2—the basic transfer of venue statute, 28 U.S.C. § 1404, provides defendants sued in *federal* courts with the opportunity to override the plaintiff's choice of an inconvenient forum, but the statute only provides relief when an alternative forum exists within another federal district within the U.S. In cases involving either foreign parties or foreign events, however, there may be no federal district with proper venue and personal jurisdiction over the defendant other than the one chosen by the plaintiff. If so, transfer of venue will not be possible. Instead, the option will be either to retain the case, or to dismiss it in favor of having the plaintiff refile in a foreign jurisdiction. Similar problems may arise if suit is filed in a state court, and no other state court would be a more convenient forum, as opposed to a foreign forum.

As discussed in Chapter 2, transfer of venue within the federal judicial system is controlled by various statutorily based factors, such as the convenience of the parties, the witnesses, and the relevant judicial systems. Although *forum non conveniens* is not itself governed by statute in the federal courts, there is a rough similarity in the methodology by which *forum non conveniens* motions and transfer of venue motions are decided, as noted in the decision that follows. In addition, keep in mind that the consequences of transfer of venue and *forum non conveniens* dismissal can be quite different. With transfer of venue, the litigation remains in the U.S., whereas with a *forum non conveniens* dismissal from a federal court, it likely will not. In addition, transfer of venue under § 1404 does not result in a change in the law that would have been applied in the district court in which the case was originally filed. See Van Dusen v. Barrack, 376 U.S. 612 (1964) (involving transfer of a diversity case brought in federal court). But in *forum non conveniens* dismissals, there is no similar automatic transfer of the law along with the case once it is refiled abroad.

Foreign defendants sued in the U.S.—who may be anxious about litigation in American courts—commonly seek to have cases dismissed on *forum non conveniens* grounds. Yet in the decision that follows, a different (but not uncommon) scenario is presented: a U.S. defendant is sued in the U.S. by a foreign plaintiff over actions that occurred abroad.

Piper Aircraft Company v. Reyno

Supreme Court of the United States, 1981.

454 U.S. 235.

JUSTICE MARSHALL delivered the opinion of the Court. * * *

I

A

In July 1976, a small commercial aircraft crashed in the Scottish highlands during * * * a charter flight from Blackpool to Perth. The pilot and five passengers were killed instantly. The decedents were all Scottish subjects and residents, as are their heirs and next of kin. There were no eyewitnesses to the accident. At the time of the crash the plane was subject to Scottish air traffic control.

The aircraft, a twin-engine Piper Aztec, was manufactured in Pennsylvania by petitioner Piper Aircraft Co. (Piper). The propellers were manufactured in

Ohio by petitioner Hartzell Propeller, Inc. (Hartzell). At the time of the crash the aircraft was registered in Great Britain and was owned and maintained by Air Navigation and Trading Co., Ltd. (Air Navigation). It was operated by McDonald Aviation, Ltd. (McDonald), a Scottish air taxi service. Both Air Navigation and McDonald were organized in the United Kingdom. The wreckage of the plane is now in a hangar in Farnsborough, England. * * *

* * * [A] California probate court appointed respondent Gaynell Reyno administratrix of the estates of the five passengers. Reyno is not related to and does not know any of the decedents or their survivors; she was a legal secretary to the attorney who filed this lawsuit. Several days after her appointment, Reyno commenced separate wrongful-death actions against Piper and Hartzell in the Superior Court of California, claiming negligence and strict liability. Air Navigation, McDonald, and the estate of the pilot are not parties to this litigation. The survivors of the five passengers whose estates are represented by Reyno filed a separate action in the United Kingdom against Air Navigation, McDonald, and the pilot's estate. Reyno candidly admits that the action against Piper and Hartzell was filed in the United States because its laws regarding liability, capacity to sue, and damages are more favorable to her position than are those of Scotland. Scottish law does not recognize strict liability in tort. Moreover, it permits wrongful-death actions only when brought by a decedent's relatives. The relatives may sue only for "loss of support and society."

On petitioners' motion, the suit was removed to the United States District Court for the Central District of California. Piper then moved for transfer to the United States District Court for the Middle District of Pennsylvania, pursuant to §1404(a). Hartzell moved to dismiss for lack of personal jurisdiction, or in the alternative, to transfer.[5] * * * [T]he District Court transferred the case to the Middle District of Pennsylvania. * * *

B

* * * [A]fter the suit had been transferred, both Hartzell and Piper moved to dismiss the action on the ground of forum non conveniens. The District Court granted these motions * * * and relied on the balancing test set forth by this Court in Gulf Oil Corp. v. Gilbert, 330 U.S. 501 (1947), and its companion case, Koster v. Lumbermens Mut. Cas. Co., 330 U.S. 518 (1947). In those decisions, the Court stated that a plaintiff's choice of forum should rarely be disturbed. However, when an alternative forum has jurisdiction to hear the case, and when trial in the chosen forum would "establish . . . oppressiveness and vexation to a defendant . . . out of all proportion to plaintiff's convenience," or when the "chosen forum [is] inappropriate because of considerations affecting the court's own administrative and legal problems," the court may, in the exercise of its sound discretion, dismiss the case. *Koster.* To guide trial court discretion, the Court provided a list of "private interest factors" affecting the convenience of the litigants, and a list of "public interest factors" affecting the convenience of the fo-

---

[5] The District Court concluded that it could not assert personal jurisdiction over Hartzell consistent with due process. However, it decided not to dismiss Hartzell because the corporation would be amenable to process in Pennsylvania.

rum. *Gilbert.*[6]

* * * [T]he District Court * * * began by observing that an alternative forum existed in Scotland; Piper and Hartzell had agreed to submit to the jurisdiction of the Scottish courts and to waive any statute of limitations defense that might be available. It then stated that plaintiff's choice of forum was entitled to little weight. The court recognized that a plaintiff's choice ordinarily deserves substantial deference. It noted, however, that Reyno "is a representative of foreign citizens and residents seeking a forum in the United States because of the more liberal rules concerning products liability law," and that "the courts have been less solicitous when the plaintiff is not an American citizen or resident, and particularly when the foreign citizens seek to benefit from the more liberal tort rules provided for the protection of citizens and residents of the United States."

The District Court next examined several factors relating to the private interests of the litigants, and determined that these factors strongly pointed towards Scotland as the appropriate forum. Although evidence concerning the design, manufacture, and testing of the plane and propeller is located in the United States, the connections with Scotland are otherwise "overwhelming." The real parties in interest are citizens of Scotland, as were all the decedents. Witnesses who could testify regarding the maintenance of the aircraft, the training of the pilot, and the investigation of the accident — all essential to the defense — are in Great Britain. Moreover, all witnesses to damages are located in Scotland. Trial would be aided by familiarity with Scottish topography, and by easy access to the wreckage.

The District Court reasoned that because crucial witnesses and evidence were beyond the reach of compulsory process, and because the defendants would not be able to implead potential Scottish third-party defendants, it would be "unfair to make Piper and Hartzell proceed to trial in this forum." The survivors had brought separate actions in Scotland against the pilot, McDonald, and Air Navigation. "[I]t would be fairer to all parties and less costly if the entire case was presented to one jury with available testimony from all relevant witnesses." Although the court recognized that if trial were held in the United States, Piper and Hartzell could file indemnity or contribution actions against the Scottish defendants, it believed that there was a significant risk of inconsistent verdicts.[7]

---

[6] The factors pertaining to the private interests of the litigants included the "relative ease of access to sources of proof; availability of compulsory process for attendance of unwilling, and the cost of obtaining attendance of willing, witnesses; possibility of view of premises, if view would be appropriate to the action; and all other practical problems that make trial of a case easy, expeditious and inexpensive." The public factors bearing on the question included the administrative difficulties flowing from court congestion; the "local interest in having localized controversies decided at home"; the interest in having the trial of a diversity case in a forum that is at home with the law that must govern the action; the avoidance of unnecessary problems in conflict of laws, or in the application of foreign law; and the unfairness of burdening citizens in an unrelated forum with jury duty.

[7] The District Court explained that inconsistent verdicts might result if petitioners were held liable on the basis of strict liability here, and then required to prove negligence in an indemnity ac-

The District Court concluded that the relevant public interests also pointed strongly towards dismissal. The court determined that Pennsylvania law would apply to Piper and Scottish law to Hartzell if the case were tried in the Middle District of Pennsylvania.[8] As a result, "trial in this forum would be hopelessly complex and confusing for a jury." In addition, the court noted that it was unfamiliar with Scottish law and thus would have to rely upon experts from that country. The court also found that the trial would be enormously costly and time-consuming; that it would be unfair to burden citizens with jury duty when the Middle District of Pennsylvania has little connection with the controversy; and that Scotland has a substantial interest in the outcome of the litigation.

In opposing the motions to dismiss, respondent contended that dismissal would be unfair because Scottish law was less favorable. The District Court explicitly rejected this claim. It reasoned that the possibility that dismissal might lead to an unfavorable change in the law did not deserve significant weight; any deficiency in the foreign law was a "matter to be dealt with in the foreign forum."

C

[On appeal, the Third Circuit reversed and remanded for trial. It rejected the District Court's balancing of the private and public interest factors. In addition, it appeared as though the Court of Appeals would have reversed even if the District Court had properly balanced the public and private interests, concluding that dismissal is automatically barred if it would lead to a change in the applicable law unfavorable to the plaintiff. A 4-3 U.S. Supreme Court would reverse.]

II

The Court of Appeals erred in holding that plaintiffs may defeat a motion to dismiss on the ground of forum non conveniens merely by showing that the substantive law that would be applied in the alternative forum is less favorable to the plaintiffs than that of the present forum. The possibility of a change in substantive law should ordinarily not be given conclusive or even substantial weight in the forum non conveniens inquiry.[13]

---

tion in Scotland. Moreover, even if the same standard of liability applied, there was a danger that different juries would find different facts and produce inconsistent results.

[8] Under *Klaxon*, a court ordinarily must apply the choice-of-law rules of the State in which it sits. However, where a case is transferred pursuant to §1404(a), it must apply the choice-of-law rules of the State from which the case was transferred. *Van Dusen v. Barrack.* Relying on these two cases, the District Court concluded that California choice-of-law rules would apply to Piper, and Pennsylvania choice-of-law rules would apply to Hartzell. It further concluded that California applied a "governmental interests" analysis in resolving choice-of-law problems, and that Pennsylvania employed a "significant contacts" analysis. The court used the "governmental interests" analysis to determine that Pennsylvania liability rules would apply to Piper, and the "significant contacts" analysis to determine that Scottish liability rules would apply to Hartzell.

[13] * * * In previous forum non conveniens decisions, the Court has left unresolved the question whether under Erie R. Co. v. Tompkins, 304 U.S. 64 (1938), state or federal law of forum non conveniens applies in a diversity case. The Court did not decide this issue because the same result would have been reached in each case under federal or state law. The lower courts * * * [herein]

* * *

[B]y holding that the central focus of the forum non conveniens inquiry is convenience, *Gilbert* implicitly recognized that dismissal may not be barred solely because of the possibility of an unfavorable change in law. Under *Gilbert*, dismissal will ordinarily be appropriate where trial in the plaintiff's chosen forum imposes a heavy burden on the defendant or the court, and where the plaintiff is unable to offer any specific reasons of convenience supporting his choice.[15] If substantial weight were given to the possibility of an unfavorable change in law, however, dismissal might be barred even where trial in the chosen forum was plainly inconvenient.

The Court of Appeals' decision is inconsistent with this Court's earlier forum non conveniens decisions in another respect. Those decisions have repeatedly emphasized the need to retain flexibility. In *Gilbert*, the Court refused to identify specific circumstances which will justify or require either grant or denial of remedy. * * * If central emphasis were placed on any one factor, the forum non conveniens doctrine would lose much of the very flexibility that makes it so valuable.

In fact, if conclusive or substantial weight were given to the possibility of a change in law, the forum non conveniens doctrine would become virtually useless. Jurisdiction and venue requirements are often easily satisfied. As a result, many plaintiffs are able to choose from among several forums. Ordinarily, these plaintiffs will select that forum whose choice-of-law rules are most advantageous. Thus, if the possibility of an unfavorable change in substantive law is given substantial weight in the forum non conveniens inquiry, dismissal would rarely be proper.

Except for the court below, every Federal Court of Appeals that has considered this question after *Gilbert* has held that dismissal on grounds of forum non conveniens may be granted even though the law applicable in the alternative forum is less favorable to the plaintiff's chance of recovery. * * *

The Court of Appeals' approach is not only inconsistent with the purpose of the forum non conveniens doctrine, but also poses substantial practical problems. If the possibility of a change in law were given substantial weight, deciding motions to dismiss on the ground of forum non conveniens would become quite difficult. Choice-of-law analysis would become extremely important, and the courts would frequently be required to interpret the law of foreign jurisdictions. First, the trial court would have to determine what law would apply if the case were tried in the chosen forum, and what law would apply if the case were tried in the alternative forum. It would then have to compare the rights, remedies, and procedures available under the law that would be applied in each fo-

---

reached the same conclusion: Pennsylvania and California law on forum non conveniens dismissals are virtually identical to federal law. Thus, here also, we need not resolve the *Erie* question.

[15] In other words, *Gilbert* held that dismissal may be warranted where a plaintiff chooses a particular forum, not because it is convenient, but solely in order to harass the defendant or take advantage of favorable law. This is precisely the situation in which the Court of Appeals' rule would bar dismissal.

rum. Dismissal would be appropriate only if the court concluded that the law applied by the alternative forum is as favorable to the plaintiff as that of the chosen forum. The doctrine of forum non conveniens, however, is designed in part to help courts avoid conducting complex exercises in comparative law. * * *

Upholding the decision of the Court of Appeals would result in other practical problems. At least where the foreign plaintiff named an American manufacturer as defendant,[17] a court could not dismiss the case on grounds of forum non conveniens where dismissal might lead to an unfavorable change in law. The American courts, which are already extremely attractive to foreign plaintiffs,[18] would become even more attractive. The flow of litigation into the United States would increase and further congest already crowded courts.[19]

The Court of Appeals based its decision, at least in part, on an analogy between dismissals on grounds of forum non conveniens and transfers between federal courts pursuant to §1404(a). In *Van Dusen v. Barrack*, this Court ruled that a §1404(a) transfer should not result in a change in the applicable law. * * * [T]he court below held that that principle is also applicable to a dismissal on the ground of forum non conveniens. Congress enacted §1404(a) to permit change of venue between federal courts. Although the statute was drafted in accordance with the doctrine of forum non conveniens, it was intended to be a revision rather than a codification of the common law. District courts were given more discretion to transfer under §1404(a) than they had to dismiss on grounds of forum non conveniens. The reasoning employed in *Van Dusen v. Barrack* is simply inapplicable to dismissals on grounds of forum non conveniens. That case did not discuss the common-law doctrine. Rather, it focused on the construction and

---

[17] In fact, the defendant might not even have to be American. A foreign plaintiff seeking damages for an accident that occurred abroad might be able to obtain service of process on a foreign defendant who does business in the United States. Under the Court of Appeals' holding, dismissal would be barred if the law in the alternative forum were less favorable to the plaintiff—even though none of the parties are American, and even though there is absolutely no nexus between the subject matter of the litigation and the United States.

[18] First, * * * strict liability remains primarily an American innovation. Second, the tort plaintiff may choose, at least potentially, from among 50 jurisdictions if he decides to file suit in the United States. Each of these jurisdictions applies its own set of malleable choice-of-law rules. Third, jury trials are almost always available in the United States, while they are never provided in civil law jurisdictions. Fourth, unlike most foreign jurisdictions, American courts allow contingent attorney's fees, and do not tax losing parties with their opponents' attorney's fees. Fifth, discovery is more extensive in American than in foreign courts.

[19] In holding that the possibility of a change in law unfavorable to the plaintiff should not be given substantial weight, we also necessarily hold that the possibility of a change in law favorable to defendant should not be considered. Respondent suggests that Piper and Hartzell filed the motion to dismiss, not simply because trial in the United States would be inconvenient, but also because they believe the laws of Scotland are more favorable. She argues that this should be taken into account in the analysis of the private interests. We recognize, of course, that Piper and Hartzell may be engaged in reverse forum-shopping. However, this possibility ordinarily should not enter into a trial court's analysis of the private interests. If the defendant is able to overcome the presumption in favor of plaintiff by showing that trial in the chosen forum would be unnecessarily burdensome, dismissal is appropriate—regardless of the fact that defendant may also be motivated by a desire to obtain a more favorable forum.

application of §1404(a). Emphasizing the remedial purpose of the statute, Barrack concluded that Congress could not have intended a transfer to be accompanied by a change in law. The statute was designed as a "federal housekeeping measure," allowing easy change of venue within a unified federal system. The Court feared that if a change in venue were accompanied by a change in law, forum-shopping parties would take unfair advantage of the relaxed standards for transfer. The rule was necessary to ensure the just and efficient operation of the statute.

We do not hold that the possibility of an unfavorable change in law should never be a relevant consideration in a forum non conveniens inquiry. Of course, if the remedy provided by the alternative forum is so clearly inadequate or unsatisfactory that it is no remedy at all, the unfavorable change in law may be given substantial weight; the district court may conclude that dismissal would not be in the interests of justice.[22] In these cases, however, the remedies that would be provided by the Scottish courts do not fall within this category. Although the relatives of the decedents may not be able to rely on a strict liability theory, and although their potential damages award may be smaller, there is no danger that they will be deprived of any remedy or treated unfairly.

III

The Court of Appeals also erred in rejecting the District Court's *Gilbert* analysis. The Court of Appeals stated that more weight should have been given to the plaintiff's choice of forum, and criticized the District Court's analysis of the private and public interests. However, the District Court's decision regarding the deference due plaintiff's choice of forum was appropriate. Furthermore, we do not believe that the District Court abused its discretion in weighing the private and public interests.

A

The District Court acknowledged that there is ordinarily a strong presumption in favor of the plaintiff's choice of forum, which may be overcome only when the private and public interest factors clearly point towards trial in the alternative forum. It held, however, that the presumption applies with less force when the plaintiff or real parties in interest are foreign.

The District Court's distinction between resident or citizen plaintiffs and foreign plaintiffs is fully justified. In *Koster,* the Court indicated that a plaintiff's choice of forum is entitled to greater deference when the plaintiff has chosen the home forum.[23] When the home forum has been chosen, it is reasonable

---

[22] At the outset of any forum non conveniens inquiry, the court must determine whether there exists an alternative forum. Ordinarily, this requirement will be satisfied when the defendant is "amenable to process" in the other jurisdiction. In rare circumstances, however, where the remedy offered by the other forum is clearly unsatisfactory, the other forum may not be an adequate alternative, and the initial requirement may not be satisfied. Thus, for example, dismissal would not be appropriate where the alternative forum does not permit litigation of the subject matter of the dispute.

[23] In *Koster,* we stated that "[i]n any balancing of conveniences, a real showing of convenience by a plaintiff who has sued in his home forum will normally outweigh the inconvenience the defend-

to assume that this choice is convenient. When the plaintiff is foreign, however, this assumption is much less reasonable. Because the central purpose of any forum non conveniens inquiry is to ensure that the trial is convenient, a foreign plaintiff's choice deserves less deference.

B

The forum non conveniens determination is committed to the sound discretion of the trial court. It may be reversed only when there has been a clear abuse of discretion; where the court has considered all relevant public and private interest factors, and where its balancing of these factors is reasonable, its decision deserves substantial deference. Here, the Court of Appeals expressly acknowledged that the standard of review was one of abuse of discretion. In examining the District Court's analysis of the public and private interests, however, the Court of Appeals seems to have lost sight of this rule, and substituted its own judgment for that of the District Court.

(1)

In analyzing the private interest factors, the District Court stated that the connections with Scotland are "overwhelming." This characterization may be somewhat exaggerated. Particularly with respect to the question of relative ease of access to sources of proof, the private interests point in both directions. As respondent emphasizes, records concerning the design, manufacture, and testing of the propeller and plane are located in the United States. She would have greater access to sources of proof relevant to her strict liability and negligence theories if trial were held here. However, the District Court did not act unreasonably in concluding that fewer evidentiary problems would be posed if the trial were held in Scotland. A large proportion of the relevant evidence is located in Great Britain.

The Court of Appeals found that the problems of proof could not be given any weight because Piper and Hartzell failed to describe with specificity the evidence they would not be able to obtain if trial were held in the United States. It suggested that defendants seeking forum non conveniens dismissal must submit affidavits identifying the witnesses they would call and the testimony these witnesses would provide if the trial were held in the alternative forum. Such detail is not necessary. Piper and Hartzell have moved for dismissal precisely because many crucial witnesses are located beyond the reach of compulsory process, and thus are difficult to identify or interview. Requiring extensive investigation would defeat the purpose of their motion. Of course, defendants must provide enough information to enable the District Court to balance the parties' interests. Our examination of the record convinces us that sufficient information was pro-

---

ant may have shown." As the District Court correctly noted in its opinion, the lower federal courts have routinely given less weight to a foreign plaintiff's choice of forum.

A citizen's forum choice should not be given dispositive weight, however. Citizens or residents deserve somewhat more deference than foreign plaintiffs, but dismissal should not be automatically barred when a plaintiff has filed suit in his home forum. As always, if the balance of conveniences suggests that trial in the chosen forum would be unnecessarily burdensome for the defendant or the court, dismissal is proper.

vided here. Both Piper and Hartzell submitted affidavits describing the evidentiary problems they would face if the trial were held in the United States.

The District Court correctly concluded that the problems posed by the inability to implead potential third-party defendants clearly supported holding the trial in Scotland. Joinder of the pilot's estate, Air Navigation, and McDonald is crucial to the presentation of petitioners' defense. If Piper and Hartzell can show that the accident was caused not by a design defect, but rather by the negligence of the pilot, the plane's owners, or the charter company, they will be relieved of all liability. It is true, of course, that if Hartzell and Piper were found liable after a trial in the United States, they could institute an action for indemnity or contribution against these parties in Scotland. It would be far more convenient, however, to resolve all claims in one trial. The Court of Appeals rejected this argument. Forcing petitioners to rely on actions for indemnity or contributions would be "burdensome" but not "unfair." Finding that trial in the plaintiff's chosen forum would be burdensome, however, is sufficient to support dismissal on grounds of forum non conveniens.

(2)

The District Court's review of the factors relating to the public interest was also reasonable. On the basis of its choice-of-law analysis, it concluded that if the case were tried in the Middle District of Pennsylvania, Pennsylvania law would apply to Piper and Scottish law to Hartzell. It stated that a trial involving two sets of laws would be confusing to the jury. It also noted its own lack of familiarity with Scottish law. Consideration of these problems was clearly appropriate under *Gilbert*; in that case we explicitly held that the need to apply foreign law pointed towards dismissal. The Court of Appeals found that the District Court's choice-of-law analysis was incorrect, and that American law would apply to both Hartzell and Piper. Thus, lack of familiarity with foreign law would not be a problem. Even if the Court of Appeals' conclusion is correct, however, all other public interest factors favored trial in Scotland.

Scotland has a very strong interest in this litigation. The accident occurred in its airspace. All of the decedents were Scottish. Apart from Piper and Hartzell, all potential plaintiffs and defendants are either Scottish or English. As we stated in *Gilbert*, there is "a local interest in having localized controversies decided at home." Respondent argues that American citizens have an interest in ensuring that American manufacturers are deterred from producing defective products, and that additional deterrence might be obtained if Piper and Hartzell were tried in the United States, where they could be sued on the basis of both negligence and strict liability. However, the incremental deterrence that would be gained if this trial were held in an American court is likely to be insignificant. The American interest in this accident is simply not sufficient to justify the enormous commitment of judicial time and resources that would inevitably be required if the case were to be tried here.

IV

The Court of Appeals erred in holding that the possibility of an unfavorable change in law bars dismissal on the ground of forum non conveniens. It also erred in rejecting the District Court's *Gilbert* analysis. The District Court properly decided that the presumption in favor of the respondent's forum choice applied with less than maximum force because the real parties in interest are foreign. It did not act unreasonably in deciding that the private interests pointed towards trial in Scotland. Nor did it act unreasonably in deciding that the public interests favored trial in Scotland. Thus, the judgment of the Court of Appeals is

 Reversed.

[Justice Powell and Justice O'Connor took no part in the decision of these cases.]

[The "statement" of Justice White, concurring in part and dissenting in part, is omitted. The dissenting opinion of Justice Stevens, with whom Justice Brennan joined, is also omitted.]

NOTES AND QUESTIONS FOR DISCUSSION

1. When, if ever, should foreign plaintiffs have access to American federal courts to litigate their grievances over events that occur abroad and caused by American defendants or products? Should such actions presumptively have to be brought abroad, where the injury occurred? *Piper* suggests that a change in the nationality of the plaintiff might have changed the proper-forum analysis. Why should that be? Will the applicable law change in such a case; or the parties' access to evidence; or the impact on the American judicial system?

 The *Piper* Court suggests that convenience could not be the real reason for a foreign plaintiff's choice of an American forum. The Court seems to suppose that such plaintiffs bring suits in the U.S merely to take advantage of the benefits of American tort law. Cf. Smith Kline & French Labs. Ltd. v. Bloch, [1983] 1 W.L.R. 730 (C.A. 1982) (noting that, because of the "fabulous damages" in American jury trials, "[a]s a moth is drawn to the light, so is a litigant drawn to the United States"). On the other hand, the *Piper* Court also stated that it would not consider the fact that the defendants' desire to have the litigation go forward in Scotland was motivated by the fact of more favorable tort law for the defendants there. As the Court put it: "[The possibility that Piper and Hartzell may be engaged in 'reverse forum shopping'] ordinarily should not enter into a trial court's analysis of the private interests. If the defendant is able to overcome the presumption in favor of plaintiff by showing that trial in the chosen forum would be unnecessarily burdensome, dismissal is appropriate—regardless of the fact that defendant may also be motivated by a desire to obtain a more favorable forum." See *Piper*, footnote 19. Can the Court have it both ways, being suspicious of the plaintiff's motives for suing here and turning a blind eye to the defendant's motives for forcing the plaintiff to sue elsewhere?

2. *Forum non conveniens* dismissal will not be granted unless there is some adequate available alternative forum. Sometimes this inquiry will focus generally on the institutional adequacy of the relevant forum's judicial system in which the litigation will likely go forward. For example, doubts about whether the Indian court system could handle the myriad claims arising out of a 1984 Union Carbide gas plant disaster in Bhopal, India were raised as an argument against dismissal of a suit brought by Indian victims against Union Carbide in New York, but they were ultimately rejected. See *In re* Union Carbide Gas Plant Disaster at Bhopal, India, 634 F. Supp. 842 (S.D.N.Y. 1986), rev'd in part on other grounds, *In re* Union Carbide Gas Plant Disaster, 809 F.2d 195 (2d Cir.), cert. denied, 484 U.S. 871 (1987). Compare Bhatnagar v. Surrendra Overseas Ltd., 52 F.3d 1220, 1226 (3d Cir. 1995) (concluding that because India's civil justice system had "was almost on the verge of collapse" and resolution of the suit might be delayed 25 years, *forum non conveniens* dismissal was not warranted).

3. Other times, the focus is not on the structural aspects of the foreign legal system but on the specifics of the adequacy of remedy (as in *Piper* itself). How inadequate does the remedy in a foreign jurisdiction need to be before *forum non conveniens* dismissal will become inappropriate? In *Piper*, the claim of strict product liability that would have been available to the plaintiffs in the U.S. was entirely unavailable in Scotland against Piper and Hartzell. All that was apparently available against them was a negligence claim. Why shouldn't that be a "substantial" factor in the analysis? Is it sufficient if there is *some* compensatory remedy that is theoretically available against *some* parties for the event complained of (such as a negligence-based claim)? Note also that in the U.S., a jury trial would have been available to the plaintiffs, and wrongful death damages would not have been limited to "loss of support and society" as they would be under Scottish law, pursuant to which only relatives would have had capacity to sue. Cf. Lockman Foundation v. Evangelical Alliance Mission, 930 F.2d 764, 768 (9th Cir. 1991) (ruling that even when the plaintiff is American, lack of a jury trial in foreign forum does not make foreign forum inadequate).

On the problem of adequacy of remedy, consider the decision in De Melo v. Lederle Labs., 801 F.2d 1058 (8th Cir. 1986). There, the Eighth Circuit upheld a trial court's decision to dismiss a product liability suit on *forum non conveniens* grounds brought by a Brazilian citizen who became blinded after taking a drug manufactured by the wholly owned Brazilian subsidiary of Lederle Labs.—a U.S. corporation. The plaintiff had alleged that Lederle was wholly responsible for the design and manufacture of the product (which it also produced in the U.S.) and that it had been responsible for the mislabeling of the drugs that were manufactured by their Brazilian subsidiary and for Lederle's failure to warn of possible side effects such as blindness. Moreover, all evidence relative to the design and labeling was in the U.S., although evidence of manufacture was in both the U.S. and Brazil, and evidence relative to the plaintiff's treatment and damages was in Brazil only. The Eighth Circuit also rejected the plaintiffs' argument that she would be unable to obtain any recovery in Brazil, noting that free legal assistance was a possible avenue, even if it was unclear whether contingent fee arrangements were possible in Brazil for those who could not afford an attorney. Brazilian law allowed for recovery of certain out of pocket losses, but did not allow for the recovery of damages for pain and suffering or for recovery of punitive damages. Nevertheless, the Eighth Circuit found that these limits did not make potential recovery "so paltry as to render the available remedy illusory."

4. As discussed in the next chapter (Chapter 6), pre-trial discovery in non-U.S. courts tends to be much less extensive than it would be in a U.S. court. How should this impact the "adequacy" inquiry or the propriety of ordering dismissal? *Piper* itself indicated that a court could condition dismissal on the defendant's willingness to submit to discovery in the foreign forum. *Piper*, 454 U.S. at 257 n.25. See also Coakes v. Arabian American Oil Co., 831 F.2d 527, 574-75 (5th Cir. 1987) (conditioning dismissal on defendant's willingness to submit to American style discovery of nonparty sources).

But there are limits. For example, in *IN RE* **UNION CARBIDE GAS PLANT DISASTER, 809 F.2d 195 (2d Cir.)**, cert. denied, 484 U.S. 871 (1987)—a mass tort case concerning an explosion at a Union Carbide plant in Bhopal, India—a New York federal district court sought to condition dismissal on the defendant's (but apparently not the plaintiff's) agreement to submit to discovery in the Indian court pursuant to the Federal Rules. The Second Circuit rejected the particular arrangement as an improper interference with foreign judicial proceedings, although it did allow the district court to condition dismissal on the defendant's waiver of statute of limitations and jurisdictional defenses. The Second Circuit also overturned the district court's insistence that Union Carbide Corporation [UCC] agree in advance to pay any judgment issued by the Indian courts, yet it also rejected UCC's argument that the trial court maintain ongoing oversight over the Indian proceedings to protect against potential due process violations by the Indian courts:

> UCC's proposed remedy is not only impractical but evidences an abysmal ignorance of basic jurisdictional principles, so much so that it borders on the frivolous. The district court's jurisdiction is limited to proceedings before it in this country. Once it dismisses those proceedings on grounds of *forum non conveniens* it ceases to have any further jurisdiction over the matter unless and until a proceeding may some day be brought to enforce here a final and conclusive Indian money judgment. Nor could we, even if we attempted to retain some sort of supervisory jurisdiction, impose our due process requirements upon Indian courts, which are governed by their laws, not ours. The concept of shared jurisdictions is both illusory and unrealistic. The parties cannot simultaneously submit to both jurisdictions the resolution of the pre-trial and trial issues when there is only one consolidated case pending in one court. Any denial by the Indian courts of due process can be raised by UCC as a defense to the plaintiffs' later attempt to enforce a resulting judgment against UCC in this country. * * *

> We also believe that the district court erred in requiring UCC to consent (which UCC did under protest and subject to its right of appeal) to broad discovery of it by the plaintiffs under the Federal Rules of Civil Procedure when UCC is confined to the more limited discovery authorized under Indian law. We recognize that under some circumstances, such as when a moving defendant unconditionally consents thereto or no undiscovered evidence of consequence is believed to be under the control of a plaintiff or co-defendant, it may be appropriate to condition a

forum non conveniens dismissal on the moving defendant's submission to discovery under the Federal Rules without requiring reciprocal discovery by it of the plaintiff. *See, e.g., Piper Aircraft v. Reyno, supra*, 454 U.S. at 257 n.25 (suggesting that district courts can condition dismissal upon a defendant's agreeing to provide all relevant records); * * * *Boskoff v. Transportes Aereos Portugueses*, 17 Av. Cas. (CCH) 18,613, at 18,616 (N.D. Ill. 1983) (accepting defendant's voluntary commitment to provide discovery in foreign forum according to Federal Rules). Basic justice dictates that both sides be treated equally, with each having equal access to the evidence in the possession or under the control of the other. Application of this fundamental principle in the present case is especially appropriate since the UOI, as the sovereign government of India, is expected to be a party to the Indian litigation, possibly on both sides.

809 F.2d at 805,

5. With *Piper* (and *Lederle, supra* Note 3), compare a case seemingly very much like *Piper*: Lacey v. Cessna Aircraft Co., 932 F.2d 170 (3d Cir. 1991). *Lacey* was a product liability suit filed in the Western District of Pennsylvania, brought by an Australian plaintiff over an air crash that occurred in British Columbia (Canada), against Cessna, a Kansas aircraft manufacturer, and Hanlon & Wilson, the Pennsylvania manufacturer of the aircraft's exhaust system. Although the district court dismissed on the basis of *Piper*, the Third Circuit reversed. It concluded that if the suit were litigated in Canada, even though certain discovery could be conducted in the U.S. under the Hague Convention (see Chapter 6), no discovery other than for use at trial was permitted under Canadian law of nonparty witnesses or their employees. Thus, it was not possible in Canada to compel discovery of all relevant documents in the hands of third parties outside of the province in which the Canadian court sat. The fact that the defendants agreed to make available relevant witnesses and documents within their control did nothing to satisfy the plaintiff's need for such third-party discovery. And the fact that defendants argued that pilot error and negligent maintenance (evidence of which was available in Canada) were the causes of the accident could not, at the pre-trial stage, undermine the plaintiff's theory of liability.

In addition, in contrast to the district court, the court of appeals thought that Pennsylvania law would be applicable to substantial portions of the plaintiff's claim (e.g., the product liability claim against Hanlon & Wilson). The Third Circuit also concluded that even though a foreign plaintiff's choice of an American forum might not always, after *Piper*, be entitled to the same deference as an American plaintiff's choice, it was nevertheless entitled "some weight." Consequently, because the relevant public and private considerations were in equipoise, or at most tilted only slightly toward dismissal, the presumption in favor of the plaintiff's choice should have controlled, and it was an abuse of discretion for the district court to dismiss. Is *Lacey* consistent with *Piper*?

Guidi v. Inter-Continental Hotels, Corp.

United States Court of Appeals, Second Circuit, 2000.
224 F.3d 142.

OAKES, SENIOR CIRCUIT JUDGE.

Karen Guidi, Eve Hoffman, Merrill Kramer, and Lois Kramer ("Plaintiffs") sued Inter-Continental Hotels Corporation and other defendants (collectively "IHC") on personal injury and wrongful death claims arising from a shooting in an Egyptian hotel managed by IHC. The United States District Court for the Southern District of New York, Loretta A. Preska, Judge, dismissed Plaintiffs' action on the ground of *forum non conveniens*, concluding that Egypt was the better forum for their suit. Plaintiffs now appeal this dismissal, arguing that the District Court applied the wrong legal standard for determining the proper forum in this case and mistakenly relied on the existence of related litigation in favor of the Egyptian forum. Because we agree with Plaintiffs that the District Court erred in concluding that their action should be heard in Egypt, we reverse.

BACKGROUND

In October 1993, Robert Guidi, Coby Hoffman, and Merrill Kramer were in Egypt on business. While eating dinner in the restaurant of the Semiramis Inter-Continental Hotel, which at the time was managed by IHC, all three men were shot by an Egyptian gunman named Farahat who had entered the hotel without triggering the suspicions of hotel security. In addition to the three Americans, Farahat shot a Syrian lawyer, a French lawyer, and an Italian judge. Of his six victims, four died, including Robert Guidi and Coby Hoffman.

Immediately after the shooting, Farahat surrendered to hotel security and the Egyptian police. His claimed motivation for the shootings was religious extremism directed against foreigners. In the criminal prosecution that followed, Farahat was adjudged insane and committed to a government hospital in January 1994. He escaped from the hospital in September 1997 and the same day, with the help of at least one other person, killed ten more people in an attack on a tour bus.

Plaintiffs filed suit against IHC on October 20, 1995, joining the wrongful death claims of Guidi's and Hoffman's widows with the personal injury claims of Kramer and his wife. At the time of suit, Mrs. Guidi and Mrs. Hoffman were residents of New Jersey and the Kramers resided in Maryland. Because IHC is a Delaware company with its principal place of business in New York City and diversity existed between the parties, Plaintiffs elected to bring their action in the Southern District of New York. On July 7, 1996, IHC moved for dismissal on the ground of *forum non conveniens*, arguing that information critical to its defense could be obtained only in Egypt, that the cost of defending itself in New York would be prohibitive, that it would be unable to implead Egyptian third parties, and that an Egyptian court would better be able to apply Egyptian tort law. Plaintiffs opposed IHC's motion on several fronts, including that American plaintiffs should not be compelled to sue an American defendant in a foreign country and that Plaintiffs were emotionally unable to travel to Egypt for a trial.

In January 1997, IHC submitted supplemental information to the District Court which indicated that the families of the Italian judge and the French lawyer, whom Farahat had killed in the same incident that gave rise to this case, had commenced wrongful death actions in the Egyptian courts.

On July 17, 1997, the District Court granted IHC's motion to dismiss. Applying the *forum non conveniens* balancing test outlined by the Supreme Court in Gulf Oil Corp. v. Gilbert, 330 U.S. 501 (1947), the court found that with respect to the private interests of the litigants, the balance slightly favored the Egyptian forum because a viewing of the premises would be possible there and because IHC would be able to implead the Egyptian government as a third party. Turning to the public interest factors presented by the case, the court found that (1) the Southern District of New York has an overburdened docket; (2) Egypt has a greater interest in the litigation than New York because it is committed to protecting its tourist industry; (3) an Egyptian court would be more familiar with Egyptian law and have a greater interest in its application; and (4) most significantly, there were two related lawsuits pending in Egypt at the time of dismissal. The court concluded that these public interest factors decisively favored the Egyptian forum, and dismissed the case on that basis.

In November 1997, Plaintiffs [renewed their motion] providing evidence of increasing terrorist activity against tourists in Egypt since the time of the dismissal. Plaintiffs' evidence included the escape and subsequent killing of nine tourists by Farahat in September 1997, as well as the terrible attack at Luxor in November 1997 that resulted in the deaths of more than 50 foreigners. Plaintiffs' motion was denied by an order dated April 16, 1999.

* * * [On appeal] plaintiffs argue primarily that the district court applied an incorrect legal standard for cases in which an American plaintiff seeks an American forum and relied excessively on the existence of related litigation in Egypt. Plaintiffs also question the district court's failure to give proper weight to the emotional toll and threats to personal safety faced by Plaintiffs if forced to bring their action in Egypt.

DISCUSSION

We have recognized that our review of a *forum non conveniens* dismissal is limited to whether a district court abused its broad discretion to dismiss on such grounds. Peregrine Myanmar Ltd. v. Segal, 89 F.3d 41, 46 (2d Cir. 1996); Scottish Air Int'l, Inc. v. British Caledonian Group, PLC, 81 F.3d 1224, 1232 (2d Cir. 1996). Our limited review, however, encompasses "the right to determine whether the district court reached an erroneous conclusion on either the facts or the law." R. Maganlal & Co. v. M.G. Chem. Co., 942 F.2d 164, 167 (2d Cir. 1991) (internal quotation omitted).

Plaintiffs believe that the district court abused its discretion in at least two ways by deciding that Egypt was the better forum for this case. First, Plaintiffs argue that the district court failed to apply the *forum non conveniens* standard articulated in Koster v. Lumbermens Mut. Cas. Co., 330 U.S. 518, 524 (1947), which Plaintiffs assert should control in a case such as theirs in which an American plaintiff has chosen to sue in his home forum. Second, Plaintiffs contest the significance given by the district court to the related wrongful death cases pending in Egypt at the time of its decision, and argue that the district court confused *forum non conveniens* with transfer to another federal court under 28 U.S.C. § 1404(a). We agree with Plaintiffs on both points. Moreover, we believe that the special circumstances presented by this case—specifically, the emotional burden on Plaintiffs of returning to the country where they or their loved ones were shot in an act of religious terrorism—provide additional weight for favoring Plaintiffs' choice of their home forum for this litigation.

I

Plaintiff's Choice of Forum under *Koster* and *Gilbert*

In 1947, the Supreme Court decided the companion cases *Koster*, 330 U.S. 518 (1947), and Gilbert v. Gulf Oil, 330 U.S. 501 (1947). In these two cases, the Court laid out the approach to *forum non conveniens* that is still followed in federal courts today.[2] See, e.g., Piper Aircraft Co. v. Reyno, 454 U.S. 235, 241 (1981)[.] In *Gilbert*, which involved a plaintiff who brought suit outside his home forum, the Court set forth a balancing test of private and public interests to guide courts' discretion in determining whether a more convenient forum exists. See id. at 508-09. While *Gilbert* acknowledged generally that "the plaintiff's choice of forum should rarely be disturbed," id. at 508, *Koster*, which involved a plaintiff who had chosen to sue in his home forum, more explicitly stated that:

> Where there are only two parties to a dispute, there is good reason why it should be tried in the plaintiff's home forum if that has been his choice. He should not be deprived of the presumed advantages of his home jurisdiction except upon a clear showing of facts which either (1) establish such oppressiveness and vexation to a defendant as to be out of all proportion to plaintiff's convenience, which may be shown to be slight or nonexistent, or (2) make trial in the chosen forum inappropriate because of considerations affecting the court's own administrative and legal problems. In any balancing of conveniences, a real showing of convenience by a plaintiff who has sued in his home forum will normally outweigh the inconvenience the defendant may have shown.

330 U.S. at 524. Thus, *Koster* is "a consistent pragmatic application of *Gilbert*," Alcoa Steamship Co. v. N/V Nordic Regent, 654 F.2d 147, 152 (2d Cir. 1980), in the home forum context.

The Supreme Court has recognized that a district court may, in the exercise of its sound discretion, dismiss a case "when an alternative forum has jurisdiction to hear the case, and when trial in the chosen forum would 'establish . . . oppressiveness and vexation to a defendant . . . out of all proportion to plaintiffs convenience,' or when the 'chosen forum [is] inappropriate because of considerations affecting the court's own administrative and legal problems.'" *Piper Aircraft*, 454 U.S. at 255 & n. 23. Although a citizen's choice of forum is not dis-

---

[2] As the Supreme Court has noted, the enactment of 28 U.S.C. § 1404 (1998), which controls interstate transfers of cases in federal courts, had the effect of limiting *forum non conveniens* analyses to cases such as this one where the alternative forum is the court of another country. See American Dredging Co., v. Miller, 510 U.S. 443, 449 n.2 (1994).

positive for the purposes of *forum non conveniens,* a plaintiff's choice of forum is entitled to greater deference when the plaintiff has chosen the home forum. *See id.*[3] Here, the district court did not accord such deference, or even mention *Koster,* in its application of the *Gilbert* private and public interest factors. This omission and consequent failure to grant Plaintiff's choice of an American forum significant deference was unsound.

In this case, Plaintiffs argue—and we agree—that their "home forum" as American citizens is a United States court, such as the courts of the Southern District of New York. Under the standard articulated in *Koster,* Plaintiffs' decision to sue in New York should not be disturbed if that forum is not so oppressive and vexatious to IHC as to overwhelm the convenience to Plaintiffs of suing in their home forum. See 330 U.S. at 524. Additionally, the convenience of the New York forum to Plaintiffs must be real and substantial, as opposed to slight or nonexistent. See id. These criteria are easily met in this case: IHC is a corporate defendant with its principal place of business in New York and is being sued for a relatively simple tort violation. Plaintiffs, in contrast, are ordinary American citizens for whom litigating in Egypt presents an obvious and significant inconvenience, especially considering their adverse experience with that country to date. This is not a case where the plaintiff is a corporation doing business abroad and can expect to litigate in foreign courts. See *Reid-Walen,* 933 F.2d at 1395 (courts partially discount citizenship when plaintiff does extensive foreign business); Contact Lumber Co. v. P.T. Moges Shipping Co., 918 F.2d 1446, 1449-50 (9th Cir. 1990) (same).

Under the circumstances presented here, we can see no reason to make an exception to the holding in *Koster* that "a real showing of convenience by a plaintiff who has sued in his home forum will normally outweigh the inconvenience the defendant may have shown." See 330 U.S. at 524.

Indeed, the district court, in its analysis of the private interest factors under *Gilbert,* concluded that the degree of inconvenience to IHC of litigating in the United States did not offer a basis for dismissing the case. After considering IHC's arguments regarding its need to implead Egypt as a third party, the availability of witnesses and evidence, the cost of obtaining depositions, and the possibility of a jury view in Egypt, the district court found that these factors "did not strongly favor" the Egyptian forum. * * * IHC therefore did not carry its burden under *Gilbert* and *Koster* to demonstrate that the balance of conveniences tipped strongly in its favor.

In the balancing of conveniences, we believe that the substantial and unusual emotional burden on Plaintiffs if they were required to travel to Egypt provides additional support for keeping the case in their chosen forum of New York.

---

[3] We held in *Alcoa* that the American citizenship of a plaintiff does not justify creating a special rule in *forum non conveniens* cases, and that the *Gilbert* standard is the proper standard to apply. 654 F.2d at 159. *Piper Aircraft,* however, establishes that *Koster* retains its vitality in the balancing of conveniences required under *Gilbert.* Our holding today does not contravene our holding in *Alcoa,* but rather follows *Piper Aircraft*'s dictate that a heightened deference should be given in the balancing of conveniences to an American citizen's choice of his or her home forum.

Plaintiffs are atypical in that they are either the widows or the victim of a murderous act directed specifically against foreigners. Understandably, they are strongly adverse to litigating in a country where foreigners have been the target of hostile attacks, and have concerns for their own safety if required to travel there to bring their suit. Plaintiffs have supplied us with ample evidence of terrorist attacks occurring after the events giving rise to their action—including the subsequent killing of nine foreign tourists by the very man who attacked Plaintiffs—which give credence to Plaintiffs' uncertainty as to the safety of American visitors to Egypt insofar as fear of religious extremism is concerned.

In its *forum non conveniens* analysis, the district court did not even mention, much less give any weight to, the emotional burden faced by Plaintiffs if the case were to be heard in Egypt. In the subsequent Fed.R.Civ.P. 60(b) motion filed by Plaintiffs on this specific point, the district court affirmed its decision to dismiss the case in favor of the Egyptian forum and rejected the argument that Plaintiffs' concerns tilted the balance in favor of keeping the case in New York. For the purposes of *forum non conveniens,* however, "the ultimate inquiry is where trial will best serve the convenience of the parties *and the ends of justice."* *Koster,* 330 U.S. at 527 (emphasis added); *see also Maganlal,* 942 F.2d at 167. We believe that justice is best served in this case by acknowledging the unique and heavy burden placed on Plaintiffs if they are required to litigate in Egypt. In balancing the interests at stake for the purposes of *forum non conveniens,* the district court should have taken into account the unusual circumstances of Plaintiffs that weigh strongly in favor of the New York forum.

Because the district court gave inadequate significance to Plaintiffs' choice of forum as American citizens and failed to consider Plaintiffs' emotional burden of having to travel to Egypt for trial in its balancing, we find that its determination that Egypt was the better forum for this litigation was erroneous. Plaintiffs' decision to bring their suit in New York rather than in a foreign country should not be disturbed.

II

The Related Litigation

In its weighing of the *Gilbert* public interest factors to determine the best forum for this case, the district court stated that the strongest public interest factor in favor of the Egyptian forum was the related litigation pending there at the time of its decision. The district court found that because the families of two other hotel guests who were killed by Farahat had brought suit in Egypt, although not against IHC, it would be most efficient if Plaintiffs' claims were heard in Egypt as well. To support its finding, the district court cited several cases based on 28 U.S.C. § 1404(a) which hold that related litigation in the transferee forum weighs heavily in favor of transfer.

The district court's reliance on 28 U.S.C. § 1404(a), which controls the transfer of cases among the federal courts within the United States, was not correct. As the Supreme Court recognized in *Piper Aircraft,* "§ 1404(a) transfers are different than dismissals on the ground of *forum non conveniens* . . . . District courts are given more discretion to transfer under § 1404(a) . . . [because] the statute was designed as a 'federal housekeeping measure,' allowing easy change of venue within a unified federal system." 454 U.S. at 253-54 (quoting Van Dusen v. Barrack, 376 U.S. 612, 613 (1964)). When, as here, the alternative forum is the court of a foreign country, the law of § 1404(a) has no application because "the differences between trial in an American court and a foreign court will almost inevitably be greater than those between trial in two federal courts in the United States." Nalls v. Rolls-Royce Ltd., 702 F.2d 255, 261 (D.C. Cir. 1983).

The existence of related litigation, while of major significance in § 1404(a) cases, is not listed as a relevant factor in the *forum non conveniens* analysis laid out in *Gilbert*. Moreover, we can find no case that gives such litigation the significance accorded by the district court here, when the parties in the related action are completely different from the parties at bar. In the two *forum non conveniens* cases cited by the district court to support its decision, the parties to the American and foreign actions were identical and there was the likelihood of "significant duplication of legal efforts on behalf of all the parties." C-Cure Chem. Co. v. Secure Adhesives Corp., 571 F. Supp. 808, 822 (W.D.N.Y. 1983); see also Ocean Shelf Trading, Inc. v. Flota Mercante Grancolombiana S.A., 638 F. Supp. 249, 253 (S.D.N.Y. 1986). The private interests of the litigants—relevant under *Gilbert*—were therefore implicated in these cases in a manner not present here. We are not persuaded that such cases, in the absence of more apposite authority, require us to uphold the reasoning of the district court that Plaintiffs' case would be more efficiently heard in Egypt.

Although we are unwilling to say that the existence of related litigation in another country should never be considered for the purposes of *forum non conveniens,* we conclude that it was unsound for the district court to rely on § 1404(a) in giving the Egyptian litigation such decisive weight in this case.

CONCLUSION

For the foregoing reasons, we find that the district court abused its discretion in deciding that Egypt was the better forum for this litigation. * * *

NOTES AND QUESTIONS FOR DISCUSSION

1. Given *Guidi,* would the French or Jordanian plaintiffs be able to join the New York suit against ICH? Or, because they would not be able to take advantage of the so-called *Koster* presumption, would their claims have to be dismissed on *forum non conveniens* grounds? In answering, consider the relevance of the fact that there is already a suit pending in the U.S. against ICH on these same events that occurred abroad.

2. The Court in *Guidi* stated that the pending civil litigation in Egypt over the same events was not a factor referred to in *Gilbert* (although lower courts had considered the presence of parallel litigation in relation to transfer of venue under § 1404). But it stopped short of saying that such pending litigation should *never* be considered in *forum non conveniens* analysis. Note that the Court in *Piper* took account of the fact that parallel litigation was pending in the United Kingdom over other potential tortfeasors (the pilot's estate, the air taxi service, and the plane's owner) whom Piper and Hartzell would have liked to have impleaded but could not, given the lack of personal jurisdiction over them in Pennsylvania. See also Calavo Growers of Cal. v. Generali Belgium, 632 F.2d 963, 967-68 (2d Cir. 1980), cert. denied, 449 U.S. 1084 (1981) (factoring in the judicial economy that could be achieved when related suit was pending in foreign forum). By contrast, is the emotional distress of having to return to the scene of the tort a factor mentioned by *Gilbert*?

3. In **Iragorri v. United Technologies Corp., 274 F.3d 65 (2d Cir. 2001)** (en banc), the Second Circuit (post-*Guidi*) purported to clarify the degree of deference a district court should accord a U.S. plaintiff's choice of a U.S. forum when the forum chosen is different from that in which the plaintiff resides. The court noted that when the plaintiff sues in her home forum, then, under *Koster*, the choice is entitled to "great deference." At the other extreme, under *Piper*, a foreign plaintiff's choice of a U.S. forum, said the appeals court, gets "less deference." From this, the Second Circuit reasoned that "the greater the plaintiff's or the lawsuit's bona fide connection to the United States and to the forum of choice and the more it appears that considerations of convenience favor the conduct of the lawsuit in the United States, the more difficult it will be for the defendant to gain dismissal for *forum non conveniens*." Id. at 72. What, if anything, does this suggestion add? Would it change the result in *Guidi*?

4. Note that whenever a foreign plaintiff sues a U.S. corporation over events occurring abroad, many of the private and public factors referred to by *Gilbert* will be less than conclusive. Insofar as party convenience is concerned, the plaintiff alleges inconvenience in having to litigate abroad, while the defendant alleges inconvenience in having to litigate in the U.S. And yet the real conveniences may be exactly the opposite in many respects—i.e., it might be simpler for the domestic corporation to litigate in the states and for the foreign plaintiff to litigate abroad. In a product liability case, moreover, there may often be evidence in the U.S respecting such matters as design defect, while there will be evidence of the accident and plaintiff's injury abroad. And there will often be more than one forum that is likely to have a concern in the litigation in terms of applicable law.

Given these considerations, many *forum non conveniens* motions present close enough questions that their outcome may be hard to predict. And in any close case of *forum non conveniens*, the district judge's decision would likely be upheld on appeal no matter which way she rules, even if the court of appeals would have come out differently in the first instance. Suppose, for example, in *Piper*, that the district court, on the same facts, had come to the opposite conclusion, and had denied dismissal on *forum non conveniens* grounds. Would or should an appellate court reverse that determination as beyond the discretion of the district court? How does the uncertainty that might inhere in such *forum non conveniens* issues impact business planning in a global economy?

5. In Pollux Holding Ltd. v. Chase Manhattan Bank, 329 F.3d 64 (2d Cir. 2003), cert. denied, 540 U.S. 1149 (2004) two Liberian investment companies that handled certain Greek citizens' bank accounts sued the defendant, a New York bank, in New York for investment losses. Greece and the U.S. were parties to a treaty providing that Greek citizens be accorded the same right of access to U.S. courts as that accorded American citizens. See Chapter 8, Section A. But the Second Circuit concluded that because the plaintiffs were not the Greek customers of the Liberian companies but rather were the Liberian companies themselves, the treaty was inapplicable. The court noted, however, that even when such treaties are applicable, foreign nationals of the signatory country are entitled to no more deference regarding their choice of a U.S. forum than is afforded a U.S. citizen living abroad.

But the appeals court rejected a *per se* rule favoring litigation in a defendant's home forum. Rather, the court concluded that "a plaintiff's choice to initiate suit in the defendant's home forum—as opposed to any other where the defendant is also amenable to suit—only merits heightened deference to the extent that the plaintiff and the case possess *bona fide* connections to, and convenience factors favor, that forum." *Pollux*, 329 F.3d at 74. Since the plaintiffs offered no proof that they had connections to the U.S. and failed to demonstrate that New York was convenient for them (insofar as nearly all of their interactions with the bank occurred at its London branch), the court held that their choice of the defendant's home forum did not merit the same substantial deference afforded to a suit initiated in a plaintiff's home forum. Upon finding that the trial court had properly determined England to be an adequate alternative forum and had properly weighed the prescribed private and public interest factors, the circuit court upheld the lower court's decision to dismiss the complaint.

6. Choice of forum clauses and *forum non conveniens*. How will the presence of a forum selection clause in an agreement between the parties impact the *forum non conveniens* calculus? Obviously, if the forum selected is also the forum in which suit has been filed, the likelihood of successful dismissal is reduced. And if the choice of forum clause selects a forum other than the forum in which suit was filed, the odds of a successful motion for dismissal increase. Of course, all of this *might* depend on whether—if the underlying claim is not one arising under federal law (e.g., it is a case premised on alienage diversity and nonfederal law)—the state in which suit has been brought would, under its own choice of law rules, consider the forum selection clause to be enforceable. Cf. Klaxon Co. v. Stentor Electric Mfg. Co., 313 U.S. 487 (1941) (instructing federal courts to apply the choice of law rules that would be applied by the state courts in the state in which they sit). See generally Chapter 7, Section B.

In the transfer of venue setting, the Supreme Court concluded that the nonenforceability of a choice of forum clause under the law of the state in which the federal diversity court sat would not only *not* be a hurdle to transfer of venue to the selected forum's federal district court under 28 U.S.C. § 1404, but the clause could be considered as some evidence of what constituted convenience of the parties. See Stewart Organization, Inc. v. Ricoh Corp., 487 U.S. 22 (1988). The Court did so largely because the federal transfer of venue statute trumped what might otherwise have been the applicable state law under the *Erie* doctrine. How should the fact that *forum non conveniens* is not governed by statute but only by judge-made law bear on the same question if presented in a motion to dismiss on *forum non conveniens* grounds rather than to transfer venue? Should the fact that such dismissals largely relate to the procedures of the federal courts mean that state law to the contrary can confidently be ignored, even if a different result would have been reached had the case remained in a state court?

7. Federal statutory claims and *forum non conveniens*. *Piper* and *Guidi* involved tort claims arising under some relevant state law or foreign law. Should *forum non conveniens* also be available in an action based, for example, on a federal statute? Presumably if the underlying federal statute (on which the claim is based) is explicit about the doctrine's availability (or unavailability), the statute will control. But what if—as will usually be the case—the statute is silent? Should a court presume that Congress would want American courts to apply procedural doctrines like *forum non conveniens* to federal statutory claims unless it says otherwise? Or should it entertain the opposite presumption, or perhaps neither presumption? For examples of successful *forum non conveniens* motions made in lawsuits involving federal statutory claims, see, e.g., Alfadda v. Fenn, 159 F.3d 41 (2d Cir. 1998) (dismissing federal securities claims on convenience grounds); Howe v. Goldcorp Investments Ltd., 946 F.2d 944 (1991), cert. denied, 502 U.S. 1095 (1992) (same); Capital Currency Exchange, N.V. v. National Westminster Bank PLC, 155 F.3d 603 (2d Cir. 1998) (antitrust action). Some cases, however, have suggested that there might be public policy objections to *forum non conveniens* dismissal in such cases. See, e.g., Laker Airways Ltd. v. Pan American World Airways, 568 F. Supp. 811 (D.D.C. 1983), aff'd, 731 F.2d 909 (D.C. Cir. 1984) (antitrust). For a survey of the problem, see Lonny S. Hoffman & Keith A. Rowley, *Forum Non Conveniens in Federal Statutory Cases*, 49 Emory L.J. 1137 (2000). Should claims under the Alien Tort Statute, 28 U.S.C. § 1350 (see Chapter 2) be immune from forum non conveniens analysis? See generally Short, *Is the Alien Tort Statute Sacrosanct? Retaining Forum Non Conveniens in Human Rights Litigation*, 33 N.Y.U. J. Int'l L. & Pol. 1001 (2001).

8. State courts and *forum non conveniens*. The *forum non conveniens* principles associated with *Piper* and *Guidi* are generally thought to be procedural principles applied in the federal courts, as a matter of federal common law. See *In re* Air Crash Disaster Near New Orleans, La., 821 F.2d 1147 (5th Cir. 1987). (Note however, that the *Piper* Court (in footnote 13) did not answer the question whether, in a case *not* governed by federal law, *forum non conveniens* doctrine in the federal courts had to map state doctrine, if different.) State courts have their own *forum non conveniens* rules that allow them to decline to entertain suits over which they might otherwise have good personal and subject matter jurisdiction. And it is doubtful that state courts are under any obligation as a matter of federal law to grant *forum non conveniens* dismissals where a federal court would do so in a case arising under federal law. Cf. American Dredging Co. v. Miller, 510 U.S. 443 (1994) (holding that *forum non conveniens* rules applicable to an admiralty case in federal court would not have to be applied to the same case in a state court in the same state).

Moreover, some states have either very weak *forum non conveniens* rules, or none to speak of. See, e.g., Dow Chemical Co. v. Alfaro, 786 S.W.2d 674 (Tex. 1990), cert. denied, 498 U.S. 1024 (1991) (concluding that Texas law, as it then stood, would not permit *forum non conveniens* dismissals; upholding exercise of jurisdiction in suit brought by Costa Rican plaintiff against U.S. pesticide manufacturers for personal injuries caused in Costa Rica); Friedrich Juenger, *Forum Shopping, Domestic and International,* 63 Tul. L. Rev. 553 (1989). Is a foreign defendant nevertheless safe from unreasonable exertions of personal jurisdiction insofar as the states are bound by the due process limits of *International Shoe* and its offspring? Or is this protection too uncertain and too little? See Alex Wilson Albright, *In Personam Jurisdiction: A Confused and Inappropriate Substitute for Forum Non Conveniens,* 71 Tex. L. Rev. 351 (1992).

9. Three points are worth emphasizing in connection with judicial review of federal trial court *forum non conveniens* decisions. *First,* as indicated in Note 4, appellate review is generally based on an abuse of standard, meaning that district court rulings are seldom overturned. *Second,* only the granting (but not the denial) of a motion to dismiss on *forum non conveniens* grounds is immediately appealable under the final judgment rule, 28 U.S.C. § 1291. See Van Cauwenberghe v. Baird, 486 U.S. 495 (1988); cf. Lauro Lines s.r.l. v. Chasser, 490 U.S. 495 (1989) (discussed in Chapter 1) (holding that refusal to dismiss lawsuit based on forum selection clause was not immediately appealable under the "collateral order doctrine"). Review of a refusal to grant dismissal can ordinarily come only after trial; and then, the defendant must show that its right to a fair trial was "substantially prejudice[d]," not simply that it had been put to inconvenience. See Indasu Int'l, C.A. v. Citibank, N.A., 861 F.2d 375, 380 (2d Cir. 1988). By contrast, neither the grant *nor* the denial of transfer of venue to another federal court will ordinarily be considered a final judgment. Thus, denial of a motion to dismiss on *forum non conveniens* grounds can usually only be had through the extraordinary (and discretionary) device of mandamus. *Third,* as a matter of sequencing, a district court need not decide a disputed question of subject matter jurisdiction ahead of a question of *forum non conveniens.* See Sinochem Int'l Co. Ltd. v. Malaysia Int'l Shipping Corp., 549 U.S. 422 (2007) (upholding dismissal on *forum non conveniens* grounds and concluding that a district court did not have to resolve the subject matter jurisdiction question first).

10. Sour Grapes? Suppose a U.S. defendant product manufacturer successfully moves for dismissal of a product liability on *forum non conveniens* grounds, and the action is thereafter brought in a foreign jurisdiction. Suppose further that in the course of arguing for dismissal, the defendant argued that the foreign jurisdiction was up to the task procedurally, remedially, and that such trial would not lack fundamental fairness. After litigation on the merits, however, the defendant suffers a substantial money judgment, and the plaintiff then seeks to enforce the foreign judgment back in the U.S. Should the defendant now be permitted to argue that the judgment should not be enforced because of some fundamental procedural or remedial failing, or because the trial failed to comply with fundamental fairness? Or, having got what it asked for, should the defendant be estopped from making such arguments, and if so, when? And consider whether it should matter that the failing is one that was systematic and could have been predicted, as opposed to being an ad hoc deviation from seemingly acceptable procedures? See generally Christopher A. Whytock & Cassandra Burke Robertson, *Forum Non Conveniens and the Enforcement of Foreign Judgments,* 111

Colum. L. Rev. 1444 (2011) (noting that, under current doctrine, the same foreign judiciary may be adequate for a *forum non conveniens* dismissal, but inadequate for purposes of enforcing an ensuing foreign judgment).

A COMPARATIVE NOTE ON FORUM NON CONVENIENS

In Europe, discretionary refusals to entertain properly invoked jurisdiction are frowned upon. See Joachim Zekoll, *The Role and Status of American Law in the Hague Judgments Convention Project*, 61 Alb. L. Rev. 1283 (1998). In the U.S., transfer of venue and *forum non conveniens* are both safety-valve mechanisms that can mitigate the harsh effects of transient jurisdiction, or an overly broad invocation of general jurisdiction, by redirecting the lawsuit to a forum with a greater connection to the litigation. Would a better approach be to tighten up on the options available for the exercise of personal jurisdiction in the first instance (e.g., abandonment of "tag" jurisdiction and some states' "doing business" version of general jurisdiction) and simultaneously dispense with *forum non conveniens*?

Consider whether dismissing an action on grounds of *forum non conveniens* is a legitimate means of guarding against forum shopping. In other words, why should federal courts not be obligated to adjudicate a case in which they have subject matter and personal jurisdiction over the defendant? Note that outside of the U.S., most legal systems do not permit their courts to dismiss any action for reasons of "inconvenience," at least when judicial jurisdiction has been established. This is so even when another forum would appear to be clearly more appropriate. Assuming that forum shopping also occurs in these systems, why is it that they do not provide a remedy against it? Conversely, what is the legal basis for applying the *forum non conveniens* doctrine in the U.S.? In the federal courts, transfer of venue is governed by statute; but as noted above, no similar statute calls for or permits dismissal on *forum non conveniens* grounds. Rather, it is based on federal judge-made law. Is the idea that every procedural system has the inherent power to reject cases that it considers would be far more appropriately litigated elsewhere? If so, how does that square with separation of powers and the "virtually unflagging" command of Congress to permit a litigant to go forward in a federal court when jurisdiction is properly invoked?

Those systems that do at least recognize the doctrine are perhaps less concerned about forum shopping than American courts and dismiss actions only in exceptional circumstances. The English judge Lord Denning put it this way:

> No one who comes to these courts asking for justice should come in vain. * * * It may be very inconvenient to the defendant to have to contest the action here. But inconvenience falling short of injustice is not sufficient to stay the action. * * * This right to come here is not confined to Englishmen. It extends to any friendly foreigner. He can seek the aid of our courts if he desires to do so. You may call this "forum-shopping" if you please, but if the forum is England, it is a good place to shop in, both for the quality of the goods and the speed of service.

Owners of the Motor Vessel "Atlantic Star" v. Owner of the Motor Vessel "Bona Spes," [1973] Q.B. 364, 381-82. Although the House of Lords ultimately reversed this decision and did invoke the *forum non conveniens* doctrine (1974 A.C. 436, 454), it significantly circumscribed its use and refused to apply the doctrine in subsequent cases, even though those cases would have been good candidates for dismissal under American law. See, e.g., Connelly v. R.T.Z. Corp., [1997] 4 All ER 335, 344 (House of Lords).

Nevertheless, there may be external limits on England's ability to apply its own *forum non conveniens* law. The Brussels Regulation (See Appendix D; see also Chapter 1, Section G) does not permit the dismissal of actions on grounds of *forum non conveniens*. That was determined by the European Court of Justice in 2005 in the following decision:

OWUSU v. JACKSON, Case C-281/02, 2005 E.C.R. I-01445. In *Owusu*, suit was filed in England by a British subject over personal injuries he received while on vacation in Jamaica and in which Jamaican law would apply. The question whether the case might be dismissed on *forum non conveniens* grounds—consistent with English practice—was eventually referred to the ECJ, which stated in relevant part:

> 37. It must be observed, first, that Article 2 of the Brussels Convention is mandatory in nature and that, according to its terms, there can be no derogation from the principle it lays down except in the cases expressly provided for by the Convention * * * . It is common ground that no exception on the basis of the forum non conveniens doctrine was provided for by the authors of the Convention, although the question was discussed when the Convention of 9 October 1978 on the Accession of Denmark, Ireland and the United Kingdom was drawn up, as is apparent from the report on that Convention by Professor Schlosser (OJ 1979 C 59, p. 71, paragraphs 77 and 78).

> 38. Respect for the principles of legal certainty, which is one of the objectives of the Brussels Convention (see, inter alia, Case C-440/97 *GIE Groupe Concorde and Others* [1999] ECRT I6307, paragraph 24), would not be fully guaranteed if the court having jurisdiction under the Convention had to be allowed to apply the forum non conveniens doctrine.

> 39. According to its preamble, the Brussels Convention is intended to strengthen in the Community the legal protection of persons established therein, by laying down common rules on jurisdiction to guarantee certainty as to the allocation of jurisdiction among the various national courts before which proceedings in a particular case may be brought.

> 40. The Court has thus held that the principle of legal certainty requires, in particular, that the jurisdictional rules which derogate from the general rule laid down in Article 2 of the Brussels Convention should be interpreted in such a way as to enable a normally well-informed defend-

ant reasonably to foresee before which courts, other than those of the State in which he is domiciled, he may be sued.

41. Application of the forum non conveniens doctrine, which allows the court seised a wide discretion as regards the question whether a foreign court would be a more appropriate forum for the trial of an action, is liable to undermine the predictability of the rules of jurisdiction laid down by the Brussels Convention, in particular that of Article 2, and consequently to undermine the principle of legal certainty, which is the basis of the Convention.

42. The legal protection of persons established in the Community would also be undermined. First, a defendant, who is generally better placed to conduct his defence before the courts of his domicile, would not be able, in circumstances such as those of the main proceedings, reasonably to foresee before which other court he may be sued. Second, where a plea is raised on the basis that a foreign court is a more appropriate forum to try the action, it is for the claimant to establish that he will not be able to obtain justice before that foreign court or, if the court seised decides to allow the plea, that the foreign court has in fact no jurisdiction to try the action or that the claimant does not, in practice, have access to effective justice before that court, irrespective of the cost entailed by the bringing of a fresh action before a court of another State and the prolongation of the procedural time-limits.

43. Moreover, allowing forum non conveniens in the context of the Brussels Convention would be likely to affect the uniform application of the rules of jurisdiction contained therein in so far as that doctrine is recognized only in a limited number of Contracting States, whereas the objective of Brussels Convention is precisely to lay down common rules to the exclusion of derogating national rules.

44. The defendants in the main proceedings emphasize the negative consequences which would result in practice from the obligation the English courts would then be under to try this case, inter alia as regards the expense of the proceedings, the possibility of recovering their costs in England if the claimant's action is dismissed, the logistical difficulties resulting from the geographical distance, the need to assess the merits of the case according to Jamaican standards, the enforceability in Jamaica of a default judgment and the impossibility of enforcing cross-claims against the other defendants.

45. In that regard, genuine as those difficulties may be, suffice it to observe that such considerations, which are precisely those which may be taken into account when forum non conveniens is considered, are not such as to call into question the mandatory nature of the fundamental rule of jurisdiction contained in Article 2 of the Brussels Convention, for the reasons set out above.

46. In the light of all the foregoing considerations, the answer to the first question must be that the Brussels Convention precludes a court of

a Contracting State from declining the jurisdiction conferred on it by Article 2 of that convention on the ground that a court of a non-Contracting State would be a more appropriate forum for the trial of the action even if the jurisdiction of no other Contracting State is in issue or the proceedings have no connecting factors to any other Contracting State. * * *

Questions: Is the value of "certainty" in litigation—which the *Owusu* Court emphasized—always or even usually one that ought to trump the value of having litigation go forward in a substantially more convenient forum than the one in which it has been brought? Doesn't abandonment of the doctrine of *forum non conveniens* give far too much power to plaintiffs to pick their forum, and thus contributes more to surprise than to predictability? In non-U.S. systems, the bases for personal jurisdiction may be narrower than those available in the U.S. Does this sufficiently mitigate any possible problem in abandoning *forum non conveniens*?

Note that, even before *Owusu*, the Brussels Regulation was treated as mirroring the prevailing opinion in most civil law nations that the plaintiff's choice of a particular forum should not be disturbed as long as a jurisdictional rule permits this choice. As one of us has explained:

> This solution is seen as providing legal certainty and avoiding costly, and potentially offensive litigation over the adequacy of the courts involved. Since [the Regulation provides a list of] fair jurisdictional bases, predictability does not come at the expense of party convenience. The principle of *lis pendens* [also embedded in the Regulation], further strengthens these values in that it prevents parallel litigation and conflicting results in different contracting states. If a case in one contracting state involves the same cause of action and the same parties as a case pending before a court in another contracting state, the second court must either dismiss the proceedings or issue a stay until the jurisdiction of the first court is established. Thus, the interplay between accepted jurisdictional bases and the preference of the forum first seized render the concept of forum non conveniens in large part irrelevant.

Zekoll, *supra*, 61 Alb. L. Rev. at 1297-1298. Persuasive? Would this solution be an alternative to the *forum non conveniens* doctrine as applied by American courts? Proposals for an international agreement on the reciprocal enforcement of foreign judgments would provide for exactly that. See Chapter 8.

B. Abstention *(Lis Pendens)* and Parallel Litigation

A party sued in a U.S. forum might prefer that litigation go forward in a foreign jurisdiction. As just discussed, one way of addressing the problem is for the defendant to seek dismissal of the U.S. proceedings on *forum non conveniens* grounds. But such dismissal may not always be likely or forthcoming. The party sued might therefore attempt to bring a reactive suit of its own in the preferred foreign forum, assuming jurisdiction can be satisfied. For example, the party sued in the U.S. might attempt to bring—in a foreign court—something in the nature of a declaratory judgment of non-liability on the underlying transaction; or perhaps the party sued in the U.S. has a counterclaim that it might attempt to bring as an affirmative claim in a foreign jurisdiction. The result is the possibility of duplicative or parallel litigation—one lawsuit here and one lawsuit abroad over the same matters. Similar problems might arise when a party initially sued abroad would prefer to have the case proceed in the U.S.

Perhaps there is little to prevent the possibility of the filing of parallel lawsuits in the first instance. But should something prevent their continued maintenance once both have been filed? One possible solution to such problems might lie in the ability of one court to issue an injunction against the proceedings in the other. In the global setting, such cross-border injunctions have the clear potential for international friction. Also, if one assumes that each court has good jurisdiction over the case, how does one conclude which proceeding ought to be privileged to proceed at the expense of the other? And what if each jurisdiction—jealous to guard its properly invoked jurisdiction—issues an injunction to the other? Another possibility for resolving the parallel litigation problem might be found in the willingness of one court system to defer to the proceedings of another court system through abstention—i.e., by staying or dismissing its own proceedings. Outside the U.S., many countries adhere to a notion of *lis alibi pendens* ["litigation pending elsewhere"]—a notion that if a parallel suit has been filed elsewhere first, and the first court has determined that it has jurisdiction, then the first-filed proceeding should ordinarily have priority. But once again, if both litigants are proceeding in courts pursuant to lawful jurisdictional grants, why should either court deny the party who has brought their later-filed action the ability to go forward with their suit? And how would a court decide that one proceeding should go forward at the expense of another? Finally, if the court wishing to abstain in deference to foreign proceedings is a U.S. federal court, consider what the authority is for doing so (or, in the alternative scenario, for issuing an antisuit injunction to halt a foreign proceeding).

BACKGROUND NOTE ON ABSTENTION AND PARALLEL LITIGATION IN THE PURELY DOMESTIC (U.S.) SETTING

The problem of parallel litigation within the U.S. is familiar to most U.S. lawyers. Such problems can arise in three different settings. First, the duplicative litigation may involve a federal court proceeding and a state court proceeding. Second, the duplicative litigation may involve two federal court proceedings. And third, duplicative litigation may involve two state court proceedings. An important question to consider is the extent to which these domestic practices can or should apply to the same sorts of problems of duplicative civil litigation at the international level, and which of these three settings (if any) provides the most appropriate model.

1. Federal-state parallel litigation. When state and federal courts would have concurrent jurisdiction over a claim, it becomes possible for lawsuits between the same parties to be filed in either system. Removal of cases from state to federal court (coupled with transfer of venue) is sometimes an available option for consolidating litigation that is pending simultaneously in state and federal courts. But there are limits on removal. [For example, in diversity of citizenship litigation, a defendant may not remove if he is a citizen of the state in which he has been sued. And there are ways for plaintiffs to defeat removal in diversity litigation, by suing a nondiverse party along with the diverse parties who might otherwise have been able to remove. Consequently, removal is not a sure-fire way to get a case into federal court, such that it might be consolidated with other related cases via transfer of venue.]

In addition, intercourt injunctions are rarely available in the state-federal setting. The Anti-Injunction Act, 28 U.S.C. § 2283 will usually stand in the way of any federal court injunction of an ongoing state court proceeding, unless the case fits one of a handful of exceptions to the Act. And supremacy concerns will usually operate to prevent state court injunctions of pending federal proceedings. See Donovan v. City of Dallas, 377 U.S. 408 (1964).

On the other hand, abstention—a self-imposed stay of a court's own proceedings—is theoretically possible from either system. State courts have a variety of *lis pendens* rules that enable them to arrest their own proceedings in favor of other proceedings. Often these rules are no more complex than favoring the suit that was filed first in time. Sometimes, however, such rules are quite weak, making it difficult to grant a stay in deference to parallel federal litigation so long as jurisdiction has been properly invoked in the state court forum. And state rules regarding *forum non conveniens* may be strong, weak, or nonexistent.

As for federal courts, matters are complex. On the one hand, the Supreme Court has said that federal courts are under a "virtually unflagging obligation" to entertain jurisdiction that the plaintiff has properly invoked. **Colorado River Water Conservation Dist. v. United States, 424 U.S. 800, 817 (1976).** That admonition would suggest that federal courts would rarely abstain and halt their own proceedings in deference to parallel state court litigation. On the other hand, in the very case that articulated the virtually-unflagging-obligation rule, the Court did indeed abstain from hearing the case brought before it, based on a laundry list of potential considerations:

> It has been held, for example, that the court first assuming jurisdiction over property may exercise that jurisdiction to the exclusion of other courts. . . . In assessing the appropriateness of dismissal in the event of an exercise of concurrent jurisdiction, a federal court may also consider such factors as the inconvenience of the federal forum . . . , the desirability of avoiding piecemeal litigation . . . ; and the order in which jurisdiction was obtained by the concurrent forums . . . . No one factor is necessarily determinative; a carefully considered judgment taking into account both the obligation to exercise jurisdiction and the combination of factors counselling against that exercise is required. . . . Only the clearest of justifications will warrant dismissal.

Id. at 818-19.

Since the decision in *Colorado River*, the Court has added further considerations, including whether there were issues of federal law that needed to be resolved and the comparative extent to which proceedings have progressed in the two forums. The predictable result of serving up such a multi-factored approach is that lower federal district courts rather routinely stay their proceedings in deference to parallel state court litigation—the basic admonition not to do so except in extraordinary circumstances notwithstanding. (In the domestic setting, therefore, results are quite hard to predict, although it may be that federal appellate courts are a bit more willing to heed *Colorado River*'s basic command than are the district courts, who would otherwise have to try the cases that they could get rid of through abstention.)

Colorado River's "virtually unflagging obligation" to exercise jurisdiction is inapplicable, however, when the federal proceeding is one in which the plaintiff seeks a declaratory judgment regarding a matter that that very same party has raised defensively in a parallel state court proceeding. For example, an insured might sue his insurer in state court for recovery on a policy. The insurance company might raise a defense of non-liability on the policy in the state court and simultaneously seek a declaratory judgment in a federal court to that same effect, suing the party that sued the company in state court. Federal jurisdiction in the declaratory judgment action will often be premised on diversity of citizenship. (The state court proceeding might not be removable by the insurance company because, for example, the plaintiff may have joined a co-citizen as a defendant in the state court action.) In Wilton v. Seven Falls Co., 515 U.S. 277 (1995), the Supreme Court indicated that abstention would be proper in such a case, even if the federal declaratory proceeding was filed first, *Colorado River* notwithstanding. The *Wilton* ruling seems to be premised on the fact that the Court read the declaratory judgment statute as making the declaratory remedy a matter of judicial discretion. 28 U.S.C. § 2201. Because the remedy was discretionary, the Court seemed to treat the continued exercise of declaratory jurisdiction as also being discretionary. *Wilton* also relied on an older pre-*Colorado River* decision in Brillhart v. Excess Ins. Co., 316 U.S. 491 (1942), that had held something similar. The *Wilton* Court thus concluded that although "the normal principle [is] that federal courts should adjudicate claims within their jurisdiction," the district court had not abused its discretion in dismissing the first-filed federal declaratory action. 515 U.S. at 288-90. *Wilton* also concluded that *Brillhart* had not been superseded by *Colorado River*.

A similar observation was made in Quackenbush v. Allstate Ins. Co., 517 U.S. 706, 707 (1996), where the Court suggested that the federal courts' ability to abstain (on the basis of the Court's more categorical abstention doctrines) was limited to "cases in which the court has discretion to grant or deny relief." But it is doubtful whether the sort of abstention that *Colorado River* might sometimes countenance would be limited to federal court lawsuits seeking equitable relief, *Quackenbush* notwithstanding. In other words, *Colorado River* might allow for parallel litigation abstention even in damages actions, at least in the sort of exceptional circumstances contemplated by *Colorado River*.

2. Federal-federal parallel litigation. Federal courts use a somewhat different approach to the problem of abstention in the parallel litigation setting when the litigation is proceeding simultaneously in two different federal courts.

To be sure, transfer of venue of one of the lawsuits may be one way to achieve an end to parallel litigation, at least where transfer's preconditions are met. And there are other mechanisms for complex litigation that allow for *pretrial* consolidation of federal cases filed in different federal district courts over the same events or transactions, see 28 U.S.C. § 1407, or more rarely, for consolidation for trial in some single incident mass disaster cases, see 28 U.S.C. § 1369, et seq. (Multiparty Multiforum Trial Jurisdiction Act of 2002). But in the more typical setting, the question whether one federal court will stay its proceedings in deference to similar proceedings in another federal court (or, alternatively, whether a federal court will enjoin proceedings in anther federal court) is largely one of discretion, unaided by any sort of strong presumption in favor of exercising jurisdiction, such as that in *Colorado River.*

The standard for such intra-federal system stays was developed from the Supreme Court's decision in Kerotest Mfg. Co. v. C-O-Two Fire Equipment Co., 342 U.S. 180 (1952), in which the Court concluded that the question whether to grant an intercourt injunction or to stay its own proceedings is committed to the discretion of "the lower courts" as a matter of their "wise judicial administration." Nevertheless, most lower courts since *Kerotest* have effectively adopted a first-in-time rule, under which the federal court that first acquired jurisdiction over the dispute is given a presumptive, albeit not conclusive, right to proceed free from interference by another federal court. See, e.g., Semmes Motors, Inc. v. Ford Motor Co., 429 F.2d 1197, 1203 (2d Cir. 1970). The presumption can be overcome only by a fairly strong showing that the later-filed suit is, on balance, to be preferred; and the calculus for a court issuing a stay of its own proceedings is to be similarly made.

Is a priority rule consistent with the Supreme Court's emphasis on flexibility in deciding such questions? Consider the Court explanation for the difference:

> Generally, as between state and federal courts, the rule is that "the pendency of an action in the state court is no bar to proceedings concerning the same matter in the Federal court having jurisdiction." * * * As between federal district courts, however, though no precise rule has evolved, the general principle is to avoid duplicative litigation. * * * This difference in general approach between state-federal concurrent jurisdiction and wholly federal concurrent jurisdiction stems from the virtually unflagging obligation of the federal courts to exercise the jurisdiction given them. * * * Given this obligation, and the absence of weightier considerations of constitutional adjudication and state-federal relations, the circumstances permitting the dismissal of a federal suit due to the presence of a concurrent state proceeding for reasons of wise judicial administration are considerably more limited than the circumstances appropriate for abstention.

Colorado River, 424 U.S. at 817-18.

3. State-state parallel litigation. Still less predictable is the problem of abstention (and intercourt injunctions) when litigation is pending in two or more *state* courts simultaneously. As noted above, different states have different approaches to the problem of *lis pendens*. So it is theoretically possible for neither state to abstain, or for one to abstain in deference to the other. (One can only hope that both do not abstain simultaneously!) Intercourt injunctions are also a possibility, and as between states, there is no Anti-Injunction Act to contend with. Nevertheless, the Supreme Court has indicated that states do not need to honor a sister state injunction purporting to bar their proceedings. Baker v. General Motors Corp., 522 U.S. 222 (1998). But it remains true that the party enjoined from litigating elsewhere could be held in contempt by the injunction-issuing court for having violated the injunction.

Of course, the larger question still remains: How do these various approaches to the problem of parallel litigation in the all-domestic setting translate (if at all) to the question of intercourt injunctions and abstention in the setting of transnational civil litigation? Although concerns of federalism are absent in such settings, there is a concern that is *not* present in the all-domestic setting—a concern for comity or respect for judicial proceedings of a foreign country. Consider whether that factor should result in a greater willingness on the part of federal courts (or state courts) to defer to parallel foreign country litigation, or to refuse to enjoin such litigation.

Royal and Sun Alliance Ins. Co. of Canada v. Century Int'l Arms, Inc.

United States Court of Appeals, Second Circuit, 2006.
466 F.3d 88.

Gerald E. Lynch, District Judge[*]:

Plaintiff-appellant Royal and Sun Alliance Insurance Company of Canada ("RSA") seeks damages from defendants-appellees Century International Arms, Inc. and Century Arms, Inc. (collectively "Century America") for the reimbursement of defense expenses and the payment of deductibles it claims to be owed under various insurance policies. Century America moved to dismiss the complaint in deference to a pending action previously filed by RSA in Canada against Century America's Canadian affiliate, Century International Arms Ltd. ("Century Canada"), based on the same insurance policies and the same factual allegations. The United States District Court for the Southern District of New York (Deborah A. Batts, Judge), granted defendants' motion, concluding that considerations of comity warranted dismissal of RSA's action against Century America.

On appeal, RSA argues that the dismissal was improper because the district court failed to give proper weight to the "virtually unflagging obligation . . . to exercise the jurisdiction given [it]." Colorado River Water Conservation Dist. v.

---

[*] The Honorable Gerard E. Lynch, of the United States District Court for the Southern District of New York, sitting by designation.

United States, 424 U.S. 800, 817 (1976). We agree and therefore vacate and remand for further proceedings.

BACKGROUND

Century America is in the business of manufacturing and distributing firearms and munitions. In connection with that business, Century America and its affiliate Century Canada obtained liability insurance policies from RSA for the time period between June 12, 1991, and March 25, 1994. During the policy period, Century America was sued by a number of individuals who alleged that they had suffered injuries caused by defects in Century America's products. RSA defended these lawsuits pursuant to the terms of the insurance policies, and eventually negotiated settlements with the various plaintiffs and paid the settlement amounts on behalf of Century America. At the conclusion of the actions, RSA requested reimbursement for defense expenses and deductibles it claimed to be owed under the policies. No payment was received.

RSA and Century Canada are both Canadian corporations, and under the insurance policies Century Canada is named as the first insured party while Century America is listed as an additional insured. Accordingly, when RSA did not receive the money it believed it was owed under the policies, RSA filed an action in Superior Court, Province of Quebec, District of Montreal, Canada, against Century Canada, seeking payment for its expenses and deductibles. In its response to the Canadian action, Century Canada asserted that the expenses and deductibles for which RSA sought reimbursement "relate[d] to events which occurred in the United States and claims asserted against name[d] insureds other than . . . [Century Canada]," Joint Appx. at 42, and that under the terms of the policies, the rights and obligations of RSA, Century Canada, and Century America apply "[s]eparately to each insured against whom claim is made or 'action' is brought," id. at 41.

Given Century Canada's averment that RSA had, in effect, sued the wrong insured party in the Canadian action, RSA filed the present complaint in the Southern District of New York against Century America. Soon after the case was filed, Century America moved to dismiss the complaint in favor of RSA's pending action against Century Canada. The district court granted Century America's motion to dismiss, stating that it had "the inherent power to stay or dismiss an action based on the pendency of a related proceeding in a foreign jurisdiction," but recognizing that its discretion was "limited by its obligation to exercise jurisdiction." In exercising its discretion, the district court concluded that the existence of a parallel proceeding in Canada involving Century America's affiliate, coupled with Century America's consent to jurisdiction in Canada, militated in favor of dismissal. This appeal followed.

DISCUSSION

We review a district court's dismissal of an action based on considerations of international comity for abuse of discretion. JP Morgan Chase Bank v. Altos Hornos De Mexico, S.A., 412 F.3d 418, 422-23 (2d Cir. 2005). However, because we are reviewing a court's decision to abstain from exercising jurisdiction, our review is "more rigorous" than that which is generally employed under the abuse-of-discretion standard. Hachamovitch v. DeBuono, 159 F.3d 687, 693 (2d Cir. 1998). "In review of decisions to abstain, there is little practical distinction between review for abuse of discretion and review *de novo*." Id. Of course, we review *de novo* a district court's conclusions of law. *JP Morgan Chase Bank*, 412 F.3d at 423.

Century America argues that the district court's decision was supported by the doctrine of international comity abstention. International comity is "the recognition which one nation allows within its territory to the legislative, executive or judicial acts of another nation, having due regard both to international duty and convenience." Hilton v. Guyot, 159 U.S. 113, 163-64 (1895). While the doctrine can be stated clearly in the abstract, in practice we have described its boundaries as "amorphous" and "fuzzy." *JP Morgan Chase Bank*, 412 F.3d at 423, quoting Harold G. Maier, *Extraterritorial Jurisdiction at a Crossroads: An Intersection Between Public and Private International Law*, 76 Am. J. Int'l L. 280, 281 (1982). In addition to its imprecise application, even where the doctrine clearly applies it "is not an imperative obligation of courts but rather is a discretionary rule of 'practice, convenience, and expediency.'" Id., quoting Pravin Banker Assocs., Ltd. v. Banco Popular Del Peru, 109 F.3d 850, 854 (2d Cir. 1997).

Often, a party invoking the doctrine of international comity seeks the recognition of a foreign judgment. In this case, however, Century America argues that concerns of comity favor the recognition of a pending foreign proceeding that has yet to reach final judgment, and that proper deference to that proceeding requires abstention in domestic courts. This type of comity has been termed the "comity of the courts." See Joseph Story, Commentaries on the Conflict of Laws § 38 (1834) (distinguishing between the comity of the courts and the comity of nations), cited in Hartford Fire Ins. Co. v. California, 509 U.S. 764, 817 (1993) (Scalia, J., dissenting).

Generally, concurrent jurisdiction in United States courts and the courts of a foreign sovereign does not result in conflict. China Trade & Dev. Corp. v. M.V. Choong Yong, 837 F.2d 33, 36 (2d Cir. 1987). Rather, "'[p]arallel proceedings in the same in personam claim should ordinarily be allowed to proceed simultaneously, at least until a judgment is reached in one which can be pled as res judicata in the other.'" Id., quoting Laker Airways, Ltd. v. Sabena Belgian World Airlines, 731 F.2d 909, 926-27 (D.C. Cir. 1984), citing *Colorado River*, 424 U.S. at 817. The mere existence of parallel foreign proceedings does not negate the district courts' "virtually unflagging obligation . . . to exercise the jurisdiction given them." *Colorado River*, 424 U.S. at 817.

We have recognized one discrete category of foreign litigation that generally requires the dismissal of parallel district court actions—foreign bankruptcy proceedings. A foreign nation's interest in the "equitable and orderly distribution of a debtor's property" is an interest deserving of particular respect and deference, and accordingly we have followed the general practice of American courts and regularly deferred to such actions. * * *

Outside the bankruptcy context, we have yet to articulate a list of factors a district court should consider when exercising its discretion to abstain in deference to pending litigation in a foreign court. However, whatever factors weigh in favor of abstention, "[o]nly the clearest of justifications will warrant dismissal." *Colorado River*, 424 U.S. at 819. The task of a district court evaluating a request for dismissal based on a parallel foreign proceeding is not to articulate a justification *for* the exercise of jurisdiction, but rather to determine whether circumstances exist that justify the surrender of that jurisdiction. Moses H. Cone Mem'l Hosp. v. Mercury Constr. Corp., 460 U.S. 1, 25-26 (1983); see also *Colorado River*, 424 U.S. at 813 ("Abstention from the exercise of federal jurisdiction is the exception, not the rule."). The exceptional circumstances that would support such a surrender must, of course, raise considerations which are not generally present as a result of parallel litigation, otherwise the routine would be considered exceptional, and a district court's unflagging obligation to exercise its jurisdiction would become merely a polite request.

Appellees contend that the above standards, articulated by the Supreme Court in *Colorado River* and *Moses H. Cone*, do not apply to the present matter because those cases involved abstention in favor of parallel state proceedings while the parallel action here at issue is pending in a foreign jurisdiction. Appellees' effort to distinguish these precedents is accurate, as far as it goes, but it does not go far. The factors a court must weigh in exercising its discretion to abstain in deference to parallel proceedings will indeed differ depending on the nature of the proceedings. For example, if the parallel proceeding is in a foreign jurisdiction, the district court need not consider the balance between state and federal power dictated by our Constitution. Conversely, if the parallel proceeding is in a state court, the district court need not concern itself with issues of international relations. However, while the relevant factors to be considered differ depending on the posture of the case, the starting point for the inquiry remains unchanged: a district court's "virtually unflagging obligation" to exercise its jurisdiction. *Colorado River*, 424 U.S. at 817. In weighing the considerations for and against abstention, a court's "heavy obligation to exercise jurisdiction" exists regardless of what factors are present on the other side of the balance. *Id.* at 820; see also Finova Capital Corp. v. Ryan Helicopters U.S.A., Inc., 180 F.3d 896, 898 (7th Cir. 1999) (applying "the same general principles" of *Colorado River* to international abstention); Ingersoll Milling Mach. Co. v. Granger, 833 F.2d 680, 685 (7th Cir. 1987) (stating that *Colorado River* and *Moses H. Cone* serve as a "helpful guide" when applied to cases of international abstention); cf. Bigio v. Coca-Cola Co., 239 F.3d 440, 454 (2d Cir. 2000) (as amended) ("When a court dismisses a complaint in favor of a foreign forum pursuant to the doctrine of international comity, it declines to exercise jurisdiction it admittedly has.").

The Supreme Court has recognized that a decision to abstain from exercising jurisdiction based on the existence of parallel litigation "does not rest on a mechanical checklist, but on a careful balancing of the important factors . . . as they apply in a given case, with the balance heavily weighted in favor of the exercise of jurisdiction." *Moses H. Cone*, 460 U.S. at 16. "No one factor is necessarily determinative; a carefully considered judgment taking into account both the obligation to exercise jurisdiction and the combination of factors counselling against that exercise is required." *Colorado River,* 424 U.S. at 818-19, citing *Landis v. N. Am. Co.,* 299 U.S. 248, 254-55 (1936); see also *Moses H. Cone,* 460 U.S. at 15 (stating that *Colorado River* did not "prescribe a hard-and-fast rule for dismissals of this type, but instead described some of the factors relevant to the decision").

In the context of parallel proceedings in a foreign court, a district court should be guided by the principles upon which international comity is based: the proper respect for litigation in and the courts of a sovereign nation, fairness to litigants, and judicial efficiency. See Turner Entm't Co. v. Degeto Film GmbH, 25 F.3d 1512, 1518 (11th Cir. 1994); see also United Feature Syndicate, Inc. v. Miller Features Syndicate, Inc., 216 F. Supp. 2d 198, 212 (S.D.N.Y. 2002). Proper consideration of these principles will no doubt require an evaluation of various factors, such as the similarity of the parties, the similarity of the issues, the order in which the actions were filed, the adequacy of the alternate forum, the potential prejudice to either party, the convenience of the parties, the connection between the litigation and the United States, and the connection between the litigation and the foreign jurisdiction. See, e.g., *Finova Capital Corp.,* 180 F.3d at 898-99; see also *Bigio,* 239 F.3d at 454. This list is not exhaustive, and a district court should examine the "totality of the circumstances," *Finova Capital Corp.,* 180 F.3d at 900, to determine whether the specific facts before it are sufficiently exceptional to justify abstention.

In the present case, the district court did not identify any exceptional circumstances that would support abstention, and therefore the dismissal of the action was an abuse of discretion. The district court's decision to dismiss the action was based on four factors: the existence of the Canadian action against Century Canada, Century America's consent to jurisdiction in Canada, the affiliation between Century America and Century Canada, and the adequacy of Canadian judicial procedures. These factors led the district court to conclude that the action in Canada was a parallel action that provided an adequate forum for RSA's claims, and that therefore a dismissal of the case was warranted.

The district court's conclusion that the Canadian action is adequate and parallel merits a brief discussion. Century Canada and Century America are affiliated but separate entities. For two actions to be considered parallel, the parties in the actions need not be the same, but they must be substantially the same, litigating substantially the same issues in both actions. See Dittmer v. County of Suffolk, 146 F.3d 113, 118 (2d Cir. 1998); see also Schneider Nat'l Carriers, Inc. v. Carr, 903 F.2d 1154, 1156 (7th Cir. 1990) ("Suits are parallel if substantially the same parties are litigating substantially the same issues simultaneously in two fora."). Whether Century Canada and Century America are substantially the same party for purposes of the relevant insurance policies was an issue raised in the Canadian action, where Century Canada asserted that it is not responsible for the obligations of Century America under the policies. The district court recognized that this issue was unsettled, but concluded that the question of which company is liable to RSA should be resolved in Canada. The fact that Century America is not a party to the Canadian action did not, in the district court's view, present a problem for the unified adjudication of RSA's claims because Century America had consented to the jurisdiction of the Canadian courts.

On appeal, RSA argues that Century America's consent to jurisdiction is small beer, because the statute of limitations has expired on RSA's potential claim against Century America in Canada. This issue was not raised or addressed in the district court, but neither the district court nor RSA can be faulted for any oversight. In response to Century America's motion, RSA had argued that Century America was not subject to the jurisdiction of the Canadian courts; Century America did not consent to jurisdiction in Canada until its reply brief in the district court. Accordingly, RSA was not afforded an opportunity to respond regarding other reasons why Canada might not be an adequate forum, such as the statute of limitations, and the issue was never presented to the district court for consideration.

Whether a statute of limitations renders a foreign jurisdiction inadequate for purposes of international comity abstention is a question we have not previously addressed. In the context of a motion to dismiss for *forum non conveniens*, a foreign jurisdiction is not adequate unless it "will permit [the plaintiff] to litigate the subject matter of its dispute." Norex Petroleum Ltd. v. Access Indus., Inc., 416 F.3d 146, 159 (2d Cir. 2005). However, while "abstention doctrines and the doctrine of *forum non conveniens* proceed from a similar premise . . . [,] abstention doctrine is of a distinct historical pedigree, and the traditional considerations behind dismissal for *forum non conveniens* differ markedly from those informing the decision to abstain." Quackenbush v. Allstate Ins. Co., 517 U.S. 706, 722-23 (1996).

In any event, we need not decide whether Century Canada and Century America are sufficiently similar to support a finding that the Canadian action is parallel to this case. Nor need we decide whether statute-of-limitations problems render a foreign forum inadequate in the context of international comity abstention. Even if we were to adopt the district court's conclusions that the Canadian action is a parallel action and that Canada provides an adequate forum for RSA's claims against Century America, those conclusions do not support the district court's dismissal of the action.

The existence of a parallel action in an adequate foreign jurisdiction must be the beginning, not the end, of a district court's determination of whether abstention is appropriate. As we explained above, circumstances that routinely exist in connection with parallel litigation cannot reasonably be considered exceptional circumstances, and therefore the mere existence of an adequate parallel action, by itself, does not justify the dismissal of a case on grounds of international comity abstention. Rather, additional circumstances must be present—such as a foreign nation's interest in uniform bankruptcy proceedings—that outweigh the district court's general obligation to exercise its jurisdiction. The district court did not identify any such special circumstances.

Finally, both parties address the question of whether, as an alternative to dismissing the action, the district court should have considered staying proceedings in deference to the Canadian litigation. Because the propriety of a temporary stay was not raised in the district court, we do not decide whether the entry of such a stay would have been appropriate. However, on remand the district court may consider the propriety of a stay based on the pending Canadian action.

In the context of abstention in deference to parallel state-court litigation, the Supreme Court has cautioned that "a stay is as much a refusal to exercise federal jurisdiction as a dismissal," because the decision to grant a stay "necessarily contemplates that the federal court will have nothing further to do in resolving any substantive part of the case." *Moses H. Cone*, 460 U.S. at 28. However, a measured temporary stay need not result in a complete forfeiture of jurisdiction. As a lesser intrusion on the principle of obligatory jurisdiction, which might permit the district court a window to determine whether the foreign action will in fact offer an efficient vehicle for fairly resolving all the rights of the parties, such a stay is an alternative that normally should be considered before a comity-based dismissal is entertained.

For example, *in Pravin Banker Associates,* we approved of the district court's measured response to the existence of parallel proceedings in *Peru.* 109 F.3d 850 (2d Cir. 1997). Initially, the district court granted a six-month stay to allow for "the orderly completion of [one defendant's] Peruvian liquidation proceedings." Id. at 853. However, at the conclusion of the stay and an additional two-month stay granted by the district court a defendant moved for "an indefinite stay to allow [defendant] Peru to complete its efforts to renegotiate its foreign debt." Id. at 855. The district court denied the defendant's motion, and we agreed with the court's decision, because an indefinite stay would have prejudiced the interests of the United States. Similarly, other Courts of Appeals have expressed a preference for measured stays of proceedings, where appropriate, in deference to parallel foreign litigation, instead of the more drastic measure of dismissal. See, e.g., Posner v. Essex Ins. Co., 178 F.3d 1209, 1224 (11th Cir. 1999) (holding that district court should have entered a stay instead of dismissal and noting that the Eleventh Circuit's jurisprudence "does not dictate that we should dismiss cases with respect to which foreign jurisdictions are conducting parallel proceedings"); *Turner Entm't Co.,* 25 F.3d at 1523 ("[A]t this stage of the litigation, the appropriate resolution is a stay rather than a dismissal of the American action."); *Ingersoll Milling Mach. Co.,* 833 F.2d at 686 ("Moreover, it is not insignificant—indeed, it is very significant—that the district court's action in this case was a decidedly measured one. The court did not dismiss the action; it simply stayed further proceedings . . . .").

Accordingly, on remand the district court may consider whether its obligation to exercise jurisdiction over this action could be satisfied despite the entry of a brief stay to allow the Canadian court to determine if, for example, Century Canada is liable for the money RSA claims to be owed under the policies. We do not now decide that such a stay would necessarily be appropriate, or that other bases for a temporary stay would not be proper. Those questions are left to the district court in the first instance.

CONCLUSION

The factors relied upon by the district court in granting Appellee's motion to dismiss are not sufficient to overcome the virtually unflagging obligation of a district court to exercise the jurisdiction conferred on it by Congress. The record contains no evidence of any exceptional circumstances that would justify abstention from jurisdiction. Accordingly, we hold that the district court abused its discretion by dismissing the action. * * *

NOTES AND QUESTIONS FOR DISCUSSION

1. Should *Colorado River*'s strong presumption in favor of the exercise of federal court jurisdiction in the face of parallel state proceedings be equally applicable in the setting of parallel foreign litigation? A possible argument in favor of such a view is that if Congress has provided for the jurisdiction, and absent "exceptional circumstances," courts should exercise their jurisdiction when properly invoked. Could one argue, however, that international comity concerns are a stronger ground for abstention than the federalism concerns present in the domestic parallel litigation setting (and which ordinarily do *not* weigh in favor of abstention)? For a negative answer, see Neuchatel Swiss Gen. Ins. Co. v. Lufthansa Airlines, 925 F.2d 1193, 1195 (9th Cir. 1991) ("[T]he fact that the parallel proceedings are pending in a foreign jurisdiction rather than in a state court is immaterial. We reject the notion that a federal court owes greater deference to foreign courts than to our own state courts.").

2. How does the *Royal & Sun Alliance* court's language of "unflagging" jurisdictional obligation in the setting of international abstention comport with the federal courts' willingness to allow for dismissal on *forum non conveniens* grounds? Does the latter require "exceptional circumstances" before dismissal can be granted? The court states that *forum non conveniens* has different roots than abstention and that their prerequisites "differ markedly." Is the court's effort at a sharp distinction persuasive? To be sure, *forum non conveniens* may be a ground for dismissal whether or not there is pending litigation elsewhere. But in the transnational setting of parallel litigation, both the *Colorado River* abstention doctrine and *forum non conveniens* doctrine argue that litigation should go forward in a foreign rather than a federal forum. Why *shouldn't* the standards between the two doctrines be roughly similar? Indeed, could it be argued that international comity is more greatly implicated (thus making the argument for abstention stronger) when there is an already pending foreign proceeding?

3. The *Royal & Sun Alliance* court makes clear that the risk of duplicative proceedings is *not* an extraordinary circumstance warranting a federal court's dismissing or staying its proceedings. Why not? In *Colorado River*, the Supreme Court mentioned the desirability of avoiding "piecemeal" litigation. Presumably, however, the Court is referring to something more than the fact that "duplicative" litigation would result if a federal court did not abstain in favor of parallel state court litigation. That is because *Colorado River*'s requirement of extraordinary circumstances already supposes that there is duplicative litigation and that, in and of itself, is not an exceptional circumstance sufficient to warrant abstention. The reference to "piecemeal" litigation therefore must have to do with a concern that the federal court might be able to resolve only a portion of the relevant contest—because, for example, of problems respecting joinder of parties and claims—whereas an ongoing state court lawsuit might yield a more complete or comprehensive resolution of the dispute. See Evans Transp. Co. v. Scullin Steel Co., 693 F.2d 715, 717 (7th Cir. 1982) ("[I]t is not enough, to justify abstention, that a failure to stay the federal suit may result in judicial diseconomy—in having two active lawsuits instead of one. That will always be possible when there is a parallel state suit pending.").

4. The court assumes, as do most federal courts, that *Colorado River* is the proper benchmark for abstention in the transnational civil litigation setting. But why isn't the *Kerotest* decision the proper benchmark? Recall that *Kerotest* deals with the problem of parallel litigation in two federal courts, in which stays are left to the discretion of the district judge, and without *Colorado River*'s strong presumption to exercise jurisdiction. As previously noted, *Kerotest* has evolved into a rule that presumptively privileges the first-filed federal lawsuit. Should the better presumption be one of abstention in deference to a first-filed foreign proceeding where jurisdiction is unproblematic? See Austen L. Parrish, *Duplicative Foreign Litigation*, 78 Geo. Wash. L. Rev. 237, 270 (2010) (suggesting such a proposal, provided foreign jurisdiction comports with U.S. standards). Some courts seem to apply a less restrictive view of the prospect for abstention than do courts like *Royal & Sun Alliance*. See, e.g., Turner Entertainment Co. v. Degeto Film GmbH, 25 F.3d 1512 (11th Cir. 1994) (noting, however, that foreign litigation was already at the appellate stage). And, of course, courts outside the U.S. are much more inclined to stay their own proceedings in deference to a first-filed action elsewhere. Should U.S. courts attempt to conform their abstention practices to those of other legal systems?

5. Abstention by federal courts in the international litigation setting, like in the all-domestic setting, will inevitably be an ad hoc determination that considers a variety of factors, no one of which will be dispositive. Predictability, therefore, will be in short supply. A full laundry list of relevant factors listed by the court in Finova Capital Corp. v. Ryan Helicopters U.S.A., Inc., 180 F.3d 896, 899 (7th Cir. 1999)), from which the *Royal & Sun Alliance* court seemed to draw, included the following:

- The identity of the court that first assumed jurisdiction over the property.
- The relative inconvenience of the federal forum.
- The need to avoid piecemeal litigation.
- The order in which the respective proceedings were filed.
- Whether federal or foreign law provides the rule of decision.
- Whether the foreign action protects the federal plaintiff's rights.
- The relative progress of the federal and foreign proceedings.
- The vexatious or contrived nature of the federal court claim.
- The similarity of the identity of the parties and issues.
- The comparative nexus between the U.S. and foreign forums and the issues involved.
- The totality of the circumstances.

Are there any additional factors that might be added to this list (as if there were not enough already)? Suppose there are doubts whether the foreign court, although possessed of jurisdiction under its law, would be able to render a judgment that would be enforced in the U.S—for example, because of public policy concerns with the potential judgment or due process concerns with the exercise of personal jurisdiction. See Chapter 8. Or suppose that the foreign court has already issued a judgment, but enforcement has not yet been sought?

6. Interestingly, one of the more important factors regarding international abstention—and not mentioned in *Colorado River*, but certainly relevant to *forum non conveniens* analysis—is the extent to which the foreign proceedings will protect the rights of the parties. And while federal courts may not always put much stock in the first-filed factor mentioned by *Colorado River* (but see Ontario, Inc. v. World Imports U.S.A., Inc.145 F. Supp. 2d 288, 291 (W.D.N.Y. 2001)), the extent of proceedings in the foreign forum seems to be an important consideration for many courts. See, e.g., *Turner Entertainment, supra*; *Goldhammer v. Dunkin' Donuts, Inc.*, 59 F. Supp. 2d 248, 255 (D. Mass. 1999); but see *Neuchatel Swiss Gen. Ins.*, 925 F.2d at 1195 ("[T]he mere fact that parallel proceedings may be further along does not make a case 'exceptional' for the purpose of invoking the *Colorado River* exception to the general rule that federal courts must exercise their jurisdiction concurrently with courts of other jurisdictions").

A COMPARATIVE NOTE ON LIS PENDENS

As noted above in connection with the discussion of *forum non conveniens*, the European perspective is that the court of a member state that first acquires good jurisdiction will not dismiss its proceedings even though another forum may be substantially more convenient. In addition, a court will not stay its own proceedings in deference to a later-filed proceeding, and other member state courts are generally obligated to dismiss later-filed parallel actions. Council Regulation (EC) 44/2001 on Jurisdiction and the Recognition and Enforcement of Judgments in Civil and Commercial Matters (see Appendix D):

Section 9. Lis pendens—related actions.

Article 27:

1. Where proceedings involving the same cause of action and between the same parties are brought in the courts of different Member States, any court other than the court first seised shall of its own motion stay its proceedings until such time as the jurisdiction of the court first seised is established.

2. Where the jurisdiction of the court first seised is established, any court other than the court first seised shall decline jurisdiction in favour of that court.

This approach means that some relatively predictable, and usually suitable rules will apply, at least when the suits involve the same parties and the same cause of action. A somewhat less absolute set of rules applies when the proceedings are "related" but do not involve the "same" parties or cause of action. See Art. 28.

The inflexible first-come-first-served approach of Article 27 has created some substantial problems, however, because the adjudicatory speed in a few EU-Member States is far below that of most other European legal systems. See Elisabetta Silvestri, *The Never-Ending Reforms of Italian Civil Justice*, http://unipv.academia.edu/ElisabettaSilvestri/Papers/825268. In Italy, for example, the average time it takes to render a final court decision in civil cases exceeds seven years. Id. Given this length of civil court proceedings, the ironclad rule of Article 27 can give rise to abusive dilatory practices. Consider the following problem:

> Company A has its seat in the Netherlands. It agreed to purchase certain goods for a certain price from company B which has its seat in France. Company A received the goods but failed to pay the purchase price, and now has every reason to expect Company B to file suit in the Netherlands. In order to preempt this lawsuit from being adjudicated in the Netherlands, Company A quickly files a suit in Italy asking for a declaratory judgment of no liability. As a consequence, under Article 27, no Dutch court could adjudicate this matter until and unless the Italian court concludes that it does not have jurisdiction. This procedural decision alone, however, may take years during which the creditor has no access to the funds it is entitled to under the purchase contract.

This strict priority-based practice, which has become known as the "Italian Torpedo," even enables a party successfully to torpedo an exclusive forum selection agreement that it entered into pursuant to Article 23 of the Brussels Regulation. According to the European Court of Justice, the *lis pendens* principle adhered to under Article 27 trumps any forum selection agreement. Specifically, the Court held that the rule "must be interpreted as meaning that a court second seised whose jurisdiction has been claimed under an agreement conferring jurisdiction must nevertheless stay proceedings until the court first seised has declared that it has no jurisdiction." (Decision of the ECJ of December 9, 2003, Case C-116/02 Erich Gasser GmbH v. MISAT s.r.l., 2003 E.C.R. I-14693, I-14741, ¶ 54). See Steven B. Burbank, *International Civil Litigation in U.S. Courts; Becoming a Paper Tiger?* 33 U. Pa. J. Int'l L. 663, 663-64 (2011) (noting the "Italian torpedo" and noting the "sclerotic" state of the Italian court system as one "in need of angioplasty"). Thus, in the above example, nothing would change even if both parties had agreed to litigate any and all disputes arising out of or relating to the purchase contract exclusively in Dutch courts.

In the meantime, however, the European Union has come to realize that the strict *lis pendens* rule can produce undesirable results. In 2010, the European Commission published a reform proposal aimed at addressing the above problems as well as others that occur as a result of the strict interpretation of Article 27. See Proposal for a Regulation of the European Parliament and of the Council on jurisdiction and the recognition and enforcement of judgments in civil and commercial matters of December 14, 2010, COM(2010) 748 final. On December 6, 2012, the Council of the EU Justice Ministers adopted a recast version of the Brussels I Regulation. (Regulation (EU) 1215/2012 of the European Parliament and of the Council of 12 December 2012 on jurisdiction and the recognition and enforcement of judgments in civil and commercial matters (recast). Official Journal, OJ 20 December 2012, L 351/1).

With respect to the relationship between exclusive forum selection agreements and *lis pendens* Article 31 para. 2 and 3 of the revised Regulation provide that:

> 2. . . . where a court of a Member State on which an agreement as referred to in Article 25 [which stipulates the requirements for forum selection agreements] confers exclusive jurisdiction is seised, any court of another Member State shall stay the proceedings until such time as the court seised on the basis of the agreement declares that it has no jurisdiction under the agreement.
>
> 3. Where the court designated in the agreement has established jurisdiction in accordance with the agreement, any court of another Member State shall decline jurisdiction in favour of that court.

Thus, if the parties have agreed to confer exclusive jurisdiction on a particular court, that court may hear the case even if another court was first seised. All other courts must decline jurisdiction and terminate their proceedings once the designated court has concluded that it has jurisdiction.

These new provisions, which will only apply as of January 10, 2015, (see Art.81), are in line with the objectives of the 2005 Hague Choice of Court Convention, a project we summarize as follows:

NOTE ON THE HAGUE CHOICE OF COURT CONVENTION

The Hague Convention of 30 June 2005 on Choice of Court Agreements is a proposal designed to promote the effectiveness of forum selection clauses between parties to international business transactions. See Chapter 7; see also Appendix C. It would apply to "exclusive" choice of court agreements (i.e., forum selection clauses) in international "civil and commercial" transactions, primarily between businesses, and excluding a great number of matters such as personal injury, antitrust and most intellectual property litigation apart from copyright. Although largely designed to ensuring the enforcement of judgments in cases brought in chosen courts consistent with the Convention, it also includes provisions that bear on the question of *forum non conveniens* dismissal and abstention in the face of parallel proceedings.

If the chosen court concludes that the Convention applies to the choice of court agreement (forum selection clause), it is obligated to exercise jurisdiction over the case, and shall not dismiss, even "on the ground that the dispute should be decided in the court of another state." Art. 5. In the face of a choice of court agreement, other states "shall suspend or dismiss" actions brought before them (Art. 6), subject to a handful of fairly limited exceptions, but including a public policy exception where "giving effect to the agreement would lead to a manifest injustice or would be manifestly contrary to the public policy of the State of the court seised."

As yet, the Convention has not entered into force, although the U.S. signed it on Jan. 19, 2009, as did the E.U. in April 2009. Both have indicated their intention to ratify the treaty. Note that if the Convention should go into effect, it would be binding on state court practice as well as on the federal courts.

C. INTERNATIONAL ANTISUIT INJUNCTIONS AND PARALLEL LITIGATION

1. The Approach(es) of U.S. Courts

As noted above, in the purely domestic setting, a combination of rules and statutes generally operates to prevent one court from enjoining another in the parallel litigation setting—whether it is a federal injunction of a state proceedings, or the reverse. There is no statute that speaks to the question of intercourt injunctions as between U.S. and foreign courts in the international parallel litigation setting, however. As a result, the rules respecting such injunctions are judge-made. These rules for antisuit injunctions have largely developed in the lower courts, because the Supreme Court has yet to weigh-in on the problem. Consider the freedom with which a federal court ought to grant a request for an injunction of foreign proceedings.

Kaepa, Inc. v. Achilles Corp.

United States Court of Appeals, Fifth Circuit, 1996.

76 F.3d 624.

JACQUES WIENER, CIRCUIT JUDGE.

The primary issue presented by this appeal is whether the district court erred by enjoining Defendant-Appellant Achilles Corporation from prosecuting an action that it filed in Japan as plaintiff, which essentially mirrored a lawsuit previously filed by Plaintiff-Appellee Kaepa, Inc. in state court and then being prosecuted in federal district court by Kaepa. Given the private nature of the dispute, the clear indications by both parties that claims arising from their contract should be adjudicated in this country, and the duplicative and vexatious nature of the Japanese action, we conclude that the district court did not abuse its discretion by barring the prosecution of the foreign litigation. Accordingly, we affirm the grant of the antisuit injunction.

I. FACTS AND PROCEEDINGS

This case arises out of a contractual dispute between two sophisticated, private corporations: Kaepa, an American company which manufactures athletic shoes; and Achilles, a Japanese business enterprise with annual sales that approximate one billion dollars. In April 1993, the two companies entered into a distributorship agreement whereby Achilles obtained exclusive rights to market

Kaepa's footwear in Japan. The distributorship agreement expressly provided that Texas law and the English language would govern its interpretation, that it would be enforceable in San Antonio, Texas, and that Achilles consented to the jurisdiction of the Texas courts. [The district court held that this clause permitted jurisdiction in Texas, and required that the agreement be interpreted under United States law and the English language. Neither party challenged this ruling.]

Kaepa grew increasingly dissatisfied with Achilles's performance under the contract. Accordingly, in July of 1994, Kaepa filed suit in Texas state court, alleging (1) fraud and negligent misrepresentation by Achilles to induce Kaepa to enter into the distributorship agreement, and (2) breach of contract by Achilles. Thereafter, Achilles removed the action to federal district court, and the parties began a laborious discovery process which to date has resulted in the production of tens of thousands of documents. In February 1995, after appearing in the Texas action, removing the case to federal court, and engaging in comprehensive discovery, Achilles brought its own action in Japan, alleging mirror-image claims: (1) fraud by Kaepa to induce Achilles to enter into the distributorship agreement, and (2) breach of contract by Kaepa.

Back in Texas, Kaepa promptly filed a motion asking the district court to enjoin Achilles from prosecuting its suit in Japan (motion for an antisuit injunction). Achilles in turn moved to dismiss the federal court action on the ground of forum non conveniens. The district court denied Achilles's motion to dismiss and granted Kaepa's motion to enjoin, ordering Achilles to refrain from litigating the Japanese action and to file all of its counterclaims with the district court. Achilles timely appealed the grant of the antisuit injunction. [Achilles did not challenge the denial of its motion to dismiss.]

II. ANALYSIS

A. Propriety of the Antisuit Injunction

Achilles's primary argument is that the district court failed to give proper deference to principles of international comity when it granted Kaepa's motion for an antisuit injunction. We review the decision to grant injunctive relief for abuse of discretion. Under this deferential standard, findings of fact are upheld unless clearly erroneous, whereas legal conclusions "'are subject to broad review and will be reversed if incorrect.'" Apple Barrel Productions, Inc. v. Beard, 730 F.2d 384, 386 (5th Cir. 1984) (quoting Commonwealth Life Insurance Co. v. Neal, 669 F.2d 300, 304 (5th Cir. 1982)).

It is well settled among the circuit courts—including this one—which have reviewed the grant of an antisuit injunction that the federal courts have the power to enjoin persons subject to their jurisdiction from prosecuting foreign suits. The circuits differ, however, on the proper legal standard to employ when determining whether that injunctive power should be exercised. We have addressed the propriety of an antisuit injunction on two prior occasions * * *. Emphasizing in both cases the need to prevent vexatious or oppressive litigation, we concluded that a district court does not abuse its discretion by issuing an antisuit injunction when it has determined "that allowing simultaneous prosecution of the same action in a foreign forum thousands of miles away would result in 'inequitable hardship' and 'tend to frustrate and delay the speedy and efficient determination of the cause.'"[9] The Seventh and the Ninth Circuits have either adopted or "inclined toward" this approach, but other circuits have employed a standard that elevates principles of international comity to the virtual exclusion of essentially all other considerations.

Achilles urges us to give greater deference to comity and apply the latter, more restrictive standard. We note preliminarily that, even though the standard espoused in *Unterweser* and *Bethell* focuses on the potentially vexatious nature of foreign litigation, it by no means excludes the consideration of principles of comity. We decline, however, to require a district court to genuflect before a vague and omnipotent notion of comity every time that it must decide whether to enjoin a foreign action.

In the instant case, for example, it simply cannot be said that the grant of the antisuit injunction actually threatens relations between the United States and Japan. First, no public international issue is implicated by the case: Achilles is a private party engaged in a contractual dispute with another private party. Second, the dispute has been long and firmly ensconced within the confines of the United States judicial system: Achilles consented to jurisdiction in Texas; stipulated that Texas law and the English language would govern any dispute; appeared in an action brought in Texas; removed that action to a federal court in Texas; engaged in extensive discovery pursuant to the directives of the federal court; and only then, with the federal action moving steadily toward trial, brought identical claims in Japan. Under these circumstances, we cannot conclude that the district court's grant of an antisuit injunction in any way trampled on notions of comity.

On the contrary, the facts detailed above strongly support the conclusion that the prosecution of the Japanese action would entail "an absurd duplication of effort" and would result in unwarranted inconvenience, expense, and vexation. Achilles's belated ploy of filing as putative plaintiff in Japan the very same claims against Kaepa that Kaepa had filed as plaintiff against Achilles smacks of cynicism, harassment, and delay. Accordingly, we hold that the district court did not abuse its discretion by granting Kaepa's motion for an antisuit injunction.[14]

---

[9] *In re* Unterweser Rederei, GmbH, 428 F.2d 888, 890, 896 (5th Cir. 1970) (noting as well that antisuit injunctions have been granted when foreign litigation would (1) frustrate a policy of the forum issuing the injunction; (2) be vexatious or oppressive; (3) threaten the issuing court's in rem or quasi in rem jurisdiction; or (4) prejudice other equitable considerations); see also Bethell v. Peace, 441 F.2d 495, 498 (5th Cir. 1971) ("The court was within its discretion in relieving the plaintiff of expense and vexation of having to litigate in a foreign court.").

[14] The parties also debated the applicability of Federal Rule of Civil Procedure 13(a) to claims brought in foreign courts. Rule 13(a) governs compulsory counterclaims and provides in relevant part: "A pleading shall state as a counterclaim any claim which at the time of serving the pleading the pleader has against any opposing party, if it arises out of the transaction or occurrence that is the subject matter of the opposing party's claim . . . ." Fed. R. Civ. P. 13(a).

Achilles concedes that under Rule 13, the Japanese action constitutes a compulsory counterclaim. Nonetheless, Achilles argues that Rule 13 does not apply to claims brought in foreign courts and thus cannot be relied on as a basis for prohibiting the prosecution of the Japanese action. As

B. *Rule 65 Requirements*

Achilles also argues that the district court erred by failing to meet several requirements of Federal Rule of Civil Procedure 65 before issuing the antisuit injunction. Rule 65(a)(1) provides that "no preliminary injunction shall be issued without notice to the adverse party." We have interpreted the notice requirement of Rule 65(a)(1) to mean that "where factual disputes are presented, the parties must be given a fair opportunity and a meaningful hearing to present their differing versions of those facts before a preliminary injunction may be granted." If no factual dispute is involved, however, no oral hearing is required; under such circumstances the parties need only be given "ample opportunity to present their respective views of the legal issues involved." In the instant case, the district court did not rely on any disputed facts in determining whether it could properly grant an antisuit injunction. Moreover, both parties presented comprehensive memoranda in support of their positions on the issue. Accordingly, the district court did not violate Rule 65(a)(1) by failing to conduct an oral hearing before granting the antisuit injunction. * * *

III. CONCLUSION

For the foregoing reasons, the district court's grant of Kaepa's motion to enjoin the litigation of Achilles's action in Japan is AFFIRMED.

EMILIO M. GARZA, CIRCUIT JUDGE, dissenting:

International comity represents a principle of paramount importance in our world of ever increasing economic interdependence. Admitting that "comity" may be a somewhat elusive concept does not mean that we can blithely ignore its cautionary dictate. Unless we proceed in each instance with respect for the independent jurisdiction of a sovereign nation's courts, we risk provoking retaliation in turn, with detrimental consequences that may reverberate far beyond the particular dispute and its private litigants. Amicable relations among sovereign nations and their judicial systems depend on our recognition, as federal courts, that we share the international arena with co-equal judicial bodies, and that we therefore act to deprive a foreign court of jurisdiction only in the most extreme circumstances. Because I feel that the majority's opinion does not grant the principle of international comity the weight it deserves, I must respectfully dissent.

I

A

I do not quarrel with the well established principle, relied on by the majority, that our courts have the power to control the conduct of persons subject to their

---

we have decided on other grounds that the district court properly exercised its authority in enjoining the Japanese action, we need not address whether Rule 13 governs foreign suits. We note, however, that our holding today is consistent with the purpose of Rule 13, which is to "'prevent multiplicity of actions and to achieve resolution in a single suit of all disputes arising out of common matters.'" Seattle Totems Hockey Club, Inc. v. National Hockey League, 652 F.2d 852, 854 (9th Cir. 1981) (quoting Southern Construction Co. v. Pickard, 371 U.S. 57 (1962)).

jurisdiction, even to the extent of enjoining them from prosecuting in a foreign jurisdiction. I write to emphasize, however, that under concurrent jurisdiction, "parallel proceedings on the same in personam claim should ordinarily be allowed to proceed simultaneously, at least until a judgment is reached in one which can be pled as *res judicata* in the other." Laker Airways Ltd. v. Sabena, Belgian World Airlines, 235 U.S. App. D.C. 207, 731 F.2d 909, 926-27 (D.C. Cir. 1984).[3] The filing of a second parallel action in another jurisdiction does not necessarily conflict with or prevent the first court from exercising its legitimate concurrent jurisdiction. 731 F.2d at 926. In the ordinary case, both forums should be free to proceed to a judgment, unhindered by the concurrent exercise of jurisdiction in another court.

The issuance of an antisuit injunction runs directly counter to this principle of tolerating parallel proceedings. An antisuit injunction "conveys the message . . . that the issuing court has so little confidence in the foreign court's ability to adjudicate a given dispute fairly and efficiently that it is unwilling even to allow the possibility." Gau Shan Co. v. Bankers Trust Co., 956 F.2d 1349, 1355 (6th Cir. 1992). It makes no difference that in formal terms the injunction is only addressed to the parties. The antisuit injunction operates to restrict the foreign court's ability to exercise its jurisdiction as effectively as if it were addressed to the foreign court itself. * * * Enjoining the parties from litigating in a foreign court will necessarily compromise the principles of comity, and may lead to undesirable consequences. For example, the foreign court may react by issuing a similar injunction, thereby preventing any party from obtaining a remedy. *Laker Airways,* 731 F.2d at 927. The foreign court may also be less inclined to enforce a judgment by our courts. The refusal to enforce a foreign judgment, however, is less offensive than acting to prevent the foreign court from hearing the matter in the first place. Id. at 931.

Antisuit injunctions intended to carve out exclusive jurisdiction may also have unintended, widespread effects on international commerce. Without "an atmosphere of cooperation and reciprocity between nations," the ability to predict future consequences of international transactions will inevitably suffer. Id. To operate effectively and efficiently, international markets require a degree of predictability which can only be harmed by antisuit injunctions and the resulting breakdown of cooperation and reciprocity between courts of different nations. The attempt to exercise exclusive jurisdiction over international economic affairs is essentially an intrusion into the realm of international economic *policy* that should appropriately be left to our legislature and the treaty making process. As the court in *Laker Airways* stated, "Absent an explicit directive from Congress, this court has neither the authority nor the institutional resources to weigh the policy and political factors that must be evaluated when resolving competing claims of jurisdiction. In contrast, diplomatic and executive channels are, by definition, designed to exchange, negotiate, and reconcile the problems which ac-

[3]   See also Princess Lida of Thurn and Taxis v. Thompson, 305 U.S. 456, 466 (1939) ("It is settled that where the judgment sought is strictly *in personam*, both the state court and the federal court, having concurrent jurisdiction, may proceed with the litigation at least until judgment is obtained in one of them which may be set up as res judicata in the other.").

company the realization of national interests within the sphere of international association." *Laker Airways,* 731 F.2d at 955.

The majority appears to require an affirmative showing that the granting of an antisuit injunction in this case would immediately and concretely affect adversely the relations between the United States and Japan. Unless there is evidence that this antisuit injunction would "actually threaten" the relations between the two countries, the majority is comfortable to assume otherwise. Cf. Allendale Mut. Ins. Co. v. Bull Data Systems, Inc., 10 F.3d 425, 431-33 (7th Cir. 1993) (requiring evidence of concrete harm to the foreign relations of the United States). Some courts have gone so far as to suggest that we might expect, for example, a representative of the foreign nation to convey their country's concern regarding the issuance of an antisuit injunction in that case. See, e.g., id. at 431; Philips Medical Sys. Int'l B.V. v. Bruetman, 8 F.3d 600, 605 (7th Cir. 1993). Insisting on evidence of immediate and concrete harm, in the form of a diplomatic protest or otherwise, is both unrealistic and shortsighted. As with most transnational relations, the potential harm to international comity caused by the issuance of a specific antisuit injunction will be as difficult to predict, as it will be to remedy. It is precisely this troubling uncertainty, and the recognition that our courts are ill equipped to weigh these types of international policy considerations, that cautions us to make the respectful deference underlying international comity the rule rather than the exception.

B

In holding that the district court in this case did not abuse its discretion by enjoining Achilles, a Japanese corporation, from proceeding with its lawsuit filed in the sovereign nation of Japan, the majority appears to rely primarily on the duplicative nature of the Japanese suit and the resulting "unwarranted inconvenience, expense, and vexation." The inconvenience, expense and vexation, however, are factors likely to be present whenever there is an exercise of concurrent jurisdiction by a foreign court. * * * The majority's standard can be understood to hold, therefore, that "a duplication of the parties and issues, alone, is sufficient to justify a foreign antisuit injunction." *Gau Shan Co.,* 956 F.2d at 1353; *see also Laker Airways,* 731 F.2d at 928 (concluding that this rationale "is *prima facie* inconsistent with the rule permitting parallel proceedings in concurrent in personam actions"). Under this standard, concurrent jurisdiction involving a foreign tribunal will rarely, if ever, withstand the request for an antisuit injunction.

By focusing on the potential hardship to Kaepa of having to litigate in two forums,[7] the majority applies an analysis that is more appropriately brought to

---

[7] I also believe the majority errs by relying on two other factors in this case. The majority reasons that the "clear indications by both parties that claims arising from their contract should be adjudicated in this country" lends support to the conclusion that the district court did not abuse its discretion by enjoining the foreign litigation. The majority reaches this conclusion even though the district court found that the jurisdictional language in the parties' agreement was *permissive* of Texas jurisdiction, rather than *exclusive.* The majority also appears to overlook the fact that this dispute involves experienced and sophisticated businessmen who were perfectly capable of negotiating an

bear in the context of a motion to dismiss for *forum non conveniens.*[8] *See Laker Airways,* 731 F.2d at 928. Considerations that are appropriate in deciding whether to decline jurisdiction are not as persuasive when deciding whether to deprive another court of jurisdiction. "The policies of avoiding hardships to the parties and promoting the economies of consolidation litigation 'do not outweigh the important principles of comity that compel deference and mutual respect for concurrent foreign proceedings. Thus, the better rule is that duplication of parties and issues alone is not sufficient to justify issuance of an antisuit injunction.'" *Gau Shan Co.,* 956 F.2d at 1355 (quoting *Laker Airways,* 731 F.2d at 928); * * * A dismissal on grounds of *forum non conveniens* by either court in this case would satisfy the majority's concern with avoiding hardship to the parties, without harming the interests of international comity. The district court is not in a position, however, to make the *forum non conveniens* determination on behalf of the Japanese court. In light of the important interests of international comity, the decision by a United States court to deprive a foreign court of jurisdiction must be supported by far weightier factors than would otherwise justify that court's decision to decline its own jurisdiction on *forum non conveniens* grounds.

C

Accordingly, I believe that the standard followed by the Second, Sixth, and D.C. Circuits more satisfactorily respects the principle of concurrent jurisdiction and safeguards the important interests of international comity. Under this stricter standard, a district court should look to only two factors in determining whether to issue an antisuit injunction: (1) whether the foreign action threatens the jurisdiction of the district court; and (2) whether the foreign action was an attempt to evade important public policies of the district court.[10] *Gau Shan Co.,* 956 F.2d at 1355; *China Trade,* 837 F.2d at 36; *Laker Airways,* 731 F.2d at 927. Neither of these factors are present in this case.

"Courts have a duty to protect their legitimately conferred jurisdiction to the extent necessary to provide full justice to litigants." *Laker Airways,* 731 F.2d at 927. Where the concurrent proceeding effectively threatens to paralyze the jurisdiction of the court, or where the foreign court is attempting to carve out exclusive jurisdiction over the action, an antisuit injunction may legitimately be necessary to protect the court's jurisdiction. In those rare cases where the foreign

---

exclusive forum clause had they desired one. See Bremen v. Zapata, 407 U.S. 1, 12-13 (1972) ("There are compelling reasons why a freely negotiated private international agreement, unaffected by fraud, undue influence, or overweening bargaining power, such as that involved here, should be given effect."). Therefore, if anything, the district court's action—in reserving exclusive jurisdiction over this suit—runs directly counter to the parties' intentions, as evinced by their freely negotiated contract. * * * I am also not persuaded by the majority's reliance on the inference that Achilles' actions, by filing their action in Japan some seven or eight months after they were sued in Texas, "smacks of cynicism, harassment, and delay." See China Trade & Dev. Corp. v. M.V. Choong Yong, 837 F.2d 33, 34-35 (2nd Cir. 1987) (vacating injunction even though second suit was filed almost two-and-a-half years after initial suit) * * *. I do not believe that Achilles' impure motives, if any, should outweigh the important interests of international comity at issue in this case. * * *

action is interdictory rather than parallel, the issuance of an antisuit injunction is primarily a defensive action not inconsistent with the principles of international comity. The court in *Laker Airways* affirmed the issuance of an antisuit injunction where the foreign action "was instituted by the foreign defendants for the sole purpose of terminating the United States claim." Id. at 915. In fact, the British Court of Appeals had enjoined the plaintiff from pursuing its claims against British defendants in a United States court under United States law. Id. Significantly, the United States district court in *Laker Airways* also made clear that its injunction was intended solely to protect its jurisdiction by preventing the defendants from taking any action before a foreign court or governmental authority that would interfere with the litigation pending before the district court. Id. at 919. The injunction was not intended to prevent all concurrent proceedings in foreign courts, only those which directly threatened the district court's jurisdiction. There is no evidence in this case that Achilles' action in Japan in any way threatens the district court's exercise of its concurrent jurisdiction. While the Japanese action may eventually proceed to a judgment which can be pled as *res judicata* in the district court, no attempt has been made to carve out exclusive jurisdiction on behalf of the foreign tribunal.

As an example of where a court may need to act in order to protect its jurisdiction, a long-standing exception to the rule tolerating concurrent jurisdiction has been recognized for proceedings *in rem* or *quasi in rem*. *China Trade,* 837 F.2d at 36. Because the second action may pose an inherent threat to the court's basis for jurisdiction, an antisuit injunction may be appropriate in an *in rem* or *quasi in rem* proceeding. *Id.* "Where jurisdiction is based on the presence of property within the court's jurisdictional boundaries, a concurrent proceeding in a foreign jurisdiction poses the danger that the foreign court will order the transfer of the property out of the jurisdictional boundaries of the first court, thus depriving it of jurisdiction over the matter. This concern of course is not present in this *in personam* proceeding." *Gau Shan Co.,* 956 F.2d at 1358. Likewise, this concern is not present in the current *in personam* proceeding, the focus of which is a distribution agreement. I note that *In re Unterweser Reederei, GmbH,* relied on by the majority, was an *in rem* proceeding, justifying the more permissive standard applied to the issuance of an antisuit injunction in that case.

Under the second factor of the stricter standard, an antisuit injunction may also be appropriate where a party seeks to evade important policies of the forum by bringing suit in a foreign court. *Gau Shan Co.,* 956 F.2d at 1357. "While an injunction may be appropriate when a party attempts to evade compliance with a statute of the forum that effectuates important public policies, an injunction is not appropriate merely to prevent a party from seeking 'slight advantages in the substantive or procedural law to be applied in a foreign court.'" *China Trade,* 837 F.2d at 37 (quoting *Laker Airways,* 731 F.2d at 931, n.73). The policy favoring the resolution in a single lawsuit of all disputes arising out of a common matter does not, as noted earlier, outweigh the important interests of international comity. Rather, the principle enunciated under the second factor is "similar to the rule that a foreign judgment not entitled to full faith and credit under the Constitution will not be enforced within the United States when contrary to the crucial public policies of the forum in which enforcement is requested." *Laker Airways,* 731 F.2d at 931. Under this principle, a court is not required to give effect to a judgment that does violence to the forum's own fundamental interests. *Id.* Since the issuance of an antisuit injunction is a much greater and more direct interference with a foreign country's judicial process than is the refusal to enforce a judgment, it follows that an antisuit injunction should only be issued in the most extreme circumstances. Although the majority questions the purity of Achilles' motives in filing suit in Japan, there is no evidence that Achilles is attempting to evade any important policy of the United States forum.

II

Because neither factor supports the issuance of an antisuit injunction in this case, I believe the district court abused its discretion by enjoining Achilles from prosecuting an action filed in Japan. Accordingly, I respectfully dissent.

Quaak v. Klynveld Peat Marwick Goerdeler Bedrijfsrevisoren

United States Court of Appeals, First Circuit, 2004.

361 F.3d 11.

Selya, Circuit Judge.

* * *

The genesis of the problem in this case lies with an auditing engagement accepted by Klynveld Peat Marwick Goerdeler Bedrijfsrevisoren (KPMG-B), a Belgian firm that served as the auditor for a publicly-traded company, Lernout & Hauspie Speech Products, N.V. (L&H). L&H's collapse precipitated a flood of actions against KPMG-B and others in the courts of this country, alleging massive securities fraud. KPMG-B refused to produce relevant auditing records and associated work papers, asserting that to do so would violate Belgian law. A magistrate judge rejected this assertion and ordered production.

In response, KPMG-B repaired to a Belgian court requesting that substantial penalties be imposed on those who might "take any step of a procedural or other nature in order to proceed with the discovery-procedure." The plaintiffs in the pending American litigation (who had obtained the turnover order in the first instance) implored the district court to enjoin KPMG-B from pursuing the Belgian action. The district court obliged. * * * KPMG-B immediately appealed. We issued a partial stay of the antisuit injunction and expedited the appeal. We now affirm the district court's order.

I. BACKGROUND

* * * KPMG-B is a target of an ongoing criminal investigation in Belgium, which arises out of the L&H fiasco. It is also a principal defendant in the aforedescribed securities fraud litigation. KPMG-B has not disputed the district court's in personam jurisdiction. It did seek to secure dismissal of the securities fraud litigation on forum non conveniens grounds, but failed in that effort. At the same time, the district court determined that the consolidated complaint against

KPMG-B satisfied the stringent pleading requirements of the Private Securities Litigation Reform Act of 1995 (PSLRA), 15 U.S.C. § 78u-4(b)(2), and Federal Rule of Civil Procedure 9(b).

Once past these threshold issues, the securities fraud plaintiffs embarked on pretrial discovery. In September of 2002, they served document requests for KPMG-B's work papers. The plaintiffs did not get very far; KPMG-B refused to comply with the requests, asseverating that Belgian law prohibited it from divulging the information sought. While this game of cat and mouse was taking place, the plaintiffs, acting on KPMG-B's advice, became civil co-prosecutors in the ongoing Belgian criminal investigation. Through this participation, they were able to examine all the documents that were not deemed confidential by the Belgian prosecutor, but they were not permitted to copy documents for use in the securities fraud litigation.

Tantalized by their glimpse of the work papers, the securities fraud plaintiffs moved to compel their production. A magistrate judge took briefing and heard argument on the applicability of and exceptions to the Belgian secrecy law [which prohibits auditors fro disclosing confidential client information]. On November 13, 2003, he rejected KPMG-B's arguments and ordered production of the work papers on or before the close of business on December 1, 2003.

On November 27, 2003—Thanksgiving day—KPMG-B filed an ex parte petition with a court in Brussels, seeking to enjoin the securities fraud plaintiffs from "taking any step" to proceed with the requested discovery. To ensure compliance, they asked the Belgian court to impose a fine of one million Euros for each violation of the proposed injunction. The Belgian court refused to act ex parte; instead, it directed that notice be provided to the securities fraud plaintiffs and scheduled a hearing for December 16, 2003. On December 1, KPMG-B gave notice of the institution of the Belgian action to the securities fraud plaintiffs. It also filed an objection to the magistrate judge's decision. That objection is still pending in the district court (there is, among other things, a disagreement as to its timeliness). Finally, KPMG-B moved to stay the turnover order.

Faced with the threat of extravagant fines, the securities fraud plaintiffs sought the district court's protection. On December 9, the judge issued a report and recommendation urging the entry of an order enjoining KPMG-B from proceeding with its Belgian action. The district judge held a hearing two days later and issued an antisuit injunction * * * . Hot on the heels of this order, the judge denied KPMG-B's motion to stay the turnover order, branding that motion untimely. KPMG-B immediately appealed the entry of the antisuit injunction. We granted a limited stay of the injunction, permitting KPMG-B to appear at the December 16 hearing in Brussels for the sole purpose of requesting a continuance. The Belgian court has been fully cooperative, and the foreign action has been continued periodically during the pendency of this expedited appeal. There has been no further action with regard to the turnover order itself.

II. STANDARD OF REVIEW

A grant of a preliminary injunction typically receives deferential review. The trial court's order will stand unless it "mistook the law, clearly erred in its factual assessments, or otherwise abused its discretion in granting the interim relief." *Id.* In our view, however, international antisuit injunctions—which involve important considerations of comity—warrant a heightened level of appellate review. Consequently, we deem it appropriate to conduct an independent review of the justification for the issuance of an international antisuit injunction. This is an "intermediate level of scrutiny, more rigorous than the abuse-of-discretion or clear-error standards, but stopping short of plenary or *de novo* review." United States v. Tortora, 922 F.2d 880, 883 (1st Cir. 1990). Given our chosen standard of review, we cede a modest degree of deference to the trier's exercise of discretion, but "we will not hesitate to act upon our independent judgment if it appears that a mistake has been made." El Dia, Inc. v. Hernandez Colon, 963 F.2d 488, 492 (1st Cir. 1992).

III. ANALYSIS

Determining the appropriateness of an international antisuit injunction is a highly nuanced exercise. An inquiring court must find a way to accommodate conflicting, mutually inconsistent national policies without unduly interfering with the judicial processes of a foreign sovereign. See Laker Airways Ltd. v. Sabena, Belgian World Airlines, 731 F.2d 909, 916 (D.C. Cir. 1984). This task is particularly formidable given the absence of guidance from the Supreme Court and the paucity of precedent in this circuit; the Justices have not spoken to the criteria for granting an international antisuit injunction and this court has passed on that question only once (and then, glancingly). * * * We begin our analysis by articulating the standards that ought to govern the question. We then apply those standards to the case at hand.

A. *Articulating the Standards.*

It is common ground that federal courts have the power to enjoin those subject to their personal jurisdiction from pursuing litigation before foreign tribunals. See, e.g., Kaepa, Inc. v. Achilles Corp., 76 F.3d 624, 626 (5th Cir. 1996); China Trade & Dev. Corp. v. M.V. Choong Yong, 837 F.2d 33, 35 (2d Cir. 1987). The exercise of that power must be tempered, however, by the accepted proposition that parallel proceedings on the same in personam claim generally should be allowed to proceed simultaneously. *Laker Airways,* 731 F.2d at 926. The decisional calculus must take account of this presumption in favor of concurrent jurisdiction. It also must take account of considerations of international comity. After all, even though an international antisuit injunction operates only against the parties, it effectively restricts the jurisdiction of a foreign sovereign's courts.

Federal courts have been consentient in endorsing these principles. Beyond that point, however, the waters grow murky. The courts of appeals have differed as to the legal standards to be employed in determining whether the power to enjoin an international proceeding should be exercised. Two basic views have emerged. For ease in reference, we shall call the more permissive of these views the liberal approach and the more restrictive of them the conservative approach. *See* Note, *Antisuit Injunctions and International Comity*, 71 Va. L. Rev. 1039, 1049-51 (1985) (using this nomenclature).

The liberal approach has been championed by two courts of appeals: the Fifth Circuit, *Kaepa,* 76 F.3d at 627, and the Ninth Circuit, Seattle Totems Hockey Club, Inc. v. Nat'l Hockey League, 652 F.2d 852, 855-56 (9th Cir. 1981). In addition, the Seventh Circuit has pronounced itself "inclined toward" the liberal view. Philips Med. Sys. Int'l v. Bruetman, 8 F.3d 600, 605 (7th Cir. 1993). Under this approach, an international antisuit injunction is appropriate whenever there is a duplication of parties and issues and the court determines that the prosecution of simultaneous proceedings would frustrate the speedy and efficient determination of the case. We do not mean to suggest that courts employing the liberal approach do not give weight to considerations of international comity. For the most part, they do—but they tend to define that interest in a relatively narrow manner and to assign it only modest weight. See, e.g., *Kaepa,* 76 F.3d at 627 (noting that an international antisuit injunction does not "actually threaten relations" between the two involved nations).

Four courts of appeals have espoused the conservative approach for gauging the propriety of international antisuit injunctions. See Stonington Partners, Inc. v. Lernout & Hauspie Speech Prods., 310 F.3d 118, 126 (3d Cir. 2002); Gau Shan Co. v. Bankers Trust Co., 956 F.2d 1349, 1355 (6th Cir. 1992); *China Trade,* 837 F.2d at 36 (2d Cir.); *Laker Airways*, 731 F.2d at 927 (D.C. Cir.). Under this approach, the critical questions anent the issuance of an international antisuit injunction are whether the foreign action either imperils the jurisdiction of the forum court or threatens some strong national policy. This approach accords appreciably greater weight to considerations of international comity.

We reject the liberal approach. We deem international comity an important integer in the decisional calculus—and the liberal approach assigns too low a priority to that interest. In the bargain, it undermines the age-old presumption in favor of concurrent parallel proceedings—a value judgment that leaves us uneasy—and presumes that public policy always favors allowing a suit pending in an American court to go forward without any substantial impediment. To cinch matters, this approach gives far too easy passage to international antisuit injunctions. We understand that the judicial process is a cornerstone of the American way of life—but in an area that raises significant separation of powers concerns and implicates international relations, we believe that the law calls for a more cautious and measured approach.

The conservative approach has more to commend it. First, it recognizes the rebuttable presumption against issuing international antisuit injunctions (and, thus, honors the presumption favoring the maintenance of parallel proceedings). Second, it is more respectful of principles of international comity. Third, it compels an inquiring court to balance competing policy considerations. Last—but far from least— * * * issuing an international antisuit injunction is a step that should "be taken only with care and great restraint" and with the recognition that international comity is a fundamental principle deserving of substantial deference.

We stop short, however, of an uncritical acceptance of the conservative approach. The recent expositions of that approach have come to regard the two main rationales upon which international antisuit injunctions may be grounded—preservation of jurisdiction and protection of important national policies—as exclusive. * * * We are uncomfortable with this gloss, for it evinces a certain woodenness. In our view, the sensitive and fact-specific nature of the inquiry counsels against the use of inflexible rules.

We therefore reject this reworking of the conservative approach and instead endorse its traditional version. That version is not only more flexible but also more consistent with *Laker Airways*—which we regard as the seminal opinion in this field of law. The *Laker Airways* court did not suggest that its two stated rationales were the only ones that could justify issuing an international antisuit injunction. 731 F.2d at 927 (noting that "injunctions are most often necessary" to protect the court's jurisdiction or to prevent evasion of the nation's important policies). Rather, the court indicated that it was prudent to use a wider-angled lens, making clear that the equitable considerations surrounding each request for an injunction should be examined carefully. *Id.*

In order to provide guidance for the district courts, we spell out the manner in which our preferred approach operates. The gatekeeping inquiry is, of course, whether parallel suits involve the same parties and issues. Unless that condition is met, a court ordinarily should go no further and refuse the issuance of an international antisuit injunction. See, e.g., *China Trade,* 837 F.2d at 36; *Laker Airways*, 731 F.2d at 928; see also George A. Bermann, *The Use of Anti-Suit Injunctions in International Litigation*, 28 Colum. J. Transnat'l L. 589, 626 (1990) (stating that courts generally "will not consider issuing antisuit injunctions" unless there are "parallel local and foreign actions between the same parties over the same claim"). If—and only if—this threshold condition is satisfied should the court proceed to consider all the facts and circumstances in order to decide whether an injunction is proper. In this analysis, considerations of international comity must be given substantial weight—and those considerations ordinarily establish a rebuttable presumption against the issuance of an order that has the effect of halting foreign judicial proceedings.

We acknowledge that the task of determining when a litigant has overcome this presumption is a difficult one. That is partly because comity is an elusive concept. The Supreme Court has defined it as "the recognition which one nation allows within its territory to the legislative, executive or judicial acts of another nation, having due regard both to international duty and convenience, and to the rights of its own citizens or of other persons who are under the protection of its laws." Hilton v. Guyot, 159 U.S. 113, 164 (1895). Judge Aldrich trenchantly described it as "a blend of courtesy and expedience." *Canadian Filters,* 412 F.2d at 578. Whatever definition is employed, it is pellucid that comity is not a matter of rigid obligation, but, rather, a protean concept of jurisdictional respect. And to complicate matters, comity, like beauty, sometimes is in the eye of the beholder.

We hasten to add that although the definition of comity may be tenebrous, its importance could not be more clear. In an increasingly global economy, commercial transactions involving participants from many lands have become common fare. This world economic interdependence has highlighted the importance of comity, as international commerce depends to a large extent on "the ability of merchants to predict the likely consequences of their conduct in overseas markets." *Gau Shan,* 956 F.2d at 1355. This predictability, in turn, depends on cooperation, reciprocity, and respect among nations. That helps to explain the enduring need for a presumption—albeit a rebuttable one—against the issuance of international antisuit injunctions.

In the final analysis, rebutting this presumption involves a continual give and take. In the course of that give and take, the presumption may be counterbalanced by other facts and factors particular to a specific case. These include (but are by no means limited to) such things as: the nature of the two actions (i.e., whether they are merely parallel or whether the foreign action is more properly classified as interdictory); the posture of the proceedings in the two countries; the conduct of the parties (including their good faith or lack thereof); the importance of the policies at stake in the litigation; and, finally, the extent to which the foreign action has the potential to undermine the forum court's ability to reach a just and speedy result.

Seen in this light, we agree that either the preservation of jurisdiction or the safeguarding of important national policies may afford a sufficient basis for the issuance of an international antisuit injunction. We do not, however, attach talismanic significance to concepts such as jurisdiction-stripping and insults to public policy. Instead, we hold that in every case a district court should examine the totality of the circumstances in deciding whether a particular case warrants the issuance of an international antisuit injunction. * * * If, after giving due regard to the circumstances (including the salient interest in international comity), a court supportably finds that equitable considerations preponderate in favor of relief, it may issue an international antisuit injunction.

B. *Applying the Standards.*

Against this backdrop, we ponder whether the district court acted within the realm of its discretion when it enjoined KPMG-B from pursuing the Belgian litigation. We conclude that it did.   * * *

We need not belabor the obvious. The parties and issues are substantially similar, thus satisfying the gatekeeping inquiry. The district judge acknowledged the importance of comity concerns in her published opinion. A reading of the hearing transcript leaves no doubt that she was fully aware of the potential ramifications with respect to international comity and that she gave heavy weight to those concerns. However, she placed on the opposite pan of the scale the character of the foreign action, the public policy favoring the safeguarding of investors from securities fraud, the need to protect the court's own processes, and the balance of the equities.. In the end, the court determined that those factors counterbalanced comity concerns in the peculiar circumstances of this case. Having conducted an independent review, we find that determination fully supportable.

The essential character of the Belgian action is easily discerned. In it, KPMG-B seeks to impose huge financial penalties on the securities fraud plaintiffs should they take any steps to enforce the district court's turnover order. This attempt to chill legitimate discovery by in terrorem tactics can scarcely be viewed as anything but an effort to "quash the practical power of the United States courts." *Laker Airways,* 731 F.2d at 938; see United States v. Davis, 767

F.2d 1025, 1029 (2d Cir. 1985) (upholding injunction of foreign proceeding where the "sole purpose" of instituting that proceeding "was to block compliance with a legitimate trial subpoena"). Thus, the foreign action is plainly interdictory in nature.

Where, as here, a party institutes a foreign action in a blatant attempt to evade the rightful authority of the forum court, the need for an antisuit injunction crests. Fairly read, KPMG-B's petition to the Belgian tribunal seeks to arrest the progress of the securities fraud action by thwarting the very discovery that the district court, which is intimately familiar with the exigencies of the underlying case, has deemed essential to the continued prosecution of the action against *any* of the defendants. In technical terms, this may not constitute a frontal assault on the district court's jurisdiction, but the practical effect is the same. That is a matter of considerable import: a court has a right—indeed, a duty—to preserve its ability to do justice between the parties in cases that are legitimately before it. * * *

The equities also counsel in favor of affirming the district court's order. This is not a case in which a trial court is enabling a fishing expedition. The securities fraud plaintiffs have survived the PSLRA's heightened pleading requirements and, moreover, they have actually seen the documents that they seek. Consequently, they know that they are not fishing in an empty stream.

In weighing the equities, we also think it noteworthy that KPMG-B, not the securities fraud plaintiffs or the district court, set the stage for a crisis of comity. If KPMG-B had not filed a foreign petition calculated to generate interference with an ongoing American case, the district court would have had no need to issue a defensive injunction that sought only to preserve the court's ability to adjudicate the claims before it according to the law of the United States. And, finally, KPMG-B's actions are harder to accept because it had available to it other options for seeking resolution of its client confidentiality concerns. The most obvious choice was to pursue and exhaust its position in the federal judicial system before attempting to sidetrack that system. Alternatively, it could have sought clarification from the Belgian courts without raising the stakes to a level that necessarily precipitated a direct conflict with the pending securities fraud action. It eschewed these options. Having called the tune, it hardly seems inequitable that KPMG-B must now pay the piper.

KPMG-B's remaining arguments need not occupy us for long. First, it posits that the district court erred when it entered the antisuit injunction prior to reviewing the magistrate judge's turnover order (including his assessment of the Belgian law issue). This argument is hopeless.

District courts have broad discretion in determining the sequence of their rulings. * * * Here, moreover, KPMG-B left the district court no practical alternative. By electing to file its petition in Belgium before it lodged an objection to the magistrate judge's decision, KPMG-B effectively dictated the sequence of subsequent events.

KPMG-B next contends that the lower court erred as a matter of law by failing to give due regard to the possible use of letters rogatory as a means of securing the requested documents. This contention lacks force.

While letters rogatory are among the discovery devices available in a federal court, parties are not required to resort to them come what may. See Société Nationale Industrielle Aérospatiale v. United States Dist. Court, 482 U.S. 522, 543-44 (1987). The transcripts of the relevant hearings make it crystal clear that, in this instance, the district court fully considered, and flatly rejected, the argument that letters rogatory would serve as a satisfactory substitute for a turnover order. * * *

Nor can we accept KPMG-B's related contention that, as a matter of law, no international antisuit injunction can issue if the forum court's goal can be achieved in some other way. While we encourage trial courts to search out alternatives that might avoid the need to issue antisuit injunctions, we will not force them to exhaust remote possibilities. Here, there is no compelling justification for overriding the district court's considered judgment that letters rogatory are not a reasonably equivalent alternative to the turnover order.

Finally, KPMG-B asserts that because the securities fraud plaintiffs will eventually gain access to the requested documents even in the absence of a turnover order, the injunction was improvidently issued. This assertion elevates hope over likelihood.

KPMG-B's thesis is, in substance, that the work papers will be made available by the Belgian prosecutor at the conclusion of the criminal investigation. But there is a rub: we have no reliable way of knowing when that investigation will end and, in all events, the record is unclear as to whether the outcome of the investigation will (or will not) affect the availability of the work papers. We do not think that a district court must bring the resolution of a case within its jurisdiction to a dead halt in the hope that the resolution of a foreign criminal proceeding at an uncertain future date may alleviate the need for a discovery order.

IV. CONCLUSION

We do not mean to minimize the potential difficulty of the situation that KPMG-B faces. To some extent, however, that situation is the natural consequence of its decision to ply its wares in the lucrative American marketplace. Having elected to establish a major presence in the United States, KPMG-B must have anticipated that it would be subject to suit in this country (and, thus, subject to pretrial discovery rules that are pandemic to the American justice system). See Restatement (Third) of Foreign Relations Law § 442, reporters' note 1 (1987) (noting "that persons who do business in the United States . . . are subject to the burdens as well as the benefits of United States law, including the laws on discovery"). While courts should "take care to demonstrate due respect for any special problem confronted by [a] foreign litigant on account of its nationality," *Société Nationale,* 482 U.S. at 546, a foreign national that chooses to engage in business in the United States likewise must demonstrate due respect for the operation of the American judicial system.

We need go no further. For the foregoing reasons, we hold that the district court acted within the encincture of its discretion in enjoining KPMG-B from pursuing its Belgian litigation. In the last analysis, an international antisuit injunction, like any other injunction, is an equitable remedy designed "to bring the scales into balance." Rosario-Torres v. Hernandez-Colon, 889 F.2d 314, 323 (1st Cir. 1989) (en banc). In this case, the district court acted defensively to protect its own authority from an interdictory strike and we are confident that, in doing so, the court kept the balance steady and true.

We affirm the district court's injunction order and vacate the partial stay of that order previously issued by this court. * * *

NOTES AND QUESTIONS FOR DISCUSSION

1. The Fifth Circuit in *Kaepa* and the First Circuit in *Quaak* purport to take more and less liberal approaches to the problem of granting antisuit injunctions in the international setting. Yet both courts grant the requested injunction. Do the differences in approach matter? Would the Court in *Quaak* not have granted the injunction in *Kaepa*? Is one court's general approach to the problem preferable to the other, and if so, why? As both courts note, there remains a split of authority regarding the ease with which federal courts should grant injunctions against parties preventing them from proceeding with parallel litigation in a foreign forum.

2. The premise of any antisuit injunction issuing from a U.S. court is the presence before that court of the party who has begun litigation abroad. The injunction, if obtained, does not enjoin the foreign proceedings themselves; rather it enjoins the party who has filed those proceedings. So, the enjoined party is bound—on penalty of contempt—to obey the U.S. court's decree. But the foreign court is not bound. And if a party is so inclined, and is willing to risk it, he might seek similar relief from the foreign court to enjoin the U.S. proceedings.

3. One of the most famous examples of antisuit injunctions and counter injunctions occurred in **Laker Airways Ltd. v. Sabena, Belgian World Airlines, 731 F.2d 909, 916 (D.C. Cir. 1984)**, discussed at length in Judge Garza's dissent in *Kaepa*. Suit was initially brought in the U.S. by Laker against various competitor airlines (some of them British, some U.S., and others), alleging violations of federal (U.S.) antitrust laws. Suit was then brought in the U.K. against Laker by some of the defendants to Laker's U.S. action, seeking an injunction against Laker's U.S. suit. Both courts eventually issued injunctions against the other, although the House of Lords later held the U.K. injunction to be improper. [1985] A.C. 58 (H.L.).

4. As just noted, the injunction requested and received by Laker from the federal courts was in connection with litigation under federal antitrust laws. Should the public law dimension of such proceedings (such as the Securities Act proceedings in *Quaak*) weigh in favor of injunctive relief against parallel litigation abroad, international comity concerns notwithstanding? Are such laws more reflective of strong public policy concerns to allow the U.S. proceedings to go forward, unmolested by parallel proceedings that are not likely to consider the federal public law provisions? Consider the statement of the D.C. Circuit in *Laker*, which upheld the district court's injunction of the U.K. proceedings.

> "Comity" summarizes in a brief word a complex and elusive concept—the degree of deference that a domestic forum must pay to the act of a foreign government not otherwise binding on the forum. . . . However, there are limitations to the application of comity. When the foreign act is inherently inconsistent with the policies underlying comity, domestic recognition could tend either to legitimize the aberration or to encourage retaliation, undercutting the realization of the goals served by comity. No nation is under an unremitting obligation to enforce foreign interests which are fundamentally prejudicial to those of the domestic forum. Thus, from the earliest times, authorities have recognized that the obligation of comity expires when the strong public policies of the forum are vitiated by the foreign act.

731 F.2d at 937.

5. Unlike in the purely domestic setting, antisuit injunctions issued by federal courts are not governed or restricted by statute. As noted earlier in this chapter, the Anti-injunction statute (28 U.S.C. § 2283) generally bars federal court injunctions of parallel state court proceedings, but it has exceptions that affirmatively allow injunctions that are "in aid of" the federal court's jurisdiction, "to protect or effectuate" judgments that the federal courts has entered, or when "expressly authorized" by Congress. Courts espousing the restrictive view sometimes seem willing to uphold injunctions in similarly narrow circumstances. See, e.g., China Trade & Dev. Corp. v. M.V. Choong Yong, 837 F.2d 33, 36-37 (2d Cir. 1987) (observing that there was no threat to U.S. jurisdiction in pendency of parallel foreign proceedings).

6. Should the threat that a foreign court judgment may be first in time be a reason for issuing an injunction, under any of the approaches to antisuit injunctions? Note that parallel proceedings inevitably raise the threat that one of the injunctions will have preclusive fallout on the other. But because preclusion is itself subject to public policy objections in the international setting, perhaps there is less of a concern than there would be in the purely domestic setting. Note that under the anti-injunction statute, the threat of first in time preclusive fallout from a parallel state court proceeding was generally *not* considered to be sufficient to trigger any of the statute's exceptions. Consequently, there would seem to be even less argument for an injunction simply to preserve the U.S. forum's ability to decide a case free and clear of possible preclusive fallout from the parallel foreign proceedings.

7. Finally, note that antisuit injunctions as between member states of the E.U. are largely a nonissue, given the *lis pendens* rule of the Brussels Regulation. See Appendix D. As the case below illustrates, the European Court of Justice has made it clear that it will not even permit the exceptional grant of an antisuit injunction against a party who is acting in bad faith with a view to frustrating the existing proceedings. Note that although this decision is based on the Brussels Convention which preceded the Brussels Regulation, both bodies of law are identical with respect to the *lis pendens* rule and its ramifications. Therefore, the decision excerpted below applies with equal force to the issue of antisuit injunction under the Regulation.

2. The Approach(es) of European Courts

Gregory Paul Turner v. Felix Fareed Ismail Grovit and Others

Court of Justice of the European Communities, 2004.

Case C-159/02, 2004 E.C.R. I-03565.

* * *

The dispute in the main proceedings * * *

3.   Mr. Turner, a British citizen domiciled in the United Kingdom, was recruited in 1990 as solicitor to a group of undertakings by one of the companies belonging to that group.

4.   The group, known as Chequepoint Group, is directed by Mr. Grovit and its main business is running *bureaux de change*. It comprises several companies established in different countries, one being China Security Ltd, which initially recruited Mr. Turner, Chequepoint UK Ltd., which took over Mr. Turner's contract at the end of 1990, Harada, established in the United Kingdom, and Changepoint, established in Spain.

5.   Mr. Turner carried out his work in London (United Kingdom). However, in May 1997, at his request, his employer allowed him to transfer his office to Madrid (Spain).

6.   Mr. Turner started working in Madrid in November 1997. On 16 November 1998, he submitted his resignation to Harada, the company to which he had been transferred on 31 December 1997.

7.   On 2 March 1998 Mr. Turner brought an action in London against Harada before the Employment Tribunal. He claimed that he had been the victim of efforts to implicate him in illegal conduct, which, in his opinion, were tantamount to unfair dismissal.

8.   The Employment Tribunal dismissed the objection of lack of jurisdiction raised by Harada. Its decision was confirmed on appeal. Giving judgment on the substance, it awarded damages to Mr. Turner.

9.   On 29 July 1998, Changepoint brought an action against Mr. Turner before a court of first instance in Madrid. The summons was served on Mr. Turner around 15 December 1998. Mr. Turner did not accept service and protested the jurisdiction of the Spanish court.

10. In the course of the proceedings in Spain, Changepoint claimed damages of ESP 85 million from Mr. Turner as compensation for losses allegedly resulting from Mr. Turner's professional conduct.

11. On 18 December 1998 Mr. Turner asked the High Court of Justice of England and Wales to issue an injunction under section 37(1) of the Supreme Court Act 1981, backed by a penalty, restraining Mr. Grovit, Harada and Changepoint from pursuing the proceedings commenced in Spain. An interlocutory injunction was issued in those terms on 22 December 1998. On 24 February 1999, the High Court refused to extend the injunction.

12. On appeal by Mr. Turner, the Court of Appeal (England and Wales) on 28 May 1999 issued an injunction ordering the defendants not to continue the proceedings commenced in Spain and to refrain from commencing further proceedings in Spain or elsewhere against Mr. Turner in respect of his contract of employment. In the grounds of its judgment, the Court of Appeal stated, in particular, that the proceedings in Spain had been brought in bad faith in order to vex Mr. Turner in the pursuit of his application before the Employment Tribunal.

13. On 28 June 1999, in compliance with that injunction, Changepoint discontinued the proceedings pending before the Spanish court.

14. Mr. Grovit, Harada and Changepoint then appealed to the House of Lords, claiming in essence that the English courts did not have the power to make restraining orders preventing the continuation of proceedings in foreign jurisdictions covered by the Convention.

The order for reference and the questions submitted to the [European] Court [of Justice]

15. According to the order for reference, the power exercised by the Court of Appeal in this case is based not on any presumed entitlement to delimit the jurisdiction of a foreign court but on the fact that the party to whom the injunction is addressed is personally amenable to the jurisdiction of the English courts.

16. According to the analysis made in the order for reference, an injunction of the kind issued by the Court of Appeal does not involve a decision upon the jurisdiction of the foreign court but rather an assessment of the conduct of the person seeking to avail himself of that jurisdiction. However, in so far as such an injunction interferes indirectly with the proceedings before the foreign court, it can be granted only where the claimant shows that there is a clear need to protect proceedings pending in England.

17. The order for reference indicates that the essential elements which justify the exercise by the Court of Appeal of its power to issue an injunction in this case were that:

> – the applicant was a party to existing legal proceedings in England;

> – the defendants had in bad faith commenced and proposed to prosecute proceedings against the applicant in another jurisdiction for the purpose of frustrating or obstructing the proceedings in England;

> – the Court of Appeal considered that in order to protect the legitimate interest of the applicant in the English proceedings it was necessary to grant the applicant an injunction against the defendants.

18. Taking the view, however, that the case raised a problem of interpretation of the Convention, the House of Lords stayed its proceedings pending a preliminary ruling from the Court of Justice on the following question:

> "Is it inconsistent with the [Brussels] Convention * * * to grant restraining orders against defendants who are threatening to commence or continue legal proceedings in another Convention country when those defendants are acting in bad faith with the intent and purpose of frustrating or obstructing proceedings properly before the English courts?"

The question referred to the Court

19. By its question, the national court seeks in essence to ascertain whether the Convention precludes the grant of an injunction by which a court of a Contracting State prohibits a party to proceedings pending before it from commencing or continuing legal proceedings before a court in another Contracting State even where that party is acting in bad faith in order to frustrate the existing proceedings.

* * *

Findings of the Court

24. At the outset, it must be borne in mind that the Convention is necessarily based on the trust which the Contracting States accord to one another's legal systems and judicial institutions. It is that mutual trust which has enabled a compulsory system of jurisdiction to be established, which all the courts within the purview of the Convention are required to respect, and as a corollary the waiver by those States of the right to apply their internal rules on recognition and enforcement of foreign judgments in favour of a simplified mechanism for the recognition and enforcement of judgments. * * *

25. It is inherent in that principle of mutual trust that, within the scope of the Convention, the rules on jurisdiction that it lays down, which are common to all the courts of the Contracting States, may be interpreted and applied with the same authority by each of them. * * *

26. Similarly, otherwise than in a small number of exceptional cases listed in the first paragraph of Article 28 of the Convention, which are limited to the stage of recognition or enforcement and relate only to certain rules of special or exclusive jurisdiction that are not relevant here, the Convention does not permit the jurisdiction of a court to be reviewed by a court in another Contracting State * * * .

27. However, a prohibition imposed by a court, backed by a penalty, restraining a party from commencing or continuing proceedings before a foreign court undermines the latter court's jurisdiction to determine the dispute. Any injunction prohibiting a claimant from bringing such an action must be seen as constituting interference with the jurisdiction of the foreign court which, as such, is incompatible with the system of the Convention.

28. Notwithstanding the explanations given by the referring court and contrary to the view put forward by Mr. Turner and the United Kingdom Government, such interference cannot be justified by the fact that it is only indirect and

is intended to prevent an abuse of process by the defendant in the proceedings in the forum State. In so far as the conduct for which the defendant is criticised consists in recourse to the jurisdiction of the court of another Member State, the judgment made as to the abusive nature of that conduct implies an assessment of the appropriateness of bringing proceedings before a court of another Member State. Such an assessment runs counter to the principle of mutual trust which, as pointed out in paragraphs 24 to 26 of this judgment, underpins the Convention and prohibits a court, except in special circumstances which are not applicable in this case, from reviewing the jurisdiction of the court of another Member State.

29. Even if it were assumed, as has been contended, that an injunction could be regarded as a measure of a procedural nature intended to safeguard the integrity of the proceedings pending before the court which issues it, and therefore as being a matter of national law alone, it need merely be borne in mind that the application of national procedural rules may not impair the effectiveness of the Convention * * *. However, that result would follow from the grant of an injunction of the kind at issue which, as has been established in paragraph 27 of this judgment, has the effect of limiting the application of the rules on jurisdiction laid down by the Convention.

30. The argument that the grant of injunctions may contribute to attainment of the objective of the Convention, which is to minimise the risk of conflicting decisions and to avoid a multiplicity of proceedings, cannot be accepted. First, recourse to such measures renders ineffective the specific mechanisms provided for by the Convention for cases of *lis alibi pendens* and of related actions. Second, it is liable to give rise to situations involving conflicts for which the Convention contains no rules. The possibility cannot be excluded that, even if an injunction had been issued in one Contracting State, a decision might nevertheless be given by a court of another Contracting state. Similarly, the possibility cannot be excluded that the courts of two Contracting States that allowed such measures might issue contradictory injunctions.

31. Consequently, the answer to be given to the national court must be that the Convention is to be interpreted as precluding the grant of an injunction whereby a court of a Contracting State prohibits a party to proceedings pending before it from commencing or continuing legal proceedings before a court of another Contracting State, even where that party is acting in bad faith with a view to frustrating the existing proceedings. * * *

NOTES AND QUESTIONS FOR DISCUSSION

1. As in other cases involving issues under the *lis pendens* rule, the ECJ repeatedly refers to the "principle of mutual trust which . . . underpins the Convention and prohibits a court, except in special circumstances which are not applicable in this case, from reviewing the jurisdiction of the court of another Member State." What exactly does the court mean by the phrase "mutual trust"? Is a categorical principle of priority always appropriate, even in a case such as *Turner*, which involves a flagrant abuse of process? Is it appropriate to adhere to the strict *lis pendens* principle on the ground of "mutual trust" between the member states

given the vastly disparate degrees of judicial productivity and adjudicatory speed in certain legal systems (such as Italy's)?

2.   As discussed in Section A of this chapter, U.S. federal courts are generally barred from issuing injunctions against state court proceedings, even when an injunction would reduce the risk of conflicting outcomes and eliminate duplicative litigation.   But the anti-injunction statute, 28 U.S.C. § 2283, nevertheless expressly includes an exception that would permit an injunction to "protect or effectuate" judgments already entered by a federal court. Consequently, under this "relitigation exception," § 2283 would not bar an injunction to prevent a losing party from filing a later suit attempting to relitigate matters already resolved in a prior suit, or even when the later suit involved a transactionally related claim that could have been brought the original proceeding but was not. See Parsons Steel v. First Alabama Bank, 474 U.S. 518 (1986). This general approach shows that even in a regime that otherwise prohibits antisuit injunctions (out of a notion of harmonious state-federal relations—a kind of "mutual trust"), there may be settings in which other values trump the values that undergird the otherwise robust antisuit injunction rule. Is it preferable to have such a safety valve even in a regime that is otherwise hostile to antisuit injunctions?   Or are the supremacy concerns (regarding federal court orders) that are reflected in the allowance of federal court injunctions against state courts under § 2283's relitigation exception something that is absent as among co-equal member states of the E.U.?

3.   As the U.S. is not a party to the Brussels Convention or Regulation, the rule articulated in *Turner* would not prevent, for example, a U.K. court from issuing an antisuit injunction against a U.S. proceeding. As discussed in Note 3, following *Kaepa* and *Quaak*, above, the U.K. courts famously did just that (until later reversed by the House of Lords) in the *Laker Airways* litigation. Consider the following post-*Laker Airways* decision by the House of Lords:

Airbus Industrie G.I.E. v. Patel

U.K. House of Lords, 1998.

[1998] UKHL 12; 1 AC 119 (H.L.)

LORD GOFF.

This appeal is concerned with the circumstances in which an English court may grant what is usually called an "anti-suit injunction." The proceedings in question have arisen from a very serious air crash which occurred at Bangalore airport on 14 February 1990. An Airbus A-320 aircraft crashed when coming in to land. Many of the passengers died and the remainder were injured. Among the passengers on board were two families of Indian origin who were British citizens with homes in London. Four of them were killed, and the remaining four were injured. They are, or are represented by, the six appellants in the appeal * * *. Following the publication in December 1990 of the Report of a Court of Inquiry in India, in which the cause of the crash was identified as error on the part of the pilots (both of whom were killed in the crash), proceedings were commenced in India on 12 February 1992 against I.A.C. [India Airline Corporation], and also against Hindustan Aeronautics Ltd. ("H.A.L."), the airport authority at Bangalore airport. H.A.L. was criticised by the Court of Inquiry for failing to make adequate arrangements for dealing with accidents, and in particular for extinguishing fires such as that which broke out in the aircraft when it crashed; the Court considered that, if such arrangements had been in place, the loss of life and the injuries suffered would not have been so severe. On 6 March 1992 the appellants settled their claim against I.A.C. for the full amount recoverable up to the limit of I.A.C.'s liability. * * *

Meanwhile in February 1992 the appellants also commenced proceedings in Texas, where they sued a number of parties who might have had some connection with the aircraft or its operation. These included the respondent company, Airbus Industrie G.I.E. ("Airbus"), which designed and assembled the aircraft at Toulouse in France. Similar proceedings were brought in Texas in respect of three American passengers who died in the same crash.[*] The two sets of proceedings were later consolidated. In response to these proceedings in Texas, on 21 November 1992 Airbus brought proceedings in the Bangalore City Civil Court against, inter alia, the appellants and the American claimants, and on 22 April 1995 the presiding judge made a number of declarations designed to deter the defendants in those proceedings (i.e. the appellants and the American claimants) from pursuing their claims in Texas. These included a declaration that the appellants were not entitled to proceed against Airbus in any court in the world other than in India/Bangalore, and an injunction which purported to restrain the appellants from claiming damages from Airbus in any court in the world except the courts in India/Bangalore. However, since the appellants were not within the Indian jurisdiction, the injunction had little deterrent effect.

Airbus then issued an originating summons in this country with the purpose of (1) enforcing the Bangalore judgment against the appellants, and (2) obtaining an injunction from the English High Court restraining the appellants, who are resident in England, from continuing with their action against Airbus in Texas on the grounds that pursuit of that action by the appellants would be contrary to justice and/or vexatious or oppressive. [The trial judge refused the injunction sought by Airbus, but the Court of Appeal reversed. Appellants then appealed to the House of Lords.]

> * * *

The underlying principles

This part of the law is concerned with the resolution of clashes between jurisdictions. Two different approaches to the problem have emerged in the world today, one associated with the civil law jurisdictions of continental Europe, and the other with the common law world. Each is the fruit of a distinctive legal history, and also reflects to some extent cultural differences which are beyond the

---

[*] [The claim against Airbus in Texas was based largely on a principle of strict liability, and remedies included a power to award punitive damages. Contingency fees were available in Texas, and Texas at the time had no doctrine of *forum non conveniens*.—eds.]

scope of an opinion such as this. On the continent of Europe, in the early days of the European Community, the essential need was seen to be to avoid any such clash between member States of the same community. A system, developed by distinguished scholars, was embodied in the Brussels Convention, under which jurisdiction is allocated on the basis of well-defined rules. This system achieves its purpose, but at a price. The price is rigidity, and rigidity can be productive of injustice. The judges of this country, who loyally enforce this system, not only between United Kingdom jurisdictions and the jurisdictions of other member States, but also as between the three jurisdictions within the United Kingdom itself, have to accept the fact that the practical results are from time to time unwelcome. This is essentially because the primary purpose of the Convention is to ensure that there shall be no clash between the jurisdictions of member States of the Community.

In the common law world, the situation is precisely the opposite. There is, so to speak, a jungle of separate, broadly based, jurisdictions all over the world. In England, for example, jurisdiction is founded on the presence of the defendant within the jurisdiction, and in certain specified (but widely drawn) circumstances on a power to serve the defendant with process outside the jurisdiction. But the potential excesses of common law jurisdictions are generally curtailed by the adoption of the principle of forum non conveniens—a self-denying ordinance under which the court will stay (or dismiss) proceedings in favour of another clearly more appropriate forum. This principle, which has no application as between states which are parties to the Brussels Convention, appears to have originated in Scotland * * * and to have been developed primarily in the United States; but, at least since the acceptance of the principle in England by your Lordships' House in *Spiliada Maritime Corporation v. Cansulex Ltd.* [1987] A.C. 460, it has become widely accepted throughout the common law world * * *. The principle is directed against cases being brought in inappropriate jurisdictions and so tends to ensure that, as between common law jurisdictions, cases will only be brought in a jurisdiction which is appropriate for their resolution. The purpose of the principle is therefore different from that which underlies the Brussels Convention. It cannot, and does not aim to, avoid all clashes between jurisdictions; indeed parallel proceedings in different jurisdictions are not of themselves regarded as unacceptable. In that sense the principle may be regarded as an imperfect weapon; but it is both flexible and practical and, where it is effective, it produces a result which is conducive to practical justice. It is however dependent on the voluntary adoption of the principle by the state in question; and, as the present case shows, if one state does not adopt the principle, the delicate balance which the universal adoption of the principle could achieve will to that extent break down.

It is at this point that, in the present context, the jurisdiction to grant an anti-suit injunction becomes relevant. This jurisdiction has a long history, finding its origin in the grant of common injunctions by the English Court of Chancery to restrain the pursuit of proceedings in the English courts of common law, * * *. The principles upon which the jurisdiction may be exercised have recently been examined and restated by the Privy Council in *Société Nationale Industrielle*

Aerospatiale v. Lee Kui Jak [1987] A.C. 871, and * * * the principles there stated have found broad acceptance in the Supreme Court of Canada (see *Amchem Products Inc. v. Workers' Compensation Board* (1993) 102 D.L.R. (4th) 96 * * * and the High Court of Australia (see the judgment of the majority of the Court in *CSR Ltd. v. Cigna Insurance Australia Ltd. and others* (1997) 146 A.L.R. 402); and a similar jurisdiction is exercised by the Indian courts, as the present litigation shows. The broad principle underlying the jurisdiction is that it is to be exercised when the ends of justice require it. Generally speaking, this may occur when the foreign proceedings are vexatious or oppressive. Historically these terms have different meanings (see *Aerospatiale* * * *); but *Amchem Products* * * * expressed a preference for a formulation of the principle based simply on the ends of justice, without reference to vexation or oppression. But, as was stressed in *Aerospatiale*, in exercising the jurisdiction regard must be had to comity, and so the jurisdiction is one which must be exercised with caution. This aspect of the jurisdiction has been stressed both by the Supreme Court of Canada * * * and by the High Court of Australia * * * and it is, in my opinion, of particular relevance in the present case.

I must stress again that, as between common law jurisdictions, there is no system as such, comparable to that enshrined in the Brussels Convention. The basic principle is that each jurisdiction is independent. There is therefore, as I have said, no embargo on concurrent proceedings in the same matter in more than one jurisdiction. There are simply these two weapons, a stay (or dismissal) of proceedings and an anti-suit injunction. Moreover, each of these has its limitations. The former depends on its voluntary adoption by the state in question, and the latter is inhibited by respect for comity. It follows that, although the availability of these two weapons should ensure that practical justice is achieved in most cases, this may not always be possible.

The problem in the present case

* * * [T]he first and crucial question which arises in the present case is whether the English court will grant an anti-suit injunction in circumstances where there is no relevant connection between the English jurisdiction and the proceedings in question other than that the appellants, who are resident in this country, are subject to the jurisdiction and so can effectively be restrained by an injunction granted by an English court.

* * * [This] question may arise not only in cases such as the present, usually described as "alternative forum cases" (the two most relevant jurisdictions here being India and Texas), but also in what have been called "single forum cases," in which (for example) the English court is asked to grant an anti-suit injunction to restrain a party from proceeding in a foreign court which alone has jurisdiction over the relevant dispute. * * * [I]n both categories of case, the basis of the jurisdiction has been traditionally stated in broad terms which are characteristic of the remedy of injunction as used in our domestic law. In alternative forum cases, it has been stated that the jurisdiction will be exercised as the ends of justice require, and in particular where the pursuit of the relevant proceedings is vexatious or oppressive; in single forum cases, it is said that an injunction may

be granted to restrain the pursuit of proceedings overseas which is unconscionable. The focus is, therefore, on the character of the defendant's conduct, as befits
an equitable remedy such as an injunction. In particular, although it has frequently been stated that comity requires that the jurisdiction to grant an anti-suit
injunction should be exercised with caution, no requirement has been imposed
specifically to prevent the grant of an anti-suit injunction in circumstances which
amount to a breach of comity. The present case raises for the first time, and in a
stark form, the question whether such a requirement should be recognised and, if
so, what form it should take.

In alternative forum cases, in which the choice is between the English forum
and some other forum overseas, an anti-suit injunction will normally only be
applied for in an English court where England is the natural forum for the resolution of the dispute; and, if so, there will be no infringement of comity. England
was assumed to be the natural forum in a passage in the judgment of the Privy
Council in *Aerospatiale*, which was delivered by myself. There, with reference
in particular to cases such as the present, I said:

> "Their Lordships refer, in particular, to the fact that litigants may now
> be encouraged to proceed in foreign jurisdictions, having no connection
> with the subject matter of the dispute, which exercise an exceptionally
> broad jurisdiction and which offer great inducements, in particular great-
> ly enhanced, even punitive, damages, that they may tempt litigants to
> pursue their remedies there. In normal circumstances, application of the
> now very widely recognised principle of forum non conveniens should
> ensure that the foreign court will itself, where appropriate, decline to ex-
> ercise its own jurisdiction . . . But a stay may not be granted; and if, in
> particular, the English court concludes that it is the natural forum for the
> adjudication of the relevant dispute, and that by proceeding in the for-
> eign court the plaintiff is acting oppressively, the English court may, in
> the interests of justice, grant an injunction restraining the plaintiff from
> pursuing the proceedings in the foreign court."

It is to be observed that the example there given presupposes that the English
court is the natural forum for the adjudication of the dispute, though it is not
stated in terms whether that is a prerequisite of the exercise of the jurisdiction in
an alternative forum case[.] * * * In a later passage in the same judgment I did
however state that, as a general rule, the court granting the injunction must conclude that it is the natural forum for the trial of the action. * * *

[In the] United States * * * the situation is more complicated. The principle
of forum non conveniens has long been recognised in the United States[.] The
jurisdiction to grant an anti-suit injunction is likewise recognised in the United
States[.] * * *

[In *Laker Airways Ltd. v. Sabena, Belgian World Airlines* (1984) 731 F.2d.
909)] Judge Wilkey stated that anti-suit injunctions are most often necessary (a)
to protect the jurisdiction of the enjoining court, or (b) to prevent the litigant's
evasion of the important public policies of the forum. Judge Wilkey's judgment
has been most influential in the United States, but there has nevertheless developed a division of opinion among the Circuits as to the circumstances in which

an anti- suit injunction may be granted. * * * One approach, * * * "the stricter standard," * * * is derived from Judge Wilkey's judgment in the *Laker* case. It requires that the court should have regard to comity, and should only grant an anti-suit injunction to protect its own jurisdiction or to prevent evasion of its public policies[.] * * * [Under the] other approach, embodying what has been called a laxer standard, * * * an anti-suit injunction will be granted if the foreign proceedings are vexatious, oppressive or will otherwise cause inequitable hardship. In deciding whether to grant an injunction, the court will take into account the effect on a foreign sovereign's jurisdiction as one factor relevant to the grant of relief (see *Philips Medical Systems International N.V. v. Bruetman* (1993) 8 F.3d. 600, 605, *per* Judge Posner), but will require evidence that comity is likely to be impaired (see *Allendale Mutual Insurance v. Bull Data Systems* (1993) 10 F.3d. 425, 431, *per* Judge Posner).

Single forum cases

Before I attempt to formulate the principle applicable in the present case, I find it useful to return to the single forum cases which arose out of the Laker Airways litigation in this country. There are two decisions in question. In the first case, *British Airways Board v. Laker Airways Ltd.* [1985] A.C. 58, * * * the House of Lords held that British Airways and British Caledonian Airways were not entitled to an injunction [of U.S. proceedings]. These two airlines had, by becoming parties to the applicable agreement between the United Kingdom and United States Governments regulating transatlantic air traffic between the two countries, accepted that they were subject to the private law of both countries; and for that reason they failed to establish that Laker Airways' conduct in instituting the proceedings against them in the United States was unconscionable. The second case, *Midland Bank Plc. v. Laker Airways Ltd.* [1986] Q.B. 689, is of more relevance to the present case. Laker Airways had joined the Midland Bank (together with another bank) to its anti-trust proceedings in the United States on the basis that the bank, having been involved in mounting a financial rescue operation for Laker Airways, had withdrawn its support in circumstances which suggested that the bank was party to the conspiracy to put Laker Airways out of business. The Court of Appeal granted the bank an anti-suit injunction to restrain Laker Airways from proceeding against the bank in the anti-trust suit in the United States. The basis for so doing appears to have been that the dealings between the two parties were part of the domestic business of the bank, which took place subject to English law and in an English context. * * *:

> ". . . it is legitimate to look very closely at the suggestion that a resident in country A who has a series of dealings in country A with another resident of country A and who conducts his dealings in accordance with and subject to the law of country A is at the same time exposing himself to a potential liability in country B because the way in which he conducts the dealings may offend some law in country B. 'This question may arise in many different situations, often in fields far removed from antitrust legislation. Where the question does arise, then, in my judgment, the court has jurisdiction to consider whether it is just and equitable for the party affected to be brought before the courts of country B. . .

.' In my view, the dealings between the plaintiff banks and Laker Airways were . . . part of the domestic business of the banks. The dealings took place subject to English law and in an English context . . . the plaintiff banks did not at any stage subject the relevant banking dealings and operations to the scrutiny or control of the United States authorities. Accordingly, in my judgment, the English court has jurisdiction to intervene to prevent the plaintiff banks from being subjected to proceedings in the New York court."

Your Lordships' House is not here concerned to consider whether that case was correctly decided. Moreover it was not a case in which our present problem arises. That would have happened if the bank in that case had been a bank which carried on business in a third country, for example India, and all the relevant business had been transacted in India subject to Indian law. The question would then have arisen whether an English court should be prepared, in such circumstances, to grant an injunction restraining Laker Airways from joining the Indian bank to its anti-trust suit in the United States, simply because Laker Airways was a company carrying on business in England and so amenable to being sued in this country; and my immediate reaction is that it would be surprising if that question was to be answered in the affirmative. At all events it is striking that, in *Midland Bank Plc. v. Laker Airways Ltd.*, the injunction was granted in circumstances where the relevant transaction was overwhelmingly English in character. It can therefore be said that, on this basis, the decision was consistent with comity, though the point was not articulated in the judgments because it did not arise for consideration; and, by parity of reasoning, it can be said that the grant of an injunction at the suit of British Airways and British Caledonian to restrain Laker from proceeding against them in the United States could not be justified in this way. These single forum cases demonstrate that any limiting principle requiring respect for comity cannot simply be expressed by reference to the question whether the English court may be the natural forum for the dispute. Such a principle would have to be stated on a wider basis. I wish to stress however that, in attempting to formulate the principle, I shall not concern myself with those cases in which the choice of forum has been, directly or indirectly, the subject of a contract between the parties. Such cases do not fall to be considered in the present case.

Comity

* * * As a general rule, before an anti-suit injunction can properly be granted by an English court to restrain a person from pursuing proceedings in a foreign jurisdiction in cases of the kind under consideration in the present case, comity requires that the English forum should have a sufficient interest in, or connection with, the matter in question to justify the indirect interference with the foreign court which an anti-suit injunction entails.

In an alternative forum case, this will involve consideration of the question whether the English court is the natural forum for the resolution of the dispute. The proper approach in such cases was considered in some depth * * * in the *Amchem Products* case, * * *

"The first step in applying the [*Aerospatiale*] analysis is to determine whether the domestic forum is the natural forum, that is the forum that on the basis of relevant factors has the closest connection with the action and the parties. I would modify this slightly to conform with the test relating to forum non conveniens. Under this test the court must determine whether there is another forum that is clearly more appropriate. The result of this change in stay applications is that where there is no one forum that is the most appropriate, the domestic forum wins out by default and refuses a stay, provided it is an appropriate forum. In this step of the analysis, the domestic court as a matter of comity must take cognizance of the fact that the foreign court has assumed jurisdiction. If, applying the principles relating to forum non conveniens outlined above, the foreign court could reasonably have concluded that there was no alternative forum that was clearly more appropriate, the domestic court should respect that decision and the application should be dismissed. Where there is a genuine disagreement between the courts of our country and another, the courts of this country should not arrogate to themselves the decision for both jurisdictions. In most cases it will appear from the decision of the foreign court whether it acted on principles similar to those that obtain here, but, if not, then the domestic court must consider whether the result is consistent with those principles. In a case in which the domestic court concludes that the foreign court assumed jurisdiction on a basis that is inconsistent with principles relating to forum non conveniens and that the foreign court's conclusion could not reasonably have been reached had it applied those principles, it must go then to the second step of the [*Aerospatiale*] test" (i.e., whether to grant an injunction on the ground that the ends of justice require it)."

His exposition is of considerable interest; for present purposes, however, it is not necessary for me to give the matter detailed consideration.

In a single forum case this approach, as I have pointed out, can have no application. In such a case it may however be possible to establish a sufficient connection with the English forum. In particular this may, as the *Midland Bank* case suggests, involve consideration of the extent to which the relevant transactions are connected with the English jurisdiction or it may, as Judge Wilkey's statement of principle suggests, involve consideration of the question whether an injunction is required to protect the policies of the English forum.

The general principle which I have outlined above is, I understand, consistent with the approach adopted by the Supreme Court of Canada in the *Amchem Products* case. It is also close to the stricter approach adopted by the Second Circuit, the Sixth Circuit and the District of Columbia Circuit in the United States. It may be said that the traditional way in which the principles applicable in cases of anti-suit injunctions have been formulated in this country corresponds to the "laxer" approach applied in the Fifth, Seventh and Ninth Circuits, in that the latter refers to vexation, oppression and inequitable hardship. But, as I see it, the problem which has arisen in such an acute form in the present case requires the English courts to identify, for the first time, the limits which comity imposes on the exercise of the jurisdiction to grant anti-suit injunctions. In truth, the solution which I prefer gives (as does the statement of the law by Judge Wilkey) due recognition to comity but, subject to that, maintains (as do the statements of the law by Judge Posner) the traditional basis of the jurisdiction as being to intervene as the ends of justice may require.

In any event, however, I am anxious that the principle which I have stated should not be interpreted too rigidly. I have therefore expressed it as a general rule. This is consistent with my statement of the law in *Aerospatiale*, an alternative forum case, to the effect that "as a general rule" the court granting the injunction must conclude that it is the natural forum for the trial of the action (see [1987] A.C. 871, 896). It is also consistent with Judge Wilkey's statement that anti-suit injunctions are "most often" necessary for the two purposes which he specified. Indeed there may be extreme cases, for example where the conduct of the foreign state exercising jurisdiction is such as to deprive it of the respect normally required by comity, where no such limit is required to the exercise of the jurisdiction to grant an anti-suit injunction. In the present case [the district court] attached particular importance to the fact that, at the material time, the State of Texas did not recognise the principle of forum non conveniens. For my part, however, I cannot accept that this was sufficient to entitle the English court to intervene in the present case, bearing in mind that the principle is by no means universally accepted, and in particular is not accepted in most civil law countries.

The present case

I ask myself therefore whether there is any other aspect of the present case which would render the intervention of the English court consistent with comity. The facts upon which Airbus particularly relies are that there is a forum other than Texas, viz. India, which is indeed the natural forum for the dispute, but which is unable to grant effective injunctive relief restraining the appellants from proceeding in Texas because they are outside the jurisdiction of the Indian courts; however, since the appellants are amenable to the jurisdiction of the English courts, Airbus is in effect seeking the aid of the English courts to prevent the pursuit by the appellants of their proceedings in Texas, which may properly be regarded as oppressive but which the Indian courts are powerless to prevent.

I must first point out that, for the English court to come to the assistance of an Indian court, the normal process is for the English court to do so by enforcing a judgment of the Indian court. However, as the present proceedings have demonstrated, that is not possible here. An attempt was made by Airbus to persuade [the trial judge] to enforce, or at least to recognise, the Indian judgment; but he declined to do so, and Airbus has not appealed from that part of [the trial court's] decision. So Airbus is relying simply on the English court's power of itself, without direct reliance on the Indian court's decision, to grant an injunction in this case where, unusually, the English jurisdiction has no interest in, or connection with, the matter in question. I am driven to say that such a course is not open to the English courts because, for the reasons I have given, it would be inconsistent with comity. In a world which consists of independent jurisdictions, interference, even indirect interference, by the courts of one jurisdiction with the exercise of the jurisdiction of a foreign court cannot in my opinion be justified by the fact that a third jurisdiction is affected but is powerless to intervene. The basic principle is that only the courts of an interested jurisdiction can act in the matter; and if they are powerless to do so, that will not of itself be enough to justify the courts of another jurisdiction to act in their place. Such are the limits of a system which is dependent on the remedy of an anti-suit injunction to curtail the excesses of a jurisdiction which does not adopt the principle, widely accepted throughout the common law world, of forum non conveniens.

Conclusion

For the reasons I have given, I would allow the appeal on the first issue, and set aside the injunction ordered by the Court of Appeal. * * *

[LORDS SLYNN, STEYN, CLYDE, HUTTON concur.]

NOTES AND QUESTIONS FOR DISCUSSION

1. Make sure you understand the *Airbus* court's distinction between "alternative forum" and "single forum" cases. How, exactly, would you describe it? Assuming one can successfully distinguish between the two, consider the results that flow from that determination. How will the availability of the antisuit injunction differ depending on whether the setting is a single forum case versus an alternative forum case?

2. The House of Lords gives high marks to Judge Wilkie's opinion in the *Laker Airline* litigation, which it describes as representing the narrower two views respecting the availability of antisuit injunctions in the United States. Obviously, the House of Lords denied the requested injunctive relief in *Airbus*. But does the opinion really represent a general acceptance of the narrower view, or is it qualified in some respect (and if so, how)?

3. Airbus had initially attempted to have the English courts recognize and enforce the injunction issued by the Indian court, but it failed in the lower courts, and it did not appeal the issue to the House of Lords. Why not? Is the problem with the judgment the lack of personal jurisdiction in India over certain of the objects of the Indian court's injunction? Consider what the result might have been if personal jurisdiction had been present over one or more of the parties who were plaintiffs in the U.S. proceedings. Assuming there had been no problems with personal jurisdiction in the court that issued the antisuit injunction, should courts ordinarily provide judicial assistance to antisuit injunctions issued by other countries?

4. Note that other countries, typically common law countries, have developed one form or another of rules for dealing with antisuit injunctions. *Patel*'s discussion of the Amchem Prods. Inc. v. British Columbia (Workers' Compen. Bd.), [1993] 1 S.C.R. 897 (Can.), indicates that Canadian courts seek to insure that the forum with the closest connection to the dispute will be able to hear a case. Id. at 912. At the same time, however, the decision indicates that Canadian courts will grant an antisuit injunction only to prevent a "serious injustice," and it denied an antisuit injunction against a Texas product liability suit brought by Canadian plaintiffs Id. at 914. Are those positions consistent? For Australia, see

CSR Ltd. v. Cigna Ins. Australia Ltd. (1997), 189 CLR 345, 391-92 (Austl.) (indicating that antisuit injunctions would be proper "to protect the integrity of the court's processes" or to "restrain unconscionable conduct or the unconscientious exercise of legal rights").

CHAPTER 6

Taking Evidence Abroad

A. INTRODUCTION

1. An Overview of Discovery in American Courts

Civil litigation in the United States builds on the principle that parties to an action are generally entitled to obtain all relevant, but unprivileged, information that other parties or non-parties possess or control. This principle manifests itself in liberal discovery procedures aimed at the full disclosure of facts. This is particularly true in the federal courts and is often true in the state courts. Indeed, no other civil procedural system grants litigants more access to evidence held by the opponent or non-parties, than do American discovery rules. Whether based on state or federal law, these rules enable plaintiffs to press claims that initially may have only modest evidentiary support, and that would not give rise to litigation in systems with less access to information held by the opposing party or witnesses. The threat of plaintiff's finding a "smoking gun" through the discovery process may induce settlement of the case. Actual discovery of such evidence expedites the settlement process and may lead to jury verdicts that would be inconceivable absent such devices.

Contrary to most other legal systems, the American discovery rules leave it largely to the parties and their lawyers, rather than judges, actively to engage in sometimes far-reaching fact-finding with little or no immediate judicial supervision. Parties subject to overly intrusive discovery requests can move the court to obtain a protective order that may curtail or avoid particular requests. See Rule 26(c), Fed. R. Civ. P. (We will make reference to the Federal Rules of Civil Procedure because they serve as model for many of the state discovery rules.) But given that the system is geared towards providing broad access to information held by others, most discovery requests will survive such challenges.

If the target of discovery resists it, the party seeking discovery can move for a court order compelling the target to disclose the requested information and to be subjected to sanctions if the court finds that there was no reason to withhold the information. Rule 37, Fed. R. Civ. P. Because discovery is a costly tool, and because either party must generally bear its own expenses, there are potential downsides to this type of fact development. For example, the resources expended by the defendant in complying with evidentiary requests, and in pursuing his own, may not be worth the ultimate possibility of success and may force him to settle for the nuisance value of the suit. Conversely, this sometimes expensive tool is often unavailable to plaintiffs with small or even medium-sized

449

claims. Because the prospective verdict might not even cover the costs needed to engage in meaningful discovery, and absent a general provision for fee shifting (which is the standard practice in U.S. courts—although there are exceptions), plaintiffs may be prevented from pursuing meritorious claims. However, when parties command sufficient resources and the stakes are high, discovery can entail many months of pretrial work involving scores of lawyers on either side.

In keeping with its primary goals—enabling parties to substantiate their claims with evidence held by others and avoiding uncorrectable surprises at trial—the scope of discovery is quite broad. Fed. R. Civ. P. 26(b)(1) provides that nonprivileged information is discoverable if it is relevant to a party's claim or defense, and for good cause, the court may order discovery of any nonprivileged matter relevant to the subject matter involved in the action. In addition, "relevant information need not be admissible at the trial if the discovery appears reasonably calculated to lead to the discovery of admissible evidence." Id. Thus, except in matters of privilege, evidence law canons do not play a controlling role in the field of discovery.

Under the current Federal Rules, the discovery process begins very early in the litigation process with a planning conference. See Rule 26(f), Fed. R. Civ. P. Some discovery is mandatory, requiring disclosures by the parties. See Rule 26(a), Fed. R. Civ. P. Initial disclosures required of each party include (1) names and addresses of those likely to have discoverable information relevant to the pleadings, (2) a listing of relevant documents or property in the control of the parties, (3) damage computations and their basis, and (4) insurance documentation. Once this meeting has been concluded, discovery begins. There are also provisions for disclosure of the identity of expert witnesses that a party may use at trial. Other pretrial disclosures include the names of those witnesses whom a party expects to call or may call at trial, as well the documents and exhibits a party expects to offer or may offer.

Among a variety of fact-gathering tools, three methods are most frequently employed. These are written interrogatories, depositions, and production of documents and things (as well as inspection of land). See Rules 28, 30, 33, 34, Fed. R. Civ. P. Interrogatories are written questions to be answered under oath, and may be directed only to the parties involved in the litigation. But through such a device, for example, plaintiffs in products liability litigation may be able to force defendants to reveal the identity of all individuals participating in the design of the product.

Once this information is available, plaintiffs may depose these individuals to obtain additional information. Such depositions are typically taken in the offices of law firms rather than courtrooms, and they are conducted by the attorneys for the parties. Private companies, commissioned by the court, provide reporters who transcribe everything that has been said during deposition into a verbatim transcript. The lawyer "defending" the deponent will register objections to questions that would lead to the revelation of privileged information. In the extreme, the lawyer will instruct the deponent not to answer a question, which could lead to requests for a court order aimed at compelling the witness to respond. But more often than not, the deponents will respond during deposition and the ultimate admissibility of their responses will be decided only at trial.

Requests for production of documents is another cornerstone in pretrial discovery proceedings. Taking again the products liability example, plaintiffs will regularly request—and ordinarily obtain—design, engineering, and manufacturing drawings of the product at issue. Plaintiffs in this type of litigation will also have access to documents concerning allegations, reports, or complaints of previous injuries associated with the product.

Depositions and requests for documents may be addressed to both parties and non-party witnesses. While uncooperative non-party witnesses can only be compelled to provide evidence in their control through a subpoena, subpoenas will generally issue as a matter of course if asked for and can even be issued by the attorney as an officer of the court in which the attorney is authorized to practice. See Rule 45(a), Fed. R. Civ. P.

2. Foreign Methods of Obtaining Evidence

The rules governing civil procedure outside the U.S. differ from one system to another. This observation remains accurate despite strong recent trends towards greater regional, particularly European, harmonization of these rules, and it continues to apply to the means and methods of obtaining evidence in foreign civil litigation systems. (For a comprehensive account of European developments see Helen E. Hartnell, *EUstitia: Institutionalizing Justice in the European Union*, 23 Nw. J. Int'l L. & Bus. 65 (2002).) These differences notwithstanding, foreign rules, even those in other common law jurisdictions, have two things in common that put them in stark contrast with their American counterparts. First, access to information is significantly more restricted in other procedural systems, so much so that it would be seriously misleading in most instances to call these procedures "discovery." Second, foreign procedures for actually obtaining evidence are widely seen as an exercise of judiciary powers that are strictly controlled by judges rather than private litigants. In short, U.S. attorneys request and routinely receive information in U.S. litigation to an extent inconceivable to most of their colleagues abroad.

A short account of the German approach to developing a case in civil litigation illustrates the fact-finding approach in civil law jurisdictions. In the German judicial system, the suit is formally instituted after the court to which the plaintiff has submitted the complaint has effectuated service of process on the defendant. The initial brief is considerably more specific than corresponding pleadings in American litigation. Each averment for which the plaintiff carries the burden of proof must be quite detailed and accompanied by a concrete offer of proof. The court asks the defendant to submit a response to the allegations in the complaint and often schedules an early initial hearing that, particularly in more complex cases, is only the first of several conferences. Instead of an initial hearing, the court may require the parties to submit further written information before the first conference is held. In either event, trial is not a single continuous event, but consists of a series of meetings and written exchanges between the judge and the attorneys. This sequence is designed to streamline the proceedings in accordance with the particular needs of the individual case. Such conferences are largely dominated by the presiding judge, who continuously develops the case by screening the proffered evidence and signaling what further evidence is needed (and what is dispensable or irrelevant), establishing deadlines for submitting evidence, and by ruling on the manner of presentation. In short, the judge commands much control over the development of the case and, upon a finding that the matter is ripe for a decision on the merits, will render the judgment without a jury.

Despite this strong position of the judge, the German and other European rules are embedded in a genuinely adversarial rather than inquisitorial system of civil procedure, because judges are bound to rest their decisions only on facts alleged by the parties. Lawyers in this type of adversary system are by no means passive bystanders. They have the opportunity, and obligation, to represent their clients' interests vigorously, in factual and legal respects, during court hearings and through written submissions. However, there is little room for courtroom drama, given the role of judges as powerful case managers and fact finders without jury input, and considering the restraint of access to information held by others, as well as the lack of an all-decisive single-event trial. Not surprisingly, many procedural features familiar to American litigants are unknown in foreign jurisdictions. There is little or no witness preparation. Lawyers may ask witnesses questions during court hearings, in addition to judges asking questions, but such questioning does not amount to an American-style cross-examination. Verbatim transcripts are unusual, experts are typically appointed by the court rather than hired by the parties, and, most importantly for present purposes, most systems do not permit pretrial discovery conducted by private litigants. For a fuller account, see Joachim Zekoll, *Recognition and Enforcement of American Products Liability Awards in the Federal Republic of Germany*, 37 Am. J. Comp. L. 301, 331 (1989).

3. American Discovery and Foreign Perceptions

The stark contrast between American discovery proceedings and foreign methods of obtaining evidence is a source of constant tension in transnational litigation settings. What is considered normal for litigants before American courts—to substantiate their legal claims by employing potentially far-reaching discovery methods—is regularly perceived as an unacceptable fishing expedition elsewhere. To vest private parties with the power largely to control the fact gathering process (as opposed to having fact gathering done by governmental personnel) further exacerbates the tensions between the U.S. and non-U.S. judicial systems. The view that the American discovery process is incompatible with basic notions of procedural fairness is not only held in civil law systems, but also is shared widely by other common law systems as well. While they do allow for some discovery, they provide for much less disclosure than American procedures and require far more specific requests. These limitations pose problems to plaintiffs with cases pending before U.S. courts whose claims depend on access to evidence located abroad. Conversely, those who are the target of American discovery requests perceive them as an encroachment on sovereign interests and privacy rights. For a comparative perspective of U.S.

versus foreign methods of discovery, and the possible reasons for the divergence, see Stephen N. Subrin, *Discovery in Global Perspective: Are We Nuts?* 52 DePaul L. Rev. 299 (2002).

B. THE HAGUE EVIDENCE CONVENTION

To increase international judicial assistance on mutually acceptable terms, the U.S. initiated negotiations at the Hague Conference on Private International Law. In 1968, the Hague Conference presented the final text of the Hague Convention on the Taking of Evidence Abroad in Civil and Commercial Matters ("Evidence Convention" or "Convention"). In 1972, it entered into force in the U.S., which was one of the original contracting states. The Convention attempts to bridge the gap between the U.S. and other legal systems. It provides a set of rules and procedures that does not impinge upon the sovereignty of the state in which the evidence is located, while yielding evidence that can be used in the country requesting discovery. The Convention is set out in Appendix B.

1. Overview of the Hague Evidence Convention Procedures

The principal mechanisms designed to achieve the Evidence Convention's goals are (1) the Letter of Request procedure and (2) the creation of a so-called Central Authority in every contracting state. The Convention requires every contracting state to designate a Central Authority that will receive Letters of Request coming from a judicial authority of another contracting state. The Central Authority will forward that request to the court in the receiving state that is competent to execute it (Art. 2). After execution the evidence obtained will be sent back to the issuing authority of the requesting state (Art. 13). The Convention is rather specific about the content of the Letter of Request (Art. 3) and failure to comply with these requirements may result in the rejection of, or delay in, the execution of the request (Art. 5). On the other hand, a Letter of Request that meets these formal requirements must, in principle, be executed (Art. 12) expeditiously (Art. 9, III). Two narrow exceptions apply, in cases in which the execution does not fall within the functions of the judiciary in the requested state or when that state considers that the execution would violate its sovereign or security interests. (As to the sovereign or security interests exception, see Section B.3, below). In executing the request, the requested authority must employ the same measure of compulsion to uncooperative witnesses as it would in a domestic case (Art. 10) and it will ordinarily apply its own law as to the methods and procedures (Art. 9, I). Special methods and procedures may be used, unless they are incompatible with the internal law of the State of execution or are impossible or impracticable to perform in light of the internal practice and procedure of that state (Art. 9, II). For example, cross-examination of witnesses and verbatim transcripts (which are basic features of the U.S. litigation process) are unknown in most civil-law systems, and would be considered special methods and procedures. Given that civil law courts are not accustomed to performing such functions, Article 9 may not be of much help from the U.S. perspective.

Two further procedures complement the Letter of Request approach: A diplomatic officer or consular agent of a contracting state may, without compulsion, take evidence in the territory of another contracting state (Arts. 15-16); evidence may also be obtained, without compulsion, through a "commissioner," appointed by the requesting state, in the territory of the requested state (Art.17). The latter option is particularly attractive for U.S. litigants because attorneys well acquainted with U.S. discovery proceedings can serve as commissioners. However, the lack of compulsion and other strict limitations render these methods less effective than they appear at first sight. In particular, a contracting state has the right to declare that it will not permit the taking of evidence by these alternative methods (Art. 33). For example, Germany has made a reservation with respect to the taking of evidence by diplomatic officers or consular agents and has declared that the taking of evidence by private commissioners requires prior approval of the German Central Authority.

2. Privileges Against Testifying Under the Convention

An important limitation for the party seeking evidence under the Convention has to do with the privileges on which a witness may rely. Reluctant witnesses may either invoke the privileges and duties to refuse to give evidence under the law of the state of execution *or* under the law of the requesting state (Art. 11). The right of witnesses to rely on privileges under the law where the evidence is located can severely hamper the attempt to conduct discovery. For example, Germany has broad testimonial privileges, such as the refusal to testify under §§ 383 and 384 of the German Code of Civil Procedure ("ZPO"):

§ 383. [Refusal to testify]

(1) The following are entitled to refuse to testify:

1. the person engaged to be married to a party;
2. the spouse of a party, even when the marriage no longer subsists;
3. those who are or were related in the direct line to a party or related by marriage, collaterally related to the third degree;
4. clergymen with respect to matters entrusted to them in the exercise of their pastoral duties;
5. persons who collaborate in the preparation, production or distribution of periodicals or broadcasts in their professional capacity, or did so in the past, concerning the person of the editor, contributor or source of contribution with regard to contributions and documents, as well as concerning information related to them with regard to their activities, insofar as it deals with contributions, documents and information for the editorial part;
6. persons to whom matters are entrusted by virtue of their office, profession or trade, which are to be kept secret due to their nature or by law, with respect to the facts to which the duty of secrecy pertains.

(2) The persons indicated in nos. 2 and 3 above shall be informed of their right to refuse to testify before they are examined.

(3) The examination of persons, indicated in nos. 4 to 6 above shall, also when testifying is not refused, not be directed to facts with regard to which it is apparent that evidence cannot be given without the violation of the duty of secrecy.

§ 384. [Refusal to answer certain questions]

Testimony may be refused:

1. concerning questions, the answering of which would result for the witness or a person related to him in the manner indicated in § 383 nos. 1 to 3 a direct financial loss;

2. concerning questions, the answer to which would disgrace the witness or a person related to him in the manner indicated in § 383 nos. 1 to 3 or would involve the jeopardy of his prosecution for a crime or infraction;

3. concerning questions which the witness could not answer without disclosing an act or trade secret.

According to Article 11 of the Convention, these domestic legal privileges will prevail. And notably, the German concept of trade secret in ZPO § 384 no.3 has been interpreted particularly broadly by the courts. It encompasses all economically relevant facts to the operation of a business such as sources of product purchases, product purchase prices, price calculation, and customers. Given this broad protective scope, many requests emanating from the U.S., whether based on depositions, interrogatories, or document discovery, would be rejected.

3. Subject Matter Scope of the Hague Evidence Convention

The Evidence Convention applies only to "civil or commercial matters" (Art. 1). As in older Hague Conventions (The Hague Conventions on Civil Procedure of 1905 and 1952 and the Hague Service Convention of 1964), these terms are not defined and give rise to divergent interpretations. Although all contracting states agree that purely criminal matters fall outside the scope of the Convention, there are conflicting views on other areas. There is disagreement, for example, on whether matters of administrative law qualify as "civil or commercial." The U.S. delegate to a Special Commission, which was set up to study the scope of the Convention in 1978, indicated that the U.S. Central Authority would honor requests for evidence to be used in foreign administrative proceedings, including fiscal matters. Conversely, civil law jurisdictions like France and Germany would not be likely to honor a request for evidence to be used before an administrative court or agency.

It is likewise unclear under the Hague Evidence Convention whether bankruptcy proceedings are "civil or commercial matters." There is also some doubt as to whether certain types of damages available under American law qualify. With respect to antitrust treble damages, for example, a German court has held that such claims must be considered a civil or commercial matter and must be dealt with under the Hague Evidence Convention. See Decision of the Munich Court of Appeals, November 27, 1980 reprinted in translation in 20 Int'l Legal Materials [I.L.M.] 1025, 1031-1032 (1981). Even though such damages are unknown in German civil proceedings, the court focused, among other things, on the fact that the claim was made by a private party in American civil proceedings. In interpreting the identical scope of application of the Hague Service Convention, a German court held that American punitive damages constitute a civil or commercial matter, despite their underlying purpose to punish the defendant for the wrongdoing he committed. See Decision of the Munich Court of Appeals, May 9, 1989, reprinted in translation in 29 I.L.M. 1570 (1989).

In a later decision, the German Federal Constitutional Court held that a party cannot resist service of punitive damages claims on public policy grounds. Specifically, the Court held that the sovereign and security interest exceptions of the Service Convention (Article 13), cannot be invoked against service of punitive damages claims under the Hague Service Convention. See Decision of the Federal Constitutional Court, December 7, 1994, reprinted in translation in 34 I.L.M. 975 (1995). See Chapter 4, Section E. One of the reasons advanced for this holding is that "such a restriction on the flow of judicial assistance is fundamentally all the less necessary insofar as the outcome of the proceedings is, at the time of service, still completely open." Id. at 991. Given that the sovereign and security interest exceptions contained in Article 12 of the Evidence Convention are identical, public policy objections to requests to take evidence under the Convention would likely fail as well. Note, however, that if such damages become part of an American judgment, they will probably not be enforced in Germany. See Chapter 8.

4. The Exclusion of Pretrial Discovery Documents

The single most important limitation of the Convention, from the American perspective, is the right of "contracting states" to declare that they will not execute letters of request issued for the purpose of obtaining pretrial discovery of documents (Art. 23). All but three states (Czechoslovakia, Israel, and the U.S.) have made use of this option, which was adopted on the initiative of the British delegation. In exercising this option, however, contracting states have adopted different approaches. Some states have declared that they will decline to execute any request for pretrial discovery of documents,[*] while others permit execution, provided the requests meet strict specificity and relevancy standards.

---

[*] Upon signing the treaty, Germany declared "that it will not, in its territory, execute Letters of Request issued for the purpose of obtaining pre-trial discovery of documents as known in Common Law countries." See Bekanntmachung über das Inkrafttreten des Haager Übereinkommens über die Beweisaufnahme im Ausland in Zivil- und Handelssachen (Promulgation of the Entering into Force of the Hague Convention on the Taking of Evidence Abroad in Civil or Commercial Matters) at B.5., BGBl II S. 780 (Federal Gazette Vol. 2, p. 780),

Switzerland's declaration is an example of the latter category. In issuing a reservation under Article 23, Switzerland declared that it will not execute requests for pretrial discovery of documents if:

1. The request has no direct and necessary link with the proceedings;
2. A person is required to indicate what documents were in his possession or at his disposal;
3. A person is required to produce documents other than those mentioned in the request; or
4. Interests worthy of protection of concerned persons are endangered.

Even though Switzerland's declaration does not amount to a blanket denial of document discovery, it falls far short of what is permissible and customary under American procedural rules. Compare Rule 26, Fed. R. Civ. P. Article 23 thus affects one of the core methods of the American discovery system, and calls into question the usefulness of the Evidence Convention for evidence-seeking litigants with cases pending before American courts.

5. *The Exclusivity of the Hague Evidence Convention*

Given the exclusion or limitations of document discovery and other strictures of the Evidence Convention, parties suing in American courts have shown little interest in seeking resort to the sort of judicial assistance offered by the Convention. Instead, plaintiffs in international civil litigation pending before American courts regularly attempt to bypass the Convention and to avail themselves of the far-reaching discovery methods employed in ordinary domestic litigation. American courts faced with the question of whether these plaintiffs *must* use the Convention procedures initially arrived at conflicting conclusions. Some held that the Convention did not preempt American rules and considered it a merely optional device, while others required that the party seeking evidence resort to American law only *after* having first tried unsuccessfully to obtain evidence through the Convention procedures. See, e.g., Philadelphia Gear Corp. v. American Pfauter Corp. 100 F.R.D. 58, 60 n.3 (E.D. Pa 1983) (holding that a party seeking evidence abroad must first attempt to obtain it pursuant to the Hague Evidence Convention, rather than by way of the Federal Rules of Civil Procedure); cf. Wilson v. Lufthansa German Airlines, 489 N.Y.S.2d 575 (N.Y. App. Div. 1985) (holding that resort to the procedures outlined in the Hague Evidence Convention was not mandated in the instant case); but see Umana v. SCM S.p.A., 737 N.Y.S.2d 556 (N.Y. App. Div. 2002) (holding that the trial court order to use the Convention as a first instance of securing evidence was a provident use of discretion). In 1987, the U.S. Supreme had the opportunity finally to decide this question:

June 21 1979. Denmark, Finland, France, Luxembourg, Norway, Portugal and Sweden also have issued declaration unequivocally rejecting document discovery requests.

Société Nationale Industrielle Aérospatiale v. U.S. District Court

Supreme Court of the United States, 1987.

482 U.S. 522.

JUSTICE STEVENS delivered the opinion of the Court.

The question presented in this case concerns the extent to which a federal district court must employ the procedures set forth in the [Hague Evidence] Convention when litigants seek answers to interrogatories, the production of documents, and admissions from a French adversary over whom the court has personal jurisdiction.

I

The two petitioners are corporations owned by the Republic of France. They are engaged in the business of designing, manufacturing, and marketing aircraft. One of their planes, the "Rallye," was allegedly advertised in American aviation publications as "the World's safest and most economical STOL [short takeoff and landing] plane." On August 19, 1980, a Rallye crashed in Iowa, injuring the pilot and a passenger.   Dennis Jones, John George, and Rosa George brought separate suits based upon this accident in the United States District Court for the Southern District of Iowa, alleging that petitioners had manufactured and sold a defective plane and that they were guilty of negligence and breach of warranty. Petitioners answered the complaints, apparently without questioning the jurisdiction of the District Court. With the parties' consent, the cases were consolidated and referred to a Magistrate.   See 28 U.S.C. § 636(c)(1).

Initial discovery was conducted by both sides pursuant to the Federal Rules of Civil Procedure without objection. [Subsequently], however, petitioners filed a motion for a protective order.   The motion alleged that because petitioners are "French corporations, and the discovery sought can only be found in a foreign state, namely France," the Hague Convention dictated the exclusive procedures that must be followed for pretrial discovery. In addition, the motion stated that under French penal law, the petitioners could not respond to discovery requests that did not comply with the Convention.[6] [The trial court denied the defendants' motion and, agreeing with that decision, the Court of Appeals for the Eighth Circuit held that] "when the district court has jurisdiction over a foreign litigant the Hague Convention does not apply to the production of evidence in that litigant's possession, even though the documents and

---

[6] Article 1A of the French "blocking statute," French Penal Code Law No. 80-538, provides: "Subject to treaties or international agreements and applicable laws and regulations, it is prohibited for any party to request, seek or disclose, in writing, orally or otherwise, economic, commercial, industrial, financial or technical documents or information leading to the constitution of evidence with a view to foreign judicial or administrative proceedings or in connection therewith." * * *

information sought may physically be located within the territory of a foreign signatory to the Convention." The Court of Appeals disagreed with petitioners' argument that this construction would render the entire Hague Convention "meaningless," noting that it would still serve the purpose of providing an improved procedure for obtaining evidence from nonparties. * * *

    * * *

III

In arguing their entitlement to a protective order, petitioners correctly assert that both the discovery rules set forth in the Federal Rules of Civil Procedure and the Hague Convention are the law of the United States. This observation, however, does not dispose of the question before us; we must analyze the interaction between these two bodies of federal law. Initially, we note that at least four different interpretations of the relationship between the federal discovery rules and the Hague Convention are possible. Two of these interpretations assume that the Hague Convention by its terms dictates the extent to which it supplants normal discovery rules. First, the Hague Convention might be read as requiring its use to the exclusion of any other discovery procedures whenever evidence located abroad is sought for use in an American court. Second, the Hague Convention might be interpreted to require first, but not exclusive, use of its procedures. Two other interpretations assume that international comity, rather than the obligations created by the treaty, should guide judicial resort to the Hague Convention. Third, then, the Convention might be viewed as establishing a supplemental set of discovery procedures, strictly optional under treaty law, to which concerns of comity nevertheless require first resort by American courts in all cases. Fourth, the treaty may be viewed as an undertaking among sovereigns to facilitate discovery to which an American court should resort when it deems that course of action appropriate, after considering the situations of the parties before it as well as the interests of the concerned foreign state.

In interpreting an international treaty, we are mindful that it is "in the nature of a contract between nations," Trans World Airlines, Inc. v. Franklin Mint Corp., 466 U.S. 243, 253 (1984), to which "[g]eneral rules of construction apply." We therefore begin "with the text of the treaty and the context in which the written words are used." Air France v. Saks, 470 U.S. 392, 397 (1985). The treaty's history, "'the negotiations, and the practical construction adopted by the parties'" may also be relevant. We reject the first two of the possible interpretations as inconsistent with the language and negotiating history of the Hague Convention. The preamble of the Convention specifies its purpose "to facilitate the transmission and execution of Letters of Request" and to "improve mutual judicial co-operation in civil or commercial matters." The preamble does not speak in mandatory terms which would purport to describe the procedures for all permissible transnational discovery and exclude all other existing practices. The text of the Evidence Convention itself does not modify the law of any contracting state, require any contracting state to use the Convention procedures, either in requesting evidence or in responding to such requests, or compel any contracting state to change its own evidence-gathering procedures.[16]

The Convention contains three chapters. Chapter I, entitled "Letters of Requests," and chapter II, entitled "Taking of Evidence by Diplomatic Officers, Consular Agents and Commissioners," both use permissive rather than mandatory language. Thus, Article 1 provides that a judicial authority in one contracting state "may" forward a letter of request to the competent authority in another contracting state for the purpose of obtaining evidence. Similarly, Articles 15, 16, and 17 provide that diplomatic officers, consular agents, and commissioners "may . . . without compulsion," take evidence under certain conditions. The absence of any command that a contracting state must use Convention procedures when they are not needed is conspicuous.

Two of the Articles in chapter III, entitled "General Clauses," buttress our conclusion that the Convention was intended as a permissive supplement, not a pre-emptive replacement, for other means of obtaining evidence located abroad. Article 23 expressly authorizes a contracting state to declare that it will not execute any letter of request in aid of pretrial discovery of documents in a common-law country. Surely, if the Convention had been intended to replace completely the broad discovery powers that the common-law courts in the United States previously exercised over foreign litigants subject to their jurisdiction, it would have been most anomalous for the common-law contracting parties to agree to Article 23, which enables a contracting party to revoke its consent to the treaty's procedures for pretrial discovery. In the absence of explicit textual support, we are unable to accept the hypothesis that the common-law contracting states abjured recourse to all pre-existing discovery procedures at the same time that they accepted the possibility that a contracting party could unilaterally abrogate even the Convention's procedures. Moreover, Article 27 plainly states that the Convention does not prevent a contracting state from using more liberal methods of rendering evidence than those authorized by the Convention. Thus, the text of the Evidence Convention, as well as the history of its proposal and ratification by the United States, unambiguously supports the conclusion that it was intended to establish optional procedures that would facilitate the taking of evidence abroad. * * *

---

[16] The Hague Conference on Private International Law's omission of mandatory language in the preamble is particularly significant in light of the same body's use of mandatory language in the preamble to the Hague Service Convention [.] Article 1 of the Service Convention provides: "The present Convention shall apply in all cases, in civil or commercial matters, where there is occasion to transmit a judicial or extra judicial document for service abroad." * * * [T]he Service Convention was drafted before the Evidence Convention, and its language provided a model exclusivity provision that the drafters of the Evidence Convention could easily have followed had they been so inclined. * * *

We conclude accordingly that the Hague Convention did not deprive the District Court of the jurisdiction it otherwise possessed to order a foreign national party before it to produce evidence physically located within a signatory nation.

IV

While the Hague Convention does not divest the District Court of jurisdiction to order discovery under the Federal Rules of Civil Procedure, the optional character of the Convention procedures sheds light on one aspect of the Court of Appeals' opinion that we consider erroneous. That court concluded that the Convention simply "does not apply" to discovery sought from a foreign litigant that is subject to the jurisdiction of an American court. Plaintiffs argue that this conclusion is supported by two considerations. First, the Federal Rules of Civil Procedure provide ample means for obtaining discovery from parties who are subject to the court's jurisdiction, while before the Convention was ratified it was often extremely difficult, if not impossible, to obtain evidence from nonparty witnesses abroad. Plaintiffs contend that it is appropriate to construe the Convention as applying only in the area in which improvement was badly needed. Second, when a litigant is subject to the jurisdiction of the district court, arguably the evidence it is required to produce is not "abroad" within the meaning of the Convention, even though it is in fact located in a foreign country at the time of the discovery request and even though it will have to be gathered or otherwise prepared abroad.

Nevertheless, the text of the Convention draws no distinction between evidence obtained from third parties and that obtained from the litigants themselves; nor does it purport to draw any sharp line between evidence that is "abroad" and evidence that is within the control of a party subject to the jurisdiction of the requesting court. Thus, it appears clear to us that the optional Convention procedures are available whenever they will facilitate the gathering of evidence by the means authorized in the Convention. Although these procedures are not mandatory, the Hague Convention does "apply" to the production of evidence in a litigant's possession in the sense that it is one method of seeking evidence that a court may elect to employ.

V

Petitioners contend that even if the Hague Convention's procedures are not mandatory, this Court should adopt a rule requiring that American litigants first resort to those procedures before initiating any discovery pursuant to the normal methods of the Federal Rules of Civil Procedure. The Court of Appeals rejected this argument because it was convinced that an American court's order ultimately requiring discovery that a foreign court had refused under Convention procedures would constitute "the greatest insult" to the sovereignty of that tribunal. We disagree with the Court of Appeals' view. It is well known that the scope of American discovery is often significantly broader than is permitted in other jurisdictions, and we are satisfied that foreign tribunals will recognize that the final decision on the evidence to be used in litigation conducted in American courts must be made by those courts. We therefore do not believe that an American court should refuse to make use of Convention procedures because of a concern that it may ultimately find it necessary to order the production of evidence that a foreign tribunal permitted a party to withhold.

Nevertheless, we cannot accept petitioners' invitation to announce a new rule of law that would require first resort to Convention procedures whenever discovery is sought from a foreign litigant. Assuming, without deciding, that we have the lawmaking power to do so, we are convinced that such a general rule would be unwise. In many situations the Letter of Request procedure authorized by the Convention would be unduly time consuming and expensive, as well as less certain to produce needed evidence than direct use of the Federal Rules. A rule of first resort in all cases would therefore be inconsistent with the overriding interest in the "just, speedy, and inexpensive determination" of litigation in our courts. See Fed. Rule Civ. Proc. 1.

Petitioners argue that a rule of first resort is necessary to accord respect to the sovereignty of states in which evidence is located. It is true that the process of obtaining evidence in a civil-law jurisdiction is normally conducted by a judicial officer rather than by private attorneys. Petitioners contend that if performed on French soil, for example, by an unauthorized person, such evidence-gathering might violate the "judicial sovereignty" of the host nation. Because it is only through the Convention that civil-law nations have given their consent to evidence-gathering activities within their borders, petitioners argue, we have a duty to employ those procedures whenever they are available. We find that argument unpersuasive. If such a duty were to be inferred from the adoption of the Convention itself, we believe it would have been described in the text of that document. Moreover, the concept of international comity requires in this context a more particularized analysis of the respective interests of the foreign nation and the requesting nation than petitioners' proposed general rule would generate.[28] We therefore decline to hold as a blanket matter that comity requires resort to Hague Evidence Convention procedures without prior scrutiny in each case of the particular facts, sovereign interests, and likelihood that resort to those procedures will prove effective.

---

[28] The nature of the concerns that guide a comity analysis is suggested by the Restatement of Foreign Relations Law of the United States (Revised) § 437(1)(c) (Tent. Draft No. 7, 1986) (approved May 14, 1986) (Restatement). While we recognize that § 437 [now § 442—eds.] of the Restatement may not represent a consensus of international views on the scope of the district court's power to order foreign discovery in the face of objections by foreign states, these factors are relevant to any comity analysis:

    "(1) the importance to the . . . litigation of the documents or other information requested;

    "(2) the degree of specificity of the request;

    "(3) whether the information originated in the United States;

    "(4) the availability of alternative means of securing the information; and

    "(5) the extent to which noncompliance with the request would undermine important interests of the United States, or compliance with the request would undermine important interests of the state where the information is located." Ibid.

Some discovery procedures are much more "intrusive" than others. In this case, for example, an interrogatory asking petitioners to identify the pilots who flew flight tests in the Rallye before it was certified for flight by the Federal Aviation Administration, or a request to admit that petitioners authorized certain advertising in a particular magazine, is certainly less intrusive than a request to produce all of the "design specifications, line drawings and engineering plans and all engineering change orders and plans and all drawings concerning the leading edge slats for the Rallye type aircraft manufactured by the Defendants." Even if a court might be persuaded that a particular document request was too burdensome or too "intrusive" to be granted in full, with or without an appropriate protective order, it might well refuse to insist upon the use of Convention procedures before requiring responses to simple interrogatories or requests for admissions. The exact line between reasonableness and unreasonableness in each case must be drawn by the trial court, based on its knowledge of the case and of the claims and interests of the parties and the governments whose statutes and policies they invoke.

American courts, in supervising pretrial proceedings, should exercise special vigilance to protect foreign litigants from the danger that unnecessary, or unduly burdensome, discovery may place them in a disadvantageous position. Judicial supervision of discovery should always seek to minimize its costs and inconvenience and to prevent improper uses of discovery requests. When it is necessary to seek evidence abroad, however, the district court must supervise pretrial proceedings particularly closely to prevent discovery abuses. For example, the additional cost of transportation of documents or witnesses to or from foreign locations may increase the danger that discovery may be sought for the improper purpose of motivating settlement, rather than finding relevant and probative evidence. Objections to "abusive" discovery that foreign litigants advance should therefore receive the most careful consideration. In addition, we have long recognized the demands of comity in suits involving foreign states, either as parties or as sovereigns with a coordinate interest in the litigation. American courts should therefore take care to demonstrate due respect for any special problem confronted by the foreign litigant on account of its nationality or the location of its operations, and for any sovereign interest expressed by a foreign state. We do not articulate specific rules to guide this delicate task of adjudication.

VI

In the case before us, the Magistrate and the Court of Appeals correctly refused to grant the broad protective order that petitioners requested. The Court of Appeals erred, however, in stating that the Evidence Convention does not apply to the pending discovery demands. This holding may be read as indicating that the Convention procedures are not even an option that is open to the District Court. It must be recalled, however, that the Convention's specification of duties in executing states creates corresponding rights in requesting states; holding that the Convention does not apply in this situation would deprive domestic litigants of access to evidence through treaty procedures to which the contracting states have assented. Moreover, such a rule would deny the foreign litigant a full and fair opportunity to demonstrate appropriate reasons for employing Convention procedures in the first instance, for some aspects of the discovery process.

JUSTICE BLACKMUN, with whom JUSTICE BRENNAN, JUSTICE MARSHALL, and JUSTICE O'CONNOR join, concurring in part and dissenting in part.

Some might well regard the Court's decision in this case as an affront to the nations that have joined the United States in ratifying the Hague Convention. * * * The Court ignores the importance of the Convention by relegating it to an "optional" status, without acknowledging the significant achievement in accommodating divergent interests that the Convention represents. Experience to date indicates that there is a large risk that the case-by-case comity analysis now to be permitted by the Court will be performed inadequately and that the somewhat unfamiliar procedures of the Convention will be invoked infrequently. I fear the Court's decision means that courts will resort unnecessarily to issuing discovery orders under the Federal Rules of Civil Procedure in a raw exercise of their jurisdictional power to the detriment of the United States' national and international interests. The Court's view of this country's international obligations is particularly unfortunate in a world in which regular commercial and legal channels loom ever more crucial.

I do agree with the Court's repudiation of the positions at both extremes of the spectrum with regard to the use of the Convention. Its rejection of the view that the Convention is not "applicable" at all to this case is surely correct: the Convention clearly applies to litigants as well as to third parties, and to requests for evidence located abroad, no matter where that evidence is actually "produced." The Court also correctly rejects the far opposite position that the Convention provides the exclusive means for discovery involving signatory countries. I dissent, however, because I cannot endorse the Court's case-by-case inquiry for determining whether to use Convention procedures and its failure to provide lower courts with any meaningful guidance for carrying out that inquiry. In my view, the Convention provides effective discovery procedures that largely eliminate the conflicts between United States and foreign law on evidence gathering. I therefore would apply a general presumption that, in most cases, courts should resort first to the Convention procedures. An individualized analysis of the circumstances of a particular case is appropriate only when it appears that it would be futile to employ the Convention or when its procedures prove to be unhelpful.

I

Even though the Convention does not expressly require discovery of materials in foreign countries to proceed exclusively according to its procedures, it cannot be viewed as merely advisory. The differences between discovery practices in the United States and those in other countries are significant, and "[n]o aspect of the extension of the American legal system beyond the territorial frontier of the United States has given rise to so much friction as the request for documents associated with investigation and litigation in the United States." Restatement of Foreign Relations Law of the United States (Revised) § 437, Reporters' Note 1, p. 35 (Tent. Draft No. 7, Apr. 10, 1986). Of particular import is the fact that discovery conducted by the parties, as is common in the United States, is alien to the legal systems of civil-law nations, which typically regard evidence gathering as a judicial function.

The Convention furthers important United States interests by providing channels for discovery abroad that would not be available otherwise. * * *

The Convention also serves the long-term interests of the United States in helping to further and to maintain the climate of cooperation and goodwill necessary to the functioning of the international legal and commercial systems. It is not at all satisfactory to view the Convention as nothing more than an optional supplement to the Federal Rules of Civil Procedure, useful as a means to "facilitate discovery" when a court "deems that course of action appropriate." Unless they had expected the Convention to provide the normal channels for discovery, other parties to the Convention would have had no incentive to agree to its terms. * * *

II

By viewing the Convention as merely optional and leaving the decision whether to apply it to the court in each individual case, the majority ignores the policies established by the political branches when they negotiated and ratified the treaty. The result will be a duplicative analysis for which courts are not well designed. The discovery process usually concerns discrete interests that a court is well equipped to accommodate—the interests of the parties before the court coupled with the interest of the judicial system in resolving the conflict on the basis of the best available information. When a lawsuit requires discovery of materials located in a foreign nation, however, foreign legal systems and foreign interests are implicated as well. The presence of these interests creates a tension between the broad discretion our courts normally exercise in managing pretrial discovery and the discretion usually allotted to the Executive in foreign matters.

It is the Executive that normally decides when a course of action is important enough to risk affronting a foreign nation or placing a strain on foreign commerce. It is the Executive, as well, that is best equipped to determine how to accommodate foreign interests along with our own. * * *

Not only is the question of foreign discovery more appropriately considered by the Executive and Congress, but in addition, courts are generally ill equipped to assume the role of balancing the interests of foreign nations with that of our own. Although transnational litigation is increasing, relatively few judges are experienced in the area and the procedures of foreign legal systems are often poorly understood. As this Court recently stated, it has "little competence in determining precisely when foreign nations will be offended by particular acts." Container Corp. v. Franchise Tax Bd., 463 U.S. 159, 194 (1983). A pro-forum bias is likely to creep into the supposedly neutral balancing process and courts not surprisingly often will turn to the more familiar procedures established by their local rules. In addition, it simply is not reasonable to expect the Federal Government or the foreign state in which the discovery will take place to participate in every individual case in order to articulate the broader international and foreign interests that are relevant to the decision whether to use the Convention. Indeed, the opportunities for such participation are limited.

Exacerbating these shortcomings is the limited appellate review of interlocutory discovery decisions, which prevents any effective case-by-case correction of erroneous discovery decisions.

III

* * * In most cases in which a discovery request concerns a nation that has ratified the Convention there is no need to resort to comity principles; the conflicts they are designed to resolve already have been eliminated by the agreements expressed in the treaty. The analysis set forth in the Restatement (Revised) of Foreign Relations Law of the United States is perfectly appropriate for courts to use when no treaty has been negotiated to accommodate the different legal systems. It would also be appropriate if the Convention failed to resolve the conflict in a particular case. The Court, however, adds an additional layer of so-called comity analysis by holding that courts should determine on a case-by-case basis whether resort to the Convention is desirable. Although this analysis is unnecessary in the absence of any conflicts, it should lead courts to the use of the Convention if they recognize that the Convention already has largely accommodated all three categories of interests relevant to a comity analysis—foreign interests, domestic interests, and the interest in a well-functioning international order.

A

* * * [T]he Court's view of the Convention rests on an incomplete analysis of the sovereign interests of foreign states. The Court acknowledges that evidence is normally obtained in civil-law countries by a judicial officer, but it fails to recognize the significance of that practice. Under the classic view of territorial sovereignty, each state has a monopoly on the exercise of governmental power within its borders and no state may perform an act in the territory of a foreign state without consent.[13] * * *

Some countries also believe that the need to protect certain underlying substantive rights requires judicial control of the taking of evidence. * * *

The United States recently recognized the importance of these sovereignty principles by taking the broad position that the Convention "must be interpreted to preclude an evidence taking proceeding in the territory of a foreign state party if the Convention does not authorize it and the host country does not otherwise permit it." Brief for United States as Amicus Curiae in Volkswagenwerk Aktiengesellschaft v. Falzon, O.T. 1983, No. 82-1888, p. 6. Now, however, it appears to take a narrower view of what constitutes an "evidence taking procedure," merely stating that "oral depositions on foreign soil . . . are improper without the consent of the foreign nation." I am at a loss to understand why gathering documents or information in a foreign country, even if for ultimate production in the United States, is any less an imposition on sovereignty than the

---

[13] Many of the nations that participated in drafting the Convention regard nonjudicial evidence taking from even a willing witness as a violation of sovereignty. * * *

taking of a deposition when gathering documents also is regarded as a judicial function in a civil-law nation.

Use of the Convention advances the sovereign interests of foreign nations because they have given consent to Convention procedures by ratifying them. This consent encompasses discovery techniques that would otherwise impinge on the sovereign interests of many civil-law nations. In the absence of the Convention, the informal techniques provided by Articles 15-22 of the Convention—taking evidence by a diplomatic or consular officer of the requesting state and the use of commissioners nominated by the court of the state where the action is pending—would raise sovereignty issues similar to those implicated by a direct discovery order from a foreign court. "Judicial" activities are occurring on the soil of the sovereign by agents of a foreign state. These voluntary discovery procedures are a great boon to United States litigants and are used far more frequently in practice than is compulsory discovery pursuant to letters of request.[16]

Civil-law contracting parties have also agreed to use, and even to compel, procedures for gathering evidence that are diametrically opposed to civil-law practices * * *.[1] These methods for obtaining evidence, which largely eliminate conflicts between the discovery procedures of the United States and the laws of foreign systems, have the consent of the ratifying nations. The use of these methods thus furthers foreign interests because discovery can proceed without violating the sovereignty of foreign nations.

B

The primary interest of the United States in this context is in providing effective procedures to enable litigants to obtain evidence abroad. This was the very purpose of the United States' participation in the treaty negotiations and, for the most part, the Convention provides those procedures. * * *

There is also apprehension that the Convention procedures will not prove fruitful. Experience with the Convention suggests otherwise—contracting parties have honored their obligation to execute letters of request expeditiously and to use compulsion if necessary. * * * By and large, the concessions made by parties to the Convention not only provide United States litigants with a means for obtaining evidence, but also ensure that the evidence will be in a form admissible in court.

---

[16] According to the French Government, the overwhelming majority of discovery requests by American litigants are "satisfied willingly . . . before consular officials and, occasionally, commissioners, and without the need for involvement by a French court or use of its coercive powers." Brief for Republic of France as Amicus Curiae 24. * * *

[1] In France, the Nouveau Code de Procedure Civile, Arts. 736-748 (76th ed. Dalloz 1984), implements the Convention by permitting examination and cross-examination of witnesses by the parties and their attorneys, Art. 740, permitting a foreign judge to attend the proceedings, Art. 741, and authorizing the preparation of a verbatim transcript of the questions and answers at the expense of the requesting authority, Arts. 739, 748.

There are, however, some situations in which there is legitimate concern that certain documents cannot be made available under Convention procedures. Thirteen nations have made official declarations pursuant to Article 23 of the Convention, which permits a contracting state to limit its obligation to produce documents in response to a letter of request. These reservations may pose problems that would require a comity analysis in an individual case, but they are not so all-encompassing as the majority implies—they certainly do not mean that a "contracting party could unilaterally abrogate . . . the Convention's procedures."   First, the reservations can apply only to letters of request for documents. Thus, an Article 23 reservation affects neither the most commonly used informal Convention procedures for taking of evidence by a consul or a commissioner nor formal requests for depositions or interrogatories.   Second, although Article 23 refers broadly to "pre-trial discovery," the intended meaning of the term appears to have been much narrower than the normal United States usage. The contracting parties for the most part have modified the declarations made pursuant to Article 23 to limit their reach.   Indeed, the emerging view of this exception to discovery is that it applies only to "requests that lack sufficient specificity or that have not been reviewed for relevancy by the requesting court." Thus, in practice, a reservation is not the significant obstacle to discovery under the Convention that the broad wording of Article 23 would suggest.

> * * *

The approach I propose is not a rigid per se rule that would require first use of the Convention without regard to strong indications that no evidence would be forthcoming.   All too often, however, courts have simply assumed that resort to the Convention would be unproductive and have embarked on speculation about foreign procedures and interpretations. When resort to the Convention would be futile, a court has no choice but to resort to a traditional comity analysis. But even then, an attempt to use the Convention will often be the best way to discover if it will be successful, particularly in the present state of general inexperience with the implementation of its procedures by the various contracting states. * * *

NOTES AND QUESTIONS FOR DISCUSSION

1. The majority of the *Aérospatiale* Court held the Convention to be merely optional and left it to the lower courts to decide on a case-by-case basis whether to use the Convention procedures. What exactly are the criteria that lower courts are supposed to employ for their decision, and how do they differ from those of the dissent?

2. Rejecting petitioners' interpretation that the application of the Convention is mandatory, or at least subject to a first-use status requirement, the majority offered several reasons:

a. Lack of mandatory language

Article 1 of the Hague Evidence Convention (see Appendix B) provides that a contracting state *may* request the competent authority of another Contracting state to obtain evidence or to perform some other judicial act. By contrast,

Article 1 of the Hague Service Convention stipulates that it *shall* apply in all civil or commercial cases where there is occasion to transmit documents for service abroad. But does the use of the word "may" in the Evidence Convention really support the majority's position that it is a purely optional device? Couldn't it be argued that Article 1 merely prescribes what is permissible under the Convention but that the Convention as such is mandatory in nature? If so, consider how one might explain the mandatory language in the Service Convention. What do you think were the expectations of the states negotiating the Evidence Convention?

b. Exclusion of document discovery

According to Article 23, every contracting state may declare at the time of signature that it will not execute letters of request issued for the purpose of obtaining pre-trial discovery of documents. Most contracting states have made such a declaration and refuse to execute such requests. The *Aérospatiale* majority concluded that the U.S. could not possibly have intended to be bound by an instrument that would empower other contracting states to eliminate document discovery, a procedural device of pivotal importance to the American litigation process. Is this argument persuasive? Is the intent of the U.S., presumed by the Court, of any relevance for the interpretation of the Convention?

c. Alternative methods provided by the Convention itself

The holding of the majority also rests on its interpretation of Article 27 of the Convention which permits contracting states to use less restrictive evidence-gathering methods than provided by the Convention. Is this argument persuasive? Consider the following counter-argument, advanced by the four justices who dissented from the majority's case-by-case analysis, and who would have applied a presumption, in most cases, that required initial resort to the Convention's procedures:

> Article 27 of the Convention is not to the contrary. The only logical interpretation of this Article is that a state receiving a discovery request may permit less restrictive procedures than those designated in the Convention. The majority finds plausible a reading that authorizes both a requesting and a receiving state to use methods outside the Convention. If this were the case, Article 27(c), which allows a state to permit methods of taking evidence that are not provided in the Convention, would make the rest of the Convention wholly superfluous. If a requesting state could dictate the methods for taking evidence in another state, there would be no need for the detailed procedures provided by the Convention.

482 U.S. at 551 n.2. Does the majority persuasively respond to this part of the dissent?

d. Fairness considerations

In a footnote, the majority points to what it perceives as "three unacceptable asymmetries" that would ensue if the Convention were the exclusive means of obtaining evidence:

       * * * First, within any lawsuit between a national of the United States and a national of another contracting party, the foreign party could obtain discovery under the Federal Rules of Civil Procedure, while the domestic party would be required to resort first to the procedures of the Hague Convention. This imbalance would run counter to the fundamental maxim of discovery that "[m]utual knowledge of all the relevant facts gathered by both parties is essential to proper litigation." Hickman v. Taylor, 329 U.S. 495, 507 (1947).

       Second, a rule of exclusivity would enable a company which is a citizen of another contracting state to compete with a domestic company on uneven terms, since the foreign company would be subject to less extensive discovery procedures in the event that both companies were sued in an American court. Petitioners made a voluntary decision to market their products in the United States. They are entitled to compete on equal terms with other companies operating in this market. But since the District Court unquestionably has personal jurisdiction over petitioners, they are subject to the same legal constraints, including the burdens associated with American judicial procedures, as their American competitors. A general rule according foreign nationals a preferred position in pretrial proceedings in our courts would conflict with the principle of equal opportunity that governs the market they elected to enter.

       Third, since a rule of first use of the Hague Convention would apply to cases in which a foreign party is a national of a contracting state, but not to cases in which a foreign party is a national of any other foreign state, the rule would confer an unwarranted advantage on some domestic litigants over others similarly situated.

482 U.S. at 540 n.25.

       Are these concerns warranted? The minority took issue with the first two "asymmetries" by pointing to Rule 26(c), Fed. R. Civ. P., which permits a court to (in the language of the Rule as it then existed) "make any order which justice requires" to limit discovery, including an order permitting discovery only on specified terms and conditions, by a particular discovery method, or with limitation in scope to certain matters. This provision, and its state law equivalents, thus vests courts with the discretionary power to prevent the imbalances that the majority envisaged. Furthermore, consider whether the majority's focus on the parties' nationality is justified. The dissent argued that it is not and that mandatory use of the Convention could equally affect a foreign litigant trying to secure evidence from a foreign branch of an American litigant.

3. The minority also expressed disagreement with the Court's third fairness concern—that a domestic litigant suing a national of a state that is not a party to the Convention would have an advantage over a litigant suing a national of a contracting state:

This statement completely ignores the very purpose of the Convention. The negotiations were proposed by the United States in order to facilitate discovery, not to hamper litigants. Dissimilar treatment of litigants similarly situated does occur, but in the manner opposite to that perceived by the Court. Those who sue nationals of noncontracting states are disadvantaged by the unavailability of the Convention procedures. This is an unavoidable inequality inherent in the benefits conferred by any treaty that is less than universally ratified.

482 U.S at 556. Do you agree? Or should this imbalance make a difference in determining the status of the Convention?

C. U.S. DISCOVERY CONDUCTED ABROAD

A Case Illustration:

Suppose that a U.S. court (state or federal) has ordered discovery, such as depositions and inspection of premises, to be conducted on foreign soil, without using the Convention procedures. Consider the following order issued by a California superior court judge in a products liability action against Volkswagen AG in Germany:

1. Premises.

a. Access: Claimants' representatives are to have access to the VWAG facilities at Wolfsburg during normal working hours on five consecutive days to inspect and photograph the premises, inspect and copy writings, and informally interview VWAG personnel. During claimants' inspection of facilities VWAG will provide a guide. Claimants may stay after normal working hours until 10:00 p.m. to examine and copy writings only, and during that time VWAG may designate a monitor at claimants' expense * * * .

2. Writings.

a. Access to technical library and plant and records: Claimants' representatives shall have access to VWAG's technical library and plant and records "relating to the Type II vehicles and predecessor and successor vehicles within its type, including the currently produced Vanagon model," subject to relevancy, trade-secret, and personnel-record limitations.

b. Inspecting and copying writings: Claimants' representatives may inspect and copy writings "which plaintiffs shall designate as bearing upon the design, testing, modification and analysis of the crashworthiness of the front end of the Type II vehicles and predecessor and successor vehicles within its type from the outset of production through the 'Vanagon' model currently produced."

Ultimately, these orders were vacated by a California appeals court which held that under these circumstances, the Hague Convention procedures should prevail. See Volkswagenwerk A.G. v. Superior Court, 123 Cal. App. 3d 840,

176 Cal. Rptr. 874 (1981). Most courts appear to share this position. See, e.g., Graco, Inc. v. Kremlin, Inc., 101 F.R.D. 503 (N.D. Ill. 1984).

The U.S. Department of Justice advanced the following rationale for this position:

> The United States played a dominant role in the negotiation of both the [Hague] Service and Evidence Conventions, and encouraged foreign states to join both, largely on the strength of representations concerning substantial reforms in United States law and procedures. . . . [T]he Evidence Convention deals comprehensively with the methods available to United States courts and litigants to obtain proceedings abroad for taking evidence. . . . The parties to the Convention contemplated that proceedings not authorized by the Convention would not be permitted. The Convention accordingly must be interpreted to preclude an evidence taking proceeding in the territory of a foreign state party if the Convention does not authorize it and the host country does not otherwise permit it. Appellees do not appear to argue to the contrary.

U.S. Brief Submitted to the Supreme Court in Response to the Court's Invitation in Volkswagenwerk A.G. v. Falzon, 23 I.L.M. 412, 414-415 (1984). The case involved a products liability suit, in which a Michigan trial court had entered two orders directing that depositions be taken of German nationals in the Federal Republic of Germany.

In another decision, a personal injury action, in which a New York trial court had entered an order requiring a French defendant to answer interrogatories propounded by the plaintiffs, the Justice Department took a different view:

> We recognize that in our brief in *Volkswagenwerk, A.G. v. Falzon*, we stated: "The parties to the Convention contemplated that proceedings not authorized by the Convention would not be permitted . . . ." After further reflection, we believe that that statement requires clarification to the extent that it could be construed to mean that the Convention is exclusive. We note that the above statement was not necessary to our argument that the trial court's order in *Falzon* was unlawful.

U.S. Brief Submitted to the Supreme Court in Response to the Court's Invitation in Club Méditerranée v. Dorin, 23 I.L.M. 1332, 1338 n.10 (1984).

Apparently, the Justice Department distinguished its position in *Falzon* on the ground that the depositions ordered in that case amounted to discovery proceedings *in the territory of a foreign state*, while the court in *Club Méditerranée* had ordered responses to interrogatories. Is this distinction meaningful? Are foreign sovereign interests less implicated when litigants request answers to interrogatories to be given from a foreign country as opposed to depositions conducted on foreign soil? How would the majority of Justices in *Aérospatiale* decide this question? Note that in *Aérospatiale*, the plaintiffs served a request for the production of documents pursuant to Rule 34, a set of interrogatories pursuant to Rule 33, and requests for admission pursuant to Rule 36. Such requests have been characterized as involving discovery of evidence *from* the territory of another signatory nation rather than obtaining evidence *within* a foreign territory. See Bruno A. Ristau, *International Judicial Assistance* Vol. 1, 308 (2000).

D. THE PERSONAL JURISDICTION REQUIREMENT

The holding in *Aérospatiale*, that the Convention is a merely optional device which does not supersede American discovery rules, rests on the assumption that the district court had personal jurisdiction over the French defendants. This holding raises two important questions in those cases in which a court does not have personal jurisdiction over a person who is in possession of the evidence that is the object of discovery. First, is use of the Convention mandatory when a litigant seeks evidence from such a non-party witness? Second, if jurisdiction is a prerequisite for the invocation of American discovery rules, must a party seeking to establish jurisdiction over a foreign defendant resort to the Hague Evidence Convention?

1. *Nonparty Witnesses*

Rule 45, Fed. R. Civ. P., prescribes strict territorial limits for non-party witnesses and does not permit the issuance of a subpoena against persons not subject to the personal jurisdiction of an American court. Thus, in cases in which there is no legal basis for compelling an uncooperative witness to give evidence, the Convention would appear to be the only means. Indeed, some courts have argued that the inability to obtain evidence from nonparty witnesses under American discovery rules was one central reason for creating the Convention. See, e.g., *In re* Anschuetz & Co., GmbH, 754 F.2d 602, 611 (1985) ("[A]n unwilling non-party witness simply cannot be reached, if outside the court's jurisdiction, unless authorities in the witness' state use their authority to compel the giving of evidence. An international agreement provides a framework for the invocation of a foreign authority's compulsory powers, making accessible evidence which otherwise would not have been accessible.") (internal citation omitted). State courts also hold that use of the Convention procedures is mandatory for discovery directed at non-party witnesses holding evidence abroad. See, e.g., Intercontinental Credit Corporation v. Roth, 595 N.Y.S. 2d 602 (1991).

2. *Jurisdictional Discovery*

It is well established that, in principle, a trial court has jurisdiction to determine its jurisdiction. See Ins. Corp. of Ireland, Ltd. v. Compagnie des Bauxites de Guinée, 456 U.S. 694, 706 (1982) ("By submitting to the jurisdiction of the court for the limited purpose of challenging jurisdiction, the defendant agrees to abide by that court's determination on the issue of jurisdiction"). See also Chapter 1, Section F (discussing *Ins. Corp. of Ireland*). However, the Supreme Court has not provided guidance on the specific question whether discovery located abroad and sought to establish personal jurisdiction over a defendant must proceed under the Evidence Convention or whether there is discretion to order such discovery under the Federal Rules of Civil Procedure.

Lower courts are split, with a clear majority holding that there is no requirement to use the Convention procedures. Compare, e.g., *In re* Automotive Refinishing Paint Antitrust Litig., 358 F.3d 288, 302-04 (3d Cir. 2004) (stating that the Convention procedures do not divest district court of the authority to order discovery under the Federal Rules); *In re* Vitamins Antitrust Litig., 120 F. Supp. 2d 45, 49 (D.D.C. 2000) (stating that jurisdictional discovery need not first be made under Hague Convention); Rich v. KIS California, Inc., 121 F.R.D. 254, 260 (M.D.N.C. 1988) (holding that *Aérospatiale* "did not carve out any exception for disputes involving personal jurisdiction" and that "[s]ufficient protection is given by the Supreme Court's admonishment to district courts to be particularly sensitive to claims of abuse of discovery made by foreign litigants"); with Knight v. Ford Motor Co., 615 A.2d 297, 301 n.11 (N.J. Super. Ct. Law Div. 1992) ("[I]f jurisdiction does not exist over a foreign party . . . , the Convention may provide the only recourse for obtaining evidence."). See also MeadWestvaco Corp. v. Rexam PLC, 2010 WL 5574325 (E.D. Va. Dec. 14, 2010). See generally, Patrick J. Borchers, *The Incredible Shrinking Hague Evidence Convention*, 38 Tex. Int'l L.J. 73, 82 (2003) (stating that the "heavy preponderance" of post-*Aérospatiale* decisional law "simply authorizes discovery under local procedures with only a passing nod to the Evidence Convention").

Which view is more persuasive? Could it be argued that a rule of first-resort is more compelling for jurisdictional discovery than for discovery directed at the merits of a case, because the comity interests of the foreign nations are higher before foreign defendants are conclusively found to be subject to the American court's jurisdiction? In *In re Vitamins Antitrust Litigation, supra,* the court stated that—at least in cases in which plaintiffs had established a prima facie basis for jurisdiction—"foreign signatory nations would [not] be any more offended by . . . jurisdictional discovery than they would be by the broader, merits-related discovery allowed by *Aérospatiale*." 120 F. Supp. 2d at 51. See also, *Rich*, 121 F.R.D. at 259 ("The fact defendant is a foreign litigant does not require deviation from the principle that discovery under the Federal Rules . . . may be employed to establish personal jurisdiction over it"). Convinced? For a critique of the lower courts' post-*Aérospatiale* treatment of jurisdictional discovery in the lower courts (and an argument that a rule of first-resort is indeed more compelling when personal jurisdiction is not yet settled), see Kathleen Braun Gilchrist, Note, *Rethinking Jurisdictional Discovery under the Hague Evidence Convention*, 44 Vand. J. Transnat'l L. 155 (2011).

E. POST-*AÉROSPATIALE* DECISIONAL LAW

The Supreme Court qualified its holding in *Aérospatiale* by introducing a three-prong test that lower courts must employ to ascertain whether discovery requests should (under certain circumstances) nevertheless proceed under the Hague Evidence Convention. This test calls for a consideration of the particular facts of the case, the sovereign interests involved, and the likelihood that resort to the Convention will prove effective. *Aérospatiale*, 482 U.S. at 544. A large majority of lower courts employing this test have ruled against the use of the Convention. The opinion in *Valois*, excerpted below, provides a summary of post-*Aérospatiale* decisions and presents an interesting compromise solution.

Valois of America, Inc. v. Risdon Corp.

Unites States District Court, District of Connecticut, 1997.
183 F.R.D. 344.

MARGOLIS, UNITED STATES MAGISTRATE JUDGE.

[Plaintiff, Valois of America, Inc. ("Valois America") filed suit against defendant Risdon Corporation ("Risdon") seeking a declaratory judgment that a patent of Risdon is invalid and is not infringed by Valois America's Seal Tight pump assembly. Risdon filed counterclaims and third-party complaints against Valois and Valois America's France-based manufacturing division, Valois S.A. ("Valois France"). The counterclaim alleged that both Valois America and Valois France infringed the patent in question. Risdon seeks monetary damages and preliminarily and permanently to enjoin Valois America and Valois France from making, using or selling the Valois Seal Tight spray pump assembly. Risdon served upon Valois France a large number of discovery requests, and Valois France sought a protective order that discovery from it be taken under the Hague Evidence Convention.]

The Hague Convention was addressed extensively by the United States Supreme Court ten years ago in Société Nationale Industrielle Aérospatiale v. United States District Court ["*Société Nationale*"], which involved personal injury lawsuits brought against the French manufacturers of aircraft that had crashed. Like here, the French companies filed a motion for a protective order that discovery be had only under the Hague Convention, and not the Federal Rules of Civil Procedure. The Supreme Court held that the Hague Convention did not preempt the Federal Rules with respect to discovery from foreign litigants. Instead, the parties could avail themselves of the procedures set forth in the Hague Convention as a supplementary measure. * * *

A party which seeks the application of the Hague Convention procedures rather than the Federal Rules bears the burden of persuading the trial court. *In re* Perrier Bottled Water Lit., 138 F.R.D. 348, 354 (D.Conn. 1991) (product liability action against French companies); Rich v. KIS California, Inc., 121 F.R.D. 254, 257-58 & n.3 (M.D.N.C. 1988) (breach of contract action against French corporation). See also Doster v. Schenk, 141 F.R.D. 50, 51-52 & n.3 (M.D.N.C. 1991) (personal injury action against German contractor); Benton Graphics v. Uddeholm Corp., 118 F.R.D. 386, 388-89 & n.2 (D.N.J. 1987) (breach of contract action against Swedish corporations). But see Hudson v. Hermann Pfauter GmbH & Co., 117 F.R.D. 33, 38 (N.D.N.Y. 1987) (in product liability action against German manufacturer, court held that burden is on party opposing use of Hague Convention).

In *Perrier*, the late Judge Daly applied the "three-pronged inquiry" set forth in *Société Nationale*, namely (1) the examination of the particular facts of the case, particularly with regard to the nature of the discovery requested; (2) the sovereign interests in issue; and (3) the likelihood that the Hague Convention procedures will prove effective. 138 F.R.D. at 354. See also *Doster*, 141 F.R.D. at 52; *Rich,* 121 F.R.D. at 257; *Benton Graphics*, 118 F.R.D. at 388.

With respect to the first prong, Judge Daly found plaintiffs' discovery requests to be "excessive," "abusive," "immaterial," "intrusive," and seeking "an extraordinary volume of information, much of it irrelevant to the cases at hand." *Perrier*, 138 F.R.D. at 354-55. With respect to the second prong, Judge Daly described France's expression of its dislike of the Federal Rules of Civil Procedure as "most emphatic," which expression "weighs heavily in favor" of the utilizing the Hague Convention. Id. at 355. Turning to the third prong, Judge Daly ruled that any inconveniences occasioned by the more time-consuming Hague Convention procedures "pale beside the importance of respecting France's sovereign interests, and the Court's concern for fairness to foreign litigants." Id. Judge Daly thus concluded that all three prongs of the *Société Nationale* test suggested utilization of the Hague Convention procedures. Id. at 356.

The same result was found in *Hudson*, where plaintiffs' first set of interrogatories contained ninety-two interrogatories, many of which contained subparts; Chief District Judge Munson observed that such interrogatories "cannot be described as 'unintrusive.'" 117 F.R.D. at 34. With respect to the second and third prongs, Chief Judge Munson concluded "the major obstacle" to effective use of the Hague Convention was its lack of familiarity by attorneys and courts. Id. at 38. He continued, "To assume that the 'American' rules are superior to those procedures agreed upon by the signatories of the Hague Convention without first seeing how effective [Hague] Convention procedures will be in practice would reflect the same parochial biases that the [Hague] Convention was designed to overcome." Id. at 38-39. Thus, under these circumstances, the court concluded that use of Hague Convention procedures "seems desirable." Id. at 40.

The court reached the opposite conclusion in *Rich*, where plaintiffs had narrowed their discovery requests to ten interrogatories limited to the issue of personal jurisdiction, the Magistrate Judge gave little "deference" to France's dislike of American discovery procedures, and defendants failed to demonstrate that the Hague Convention Procedures would be more effective than the use of the Federal Rules. 121 F.R.D. at 258. The judge thus concluded that "use of the Federal Rules of Civil Procedure is in the best overall interest." Id. at 260.

In many of the post-*Société Nationale* decisions addressing this issue, except *Perrier* and *Hudson*, the judges were unwilling to attach much significance to the sovereign interests involved, finding no important interest to be offended by use of the Federal Rules, and instead recognized that use of the Hague Convention could involve considerable time and expense. *Doster*, 141 F.R.D. at 53-54; Haynes v. Kleinwefers, 119 F.R.D. 335, 338 (E.D.N.Y. 1988) (product liability claim against German manufacturer); *Benton Graphics*, 118 F.R.D. at 391-92.

The critical prong of the *Société Nationale* analysis, then, is the first one. In

Doster, the Magistrate Judge emphasized this country's "strong interest" in the product liability actions, based upon injuries from the German defendant's construction activities in this country. 141 F.R.D. at 52. The German corporation was not "surprised or disadvantaged by litigation under the Federal Rules of Civil Procedure." Id. Plaintiffs had served about twenty interrogatories, five requests for admissions, and twelve requests for production of documents. After his review of these requests, the judge found them to be "fairly standard for these types of cases," "routine," "not overly burdensome in amount or scope," and "not . . . potentially harassing or of . . . a sensitive nature." Id. at 53. "More importantly, both plaintiffs have expressed their willingness to cooperate with defendant's counsel to narrow the scope of discovery and reduce the intrusive nature of the requests." Id. Under these circumstances, the Magistrate Judge ordered that the parties proceed, at least initially, under the Federal Rules of Evidence. Id. at 54-55.

The same conclusion was reached in *Benton Graphics*, where defendants "have largely failed to specifically identify their objections," thus making it "impossible for [the Court] to determine which, if any, requests are overbroad and burdensome." 118 F.R.D. at 390. However, after her review of plaintiff's interrogatories, the Magistrate Judge determined that "a number of the requests are not 'simple' and may require streamlining if [the case was] to proceed under the federal rules." Id. The Magistrate Judge instructed counsel to confer to limit and resolve the scope of discovery requests, ensuring that they were reasonable, not overly burdensome, and not too intrusive. Id. * * *

Valois France additionally relies upon the French "blocking statute," French Penal Code Law No. 80-538, which provides:

> Subject to treaties or international agreements and applicable laws and regulations, it is prohibited for any party to request, seek, or disclose, in writing, orally or otherwise, economic, commercial, industrial, financial or technical documents or information leading to the constitution of evidence with a view to foreign judicial of administrative proceedings or in connection therewith.

In *Société Nationale*, the Supreme Court minimized the effect of this statute upon litigation pending in the United States:

> The French "blocking statute" . . . does not alter our conclusion. It is well settled that such statutes do not deprive an American court of the power to order a party subject to its jurisdiction to produce evidence even though the act of production may violate that statute. Nor can the enactment of such a statute by a foreign nature require American courts to engraft a rule of first resort onto the Hague Convention, or otherwise to provide the nationals of such a country with a preferred status in our court. . . . 482 U.S. at 544-45 n.29 (citations omitted).

As previously mentioned, the late Judge Daly placed great emphasis upon this French "blocking statute," in describing France as "most emphatic" in its preference for Hague Convention procedures over the American rules. Perrier, 138 F.R.D. at 355. In citing footnote 29 of the *Société Nationale* decision, the Magistrate Judge in *Rich* did not give this statute much weight:

[T]his statute, which is solely designed to protect French businesses from foreign discovery, is both overly broad and vague and need not be given the same deference as a substantive rule of law. In general, broad blocking statutes, including those which purport to impose criminal sanctions, which have such extraordinary extraterritorial effect, do not warrant much deference. 121 F.R.D. at 258.

This case presents a closer question than those addressed above. With regard to the second prong in *Société Nationale*, like the Supreme Court in *Société Nationale* and the Magistrate Judge in *Rich*, and contrary to *Perrier*, this judicial officer does not give substantial deference to France's preference for the Hague Convention, as expressed in its "blocking statute." With regard to the third prong, as recognized in *Doster*, 141 F.R.D. at 54, *Perrier*, 138 F.R.D. at 355, *Rich*, 121 F.R.D. at 258, *Haynes*, 119 F.R.D. at 338, and *Benton Graphics*, 118 F.R.D. at 391, and contrary to the position taken in *Hudson*, 117 F.R.D. at 38-39, it is generally recognized that procedures under the Hague Convention are far more cumbersome than under the Federal Rules of Civil Procedures.

The critical examination then is the first prong of the *Société Nationale* inquiry, namely "the particular facts of the case, particularly with regard to the nature of the discovery requested." * * * As in *Perrier, Hudson, Doster*, and *Benton Graphics*, Risdon's requests for production, interrogatories, and requests for admission, which collectively contain ninety-six items, are hardly "unintrusive." The Court need not decide whether Risdon's discovery requests are reasonable under the Federal Rules, if they were submitted to an American litigant. Given the concerns articulated by the Supreme Court in *Société Nationale*, they clearly are "too burdensome and too 'intrusive.'" 482 U.S. at 545. However, Valois France's counsel has expressed a willingness to cooperate with Risdon's counsel in attempting to resolve their differences. Thus, this case resembles *Doster* and *Benton Graphics*, in that the better approach is to have counsel confer further, in an attempt to limit and resolve the scope of discovery requests, so as to ensure that such requests to Valois France are reasonable, not overly burdensome, and not too intrusive. If Risdon continues to insist upon burdensome and intrusive discovery from Valois France, then resort to the Hague Convention procedures ultimately may be appropriate.

Therefore, counsel for Risdon and Valois France are instructed to confer with one another, for the purposes indicated above. If no amicable resolution of this issue is reached, after counsel confer with one another in a professional and reasonable manner, then on or before August 22, 1997, either counsel may file supplemental briefs, which shall relate, in detail, those discovery requests as to which no agreement was reached and each party's position with respect to such discovery requests. The Judge will thereafter issue a Supplemental Ruling, which decides whether Risdon's discovery from Valois France will continue under the Federal Rules of Civil Procedure or under the Hague Convention. For the reasons stated above, Valois France's motion for protective order is denied without prejudice to renewal at a later time, if counsel are unable to resolve their differences over the extent of Risdon's discovery from Valois France.

NOTES AND QUESTIONS FOR DISCUSSION

1. The parties in *Valois* apparently reached a compromise. Following the above ruling, discovery (including depositions) was taken in France. See Valois of America, Inc. v. Risdon Corp., 1998 WL 1661397 (D.Conn. Dec. 18, 1998).

2. The court in *Valois* held that a party seeking the application of the Hague Evidence Convention procedures bears the burden of demonstrating the necessity of using those procedures. Thus, it is for the proponent of the Convention procedures to prove that the particular facts, the sovereign interests and the effectiveness of the Convention warrant its application. Most lower courts agree with this allocation of the burden of proof, and although the Supreme Court did not specifically address this important question, some courts point to the following language in *Aérospatiale* to support their position:

> The Court of Appeals erred, however, in stating that the Evidence Convention does not apply to the pending discovery demands. This holding may be read as indicating that the Convention procedures are not even an option that is open to the District Court. . . . [S]uch a rule would deny the foreign litigant a full and fair opportunity to demonstrate appropriate reasons for employing Convention procedures in the first instance, for some aspects of the discovery process.

Aérospatiale, 482 U.S. at 547. Does this language indicate that the Court requires the proponent of the Convention to prove *each* of the three factors—the particular facts, the sovereign interests, and the efficacy of the Convention? If so, do you find it convincing? Not all courts agree with this allocation of the burden of proof, however. For example, the court in Husa v. Laboratories Servier SA, 740 A.2d 1092, 1096 (N.J. Super. Ct. App. Div. 1999) held that:

> New Jersey courts should utilize international agreements which facilitate the conduct of cross-border litigation in the absence of demonstrable prejudice to legitimate interests. Implementation of the Convention will demonstrate our cosmopolitan approach to litigation arising out of the global economy and our sensitivity to the concerns of our trading partners.

See also Hudson v. Hermann Pfauter GmbH & Co., 117 F.R.D. 33, 38 (N.D.N.Y. 1987) (finding "that the burden should be placed on the party opposing the use of Convention procedures to demonstrate that those procedures would frustrate [legitimate American] interests").

3. The first factor—the particular facts of the case—often leads lower courts to examine the breadth and intrusiveness of the American discovery requests. If these requests are perceived as unduly broad and burdensome, they will be curtailed either by court order or voluntarily, sometimes upon the recommendation of the court, by the requesting party. See Rich v. KIS California, Inc., 121 F.R.D. 254, 258 (M.D.N.C. 1988) ("Because plaintiffs have pared their discovery requests to ten interrogatories limited to the issue of personal jurisdiction, defendants cannot show that the information sought is intrusive."). It appears, however, that American standards and practices, rather than international concerns dominate this question.

4. Note that most courts expect litigants who seek to invoke the Evidence Convention to identify specific sovereign interests that the application of the Federal Rules would imperil. The statement that a contracting state views American discovery as fishing expeditions which by their very nature violate foreign sovereign interests has been rejected as too vague and unspecific. See, e.g., Benton Graphics v. Uddeholm Corp. 118 F.R.D. 386 (D.N.J. 1987). But query what constitutes a "specific sovereign interest"? Given that the very concerns over the breath of the American proceedings prompted other nations to participate in the negotiation of the Convention, isn't it specific enough for litigants to voice foreign sovereign interests in this way? There are several decisions in which American courts have acknowledged the legitimacy of foreign concerns. See, e.g., *In re* Vitamins Antitrust Litig., 120 F. Supp. 2d 45, 53 (D.D.C. 2000) ("Clearly, these signatory nations have a strong interest in protecting their citizens from what they may perceive as unduly burdensome discovery under evidence laws foreign to and incompatible with their own procedures."). However, such concerns rarely convince courts to use the Convention procedures. Typically, these courts find that American interests in conducting American-style discovery outweigh foreign sovereignty interests.

5. The third prong of the test—the efficacy of the Convention—also poses great problems to litigants asking American courts to apply the Evidence Convention. They have to show, typically by way of specific expert testimony, how the use of the Convention procedure will prove to be effective. Given the limitations described above (particularly the Article 23 exclusion of document discovery), proponents have often been unable to convince courts of the efficacy of the Convention. Further compounding the difficulties of those seeking application of the Convention is the tendency of American courts to measure "effectiveness" by domestic expectations rather than by the international standard embodied in the Convention. Proponents of the Convention also find themselves in a somewhat paradoxical situation when they attempt to establish the effectiveness of the Convention procedures. On the one hand, they must argue that these procedures will yield results that match American expectations. On the other hand, the first two factors of the analysis force proponents to complain about the particular burden of the discovery requests and the violation of particular sovereign interests that American style discovery would entail.

6. Courts favoring the use of the Convention procedures sometimes take a different perspective on the issue of effectiveness. Consider the following:

> It appears that the major obstacle to the effective use of Convention procedures by litigants and the courts is the fact that we are less familiar with those procedures than with the discovery provisions of the Federal Rules. Consequently, use of the Convention procedures will, at least initially, result in greater expenditures of time and money for attorneys pursuing causes of action against foreign parties on behalf of their clients and could require an increased commitment of judicial resources. Nonetheless, these inconveniences alone do not outweigh the important purposes served by the Hague Convention. Further, as judges and lawyers become more familiar with the discovery rules of the

Convention, it is quite possible that its procedures will prove just as effective and cost-efficient as those of the Federal Rules. To assume that the "American" rules are superior to those procedures agreed upon by the signatories of the Hague Convention without first seeing how effective Convention procedures will be in practice would reflect the same parochial biases that the Convention was designed to overcome.

Hudson v. Hermann Pfauter GmbH & Co., 117 F.R.D. 33, 38-39 (N.D.N.Y. 1987). Is this view of "prospective" effectiveness convincing? Should litigants initially "pay the price" for the lack of familiarity so that the experience gained inures to the benefit of those who litigate later?

7. As an international treaty, the Supremacy Clause governs the domestic (U.S.) status of the Convention. State courts and lower federal courts are thus bound by the Supreme Court's holding that the Convention is an optional, rather than mandatory, device. But what exactly is the effect of being bound by this interpretation? It would seem clear that lower courts cannot be more restrictive than the Supreme Court was. In other words, they cannot hold, as the Court of Appeals in *Aérospatiale* did, that the Convention has no application at all. But are lower courts free to interpret the Convention more liberally, for example, by imposing a first-use requirement? Consider the following statement:

> We are, of course, bound by the majority's construction of the Convention in *Aérospatiale*. Thus, we deem it to be an optional method of evidence gathering. In the present case, however, the choice is between the Convention and New Jersey procedural and substantive law. Consequently, we perceive no conflict with federal supremacy, if, in exercising the option to resort to the Convention, we are more generous in our use of the Convention's procedures than the United States' courts. Moreover, because the present litigation is in a state court, we are not concerned with issues regarding the distribution of power among the three branches of the federal government.

Husa v. Laboratories Servier, S.A., 740 A.2d 1092, 1095 (N.J. Super Ct. App. Div. 1999). Is the New Jersey court's decision consistent with *Aérospatiale*?

8. For a sampling of commentary on how *Aérospatiale* has been implemented in the lower courts, see, e.g., Borchers, *supra* (Section D); Steven F. Black, *United States Transnational Discovery: The Rise and Fall of the Hague Evidence Convention*, 40 Int'l & Comp. L.Q. 901 (1991); Gary B. Born & Scott Honig, *Comity and the Lower Courts: Post-Aérospatiale Applications of the Hague Evidence Convention*, 24 Int'l Law. 393 (1990).

F. FOREIGN BLOCKING STATUTES

Over the past half century, the number of American court orders mandating disclosure of evidence located abroad has steadily increased. This increase is in part due to the extraterritorial application of U.S. antitrust laws to conduct occurring abroad. Since the mid 1940s, American courts have invoked the so-called effects doctrine to suspected cartels formed outside of the United States. See United States v. Aluminum Co. of America, 148 F.2d 416 (2d. Cir. 1945). In essence, this doctrine applies to foreign anticompetitive conduct that had some substantial effect on U.S. commerce. See Hartford Fire Ins. Co. v. California, 509 U.S. 764 (1993). In order to prove the existence of such cartels—typically price-fixing agreements—U.S. litigants often launch sweeping court-sanctioned discovery requests aimed at building their case with evidence located outside the U.S. Mostly in response to this development, which is viewed as a transgression of their sovereignty, a number of foreign nations enacted blocking statutes that prohibit their citizens and corporations to comply with U.S. discovery orders. (Some foreign statutes, such as Swiss bank secrecy laws, were enacted for other reasons, long before American courts issued extraterritorial discovery orders.) Several of these statutes impose criminal sanctions for those who violate them.

Parties or non-party witnesses to whom a court order or subpoena is addressed therefore face a dilemma: If they do not disclose the information as ordered, they may be subject to sanctions under Rules 37 and 45 of the Federal Rules of Civil Procedure. These sanctions can be severe and may include a finding of contempt of court resulting in hefty fines, if not imprisonment. Disobedient parties may even suffer a default judgment or dismissal of their claim. On the other hand, compliance with the American order carries the risk of civil or criminal liability under foreign domestic blocking statutes.

How, then, are these frictions resolved? American courts have long held that these blocking statutes cannot prevent them from issuing discovery orders. See, e.g., *In re* Air Crash at Taipei, Taiwan on October 31, 2000, 211 F.R.D. 374 (C.D. Cal. 2002). Considering a French blocking statute, the Court in *Aérospatiale* only offered a footnote, albeit a lengthy one, on this matter:

> The French "blocking statute" * * * does not alter our conclusion. It is well settled that such statutes do not deprive an American court of the power to order a party subject to its jurisdiction to produce evidence even though the act of production may violate that statute. * * * It is clear that American courts are not required to adhere blindly to the directives of such a statute. Indeed, the language of the statute, if taken literally, would appear to represent an extraordinary exercise of legislative jurisdiction by the Republic of France over a United States district judge, forbidding him or her to order any discovery from a party of French nationality, even simple requests for admissions or interrogatories that the party could respond to on the basis of personal knowledge. It would be particularly incongruous to recognize such a preference for corporations that are wholly owned by the enacting nation. Extraterritorial assertions of jurisdiction are not one-sided. While the District Court's discovery orders arguably have some impact in France, the French blocking statute asserts similar authority over acts to take place in this country. The lesson of comity is that neither the discovery order nor the blocking statute can have the same omnipresent effect that it would have in a world of only one sovereign. The blocking statute thus is relevant to the court's particularized comity analysis only to the extent that its terms and its enforcement identify the nature of the sovereign interests in nondisclosure of specific kinds of material.

Aérospatiale, 482 U.S. at 544 n.29. As the Court implied, this was not the first decision that favored the application of domestic discovery rules over deference to a conflicting foreign statute. In the following decision the Supreme Court held that that the illegality of disclosure of materials under foreign law would not prevent an American court from issuing the order.

Société Internationale Pour Participations Industrielles et Commerciales, S.A. v. Rogers

Supreme Court of the United States, 1958.

357 U.S. 197.

MR. JUSTICE HARLAN delivered the opinion of the Court.

The question before us is whether, in the circumstances of this case, the District Court erred in dismissing, with prejudice, a complaint in a civil action as to a plaintiff that had failed to comply fully with a pretrial production order.

This issue comes to us in the context of an intricate litigation. Section 5(b) of the Trading with the Enemy Act, sets forth the conditions under which the United States during a period of war or national emergency may seize ". . . any property or interest of any foreign country or national . . . ." Acting under this section, the Alien Property Custodian during World War II assumed control of assets which were found by the Custodian to be "owned by or held for the benefit of" I.G. Farbenindustrie, a German firm and a then enemy national. These assets, valued at more than $100,000,000, consisted of cash in American banks and approximately 90% of the capital stock of General Aniline & Film Corporation, a Delaware corporation. In 1948 petitioner, a Swiss holding company also known as I.G. Chemie or Interhandel, brought suit under § 9(a) of the Trading with the Enemy Act against the Attorney General, as successor to the Alien Property Custodian, and the Treasurer of the United States, to recover these assets. This section authorizes recovery of seized assets by "(a)ny person not an enemy or ally of enemy" to the extent of such person's interest in the assets. Petitioner claimed that it had owned the General Aniline stock and cash at the time of vesting and hence, as the national of a neutral power, was entitled under § 9(a) to recovery.

The Government both challenged petitioner's claim of ownership and asserted that in any event petitioner was an "enemy" within the meaning of the Act since it was intimately connected with I.G. Farben and hence was affected with "enemy taint" despite its "neutral" incorporation. More particularly, the Government alleged that from the time of its incorporation in 1928, petitioner had conspired with I.G. Farben, H. Sturzenegger & Cie, a Swiss banking firm, and others "(t)o conceal, camouflage, and cloak the ownership, control and domination by I.G. Farben of properties and interests located in countries, including the United States, other than Germany, in order to avoid seizure and confiscation in the event of war between such countries and Germany."

At an early stage of the litigation the Government moved under Rule 34 of the Federal Rules of Civil Procedure for an order requiring petitioner to make available for inspection and copying a large number of the banking records of Sturzenegger & Cie. * * * In support of its motion the Government alleged that the records sought were relevant to showing the true ownership of the General Aniline stock and that they were within petitioner's control because petitioner and Sturzenegger were substantially identical. Petitioner did not dispute the general relevancy of the Sturzenegger documents but denied that it controlled them. The District Court granted the Government's motion, holding, among other things, that petitioner's "control" over the records had been prima facie established.

Thereafter followed a number of motions by petitioner to be relieved of production on the ground that disclosure of the required bank records would violate Swiss penal laws and consequently might lead to imposition of criminal sanctions, including fine and imprisonment, on those responsible for disclosure. The Government in turn moved under Rule 37(b)(2) of the Federal Rules of Civil Procedure to dismiss the complaint because of petitioner's noncompliance with the production order. During this period the Swiss Federal Attorney, deeming that disclosure of these records in accordance with the production order would constitute a violation of Article 273 of the Swiss Penal Code, prohibiting economic espionage, and Article 47 of the Swiss Bank Law, relating to secrecy of banking records, "confiscated" the Sturzenegger records. This "confiscation" left possession of the records in Sturzenegger and amounted to an interdiction on Sturzenegger's transmission of the records to third persons. The upshot of all this was that the District Court, before finally ruling on petitioner's motion for relief from the production order and on the Government's motion to dismiss the complaint, referred the matter to a Special Master for findings as to the nature of the Swiss laws claimed by petitioner to block production and as to petitioner's good faith in seeking to achieve compliance with the court's order.

* * *

[The] findings of the Master (that the Swiss Government had acted in accordance with its own established doctrines and that the plaintiff had shown good faith) were confirmed by the District Court. Nevertheless the court, in February 1953, granted the Government's motion to dismiss the complaint and filed an opinion wherein it concluded that: (1) apart from considerations of Swiss law petitioner had control over the Sturzenegger records; (2) such records might prove to be crucial in the outcome of this litigation; (3) Swiss law did not furnish an adequate excuse for petitioner's failure to comply with the production order, since petitioner could not invoke foreign laws to justify disobedience to orders entered under the laws of the forum; and (4) that the court in these circumstances had power under Rule 37(b)(2), as well as inherent power, to dismiss the complaint. However, in view of statements by the Swiss Government, following petitioner's intercession, that certain records not deemed to violate the Swiss laws would be released, and in view of efforts by petitioner to secure waivers from those persons banking with the Sturzenegger firm who were protected by the Swiss secrecy laws, and hence whose waivers might lead the Swiss Government to permit production, the court suspended the effective date of its dismissal order for a limited period in order to permit petitioner to continue efforts to obtain waivers and Swiss consent for production.

By October 1953, some 63,000 documents had been released by this process and tendered the Government for inspection. * * * However, since full production appeared impossible, the District Court in November 1953 entered a final dismissal order. This order was affirmed by the Court of Appeals, which accepted the findings of the District Court as to the relevancy of the documents, control of them by petitioner, and petitioner's good-faith efforts to comply with the production order. The court * * * did, however, modify the dismissal order to allow petitioner an additional six months in which to continue its efforts.

During this further period of grace, additional documents, with the consent of the Swiss Government and through waivers, were released and tendered for inspection, so that by July of 1956, over 190,000 documents had been procured. * * *

The District Court, however, * * * directed final dismissal of the action. The Court of Appeals affirmed, but at the same time observed: "That [petitioner] and its counsel patiently and diligently sought to achieve compliance * * * is not to be doubted." Because this decision raised important questions as to the proper application of the Federal Rules of Civil Procedure, we granted certiorari.

I.

We consider first petitioner's contention that the District Court erred in issuing the production order because the requirement of Rule 34, that a party ordered to produce documents must be in "control" of them, was not here satisfied. Without intimating any view upon the merits of the litigation, we accept as amply supported by the evidence the findings of the two courts below that, apart from the effect of Swiss law, the Sturzenegger documents are within petitioner's control. The question then becomes: Do the interdictions of Swiss law bar a conclusion that petitioner had "control" of these documents within the meaning of Rule 34?

* * *

In its broader scope, the problem before us requires consideration of the policies underlying the Trading with the Enemy Act. If petitioner can prove its record title to General Aniline stock, it certainly is open to the Government to show that petitioner itself is the captive of interests whose direct ownership would bar recovery. This possibility of enemy taint of nationals of neutral powers, particularly of holding companies with intricate financial structures, which asserted rights to American assets was of deep concern to the Congress when it broadened the Trading with the Enemy Act in 1941 " . . . to reach enemy interests which masqueraded under those innocent fronts." * * *

In view of these considerations, to hold broadly that petitioner's failure to produce the Sturzenegger records because of fear of punishment under the laws of its sovereign precludes a court from finding that petitioner had "control" over them, and thereby from ordering their production, would undermine congressional policies made explicit in the 1941 amendments, and invite efforts to place ownership of American assets in persons or firms whose sovereign assures secrecy of records. The District Court here concluded that the

Sturzenegger records might have a vital influence upon this litigation insofar as they shed light upon petitioner's confused background. Petitioner is in a most advantageous position to plead with its own sovereign for relaxation of penal laws or for adoption of plans which will at the least achieve a significant measure of compliance with the production order, and indeed to that end it has already made significant progress. United States courts should be free to require claimants of seized assets who face legal obstacles under the laws of their own countries to make all such efforts to the maximum of their ability where the requested records promise to-bear out or dispel any doubt the Government may introduce as to true ownership of the assets.

We do not say that this ruling would apply to every situation where a party is restricted by law from producing documents over which it is otherwise shown to have control. Rule 34 is sufficiently flexible to be adapted to the exigencies of particular litigation. The propriety of the use to which it is put depends upon the circumstances of a given case, and we hold only that accommodation of the Rule in this instance to the policies underlying the Trading with the Enemy Act justified the action of the District Court in issuing this production order.

* * *

III.

We turn to the remaining question, whether the District Court properly exercised its powers under Rule 37(b) by dismissing this complaint despite the findings that petitioner had not been in collusion with the Swiss authorities to block inspection of the Sturzenegger records, and had in good faith made diligent efforts to execute the production order.

* * *

The provisions of Rule 37 which are here involved must be read in light of the provisions of the Fifth Amendment that no person shall be deprived of property without due process of law * * *.

* * *

The findings below, and what has been shown as to petitioner's extensive efforts at compliance, compel the conclusion on this record that petitioner's failure to satisfy fully the requirements of this production order was due to inability fostered neither by its own conduct nor by circumstances within its control. It is hardly debatable that fear of criminal prosecution constitutes a weighty excuse for nonproduction, and this excuse is not weakened because the laws preventing compliance are those of a foreign sovereign. Of course this situation should be distinguished from one where a party claims that compliance with a court's order will reveal facts which may provide the basis for criminal prosecution of that party under the penal laws of a foreign sovereign thereby shown to have been violated. * * * Here the findings below establish that the very fact of compliance by disclosure of banking records will itself constitute the initial violation of Swiss laws. In our view, petitioner stands in the position of an American plaintiff subject to criminal sanctions in Switzerland because production of documents in Switzerland pursuant to the order of a United States court might violate Swiss laws. Petitioner has sought no privileges because of its foreign citizenship which are not accorded domestic litigants in United States courts. It does not claim that Swiss laws protecting banking records should here be enforced. It explicitly recognizes that it is subject to procedural rules of United States courts in this litigation and has made full efforts to follow these rules. It asserts no immunity from them. It asserts only its inability to comply because of foreign law.

In view of the findings in this case, the position in which petitioner stands in this litigation, and the serious constitutional questions we have noted, we think that Rule 37 should not be construed to authorize dismissal of this complaint because of petitioner's noncompliance with a pretrial production order when it has been established that failure to comply has been due to inability, and not to willfulness, bad faith, or any fault of petitioner.

This is not to say that petitioner will profit through its inability to tender the records called for. In seeking recovery of the General Aniline stock and other assets, petitioner recognizes that it carries the ultimate burden of proof of showing itself not to be an "enemy" within the meaning of the Trading with the Enemy Act. The Government already has disputed its right to recovery by relying on information obtained through seized records of I.G. Farben, documents obtained through petitioner, and depositions taken of persons affiliated with petitioner. It may be that in a trial on the merits, petitioner's inability to produce specific information will prove a serious handicap in dispelling doubt the Government might be able to inject into the case. It may be that in the absence of complete disclosure by petitioner, the District Court would be justified in drawing inferences unfavorable to petitioner as to particular events. So much indeed petitioner concedes. But these problems go to the adequacy of petitioner's proof and should not on this record preclude petitioner from being able to contest on the merits.

On remand, the District Court possesses wide discretion to proceed in whatever manner it deems most effective. It may desire to afford the Government additional opportunity to challenge petitioner's good faith. It may wish to explore plans looking towards fuller compliance. Or it may decide to commence at once trial on the merits. We decide only that on this record dismissal of the complaint with prejudice was not justified.

[Reversed and remanded.]

MR. JUSTICE CLARK took not part in the consideration or decision of this case.

NOTES AND QUESTIONS FOR DISCUSSION

1. How *should* courts react to parties or non-party witnesses who claim that a foreign blocking statute prevents them from complying with the discovery order? In *Rogers*, the Supreme Court held that parties attempting in good faith to obtain a waiver under foreign law should then at least not suffer the ultimate sanction of a dismissal of their action. The Restatement (Third) of Foreign Relations Law of the United States § 442 (1987) appears to have adopted this part of the Court's holding:

§ 442(1).

(a) A court or agency in the United States, when authorized by statute or rule of court, may order a person subject to its jurisdiction to produce documents, objects, or other information relevant to an action or investigation, even if the information or the person in possession of the information is outside the United States.

(b) Failure to comply with an order to produce information may subject the person to whom the order is directed to sanctions, including finding of contempt, dismissal of a claim or defense, or default judgment, or may lead to a determination that the facts to which the order was addressed are as asserted by the opposing party.

(c) In deciding whether to issue an order directing production of information located abroad, and in framing such an order, a court or agency in the United States should take into account the importance to the investigation or litigation of the documents or other information requested; the degree of specificity of the request; whether the information originated in the United States; the availability of alternative means of securing the information; and the extent to which noncompliance with the request would undermine important interests of the United States, or compliance with the request would undermine important interests of the state where the information is located.

(2). If disclosure of information located outside the United States is prohibited by a law, regulation, or order of a court or other authority of the state in which the information or prospective witness is located, or of the state of which a prospective witness is a national,

(a) a court or agency in the United States may require the person to whom the order is directed to make a good faith effort to secure permission from the foreign authorities to make the information available;

(b) a court or agency should not ordinarily impose sanctions of contempt, dismissal, or default on a party that has failed to comply with the order for production, except in cases of deliberate concealment or removal of information or of failure to make a good faith effort in accordance with paragraph (a);

(c) a court or agency may, in appropriate cases, make findings of fact adverse to a party that has failed to comply with the order for production, even if that party has made a good faith effort to secure permission from the foreign authorities to make the information available and that effort has been unsuccessful.

2. Consider a few of the details of the provisions just quoted from the Restatement.

- Note first that § 442(1)(c) lists a number of balancing factors, including the specificity of the request and the availability of alternative means of securing the information. Some courts look to these and other factors of

Subsection 1(c) to decide whether or not to issue an international discovery order. See, e.g., White v. Kenneth Warren & Son, Ltd., 203 F.R.D. 369 (N.D. Ill. 2001) (denying discovery directed at evidence located in England). The Supreme Court in *Aérospatiale* acknowledged "these factors as relevant to any comity analysis,"[*] but in the end relied on a different set of criteria to determine that a unilateral order mandating the disclosure of information located abroad was appropriate. What is different under the Restatement?

- Next, note that § 442(2) addresses the dilemma that litigants face who cannot comply with the American discovery order without violating domestic law of their home state. In line with *Rogers*, § 442(2)(a) endorses a good faith requirement that courts may impose on such litigants. Subsections (b) and (c) delineate the kind of sanctions that may be imposed if the litigant subject to the discovery order made a good faith effort but was unsuccessful. If good faith has been shown, the sanctions of contempt, dismissal, or default should not be an option. However, under Subsection (c) the sanction of adverse fact findings might still be imposed, even if the party undertook a good faith effort.

- Finally, while courts have adopted the good faith requirement, enunciated in *Rogers* and embodied in § 442(2) as criterion for the imposition of sanctions, there are uncertainties as to how this and other factors apply at the sanction stage.

The following two decisions illustrate some of problems that arise in the sort of conflicts just noted. The decision in *Richmark Corp. v. Timber Falling Consultants*, below, stands for the proposition that a party claiming good faith must show an affirmative request for dispensation from the foreign secrecy laws. The decision *In re Marc Rich & Co., A.G.*, illustrates the conundrum that parties face when foreign governments get actively involved in the discovery dispute by enforcing their secrecy laws.

Richmark Corp. v. Timber Falling Consultants

United States Court of Appeals, Ninth Circuit, 1992.
959 F.2d 1468.

DOROTHY NELSON, CIRCUIT JUDGE.

This case presents a number of difficult questions regarding a sensitive area of law and foreign relations. Timber Falling Consultants, Inc. (TFC) won a default judgment for fraud and breach of contract against Beijing Ever Bright

---

[*] Note that the Supreme Court in *Aérospatiale* cited to §437 of the draft version of the Restatement which was later renumbered to become § 442.

Industrial Co. (Beijing), a corporation organized under the laws of the People's Republic of China (PRC) and an arm of the PRC government. As part of an effort to execute that judgment, TFC sought discovery of Beijing's assets worldwide. Beijing resisted those discovery efforts, and refused to comply when ordered to do so by the district court. The district court imposed discovery sanctions, held Beijing in contempt, and ordered contempt fines of $10,000 a day. Beijing contends that PRC secrecy laws prevent it from complying with the discovery order and that it would be subject to prosecution in the PRC were it to comply. It appeals the discovery order, the discovery sanction, the contempt order, and the district court's refusal to vacate the contempt order * * *.

* * *

DISCUSSION

I. Propriety of Discovery Orders and Sanctions

Beijing contends that the state secrecy laws prohibit it from disclosing the information the district court ordered it to provide, that it would be subject to criminal prosecution if it did disclose such information, and that this prohibition necessitates the reversal of the discovery order and the contempt sanctions against it. The district court explicitly accepted Beijing's contention that the PRC's State Secrets Act barred disclosure of the information in question. We do so as well. * * *

[Applying the balancing test of § 442(1)(c), the Ninth Circuit nevertheless decided to uphold the district court's order compelling discovery. With respect to Beijing's good faith effort and the propriety of contempt sanctions, the Ninth Circuit wrote:]

Beijing next contends that, even if the discovery order was valid, the contempt sanction should be vacated because Beijing has attempted in good faith to comply with the court's orders. It is true that contempt is inappropriate where a party has taken "all the reasonable steps" it can take to comply. The Restatement (Third) of Foreign Relations Law §442(2)(b) provides that "a court or agency should not ordinarily impose sanctions of contempt . . . on a party that has failed to comply with the order for production, except in cases of deliberate concealment or removal of information or of failure to make a good faith effort" to secure permission from the foreign government to disclose the information.

In [United States v. Vetco, Inc., 691 F.2d 1281 (9th Cir. 1981)] we required a foreign corporation asserting a blocking statute as a defense to make an *affirmative showing* of its good faith in seeking permission to disclose the information. [Id.] at 1287 * * *

Beijing has made no such affirmative showing here. The district court did not find that Beijing acted in good faith in attempting to obtain a waiver. Nor is good faith evident from the record. Beijing fought disclosure for several months before raising the foreign law problem, even after the district court issued an order on October 15, 1990 compelling disclosure. Beijing's effort to seek a waiver consisted of a letter to the Ministry of Justice on January 28, 1991, in which it noted the "broad scope" of the discovery order, pointed out to the Ministry the legal provision it felt barred disclosure, and asked whether it was permitted to disclose the information under the State Secrets Act. While Beijing did ask whether there was "a procedure through which Beijing Ever Bright may seek the permission of the government to disclose the information it is not presently permitted to disclose," it did not in fact seek such permission, but rather requested only "guidance" on the legal question. In spite of this, Beijing asserted that the State Secrets Act prevented it from complying in February 1991, two months *before* the Ministry even responded to this request. Beijing does not appear to have made a good faith effort to clarify PRC law or to seek a waiver of the secrecy statutes before refusing to comply with the district court order. For these reasons, the district court acted within its discretion in sanctioning Beijing for its noncompliance. * * * [Affirmed.]

In re Marc Rich & Co. A.G.

United States Court of Appeals, Second Circuit, 1984.
736 F.2d 864.

Oakes, Circuit Judge.

Marc Rich & Co., A.G. ("Rich"), appeals from the denial by the United States District Court for the Southern District of New York, Leonard B. Sand, Judge, of its motion to terminate fines of $50,000 per day as sanctions for civil contempt. The fines were imposed by the district court on September 13, 1982, for Rich's failure to comply with a grand jury subpoena duces tecum, which required Rich to produce all documents "pertaining to any and all foreign and domestic oil transactions for the years 1980 and 1981." In May, 1983, the court of appeals affirmed the court's judgment of contempt. * * * The only issue raised and decided on that appeal was whether the district court had personal jurisdiction over Rich.

In June, 1983, Rich moved to vacate the contempt judgment on the ground that Swiss court orders prohibited compliance with the subpoena. The motion was denied, and Rich appealed. Shortly thereafter, in August, 1983, Rich agreed to comply with the subpoena, withdrew its appeal with prejudice, and agreed "not [to] raise at any time in any court the claim that any law of Switzerland prevents the Company from producing the documents . . . ." This agreement became part of the court's order.

Subsequently Swiss authorities ordered Rich not to comply with the subpoena, and, on three occasions (August 13, 1983, November 22, 1983, and February 9, 1984) Swiss officials seized various documents responsive to the subpoena. In response, Rich moved three more times to vacate the judgment of contempt. The present case involves the last two of these motions. Rich argues that it should be released of contempt because of the "unequivocal statements and compulsory actions of the Swiss government prohibiting and preventing" its further compliance with the subpoena.

The Government of Switzerland has appeared in this appeal as amicus curiae on behalf of Rich. The Swiss have taken the position that there is a clear conflict between the public laws of Switzerland and those of the United States, and that efforts to force compliance with the subpoena despite Swiss law violate Swiss sovereignty and international comity. The Government of Switzerland maintains, however, that the United States can obtain documents in its possession or under its control upon application under the Swiss Federal Act on Mutual Assistance in Criminal Matters (1981). It has apparently made known this position to the United States Department of State and others.

Civil contempt is a coercive sanction, and thus a person held in civil contempt must be able to comply with the court order at issue. * * * Individuals unable to comply, because of their own bad faith actions or otherwise, may be subject to criminal sanctions, but may not be held in civil contempt. The burden of proving "plainly and unmistakably" that compliance is impossible rests with the contemnor. * * *

We face two different issues in deciding whether Rich should continue to be held in civil contempt: (1) Has Rich proved that it is no longer in possession or control of documents responsive to the subpoena and thus no longer able to comply? (2) If Rich still possesses or controls such documents, are Swiss laws or orders sufficient to excuse noncompliance and thus to serve as the basis for vacating the judgment of contempt?

Prior to the February 9 seizure by the Swiss, Rich had clearly not demonstrated that further compliance with the subpoena was impossible. Judge Sand made it perfectly clear that Rich simply had to produce appropriate affidavits attesting to the impossibility of compliance and the judgment would be lifted. Rich has never done so. Thus, we think the district court was correct in its ruling of January 27, 1984, denying Rich's motion to vacate. Moreover, we think that Judge Sand properly declined to rule on whether Rich's situation had changed after the February seizure. There was a pending appeal of his earlier ruling, which involved at least some of the same issues, and Rich would not be prejudiced by waiting for consideration of its post-February 9 position.

Finally, we think that Rich is barred from relying on Swiss law or orders of the Swiss Government as an excuse for its noncompliance with the subpoena. In the first place, Rich's agreement of August, 1983, stated unequivocally that it would not rely on Swiss law in refusing to comply with the subpoena. Rich's argument that the parties never contemplated that the Swiss Government would seize the documents or "issue its own orders" is not persuasive. We think any orders of the Swiss authorities are fairly covered by the 1983 waiver. Of course, if the seizures have made further compliance impossible, the agreement would not bar Rich from asserting that fact as a defense.

In addition, consideration of Swiss law and orders is now barred by res judicata. Rich did not raise the issue of Swiss law on its first appeal to the Second Circuit, and thus the district court's ruling on this matter stands. The effect of direct Swiss orders is a separate issue, but res judicata applies nonetheless because of Rich's failure to appeal other rulings. Rich's first motion to vacate, in June, 1983, was based on an order of the Swiss courts. Rich withdrew its appeal on this issue with prejudice. In addition, Rich did not appeal the denial of its second motion to vacate in October, 1983, in which the district court again rejected Swiss orders as an excuse for noncompliance. Since Rich has had numerous opportunities to bring this issue to the court of appeals and has not done so, the principle of res judicata bars it from doing so now.

Recognizing that on the merits the question of noncompliance with the subpoena at the present time is a close one, that the circumstances since the issuance of the order of January 27, 1984, may have changed, and that there are ongoing negotiations between the governments of Switzerland and the United States, we remand the cause for the district court's consideration of the motion to vacate made following the February seizure of documents, and for an evidentiary hearing on the question whether all of the documents Rich has not produced that are subject to the subpoena are now or have been since February 9, 1984, or some other date, in the possession of the Swiss Government. Orders of January 27, 1984, and March 8, 1984, affirmed; cause remanded.

NOTES AND QUESTIONS FOR DISCUSSION

1. As in *Richmark*, most courts require that the target of the discovery order make an *affirmative* showing of its good faith in seeking a waiver from the foreign blocking statute. Is this appropriate? As a general matter, why shouldn't the American court defer to foreign law—given that it is an expression of the foreign state's public and sovereign interests and considering that compliance with the American order exposes the party to the risk of criminal prosecution in the foreign state? Note that, contrary to § 442, the Restatement seems to suggest just that by providing in another Section: "In general, a state may not require a person (a) to do an act in another state that is prohibited by the law of that state . . . or (b) to refrain from an act in another state that is required by the law of that state . . . ." § 441(1)(a)&(b). This section is an expression of the so-called foreign sovereign compulsion doctrine which protects persons caught between conflicting commands. It defers to the law of the state which prohibits or compels the act. For example, the doctrine may act as a defense against claims under American antitrust law, when a foreign state compels certain trade practices and companies have no choice but to obey. Trugman-Nash, Inc. v. New Zealand Dairy Board, 954 F. Supp. 733 (S.D.N.Y. 1997); Interamerican Refining Corp. v. Texaco Maracaibo, Inc.; 307 F. Supp. 1291 (D. Del. 1970).

2. Is the foreign sovereign compulsion doctrine under § 441 compatible with American case law or § 442 which force parties to do what they are prohibited from doing on foreign territory under foreign law? It has been argued that the foreign sovereign compulsion doctrine set out in § 441 applies to conflicts of substantive laws, as in the antitrust setting, and that conflicts of a procedural nature, particularly over the discoverability of evidence, justify less deference to the law of foreign states. Restatement (Third) of Foreign Relations Law of the United States § 442 (1987) comment (e). What is the reason for this distinction? Is it compelling or even convincing?

3. One reason for the meager respect American courts pay foreign blocking statutes stems from the suspicion that these laws are merely "on the books," but are not actually enforced against those who eventually comply with American discovery orders. And upon finding that these suspicions are warranted, American courts have not hesitated to impose sanctions for failure to make discovery. See, e.g., Remington Products, Inc. v. North American Philips Corp.,

107 F.R.D. 642 (D. Conn. 1985) (holding that the Dutch blocking statute was never enforced, and was not concerned with the secrecy of business records, but rather sought to block the extraterritorial reach of U.S. antitrust laws).

4. Recall that under Subsection (2)(c) of the Restatement even a good faith effort may not shield a party from sanctions. Courts may, "in appropriate cases, make findings of facts adverse to the party" that tried but failed to obtain a waiver. Can you imagine a case in which this sanction would be appropriate?

5. While it is not entirely clear what it takes to make a good faith effort so as to avoid or vacate the most severe sanctions, it is well settled that the standards are rather strict. In *Richmark*, the Chinese corporation asked its government whether state secrecy laws prohibited it from disclosing the requested information and received the response that this information was classified as a state secret and could not be disclosed. The court held that this request did not amount to a good faith effort. What else could the company have done?

6. There is consensus that the good faith defense is not available when parties solicit the foreign authority to enforce the domestic secrecy law. See Restatement (Third) of Foreign Relations Law of the United States §442 (1987), comment (h):

> Evidence that parties or targets have actively sought a prohibition against disclosure, or that the information was deliberately moved to a state with blocking legislation, may be regarded as evidence of bad faith and justification for sanctions in accordance with Subsection (2)(b). Merely notifying the authorities of another state or consulting with them about a request for discovery is not evidence of bad faith.

Does this section provide a workable solution for a finding of good faith or its absence and for the corresponding choice of sanctions? What if "merely notifying the authorities of a foreign state" inevitably triggers an enforcement mechanism which effectively forecloses any possibility of complying with the American order? Is it bad faith, justifying contempt sanctions, if the party subject to the order anticipated this reaction of the foreign authorities?

7. Consider whether a targeted party would be acting in bad faith if the foreign government reacts to such notification by submitting an amicus curiae brief in support of that party. Would it make a difference if the party requested this type of governmental reaction? American courts do not appear to view such interventions as bad faith. Quite the contrary, at an earlier stage of the discovery dispute—when courts decide on whether to issue a disclose order in the first place—some courts expect precisely this kind of initiative. These courts take it as an expression of foreign sovereign interests that they balance against the interests in obtaining discovery. And the absence of such expression may tip the balance in favor of ordering discovery. For example, in one case before the Second Circuit, a domestic bank refused to comply with a Grand Jury subpoena duces tecum requiring the production of documents in the possession of a German branch of the bank on the ground that compliance would violate German bank secrecy law. Holding that the interests of the U.S. in enforcing the subpoena outweighed the German interests in its bank secrecy laws, the court reasoned in part as follows:

> We are fully aware that when foreign governments, including Germany, have considered their vital national interests threatened, they have not hesitated to make known their objections to the enforcement of a subpoena to the issuing court * * *. So far as appears, both the United States and German governments have voiced no opposition to Citibank's production of the subpoenaed records.

United States v. First National City Bank, 396 F.2d 897, 904 (2d Cir. 1968). Is it consistent for American courts to encourage this type of governmental action but to hold parties in bad faith when they cite to sanctions that foreign penal law entails for complying with the American order?

8. Suppose First National City Bank had enlisted German authorities to support its case and, in response, the German authorities not only submitted an amicus curiae brief but also enjoined the bank's German branch office from releasing any files. Could that have been construed as bad faith on the part of the bank? Is that what happened in *Marc Rich*? In *Marc Rich*, the court upheld the initial contempt order in part because Rich had agreed to comply with the subpoena and to refrain from raising Swiss secrecy law in defense against the subpoena. Is it possible for private litigants to "waive" foreign public laws and their enforcement? *Should* it be possible?

9. The Swiss authorities had enjoined Rich from complying with the subpoena and, on three occasions, had seized documents responsive to the subpoena. While the court acknowledged that the last seizure (on February 9, 1984) may have made it impossible for Rich to comply, and thus may have been grounds for vacating the contempt order, the court nevertheless found that Rich had failed to show the impossibility of complying with the subpoena prior to that date. Is there anything in the opinion that explains why the first two seizures, coupled with the Swiss order not to comply, were not held sufficient for lifting the contempt?

10. Note the *Marc Rich* court's reference to the "ongoing negotiations between the governments of Switzerland and the United States." It appears, however, that the Swiss government, frustrated with the coercive unilateral actions of American authorities, never actually released the seized documents to the U.S. Is there a more promising way to obtain crucial evidence in such government-initiated litigation? For an alternative to unilateral discovery orders and a call for early involvement of and cooperation between public authorities on either side, see James I. K. Knapp, *Mutual Legal Assistance Treaties as a Way to Pierce Bank Secrecy,* 20 Case W. Res. J. Int'l L. 405 (1988).

11. The *Marc Rich* controversy was finally settled by a plea bargain in which the Rich Companies agreed to pay several hundred million dollars in fines for tax evasion and back taxes to the U.S. government. Marc Rich himself was also famously pardoned in the waning hours of the administration of President Bill Clinton.

G. U.S. DISCOVERY AND EVIDENCE PRODUCTION FOR FOREIGN AND INTERNATIONAL TRIBUNALS

U.S. courts may provide assistance to foreign and international tribunals and to litigants before those tribunals. One statute, for example, gives the State Department the power to receive letters rogatory[*] issued by, or other requests made by, such tribunals and to transmit them to the U.S. tribunal, officer or agency to whom it is addressed. 28 U.S.C. § 1781(a)(1). But the statute does not preclude the transmittal of such matters directly from a foreign or international tribunal to the U.S. tribunal officer or agency to whom it is addressed. Id. at § 1781(b)(1). In addition, under 28 U.S.C. § 1696(a), a federal district court may order service upon a person residing in the district of "any document issued in connection with a proceeding in a foreign or international tribunal," including letters rogatory and other requests. But the provision also does not preclude service of such a document without court order. See id. at § 1696(b).

Another statute, 28 U.S.C. § 1782, pursues the twin aims of providing efficient means of assistance to participants in international litigation in U.S. courts and encouraging foreign countries (by example) to provide similar means of assistance to U.S. courts.

28 U.S.C. § 1782. Assistance to foreign and international tribunals and to litigants before such tribunals

(a) The district court of the district in which a person resides or is found may order him to give his testimony or statement or to produce a document or other thing for use in a proceeding in a foreign or international tribunal, including criminal investigations conducted before formal accusation. The order may be made pursuant to a letter rogatory issued, or request made, by a foreign or international tribunal or upon the application of any interested person and may direct that the testimony or statement be given, or the document or other thing be produced, before a person appointed by the court. * * * The order may prescribe the practice and procedure, which may be in whole or part the practice and procedure of the foreign country or the international tribunal, for taking the testimony or statement or producing the document or other thing. To the extent that the order does not prescribe otherwise, the testimony or statement shall be taken, and the document or other thing produced, in accordance with the Federal Rules of Civil Procedure.

---

[*] "[A] *letter rogatory* is the request by a domestic court to a foreign court to take evidence from a certain witness." Harry Leroy Jones, *International Judicial Assistance: Procedural Chaos and a Program for Reform,* 62 Yale L.J. 515, 519 (1953).

A person may not be compelled to give his testimony or statement or to produce a document or other thing in violation of any legally applicable privilege.

(b) This chapter does not preclude a person within the United States from voluntarily giving his testimony or statement, or producing a document or other thing, for use in a proceeding in a foreign or international tribunal before any person and in any manner acceptable to him.

Some of the language of the statute is mandatory; some is permissive. We offer two decisions interpreting § 1782. The first of them deals with the interpretation of the statute and the obligations that it imposes. The second deals with the question of the extent to which a court may exercise discretion under the statute.

Intel Corp. v. Advanced Micro Devices, Inc.

Supreme Court of the United States, 2004.
542 U.S. 241.

JUSTICE GINSBURG delivered the opinion of the Court.

This case concerns the authority of federal district courts to assist in the production of evidence for use in a foreign or international tribunal. In the matter before us, respondent Advanced Micro Devices, Inc. (AMD) filed an antitrust complaint against petitioner Intel Corporation (Intel) with the Directorate-General for Competition of the Commission of the European Communities (European Commission or Commission). In pursuit of that complaint, AMD applied to the United States District Court for the Northern District of California, invoking 28 U.S.C. § 1782(a) for an order requiring Intel to produce potentially relevant documents. Section 1782(a) provides that a federal district court "may order" a person "resid[ing]" or "found" in the district to give testimony or produce documents "for use in a proceeding in a foreign or international tribunal . . . upon the application of any interested person."

Concluding that § 1782(a) did not authorize the requested discovery, the District Court denied AMD's application. The Court of Appeals for the Ninth Circuit reversed that determination and remanded the case, instructing the District Court to rule on the merits of AMD's application. In accord with the Court of Appeals, we hold that the District Court had authority under § 1782(a) to entertain AMD's discovery request. The statute, we rule, does not categorically bar the assistance AMD seeks: (1) A complainant before the European Commission, such as AMD, qualifies as an "interested person" within § 1782(a)'s compass; (2) the Commission is a § 1782(a) "tribunal" when it acts as a first-instance decisionmaker; (3) the "proceeding" for which discovery is sought under § 1782(a) must be in reasonable contemplation, but need not be "pending" or "imminent"; and (4) § 1782(a) contains no threshold requirement that evidence sought from a federal district court would be discoverable under the law governing the foreign proceeding. We caution, however, that § 1782(a) authorizes, but does not require, a federal district court to provide judicial assistance to foreign or international tribunals or to "interested person[s]" in proceedings abroad. Whether such assistance is appropriate in this case is a question yet unresolved. To guide the District Court on remand, we suggest considerations relevant to the disposition of that question.

I

A

Section 1782 is the product of congressional efforts, over the span of nearly 150 years, to provide federal-court assistance in gathering evidence for use in foreign tribunals. Congress first provided for federal-court aid to foreign tribunals in 1855; requests for aid took the form of letters rogatory forwarded through diplomatic channels. See Act of Mar. 2, 1855, ch. 140, § 2, 10 Stat. 630 (circuit court may appoint "a United States commissioner designated . . . to make the examination of witnesses" on receipt of a letter rogatory from a foreign court); Act of Mar. 3, 1863, ch. 95, § 1, 12 Stat. 769 (authorizing district courts to respond to letters rogatory by compelling witnesses here to provide testimony for use abroad in "suit[s] for the recovery of money or property"). In 1948, Congress substantially broadened the scope of assistance federal courts could provide for foreign proceedings. That legislation, codified as § 1782, eliminated the prior requirement that the government of a foreign country be a party or have an interest in the proceeding. The measure allowed district courts to designate persons to preside at depositions "to be used in *any civil action* pending in any court in a foreign country with which the United States is at peace." * * * The next year, Congress deleted "civil action" from § 1782's text and inserted "judicial proceeding." * * *

In 1958, prompted by the growth of international commerce, Congress created a Commission on International Rules of Judicial Procedure (Rules Commission) to "investigate and study existing practices of judicial assistance and cooperation between the United States and foreign countries with a view to achieving improvements." * * * Six years later, in 1964, Congress unanimously adopted legislation recommended by the Rules Commission; legislation included a complete revision of § 1782. * * *

As recast in 1964, § 1782 provided for assistance in obtaining documentary and other tangible evidence as well as testimony. Notably, Congress deleted the words "in any judicial proceeding *pending* in any court in a foreign country," and replaced them with the phrase "in a proceeding in a foreign or international tribunal." While the accompanying Senate Report does not account discretely for the deletion of the word "pending," it explains that Congress introduced the word "tribunal" to ensure that "assistance is not confined to proceedings before conventional courts," but extends also to "administrative and quasi-judicial proceedings." S. Rep. No. 1580, 88th Cong., 2d Sess., p. 7 (1964); see H. R. Rep. No. 1052, 88th Cong., 1st Sess., p. 9 (1963) (same). Congress further amended § 1782(a) in 1996 to add, after the reference to "foreign or international tribunal," the words "including criminal investigations conducted before formal accusation." National Defense Authorization Act for Fiscal Year 1996, Pub. L. 104-106, § 1342(b), 110 Stat. 486. * * *

B

AMD and Intel are "worldwide competitors in the microprocessor industry." 292 F.3d 664, 665 (CA9 2002). In October 2000, AMD filed an antitrust complaint with the Directorate-General for Competition (DG-Competition) of the European Commission. "The European Commission is the executive and administrative organ of the European Communities." The Commission exercises responsibility over the wide range of subject areas covered by the European Union treaty; those areas include the treaty provisions, and regulations thereunder, governing competition. The DG-Competition, operating under the Commission's aegis, is the European Union's primary antitrust law enforcer. Within the DG-Competition's domain are anticompetitive agreements (Art. 81) and abuse of dominant market position (Art. 82).

AMD's complaint alleged that Intel, in violation of European competition law, had abused its dominant position in the European market through loyalty rebates, exclusive purchasing agreements with manufacturers and retailers, price discrimination, and standard-setting cartels. AMD recommended that the DG-Competition seek discovery of documents Intel had produced in a private antitrust suit [filed in an Alabama federal court]. After the DG-Competition declined to seek judicial assistance in the United States, AMD, pursuant to § 1782(a), petitioned the District Court for the Northern District of California for an order directing Intel to produce documents discovered in the [Alabama federal court] litigation and on file in the [Alabama] federal court. AMD asserted that it sought the materials in connection with the complaint it had filed with the European Commission.

[The California federal district court denied the discovery application of AMD, but the Ninth Circuit reversed and remanded the case for disposition on the merits. On remand, the district court concluded that the application was "overbroad" and ordered AMD to make a more specific request. The district court proceedings were eventually stayed pending Intel's petition for certiorari to the U.S. Supreme Court to review the Ninth Circuit's ruling regarding discovery.]

We granted certiorari, in view of the division among the Circuits on the question whether § 1782(a) contains a foreign-discoverability requirement. We now hold that § 1782(a) does not impose such a requirement. We also granted review on two other questions. First, does § 1782(a) make discovery available to complainants, such as AMD, who do not have the status of private "litigants" and are not sovereign agents? Second, must a "proceeding" before a foreign "tribunal" be "pending" or at least "imminent" for an applicant to invoke § 1782(a) successfully? * * * Answering "yes" to the first question and "no" to the second, we affirm the Ninth Circuit's judgment.

II

To place this case in context, we sketch briefly how the European Commission, acting through the DG-Competition, enforces European competition laws and regulations. The DG-Competition's "overriding responsibility" is to conduct investigations into alleged violations of the European Union's competition prescriptions. On receipt of a complaint or *sua* *sponte*, the DG-Competition conducts a preliminary investigation. In that investigation, the DG-Competition "may take into account information provided by a complainant, and it may seek information directly from the target of the complaint." "Ultimately, DG Competition's preliminary investigation results in a formal written decision whether to pursue the complaint. If [the DG-Competition] declines to proceed, that decision is subject to judicial review" by the Court of First Instance and, ultimately, by the court of last resort for European Union matters, the Court of Justice for the European Communities (European Court of Justice). * * *

If the DG-Competition decides to pursue the complaint, it typically serves the target of the investigation with a formal "statement of objections" and advises the target of its intention to recommend a decision finding that the target has violated European competition law. The target is entitled to a hearing before an independent officer, who provides a report to the DG-Competition. Once the DG-Competition has made its recommendation, the European Commission may "dismis[s] the complaint, or issu[e] a decision finding infringement and imposing penalties." The Commission's final action dismissing the complaint or holding the target liable is subject to review in the Court of First Instance and the European Court of Justice.

Although lacking formal "party" or "litigant" status in Commission proceedings, the complainant has significant procedural rights. Most prominently, the complainant may submit to the DG-Competition information in support of its allegations, and may seek judicial review of the Commission's disposition of a complaint. * * *

III

As "in all statutory construction cases, we begin [our examination of § 1782] with the language of the statute." * * * The language of § 1782(a), confirmed by its context, our examination satisfies us, warrants this conclusion: The statute authorizes, but does not require, a federal district court to provide assistance to a complainant in a European Commission proceeding that leads to a dispositive ruling, *i.e.*, a final administrative action both responsive to the complaint and reviewable in court. Accordingly, we reject the categorical limitations Intel would place on the statute's reach.

A

We turn first to Intel's contention that the catalog of "interested person[s]" authorized to apply for judicial assistance under § 1782(a) includes only "litigants, foreign sovereigns, and the designated agents of those sovereigns," and excludes AMD, a mere complainant before the Commission, accorded only "limited rights." Highlighting § 1782's caption, "[a]ssistance to foreign and international tribunals and to *litigants* before such tribunals," Intel urges that the statutory phrase "any interested person" should be read, correspondingly, to reach only "litigants." (internal quotation marks omitted, emphasis in original).

The caption of a statute, this Court has cautioned, "cannot undo or limit that which the [statute's] text makes plain." *Trainmen* v. *Baltimore & Ohio R. Co.,* 331 U.S. 519, 529 (1947). The text of § 1782(a), "upon the application of any interested person," plainly reaches beyond the universe of persons designated "litigant." No doubt litigants are included among, and may be the most common example of, the "interested person[s]" who may invoke § 1782; we read § 1782's caption to convey no more. * * *

The complainant who triggers a European Commission investigation has a significant role in the process. As earlier observed, in addition to prompting an investigation, the complainant has the right to submit information for the DG-Competition's consideration, and may proceed to court if the Commission discontinues the investigation or dismisses the complaint. Given these participation rights, a complainant "possess[es] a reasonable interest in obtaining [judicial] assistance," and therefore qualifies as an "interested person" within any fair construction of that term. * * *

B

We next consider whether the assistance in obtaining documents here sought by an "interested person" meets the specification "for use in a foreign or international tribunal." Beyond question the reviewing authorities, both the Court of First Instance and the European Court of Justice, qualify as tribunals. But those courts are not proof-taking instances. Their review is limited to the record before the Commission. Hence, AMD could "use" evidence in the reviewing courts only by submitting it to the Commission in the current, investigative stage.

Moreover, when Congress established the Commission on International Rules of Judicial Procedure in 1958, it instructed the Rules Commission to recommend procedural revisions "for the rendering of assistance to foreign courts *and quasi-judicial agencies.*" § 2, 72 Stat. 1743 (emphasis added). Section 1782 had previously referred to "any judicial proceeding." The Rules Commission's draft, which Congress adopted, replaced that term with "a proceeding in a foreign or international tribunal." Congress understood that change to "provid[e] the possibility of U. S. judicial assistance in connection with [administrative and quasi-judicial proceedings abroad]." S. Rep. No. 1580, at 7–8 [.] * * * We have no warrant to exclude the European Commission, to the extent that it acts as a first-instance decisionmaker, from § 1782(a)'s ambit.

C

Intel also urges that AMD's complaint has not progressed beyond the investigative stage; therefore, no adjudicative action is currently or even imminently on the Commission's agenda.

Section 1782(a) does not limit the provision of judicial assistance to "pending" adjudicative proceedings. In 1964, when Congress eliminated the requirement that a proceeding be "judicial," Congress also deleted the requirement that a proceeding be "pending." "When Congress acts to amend a statute, we presume it intends its amendment to have real and substantial effect." * * * The legislative history of the 1964 revision is in sync; it reflects Congress' recognition that judicial assistance would be available "whether the foreign or international proceeding *or investigation* is of a criminal, civil, administrative, or other nature." S. Rep. No. 1580, at 9 (emphasis added).

In 1996, Congress amended § 1782(a) to clarify that the statute covers "criminal investigations conducted before formal accusation." See § 1342(b), 110 Stat. 486 [.] Nothing suggests that this amendment was an endeavor to rein in, rather than to confirm, by way of example, the broad range of discovery authorized in 1964. See S. Rep. No. 1580, at 7 ("[T]he [district] court[s] have discretion to grant assistance when proceedings are pending before investigating magistrates in foreign countries.").

In short, we reject the view, * * * that § 1782 comes into play only when adjudicative proceedings are "pending" or "imminent." Instead, we hold that § 1782(a) requires only that a dispositive ruling by the Commission, reviewable by the European courts, be within reasonable contemplation. * * *

D

We take up next the foreign-discoverability rule on which lower courts have divided: Does § 1782(a) categorically bar a district court from ordering production of documents when the foreign tribunal or the "interested person" would not be able to obtain the documents if they were located in the foreign jurisdiction?

We note at the outset, and count it significant, that § 1782(a) expressly shields privileged material: "A person may not be compelled to give his testimony or statement or to produce a document or other thing in violation of any legally applicable privilege." Beyond shielding material safeguarded by an applicable privilege, however, nothing in the text of § 1782 limits a district court's production-order authority to materials that could be discovered in the foreign jurisdiction if the materials were located there. "If Congress had intended to impose such a sweeping restriction on the district court's discretion, at a time when it was enacting liberalizing amendments to the statute, it would have included statutory language to that effect." *In re Application of Gianoli Aldunate*, 3 F.3d 54, 59 (CA2 1993) [.] * * *

Nor does § 1782(a)'s legislative history suggest that Congress intended to impose a blanket foreign-discoverability rule on the provision of assistance under § 1782(a). The Senate Report observes in this regard that § 1782(a) "leaves the issuance of an appropriate order to the discretion of the court which, in proper cases, may refuse to issue an order or may impose conditions it deems desirable." S. Rep. No. 1580, at 7.

Intel raises two policy concerns in support of a foreign-discoverability limitation on § 1782(a) aid—avoiding offense to foreign governments, and maintaining parity between litigants. * * * While comity and parity concerns may be important as touchstones for a district court's exercise of discretion in particular cases, they do not permit our insertion of a generally applicable foreign-discoverability rule into the text of § 1782(a).

We question whether foreign governments would in fact be offended by a domestic prescription permitting, but not requiring, judicial assistance. A foreign nation may limit discovery within its domain for reasons peculiar to its own legal practices, culture, or traditions—reasons that do not necessarily signal objection to aid from United States federal courts. * * * A foreign tribunal's reluctance to order production of materials present in the United States similarly may signal no resistance to the receipt of evidence gathered pursuant to § 1782(a). See *South Carolina Ins. Co. v Assurantie Maatschappij "De Zeven Provincien" N.V.*, [1987] 1 App. Cas. 24 (House of Lords ruled that nondiscoverability under English law did not stand in the way of a litigant in English proceedings seeking assistance in the United States under § 1782). When the foreign tribunal would readily accept relevant information discovered in the United States, application of a foreign-discoverability rule would be senseless. The rule in that situation would serve only to thwart § 1782(a)'s objective to assist foreign tribunals in obtaining relevant information that the tribunals may find useful but, for reasons having no bearing on international comity, they cannot obtain under their own laws.

Concerns about maintaining parity among adversaries in litigation likewise do not provide a sound basis for a cross-the-board foreign-discoverability rule. When information is sought by an "interested person," a district court could condition relief upon that person's reciprocal exchange of information. * * * Moreover, the foreign tribunal can place conditions on its acceptance of the information to maintain whatever measure of parity it concludes is appropriate. See *In re Application of Euromepa, S.A.*, 51 F.3d 1095, 1101 n.14 (2d Cir. 1995).

We also reject Intel's suggestion that a § 1782(a) applicant must show that United States law would allow discovery in domestic litigation analogous to the foreign proceeding. * * * Section 1782 is a provision for assistance to tribunals abroad. It does not direct United States courts to engage in comparative analysis to determine whether analogous proceedings exist here. Comparisons of that order can be fraught with danger. For example, we have in the United States no close analogue to the European Commission regime under which AMD is not free to mount its own case in the Court of First Instance or the European Court of Justice, but can participate only as complainant, an "interested person," in Commission-steered proceedings. * * *

IV

As earlier emphasized, * * * a district court is not required to grant a § 1782(a) discovery application simply because it has the authority to do so. * * * We note below factors that bear consideration in ruling on a § 1782(a) request.

First, when the person from whom discovery is sought is a participant in the foreign proceeding (as Intel is here), the need for § 1782(a) aid generally is not as apparent as it ordinarily is when evidence is sought from a nonparticipant in the matter arising abroad. A foreign tribunal has jurisdiction over those appearing before it, and can itself order them to produce evidence. * * * In contrast, nonparticipants in the foreign proceeding may be outside the foreign tribunal's jurisdictional reach; hence, their evidence, available in the United States, may be unobtainable absent § 1782(a) aid.

Second, as the 1964 Senate Report suggests, a court presented with a § 1782(a) request may take into account the nature of the foreign tribunal, the character of the proceedings underway abroad, and the receptivity of the foreign government or the court or agency abroad to U.S. federal-court judicial assistance. See S. Rep. No. 1580, at 7. Further, the grounds Intel urged for categorical limitations on § 1782(a)'s scope may be relevant in determining whether a discovery order should be granted in a particular case. Specifically, a district court could consider whether the § 1782(a) request conceals an attempt to circumvent foreign proof-gathering restrictions or other policies of a foreign country or the United States. Also, unduly intrusive or burdensome requests may be rejected or trimmed. * * *

Intel maintains that, if we do not accept the categorical limitations it proposes, then, at least, we should exercise our supervisory authority to adopt rules barring § 1782(a) discovery here. * * * We decline, at this juncture, to adopt supervisory rules. Any such endeavor at least should await further experience with § 1782(a) applications in the lower courts. The European Commission has stated in *amicus curiae* briefs to this Court that it does not need or want the District Court's assistance. It is not altogether clear, however, whether the Commission, which may itself invoke § 1782(a) aid, means to say "never" or "hardly ever" to judicial assistance from United States courts. Nor do we know whether the European Commission's views on § 1782(a)'s utility are widely shared in the international community by entities with similarly blended adjudicative and prosecutorial functions.

Several facets of this case remain largely unexplored. Intel and its *amici* have expressed concerns that AMD's application, if granted in any part, may yield disclosure of confidential information, encourage "fishing expeditions," and undermine the European Commission's Leniency Program. Yet no one has suggested that AMD's complaint to the Commission is pretextual. Nor has it been shown that § 1782(a)'s preservation of legally applicable privileges, and the controls on discovery available to the District Court, see, e.g., Fed. Rule Civ. Proc. 26(b)(2) and (c), would be ineffective to prevent discovery of Intel's business secrets and other confidential information.

On the merits, this case bears closer scrutiny than it has received to date. Having held that § 1782(a) authorizes, but does not require, discovery assistance, we leave it to the courts below to assure an airing adequate to determine what, if any, assistance is appropriate. [Affirmed.]

JUSTICE O'CONNOR took no part in the consideration or decision of this case.

JUSTICE SCALIA, concurring in the judgment. [Omitted.]

JUSTICE BREYER, dissenting.

The Court reads the scope of 28 U.S.C. § 1782 to extend beyond what I believe Congress might reasonably have intended. Some countries allow a private citizen to ask a court to review a criminal prosecutor's decision not to prosecute. On the majority's reading, that foreign private citizen could ask an American court to help the citizen obtain information, even if the foreign prosecutor were indifferent or unreceptive. Many countries allow court review of decisions made by any of a wide variety of nonprosecutorial, nonadjudicative bodies. On the majority's reading, a British developer, hoping to persuade the British Housing Corporation to grant it funding to build a low-income housing development, could ask an American court to demand that an American firm produce information designed to help the developer obtain the British grant. * * * This case itself suggests that an American firm, hoping to obtain information from a competitor, might file an antitrust complaint with the European antitrust authorities, thereby opening up the possibility of broad American discovery—contrary to the antitrust authorities' desires.

One might ask why it is wrong to read the statute as permitting the use of America's court processes to obtain information in such circumstances. One might also ask why American courts should not deal *case by case* with any problems of the sort mentioned. The answer to both of these questions is that discovery and discovery-related judicial proceedings take time, they are expensive, and cost and delay, or threats of cost and delay, can themselves force parties to settle underlying disputes. * * * To the extent that expensive, time-consuming battles about discovery proliferate, they deflect the attention of foreign authorities from other matters those authorities consider more important; they can lead to results contrary to those that foreign authorities desire; and they can promote disharmony among national and international authorities, rather than the harmony that § 1782 seeks to achieve. They also use up domestic judicial resources and crowd our dockets.

    * * *

I respectfully dissent from the Court's contrary determination.

NOTES AND QUESTIONS FOR DISCUSSION

1. Is *Intel*'s reading of § 1782 a fair one? Or is it, as Justice Breyer asks, one that Congress did not likely intend? Consider the possibility, as a matter of statutory interpretation, that Congress should be presumed to desire to have its statutes construed in a manner that would promote harmonious international relations. Is there sufficient ambiguity in the statute to allow such a presumption to operate? However one answers that question, the ball is now in Congress's court. Should it amend § 1782?

2. In his dissent, Justice Breyer suggested the creation of two "categorical" exceptions to the discretion that would otherwise be available to the district courts under § 1782:

> First, when a foreign entity possesses few tribunal-like characteristics, so that the applicability of the statute's word "tribunal" is in serious doubt, then a court should pay close attention to the foreign entity's own view of its "tribunal"-like or non-"tribunal"-like status. By paying particular attention to the views of the very foreign nations that Congress sought to help, courts would better achieve Congress' basic cooperative objectives in enacting the statute. * * *

> Second, a court should not permit discovery where both of the following are true: (1) A private person seeking discovery would not be entitled to that discovery under foreign law, *and* (2) the discovery would not be available under domestic law in analogous circumstances. The

Federal Rules of Civil Procedure, for example, make only limited provisions for nonlitigants to obtain certain discovery. See Fed. Rule Civ. Proc. 27. The limitations contained in the Rules help to avoid discovery battles launched by firms simply seeking information from competitors. Where there is benefit in permitting such discovery, and the benefit outweighs the cost of allowing it, one would expect either domestic law or foreign law to authorize it. If, notwithstanding the fact that it would not be allowed under either domestic or foreign law, there is some special need for the discovery in a particular instance, one would expect to find foreign governmental or intergovernmental authorities making the case for that need. Where *none* of these circumstances is present, what benefit could offset the obvious costs to the competitor and to our courts? I cannot think of any.

542 U.S. at 269-70 (dissenting opinion). Are either of these limits desirable, and if so, why did the majority reject the possibility of such categorical limits? Justice Breyer also concluded that "application of either of these limiting principles would require dismissal of this discovery proceeding." Was he right about that? For a critique of *Intel*, see, e.g., Marat A. Massen, Note, *Discovery for Foreign Proceedings After* Intel v. Advanced Micro Devices: *A Critical Analysis of 28 U.S.C. § 1782 Jurisprudence*, 83 S. Cal. L. Rev. 875, 915-25 (2010).

3. The opinion in *Intel* leaves it open to the district court whether to order the discovery there requested. On remand, how should that discretion be exercised? Note that the majority suggests that Justice Breyer's concerns (which he would have made into categorical restrictions on the exercise of discretion) would nevertheless be relevant to the exercise of discretion under § 1782. If so, did the *Intel* Court accomplish much, insofar as a district court could reject discovery for the very reasons Justice Breyer would have them reject it—provided the district court is careful to say that they are exercising their discretion (rather than interpreting a limitation in the statute)?

4. In light of question #3, consider the reasoning of the following (pre-*Intel*) decision on the question of the proper exercise of discretion under § 1782:

In re Application for an Order Permitting Metallgesellschaft AG to take Discovery

United States Court of Appeals, Second Circuit, 1997.
121 F.3d 77.

WALKER, CIRCUIT JUDGE.

Metallgesellschaft AG ("MG"), a German industrial and trading company, appeals from a final judgment of the United States District Court for the Southern District of New York (Thomas P. Griesa, Chief Judge), denying MG's application to compel discovery from Siegfried Hodapp pursuant to 28 U.S.C. § 1782(a) and vacating a prior subpoena issued by the same court ordering discovery in aid of a foreign proceeding. We agree with MG that the district court abused its discretion in refusing discovery. We reverse and remand.

I. BACKGROUND

MG applied for discovery pursuant to 28 U.S.C. § 1782(a) from Hodapp, a New York resident and the former president of MG's principal subsidiary in the United States. Hodapp is suing MG in the Labor Court ("Arbeitsgericht") in Frankfurt, Germany, for breach of his employment contract with MG alleging that MG failed to pay severance remuneration during an 18-month period following his dismissal by the company. In response, MG has asserted that Hodapp has forfeited his right to such compensation under German law because he was in commercial competition with MG during the period following his dismissal. It was discovery relevant to this defense that MG sought pursuant to 28 U.S.C. § 1782(a). On March 25, 1997, the district court granted MG's application.

On April 9, 1997, the date for Hodapp's deposition and document production, Hodapp refused to testify or to produce documents, claiming a privilege under German law. MG promptly moved to compel Hodapp's compliance with the court's order, and on April 10, 1997, the district court heard the parties' arguments in chambers. Later that day, the district court vacated its formerly-issued subpoena for reasons stated on the record. The district court was of the view (1) that, generally speaking, it was preferable for discovery issues to be raised and resolved before the foreign tribunal in which the action was pending and (2) that the information sought by MG would not have been available to it had it been sought from the German court. The court also noted that the parties were scheduled to appear before the German Labor Court on April 18, 1997, where the matter could be raised for the foreign tribunal's consideration. MG appeals from the dismissal of its § 1782(a) application.

II. DISCUSSION

* * *

Under § 1782, once the statutory requirements are met, a district court is free to grant discovery in its discretion. * * * The parties do not dispute that the statutory requirements of § 1782 are satisfied [.] The only open question is whether the district court abused its discretion in denying discovery.

The permissive language of § 1782 vests district courts with discretion to grant, limit, or deny discovery. However, on several occasions recently, we have circumscribed that discretion. * * * Underlying these decisions is our view that district courts must exercise their discretion under § 1782 in light of the twin aims of the statute: "providing efficient means of assistance to participants in international litigation in our federal courts and encouraging foreign countries by example to provide similar means of assistance to our courts . . . . " * * * In stating its views, the district court did not advert to these objectives, explicitly or implicitly, and in fact the reasons the court did give were at odds with these goals. Specifically, the district court remarked:

> I have decided to not order the discovery here and I have decided to vacate the subpoena because I believe, on balance, this kind of discovery would not be afforded at this juncture in the German court if the matter

were before the German court. I also believe that it is better to have these discovery issues come up on the 18th of April in the German court and be decided by the German court.

We have rejected any requirement that evidence sought in the United States pursuant to § 1782(a) be discoverable under the laws of the foreign country that is the locus of the underlying proceeding. * * * Similarly, we have held that a district court may not refuse a request for discovery pursuant to § 1782 because a foreign tribunal has not yet had the opportunity to consider the discovery request. * * * The district court abused its discretion by imposing such extra-statutory requirements and, as noted, by failing to take into consideration the twin aims of the statute in reaching its decision.

Hodapp contends that the district court acted properly in considering the foreign discoverability of the material sought in exercising its discretion. In doing so, Hodapp relies on language in [*In re Application of Gianoli*, 3 F.3d 54, 60 (2d Cir. 1993)] where we observed that "district judges may well find that in appropriate cases a determination of discoverability under the laws of the foreign jurisdiction is a useful tool in the exercise of discretion under section 1782." However, this language was not meant to authorize denial of discovery pursuant to § 1782 solely because such discovery is unavailable in the foreign court, but simply to allow consideration of foreign discoverability (along with many other factors) when it might otherwise be relevant to the § 1782 application. For example, if it were clear that discovery were equally available in both foreign and domestic jurisdictions, a district court might rely on this evidence to conclude that the § 1782 application was duplicative, see Fed.R.Civ.P. 26(b)(2), or was brought vexatiously, see *In re* Request for Assistance from Ministry of Legal Affairs of Trinidad and Tobago, 848 F.2d 1151, 1156 (11th Cir. 1988) (noting that "[i]f the judge . . . suspects that the [§ 1782 discovery] request is a 'fishing expedition' or a vehicle for harassment, the district court should deny the request").

In the present case, however, the district court considered discoverability under foreign law as more than merely, * * * a "useful tool[;]" it was the beginning and end of the inquiry. As we [have previously] declared: foreign discoverability cannot be used, consistent with the language and purpose of § 1782, as such a blunt instrument.

Moreover, even if the district court were animated by a concern that permitting discovery in this jurisdiction would alter the balance created by the procedural rules of the German court, recently, we have made the point that although American-style discovery for one party may skew foreign litigation, "it is far preferable for a district court to reconcile whatever misgivings it may have about the impact of its participation in the foreign litigation by issuing a closely tailored discovery order rather than by simply denying relief outright." *In re* Application of Euromepa, S.A., 51 F.3d 1095, 1101 (2d Cir. 1995). The district court did not follow this guidance. Instead of tailoring discovery pursuant to its authority under Fed. R. Civ. P. 26 or imposing reciprocal discovery obligations, the district court denied discovery outright.

We can understand how a district court might conclude, almost instinctively, that "it is better to have these discovery issues come up on the 18th of April in the German court and be decided be the German court." After all, that foreign tribunal has the greatest interest in the case. However, through § 1782 Congress has seen fit to authorize discovery which, in some cases, would not be available in foreign jurisdictions, as a means of improving assistance by our courts to participants in international litigation and encouraging foreign countries by example to provide similar means of assistance to our courts. If district courts were free to refuse discovery based upon its unavailability in a foreign court or because the foreign court had not first passed on the discoverability of the material sought, § 1782 would be irrelevant to much international litigation, frustrating its underlying purposes.

Hodapp also argues at some length that the district court was required to deny discovery because, under § 1782(a), "[a] person may not be compelled to give his testimony or statement or to produce a document or other thing in violation of any legally applicable privilege." This argument is unavailing because—contrary to Hodapp's assertion—the district court did not base its decision on the existence of a privilege under German law. The court made no mention of the matter. Anyway, as is evident from the parties' briefs and oral argument, whether such a privilege exists under German law is far from clear. To require the district court to determine such an issue would involve it in a "speculative foray[] into legal territories unfamiliar to federal judges." * * * Such a foray would result in "'an unduly expensive and time-consuming fight about foreign law,'" * * * undermining the twin aims of the statute. Thus, absent "authoritative proof that a foreign tribunal would reject the evidence obtained with the aid of section 1782," *Euromepa*, 51 F.3d at 1100—in this instance presumably because of a violation of the alleged privilege—a district court should not refrain from granting the assistance afforded under the Act based simply on allegations to that effect.

No such "authoritative proof" was forthcoming, notwithstanding Hodapp's opportunity to request a ruling from the Labor Court in Frankfurt at the April 18th hearing. * * * In the face of this inaction, we will not speculate—particularly on the basis of an ambiguous affidavit submitted by Hodapp's German counsel—whether Hodapp enjoys a privilege under German law entitling him to refuse to comply with a discovery order under § 1782.

III. CONCLUSION

We have considered Hodapp's remaining arguments and find them to be without merit. For the foregoing reasons, we *reverse* the judgment of the district court and *remand* for proceedings not inconsistent with this opinion.

NOTES AND QUESTIONS FOR DISCUSSION

1. Clearly, if the district court in *Metallgesellschaft* meant to hold that it could not allow the requested discovery as a matter of § 1782, simply because such discovery would not have been allowed in the foreign tribunal, it was in error after *Intel*. But as the *Intel* Court notes, it would not be irrelevant to the exercise of the district court's discretion under § 1782 that a foreign court would not allow the particular discovery. And note further that the question of the propriety of a particular exercise of discretion by a district court under § 1782—which was all that was at issue in *Metallgesellcshaft*—was a question with which the Supreme Court in *Intel* did not purport to deal.

2. In the course of its opinion, the Second Circuit stated that it had, in the past, circumscribed the discretion of the district courts in connection with requests under § 1782. See, e.g., Euromepa S.A. v. R. Esmerian, Inc., 51 F.3d 1095, 1099-1100 (2d Cir. 1995); *In re* Application of Gianoli, 3 F.3d 54, 58-60 (2d Cir. 1993); *In re* Application of Malev Hungarian Airlines, 964 F.2d 97, 100-01 (2d Cir. 1992). Those decisions, like *Metallgesellschaft* itself, were rendered prior to *Intel*. Do they survive *Intel*? Or does the Second Circuit's "circumscrib[ing]" of discretion look too much like the categorical exceptions brought up by Justice Breyer in his *Intel* dissent (and which the majority rejected)?

3. If discovery orders pursuant to § 1782 are discretionary, what kind of additional factors should inform the trial court's decision to grant or deny a particular request? Presumably, these discretionary factors include the two categorical exceptions articulated by Justice Breyer in his *Intel* dissent (so long as they are not mandatory). But what else? For an interesting example of a court that denied the request, even though all requirements of the statute were met, see *In re* Application of Schmitz, 259 F. Supp. 2d 294 (S.D.N.Y. 2003).

4. The Second Circuit in *Metallgesellschaft* seemed unimpressed by the argument that questions of privilege were presented and demanded a very strong showing that such might be the case before the court would exercise its discretion in a manner that denied discovery. Should it be considered an abuse of discretion to err on the side of caution in such circumstances (and deny discovery), given the potentially irreparable harm to individual rights that might be involved in erroneous disclosure of privileged information as well as the interests of foreign tribunals?

5. Finally, note that one of the goals of § 1782 is to encourage other countries, by our own example, to render similar assistance in connection with discovery in U.S. courts. After what you have learned about the way in which foreign legal systems tend to view American discovery requests, do you think that this goal can realistically be achieved by providing such unilateral assistance?

CHAPTER 7

International Litigation and Choice of Law

A. An Overview of American Choice of Law

Choice of law rules determine the law that will apply to a transaction that implicates more than one state or country. Absent an agreement between the parties respecting the applicable law, the relevant choice of law rules are those of the forum in which suit has been brought. A forum's choice of law rules, however, may point to the law of another jurisdiction or to its own law. Indeed, as discussed in this chapter, even when the parties have contractually chosen the relevant law, the forum's choice of law rules may speak to the question whether the choice of law clause is enforceable.

When a suit is tried in a court in the U.S., the relevant choice of law rules are usually state law—i.e., the choice of law rules of the forum state in which suit has been brought. That is true in the purely domestic (U.S.) setting involving U.S. parties and U.S. events, but it is also true even when the underlying suit implicates foreign parties or foreign events. That is because there is no general federal choice of law statute telling states what their choice of law rules must be, even though Congress may have the power to enact such a statute. Consequently, for a case not arising under federal law, state law choice of law rules will determine which state or country's law to apply in a transaction implicating more than one state or country. Moreover, as discussed later in this chapter, even if a case is brought in a federal court, the choice of law rules of the state in which the federal court sits will ordinarily apply in cases not otherwise governed by federal law.

1. Traditional Choice of Law Rules

Over time, different U.S. states have developed different choice of law rules. Those rules also reflect the evolution of American choice of law methodologies over time. A number of states still adhere to what might be called "traditional" choice of law rules. Those rules—often associated with the Restatement (First) of the Conflict of Laws (1934), and its reporter, Professor Joseph Beale—tend to focus on isolating a specific act or event that will dictate the jurisdiction whose law will apply. For example, in tort cases, the law of the place of the injury ("lex loci delicti")—the last act necessary to create tort liability—will typically apply, even if that is different from the place where the wrongful act occurred. And in the contracts setting, the law of the place of the last act necessary to create a contract ("lex loci contractus")—such as place of acceptance—would typically apply. And in real property cases, the "situs" of the property would control. Traditional choice of law rules were sometimes called "jurisdiction selecting" rules because they tended to identify a single solitary jurisdiction whose law would apply depending on the location of some relevant last act.

Such rules were relatively predictable in run-of-the-mill cases. And to the extent that all states adhered to traditional choice of law rules, which they once did, interstate (and international) actors could generally predict whose law might apply to most transactions or events. Nevertheless, the traditional approach could produce awkward results in at least some cases. For example, in Alabama Great Southern Railway Co. v. Carroll, 97 Ala. 126, 11 So. 803 (1892), an Alabama railroad employee sued his Alabama employer in an Alabama court over an act of negligence that occurred in Alabama, where, under Alabama law, employees could sue their employers for their fellow employee's negligence. The injury, however, occurred in Mississippi which did not provide for employer liability for fellow employee negligence. Although Mississippi had very little interest in applying its law to this otherwise all-Alabama dispute, the result under traditional choice of law rules mechanically pointed to Mississippi.

In addition, under traditional choice of law rules, there might be some room for argument relating to issues of "characterization." Depending on how a transaction or event was characterized, different relevant last acts might be implicated, and thus, potentially different states' laws. For example, a suit between two spouses over injuries resulting from an automobile accident might be characterized as a tort suit, thus triggering the inter-spousal immunities laws (if any) of the place of the injury. On the other hand, the same suit might be characterized as one implicating family law or domestic relations, thus triggering the inter-spousal immunity law of the marital domicile, which might be different from that of the place of the injury. See, e.g., Haumschild v. Continental Cas. Co., 7 Wis.2d 130, 95 N.W.2d 814 (1959) (applying law of marital domicile rather than law of the place of the tort). Such characterization questions might produce good faith differences among states applying traditional choice of law rules. But result-oriented judges could manipulate such questions of characterization to choose the law that produced the desired (choice of law) outcome.

Similar room for argument could arise with respect to questions of "localization"—i.e., determining where the relevant last act occurred that created rights under tort law or contract law. To illustrate: In a breach of contract case, there might be a dispute over what sort of contract was at issue, and thus, a question as to where the last act occurred to create a contract (if any). According to the First Restatement, if the contract was an "informal unilateral contract," the place of contracting would be the place where the event took place that would make the contract binding—e.g., the offeree's acting in reliance on the offer. Id. § 323. On the other hand, if the contract was a "formal contract" that became effective on delivery, the place of contracting was where the delivery was made. Id. § 312. And depending on where that relevant last act occurred, the law of that state would be applicable to the contract. Of course, the forum court has to determine antecedently what sort of contract was at issue, and to do so, it might apply "general" contract principles, or perhaps its own contract law (even if it ultimately concludes that another state's contract law will apply to the contract). Again, such localization questions might produce good faith differences among states applying traditional choice of law rules. But result-oriented judges could manipulate such questions of characterization to choose the law that produced the desired (choice of law) outcome.

In addition, there could be a limited opportunity under traditional choice of law rules to avoid applying otherwise relevant law through invocation of the doctrine of "renvoi"—meaning: to send back. Usually, when courts look to foreign law, they look only to the "local" (or internal) law of the sister state jurisdiction whose law is chosen, rather than to their "whole law," which would include the sister state's choice of law rules as well. When renvoi is invoked by the forum court, however, the court looks not just to sister state law that the sister state might apply in a purely domestic setting—the usual practice when one state choses the law of another state—but looks to the whole law of the sister state, including the sister state's choice of law rules. Those rules, in turn, might look back, for example, to the law of the forum. However, application of renvoi was not frequent in traditional choice of law jurisdictions, although it was often applied, for example, in cases involving real property. Application of renvoi in such settings would enable the forum to decide the case the very same way the sister state would have decided it if it had heard it. Arguably, property cases called for such a heightened degree of uniformity of outcome in a way that other cases did not.

In routine cases, these traditional choice of law rules had predictable application in the domestic as well as the transnational setting. For example, if suit were brought in a First Restatement state over injuries arising out of an automobile accident in France, the courts of that state would likely apply French tort law. (In extreme cases, when the place of the tort was not a "civilized" country or had "no law that civilized countries would recognize as adequate," courts could look elsewhere for their rule of decision. See Cuba R.R. v. Crosby, 222 U.S. 473, 478-479 (1912) (Holmes, J.). Of course, it was also part of traditional choice of law rules that the forum could apply its own procedures, its own statute of limitations, and in some instances its own remedies, even when enforcing an out-of-state cause of action. Moreover, even in those jurisdictions that have abandoned the traditional choice of law rules, there remains considerable power in the forum to apply most of its own procedural and remedial rules.

Finally, it was possible for a First Restatement court to choose not to entertain the sister state (or foreign country) cause of action at all, if the court found that the foreign law to which its choice of law rules pointed would be repugnant to the forum's public policy. For example, a court would not have to enforce a gambling contract, if it thought that doing so would violate the forum's strong sense of public policy. Nevertheless, even though all law is the expression of a state's public policy, the public policy objection generally would not be triggered simply because the law of the sister state (or foreign country) was different from the law of the forum. See, e.g., Loucks v. Standard Oil Co. of New York, 224 N.Y. 99, 111, 120 N.E. 198, 201 (1918) ("We are not so provincial as to say that every solution of a problem is wrong because we deal with it otherwise at home."). Neither the Constitution's Full Faith and Credit Clause nor its implementing statute have been read to prohibit a state from asserting a bona fide public policy objection to enforcing sister state law in the first instance. And whatever obligation might exist for state courts to open their doors to sister state obligations as a matter of full faith and credit, neither the Clause nor its implementing statute applies when the issue is whether a state will close its doors to a claim arising under foreign country law. Consequently, a state court's choice whether to hear a foreign cause of action is ordinarily a question of "comity," entrusted to the discretion of the forum court. For a more detailed treatment of traditional choice of law rules (as well as the other approaches to choice of law discussed below), see Kermit Roosevelt, Conflict of Laws 3-32 (2011) (discussing "The Traditional Approach"); id at 33-107 (discussing "Modern Approaches").

2. Interest Analysis and the Conflicts Revolution

Nearly all states once adhered to traditional choice of law rules. Today, however, fewer than a dozen continue to do so, either in the area of torts, or contract, or both. Beginning in the 1950s and '60s, there was a revolution in American conflict of laws that saw the gradual abandonment of the traditional rules, particularly in the areas of tort and contract. Scholars criticized the traditional approach for being too mechanical and productive of odd results (as in *Alabama Great Southern, supra*). At the same time—and perhaps inconsistently—scholars also criticized the traditional approach as being too manipulable (as in *Haumschild, supra*), and thus not providing all the certainty that was supposed to be a virtue of the older approach. Critics urged instead that states assess the "interests" of the different jurisdictions in having their law apply in the particular case, rather than focusing exclusively on the place of the last relevant act.

One of the earliest courts to adopt a form of governmental interest analysis was the New York Court of Appeals in Babcock v. Jackson, 12 N.Y.2d 473, 191 N.E.2d 279 (1963). *Babcock* was itself a transnational case. There, two New Yorkers were involved in a single car accident while in Ontario, Canada on a weekend trip. Under Ontario law—the place of the tort—passenger-guests could not sue their driver-hosts for negligence because of Ontario's "guest statute"; under New York law there was no such impediment to suit. The purpose behind the guest statute may have been a concern that suits between guests and their hosts could be less than adversarial or even fraudulent, to the detriment of those who insured Ontario risks. Under New York tort law, guests could freely sue their hosts for negligence under ordinary negligence rules. The purpose of the latter rule—the usual rule of negligence—was to foster compensation to accident victims (especially New York victims) and to deter bad driving on New York roads. It is not as though New York was unconcerned about the potential for fraudulent litigation; it was just that it subordinated that concern to the other concerns of compensation and deterrence. If there was fraud, it could be policed on an ad hoc rather than categorical basis.

The guest-versus-host suit in *Babcock* was brought in a New York court and appealed to New York's highest court. Had the high court applied traditional choice of law rules, it would have applied the Ontario guest statute (as the law of the place of the tort), and denied recovery. But the court instead looked to the interests of the relevant jurisdictions in applying their law regarding guest recovery. It found that Ontario had little or no interest in applying its guest statute because there was no Ontario insured risk. On the other hand, New York had an interest in allowing recovery as between its co-domiciliaries under the ordinary rule of negligence. As a result, New York was the primary jurisdiction interested in having its law apply, and consequently, the court applied New York law allowing guests to sue their hosts. At the same time, the court indicated that the standard of care that would be applied in such a case would be that of Ontario. Here, Ontario had a regulatory interest in having its negligence law and standard of care apply to govern the behavior of parties on Ontario roads. At the same time, because the accident did not occur on New York roads, New York had no regulatory interest in applying its own law of negligence. The *Babcock* court's decision to apply New York law to some of the case, and Ontario law to some of the case is what is known as "dépeçage"—meaning: to carve up.

Over time, a handful of states began to adopt interest analysis at the expense of traditional choice of law rules. Perhaps the foremost advocate of interest analysis—Professor Brainerd Currie—would have called a case such as *Babcock* a "false conflict." In other words, only one state had any real interest in having its law respecting guest recovery apply. And in the setting of a false conflict, Currie would apply the law of the only interested sovereign. Currie viewed his approach as a form of statutory interpretation (even when the rule in question was a common law rule). And, under the purposivist approach to statutory interpretation in vogue at the time Currie wrote, the task of the court was to imagine whether the legislature would have wanted its law to apply, and therefore to inquire into the purposes underlying the respective states' laws to see if they were implicated on the facts of the particular case.

The problem for Currie and for interest analysis more generally was what to do when more than one state had an interest in having its law apply—a "true conflict." At first, Currie suggested that if the forum had any interest in applying its law it should do so, even if some other forum might also have an interest in applying its own law. Currie thought that courts (as opposed to legislatures) should not engage in balancing or the weighing of competing interests, and that for a forum to apply its own law in the event of a true conflict was somehow the natural thing to do and what the forum legislature would have wanted. In short, Currie would have a forum court apply sister state or foreign law only when the sister state or foreign country had an interest in having its law apply *and* the forum had none. Of course, solving true conflicts in favor of the forum created rather substantial opportunities for forum shopping, not just to secure a possibly more convenient forum, but one with the best law for the plaintiff.

Currie—and the courts that followed him—later relented somewhat, and concluded that perhaps a more moderate and restrained analysis of the forum's interest in applying its own law might indicate that the forum would not really want its law to apply after all. As a result, an interest analysis court could turn an apparent true conflict into a false conflict, such that the law of the only interested state could apply. See, e.g., Bernkrant v. Fowler, 55 Cal.2d 588, 360 P.2d 906 (1961). (Interestingly, doubts about whether a state would want to apply its law extraterritorially figured into this more moderate and restrained analysis, although interest analysis generally rejects the territorially based premises of the First Restatement.) Still later variants of interest analysis sought to ascertain, in the case of a potential true conflict, which state's interests would be more severely impaired if its law were not applied, and to apply that state's law. Bernhard v. Harrah's Club, 16 Cal.3d 313, 546 P.2d 719 (1976). This sort of "comparative impairment" analysis is a staple of choice of law analysis of California courts in tort cases—one of the few courts still to engage in what might be called a relatively pure form of interest analysis in the area of tort law. Nevertheless, even with these qualifications, it remains true that forum law stands a far greater chance of applying under interest analysis than would have been true under a traditional approach.

3. The Restatement (Second) of Conflict of Laws

Although only a few courts apply what might be called a pure form of interest analysis, interest analysis and its critiques of the traditional approach were influential in the American Law Institute's shaping of the Restatement (Second) of the Conflict of Laws (1971). The Restatement is something of an amalgam of traditional rules and the approach of interest analysis, and it has been adopted by a plurality of the states. The goal of the Second Restatement is generally to identify the state with the "most significant relationship" to the occurrence and the parties, and to apply that state's law. Moreover, the Restatement dictates that this inquiry should be made on an issue-by-issue basis. In identifying the state with the most significant relationship to a particular issue, the Restatement provides a multitude of factors for courts to consider in identifying that state. Indeed, for every case in which the forum legislature has not supplied a statutory choice of law rule (which it rarely has), courts must resort to the general "Choice of Law Principles" in § 6 of the Restatement to determine the state with the most significant relationship. Those principles are as follows:

 (a) The needs of the interstate and international systems;

 (b) The relevant policies of the forum;

 (c) The relevant policies of other interested states and the relative interests of those states in the determination of the particular issue;

 (d) The protection of justified expectations;

 (e) The basic policies underlying the particular field of law;

 (f) Certainty, predictability and uniformity of result; and

 (g) Ease in the determination and application of the law to be applied.

Note that factors (c), (d) and (e) effectively require a kind of interest analysis to be done, whereas the other factors were ones that interest analysis generally would not take into account, and which were most clearly advanced by traditional choice of law rules. Nevertheless, by turning away from the more mechanical and territorialist rules of the First Restatement, the Second Restatement embraces interest analysis and its case by case approach. On the other hand, it endorses what interest analysis does not, which is a kind of weighing or comparing of relative interests.

Complicating matters is the fact that in applying these general principles to determine the state with the most significant relationship, courts must "take[] into account" various "contacts" associated with particular causes of action. For example, under § 145(2), relevant contacts to be considered in tort cases include:

(a) The place where the injury occurred;

(b) The place where the conduct causing the injury occurred;

(c) The domicile, residence, nationality, place of incorporation and place of business of the parties; and

(d) The place where the relationship, if any, between the parties is centered.

Contract cases have their own list of "contacts" to consider. See id. at § 188. Unfortunately, the Second Restatement does not indicate exactly how such laundry lists of "contacts" should mesh with the laundry list of general "choice-of-law principles" under § 6. Rather, the Restatement merely says that such "contacts [are] to be taken into account in applying the principles of § 6 to determine the law applicable"—i.e., to determine the law of the state with the most significant relationship to the parties and the occurrence with respect to a particular issue. See id. at § 188(2). As a result, many complain that the Second Restatement is just a grab bag of factors that may lead a court to reach any result that it wishes. See, e.g., Douglas Laycock, *Equal Citizens of Equal and Territorial States: The Constitutional Foundations of Choice of Law*, 92 Colum. L. Rev. 249, 253 (1992) (referring to what the Second Restatement has produced as "mush").

Nevertheless, the Second Restatement also borrows from traditional rules in a number of areas by creating categorical presumptions for certain kinds of claims. Such presumptions have the potential to make the Second Restatement somewhat more predictable than it otherwise could be. For example, in a personal injury case, there is a presumption—consistent with traditional conflicts rules—that the law of the place of the injury will apply. Id. at § 146. And in a case of a contract for the rendition of services, there is a presumption that the law of the place where the services are to be performed will apply. See id. at § 196. But such presumptions are only presumptions, and the Second Restatement indicates that the presumptive law will not apply if "some other state has a more significant relationship under the principles stated in § 6 to the transaction and the parties." Id. So, the presumption itself is ultimately subject to the multifactor considerations of the Restatement, and that might mean that the presumption will ultimately have little or no weight. But some courts have seen the presumptions as more than a starting point or tie-breaker, and have indicated that the presumption should be considered a strong one. See, e.g., Townsend v. Sears, Roebuck & Co., 227 Ill.2d 147, 162, 879 N.E.2d 893, 902 (2007) ("[T]he

bench and bar have overemphasized the general sections of the Second Restatement of Conflict of Laws and have undervalued the specific presumptive
rules."). In so doing, many of the virtues of the traditional rules have been put
back into place. But not all causes of actions have such a presumption, and
there is disagreement over the force such presumptions ought to have. In any
event, the Second Restatement, despite its critics, is now the dominant approach
to choice of law in the U.S.

B. AMERICAN CHOICE OF LAW IN THE TRANSNATIONAL SETTING

We have offered this rather extensive introduction to American choice of
law practices because even in the transnational litigation setting, state courts
faced with questions of choice of law will ordinarily apply the general choice of
law methodology that they would apply in a purely domestic case. Indeed, as
discussed below, even if the parties have contractually agreed upon the law to be
applied to their transaction in the event of a dispute, the enforceability of such an
agreement will be determined by the ordinary choice of law rules of the forum.
Of course, the multifactored analysis of the Second Restatement has the flexibility to take international concerns into account, insofar as the systemic interests
associated with international civil litigation may be somewhat different than
those associated with purely domestic litigation.

In the decision that follows, a *federal* court was called upon to determine the
relevant tort law to be applied to an injury that occurred in an American-owned
hotel in Mexico. In such cases—i.e., in cases not governed by federal law—
federal courts are typically exercising jurisdiction under the rubric of diversity of
citizenship (or alienage diversity). And the choice of law rules that federal
courts apply in such cases are the choice of law rules that would be applied by
the state courts in the state in which the federal court sits. In Klaxon Co. v.
Stentor Electric Mfg. Co., 313 U.S. 487 (1941), the Supreme Court determined
that, just as federal courts were obligated to apply the substantive law of the
state in which they sit under the rule of Erie Railroad Co. v. Tompkins, 304 U.S.
64 (1938), they are obliged to apply the choice of law rules of the state in which
they sit as well. This meant, for example, that if a Texas state court, as a matter
of its own choice of law rules, would apply Florida law to a case before it, then a
federal court in Texas hearing the case must do the same. Although *Klaxon* has
been ably criticized on various grounds, its rule remains very much in place.
And *Klaxon* is no less applicable in international civil litigation. See Day &
Zimmerman, Inc. v. Challoner, 423 U.S. 3, 4 (1975) ("A federal court in a
diversity case is not free to engraft onto those state rules exceptions or
modifications which may commend themselves to the federal court, but which
have not commended themselves to the State in which the federal court sits.").
And if the Texas state court would apply English law to a transaction, the Texas
federal court must do likewise.

In short, in international civil litigation in which the underlying claim is not
governed by federal law, choice of law rules will not vary depending on whether
a case is brought in a state court of a particular state or a federal court in that

state. Of course, choice of law rules still differ from state to state, and federal courts will thus apply different choice of law rules from one another, depending on the state in which they sit. Consequently, the opportunities for law-shopping are not insignificant, even within the U.S. By contrast, when a case is governed by federal law—for example, by a federal statute—the choice of law analysis works differently, and is usually framed in terms of the extraterritorial scope of the statute. See Caleb Nelson, *State and Federal Models of the Interaction between Statutes and Unwritten Law*, 80 U. Chi. L. Rev. (forthcoming, 2013). We discuss issues surrounding the extraterritorial application of federal statutes in Section F of this chapter.

Spinozzi v. ITT Sheraton Corp.

United States Court of Appeals, Seventh Circuit, 1999.
174 F.3d 842.

POSNER, CHIEF JUDGE.

Dr. Thomas Spinozzi, a dentist who lives and works in Illinois, and his wife Linda went to Acapulco on vacation. They stayed at a Sheraton hotel. Dr. Spinozzi fell into a maintenance pit on the hotel grounds and was seriously injured. He and his wife (the wife claiming loss of consortium) brought suit in a federal district court in Illinois, under the diversity jurisdiction, against the Mexican corporation that owns the hotel, and three affiliates of that corporation. The suit alleges negligence. It was dismissed on summary judgment. The district judge held that under Illinois conflict of laws principles, which of course bind him in this diversity suit, Klaxon v. Stentor Electric Mfg. Co., 313 U.S. 487 (1941), Mexican law governs the substantive issues; and that law, he concluded, bars the plaintiff's claims, mainly because it makes contributory negligence a complete defense to negligence liability and the uncontested facts showed that Dr. Spinozzi had been contributorily negligent. The Spinozzis' appeal challenges both the conflicts ruling—they contend that Illinois rather than Mexican tort law applies—and the ruling that Dr. Spinozzi was contributorily negligent as a matter of law.

The ownership structure of the Sheraton Acapulco Resort is complex, but to simplify the opinion we shall assume, favorably to the plaintiffs, that it is owned and operated by ITT Sheraton Corporation ("Sheraton"), a Delaware corporation with its principal place of business in Massachusetts, and forget the other defendants. Sheraton advertises its hotels all over the world, including Illinois, and it was in response to an advertisement in Illinois that the Spinozzis decided to stay at the Sheraton Acapulco. In fact, because Mrs. Spinozzi is a travel agent, Sheraton granted the Spinozzis a special rate to induce them to stay at the hotel. The plaintiffs argue that by its promotional activities in Illinois directed particularly to the small group (travel agents and their spouses) to which the Spinozzis belong, Sheraton should be taken to have "caused" in Illinois the injury to Dr. Spinozzi. And this injury-causing activity in Illinois, when taken in conjunction with the fact that the plaintiffs are Illinois residents, establishes (the plaintiffs argue) that the preponderance of "contacts" between the plaintiffs and either Illinois or Mexico was with Illinois, and not, as one might suppose from the location of the accident, with Mexico.

Under the *ancien régime* of conflict of laws, this argument would have been a nonstarter. The rule was simple: the law applicable to a tort suit was the law of the place where the tort occurred, more precisely the place where the last act, namely the plaintiff's injury, necessary to make the defendant's careless or otherwise wrongful behavior actually tortious, occurred, Restatement of Conflicts §§ 377-378 (1934); 2 Joseph H. Beale, A Treatise on the Conflict of Laws § 377.2, pp. 1287-88 (1935), and here that place was Mexico. This and other simple rules of conflict of laws came to seem too rigid, mainly because of such anomalies as suits between citizens of the same state when it was not the state where the accident had occurred. See, e.g., Babcock v. Jackson, 12 N.Y.2d 473, 191 N.E.2d 279 (1963). But the search for flexibility led, alas, to standards that were nebulous, such as the "most significant relationship" test of the Second Restatement that is orthodox in Illinois, Ingersoll v. Klein, 46 Ill.2d 42, 262 N.E.2d 593 (1970), and a number of other states. * * * [S]ee Restatement (Second) of Conflict of Laws § 145(1) (1971).

Often, however, the simple old rules can be glimpsed through modernity's fog, though spectrally thinned to presumptions—in the latest lingo, "default rules." For in the absence of unusual circumstances, the highest scorer on the "most significant relationship" test is—the place where the tort occurred. *Ingersoll v. Klein, supra*, 262 N.E.2d at 595; Ferguson v. Kasbohm, 131 Ill.App.3d 424, 475 N.E.2d 984, 987 (1985); Kuehn v. Childrens Hospital, 119 F.3d 1296, 1301 (7th Cir.1997); In re Air Crash Disaster Near Chicago, 644 F.2d 594, 611, 628-29 (7th Cir.1981); *Travelers Indemnity Co. v. Lake, supra*, 594 A.2d at 47; Pevoski v. Pevoski, 371 Mass. 358, 358 N.E.2d 416, 417 (1976); Restatement (Second) of Conflict of Laws, *supra*, § 145 comment e, § 146. For that is the place that has the greatest interest in striking a reasonable balance among safety, cost, and other factors pertinent to the design and administration of a system of tort law. Most people affected whether as victims or as injurers by accidents and other injury-causing events are residents of the jurisdiction in which the event takes place. So if law can be assumed to be generally responsive to the values and preferences of the people who live in the community that formulated the law, the law of the place of the accident can be expected to reflect the values and preferences of the people most likely to be involved in accidents—can be expected, in other words, to be responsive and responsible law, law that internalizes the costs and benefits of the people affected by it.

Only a tiny fraction of hotel guests in Mexico are from Illinois. Illinois residents may want a higher standard of care than the average hotel guest in Mexico, but to supplant Mexican by Illinois tort law would disserve the general welfare because it would mean that Mexican safety standards (insofar as they are influenced by tort suits) were being set by people having little stake in those standards. Of course the plaintiffs do not argue that Illinois tort law should govern all accidents in Mexican hotels. They argue for something that is even worse—that each guest be permitted to carry with him the tort law of his state or country, provided that he is staying in a hotel that had advertised there. The domicile of the hotel's owner would be irrelevant. If a French citizen were injured in a hotel in Mexico owned by a German corporation that had advertised in France, the law applicable to his suit against the German corporation would be French law. If in the course of a year citizens of a hundred different countries and U.S. states stayed at the Sheraton Acapulco Resort, Sheraton would be subject to a hundred different bodies of tort law. Inconsistent duties of care might be imposed. *Kuehn v. Childrens Hospital, supra*, 119 F.3d at 1302. A resort might have a system of firewalls that under the law of some states or nations might be considered essential to safety and in others might be considered a safety hazard. Suppose the resort burned down and dozens of injured guests sued: according to the plaintiffs' notion of conflict of laws, each claim would be governed by a different tort regime if each plaintiff was from a different state or country. If the regimes were incompatible, it might be impossible for Sheraton to escape liability to some of the plaintiffs no matter how careful it had been. Negligence would be strict liability.

Uniformity of tort law and consequent avoidance of anomalies cannot, we recognize, be achieved by an interpretation just of Illinois' conflict of law rules. Guests of the Sheraton Acapulco Resort who come from somewhere else and sue in their home court will be governed by the conflict of laws rules applied by that court, which may differ from Illinois. But there might be general agreement that the law of the place of the injury is presumptively the right law to apply to issues of duty of care, for the reasons that we have suggested. "[A] state may not exercise jurisdiction to prescribe law with respect to a person or activity having connections with another state when the exercise of such jurisdiction is unreasonable." Restatement (Third) of the Foreign Relations Law of the United States § 403(1) (1987). It is unreasonable that the Illinois courts should be setting safety standards for hotels in Mexico.

Sheraton could, it is true, include in all its contracts with its guests a forum-selection clause that would require the guest to sue in a jurisdiction in which lex loci delicti (the law of the place of the accident) was the default rule. Id., § 421 comment h; Carnival Cruise Lines, Inc. v. Shute, 499 U.S. 585, 593 (1991). It might, for that matter, specify the jurisdiction whose tort law would govern in the event of an accident; contractual choice of tort law provisions are generally enforceable. Chan v. Society Expeditions, Inc., 123 F.3d 1287, 1296-98 (9th Cir.1997); *Kuehn v. Childrens Hospital, supra*, 119 F.3d at 1301-02. Sheraton has followed neither course, and this undermines its claim to be concerned with being subjected to the different and even conflicting tort laws of dozens or hundreds of different jurisdictions. Id. at 1302. But that cannot be the end of the analysis. There is no rule that there shall be no conflict of laws analysis—that the law of the jurisdiction where the suit is brought (lex fori) shall apply—unless the parties could have negotiated a choice of law clause yet failed to do so. So we must forge on.

Whenever a legal claim, whether technically it is a contract claim or a tort claim, arises out of a voluntary relationship between injurer and victim, a court applying the Second Restatement's test should ask what body of law the parties would have expected to govern an accident arising out of that relationship. *Esser v. McIntyre*, 169 Ill.2d 292, 661 N.E.2d 1138, 1142 (1996); Restatement (2d) of Conflict of Laws, *supra*, § 6(2)(d) and comment g. (If the simple rules of the First Restatement were still in force, they would know!) We doubt that Dr. Spinozzi would have thought he was carrying his domiciliary law with him, like a turtle's house, to every foreign country he visited. To change the zoological metaphor, he would not, eating dinner with a Mexican in Acapulco, feel himself cocooned in Illinois law, like citizens of imperial states in the era of colonialism who were granted extraterritorial privileges in weak or dependent states. Law is largely territorial, and people have at least a vague intuition of this. They may feel safer in foreign hotels owned by American chains, but they do not feel that they are on American soil and governed by American law.

It would be different (though we cannot find a case on the point) if Sheraton had promised the Spinozzis a tort regime, in the event of an accident, that would be as favorable to them as Illinois tort law; or if it had induced them to stay at the Sheraton Acapulco Resort by representations concerning safety that might have led them to believe they would have the same legal protection in Mexico as in Illinois. No such representations are alleged. That is why the implication of the plaintiffs' position is, as their lawyer acknowledged at argument, that every foreign guest of a Mexican hotel is governed by his home country's tort law, provided only that the hotel was advertised in his country—the usual case, since it is hard to attract guests without advertising in the country where they live.

The plaintiffs emphasize that the growth in international travel and communications is shrinking the globe in a human sense. But the implication for conflict of laws is the opposite of what they think. It is not that the place of the accident is of diminishing relevance to the choice of law, but that it is of increasing relevance. For in the absence of a choice of law clause in the contract between the injurer and the victim, lex loci delicti is the only choice of law that won't impose potentially debilitating legal uncertainties on businesses that cater to a multinational clientele while selecting the rule of decision most likely to optimize safety.

The plaintiffs' backup position is that a defense of contributory negligence is repugnant to the public policy of Illinois, and therefore an Illinois court would not enforce that defense even if it would apply the rest of Mexico's tort law to an accident such as this. States do refuse to enforce foreign law that is particularly obnoxious to them. E.g., *Nelson v. Hix*, 122 Ill.2d 343, 522 N.E.2d 1214, 1218 (1988); *Lyons v. Turner Construction Co.*, 195 Ill.App.3d 36, 551 N.E.2d 1062, 1065 (1990); * * *. But obviously the mere fact that foreign and domestic law differ on some point is not enough to invoke the exception. Otherwise in every case of an actual conflict the court of the forum state would choose its own law; there would be no law of conflict of laws.

The danger of the public policy exception is provincialism: an inability to recognize that a different jurisdiction (especially a foreign country) need not be benighted to have a different approach to a particular legal problem. Recognizing this danger, the courts insist, as in the *Lyons* case, that application of foreign law yield an "evil or repugnant result" for the public policy exception to apply.

551 N.E.2d at 1065. In that case the Illinois legislature had declared the rule applied by another state "void as against public policy and wholly unenforceable," id., and the court took this as an authoritative declaration that the rule was indeed repugnant to the public policy of Illinois. *Nelson v. Hix, supra,* states the test this way: Illinois courts will not apply foreign law that is "clearly contrary to the public morals, natural justice or the general interest of the citizens of this State." 522 N.E.2d at 1218. The foreign law in that case was Canadian law permitting spouses to sue each other in tort, which Illinois law at the time forbade; the Illinois court applied the Canadian law.

Some years ago, by decision of its highest court, Illinois joined the accelerating trend toward replacing contributory negligence by comparative negligence, that is, reducing contributory negligence from a complete defense to a partial defense. Alvis v. Ribar, 85 Ill.2d 1, 421 N.E.2d 886 (1981). But it did not do so because it thought contributory negligence, like polygamous marriage, deeply offensive; it thought it outmoded and inferior to comparative negligence. It did use some strong language, calling it for example "repulsive," 421 N.E.2d at 895, but if it had really meant this, it would not have made its decision prospective only, as it did. * * * The Illinois courts have not had occasion to decide whether their preference for comparative over contributory negligence should override the different preference of the state whose law would normally govern the accident in question. Other jurisdictions have divided over the issue. * * *

We think it unlikely that Illinois would refuse to apply Mexican law in this case. When the rule of *Alvis* came to be codified, 735 ILCS 5/21116(c), the Illinois legislature curtailed it, retaining contributory negligence as a complete bar in all cases in which the victim is found to be more than 50 percent responsible for the accident. In light of this provision it is no surprise that the legislation is notably devoid of the "void as against public policy and wholly unenforceable" language that was decisive in *Lyons*. Granted, the statute in *Lyons* was intended to create a contract defense, but it could have made the contracts to which the defense applied merely voidable.

To apply the public policy exception to the issue of contributory negligence would be to pull on one thread in a complex legal tapestry, a problem that has been discussed extensively in relation to statutes of limitations. Walker v. Armco Steel Corp., 446 U.S. 740, 750-53 (1980); Board of Regents v. Tomanio, 446 U.S. 478, 485-86 (1980); Johnson v. Railway Express Agency, 421 U.S. 454, 464 (1975); * * *. A statute of limitations typically consists not only of a specified period of years but also of accrual and tolling rules (which are often common law grafts on the statute), and those rules are reciprocals of the length of the period. A short limitations period can be offset by generous accrual and tolling rules, and a long limitations period offset by miserly ones. *Walker,* which involved state accrual rules, is particularly pertinent because of the emphasis the Court placed on the inappropriateness under the *Erie* doctrine (itself a conflict of laws rule) of engrafting the forum state's accrual rules on the foreign state's limitations period. Negligence and contributory negligence bear much the same relation to each other as the specified length of the limitations period and the accrual and tolling rules that transform that fixed length into a varying standard.

A state or nation might decide to adopt a high standard of care for potential injurers but offset it by making victims' negligence a complete rather than merely partial defense.

Sometimes it is appropriate to apply the law of more than one jurisdiction, the procedure known in conflicts-speak as "dépeçage." *In re Air Crash Disaster Near Chicago, supra*, 644 F.2d at 611. But these are cases in which the issues to which the different laws are applied are separable, id. at 611 n.14—for example, capacity and damages, or negligence and a guest statute (as in *Babcock v. Jackson, supra*, 240 N.Y.S.2d 743, 191 N.E.2d at 285) designed to reduce fraud against insurers-rather than parts of an integrated liability standard, as here. It is especially questionable to take a piece of the standard from the common law and another piece from the civil law of a foreign country (Mexico is a civil law, not a common law, jurisdiction), and ask a jury to apply this unnatural hybrid to the facts.

[The court then concluded that summary judgment against Dr. Spinozzi was proper based on Mexican law.]

NOTES AND QUESTIONS FOR DISCUSSION

1. Did the *Spinozzi* court faithfully apply the Second Restatement? The Seventh Circuit was applying Illinois choice of law in a diversity case filed in Illinois, as called for by the decision in *Klaxon, supra*. The court starts with the Second Restatement's presumption in § 146 that the law of the place of the tort (lex loci delicti) will apply in a personal injury case, which in *Spinozzi* meant Mexican tort law. And the court then spends a lot of time explaining why that traditional rule makes sense. But did the court take the time to consider the other contacts that courts are to consider in tort cases under § 145(2)—set out above—in light of the multiple overarching choice of law principles in § 6? Didn't it arguably give close to conclusive weight to the lex loci presumption?

2. Whether or not *Spinozzi* was faithful to the Second Restatement, did the court nevertheless reach the right result? Obviously the result reached in *Spinozzi* would have been the same result that would have been reached under the traditional approach of the First Restatement, as the court is happy to note on more than one occasion. Consider whether the outcome would have been any different under a pure governmental interest analysis approach. Would Illinois have had no interest in applying its rule of contributory negligence?

3. To what extent did the foreignness of the tort matter to the *Spinozzi* court? The Second Restatement seems to suppose that its analysis is to be applied in cases that implicate transnational litigation as well as domestic litigation, insofar as the general choice of law considerations of § 6 specifically reference the needs of the "interstate and international system." Should a U.S. forum's choice of law rules take greater account of the fact that foreign law and not just sister state law is the law that is arguably relevant to a particular transaction?

4. The *Spinozzi* court reasons that the lex loci rule is efficient because variations in tort law across different peoples and geographical areas is itself efficient. The suggestion is that because "most" victims and injurers will be residents of the place of the tort, the law of the place of the tort can be expected to be "responsive to the values and preferences of the people who live in the community" and will best "internalize the costs and benefits of the people affected by it." Is this "comparative regulatory advantage" argument persuasive? Professors Goldsmith and Sykes express doubt whether tort rules will necessarily be responsive to the needs of their political communities in less developed counties in the same way as in highly developed countries. See Jack L. Goldsmith & Alan O. Sykes, *Lex Loci Delictus* [sic] *and Global Economic Welfare: Spinozzi v. ITT Sheraton Corp.*, 120 Harv. L. Rev. 1137, 1139-43 (2007). Instead, they argue that the lex loci rule is efficient for another reason: the advancement of global economic welfare. Absent such a rule, U.S. businesses will be at a competitive disadvantage in foreign countries because local businesses will not have to fear the added costs of American tort law (as will U.S. businesses). See id. at 1143-47 (stating that failure to follow the lex loci rule would amount to a "discriminatory tax on U.S. corporations that operate in foreign jurisdictions").

5. Consider *Spinozzi*'s argument for the lex loci rule based on party expectations. Even if the party-expectation rationale extends to the relevant standard of care—i.e., that of the place of the tort—does the rationale extend to such things as contributory negligence rules that allocate losses between parties but do not directly regulate behavior? Note that although the Second Restatement includes party expectations as a relevant factor, it actually suggests that party expectations might carry little weight in negligence cases, where "parties act without thought to the legal consequences of their conduct or the law that may be applied. In such situations, the parties have no justified expectations to protect . . . ." Restatement (Second) of Conflict of Laws, § 6, comment g. How does that language square with the considerable emphasis on party expectations in *Spinozzi* itself?

6. Who bears the burden of raising the applicability of foreign law and proving its content? It is apparently "hornbook law" that forum law will apply in the absence of a showing as to the content of foreign law, at least in a cases that appear to involve foreign law, and thus the burden is on the party who wishes to rely on foreign law to raise the point of its applicability and to prove its content. Peter Hay, et al., Conflict of Laws § 12.19 (5th ed. 2010) ("[W]here foreign law is not proved the court applies . . . local law.") (quoting an English treatise). But is that the right place to start? Sometimes it might be clear from the face of the plaintiff's complaint that forum law obviously does not apply and that foreign law does. For example, in a traditional choice of law jurisdiction, alleging a tort claim over a vehicular accident between two Americans that took place in Saudi Arabia would fairly suggest that forum law will not apply, as opposed to the law of the place of the tort. Cf. Walton v. Arabian American Oil Co., 233 F.2d 541 (2d Cir. 1956) (dismissing action when plaintiff ultimately failed to establish the content of Saudi law). In such a case, perhaps it makes sense that if the plaintiff wishes to have *forum* law apply, then the plaintiff should have the burden of persuading the court that foreign law should *not* apply, and failing that, to prove the content of foreign law in order to withstand a motion to dismiss for failure to state a claim. See Larry Kramer, *Interest Analysis and the Presumption of Fo-*

rum Law, 56 U. Chi. L. Rev. 1301 (1989). But often the applicability of non-forum law may not be easy to ascertain from the pleadings. In those sorts of cases, should there be a presumption that forum law applies unless and until the party who wishes to rely on foreign law raises the point and establishes its content? See Brainerd Currie, Selected Essays on the Conflict of Laws 9, 46-48 (1963) (arguing that this is the "normal and natural" thing for the forum to do). How persuasive is the argument for such a forum-law presumption more generally? Shouldn't such a presumption exist, if at all, only under a peculiar choice of law methodology that routinely defaults to forum law (such as Currie's)? Or can failure to raise or prove foreign law be seen an as implicit choice between the parties to have forum law apply?

7. In federal courts, under Rule 44.1, Fed. R. Civ. P., "A party who intends to raise an issue about a foreign country's law must give notice by a pleading or other writing." In ascertaining the content of foreign law, a court "may consider any relevant material or source, including testimony, whether or not submitted by a party or admissible under the Federal Rules of Evidence." Id. In addition, the court's determination of the content of foreign law "shall be treated as a ruling on a question of law." Formerly, such a determination was treated as a question of fact, and it still is in some states that have not adopted a variant of Rule 44.1. Reasonable notice does not require that the "precise content of foreign law" be specifically detailed, however, as opposed to generally informing the court and the opposing party of the law that is relevant to some or all of the claim or defense. See, e.g., Rationis Enterprises Inc. of Panama v. Hyundai Mipo Dockyard Co., Ltd., 426 F.3d 580, 586 (2d Cir. 2005). But reasonable notice means that it must generally be given pre-trial, for example in the pleadings or perhaps as late as summary judgment. See Hidden Brook Air, Inc. v. Thabet Aviation Int'l, Inc., 241 F. Supp. 2d 246, 277 (S.D.N.Y. 2002) (noting authorities). Noncompliance with Rule 44.1 has apparently been read as a waiver of the claim that foreign law should apply. See George A. Bermann, Transnational Litigation 258 (2003) (gathering authority).

8. From the perspective of foreign parties—particularly foreign party defendants—is it tolerable that there should potentially be 50 different choice of law regimes that might be applicable to a particular transaction or event that touches the U.S. or a U.S. party, depending on the state in which suit is ultimately brought? Or is this just one of the costs of our (American) federalism? Consider whether there might be an argument that when a case implicates either foreign parties or foreign transactions that are the subject of suit, the *Klaxon* rule should be inoperative, and that uniform federal choice of law rules should apply. If you find that possibility attractive, should the displacement of *Klaxon* in such cases be a task for Congress or the courts?

C. CONSTITUTIONAL LIMITS ON AMERICAN CHOICE OF LAW

States do not have unlimited ability to apply their own law, or the law of any particular jurisdiction. Starting in the late nineteenth century, the Supreme Court began to apply the Fourteenth Amendment's Due Process Clause to prohibit extraterritorial applications of forum state law. See James Y. Stern, Note, *Choice of Law, the Constitution, and* Lochner, 94 Va. L. Rev. 1509 (2008). And beginning in the twentieth century, the Court also began to apply the Full Faith and Credit Clause to compel states to apply sister state law in some cases. See, e.g., Bradford Elec. Light Co. v. Clapper, 286 U.S. 145 (1932). Interestingly, the problem of constitutional limits on choice of law does not seem to have presented much of a problem prior to this time, perhaps in part because traditional choice of law rules tended to conform to the idea that a sovereign's law could not apply extra-territorially. The Fourteenth Amendment's Due Process Clause, moreover, did not materialize until after the Civil War, and for the nation's first 100 years, there was very little suggestion that the unimplemented Full Faith and Credit Clause dictated the effect that the laws of one state would have in another. Moreover, unlike with sister-state judgments, Congress did not get around to implementing the constitutional requirement of full faith and credit to sister state laws until 1948.

In the international litigation setting, however, there is no full faith and credit obligation to apply foreign law in U.S. courts. Thus, Due Process alone provides a limit to the application of forum state law (or any jurisdiction's law) to a lawsuit that may implicate foreign parties or foreign events. But as discussed in the notes that follow the case below, the Supreme Court's current approach to the limits on the ability of a forum state to apply its own law as a matter of Due Process largely collapses into the Court's analysis of the limits imposed by the Full Faith and Credit Clause. Moreover, those limits have proved to be few and far between.

Home Insurance Co. v. Dick

Supreme Court of the United States, 1930.
281 U.S. 397.

MR. JUSTICE BRANDEIS delivered the opinion of the Court.

Dick, a citizen of Texas, brought this action in a court of that state against Compania General Anglo-Mexicana de Seguros S.A., a Mexican corporation, to recover on a policy of fire insurance for the total loss of a tug. Jurisdiction was asserted *in rem* through garnishment, by ancillary writs issued against the Home Insurance Company and Franklin Fire Insurance Company, which reinsured, by contracts with the Mexican corporation, parts of the risk which it had assumed. The garnishees are New York corporations. Upon them, service was effected by serving their local agents in Texas appointed pursuant to Texas statutes, which require the appointment of local agents by foreign corporations seeking permits to do business within the state.

The controversy here is wholly between Dick and the garnishees. The defendant has never been admitted to do business in Texas, has not done any business there, and has not authorized anyone to receive service of process or enter an appearance for it in this cause. It was cited [i.e., constructively served] by publication, in accordance with a Texas statute, attorneys were appointed for it by the trial court, and they filed on its behalf an answer which denied liability. But there is no contention that thereby jurisdiction *in personam* over it was acquired. Dick's claim is that, since the obligation of a reinsurer to pay the original insurer arises upon the happening of the loss, and is not conditional upon prior payment of the loss by the insurer, * * * the New York companies are indebted to the Mexican company, and these debts are subject to garnishment in a proceeding against the latter *quasi in rem,* even though it is not suable *in personam.* The garnishees concede that inability to sue the Mexican corporation in Texas *in personam* is not material if a cause of action against it existed at the time of garnishment and there was within the state a *res* belonging to it. But they deny the existence of the cause of action or of the *res.*

Their defense rests upon the following facts: this suit was not commenced till more than one year after the date of the loss. The policy provided:

> "It is understood and agreed that no judicial suit or demand shall be entered before any tribunal for the collection of any claim under this policy unless such suits or demands are filed within one year counted as from the date on which such damage occurs."

This provision was in accord with the Mexican law to which the policy was expressly made subject. It was issued by the Mexican company in Mexico to one Bonner, of Tampico, Mexico, and was there duly assigned to Dick prior to the loss. It covered the vessel only in certain Mexican waters. The premium was paid in Mexico, and the loss was "payable in the City of Mexico in current funds of the United States of Mexico, or their equivalent elsewhere." At the time the policy was issued, when it was assigned to him, and, until after the loss, Dick actually resided in Mexico, although his permanent residence was in Texas. The contracts of reinsurance were effected by correspondence between the Mexican company in Mexico and the New York companies in New York. Nothing thereunder was to be done, or was in fact done, in Texas.

In the trial court, the garnishees contended that, since the insurance contract was made and was to be performed in Mexico, and the one-year provision was valid by its laws, Dick's failure to sue within one year after accrual of the alleged cause of action was a complete defense to the suit on the policy; that this failure also relieved the garnishees of any obligation as reinsurers, the same defense being open to them, *New York state Marine Ins. Co. v. Protection Ins. Co.,* 1 Story, 458, 460, and that they consequently owed no debt to the Mexican company subject to garnishment. To this defense, Dick demurred on the ground that Article 5545 of the Texas Revised Civil Statutes (1925) provides:

> "No person, firm, corporation, association or combination of whatsoever kind shall enter into any stipulation, contract, or agreement, by reason whereof the time in which to sue thereon is limited to a shorter period than two years. And no stipulation, contract, or agreement for any such shorter limitation in which to sue shall ever be valid in this State."

The trial court sustained Dick's contention and entered judgment against the garnishees. On appeal, * * * and in the supreme court of the state * * *, the garnishees asserted that, as construed and applied, the Texas statute violated the due process clause of the Fourteenth Amendment and the contract clause. Both courts treated the policy provision as equivalent to a foreign statute of limitation; held that Article 5545 related to the remedy available in Texas courts; concluded that it was validly applicable to the case at bar, and affirmed the judgment of the trial court. The garnishees appealed to this Court on the ground that the statute, as construed and applied, violated their rights under the federal Constitution. Dick moved to dismiss the appeal for want of jurisdiction. * * *

First. [The Court concluded that the appeal was properly before it. In so doing, it rejected the argument that no federal question was presented because Texas was merely applying its forum statute of limitations—a purely procedural question of state law.] The statute is not simply one of limitation. It does not merely fix the time in which the aid of the Texas courts may be invoked. Nor does it govern only the remedies available in the Texas courts. It deals with the powers and capacities of persons and corporations. It expressly prohibits the making of certain contracts. As construed, it also directs the disregard in Texas of contractual rights and obligations wherever created and assumed, and it commands the enforcement of obligations in excess of those contracted for. Therefore, the objection that, as applied to contracts made and to be performed outside of Texas, the statute violates the federal Constitution raises federal questions of substance, and the existence of the federal claim is not disproved by saying that the statute, or the one-year provision in the policy, relates to the remedy and not to the substance. * * * The case is properly here on appeal. * * *

Second. The Texas statute as here construed and applied deprives the garnishees of property without due process of law. A state may, of course, prohibit and declare invalid the making of certain contracts within its borders. Ordinarily, it may prohibit performance within its borders, even of contracts validly made elsewhere, if they are required to be performed within the state and their performance would violate its laws. But, in the case at bar, nothing in any way relating to the policy sued on, or to the contracts of reinsurance, was ever done or required to be done in Texas. All acts relating to the making of the policy were done in Mexico. All in relation to the making of the contracts of reinsurance were done there or in New York. And likewise, all things in regard to performance were to be done outside of Texas. Neither the Texas laws nor the Texas courts were invoked for any purpose except by Dick in the bringing of this suit. The fact that Dick's permanent residence was in Texas is without significance. At all times here material, he was physically present and acting in Mexico. Texas was therefore without power to affect the terms of contracts so made. Its attempt to impose a greater obligation than that agreed upon and to seize property in payment of the imposed obligation violates the guaranty against deprivation of property without due process of law. * * *

The cases relied upon, in which it was held that a state may lengthen its statute of limitations, are not in point. * * * In those cases, the parties had not stipulated a time limit for the enforcement of their obligations. It is true that a state may extend the time within which suit may be brought in its own courts if, in doing so, it violates no agreement of the parties. And, in the absence of a contractual provision, the local statute of limitation may be applied to a right created in another jurisdiction even where the remedy in the latter is barred. In such cases, the rights and obligations of the parties are not varied. When, however, the parties have expressly agreed upon a time limit on their obligation, a statute which invalidates the agreement and directs enforcement of the contract after the time has expired increases their obligation and imposes a burden not contracted for.

It is true also that a state is not bound to provide remedies and procedure to suit the wishes of individual litigants. It may prescribe the kind of remedies to be available in its courts and dictate the practice and procedure to be followed in pursuing those remedies. Contractual provisions relating to these matters, even if valid where made, are often disregarded by the court of the forum, pursuant to statute or otherwise. But the Texas statute deals neither with the kind of remedy available nor with the mode in which it is to be pursued. It purports to create rights and obligations. It may not validly affect contracts which are neither made nor are to be performed in Texas.

Third. Dick urges that Article 5545 of the Texas law is a declaration of its public policy, and that a state may properly refuse to recognize foreign rights which violate its declared policy. Doubtless a state may prohibit the enjoyment by persons within its borders of rights acquired elsewhere which violate its laws or public policy, and, under some circumstances, it may refuse to aid in the enforcement of such rights. * * * But the Mexican corporation never was in Texas, and neither it nor the garnishees invoked the aid of the Texas courts or the Texas laws. The Mexican corporation was not before the court. The garnishees were brought in by compulsory process. Neither has asked favors. They ask only to be let alone. We need not consider how far the state may go in imposing restrictions on the conduct of its own residents, and of foreign corporations which have received permission to do business within its borders, or how far it may go in refusing to lend the aid of its courts to the enforcement of rights acquired outside its borders. It may not abrogate the rights of parties beyond its borders having no relation to anything done or to be done within them.

Fourth. Finally, it is urged that the federal Constitution does not require the states to recognize and protect rights derived from the laws of foreign countries—that as to them the full faith and credit clause has no application. *See Aetna Life Ins. Co. v. Tremblay,* 223 U. S. 185. The claims here asserted are not based upon the full faith and credit clause. * * * They rest upon the Fourteenth Amendment. Its protection extends to aliens. Moreover, the parties in interest here are American companies. The defense asserted is based on the provision of the policy and on their contracts of reinsurance. The courts of the state confused this defense with that based on the Mexican Code. They held that, even if the effect of the foreign statute was to extinguish the right, Dick's removal to Texas prior to the bar of the foreign statute removed the cause of action from Mexico, and subjected it to the Texas statute of limitation. And they applied the same rule to the provision in the policy. Whether or not that is a sufficient answer to the defense based on the foreign law we may not consider, for no issue under the full faith and credit clause was raised. But, in Texas, as elsewhere, the contract was subject to its own limitations.

Fifth. [The Court refused to consider the claim under the Contracts Clause, U.S. Const. art. I, §10, cl. 1, insofar as it found the state's action unconstitutional as a matter of Due Process.]

Reversed.

NOTES AND QUESTIONS FOR DISCUSSION

1. Exactly what in the text of the Fourteenth Amendment's Due Process Clause prohibits the application of Texas law to the Mexican contract in this case? ("No state shall . . . deprive any person of life, liberty, or property, without due process of law"). The linkage of the Due Process Clause with extraterritorial assertions of *judicial* jurisdiction had been cemented in the famous nineteenth century case of Pennoyer v. Neff, 95 U.S. 714 (1877). And late in that same century, due process limitations became linked to extraterritorial assertions of legislative jurisdiction. In Allgeyer v. Louisiana, 165 U.S. 578 (1897), for example, the Supreme Court held that Louisiana could not apply its statute outlawing a particular contract of insurance entered into by one of its citizens, when the contract was deemed to have been made in New York, where the contract was lawful. *Allgeyer* has achieved fame as one of the Supreme Court's early substantive due process/liberty of contract cases. But it was fundamentally a conflict of laws case, in which the Court concluded that the exercise of a state's legislative jurisdiction was impermissibly extraterritorial. But again, how does a limit on the extraterritorial exercise of legislative (or judicial) jurisdiction find a home in the Due Process Clause? See Kermit Roosevelt, Conflict of Laws 109 n.4 (2010); Michael G. Collins, *October Term 1896—Embracing Due Process*, 45 Am. J. Legal Hist. 71 (2001).

2. The Court's decision in *Home Insurance* is susceptible of more than one reading. On the one hand, it echoes the territorialist view of legislative jurisdiction described in Note 1, by suggesting that the application of Texas law to the dispute would be impermissibly extraterritorial. Certainly that was the approach of a number of the Court's post-*Allgeyer* due process cases that disabled states from applying their law to contracts lawfully entered into in another state. See, e.g., New York Life Ins. Co. v. Dodge, 246 U.S. 357 (1918); see generally Stern, *supra.* On the other hand, the decision also seems to focus on the contacts that Texas had to the litigation, suggesting perhaps that Texas might have been able to apply its law to this Mexican contract, had there been additional contacts. Cf. *Dodge,* 246 U.S. at 382 (Brandeis, J., dissenting) ("There is no constitutional limitation by virtue of which a statute enacted by a state in the exercise of its police power is necessarily void, if, in its operation, the contracts made in another state may be affected.").

3. The modern Court seems to have read *Home Insurance* in the second of the two ways just suggested—i.e., as a case in which a forum state attempted to apply its law, even though the forum lacked any meaningful contacts with the parties and the underlying events. In a series of New Deal era worker compensation cases, the Court shifted its focus away from Due Process toward the Full Faith and Credit Clause, and ultimately concluded that the Clause did not prevent states from applying their own law to the exclusion of sister state law, so long as it had an interest in doing so and the application of forum law was not unreasonable under the circumstances. Compare Pacific Employers Ins. Co. v. Indus. Acc. Comm'n, 306 U.S. 493 (1939) (indicating that it was not relevant that a sister-state might also have a legitimate interest in applying its law to the events in question), with Alaska Packers Ass'n v. Indus. Acc. Comm'n, 294 U.S. 532 (1935) (indicating that the Court's role in conflicts cases was to ascertain the state with the "greater" or "superior" "interest" in having its law apply). That essentially became the position of the modern Court, which concluded that the constitutional limits on state choice of law—as a matter of *both* due process and full faith and credit—required only that a state have "a significant contact or significant aggregation of contacts [with the parties and the occurrence or transaction], creating state interests, such that choice of its law is neither arbitrary nor fundamentally unfair." Allstate Ins. Co. v. Hague, 449 U.S. 302, 313 (1981). *Home Insurance* was treated as a case in which a state (Texas) had "only an insignificant contact with the parties and the occurrence or transaction"—i.e., the "nominal residence" of the plaintiff. Was that a fair characterization of *Home Insurance* or its facts?

4. *Hague*'s facts indicate how weak the Court's due process/full faith and credit inquiry really is. *Hague* was a purely domestic case, in which a Wisconsin insured was in a Wisconsin accident with another domiciliary of Wisconsin, in which the insured was killed. The insured worked across the border in Minnesota, but he was not in Minnesota at the time of the accident, nor going to or from work there. He had three insurance policies that he had purchased in Wisconsin from Allstate Insurance on three different vehicles of his, all garaged in Wisconsin. His widow, who remarried and moved to Minnesota after the accident, sought to "stack" all of her former spouse's policies in a suit that she brought against Allstate so that she could recover under the higher policy limits of all three added together—something that Minnesota law allowed and that Wisconsin law did not. The question was: Could the Minnesota courts constitutionally apply Minnesota's stacking law (which they did) to these events? Focusing on Minnesota's "contacts," a plurality of four Justices of the U.S. Supreme Court found (1) that because the insured was employed by a Minnesota employer, Minnesota had an interest in the "safety and well-being" of the insured; (2) that Allstate did business in Minnesota and could not be surprised by the application of Minnesota law if sued there; and (3) that Minnesota had an interest in maximal compensation to one of its residents "to keep her 'off welfare rolls' and able 'to meet financial obligations.'" Those contacts were sufficient for the plurality to uphold the application of Minnesota law, even though—as the dissent noted—the plurality failed to explain how Minnesota's interests under (1) and (2) were furthered by application of the stacking rule. (The dissent also argued that the post-event move to Minnesota (contact (3)) should not count as a relevant contact under the Court's earlier precedents.) A fifth Justice indicated that a state should be able to apply its own law "unless that choice threatens the federal interest in national unity," thus providing a majority for upholding the constitutionality of Minnesota's application of its stacking rule.

5. Insofar as *Hague* concludes that the test under due process is the same as that under full faith and credit, and because the test is so weak, it means that there will be few constitutional limits on states applying their own law in transnational litigation, as long as the state has some nexus to the parties or the events in question. Indeed, in only one post-*Hague* case has the Court rejected a state's application of its own law as violative of the Constitution. See Phillips Petroleum Co. v. Shutts, 472 U.S. 797 (1985). In *Shutts*, the Court held that Kansas could not apply its own rule of interest on delayed payments on oil and gas leases (in a nation-wide class action brought in a Kansas court), at least as to non-Kansas parties with non- Kansas leases. Importantly, in *Shutts*, the Court seemed to demand—unlike the plurality in *Hague*—that the forum state not simply have "interests" in the abstract as a precondition to applying its own law, but that those interests would actually be furthered by application of its law in the particular case.

6. Even though the Court in *Hague* and *Shutts* merged the tests for due process and full faith and credit—and turned both of them into a focus on contacts—is it possible that some contacts may be more relevant for due process purposes, and others for full faith and credit? For example, some contacts (or the lack thereof) might seem to be especially related to concerns of unfair surprise —a classic sort of due process concern. Other contacts seem to focus on the regulatory interest of a state in applying its own law, arguably more of a full faith and credit concern. To the extent that only due process and not full faith and credit is a limit on the application of forum law in the international setting, does that mean that only those contacts that relate to considerations such as unfair surprise should be relevant? Or should the contacts that bear on a state's regulatory interest in applying its own law—which, under the Court's analysis, seems to have migrated from due process to full faith and credit—still be a relevant part of the due process analysis, insofar as the Court now lumps them together?

7. Finally, note that in the personal jurisdiction context, the Supreme Court has considered foreignness of a party defendant to be a particular concern to its "fairness" analysis under due process, at least when minimum contacts are otherwise present. See Asahi Metal Indus. Co. Ltd. v. Superior Court, 480 U.S. 102 (1987) (discussed in Chapter 1). Does this suggest that when considering the limits that due process might impose on a state's choice of law in the transnational setting, the foreignness of the defendant should weigh in the balance in assessing the fairness of the application of law, and in a way that it might not for an out of state (U.S.) defendant?

D. INTERNATIONAL CHOICE OF LAW CLAUSES

The approach to choice of law (and the constitutional limits thereon) presented in Sections A-C, are operative in U.S. courts when there has been no agreement between the parties as to the law that will apply to their transaction in the event of a dispute. Parties to international contractual transactions, for example, will often prefer the greater certainty and predictability that a choice of law clause in the contract between them can provide. See Erin A. O'Hara and

Larry E. Ribstein, The Law Market 4-5 (2009). In this regard, the concerns are not unlike those that lead parties to contract for their preferred forum. See Chapter 1, Section I. Indeed, parties may wish to contract for both—for choice of forum as well as choice of law. Of course, the choice of law option is less likely to be available in connection with transactions in which the first meeting of the parties is the event over which suit is brought—such as a personal injury suit arising out of an automobile accident. But where the opportunity presents itself, the incentives to agree in advance on the applicable law are clear, especially when a given transaction may implicate more than one country and its laws.

Interestingly, the First Restatement of Conflicts was unfriendly to the enforcement of choice of law clauses that would oust the law that would otherwise apply to the contract under the law of the jurisdiction selected by the First Restatement's choice of law rules. The older view seems to have been that overriding the law that would otherwise be applicable under traditional choice of law rules was somehow a "legislative act" that private parties could not perform.

Nevertheless, even when traditional choice of law rules were dominant, courts found ways to enforce contractual agreements as to choice of law, particularly in the transnational setting. For example, in Siegelman v. Cunard White Star Ltd., 221 F.2d 189 (2d Cir. 1955), the court had before it a choice of law clause that designated English law in a passenger ticket for a transatlantic ocean voyage on board an English ocean liner for all claims arising out of the voyage. The question was whether a low level agent of the defendant shipping company could orally waive a condition in the ticket that limited a passenger's personal injury suits to a year from the date of the accident (and upon which oral waiver plaintiff relied to his detriment). If federal admiralty law applied to the contract, the waiver would be valid; if English law applied, the waiver would be invalid. The court noted (as a matter of choice of law rules under admiralty law) that it should be relatively easy to enforce the "parties' intention" to have a particular jurisdiction's law govern questions of the "interpretation of the contract." "Stipulating the governing law for this purpose is much like stipulating that words of the contract have the meanings given in a particular dictionary." Id. at 195. English law might therefore displace the default rule of interpretation that would otherwise apply under the federal courts' admiralty precedents. The court also noted, however, it might be more difficult for the parties to "stipulate the law by which the validity of their contract is to be judged" (and citing the First Restatement). Id. Although the court thought the question to be close, it found the issue of the agent's oral waiver of the contract's conditions to be "more closely akin to a question of validity." Id. Nevertheless, the court enforced the choice of law provision in the ticket and applied English law, meaning that the anti-waiver provision of the contract was upheld. The trial court's dismissal of the passenger's suit was therefore upheld, because suit was filed too late.

1. Validating and Interpreting Choice of Law Clauses

As *Siegelman* indicates, and despite a general sense that it might generally be desirable for parties to be able to choose the law applicable to their transaction, a choice of law provision in an agreement between parties is itself an agreement that must be validated by *some* law. The choice of law agreement in *Siegelman* was enforced because it complied with the court's assessment of what the choice of law rules of admiralty would allow—even if enforcing the choice of law clause would mean that English contract law would apply rather than the contract law as ordinarily applied by federal admiralty courts. A forum's choice of law rules are therefore still relevant in assessing the law to be applied to a choice of law clause to determine whether it ought to be enforced as a valid agreement.

Nedlloyd Lines B.V. v. Seawinds Ltd.

Supreme Court of California, 1992.

3 Cal.4th 459; 834 P.2d 1148.

BAXTER, J.

We granted review to consider the effect of a choice-of-law clause in a contract between commercial entities to finance and operate an international shipping business. In our order granting review, we limited our consideration to the question whether and to what extent the law of Hong Kong, chosen in the parties' agreement, should be applied in ruling on defendant's demurrer to plaintiff's complaint.

We conclude the choice-of-law clause, which requires that the contract be "governed by" the law of Hong Kong, a jurisdiction having a substantial connection with the parties, is fully enforceable and applicable to claims for breach of the implied covenant of good faith and fair dealing and for breach of fiduciary duties allegedly arising out of the contract. Our conclusion rests on the choice-of-law rules derived from California decisions and the Restatement Second of Conflict of Laws, which reflect strong policy considerations favoring the enforcement of freely negotiated choice-of-law clauses. Based on our conclusion, we will reverse the judgments of the Court of Appeal and remand for further proceedings.

STATEMENT OF FACTS AND PROCEEDINGS BELOW

Plaintiff and real party in interest Seawinds Limited (Seawinds) is a shipping company, currently undergoing reorganization under chapter 11 of the United States Bankruptcy Code, whose business consists of the operation of three container ships. Seawinds was incorporated in Hong Kong in late 1982 and has its principal place of business in Redwood City, California. Defendants and petitioners Nedlloyd Lines B.V., Royal Nedlloyd Group N.V., and KNSM Lines B.V. (collectively referred to as Nedlloyd) are interrelated shipping companies incorporated in the Netherlands with their principal place of business in Rotterdam.

In March 1983, Nedlloyd and other parties (including an Oregon corporation, a Hong Kong corporation, a British corporation, three individual residents of California, and a resident of Singapore) entered into a contract with Seawinds to purchase shares of Seawinds's stock. The contract, which was entitled

"Shareholders' Agreement in Respect of Seawinds Limited," stated that its purpose was "to establish [Seawinds] as a joint venture company to carry on a transportation operation." The agreement also provided that Seawinds would carry on the business of the transportation company and that the parties to the agreement would use "means reasonably available" to ensure the business was a success.

The shareholders' agreement between the parties contained the following choice-of-law and forum selection provision: "This agreement shall be governed by and construed in accordance with Hong Kong law and each party hereby irrevocably submits to the non-exclusive jurisdiction and service of process of the Hong Kong courts."

In January 1989, Seawinds sued Nedlloyd, alleging in essence that Nedlloyd breached express and implied obligations under the shareholders' agreement by: "(1) engaging in activities that led to the cancellation of charter hires that were essential to Seawinds' business; (2) attempting to interfere with a proposed joint service agreement between Seawinds and the East Asiatic Company, and delaying its implementation; (3) making and then reneging on commitments to contribute additional capital, thereby dissuading others from dealing with Seawinds, and (4) making false and disparaging statements about Seawinds' business operations and financial condition." Seawinds's original and first amended complaint included causes of action for breach of contract, breach of the implied covenant of good faith and fair dealing (in both contract and tort), and breach of fiduciary duty. This matter comes before us after trial court rulings on demurrers to Seawinds's complaints.

Nedlloyd demurred to Seawinds's original complaint on the grounds that it failed to state causes of action for breach of the implied covenant of good faith and fair dealing (either in contract or in tort) and breach of fiduciary duty. In support of its demurrer, Nedlloyd contended the shareholders' agreement required the application of Hong Kong law to Seawinds's claims. In opposition to the demurrer, Seawinds argued that California law should be applied to its causes of action. * * *

DISCUSSION

I. THE PROPER TEST

We have not previously considered the enforceability of a contractual choice-of-law provision.

We have, however, addressed the closely related issue of the enforceability of a contractual choice-of-forum provision, and we have made clear that, "No satisfying reason of public policy has been suggested why enforcement should be denied a forum selection clause appearing in a contract entered into freely and voluntarily by parties who have negotiated at arm's length." (*Smith, Valentino & Smith, Inc. v. Superior Court* (1976) 17 Cal.3d 491, 495-496 (*Smith*).) The forum selection provision in *Smith* was contained within a choice-of-law clause, and we observed that, "Such choice of law provisions are usually respected by California courts." We noted this result was consistent with the modern approach of section 187 of the Restatement Second of Conflict of Laws (Restatement). Prior Court of Appeal decisions, although not always explicitly referring to the Restatement, also overwhelmingly reflect the modern, mainstream approach adopted in the Restatement.

We reaffirm this approach. In determining the enforceability of arm's-length contractual choice-of-law provisions, California courts shall apply the principles set forth in Restatement section 187, which reflects a strong policy favoring enforcement of such provisions. * * *

[T]he proper approach under Restatement section 187, subdivision (2) is for the court first to determine either: (1) whether the chosen state has a substantial relationship to the parties or their transaction, or (2) whether there is any other reasonable basis for the parties' choice of law. If neither of these tests is met, that is the end of the inquiry, and the court need not enforce the parties' choice of law.[4] If, however, either test is met, the court must next determine whether the chosen state's law is contrary to a *fundamental* policy of California.[5] If there is no such conflict, the court shall enforce the parties' choice of law. If, however, there is a fundamental conflict with California law, the court must then determine whether California has a "materially greater interest than the chosen state in the determination of the particular issue . . . ." (Rest., § 187, subd. (2).) If California has a materially greater interest than the chosen state, the choice of law shall not be enforced, for the obvious reason that in such circumstance we will decline to enforce a law contrary to this state's fundamental policy.[6] We now apply the Restatement test to the facts of this case.

II. Application of the Test in this Case

* * *

B. *Implied covenant of good faith and fair dealing*

1. *Substantial relationship or reasonable basis*

As to the first required determination, Hong Kong—"the chosen state"—clearly has a "substantial relationship to the parties." (Rest., § 187, subd. (2)(a).)

---

[4] As noted above, a different result might obtain under Restatement section 187, subdivision (1), which appears to allow the parties *in some circumstances* to specify the law of a state that has no relation to the parties or their transaction. * * *

[5] To be more precise, we note that Restatement section 187, subdivision (2) refers not merely to the forum state—for example, California in the present case—but rather to the state ". . . which, under the rule of § 188, would be the state of the applicable law in the absence of an effective choice of law by the parties." For example, there may be an occasional case in which California is the forum, and the parties have chosen the law of another state, but the law of yet a third state, rather than California's, would apply absent the parties' choice. In that situation, a California court will look to the fundamental policy of the third state in determining whether to enforce the parties' choice of law. The present case is not such a situation.

[6] There may also be instances when the chosen state has a materially greater interest in the matter than does California, but enforcement of the law of the chosen state would lead to a result contrary to a fundamental policy of California. In some such cases, enforcement of the law of the chosen state may be appropriate despite California's policy to the contrary. (S. A. Empresa, etc. v. Boeing Co., 641 F.2d 746, 749 (9th Cir. 1981)). Careful consideration, however, of California's policy and the other state's interest would be required. No such question is present in this case, and we thus need not and do not decide how Restatement section 187 would apply in such circumstances.

The shareholders' agreement, which is incorporated by reference in Seawinds' first amended complaint, shows that Seawinds is incorporated under the laws of Hong Kong and has a registered office there. The same is true of one of the shareholder parties to the agreement—Red Coconut Trading Co. The incorporation of these parties in Hong Kong provides the required "substantial relationship." (*Id.*,) com. f [substantial relationship present when "one of the parties is domiciled" in the chosen state][.]

Moreover, the presence of two Hong Kong corporations as parties also provides a "reasonable basis" for a contractual provision requiring application of Hong Kong law. "If one of the parties resides in the chosen state, the parties have a reasonable basis for their choice." The reasonableness of choosing Hong Kong becomes manifest when the nature of the agreement before us is considered. A state of incorporation is certainly at least one government entity with a keen and intimate interest in internal corporate affairs, including the purchase and sale of its shares, as well as corporate management and operations. (See Corp. Code, § 102 [applying California's general corporation law to domestic corporations].)

2. *Existence of fundamental public policy*

We next consider whether application of the law chosen by the parties would be contrary to "a fundamental policy" of California. We perceive no fundamental policy of California requiring the application of California law to Seawinds's claims based on the implied covenant of good faith and fair dealing. The covenant is not a government regulatory policy designed to restrict freedom of contract, but an implied promise inserted in an agreement to carry out the presumed intentions of contracting parties. * * *

Seawinds directs us to no authority exalting the *implied* covenant of good faith and fair dealing over the *express* covenant of these parties that Hong Kong law shall govern their agreement. We have located none. Because Seawinds has identified no fundamental policy of our state at issue in its essentially contractual dispute with Nedlloyd, the second exception to the rule of section 187 of the Restatement does not apply.

C. *Fiduciary duty cause of action*

1. *Scope of the choice-of-law clause*

Seawinds contends that, whether or not the choice-of-law clause governs Seawinds's implied covenant claim, Seawinds's fiduciary duty claim is somehow independent of the shareholders' agreement and therefore outside the intended scope of the clause. Seawinds thus concludes California law must be applied to this claim. We disagree.

When two sophisticated, commercial entities agree to a choice-of-law clause like the one in this case, the most reasonable interpretation of their actions is that they intended for the clause to apply to all causes of action arising from or related to their contract. Initially, such an interpretation is supported by the plain meaning of the language used by the parties. The choice-of-law clause in the shareholders' agreement provides: "This agreement shall be *governed by* and construed in accordance with Hong Kong law and each party hereby irrevocably submits to the non-exclusive jurisdiction and service of process of the Hong Kong courts." (Italics added.)[7]

The phrase "governed by" is a broad one signifying a relationship of absolute direction, control, and restraint. Thus, the clause reflects the parties' clear contemplation that "the agreement" is to be completely and absolutely controlled by Hong Kong law. No exceptions are provided. In the context of this case, the agreement to be controlled by Hong Kong law is a shareholders' agreement that expressly provides for the purchase of shares in Seawinds by Nedlloyd and creates the relationship between shareholder and corporation that gives rise to Seawinds's cause of action. Nedlloyd's fiduciary duties, if any, arise from—and can exist only because of—the shareholders' agreement pursuant to which Seawinds's stock was purchased by Nedlloyd.

In order to control completely the agreement of the parties, Hong Kong law must also govern the stock purchase portion of that agreement and the legal duties created by or emanating from the stock purchase, including any fiduciary duties. If Hong Kong law were not applied to these duties, it would effectively control only part of the agreement, not all of it. Such an interpretation would be inconsistent with the unrestricted character of the choice-of-law clause.

Our conclusion in this regard comports with common sense and commercial reality. When a rational businessperson enters into an agreement establishing a transaction or relationship and provides that disputes arising from the agreement shall be governed by the law of an identified jurisdiction, the logical conclusion is that he or she intended that law to apply to *all* disputes arising out of the transaction or relationship. We seriously doubt that any rational businessperson, attempting to provide by contract for an efficient and business-like resolution of possible future disputes, would intend that the laws of multiple jurisdictions would apply to a single controversy having its origin in a single, contract-based relationship. Nor do we believe such a person would reasonably desire a protracted litigation battle concerning only the threshold question of what law was to be applied to which asserted claims or issues. Indeed, the manifest purpose of a choice-of-law clause is precisely to avoid such a battle.

Seawinds's view of the problem—which would require extensive litigation of the parties' supposed intentions regarding the choice-of-law clause to the end that the laws of multiple states might be applied to their dispute—is more likely the product of postdispute litigation strategy, not predispute contractual intent. If commercially sophisticated parties (such as those now before us) truly intend the result advocated by Seawinds, they should, in fairness to one another and in the interest of economy in dispute resolution, negotiate and obtain the assent of

---

[7] As we have noted, the choice-of-law clause states: "This agreement shall be governed by and *construed in accordance with Hong Kong law* . . . ." (Italics added.) The agreement, of course, includes the choice-of-law clause itself. Thus the question of whether that clause is ambiguous as to its scope (i.e., whether it includes the fiduciary duty claim) is a question of contract interpretation that in the normal course should be determined pursuant to Hong Kong law. The parties in this case, however, did not request judicial notice of Hong Kong law on this question of interpretation (Evid. Code, § 452, subd. (f)) or supply us with evidence of the relevant aspects of that law (Evid. Code, § 453, subd. (b)). The question therefore becomes one of California law.

their fellow parties to explicit contract language specifying what jurisdiction's law applies to what issues. * * *

For the reasons stated above, we hold a valid choice-of-law clause, which provides that a specified body of law "governs" the "agreement" between the parties, encompasses all causes of action arising from or related to that agreement, regardless of how they are characterized, including tortious breaches of duties emanating from the agreement or the legal relationships it creates.

2. *Enforceability of chosen law as to fiduciary duty claim*

Applying the test we have adopted, we find no reason not to apply the parties' choice of law to Seawinds's cause of action for breach of fiduciary duty. As we have explained, Hong Kong, the chosen state, has a "substantial relationship to the parties" because two of those parties are incorporated there. Moreover, their incorporation in that state affords a "reasonable basis" for choosing Hong Kong law.

Seawinds identifies no fundamental public policy of this state that would be offended by application of Hong Kong law to a claim by a Hong Kong corporation against its allegedly controlling shareholder. We are directed to no California statute or constitutional provision designed to preclude freedom of contract in this context. Indeed, even in the absence of a choice-of-law clause, Hong Kong's overriding interest in the internal affairs of corporations domiciled there would in most cases require application of its law. (See Rest., § 306 [obligations owed by majority shareholder to corporation determined by the law of the state of incorporation except in unusual circumstances not present here].) * * *

For strategic reasons related to its current dispute with Nedlloyd, Seawinds seeks to create a fiduciary relationship by disregarding the law Seawinds voluntarily agreed to accept as binding—the law of a state that also happens to be Seawinds's own corporate domicile. To allow Seawinds to use California law in this fashion would further no ascertainable fundamental policy of California; indeed, it would undermine California's policy of respecting the choices made by parties to voluntarily negotiated agreements. * * *

LUCAS, C. J., ARABIAN, J., and GEORGE, J., concurred.

PANELLI, J., KENNARD, J., concurring and dissenting.

I generally concur in the majority opinion's explanation of the standards controlling when a contractual choice-of-law provision will be honored by the courts of this state and with the majority's application of these standards to Seawinds's cause of action for breach of the covenant of good faith and fair dealing. I write separately to express my disagreement with the majority's conclusion, based on the record before us, that the choice-of-law clause in this case governs Seawinds's cause of action for breach of fiduciary duty. In my view, the majority's analysis of the scope of the choice-of-law clause is unsound.

The choice-of-law clause in this case reads * * * : "This agreement shall be governed by and construed in accordance with Hong Kong law . . . ." The majority determines that the scope of the choice-of-law clause, which was incorporated into the first amended complaint by attachment, extends to related, *noncon-*

tractual causes of action, such as Seawinds's breach of fiduciary duty claim. In so doing, the majority opinion adopts the rule that "[w]hen two sophisticated, commercial entities agree to a choice-of-law clause like the one in this case, the most reasonable interpretation of their actions is that they intended for the clause to apply to all causes of action arising from or related to their contract." Without citing any authority, the majority opinion announces a binding rule of contractual interpretation, based solely upon "common sense and commercial reality."

The problem with the majority's approach is that it ignores controlling California law. On demurrer, a pleading must be liberally construed. (Code Civ. Proc., § 452.) The accepted rule of contractual construction on demurrer is that "[w]here a written contract is pleaded by attachment to and incorporation in a complaint, and where the complaint fails to allege that the terms of the contract have any special meaning, a court will construe the language of the contract on its face to determine whether, as a matter of law, the contract is reasonably subject to a construction sufficient to sustain a cause of action . . . ." * * * In this case, the language of the incorporated contract easily can be read to apply only to contractual causes of action: *"This agreement* shall be governed . . . by Hong Kong law."

In my view, the majority's mistaken construction of the choice-of-law clause is clear when the language used in the present contract is compared, as Nedlloyd urges us to do, with the language construed by this court in *Smith, Valentino & Smith, Inc. v. Superior Court* (1976) 17 Cal.3d 491. In that case, this court determined that claims for unfair competition and intentional interference with advantageous business relationships were governed by a choice-of-forum clause as "'actions or proceedings instituted by . . . [Smith] under this Agreement with respect to any matters arising under *or growing out of this agreement* . . . .'" In contrast to the language used by Nedlloyd and Seawinds in their agreement, the contractual language, "arising under or growing out of this agreement," which was used in *Smith*, explicitly shows an intent to embrace related noncontractual claims, as well as contractual claims. Although similar language was readily available to them, the sophisticated parties in the present case did not draft their choice-of-law clause to clearly encompass related noncontractual causes of action.[2] Therefore, on demurrer and in the absence of parol evidence, I cannot fairly construe the contractual language at issue here to be consistent with the interpretation proposed by Nedlloyd and adopted in the majority opinion. To do so would violate the statutory canon of contract interpretation that "[t]he language of a contract is to govern its interpretation, if the language is clear and explicit, and does not involve an absurdity." (Civ. Code, § 1638.)

Finally, the majority's rule effectively subordinates the intent of the contracting parties to the need for predictability in commercial transactions. The majority strikes this balance despite the fact that our Legislature has commanded otherwise. Under California law, "[a] contract must be so interpreted as to give

---

[2] Despite the majority's artfully crafted argument, the words "governed by" do not assist in defining what causes of action the choice-of-law clause was intended to address. Rather, the parties defined the scope of their choice-of-law clause by choosing the phrase "[t]his agreement."

effect to the mutual intention of the parties as it existed at the time of contract-ing, so far as the same is ascertainable and lawful." (Civ. Code, § 1636.) In con-trast to this legislative command, the majority conclusively presumes that choice-of-law clauses entered into between or among commercial entities apply to related noncontractual causes of action regardless of whether the intent of the parties or the contract language (as in this case) shows otherwise. I believe that the departure by the majority from established California law is unwarranted and is unnecessary to further the goals of predictability in the enforcement of con-tracts and protection of the justified expectations of contracting parties. These goals can be adequately protected within the framework of the current law gov-erning contractual interpretation by enforcing choice-of-law clauses in a manner consistent with the language of the contract and the intent of the parties.

I am keenly aware of the need for predictability in the enforcement of com-mercial contracts. Nevertheless, although courts and litigants may wish the law were otherwise, not every issue can be conclusively determined at the pleading stage. On the present record, the scope of the choice-of-law clause must be con-strued in favor of Seawinds.

NOTES AND QUESTIONS FOR DISCUSSION

1. Was the *Seawinds* court correct in reading the choice of law clause to cover noncontractual claims arising out of the relationship between the parties in con-nection with the agreement? The dissent makes a comparison to the court's treatment of language of forum selection clauses, noting that clearer language is usually needed for such clauses to apply to related noncontractual claims. Is there a difference between the two sorts of clauses that might warrant the majori-ty's approach? Consider what sort of language might have made it clearer that the scope of the choice of law clause was indeed meant to cover such claims. What about: "all disputes arising out of *or related to* this contract shall be gov-erned by the law of Hong Kong"? See George A. Bermann, Transnational Liti-gation 216-17 (2003) (emphasis added) (noting that such language would be broad enough to cover not just all aspects of contractual claims "but also other private law claims between the parries bearing a relation to the contract, such as tort, product liability, restitution and the like"). As discussed in the notes that follow, *the validity* of the Hong Kong choice of law clause was decided in *Sea-winds* by looking to forum (California) choice of law principles. But whose law did the *Seawinds* court apply to the question of the interpretation of the clause's scope, so as to include noncontractual claims? If the choice of law clause is val-id, shouldn't Hong Kong law be applied to the question of its scope? See Re-statement (Second) of Conflict of Laws § 204(b) (arguably so suggesting).

2. The *Seawinds* opinion presents a sophisticated analysis of the enforceability of choice of law clauses from the perspective of the Second Restatement. In-deed, the Restatement's provisions on choice of law clauses is followed even by a number of states that do not ordinarily adhere to the Restatement, such as Cali-fornia. However, it is probably fair to say that many courts do very little analy-sis of choice of law clauses when determining their enforceability, other than to invoke general policy of accommodating party autonomy, to refer to the presumptive enforceability of such clauses, and then (sometimes) to see if forum public policy would somehow be violated by enforcing the substantive law that the choice of law clause would provide. In short, those courts tend to apply their own law to the question of the validity of such clauses, without regard to the contract law of the place where the contract was made or the contract law that would otherwise apply pursuant to the forum's choice of law rules.

3. The Second Restatement's approach to the problem under § 187 is actually somewhat involved, and hardly guarantees the enforceability of such clauses, although it is generally hospitable to them.

- Section 187(1) provides that a choice of law clause respecting a particular issue in a contract is enforceable "if the particular issue is one which the parties could have resolved by an explicit provision in their agreement directed to that issue." In other words, if the choice of law provision simply provides for a particular law to apply in place of default rules of contract law that would otherwise apply (under ordinary choice of law rules, absent a choice of law clause), life is simple. The choice of law clause will be enforced. That is because default rules ordinarily only come into play in the absence of some express provision of the parties—e.g., as to what would constitute "substantial completion" of a construction project. Applying a particular jurisdiction's law of substantial completion by contractual choice (e.g., Florida law will determine whether there has been substantial completion) is therefore a kind of short hand to fill in the gaps that the otherwise applicable contract default rules would fill. Indeed, in such cases, there does not even need to be a relationship between the parties or the transaction and the jurisdiction whose law is chosen.

- Section 187(2)—at issue in *Seawinds*—provides that "even if the particular issue is one which the parties could not have resolved by an explicit provision in their agreement directed to that issue," the choice of law clause might nevertheless be enforced. This provision deals with so-called mandatory rules (as opposed to default rules), that parties ordinarily cannot contract around. (The distinction is the same as that noted in *Siegelman, supra*, between choosing law to help *interpret* the contract, and choosing law to determine the *validity* of the contract.) But the Restatement allows parties to do so subject to a few provisos. First, as noted in *Seawinds*, there needs to be a reasonable nexus between the jurisdiction whose law has been chosen and the parties or the events in question. Second, the court must ascertain the law that would otherwise be applicable even in the absence of a choice of law clause. Third, once that law is determined, the court must ascertain whether some fundamental policy of that jurisdiction would be offended by application of the chosen law. And fourth, if such a policy would be offended, then the court must ascertain whether the offended jurisdiction has a "materially greater" interest in having its law apply over the chosen law.

In short, under the Second Restatement, a choice of law clause attempting to get around a mandatory rule—such as a rule of contract invalidity—will generally be enforced only if it would not violate the public policy of the jurisdiction whose law would otherwise be applicable in the absence of any such clause. Note also that under the Restatement § 187(3), choice of law clauses will ordinarily be interpreted as not referring to the "whole law" of the chosen state, but to its internal law. In other words, the notion of renvoi (see above at Section A.1) is presumptively rejected, although parties are free to make clear that they wish to incorporate it.

4. As an illustration of the Restatement's limitations noted above, domestic courts have often refused to enforce choice of law clauses that would have validated covenants not to complete in a jurisdiction where such covenants run afoul of public policy, and even if they were lawful in the jurisdiction in which the contract was entered into. See, e.g., DeSantis v. Wackenhut Corp., 793 S.W.2d 670 (Tex. 1990), cert. denied, 498 U.S. 1048 (1991) (refusing to enforce Florida choice of law clause that would have validated covenant not to complete which was illegal in the forum state which was also the state in which the covenant would have been enforced). Should courts following the Second Restatement be more hospitable to enforcement of choice of law clauses in the international setting than in the domestic setting?

5. Another possible example of non-enforcement of choice of law clauses might arise when the law chosen would run afoul of a state's regulatory statute designed to protect particular parties from financial overreaching by other parties. But consider the result in the transnational case of Tele-Save Merchandising Co. v. Consumers Distributors, 814 F.2d 1120 (6th Cir. 1987). Tele-Save, an Ohio corporation, entered into a franchise agreement with a large Canadian corporation, Consumers Distributors, which operated a chain of retail catalog stores, and which had a large office in New Jersey. Tele-Save was to open a store in Ohio and offer Consumers' products for sale. The contract between them stated that New Jersey law would apply to any disputes arising out of the contract. Suit was eventually brought by Tele-Save in a federal court in Ohio, after Consumers terminated the franchise early on. Tele-Save alleged a breach of contract and alleged that Consumers violated various provisions of the Ohio Franchise Act, including making false and misleading statements to induce the deal and by failing to provide the kind of notice required by Ohio law prior to termination of the contract. Tele-Save argued for various reasons that the New Jersey choice of law clause should be ignored and that the Ohio Franchise Act should be applied. The federal district court and the court of appeals disagreed, and applied New Jersey law, as argued by the Canadian defendant, and in accordance with the choice of law clause.

Among other things, Tele-Save argued that the language of the Franchise Act provided that "any waiver by a purchaser of [various sections of the Act Tele-Save alleged Consumers had violated] is contrary to public policy and is void and unenforceable." Id. at 1123. The federal appeals court seemed to conclude, however, that the Act's no-waiver language did not mean generally to disallow choice-of law clauses that ousted Ohio law and substituted some other state's law. The court found that Ohio was generally favorable to choice of law provisions otherwise, and that such provisions would be dishonored only when the law chosen was repugnant to Ohio's public policy. In addition to noting that the contract had been freely negotiated between savvy business parties, the court stated that even if Ohio's franchise law represented fundamental policy of Ohio in some respect, the "fundamental policy" exception of the Restatement was still not triggered by any of the provisions of the contract. New Jersey law provided common law remedies for breach of contract and for fraud, even though those remedies may not have been quite as protective as the Ohio Act. The differences in available remedies to franchisees under the two states' laws were not such that the court could conclude that New Jersey law ran afoul of Ohio's public policy within the meaning of the Restatement. Note that *Tele-Save* was decided by the federal courts applying the Second Restatement as a matter of Ohio choice of law rules. How persuasive was its conclusion that Ohio public policy would not be violated by non-application of Ohio franchise law? Is it realistic to suppose that an Ohio state court would have come out the same way?

6. In Richards v. Lloyd's of London, 135 F.3d 1289 (9th Cir. 1998) (en banc) (see Chapter I, Section I), the plaintiffs—Americans who had entered into underwriting agreements with Lloyd's of London—brought claims against Lloyd's based on federal securities and antiracketeering laws. The Ninth Circuit upheld an exclusive choice of forum clause in favor of England, as well as a choice of law clause designating English law. The court concluded that both clauses should be governed by the pro-enforcement principles of The Bremen v. Zapata Off-Shore, 407 U.S. 1 (1972), a choice of forum decision. Of course, even *The Bremen* observed that a choice clause need not be enforced "if enforcement would contravene a strong public policy of the forum in which suit is brought." Id. at 12-13, 15. The *Richards* plaintiffs argued that application of English law would violate federal public policy because Lloyd's would be immunized as against many of the claims that would have been available under federal securities laws, and that overall, fewer remedies would be available to the plainitffs under English law. The *Richards* court agreed that if "English law [was] so deficient that the [plaintiffs] would be deprived of any reasonable recourse," the choice clause would not be enforceable. Nevertheless, it rejected the public policy objection, noting that "English law provides the Names with sufficient protection," including claims against individual "Members" of Lloyd's for negligent misrepresentation, fraud, and breach of fiduciary duty. And the court noted that a claim of fraud might also be available against Lloyd's itself. *Richards'* approach to such U.S. public policy issues in the setting of choice of law clauses is shared by other federal courts. See, e.g., Roby v. Corporation of Lloyd's, 996 F.2d 1353, 1364-66 (2nd Cir.), cert. denied, 510 U.S. 945 (1993).

Note, however, that *Richards* and other courts have to step around Mitsubishi Motors Corp. v. Soler Chrysler-Plymouth, Inc., 473 U.S. 614, 634 (1985), an antitrust case, in which Supreme Court stated (albeit in dicta) that "in the event the choice-of-forum and choice-of-law clauses operated in tandem as a prospective waiver of a party's right to pursue statutory remedies for antitrust violations, we would have little hesitation in condemning the agreement as against public policy." Why wasn't *Mitsubushi* controlling in a case such as *Richards*?

2. The Interrelationship between Choice of Law and Choice of Forum Clauses

In Chapter 1, we discussed forum selection clauses and their enforceability in international civil litigation. Left unanswered was the question of whose law should govern such clauses. As with choice of law clauses, courts sometimes pay little attention to the issue, but there are a variety of approaches, some of which view choice of forum clauses as a creature of federal procedural common law, federal substantive common law, or state law. But what if a contract contains *both* a choice of forum clause as well as a choice of law clause? Should the choice of law clause control the interpretation of the choice of forum clause, if there is some question about its interpretation or scope? And what if the choice of law clause would validate a choice of forum clause that might otherwise be invalid? Some of these issues are considered in the case that follows.

Albemarle Corp. v. AstraZenica U.K., Ltd.

United States Court of Appeals, Fourth Circuit, 2010.

628 F.3d 643.

NIEMEYER, CIRCUIT JUDGE.

In this case, we address how to interpret a forum selection clause that makes an international contract "subject to jurisdiction" in the United Kingdom.

Astra Zenica UK, Ltd, a United Kingdom corporation, agreed in a 2005 contract to purchase a substantial portion of its needs for di-isopropyl-phenol ("DIP") from Albemarle International Corporation, a Virginia corporation. Albemarle International Corporation was the global marketing arm of a Virginia corporation (both corporations, collectively "Albemarle"), and Albemarle Corporation manufactured DIP in its plant in South Carolina. AstraZeneca used DIP to manufacture the drug Diprivan, a fast-acting anesthetic, at its plant in England. In the 2005 contract, AstraZenica also agreed that if it ceased using DIP in favor of propofol, a derivative of DIP, it would give Albemarle the right of first refusal to supply AstraZeneca with propofol. When AstraZenica did elect a year later to use propofol in lieu of DIP, Albemarle contends that AstraZenica breached its duty to give Albemarle the right of first refusal, and Albemarle commenced this action in South Carolina, alleging that AstraZenica breached the 2005 contract.

Based on a forum selection clause in the 2005 contract, which provided that the contract was "subject to" the jurisdiction of the English High Court, AstraZeneca filed a motion to dismiss this action for improper venue. The district court granted the motion and dismissed the complaint, applying English law, which the contract specified was applicable, to hold that the forum selection clause was mandatory and exclusive, even though such a clause would likely be construed under federal case law to be permissive.

We affirm. Resting on the traditional proposition that we should give effect to parties' expectations as manifested in their legitimate agreements, we apply

English law to construe the forum selection clause and conclude that under English law, the clause requires that this litigation be pursued in the designated English court. We also conclude that enforcing the forum selection clause in this manner is not unreasonable, as unreasonableness is detailed in *The Bremen v. Zapata Off-Shore Co.*, 407 U.S. 1, 15-18 (1972).

I

In the [2005] * * * contract, AstraZeneca agreed to purchase at least 80% of its requirements for DIP from Albemarle. To manufacture Diprivan, AstraZeneca distilled the DIP to obtain propofol, the active ingredient in Diprivan. In the 2005 contract AstraZenica agreed that if it decided to bypass its own distilling process and purchase propofol directly for its manufacturing of Diprivan, it would give Albemarle the right of first refusal to sell AstraZeneca propofol "under mutually acceptable terms and conditions."

About a year later, in June 2006, AstraZenica notified Albemarle that it intended to cease purchasing DIP and instead to purchase propofol directly from a third party. After AstraZenica provided Albemarle with a copy of its purchase agreement with the third party and Albemarle made a competing offer to sell propofol to AstraZenica, AstraZenica refused to purchase propofol from Albemarle.

Albemarle commenced this breach of contract action against AstraZenica in the Court of Common Pleas in Orangeburg, South Carolina, and AstraZenica, invoking diversity jurisdiction, removed the case to federal court. AstraZeneca then filed a motion to dismiss for improper venue * * *. In support of its motion, AstraZenica pointed to the choice of law and forum selection clauses which provided simply that the contract "shall be subject to English Law and the jurisdiction of the English High Court." In response to the motion, Albemarle argued that the forum selection clause was only permissive and did not exclude a South Carolina court as an appropriate forum. It also filed a motion seeking to enjoin AstraZenica from pursuing litigation concerning the contract in England. * * *

[In 2009, the district court initially denied AstraZenica's motion to dismiss, finding that federal common law applied to the construction of the forum selection clause in the 2005 contract and that, under federal law, this form of forum selection clause was only permissive and not exclusive. (The court also entered an injunction barring AstraZenica from pursuing claims on the 2005 contract in England.) Six months later, however, the district court granted AstraZenica's motion for reconsideration and also granted its motion to dismiss. Instead of relying on federal law to assess the validity of the forum selection clause, the district court reasoned that English law applied because the parties had agreed that English law should apply to the contract generally. Under English law (unlike under federal common law) the forum selection clause was "mandatory." It also concluded that enforcing the forum selection clause would not violate any "strong public policy" of the forum state, South Carolina. The court also ruled that the 2008 contract did not supersede the 2005 contract. Albemarle appealed.]

II

[The Court first rejected Albemarle's argument that the 2008 contract had superseded the 2005 forum selection clause.]

III

For its principal argument, Albemarle contends that the district court erred in enforcing the forum selection clause under English law rather than under American federal common law. It argues that federal law applies because seeking to enforce a forum selection clause in a federal court implicates venue rules and statutes that are part of the federal law, as, for example, Federal Rule of Civil Procedure 12(b)(3), 28 U.S.C. § 1391, and 28 U.S.C. § 1406(a). *See Wong v. PartyGaming Ltd.*, 589 F.3d 821, 827 (6th Cir. 2009) (noting that six circuits have held that "the enforceability of a forum selection clause implicates federal procedure and should therefore be governed by federal law," and adopting that rule); *Manetti-Farrow, Inc. v. Gucci America, Inc.*, 858 F.2d 509, 513 (9th Cir. 1988) ("[B]ecause enforcement of a forum clause necessarily entails interpretation of the clause before it can be enforced, federal law also applies to interpretation of forum selection clauses"). It then continues with its argument that under federal law the general maxim is that "an agreement conferring jurisdiction in one forum will not be interpreted as excluding jurisdiction elsewhere unless it contains specific language of exclusion." *IntraComm, Inc. v. Bajaj*, 492 F.3d 285, 290 (4th Cir. 2007) (emphasis omitted) (*quoting John Boutari & Son, Wines & Spirits, S.A. v. Attiki Importers & Distribs. Inc.*, 22 F.3d 51, 53 (2d Cir. 1994)). In sum, Albemarle asserts that federal law would hold that a forum selection clause, as written in the 2005 contract—providing that the contract is "subject to . . . the jurisdiction of the English High Court"—*permits* the English court to entertain the case but does not *require* that the litigation take place there, because the language does not exclude other jurisdictions and forums.

AstraZeneca agrees that federal law applies when a federal court construes a forum selection clause, but it argues that federal law also requires that a court give effect to the parties' intent as expressed in the parties' choice of law. *See Sterling Forest Assoc., Ltd. v. Barnett-Range Corp.*, 840 F.2d 249, 251 (4th Cir. 1988) (analyzing parties' intent to hold that forum selection clause mandated bringing the action in California); *Yakin v. Tyler Hill Camp, Inc.*, 566 F.3d 72, 76 (2d Cir. 2009) ("[W]e are obliged to give effect to the parties' intentions regarding venue"); *Mazda Motors of Am., Inc. v. M/V Cougar ACE*, 565 F.3d 573, 580 (9th Cir. 2009) (same). It observes that since the parties specified that English law was to apply, the forum selection clause must be taken as English law would construe it, and that, under English law, the English forum is mandatory, not permissive. *See Yavuz v. 61 MM, Ltd.*, 465 F.3d 418, 431 (10th Cir. 2006) (holding that the law that the parties chose to govern the contract should be applied to construe a forum selection clause in that contract).

We find much of the parties' discussion is unhelpful. Albemarle largely addresses naked forum selection clauses where no choice of law is indicated. AstraZeneca, by contrast, collapses the analysis of the forum selection clause with the discussion of the choice of law clause. While the parties do not appear to be in any serious disagreement about the controlling legal principles, they do disagree over the analysis to be undertaken. We analyze this contract as one that contains both a choice of law clause and a forum selection clause.

We begin by noting that when parties to a contract confer jurisdiction and venue on a particular court, as a general matter federal common law directs courts to favor enforcement of the agreement, so long as it is not unreasonable. *See The Bremen*, 407 U.S. at 10. "Forum-selection clauses [had] historically not been favored by American courts" because the effect of enforcing them "was to 'oust the jurisdiction' of the court." *Id.* at 9. This historical reluctance to enforce such clauses was not unlike the historical reluctance to enforce arbitration clauses. *See, e.g., Scherk v. Alberto-Culver Co.*, 417 U.S. 506, 519 (1974) (observing that an agreement to arbitrate is in effect a type of forum selection clause). Rejecting the historical judicial bias and giving effect to privately negotiated agreements, the *Bremen* Court held:

> Thus, in the light of present-day commercial realities and expanding international trade we conclude that the forum clause should control absent a strong showing that it should be set aside. . . . The correct approach would have been to enforce the forum clause specifically unless Zapata could clearly show that enforcement would be unreasonable and unjust, or that the clause was invalid for such reasons as fraud or overreaching.

The Bremen, 407 U.S. at 15.

Even though *The Bremen* was an admiralty case, its rationale is applicable to forum selection clauses generally. *See, e.g., Bryant Elec. Co. v. City of Fredericksburg*, 762 F.2d 1192, 1196 (4th Cir. 1985) ("[T]his Court has applied [*The Bremen's*] reasoning in diversity cases not involving international contracts"); *Mercury Coal & Coke, Inc. v. Mannesmann Pipe & Steel Corp.*, 696 F.2d 315, 317-18 (4th Cir. 1982); *see also Stewart Org., Inc. v. Ricoh*, 487 U.S. 22, 33 (1988) (Kennedy, J., concurring) ("Although our opinion in *The Bremen* involved a Federal District Court sitting in admiralty, its reasoning applies with much force to federal courts sitting in diversity" (internal citation omitted)).

These cases apply federal common law favoring the enforcement of forum selection clauses when interpreting contracts that contain forum selection clauses, because forum selection clauses implicate the appropriate venue of a court. The appropriate venue of an action is a procedural matter that is governed by federal rule and statutes. *See, e.g.,* Fed. R. Civ. P. 12(b)(3); 28 U.S.C. § 1391; 28 U.S.C. § 1406(a); *see also Manetti-Farrow*, 858 F.2d at 513 (noting that federal law was enacted to address venue, and applying state law concerning venue would render the federal law "nugatory"); *cf. Stewart*, 487 U.S. at 32 (holding that 28 U.S.C. § 1404(a), which governs the transfer of venue among federal courts, is "doubtless capable of classification as a procedural rule"). Thus, when a court is analyzing a forum selection clause, which changes the default venue rules applicable to the agreement, that court will apply federal law and in doing so, give effect to the parties' agreement. *See The Bremen*, 407 U.S. at 12-13 ("There are compelling reasons why a freely negotiated private international agreement, unaffected by fraud, undue influence, or overweening bargaining power, such as that involved here, should be given full effect"); *Wong*, 589 F.3d at 828 ("We therefore hold that in this diversity suit, the enforceability of the forum selection clause is governed by federal law"); *Manetti-Farrow*, 858 F.2d at 513 ("[B]ecause enforcement of a forum clause necessarily entails interpretation of the clause before it can be enforced, federal law also applies to interpretation of forum selection clauses"). *But see Abbott Labs. v. Takeda Pharm. Co.*, 476 F.3d 421, 423 (7th Cir. 2007) ("Simplicity argues for determining the validity . . . of a forum selection clause . . . by reference to the law of the jurisdiction whose law governs the rest of the contract").

Following the majority rule, we thus conclude that a federal court interpreting a forum selection clause must apply federal law in doing so. As an agreement purporting to modify or waive the venue of a federal court, a forum selection clause implicates what is recognized as a procedural matter governed by federal law—the proper venue of the court. Using this reasoning, the Supreme Court applied federal law in enforcing a forum selection clause in a federal suit where a motion to transfer venue under 28 U.S.C. § 1404 had been filed. *See Stewart*, 487 U.S. at 32.

When construing forum selection clauses, federal courts have found dispositive the particular language of the clause and whether it authorizes another forum as an *alternative* to the forum of the litigation or whether it makes the designated forum *exclusive*. *See IntraComm*, 492 F.3d at 290 (ruling that a clause providing that either party "shall be free" to pursue its rights in a specified court did not preclude jurisdiction or venue in the forum court). As we said in *IntraComm*, "A general maxim in interpreting forum selection clauses is that 'an agreement *conferring* jurisdiction in one forum will not be interpreted as *excluding* jurisdiction elsewhere unless it contains specific language of exclusion.'" *Id.* (*quoting John Boutari & Son*, 22 F.3d at 53).

The language of the forum selection clause in this case, taken by itself and out of context, appears to make the designation of the English court permissive, as we construed a similar clause in *IntraComm*. That conclusion would be consistent with the principle of federal common law to make such clauses permissive unless they contain specific language of exclusion. But in this case the clause taken in context does contain what amounts, in effect, to language of exclusion. The clause here includes language that English law, not American federal law, must be applied. *See Yavuz*, 465 F.3d at 430 (holding that a court must honor the forum selection clause "as construed under the law specified in the agreement's choice-of-law provision"). And applying English law makes a difference, as the parties have recognized and stipulated. Under English law, when the parties designate the English High Court as an appropriate forum, the designation is mandatory and exclusive. The district court observed in this case, "[Albemarle] candidly concede[s] that the forum selection clause at issue would be considered to be mandatory under English law."

Moreover, the parties' stipulation about the effect of English law seems to be supported. *See* Commission Regulation 44/2001, art. 23, 2001 O.J. (L 12) 1 (EU), *amended by* 2002 307/28 (L 225) 2. This was directly confirmed recently by the English High Court, which ruled on the very contract before us: "As a matter of English law, which is the applicable law, that clause [in the same contract that is before us] would be construed as being an exclusive jurisdiction clause, as was conceded by Albemarle in the 2008 Action in light of Article 23.1 of the Judgements Regulation (No. 44/2001)." *AstraZeneca UK Ltd. v. Albemarle Int'l Corp.*, 34 [2010] EWHC 1028 (comm), [43].

IV

Of course, we will give effect to the parties' selection of the English forum only if it would not be unreasonable to do so. Under *The Bremen*, a forum selection clause may be found unreasonable if:

> (1) [its] formation was induced by fraud or overreaching; (2) the complaining party "will for all practical purposes be deprived of his day in court" because of the grave inconvenience or unfairness of the selected forum; (3) the fundamental unfairness of the chosen law may deprive the plaintiff of a remedy; or (4) [its] enforcement would contravene a strong public policy of the forum state.

Allen v. Lloyd's of London, 94 F.3d 923, 928 (4th Cir. 1996) (summarizing the *The Bremen* definition).

In this case, Albemarle contends that enforcement of the forum selection clause would violate a strong public policy of South Carolina, namely South Carolina's disfavor of such clauses as indicated in S.C. Code Ann. § 15-7-120(A), which reads:

> Notwithstanding a provision in a contract requiring a cause of action arising under it to be brought in a location other than as provided in this title and the South Carolina Rules of Civil Procedure for a similar cause of action, the cause of action alternatively may be brought in the manner provided in this title and the South Carolina Rules of Civil Procedure for such causes of action.

In effect, this statute makes all forum selection clauses permissive and thus would overrule the forum selection clause in this case, that makes the English forum exclusive. We reject Albemarle's public policy argument at several levels.

First, insofar as the South Carolina statue would purport to impose South Carolina procedural rules on a federal court, it would be preempted by federal law. Federal law explicitly regulates the appropriate venue in cases filed in federal court, and to the extent that a forum selection clause is invoked to change venue, federal law applies, as we have discussed above.

Second, state reluctance to recognize and enforce forum selection clauses was specifically addressed and countered by the Supreme Court's holding in *The Bremen*. In *The Bremen*, the Court acknowledged that "[m]any courts, federal and state, have declined to enforce [forum selection] clauses on the ground that they were 'contrary to public policy' or that their effect was to 'oust the jurisdiction' of the court." 407 U.S. at 9. But it rejected that rationale, noting that these courts' approach was based on the "provincial attitude regarding the fairness of other tribunals." *Id.* at 12. The Court thus held that, contrary to judicial disfavor of forum selection clauses such as that manifested in the South Carolina statute, in federal court, forum selection clauses enjoy a presumption of enforceability.

Third, we can find virtually no evidence to indicate that S.C. Code Ann. § 15-7-120(A), overriding exclusive forum selection clauses in favor of applying state procedural rules for venue, manifests a strong public policy of South Carolina. We could find no South Carolina court that has so held. Indeed, we have cases in which South Carolina courts have enforced forum selection clauses in contracts, notwithstanding the existence of § 15-7-120(A). * * * And following South Carolina's cases, federal courts sitting in South Carolina have enforced forum selection clauses, notwithstanding the statute. * * *

Fourth and finally, it can hardly be a strong public policy to countermand the very policy that the Supreme Court adopted in *The Bremen*. *The Bremen* would have little effect if states could effectively override the decision by expressing disagreement with the decision's rationale. Classifying South Carolina's statute as manifesting a strong public policy within *The Bremen's* reasoning would allow the very "provincial attitude" rejected by *The Bremen* to override the federal policy of favoring a contractual choice of forum.

V

If we were, in this case, to exclude the federal interests from our analysis—interests represented by federal venue rules and statutes and by the policy articulated in *The Bremen*—a traditional conflicts-of-laws analysis would apply, and in a diversity case involving breach of contract, that would begin with the Supreme Court's decision in *Klaxon Co. v. Stentor Elec. Mfg. Co.*, 313 U.S. 487 (1941). In *Klaxon*, the Court stated, "The conflict of laws rules to be applied by [a] federal court . . . must conform to those prevailing in [the] state courts. Otherwise, the accident of diversity of citizenship would constantly disturb equal administration of justice in coordinate state and federal courts sitting side by side." *Id.* at 496 (*citing Erie R.R. Co. v. Tompkins*, 304 U.S. 64, 74-77 (1938)). Thus, for an action filed in South Carolina, South Carolina law would be consulted for its choice of law rules, and under those rules, South Carolina law would give effect to the parties' choice of law as specified in the contract. *See* S.C. Code Ann. § 36-1-105(1) (providing, as applicable here, "When a transaction bears a reasonable relation to this State and also to another state or nation the parties may agree that the law either of this State or of another state or nation shall govern their rights and duties").

In this case, the parties agreed to the application of English law, which would make the English forum exclusive and would override South Carolina's statute making all forum selection clauses permissive, *see* S.C. Code § 15-7-120(A), unless that statute manifested a strong public policy. But under state law, a state provision establishing, as a procedural matter, that the South Carolina venue rules trump any contractual agreement selecting an exclusive forum outside of South Carolina is not the type of provision that South Carolina courts have recognized as establishing a strong public policy of the State that would overrule the parties choice of law outside South Carolina. *See Nash v. Tindall Corp.*, 375 S.C. 36, 650 S.E.2d 81, 83-84 (S.C. Ct. App. 2007) (defining the public policy of the State to implicate foreign law when it "is against good morals or natural justice," such as "prohibited marriages, wagers, lotteries, racing, contracts for gaming or the sale of liquors, and others").

So whether we give effect to the parties' agreement as a matter of federal venue law or import the conflicts of laws rules from South Carolina, we end up in the same place, concluding that the parties agreed to the application of English law. Thus, even while federal law may have required a construction rendering the forum selection clause permissive, English law must be applied, and it takes the clause as mandatory.

For the reasons given, we affirm the district court's ruling dismissing this case, based on enforcement of the parties' forum selection and choice of law clauses.

VI

The parties here have negotiated for and agreed to a contractual provision which provides that this "contract shall be subject to English law and the jurisdiction of the English High Court." While an agreement to be *subject to the jurisdiction* of the English High Court could reasonably be taken to mean that the parties only authorize litigation there but do not exclude other appropriate forums, for the agreement to be *subject to English law*, of necessity, excludes the application of other law. And if English law construes the forum selection clause to mean that litigation must be conducted in the English High Court exclusively, as the parties agree that it does, then the entire contractual provision's meaning becomes free of ambiguity.

In agreeing to these provisions, the parties undoubtedly accepted that litigation on disputes arising under the 2005 contract would be conducted in England, just as they accepted that litigation on disputes arising under the 2008 contract would be conducted in South Carolina. It, therefore, cannot be surprising to them that we enforce the 2005 contract that way, especially in light of our longstanding tradition of favoring the enforcement of contracts according to their terms.

The Supreme Court's discussion in *The Bremen* sets forth the reasons for this fundamental policy. Enforcement gives effect to the legitimate expectations of the parties and eliminates uncertainty and unexpected inconvenience. Indeed, the Court pointed out then that "[t]he elimination of all such uncertainties by agreeing in advance on a forum acceptable to both parties is an indispensable element in international trade, commerce, and contracting." *The Bremen*, 407 U.S. at 13-14; *see also Scherk*, 417 U.S. at 516 ("A contractual provision specifying in advance the forum in which disputes shall be litigated and the law to be applied is, therefore, an almost indispensable precondition to achievement of the orderliness and predictability essential to any international business transaction").

For the reasons given, we affirm the judgment of the district court.

NOTES AND QUESTIONS FOR DISCUSSION

1. In *The Bremen*, the Supreme Court articulated a rule of general hospitality to the enforcement of forum selection clauses as a matter of federal admiralty law. A harder question is whether federal common law (as opposed to state law) should govern the enforceability (and interpretation) of choice of forum provisions in international agreements. Assuming that a case arises under state law or foreign country law (as opposed to federal law), and assuming the absence of a choice of *law* clause, is there no argument that the relevant applicable law should be state law, under the doctrine of Erie Railroad v. Tompkins, 304 U.S. 64 (1938)? And if state law applies, is that a problem for international actors?

2.   The *AstraZenica* court states that, in the absence of a choice of law clause, a choice of forum clause in an international agreement should be governed by federal common law. (Of course, neither party had suggested otherwise, and indeed, both parties endorsed the idea that federal common law should apply.) The court comes to its conclusion because it sees the enforceability of forum selection clauses as a question of federal procedure. Is the court's reasoning persuasive? In addition to various other lower court authorities (which are divided), the court cites the federal transfer of venue statute, which, of course, is inapplicable if transfer is not sought to another federal district, and it was not in *AstraZenica*. It cites Rule 12(b)(3), Fed. R. Civ. P., for cases in which venue is bad, which is arguably inapplicable if venue is good under the venue statutes, as it was in *Astra Zenica*. Are you persuaded that these statutes and Rules speak to the question in a way that, under Hanna v. Plumer, 380 U.S. 460 (1965), permits them to trump potentially applicable state law?

3.   Absent a federal statute or rule that speaks to the question, *Erie* requires that a judge-made federal practice be considered in light of competing state law which may reflect important state policies that may be substantive in nature. Is it possible that a state law which generally prohibits enforcement of forum selection clauses could have a substantive dimension to it? If so, how would you articulate it? Alternatively, consider whether state law regarding enforcement of forum selection clauses should generally be subordinated to federal procedural interests in dismissals on *forum non conveniens* grounds. Is it fair to call a federal procedural common law policy favoring enforcement of forum selection clauses an aspect of *forum non conveniens* doctrine?

4.   The Fourth Circuit concludes that the presence of a choice of law clause trumps whatever federal common law would otherwise apply in connection with the interpretation of the choice of forum provision. Surely the court was right to consider the possibility that the choice of law clause might govern the choice of forum clause. But did it perhaps forget a step? Note that the court failed to consider what law might govern the validity of the choice of law clause itself. As earlier cases in this chapter show, choice of law clauses are not enforceable on their own authority. They must be valid under some law other than the choice of law clause itself. Did *AstraZenica* implicitly treat this as a question of federal common law? If state law should have applied to the question of the enforceability of the choice of law clause, which state's law would that be?

E. THE EUROPEAN PERSPECTIVE ON CHOICE OF LAW

So far, this chapter has emphasized the U.S. approach to questions of conflict of laws and the extraterritorial reach of U.S. federal statutes. In this section we focus on the European approach to conflict of laws problems. We begin with an excerpt from Prof. Matthias Reimann on the European outlook on conflicts generally. Thereafter, we turn our attention to specific agreements within the European Union [E.U.] and how courts have approached them.

Matthias Reimann, Conflict of Laws in Western Europe 3-17 (1995):

European conflicts law is primarily rooted in and characterized by the civil law culture. To be sure, the countries beyond the Channel have common law systems or are, as in the case of Scotland, hybrid jurisdictions. As these countries acceded to the EC [European Community], common law elements became part of the European conflicts scene. As a result, occasional compromises and mutual adjustments between common and civil law conflicts rules became necessary. Nonetheless, the civilian approach has continued to dominate. The reason is not only that in Europe, the common law countries are in the minority, but also, and more importantly, that the continental conflicts regimes were already firmly in place on the European level at the time of the common law members' integration into the EC. * * *

1. The Sources of Law

Like most areas of modern Western law, European conflicts law is a medley of statutory rules, case law, and academic writings. While in theory only statutes are binding in the civil law culture (i.e. in most of Western Europe), in practice, appellate decisions are followed almost as a matter of course, and scholars wield considerable influence. Thus, in practice, the situation looks roughly like the U.S. scene, at least at first glance. Yet, an American lawyer should be aware that there are in fact significant differences. They concern the respective emphasis on the various sources of law and the conception of statutes. These differences are matters of degree but are of considerable practical relevance.

a. The Primacy of Conventions and Statutes

In contrast to her American colleague, a European conflicts lawyer seeks rules primarily in conventions and statutes; other sources take second place.

While it has, of course, long ceased to be true that Anglo-American law consists mainly of cases whereas continental law is statutory, this traditional distinction still matters. It continues to shape the views of the relative importance of legal sources in the two systems. For continental lawyers, the primacy of statutory law is assumed and is welcome, while Americans shy away from statutes and feel more at home with cases, especially, as every teacher knows, in law school.

Moreover, the traditional distinction continues to hold particularly true in conflicts law. In the United States, statutory rules on jurisdiction, choice of law, or recognition of judgments are few and of limited importance; they mostly supplement an area dominated by case law. In Western Europe, in contrast, most basic rules are legislatively enacted. It is true that there are subjects and countries where statutory conflicts law is scarce and case law reigns supreme, especially in choice of law. Yet this is the exception, not, as in the United States, the rule.

In fact, conflict of laws is one of the few areas in which the traditional distinction between common law as a realm of cases and civil law as a world of statutes has recently become more, rather than less, pronounced. * * *

Not only do statutory rules govern most of European conflicts law, but they also enjoy greater respect than their counterparts in the United States. In continental Europe, statutes have since the middle ages been regarded not merely as one legal source among others but as the paramount texts and thus the unquestionable basis of all, legal discourse. In the civil law tradition, law is regarded as coming primarily from the legislator, instead of from the courts, and thus in statutory form. Statutes thereby enjoy utmost respect.

This respect manifests itself in two seemingly contradictory ways: as befits the civilian tradition, judges normally follow statutory commands quite strictly, but at the same time, they often expand the meaning of statutory rules rather liberally.

On the one hand, the wording of statutes and conventions is taken very seriously. It is the point of departure of all legal analysis in Western Europe. Drafted with care and precision, statutory language is considered to provide the answers in most cases. Thus, where statutory provisions plainly apply, they decide an issue without further ado. Where they leave room for disagreement, they are the constant and most important point of reference. Gaps are filled and doubts resolved primarily by extrapolation from other parts or from the overall structure of the act. Case law and scholarly opinion may aid the interpretation, but they will, as a rule, serve a mere auxiliary function.

On the other hand, continental judges and scholars tend to read statutes broadly and to reason from them, like an American judge does from a case, by analogy. In other words, they begin with the statute's exact wording, but they do not end with it. Instead, they consider the statute in order to give general guidance for similar cases, interpret it teleologically, and assume that the decision that comes closest to the spirit of the statute is normally the best. All this evinces both deference to the legislator and trust that statutory rules embody reasonable and useful principles.

b. Case Law and Scholarship

This is not to belittle the role of case law and scholarly views. Both play a significant role in European conflicts law as well. In the absence of enacted rules, case law governs whole areas. In some countries, for example in Scandinavia, choice of law is mostly a matter of case law, and in others, like Belgium or France, substantial areas are left to it. Yet, even here the courts rarely endorse general theories or innovate approaches. They rather go about the business of deciding cases in an unpretentious and traditional manner that strikes an American observer as uninspired, if not boring.

Academic opinion also has long held a prominent place, especially in choice of law. In contrast to the judge-made common law, the civil law has been developed largely by scholars ever since the days of the Roman emperors and particularly since the high middle ages. Even today, academic writing often precedes and thus prepares the way for both statutes and court decisions, so that the jurists' views enjoy great respect in legislatures and courts. Academic writers have an even greater impact in continental Europe than in the United States partially because the European academic literature is not nearly as preoccupied with grand theoretical issues as American conflicts scholarship, but rather is more focused on the concrete practical problems that courts face. It is thus likely to strike an American observer as rule-oriented and theoretically barren. Yet, it can also, particularly in the general parts of the great treatises, be abstract and dogmatic in the sense of being preoccupied with the definition, interpretation, and ordering of general concepts the practical importance of which is not always clear. * * *

2. The Importance of Rules and the Method of Analysis

European conflicts law differs from its American counterpart in its drive for clarity of concepts and precision of rules, in its ambition to reach results by logical deduction from them, and in its desire to maintain a logical coherence among them.

a. The Preference for Rules

In modern American conflicts law, both in choice of law and personal jurisdiction, the emphasis has shifted from rules and bright-line tests to approaches and multifactor analysis, i.e. to more general and open-ended methodologies. In contrast, European conflicts lawyers continue to look primarily for and to rules. In style, most European conflicts law thus reminds an American observer of a Restatement: it tends to be blackletter. This is particularly true where statutes govern, but even in case law or scholarly opinion, one is likely to find unambiguously stated rules that provide for apparently clear results. For example, both French and German case law have established the rule that torts cases are governed by the place of the wrong, although they admit of exceptions.

Sometimes these rules build on open-ended criteria, like the "strongest connection" between an issue and a national law, and thus require comparisons or call for value judgments. Here, they remind an American lawyer of criteria such as "the most significant relationship" in a Second Restatement. As in the Second Restatement, such general criteria are often made concrete through reference to specific factors. The employment of such open-ended criteria within conflicts rules is a more recent phenomenon in Europe. While it has, so far, affected only a few, albeit important areas (mainly choice of law in contracts cases), it may indicate a trend towards greater use of general criteria. For the time being, however, such criteria are still the exception to the rule of using rather unambiguous factors such as nationality, domicile, and the place of certain events. Moreover, continental lawyers, feeling bound by legislative commands, on the whole tend to apply even open-ended rules more conscientiously than their American colleagues. Similarly, while exception clauses, such as public policy, are very common, they are normally not used to undermine the system of rules. Manipulation for the sake of a particular result is not unknown in Europe either, but it is less frequent, less accepted, and certainly less openly recognized.

In the continental European view, rules should ideally yield results by direct application to the facts, i.e., by logical categorization of the fact-situation under the criteria set forth by the rule. Sometimes, of course, rules provide no clear answers. Yet, in contrast to their American colleagues, Europeans assume that this is the exception. Since they take rules more seriously and attribute greater authority to them than Americans, they rarely make reference to criteria outside of the rules, or at least rarely admit it. Beneath these respective attitudes lie different conceptions of the nature and function of rules generally. Since the days of Legal Realism, the American credo has become that "rules guide, but they do not control decision." The European assumption is that rules do control decisions-at least in the vast majority of cases.

b. Beyond Rules

This does not mean that interests, practical concerns, and desirability of results play no role in European conflicts law. These factors are simply considered at a different stage in the lawmaking process and in a more generalized fashion than in the United States. In the United States, they usually come into play more or less ad hoc when courts decide individual disputes. European conflicts law, in contrast, tends to typify and generalize them and to incorporate them into (mostly statutory) rules. As a result of having already been taken into account at the rule-making stage, they are normally not, as in the United States, open for debate in each case. * * *

As a result of this orientation toward rules and preference for deductive reasoning, European conflicts law places utmost importance on precise knowledge of rules and principles, their interplay, and the technique of their application. In contrast, the ability to argue general policies, interests, or fairness plays a minor role, at least in the individual case. Consequently, an American observer will find much of European conflicts law amazingly clear and straightforward, yet suspiciously rigid and dogmatic: just as a European jurist is likely to see the American conflicts process as hopelessly confused by multifactor tests and unprincipled ad hoc decisions. Whatever the merits of the respective methods, an American lawyer looking at European conflicts law should accept this difference lest she underestimate the significance of rules and misunderstand the intellectual disposition of her continental colleagues.

3. The Values of the Legal Order

The prevalence of statutes and the emphasis on rules indicate already that the European values of the legal order differ from those cherished in the United States. The United States is a country of immigrants with a diverse culture and a relatively short history. As a result, American society is committed to flexibility, change, and individualism. European nations including the common law jurisdictions, in contrast, are mostly old countries with more homogenous populations and long traditions. As a result, Western European society values stability, consistency, and social welfare. Of course, the differences are matters of degree and may be diminishing, but they are still reflected in the legal culture generally, and in conflicts law in particular. As a general matter, European conflicts law is marked by comparatively greater preference for certainty, logical consistency, and stability of rules, and for predictability of results over justice in the individual case. It is worthwhile to consider these preferences in turn.

a. Certainty

The certainty of rules is deemed more important than their flexibility in continental Europe. This is one reason why statutes are normally preferable to other sources. This preference is primarily responsible for the current European trend to codify choice-of-law for the same reason, blackletter rules are, in principle, desirable, not deplorable. The clearer rules cut, the better. The underlying assumption is that if a rule incorporates the appropriate policies and interests and is well-drafted, its blackletter character will not lead to unjust results, except in extreme, and thus rare, cases. * * *

b. Consistency

Rules are designed to be logically consistent and systematically organized, as befits a continental codification. They purport to build on clearly understood concepts and to use a precise uniform and thus reliable terminology. They should not contradict or cast doubt on each other and should contain no unintended gaps. * * *

c. Stability

It is important to Europeans that rules be stable and not subject to frequent innovation * * * [C]hange is approached with a circumspection bordering on hesitancy not only by legislatures, but also by courts and scholars. * * * Thus, from an American perspective, the European conflicts scene looks rather conservative, if not old-fashioned. It is important to recognize that this rarely results from lack of imagination but mostly reflects a conscious preference for stability over experimentation.

d. Predictability

The certainty, stability, and consistency of conflicts rules is meant to promote the predictability of results. Like American lawyers, European jurists recognize that complete predictability is unattainable. Since the uncertainty and stability of rules must be balanced against fairness in the individual case, European conflicts lawyers readily acknowledge that some flexibility of norms is desirable even at the expense of predictability of outcomes. But American and European conflicts regimes, again, often strike different balances. * * *

For an American conflicts lawyer dealing with transatlantic conflicts cases, the different values result in advantages as well as pitfalls.

One [sic] the one hand, the relative clarity, consistency, and stability of rules, and the emphasis on predictability of results, make European conflicts law more easily accessible to American lawyers than the more uncertain, fluctuating, and disparate American law is to her Swiss or Italian colleague. A half hour of studying the Rome Convention may enable an American lawyer to understand the basics of Western European choice of law rules in contracts and to predict the outcomes of all but the very difficult cases with a high degree of certainty. In contrast, a European lawyer, after having spent half an hour on American choice of law rules, has at best understood that she better not venture any prediction.

On the other hand, the values underlying and the characteristic features shaping European conflicts law require that American lawyers change their ways of thinking and adjust to the premises and predilections of the civil law culture. If they fail to take rules seriously and to handle them carefully, if they insist on emphasizing policies and interests in individual cases, and if they disregard the goals of certainty and predictability, they are bound to misinterpret and mishandle European conflicts law. They will also alienate European colleagues as well as judges and thus, inevitably, hurt their client's case.

NOTE ON SUBSEQUENT DEVELOPMENTS IN THE EUROPEAN UNION

The European perspective on private international law—i.e., the methodological, rule-oriented approach as summarized above by Prof. Reimann—has not changed significantly since 1995. Almost 15 years later, however, in 2009, this area became further unified in the E.U. First, Regulation (EC) No 864/2007 of the European Parliament and of the Council of 11 July 2007 on the Law Applicable to Non-Contractual obligations (*OJ* 2007, L 199/40—the so-called "Rome II Regulation") entered into force. Subsequently, Regulation (EC) No 593/2008 of the European Parliament and of the Council of 17 June 2008 on the Law Applicable to Contractual Obligations, (*OJ* 2008, L 177/6—the so-called "Rome I Regulation") went into force. Rome I replaced the 1980 Rome Convention [Rome Convention on the Law Applicable to Contractual Obligations, (originally enacted June 19, 1980) 2005 O.J. (C 334) 1], which governed contractual obligations at the time the above text was authored. Both Regulations apply in most, but not in all E.U. Member States. For details see, Volker Behr, *Rome I Regulation—A Mostly Unified Private International Law of Contractual Relationships within Most of the European Union*, 29, J. L. & Comm. 233 (2011).[*]

The Rome I Regulation applies to situations involving a conflict of laws, to contractual obligations in civil and commercial matters. It does not apply to revenue, customs or administrative matters. Art 1.1. There are a number of other areas that are excluded from the substantive scope of Rome I, such as questions involving the status or legal capacity of natural persons and arbitration agreements as well as agreements on the choice of court. As do most other legal systems, the Rome I Regulation provides as a basic rule that transnational contracts "be governed by the law chosen by the parties." Art. 3.1. Thus, the principle of party autonomy renders choice of law clauses generally enforceable. Article 4 provides hard and fast rules to determine the applicable law in the absence of choice. For example, a contract for the sale of goods shall be governed by the law of the country where the seller has his habitual residence. Art. 4.1(a). Again, in principle, the parties are free—and are actually encouraged—to agree in advance on what law should govern their transaction.

There are exceptions to this rule, however: As with forum selection clauses, systemically weaker parties, such as consumers, will be bound by choice of law

---

[*] For the text of Rome I, see http://eur-lex.europa.eu/ LexUriServ/LexUriServ.do?uri=OJ:L:2008: 177:0006:0016:EN:PDF

clauses only under certain circumstances, as stipulated in Article 6 of the Rome I Regulation.

Article 6 (ROME I)

Consumer contracts

1. Without prejudice to Articles 5 and 7, a contract concluded by a natural person for a purpose which can be regarded as being outside his trade or profession (the consumer) with another person acting in the exercise of his trade or profession (the professional) shall be governed by the law of the country where the consumer has his habitual residence, provided that the professional:

(a) pursues his commercial or professional activities in the country where the consumer has his habitual residence, or

(b) by any means, directs such activities to that country or to several countries including that country, and the contract falls within the scope of such activities.

2. Notwithstanding paragraph 1, the parties may choose the law applicable to a contract which fulfills the requirements of paragraph 1, in accordance with Article 3. Such a choice may not, however, have the result of depriving the consumer of the protection afforded to him by provisions that cannot be derogated from by agreement by virtue of the law which, in the absence of choice, would have been applicable on the basis of paragraph 1.

3. If the requirements in points (a) or (b) of paragraph 1 are not fulfilled, the law applicable to a contract between a consumer and a professional shall be determined pursuant to Articles 3 and 4.

4. Paragraphs 1 and 2 shall not apply to:

(a) a contract for the supply of services where the services are to be supplied to the consumer exclusively in a country other than that in which he has his habitual residence;

(b) a contract of carriage other than a contract relating to package travel within the meaning of Council Directive 90/314/EEC of 13 June 1990 on package travel, package holidays and package tours (1);

(c) a contract relating to a right *in rem* in immovable property or a tenancy of immovable property other than a contract relating to the right to use immovable properties on a timeshare basis within the meaning of Directive 94/47/EC;

(d) rights and obligations which constitute a financial instrument and rights and obligations constituting the terms and conditions governing the issuance or offer to the public and public take-over bids of transferable securities, and the subscription and redemption of units in collective investment undertakings in so far as these activities do not constitute provision of a financial service;

(e) a contract concluded within the type of system falling within the scope of Article 4(1)(h).

In contrast to the Rome I Regulation, the Rome II Regulation[*] covers situations involving cross-border conflict of laws in *non*-contractual obligations in civil and commercial matters. Art. 1.1. Similar to Rome I, Rome II does not apply to revenue, customs, or administrative matters, or to the liability of a Member State for acts and omissions in the exercise of State authority. Id. As with Rome I, there are a number of areas that are excluded from the substantive scope of Rome II. Perhaps most notable is the exclusion of non-contractual obligations arising out of violations of privacy and rights relating to personality, including defamation. Art. 1.2.(g). Such matters therefore continue to be governed by the preexisting domestic conflicts rules of the Member States. Non-contractual obligations mean primarily torts but include, among other things, claims based on unjust enrichment (Art. 2.1), and they encompass "non-contractual obligations that are likely to arise." Art. 2.2. The latter provision of Rome II on future torts corresponds with (and actually mirrors) the personal jurisdiction rule of Article 5.3 of the Brussels Regulation which we discuss more generally in Chapter 1.

The general principle for determining which law applies is set out in Article 4.1 of Rome II. According to that provision,

> Unless otherwise provided for in this Regulation, the law applicable to a non-contractual obligation arising out of a tort/delict shall be the law of the country in which the damage occurs irrespective of the country in which the event giving rise to the damage occurred and irrespective of the country or countries in which the indirect consequences of that event occur.

The remainder of Article 4 of Rome II provides for derogations from this rule as follows: According to Article 4.2, "where the person claimed to be liable and the person sustaining damage both have their habitual residence in the same country at the time when the damage occurs, the law of that country shall apply." And, pursuant to Article 4.3,

> Where it is clear from all the circumstances of the case that the tort/delict is manifestly more closely connected with a country other than that indicated in paragraphs 1 or 2, the law of that other country shall apply. A manifestly closer connection with another country might be based in particular on a preexisting relationship between the parties, such as a contract, that is closely connected with the tort/delict in question.

Subsequent provisions set out rules for specific torts, such as product liability suits (Art. 5), and suits over unfair competition (Art. 6).

As in Rome I, parties deemed to be in a systemically weaker position enjoy special protections. For example, Article 14 of the Rome II Regulation provides

---

[*] See http://eur-lex.europa.eu/LexUriServ/site/en/oj/2007/l_199/l_19920070731en00400049.pdf

that a choice of law clause is generally valid and enforceable, if the parties entered into the agreement after the event giving rise to the damage occurred. Alternatively, according to Article 14, agreements are valid and enforceable if they were entered into before the event rise to the damage occurred if they were freely negotiated and if all parties involved are pursuing a commercial activity. By implication, then, consumers cannot validly enter into a choice of law agreement before the event giving rise to the damages occurred. For a more detailed discussion of the Rome II Regulation, see Symeon Symeonides, *Rome II and Tort Conflicts: A Missed Opportunity,* 56 Am. J. Comp. L. 173 (2008).

F. The Extraterritorial Application of U.S. Statutes

Thus far, we have dealt with the problem of choice of law, primarily in areas such as tort and contract that are often not governed by statute. But many federal statutes may be relevant to transnational litigation, such as federal antitrust laws, or securities laws. Moreover, these statutes are often written in very broad language. The antitrust statute, for example, purports to outlaw "every" agreements in restraint of trade. Does that mean that an agreement in restraint of trade entered into by two French nationals to restrain trade in certain goods or services available only within France would be subject to U.S. law? Here the issue is whether the federal statute has extraterritorial reach, and if so, to what extent. And the analysis usually involves a question of statutory interpretation to ascertain congressional meaning.

Historically, since the emergence of nation states, the exercise of judicial, prescriptive and enforcement jurisdiction has been closely linked to the concept of territoriality and a simple (if not simplistic) syllogism reveals the reason for this nexus: the assertion of jurisdiction is an expression of state sovereignty; territoriality is an indispensable ingredient of state sovereignty; hence, jurisdiction must be closely related to, if not anchored in, territoriality. This finding was inherent in Ulrich Huber's 17th century work: *De Conflictu Legum Diversarum in Diversis Imperiis.* See Ernest G Lorenzen, "*Huber's* De Conflictu Legum," *in* Albert Kocourek (ed.), Celebration Legal Essays, To Mark the Twenty-fifth Year of Service of John H. Wigmore 200 (1919). And it was introduced to the jurisprudence of the United States by Justice Story in a Supreme Court decision nearly 190 years ago that produced at least two rules: first, every state may exercise control over persons, things and conduct within its territory; and second, no state has such regulatory power over persons, things and conduct outside its territory. See The Apollon, 22 U.S. (9 Wheat.) 362, 370 (1824) ("The laws of no nation can justly extend beyond its own territories except so far as regards its own citizens.").

In times when geographical space, distance and borders limited human activity, these rules were perceived as both workable and, for the most part, legitimate. But they were never absolute. See *The Case of the S.S. Lotus-France v. Turkey* (1927) PCIJ Reports, Series A, No. 10, in which the Permanent Court of International Justice held that a state may sanction a person's conduct who acted abroad but produced local injury. As territorial boundaries lost in significance, however, this perception changed. With markets no longer confined to national borders and with foreign conduct affecting local interests, jurisdictional rules premised on the concept of territoriality were increasingly criticized as providing neither workable nor fair solutions. Prompted by the need to adequately address these developments, changes did occur, such as the extension of domestic jurisdictional rules to conduct occurring in foreign locales when that activity produced local damages. For a recent and multidisciplinary account of the developments in this field, see Hannah L. Buxbaum, *Territory, Territoriality, and the Resolution of Jurisdictional Conflict*, 57 Am. J. Comp. L. 631, 632-636 (2009).

In what follows, we will examine the "extraterritorial" reach of the U.S. antitrust and securities laws, as well as the approach of the European Court of Justice with respect to foreign anticompetitive conduct affecting European interests.

1. The Extraterritorial Reach of U.S. Antitrust Laws

We begin by retracing the antitrust developments in the U.S. The most relevant statutory provisions in this field are found in the Sherman Act and the Clayton Act. According to section 1 of the Sherman Act, "Every contract, combination in the form of trust or otherwise, or conspiracy, in restraint of trade or commerce among the several States, or with foreign nations, is declared to be illegal." 15 U.S.C. § 1. Section 2 provides that "[e]very person who shall monopolize, or attempt to monopolize, or combine or conspire with any other person or persons, to monopolize any part of the trade or commerce among the several States, or with foreign nations, shall be deemed guilty of a felony . . . ." Id. § 2. Section 4 of the Clayton Act operationalizes the provisions of the Sherman Act, among other things, by vesting private plaintiffs with the right to sue defendants for treble damages and attorney fees if they have violated the antitrust provisions of the Sherman Act to the plaintiff's alleged injury. 15 U.S.C. § 15.

American Banana Co. v. United Fruit Co.

Supreme Court of the United States, 1909.

213 U.S. 347.

MR. JUSTICE HOLMES delivered the opinion of the court:

This is an action brought to recover threefold damages under the [Sherman Act] to protect trade against monopolies. * * *

The allegations of the complaint may be summed up as follows: The plaintiff is an Alabama corporation, organized in 1904. The defendant is a New Jersey corporation, organized in 1899. Long before the plaintiff was formed, the defendant, with intent to prevent competition and to control and monopolize the banana trade, bought the property and business of several of its previous competitors, with provision against their resuming the trade, made contracts with others, including a majority of the most important, regulating the quantity to be purchased and the price to be paid, and acquired a controlling amount of stock in still others. For the same purpose it organized a selling company, of which it held the stock that by agreement sold at fixed prices all the bananas of the combining parties. By this and other means it did monopolize and restrain the trade and maintained unreasonable prices. The defendant being in this ominous attitude, one McConnell, in 1903, started a banana plantation in Panama, then part of the United States of Columbia, and began to build a railway (which would afford his only means of export), both in accordance with the laws of the United States of Columbia. He was notified by the defendant that he must either combine or stop. Two months later, it is believed at the defendant's instigation, the governor of Panama recommended to his national government that Costa Rica be allowed to administer the territory through which the railroad was to run, and this although that territory had been awarded to Colombia under an arbitration agreed to by treaty. The defendant, and afterwards, in September, the government of Costa Rica, it is believed by the inducement of the defendant, interfered with McConnell. In November, 1903, Panama revolted and became an independent republic, declaring its boundary to be that settled by the award. In June, 1904, the plaintiff bought out McConnell and went on with the work, as it had a right to do under the laws of Panama. But in July, Costa Rican soldiers and officials, instigated by the defendant, seized a part of the plantation and a cargo of supplies and have held them ever since, and stopped the construction and operation of the plantation and railway. In August one Astua, by *ex parte* proceedings, got a judgment from a Costa Rican court, declaring the plantation to be his, although, it is alleged, the proceedings were not within the jurisdiction of Costa Rica, and were contrary to its laws and void. Agents of the defendant then bought the lands from Astua. The plaintiff has tried to induce the government of Costa Rica to withdraw its soldiers, and also has tried to persuade the United States to interfere, but has been thwarted in both by the defendant and has failed. The government of Costa Rica remained in possession down to the bringing of the suit.

As a result of the defendant's acts the plaintiff has been deprived of the use of the plantation, and the railway, the plantation, and supplies have been injured. The defendant also, by outbidding, has driven purchasers out of the market and has compelled producers to come to its terms, and it has prevented the plaintiff from buying for export and sale. This is the substantial damage alleged. There is thrown in a further allegation that the defendant has "sought to injure" the plaintiff's business by offering positions to its employees, and by discharging and threatening to discharge persons in its own employ who were stockholders of the plaintiff. But no particular point is made of this. It is contended, however, that, even if the main argument fails and the defendant is held not to be answerable for acts depending on the co-operation of the government of Costa Rica for their effect, a wrongful conspiracy resulting in driving the plaintiff out of business is to be gathered from the complaint, and that it was entitled to go to trial upon that.

It is obvious that, however stated, the plaintiff's case depends on several rather startling propositions. In the first place, the acts causing the damage were done, so far as appears, outside the jurisdiction of the United States, and within that of other states. It is surprising to hear it argued that they were governed by the act of Congress.

No doubt in regions subject to no sovereign, like the high seas, or to no law that civilized countries would recognize as adequate, such countries may treat some relations between their citizens as governed by their own law, and keep, to some extent, the old notion of personal sovereignty alive. * * * They go further, at times, and declare that they will punish anyone, subject or not, who shall do certain things, if they can catch him, as in the case of pirates on the high seas. In cases immediately affecting national interests they may go further still and may make, and, if they get the chance, execute, similar threats as to acts done within another recognized jurisdiction. * * * But the general and almost universal rule is that the character of an act as lawful or unlawful must be determined wholly by the law of the country where the act is done. * * * This principle was carried to an extreme in Milliken v. Pratt, 125 Mass. 374, 28 Am. Rep. 241. For another jurisdiction, if it should happen to lay hold of the actor, to treat him according to its own notions rather than those of the place where he did the acts, not only would be unjust, but would be an interference with the authority of another sovereign, contrary to the comity of nations, which the other state concerned justly might resent. * * *

Law is a statement of the circumstances, in which the public force will be brought to bear upon men through the courts. But the word commonly is confined to such prophecies or threats when addressed to persons living within the power of the courts. A threat that depends upon the choice of the party affected to bring himself within that power hardly would be called law in the ordinary sense. We do not speak of blockade running by neutrals as unlawful. And the usages of speech correspond to the limit of the attempts of the lawmaker, except in extraordinary cases. It is true that domestic corporations remain always within the power of the domestic law; but, in the present case, at least, there is no ground for distinguishing between corporations and men.

The foregoing considerations would lead, in case of doubt, to a construction of any statute as intended to be confined in its operation and effect to the territorial limits over which the lawmaker has general and legitimate power. "All legislation is prima facie territorial." Ex parte Blain, L. R. 12 Ch. Div. 522, 528; State v. Carter, 27 N. J. L. 499; People v. Merrill, 2 Park. Crim. Rep. 590, 596. Words having universal scope, such as "every contract in restraint of trade," "every person who shall monopolize," etc., will be taken, as a matter of course, to mean only everyone subject to such legislation, not all that the legislator subsequently may be able to catch. In the case of the present statute, the improbability of the United States attempting to make acts done in Panama or Costa Rica criminal is obvious, yet the law begins by making criminal the acts for which it gives a right to sue. We think it entirely plain that what the defendant did in Panama or Costa Rica is not within the scope of the statute so far as the present suit is concerned. Other objections of a serious nature are urged, but need not be discussed.

For again, not only were the acts of the defendant in Panama or Costa Rica not within the Sherman Act, but they were not torts by the law of the place, and therefore were not torts at all, however contrary to the ethical and economic postulates of that statute. The substance of the complaint is that, the plantation being within the *de facto* jurisdiction of Costa Rica, that state took and keeps possession of it by virtue of its sovereign power. But a seizure by a state is not a thing that can be complained of elsewhere in the courts. The fact, if it be one, that *de jure* the estate is in Panama, does not matter in the least; sovereignty is pure fact. The fact has been recognized by the United States, and, by the implications of the bill, is assented to by Panama.

The fundamental reason why persuading a sovereign power to do this or that cannot be a tort is not that the sovereign cannot be joined as a defendant or because it must be assumed to be acting lawfully. * * * The fundamental reason is that it is a contradiction in terms to say that, within its jurisdiction, it is unlawful to persuade a sovereign power to being about a result that it declares by its conduct to be desirable and proper. It does not, and foreign courts cannot, admit that the influences were improper or the results bad. It makes the persuasion lawful by its own act. The very meaning of sovereignty is that the decree of the sovereign makes law. * * * In the case of private persons, it consistently may assert the freedom of the immediate parties to an injury and yet declare that certain persuasions addressed to them are wrong. * * *

The acts of the soldiers and officials of Costa Rica are not alleged to have been without the consent of the government, and must be taken to have been done by its order. It ratified them, at all events, and adopted and keeps the possession taken by them. * * * The injuries to the plantation and supplies seem to have been the direct effect of the acts of the Costa Rican government, which is holding them under an adverse claim of right. The claim for them must fall with the claim for being deprived of the use and profits of the place. As to the buying at a high price, etc., it is enough to say that we have no ground for supposing that it was unlawful in the countries where the purchases were made. Giving to this complaint every reasonable latitude of interpretation we are of opinion that it alleges no case under the act of Congress, and discloses nothing that we can suppose to have been a tort where it was done. A conspiracy in this country to do acts in another jurisdiction does not draw to itself those acts and make them unlawful, if they are permitted by the local law.

Further reasons might be given why this complaint should not be upheld, but we have said enough to dispose of it and to indicate our general point of view.

NOTES AND QUESTIONS FOR DISCUSSION

1. Consider the role played by the "universal" principle of extraterritoriality in Justice Holmes's opinion in *American Banana*. Is the Court using the principle as a canon of statutory interpretation, to assess the likely intent of Congress? Or is the principle one that operates independently of any likely congressional intent? Suppose Congress had been clearer in the words of the statute about its intent for contracts such as those at issue in *American Banana* to be covered by the antitrust laws. Would the extraterritoriality principle block such application?

2. Around the same time as *American Banana*, the Supreme Court's approach to personal jurisdiction and choice of law was also grounded in notions of territoriality. Was the source of law respecting territorial limits in those other two areas the same as it was for the limit associated with the reach of federal statutes? If territorialism no longer operates to limit personal jurisdiction and choice of law in the way that it once did, could one predict a corresponding demise of territoriality as a limit on the scope of federal statutes in the modern era?

3. The Supreme Court adhered to *American Banana*'s strict territoriality presumption in subsequent decisions, including in areas outside of the antitrust laws. See, e.g., Jackson v. The Archimedes, 275 U.S. 463, 467-468 (1928) (citing to *American Banana* in support of its holding that the legal prohibition of paying seamen wages in advance would not apply to advancements by foreign vessels in foreign ports). It was only towards the end of World War II that the Sherman Act was applied in an extraterritorial manner. Ironically, the decision which is credited with opening the world to expansive, trans-border antitrust liability was not issued by the U.S. Supreme Court. Due to a lack of a quorum on the Court because of judicial recusals, the case was referred to a Second Circuit Court of Appeals panel to act as a court of last resort—a unique occurrence in the Supreme Court's history. Judge Learned Hand authored the opinion which outlasted in impact those of many of his colleagues on the Supreme Court bench.

United States v. Aluminum Co. of America

United States Court of Appeals, Second Circuit, 1945.
148 F.2d 416.

L. HAND, CIRCUIT JUDGE.

[In an antitrust action it brought initially against 63 defendants, the U.S. Government claimed "that the defendant, Aluminum Company of America [Alcoa], was monopolizing interstate and foreign commerce, particularly in the manufacture and sale of 'virgin' aluminum ingot, and . . . that that company and the defendant, Aluminum Limited [Limited], had entered into a conspiracy in restraint of such commerce." Alcoa was a U.S. company and Aluminum, Ltd. (Limited), a Canadian corporation. The extraterritoriality issue involved in this case was whether Limited and Alcoa had violated § 1 of the Sherman Act by becoming members of an international cartel (the "Alliance") among foreign aluminum producers.]

[W]e conclude that 'Alcoa' was not a party to the 'Alliance,' and did not join in any violation of Sec. 1 of the Act, so far as concerned foreign commerce.

Whether 'Limited' itself violated that section depends upon the character of the 'Alliance.' It was a Swiss corporation, created in pursuance of an agreement entered into on July 3, 1931, the signatories to which were a French corporation, two German, one Swiss, a British, and 'Limited.' The original agreement, or 'cartel,' provided for the formation of a corporation in Switzerland which should issue shares, to be taken up by the signatories. This corporation was from time to time to fix a quota of production for each share, and each shareholder was to be limited to the quantity measured by the number of shares it held, but was free to sell at any price it chose. The corporation fixed a price every year at which it would take off any shareholder's hands any part of its quota which it did not sell. No shareholder was to 'buy, borrow, fabricate or sell' aluminum produced by anyone not a shareholder except with the consent of the board of governors, but that must not be 'unreasonably withheld.' Nothing was said as to whether the arrangement extended to sales in the United States; but Article X, known as the 'Conversion Clause,' provided that any shareholder might exceed his quota to the extent that he converted into aluminum in the United States or Canada any ores delivered to him in either of those countries by persons situated in the United States. * * *

The agreement of 1936 abandoned the system of unconditional quotas, and substituted a system of royalties. Each shareholder was to have a fixed free quota for every share it held, but as its production exceeded the sum of its quotas, it was to pay a royalty, graduated progressively in proportion to the excess; and these royalties the 'Alliance' divided among the shareholders in proportion to their shares. This agreement—unlike the first—did not contain an express promise that the 'Alliance' would buy any undisposed of stocks at a fixed price, although perhaps § 3 of Subdivision A, of Part X may have impliedly recognized such an obligation. Probably, during the two years in which the shareholders operated under this agreement, that question did not arise for the demand for aluminum was very active. Nevertheless, we understand from 'Limited's' answer to an interrogatory that the last price fixed under the agreement of 1931 was understood to remain in force. Although this agreement, like its predecessor, was silent as to imports into the United States, when that question arose during its preparation, as it did, all the shareholders agreed that such imports should be included in the quotas. The German companies were exempted from royalties—for obvious reasons—and that, it would seem, for practical purposes put them out of the 'cartel' for the future, for it was scarcely possible that a German producer would be unable to dispose of all its production, at least within any future period that would be provided for. The shareholders continued this agreement unchanged until the end of March, 1938, by which time it had become plain that, at least for the time being, it was no longer of service to anyone. Nothing was, however, done to end it, although the German shareholders of course became enemies of the French, British and Canadian shareholders in 1939. The 'Alliance' itself has apparently never been dissolved; and indeed it appeared on the 'Proclaimed List of Blocked Nationals' of September 13, 1944.

Did either the agreement of 1931 or that of 1936 violate § 1 of the Act? The answer does not depend upon whether we shall recognize as a source of liability a liability imposed by another state. On the contrary we are concerned only with whether Congress chose to attach liability to the conduct outside the United States of persons not in allegiance to it. That being so, the only question open is whether Congress intended to impose the liability, and whether our own Constitution permitted it to do so: as a court of the United States, we cannot look beyond our own law. Nevertheless, it is quite true that we are not to read general words, such as those in this Act, without regard to the limitations customarily observed by nations upon the exercise of their powers; limitations which generally correspond to those fixed by the 'Conflict of Laws.' We should not impute to Congress an intent to punish all whom its courts can catch, for conduct which has no consequences within the United States. * * * On the other hand, it is settled law—as 'Limited' itself agrees—that any state may impose liabilities, even upon persons not within its allegiance, for conduct outside its borders that has consequences within its borders which the state reprehends; and these liabilities other states will ordinarily recognize. * * * It may be argued that this Act extends further. Two situations are possible. There may be agreements made beyond our borders not intended to affect imports, which do affect them, or which affect exports. Almost any limitation of the supply of goods in Europe, for example, or in South America, may have repercussions in the United States if there is trade between the two. Yet when one considers the international complications likely to arise from an effort in this country to treat such agreements as unlawful, it is safe to assume that Congress certainly did not intend the Act to cover them. Such agreements may on the other hand intend to include imports into the United States, and yet it may appear that they had no effect upon them. That situation might be thought to fall within the doctrine that intent may be a substitute for performance in the case of a contract made within the United States; or it might be thought to fall within the doctrine that a statute should not be interpreted to cover acts abroad which have no consequence here. We shall not choose between these alternatives; but for argument we shall assume that the Act does not cover agreements, even though intended to affect imports or exports, unless its performance is shown actually to have had some effect upon them. Where both conditions are satisfied, the situation certainly falls within such decisions as United States v. Pacific & Artic R. & Navigation Co., 228 U.S. 87; Thomsen v. Cayser, 243 U.S. 66 (1917), and United States v. Sisal Sales Corporation, 274 U.S. 268. (United States v. Nord Deutcher Lloyd, 223 U.S. 512, illustrates the same conception in another field.) It is true that in those cases the persons held liable had sent agents into the United States to perform part of the agreement; but an agent is merely an animate means of executing his principal's purposes, and, for the purposes of this case, he does not differ from an inanimate means; besides, only human agents can import and sell ingot.

Both agreements would clearly have been unlawful, had they been made within the United States; and it follows from what we have just said that both were unlawful, though made abroad, if they were intended to affect imports and did affect them. Since the shareholders almost at once agreed that the agreement of 1931 should not cover imports, we may ignore it and confine our discussion to that of 1936: indeed that we should have to do anyway, since it superseded the earlier agreement. * * *

The judge also found that the 1936 agreement did not 'materially affect the * * * foreign trade or commerce of the United States'; apparently because the imported ingot was greater in 1936 and 1937 than in earlier years. We cannot accept this finding, based as it was upon the fact that, in 1936, 1937 and the first quarter of 1938, the gross imports of ingot increased. It by no means follows from such an increase that the agreement did not restrict imports; and incidentally it so happens that in those years such inference as is possible at all, leads to the opposite conclusion. It is true that the average imports—including 'Alcoa's'—for the years 1932-1935 inclusive were about 15 million pounds, and that for 1936, 1937 and one-fourth of 1938 they were about 33 million pounds;

but the average domestic ingot manufacture in the first period was about 96 million and in the second about 262 million; so that the proportion of imports to domestic ingot was about 15.6 per cent for the first period and about 12.6 per cent for the second. We do not mean to infer from this that the quota system of 1936 did in fact restrain imports, as these figures might suggest; but we do mean that nothing is to be inferred from the gross increase of imports. We shall dispose of the matter therefore upon the assumption that, although the shareholders intended to restrict imports, it does not appear whether in fact they did so. Upon our hypothesis the plaintiff would therefore fail, if it carried the burden of proof upon this issue as upon others. We think, however, that, after the intent to affect imports was proved, the burden of proof shifted to 'Limited.' In the first place a depressant upon production which applies generally may be assumed, certeris paribus, to distribute its effect evenly upon all markets. Again, when the parties took the trouble specifically to make the depressant apply to a given market, there is reason to suppose that they expected that it would have some effect, which it could have only by lessening what would otherwise have been imported. If the motive they introduced was over-balanced in all instances by motives which induced the shareholders to import, if the United States market became so attractive that the royalties did not count at all and their expectations were in fact defeated, they to whom the facts were more accessible than to the plaintiff ought to prove it, for a prima facie case had been made. Moreover, there is an especial propriety in demanding this of 'Limited,' because it was 'Limited' which procured the inclusion in the agreement of 1936 of imports in the quotas. [Finding that this assumed restriction was bound to affect prices in the United States, the Court concluded that Limited's foreign conduct did constitute a violation of § 1 of the Sherman Act.]

NOTES AND QUESTIONS FOR DISCUSSION

1. The *Alcoa* decision fundamentally changed the operation of the Sherman Act. Since *Alcoa*, American courts apply U.S. antitrust law to any agreement or transaction with significant impact (i.e. "direct and substantial effect") on the U.S. economy, no matter where that agreement or transaction occurred. It thereby effectively did away with the territoriality restriction in its classical sense and replaced it with the new effects doctrine. It is needless to say that this decision forever changed the face of international law. It began the struggle between the United States and, in particular, its European allies, over the proper reach of competition laws.

2. The most dogged adversary of the U.S. in this struggle ironically was its closest ally on all other fronts: the United Kingdom. What had changed between *United Fruit* and *Alcoa*? The U.S. was emerging as the only remaining great power of the Western Hemisphere. U.S. troops were stretched over the far reaches of the globe, the U.S. had clearly awoken from an isolationist slumber. Yet more than just political reality had changed. Throughout the 1920s and 30s and certainly in the middle of the 1940s, the global economy, too, had changed. The 1920s (before the stock market crash) could be called a first era of globalization, but in 1929, it ended abruptly. Yet the global mindset and the inherent dangers for the domestic economy from foreign influences remained a background for economic decision-making in the public and private sector. The U.S. had become aware of foreign influences on its market now more acutely than ever. It also wished to avoid an economic meltdown and the ensuing consequences. One means of achieving this goal was to apply competition laws beyond the scope of national frontiers. And while *Alcoa* allows just this, it was the post-*Alcoa* Justice Department which made the most ample and most notorious use of the new reach of the Sherman Act. Indeed, "[i]n actual litigation, jurisdiction has not often been found lacking. Up to May 1973, the Department of Justice filed some 248 foreign trade antitrust cases; not one was lost for want of jurisdiction over the activities claimed to violate the law." Timberlane Lumber Co. v. Bank of America N.T. & S.A., 549 F.2d 597, 609 n.12 (9th Cir. 1976), citing to Wilbur Fugate, Foreign Commerce and the Antitrust Laws, App.B. at 498 (2d ed. 1973).

3. The new assertion of legislative power by the U.S. was not at all welcomed by Europe and other trading partners of the U.S. Most vociferously of all, the United Kingdom protested the use of the effects doctrine. See, e.g., A.V. Lowe, *Blocking Extraterritorial Jurisdiction: The British Protection of Trading Interests Act*, 1980, 75 Am. J. Int'l L. 257 (1981) (tracing the development of this protest which culminated in the 1980 enactment of the British Protection of Trading Interests Act.) Although the Act is neutral in its wording, it clearly aims at the reach of American antitrust laws by providing, inter alia, for the nonenforcement of foreign judgments that are premised on the extraterritorial application of substantive laws and by creating a "claw-back" remedy which grants recovery of the non-compensatory parts of multiple (i.e., treble) damages awards handed down by foreign (i.e., American) courts.

4. While these objections fell on deaf ears in the U.S. in the first decades of the effects doctrine, the mounting protest from foreign nations did create an awareness of such problems among some courts in the U.S. This unease found its most influential expression in a 1976 decision by the Ninth Circuit Court of Appeals, which follows.

Timberlane Lumber Co. v. Bank of America N.T. & S.A.

United States Court of Appeals, Ninth Circuit, 1976.

549 F.2d 597.

CHOY, CIRCUIT JUDGE.

Four separate actions, arising from the same series of events, were dismissed by the same district court and are consolidated here on appeal. The principal action is Timberlane Lumber Co. v. Bank of America (Timberlane action), an antitrust suit alleging violations of sections 1 and 2 of the Sherman Act (15 U.S.C. §§ 1, 2). * * * This action raises important questions concerning the application of American antitrust laws to activities in another country, including actions of foreign government officials. The district court dismissed the Timberlane action under the act of state doctrine and for lack of subject matter jurisdiction. The other three are diversity tort suits brought by employees of one of the Timberlane plaintiffs for individual injuries allegedly suffered in the course of the extended anti-Timberlane drama. Having dismissed the Timberlane action, the district court dismissed these three suits on the ground of forum non conveniens. We vacate the dismissals of all four actions and remand. * * *

The basic allegation of the Timberlane plaintiffs is that officials of the Bank of America and others located in both the United States and Honduras conspired to prevent Timberlane, through its Honduras subsidiaries, from milling lumber in Honduras and exporting it to the United States, thus maintaining control of the Honduran lumber export business in the hands of a few select individuals financed and controlled by the Bank. The intent and result of the conspiracy, they contend, was to interfere with the exportation to the United States, including Puerto Rico, of Honduran lumber for sale or use there by the plaintiffs, thus directly and substantially affecting the foreign commerce of the United States. * * *

There is no doubt that American antitrust laws extend over some conduct in other nations.* * * [T]he Sherman Act and with it other antitrust laws has been applied to extraterritorial conduct. See, e.g., * * * United States v. Aluminum Co. of America, 148 F.2d 416, (2d Cir. 1945) (the "Alcoa" case) * * *.

That American law covers some conduct beyond this nation's borders does not mean that it embraces all, however. Extraterritorial application is understandably a matter of concern for the other countries involved. Those nations have sometimes resented and protested, as excessive intrusions into their own spheres, broad assertions of authority by American courts. * * * Our courts have recognized this concern and have, at times, responded to it, even if not always enough to satisfy all the foreign critics. * * * In any event, it is evident that at some point the interests of the United States are too weak and the foreign harmony incentive for restraint too strong to justify an extraterritorial assertion of jurisdiction.

What that point is or how it is determined is not defined by international law. * * * Nor does the Sherman Act limit itself. In the domestic field the Sherman Act extends to the full reach of the commerce power. * * * To define it somewhat more modestly in the foreign commerce area courts have generally, and logically, fallen back on a narrower construction of congressional intent. * * *

It is the effect on American foreign commerce which is usually cited to support extraterritorial jurisdiction. *Alcoa* set the course, when Judge Hand declared [in *Alcoa*].: "[I]t is settled law . . . that any state may impose liabilities, even upon persons not within its allegiance, for conduct outside its borders that has consequences within its borders which the state reprehends; and these liabilities other states will ordinarily recognize." Despite its description as "settled law," Alcoa's assertion has been roundly disputed by many foreign commentators as being in conflict with international law, comity, and good judgment. Nonetheless, American courts have firmly concluded that there is some extraterritorial jurisdiction under the Sherman Act.

Even among American courts and commentators, however, there is no consensus on how far the jurisdiction should extend. The district court here concluded that a "direct and substantial effect" on United States foreign commerce was a prerequisite, without stating whether other factors were relevant or considered. * * *

The effects test by itself is incomplete because it fails to consider other nations' interests. Nor does it expressly take into account the full nature of the relationship between the actors and this country. Whether the alleged offender is an American citizen, for instance, may make a big difference; applying American laws to American citizens raises fewer problems than application to foreigners. * * *

A tripartite analysis seems to be indicated. * * * [T]he antitrust laws require in the first instance that there be some effect actual or intended on American foreign commerce before the federal courts may legitimately exercise subject matter jurisdiction under those statutes. Second, a greater showing of burden or restraint may be necessary to demonstrate that the effect is sufficiently large to present a cognizable injury to the plaintiffs and, therefore, a civil violation of the antitrust laws. * * * Third, there is the additional question which is unique to the international setting of whether the interests of, and links to, the United States including the magnitude of the effect on American foreign commerce are sufficiently strong, vis-a-vis those of other nations, to justify an assertion of extraterritorial authority. * * *

What we prefer [regarding the third component of the tripartite analysis] is an evaluation and balancing of the relevant considerations in each case in the words of Kingman Brewster, a "jurisdictional rule of reason." * * *

The elements to be weighed [in assessing the third component] include the degree of conflict with foreign law or policy, the nationality or allegiance of the parties and the locations or principal places of businesses or corporations, the extent to which enforcement by either state can be expected to achieve compliance, the relative significance of effects on the United States as compared with those elsewhere, the extent to which there is explicit purpose to harm or affect American commerce, the foreseeability of such effect, and the relative importance to the violations charged of conduct within the United States as compared with conduct abroad. A court evaluating these factors should identify the potential degree of conflict if American authority is asserted. A difference in law or policy is one likely sore spot, though one which may not always be present. Nationality is another; though foreign governments may have some concern for the treatment of American citizens and business residing there, they primarily care about their own nationals. Having assessed the conflict, the court should then determine whether in the face of it the contacts and interests of the United States are sufficient to support the exercise of extraterritorial jurisdiction.

We conclude, then, that the problem should be approached in three parts: Does the alleged restraint affect, or was it intended to affect, the foreign commerce of the United States? Is it of such a type and magnitude so as to be cognizable as a violation of the Sherman Act? As a matter of international comity and fairness, should the extraterritorial jurisdiction of the United States be asserted to cover it? The district court's judgment found only that the restraint involved in the instant suit did not produce a direct and substantial effect on American foreign commerce. That holding does not satisfy any of these inquiries.

NOTES AND QUESTIONS FOR DISCUSSION

1. On remand, the district court applied the tripartite test and found that Timberlane's complaint should be dismissed because maintaining the action would violate the comity-based "jurisdictional rule of reason" enunciated by the court of appeals. Timberlane appealed that decision which was, however, affirmed. 749 F.2d 1378 (9th Cir. 1984).

2. The *Timberlane* decision provides an unprecedented international comity approach to the application of U.S. antitrust laws abroad. It appears designed to set limits to the exercise of jurisdiction over a dispute which should more properly have been resolved elsewhere. Note how the Supreme Court defined comity in its seminal decision on foreign judgment recognition:

> "Comity," in the legal sense, is neither a matter of absolute obligation, on the one hand, nor of mere courtesy and good will, upon the other. But it is the recognition which one nation allows within its territory to the legislative, executive or judicial acts of another nation, having due regard both to international duty and convenience, and to the rights of its own citizens or of other persons who are under the protection of its laws.

Hilton v. Guyot 159 U.S. 113, 143 (1895). See Chapter 8, Section B.

Does this help to explain the reference to comity in a setting like *Timberlane* which involves the curtailment of the extraterritorial application of domestic law? The court in *Timberlane* sought to remedy the normative overreach of previous decisions. It attempted to bring into reasonable confines the exercise of federal jurisdiction over foreign transactions. While the court in *Timberlane* found little, if any, affirmation in any subsequent opinion of the Supreme Court, it certainly had some impact on the development of jurisdictional doctrine in in the field of American antitrust law. But see F. Hoffman-La Roche Ltd. v. Empagran, S.A., 542 U.S. 155 (2004), discussed at subsection 3, below.

3. *Timberlane's* third prong, the jurisdictional "rule of reason," is what distinguished it from previous court decisions. It involves a test which required, in essence, the court to balance foreign sovereign interests in the case against those of the U.S. If the U.S. had a greater public interest than the foreign sovereign, jurisdiction would be deemed proper. If, however, the foreign state had a greater interest in adjudicating the matter, a federal court would have to stay its proceedings. Was the *Timberlane* court trying to resolve the question of the extraterritorial reach of the antitrust statute by engaging in a kind of governmental interest analysis that is usually reserved for conflict of laws? Identify the factors of *Timberlane's* rule of reason and compare them with the following Restatement provisions that were adopted almost 10 years after Judge Choy wrote the opinion in *Timberlane*:

RESTATEMENT (THIRD) OF FOREIGN RELATIONS LAW OF THE UNITED STATES (1987).

§ 402. Bases of Jurisdiction to Prescribe

Subject to § 403, a state has jurisdiction to prescribe law with respect to

(1) (a) conduct that, wholly or in substantial part, takes place within its territory;

(b) the status of persons, or interests in things, present within its territory;

(c) conduct outside its territory that has or is intended to have substantial effect within its territory;

(2) the activities, interests, status, or relations of its nationals outside as well as within its territory; and

(3) certain conduct outside its territory by persons not its nationals that is directed against the security of the state or against a limited class of other state interests.

§ 403. Limitations on Jurisdiction to Prescribe

(1) Even when one of the bases for jurisdiction under § 402 is present, a state may not exercise jurisdiction to prescribe law with respect to a person or activity having connections with another state when the exercise of such jurisdiction is unreasonable.

(2) Whether exercise of jurisdiction over a person or activity is unreasonable is determined by evaluating all relevant factors, including, where appropriate:

(a) the link of the activity to the territory of the regulating state, i.e., the extent to which the activity takes place within the territory, or has substantial, direct, and foreseeable effect upon or in the territory;

(b) the connections, such as nationality, residence, or economic activity, between the regulating state and the person principally responsible for the activity to be regulated, or between that state and those whom the regulation is designed to protect;

(c) the character of the activity to be regulated, the importance of regulation to the regulating state, the extent to which other states regulate such activities, and the degree to which the desirability of such regulation is generally accepted.

(d) the existence of justified expectations that might be protected or hurt by the regulation;

(e) the importance of the regulation to the international political, legal, or economic system;

(f) the extent to which the regulation is consistent with the traditions of the international system;

(g) the extent to which another state may have an interest in regulating the activity; and

(h) the likelihood of conflict with regulation by another state.

(3) When it would not be unreasonable for each of two states to exercise jurisdiction over a person or activity, but the prescriptions by the two states are in conflict, each state has an obligation to evaluate its own as well as the other state's interest in exercising jurisdiction, in light of all the relevant factors, including those set out in Subsection (2); a state should defer to the other state if that state's interest is clearly greater.

Is the approach of the Restatement (Third) essentially the same that Judge Choy employs in *Timberlane*? Whatever your decision, note that both tests involve an exercise of interest balancing. While *Timberlane* was celebrated by some for its comity-based concerns for foreign sensitivities (and foreign sovereign interests), it also attracted a large group of critics. The criticism focused on whether evaluating and weighing foreign political and economic interests would entail tasks that the judiciary is neither equipped nor authorized to perform. See, e.g., *In re* Uranium Antitrust Litigation, 480 F. Supp. 1138, 1148 (N.D. Ill. 1979), which discussed the balancing problem at about the same time as *Timberlane was* pending:

> To summarize the preceding discussion, we have concluded that we possess the power to enter an order against defendants under Rule 37(a) compelling them to produce documents located abroad if the particular defendant is within the personal jurisdiction of this court and has control over the requested documents. *Société* [Nationale Industrielle Aérospatiale v. Z.S. District Court, 482 U.S. 522 (1987)] teaches that the decision whether to exercise that power is a discretionary one which is informed by three main factors: 1) the importance of the policies underlying the United States statute which forms the basis for the plaintiffs' claims; 2) the importance of the requested documents in illuminating key elements of the claims; and 3) the degree of flexibility in the foreign nation's application of its nondisclosure laws. Relying on the Court's additional suggestion that each case must depend upon its particular facts, several defendants urge that we consider several other factors that we have not yet discussed. However, in the circumstances of this case, we find that these other factors are of limited or no utility.

> Several defendants cite the Restatement, Second, Foreign Relations Law of the United States, § 40(a) [which was the predecessor of § 403 of the Third Restatement]or rely on broad notions of "international comity" for the proposition that we should balance the vital national interests of the United States and the foreign countries to determine which interests predominate. Aside from the fact that the judiciary has little expertise, or perhaps even authority, to evaluate the economic and social policies of a foreign country, such a balancing test is inherently unworkable in this case. The competing interests here display an irreconcilable conflict on precisely the same plane of national policy. Westinghouse seeks to enforce this nation's antitrust laws against an alleged international marketing arrangement among uranium producers, and to

that end has sought documents located in foreign countries where those producers conduct their business. In specific response to this and other related litigation in the American courts, three foreign governments have enacted nondisclosure legislation which is aimed at nullifying the impact of American antitrust legislation by prohibiting access to those same documents. It is simply impossible to judicially "balance" these totally contradictory and mutually negating actions.

In re Uranium Antitrust Litigation, 480 F. Supp. at 1148.

How exactly does *Uranium Antitrust* differ from *Timberlane*? Is one decision's analysis preferable to the other, or more practical? Consider whether there are any indications in the Restatement or in *Timberlane* as to the relative weight of comity factors. For example, what should weigh more: the "degree of the conflict," or "the nationality . . . of the parties"?

More than 15 years after the Ninth Circuit's decision in *Timberlane*, the U.S. Supreme Court had the opportunity to decide whether it would adopt *Timberlane*'s comity-based limitations on the reach of U.S. antitrust law. The case is excerpted below. Make sure to read and compare carefully the majority opinion and the dissent.

Hartford Fire Ins. Co. v. California

Supreme Court of the United States, 1993.

509 U.S. 764.

JUSTICE SOUTER announced the judgment of the Court and delivered the opinion of the Court with respect to Parts I, II-A, III, and IV, and an opinion concurring in the judgment with respect to Part II-B.

The Sherman Act makes every contract, combination, or conspiracy in unreasonable restraint of interstate or foreign commerce illegal. 26 Stat. 209, as amended, 15 U.S.C. § 1. These consolidated cases present questions about the application of that Act to the insurance industry, both here and abroad. The plaintiffs (respondents here) allege that both domestic and foreign defendants (petitioners here) violated the Sherman Act by engaging in various conspiracies to affect the American insurance market. * * * [A] group of foreign defendants argues that * * * international comity requires the District Court to refrain from exercising jurisdiction over certain claims against it. We hold that * * * , even assuming it applies, the principle of international comity does not preclude District Court jurisdiction over the foreign conduct alleged.

I.

The two petitions before us stem from consolidated litigation comprising the complaints of 19 States and many private plaintiffs alleging that the defendants, members of the insurance industry, conspired in violation of § 1 of the Sherman

Act to restrict the terms of coverage of commercial general liability (CGL) insurance available in the United States. * * *

A.

According to the complaints, the object of the conspiracies was to force certain primary insurers (insurers who sell insurance directly to consumers) to change the terms of their standard CGL insurance policies to conform with the policies the defendant insurers wanted to sell. The defendants wanted four changes. * * *

The Fifth Claim for Relief in the * * * Complaint charge[s] a conspiracy among a group of London reinsurers [in violation of § 1 of the Sherman Antitrust Act.] * * *

After the actions had been consolidated for litigation in the Northern District of California, the defendants moved to dismiss for failure to state a cause of action, or, in the alternative, for summary judgment. The District Court granted the motions to dismiss. * * * The District Court also dismissed the three claims that named only certain London-based defendants, invoking international comity and applying the Ninth Circuit's decision in *Timberlane Lumber Co.* * * *

The Court of Appeals reversed. * * * [Regarding] the three claims brought solely against foreign defendants, the court applied its *Timberlane* analysis, but concluded that the principle of international comity was no bar to exercising Sherman Act jurisdiction.

* * *

III

* * * [T]he District Court undoubtedly had jurisdiction of these Sherman Act claims, as the London reinsurers apparently concede. See Tr. of Oral Arg. 37 ("Our position is not that the Sherman Act does not apply in the sense that a minimal basis for the exercise of jurisdiction doesn't exist here. Our position is that there are certain circumstances, and that this is one of them, in which the interests of another State are sufficient that the exercise of that jurisdiction should be restrained"). Although the proposition was perhaps not always free from doubt, see *American Banana Co. v. United Fruit Co.,* it is well established by now that the Sherman Act applies to foreign conduct that was meant to produce and did in fact produce some substantial effect in the United States. * * * Such is the conduct alleged here: that the London reinsurers engaged in unlawful conspiracies to affect the market for insurance in the United States and that their conduct in fact produced substantial effect.[23]

---

[23] Under § 402 of the Foreign Trade Antitrust Improvements Act of 1982 (FTAIA), 96 Stat. 1246, 15 U.S.C. § 6a, the Sherman Act does not apply to conduct involving foreign trade or commerce, other than import trade or import commerce, unless "such conduct has a direct, substantial, and reasonably foreseeable effect" on domestic or import commerce. § 6a(1)(A). The FTAIA was intended to exempt from the Sherman Act export transactions that did not injure the United States economy, see H.R. Rep. No. 97-686, pp. 2-3, 9-10 (1982); P. Areeda & H. Hovenkamp, Antitrust Law ¶ 236'a, pp. 296-297 (Supp. 1992); and it is unclear how it might apply to the conduct alleged here. Also unclear is whether the Act's "direct, substantial, and reasonably foreseeable effect" standard amends existing law or merely codifies it. See *id.,* ¶ 236'a, p. 297. We need not address

According to the London reinsurers, the District Court should have declined to exercise such jurisdiction under the principle of international comity.[24] The Court of Appeals agreed that courts should look to that principle in deciding whether to exercise jurisdiction under the Sherman Act. This availed the London reinsurers nothing, however. To be sure, the Court of Appeals believed that "application of [American] antitrust laws to the London reinsurance market 'would lead to significant conflict with English law and policy,'" and that "[s]uch a conflict, unless out-weighed by other factors, would by itself be reason to decline exercise of jurisdiction." But other factors, in the court's view, including the London reinsurers' express purpose to affect United States commerce and the substantial nature of the effect produced, out-weighed the supposed conflict and required the exercise of jurisdiction in this litigation.

When it enacted the FTAIA, Congress expressed no view on the question whether a court with Sherman Act jurisdiction should ever decline to exercise such jurisdiction on grounds of international comity. See H.R. Rep. No. 97-686, p. 13 (1982) ("If a court determines that the requirements for subject matter jurisdiction are met, [the FTAIA] would have no effect on the court['s] ability to employ notions of comity * * * or otherwise to take account of the international character of the transaction") (citing *Timberlane*). We need not decide that question here, however, for even assuming that in a proper case a court may decline to exercise Sherman Act jurisdiction over foreign conduct (or, as JUSTICE SCALIA would put it, may conclude by the employment of comity analysis in the first instance that there is no jurisdiction), international comity would not counsel against exercising jurisdiction in the circumstances alleged here.

The only substantial question in this litigation is whether "there is in fact a true conflict between domestic and foreign law." *Société Nationale Industrielle Aérospatiale v. United States Dist. Court for Southern Dist. of Iowa,* 482 U.S. 522, 555 (1987) (BLACKMUN, J., concurring in part and dissenting in part). The London reinsurers contend that applying the Act to their conduct would conflict significantly with British law, and the British Government, appearing before us as *amicus curiae*, concurs. They assert that Parliament has established a com-

---

these questions here. Assuming that the FTAIA's standard affects this litigation, and assuming further that that standard differs from the prior law, the conduct alleged plainly meets its requirements.

[24] JUSTICE SCALIA contends that comity concerns figure into the prior analysis whether jurisdiction exists under the Sherman Act. This contention is inconsistent with the general understanding that the Sherman Act covers foreign conduct producing a substantial intended effect in the United States, and that concerns of comity come into play, if at all, only after a court has determined that the acts complained of are subject to Sherman Act jurisdiction. See *United States v. Aluminum Co. of America,* 148 F.2d 416, 444 (CA2 1945) ("It follows from what we have . . . said that [the agreements at issue] were unlawful [under the Sherman Act], though made abroad, if they were intended to affect imports and did affect them"); *Mannington Mills, Inc. v. Congoleum Corp.,* 595 F.2d 1287, 1294 (CA3 1979) (once court determines that jurisdiction exists under the Sherman Act, question remains whether comity precludes its exercise); H. R. Rep. No. 97-686, *supra,* at 13. But cf. *Timberlane Lumber Co. v. Bank of America, N.T. & S.A.,* 549 F.2d 597, 613 (CA9 1976); 1 J. Atwood & K. Brewster, Antitrust and American Business Abroad 166 (1981). In any event, the parties conceded jurisdiction at oral argument, and we see no need to address this contention here.

prehensive regulatory regime over the London reinsurance market and that the conduct alleged here was perfectly consistent with British law and policy. But this is not to state a conflict. "The fact that conduct is lawful in the state in which it took place will not, of itself, bar application of the United States antitrust laws," even where the foreign state has a strong policy to permit or encourage such conduct. Restatement (Third) Foreign Relations Law § 415, Comment *j*; * * * . No conflict exists, for these purposes, "where a person subject to regulation by two states can comply with the laws of both." * * * Since the London reinsurers do not argue that British law requires them to act in some fashion prohibited by the law of the United States, or claim that their compliance with the laws of both countries is otherwise impossible, we see no conflict with British law. * * * We have no need in this litigation to address other considerations that might inform a decision to refrain from the exercise of jurisdiction on grounds of international comity.

IV

The judgment of the Court of Appeals is affirmed in part and reversed in part, and the cases are remanded for further proceedings consistent with this opinion.

SCALIA, J., delivered a dissenting opinion with respect to Part II, in which O'CONNOR, KENNEDY, and THOMAS, JJ. have joined.

* * *

II

Petitioners, * * * various British corporations and other British subjects, argue that certain of the claims against them constitute an inappropriate extraterritorial application of the Sherman Act. It is important to distinguish two distinct questions raised by this petition: whether the District Court had jurisdiction, and whether the Sherman Act reaches the extraterritorial conduct alleged here. On the first question, I believe that the District Court had subject-matter jurisdiction over the Sherman Act claims against all the defendants (personal jurisdiction is not contested). Respondents asserted nonfrivolous claims under the Sherman Act, and 28 U.S.C. § 1331 vests district courts with subject-matter jurisdiction over cases "arising under" federal statutes. As precedents such as *Lauritzen v. Larsen,* 345 U.S. 571 (1953), make clear, that is sufficient to establish the District Court's jurisdiction over these claims. *Lauritzen* involved a Jones Act claim brought by a foreign sailor against a foreign shipowner. The shipowner contested the District Court's jurisdiction, apparently on the grounds that the Jones Act did not govern the dispute between the foreign parties to the action. Though ultimately agreeing with the shipowner that the Jones Act did not apply, the Court held that the District Court had jurisdiction.

> "As frequently happens, a contention that there is some barrier to granting plaintiff's claim is cast in terms of an exception to jurisdiction of subject matter. A cause of action under our law was asserted here, and the court had power to determine whether it was or was not well founded in law and in fact." 345 U.S. at 575.

The second question—the extraterritorial reach of the Sherman Act—has nothing to do with the jurisdiction of the courts. It is a question of substantive law turning on whether, in enacting the Sherman Act, Congress asserted regulatory power over the challenged conduct. * * * If a plaintiff fails to prevail on this issue, the court does not dismiss the claim for want of subject-matter jurisdiction—want of power to adjudicate; rather, it decides the claim, ruling on the merits that the plaintiff has failed to state a cause of action under the relevant statute. * * *

There is, however, a type of "jurisdiction" relevant to determining the extraterritorial reach of a statute; it is known as "legislative jurisdiction," * * * or "jurisdiction to prescribe". * * * This refers to "the authority of a state to make its law applicable to persons or activities," and is quite a separate matter from "jurisdiction to adjudicate" * * * There is no doubt, of course, that Congress possesses legislative jurisdiction over the acts alleged in this complaint: Congress has broad power under Article I, § 8, cl. 3, "to regulate Commerce with foreign Nations," and this Court has repeatedly upheld its power to make laws applicable to persons or activities beyond our territorial boundaries where United States interests are affected. See *Ford v. United States,* 273 U.S. 593, 621-623 (1927); *United States v. Bowman,* 260 U.S. 94, 98-99 (1922); *American Banana,* at 356. But the question in this litigation is whether, and to what extent, Congress *has* exercised that undoubted legislative jurisdiction in enacting the Sherman Act.

Two canons of statutory construction are relevant in this inquiry. The first is the "longstanding principle of American law 'that legislation of Congress, unless a contrary intent appears, is meant to apply only within the territorial jurisdiction of the United States.'" *Aramco,* at 248 (quoting *Foley Bros., Inc. v. Filardo*, 336 U.S. 281, 285 (1949)). Applying that canon in *Aramco*, we held that the version of Title VII of the Civil Rights Act of 1964 then in force, 42 U.S.C. §§ 2000e to 2000e-17 (1988 ed.), did not extend outside the territory of the United States even though the statute contained broad provisions extending its prohibitions to, for example, "'any activity, business, or industry in commerce.'" *Id.,* at 249 (quoting 42 U.S.C. § 2000e(h)). We held such "boilerplate language" to be an insufficient indication to override the presumption against extraterritoriality. The Sherman Act contains similar "boilerplate language," and if the question were not governed by precedent, it would be worth considering whether that presumption controls the outcome here. We have, however, found the presumption to be overcome with respect to our antitrust laws; it is now well established that the Sherman Act applies extraterritorially. See *Matsushita Elec. Industrial Co. v. Zenith Radio Corp.,* 475 U.S. 574, 582, n.6 (1986); *Continental Ore Co. v. Union Carbide & Carbon Corp.,* 370 U.S. 690, 704 (1962); see also *United States v. Aluminum Co. of America,* 148 F.2d 416 (CA2 1945).

But if the presumption against extraterritoriality has been overcome or is otherwise inapplicable, a second canon of statutory construction becomes relevant: "An act of congress ought never to be construed to violate the law of nations if any other possible construction remains." *Murray v. Schooner Charming Betsy,* 6 U.S. 64 (1804) (Marshall, C.J.). This canon is "wholly independent" of the presumption against extraterritoriality. *Aramco,* at 264 (Marshall, J., dissenting). It is relevant to determining the substantive reach of a statute because "the law of nations," or customary international law, includes limitations on a nation's exercise of its jurisdiction to prescribe. See Restatement (Third) §§ 401-416. Though it clearly has constitutional authority to do so, Congress is generally presumed not to have exceeded those customary international-law limits on jurisdiction to prescribe.

Consistent with that presumption, this and other courts have frequently recognized that, even where the presumption against extraterritoriality does not apply, statutes should not be interpreted to regulate foreign persons or conduct if that regulation would conflict with principles of international law. For example, in *Romero v. International Terminal Operating Co.*, 358 U.S. 354 (1959), the plaintiff, a Spanish sailor who had been injured while working aboard a Spanish-flag and Spanish-owned vessel, filed a Jones Act claim against his Spanish employer. The presumption against extraterritorial application of federal statutes was inapplicable to the case, as the actionable tort had occurred in American waters. The Court nonetheless stated that, "in the absence of a contrary congressional direction," it would apply "principles of choice of law that are consonant with the needs of a general federal maritime law and with due recognition of our self-regarding respect for the relevant interests of foreign nations in the regulation of maritime commerce as part of the legitimate concern of the international community." * * * "The controlling considerations" in this choice-of-law analysis were "the interacting interests of the United States and of foreign countries."

Romero referred to, and followed, the choice-of-law analysis set forth in *Lauritzen v. Larsen*, 345 U.S. 571 (1953). As previously mentioned, *Lauritzen* also involved a Jones Act claim brought by a foreign sailor against a foreign employer. The *Lauritzen* Court recognized the basic problem: "If [the Jones Act were] read literally, Congress has conferred an American right of action which requires nothing more than that plaintiff be 'any seaman who shall suffer personal injury in the course of his employment.'" The solution it adopted was to construe the statute "to apply only to areas and transactions in which *American law would be considered operative under prevalent doctrines of international law.*" (emphasis added). To support application of international law to limit the facial breadth of the statute, the Court relied upon—of course—Chief Justice Marshall's statement in *Schooner Charming Betsy*. It then set forth "several factors which, alone or in combination, are generally conceded to influence choice of law to govern a tort claim." * * * See also *McCulloch v. Sociedad Nacional de Marineros de Honduras*, 372 U.S. 10, 21-22 (1963) (applying *Schooner Charming Betsy* principle to restrict application of National Labor Relations Act to foreign-flag vessels).

Lauritzen, Romero, and *McCulloch* were maritime cases, but we have recognized the principle that the scope of generally worded statutes must be construed in light of international law in other areas as well. More specifically, the principle was expressed in *United States v. Aluminum Co. of America*, 148 F.2d 416 (CA2 1945), the decision that established the extraterritorial reach of the Sherman Act. In his opinion for the court, Judge Learned Hand cautioned "we are not to read general words, such as those in [the Sherman] Act, without regard to the limitations customarily observed by nations upon the exercise of their powers; limitations which generally correspond to those fixed by the 'Conflict of Laws.'"

More recent lower court precedent has also tempered the extraterritorial application of the Sherman Act with considerations of "international comity." The "comity" they refer to is not the comity of courts, whereby judges decline to exercise jurisdiction over matters more appropriately adjudged elsewhere, but rather what might be termed "prescriptive comity": the respect sovereign nations afford each other by limiting the reach of their laws. That comity is exercised by legislatures when they enact laws, and courts assume it has been exercised when they come to interpreting the scope of laws their legislatures have enacted. It is a traditional component of choice-of-law theory. See J. Story, Commentaries on the Conflict of Laws § 38 (1834) (distinguishing between the "comity of the courts" and the "comity of nations," and defining the latter as "the true foundation and extent of the obligation of the laws of one nation within the territories of another"). Comity in this sense includes the choice-of-law principles that, "in the absence of contrary congressional direction," are assumed to be incorporated into our substantive laws having extraterritorial reach. *Romero,* at 382-383; see also *Lauritzen,* at 578-579; *Hilton v. Guyot,* 159 U.S. 113, 162-166 (1895). Considering comity in this way is just part of determining whether the Sherman Act prohibits the conduct at issue.[9]

In sum, the practice of using international law to limit the extraterritorial reach of statutes is firmly established in our jurisprudence. In proceeding to apply that practice to the present cases, I shall rely on the Restatement (Third) for the relevant principles of international law. Its standards appear fairly supported in the decisions of this Court construing international choice-of-law principles (*Lauritzen, Romero,* and *McCulloch*) and in the decisions of other federal courts, especially *Timberlane.* Whether the Restatement precisely reflects international law in every detail matters little here, as I believe this litigation would be resolved the same way under virtually any conceivable test that takes account of foreign regulatory interests.

Under the Restatement, a nation having some "basis" for jurisdiction to prescribe law should nonetheless refrain from exercising that jurisdiction "with respect to a person or activity having connections with another state when the exercise of such jurisdiction is unreasonable." Restatement (Third) § 403(1). The "reasonableness" inquiry turns on a number of factors. * * * Rarely would these factors point more clearly against application of United States law. The activity relevant to the counts at issue here took place primarily in the United Kingdom,

---

[9] Some antitrust courts, including the Court of Appeals in the present cases, have mistaken the comity at issue for the "comity of courts," which has led them to characterize the question presented as one of "abstention," that is, whether they should "exercise or decline jurisdiction." *Mannington Mills, Inc. v. Congoleum Corp.,* 595 F.2d 1287, 1294, 1296 (CA3 1979); see also *In re Insurance Antitrust Litigation,* 938 F.2d 919, 932 (CA9 1991). As I shall discuss, that seems to be the error the Court has fallen into today. Because courts are generally reluctant to refuse the exercise of conferred jurisdiction, confusion on this seemingly theoretical point can have the very practical consequence of greatly expanding the extraterritorial reach of the Sherman Act.

and the defendants in these counts are British corporations and British subjects having their principal place of business or residence outside the United States. Great Britain has established a comprehensive regulatory scheme governing the London reinsurance markets, and clearly has a heavy "interest in regulating the activity". Considering these factors, I think it unimaginable that an assertion of legislative jurisdiction by the United States would be considered reasonable, and therefore it is inappropriate to assume, in the absence of statutory indication to the contrary, that Congress has made such an assertion.

It is evident from what I have said that the Court's comity analysis, which proceeds as though the issue is whether the courts should "decline to exercise . . . jurisdiction," rather than whether the Sherman Act covers this conduct, is simply misdirected. I do not at all agree, moreover, with the Court's conclusion that the issue of the substantive scope of the Sherman Act is not in the cases. To be sure, the parties did not make a clear distinction between adjudicative jurisdiction and the scope of the statute. Parties often do not, as we have observed (and have declined to punish with procedural default) before. It is not realistic, and also not helpful, to pretend that the only really relevant issue in this litigation is not before us. In any event, if one erroneously chooses, as the Court does, to make adjudicative jurisdiction (or, more precisely, abstention) the vehicle for taking account of the needs of prescriptive comity, the Court still gets it wrong. It concludes that no "true conflict" counseling nonapplication of United States law (or rather, as it thinks, United States judicial jurisdiction) exists unless compliance with United States law would constitute a *violation* of another country's law. That breathtakingly broad proposition, which contradicts the many cases discussed earlier, will bring the Sherman Act and other laws into sharp and unnecessary conflict with the legitimate interests of other countries—particularly our closest trading partners.

In the sense in which the term "conflict" was used in *Lauritzen,* and is generally understood in the field of conflicts of laws, there is clearly a conflict in this litigation. The petitioners here, like the defendant in *Lauritzen,* were not compelled by any foreign law to take their allegedly wrongful actions, but that no more precludes a conflict-of-laws analysis here than it did there. Where applicable foreign and domestic law provide different substantive rules of decision to govern the parties' dispute, a conflict-of-laws analysis is necessary. See generally R. Weintraub, Commentary on Conflict of Laws 2-3 (1980); Restatement (First) of Conflict of Laws § 1, Comment *c* and Illustrations (1934).

Literally the *only* support that the Court adduces for its position is § 403 of the Restatement (Third)—or more precisely Comment *e* to that provision, which states:

> "Subsection (3) [which says that a State should defer to another state if that State's interest is clearly greater] applies only when one state requires what another prohibits, or where compliance with the regulations of two states exercising jurisdiction consistently with this section is otherwise impossible. It does not apply where a person subject to regulation by two states can comply with the laws of both . . . ."

The Court has completely misinterpreted this provision. Subsection (3) of § 403 (requiring one State to defer to another in the limited circumstances just described) comes into play only after subsection (1) of § 403 has been complied with—*i.e.*, after it has been determined that the exercise of jurisdiction by *both* of the two States is not "unreasonable." That prior question is answered by applying the factors (*inter alia*) set forth in subsection (2) of § 403, that is, precisely the factors that I have discussed in text and that the Court rejects.[11]

I would reverse the judgment of the Court of Appeals on this issue, and remand to the District Court with instructions to dismiss for failure to state a claim on the three counts at issue. * * *

NOTES AND QUESTIONS FOR DISCUSSION

1. *Hartford Fire* repudiated the *Timberlane* approach. It was also the first case addressing (at least to some extent—see *Hartford Fire, supra* at footnote 23) the question how far abroad the Foreign Trade Antitrust Improvement Act, 15 U.S.C. § 6a (2000) (FTAIA), can reach. The FTAIA is the most important statute regulating the applicability of the Sherman Act to foreign conduct. Enacted in 1982, the FTAIA provides in relevant part:

Section 6a. Conduct involving trade or commerce with foreign nations

Sections 1 to 7 of this title shall not apply to conduct involving trade or commerce (other than import trade or import commerce) with foreign nations unless—

(1) such conduct has a direct, substantial, and reasonably foreseeable effect—

    (A) on trade or commerce which is not trade or commerce with foreign nations, or on import trade or import commerce with foreign nations; or

    (B) on export trade or export commerce with foreign nations, of a person engaged in such trade or commerce in the United States; and

(2) such effect gives rise to a claim under the provisions of sections 1 to 7 of this title, other than this section.

If sections 1 to 7 of this title apply to such conduct only because of the operation of paragraph (1)(B), then sections 1 to 7 of this title shall apply to such conduct only for injury to export business in the United States.

---

[11] The Court skips directly to subsection (3) of § 403, apparently on the authority of Comment *j* to § 415 of the Restatement (Third). But the preceding commentary to § 415 makes clear that "any exercise of [legislative] jurisdiction under this section is subject to the requirement of reasonableness" set forth in § 403(2). Restatement (Third) § 415, Comment *a*. Comment *j* refers back to the conflict analysis set forth in § 403(3), which, as noted above, comes after the reasonableness analysis of § 403(2).

2. How do you interpret the FTAIA with a view towards the facts in *Hartford Fire*? Did it require the outcome in *Hartford Fire*? In its Report, the House of Representatives made the following comment concerning the FTAIA:

> Moreover, the Bill is intended neither to prevent nor to encourage additional judicial recognition of the special international characteristics of transactions. If a court determines that the requirements for subject matter jurisdiction are met, this bill would have no effect on the courts' ability to employ notions of comity, see, e.g. *Timberlane Lumber Co. v. Bank of America*, 549 F.2d 1287 (3rd Cir. 1979) [sic], or otherwise to take account of the international character of the transaction. Similarly, the bill is not intended to restrict the application of American laws to extraterritorial conduct where the requisite effects exist or to the extraterritorial pursuit of evidence in appropriate cases.

H.R. Rep. 97-686 at 13 (1982). Does the Report support the *Timberlane* approach? Or is it more interested in achieving the result of the decision in *Uranium Antitrust, supra*? Is it a fair interpretation to say that the FTAIA leaves to the court's discretion to apply the *Timberlane* test and hence gives it its implicit imprimatur?

3. Public international law distinguishes between prescriptive jurisdiction, judicial jurisdiction, and enforcement jurisdiction. Prescriptive jurisdiction circumscribes the applicability of domestic laws abroad. Traditionally, there have been two main sources on which prescriptive jurisdiction could be based: territoriality and citizenship. As stated above, American courts heavily (but not exclusively) rely on the effects doctrine to apply domestic laws to foreign conduct. Most relevant to the current context, it forms the basis on which the U.S. courts exercise their jurisdiction over foreign transactions in antitrust suits. In its classical formulation, the effects doctrine states that if there are direct, substantial, and reasonably foreseeable effects from anticompetitive conduct abroad, U.S. laws may be applied to the transaction. Again, the effects doctrine has been criticized abroad as an illegitimate exercise of power by the U.S. courts and Congress. In this context, consider Justice Scalia's use of prescriptive jurisdiction in his *Hartford Fire* dissent. Wouldn't a consistent prescriptive jurisdiction analysis vitiate the application of U.S. laws to foreign conduct entirely? What, in Justice Scalia's opinion, is the proper test for the application of U.S. laws abroad? The majority opinion does not engage in the prescriptive jurisdiction analysis at all. Considering the international challenges to the American effects doctrine, which position strikes you as more consistent with U.S. jurisprudence: the dissent, which tries to reconcile international sentiments and U.S. law, or the majority which simply continues in its historically based rejection of international legal standards?

4. Justice Scalia's dissent draws a distinction between subject matter jurisdiction and prescriptive comity analysis. Yet he relies heavily on Chief Justice Marshall's *Charming Betsy* decision in which Marshall held that U.S. law was to be construed consistently with international law unless Congress explicitly instructed the courts to do otherwise. Does this canon of statutory construction introduce a dormant prescriptive jurisdiction element into U.S. subject matter jurisdiction in transnational cases?

5. According to the majority in *Hartford Fire*, considerations of comity could be used as tools to limit the applicability of American law to conduct abroad only if there were a conflict—i.e., only if foreign law requires the conduct forbidden by American law could domestic courts conceivably be forced to dismiss the action on grounds of comity. In the antitrust context, does this mean that the foreign statute must mandate the defendant to be anticompetitive? If that seems unsatisfactory, consider how you would formulate an alternative definition of a conflict between a domestic and a foreign regulatory regime. On this point, how does Justice Scalia's view differ from that of Justice Souter?

6. Considering today's global economy, does the international recalcitrance towards the effects doctrine make any sense any longer? Would the classical understanding of international law allow modern multinational corporations to circumnavigate domestic competition policies by moving their management and production sights overseas? Consider what corrective would be required to improve international rules of prescriptive jurisdiction to account for the economic changes of the last fifty years without giving up its fundamental commitment to the sovereign prerogative of the state to make its own competition laws.

7. The U.S. has entered into a number of international treaties designed to ameliorate the tensions that the application of U.S. antitrust law may produce. As between the U.S. and the E.U., for example, there has been an agreement since 1991 regarding the application of their respective competition laws in certain government-initiated lawsuits. See "Agreement Between the Government of the United States of America and the European Communities on the Application of Positive Comity Principles in the Enforcement of their Competition Laws." (http://www.justice.gov/atr/public/international/docs/1781.htm) The Agreement provides, among other things, that the parties grant each other "positive comity" which means the following according to Article III of the Agreement:

> The competition authorities of a Requesting Party may request the competition authorities of a Requested Party to investigate and, if warranted, to remedy anticompetitive activities in accordance with the Requested Party's competition laws. Such a request may be made regardless of whether the activities also violate the Requesting Party's competition laws, and regardless of whether the competition authorities of the Requesting Party have commenced or contemplate taking enforcement activities under their own competition laws.

Article IV (Deferral or Suspension of Investigations in Reliance On Enforcement Activity by the Requested Party) provides:

> **1.** The competition authorities of the Parties may agree that the competition authorities of the Requesting Party will defer or suspend pending or contemplated enforcement activities during the pendency of enforcement activities of the Requested Party.

> **2.** The competition authorities of a Requesting Party will normally defer or suspend their own enforcement activities in favor of enforcement ac-

tivities by the competition authorities of the Requested Party when the following conditions are satisfied:

a. The anticompetitive activities at issue:

i. do not have a direct, substantial and reasonably foreseeable impact on consumers in the Requesting Party's territory, or

ii. where the anticompetitive activities do have such an impact on the Requesting Party's consumers, they occur principally in and are directed principally towards the other Party's territory;

b. The adverse effects on the interests of the Requesting Party can be and are likely to be fully and adequately investigated and, as appropriate, eliminated or adequately remedied pursuant to the laws, procedures, and available remedies of the Requested Party. The Parties recognize that it may be appropriate to pursue separate enforcement activities where anticompetitive activities affecting both territories justify the imposition of penalties within both jurisdictions; and

c. The competition authorities of the Requested Party agree that in conducting their own enforcement activities, they will:

i. devote adequate resources to investigate the anticompetitive activities and, where appropriate, promptly pursue adequate enforcement activities;

ii. use their best efforts to pursue all reasonably available sources of information, including such sources of information as may be suggested by the competition authorities of the Requesting Party;

iii. inform the competition authorities of the Requesting Party, on request or at reasonable intervals, of the status of their enforcement activities and intentions, and where appropriate provide to the competition authorities of the Requesting Party relevant confidential information if consent has been obtained from the source concerned. The use and disclosure of such information shall be governed by Article V;

iv. promptly notify the competition authorities of the Requesting Party of any change in their intentions with respect to investigation or enforcement;

v. use their best efforts to complete their investigation and to obtain a remedy or initiate proceedings within six months, or such other time as agreed to by the competition authorities of the Parties, of the deferral or suspension of enforcement activities by the competition authorities of the Requesting Party;

vi. fully inform the competition authorities of the Requesting Party of the results of their investigation, and take into account the views of the competition authorities of the Requesting Party, prior to any settlement, initiation of proceedings, adoption of remedies, or termination of the investigation; and

vii. comply with any reasonable request that may be made by the competition authorities of the Requesting Party.

When the above conditions are satisfied, a Requesting Party which chooses not to defer or suspend its enforcement activities shall inform the competition authorities of the Requested Party of its reasons.

3. The competition authorities of the Requesting Party may defer or suspend their own enforcement activities if fewer than all of the conditions set out in paragraph 2 are satisfied.

4. Nothing in this Agreement precludes the competition authorities of a Requesting Party that choose to defer or suspend independent enforcement activities from later initiating or reinstituting such activities. In such circumstances, the competition authorities of the Requesting Party will promptly inform the competition authorities of the Requested Party of their intentions and reasons. If the competition authorities of the Requested Party continue with their own investigation, the competition authorities of the two Parties shall, where appropriate, coordinate their respective investigations under the criteria and procedures of Article IV of the 1991 Agreement.

These agreements only apply to public antitrust actions instituted by the Department of Justice or Federal Trade Commission, or the E.U. Commission. They do not expressly address jurisdictional standards to be applied in private antitrust actions. Nonetheless, shouldn't these factors also inform courts sitting in judgment over lawsuits initiated by private parties? If this were so, would *Hartford Fire* have been decided differently? What would be the value of a uniform standard in the public and private arenas?

2. *A Comparative Perspective on Extraterritoriality*

The following case presents the opportunity to engage in a comparative law exercise. It is the landmark decision by the European Court of Justice on the applicability of E.U. antitrust law to foreign conduct with an impact on European interests.

A. Ahlström Osakeyhtiö et al. v. Commission of the European Communities

Court of Justice of the European Communities, 1988.

Joined Cases 89, 104, 114, 116, 117 & 125 to 129/85, 1988 E.C.R. I-05193.

Grounds

1. By applications lodged at the Court Registry between 4 and 30 April 1985, wood pulp producers and two associations of wood pulp producers, all having their registered offices outside the Community, brought an action under the second paragraph of Article 173 of the EEC Treaty for the annulment of Decision IV/29.725 of 19 December 1984 (Official Journal 1985, L 85, p. 1), in

which the Commission had established that they had committed infringements of Article 85 [101][*] of the Treaty and imposed fines on them .

2. The alleged infringements consisted of: concertation between those producers on prices announced each quarter to customers in the Community and on actual transaction prices charged to such customers (Article 1(1) and (2) of the decision); price recommendations addressed to its members by the Pulp, Paper and Paperboard Export Association of the United States (formerly named Kraft Export Association and hereinafter referred to as "KEA"), an association of a number of United States producers (Article 1(3)). * * *

3. In paragraph 79 of the contested decision the Commission set out the grounds which in its view justify the Community's jurisdiction to apply Article [101] of the Treaty to the concertation in question. It stated first that all the addressees of the decision were either exporting directly to purchasers within the Community or were doing business within the Community through branches, subsidiaries, agencies or other establishments in the Community. It further pointed out that the concertation applied to the vast majority of the sales of those undertakings to and in the Community. Finally it stated that two-thirds of total shipments and 60% of consumption of the product in question in the Community had been affected by such concertation. The Commission concluded that: "The effect of the agreements and practices on prices announced and/or charged to customers and on resale of pulp within the EEC was therefore not only substantial but intended, and was the primary and direct result of the agreements and practices."

* * *

6. All the applicants which have made submissions regarding jurisdiction maintain first of all that by applying the competition rules of the Treaty to them the Commission has misconstrued the territorial scope of Article [101]. They note that in its judgment of 14 July 1972 in Case 48/69 ICI v. Commission ((1972)) ECR 619 the Court did not adopt the "effects doctrine" but emphasized

---

[*] [Note that Article 85 is now Article 101 of the Consolidated version of the Treaty on the Functioning of the European Union. Article 101 reads in pertinent part:

 1. The following shall be prohibited as incompatible with the internal market: all agreements between undertakings, decisions by associations of undertakings and concerted practices which may affect trade between Member States and which have as their object or effect the prevention, restriction or distortion of competition within the internal market, and in particular those which:

    (a) directly or indirectly fix purchase or selling prices or any other trading conditions;
    (b) limit or control production, markets, technical development, or investment;
    (c) share markets or sources of supply;
    (d) apply dissimilar conditions to equivalent transactions with other trading parties, thereby placing them at a competitive disadvantage;
    (e) make the conclusion of contracts subject to acceptance by the other parties of supplementary obligations which, by their nature or according to commercial usage, have no connection with the subject of such contracts.

 2. Any agreements or decisions prohibited pursuant to this Article shall be automatically void.—eds.]

that the case involved conduct restricting competition within the common market because of the activities of subsidiaries which could be imputed to the parent companies. The applicants add that even if there is a basis in Community law for applying Article [101] to them, the action of applying the rule interpreted in that way would be contrary to public international law which precludes any claim by the Community to regulate conduct restricting competition adopted outside the territory of the Community merely by reason of the economic repercussions which that conduct produces within the Community.

* * *

8. Certain Canadian applicants also maintain that by imposing fines on them and making reduction of those fines conditional on the producers giving undertakings as to their future conduct the Commission has infringed Canada's sovereignty and thus breached the principle of international comity.

Incorrect assessment of the territorial scope of Article [101] of the Treaty and incompatibility of the decision with public international law

* * *

11. In so far as the submission concerning the infringement of Article 85 of the Treaty itself is concerned, it should be recalled that that provision prohibits all agreements between undertakings and concerted practices which may affect trade between Member States and which have as their object or effect the restriction of competition within the common market.

12. It should be noted that the main sources of supply of wood pulp are outside the Community, in Canada, the United States, Sweden and Finland and that the market therefore has global dimensions. Where wood pulp producers established in those countries sell directly to purchasers established in the Community and engage in price competition in order to win orders from those customers, that constitutes competition within the common market.

13. It follows that where those producers concert on the prices to be charged to their customers in the Community and put that concertation into effect by selling at prices which are actually coordinated, they are taking part in concertation which has the object and effect of restricting competition within the common market within the meaning of Article 85 of the Treaty.

14. Accordingly, it must be concluded that by applying the competition rules in the Treaty in the circumstances of this case to undertakings whose registered offices are situated outside the Community, the Commission has not made an incorrect assessment of the territorial scope of Article 85.

15. The applicants have submitted that the decision is incompatible with public international law on the grounds that the application of the competition rules in this case was founded exclusively on the economic repercussions within the common market of conduct restricting competition which was adopted outside the Community.

16. It should be observed that an infringement of Article 85, such as the conclusion of an agreement which has had the effect of restricting competition within the common market, consists of conduct made up of two elements, the

formation of the agreement, decision or concerted practice and the implementation thereof. If the applicability of prohibitions laid down under competition law were made to depend on the place where the agreement, decision or concerted practice was formed, the result would obviously be to give undertakings an easy means of evading those prohibitions. The decisive factor is therefore the place where it is implemented.

17. The producers in this case implemented their pricing agreement within the common market. It is immaterial in that respect whether or not they had recourse to subsidiaries, agents, sub-agents, or branches within the Community in order to make their contacts with purchasers within the Community.

18. Accordingly the Community's jurisdiction to apply its competition rules to such conduct is covered by the territoriality principle as universally recognized in public international law.

19. As regards the argument based on the infringement of the principle of non-interference, it should be pointed out that the applicants who are members of KEA have referred to a rule according to which where two States have jurisdiction to lay down and enforce rules and the effect of those rules is that a person finds himself subject to contradictory orders as to the conduct he must adopt, each State is obliged to exercise its jurisdiction with moderation. The applicants have concluded that by disregarding that rule in applying its competition rules the Community has infringed the principle of non-interference.

20. There is no need to enquire into the existence in international law of such a rule since it suffices to observe that the conditions for its application are in any event not satisfied. There is not, in this case, any contradiction between the conduct required by the United States and that required by the Community since the Webb Pomerene Act merely exempts the conclusion of export cartels from the application of United States anti-trust laws but does not require such cartels to be concluded.

21. It should further be pointed out that the United States authorities raised no objections regarding any conflict of jurisdiction when consulted by the Commission pursuant to the OECD Council Recommendation of 25 October 1979 concerning Cooperation between Member Countries on Restrictive Business Practices affecting International Trade (Acts of the Organization, Vol. 19, p. 376).

22. As regards the argument relating to disregard of international comity, it suffices to observe that it amounts to calling in question the Community's jurisdiction to apply its competition rules to conduct such as that found to exist in this case and that, as such, that argument has already been rejected.

23. Accordingly it must be concluded that the Commission's decision is not contrary to Article [101] of the Treaty or to the rules of public international law relied on by the applicants. * * *

On those grounds, **THE COURT**, * * *

Rejects the submission relating to the incorrect assessment of the territorial scope of Article [101] of the Treaty and the incompatibility of Commission Decision IV/29.725 of 19 December 1984 with public international law * * *.

NOTES AND QUESTIONS FOR DISCUSSION

1. Consider how you would articulate the holding in this case. Is the decision of the E.U. Commission different from that of the ECJ? Note the similarity between the Commission's approach and that of the Court in *Alcoa, supra.* Does the ECJ adopt the effects test as expressed in *Alcoa*? Or does it adhere to the traditional territoriality principle? Of central importance for the holding of the ECJ was that the agreement of the foreign producers was "implemented" in the European Union. Is it clear what the Court means by implementation?

2. Reread paragraph 20 of the ECJ's decision. Can it fairly be characterized as a restatement of Justice Souter's definition of a conflict in *Hartford Fire*? If not, how do they differ? Consider as well how the ECJ would have decided a case involving facts like those in *Hartford Fire*—with acts/omissions on the part of non-European defendants outside Europe. Do you think that under the *Hartford Fire* facts, the ECJ would have viewed the agreement as having been "implemented" within the European Union?

3. Section 130(2) of the German Act against Restraints on Competition (Gesetz gegen Wettbewerbsbeschranjunken [GWB]), reads as follows:

* * *

> (2) This Act shall apply to all restraints of competition having an effect within the area of application of this Act, [even] if they were caused outside the area of application of this Act.

This provision clearly sets out an effects test. Note, however, that under German and European Union law, actions against anticompetitive behavior are initiated by the Federal Cartel Office or the European Commission, and are thus public in nature. In the U.S., the situation is largely the reverse: Most suits are initiated by private parties suing for treble damages, a type of award that is unavailable under German and European law. There are initiatives, however, to increase the number of private actions within the European Union. Since 2003, the European Commission has taken several steps aimed at encouraging private lawsuits against antitrust violations. Most recently, the Commission Work Programme 2012 presented a legislative initiative on actions for damages for breaches of antitrust law. One of the objectives is to "ensure effective damages actions before national courts for breaches of E.U. antitrust rules."[*]

4. Finally, note that in Germany and other European nations, as well as in the European Court of Justice, professional judges rather than juries determine the issues of liability and the amount of damages. Perhaps then, it is the procedural setting and its consequences, rather than the doctrinal basis—i.e., the effect principle as opposed to the territoriality principle—that causes so much dismay and mistrust directed at the American system. On the different dynamics of U.S. and European antitrust law, see generally David J. Gerber, Law and Competition in Twentieth Century Europe (1988).

---

[*] See http://ec.europa.eu/competition/antitrust/actionsdamages/documents.html

5. The decision that follows—F. Hoffman-La Roche, Ltd. v. Empagran S.A.—is the most recent Supreme Court decision on the question of how far the U.S. antitrust laws can reach abroad. The decision has produced significant confusion among antitrust scholars and practitioners. There are several readings that the decision could be given: it could be considered to overturn *Hartford Fire* in favor of the dissent in that case; it could also be read as a sign that the Court is not yet willing to go to the lengths of the dissent in *Hartford Fire*, but is looking for a middle ground between the dissent and the majority; finally, the case could also be read as a mere technical ruling stating that where the claimants have suffered a harm independent from the one experienced in the U.S., *Hartford Fire* does not apply.

F. Hoffman-La Roche, Ltd. v. Empagran, S.A.

Supreme Court of the United States, 2004.

542 U.S. 155.

JUSTICE BREYER delivered the opinion of the Court.

The Foreign Trade Antitrust Improvements Act of 1982 (FTAIA) excludes from the Sherman Act's reach much anticompetitive conduct that causes only foreign injury. It does so by setting forth a general rule stating that the Sherman Act "shall not apply to conduct involving trade or commerce . . . with foreign nations." * * * It then creates exceptions to the general rule, applicable where (roughly speaking) that conduct significantly harms imports, domestic commerce, or American exporters. * * *

The issue before us concerns (1) significant foreign anticompetitive conduct with (2) an adverse domestic effect and (3) an independent foreign effect giving rise to the claim. In more concrete terms, this case involves vitamin sellers around the world that agreed to fix prices, leading to higher vitamin prices in the United States and independently leading to higher vitamin prices in other countries such as Ecuador. We conclude that, in this scenario, a purchaser in the United States could bring a Sherman Act claim under the FTAIA based on domestic injury, but a purchaser in Ecuador could not bring a Sherman Act claim based on foreign harm.

I

The plaintiffs in this case originally filed a class-action suit on behalf of foreign and domestic purchasers of vitamins under, *inter alia,* § 1 of the Sherman Act, 26 Stat. 209, as amended, 15 U.S.C. § 1, and §§ 4 and 16 of the Clayton Act, 38 Stat. 731, 737, as amended, 15 U.S.C. §§ 15, 26. Their complaint alleged that petitioners, foreign and domestic vitamin manufacturers and distributors, had engaged in a price-fixing conspiracy, raising the price of vitamin products to customers in the United States and to customers in foreign countries.

As relevant here, petitioners moved to dismiss the suit as to the *foreign* purchasers (the respondents here), five foreign vitamin distributors located in Ukraine, Australia, Ecuador, and Panama, each of which bought vitamins from petitioners for delivery outside the United States. * * * Respondents have never asserted that they purchased any vitamins in the United States or in transactions in United States commerce, and the question presented assumes that the relevant "transactions occurr[ed] entirely outside U.S. commerce." The District Court dismissed their claims. It applied the FTAIA and found none of the exceptions applicable. Thereafter, the *domestic* purchasers transferred their claims to another pending suit and did not take part in the subsequent appeal. * * *

A divided panel of the Court of Appeals reversed. The panel concluded that the FTAIA's general exclusionary rule applied to the case, but that its domestic-injury exception also applied. It basically read the plaintiffs' complaint to allege that the vitamin manufacturers' price-fixing conspiracy (1) had "a direct, substantial, and reasonably foreseeable effect" on ordinary domestic trade or commerce, *i.e.,* the conspiracy brought about higher domestic vitamin prices, and (2) "such effect" gave "rise to a [Sherman Act] claim," *i.e.,* an injured *domestic* customer could have brought a Sherman Act suit. Those allegations, the court held, are sufficient to meet the exception's requirements.

The court assumed that the foreign effect, *i.e.,* higher prices in Ukraine, Panama, Australia, and Ecuador, was independent of the domestic effect, *i.e.,* higher domestic prices. But it concluded that, in light of the FTAIA's text, legislative history, and the policy goal of deterring harmful price-fixing activity, this lack of connection does not matter. The District of Columbia Circuit denied rehearing *en banc* by a 4-to-3 vote.

[We granted certiorari.]

II

The FTAIA seeks to make clear to American exporters (and to firms doing business abroad) that the Sherman Act does not prevent them from entering into business arrangements (say, joint-selling arrangements), however anticompetitive, as long as those arrangements adversely affect only foreign markets. * * * It does so by removing from the Sherman Act's reach, (1) export activities and (2) other commercial activities taking place abroad, *unless* those activities adversely affect domestic commerce, imports to the United States, or exporting activities of one engaged in such activities within the United States.

* * *

IV

We turn now to the basic question presented, that of the exception's application. Because the underlying antitrust action is complex, potentially raising questions not directly at issue here, we reemphasize that we base our decision upon the following: The price-fixing conduct significantly and adversely affects both customers outside the United States and customers within the United States, but the adverse foreign effect is independent of any adverse domestic effect. In these circumstances, we find that the FTAIA exception does not apply (and thus the Sherman Act does not apply) for two main reasons.

First, this Court ordinarily construes ambiguous statutes to avoid unreasonable interference with the sovereign authority of other nations. See, *e.g., McCulloch v. Sociedad Nacional de Marineros de Honduras,* 372 U.S. 10, 20-22 (1963) (application of National Labor Relations Act to foreign-flag vessels);

Romero v. International Terminal Operating Co., 358 U.S. 354, 382-383 (1959) (application of Jones Act in maritime case); *Lauritzen v. Larsen,* 345 U.S. 571, 578 (1953) (same). This rule of construction reflects principles of customary international law—law that (we must assume) Congress ordinarily seeks to follow. See Restatement (Third) of Foreign Relations Law of the United States §§ 403(1), 403(2) (1986) (hereinafter Restatement) (limiting the unreasonable exercise of prescriptive jurisdiction with respect to a person or activity having connections with another State); *Murray v. Schooner Charming Betsy,* 2 Cranch 64, 118, 2 L.Ed. 208 (1804) ("[A]n act of Congress ought never to be construed to violate the law of nations if any other possible construction remains"); *Hartford Fire Insurance Co. v. California,* 509 U.S. 764, 817 (1993) (SCALIA, J., dissenting) (identifying rule of construction as derived from the principle of "prescriptive comity").

This rule of statutory construction cautions courts to assume that legislators take account of the legitimate sovereign interests of other nations when they write American laws. It thereby helps the potentially conflicting laws of different nations work together in harmony—a harmony particularly needed in today's highly interdependent commercial world.

No one denies that America's antitrust laws, when applied to foreign conduct, can interfere with a foreign nation's ability independently to regulate its own commercial affairs. But our courts have long held that application of our antitrust laws to foreign anticompetitive conduct is nonetheless reasonable, and hence consistent with principles of prescriptive comity, insofar as they reflect a legislative effort to redress *domestic* antitrust injury that foreign anticompetitive conduct has caused. See *United States v. Aluminum Co. of America,* 148 F.2d 416, 443-444 (CA2 1945) (L.Hand, J.); 1 P. Areeda & D. Turner, Antitrust Law ¶ 236 (1978).

But why is it reasonable to apply those laws to foreign conduct *insofar as that conduct causes independent foreign harm and that foreign harm alone gives rise to the plaintiff's claim?* Like the former case, application of those laws creates a serious risk of interference with a foreign nation's ability independently to regulate its own commercial affairs. But, unlike the former case, the justification for that interference seems insubstantial. See Restatement § 403(2) (determining reasonableness on basis of such factors as connections with regulating nation, harm to that nation's interests, extent to which other nations regulate, and the potential for conflict). Why should American law supplant, for example, Canada's or Great Britain's or Japan's own determination about how best to protect Canadian or British or Japanese customers from anticompetitive conduct engaged in significant part by Canadian or British or Japanese or other foreign companies?

We recognize that principles of comity provide Congress greater leeway when it seeks to control through legislation the actions of *American* companies, see Restatement § 402; and some of the anticompetitive price-fixing conduct alleged here took place in *America.* But the higher foreign prices of which the foreign plaintiffs here complain are not the consequence of any domestic anticompetitive conduct *that Congress sought to forbid,* for Congress did not seek to forbid any such conduct insofar as it is here relevant, *i.e.,* insofar as it is intertwined with foreign conduct that causes independent foreign harm. Rather Congress sought to *release* domestic (and foreign) anticompetitive conduct from Sherman Act constraints when that conduct causes foreign harm. Congress, of course, did make an exception where that conduct also causes domestic harm. * * * But any independent domestic harm the foreign conduct causes here has, by definition, little or nothing to do with the matter.

We thus repeat the basic question: Why is it reasonable to apply this law to conduct that is significantly foreign *insofar as that conduct causes independent foreign harm and that foreign harm alone gives rise to the plaintiff's claim?* We can find no good answer to the question.

The Areeda and Hovenkamp treatise notes that under the Court of Appeals' interpretation of the statute

> "a Malaysian customer could . . . maintain an action under United States law in a United States court against its own Malaysian supplier, another cartel member, simply by noting that unnamed third parties injured [in the United States] by the American [cartel member's] conduct would also have a cause of action. Effectively, the United States courts would provide worldwide subject matter jurisdiction to any foreign suitor wishing to sue its own local supplier, but unhappy with its own sovereign's provisions for private antitrust enforcement, provided that a different plaintiff had a cause of action against a different firm for injuries that were within U.S. [other-than-import] commerce. It does not seem excessively rigid to infer that Congress would not have intended that result."

P. Areeda & H. Hovenkamp, Antitrust Law ¶ 273, pp. 51-52 (Supp.2003). We agree with the comment. We can find no convincing justification for the extension of the Sherman Act's scope that it describes.

Respondents reply that many nations have adopted antitrust laws similar to our own, to the point where the practical likelihood of interference with the relevant interests of other nations is minimal. Leaving price fixing to the side, however, this Court has found to the contrary. See, *e.g., Hartford Fire,* 509 U.S. at 797-799 (noting that the alleged conduct in the London reinsurance market, while illegal under United States antitrust laws, was assumed to be perfectly consistent with British law and policy); * * * .

Regardless, even where nations agree about primary conduct, say price fixing, they disagree dramatically about appropriate remedies. The application, for example, of American private treble-damages remedies to anticompetitive conduct taking place abroad has generated considerable controversy. See, *e.g.,* 2 ABA Section of Antitrust Law, Antitrust Law Developments 1208-1209 (5th ed. 2002). And several foreign nations have filed briefs here arguing that to apply our remedies would unjustifiably permit their citizens to bypass their own less generous remedial schemes, thereby upsetting a balance of competing considerations that their own domestic antitrust laws embody. *E.g.,* Brief for Federal Republic of Germany et al. as *Amici Curiae* 2 (setting forth German interest "in seeing that German companies are not subject to the extraterritorial reach of the United States' antitrust laws by private foreign plaintiffs—whose injuries were sustained in transactions entirely outside United States commerce—seeking treble damages in private lawsuits against German companies"); Brief for Government of Canada as *Amicus Curiae* 14 ("treble damages remedy would supersede" Canada's "national policy decision"); Brief for Government of Japan as *Amicus Curiae* 10 (finding "particularly troublesome" the potential "interfere[nce] with Japanese governmental regulation of the Japanese market").

These briefs add that a decision permitting independently injured foreign plaintiffs to pursue private treble-damages remedies would undermine foreign nations' own antitrust enforcement policies by diminishing foreign firms' incentive to cooperate with antitrust authorities in return for prosecutorial amnesty. Brief for Federal Republic of Germany et al. as *Amici Curiae* 28-30; Brief for Government of Canada as *Amicus Curiae* 11-14. See also Brief for United States as *Amicus Curiae* 19-21 (arguing the same in respect to American antitrust enforcement).

Respondents alternatively argue that comity does not demand an interpretation of the FTAIA that would exclude independent foreign injury cases *across the board.* Rather, courts can take (and sometimes have taken) account of comity considerations case by case, abstaining where comity considerations so dictate. Cf., *e.g., Hartford Fire, supra,* at 797, n.24 * * *.

In our view, however, this approach is too complex to prove workable. The Sherman Act covers many different kinds of anticompetitive agreements. Courts would have to examine how foreign law, compared with American law, treats not only price fixing but also, say, information-sharing agreements, patent-licensing price conditions, territorial product resale limitations, and various forms of joint venture, in respect to both primary conduct and remedy. The legally and economically technical nature of that enterprise means lengthier proceedings, appeals, and more proceedings—to the point where procedural costs and delays could themselves threaten interference with a foreign nation's ability to maintain the integrity of its own antitrust enforcement system. Even in this relatively simple price-fixing case, for example, competing briefs tell us (1) that potential treble-damage liability would help enforce widespread anti-price-fixing norms (through added deterrence) and (2) the opposite, namely that such liability would hinder antitrust enforcement (by reducing incentives to enter amnesty programs). Compare, *e.g.,* Brief for Certain Professors of Economics as *Amici Curiae* 2-4 with Brief for United States as *Amicus Curiae* 19-21. How could a court seriously interested in resolving so empirical a matter—a matter potentially related to impact on foreign interests—do so simply and expeditiously?

We conclude that principles of prescriptive comity counsel against the Court of Appeals' interpretation of the FTAIA. Where foreign anticompetitive conduct plays a significant role and where foreign injury is independent of domestic effects, Congress might have hoped that America's antitrust laws, so fundamental a component of our own economic system, would commend themselves to other nations as well. But, if America's antitrust policies could not win their own way in the international marketplace for such ideas, Congress, we must assume, would not have tried to impose them, in an act of legal imperialism, through legislative fiat.

Second, the FTAIA's language and history suggest that Congress designed the FTAIA to clarify, perhaps to limit, but not *to expand* in any significant way, the Sherman Act's scope as applied to foreign commerce. See House Report, at 2-3, U.S.Code Cong. & Admin.News 1982, 2487, 2487-2488. And we have found no significant indication that at the time Congress wrote this statute courts would have thought the Sherman Act applicable in these circumstances. * * *

Finally, respondents point to policy considerations that we have previously discussed, namely, that application of the Sherman Act in present circumstances will (through increased deterrence) help protect Americans against foreign-caused anticompetitive injury. As we have explained, however, the plaintiffs and supporting enforcement-agency *amici* have made important experience-backed arguments (based upon amnesty-seeking incentives) to the contrary. We cannot say whether, on balance, respondents' side of this empirically based argument or the enforcement agencies' side is correct. But we can say that the answer to the dispute is neither clear enough, nor of such likely empirical significance, that it could overcome the considerations we have previously discussed and change our conclusion.

For these reasons, we conclude that petitioners' reading of the statute's language is correct. That reading furthers the statute's basic purposes, it properly reflects considerations of comity, and it is consistent with Sherman Act history.

VI

We have assumed that the anticompetitive conduct here independently caused foreign injury; that is, the conduct's domestic effects did not help to bring about that foreign injury. Respondents argue, in the alternative, that the foreign injury was not independent. Rather, they say, the anticompetitive conduct's domestic effects were linked to that foreign harm. Respondents contend that, because vitamins are fungible and readily transportable, without an adverse domestic effect (*i.e.,* higher prices in the United States), the sellers could not have maintained their international price-fixing arrangement and respondents would not have suffered their foreign injury. They add that this "but for" condition is sufficient to bring the price-fixing conduct within the scope of the FTAIA's exception.

The Court of Appeals, however, did not address this argument, and, for that reason, neither shall we. Respondents remain free to ask the Court of Appeals to consider the claim. The Court of Appeals may determine whether respondents properly preserved the argument, and, if so, it may consider it and decide the related claim.

For these reasons, the judgment of the Court of Appeals is vacated, and the case is remanded for further proceedings consistent with this opinion.

It is so ordered.

JUSTICE O'CONNOR took no part in the consideration or decision of this case.

JUSTICE SCALIA with whom JUSTICE THOMAS joins, concurring in the judgment.

I concur in the judgment of the Court because the language of the statute is readily susceptible of the interpretation the Court provides and because only that interpretation is consistent with the principle that statutes should be read in accord with the customary deference to the application of foreign countries' laws within their own territories.

NOTES AND QUESTIONS FOR DISCUSSION

1. Note that, on remand, the D.C. Circuit Court of Appeals had to address plaintiffs' arguments "that, because vitamins are fungible and readily transportable, without an adverse domestic effect (*i.e.,* higher prices in the United States), the sellers could not have maintained their international price-fixing arrangement and respondents would not have suffered their foreign injury [and] that this 'but for' condition is sufficient to bring the price-fixing conduct within the scope of the FTAIA's exception."

The Court of Appeals rejected these arguments stating that actual ("but-for") causation would not suffice to make the foreign injuries dependent on domestic antitrust law violations. Requiring instead a proximate cause standard, the Court stated:

> Applying the proximate cause standard, we conclude the domestic effects the appellants cite did not give rise to their claimed injuries so as to bring their Sherman Act claim within the FTAIA exception. While maintaining super-competitive prices in the United States may have facilitated the appellees' scheme to charge comparable prices abroad, this fact demonstrates at most but-for causation. It does not establish, as in the cases the United States cites, that the U.S. effects of the appellees' conduct—i.e., increased prices in the United States—proximately caused the foreign appellants' injuries. Nor do the appellants otherwise identify the kind of direct tie to U.S. commerce found in the cited cases. Although the appellants argue that the vitamin market is a single, global market facilitated by market division agreements so that their injuries arose from the higher prices charged by the global conspiracy (rather than from super-competitive prices in one particular market), they still must satisfy the FTAIA's requirement that the U.S. effects of the conduct give rise to their claims. The but-for causation the appellants proffer establishes only an indirect connection between the U.S. prices and the prices they paid when they purchased vitamins abroad."

Empagran S.A. v. F. Hoffman-La Roche, Ltd., 417 F.3d 1267, 1271 (D.C. Cir. 2005).

2. The Supreme Court's opinion in *Hoffman-La Roche* stands in considerable contrast in its reasoning to the previous decision by the Court in *Hartford Fire.* Indeed, the decision in *Hartford Fire* is typically cited for the proposition that international comity is irrelevant in the application of U.S. antitrust laws to foreign conduct. Review *Hartford Fire* and re-assess whether comity analysis has returned for good. Does Justice Breyer seek to reinstate the inquiry from *Timberlane* to test for international comity in international antitrust cases?

3. Consider whether the *Hoffman-La Roche* Court adopts the approach of § 403 of the Restatement (Third) for future cases, or merely references it in this particular context. Consider also how the use of the Restatement in *Hoffman La Roche* compares to the use of the Restatement in *Hartford Fire*. Does it more resemble the dissent of Justice Scalia in *Hartford Fire* or the opinion of the majority?

4. Justice Scalia authored a short, yet pointed concurrence in *Hoffman La Roche*. What, if anything, does the concurrence tell you about the Court's attitude towards its previous holding in *Hartford Fire*? Is the previous holding implicitly overruled, or did the Court make an exception from *Hartford Fire* that is limited to instances in which the plaintiff can only assert an action independent from harm in the United States?

5. In the context of the global economy, is it possible to argue that a conspiracy to fix prices in the vitamin market can ever truly be local? Bear in mind the low transportation costs of vitamins and the low tariffs for imports into the U.S. Nonetheless, Justice Breyer was not convinced:

> We thus repeat the basic question: Why is it reasonable to apply this law to conduct that is significantly foreign *insofar as that conduct causes independent foreign harm and that foreign harm alone gives rise to the plaintiff's claim?* We can find no good answer to the question.

Hoffman-La Roche, 542 U.S. at 166. Can you find an answer to the question, based on what the Court refers to as "added deterrence"? Compare the following excerpt of one of the Amicus Curiae briefs which attempts to provide an answer that Justice Breyer did not find:

> Petitioners' view that regulation in each country must be limited to injuries suffered in that country would lead to underregulation. "If foreign plaintiffs were not permitted to seek a remedy for their antitrust injuries, persons doing business both in this country and abroad might be tempted to enter into anticompetitive conspiracies affecting American consumers in the expectation that the illegal profits they could safely extort abroad would offset any liability to plaintiffs at home. If, on the other hand, potential antitrust violators must take into account the full costs of their conduct, American consumers are benefited by the maximum deterrent effect of treble damages upon all potential violators." * * *
>
> Amici curiae for foreign governments submit that the danger of underdeterrence does not exist, because they themselves regulate price-fixing cartels heavily. * * * To the extent that effective regulation exists in a foreign market, the risk of underdeterrence, and thus the U.S. interest in regulation, are reduced *with regard to that market*. But amici curiae overlook the fact that there are other markets, especially in developing countries, where such regulation is absent. * * * This failure to consider other countries is widespread: "[M]ost prior studies of the impact of these cartels have focused on the better-documented effects on

wealthy, industrialized countries." Yet the effects on those countries, and therefore the risk of underdeterrence, are substantial. A recent study shows that "cartels have adversely affected a not insignificant portion of the trade, and therefore the trade balance and consumption, of developing countries" and finds that in 1997 alone "the total value of potentially 'cartel-affected' imports to developing countries was $51.1 billion."

Brief of Amici Curiae Law Professors Ralf Michaels, Hannah Buxbaum and Horatia Muir Watt in Support of Respondents, 2004 WL 542780, at 14-15. Does the Court acknowledge the issue of underdeterrence that its holding may produce in a global economy? How might one respond to the points made by the Amici?

3.   *The Extraterritorial Reach of Federal Securities Laws*

As with antitrust law, U.S. federal courts have not reached consistent results in applying the federal securities laws extraterritorially. Particularly problematic in this context have been Section 10(b) of the Securities Exchange Act of 1934 and Rule 10b-5 adopted by the Securities and Exchange Commission (SEC) under Section 10(b). Both provisions lack guidance as to when they apply in transnational disputes. Section 10(b) reads in part:

> It shall be unlawful for any person, directly or indirectly, by the use of any means or instrumentality of interstate commerce or of the mails, or of any facility of any national securities exchange . . . [t]o use or employ, in connection with the purchase or sale of any security registered on a national securities exchange or any security not so registered, . . . any manipulative or deceptive device or contrivance in contravention of such rules and regulations as the [Securities and Exchange] Commission may prescribe . . . .

15 U.S.C. § 78j(b).

Pursuant to Rule 10b-5 of the SEC, it is unlawful:

> [F]or any person, directly or indirectly, by the use of any means or instrumentality of interstate commerce, or of the mails or of any facility of any national securities exchange,
>
> > (a) To employ any device, scheme, or artifice to defraud,
> >
> > (b) To make any untrue statement of a material fact or to omit to state a material fact necessary in order to make the statements made, in the light of the circumstances under which they were made, not misleading, or
> >
> > (c) To engage in any act, practice, or course of business which operates or would operate as a fraud or deceit upon any person, in connection with the purchase or sale of any security.

17 C.F.R. 240.10b-5.

The breadth and vagueness of Section 10(b) and Rule 10b-5 have made it difficult to predict the exact reach of these provisions in transnational litigation contexts. Led by the U.S. Court of Appeals for the Second Circuit, however, most courts have opted in favor of generously applying these norms extraterritorially. The leading precedent for this approach was Schoenbaum v. Firstbrook, 405 F.2d 200 (2d Cir. 1968), in which the Second Circuit opined that "Congress intended the Exchange Act to have extraterritorial application in order to protect domestic investors who have purchased foreign securities on American exchanges and to protect the domestic securities market from the effects of improper foreign transactions in American securities." Id. at 206. Under this case law, liability could be imposed either by a showing of substantial "conduct" of the defendant in the U.S. or by proving significant "effects" of the illegal foreign activity within the U.S. The history and development of the conduct-and-effects approaches, which hailed defendants into American courts even under rather attenuated circumstances, are recounted in the U.S. Supreme Court opinion of *Morrison v. National Australia Bank Ltd.*, which is reproduced immediately below. In reading it, try to compare the conduct-and-effects approaches with the new test and limits that the Supreme Court introduced as benchmarks for the extraterritorial application of the U.S. securities laws.

Morrison v. National Australia Bank Ltd.

Supreme Court of the United States, 2010.

130 S.Ct. 2869.

JUSTICE SCALIA delivered the opinion of the Court.

We decide whether § 10(b) of the Securities Exchange Act of 1934 provides a cause of action to foreign plaintiffs suing foreign and American defendants for misconduct in connection with securities traded on foreign exchanges.

I

Respondent National Australia Bank Limited (National) was, during the relevant time, the largest bank in Australia. Its Ordinary Shares—what in America would be called "common stock"—are traded on the Australian Stock Exchange Limited and on other foreign securities exchanges, but not on any exchange in the United States. There are listed on the New York Stock Exchange, however, National's American Depositary Receipts (ADRs), which represent the right to receive a specified number of National's Ordinary Shares.

The complaint alleges the following facts, which we accept as true. In February 1998, National bought respondent HomeSide Lending, Inc., a mortgage servicing company headquartered in Florida. HomeSide's business was to receive fees for servicing mortgages. * * * The rights to receive those fees, so-called mortgage-servicing rights, can provide a valuable income stream. * * * How valuable each of the rights is depends, in part, on the likelihood that the mortgage to which it applies will be fully repaid before it is due, terminating the need for servicing. HomeSide calculated the present value of its mortgage-servicing rights by using valuation models designed to take this likelihood into account. It recorded the value of its assets, and the numbers appeared in National's financial statements.

From 1998 until 2001, National's annual reports and other public documents touted the success of HomeSide's business, and respondents Frank Cicutto (National's managing director and chief executive officer), Kevin Race (HomeSide's chief operating officer), and Hugh Harris (HomeSide's chief executive officer) did the same in public statements. But on July 5, 2001, National announced that it was writing down the value of HomeSide's assets by $450 million; and then again on September 3, by another $1.75 billion. The prices of both Ordinary Shares and ADRs slumped. After downplaying the July write-down, National explained the September write-down as the result of a failure to anticipate the lowering of prevailing interest rates (lower interest rates lead to more refinancings, *i.e.,* more early repayments of mortgages), other mistaken assumptions in the financial models, and the loss of goodwill. According to the complaint, however, HomeSide, Race, Harris, and another HomeSide senior executive who is also a respondent here had manipulated HomeSide's financial models to make the rates of early repayment unrealistically low in order to cause the mortgage-servicing rights to appear more valuable than they really were. The complaint also alleges that National and Cicutto were aware of this deception by July 2000, but did nothing about it.

As relevant here, petitioners Russell Leslie Owen and Brian and Geraldine Silverlock, all Australians, purchased National's Ordinary Shares in 2000 and 2001, before the write-downs. They sued National, HomeSide, Cicutto, and the three HomeSide executives in the United States District Court for the Southern District of New York for alleged violations of §§ 10(b) and 20(a) of the Securities and Exchange Act of 1934, 48 Stat. 891, 15 U.S.C. §§ 78j(b) and 78t(a), and SEC Rule 10b-5, 17 CFR § 240.10b-5 (2009), promulgated pursuant to § 10(b). * * *

Respondents moved to dismiss for lack of subject-matter jurisdiction under Federal Rule of Civil Procedure 12(b)(1) and for failure to state a claim under Rule 12(b)(6). The District Court granted the motion on the former ground, finding no jurisdiction because the acts in this country were, "at most, a link in the chain of an alleged overall securities fraud scheme that culminated abroad." * * * The Court of Appeals for the Second Circuit affirmed on similar grounds. The acts performed in the United States did not "compris[e] the heart of the alleged fraud." We granted certiorari.

II

Before addressing the question presented, we must correct a threshold error in the Second Circuit's analysis. It considered the extraterritorial reach of § 10(b) to raise a question of subject-matter jurisdiction, wherefore it affirmed the District Court's dismissal under Rule 12(b)(1).

But to ask what conduct § 10(b) reaches is to ask what conduct § 10(b) prohibits, which is a merits question. Subject-matter jurisdiction, by contrast, "refers to a tribunal's '"power to hear a case."'" * * * It presents an issue quite separate from the question whether the allegations the plaintiff makes entitle him to relief. The District Court here had jurisdiction under 15 U.S.C. § 78aa to adjudicate the question whether § 10(b) applies to National's conduct. * * *

III

A

It is a "longstanding principle of American law 'that legislation of Congress, unless a contrary intent appears, is meant to apply only within the territorial jurisdiction of the United States.'" * * * This principle represents a canon of construction, or a presumption about a statute's meaning, rather than a limit upon Congress's power to legislate, * * *. It rests on the perception that Congress ordinarily legislates with respect to domestic, not foreign matters. Thus, "unless there is the affirmative intention of the Congress clearly expressed" to give a statute extraterritorial effect, "we must presume it is primarily concerned with domestic conditions." * * * The canon or presumption applies regardless of whether there is a risk of conflict between the American statute and a foreign law, * * *. When a statute gives no clear indication of an extraterritorial application, it has none.

Despite this principle of interpretation, long and often recited in our opinions, the Second Circuit believed that, because the Exchange Act is silent as to the extraterritorial application of § 10(b), it was left to the court to "discern" whether Congress would have wanted the statute to apply. This disregard of the presumption against extraterritoriality did not originate with the Court of Appeals panel in this case. It has been repeated over many decades by various courts of appeals in determining the application of the Exchange Act, and § 10(b) in particular, to fraudulent schemes that involve conduct and effects abroad. That has produced a collection of tests for divining what Congress would have wanted, complex in formulation and unpredictable in application.

As of 1967, district courts at least in the Southern District of New York had consistently concluded that, by reason of the presumption against extraterritoriality, § 10(b) did not apply when the stock transactions underlying the violation occurred abroad. See *Schoenbaum v. Firstbrook,* 268 F.Supp. 385, 392 (1967) * * *. *Schoenbaum* involved the sale in Canada of the treasury shares of a Canadian corporation whose publicly traded shares (but not, of course, its treasury shares) were listed on both the American Stock Exchange and the Toronto Stock Exchange. Invoking the presumption against extraterritoriality, the court held that § 10(b) was inapplicable (though it incorrectly viewed the defect as jurisdictional). The decision in *Schoenbaum* was reversed, however, by a Second Circuit opinion which held that "neither the usual presumption against extraterritorial application of legislation nor the specific language of [§] 30(b) show Congressional intent to preclude application of the Exchange Act to transactions regarding stocks traded in the United States which are effected outside the United States . . . ." It sufficed to apply § 10(b) that, although the transactions in treasury shares took place in Canada, they affected the value of the common shares publicly traded in the United States. Application of § 10(b), the Second Circuit found, was "necessary to protect American investors."

The Second Circuit took another step with *Leasco Data Processing Equip. Corp. v. Maxwell,* 468 F.2d 1326 (1972), which involved an American company that had been fraudulently induced to buy securities in England. There, unlike in

Schoenbaum, some of the deceptive conduct had occurred in the United States but the corporation whose securities were traded (abroad) was not listed on any domestic exchange. *Leasco* said that the presumption against extraterritoriality apples only to matters over which the United States would not have prescriptive jurisdiction. Congress had prescriptive jurisdiction to regulate the deceptive conduct in this country, the language of the Act could be read to cover that conduct, and the court concluded that "if Congress had thought about the point," it would have wanted § 10(b) to apply.

With *Schoenbaum* and *Leasco* on the books, the Second Circuit had excised the presumption against extraterritoriality from the jurisprudence of § 10(b) and replaced it with the inquiry whether it would be reasonable (and hence what Congress would have wanted) to apply the statute to a given situation. As long as there was prescriptive jurisdiction to regulate, the Second Circuit explained, whether to apply § 10(b) even to "predominantly foreign" transactions became a matter of whether a court thought Congress "wished the precious resources of United States courts and law enforcement agencies to be devoted to them rather than leave the problem to foreign countries." *Bersch v. Drexel Firestone, Inc.,* 519 F.2d 974, 985 (1975); * * *.

The Second Circuit had thus established that application of § 10(b) could be premised upon either some effect on American securities markets or investors *(Schoenbaum)* or significant conduct in the United States *(Leasco)*. It later formalized these two applications into (1) an "effects test," "whether the wrongful conduct had a substantial effect in the United States or upon United States citizens," and (2) a "conduct test," "whether the wrongful conduct occurred in the United States." *SEC v. Berger,* 322 F.3d 187, 192-193 (C.A.2 2003). These became the north star of the Second Circuit's § 10(b) jurisprudence, pointing the way to what Congress would have wished. Indeed, the Second Circuit declined to keep its two tests distinct on the ground that "an admixture or combination of the two often gives a better picture of whether there is sufficient United States involvement to justify the exercise of jurisdiction by an American court." *Itoba Ltd. v. Lep Group PLC,* 54 F.3d 118, 122 (1995). The Second Circuit never put forward a textual or even extratextual basis for these tests. As early as *Bersch,* it confessed that "if we were asked to point to language in the statutes, or even in the legislative history, that compelled these conclusions, we would be unable to respond," * * *.

Other Circuits embraced the Second Circuit's approach, though not its precise application. Like the Second Circuit, they described their decisions regarding the extraterritorial application of § 10(b) as essentially resolving matters of policy. While applying the same fundamental methodology of balancing interests and arriving at what seemed the best policy, they produced a proliferation of vaguely related variations on the "conduct" and "effects" tests. * * *

At least one Court of Appeals has criticized this line of cases and the interpretive assumption that underlies it. In *Zoelsch v. Arthur Andersen & Co.,* 824 F.2d 27, 32 (1987) (Bork, J.), the District of Columbia Circuit observed that rather than courts' "divining what 'Congress would have wished' if it had addressed the problem[, a] more natural inquiry might be what jurisdiction Congress in fact thought about and conferred." Although tempted to apply the presumption against extraterritoriality and be done with it, see *id.,* at 31-32, that court deferred to the Second Circuit because of its "preeminence in the field of securities law."

Commentators have criticized the unpredictable and inconsistent application of § 10(b) to transnational cases. See, *e.g.,* Choi & Silberman, Transnational Litigation and Global Securities Class-Action Lawsuits, 2009 Wis. L. Rev. 465, 467-468; Chang, Multinational Enforcement of U.S. Securities Laws: The Need for the Clear and Restrained Scope of Extraterritorial Subject-Matter Jurisdiction, 9 Fordham J. Corp. & Fin. L. 89, 106-108, 115-116 (2004); Langevoort, *Schoenbaum* Revisited: Limiting the Scope of Antifraud Protection in an Internationalized Securities Marketplace, 55 Law & Contemp. Probs. 241, 244-248 (1992). Some have challenged the premise underlying the Courts of Appeals' approach, namely that Congress did not consider the extraterritorial application of § 10(b) (thereby leaving it open to the courts, supposedly, to determine what Congress would have wanted). See, *e.g.,* Sachs, The International Reach of Rule 10b-5: The Myth of Congressional Silence, 28 Colum. J. Transnat'l L. 677 (1990) (arguing that Congress considered, but rejected, applying the Exchange Act to transactions abroad). Others, more fundamentally, have noted that using congressional silence as a justification for judge-made rules violates the traditional principle that silence means no extraterritorial application. See, *e.g.,* Note, Let There Be Fraud (Abroad): A Proposal for A New U.S. Jurisprudence with Regard to the Extraterritorial Application of the Anti-Fraud Provisions of the 1933 and 1934 Securities Acts, 28 Law & Pol'y Int'l Bus. 477, 492-493 (1997).

The criticisms seem to us justified. The results of judicial-speculation-made-law—divining what Congress would have wanted if it had thought of the situation before the court—demonstrate the wisdom of the presumption against extraterritoriality. Rather than guess anew in each case, we apply the presumption in all cases, preserving a stable background against which Congress can legislate with predictable effects.

B

Rule 10b-5, the regulation under which petitioners have brought suit was promulgated under § 10(b), and "does not extend beyond conduct encompassed by § 10(b)'s prohibition." *United States v. O'Hagan,* 521 U.S. 642, 651, 117 S.Ct. 2199, 138 L.Ed.2d 724 (1997). Therefore, if § 10(b) is not extraterritorial, neither is Rule 10b-5.

On its face, § 10(b) contains nothing to suggest it applies abroad:

> "It shall be unlawful for any person, directly or indirectly, by the use of any means or instrumentality of interstate commerce or of the mails, or of any facility of any national securities exchange . . . [t]o use or employ, in connection with the purchase or sale of any security registered on a national securities exchange or any security not so registered, . . . any manipulative or deceptive device or contrivance in contravention of such rules and regulations as the [Securities and Exchange] Commission may prescribe . . . ." 15 U.S.C. § 78j(b).

Petitioners and the Solicitor General contend, however, that three things indicate that § 10(b) or the Exchange Act in general has at least some extraterritorial application.

First, they point to the definition of "interstate commerce," a term used in § 10(b), which includes "trade, commerce, transportation, or communication . . . between any foreign country and any State." 15 U.S.C. § 78c(a)(17). But "we have repeatedly held that even statutes that contain broad language in their definitions of 'commerce' that expressly refer to '*foreign* commerce' do not apply abroad." The general reference to foreign commerce in the definition of "interstate commerce" does not defeat the presumption against extraterritoriality.

Petitioners and the Solicitor General next point out that Congress, in describing the purposes of the Exchange Act, observed that the "prices established and offered in such transactions are generally disseminated and quoted throughout the United States and foreign countries." 15 U.S.C. § 78b(2). The antecedent of "such transactions," however, is found in the first sentence of the section, which declares that "transactions in securities as commonly conducted upon securities exchanges and over-the-counter markets are affected with a national public interest." § 78b. Nothing suggests that this *national* public interest pertains to transactions conducted upon *foreign* exchanges and markets. The fleeting reference to the dissemination and quotation abroad of the prices of securities traded in domestic exchanges and markets cannot overcome the presumption against extraterritoriality.

Finally, there is § 30(b) of the Exchange Act, 15 U.S.C. § 78dd(b), which *does* mention the Act's extraterritorial application: "The provisions of [the Exchange Act] or of any rule or regulation thereunder shall not apply to any person insofar as he transacts a business in securities without the jurisdiction of the United States," unless he does so in violation of regulations promulgated by the Securities and Exchange Commission "to prevent . . . evasion of [the Act]." (The parties have pointed us to no regulation promulgated pursuant to § 30(b).) The Solicitor General argues that "[this] exemption would have no function if the Act did not apply in the first instance to securities transactions that occur abroad."

We are not convinced. In the first place, it would be odd for Congress to indicate the extraterritorial application of the whole Exchange Act by means of a provision imposing a condition precedent to its application abroad. And if the whole Act applied abroad, why would the Commission's enabling regulations be limited to those preventing "evasion" of the Act, rather than all those preventing "violation"? The provision seems to us directed at actions abroad that might conceal a domestic violation, or might cause what would otherwise be a domestic violation to escape on a technicality. At most, the Solicitor General's proposed inference is possible; but possible interpretations of statutory language do not override the presumption against extraterritoriality.

The Solicitor General also fails to account for § 30(a), which reads in relevant part as follows:

> "It shall be unlawful for any broker or dealer . . . to make use of the

mails or of any means or instrumentality of interstate commerce for the purpose of effecting on an exchange not within or subject to the jurisdiction of the United States, any transaction in any security the issuer of which is a resident of, or is organized under the laws of, or has its principal place of business in, a place within or subject to the jurisdiction of the United States, in contravention of such rules and regulations as the Commission may prescribe . . . ." 15 U.S.C. § 78dd(a).

Subsection 30(a) contains what § 10(b) lacks: a clear statement of extraterritorial effect. Its explicit provision for a specific extraterritorial application would be quite superfluous if the rest of the Exchange Act already applied to transactions on foreign exchanges—and its limitation of that application to securities of domestic issuers would be inoperative. Even if that were not true, when a statute provides for some extraterritorial application, the presumption against extraterritoriality operates to limit that provision to its terms. No one claims that § 30(a) applies here. * * *

In short, there is no affirmative indication in the Exchange Act that § 10(b) applies extraterritorially, and we therefore conclude that it does not.

IV

A

Petitioners argue that the conclusion that § 10(b) does not apply extraterritorially does not resolve this case. They contend that they seek no more than domestic application anyway, since Florida is where HomeSide and its senior executives engaged in the deceptive conduct of manipulating HomeSide's financial models; their complaint also alleged that Race and Hughes made misleading public statements there. This is less an answer to the presumption against extraterritorial application than it is an assertion—a quite valid assertion—that that presumption here (as often) is not self-evidently dispositive, but its application requires further analysis. For it is a rare case of prohibited extraterritorial application that lacks *all* contact with the territory of the United States. But the presumption against extraterritorial application would be a craven watchdog indeed if it retreated to its kennel whenever *some* domestic activity is involved in the case. The concurrence seems to imagine just such a timid sentinel, * * * but our cases are to the contrary. * * *

[W]e think that the focus of the Exchange Act is not upon the place where the deception originated, but upon purchases and sales of securities in the United States. Section 10(b) does not punish deceptive conduct, but only deceptive conduct "in connection with the purchase or sale of any security registered on a national securities exchange or any security not so registered." 15 U.S.C. § 78j(b). Those purchase-and-sale transactions are the objects of the statute's solicitude. It is those transactions that the statute seeks to "regulate* * *"; it is parties or prospective parties to those transactions that the statute seeks to "protec[t]," And it is in our view only transactions in securities listed on domestic exchanges, and domestic transactions in other securities, to which § 10(b) applies.

The primacy of the domestic exchange is suggested by the very prologue of the Exchange Act, which sets forth as its object "[t]o provide for the regulation of securities exchanges . . . operating in interstate and foreign commerce and through the mails, to prevent inequitable and unfair practices on such exchanges . . . ." 48 Stat. 881. We know of no one who thought that the Act was intended to "regulat[e]" *foreign* securities exchanges—or indeed who even believed that under established principles of international law Congress had the power to do so. The Act's registration requirements apply only to securities listed on national securities exchanges. 15 U.S.C. § 78*l* (a). * * *

Finally, we reject the notion that the Exchange Act reaches conduct in this country affecting exchanges or transactions abroad * * *. The probability of incompatibility with the applicable laws of other countries is so obvious that if Congress intended such foreign application "it would have addressed the subject of conflicts with foreign laws and procedures." Like the United States, foreign countries regulate their domestic securities exchanges and securities transactions occurring within their territorial jurisdiction. And the regulation of other countries often differs from ours as to what constitutes fraud, what disclosures must be made, what damages are recoverable, what discovery is available in litigation, what individual actions may be joined in a single suit, what attorney's fees are recoverable, and many other matters. See, *e.g.,* Brief for United Kingdom of Great Britain and Northern Ireland as *Amicus Curiae* 16-21. The Commonwealth of Australia, the United Kingdom of Great Britain and Northern Ireland, and the Republic of France have filed *amicus* briefs in this case. So have (separately or jointly) such international and foreign organizations as the International Chamber of Commerce, the Swiss Bankers Association, the Federation of German Industries, the French Business Confederation, the Institute of International Bankers, the European Banking Federation, the Australian Bankers' Association, and the Association Française des Entreprises Privées. They all complain of the interference with foreign securities regulation that application of § 10(b) abroad would produce, and urge the adoption of a clear test that will avoid that consequence. The transactional test we have adopted—whether the purchase or sale is made in the United States, or involves a security listed on a domestic exchange—meets that requirement.

B

The Solicitor General suggests a different test, which petitioners also endorse: "[A] transnational securities fraud violates [§] 10(b) when the fraud involves significant conduct in the United States that is material to the fraud's success." Neither the Solicitor General nor petitioners provide any textual support for this test. * * *

If, moreover, one is to be attracted by the desirable consequences of the "significant and material conduct" test, one should also be repulsed by its adverse consequences. While there is no reason to believe that the United States has become the Barbary Coast for those perpetrating frauds on foreign securities markets, some fear that it has become the Shangri-La of class-action litigation for lawyers representing those allegedly cheated in foreign securities markets. * * *

Section 10(b) reaches the use of a manipulative or deceptive device or contrivance only in connection with the purchase or sale of a security listed on an

American stock exchange, and the purchase or sale of any other security in the United States. This case involves no securities listed on a domestic exchange, and all aspects of the purchases complained of by those petitioners who still have live claims occurred outside the United States. Petitioners have therefore failed to state a claim on which relief can be granted. We affirm the dismissal of petitioners' complaint on this ground.

* * *

JUSTICE STEVENS, with whom JUSTICE GINSBURG joins, concurring in the judgment.

While I agree that petitioners have failed to state a claim on which relief can be granted, my reasoning differs from the Court's. I would adhere to the general approach that has been the law in the Second Circuit, and most of the rest of the country, for nearly four decades.

I

Today the Court announces a new "transactional test," for defining the reach of § 10(b) of the Securities Exchange Act of 1934 (Exchange Act), 15 U.S.C. § 78j(b), and SEC Rule 10b-5, 17 CFR § 240.10b-5(b) (2009): Henceforth, those provisions will extend only to "transactions in securities listed on domestic exchanges . . . and domestic transactions in other securities[.]" If one confines one's gaze to the statutory text, the Court's conclusion is a plausible one. But the federal courts have been construing § 10(b) in a different manner for a long time, and the Court's textual analysis is not nearly so compelling, in my view, as to warrant the abandonment of their doctrine. * * *

The Second Circuit's test became the "north star" of § 10(b) jurisprudence, not just regionally but nationally as well. With minor variations, other courts converged on the same basic approach. * * *

In light of this history, the Court's critique of the decision below for applying "judge-made rules" is quite misplaced. This entire area of law is replete with judge-made rules, which give concrete meaning to Congress' general commands. * * *

The development of § 10(b) law was hardly an instance of judicial usurpation. Congress invited an expansive role for judicial elaboration when it crafted such an open-ended statute in 1934. And both Congress and the Commission subsequently affirmed that role when they left intact the relevant statutory and regulatory language, respectively, throughout all the years that followed. * * *

Thus, while the Court devotes a considerable amount of attention to the development of the case law, it draws the wrong conclusions. The Second Circuit refined its test over several decades and dozens of cases, with the tacit approval of Congress and the Commission and with the general assent of its sister Circuits. That history is a reason we should give additional weight to the Second Circuit's "judge-made" doctrine, not a reason to denigrate it. * * *

II

The Court's other main critique of the Second Circuit's approach—apart from what the Court views as its excessive reliance on functional considerations and reconstructed congressional intent—is that the Second Circuit has "disregard[ed]" the presumption against extraterritoriality. It is the Court, however, that misapplies the presumption, in two main respects.

First, the Court seeks to transform the presumption from a flexible rule of thumb into something more like a clear statement rule. We have been here before. In the case on which the Court primarily relies, *EEOC v. Arabian American Oil Co.*, 499 U.S. 244 (1991) *(Aramco)*, Chief Justice Rehnquist's majority opinion included a sentence that appeared to make the same move. See *id.,* at 258, ("Congress' awareness of the need to make a clear statement that a statute applies overseas is amply demonstrated by the numerous occasions on which it has expressly legislated the extraterritorial application of a statute"). Justice Marshall, in dissent, vigorously objected. See *id.,* at 261 ("[C]ontrary to what one would conclude from the majority's analysis, this canon is *not* a 'clear statement' rule, the application of which relieves a court of the duty to give effect to all available indicia of the legislative will").

Yet even *Aramco*—surely the most extreme application of the presumption against extraterritoriality in my time on the Court—contained numerous passages suggesting that the presumption may be overcome without a clear directive. And our cases both before and after *Aramco* make perfectly clear that the Court continues to give effect to "*all available evidence* about the meaning" of a provision when considering its extraterritorial application, lest we defy Congress' will. Contrary to Justice Scalia's personal view of statutory interpretation, that evidence legitimately encompasses more than the enacted text. Hence, while the Court's dictum that "[w]hen a statute gives no clear indication of an extraterritorial application, it has none," makes for a nice catchphrase, the point is overstated. The presumption against extraterritoriality can be useful as a theory of congressional purpose, a tool for managing international conflict, a background norm, a tiebreaker. It does not relieve courts of their duty to give statutes the most faithful reading possible.

Second, and more fundamentally, the Court errs in suggesting that the presumption against extraterritoriality is fatal to the Second Circuit's test. For even if the presumption really were a clear statement (or "clear indication") rule, it would have only marginal relevance to this case.

It is true, of course, that "this Court ordinarily construes ambiguous statutes to avoid unreasonable interference with the sovereign authority of other nations," *F. Hoffmann-La Roche Ltd. v. Empagran S.A.,* 542 U.S. 155, 164 (2004), and that, absent contrary evidence, we presume "Congress is primarily concerned with domestic conditions," *Foley Bros., Inc. v. Filardo,* 336 U.S. 281, 285 (1949). Accordingly, the presumption against extraterritoriality "provides a sound basis for concluding that Section 10(b) does not apply when a securities fraud with no effects in the United States is hatched and executed entirely outside this country." But that is just about all it provides a sound basis for concluding. And the conclusion is not very illuminating, because no party to the litigation disputes it. No one contends that § 10(b) applies to wholly foreign frauds.

Rather, the real question in this case is how much, and what kinds of, *domestic* contacts are sufficient to trigger application of § 10(b). In developing its conduct-and-effects test, the Second Circuit endeavored to derive a solution from the Exchange Act's text, structure, history, and purpose. Judge Friendly and his colleagues were well aware that United States courts "cannot and should not expend [their] resources resolving cases that do not affect Americans or involve fraud emanating from America."

The question just stated does not admit of an easy answer. The text of the Exchange Act indicates that § 10(b) extends to at least some activities with an international component, but, again, it is not pellucid as to which ones. The Second Circuit draws the line as follows: § 10(b) extends to transnational frauds "only when substantial acts in furtherance of the fraud were committed within the United States," or when the fraud was "'intended to produce'" and did produce "'detrimental effects within'" the United States, * * *.

This approach is consistent with the understanding shared by most scholars that Congress, in passing the Exchange Act, "expected U.S. securities laws to apply to certain international transactions or conduct." It is also consistent with the traditional understanding, regnant in the 1930's as it is now, that the presumption against extraterritoriality does not apply "when the conduct [at issue] occurs within the United States," and has lesser force when "the failure to extend the scope of the statute to a foreign setting will result in adverse effects within the United States." And it strikes a reasonable balance between the goals of "preventing the export of fraud from America," protecting shareholders, enhancing investor confidence, and deterring corporate misconduct, on the one hand, and conserving United States resources and limiting conflict with foreign law, on the other.

Thus, while § 10(b) may not give any "clear indication" on its face as to how it should apply to transnational securities frauds, it does give strong clues that it should cover at least some of them. * * *

Repudiating the Second Circuit's approach in its entirety, the Court establishes a novel rule that will foreclose private parties from bringing § 10(b) actions whenever the relevant securities were purchased or sold abroad and are not listed on a domestic exchange. The real motor of the Court's opinion, it seems, is not the presumption against extraterritoriality but rather the Court's belief that transactions on domestic exchanges are "the focus of the Exchange Act" and "the objects of [its] solicitude." In reality, however, it is the "public interest" and "the interests of investors" that are the objects of the statute's solicitude. And while the clarity and simplicity of the Court's test may have some salutary consequences, like all bright-line rules it also has drawbacks. * * *

III

In my judgment, if petitioners' allegations of fraudulent misconduct that took place in Florida are true, then respondents may have violated § 10(b), and could potentially be held accountable in an enforcement proceeding brought by the Commission. But it does not follow that shareholders who have failed to allege that the bulk or the heart of the fraud occurred in the United States, or that the fraud had an adverse impact on American investors or markets, may maintain a private action to recover damages they suffered abroad. Some cases involving foreign securities transactions have extensive links to, and ramifications for, this country; this case has Australia written all over it. Accordingly, * * * I would affirm its judgment. * * *

NOTES AND QUESTIONS FOR DISCUSSION

1. *Morrison* significantly circumscribed the reach of Section 10(b) and Rule 10b-5 in private claims litigation (i.e., those brought by natural persons or companies as opposed to SEC- or DOJ-initiated public actions). The majority in *Morrison* substituted a "transactional" test for the conduct-and-effects approach of the Second Circuit. Thus, Section 10(b) applies only to fraudulent acts or omissions in connection with the purchase or sale of securities listed on a U.S. exchange and the purchase or sale of any other security in the U.S. *Morrison*, 130 S. Ct. at 2888. Conversely, *Morrison* categorically excludes the application of Rule 10(b) in so-called "f-cubed" transactions which involve the purchase of a foreign issuer's security by foreign investors on a foreign exchange.

Is that an appropriate limitation of the reach of U.S. securities laws? Consider the following doubts, expressed by Justice Stevens, who concurred in the result of *Morrison* but rejected the new transactional test as lacking adequate protection for domestic investors:

> Imagine, for example, an American investor who buys shares in a company listed only on an overseas exchange. That company has a major American subsidiary with executives based in New York City; and it was in New York City that the executives masterminded and implemented a massive deception which artificially inflated the stock price— and which will, upon its disclosure, cause the price to plummet. Or, imagine that those same executives go knocking on doors in Manhattan and convince an unsophisticated retiree, on the basis of material misrepresentations, to invest her life savings in the company's doomed securities. Both of these investors would, under the Court's new test, be barred from seeking relief under § 10(b).

Morrison, 130 S. Ct. at 2895 (concurring opinion). Do you share the concern about the potential lack of adequate protection of American investors under the new transactional approach? If so, how might Congress rewrite its statute? (See Note 4, below).

2. Does the majority in *Morrison*—by rejecting the conduct-and-effects approach—reject the Restatement's approach to prescriptive jurisdiction? Compare § 402 of the Restatement (Third) of Foreign Relations Law of the United States (1987), according to which the U.S. has authority to prescribe law with respect to:

> (1) (a) conduct that, wholly or in substantial part, takes place within its territory;
>
> (b) the status of persons, or interests in things, present within its territory;
>
> (c) conduct outside its territory that has or is intended to have substantial effect within its territory;

(2) the activities, interests, status, or relations of its nationals outside as well as within its territory; and

(3) certain conduct outside its territory by persons not its nationals that is directed against the security of the state or against a limited class of other state interests.

3. In overruling the effects test in the context of securities litigation, is the majority's decision in *Morrison* any indication that this same test may have also lost its force in the field of U.S. federal antitrust law where it has been the standard since *Alcoa* (see supra) was decided in 1945? Are there differences between the fields of securities and antitrust litigation that would justify a different treatment of the effects test? Or in the text of the particular statutes?

4. An important point noted by Justice Stevens is that "[t]he Court's opinion does not, however, foreclose the Commission from bringing enforcement actions in additional circumstances, as no issue concerning the Commission's authority is presented by this case. The Commission's enforcement proceedings not only differ from private § 10(b) actions in numerous potentially relevant respects. . . . . but they pose a lesser threat to international comity . . . ." 130 S.Ct. at 2894, n.12. Note also the Congressional response to *Morrsion*: By adding Section 929P(b) to the Dodd-Frank Wall Street Reform and Consumer Protection Act of 2010 ("Dodd-Frank"), Congress resuscitated the conduct and effects approach for civil and criminal actions brought by the SEC and the Department of Justice. Furthermore, according to Section 929Y of Dodd-Frank, the SEC undertook a study on whether and to what extent private rights of action under the Section 10(b) of the Securities Exchange Act should be extended extraterritorially on the basis of the old conduct-and-effects approach. The SEC released its study on April 11, 2012. The results do not amount to recommendations to Congress, but consist of a wide range of options on which Congress could seize. The options include, for example:

- Enacting an equivalent conduct-and-effects approach for Section 10(b) private actions as Congress created for the SEC and DOJ enforcement actions.

- Adopting the conduct-and-effects tests, but to narrow the conduct test so that a private plaintiff seeking to base a Section 10(b) private action on it must demonstrate that the plaintiff's injury resulted *directly* from conduct within the United States.

For more details, see Study on the Cross-Border Scope of the Private Right of Action Under Section 10(b) of the Securities Exchange Act of 1934.[*]

---

[*] http://www.sec.gov/news/studies/2012/929y-study-cross-border-private-rights.pdf

CHAPTER 8

Recognition and Enforcement of Judgments

A. INTRODUCTION

A final judgment on the merits normally marks the end of litigation in the jurisdiction in which this judgment was rendered. The judgment displays so-called res judicata and collateral estoppel effects—that is, it bars the relitigation of the same claims in a second court or, in many cases, relitigation of issues on which a party has previously litigated and lost. Having lost the case, the defendant will satisfy the judgment or, if he proves recalcitrant, will be compelled to satisfy it by way of enforcement proceedings.

Because it would ordinarily be pointless to bring an action against an insolvent party in the first place, it is not uncommon for plaintiffs to ascertain the liquidity of potential defendants prior to suing them. Many private companies in the United States offer services that help determine whether a defendant holds sufficient assets to satisfy a judgment, and where those assets are located. Once it is established that the defendant is in a position to satisfy a judgment, the plaintiff will have to decide where to litigate. The place at which the defendant's assets are located is one obvious choice, because it is there that a final judgment can most certainly be enforced. That choice, however, may not always be available or even desirable. It may not be available if courts in that state lack personal jurisdiction over the defendant, because the simple presence of assets is ordinarily not enough to establish personal jurisdiction in the U.S., particularly in connection with a lawsuit that is otherwise unrelated to those assets. And, even if personal jurisdiction is not a hurdle, a particular forum may not be desirable either because of the law that the forum would apply, or because of the remedies available in the forum, or because of the presence or absence of a jury.

Thus, in light of such considerations, the plaintiff might decide to initiate a lawsuit in a forum in which the defendant would be subject to personal jurisdiction, but in which he does not have adequate assets to satisfy a judgment. When that occurs, the recognition and enforcement of a resulting judgment in a second judicial system may become an issue. The difficulties associated with enforcing such a judgment vary, depending on where its enforcement is sought.

In purely domestic litigation in the U.S., the enforcement of a final judicial decree across state lines poses relatively few problems. According to the U.S.

Supreme Court, under the Commerce Clause, U.S. Const. art. I, § 8, "[the Framers] provided that the Nation was to be a common market, a 'free trade unit' in which the States are debarred from acting as separable economic entities." World-Wide Volkswagen Corp. v. Woodson, 444 U.S. 286, 293 (1980). Similar thinking arguably provided for the free movement of judgments among the states. The Full Faith and Credit Statute, 28 U.S.C. § 1738, which implements the Full Faith and Credit Clause, Art. IV, § 1 of the U.S. Constitution, imposes an obligation on state and federal courts to recognize and enforce final judgments handed down by the courts of sister states.

In order to guarantee the liberal enforcement of other states' judicial decrees, this full faith and credit obligation is subject to only a few exceptions. For example, a state court will not recognize and enforce the judgment of the sister state court when the latter lacked personal jurisdiction over the defendant, at least when the jurisdictional question was not itself litigated or somehow waived in the judgment rendering court. Similarly, recognition and enforcement will be denied when the defendant was not given adequate notice of the pendency of the original lawsuit. The want of personal jurisdiction (or notice) provides a constitutional limit on full faith and credit. Other limitations—typically subconstitutional—are noted elsewhere in this chapter, such as the traditional exception for penal judgments. On the other hand, the second court is ordinarily obligated to recognize and enforce the original judgment even if it would be contrary to the public policy of the enforcing state. Griffin v. Griffin, 327 U.S. 220 (1946); Fauntleroy v. Lum, 210 U.S. 230 (1908).

To be sure, states have traditionally been able to refuse to entertain a claim arising under sister state "laws" if the claim would run afoul of the forum state's strongly held public policy. But matters are different when it comes to enforcing a judgment from another state. In *Fauntleroy, supra,* the Supreme Court held that Mississippi was obligated to enforce a Missouri judgment that had found liability on a contract entered into in Mississippi between two Mississippi citizens, although Mississippi courts would not have enforced it in the first instance because it was illegal under Mississippi law. Even though Missouri courts may have misconstrued Mississippi law, and even though the contract was against Mississippi's public policy, enforcement of the Missouri judgment on the Mississippi contract was required. In short, the full faith and credit statute requires states to give the "same" faith and credit that the state that rendered the judgment would give to it (within the constitutional limits just noted). 28 U.S.C. § 1738. An enforcing state may not give a judgment only the effect that a similar judgment would have in the enforcing state's courts.

By contrast, international recognition and enforcement proceedings involving American courts follow different rules—rules that ordinarily do not track the obligations surrounding full faith and credit. Two scenarios are possible. Either an American court is asked to enforce a judgment of a foreign tribunal, or an American court has rendered the original judgment and the successful plaintiff ("judgment creditor") seeks enforcement in a foreign forum where the defendant's assets are located. Because full faith and credit only provides that binding effect be given to state court judgments in other courts in the U.S., it has no application in the international context. Consequently, the plaintiff's prospects of having a judgment recognized in the international civil litigation setting are much less certain than they are in a purely domestic setting.

A judgment recognition treaty between the U.S. and foreign countries could certainly solve the problem, but by and large, such treaties have been few and far between. For example, there are certain so-called Friendship Treaties in which the U.S. has agreed to treat foreign nationals pursuing their rights in American courts in a nondiscriminatory manner. See, e.g., The Friendship, Commerce and Navigation Treaty between the United States and Greece, Aug. 3, 1951, 5 U.S.T. 1829 (entered into force Oct. 13, 1954). Article VI, § 1 of that document provides in pertinent part: "Nationals and companies of either Party shall be accorded national treatment and most-favored-nation treatment with respect to access to the courts of justice . . . in all degrees of jurisdiction, both in pursuit and in defense of their rights." Id., art. VI, 5 U.S.T. at 1851. Article XXIV, § 1, defines national treatment as that treatment which is "accorded within the territories of a Party upon terms no less favorable than the treatment accorded therein, in like situations, to nationals, companies, . . ." Id., art. XXIV, 5 U.S.T. at 1907. This Treaty has been held to elevate a Greek judgment whose enforcement is sought in the U.S. to the status of an American sister state judgment entitled to full faith and credit. See Vagenas v. Continental Gin Co., 988 F.2d 104 (11th Cir.), cert. denied, 510 U.S. 947 (1993).

It might also be possible for Congress, by statute, to legislate a uniform rule of recognition of foreign judgments. But as discussed later in this chapter, Congress has done so only in the setting of enforcement of certain foreign defamation judgments. See Section D, below. Although the U.S. has signed, it has not yet ratified a Convention that would provide uniform rules of enforcement of judgments entered by courts chosen in accordance with a proposed agreement respecting enforcement of forum selection clauses. And even upon ratification, there would likely have to be legislation to enforce the Convention. Consequently, most judgment enforcement law in the U.S. has been premised on the judgments law of the state in which recognition and enforcement is sought, whether in state or federal courts.

Courts asked to enforce a foreign judgment will, to some extent at least, examine the procedural and substantive law that formed the basis for the foreign decision. Courts, including those of the U.S., do this to determine whether the foreign decree comports with domestic notions of judicial fairness. If the laws of the foreign forum are considered incompatible, enforcement of the judgment may be denied, as a matter of domestic public policy. Obviously, this approach tends to produce unfavorable results for plaintiffs whose judgments are based on legal rules that differ substantially from those of the enforcing state. Jurisdictions striving for regional integration, such as the European Union, have sought to eliminate this problem by providing mechanisms similar to the American full faith and credit provisions. In many cases judgment creditors can also rely on bilateral agreements that nations have executed to facilitate the mutual recognition and enforcement of judgments. Unlike most other nations, however, the U.S. is currently not a member of any treaty or convention facilitating the recognition and enforcement of its judgments abroad. And while the friendship treaties with other nations have been interpreted by American courts to accord a type of full faith and credit treatment to judgments emanating from such nations' courts, American judgments generally do not seem to benefit from such agreements abroad.

Substantive and procedural rules in the U.S. are perceived to differ from their foreign counterparts to such an extent that attempts to forge international accords thus far have not succeeded. In 1992, a U.S. delegation to the Hague Conference on Private International Law proposed the creation of an international convention on jurisdiction and the recognition and enforcement of foreign judgments in civil and commercial matters. This effort failed, however, largely because American and European expectations could not be reconciled. In particular, the higher average level of damage awards and the types of awards (e.g., punitive damages) in the U.S. have been met with disapproval abroad. For details see Joachim Zekoll, *Comparative Civil Procedure*, in The Oxford Handbook of Comparative Law 1327, 1342 et seq. (M. Reimann & R. Zimmermann eds., 2008). On the other hand, American courts likewise have been loath to enforce foreign judgments that do not comport with legal and constitutional principles considered to be of great importance in this country. Indeed, in the SPEECH Act of 2010, 28 U.S.C. §§ 4101-4105, Congress acted to prevent the enforcement of foreign defamation judgments that did not comport with American free-speech standards. We address the SPEECH Act as well as certain earlier state court decisions reaching similar results in Section D, below.

There are two notable exceptions to this general lack of international agreement. One is The Hague Convention of 30 June 2005 on the Choice of Court Agreements, 44 I.L.M. 1294, set out at Appendix C. This Convention introduces a uniform set of rules for the enforcement of exclusive choice of court agreements for transactions between business entities ("B2B"). Importantly, the Convention also provides for the recognition and enforcement of judgments given by a court of a contracting State designated in an exclusive choice of court agreement (Art. 8). To enter into force, however, there must be at least two contracting States (Art. 31), and so far, there is only one, Mexico, which acceded in 2007. In 2009, the E.U. and the U.S. undertook the first step towards joining as well, by signing the Convention. But as of this writing, neither the U.S. nor the E.U has ratified it.

The other exception applies to the area of arbitration—a topic that we take up in Chapter 9. The U.S. has signed a multilateral treaty for the enforcement of arbitral awards, the Convention on the Recognition and Enforcement of Foreign Arbitral Awards, *opened for signature* June 10, 1958, 21 U.S.T. 2517 (entered into force Dec. 28, 1970), *codified in* 9 U.S.C. §§201-208 (1970) (hereinafter "New York Convention"). The U.S. courts have interpreted the New York Convention as a strict and binding obligation on the U.S. to enforce arbitral awards to the fullest extent. See, e.g., Parsons & Whittemore Overseas Co., Inc. v. Société Generale de L'Industrie du Papier (RAKTA), 508 F.2d 969 (2d Cir. 1974) (holding that since the Convention was signed in order to encourage the use of arbitration, the narrowest possible reading had to be given to the exceptions to enforcement contained in the treaty). In effect, where arbitral awards are concerned, the U.S. will enforce any final disposition so long as it does not violate general principles of international law or any specific provisions of the New York Convention. Errors of law, even where apparent, do not vitiate the enforcement of an award.

In the materials that follow, we will present American court decisions denying or granting the enforcement of a foreign judgment and we will then draw comparisons with foreign cases in which plaintiffs sought the enforcement of American judgments abroad. In the absence of a treaty or multilateral convention, all of these judgments raise the same two intriguing questions: (1) What elements of the decision whose enforcement is sought abroad can fairly be said to deviate from mandatory rules of the foreign (enforcing) forum? (2) To what extent can these deviations be tolerated without unduly compromising public policy or other judicial fairness concerns of the enforcing forum? Lastly, we will provide an introduction to the mechanisms governing the recognition of judgments as among the members of the European Union.

B. Enforcing Foreign Judgments in the U.S.—Basic Considerations

1. Traditional Approaches and the Regime of Comity

Hilton v. Guyot

Supreme Court of the United States, 1895.
159 U.S. 113.

MR. JUSTICE GRAY, after stating the case, delivered the opinion of the court.
* * *

International law, in its widest and most comprehensive sense—including not only questions of right between nations, governed by what has been appropriately called the law of nations; but also questions arising under what is usually called private international law, or the conflict of laws, and concerning the rights of persons within the territory and dominion of one nation, by reason of acts, private or public, done within the dominions of another nation—is part of our law, and must be ascertained and administered by the courts of justice, as often as such questions are presented in litigation between man and man, duly submitted to their determination.

The most certain guide, no doubt, for the decision of such questions is a treaty or a statute of this country. But when, as is the case here, there is no written law upon the subject, the duty still rests upon the judicial tribunals of ascertaining and declaring what the law is, whenever it becomes necessary to do so, in order to determine the rights of parties to suits regularly brought before them. In doing this, the courts must obtain such aid as they can from judicial decisions, from the works of jurists and commentators, and from the acts and usages of civilized nations.

No law has any effect, of its own force, beyond the limits of the sovereignty from which its authority is derived. The extent to which the law of one nation, as put in force within its territory, whether by executive order, by legislative act, or by judicial decree, shall be allowed to operate within the dominion of another nation, depends upon what our greatest jurists have been content to call "the comity of nations." Although the phrase has been often criticized, no satisfactory substitute has been suggested.

"Comity," in the legal sense, is neither a matter of absolute obligation, on the one hand, nor of mere courtesy and good will, upon the other. But it is the recognition which one nation allows within its territory to the legislative, executive or judicial acts of another nation, having due regard both to international duty and convenience, and to the rights of its own citizens or of other persons who are under the protection of its laws.

* * *

[The Court then supplied a lengthy discussion of the practices of various nations and the views of various writers, foreign and domestic.] [W]e are satisfied that, where there has been opportunity for a full and fair trial abroad before a court of competent jurisdiction, conducting the trial upon regular proceedings, after due citation or voluntary appearance of the defendant, and under a system of jurisprudence likely to secure an impartial administration of justice between the citizens of its own country and those of other countries, and there is nothing to show either prejudice in the court, or in the system of laws under which it was sitting, or fraud in procuring the judgment, or any other special reason why the comity of this nation should not allow it full effect, the merits of the case should not, in an action brought in this country upon the judgment, be tried afresh, as on a new trial or an appeal, upon the mere assertion of the party that the judgment was erroneous in law or in fact. The defendants, therefore, cannot be permitted, upon that general ground, to contest the validity or the effect of the judgment sued on.

But they have sought to impeach that judgment upon several other grounds, which require separate consideration.

It is objected that the appearance and litigation of the defendants in the French tribunals were not voluntary, but by legal compulsion, and therefore that the French courts never acquired such jurisdiction over the defendants, that they should be held bound by the judgment. * * *

But it is now settled in England that, while an appearance by the defendant in a court of a foreign country, for the purpose of protecting his property already in the possession of that court, may not be deemed a voluntary appearance, yet an appearance solely for the purpose of protecting other property in that country from seizure is considered as a voluntary appearance.

The present case is not one of a person travelling through or casually found in a foreign country. The defendants, although they were not citizens or residents of France, but were citizens and residents of the State of New York, and their principal place of business was in the city of New York, yet had a storehouse and an agent in Paris, and were accustomed to purchase large quantities of goods there, although they did not make sales in France. Under such circumstances, evidence that their sole object in appearing and carrying on the litigation in the French courts was to prevent property, in their storehouse at Paris, belonging to them, and within the jurisdiction, but not in the custody, of those courts, from being taken in satisfaction of any judgment that might be recovered against them, would not, according to our law, show that those courts did not acquire jurisdiction of the persons of the defendants.

It is next objected that in those courts one of the plaintiffs was permitted to testify not under oath, and was not subjected to cross-examination by the opposite party, and that the defendants were, therefore, deprived of safeguards which are by our law considered essential to secure honesty and to detect fraud in a witness; and also that documents and papers were admitted in evidence, with which the defendants had no connection, and which would not be admissible under our own system of jurisprudence. But it having been shown by the plaintiffs, and hardly denied by the defendants, that the practice followed and the method of examining witnesses were according to the laws of France, we are not prepared to hold that the fact that the procedure in these respects differed from that of our own courts is, of itself, a sufficient ground for impeaching the foreign judgment.

It is also contended that a part of the plaintiffs' claim is affected by one of the contracts between the parties having been made in violation of the revenue laws of the United States, requiring goods to be invoiced at their actual market value. Rev. Stat. § 2854. It may be assumed that, as the courts of a country will not enforce contracts made abroad in evasion or fraud of its own laws, so they will not enforce a foreign judgment upon such a contract. But as this point does not affect the whole claim in this case, it is sufficient, for present purposes, to say that there does not appear to have been any distinct offer to prove that the invoice value of any of the goods sold by the plaintiffs to the defendants was agreed between them to be, or was, in fact, lower than the actual market value of the goods.

It must, however, always be kept in mind that it is the paramount duty of the court, before which any suit is brought, to see to it that the parties have had a fair and impartial trial, before a final decision is rendered against either party.

When an action is brought in a court of this country, by a citizen of a foreign country against one of our own citizens, to recover a sum of money adjudged by a court of that country to be due from the defendant to the plaintiff, and the foreign judgment appears to have been rendered by a competent court, having jurisdiction of the cause and of the parties, and upon due allegations and proofs, and opportunity to defend against them, and its proceedings are according to the course of a civilized jurisprudence, and are stated in a clear and formal record, the judgment is prima facie evidence, at least, of the truth of the matter adjudged; and it should be held conclusive upon the merits tried in the foreign court, unless some special ground is shown for impeaching the judgment, as by showing that it was affected by fraud or prejudice, or that, by the principles of international law, and by the comity of our own country, it should not be given full credit and effect. * * *

In the case at bar, the defendants offered to prove, in much detail, that the plaintiffs presented to the French court of first instance and to the arbitrator appointed by that court, and upon whose report its judgment was largely based, false and fraudulent statements and accounts against the defendants, by which the arbitrator and the French courts were deceived and misled, and their judgments were based upon such false and fraudulent statements and accounts. This offer, if satisfactorily proved, would, according to the decisions [of the English Courts] be a sufficient ground for impeaching the foreign judgment, and examining into the merits of the original claim.

But whether those decisions can be followed in regard to foreign judgments, consistently with our own decisions as to impeaching domestic judgments for fraud, it is unnecessary in this case to determine, because there is a distinct and independent ground upon which we are satisfied that the comity of our nation does not require us to give conclusive effect to the judgments of the courts of France; and that ground is, the want of reciprocity, on the part of France, as to the effect to be given to the judgments of this and other foreign countries.

                    * * *

By the law of France, settled by a series of uniform decisions of the Court of Cassation, the highest judicial tribunal, for more than half a century, no foreign judgment can be rendered executory in France without a review of the judgment *au fond*—to the bottom, including the whole merits of the cause of action on which the judgment rests. * * *

The reasonable, if not the necessary, conclusion appears to us to be that judgments rendered in France, or in any other foreign country, by the laws of which our own judgments are reviewable upon the merits, are not entitled to full credit and conclusive effect when sued upon in this country, but are prima facie evidence only of the justice of the plaintiffs' claim.

In holding such a judgment, for want of reciprocity, not to be conclusive evidence of the merits of the claim, we do not proceed upon any theory of retaliation upon one person by reason of injustice done to another; but upon the broad ground that international law is founded upon mutuality and reciprocity, and that by the principles of international law recognized in most civilized nations, and by the comity of our own country, which it is our judicial duty to know and to declare, the judgment is not entitled to be considered conclusive.

By our law, at the time of the adoption of the Constitution, a foreign judgment was considered as prima facie evidence, and not conclusive. There is no statute of the United States, and no treaty of the United States with France, or with any other nation, which has changed that law, or has made any provision upon the subject. It is not to be supposed that, if any statute or treaty had been or should be made, it would recognize as conclusive the judgments of any country, which did not give like effect to our own judgments. In the absence of statute or treaty, it appears to us equally unwarrantable to assume that the comity of the United States requires anything more.

If we should hold this judgment to be conclusive, we should allow it an effect to which, supposing the defendants' offers to be sustained by actual proof, it would, in the absence of a special treaty, be entitled in hardly any other country in Christendom, except the country in which it was rendered. If the judgment had been rendered in this country, or in any other outside of the jurisdiction of France, the French courts would not have executed or enforced it, except after examining into its merits. The very judgment now sued on would be held inconclusive in almost any other country than France. In England, and in the Colonies subject to the law of England, the fraud alleged in its procurement would be a sufficient ground for disregarding it. In the courts of nearly every other nation, it would be subject to reexamination, either merely because it was a foreign judgment, or because judgments of that nation would be reexaminable in the courts of France. [Reversed.]

MR. CHIEF JUSTICE FULLER, with whom concurred MR. JUSTICE HARLAN, MR. JUSTICE BREWER and MR. JUSTICE JACKSON, dissenting.

Plaintiffs brought their action on a judgment recovered by them against the defendants in the courts of France, which courts had jurisdiction over person and subject-matter, and in respect of which judgment no fraud was alleged, except in particulars contested in and considered by the French courts. The question is whether under these circumstances, and in the absence of a treaty or act of Congress, the judgment is reexaminable upon the merits. * * * [I]t seems to me that the doctrine of res judicata applicable to domestic judgments should be applied to foreign judgments as well, and rests on the same general ground of public policy that there should be an end of litigation. * * *

The principle that requires litigation to be treated as terminated by final judgment properly rendered, is as applicable to a judgment proceeded on in such an action, as to any other, and forbids the allowance to the judgment debtor of a retrial of the original cause of action, as of right, in disregard of the obligation to pay arising on the judgment and of the rights acquired by the judgment creditor thereby. * * *

I cannot yield my assent to the proposition that because by legislation and judicial decision in France that effect is not there given to judgments recovered in this country which, according to our jurisprudence, we think should be given to judgments wherever recovered (subject, of course, to the recognized exceptions,) therefore we should pursue the same line of conduct as respects the judgments of French tribunals. The application of the doctrine of res judicata does not rest in discretion; and it is for the government, and not for its courts, to adopt the principle of retorsion [i.e., reciprocity—eds.], if deemed under any circumstances desirable or necessary.

NOTES AND QUESTIONS FOR DISCUSSION

1. In *Hilton*, the Supreme Court considered the effect that a foreign court's judgment obtained by a foreign citizen against a U.S. citizen should have in a federal court proceeding to enforce the judgment. It concluded that while U.S. courts were generally under no absolute duty to enforce another country's judgments (absent a treaty or statute), principles of "comity" among nations would ordinarily control the preclusive effect that this nation would give to foreign judgments. Consequently, there is considerable discretion whether to honor the request to enforce foreign country judgments (as well as their laws).

2. Recall that in the U.S., under the full faith and credit statute, 28 U.S.C. § 1738, which implements the Constitution's Full Faith and Credit Clause, U.S. Const. art. IV, § 1, a state would ordinarily be required to enforce the jurisdictionally valid judgments of sister states. It therefore could *not* treat a sister state judgment as if it emanated from a foreign country under notions of "comity." Rather, such a judgment has to be given the same force and effect that they would have in the state that rendered the judgment in the first place. According to the modern Court, the "constitutional limitation imposed by the full faith and credit clause abolished, in large measure, the general principle of international law by which local policy is permitted to dominate rules of comity." Broderick v. Rosner, 294 U.S. 629, 643 (1935). Thus, U.S. enforcement of judgments of foreign tribunals—being governed only by notions of comity rather than full faith and credit—is much less certain than the enforcement of domestic judgments within the U.S.

3. Nevertheless, in deciding what comity required in the context of enforcement of a foreign court's judgment, the Court in *Hilton* concluded that—given a decision of a court of competent jurisdiction, where there has been a full and fair opportunity to litigate, after due notice or voluntary appearance, "under a system of jurisprudence likely to secure an impartial administration of justice between the citizens of its own country and those of other countries," and absent fraud—"the merits of that case should not, in an action brought in this country upon the judgment, be tried afresh . . . upon the mere assertion of the party that the judgment was erroneous in law or in fact." 159 U.S. at 202-03. As thus articulated, how different is such a standard from that required by full faith and credit?

4. In *Hilton*, the parties in the original French action were permitted to testify other than under oath and were not subject to cross-examination. In addition, evidence inadmissible in a U.S. proceeding was admitted in the foreign proceeding. Even though the practice followed was according to the law of France, why weren't such differences a reason for nonenforcement?

5. Because French courts would not give similar faith and credit to another nation's judgments against a French citizen, and would instead allow for relitigation of the merits in the French courts, a narrow majority in *Hilton* concluded that the U.S. courts would not automatically enforce a French judgment. The Court explained that comity incorporated a notion of reciprocity that trumped the default rule against relitigation. Note that this is an obvious difference from the faith and credit that would have to be given to a sister state judgment, because "reciprocity" is essentially commanded as a matter of federal law. Four dissenters in *Hilton* argued that the Court's reciprocity analysis should give way to ordinary principles of res judicata, and that second rounds of litigation in U.S. courts ought to be discouraged—whether or not the country that rendered the judgment would do the same for a judgment from a U.S. court. Were the *Hilton* dissenters right? Is there any argument that it would be in the nation's interest to enforce a foreign judgment unilaterally, the lack of reciprocity notwithstanding? For some classic critiques of the reciprocity requirement, see Joseph Beale, The Conflict of Laws § 434.3 (1935); Arthur Taylor von Mehren & Donald T. Trautman, *Recognition of Foreign Adjudications: A Survey and a Suggested Approach*, 81 Harv. L. Rev. 1601, 1660-62 (1968); Willis L. Reese, *The Status in This Country of Judgments Rendered Abroad*, 50 Colum. L. Rev. 783, 790-93 (1950); Comment, *Reciprocity and the Recognition of Foreign Judgments*, 36 Yale L.J. 542 (1927).

6. *Hilton* is perhaps the only U.S. Supreme Court opinion to address the recognition of foreign judgments. What was the source of law that the Court applied? Hilton was a decision rendered prior to Erie Railroad Co. v. Tompkins, 304 U.S. 64 (1938). Consequently, the law that the Court applied was likely "general" law, which, strictly speaking, was neither state law nor federal law. Indeed, pre-*Erie*, it is possible that the result in *Hilton* may have differed from whatever the relevant state's law of judgment recognition might have been. After *Erie*, how should the question be resolved? Should the *Hilton* decision now be read as creating a "federal common law" of recognition and enforcement of foreign judgments, binding even on state courts? Or should the question of the force to be given foreign judgments now be seen as a question of state law? We consider the issue in the materials that follow.

2. The Source of Law Governing Enforcement of Foreign Judgments in U.S. Courts

Johnston v. Compagnie Générale Transatlantique

Court of Appeals of New York, 1926.
242 N.Y. 381.

POUND, J.

The controversy arises over an alleged wrongful delivery of goods by the defendant, a steamship carrier, which is a foreign corporation organized under the laws of the Republic of France. Plaintiff is the assignee of triplicate bills of lading issued in New York, under which one Frank E. Webb shipped the goods from New York to Havre. Defendant delivered the goods to other parties upon presentation of a non-negotiable copy of the bill of lading which Webb retained as an office copy not used for presentation to secure the delivery of the goods.

Defendant set up as a defense an adjudication of the Tribunal of Commerce at Paris in favor of defendant upon the same cause of action, in an action brought by plaintiff thereon and established on the trial that the French judgment was the final judgment on the merits of a court of competent jurisdiction. No attempt was made to impeach it for fraud.

The courts below refused to give effect to the French judgment on the authority of *Hilton* v. *Guyot* (159 U.S. 113), decided in 1895, for the reason that by the law of France no foreign judgment can be rendered executory in France without a review of the judgment *au fond*, that is, of the whole merits of the cause of action on which the judgment rests; that for want of reciprocity the courts of this State are not bound by the judgment but will, in their discretion, examine the rights of the parties as fully and absolutely as if the matter had never been submitted to the French court; and that on the merits the French judgment was contrary to the principles of our law and should be disregarded.

The New York rule was stated in *Dunstan* v. *Higgins* (138 N.Y. 70), decided in 1893, as follows:

It is the settled law of this State that a foreign judgment is conclusive upon the merits. It can be impeached only by proof that the court in which it was rendered had not jurisdiction of the subject matter of the action or of the person of the defendant, or that it was procured by means of fraud. * * * The judgments of the courts of a sister State are entitled to full faith and credit in the courts of the other States under the Constitution of the United States, but effect is given to the judgments of the courts of foreign countries by the comity of nations which is part of our municipal law. The refusal of the foreign court to allow a commission to examine witnesses here does not affect the conclusive character of the judgment. Such applications are generally within the discretion of the court to which they are addressed and then a refusal to grant them does not constitute even a legal error subject to review. But even if it appeared in this case, as it does not, that some legal right of the defendant was denied in refusing the application that would not affect the validity or conclusive nature of the judgment, so long as it stood unreversed and not set aside. Legal errors committed upon the trial or during the progress of the cause may be corrected by appeal or motion to the proper court, but they furnish no defense to an action upon the judgment itself. Where a party is sued in a foreign country, upon a contract made there, he is subject to the procedure of the court in which the action is pending, and must resort to it for the purpose of his defense, if he has any, and any error committed must be reviewed or corrected in the usual way. So long as he has the benefit of such rules and regulations as have been adopted or are in use for the ordinary administration of justice among the citizens or subjects of the country he cannot complain, and justice is not denied to him. The presumption is that the rights and liability of the defendant have been determined according to the law and procedure of the country where the judgment was rendered.

This is the modern English doctrine and the doctrine of some, at least, of our State courts. (*Lazier* v. *Westcott*, 26 N.Y. 146; *Konitzky* v. *Meyer*, 49 N.Y. 571, 576; *MacDonald* v. *Grand Trunk Ry. Co.*, 71 N.H. 448; *Nouvion* v. *Freeman*, 15 App. Cas. 1, 9; *Godard* v. *Gray*, L. R. 6 Q. B. 139-148) and has the approval of recent text-book writers. (3 Freeman on Judgments, 3069.)

In *Hilton* v. *Guyot* the action was brought on a foreign judgment, rendered by the same court in which the judgment herein was rendered. The opinion of Judge Gray, after an exhaustive review of the subject, while fully recognizing the general rule as stated, lays down the collateral and qualifying rule that on principles of comity judgments rendered in France, by whose laws judgments of the United States courts are reviewable on their merits, are not conclusive when sued upon in the United States and are only *prima facie* evidence of the justice of plaintiff's claim. Fuller, Ch. J., wrote a dissenting opinion in which Harlan, Brewer and Jackson, JJ., concurred. He says (p. 233):

In any aspect, it is difficult to see why rights acquired under foreign judgments do not belong to the category of private rights acquired under foreign laws. Now the rule is universal in this country that private rights acquired under the laws of foreign states will be respected and enforced in our courts unless contrary to the policy or prejudicial to the interests of the state where this is sought to be done; and although the source of this rule may have been the comity characterizing the intercourse between nations, it prevails today by its own strength, and the right to the application of the law to which the particular transaction is subject to a juridical right.

No case has previously arisen in this State which necessarily involved the consideration of *Hilton* v. *Guyot*. The question here presented may be regarded as an open one in this court. Cullen, Ch. J., said in *Grubel* v. *Nassauer* (210 N.Y. 149, 151) (by way of dictum, for the question was as to the jurisdiction of the foreign court): "The judgments of the courts of no country have, necessarily, any extraterritorial effect. When they are enforced in a foreign country, which as a rule they are to a certain extent, it is solely by virtue of comity. The elaborate review of this subject by the Supreme Court of the United States in *Hilton* v. *Guyot* renders further discussion unnecessary." Very recently in *Gould* v. *Gould* (235 N.Y. 14) it was said that *Hilton* v. *Guyot* did not apply in a matrimonial action where both parties although resident in France were said to be domiciled in the State of New York. Full force and effect was given to the French decree. The court in the end, however, disposed of the case in the exercise of discretion. It seems illogical to leave the effect of a foreign judgment *in personam* in individual cases to the discretion of the court.

To what extent is this court bound by *Hilton* v. *Guyot*? It is argued with some force that questions of international relations and the comity of nations are to be determined by the Supreme Court of the United States; that there is no such thing as comity of nations between the State of New York and the Republic of France and that the decision in *Hilton* v. *Guyot* is controlling as a statement of the law. But the question is one of private rather than public international law, of private right rather than public relations and our courts will recognize private rights acquired under foreign laws and the sufficiency of the evidence establishing such rights. A right acquired under a foreign judgment may be established in this State without reference to the rules of evidence laid down by the courts of the United States. Comity is not a rule of law, but it is a rule of "practice, convenience and expediency. It is something more than mere courtesy, which implies only deference to the opinion of others, since it has a substantial value in securing uniformity of decision, and discouraging repeated litigation of the same question." (Brown, J., in *Mast, Foos & Co.* v. *Stover Mfg. Co.*, 177 U.S. 485, 488.) It, therefore, rests, not on the basis of reciprocity, but rather upon the persuasiveness of the foreign judgment. (*Loucks* v. *Standard Oil Co.*, 224 N.Y. 99, 111.) When the whole of the facts appear to have been inquired into by the French courts, judicially, honestly and with full jurisdiction and with the intention to arrive at the right conclusion, and when they have heard the facts and come to a conclusion, it should no longer be open to the party invoking the foreign court against a resident of France to ask the American court to sit as a court of appeal from that which gave the judgment. I reach the conclusion that this court is not bound to follow the *Hilton* case and reverse its previous rulings.

The reasoning of the learned justice who wrote the prevailing opinion is, however, entitled to most respectful consideration. Nor need we disregard the authority of the *Hilton* case. We may limit it to the questions actually decided. Mr. Justice Gray says: "In England, and in the Colonies subject to the law of England, the fraud alleged in its [the French judgment] procurement would be a sufficient ground for disregarding it." As this State has always permitted foreign judgments to be impeached for fraud, the preceding fifty-four pages of the opinion may be regarded as magnificent dictum, entitled to the utmost respect, but not determinative of the question.

Furthermore, the learned justice limits his discussion to the effect which a judgment, purely executory, rendered in favor of a citizen or resident of France in a suit there brought by him against a citizen of the United States may be entitled to in an action thereon in the United States. Here the plaintiff was the actor in the French court. After having sought the jurisdiction of the foreign tribunal, brought the defendant into that court and litigated the question there, he now seeks to impeach the judgment rendered against him. The principles of comity should give conclusiveness to such a judgment as a bar to the present action. Dicey on Conflict of Laws (3d ed. p. 455) states separately the rule as to foreign judgments pleaded as a defense, as follows: "A valid foreign judgment *in personam* if it is final and conclusive on the merits (but not otherwise) is a good defense to an action for the same matter when either (1) the judgment was in favor of defendant or (2) the judgment in favor of the plaintiff has been satisfied." The law of the State of New York remains unchanged and the French judgment should be given full faith and credit. [Reversed.]

NOTES AND QUESTIONS FOR DISCUSSION

1. As noted above, *Hilton v. Guyot* spoke at length about the general common law of judgment recognition, but it did not identify the source of that law. *Johnston* indicates that the relevant law is state law. After *Erie* (see Note 6 following *Hilton*), this appears to mean that a federal court sitting in a diversity of citizenship case will also be obligated to apply state judgment recognition law as well, when assessing the force to be given to a foreign judgment. Note that most suits to enforce foreign judgments pit an alien against a U.S. citizen, no treaty is applicable, and Congress has yet to address the problem by statute. Should the recognition of foreign judgments in state courts, as well as in federal courts where diversity of citizenship is present, be left to the vagaries of state law? For a critique, see Steven B. Burbank, *Federalism and Private International Law: Implementing the Hague Choice of Court Convention in the United States*, 2 J. Priv. Int'l L. 287 (2006).

2. For better or for worse, *Johnston* reflects the prevailing opinion as evidenced by the Restatement (Third) of Foreign Relations Law of the United States (1987): "[R]ecognition and enforcement of foreign country judgments is a matter of State law, and an action to enforce a foreign country judgment is not an action arising under the laws of the United States. Thus, State courts, and federal courts applying State law, recognize and enforce foreign country judgments without reference to federal rules." Section 481, comment a. See also Success Motivation Inst. of Japan Ltd. v. Success Motivation Institute, Inc., 966 F.2d 1007, 1009-10 (5th Cir. 1992) ("*Erie* applies even though some courts have found that these suits necessarily involve relations between the U.S. and foreign governments, and even though some commentators have argued that the enforceability of these judgments in the courts of the United States should be governed by reference to a general rule of federal law."). The American Law Institute (ALI) has revisited the issue in its International Jurisdiction and Judgments Project. The Reporters for the Project drafted, and then adopted, a proposal under the title: "Recognition and Enforcement of Foreign Judgments: Analysis and Proposed Federal Statute (2006)." The proposed statute would introduce a single national standard for the recognition and enforcement of foreign judgments that would preempt state law. Consider whether a centralized effort at unification is preferable to the rough uniformity obtained by the Uniform Foreign-County Money Judgments Act (discussed below)—a model act that the majority of states have adopted, albeit with various modifications.

3.   Notwithstanding cases such as *Johnston* and the Restatement, and as noted in *Success Motivation, supra*, some courts have suggested that the relevant law of judgment recognition might be federal law, not state law, while some others seem to suppose it is an open question. See, e.g., Tahan v. Hodgson, 662 F.2d 862, 868 (D.C. Cir. 1981) ("[N]otwithstanding *Erie Railroad Co. v. Tompkins*, the issue seems to be national rather than state."); John Sanderson & Co. (Wool) Pty. Ltd. v. Ludlow Jute Co., Ltd., 569 F.2d 696, 697 n.1 (1st Cir. 1978) (leaving the question open); Banque Libanaise Pour Le Commerce v. Khreich, 915 F.2d 1000, 1003 n.1 (5th Cir. 1990) (noting that "[c]ommentators have argued that the enforceability of a foreign judgment in United States' courts should therefore be governed by reference to a general rule of federal law," but applying state law); see also Restatement (Second) of Conflict of Laws § 98, comment c (1971) ("[I]t seems probable that federal law would be applied to prevent application of a State rule on the recognition of foreign nation judgments if such application would result in the disruption or embarrassment of the foreign relations of the United States." (citing Zschernig v. Miller, 389 U.S. 429 (1968))).

4.   As noted in *Banque Libanaise*, a number of commentators seem to favor a federal common law approach. See, e.g., Andreas F. Lowenfeld, *Nationalizing International Law: Essay in Honor of Louis Henkin*, 36 Colum. J. Transnat'l L. 121, 131 (1997); Donald T. Trautman, *Towards Federalizing Choice of Law*, 70 Tex. L. Rev. 1715, 1735-36 (1992); Ronald A. Brand, *Enforcement of Foreign Money-Judgments in the United States: In Search of Uniformity and International Acceptance*, 67 Notre Dame L. Rev. 253, 301-18 (1991). See also Robert C. Casad, Symposium: *Issue Preclusion and Foreign Country Judgments; Whose Law?*, 70 Iowa L. Rev. 53, 77-80 (1984) ("Although the Republic can survive without federalizing the law of foreign judgment recognition, the arguments in favor of that position are strong and the principle argument against it amounts to little more than inertia."). Consider, however, why federal law should arguably be applicable, even in the absence of congressional action. Is it because judgments recognition law is merely a matter of "procedure" that federal courts may resolve on their own? Note that if that were true, federal judgment-recognition law would apply only in federal courts, not state courts, and the enforceability of a foreign judgment might turn on the court in which enforcement was sought. Or is there an argument that the enforceability of a foreign judgment should be considered a question of federal substantive law and thus controlling on state courts as well?

5.   One of the normative arguments in favor of a uniform federal standard is that the recognition or rejection of foreign judgments involves strong federal interests in the field of international relations. See *Zschernig, supra.* Is it clear, however, that a nationwide, uniform federal rule would not run afoul of any constitutional restraints? Foreign commerce (U.S. Const., art. 1, § 8, cl. 3) and foreign relations are both matters that can be regulated by the federal government. See Chae Chan Ping v. United States, 130 U.S. 581, 606 (1889) ("For local interests the several states of the Union exist, but for national purposes, embracing our relations with foreign nations, we are but one people, one nation, one power.") But are foreign judgments articles of "commerce"? Alternatively, does the non-uniform application of state law of judgment recognition so interfere with federal interests in foreign relations that it is constitutionally preempted? Even assuming *Congress* could supply a uniform rule of judgment recognition by statute, the question remains: Is it proper for the federal *courts* to develop uniform federal common law in the absence of congressional action, simply because there may be a federal "interest" in having such a rule?

6.   Another argument in favor of a uniform standard likely comes from concerns of foreign litigants (and their countries). From the point of view of judgment creditors seeking to enforce foreign judgments in this country, will a uniform solution necessarily be a better one? Might it depend on the content of the federal law? Currently, several states have more lax standards (i.e., standards more favorable to judgment enforcement) than the ALI Proposed Federal Statute (Note 2, above), although the certainty of a truly common standard such as the ALI proposal might well reduce significantly the risks of doing business with U.S. companies. Finally, note that cases such as *Hilton* meant—pre-*Erie*—that there was indeed a uniform approach to enforcement of judgments, but only in federal courts. Just as federal courts were often free to ignore state decisional law, states were free to ignore the general common law decisions of federal courts, including the U.S. Supreme Court. Indeed, that is precisely what happened in *Johnston.*

3. Introduction to Current Approaches under State Law

Although the states are largely free to fashion their own law governing the enforcement of foreign judgments, and to apply their own procedures and enforcement mechanisms, the rules that have emerged over time are in important respects similar, and they are derived in part from the holding in *Hilton*. Most importantly, state laws espouse the principle enunciated in *Hilton* that ordinarily disallows relitigation of the merits of the foreign judgment. There is, moreover, agreement over several grounds for denying enforcement: The most important ones are lack of personal jurisdiction over the defendant and lack of due process in the foreign proceedings. Important differences continue to exist, however. For example, unlike *Hilton*, most states do not require reciprocity as a prerequisite for enforcement, while some jurisdictions still do. In an effort to harmonize this area of the law, the National Conference of Commissioners on Uniform State Laws and the American Bar Association "codified" the prevailing state law approaches in the Uniform Foreign-Country Money Judgments Recognition Act (2005) ("UFCMJA"), a revised (a slightly re-titled) version of the Uniform Foreign Money Judgments Recognition Act of 1962. As of early 2013, more than half of the states, plus the District of Columbia and the territory of the Virgin Islands, have adopted some version of the Act. And nearly 20 states have adopted the latest (2005) revisions. Nevertheless, states that have adopted the Act in one or another of its versions have done so with sometimes significant deviations from the original text. Massachusetts and Georgia, for example, have adopted the Act but included *Hilton*'s reciprocity requirement that the drafters of the Act consciously omitted to facilitate foreign judgment recognition. Consequently, it cannot be said that the uniform act is applied uniformly. Nevertheless, in many respects the Act does reflect the prevailing practices of American courts, as is evidenced by the Restatement (Third) of Foreign Relations Law of the United States (1987), which adopted most of its (original) text, verbatim.

UNIFORM FOREIGN-COUNTRY MONEY JUDGMENTS RECOGNITION ACT OF 1962 (as modified, 2005):

* * *

Sec. 3. Applicability.

(a) Except as otherwise provided in subsection (b), this [act] applies to a foreign-country judgment to the extent that the judgment:

(1) grants or denies recovery of a sum of money; and

(2) under the law of the foreign country where rendered, is final, conclusive and enforceable.

(b) This [act] does not apply to a foreign-country judgment, even if the judgment grants or denies recovery of a sum of money, to the extent that the judgment is:

(1) a judgment for taxes;

(2) a fine or other penalty; or

(3) a judgment for divorce, support, or maintenance, or other judgment rendered in connection with domestic relations.

(c) A party seeking recognition of a foreign-country judgment has the burden of establishing that this [act] applies to the foreign-country judgment.

Sec. 4. Standards for Recognition of Foreign-Country Judgments.

(a) Except as provided in subsections (b) and (c), a court of this state shall recognize a foreign-country judgment to which this [act] applies.

(b) A court of this state may not recognize a foreign-country judgment if:

(1) the judgment was rendered under a judicial system that does not provide impartial tribunals or procedures compatible with the requirements of due process of law;

(2) the foreign court did not have personal jurisdiction over the defendant; or

(3) the foreign court did not have jurisdiction over the subject matter.

(c) A court of this state need not recognize a foreign-country judgment if:

(1) the defendant in the proceeding in the foreign court did not receive notice of the proceeding in sufficient time to enable the defendant to defend;

(2) the judgment was obtained by fraud that deprived the losing party of an adequate opportunity to present a case;

(3) the judgment or the [cause of action] [claim for relief] on which the judgment is based is repugnant to the public policy of this state or of the United States;

(4) the judgment conflicts with another final and conclusive judgment;

(5) the proceeding in the foreign court was contrary to an agreement between the parties under which the dispute in question was to be determined otherwise than by proceedings in that foreign court;

(6) in the case of jurisdiction based only on personal service, the foreign court was a seriously inconvenient forum for the trial of the action;

(7) the judgment was rendered in circumstances that raise substantial doubt about the integrity of the rendering court with respect to the judgment; or

(8) the specific proceeding in the foreign court leading to the judgment was not compatible with the requirements of due process of law.

(d) A party resisting recognition of a foreign-country judgment has the burden of establishing that a ground for nonrecognition stated in subsection (b) or (c) exists.

Sec. 5. Personal Jurisdiction.

(a) A foreign country judgment may not be refused recognition for lack of personal jurisdiction if:

(1) the defendant was served with process personally in the foreign country;

(2) the defendant voluntarily appeared in the proceeding, other than for the purpose of protecting property seized or threatened with seizure in the proceeding or of contesting the jurisdiction of the court over the defendant;

(3) the defendant, before the commencement of the proceeding, had agreed to submit to the jurisdiction of the foreign court with respect to the subject matter involved;

(4) the defendant was domiciled in the foreign country when the proceeding was instituted, or was a corporation or other form of business organization that had its principal place of business in, or

was organized under the laws of, the foreign country;

(5) the defendant had a business office in the foreign country and the proceeding in the foreign court involved a [cause of action] [claim for relief] arising out of business done by the defendant through that office in the foreign country; or

(6) the defendant operated a motor vehicle or airplane in the foreign country and the proceeding involved a [cause of action] [claim for relief] arising out of that operation.

(b) The list of bases for personal jurisdiction in subsection (a) is not exclusive. And the courts of this state may recognize bases of personal jurisdiction other than those listed in subsection (a) as sufficient to support a foreign-country judgment.

* * *

Sec. 7. Effect of Recognition of Foreign-Country Judgment under this [Act].

If the court . . . finds that the foreign-country judgment is entitled to recognition under this [act] then, to the extent that the foreign-country judgment grants or denies recovery of a sum of money, the foreign judgment is:

(1) conclusive between the parties to the same extent as the judgment of a sister state entitled to full faith and credit in this state would be conclusive; and

(2) enforceable in the same manner and to the same extent as a judgment rendered in this state.

NOTES AND QUESTIONS FOR DISCUSSION

1. Section 4 of the UFCMJA distinguishes between mandatory grounds for non recognition (§ 4(b)) and discretionary grounds for non-recognition (§ 4(c)). Consider whether the distinctions make sense and whether the reasons listed in paragraph (c) should merely permit and not require denial of recognition. For example, why should a foreign judgment obtained by fraud (§ 4(c)(2)) or one that is repugnant to the public policy of the enforcing state (§ 4(c)(3)) be entitled to potentially greater respect than a judgment in which the rendering court did not have personal jurisdiction (§ 4(b)(2))?

2. Despite this comprehensive list of grounds for rejecting foreign judgments, there is a common perception (outside the U.S.) that American courts tend to be rather permissive when faced with requests to recognize and enforce foreign judgments. Section 4(a) of the Act arguably codifies this position by declaring favorable treatment of foreign judgments to be the rule, while pointing to the grounds for rejection listed in § 4 only as exceptions. Furthermore, the saving clause of § 6(b) provides that the Act does not prevent recognition of a foreign judgment in situations not covered by the Act. Just how tolerant American courts are in practice, compared to their foreign counterparts, is a difficult matter to determine. Of course, there are those American decisions that liberally recognize foreign judgments and, in line with the spirit of § 4(a) of the Act, effectively accord them a kind of full faith and credit. See § 7(1). But there are also a number of cases in which American judges have displayed a great deal of distrust towards foreign decisions. The cases that follow illustrate these conflicting trends.

C. FOREIGN JUDGMENTS AND THE REQUIREMENT OF PERSONAL JURISDICTION

It is well accepted that a foreign judgment will not be enforced if the foreign court did not have personal jurisdiction over the defendant, and section 4(b)(2) of the current UFCMJA reinforces this view. But whose jurisdictional standards shall apply to this inquiry? Those of the judgment-rendering forum? Of the judgment-recognizing forum? Or both? The following decision provides a discussion of some of these issues.

Evans Cabinet Corp. v. Kitchen Int'l, Inc.

United States Court of Appeals, First Circuit, 2010.

593 F.3d 135.

RIPPLE, CIRCUIT JUDGE.[*]

Evans Cabinet Corporation ("Evans") [a Georgia corporation with a principal place of business in Georgia] instituted this diversity action in the United States District Court for the District of Massachusetts against Kitchen International, Inc. [a Louisiana corporation with its principal place of business in Montreal, Quebec] for breach of contract and quantum meruit. Kitchen International filed a motion to dismiss based on res judicata. It claimed that the action was foreclosed because of an earlier judgment entered by the Superior Court of Quebec. After a hearing * * * the court entered judgment for Kitchen International. Evans filed a timely appeal to this court.

For the reasons set forth in the following opinion, we reverse the judgment of the district court and remand for proceedings consistent with this opinion.

I

BACKGROUND

According to the allegations of the complaint, Kitchen International and Evans entered into a contract in 2004. Evans agreed to supply Kitchen International with manufactured cabinetry for several residential construction sites on the East Coast of the United States. Kitchen International placed these orders from its headquarters in Montreal with the Georgia offices of Evans. The materials were shipped directly to the construction sites.

---

[*] Of the Seventh Circuit, sitting by designation.

According to Kitchen International, in 2004, the two parties also agreed that they would create a products showroom at Kitchen International's office in Montreal. Kitchen International claims that Paul Gatti of Evans approved the design and layout of the showroom. According to Kitchen International, later that year, Evans manufactured and shipped cabinetry, related products and sales and promotional materials to Quebec for use in the showroom. Evans denies the existence of such an agreement; it claims that it never authorized Kitchen International to build a showroom and that it did not supply products to Kitchen International for that purpose.

Various issues arose about the quality and conformity of the products that Evans had shipped to the East Coast projects. Consequently, in May 2006, Kitchen International engaged a Canadian attorney to file suit against Evans in the Superior Court of Quebec for breach of contract arising from the materials supplied by Evans. Evans was served with process and given notice of this proceeding. Evans did not answer or otherwise respond to the action, and, consequently, on May 31, 2007, the Superior Court of Quebec entered a default judgment against Evans in the amount of $ 149,354.74.

On April 23, 2007, Evans instituted this action for breach of contract and quantum meruit in the United States District Court for the District of Massachusetts. Kitchen International filed a motion to dismiss on the ground that the action was barred by res judicata by virtue of the Canadian judgment against Evans. Evans opposed the motion on the ground that the Superior Court of Quebec had lacked jurisdiction over it, and, therefore, the Quebec judgment could not be recognized by the district court. [The motion was converted to a motion for summary judgment because the issues went beyond the pleadings]. * * *

The district court, held that res judicata precluded the present action and entered summary judgment for Kitchen International.

II

DISCUSSION

A. Contentions of the Parties.

Evans submits that the district court erred in holding that its claim for damages for breach of contract or in quantum meruit were barred because of the prior default judgment entered against it by the Superior Court of Quebec. In Evans's view, the Superior Court of Quebec lacked personal jurisdiction over it, and, consequently, the default judgment was unenforceable and not subject to recognition by the district court. * * * Evans submits that there are significant unresolved factual questions concerning the nature of Evans's relevant contacts with the Province of Quebec. Evans contends that, if the district court had taken the facts in the light most favorable to its position, as the district court must do in the context of summary judgment, there would be no basis for concluding that the Quebec court could exercise personal jurisdiction over it.

Kitchen International takes a decidedly different view. It submits that the Quebec judgment must be recognized and precludes the present suit. Focusing on the summary judgment motion, it notes that the district court characterized its evidence that Evans had purposeful contacts with Quebec as "overwhelming." * * * By contrast, Evans submitted only the affidavits of Mark Trexler, Evans's

CEO, who, in Kitchen International's view, could show no involvement in the parties' agreements.

B. Threshold Matters.

* * * When sitting in diversity and asked to recognize and enforce a foreign country judgment, federal courts tend to apply the law of recognition and enforcement of the state in which they sit, as required by Erie Railroad Co. v. Tompkins, 304 U.S. 64 (1938). However, some courts and commentators have suggested that recognition and enforcement of foreign country judgments deserves application of a uniform federal body of law because suits of this nature necessarily implicate the foreign relations of the United States.[7] This question has not been decided definitively in this circuit. In John Sanderson (Wool) Pty. Ltd. v. Ludlow Jute Co., 569 F.2d 696, 697 n.1 (1st Cir. 1978), we left the question open, noting that there was no reason to decide the matter under the facts of that case because there was no appreciable difference between the federal and the state rules. We shall follow the same course in this case because we need not resolve the matter here. Neither party has suggested that the district court ought to have followed a rule other than that of Massachusetts. In any event, even if the reciprocity rule of *Hilton v. Guyot* were applicable under the facts of this case, the Massachusetts rule of recognition and enforcement also contains a reciprocity requirement. See Mass. Gen. Laws ch. 235, § 23A (subsection (7) of third paragraph); see also *John Sanderson,* 569 F.2d at 697.

C. Massachusetts Law on the Recognition of Foreign Country Judgments.

With respect to the recognition of foreign *country* judgments, Massachusetts, like many other states of the Union, has enacted a version of the [Uniform Foreign Country Money Judgments] Recognition Act. [Massachusetts General Laws chapter 235 § 23A.][*] This section clearly requires that the *rendering* court have personal jurisdiction over the defendant in order for the resulting judgment to be recognized in Massachusetts. The statute does not state explicitly, however, whether the correctness of that exercise of jurisdiction by the rendering court ought to be determined according to the law of the rendering or the enforcing jurisdiction. The district court suggested that there is currently a division of au-

---

[7] * * * According to *Hilton*, a diversity case from the *pre-Erie* era, foreign judgments shall be recognized so long as the rendering court afforded an opportunity for full and fair proceedings; the court was of competent jurisdiction over the persons and subject matter; the court conducted regular proceedings, which afforded due notice of appearance to adversary parties; and the court afforded a system of jurisprudence likely to secure an impartial administration of justice between the citizens of its own country and those of other countries. *See* 159 U.S. at 202–03. The *Hilton* rule also requires reciprocity in the recognition and enforcement of United States judgments from the jurisdiction of the rendering court. *Id.* at 210, 226–27.

[*] [The relevant provisions of the Massachusetts statute parallel those of the UFCMJA: "A foreign judgment shall not be conclusive if (1) it was rendered under a system which does not provide impartial tribunals or procedures compatible with the requirements of due process of law; (2) the foreign court did not have personal jurisdiction over the defendant; or (3) the foreign court did not have jurisdiction over the subject matter."—eds.]

thority on this question among the states that have enacted a form of the Recognition Act.[10] The district court also noted that the Supreme Judicial Court of Massachusetts has not yet spoken squarely on the matter.

The district court, faced with the ambiguity about the prevailing rule in Massachusetts with respect to the law governing personal jurisdiction in the rendering court, explicitly declined to resolve the matter and instead applied the governing rule of both jurisdictions. On appeal, neither party has contended that the district court erred in this regard. Nor has either party argued that Massachusetts would apply any other rule. Under these circumstances, we must conclude that the parties have waived any reliance on another rule and that we must decide this case by assessing the facts in light of the personal jurisdiction law of both the Province of Quebec and the Commonwealth of Massachusetts.

1. The Jurisdiction of the Superior Court of Quebec under the Law of Quebec

We turn, then, to the question of whether Kitchen International established that the Superior Court of Quebec properly exercised personal jurisdiction over

---

[10] Some states have concluded that the relevant question is only whether personal jurisdiction would have been present had the rendering court applied the law of the enforcing state. See, e.g., Genujo Lok Beteiligungs GmbH v. Zorn, 943 A.2d 573, 580 (Me. 2008) (looking only to whether the foreign jurisdiction could have established personal jurisdiction under Maine law); Sung Hwan Co. v. Rite Aid Corp., 850 N.E.2d 647, 650-51 (N.Y. 2006) (interpreting the term "personal jurisdiction" as used in an analogous New York statute to mean "whether exercise of jurisdiction by the foreign court comports with New York's concept of personal jurisdiction" and omitting any analysis of foreign law).

Other state courts instead have concluded that the proper interpretation is to ascertain first whether the rendering court could exercise personal jurisdiction over the defendant under its own laws. They then look to whether the rendering court could have exercised personal jurisdiction under the law of the forum state. The purpose of this second step is to ensure that the rendering court not only possessed jurisdiction at the time of judgment but also that the rendering court's procedures comported with United States due process standards. Under this approach, both of these requirements are necessary for a rendering court to have personal jurisdiction over the defendant within the meaning of the Recognition Act. See, e.g., Monks Own, Ltd. v. Monastery of Christ in the Desert, 168 P.3d 121, 124-27 (N.M. 2007) (adopting the approach of first ascertaining whether personal jurisdiction was satisfied under the law of the rendering foreign jurisdiction and then determining whether the judgment debtor's applicable contacts with the rendering jurisdiction satisfy the United States constitutional due process minimum); Vrozos v. Sarantopoulos, 195 Ill. App. 3d 610, 552 N.E.2d 1093, 1099-1100, 142 Ill. Dec. 352 (Ill. App. Ct. 1990) (reviewing a trial court decision concluding that a Canadian court had personal jurisdiction over the judgment debtor pursuant to United States principles of due process and remanding for consideration of whether the Canadian court also had personal jurisdiction pursuant to Canadian law of service of summons). Federal courts applying analogous state recognition acts also have adopted this approach. See K & R Robinson Enters. Ltd. v. Asian Exp. Material Supply Co., 178 F.R.D. 332, 339-42 (D. Mass. 1998). See generally Royal Bank of Canada v. Trentham Corp., 491 F. Supp. 404, 408-10 (S.D. Tex. 1980), vacated by, 665 F.2d 515 (5th Cir. 1981). The American Law Institute adopts this approach in its model federal statute on the recognition of foreign money judgments. *See* American Law Institute, *Recognition and Enforcement of Foreign Judgments: Analysis and Proposed Federal Statute* § 3 & cmt. c (2006).

Evans. [After a review of the record on summary judgment, the court of appeals concluded that "it is clear that genuine issues of fact remain to be resolved before the authority of Quebec to exercise personal jurisdiction over Evans can be established."] * * *

2. The Application of Massachusetts Standards to the Superior Court of Quebec's Exercise of Jurisdiction

* * * Here we review its determination of whether the exercise of personal jurisdiction by the Superior Court of Quebec comported with Massachusetts and federal standards.

The exercise of personal jurisdiction over a defendant such as Evans is governed by the Commonwealth's long-arm statute insofar as the exercise of jurisdiction also comports with the requirements of the federal Due Process Clause. * * * The Massachusetts long-arm statute permits the exercise of personal jurisdiction when a person has transacted business within the Commonwealth or when the person has contracted to supply services or things within the Commonwealth. This conferral of jurisdiction creates a specifically affiliating jurisdictional nexus; the personal jurisdiction conferred is only with respect to litigation *arising out of* the transaction within the Commonwealth, not with respect to the defendant's transactions that did not take place in the Commonwealth. Here, "[w]e may sidestep the statutory inquiry and proceed directly to the constitutional analysis . . . because the Supreme Judicial Court of Massachusetts has interpreted the state's long-arm statute as an assertion of jurisdiction over the person to the limits allowed by the Constitution of the United States." Daynard v. Ness, Motley, Loadholt, Richardson & Poole, 290 F.3d 42, 52 (1st Cir. 2002) (internal quotation marks omitted).

We have described in earlier cases these constitutional requirements:

> "First, the claim underlying the litigation must directly arise out of, or relate to, the defendant's forum-state activities. Second, the defendant's in-state contacts must represent a purposeful availment of the privilege of conducting activities in the forum state, thereby invoking the benefits and protections of that state's laws and making the defendant's involuntary presence before the state's courts foreseeable. Third, the exercise of jurisdiction must, in light of the Gestalt factors, be reasonable."

Foster-Miller, Inc. v. Babcock & Wilcox Canada, 46 F.3d 138, 144 (1st Cir. 1995) * * *. With respect to the "Gestalt factors," we have observed that,

> In constitutional terms, the jurisdictional inquiry is not a mechanical exercise. The Court has long insisted that concepts of reasonableness must inform a properly performed minimum contacts analysis. This means that, even where purposefully generated contacts exist, courts must consider a panoply of other factors which bear upon the fairness of subjecting a nonresident to the authority of a foreign tribunal.

Ticketmaster-New York, 26 F.3d at 209 (internal quotation marks and citations omitted). The Gestalt [i.e., fairness] factors that a court will consider include: "(1) the defendant's burden of appearing, (2) the forum state's interest in adjudicating the dispute, (3) the plaintiff's interest in obtaining convenient and effective relief, (4) the judicial system's interest in obtaining the most effective resolution of the controversy, and (5) the common interests of all sovereigns in promoting substantive social policies." *Id.*

In applying these standards, the district court held: "The Quebec Superior Court's exercise of personal jurisdiction over Plaintiff did not contravene traditional notions of fair play and substantial justice. Plaintiff had several contacts with Quebec." * * * However, as we have noted in our earlier discussion of the Quebec jurisdictional statute, the affidavits supplied by the parties were in conflict. * * *

Furthermore, even if such an argument had been made successfully, the district court's analysis of jurisdiction still is deficient. Absent from the district court's analysis is any discussion of the "Gestalt factors," which, we have made clear, a court must consider to determine the fairness of subjecting the defendant to a foreign jurisdiction. * * *

Because the district court resolved material issues of fact against Evans, the nonmoving party, the judgment must be reversed. The controverted issues of fact that Evans has raised must be resolved. Accordingly, the judgment of the district court is reversed and the case is remanded for proceedings consistent with this opinion. *Reversed and Remanded.*

NOTES AND QUESTIONS FOR DISCUSSION

1. The UFCMJA indicates that a judgment will not be enforceable if the court that rendered the judgment did not have personal jurisdiction over the defendant. Yet neither the Act (nor Massachusetts' version of it) declares *whose* law is relevant to the personal jurisdiction question. In addition to insisting that jurisdiction be good as a matter of foreign law, the First Circuit in *Evans Cabinet* (as a matter of Massachusetts law) applied domestic standards to determine whether the foreign court had personal jurisdiction over the non-appearing U.S. defendant. Why should foreign judgments be subject to a minimum contacts/fairness analysis before they will be enforceable in the U.S. if personal jurisdiction was good in the foreign court under foreign standards and the exercise of jurisdiction was not exorbitant?

2. The First Circuit's decision to apply a federal due process (minimum contacts/fairness) analysis to foreign judgments, no matter what country they come from, is representative of the practice of most courts. See, e.g., Koster v. Automark Indus., Inc. 640 F.2d 77, 79 (7th Cir. 1981) ("Whether it be Wisconsin or the Netherlands, the standard of minimum contacts is the same."). Note that just as when a court determines whether personal jurisdiction exists in the first instance (see Chapter 1), there may be disputed questions of fact for the court to resolve. In denying summary judgment, was the First Circuit suggesting that the disputed questions of fact surrounding jurisdiction over Evans Cabinet in Canada were questions for a jury? Or was it merely asking the district court to hold an evidentiary hearing and to make further findings, such as those surrounding the fairness (or "Gestalt") considerations in the due process analysis?

3. The Massachusetts long-arm statute went to the length of due process. Suppose it did not. Should an enforcing court also test the foreign judgment against its own state standards as well as federal due process standards? In Siedler v.

Jacobsen, 383 N.Y.S.2d 833 (N.Y. App. Term 1976), a lower New York court refused to recognize an Austrian judgment because personal jurisdiction did not satisfy New York's long arm statute. New York C.P.L.R. § 302. An Austrian court had entered judgment in favor of an Austrian antique dealer and against a New York purchaser for nonpayment for an item purchased in Austria. (The buyer claimed that the seller misrepresented the provenance of the antique.) According to *Siedler*, the single "casual" incident of doing business was an insufficient basis for Austria to exercise jurisdiction when judged by New York law (and the New York courts' interpretation of that law). Even if it makes sense to test foreign judgments by federal due process standards, does it make sense that they be judged by possibly idiosyncratic state long-arm laws as well? It is open to question whether *Siedler*'s analysis was correct as a matter of (constitutional) minimum contacts analysis, given that it was defendant's "casual" purposeful activities in Austria that directly gave rise to the underlying action. Is *Siedler*'s approach simply a kind of state-law based public policy objection to the enforcement of the judgment, above and beyond due process? Note that *Siedler*'s approach of looking solely to New York law was consistent with that of some other state courts and with later New York authority, as cited in footnote 10 of *Evans Cabinet*.

4.   One interesting example of the courts' general approach is Guardian Insurance Co. v. Bain Hogg International Ltd., 52 F. Supp. 2d 536 (D. V.I. 1999). The case involved a dispute between a Virgin Islands insurance company (Guardian) and a British reinsurance company (HIB). Guardian sued HIB in a U.S. court and HIB defended on the ground that a British declaratory judgment, finding that it was not liable to Guardian for a breach of any duty, should bar Guardian's suit by res judicata. The U.S. District Court for the Virgin Islands examined whether the British court had personal jurisdiction over Guardian and, employing the standard minimum contacts test, concluded that the English court's exercise of jurisdiction comported with American due process requirements. The court noted that the Uniform Act (reproduced above) does not specifically articulate a standard for finding jurisdiction, and that according to the Restatement (Third) of Foreign Relations Law of the United States § 421(1) (1987), a foreign court has jurisdiction over a party if the relationship of the state to the person involved in litigation is "reasonable."

Because Guardian had appeared in the English proceedings and had unsuccessfully challenged the jurisdiction of the British court, one might question whether it was necessary or even appropriate for the federal District Court to reevaluate the issue of jurisdiction. The Court in *Guardian*, although stating that it was performing de novo review, indicated that such review might not be necessary when, as in that case, the foreign court's reasons "do not appear to be clearly untenable and the . . . Court's assertion of jurisdiction . . . was reasonable." *Guardian*, 52 F. Supp. 2d at 542. As just noted, such an approach is supported by the Restatement:

> If the judgment debtor appeared in the rendering court for the purpose of challenging its jurisdiction and that jurisdiction was upheld, he is generally precluded from renewing the challenge in the state where recognition is sought, unless the proceeding in the foreign court was manifestly

unfair or the asserted basis for jurisdiction clearly untenable.
Restatement (Third), *supra* at § 481 (1987), comment (i).

5. *Guardian* notwithstanding, courts are split on whether a foreign court's decision on the question of personal jurisdiction should be treated as res judicata if that very question was already fully litigated abroad between the parties. (Note that within the U.S., actual litigation of the personal jurisdiction question in one U.S. court is ordinarily considered preclusive in another. See Insurance Corp. of Ireland, Ltd. v. Compagnie des Bauxites de Guinée, 456 U.S. 694, 702 n.9 (1982) ("It has long been the rule that principles of res judicata apply to jurisdictional determinations—both subject matter and personal.") *Guardian* allowed for review of the question, although it indicated that such review might not be needed if the judgment rendering court's reasons were not "untenable" and the exercise of jurisdiction was "reasonable." Would such a "reasonableness" inquiry be a weaker standard than what due process would call for? Would a possible solution be for a U.S. court to treat the foreign court's determination of its own (foreign) jurisdiction as a matter of its own (foreign) law as conclusive, but not conclusive as to whether the exercise of jurisdiction was "reasonable" (or comported with due process)? For the European approach to this issue under the Brussels Convention, see Section F, below.

6. There is consensus that if the defendant did not appear at all in the foreign proceedings and did not otherwise litigate or waive jurisdiction, the resulting default judgment is open to challenge on jurisdictional grounds. See, e.g., Restatement (Third) of Foreign Relations Law of the United States § 482 (1987), Reporter's note 3: "By analogy to practice between States in the United States, if jurisdiction of the foreign court was not contested or waived, the judgment debtor may challenge jurisdiction of the rendering court in resisting enforcement in the United States." Note that even if jurisdiction is not litigated, litigating the merits will ordinarily constitute a waiver of personal jurisdiction. Should that also be true if the jurisdictional defect is one of subject matter rather than personal jurisdiction? The answer is not altogether clear, even as between states in the U.S. See David L. Shapiro, Preclusion in Civil Actions 25-29 (2001); Restatement (Second) of Judgments §§ 11, 12, and 66 (1982).

Somportex Ltd. v. Philadelphia Chewing Gum Corp.

United States Court of Appeals, Third Circuit, 1971.

453 F.2d 435, cert. denied, 405 U.S. 1017 (1972).

ALDISERT, CIRCUIT JUDGE.

Several interesting questions are presented in this appeal from the district court's order, granting summary judgment to enforce a default judgment entered by an English court. To resolve them, a complete recitation of the procedural history of this case is necessary.

This case has its genesis in a transaction between appellant, Philadelphia Chewing Gum Corporation, and Somportex Limited, a British corporation, which was to merchandise appellant's [Philadelphia Chewing Gum's] wares in

Great Britain under the trade name "Tarzan Bubble Gum." According to the facts as alleged by appellant, there was a proposal which involved the participation of Brewster Leeds and Co., Inc., and M.S. International, Inc., third-party defendants in the court below. Brewster made certain arrangements with Somportex to furnish gum manufactured by Philadelphia; M.S. International, as agent for the licensor of the trade name "Tarzan," was to furnish the African name to the American gum to be sold in England. For reasons not relevant to our limited inquiry, the transaction never reached fruition.

Somportex filed an action against Philadelphia for breach of contract in the Queen's Bench Division of the High Court of England. Notice of the issuance of a Writ of Summons was served, in accordance with the rules and with the leave of the High Court, upon Philadelphia at its registered address in Havertown, Pennsylvania, on May 15, 1967. The extraterritorial service was based on the English version of long-arm statutes utilized by many American states.[1] Philadelphia then consulted a firm of English solicitors, who, by letter of July 14, 1967, advised its Pennsylvania lawyers:

> I have arranged with the Solicitors for Somportex Limited that they will let me have a copy of their Affidavit and exhibits to that Affidavit which supported their application to serve out of the Jurisdiction. Subject to the contents of the Affidavit, and any further information that can be provided by Philadelphia Chewing Gum Corporation after we have had the opportunity of seeing the Affidavit, it may be possible to make an application to the Court for an Order setting the Writ aside. But for such an application to be successful we will have to show that on the facts the matter does not fall within the provision of (f) and (g) [of the long-arm statute, note 1, supra] referred to above.
>
> In the meantime we will enter a conditional Appearance to the Writ in behalf of Philadelphia Chewing Gum Corporation in order to preserve the status quo.

---

[1] The English Statute provides:

> (f) If the action begun by the Writ is brought against a Defendant not domiciled or ordinarily resident in Scotland to enforce, rescind, dissolve, annul or otherwise affect a contract, or to recover damages or obtain other relief in respect of the breach of a contract, being (in either case) a contract which—
>
> (i) was made within the jurisdiction, or
>
> (ii) was made by or through an Agent trading or residing within the Jurisdiction on behalf of a principal trading or residing out of the jurisdiction, or
>
> (iii) is by the terms, or by implication, governed by the English law;
>
> (g) If the action begun by the Writ is brought against a Defendant not domiciled or ordinarily resident in Scotland or Northern Ireland, in respect of a breach committed within the Jurisdiction of a contract made within or out of Jurisdiction, and irrespective of the fact, if such be the case, that the breach was preceded or accompanied by a breach committed out of the Jurisdiction that rendered impossible the performance of so much of the Contract as ought to have been performed within the Jurisdiction[.]

On August 9, 1967, the English solicitors entered a "conditional appearance to the Writ" and filed a motion to set aside the Writ of Summons.[2] At a hearing before a Master on November 13, 1967, the solicitors appeared and disclosed that Philadelphia had elected not to proceed with the [motion] or to contest the jurisdiction of the English Court, but instead intended to obtain leave of court to withdraw appearance of counsel. The Master then dismissed Philadelphia's [motion] to set aside plaintiff's Writ of Summons. Four days later, the solicitors sought to withdraw their appearance as counsel for Philadelphia, contending that it was a conditional appearance only. On November 27, 1967, after a Master granted [their] motion, Somportex appealed. The appeal was denied after hearing before a single judge, but the Court of Appeal, reversing the decision of the Master, held that the appearance was unconditional and that the submission to the jurisdiction by Philadelphia was, therefore, effective.[3] But the court let stand

---

[2] The memorandum of conditional appearance was stamped with this formula: "This appearance is to stand as unconditional unless the defendant applies within fourteen days to set aside the writ and service thereof and obtains an order to that effect." The motion alleged:

> (1) that there was no agreement made between the Plaintiffs and Defendants on or about 17th December 1966;
>
> (2) alternatively that if there was such an agreement:
>
>> (a) it was not made within the jurisdiction of this honourable Court; or
>>
>> (b) it was not made by or through an agent trading or residing within the jurisdiction on behalf of the Defendants a principal trading or residing out of the jurisdiction; or
>>
>> (c) it was not by its terms or by implication to be governed by English law;
>
> (3) in the further alternative that if there was such an agreement there has been no breach of the said agreement committed within the jurisdiction of this honourable court;
> . . .

[3] Somportex v. Philadelphia Chewing Gum [1968], 3 All E.R. 26, 29, Lord Denning:

> In order to decide the point, I think that one has to put oneself in the position of the American company and their advisers when faced with this notice of the writ. They could have not entered an appearance at all, in which case by the law of Pennsylvania they would not be bound by any judgment. Instead of doing that, however, after consultation with a distinguished firm of lawyers in the city of London they decided to enter a conditional appearance. That was a very important step for them to take (especially if they had assets in England or were likely to bring assets into England) because it was an essential way of defending their own position. After all, if they did not enter an appearance at all, and in consequence the English courts gave judgment against them in default of appearance, that judgment could be executed against them in England in respect of assets in England. In order to guard against that eventuality, they had first to enter a conditional appearance here, then argue whether it was within the jurisdiction of the court or not. If it was outside the jurisdiction, all well and good. The writ would be set aside. They would go away free. If it was within the jurisdiction, however, their appearance became unconditional and they could fight out the case on the merits. In these circumstances it seems to me that they were very wise to enter a conditional appearance. It was a step which would be advised by any competent lawyer if there was a likelihood that assets would then or afterwards come into England.

"the original order which was made by the master on Nov. 13 dismissing the application to set aside. The writ therefore will stand. On the other hand, if the American company would wish to appeal from the order of Nov. 13, I see no reason why the time should not be extended and they can argue that matter out at a later stage if they should so wish."[4]

Thereafter, Philadelphia made a calculated decision: it decided to do nothing. It neither asked for an extension of time nor attempted in any way to proceed with an appeal from the Master's order dismissing its application to set aside the Writ. Instead, it directed its English solicitors to withdraw from the case. There being no appeal, the Master's order became final.

Somportex then filed a Statement of Claim which was duly served in accordance with English Court rules. In addition, by separate letter, it informed Philadelphia of the significance and effect of the pleading, the procedural posture of the case, and its intended course of action.[5]

Philadelphia persisted in its course of inaction; it failed to file a defense. Somportex obtained a default judgment against it in the Queen's Bench Division

---

We have, therefore, a wise course of action deliberately decided on by eminent firms in England and the United States after consulation, and I do not think that they should be allowed now to go back on it. It must be remembered that, on the faith of this entry of appearance, the English company have altered their position. They have not gone to the United States, as they might have done, and taken steps there against the American company. They have remained in this country and pursued the action here—on the faith that there was a conditional appearance entered which would become unconditional unless it was duly set aside. In the circumstances, I do not think that we should give leave to withdraw the appearance.

[4] *Ibid.* 3 All E.R. at 29, 30.

[5] [The letter read as follows:]

Accompanying this letter is the Plaintiff's Statement of Claim the service of which upon yourselves is the next step in the action after the entry of your appearance. You will observe that it contains in numbered paragraphs the material facts relied on by our Clients in support of their claim against you. Under the Rules of the Supreme Court in England, you may serve upon us as Solicitors for the Plaintiffs your Defence (should you consider that you have one) in writing within 14 days from the date of service upon you of the Statement of Claim. In view of the fact that Messrs. Clifford-Turner & Company no longer appear to be acting on your behalf, we recognise that you may have some difficulty in preparing and serving your Defence within that time. Accordingly, we are prepared voluntarily to give you an extension of time for the service of your Defence, namely a further 14 days, so that you may have 28 days in all for this purpose. Should you fail to serve your Defence before the expiry of this extended period, the Plaintiffs will proceed to obtain judgment against you in default of Defence. If however you do enter a Defence, the action will then proceed to a trial at which you will have an opportunity of contesting fully and fairly the merits of the Plaintiff's claim.

We have thought it right to draw your attention to the points mentioned above so that you may fully understand your present position in relation to the action now being prosecuted against you. Further we feel bound to inform you that in the event of judgment being obtained against you, the Plaintiffs will seek to enforce the judgment against you through the appropriate Court in Pennsylvania.

of the High Court of Justice in England for the sum of 39,562.10.10 pounds (approximately $94,000.00). The award reflected some $45,000.00 for loss of profit; $46,000.00 for loss of good will and $2,500.00 for costs, including attorneys' fees.

Thereafter, Somportex filed a diversity action in the court below, seeking to enforce the foreign judgment, and attached to the complaint a certified transcript of the English proceeding. The district court granted two motions which gave rise to this appeal: it dismissed the third-party complaints for failure to state a proper claim under F.R.C.P. 14; and it granted plaintiff's motion for summary judgment, F.R.C.P. 56(a).

[The Court of Appeals first concluded that the district court did not err in dismissing the impleader actions.]

Appellant presents a cluster of contentions supporting its major thesis that we should not extend hospitality to the English judgment. First, it contends, and we agree, that because our jurisdiction is based solely on diversity, "the law to be applied . . . is the law of the state," in this case, Pennsylvania law. Erie R. Co. v. Tompkins, 304 U.S. 64 (1938); Svenska Handelsbanken v. Carlson, 258 F. Supp. 448 (D.Mass.1966).

Pennsylvania distinguishes between judgments obtained in the courts of her sister states, which are entitled to full faith and credit, and those of foreign courts, which are subject to principles of comity. [Here, the Court referenced the Pennsylvania state courts' embrace of the principles discussed in *Hilton, supra.*]

It is by this standard, therefore, that appellant's arguments must be measured.

Appellant's contention that the district court failed to make an independent examination of the factual and legal basis of the jurisdiction of the English Court at once argues too much and says too little. The reality is that the court did examine the legal basis of asserted jurisdiction and decided the issue adversely to appellant.

Indeed, we do not believe it was necessary for the court below to reach the question of whether the factual complex of the contractual dispute permitted extraterritorial service under the English long-arm statute. In its opinion denying leave of defense counsel to withdraw, the Court of Appeal specifically gave Philadelphia the opportunity to have the factual issue tested before the courts; moreover, Philadelphia was allocated additional time to do just that. Lord Denning said: ". . . They can argue that matter out at a later stage if they should so wish." Three months went by with no activity forth-coming and then, as described by the district court, "during this three month period, defendant changed its strategy and, not wishing to do anything which might result in its submitting to the English Court's jurisdiction, decided to withdraw its appearance altogether." Under these circumstances, we hold that defendant cannot choose its forum to test the factual basis of jurisdiction. It was given, and it waived, the opportunity of making the adequate presentation in the English Court. [9]

Additionally, appellant attacks the English practice wherein a conditional appearance attacking jurisdiction may, by court decision, be converted into an unconditional one. It cannot effectively argue that this practice constitutes "some special ground . . . for impeaching the judgment," as to render the English judgment unwelcome in Pennsylvania under principles of international law and comity because it was obtained by procedures contrary or prejudicial to the host state. The English practice in this respect is identical to that set forth in both the Federal and Pennsylvania rules of civil procedure. F.R.C.P. 12(b)(2) provides the vehicle for attacking jurisdiction over the person, and, in Orange Theatre Corp. v. Rayherstz Amusement Corp., 139 F.2d 871, 874 (3d Cir. 1944), we said that Rule 12 "has abolished for the federal courts the age-old distinction between general and special appearances." Similarly, a conditional or "*de bene esse*" appearance no longer exists in Pennsylvania. [12] Monaco v. Montgomery Cab Co.,

---

[9] In *Baldwin v. Iowa State Traveling Men's Association*, 283 U.S. 522 (1931), a federal district court defendant, who had unsuccessfully conditionally appeared and then, like appellant here, failed either to file a defense or to appeal from the default judgment entered on the merits, was sued in another district court for enforcement of the default judgment. The Court emphasized that "the full faith and credit required by [Article IV, Section 1] is not involved, since neither of the courts was a state court." 283 U.S. at 524. The Court then declared:

> "The special appearance gives point to the fact that the respondent entered the Missouri court for the very purpose of litigating the question of jurisdiction over its person. It had the election not to appear at all. If, in the absence of appearance, the court had proceeded to judgment, and the present suit had been brought thereon, respondent could have raised and tried out the issue in the present action, because it would never have had its day in court with respect to jurisdiction. . . . It had also the right to appeal from the decision of the Missouri District Court, as is shown by *Harkness v. Hyde, supra*, [98 U.S. 476] and the other authorities cited. It elected to follow neither of those courses, but, after having been defeated upon full hearing in its contention as to jurisdiction, it took no further steps, and the judgment in question resulted.

> "Public policy dictates that there be an end of litigation; that those who have contested an issue shall be bound by the result of the contest, and that matters once tried shall be considered forever settled as between the parties. We see no reason why this doctrine should not apply in every case where one voluntarily appears, presents his case and is fully heard, and why he should not, in the absence of fraud, be thereafter concluded by the judgment of the tribunal to which he has submitted his cause."

283 U.S. at 525-526.

The *Baldwin* principle was reaffirmed in Durfee v. Duke, 375 U.S. 106, 111 (1963). See also, American Surety Co. v. Baldwin, 287 U.S. 156, 166 (1932), in which Mr. Justice Brandeis stated that "the principles of *res judicata* apply to questions of jurisdiction as well as to other issues."

[12] Appellant attaches much significance to the July 14, 1967, letter of its English solicitors, *supra*, wherein its American counsel were told: "we will enter a conditional Appearance to the Writ in behalf of Philadelphia Chewing Gum Corporation in order to preserve the status quo." From that it builds the argument that it cannot be said to have ever consented to have entered an appearance which would have subjected it to the court's jurisdiction. In support thereof it contends that it and its American counsel took the phrase "conditional appearance" to mean *de bene esse*. The argu-

417 Pa. 135, 208 A.2d 252 (1965), Pa.R.C.P. 1451(a)(7). A challenge to jurisdiction must be asserted there by a preliminary objection raising a question of jurisdiction. Pa.R.C.P. 1017(b) (1).

Thus, we will not disturb the English Court's adjudication. That the English judgment was obtained by appellant's default instead of through an adversary proceeding does not dilute its efficacy. In the absence of fraud or collusion, a default judgment is as conclusive an adjudication between the parties as when rendered after answer and complete contest in the open courtroom. * * * The polestar is whether a reasonable method of notification is employed and reasonable opportunity to be heard is afforded to the person affected. Restatement (Second) Conflict of Laws, § 92 (Proposed Final Draft), 1967.

* * *

Finally, appellant contends that since "it maintains no office or employee in England and transacts no business within the country" there were [insufficient] contacts there to meet the due process tests of International Shoe Co. v. Washington, 326 U.S. 310 (1965). It argues that, at best, "the only contact Philadelphia had with England was the negotiations allegedly conducted by an independent New York exporter by letter, telephone and telegram to sell Philadelphia's products in England." In Hanson v. Denckla, 357 U.S. 235, 253 (1958), Chief Justice Warren said: "The application of [the requirement of contact] rule will vary with the quality and nature of the defendant's activity, but it is essential in each case that there be some act by which the defendant purposely avails itself of the privilege of conducting business within the forum State, thus invoking the benefits and protection of its laws." We have concluded that whether the New York exporter was an independent contractor or Philadelphia's agent was a matter to be resolved by the English Court. For the purpose of the constitutional argument, we must assume the proper agency relationship. So construed, we find his activity would constitute the "quality and nature of the defendant's activity" similar

---

ment is totally without merit. We can perceive of no principle of law which removes one from the reach of a court's jurisdiction because of misunderstanding or misimpression by one counsel of advice from privately retained co-counsel. Moreover, as heretofore observed, the conditional appearance was described by Lord Denning in Somportex v. Philadelphia Chewing Gum, 3 All E.R. 26, 27: "the memorandum of conditional appearance was stamped with the usual formula: 'This appearance is to stand as unconditional unless the defendant applies within fourteen days to set aside the writ and service thereof and obtains an order to that effect.'"

It can also be said that appellant may be estopped from advancing this argument before this court. * * * In the district court, its counsel stated:

> "The English Court decided that a conditional appearance was a general appearance. We are not asking this court to redetermine that issue. We are saying that even assuming the English Court was correct, that judgment is not entitled to comity; no cases support it. Thank you."

> THE COURT: Now do you agree that the issue as to mistake in the law was litigated in the English Courts?

> COUNSEL: Yes, sir.

to that of the defendant in McGee v. International Life Ins. Co., 355 U.S. 220 (1957), there held to satisfy due process requirements.

For the reasons heretofore rehearsed we will not disturb the English Court's adjudication of jurisdiction; we have deemed as irrelevant the default nature of the judgment; we have concluded that the English compensatory damage items do not offend Pennsylvania public policy; and hold that the English procedure comports with our standards of due process.

In sum, we find that the English proceedings met all the tests enunciated in *Christoff, supra*. We are not persuaded that appellant met its burden of showing that the British "decree is so palpably tainted by fraud or prejudice as to outrage our sense of justice, or [that] the process of the foreign tribunal was invoked to achieve a result contrary to our laws of public policy or to circumvent our laws or public policy." *Christoff, supra*, 192 A.2d at 739. [Affirmed.]

NOTES AND QUESTIONS FOR DISCUSSION

1. *Somportex* did not permit the defendant to collaterally challenge the English default judgment. The court held that "[i]n the absence of fraud or collusion, a default judgment is as conclusive an adjudication between the parties as when rendered after answer and complete contest in the open courtroom." 453 F.2d at 452. Presumably that is generally true only when jurisdiction otherwise exists, or when it has been litigated or has been waived. Which, if any, of those jurisdictional pre-conditions were satisfied by the English default judgment in *Somportex*?

2. The *Somportex* court relies on the Supreme Court's decisions in Baldwin v. Iowa State Traveling Men's Association, 283 U.S. 522 (1931), and Durfee v. Duke, 375 U.S. 106 (1963), as support for its disposition of the case. In each of those cases, however, the defendant unambiguously appeared and clearly contested the question of jurisdiction and lost on that issue. And in *Durfee*, but not in *Baldwin*, the defendant went on to contest the merits. Given the facts of *Somportex*, isn't it possible to distinguish those decisions? After all, the Court of Appeals in *Somportex* states that it is not necessary for it to determine whether the English long-arm statute was actually satisfied in this case.

3. Consider the solution adopted by the ALI for recognition and enforcement of default judgments in its Proposed Federal Statute on Recognition and Enforcement of Foreign Judgments § 3(b) :

> A foreign judgment rendered in default of appearance of the defendant is entitled to recognition and enforcement, provided that the party seeking recognition satisfies the court in the United States that (i) the rendering court had jurisdiction over the defendant in accordance with the law of the state of origin of the judgment; [and] (ii) the defendant was served with initiating process in accordance with the law of the state of origin; and (iii) the rendering court had jurisdiction over the defendant on a basis not unacceptable in the United States [elsewhere under this Act].

Is this a more sensible approach? Note that jurisdiction would be policed at two levels—by jurisdiction of the judgment rendering court, and jurisdiction under U.S. standards as well. Is it fair to require the judgment creditor to have to show that the foreign court had jurisdiction if there was valid service in the foreign proceedings and the defendant had an opportunity to raise jurisdictional issues abroad?

D. FOREIGN JUDGMENTS RAISING DOMESTIC (U.S.) PUBLIC POLICY CONCERNS

1. Concerns Regarding Substantive Law

Under a regime of comity, the courts of the state asked to enforce a foreign judgment need not always do so, even when questions of jurisdiction and service are not obstacles to enforcement. A classic sort of objection to the enforcement of foreign country judgments is that it somehow runs counter to the "public policy" of the enforcing state. Indeed, section 4(c)(3) of the UFCMJA specifically provides that courts "need not" recognize a foreign judgment when "the judgment or the [cause of action] [claim for relief] on which the judgment is based is repugnant to the public policy of this state or of the United States." (Recall that a public policy objection *cannot* be raised by a U.S. state to the enforcement of a sister-state judgment. See Section A, above.) Consider the meaning of "public policy" here. Should a foreign judgment not be recognized anytime foreign substantive law is different? After all, all law is an expression of a jurisdiction's public policy. Or are public policy concerns triggered only when there is a more dramatic departure from local law? How dramatic a difference ought to be dramatic enough to overcome the party-based and system-based interests in preclusion, and the comity among nations?

Southwest Livestock & Trucking Co., Inc. v. Ramon

United States Court of Appeals, Fifth Circuit, 1999.

169 F.3d 317.

EMILIO M. GARZA, CIRCUIT JUDGE:

Defendant-Appellant, Reginaldo Ramon, appeals the district court's grant of summary judgment in favor of Plaintiffs-Appellees, Southwest Livestock & Trucking Co., Inc., Darrel Hargrove and Mary Jane Hargrove. Ramon contends that the district court erred by not recognizing a Mexican judgment, that if recognized would preclude summary judgment against him. We vacate the district court's summary judgment and remand.

I

Darrel and Mary Jane Hargrove (the "Hargroves") are citizens of the United States and officers of Southwest Livestock & Trucking Co., Inc. ("Southwest Livestock"), a Texas corporation involved in the buying and selling of livestock. In 1990, Southwest Livestock entered into a loan arrangement with Reginaldo Ramon ("Ramon"), a citizen of the Republic of Mexico. Southwest Livestock borrowed $400,000 from Ramon. To accomplish the loan, Southwest Livestock executed a "pagare"—a Mexican promissory note—payable to Ramon with interest within thirty days. Each month, Southwest Livestock executed a new pagare to cover the outstanding principal and paid the accrued interest. Over a period of four years, Southwest Livestock made payments towards the principal, but also borrowed additional money from Ramon. In October of 1994, Southwest Livestock defaulted on the loan. With the exception of the last pagare executed by Southwest Livestock, none of the pagares contained a stated interest rate. Ramon, however, charged Southwest Livestock interest at a rate of approximately fifty-two percent. The last pagare stated an interest rate of forty-eight percent, and under its terms, interest continues to accrue until Southwest Livestock pays the outstanding balance in full.

After Southwest Livestock defaulted, Ramon filed a lawsuit in Mexico to collect on the last pagare. The Mexican court granted judgment in favor of Ramon, and ordered Southwest Livestock to satisfy its debt and to pay interest at forty-eight percent. Southwest Livestock appealed, claiming that Ramon had failed to effect proper service of process, and therefore, the Mexican court lacked personal jurisdiction. The Mexican appellate court rejected this argument and affirmed the judgment in favor of Ramon.

After Ramon filed suit in Mexico, but prior to the entry of the Mexican judgment, Southwest Livestock brought suit in United States District Court, alleging that the loan arrangement violated Texas usury laws. Southwest Livestock then filed a motion for partial summary judgment, claiming that the undisputed facts established that Ramon charged, received and collected usurious interest in violation of Texas law. Ramon also filed a motion for summary judgment. By then the Mexican court had entered its judgment, and Ramon sought recognition of that judgment. He claimed that, under principles of collateral estoppel and res judicata, the Mexican judgment barred Southwest Livestock's suit. * * *

The district court * * * grant[ed] Southwest Livestock's motion for summary judgment as to liability under Texas usury law, and den[ied] Ramon's motion for summary judgment. The district court agreed that the Mexican judgment violated Texas public policy, and that Texas law applied. * * * Ramon appealed. * * *

II

We must determine first whether the district court properly refused to recognize the Mexican judgment. Our jurisdiction is based on diversity of citizenship. Hence, we must apply Texas law regarding the recognition of foreign country money-judgments. See Erie R.R. Co. v. Tompkins, 304 U.S. 64 (1938) (holding that in a diversity action, a federal court must apply the law of the forum state); Success Motivation Institute of Japan, Ltd. v. Success Motivation Institute Inc., 966 F.2d 1007, 1009-10 (5th Cir.1992) ("*Erie* applies even though some courts have found that these suits necessarily involve relations between the U.S. and foreign governments, and even though some commentators have argued that the enforceability of these judgments in the courts of the United States should be governed by reference to a general rule of federal law.").

Under the Texas Recognition Act, a court must recognize a foreign country judgment assessing money damages unless the judgment debtor establishes one of ten specific grounds for nonrecognition. See Tex. Civ. Prac. & Rem. Code Ann. § 36.005 (West 1998) * * * Southwest Livestock contends that it established a ground for nonrecognition. It notes that the Texas Constitution places a six percent interest rate limit on contracts that do not contain a stated interest rate. See Tex. Const. art. XVI, § 11. It also points to a Texas statute that states that usury is against Texas public policy. * * * Thus, according to Southwest Livestock, the Mexican judgment violates Texas public policy, and the district court properly withheld recognition of the judgment. See Tex. Civ. Prac. & Rem.Code Ann. § 36.005(b)(3) (West 1998).

We review the district court's grant of summary judgment de novo. In reviewing the district court's decision, we note that the level of contravention of Texas law has "to be high before recognition [can] be denied on public policy grounds." Hunt v. BP Exploration Co. (Libya) Ltd., 492 F. Supp. 885, 900 (N.D.Tex.1980). The narrowness of the public policy exception reflects a compromise between two axioms—res judicata and fairness to litigants—that underlie our law of recognition of foreign country judgments.

To decide whether the district court erred in refusing to recognize the Mexican judgment on public policy grounds, we consider the plain language of the Texas Recognition Act. * * * Section 36.005(b)(3) of the Texas Recognition Act permits the district court not to recognize a foreign country judgment if "the cause of action on which the judgment is based is repugnant to the public policy" of Texas. * * * This subsection of the Texas Recognition Act does not refer to the judgment itself, but specifically to the "cause of action on which the judgment is based." Thus, the fact that a judgment offends Texas public policy does not, in and of itself, permit the district court to refuse recognition of that judgment. See Norkan Lodge Co. Ltd. v. Gillum, 587 F. Supp. 1457, 1461 (N.D. Tex.1984) (noting that a "judgment may only be attacked in the event that 'the cause of action [on] which the judgment is based is repugnant to the public policy of this state,' not the judgment itself").

In this case, the Mexican judgment was based on an action for collection of a promissory note. This cause of action is not repugnant to Texas public policy. * * * Under the Texas Recognition Act, it is irrelevant that the Mexican judgment itself contravened Texas's public policy against usury. Thus, the plain language of the Texas Recognition Act suggests that the district court erred in refusing to recognize the Mexican judgment.

Southwest Livestock, however, argues that we should not interpret the Texas Recognition Act according to its plain language. Southwest Livestock contends that Texas courts will not enforce rights existing under laws of other jurisdictions when to do so would violate Texas public policy. See, e.g., Larchmont Farms, Inc. v. Parra, 941 S.W.2d 93, 95 (Tex.1997) (noting that "the basic rule is that a court need not enforce a foreign law if enforcement would be contrary to Texas public policy"). It believes that the reasoning of the Texas Supreme Court in DeSantis v. Wackenhut Corp., 793 S.W.2d 670 (Tex.1990), requires us to affirm the district court's decision not to recognize the Mexican judgment. In DeSantis, the Court refused to apply Florida law to enforce a noncompetition agreement, even though the agreement contained an express choice of Florida law provision, and Florida had a substantial interest in the transaction. The Court concluded that "the law governing enforcement of noncompetition agreements is fundamental policy in Texas, and that to apply the law of another state to determine the enforceability of such an agreement in the circumstances of a case like this would be contrary to that policy." Id. at 681. Southwest Livestock argues similarly that the law governing usury constitutes a fundamental policy in Texas, and that to recognize the Mexican judgment would transgress that policy.

We find that, contrary to Southwest Livestock's argument, *DeSantis* does not support the district court's grant of summary judgment.* * * [I]n *DeSantis* the Court refused to enforce an agreement violative of Texas public policy; it did not refuse to recognize a foreign judgment. Recognition and enforcement of a judgment involve separate and distinct inquiries. * * *

We are especially reluctant to conclude that recognizing the Mexican judgment offends Texas public policy under the circumstances of this case. The purpose behind Texas usury laws is to protect unsophisticated borrowers from unscrupulous lenders. This case, however, does not involve the victimizing of a naive consumer. Southwest Livestock is managed by sophisticated and knowledgeable people with experience in business. Additionally, the evidence in the record does not suggest that Ramon misled or deceived Southwest Livestock. Southwest Livestock and Ramon negotiated the loan in good faith and at arms length. In short, both parties fully appreciated the nature of the loan transaction and their respective contractual obligations.

Accordingly, in light of the plain language of the Texas Recognition Act, and after consideration of our decision in Woods-Tucker and the purpose behind Texas public policy against usury, we hold that Texas's public policy does not justify withholding recognition of the Mexican judgment. The district court erred in deciding otherwise.

III

For the foregoing reasons, we VACATE the district court's summary judgment, and REMAND for further proceedings.

NOTES AND QUESTIONS FOR DISCUSSION

1. In holding that the Mexican judgment was entitled to enforcement, the Fifth Circuit in *Southwest Livestock* relied on a literal reading of the Texas version of the UFCMJA. The court emphasized that the Act permits the district court not to recognize a foreign country judgment if "the cause of action on which the judgment is based is repugnant to the public policy" of Texas. It went on to hold that "[t]his subsection of the Texas Recognition Act does not refer to the judgment itself, but specifically to the 'cause of action on which the judgment is based.' Thus, the fact that a judgment offends Texas public policy does not, in and of itself, permit the district court to refuse recognition of that judgment." Is it persuasive to distinguish between the foreign cause of action (as the key criterion for the denial/grant of recognition) and the foreign judgment (as immaterial for the denial/grant of recognition)? If one distinguishes at all, why should the emphasis not be the other way round? In other words, isn't it the Mexican judgment that, by Texas standards, embodies a usurious interest rate, and isn't it the *effect of the enforcement of the judgment* containing this usurious interest rate that affects Texas' public policy interests? Does it make sense to focus on the highly abstract concept of cause of action rather than on the actual impact that the enforcement of the foreign judgment would entail?

2. The lender in *Southwest Livestock* charged effective annual interest rates between 48 and 52 percent—rates that are considered usurious under Texas law. Would the Fifth Circuit have reached a different result if the loan agreement had called for an interest rate of 250 percent? Should the court enforce a foreign judgment that orders the defendant to pay a promissory note for $20,000, an amount he lost in a poker game that is considered illegal under Texas law?

3. In DeSantis v. Wackenhut Corp., 793 S.W.2d 670 (Tex. 1990), discussed in *Southwest Livestock*, the Texas Supreme Court refused to apply foreign (Florida) law to enforce a non-competition agreement entered into in Florida, which the Texas Supreme Court considered violative of Texas public policy. It did so even though the parties had included a Florida choice of law clause in the non-competition agreement which, if applied, would have upheld the contract. Understandably, the debtor in *Southwest Livestock* relied on *DeSantis*, but the Fifth Circuit was unpersuaded. It drew a distinction between the application of foreign law in the first instance, as in *DeSantis*, and the recognition and enforcement of a foreign judgment, as in *Southwest Livestock*, stating that the latter "involve[s] separate and distinct inquiries." What is the difference, and why should a court be less willing to allow a public policy objection to foreign law in the judgment-recognition setting?

4. Not all states have such prickly standards of public policy when it comes to foreign judgments. Courts often invoke the classic statement of Justice Cardozo for the New York Court of Appeals: "We are not so provincial as to say that every solution of a problem is wrong because we deal with it otherwise at home." Loucks v. Standard Oil Co. of New York, 224 N.Y. 99, 111 (1918). See also Sung Hwan Co., Ltd. v. Rite Aid Corp., 7 N.Y.3d 78, 82 (2006) (stating that for a judgment to run afoul of New York public policy it must be "inherently vicious, wicked or immoral, and shocking to the prevailing moral sense") (quoting Intercontinental Hotels Corp., v. Golden, 15 N.Y.2d 9, 13 (1964)); Ackermann v. Levine, 788 F.2d 830, 841-42 (2d Cir. 1986) (quoting *Loucks*); CIBC Mellon Trust Co. v. Mora Hotel Corp., 100 N.Y.2d 215, 221 (2003) ("New York has traditionally been a generous forum in which to enforce judgments for money damages rendered by foreign courts."). As one federal court put it when construing the scope of the Massachusetts public policy exception:

> The public policy exception operates only in those unusual cases where the foreign judgment is "repugnant to fundamental notions of what is decent and just in the State where enforcement is sought." Tahan v. Hodgson, 662 F.2d 862, 864 (D.C. Cir. 1981); Ackermann v. Levine, 788 F.2d 830, 841 (2d Cir. 1986); See also, Restatement (Second) of the Conflict of Laws § 117 (1971). Under the "classic formulation" of the public policy exception, a judgment is contrary to the public policy of the enforcing state where that judgment "'tends clearly' to undermine the public interest, the public confidence in the administration of the law, or security for individual rights of personal liberty or of private property." *Ackermann*, 788 F.2d at 841 (quoting Somportex v. Philadelphia Chewing Gum, 453 F.2d 435, 443 (3d Cir. 1971), cert. denied, 405 U.S. 1017 (1972)).

McCord v. Jet Spray Int'l Corp. 874 F. Supp. 436 (D. Mass. 1994).

In the case that follows, public policy concerns were raised in connection with the enforcement of a defamation judgment rendered in a foreign tribunal which provided speakers with fewer free-speech protections than those offered by the U.S. Constitution and the enforcing state's constitution. In response to what some have called the problem of "libel tourism"—filing a defamation suit in a foreign jurisdiction that has weak rules favoring speakers and strong rules favoring victims—Congress recently undertook to restrict the enforcement of foreign defamation judgments in American courts in The SPEECH Act of 2010, 28 U.S.C. §§ 4101 et seq. We discuss the statute below. But we include the following case, in part because it illustrated the issues to which the federal statute was responsive and in part because it offers a model for dealing with such judgments on a state-by-state basis that is more congenial to traditional federalism values than the uniform rule for which Congress has opted.

Telnikoff v. Matusevitch

Maryland Supreme Court, 1997.

347 Md. 561, 702 A.2d 230.

ELDRIDGE, J.

[An English jury returned a £240,000 verdict in favor of the plaintiff, Telnikoff (a Russian émigré and English citizen), finding that a letter written by the defendant Matusevitch and published in the London Daily Telegraph, conveyed that Telnikoff had made statements inciting racial hatred and/or racial discrimination, and that Telnikoff was a racialist and/or anti-Semite. (By birth, Matusevitch was a U.S. citizen who had lived in Russia for 28 years but was living in Europe at the time of the original suit; he later became a Maryland resident.) Judgment was entered for the amount of the jury's verdict. Telnikoff then attempted to have the English judgment enforced against Matusevitch in several American courts in states in which Matusevitch had assets. Eventually, upon certification by the United States Court of Appeals for the District of Columbia Circuit, the Court of Appeals of Maryland had to decide whether the English libel judgment was contrary to the public policy of Maryland.]

The question before us is whether Telnikoff's English libel judgment is based upon principles which are so contrary to Maryland's public policy concerning freedom of the press and defamation actions that recognition of the judgment should be denied. * * *

While we shall rest our decision in this case upon the non-constitutional ground of Maryland public policy, nonetheless, in ascertaining that public policy, it is appropriate to examine and rely upon the history, policies, and requirements of the First Amendment and Article 40 of the Declaration of Rights. In determining non-constitutional principles of law, courts often rely upon the policies and requirements reflected in constitutional provisions. * * *

Consequently, it is appropriate to examine some of the history, policies, and requirements of the free press clauses of the First Amendment and Article 40 of the Declaration of Rights, as well as the present relationship between those provisions and defamation actions in Maryland. * * *

American and Maryland history reflects a public policy in favor of a much broader and more protective freedom of the press than ever provided for under English law. [The court went on to provide a very detailed account on the different historic developments in England and the United States.]

Despite the very strong public policy in Maryland regarding freedom of the press, the relationship between freedom of the press and defamation actions did not receive a great deal of attention prior to the Supreme Court's opinion in *New York Times Co. v. Sullivan*, 376 U.S. 254 (1964). * * * Nevertheless, prior to *New York Times Co. v. Sullivan, supra,* and its progeny, numerous English common law principles governing libel and slander actions were routinely applied in Maryland defamation cases without any consideration or mention of the constitutional free press clauses or the strong public policy favoring freedom of the press. * * *

The Supreme Court in *New York Times Co. v. Sullivan* held that the First Amendment "prohibits a public official from recovering damages for a defamatory falsehood relating to his official conduct unless he proves that the statement was made with 'actual malice'—that is, with knowledge that it was false or with reckless disregard of whether it was false or not." The Court went on to hold that such malice could not be presumed, * * * that the constitutional standard requires proof having "convincing clarity," * * * and that evidence simply supporting a finding of negligence is insufficient. * * *

The Supreme Court in *Gertz v. Robert Welch, Inc.,* 418 U.S. 323, 347 (1974), held that the "actual malice" standard of *New York Times Co. v. Sullivan* did not extend to defamation actions by persons who were neither public officials nor public figures. Nevertheless the Court went to hold that, in a defamation action by such a private person against a magazine publisher who published an article relating to a matter of public concern, the First Amendment precluded the imposition of liability for compensatory damages without fault. The Court further held that, in such a defamation action, there can be no recovery of presumed or punitive damages without a showing of actual malice, defined as "knowledge of falsity or reckless disregard for the truth." * * *

[The court went on, again in considerable detail, to state its own holdings based on *New York Times* and *Gertz* and concluded that] [t]he contrast between English standards governing defamation actions and the present Maryland standards is striking. For the most part, English defamation actions are governed by principles which are unchanged from the earlier common law period.

Thus, under English defamation law, it is unnecessary for the plaintiff to establish fault, either in the form of conscious wrongdoing or negligence. The state of mind or conduct of the defendant is irrelevant.

Moreover, under English law, defamatory statements are presumed to be false unless a defendant proves them to be true.

In England, a qualified privilege can be overcome without establishing that the defendant actually knew that the publication was false or acted with reckless disregard of whether it was false or not. It can be overcome by proof of "spite or ill-will or some other wrong or improper motive." Peter F. Carter-Ruck, Libel and Slander, 137 (1973). English law authorizes punitive or exemplary damages under numerous circumstances in defamation actions; unlike Maryland law, they are not limited to cases in which there was actual knowledge of the falsehood or reckless disregard as to truth or falsity. Id. at 172-73. Furthermore, as one scholar has pointed out, id. at 172, "in practice only one sum is awarded and it is impossible to tell to what extent the damages awarded in any particular case were intended to be compensatory and to what extent exemplary or punitive. * * *"

* * * Finally, English defamation law flatly rejects the principles set forth in *New York Times Co. v. Sullivan, supra,* and *Gertz v. Robert Welch, Inc., supra.* The basic rules are the same regardless of whether the plaintiff is a public official, public figure, or a private person, regardless of whether the alleged defamatory statement involves a matter of public concern, and regardless of the defendant's status. * * *

A comparison of English and present Maryland defamation law does not simply disclose a difference in one or two legal principles. * * * Instead, present Maryland defamation law is totally different from English defamation law in virtually every significant respect. Moreover, the differences are rooted in historic and fundamental public policy differences concerning freedom of the press and speech.

The stark contrast between English and Maryland law is clearly illustrated by the underlying litigation between Telnikoff and Matusevitch. Telnikoff, an employee of the publicly funded Radio Free Europe/Radio Liberty, was undisputably a public official or public figure. In this country, he would have had to prove, by clear and convincing evidence, that Matusevitch's letter contained false statements of fact and that Matusevitch acted maliciously in the sense that he knew of the falsity or acted with reckless disregard of whether the statements were false or not. The English courts, however, held that there was no evidence supporting Telnikoff's allegations that Matusevitch acted with actual malice, either under the *New York Times Co. v. Sullivan* definition or in the sense of ill-will, spite or intent to injure. Despite the absence of actual malice under any definition, Telnikoff was allowed to recover. He was not even required to prove negligence, which is the minimum a purely private defamation plaintiff must establish to recover under Maryland law.

In addition, Telnikoff was not required to prove that Matusevitch's letter contained a false statement of fact, which would have been required under present Maryland law. Instead, falsity was presumed, and the defendant had the risky choice of whether to attempt to prove truth. Furthermore, Telnikoff did not have to establish that the alleged defamation even contained defamatory statements of fact; the burden was upon the defendant to establish that the alleged defamatory language amounted to comment and not statements of fact. * * *

The principles governing defamation actions under English law, which were applied to Telnikoff's libel suit, are so contrary to Maryland defamation law, and to the policy of freedom of the press underlying Maryland law, that Telnikoff's judgment should be denied recognition under principles of comity. In the language of the Uniform Foreign-Money Judgments Recognition Act, § 10-704(b)(2) of the Courts and Judicial Proceedings Article, Telnikoff's English "cause of action on which the judgment is based is repugnant to the public policy of the State. . . ."

The only American case which the two parties have called to our attention, which is directly on point, reached a similar conclusion. In *Bachchan v. India Abroad Publications,* 85 N.Y.S.2d 661 (1992), an Indian national brought a libel action in the High Court of Justice in London against the New York operator of a news service which transmitted stories exclusively to India. The suit was based upon an article, written by a London reporter and transmitted by the defendant to India, in which the plaintiff's name was used in connection with an international scandal. After a jury assessed 40,000 pounds in damages against the defendant, the plaintiff sought to enforce the judgment against the defendant in New York. The defendant opposed recognition of the judgment on the ground that the judgment was "repugnant to public policy" of New York as embodied in the First Amendment to the United States Constitution and the free speech and press guarantees of the New York Constitution. After contrasting English with American defamation law, the court concluded: * * *

> "It is true that England and the United States share many common-law principles of law. Nevertheless, a significant difference between the two jurisdictions lies in England's lack of an equivalent to the First Amendment to the U.S. Constitution. The protection to free speech and the press embodied in that amendment would be seriously jeopardized by the entry of foreign libel judgments granted pursuant to standards deemed appropriate in England but considered antithetical to the protections afforded the press by the U.S. Constitution."

Moreover, recognition of English defamation judgments could well lead to wholesale circumvention of fundamental public policy in Maryland and the rest of the country. With respect to the sharp differences between English and American defamation law, Professor Smolla has observed (Rodney A. Smolla, Law of Defamation, § 1.03[3] (1996)):

> "This striking disparity between American and British libel law has led to a curious recent phenomenon, a sort of balance of trade deficit in libel litigation: Prominent persons who receive bad press in publications distributed primarily in the United States now often choose to file their libel suits in England. London has become an international libel capital. Plaintiffs with the wherewithal to do so now often choose to file suit in Britain in order to exploit Britain's strict libel laws, even when the plaintiffs and the publication have little connection to that country."

* * * "At the heart of the First Amendment," as well as Article 40 of the Maryland Declaration of Rights and Maryland public policy, "is the recognition of the fundamental importance of the free flow of ideas and opinions on matters of public interest and concern." *Hustler Magazine v. Falwell,* 485 U.S. 46, 50 (1988). The importance of that free flow of ideas and opinions on matters of

public concern precludes Maryland recognition of Telnikoff's English libel judgment.

Dissenting Opinion by CHASANOW, J.

* * * I believe Maryland public policy should not prevent enforcement of this English libel judgment. * * *

For hundreds of years, up until 1964 when the Supreme Court decided *New York Times Co.,* the Maryland common law of libel was the same as the current English libel law under which the instant English libel case was decided. * * *

It was only after New York Times Co. and its progeny that this Court abandoned hundreds of years of common-law defamation. * * * It was the Supreme Court construing the First Amendment to the United States Constitution that made us jettison the same English common law of libel that we now find so offensive. * * *

* * * I believe Maryland's public policy should not preclude enforcement of this judgment. The majority opinion devotes page after page to a stirring tribute to freedom of the press, but this case does not involve freedom of the press. This is a libel judgment obtained by one resident of England against another resident of England. The libel was contained in a letter written by the defendant. Although the letter was published by a newspaper as a letter to the editor, that only increased the damages, the libel was the letter prepared and dispatched by a private person. The letter was libelous regardless of whether the newspaper chose to reprint it. Freedom of the press is not implicated, nor was any United States interest implicated. I trust the majority is not somehow suggesting that it is freedom of speech that protects speaking, but it is freedom of the press that protects printing or writing; that simply is wrong. * * *

Matusevitch's letter was determined to be libelous by a jury; the proceedings were fair and carefully reviewed by the House of Lords, the highest court in England. There is no grave injustice in this internal English litigation. * * *

There is another public policy that should also be considered by this Court. That public policy, recognized by our legislature when it adopted the Uniform Foreign Money-Judgment Recognition Act, is to give broad and uniform recognition to foreign judgments. The Act gives our courts discretion to subordinate our State's public policy. Our interest in international good will, comity, and res judicata fostered by recognition of foreign judgments must be weighed against our minimal interest in giving the benefits of our local libel public policy to residents of another country who defame foreign public figures in foreign publications and who have no reasonable expectation that they will be protected by the Maryland Constitution. Unless there is some United States interest that should be protected, there is no good reason to offend a friendly nation like England by refusing to recognize a purely local libel judgment for a purely local defamation. In the instant case, there is no United States interest that might necessitate non-recognition or non-enforcement of the English defamation judgment. * * *

The majority makes the finding of fact that "Telnikoff . . . was undisputably a public official or public figure," * * * but fails to take into account that Telnikoff was not an American public official or public figure. Our Constitution extracts a price for notoriety. American public officials and public figures must realize that if they are defamed there is no redress under our laws unless the defamation is done with malice. This may keep some people from becoming public officials and induce others to shun notoriety, but they generally have that choice. British public officials and public figures, however, expect their law to give them protection from even non-malicious false defamatory statements. We should respect this difference between British public figures and their American counterparts in cases of purely internal English defamation by private persons. I doubt the public would find this as repugnant as does the majority of this Court. Matusevitch, at the time he falsely accused Telnikoff of being a racist hate monger, had no right to, or expectation that he would, be protected by the United States Constitution, and I doubt that the public would be outraged if we do not retroactively bestow our constitutional right to non-maliciously defame a public official on Matusevitch merely because he later moves to our country. * * *

Public policy should not require us to give First Amendment protection or Article 40 protection to English residents who defame other English residents in publications distributed only in England. Failure to make our constitutional provisions relating to defamation applicable to wholly internal English defamation would not seem to violate fundamental notions of what is decent and just and should not undermine public confidence in the administration of law. The Court does little or no analysis of the global public policy considerations and seems inclined to make Maryland libel law applicable to the rest of the world by providing a safe haven for foreign libel judgment debtors.

NOTES AND QUESTIONS FOR DISCUSSION

1. The majority in *Telnikoff* held that the English libel judgment was incompatible with Maryland's public policy and therefore unenforceable. Specifically, the majority feared that "recognition of English defamation judgments could well lead to wholesale circumvention of fundamental public policy in Maryland and the rest of the country." 347 Md. at 601. Given its reasoning, could *any* English libel judgment be enforced in Maryland? If so, under what circumstances?

2. At the time of the libel and the trial, both the plaintiff and the defendant in *Telnikoff* were Russian émigrés residing in England, and the speech in question had nothing to do with persons or events in the U.S. As the dissent asks, are American free speech interests implicated in such a case? At the time of judgment enforcement, Matusevitch was a Maryland resident. Does that suffice for Maryland to be able to assert a public policy objection to enforcement of the English judgment? Would it be a sufficient interest for purposes of such an objection that the judgment was being enforced in a state whose only connection with the litigation was the presence of assets of the judgment debtor? For doubts about *Telnikoff*, see Linda J. Silberman & Andreas F. Lowenfeld, *A Different Challenge for the ALI: Herein of Foreign Country Judgments, an International Treaty, and an American Statute*, 75 Ind. L.J. 635, 644 (2000). Consider also whether there might have been English interests involved in this litigation. Shouldn't they count as well? See Craig A. Stern, *Foreign Judgments and the Freedom of Speech: Look Who's Talking*, 60 Brook. L. Rev. 999, 1033-34 (1994) (emphasizing English "interest in applying its law of defamation" and in the integrity of English libel judgments).

3. The majority in *Telnikoff* denied recognition and enforcement of the English libel judgment on grounds derived from Maryland's public policy and the First Amendment. Consider the interrelationship between the two, given that the First Amendment itself could not possibly extend to the underlying actions. And consider what weight, if any, should be given to the dissent's argument that for hundreds of years, the Maryland common law of libel was identical with the English common law of libel.

4. The *Telnikoff* majority relied on both federal and state law in formulating its public policy objection. Yet the D.C. Circuit, which certified the question to the Maryland court, did so to get Maryland's input on the unclear question of Maryland law. Should the D.C. Circuit feel compelled to accept the Maryland Court's views of the federal constitution if, for example, it thought the Maryland courts were in error? Or is the reference to the federal constitution ultimately a question of state law? See also Sarl Louis Feraud Int'l v. Viewfinder, Inc., 489 F.3d 474, 481-82 (2d Cir. 2007) ("In deciding whether the French Judgments are repugnant to the public policy of New York, the district court should first determine the level of First Amendment protection required by New York public policy . . . . Then, it should determine whether the French intellectual property regime provides comparable protections.").

5. The *Telnikoff* majority relied in part on **Bachchan v. India Abroad Publications Inc., 585 N.Y.S.2d 661 (N.Y. Sup. Ct. 1992).** In that case, the defendant resisting the enforcement of an English defamation judgment was a New York operator of a news service that transmitted reports only to India. The defamatory story was written by a reporter in London and wired by the defendant to a news service in India which relayed the story to Indian newspapers. Two Indian newspapers published the story and copies of those newspapers were distributed in the United Kingdom. The story was further published in an issue of defendant's New York newspaper, "India Abroad." An edition of "India Abroad" was also printed in, and distributed in, the United Kingdom by the defendant's English subsidiary. The claim leading to the English defamation judgment was based on the latter (U.K.) distribution. The New York supreme court refused to recognize the English judgment on the ground that it failed to comport with the protections of the First Amendment. Based on the facts presented here, is *Bachchan* distinguishable from *Telinikoff*?

6. *Bachchan* rested its own conclusion in part on the U.S. Supreme Court decision in Philadelphia Newspapers, Inc. v. Hepps, 475 U.S. 767 (1986). There, the Court enunciated (for the first time) that the First Amendment required a reversal of the traditional burden of proof for private figures suing newspapers for articles raising issues of public concern. According to the time-honored common-law rule which was valid in the U.S. until 1986, and is still valid in England, the defendant has to prove the truth of its statement if it wishes to avoid liability for uttering a defamatory statement. The Court's new rule requires instead that the plaintiff bear the burden of showing falsity of the defendant's defamatory statement and of showing fault on the part of the defendant. Is it persuasive to argue that the English approach, long adhered to by American courts, should overnight be considered repugnant to New York's public policy? For doubts whether minor deviations from First Amendment law should trigger a public policy objection, see Joachim Zekoll, *The Role and Status of American Law in the Hague Judgments Convention Project,* 61 Alb. L. Rev. 1283, 1305 (1998).

7. As noted above, Congress chose to legislate a uniform solution to the problem of "libel tourism" in **The SPEECH Act of 2010, 28 U.S.C. §§ 4101-4105.** ("SPEECH" was the acronym for the contorted title of the statute: the "Securing the Protection of our Enduring Constitutional Heritage Act"). The Act basically provides that no court—state or federal—may recognize or enforce a defamation judgment that was rendered in a foreign court system with free speech protections less favorable than those under the federal Constitution or the relevant enforcing-state constitution, id. at § 4102(a)(1)(A), unless the party opposing enforcement would have been found liable in a domestic (U.S.) court applying federal and state constitutional provisions, id. at § 4102(a)(1)(B). Moreover, the judgment creditor has the burden of showing that the statute's prerequisites have been met. Id. at § 4102(a)(2). Consequently, states no longer have the ability to develop their own standards for enforcement of judgments covered by the Act. Finally, the statute specifically requires that federal due process requirements must be satisfied in the exercise of personal jurisdiction by the foreign court before its defamation judgment will be recognized, even if the other (free speech) provisions of the statute are satisfied. Id. at § 4102(b)(1). Although parts of the statute are directed toward "U.S. parties," the general prohibition on judgment enforcement is not limited to cases involving U.S. parties or U.S. transactions, and would thus seem to apply to a case such as *Telnikoff.*

8. The SPEECH Act raises all of the policy questions noted above in connection with the Maryland judgment in *Telnikoff*—and leaves no room for a more moderate stance towards foreign defamation judgments as suggested by the dissent in that case. In fact, the Act all but requires that foreign law and foreign courts mimic American standards as a prerequisite to judgment recognition in the U.S. Is this quasi-extraterritorial application of American law justified? If your answer is "yes," consider whether you would change your opinion if the only nexus between the foreign litigation and the American forum happened to be the presence of assets of the (foreign) judgment debtor in the forum.

9. The SPEECH Act clearly raises federalism concerns to the extent that it provides a uniform federal solution in place of a state-by-state solution. Was a uniform solution preferable to state-by-state development, as in *Telnikoff* and *Bachchan*? If only state constitutional issues are present (because the foreign judgment satisfies federal but not, for example, tougher state free-speech requirements), shouldn't a state have the *option* whether or not to enforce the judgment? Is there federal power that would allow Congress to prevent states from enforcing foreign judgments that run afoul only of state law rather than federal law? The SPEECH Act is the only federal statute to date that purports to provide for the effect to be given to a foreign judgment. Do these sorts of judgments present a compelling case for such extraordinary intervention, particularly when states seem not to have been enforcing such judgments on their own? See e.g., N.Y.C.P.L.R. § 5304(b)(8) (2009) (providing a standard somewhat similar to that of The SPEECH Act); see also 735 I.L.C.S. 5/12-621(b)(7) (2008) (Illinois) (repealed Jan. 1, 2012).

10. With the advent of the Internet, objections based on the First Amendment are likely to become more frequent and to present difficult issues in American enforcement procedures. Illustrative is **YAHOO!, INC. v. LA LIGUE CONTRE LE RACISME ET L'ANTISEMITISME, 169 F. Supp. 2d 1181 (N.D. Cal. 2001)**, which was later dismissed (on grounds not relevant here) by the Ninth Circuit. See 433 F.3d 1199 (9th Cir. 2006) (en banc). A French court had enjoined a U.S. internet service provider from disseminating offers to French users in France to buy Nazi and Third Reich related objects. In an effort to prevent the French plaintiffs from enforcing the French injunction in the U.S., Yahoo! sought and obtained a declaratory judgment from a California federal district court on the ground that enforcement of the French injunction would be irreconcilable with American free speech protections. The following excerpt from the district court's opinion illustrates how Internet activities exacerbate the already-existing tensions in this area of the law:

> As this Court and others have observed, the instant case presents novel and important issues arising from the global reach of the Internet. Indeed, the specific facts of this case implicate issues of policy, politics, and culture that are beyond the purview of one nation's judiciary. Thus it is critical that the Court define at the outset what is and is not at stake in the present proceeding. * * *

> [T]his case [is not] about the right of France or any other nation to determine its own law and social policies. A basic function of a sovereign state is to determine by law what forms of speech and conduct are acceptable within its borders. In this instance, as a nation whose citizens suffered the effects of Nazism in ways that are incomprehensible to most Americans, France clearly has the right to enact and enforce laws such as those relied upon by the French Court here. What *is* at issue here is whether it is consistent with the Constitution and laws of the United States for another nation to regulate speech by a United States resident within the United States on the basis that such speech can be accessed by Internet users in that nation. In a world in which ideas and information transcend borders and the Internet in particular renders the physical distance between speaker and audience virtually meaningless, the implications of this question go far beyond the facts of this case. The modern world is home to widely varied cultures with radically divergent value systems. There is little doubt that Internet users in the United States routinely engage in speech that violates, for example, China's laws against religious expression, the laws of various nations against advocacy of gender equality or homosexuality, or even the United Kingdom's restrictions on freedom of the press. If the government or another party in one of these sovereign nations were to seek enforcement of such laws against Yahoo! or another U.S.-based Internet service provider, what principles should guide the court's analysis?

> The Court has stated that it must and will decide this case in accordance with the Constitution and laws of the United States. It recognizes that in so doing, it necessarily adopts certain value judgments embedded in those enactments, including the fundamental judgment expressed in

the First Amendment that it is preferable to permit the non-violent expression of offensive viewpoints rather than to impose viewpoint-based governmental regulation upon speech. The government and people of France have made a different judgment based upon their own experience. In undertaking its inquiry as to the proper application of the laws of the United States, the Court intends no disrespect for that judgment or for the experience that has informed it.

Yahoo!, 169 F. Supp. 2d, at 1186-87.

Does a case such as this present a stronger argument in favor of refusing enforcement than in the defamation setting? Should it matter that the exhibition of Nazi propaganda and artifacts for sale is a violation of French *criminal* law? In the California federal district court, the two French Civil Rights organizations who were defendants in the declaratory action (i.e., the foreign plaintiffs) had objected to personal jurisdiction over them in California. Eventually, the Ninth Circuit Court of Appeals dismissed the action based in part on concerns about the ripeness of the dispute regarding enforcement of the judgment. See Yahoo!, Inc. v. La Ligue Contre Le Racisme et L'Antisemitisme 433 F.3d 1199 (9th Cir. 2006) (en banc). We discuss the personal jurisdiction dimension of *Yahoo!* in Chapter 1, Section B.

11. *Yahoo!* is not the only time U.S. judgment debtors have attempted to make a preemptive strike against enforcement of a foreign judgment in the U.S. by bringing a declaratory judgment prior to enforcement proceedings. For example, in Chevron Corp. v. Naranjo, 667 F.3d 232 (2d Cir. 2012), the Second Circuit concluded that New York's version of the UFCMJA, N.Y.C.P.L.R. §§ 5301-5309, did not allow a pre-emptive injunction against judgment creditors prohibiting their enforcement of an allegedly fraudulent (non-defamation) judgment obtained against Chevron in Ecuador. Rather, the provisions of the UFCMJA could only be enforced defensively to an enforcement action once it was actually brought. As noted in Chapter 1, Section B, however, New York has expressly provided in N.Y.C.P.L.R. § 302(d) for personal jurisdiction over certain foreign judgment creditors in actions for declaratory relief that a foreign defamation judgment is not enforceable because it did not comply with American free speech standards. What is the advantage to the judgment debtor in bringing such an anticipatory action, as opposed to waiting for the judgment creditor to enforce the action in the U.S.?

12. In the SPEECH Act, Congress expressly provided for federal court subject matter jurisdiction over declaratory judgment actions brought by "U.S. parties" seeking a pre-emptive declaration that a foreign defamation judgment did not comport with the requirements of the Act. Given that the Act's general command is not limited to foreign judgments involving U.S. parties, why is the declaratory remedy limited to such parties? Moreover, the Act requires that the foreign proceedings comply with both federal *and* state constitutional standards. Would there be a constitutional problem (absent diversity) with a federal court exercising jurisdiction over a U.S. party's declaratory judgment action to the effect that a foreign defamation judgment failed to comply with relevant *state* law, even though it may have complied with the U.S. Constitution?

2. Concerns Regarding Fair Procedures

The Society of Lloyd's v. Ashenden

United States Court of Appeals, Seventh Circuit, 2000.

233 F.3d 473.

POSNER, CIRCUIT JUDGE.

These are diversity suits brought in the federal district court in Chicago by Lloyd's, a foreign corporation * * * against American members ("names") of insurance syndicates that Lloyd's manages. 28 U.S.C. § 1332(a)(2). Lloyd's wanted to use the Illinois Uniform Foreign Money-Judgments Recognition Act, 735 ILCS 5/12-618 to 626, to collect money judgments, each for several hundred thousand dollars, that it had obtained against the defendants in an English court after the names' repeated efforts in earlier litigation to knock out the forum-selection clause in their contracts with Lloyd's had failed. * * * Pursuant to this strategy, Lloyd's filed the judgments in the district court and then issued "citations" pursuant to the Illinois procedure for executing a judgment. The filing of the judgments inaugurated this federal-court proceeding to collect them; and state law, in this case the Illinois citations statute, 735 ILCS 5/2-1402, supplies the procedure for executing a federal-court judgment. Fed. R. Civ. Pro. 69(a); *Resolution Trust Corp. v. Ruggiero,* 994 F.2d 1221, 1226 (7th Cir. 1993); 12 Charles A. Wright, Arthur R. Miller & Richard L. Marcus, *Federal Practice and Procedure* § 3012, p. 148 (1997). The statute allows the holder of a judgment to depose the judgment debtor respecting the existence, amount, and whereabouts of assets that can be seized to satisfy the judgment; to impose a lien on those assets; and to command the debtor to turn over to the judgment creditor as many of the seizable assets as may be necessary to satisfy the judgment. See *Bank of Aspen v. Fox Cartage, Inc.,* 126 Ill. 2d 307, 533 N.E.2d 1080, 1083, 127 Ill. Dec. 952 (Ill. 1989).

The defendants ignored the citations and instead asked the district court not to recognize the English judgments as being enforceable in Illinois. They argued that those judgments had denied them due process of law and therefore were not enforceable under the foreign money-judgments recognition act, which makes a judgment rendered by a court outside the United States unenforceable in Illinois if "the judgment was rendered under a *system* which does not provide impartial tribunals or procedures compatible with the requirements of due process of law." 735 ILCS 5/12-621 (emphasis added); see also 5/12-620. The district court rejected the argument and granted summary judgment for Lloyd's, declaring the judgments enforceable and so the issuance of citations proper.

We have italicized the word that defeats the defendants' argument. The judgments about which they complain were rendered by the Queen's Bench Division of England's High Court, which corresponds to our federal district courts; they were affirmed by the Court of Appeal, which corresponds to the federal courts of appeals; and the Appellate Committee of the House of Lords, which corresponds to the U.S. Supreme Court, denied the defendants' petition for review. Any suggestion that this system of courts "does not provide impartial tribunals or procedures compatible with the requirements of due process of law" borders on the risible. "The courts of England are fair and neutral forums." *Riley v. Kingsley Underwriting Agencies, Ltd.,* 969 F.2d 953, 958 (10th Cir. 1992), * * * and the English courts, especially the Supreme Court of Judicature (composed of the High Court and the Court of Appeal) and the Appellate Committee of the House of Lords, the tribunals involved in the judgments challenged here, are highly regarded for impartiality, professionalism, and scrupulous regard for procedural rights. The English judicial "system . . . is the very fount from which our system developed; a system which has procedures and goals which closely parallel our own." *In re Hashim,* 213 F.3d 1169, 1172 (9th Cir. 2000), quoting *Somportex Ltd. v. Philadelphia Chewing Gum Corp.,* 318 F. Supp. 161, 166 (E.D. Pa. 1970), aff'd, 453 F.2d 435 (3d Cir. 1971). "United States courts which have inherited major portions of their judicial traditions and procedure from the United Kingdom are hardly in a position to call the Queen's Bench a kangaroo court." *British Midland Airways Ltd. v. International Travel, Inc.,* 497 F.2d 869, 871 (9th Cir. 1974).

Not that the English concept of fair procedure is identical to ours; but we cannot believe that the Illinois statute is intended to bar the enforcement of all judgments of any foreign legal system that does not conform its procedural doctrines to the latest twist and turn of our courts regarding, for example, the circumstances under which due process requires an opportunity for a hearing in advance of the deprivation of a substantive right rather than afterwards. See *Hilton v. Guyot,* 159 U.S. 113, 205 (1895); *Ingersoll Milling Machine Co. v. Granger,* 833 F.2d 680, 687-88 (7th Cir. 1987). It is a fair guess that no foreign nation has decided to incorporate our due process doctrines into its own procedural law; and so we interpret "due process" in the Illinois statute (which, remember, is a uniform act, not one intended to reflect the idiosyncratic jurisprudence of a particular state) to refer to a concept of fair procedure simple and basic enough to describe the judicial processes of civilized nations, our peers. The statute requires only that the foreign procedure be *"compatible* with the requirements of due process of law," and we have interpreted this to mean that the foreign procedures are "fundamentally fair" and do not offend against "basic fairness." *Id.* at 687-88[.] * * *

We'll call this the "international concept of due process" to distinguish it from the complex concept that has emerged from American case law. We note that it is even less demanding than the test the courts use to determine whether to enforce a foreign arbitral award under the New York Convention, 9 U.S.C. § 201 *et seq.,* whose due process defense (that a party lacked "proper notice of the appointment of the arbitrator or of the arbitration proceedings or was otherwise unable to present his case," Article V(1) (b), 9 U.S.C. § 201) has been interpreted to mean the enforcing jurisdiction's concept of due process, albeit a rather minimal such concept. *Iran Aircraft Industries v. Avco Corp.,* 980 F.2d 141, 145-46 (2d Cir. 1992); see also *Generica Ltd. v. Pharmaceutical Basics, Inc.,* 125 F.3d 1123, 1129-31 (7th Cir. 1997).

It is true that no evidence was presented in the district court on whether England *has* a civilized legal system, but that is because the question is not open to doubt. We need not consider what kind of evidence would suffice to show that a foreign legal system "does not provide impartial tribunals or procedures compatible with the requirements of due process of law" if the challenged judgment had been rendered by Cuba, North Korea, Iran, Iraq, Congo, or some other nation whose adherence to the rule of law and commitment to the norm of due process are open to serious question, * * * as England's are not. It is anyway not a question of fact. It is not, strictly speaking, a question of law either, but it is a question about the law of a foreign nation, and in answering such questions a federal court is not limited to the consideration of evidence that would be admissible under the Federal Rules of Evidence; any relevant material or source may be consulted. Fed. R. Civ. P. 44.1; *Pittway Corp. v. United States,* 88 F.3d 501, 504 (7th Cir. 1996); 9 Charles A. Wright & Arthur R. Miller, *Federal Practice and Procedure* § 2446 (1995).

Rather than trying to impugn the English legal system en gross, the defendants argue that the Illinois statute requires us to determine whether the particular judgments that they are challenging were issued in proceedings that conform to the requirements of due process of law as it has come to be understood in the case law of Illinois and other American jurisdictions. The statute, with its reference to "system," does not support such a retail approach, which would moreover be inconsistent with providing a streamlined, expeditious method for collecting money judgments rendered by courts in other jurisdictions—which would in effect give the judgment creditor a further appeal on the merits. The process of collecting a judgment is not meant to require a second lawsuit, see *Bank of Aspen v. Fox Cartage, Inc., supra,* 533 N.E.2d at 1083; *Resolution Trust Corp. v. Ruggiero, supra,* 994 F.2d at 1226, thus converting every successful multinational suit for damages into two suits (actually three, as we'll see at the end of this opinion). But that is the implication of the defendants' argument. They claim to be free to object in the collection phase of the case to the procedures employed at the merits phase, even though they were free to challenge those procedures at that phase and indeed did so.

Even if the retail approach is valid—and we want to emphasize our belief that it is not—it cannot possibly avail the defendants here unless they are right that the approach requires subjecting the foreign proceeding to the specifics of the American doctrine of due process. They are not right. Just as no judgments of a foreign legal system would be enforceable in Illinois if the system had to conform to the specifics of the American doctrine of due process, so very few foreign judgments would be enforceable in Illinois if the proceeding in which such a judgment was rendered had to conform to those specifics. In a case decided by a foreign court system that has not adopted every jot and tittle of American due process (and no foreign court system has, to our knowledge, done that), it will be sheer accident that a particular proceeding happened to conform in every particular to our complex understanding of due process. So even the retail approach, in order to get within miles of being reasonable, would have to content itself with requiring foreign conformity to the international concept of due process.

And now let us for the sake of completeness apply that concept to the particulars of these judgments.

A bit of background (much simplified): Lloyd's, contrary to popular understanding, is not an insurer, but rather the overseer of the London insurance market. The actual insurance is written by syndicates of "names." The syndicates do not have limited liability, and so the personal assets of the names are at risk should an insured obtain a judgment for more than the assets of the syndicate that insured him. In the late 1980s and early 1990s the Lloyd's-supervised syndicates incurred huge underwriting losses that threatened to destroy the London insurance market. To ward off this disaster the governing body of Lloyd's, a Council elected primarily by the managing agents of the syndicates, created a company called "Equitas" to reinsure the risks underwritten by the syndicates. The reinsurance would both protect the insureds against being unable to collect the proceeds of their insurance policies from the syndicates and protect the names from unlimited personal liability for the underwriting losses. To finance the new company, Lloyd's levied an assessment (the reinsurance premium) against all the names. Lloyd's offered a discount on the assessment to induce the names to go along with this plan voluntarily, and 95 percent of them did. The defendants are among those who did not, and Lloyd's sued them in the High Court to collect the assessment. The suit was based on the contract with Equitas, Lloyd's Council having (pursuant to a by-law that it had adopted) appointed "substitute agents" for all the names, and these agents having signed the contract on behalf of the defendants as of the other recusant names.

In the English court the defendants opposed Lloyd's suit on the basis of two clauses which they contend would, if enforced, deny them due process of law; and they renew the contention here. The first clause, the "pay now sue later" clause as the parties call it, forbids names, in suits (such as the ones before us) by Lloyd's to collect the assessment, to set off against the claim by Lloyd's any claim the names might have against Lloyd's, such as a claim that the contract had been induced by fraud. If they want to press such a claim they have to file a separate suit. (Some have now done so, and lost. *Society of Lloyd's v. Jaffray*, 2000 WL 1629463 (Queen's Bench Division Commercial Court Nov. 3, 2000).) The second clause, the "conclusive evidence" clause, makes Lloyd's determination of the amount of the assessment "conclusive" "in the absence of manifest error." The defendants claim that the High Court refused to order Lloyd's to provide them with enough information about how the assessment had been calculated to enable them to prove manifest error.

Both clauses therefore curtail the names' procedural rights. But due process is not a fixed menu of procedural rights. How much process is due depends on the circumstances. * * * Faced with looming disaster, Lloyd's reasonably deemed it essential to obtain adequate funding for Equitas. The only potential source for such funding consisted of the names themselves. If they were entitled to set off any claims they might have against Lloyd's, the collection of the full assessment would be deferred until those claims could be adjudicated. The pay now sue later clause was designed to enable Equitas to be fully funded immediately. That would work to the benefit of the names by giving them surer, earlier, and fuller reinsurance. In exchange it was reasonable to ask them to postpone the enforcement of any claims they might have against Lloyd's. Instead Lloyd's has had to prosecute these suits and many like them to collect from the names. Were it not for the pay now sue later clause, many other names might have forced Lloyd's into collection litigation as well.

In these circumstances the clause did not violate international due process or, we add unnecessarily, domestic due process. It is the same procedure used by federal law when a firm withdraws from a multiemployer pension plan—the firm is required to pay the plan administrator's assessment of the firm's share of vested but unfunded benefits and to reserve any objections for a subsequent suit, Multiemployer Pension Plan Amendments Act, 29 U.S.C. §§ 1399(c)(2), 1401(d); *Robbins v. Pepsi-Cola Metropolitan Bottling Co.*, 800 F.2d 641, 642 (7th Cir. 1986) (per curiam)—and this procedure ("pay now, dispute later," *id.*) has survived due process challenge, see, e.g., *Debreceni v. Merchants Terminal Corp.*, 889 F.2d 1, 3-4 (1st Cir. 1989). Anyway the question is not whether Lloyd's accorded due process to the names, but whether the English courts did. All they did was enforce the clause, and they did so on the basis of an interpretation of a provision of the original contract between the names and Lloyd's that authorized Lloyd's to take measures unilaterally to prevent the society from failing. Stated differently, the courts held that the names had waived their procedural rights in advance, thus bringing the case within the rule of *D.H. Overmyer Co. v. Frick Co.*, 405 U.S. 174 (1972). That case upheld against a due process challenge similar to that mounted by the names in this case the enforcement of a cognovit note, by which a debtor consents in advance to the creditor's obtaining a judgment against him on the note without notice or hearing, and possibly even—to make the analogy to the present case even closer—with the appearance on the debtor's behalf, to confess judgment, of an attorney designated by the creditor. *Id.* at 176. The English courts' interpretation of the original contract with the names as authorizing the pay now sue later clause could not be thought so unreasonable an interpretation of that contract as to take the case out from under *Overmyer* by demonstrating the absence of a genuine waiver. And this is to assume that reasonableness in contract interpretation could ever be a component of due process, which we greatly doubt, as we're about to explain.

The rationale for the conclusive-evidence clause, and for the denial of full discovery regarding the accuracy of the assessment, is similar to the rationale for the pay now sue later clause. If the names could resist ponying up the assessment until its accuracy was determined by the normal process of litigation, with pretrial discovery followed by pretrial motions and by trial, the funding of Equitas would be delayed. But this clause does more than postpone claims by the names; it extinguishes them by shrinking the names' entitlement to a right to the rectification of only those errors that leap out from the assessment figure itself with no right to pretrial discovery to search out possible errors in the actuarial or other assumptions that generated the figure. This extinction of rights could raise a question if what we are calling international due process had a substantive component. But the defendants do not argue that it does. Though we cannot find a case on the point, the cases that deal with international due process talk only of procedural rights. See, e.g., *Wilson v. Marchington, supra,* 127 F.3d at 811. The only substantive basis that the Uniform Foreign Money-Judgments Recognition Act recognizes for not enforcing a foreign judgment is that "the cause of action on which the judgment is based is repugnant to the public policy" of Illinois, 735

ILCS 5/12-621; see, e.g., *Ingersoll Milling Machine Co. v. Granger, supra,* 833 F.2d at 686-88; cf. *Loucks v. Standard Oil of New York,* 224 N.Y. 99, 120 N.E. 198, 201 (N.Y. 1918) (Cardozo, J.), a claim the plaintiffs have abandoned in this court.

If Parliament passed a law that the Equitas premium was whatever Lloyd's Council said it was, this would not be a denial of a procedural right of any of the names, but rather a revision of the substantive terms of the names' relation to Lloyd's. But if Parliament went further and precluded the names from challenging in court the applicability of the new law to them, that would be a curtailment of their procedural rights, and doubtless a deprivation of their property without due process of law. But this is not what happened. Lloyd's appointed agents to negotiate a contract binding the names that (they argue) was disadvantageous to them. It was disadvantageous in part because it reserved to Lloyd's a very broad discretion to fix the premium for the new reinsurance. But a one-sided contract is a substantive, not a procedural, offense. (Nor, to recur for a moment to the pay now sue later clause, is an unreasonable contractual interpretation a procedural violation.) The names were free both to challenge the clause and to show if they could "manifest error" in the assessment of their liability under it. They could not show this, but only because manifest error is hard to prove. It would have to be an error that was obvious because of the disproportion between the reinsurance premium levied by Lloyd's and the risk to which the particular name would be exposed if he lacked reinsurance. Their real objection to the exclusive-evidence clause, moreover, is that it curtails pretrial discovery, and the right to pretrial discovery is not a part of the U.S. concept of due process, * * * let alone of international due process. See, e.g., Hague Convention, art. 23 (reprinted at 28 U.S.C. § 1781); *Panama Processes, S.A. v. Cities Service Co.,* 500 F. Supp. 787, 800 (S.D.N.Y. 1980), aff'd, 650 F.2d 408 (2d Cir. 1981).

And again the key question is not the fairness of Lloyd's measures but the fairness of the English court in holding that Lloyd's was authorized by its contract with the names to appoint agents to negotiate a contract that would bind the names without the names' consent. This interpretation of the original contract, like the interpretation authorizing Lloyd's to adopt the pay now sue later clause, is not so unreasonable that it could be thought a denial of international due process even if international due process had a substantive component.

We conclude that the judgments are enforceable under the foreign money-judgments statute. * * * [Affirmed.]

NOTES AND QUESTIONS FOR DISCUSSION

1. In *Ashenden*, Judge Posner notes that the Illinois foreign country money judgments statute requires a foreign judgment to be the product of a system that comports with due process, yet concludes that a foreign judgment need not comply with every aspect of due process that might apply in U.S. proceedings. What, exactly, is the distinction? Did the Illinois legislature mean to incorporate the rougher (i.e., a somewhat watered-down) notion of due process associated with what Judge Posner calls "international due process"? See also *In re* Treco, 240 F.3d 148, 157-59 (2d Cir. 2001) (concluding that Bahamian insolvency proceedings were "fair," "impartial," and "procedurally sound," despite deviations from domestic (U.S.) law).

2. The court seems concerned that if domestic due process standards were applied to foreign judgments, it would be the rare foreign judgment that would be enforceable. Does it make more sense to assume that the state legislature would *not* have wanted such a result, despite the language in the statute? If it makes sense to apply only a rough (rather than strict) due process check on foreign judgments, does it make sense for U.S. courts to refuse to enforce judgments in which the basis for personal jurisdiction failed to comport with U.S. due process standards? Or for U.S. courts to refuse enforcement of judgments with procedures even marginally less friendly to the First Amendment than those in the U.S.?

3. The right to trial by jury in civil cases in federal courts is guaranteed by the Seventh Amendment and in the state courts by state constitutional provisions. It will be infrequent that a U.S. state or federal court is asked to enforce a foreign civil judgment in which there was a right to trial by jury. Would such a failure run afoul of due process? Of rough due process?

4. *Ashenden* effectively requires a court to assess the capacity of the legal system that rendered the judgment, and it distinguishes between "civilized" systems and other less civilized systems. Is there anything problematic about a U.S. court making such an assessment of foreign legal institutions? For a suggestion that there is, see Montré D. Carodine, *Political Judging: When Due Process Goes International*, 48 Wm. & Mary L. Rev. 1159 (2007) (urging application of U.S. due process standards in individual cases rather than "international due process").

NOTE ON U.S. RECOGNITION OF FOREIGN TAX AND PENAL JUDGMENTS

The UFCMJA does not apply—inter alia—to foreign country judgments for fines, penalties, and forfeitures. In addition, according to § 483 of the Restatement (Third) of Foreign Relations Law of the United States (1987), courts in the U.S. are not required to recognize or to enforce judgments for the collection of taxes, fines, or penalties by the courts of other countries. Although it has been acknowledged that neither U.S. law nor international law would be violated if such judgments were recognized or enforced, most American courts have refused to do so. See, e.g., Her Majesty the Queen in Right of the Province of British Columbia v. Gilbertson, 597 F. 2d 1161 (9th Cir. 1979). A similar practice generally prevails even as among the states of the U.S., at least as regards sister-state judgments for fines and penalties, the Full Faith and Credit Act (and Clause) notwithstanding. Nevertheless, the Supreme Court has held that the Clause requires states to enforce sister state judgments for taxes. See Milwaukee County v. M.E. White Co., 296 U.S. 268 (1935) (leaving open question whether full faith and credit would have to be given to judgments for penalties or fines). But full faith and credit obviously cannot compel a similar result in the setting of foreign tax judgments.

What is the rationale for the nonenforcement of foreign judgments for fines, taxes, or penalties? Consider the explanation offered by Judge Learned Hand:

> To pass upon the provisions for the public order of another state is, or at any rate should be, beyond the powers of a court; it involves the relations between the states themselves, with which courts are incompetent to deal, and which are entrusted to other authorities. It may commit the domestic state to a position which would seriously embarrass its neighbor. Revenue laws fall within the same reasoning; they affect a state in matters as vital to its existence as its criminal laws. No court ought to undertake an inquiry which it cannot prosecute without determining whether those laws are consonant with its own notions of what is proper.

Moore v. Mitchell, 30 F.2d 600, 604 (2d Cir. 1929) (Hand, J., concurring), aff'd on other grounds, 281 U.S. 18 (1930).

Is the explanation convincing? Perhaps having one state enforce the penal laws of another sovereign in the first instance is problematic. But is it equally problematic, once the dispute has been reduced to a money judgment? Does a court "seriously embarrass" another state or nation by evaluating the enforceability of its penal or tax laws? If so, isn't the application of the general rule—i.e., the wholesale refusal to enforce *any* foreign judgment in the tax or penal setting—more damaging than the enforcement of some of such judgments? Consider also the following comment that perhaps casts additional doubt on the rule as it applies to tax judgments:

> Although the rule as commonly stated treats tax and penal judgments alike, the considerations concerning foreign tax judgments are different from those for penal judgments. In an age when virtually all states impose and collect taxes and when instantaneous transfer of assets can be easily arranged, the rationale for not recognizing or enforcing tax judgments is largely obsolete.

Restatement (Third), at § 483, Reporters' Note 2. See also *Milwaukee County, supra*. Despite these considerations, courts continue to decline the enforcement of foreign country tax judgments. However, courts may be inclined to enforce a portion of a judgment if it is based on acts giving rise to both criminal and civil liability. There are civil law systems, such as France, which allow an injured party to pursue civil claims by joining such claims in criminal proceedings against the defendant. Thus, the civil portion of such a decision—based, for example, on reckless conduct of the defendant—may be enforceable even though it is embodied in a penal judgment. See Reporters' Note 4 to § 483.

E. U.S. JUDGMENTS AND FOREIGN PUBLIC POLICY CONCERNS

In this section, we will focus on two American judgments whose enforcement was sought in German courts. As discussed below, German courts decide recognition and enforcement matters on the basis of German federal procedural law. In many cases, the applicable legal standards derive from international treaty obligations that Germany has assumed by way of bilateral arrangements. See, e.g., The Treaty between the Federal Republic of Germany and the State of Israel Concerning the Mutual Recognition and Enforcement of Judgments in

Civil and Commercial Matters of July 20, 1977. At other times, they arise from multilateral conventions. See, e.g., the Brussels Convention (now replaced by the Brussels Regulation) that governs the recognition and enforcement of judgments in the European Union (discussed below). In relation to money judgments emanating from American courts, however, such treaty obligations do not exist, and German procedural default rules—German (federal) Zivilprozessordnung (German Code of Civil Procedure—"ZPO"—apply instead. (Note that although we have selected two German decisions, other countries enforcing U.S. judgments would ordinarily apply their own (forum) procedural rules in deciding questions of recognition and enforcement.)

Sections 722 and 723 of the ZPO govern the enforcement phase, while ZPO § 328 addresses the recognition of foreign judgments. ZPO § 722(1) requires that the execution of a foreign judgment be authorized through a German court decision. According to ZPO § 723(1), the German court issuing this decision, must not reexamine the "legality" ("Gesetzmäßigkeit"), that is, the merits of the foreign judgment. Further, according to ZPO § 723(2), the foreign judgment must be final and its recognition must not be prohibited by any of the five reasons set out in ZPO § 328.

German Code of Civil Procedure [ZPO] § 328

(1) The recognition of a foreign court is excluded

1. if the courts of the state to which the foreign court belongs have no jurisdiction under German law;

2. if the defendant who has not argued the case on the merits and raises this plea, has not been served with the document that instituted the proceedings in the required manner or not so timely that he could defend himself;

3. if the judgment is irreconcilable with a judgment rendered here or with an earlier foreign judgment which must be recognized here …;

4. if the recognition of the judgment would lead to a result that is patently irreconcilable with fundamental principles of German law, particularly, if recognition would be irreconcilable with the Basic (i.e. Constitutional) Rights;

5. if reciprocity is not ensured. * * *

Compare this statutory scheme with the provisions of the Uniform Foreign-Country Money Judgments Recognition Act, discussed above in Section B. Does a textual comparison of these two sets of provisions indicate which regime is more lenient on foreign judgments? In what respects?

The following two cases address primarily questions of German public policy under ZPO § 328(1) No. 4. The first case involved a compensatory damages award handed down by a Massachusetts jury in a products liability action. The decision by a lower court in Berlin to reject enforcement of the award epitomizes the public policy concerns that American judgments encounter abroad. In the second case, the German Federal Supreme Court had to decide whether an American judgment containing both compensatory and punitive damages could be enforced in Germany. While finding the compensatory components of the American judgment were enforceable, and thereby articulating a much more lenient view than the lower court in Berlin, the German Supreme Court held that enforcement of the punitive damages portion would violate German public policy.

Re the Enforcement of a U.S. Judgment

Before the Landgericht (District Court), Berlin (20th Civil Chamber), 1992.
Case 20.0.314/88, 3 Int. Lit. Proc. 430.

Facts, Proceedings and Argument

In July 1967, the defendant, at that time trading as a limited partnership, supplied to another firm a machine designed to stamp information on to electronic components and powered by a motor of American manufacture. The female plaintiff was employed by the latter firm as an operator of the machine.

On 8 October 1975, in the course of her work, the plaintiff switched off the machine in order to retrieve an electronic component which had fallen inside it from the main plate. In searching for the component, she unintentionally restarted the motor and, as a result, a swiveling arm descended and trapped her right wrist against the machine's main plate.

Following immediate medical treatment for a swollen wrist, which did not involve hospitalization, the plaintiff on 14 November 1975 underwent surgery necessitated by the appearance of the symptoms of carpal tunnel syndrome. She returned to work on 6 July 1976.

In subsequent proceedings in the U.S. State of Massachusetts under a 'warranty claim' pursuant to the law of that State, the plaintiff on 24 January 1985 obtained judgment against the defendant in the Superior Court, Middlesex for the sum of $275,000 plus interest of $207,905.50, making a total award of $482,905.50. On an appeal by the defendant, the judgment was upheld by the Supreme Judicial Court of Massachusetts. The Superior Court, Middlesex, in a writ of execution, awarded the plaintiff an additional sum of $177,392.61 in respect of further interest and costs.

In 1988, the plaintiff brought an action against the defendant before the Landgericht (District Court) in Berlin, seeking an order for compulsory enforcement of the Massachusetts judgment and payment of further interest thereon at 12 per cent. per annum pursuant to that judgment.

The plaintiff relied upon the fact that the function of her right hand had been reduced by 35 per cent. and that of her right arm by 46 per cent., that her own contributory negligence had been assessed by the Massachusetts court at only 5 per cent., and that the operation in November 1975 had been necessitated by the accident.

The defendant, in resisting the order sought, drew attention to certain alleged irregularities in the authentication, translation and interpretation of the documents exhibited by the plaintiff and asserted that the Massachusetts judgment of 24

January 1985 was in various respects contrary to the German *ordre public*. Also, on the basis of an up-to-date medical report, the defendant disputed that the carpal tunnel syndrome suffered by the plaintiff was a direct or indirect consequence of the accident and asserted that the plaintiff's loss of function in the right hand was less than that relied upon by her and in any event arose out of the surgical treatment of the carpal tunnel syndrome or of inadequate post-operative treatment.

JUDGMENT

This action—admissible in accordance with sections 722 and 723 of the Code of Civil Procedure—which is directed at obtaining an order for enforcement of the judgment of 24 January 1985 is not well-founded.

In so holding, the Court proceeds on the assumption that the judgment has become final and absolute on the basis of the judgment of the Supreme Court of Massachusetts. Nor does it entertain any substantial doubts that the documents lodged represent a foreign judgment which is amenable to an order for enforcement. The judgment of 24 January 1985 in particular, which is what primarily matters, has obviously been lodged in an authenticated copy. It emerges there from that, in any event, $275,000 plus interest at 12 per cent. as from 6 October 1978, that is, as from the time when the action was filed, must be paid. Interest is then again awarded at 12 per cent. on the whole of the overall sum of $482,905.50 which is apparent from the judgment, even though that sum already contains an element of interest. Furthermore, no misgivings arise from the fact that the documents are signed by an 'Assistant' or 'Deputy Assistant' who is to be compared in his function with a judicial official. Regard is to be had solely on whether some foreign court has reached the judgment. Who is competent by virtue of his function is irrelevant, so long as an independent judge has been involved. This involvement was here ensured even at first instance by the judge.

Nor does the Court have any substantial misgivings as to the fact that individual documents have not been lodged, or have only belatedly been lodged, in authenticated German translation. Under section 184 of the Constitution of Courts Act, the language of the courts is German. It must be assumed that, as a result of the proceedings conducted in America, the defendant was already familiar with all the documents. Moreover, individual errors of translation do not preclude comprehension of the documents. Thus, for instance, there has not been incorporated into the translation of the underlying judgment of 24 January 1985 a breakdown of the total sum to be paid. The breakdown emerges, however, from the exhibited document K 1 itself.

Furthermore, the rule contained in section 328(1)(i) of the Code of Civil Procedure does not pose any obstacle to the making of an order to enforce as sought. Under this rule, such order would have to be refused, if, under German law, the foreign court had no jurisdiction. The jurisdiction of the foreign court, however, follows here from the standpoint of the special rule awarding jurisdiction to the court for the place of commission of a tort under section 32 of the Code of Civil Procedure. It is sufficient in this respect that, in any event, the injury has come about in the United States. Whenever any factual ingredient occurs at the foreign place in question, there is in this respect a foundation for the rule as to jurisdiction under section 32 of the Code of Civil Procedure. It is not decisive in this respect that, here, enforcement is being sought of the judgment relating to the 'warranty claim,' and not of the judgment relating to the 'negligence claim.' It is true that the 'warranty claim' relates to a sort of contractual liability for an assurance, and not to any tortuous liability in the narrower sense. The concept of a tortuous act within the meaning of section 32 of the Code of Civil Procedure must, however, be understood in a wider sense. It includes, for instance, claims on the basis of statutory liability for putting someone at risk. The 'warranty claim' here asserted corresponds to such a claim. It includes, irrespective of the parties to the contract site of sale, all natural and legal persons as persons entitled to claim, and personal injury as well as damage to property, and moreover permits a claim against the manufacturer. In accordance with German notions, this corresponds to a claim in tort in the wider sense.

The reciprocity of recognition of judgments is also guaranteed in relations between the Federal Republic of Germany, including West Berlin, and the U.S. State of Massachusetts. The enforcement of German judgments is not substantially more difficult in Massachusetts than, vice versa, the enforcement of an American judgment in Germany. In 1966, Massachusetts, together with eight other U.S. States, adopted the Uniform Foreign Money Recognition Act of 1962, on condition that reciprocity was guaranteed. This Act applies to foreign judgment which are final and conclusive. This corresponds to German procedure. Under the practice in Massachusetts, the foreign judgment moreover has its full effect, even when it is not a judgment which would have been given under local law. It must be proved by the production of authenticated copies of the court documents. Enforcement does not take place until a copy of the documents certified by means of the court seal is lodged. It must therefore be assumed that there is a guarantee of reciprocity. * * *

The general *ordre public* examination under section 328(1)(iv) of the Code of Civil Procedure which ultimately remains leads to the result that enforcement of the judgment of 24 January 1985 in the Federal Republic of Germany and West Berlin is not permissible. This arises from various aspects. First, it is noticeable that the judgment at first instance which is sought to be enforced does not contain any written reasoning. In the reasoning in support of the judgment on appeal, moreover, only the various objections raised by the defendant are discussed. What is, however, missing, for instance, is any general account as to how it was ascertained that the defendant was at fault and as to what circumstances played a part in the determination in relation to the respective contributions to causation. There is not a word as to the extent of the injury ascertained. While the absence of written reasons for the judgment is not in itself contrary to the German *ordre public*, the resultant uncertainties mitigate against the plaintiff as the party which was victorious in the foreign proceedings. Insofar as one can to some extent fall back upon the grounds recited in support of the appellate judgment, the latter shows that, ultimately, the conclusion is drawn from the fact of the occurrence of damage that there was a breach of duty by the defendant. This is made clear in the passage in the appellate judgment which deals with possible theories about the fault in construction. What is being discussed there is the arrangement of the on-off rocker switch or of possible protective devices projecting above it as well as a protective device over the swiveling arm of the machine. This accords with the American case law, which, contrary to the principles of a German manufacturer's liability under section 823 et seq. of the Civil Code, affirms the existence of liability once a product does not work as safely as the ordinary user/consumer is entitled to expect, or once the manufacturer fails to choose a construction which is conceivable on the basis of the possibilities for construction and which is—on balance—safe, and which can reasonably be required of him. It is then enough that—without evidence of a 'fault' having to be given—circumstances are set out which have led to the accident, in so far as grounds emerge there from for holding that the cause of the accident was a fault in the product. Therein lies something which is contrary to German *ordre public*. First, there are only conceivable—not even expressly ascertained—causes for the injury. Secondly, with regard to the conceivable causes, breach of duty is at the same time presumed. All of this is contrary to the fundamental notions of German liability and insurance law; it would, if it were to be enforceable in the Federal Republic of Germany, result in a serious encroachment upon the defendant's right of property and upon the right to conduct an established and operational commercial enterprise.

There are also further aspects which support the proposition that there is an infringement of German *ordre public*. One, in particular, is the calculation of interest, which, in violation of section 289 of the Civil Code, is carried out in such a way that interest is calculated upon interest. This emerges from the mere fact that, in the further award of interest on the amounts arising out of the judgment of 24 January 1985 as a base figure, actual amounts of interest in the sum of $207,905.50 are included as a base figure, on which then, in future, further interest at 12 per cent. is calculated. Further aspects supporting an infringement of *ordre public* arise from the size of the sum of $275,000 originally awarded. This sum is many times in excess of sums which would have been paid in a comparable case in Germany. Its composition has neither been explained in more detail nor can it be otherwise ascertained. Finally, regard must be had to the apparently arbitrary assessment of a contribution to causation of 95 per cent. against the defendant. How this has been arrived at is likewise neither explained nor can it be ascertained. So far as can be seen, the fact that the plaintiff herself switched the machine off, then reached into the machine and thereby set in motion the chain of causation which led to the injury is not gone into in more detail. The plaintiff knew the machine, on which she had apparently worked for some time. Taking account of these circumstances would under German law have led to the allocation of a considerable degree of contributory causation or of contributory blameworthiness, and possibly to the complete exclusion of liability. Finally, it remained to take account of the fact that the judgment of 24 January 1985 was clearly preceded by 'pre-trial discovery' proceedings. Such a procedure is represented by German standards as evidence obtained by investigation of the other party's case. In itself, the application of this procedure is not contrary to *ordre public*. Having regard, however, to the other aspects referred to, the result is an overall unequivocal infringement of German *ordre public*.

This leads in this case to the dismissal of the action as a whole, and not—as [sometimes] suggested—to the award of a sum which is capable of enforcement.

The awarding of a sum capable of recognition would actually lead to the result that the foreign judgment is subjected to German rules. Moreover, it follows from the above discussions that, in particular in relation to the aspect of the here criticized conclusion in the American judgment, on the basis of the fact of the occurrence of injury, the defendant was found to be responsible, and in relation to the aspect of the in any event predominant contributory fault by the plaintiff, no sum would be left over to be awarded.

Action dismissed with costs.

NOTES AND QUESTIONS FOR DISCUSSION

1. There is no treaty arrangement between the U.S. and Germany that provides for the mutual recognition of money judgments. Therefore, Federal German law—the Code of Civil Procedure (ZPO)—applies instead. Under ZPO § 723, a German court faced with an action for enforcement of a final foreign judgment may not reexamine the judgment on its merits. One exception to this principle is set forth in ZPO § 328(1) No. 4. Recognition will be denied if, particularly in view of basic constitutional rights, it would lead to a result that would be clearly incompatible with fundamental principles of German law. This public policy clause (*ordre public*) is considered a solution of last resort that only applies in extreme cases. Thus, in principle, even if a foreign court relies on rules that deviate from German law, the resulting judgment could still be held enforceable. Did the Berlin court abide by this principle in the above decision? The court cited a number of reasons for its holding, which are discussed in the following notes.

2. In Germany, as in virtually all other legal systems, cases involving civil litigation are decided by professional judges rather than juries, and judges are required to provide reasons for their decision. But what is the harm of not having written reasons accompanying a jury verdict? After all, juries do not give reasons for their their verdicts, and it had been upheld on appeal before the Massachusetts Supreme Judicial Court in Solimene v. B. Grauel & Co., K.G., 507 N.E. 2d 662 (1987). And that court *did* supply a comprehensive opinion on the issues involved in the case.

3. Why does the warranty cause of action, which does not require a showing of the defendant's fault, pose a problem for German public policy? Although it is true that the threshold for the imposition of liability tends to be lower in the U.S. than in Germany, can it really be said that fundamental German legal principles are at stake? Note that at the time the case was decided, German courts applied the principle of *res ipsa loquitur* in certain tort cases, thus requiring the defendant to prove that it acted without fault.

4. The Berlin court also took issue with the amount of damages handed down by the American tribunal. What should be the gauge for measuring excessive damages in an American court? German standards? Would this comport with the principle of refraining from reexamining the merits of the foreign decision? The amount of damages is usually a question of fact, and whether there is sufficient evidence for such an award is a question of law. Even if the amount is deemed to be incompatible with German fundamental legal principles, is it appropriate for the German court to declare the entire damages award to be unenforceable? Consider whether it might have made more sense to have enforced at least a portion of that award. What reasons does the court give for denying partial enforcement of the award?

5.   Rightly or wrongly, American discovery procedures are perceived as intrusive fishing expeditions—not only in Germany, but throughout the world. Nevertheless, is it justified to view the American way of taking evidence in domestic proceedings as an obstacle to judgment enforcement abroad? If your answer is yes, consider whether any American judgment could ever be enforced abroad. The decision by the Berlin court was appealed, and it was reportedly settled in the courthouse, outside the judges' chambers.

Re the Enforcement of a U.S. Judgment

Before the Bundesgerichtshof (German Federal Supreme Court), 1992.

Case IX ZR 149/91. *Reprinted in* [1994] I.L. Pr. 602.

[Three years after the Berlin District court had rejected enforcement of the Massachusetts judgment, the request for the enforcement of another American judgment came before the German Federal Supreme Court.[1] This case involved the enforcement of American damage award rendered against a defendant with dual American and German citizenship. The defendant had earlier been found guilty on criminal charges of sexual misconduct, and was sentenced to a long prison term in California. He avoided the criminal sentence by moving to Germany, but prior to his departure, the plaintiff-victim served a civil summons and complaint on the defendant in an action filed with the San Joaquin County Superior Court in California. The defendant failed to appear at trial, and judgment was entered in favor of the plaintiff in the amount of $750,260, of which $150,260 was for past and future medical expenses, $200,000 for anxiety, pain, and suffering, and $400,000 as punitive damages. Contrary to the Berlin District court, the German Federal Supreme Court took a significantly more lenient approach towards the American judgment. Premised on the view that German law prescribes a high level of tolerance in enforcement proceedings, the Supreme Court ruled out a blanket rejection of American judgments that are preceded by full-fledged discovery. It also held that neither the award for pain and suffering nor that for uncertain future medical expenses violated German public policy. The holding is noteworthy because a plaintiff suing under German law would not have received more than about one tenth of the pain and suffering award, and would have received no award for what are considered speculative medical costs which may or may not be incurred in the future. Although the Court thus exhibited great deference to the compensatory components of the foreign judgment, it rejected the enforcement of the punitive damages award. The central arguments of the Court are excerpted below]:

---

[1]   *Re* the Enforcement of a United States Judgment for Damages, Case IX ZR 149/91 (1992), reprinted in English in 5 Intern. Lit. Rep. 602 (1994) and 32 I.L.M. 1320 (1993).

[T]he American concept of punitive damages is characterised by the main motives of punishment and deterrence. (ALI, *Enterprise Responsibility for Personal Injury*, Vol. II, pp. 231, 236, 247, Madden, *Products Liability* (2d ed.) p. 316, Kionka, *Torts in a Nutshell* p. 374, Fleming, *The American Tort Process,* 214, Zekoll, *US-Amerikanisches Produkthaftpflichtrecht vor deutschen Gerichten*: *Produkthaftpflichtrecht,* pp. 152 *et seq.,* 156, and 37 Am. J. Comp. L. at 325 *et seq.*) It is historically derived from those motives, and they are still a factor in the quantification of such damages in present times. The only relevant precondition is the heightened degree of the fault alleged. The absence of any specific right of the injured party to claim them demonstrates the subordinate significance of his private interests. Furthermore, since there is no measurable general relationship between the sums of money to be assessed and the injury suffered, considerations of compensation are generally subordinate.

On that basis, it is clearly incompatible with essential principles of German law to grant enforcement in this country of punitive damages awarded as a lump-sum to any significant level.

The essential principles of German law include the principle of proportionality, which follows from that of the rule of law, and is also applicable in the civil legal system. Account is taken of it in civil law *inter alia* by reference to considerations of compensation in the assessment of damages: generally speaking, the equalisation of the immediate parties' property relationships upset by an unlawful infringement is the only proper objective of the civil action brought in respect of the infringement. * * *

By contrast, according to German concepts sanctions serving to punish and deter—that is to say, to protect the legal system in general—in principle fall within the state's monopoly on punishment. The state exercises the monopoly in the public interest by means of a special type of proceeding, in which on the one hand investigation by the court of its own authority is intended to provide a greater guarantee of the correctness of the decision on matters of fact, and on the other hand the rights of the defendants are more strongly protected. From the German viewpoint it would not be acceptable for a civil judgment to order the payment of a considerable sum of money which does not serve to compensate for injury, but is essentially assessed on the basis of the public interest and could possibly be imposed in addition to a criminal penalty for the same conduct.

In the final analysis that is the position in the present case. The amount of punitive damages awarded is higher than the total of all the sums awarded by way of compensation. Even that proportion of it that is ascribable to the lawyer's fee could only amount to about one-third of the "punitive damages". There is no evidence of any other injury for which compensation was required. That means that enforcement would have excessive effects for the defendant.

In the U.S. "punitive damages" awarded by courts in their discretion without a fixed relationship to the injury suffered and sometimes awarded at an excessively high level have had the effect of contributing to a rapid increase in the burden of compensation in economic terms, going to the limits of calculable and insurable risk. (*cf.* Zekoll, *Produkthaftpflichtrecht,* pp. 84, 155; Hoechst, [1983] VersR at 15; * * *).

From a German viewpoint, the motives alien to civil law and the absence of sufficiently precise and reasonable limits in the case of recognition of such judgments are calculated to destroy all the domestic standards of civil liability. On the basis of such judgments, foreign creditors could have access to the assets of debtors in this country to an extent many times greater than that available to domestic creditors, who in certain circumstances will have suffered substantially greater injury. Such preferential treatment solely for creditors from the few states in the world which allow for punitive damages as compared with all other creditors is not justified by considerations which give rise to a right to protection under the German legal system. For that reason alone the enforcement of a claim for lump-sum punitive damages (exceeding the compensation for all special and general losses) would be an insupportable consequence in Germany, so that the relatively slight connection of the present case with this country is by itself a reason to reject the application.

Accordingly, enforcement in Germany is ruled out in this respect. It is no longer necessary to decide whether the enforcement of punitive damages is contrary to German public policy for other reasons, too. In particular it is not necessary to decide whether the relatively undefined conditions for the award of "punitive damages" and for their quantification are subject to scrutiny under Article 103(2) of the Constitution, and whether the award of such damages in addition to a criminal penalty falls within the prohibition on double jeopardy from a German viewpoint (Article 103(3) of the Constitution). (*cf.* Zekoll, *Produkthaftpflichtrecht,* pp. 152 *et seq.;* Hoechst, *op. cit.,* [1983] VersR at 17).

The fact that the judgment of the Superior Court cannot be declared enforceable in Germany because of the punitive damages contained in it does not prevent its recognition in other respects. Contrary to the view set out in the appeal, the fact that the subject-matter of an enforcement order does not consist in the substantive law claim on which the foreign judgment is based but is determined by the creditor's application for the judgment to be enforced in this country does not make it necessary always to make a single order on the enforceability of a foreign judgment for the payment of damages covering the total sum awarded. If a foreign judgment allows several legally independent claims, it is also possible for each to be examined individually to see whether the conditions for its recognition are satisfied. In so far as they are not satisfied for all the claims, partial recognition for a lesser sum is possible without it being necessary for the applicant to take account of that possibility in his application. (Geimer, IZPR, n. 2294; Zoller/Geimer, *ZPO* (17th ed.) s.328, n.285; Zekoll: *Produkthaftpftichtrecht,* p. 37, and 37 Am.J.Comp.L. at 330; * * *.)

NOTES AND QUESTIONS FOR DISCUSSION

1. Despite its refusal to enforce the punitive damage award in this case, the Court suggested in dicta that such damages may be enforceable if they serve legitimate compensatory purposes:

> The position might possibly be different in so far as the imposition of punitive damages is intended to compensate by way of a lump-sum for residual economic disadvantages not specifically allowed for or difficult

to prove, or is for the purpose of depriving the tortfeasor of profits gained by his unlawful act. In this connection the passing on to the defendant of the costs of the action or other losses through non-payment which cannot be recovered independently is also a matter which generally arises for consideration.

[1994] I.L. Pr. 602, 630-631.

The "residual economic disadvantages," to which the Court refers, may include the attorney fees which successful plaintiffs owe their attorneys and which lead to a sizable reduction of the damages award. However, the Court's position is less generous than might appear at first glance. In contrast to the lower court and some commentators, the Court did not accept the proposition that one of the reasons for imposing punitive damages is invariably the intention to compensate plaintiffs for litigation costs and other incurred expenses. Consistent with its assessment of punitive damages as a means of punishing and deterring, the Court stated that it would allow enforcement only if the foreign decision provided evidence clearly indicative of the compensatory objective of the award.

The exception carved out by the Court appears, therefore, to be of relatively minor practical importance. It may apply to decisions rendered in those American jurisdictions that explicitly recognize compensation as a legitimate purpose for assessing punitive damages. Even these decisions, however, may not pass muster when they are based on general jury verdicts, because such verdicts might not spell out the basis for the award. And it is questionable whether jury instructions which designate compensation as one of several purposes would be recognized as sufficiently probative. The German Federal Court of Justice made clear that the judge in a German enforcement proceeding may not speculate as to whether compensatory motives played a role for the imposition of punitive damages. For a discussion of this decision, see Joachim Zekoll, *The Enforceability of American Money Judgments Abroad: A Landmark Decision by the German Federal Court of Justice*, 30 Colum. J. Transnat'l L. 641 (1992).

2. Finding that considerations of compensation play little or no role for the imposition of punitive damages, the German Supreme Court argued that "there is no measurable general relationship between the sums of money to be assessed and the injury suffered." Note that the U.S. Supreme Court has established, since then, heightened due process protections against excessive punitive damages. In BMW of North America, Inc. v. Gore, 517 U.S. 559 (1996), the Court held, among other things, that punitive damages awards must be both reasonable and proportionate in relation to the plaintiff's harm and to the general damages recovered. As a result, few awards exceeding a single-digit ratio between punitive and compensatory damages will satisfy due process. See also Exxon Shipping Co. v. Baker, 554 U.S. 471 (2008); State Farm Mutual Auto Ins. Co. v. Campbell, 538 U.S. 408 (2003). Reconsider the reasons the German Supreme Court advanced against enforcement. If faced with an American judgment that is in line with these more recently established American due process limits, would or should a German court enforce such a judgment? See also Phillip Morris USA v. Williams, 549 U.S. 346 (2007) (holding punitive damages award based in part on jury instructions that may have permitted jury to punish a defendant for having harmed nonparties to the litigation violated Due Process).

3. As in other civil law jurisdictions, the holding of the German Supreme Court is technically not binding on lower courts faced with similar issues. It is nevertheless safe to say that the Court's opinion will serve as an important guide post for future cases.

4. In a 1994 decision relating to The Hague Service Convention, the German Supreme Court stated in dicta that punitive damages seen in context are not necessarily a violation of German constitutional principles. The Court reasoned that they can be a means with which to shift attorney's fees, as well as a measure to make litigation affordable in especially egregious cases. See *Federal Constitutional Court Order Concerning Process of Punitive Damage Claims*, 1995 NJW 649, *reprinted and translated in* 34 I.L.M. 975, 993-994 (1995). The decision is excerpted and discussed in Chapter 4, Section E.

F. JUDGMENT RECOGNITION UNDER EUROPEAN UNION LAW

A plaintiff who has obtained a judgment in one member state of the European Union ordinarily does not encounter problems when seeking to enforce that judgment in another member state. Perhaps inspired by the full faith and credit provisions of federal law, the drafters of the EC Treaty realized that market integration in Europe not only requires the free movement of goods, persons, services and capital, but also depends on the liberal enforcement of judgments across borders. Until 2002, the Brussels Convention provided the legal framework for simple and speedy cross-border enforcement procedures. Since March 1, 2002, EU-Regulation 44/2001 (the "Brussels Regulation") has replaced the Convention. See Appendix D. Both the Convention and the Regulation pursue the twin goals of harmonizing the rules for the exercise of personal jurisdiction and those for the recognition and enforcement of judgments in the member states of the European Union.

In this section, we will discuss the cross-border recognition and enforcement of judgments in the European Union under the Brussels Convention/Regulation. While the Convention has been displaced by the Regulation, most of the changes have clarified rather than modified the recognition and enforcement provisions. It is therefore safe to predict that existing European Court of Justice case law interpreting the Convention will continue to serve as an important guidepost for deciding future recognition and enforcement disputes which will arise under the new Regulation.

The Regulation leaves no doubt about the drafters' intent to establish a simple and effective procedure designed to facilitate the "free movement" of judgments throughout the European Union. Article 32 provides a broad definition of what constitutes a judgment, "including a decree, order, decision or writ of execution, as well as the determination of costs or expenses by an officer of the court."

According to Regulation Article 33, "[a] judgment given in a Member State shall be recognised in the other Member States without any special procedure being required." Recognition does not require the finality of the judgment. However, Article 37 permits a court in which recognition is sought to stay the proceedings if the judgment is being appealed in the original forum. Articles 34 and 35 spell out the grounds for denying judgment recognition (see also Appendix D):

Article 34.

A judgment shall not be recognised:

1. if such recognition is manifestly contrary to public policy in the Member State in which recognition is sought;

2. where it was given in default of appearance, if the defendant was not duly served with the document which instituted the proceedings or with an equivalent document in sufficient time and in such a way as to enable

him to arrange for his defense, unless the defendant failed to commence proceedings to challenge the judgment when it was possible for him to do so;

3. if it is irreconcilable with a judgment given in a dispute between the same parties in the Member State in which recognition is sought;

4. if it is irreconcilable with an earlier judgment given in another Member State or in a third State involving the same cause of action and between the same parties, provided that the earlier judgment fulfils the conditions necessary for its recognition in the Member State addressed.

Article 35.

1. Moreover, a judgment shall not be recognised if it conflicts with the provisions of Sections 3, 4 or 6 of Chapter II [i.e. the special rules on insurance and consumer contracts as well as the rules on exclusive jurisdiction], or in a case provided for in Article 72.

2. In its examination of the grounds of jurisdiction referred to in the foregoing paragraph, the court or authority applied to shall be bound by the findings of fact on which the court of the Member State of origin based its jurisdiction.

3. Subject to the provisions of paragraph 1, the jurisdiction of the court of the Member State of origin may not be reviewed. The test of public policy referred to in point 1 of Article 34 may not be applied to the rules relating to jurisdiction.

Finally, Article 36 prohibits the relitigation of the merits of the foreign judgment: "Under no circumstances may a foreign judgment be reviewed as to its substance." However, the actual enforcement of the judgment in another Member State does require a second step. According to Article 38(1), "a judgment given in a Member State and enforceable in that State shall be enforced in another Member State when, on the application of any interested party, it has been declared enforceable there." This so-called *exequatur* procedure has been perceived by many observers as an unnecessary time-consuming and costly additional procedural layer. The revised Brussels I Regulation, which will apply from January 10, 2015 (see Chapter 5, Section B) abolishes the *exequatur* procedure and thus further facilitates and expedites the enforcement of foreign judgments within the European Union. However, even under the revised rules, the judgment debtor will still be entitled to raise certain procedural public policy objections to prevent the enforcement of the foreign judgment in extreme cases.

The following excerpt of the European Court of Justice decision in *Krombach v. Bamberski*, which was rendered on the basis of the almost identical Brussels Convention rules, illustrates the operation of the Brussels Regulation rules which are currently in effect:

Krombach v. Bamberski

Court of Justice of the European Communities, 2000.
Case C-7/98, 2000 E.C.R. I-01935.

The dispute in the main proceedings

* * *

12. Mr [Dieter] Krombach was the subject of a preliminary investigation in Germany following the death in Germany of a 14-year-old girl of French nationality. That preliminary investigation was subsequently discontinued.

13. In response to a complaint by Mr. [Andre] Bamberski, the father of the young girl, a preliminary investigation was opened in France, the French courts declaring that they had jurisdiction by virtue of the fact that the victim was a French national. At the conclusion of that investigation, Mr Krombach was, by judgment of the Chambre d'Accusation (Chamber of Indictments) of the Cour d'Appel de Paris (Paris Court of Appeal), committed for trial before the Cour d'Assises de Paris.

14. That judgment and notice of the introduction of a civil claim by the victim's father were served on Mr. Krombach. Although Mr. Krombach was ordered to appear in person, he did not attend the hearing. The Cour d'Assises de Paris thereupon applied the contempt procedure governed by Article 627 et seq. of the French Code of Criminal Procedure. Pursuant to Article 630 of that Code, under which no defence counsel may appear on behalf of the person in contempt, the Cour d'Assises reached its decision without hearing the defence counsel instructed by Mr. Krombach.

15. By judgment of 9 March 1995 the Cour d'Assises imposed on Mr. Krombach a custodial sentence of 15 years after finding him guilty of violence resulting in involuntary manslaughter. By judgment of 13 March 1995, the Cour d'Assises, ruling on the civil claim, ordered Mr. Krombach, again as being in contempt, to pay compensation to Mr. Bamberski in the amount of FRF 350 000.

16. On application by Mr. Bamberski, the President of a civil chamber of the Landgericht (Regional Court) Kempten (Germany), which had jurisdiction ratione loci, declared the judgment of 13 March 1995 to be enforceable in Germany. Following dismissal by the Oberlandesgericht (Higher Regional Court) of the appeal which he had lodged against that decision, Mr. Krombach brought an appeal on a point of law (Rechtsbeschwerde) before the Bundesgerichtshof in

which he submitted that he had been unable effectively to defend himself against the judgment given against him by the French court.

17. Those are the circumstances in which the Bundesgerichtshof decided to stay proceedings and to refer the following questions to the Court for a preliminary ruling:

> 1. May the provisions on jurisdiction form part of public policy within the meaning of Article 27, point 1, of the Brussels Convention [Art. 34, point 1 of the Regulation] where the State of origin has based its jurisdiction as against a person domiciled in another Contracting State * * * solely on the nationality of the injured party * * * ?

If Question 1 is answered in the negative:

> 2. May the court of the State in which enforcement is sought * * * take into account under public policy within the meaning of Article 27, point 1 of the Brussels Convention [Art. 34, point 1 of the Regulation] that the criminal court of the State of origin did not allow the debtor to be defended by a lawyer in a civil-law procedure for damages instituted within the criminal proceedings (Article II of the Protocol of 27 September 1968 on the interpretation of the Brussels Convention) because he, a resident of another Contracting State, was charged with an intentional offence and did not appear in person? * * *

The first question

29. By this question, the national court is essentially asking whether, regard being had to the public-policy clause contained in Article 27, point 1 of the Convention [Art. 34, point 1 of the Regulation], the court of the State in which enforcement is sought can, with respect to a defendant domiciled in that State, take into account the fact that the court of the State of origin based its jurisdiction on the nationality of the victim of an offence. * * *

31. Under the system of the Convention, with the exception of certain cases exhaustively listed in the first paragraph of Article 28 [Art. 35 of the Regulation], none of which corresponds to the facts of the case in the main proceedings, the court before which enforcement is sought cannot review the jurisdiction of the court of the State of origin. This fundamental principle, which is set out in the first phrase of the third paragraph of Article 28 of the Convention [Art. 35 of the Regulation], is reinforced by the specific statement, in the second phrase of the same paragraph, that 'the test of public policy referred to in point 1 of Article 27 [Art. 34 of the Regulation] may not be applied to the rules relating to jurisdiction.'

32. It follows that the public policy of the State in which enforcement is sought cannot be raised as a bar to recognition or enforcement of a judgment given in another Contracting State solely on the ground that the court of origin failed to comply with the rules of the Convention which relate to jurisdiction.

33. Having regard to the generality of the wording of the third paragraph of Article 28 of the Convention [Art. 35 of the Regulation], that statement of the law must be regarded as being, in principle, applicable even where the court of the State of origin wrongly founded its jurisdiction, in regard to a defendant

domiciled in the territory of the State in which enforcement is sought, on a rule which has recourse to a criterion of nationality.

34. The answer to the first question must therefore be that the court of the State in which enforcement is sought cannot, with respect to a defendant domiciled in that State, take account, for the purposes of the public-policy clause in Article 27, point 1, of the Convention [Art. 34, point 1 of the Regulation], of the fact, without more, that the court of the State of origin based its jurisdiction on the nationality of the victim of an offence.

The second question

35. By this question, the national court is essentially asking whether, in relation to the public-policy clause in Article 27, point 1 of the Convention [Art. 34, point 1 of the Regulation], the court of the State in which enforcement is sought can, with respect to a defendant domiciled in its territory and charged with an intentional offence, take into account the fact that the court of the State of origin refused to allow that defendant to have his defence presented unless he appeared in person.

36. By disallowing any review of a foreign judgment as to its substance, Article 29 [Art. 36 of the Regulation] * * * prohibits the court of the State in which enforcement is sought from refusing to recognise or enforce that judgment solely on the ground that there is a discrepancy between the legal rule applied by the court of the State of origin and that which would have been applied by the court of the State in which enforcement is sought had it been seised of the dispute. Similarly, the court of the State in which enforcement is sought cannot review the accuracy of the findings of law or fact made by the court of the State of origin.

37. Recourse to the public-policy clause in Article 27, point 1 of the Convention [Art. 34, point 1 of the Regulation], can be envisaged only where recognition or enforcement of the judgment delivered in another Contracting State would be at variance to an unacceptable degree with the legal order of the State in which enforcement is sought inasmuch as it infringes a fundamental principle. In order for the prohibition of any review of the foreign judgment as to its substance to be observed, the infringement would have to constitute a manifest breach of a rule of law regarded as essential in the legal order of the State in which enforcement is sought or of a right recognised as being fundamental within that legal order.

38. With regard to the right to be defended, to which the question submitted to the Court refers, this occupies a prominent position in the organisation and conduct of a fair trial and is one of the fundamental rights deriving from the constitutional traditions common to the Member States.

39. More specifically still, the European Court of Human Rights has on several occasions ruled in cases relating to criminal proceedings that, although not absolute, the right of every person charged with an offence to be effectively defended by a lawyer, if need be one appointed by the court, is one of the fundamental elements in a fair trial and an accused person does not forfeit entitlement to such a right simply because he is not present at the hearing [citing case law of the European Court of Human Rights].

40. It follows from that case-law that a national court of a Contracting State is entitled to hold that a refusal to hear the defence of an accused person who is not present at the hearing constitutes a manifest breach of a fundamental right. * * *

43. The Court has also held that, even though the Convention is intended to secure the simplification of formalities governing the reciprocal recognition and enforcement of judgments of courts or tribunals, it is not permissible to achieve that aim by undermining the right to a fair hearing.

44. [Therefore] recourse to the public-policy clause must be regarded as being possible in exceptional cases where the guarantees laid down in the legislation of the State of origin and in the Convention itself have been insufficient to protect the defendant from a manifest breach of his right to defend himself before the court of origin, as recognised by the ECHR. * * *

45. The answer to the second question must therefore be that the court of the State in which enforcement is sought can, with respect to a defendant domiciled in that State and prosecuted for an intentional offence, take account, in relation to the public-policy clause in Article 27, point 1 of the Convention [Art. 34, point 1 of the Regulation], of the fact that the court of the State of origin refused to allow that person to have his defence presented unless he appeared in person. * * *

NOTES AND QUESTIONS FOR DISCUSSION

1. According to Article 2(1) of the Convention (and the Regulation, which substitutes "Member State" for "Contracting State"), "persons domiciled in a Contracting State shall, whatever their nationality, be sued in the courts of that State." Mr. Krombach was domiciled in Germany. There are special jurisdictional rules which permit deviation from this principle. Article 5 of the Convention (and the Regulation) provides:

> A person domiciled in a Contracting State may, in another Contracting State, be sued:
>
> * * *
>
> 4. As regards a civil claim for damages or restitution which is based on an act giving rise to criminal proceedings, in the court seised of those proceedings, to the extent that that court has jurisdiction under its own law to entertain civil proceedings[.]

However, Article 3 prohibits plaintiffs from relying on certain exorbitant jurisdictional rules. They include Articles 14 and 15 of the French Civil Code that premise jurisdiction on the parties' nationality. See Chapter I, Section G.

If the French courts, by exercising jurisdiction on the basis of the victim's nationality, violated the Convention, why was such error in itself not a ground for denying the recognition of the judgment? The Court, finding no obstacle to recognition in this respect, focused on the language of Article 28 of the Convention (Art. 35 of the Regulation). Reread the text of that Article. Was it a wise decision by the drafters of the Convention to prohibit courts from reviewing the jurisdiction of the original court? By contrast, American courts called upon to enforce foreign judgments typically examine such jurisdictional questions. See Section C, above. Can you see an argument why either approach may be justified?

2. With a view towards facilitating the free movement of judgments to the greatest extent possible, the ECJ has consistently interpreted the public policy reservation in Article 27(1) of the Convention as a solution of last resort (see, e.g., Case C-145/86, Hoffmann v. Krieg, 1988 E.C.R. 645, paragraph 21; and Case C-78/95, Hendrikman and Feyen v. Magenta Druck & Verlag, 1996 E.C.R. I-4943, paragraph 23). Judgments premised on rules that merely differ from those applied in the enforcement state do not justify refusal of recognition. Instead, as formulated in paragraph 37 of the *Krombach* decision, recognition or enforcement cannot be refused unless it entailed a "manifest breach of a rule of law regarded as essential in the legal order of the State in which enforcement is sought or of a right recognised as being fundamental within that legal order." Note that the new body of law governing judgment recognition, the Brussels Regulation, embodies the Court's strict interpretation of public policy. While Article 27(1) of the Convention simply stated that a judgment must not be recognized if such recognition is contrary to the public policy of the enforcing Member State, the pertinent provision in the Regulation, Article 34(1), requires that the infringement "manifestly" violate the public policy of the Member State.

Despite the self-imposed high threshold, the Court invoked the public policy clause against the French decision in *Krombach*. It did so by drawing on its "fundamental rights" jurisprudence which, among other things, is informed by the European Convention for the Protection of Human Rights and Fundamental Freedoms (ECHR).

Although the European Union is not yet a party to the European Convention for the Protection of Human Rights and Fundamental Freedoms, Article 6(2) of the Treaty on European Union calls for such accession. Furthermore, Article 6(3) acknowledges the relevance of that Convention by providing that "[f]undamental rights, as guaranteed by the . . . Convention . . . and as they result from the constitutional traditions common to the Member States, shall constitute general principles of the Union's law." Even prior to the enactment of this provision, the Court has cited fundamental rights in a variety of cases. In this respect, it has repeatedly relied on the European Convention and constitutional traditions of the Member States. For example, in a case involving an administrative decision not to renew a contract of a female police officer in Northern Ireland for reasons of public safety, the Court invoked Articles 6 and 13 of the European Convention to hold that judicial review of such decisions must be available; see Case C-222/84, Johnston v. Chief Constable of the Royal Ulster Constabulary, 1986 E.C.R. 1651. How would an American Court resolve the public policy question in *Krombach*?

3. In the fall of 2009, Andre Bamberski arranged for the kidnapping of Dieter Krombach in Germany so that he could be tried in France for murdering his daughter. Krombach fought to have the case dismissed arguing that the German authorities' decision to drop the case for lack of evidence was conclusive in this matter and did not allow for a retrial in France. Krombach also argued that a retrial should be rejected as it would be the consequence of a crime committed through his illegal abduction. In 2011, however, a French court decided that Mr. Krombach must stand trial for the 1982 death of Mr. Bamberski's daughter.

———————————————

CHAPTER 9

International Arbitration

A. INTRODUCTION

Arbitration is a type of alternative dispute resolution (ADR) that enables parties to have their disputes resolved out of court by a binding and enforceable decision rendered by one or more private (i.e. non-governmental) arbitrators chosen by the parties. Today, a majority of transnational commercial contracts contain an arbitration clause pursuant to which the parties agree to resolve future disputes arising out of the contract by way of arbitration.

There are several reasons for the popularity of this ADR device, particularly in the international realm: Importantly, the language of arbitral proceedings may be determined by the parties. By contrast, judicial proceedings in court will be conducted in the language of the country where the case is pending. Also, as opposed to judicial proceedings which do not permit the parties to choose particular judges, parties entering into an arbitration agreement are free to choose experts as decision makers. That choice is perceived as a great advantage over ordinary litigation, particularly in complex and technical subject matter areas which are best understood by experts in the field at issue. Commercial entities, furthermore, appreciate the confidentiality of the non-public arbitration proceedings and the non-public results that they produce. Whether, as has often been argued, arbitration is actually cheaper and less lengthy than proceedings in court, may be debatable as arbitration proceedings can become quite lengthy and thus expensive as well.

One thing that particularly sets arbitration apart from court cases, however, is that arbitral awards are generally final and easily enforceable in the transnational context. There is ordinarily no appeal and the likelihood that an award will be enforced abroad is much higher than is the likelihood of the enforcement of an American court judgment outside the U.S. judicial system. The ease of enforceability of arbitral awards is, in large part, due to the 1958 Convention on the Recognition and Enforcement of Foreign Arbitral Awards (the so called "New York Convention" (see Appendix E)), an instrument drafted by the United Nations Commission on International Trade Law ("UNCITRAL"). Since its entry into force in 1959, a total of 148 nations have become parties to the Convention. As stated on the official UNCITRAL website,

> The Convention's principal aim is that foreign and non-domestic arbitral awards will not be discriminated against and it obliges Parties to ensure

693

such awards are recognized and generally capable of enforcement in their jurisdiction in the same way as domestic awards.[*]

The New York Convention has clearly met this objective. In fact, it has been a tremendously successful device, unparalleled by any other international instrument in harmonizing a significant area of the law on an essentially world-wide basis. The Convention establishes a baseline rule of recognition of arbitral awards between signatory states, making awards handed down in one state binding and enforceable in another, subject only to limited exceptions. See New York Convention, Art. III,. To implement the Convention, Congress amended the Federal Arbitration Act to make foreign awards enforceable under the terms of the Convention as a matter of federal law. See 9 U.S.C. §§ 201-208. Similar to the New York Convention, the Inter-American Convention (or Panama Convention) on International Commercial Arbitration, albeit regionally limited, provides for the transnational recognition and enforcement of arbitral awards. The Panama Convention entered into force in 1976.

An additional feature of arbitration that is often cited as an advantage over the regular litigation process is the flexibility that these non-state proceedings offer. This is particularly true with respect to the procedural rules that govern arbitration. These rules can be more or less customized so as to represent an acceptable compromise between the different legal cultures that inform the parties' expectations about procedural fairness. The degree of flexibility depends on the type of arbitration that the parties opt for. Arbitral proceedings fall into one of two basic categories—"*ad hoc*" or "institutional"—and it is the *ad hoc* category that provides the greatest freedom to tailor an idiosyncratic procedural framework that meets both parties' needs. In *ad hoc* proceedings, the parties can determine all aspects of the procedure for conducting the arbitration. As an alternative to agreeing on every single procedural rule, which may be time-consuming and conflict-laden, parties in *ad hoc* arbitration can avail themselves of already existing procedural regimes such as the rules established by UNCITRAL (the United Nations Commission on International Trade Law—http://www.uncitral.org/uncitral/uncitral_texts/arbitration.html).

"Institutional" arbitration is conducted within the procedural framework provided by one of the numerous arbitration institutions, such as the International Chamber of Commerce (http://www.iccwbo.org/products-and-services/arbitration-and-adr/) and the Dubai International Arbitration Centre (http://www.diac.ae/idias/). While these institutions offer administrative assistance and a set of basic rules, parties in institutional settings still retain considerable autonomy to craft specific procedural rules that fit their needs and fill the gaps left by the institutional procedural framework.

Over the past two decades, international arbitration has become an increasingly complex area of the law. Accompanied by ample literature and teaching materials (see, e.g., See Gary Born, International Arbitration: Cases and Materials (2011)), the subject deserves and often actually occupies its own and separate space in the American law school curriculum. In keeping with our

---

[*] http://www.uncitral.org/uncitral/en/uncitral_texts/arbitration/NYConvention.html

emphasis on courts and litigation, this chapter will only highlight a few selected issues of international arbitration and will illustrate the way in which American courts have dealt with them. Section B will examine the scope of arbitration—that is, which claims may be subject to arbitration. Section C will look at the enforceability of arbitral awards, with a particular focus on the operations of the New York Convention. Finally, in Section D, we will take a brief look at the possibilities, both here and abroad, of obtaining an antisuit injunction from a court in aid of arbitration.

B. Claims Subject to Arbitration

Vimar Seguros y Reaseguros, S.A. v. M/V Sky Reefer

Supreme Court of the United States, 1995.
515 U.S. 528.

Justice Kennedy delivered the opinion of the Court.

This case requires us to interpret the Carriage of Goods by Sea Act (COGSA), 46 U.S.C.App. § 1300 et seq., as it relates to a contract containing a clause requiring arbitration in a foreign country. The question is whether a foreign arbitration clause in a bill of lading is invalid under COGSA because it lessens liability in the sense that COGSA prohibits. Our holding that COGSA does not forbid selection of the foreign forum makes it unnecessary to resolve the further question whether the Federal Arbitration Act (FAA), 9 U.S.C. § 1 et seq., would override COGSA were it interpreted otherwise. In our view, the relevant provisions of COGSA and the FAA are in accord, not in conflict.

I

The contract at issue in this case is a standard form bill of lading to evidence the purchase of a shipload of Moroccan oranges and lemons. The purchaser was Bacchus Associates (Bacchus), a New York partnership that distributes fruit at wholesale throughout the Northeastern United States. Bacchus dealt with Galaxie Negoce, S.A. (Galaxie), a Moroccan fruit supplier. Bacchus contracted with Galaxie to purchase the shipload of fruit and chartered a ship to transport it from Morocco to Massachusetts. The ship was the M/V Sky Reefer * * *. Once the ship set sail from Morocco, Galaxie tendered the bill of lading to Bacchus according to the terms of a letter of credit posted in Galaxie's favor.

Among the rights and responsibilities set out in the bill of lading were arbitration and choice-of-law clauses. Clause 3, entitled "Governing Law and Arbitration," provided:

"(1) The contract evidenced by or contained in this Bill of Lading shall be governed by the Japanese law.

"(2) Any dispute arising from this Bill of Lading shall be referred to arbitration in Tokyo by the Tokyo Maritime Arbitration Commission (TOMAC) of The Japan Shipping Exchange, Inc., in accordance with the rules of TOMAC and any amendment thereto, and the award given by the arbitrators shall be final and binding on both parties."

When the vessel's hatches were opened for discharge in Massachusetts, Bacchus discovered that thousands of boxes of oranges had shifted in the cargo holds, resulting in over $1 million damage. Bacchus received $733,442.90 compensation from petitioner Vimar Seguros y Reaseguros (Vimar Seguros), Bacchus' marine cargo insurer that became subrogated pro tanto to Bacchus' rights. Petitioner and Bacchus then brought suit against Maritima in personam and M/V Sky Reefer in rem in the District Court for the District of Massachusetts under the bill of lading. These defendants, respondents here, moved to stay the action and compel arbitration in Tokyo under clause 3 of the bill of lading and § 3 of the FAA, which requires courts to stay proceedings and enforce arbitration agreements covered by the Act. Petitioner and Bacchus opposed the motion, arguing the arbitration clause was unenforceable under the FAA both because it was a contract of adhesion and because it violated COGSA § 3(8). The premise of the latter argument was that the inconvenience and costs of proceeding in Japan would "lesse[n] . . . liability" as those terms are used in COGSA.

The District Court rejected the adhesion argument, observing that Congress defined the arbitration agreements enforceable under the FAA to include maritime bills of lading, 9 U.S.C. § 1, and that petitioner was a sophisticated party familiar with the negotiation of maritime shipping transactions. It also rejected the argument that requiring the parties to submit to arbitration would lessen respondents' liability under COGSA § 3(8). The court granted the motion to stay judicial proceedings and to compel arbitration. [After the District Court certified an interlocutory appeal, the First Circuit affirmed.]

II

The parties devote much of their argument to the question whether COGSA or the FAA has priority. "[W]hen two statutes are capable of co-existence," however, "it is the duty of the courts, absent a clearly expressed congressional intention to the contrary, to regard each as effective." *Morton v. Mancari*, 417 U.S. 535, 551 (1974); *Pittsburgh & Lake Erie R. Co. v. Railway Labor Executives' Assn.*, 491 U.S. 490, 510 (1989). There is no conflict unless COGSA by its own terms nullifies a foreign arbitration clause, and we choose to address that issue rather than assume nullification arguendo, as the Court of Appeals did. We consider the two arguments made by petitioner. The first is that a foreign arbitration clause lessens COGSA liability by increasing the transaction costs of obtaining relief. The second is that there is a risk foreign arbitrators will not apply COGSA.

A

The leading case for invalidation of a foreign forum selection clause is the opinion of the Court of Appeals for the Second Circuit in *Indussa Corp. v. S.S. Ranborg*, 377 F.2d 200 (1967) (en banc). The court there found that COGSA invalidated a clause designating a foreign judicial forum because it "puts 'a high hurdle' in the way of enforcing liability, and thus is an effective means for carriers to secure settlements lower than if cargo [owners] could sue in a convenient forum." Id., at 203 (citation omitted). The court observed "there could be no assurance that [the foreign court] would apply [COGSA] in the same way as would an American tribunal subject to the uniform control of the Supreme Court." Id., at 203-204. * * *

The determinative provision in COGSA, examined with care, does not support the arguments advanced first in *Indussa* and now by petitioner. Section 3(8) of COGSA provides as follows:

> "Any clause, covenant, or agreement in a contract of carriage relieving the carrier or the ship from liability for loss or damage to or in connection with the goods, arising from negligence, fault, or failure in the duties and obligations provided in this section, or lessening such liability otherwise than as provided in this chapter, shall be null and void and of no effect." 46 U.S.C. App. § 1303(8).

The liability that may not be lessened is "liability for loss or damage . . . arising from negligence, fault, or failure in the duties and obligations provided in this section." The statute thus addresses the lessening of the specific liability imposed by the Act, without addressing the separate question of the means and costs of enforcing that liability. The difference is that between explicit statutory guarantees and the procedure for enforcing them, between applicable liability principles and the forum in which they are to be vindicated.

The liability imposed on carriers under COGSA § 3 is defined by explicit standards of conduct, and it is designed to correct specific abuses by carriers. In the 19th century it was a prevalent practice for common carriers to insert clauses in bills of lading exempting themselves from liability for damage or loss, limiting the period in which plaintiffs had to present their notice of claim or bring suit, and capping any damages awards per package. Thus, § 3, entitled "Responsibilities and liabilities of carrier and ship," requires that the carrier "exercise due diligence to . . . [m]ake the ship seaworthy" and "[p]roperly man, equip, and supply the ship" before and at the beginning of the voyage, § 3(1), "properly and carefully load, handle, stow, carry, keep, care for, and discharge the goods carried," § 3(2), and issue a bill of lading with specified contents, § 3(3). 46 U.S.C.App. §§ 1303(1), (2), and (3). Section 3(6) allows the cargo owner to provide notice of loss or damage within three days and to bring suit within one year. These are the substantive obligations and particular procedures that § 3(8) prohibits a carrier from altering to its advantage in a bill of lading. Nothing in this section, however, suggests that the statute prevents the parties from agreeing to enforce these obligations in a particular forum. By its terms, it establishes certain duties and obligations, separate and apart from the mechanisms for their enforcement. * * *

If the question whether a provision lessens liability were answered by reference to the costs and inconvenience to the cargo owner, there would be no principled basis for distinguishing national from foreign arbitration clauses. Even if it were reasonable to read § 3(8) to make a distinction based on travel time, airfare, and hotels bills, these factors are not susceptible of a simple and enforceable distinction between domestic and foreign forums. Requiring a Seattle cargo owner to arbitrate in New York likely imposes more costs and burdens than a foreign arbitration clause requiring it to arbitrate in Vancouver. It would be unwieldy and unsupported by the terms or policy of the statute to require courts to proceed case by case to tally the costs and burdens to particular plaintiffs in light of their means, the size of their claims, and the relative burden on the carrier.

Our reading of "lessening such liability" to exclude increases in the transaction costs of litigation also finds support in the goals of the Brussels Convention for the Unification of Certain Rules Relating to Bills of Lading, 51 Stat. 233 (1924) (Hague Rules), on which COGSA is modeled. Sixty-six countries, including the United States and Japan, are now parties to the Convention, and it appears that none has interpreted its enactment of § 3(8) of the Hague Rules to prohibit foreign forum selection clauses. The English courts long ago rejected the reasoning later adopted by the *Indussa* court. See *Maharani Woollen Mills Co. v. Anchor Line*, [1927] 29 Lloyd's List L. Rep. 169 (C.A.) (Scrutton, L.J.) ("[T]he liability of the carrier appears to me to remain exactly the same under the clause. The only difference is a question of procedure—where shall the law be enforced?—and I do not read any clause as to procedure as lessening liability"). And other countries that do not recognize foreign forum selection clauses rely on specific provisions to that effect in their domestic versions of the Hague Rules, see, e.g., Sea-Carriage of Goods Act 1924, § 9(2) (Australia); Carriage of Goods by Sea Act, No. 1 of 1986, § 3 (South Africa). In light of the fact that COGSA is the culmination of a multilateral effort "to establish uniform ocean bills of lading to govern the rights and liabilities of carriers and shippers inter se in international trade," *Robert C. Herd & Co. v. Krawill Machinery Corp.*, 359 U.S. 297, 301 (1959), we decline to interpret our version of the Hague Rules in a manner contrary to every other nation to have addressed this issue.

It would also be out of keeping with the objects of the Convention for the courts of this country to interpret COGSA to disparage the authority or competence of international forums for dispute resolution. Petitioner's skepticism over the ability of foreign arbitrators to apply COGSA or the Hague Rules, and its reliance on this aspect of *Indussa Corp. v. S.S. Ranborg*, 377 F.2d 200 (CA2 1967), must give way to contemporary principles of international comity and commercial practice. As the Court observed in *The Bremen v. Zapata Off-Shore Co.*, 407 U.S. 1 (1972), when it enforced a foreign forum selection clause, the historical judicial resistance to foreign forum selection clauses "has little place in an era when . . . businesses once essentially local now operate in world markets." Id., at 12. "The expansion of American business and industry will hardly be encouraged," we explained, "if, notwithstanding solemn contracts, we insist on a parochial concept that all disputes must be resolved under our laws and in our courts." Id., at 9. See *Mitsubishi Motors Corp. v. Soler Chrysler-Plymouth, Inc.*, 473 U.S. 614, 638 (1985) (if international arbitral institutions "are to take a central place in the international legal order, national courts will need to 'shake off the old judicial hostility to arbitration,' and also their customary and understandable unwillingness to cede jurisdiction of a claim arising under domestic law to a foreign or transnational tribunal") (citation omitted); *Scherk v. Alberto-Culver Co.*, 417 U.S. 506, 516 (1974) ("A parochial refusal by the courts of one country to enforce an international arbitration agreement" would frustrate "the orderliness and predictability essential to any international business transaction").

That the forum here is arbitration only heightens the irony of petitioner's argument, for the FAA is also based in part on an international convention, 9 U.S.C. § 201 et seq. (codifying the United Nations Convention on the Recognition and Enforcement of Foreign Arbitral Awards, June 10, 1958, [1970] 21 U.S.T. 2517, T.I.A.S. No. 6997), intended "to encourage the recognition and enforcement of commercial arbitration agreements in international contracts and to unify the standards by which agreements to arbitrate are observed and arbitral awards are enforced in the signatory countries," *Scherk, supra,* at 520, n. 15. The FAA requires enforcement of arbitration agreements in contracts that involve interstate commerce, and in maritime transactions, including bills of lading, see 9 U.S.C. §§ 1, 2, 201, 202, where there is no independent basis in law or equity for revocation., cf. *Carnival Cruise Lines, Inc. v. Shute,* 499 U.S. 585, 595 (1991) ("[F]orum-selection clauses contained in form passage contracts are subject to judicial scrutiny for fundamental fairness"). If the United States is to be able to gain the benefits of international accords and have a role as a trusted partner in multilateral endeavors, its courts should be most cautious before interpreting its domestic legislation in such manner as to violate international agreements. That concern counsels against construing COGSA to nullify foreign arbitration clauses because of inconvenience to the plaintiff or insular distrust of the ability of foreign arbitrators to apply the law.

B

Petitioner's second argument against enforcement of the Japanese arbitration clause is that there is no guarantee foreign arbitrators will apply COGSA. This objection raises a concern of substance. The central guarantee of § 3(8) is that the terms of a bill of lading may not relieve the carrier of the obligations or diminish the legal duties specified by the Act. The relevant question, therefore, is whether the substantive law to be applied will reduce the carrier's obligations to the cargo owner below what COGSA guarantees. See *Mitsubishi Motors, supra,* 473 U.S. at 637, n. 19.

Petitioner argues that the arbitrators will follow the Japanese Hague Rules, which, petitioner contends, lessen respondents' liability in at least one significant respect. The Japanese version of the Hague Rules, it is said, provides the carrier with a defense based on the acts or omissions of the stevedores hired by the shipper, Galaxie, see App. 112, Article 3(1) (carrier liable "when he or the persons employed by him" fail to take due care), while COGSA, according to petitioner, makes nondelegable the carrier's obligation to "properly and carefully . . . stow . . . the goods carried," COGSA § 3(2), 46 U.S.C.App. § 1303(2).

Whatever the merits of petitioner's comparative reading of COGSA and its Japanese counterpart, its claim is premature. At this interlocutory stage it is not established what law the arbitrators will apply to petitioner's claims or that petitioner will receive diminished protection as a result. The arbitrators may conclude that COGSA applies of its own force or that Japanese law does not apply so that, under another clause of the bill of lading, COGSA controls.

Respondents seek only to enforce the arbitration agreement. The District Court has retained jurisdiction over the case and "will have the opportunity at the award-enforcement stage to ensure that the legitimate interest in the enforcement of the . . . laws has been addressed." *Mitsubishi Motors, supra*, 473 U.S., at 638; cf. 1 Restatement (Third) of Foreign Relations Law of the United States § 482(2)(d) (1986) ("A court in the United States need not recognize a judgment of the court of a foreign state if . . . the judgment itself, is repugnant to the public policy of the United States"). Were there no subsequent opportunity for review and were we persuaded that "the choice-of-forum and choice-of-law clauses operated in tandem as a prospective waiver of a party's right to pursue statutory remedies . . . we would have little hesitation in condemning the agreement as against public policy." *Mitsubishi Motors, supra*, at 637, n. 19. Under the circumstances of this case, however, the First Circuit was correct to reserve judgment on the choice-of-law question, as it must be decided in the first instance by the arbitrator, cf. *Mitsubishi Motors*, 473 U.S., at 637, n. 19. As the District Court has retained jurisdiction, mere speculation that the foreign arbitrators might apply Japanese law which, depending on the proper construction of COGSA, might reduce respondents' legal obligations, does not in and of itself lessen liability under COGSA § 3(8).

Because we hold that foreign arbitration clauses in bills of lading are not invalid under COGSA in all circumstances, both the FAA and COGSA may be given full effect. The judgment of the Court of Appeals is affirmed, and the case is remanded for further proceedings consistent with this opinion.

It is so ordered.

[JUSTICE O'CONNOR concurred in the judgment, reserving the question whether a foreign forum selection clause, unlike the arbitration clause in this case, would entirely "divest domestic courts of jurisdiction."]

JUSTICE STEVENS, dissenting.

* * *

The Court assumes that the words "lessening such liability" must be narrowly construed to refer only to the substantive rules that define the carrier's legal obligations. Under this view, contractual provisions that lessen the amount of the consignee's net recovery, or that lessen the likelihood that it will make any recovery at all, are beyond the scope of the statute.

In my opinion, this view is flatly inconsistent with the purpose of COGSA § 3(8). That section responds to the inequality of bargaining power inherent in bills of lading and to carriers' historic tendency to exploit that inequality whenever possible to immunize themselves from liability for their own fault. A bill of lading is a form document prepared by the carrier, who presents it to the shipper on a take-it-or-leave-it basis. Characteristically, there is no arm's-length negotiation over the bill's terms; the shipper must agree to the carrier's standard-form language, or else refrain from using the carrier's services. Accordingly, if courts were to enforce bills of lading as written, a carrier could slip in a clause relieving itself of all liability for fault, or limiting that liability to a fraction of the shipper's damages, and the shipper would have no recourse. COGSA represents Congress' most recent attempt to respond to this problem. By its terms, it invalidates any clause in a bill of lading "relieving" or "lessening" the "liability" of the carrier for negligence, fault, or dereliction of duty.

When one reads the statutory language in light of the policies behind COGSA's enactment, it is perfectly clear that a foreign forum selection or arbitration clause "relieves" or "lessens" the carrier's liability. The transaction costs associated with an arbitration in Japan will obviously exceed the potential recovery in a great many cargo disputes. As a practical matter, therefore, in such a case no matter how clear the carrier's formal legal liability may be, it would make no sense for the consignee or its subrogee to enforce that liability. It seems to me that a contractual provision that entirely protects the shipper from being held liable for anything should be construed either to have "lessened" its inability or to have "relieved" it of liability.

Even if the value of the shipper's claim is large enough to justify litigation in Asia, contractual provisions that impose unnecessary and unreasonable costs on the consignee will inevitably lessen its net recovery. If, as under the Court's reasoning, such provisions do not affect the carrier's legal liability, it would appear to be permissible to require the consignee to pay the costs of the arbitration, or perhaps the travel expenses and fees of the expert witnesses, interpreters, and lawyers employed by both parties. * * *

Lurking in the background of the Court's decision today is another possible reason for holding, despite the clear meaning of COGSA and decades of precedent, that a foreign arbitration clause does not lessen liability. It may be that the Court does violence to COGSA in order to avoid a perceived conflict with another federal statute, the Federal Arbitration Act (FAA), 9 U.S.C. § 1 et seq. The FAA requires that courts enforce arbitration clauses in contracts—including those requiring arbitration in foreign countries the same way they would enforce any other contractual clause. * * *

Unfortunately, in adopting a contrary reading to avoid this conflict, the Court has today deprived COGSA § 3(8) of much of its force. The Court's narrow reading of "lessening [of] liability" excludes more than arbitration; it apparently covers only formal, legal liability. Although I agree with the Court that it is important to read potentially conflicting statutes so as to give effect to both wherever possible, I think the majority has ignored a much less damaging way to harmonize COGSA with the FAA.

Section 2 of the FAA reads:

> "A written provision in any maritime transaction . . . to settle by arbitration a controversy thereafter arising out of such contract . . . shall be valid, irrevocable, and enforceable, save upon such grounds as exist at law or in equity for the revocation of any contract." 9 U.S.C. § 2.

This language plainly intends to place arbitration clauses upon the same footing as all other contractual clauses. Thus, like any clause, an arbitration clause is enforceable, "save upon such grounds" as would suffice to invalidate any other, nonarbitration clause. The FAA thereby fulfills its policy of jettisoning the prior regime of hostility to arbitration. Like any other contractual clause, then, an arbitration clause may be invalid without violating the FAA if, for example, it is procured through fraud or forgery; there is mutual mistake or impossibility; the provision is unconscionable; or, as in this case, the terms of the clause are illegal under a separate federal statute which does not evidence a hostility to arbitration. Neither the terms nor the policies of the FAA would be thwarted if the Court were to hold today that a foreign arbitration clause in a bill of lading "lessens liability" under COGSA. COGSA does not single out arbitration clauses for disfavored treatment; it invalidates any clause that lessens the carrier's liability. Illegality under COGSA is therefore an independent ground "for the revocation of any contract," under FAA § 2. There is no conflict between the two federal statutes.

The correctness of this construction becomes even more apparent when one considers the policies of the two statutes. COGSA seeks to ameliorate the inequality in bargaining power that comes from a particular form of adhesion contract. The FAA seeks to ensure enforcement of freely negotiated agreements to arbitrate. As I have discussed, foreign arbitration clauses in bills of lading are not freely negotiated. COGSA's policy is thus directly served by making these clauses illegal; and the FAA's policy is not disserved thereby. In contrast, allowing such adhesionary clauses to stand serves the goals of neither statute. * * *

NOTES AND QUESTIONS FOR DISCUSSION

1. *Vimar Seguros* exemplifies a trend in favor of arbitration and, more generally, in favor of contractual alteration of otherwise applicable procedural rules. The latter is evident in decisions enforcing choice of forum clauses, such as The Bremen v. Zapata Off-Shore Co., 407 U.S. 1 (1972), which appears as a principal case in Chapter 1. At about the same time, the Supreme Court began a steady retreat from the principle that statutory claims could not be subject to arbitration. Some of these, like Scherk v. Alberto-Culver Co., 417 U.S. 506 (1974), arose in international business transactions and involved claims under regulatory statutes, like the Securities Exchange Act. Just as with forum selection clauses, the reasoning of these decisions has been extended outside the business context to individual claims, like those under the statutes prohibiting employment discrimination. See, e.g., Gilmer v. Interstate/Johnson Lane Corp., 500 U.S. 20 (1991).

The trend in favor of arbitration is a broad one, reversing the common law presumption that arbitration clauses were invalid as an attempted ouster of the jurisdiction of the courts. The Supreme Court has looked to the Federal Arbitration Act to find a "liberal federal policy favoring arbitration," and the "fundamental principle that arbitration is a matter of contract." AT&T Mobility LLC v. Concepcion, 131 S.Ct. 1740, 1745 (2011) (quoting earlier decisions). In international cases, the presumption in favor of arbitration finds support in the New York Convention as described in the introduction of this chapter. Although the courts now undertake a case-specific analysis, looking both to the terms of the arbitration clause and to the terms of the statute under which the claim is brought, that inquiry usually results in a finding that the claim is subject to arbitration, as in the cases cited in the preceding note. Decisions such as *Vimar*

Seguros therefore raise the question how much they depend upon the particular statute at issue to determine whether arbitration is a valid alternative to litigation.

2. The plaintiffs in *Vimar Seguros* asserted a standard claim for cargo damage under the Carriage of Goods by Seas Act (COGSA). Their claim, like the leading decisions on forum selection clauses (see Chapter 1, Section I), arose under the admiralty jurisdiction of the federal courts. Admiralty jurisdiction, from its beginnings, has implicated concerns about international trade and international relations. COGSA itself, as the Court points out, was passed to implement an international convention on carriage of goods by sea, the Hague Rules. So, too, was the Japanese version of COGSA, under which the plaintiffs were supposed to arbitrate their claims pursuant to the contract's choice-of-law provisions. Given this background of international cooperation and similar laws, the Court found little reason to prefer American litigation over Japanese arbitration. As discussed in Chapter 7, choice-of-law clauses generally are given effect, if there is some reasonable basis for the law chosen by the parties and if it does not contravene a fundamental policy of the forum. Restatement (Second) of Conflict of Laws § 187.

The only impediment to applying Japanese law in *Vimar Seguros* concerned the protective provisions in COGSA that prevented carriers, like the defendant, from reducing their obligations and liability below the floor specified in the statute. COGSA § 3(8). Given their common origin in an international agreement, how far was the Japanese version of COGSA likely to deviate from the U.S. version? The plaintiffs could point to only one feature of the Japanese law that might favor the carrier, giving it a defense based on the action of the stevedores, who loaded and unloaded the cargo, because they were hired by the plaintiffs. How compelling is this discrepancy, when it only relieves the *defendant* of liability incurred by the action of someone hired by the *plaintiff*?

The Court acknowledged the possibility that a foreign arbitration award might nevertheless be contrary to American law, but postponed consideration of this issue until the award had been rendered. The arbitrator would, in the first instance, determine the choice-of-law question, and if applicable, the content of Japanese law. That decision could then be reviewed by the district court, which reserved jurisdiction over any proceedings to enforce the arbitral award. The Court at this point invoked the general, if narrow, restriction on enforcement of foreign judgments that are "repugnant to the public policy of the United States." Restatement (Third) of Foreign Relations Law of the United States § 482(2)(d). This issue, discussed in Chapter 8, also comes up in the next case in this chapter.

3. Preliminary questions of forum selection and choice-of-law lie just beneath the surface of the opinion in *Vimar Seguros*. The Court presumes, as do most courts confronted with a request to stay judicial proceedings and order arbitration, that it has the power to decide whether the plaintiff's claim is subject to arbitration and to apply its own law in doing so. This presumption follows from the principle that a court always has the start-up power to determine the scope of its own jurisdiction. See United States v. United Mine Workers, 330 U.S. 258, 292-93 (1947). It always has "jurisdiction to determine its own jurisdiction," and with it, jurisdiction to determine whether a dispute must go to arbitration.

In the procedural posture of *Vimar Seguros*, this power seems to be almost self-evident. The plaintiffs had invoked the jurisdiction of the federal court to determine their claims under COGSA. The defendant then moved for a stay of litigation and an order compelling arbitration. At this point, the federal court had to determine whether the claim fell within the scope of the arbitration clause and whether arbitration violated COGSA or any other federal statute. Those questions could not be avoided—without circularity—by invoking the arbitration clause itself or the contractual choice-of-law clause. Other leading American decisions follow this standard procedure. See, e.g., Mitsubishi Motors Corp. v. Soler Chrysler-Plymouth, Inc., 473 U.S. 614 (1985).

It nevertheless remains possible for the arbitrator, or a foreign court where enforcement of the arbitration is sought, to re-examine those questions. The usual effect of a decision ordering arbitration is to give all issues to the arbitral tribunal, subject to the procedural law of the place or "seat" of arbitration and the substantive law chosen by the parties or, failing that, the law otherwise applicable. The enforceability of any award then depends upon the law of the forum where enforcement is sought, as discussed in the next principal case.

4. The likely consequence of the current regime favoring arbitration is to deny parties, like the plaintiffs in *Vimar Seguros*, of almost any prospects of judicial review of their claims under American law. Justice Stevens, in his dissent, finds this one-sided result contrary to COGSA. It leaves cargo owners, like the plaintiffs, at the mercy of carriers, like the defendant, who typically draft the bill of lading that constitutes the contract between the parties and that contains the disputed arbitration and choice-of-law clauses. These clauses are likely to favor the carriers who draft them, as this one did by sending the case to a distant arbitral tribunal. Should this be a concern? Or can we count on business firms to protect themselves? Often, as in this case, they do so through their insurers who become the real parties in interest by covering the loss and subrogating to the underlying claims. Are firms in international trade invariably able to protect themselves in this fashion or in some other way? Or should the risk of arbitration in a distant forum under foreign law be accepted as a risk of international business activity, better decided ex ante between the parties by contract rather than by the courts by judicial decision ex post?

C. ENFORCEMENT OF ARBITRATION AWARDS

Parsons & Whittemore Overseas Co., Inc. v. Société Général de l'Industrie du Papier (RAKTA)

United States Court of Appeals, Second Circuit, 1974.

508 F.2d 969.

J. JOSEPH SMITH, CIRCUIT JUDGE.

Parsons & Whittemore Overseas Co., Inc., (Overseas), an American corporation, appeals from the entry of summary judgment on February 25, 1974, by Judge Lloyd F. MacMahon of the Southern District of New York on the counter-claim by Société Générale de L'Industrie du Papier (RAKTA), an Egyptian corporation, to confirm a foreign arbitral award holding Overseas liable to RAKTA for breach of contract. RAKTA in turn challenges the court's concurrent order granting summary judgment on Overseas' complaint, which sought a declaratory judgment denying RAKTA's entitlement to recover the amount of a letter of credit issued by Bank of America in RAKTA's favor at Overseas' request. Jurisdiction is based on 9 U.S.C. § 203, which empowers federal district courts to hear cases to recognize and enforce foreign arbitral awards, and 9 U.S.C. 205, which authorizes the removal of such cases from state courts, as was accomplished in this instance. We affirm the district court's confirmation of the foreign [arbitral] award. * * *

In November 1962, Overseas consented by written agreement with RAKTA to construct, start up and, for one year, manage and supervise a paperboard mill in Alexandria, Egypt. The Agency for International Development (AID), a branch of the United States State Department, would finance the project by supplying RAKTA with funds with which to purchase letters of credit in Overseas' favor. Among the contract's terms was an arbitration clause, which provided a means to settle differences arising in the course of performance, and a "force majeure" clause, which excused delay in performance due to causes beyond Overseas' reasonable capacity to control.

Work proceeded as planned until May, 1967. Then, with the Arab-Israeli Six Day War on the horizon, recurrent expressions of Egyptian hostility to Americans—nationals of the principal ally of the Israeli enemy—caused the majority of the Overseas work crew to leave Egypt. On June 6, the Egyptian government broke diplomatic ties with the United States and ordered all Americans expelled from Egypt except those who would apply and qualify for a special visa.

Having abandoned the project for the present with the construction phase near completion, Overseas notified RAKTA that it regarded this postponement as excused by the force majeure clause. RAKTA disagreed and sought damages for breach of contract. Overseas refused to settle and RAKTA, already at work on completing the performance promised by Overseas, invoked the arbitration clause. Overseas responded by calling into play the clause's option to bring a dispute directly to a three-man arbitral board governed by the rules of the International Chamber of Commerce. After several sessions in 1970, the tribunal issued a preliminary award, which recognized Overseas' force majeure defense as good only during the period from May 28 to June 30, 1967. In so limiting Overseas' defense, the arbitration court emphasized that Overseas had made no more than a perfunctory effort to secure special visas and that AID's notification that it was withdrawing financial backing did not justify Overseas' unilateral decision to abandon the project. After further hearings in 1972, the tribunal made its final award in March, 1973: Overseas was held liable to RAKTA for $312,507.45 in damages for breach of contract and $30,000 for RAKTA's costs; additionally, the arbitrators' compensation was set at $49,000, with Overseas responsible for three-fourths of the sum.

Subsequent to the final award, Overseas in the action here under review sought a declaratory judgment to prevent RAKTA from collecting the award out of a letter of credit issued in RAKTA's favor by Bank of America at Overseas' request. The letter was drawn to satisfy any "penalties" which an arbitral tribunal might assess against Overseas in the future for breach of contract. RAKTA contended that the arbitral award for damages met the letter's requirement of "penalties" and counter-claimed to confirm and enter judgment upon the foreign arbitral award. Overseas' defenses to this counterclaim, all rejected by the district court, form the principal issues for review on this appeal. Four of these defenses are derived from the express language of the applicable United Nations Convention on the Recognition and Enforcement of Foreign Arbitral Awards (Convention), 330 U.N.Treaty Ser. 38, and a fifth is arguably implicit in the Convention. These include: enforcement of the award would violate the public policy of the United States, the award represents an arbitration of matters not appropriately decided by arbitration; the tribunal denied Overseas an adequate opportunity to present its case; the award is predicated upon a resolution of issues outside the scope of contractual agreement to submit to arbitration; and the award is in manifest disregard of law. In addition to disputing the district court's rejection of its position on the letter of credit, RAKTA seeks on appeal modification of the court's order to correct for an arithmetical error in sum entered for judgment, as well as an assessment of damages and double costs against Overseas for pursuing a frivolous appeal.

I. OVERSEAS' DEFENSES AGAINST ENFORCEMENT

In 1958 the Convention was adopted by 26 of the 45 states participating in the United Nations Conference on Commercial Arbitration held in New York. For the signatory state, the New York Convention superseded the Geneva Convention of 1927, 92 League of Nations Treaty Ser. 302. The 1958 Convention's basic thrust was to liberalize procedures for enforcing foreign arbitral awards: While the Geneva Convention placed the burden of proof on the party seeking enforcement of a foreign arbitral award and did not circumscribe the range of available defenses to those enumerated in the convention, the 1958 Convention clearly shifted the burden of proof to the party defending against enforcement and limited his defenses to seven set forth in Article V. [See Appendix E—eds.] * * * The United States ultimately acceded to the Convention * * * in 1970, and implemented its accession with 9 U.S.C. §§ 201-208. Under 9 U.S.C. § 208, the existing Federal Arbitration Act, 9 U.S.C. §§ 1-14, applies to the enforcement of foreign awards except to the extent to which the latter may conflict with the Convention.

A. Public Policy

Article V(2)(b) of the Convention allows the court in which enforcement of a foreign arbitral award is sought to refuse enforcement, on the defendant's motion or sua sponte, if "enforcement of the award would be contrary to the public policy of (the forum) country." The legislative history of the provision offers no certain guidelines to its construction. Its precursors in the Geneva Convention and the 1958 Convention's ad hoc committee draft extended the public policy exception to, respectively, awards contrary to "principles of the law" and awards violative of "fundamental principles of the law."

[Commentators differed on whether] the Convention's failure to include similar language signifies a narrowing of the defense.

Perhaps more probative, however, are the inferences to be drawn from the history of the Convention as a whole. The general pro-enforcement bias informing the Convention and explaining its supersession of the Geneva Convention points toward a narrow reading of the public policy defense. An expansive construction of this defense would vitiate the Convention's basic effort to remove preexisting obstacles to enforcement. Additionally, considerations of reciprocity—considerations given express recognition in the Convention itself [4]—counsel courts to invoke the public policy defense with caution lest foreign courts frequently accept it as a defense to enforcement of arbitral awards rendered in the United States.

We conclude, therefore, that the Convention's public policy defense should be construed narrowly. Enforcement of foreign arbitral awards may be denied on this basis only where enforcement would violate the forum state's most basic notions of morality and justice. Cf. 1 Restatement Second of the Conflict of Laws 117, comment c, at 340 (1971); *Loucks v. Standard Oil Co.*, 224 N.Y. 99, 111, 120 N.E. 198 (1918).

Under this view of the public policy provision in the Convention, Overseas' public policy defense may easily be dismissed. Overseas argues that various actions by United States officials subsequent to the severance of American-Egyptian relations—most particularly, AID's withdrawal of financial support for the Overseas-RAKTA contract—required Overseas, as a loyal American citizen, to abandon the project. Enforcement of an award predicated on the feasibility of Overseas' returning to work in defiance of these expressions of national policy would therefore allegedly contravene United States public policy. In equating "national" policy with United States "public" policy, the appellant quite plainly misses the mark. To read the public policy defense as a parochial device protective of national political interests would seriously undermine the Convention's utility. This provision was not meant to enshrine the vagaries of international politics under the rubric of "public policy." Rather, a circumscribed public policy doctrine was contemplated by the Convention's framers and every indication is that the United States, in acceding to the Convention, meant to subscribe to this supranational emphasis.[5]

To deny enforcement of this award largely because of the United States' falling out with Egypt in recent years would mean converting a defense intended to be of narrow scope into a major loophole in the Convention's mechanism for enforcement. We have little hesitation, therefore, in disallowing Overseas' proposed public policy defense.

---

[4] A Contracting State shall not be entitled to avail itself of the present Convention against other Contracting States except to the extent that it is itself bound to apply the Convention. Article XIV. * * *

[5] Moreover, the facts here fail to demonstrate that considered government policy forbids completion of the contract itself by a private party.

B. Non-Arbitrability

Article V(2)(a) authorizes a court to deny enforcement, on a defendant's or its own motion, of a foreign arbitral award when "the subject matter of the difference is not capable of settlement by arbitration under the law of that (the forum) country." Under this provision, a court sitting in the United States might, for example, be expected to decline enforcement of an award involving arbitration of an antitrust claim in view of domestic arbitration cases which have held that antitrust matters are entrusted to the exclusive competence of the judiciary. On the other hand, it may well be that the special considerations and policies underlying a "truly international agreement," *Scherk v. Alberto-Culver Co.*, 417 U.S. 506, 515 (1974), call for a narrower view of non-arbitrability in the international than the domestic context.

Resolution of Overseas' non-arbitrability argument, however, does not require us to reach such difficult distinctions between domestic and foreign awards. For Overseas' argument, that "United States foreign policy issues can hardly be placed at the mercy of foreign arbitrators 'who are charged with the execution of no public trust' and whose loyalties are to foreign interests," plainly fails to raise so substantial an issue of arbitrability. Resolution of Overseas' non-arbitrability argument, however, does not require us to reach such difficult distinctions between domestic and foreign awards. The mere fact that an issue of national interest may incidentally figure into the resolution of a breach of contract claim does not make the dispute not arbitrable. Rather, certain categories of claims may be non-arbitrable because of the special national interest vested in their resolution. Furthermore, even were the test for non-arbitrability of an ad hoc nature, Overseas' situation would almost certainly not meet the standard, for Overseas grossly exaggerates the magnitude of the national interest involved in the resolution of its particular claim. Simply because acts of the United States are somehow implicated in a case one cannot conclude that the United States is vitally interested in its outcome. Finally, the Supreme Court's decision in favor of arbitrability in a case far more prominently displaying public features than the instant one, *Scherk v. Alberto-Culver Co.*, *supra*, compels by analogy the conclusion that the foreign award against Overseas dealt with a subject arbitrable under United States law.

The court below was correct in denying relief to Overseas under the Convention's non-arbitrability defense to enforcement of foreign arbitral awards. There is no special national interest in judicial, rather than arbitral, resolution of the breach of contract claim underlying the award in this case.

C. Inadequate Opportunity to Present Defense

Under Article V(1)(b) of the Convention, enforcement of a foreign arbitral award may be denied if the defendant can prove that he was "not given proper notice . . . or was otherwise unable to present his case." This provision essentially sanctions the application of the forum state's standards of due process.

Overseas seeks relief under this provision for the arbitration court's refusal to delay proceedings in order to accommodate the speaking schedule of one of Overseas' witnesses, David Nes, the United States Chargé d'Affaires in Egypt at the time of the Six Day War. This attempt to state a due process claim fails for several reasons. First, inability to produce one's witnesses before an arbitral tribunal is a risk inherent in an agreement to submit to arbitration. By agreeing to submit disputes to arbitration, a party relinquishes his courtroom rights— including that to subpoena witnesses—in favor of arbitration "with all of its well known advantages and drawbacks." *Washington-Baltimore Newspaper Guild, Local 35 v. The Washington Post Co.*, 442 F.2d 1234, 1238 (D.C. Cir. 1971). Secondly, the logistical problems of scheduling hearing dates convenient to parties, counsel and arbitrators scattered about the globe argues against deviating from an initially mutually agreeable time plan unless a scheduling change is truly unavoidable. * * * Finally, Overseas cannot complain that the tribunal decided the case without considering evidence critical to its defense and within only Mr. Nes' ability to produce. In fact, the tribunal did have before it an affidavit by Mr. Nes in which he furnished, by his own account, "a good deal of the information to which I would have testified." * * *

The arbitration tribunal acted within its discretion in declining to reschedule a hearing for the convenience of an Overseas witness. Overseas' due process rights under American law, rights entitled to full force under the Convention as a defense to enforcement, were in no way infringed by the tribunal's decision.

D. Arbitration in Excess of Jurisdiction

Under Article V(1)(c), one defending against enforcement of an arbitral award may prevail by proving that:

> The award deals with a difference not contemplated by or not falling within the terms of the submission to arbitration, or it contains decisions on matters beyond the scope of the submission to arbitration . . . .

This provision tracks in more detailed form § 10(d) of the Federal Arbitration Act, 9 U.S.C. § 10(d), which authorizes vacating an award "where the arbitrators exceeded their powers." Both provisions basically allow a party to attack an award predicated upon arbitration of a subject matter not within the agreement to submit to arbitration. This defense to enforcement of a foreign award, like the others already discussed, should be construed narrowly. Once again a narrow construction would comport with the enforcement-facilitating thrust of the Convention. In addition, the case law under the similar provision of the Federal Arbitration Act strongly supports a strict reading. See, e.g., *United Steelworkers of America v. Enterprise Wheel & Car Corp.*, 363 U.S. 593 (1960).

In making this defense as to three components of the award, Overseas must therefore overcome a powerful presumption that the arbitral body acted within its powers. Overseas principally directs its challenge at the $185,000 awarded for loss of production. Its jurisdictional claim focuses on the provision of the contract reciting that "neither party shall have any liability for loss of production." The tribunal cannot properly be charged, however, with simply ignoring this alleged limitation on the subject matter over which its decision-making powers extended. Rather, the arbitration court interpreted the provision not to preclude jurisdiction on this matter. As in *United Steelworkers of America v. Enterprise Wheel & Car Corp.*, *supra*, the court may be satisfied that the arbitrator premised the award on a construction of the contract and that it is "not apparent," 363 U.S. at 598, that the scope of the submission to arbitration has been exceeded.

The appellant's attack on the $60,000 awarded for start-up expenses and $30,000 in costs cannot withstand the most cursory scrutiny. In characterizing the $60,000 as "consequential damages" (and thus proscribed by the arbitration agreement), Overseas is again attempting to secure a reconstruction in this court of the contract—an activity wholly inconsistent with the deference due arbitral decisions on law and fact. See generally, *Bernhardt v. Polygraphic Company of America, Inc.*, 350 U.S. 198, 203 & n. 4 (1956). The $30,000 in costs is equally unassailable, for the appellant's contention that this portion of the award is inconsistent with guidelines set by the International Chamber of Commerce is twice removed from reality. First of all, contrary to Overseas' representations, these guidelines * * * do not require, as a pre-condition to an award of expenses, express authority for such an award in the arbitration clause. The arbitration agreement's silence on this matter, therefore, is not determinative in the case under review. Secondly, since the parties in fact complied with the Guide's advice to reach agreement on this matter prior to arbitration—i.e., the request by each for such an award for expenses amounts to tacit agreement on this point—any claim of fatal deviation from the Guide is disingenuous to say the least.

Although the Convention recognizes that an award may not be enforced where predicated on a subject matter outside the arbitrator's jurisdiction, it does not sanction second-guessing the arbitrator's construction of the parties' agreement. The appellant's attempt to invoke this defense, however, calls upon the court to ignore this limitation on its decision-making powers and usurp the arbitrator's role. The district court took a proper view of its own jurisdiction in refusing to grant relief on this ground.

E. Award in "Manifest Disregard" of Law

Both the legislative history of Article V and the statute enacted to implement the United States' accession to the Convention[6] are strong authority for treating as exclusive the bases set forth in the Convention for vacating an award. On the other hand, the Federal Arbitration Act, specifically 9 U.S.C. § 10, has been read to include an implied defense to enforcement where the award is in "manifest disregard" of the law. *Wilko v. Swan*, 346 U.S. 427, 436 (1953).

This case does not require us to decide, however, whether this defense stemming from dictum in *Wilko, supra*, obtains in the international arbitration context. For even assuming that the "manifest disregard" defense applies under the Convention, we would have no difficulty rejecting the appellant's contention that such "manifest disregard" is in evidence here. Overseas in effect asks this court to read this defense as a license to review the record of arbitral proceedings for errors of fact or law—a role which we have emphatically declined to assume in the past and reject once again. * * *

Insofar as this defense to enforcement of awards in "manifest disregard" of law may be cognizable under the Convention, it, like the other defenses raised

---

[6] "The court shall confirm the award unless it finds one of the grounds for refusal or deferral of recognition or enforcement specified in the said Convention." 9 U.S.C. § 207.

by the appellant, fails to provide a sound basis for vacating the foreign arbitral award. We therefore affirm the district court's confirmation of award. * * *

We affirm the district court's confirmation of the foreign arbitral award.

NOTES AND QUESTIONS FOR DISCUSSION

1. The multiple defenses advanced in *Parsons & Whittemore* against enforcement of the arbitration award all failed. The court considered and rejected several arguments against enforcement based on the purported inconsistency of the award with American law. Public policy, non-arbitrability, and manifest disregard of the law were all asserted as grounds for refusing enforcement of the award. In addition, the losing party also argued that it was denied a fair opportunity to be heard in the arbitration and that the arbitration board had exceeded its jurisdiction under the arbitration agreement. Which of these grounds were most promising, either on the facts of this case or in similar cases?

Arguments based on inconsistency of the award with substantive law takes different forms under the New York Convention and the Federal Arbitration Act. Under Article V.2., the Convention makes an award unenforceable if, under the law of the country where enforcement is sought, the dispute "is not capable of settlement by arbitration" or enforcement "would be contrary to the public policy of that country." Decisions under § 10 of the Federal Arbitration Act have denied enforcement of arbitration awards made "in manifest disregard" of the law. All three defenses, although framed in general terms, usually succeed only when the arbitration award conflicts with a specific provision of the enforcing nation's law. The courts have retained a degree of flexibility in evaluating arbitration awards, but they have seldom refused enforcement in the absence of specific legislation or judicial decisions under domestic law.

The "public policy" exception is illustrative. Although frequently invoked, it rarely meets with success, and even then, it is primarily as to procedural issues. See Gary Born, International Arbitration: Cases and Materials 1197-98 (2011). Under Article V.1. of the New York Convention, procedural defects in the arbitration process already are grounds for refusing to enforce an award. In *Parsons & Whittemore*, the defense based on lack of opportunity to be heard relied upon the provision for cases in which a party "was otherwise unable to present his case." Art. V.1(b). If, as the court held, the losing party could not successfully invoke that provision, what chance did it have in invoking the "public policy" defense? The court recognizes the narrowness of this defense by citing Loucks v. Standard Oil Co. of New York, 224 N.Y. 99, 120 N.E. 198 (1918), a case on enforcement of foreign judgments where Judge Cardozo famously observed: "We are not so provincial as to say that every solution of a problem is wrong because we deal with it otherwise at home." 224 N.Y. at 111, 120 N.E. at 201. See Chapter 7, Section A. Should the "public policy" exception be equally narrow for arbitration awards as for foreign judgments?

Much the same question can be asked of the implied defense under the Federal Arbitration Act where an arbitration award is "in manifest disregard of the law." Like the "public policy" defense, it is broad in scope but narrow in application, leaving intact the broad deference usually accorded to arbitrators. As the court emphasizes in *Parsons & Whittemore*, the defense cannot be read "as a license to review the record of the arbitral proceedings for errors of fact or law." Moreover, while the defense "in manifest disregard of the law" is available under the Federal Arbitration Act which governs the recognition and enforcement of domestic awards, several courts have held that the defense may *not* be invoked under the New York Convention. For example, a federal court recently held as follows:

> [T]he text of the Convention [does not] suggest that an arbitrator's "manifest disregard of the law" can serve as an independent and additional ground for denying confirmation of an arbitral award. Under Article V of the Convention, the Court's refusal to confirm an arbitral award is limited to "only" those situations where a "party furnishes . . . proof that" one of the enumerated provisions applies. Nowhere in the seven enumerated provisions listed under Article V is an arbitrator's "manifest disregard of the law" a ground upon which the Court may deny confirmation of the Award; by negative implication, that basis, along with any other potential grounds for refusing confirmation of an arbitral award, are excluded. * * * Such a narrow reading of the New York Convention comports with the context in which the Convention was enacted, as a broad construction of the Convention would do nothing more than erect additional hurdles to confirmation of arbitral awards, which in turn would contravene the "principal purpose" of the Convention, i.e., "to encourage the recognition and enforcement of commercial arbitration agreements in international contracts." * * * Thus, the Court cannot envision how an arbitrator's "manifest disregard of the law" can serve as an independent ground to deny confirmation of the Award in the face of the Convention's plain language.

International Trading and Indus. Inv. Co. v. DynCorp Aerospace Technology, 763 F. Supp. 2d 12, 28 (D.D.C. 2011) (citations omitted).

Even courts that do allow the defense under the New York Convention do so only exceptionally because "[i]t is not enough . . . to show that the panel committed an error—or even a serious error." Lagstein v. Certain Underwriters at Lloyd's, London 607 F.3d 634 at 641 (9th Cir. 2010) (quoting Stolt-Nielsen S.A. v. AnimalFeeds Int'l Corp., 130 S.Ct. 1758, 1767 (2010)). Rather, "'[m]anifest disregard of the law' means something more than just an error in the law or a failure on the part of the arbitrators to understand or apply the law. . . . To vacate an arbitration award on this ground, '[i]t must be clear from the record that the arbitrators recognized the applicable law and then ignored it.'" *Id.* (Citations omitted).

2. Another defense along the same lines appeals to some provision of law that removes a subject entirely from arbitration, making it "not capable of settlement by arbitration." (Note that such a defense also implicates the types of claims that are subject to arbitration, as discussed in Section B of this chapter.) A statute specifically requiring adjudication of a claim would meet this requirement, as would categories of litigation, such as criminal prosecutions, reserved to the courts for constitutional reasons. Before the current trend in favor of arbitration became established in the last decades of the twentieth century, numerous decisions reserved a variety of claims for the courts. *Vimar Seguros* referred to, and overruled, one such decision concerned with claims under COGSA, and *Parsons & Whittemore* cited a decision, now also limited, that prevented arbitration of antitrust claims. The limited decision, Mitsubishi Motors Corp. v. Soler Chrysler-Plymouth, Inc., 473 U.S. 614 (1985), now allows arbitration of antitrust claims arising in international trade. The trend in favor of arbitration has dramatically reduced the scope of this exception, both in ordering arbitration in the first instance and in enforcing any resulting arbitration award.

3. The "public policy" defense, and variations upon it, all refer to the law of "the country where recognition and enforcement is sought." New York Convention Art. V.2. See Appendix E. This follows the general principle that the award must be enforced "in accordance with the rules of procedure of the territory where the award is relied upon." Art. III. Other defenses to enforcement, however, refer to different sources of law. Thus the validity of the agreement to arbitrate is determined "under the law to which the parties have subjected it or, failing any indication thereon, under the law of the country where the award was made," Art. V.1(a); and composition of the arbitration panel and the arbitration procedures must be "in accordance with the law of the country where the arbitration took place." Art. V.1(d).

It remains possible that these primary references to the applicable law could incorporate references to choice of law rules, which would ultimately result in application of the law of a different state. That possibility remains remote in most enforcement cases because little appears to be gained by referring the dispute to foreign law. Nevertheless, in rare cases, courts have referred to foreign law in determining whether an award is contrary to "public policy." Victrix Steamship Co. S.A. v. Salen Dry Cargo A.B., 825 F.2d 709 (2d Cir. 1987) (arbitration award not enforced because contrary to Swedish bankruptcy law). Any such reference to foreign law, if made, would have to conform to the principles of choice of law discussed earlier in Chapter 7.

A broadly similar analysis applies to the incorporation of international law in the law of the enforcing state. As a matter of American law, the New York Convention governs the enforcement of foreign arbitration awards only because it has been incorporated in federal law by § 201 of the Federal Arbitration Act. By the same token, general principles of international law, to the extent they have become American law, could support application of the "public policy" exception. Again, however, decisions to this effect are rare. See Born, *supra* (Note 1) at 1194.

4. A basic principle of arbitration makes it "a matter of contract," so that fundamental changes in the disputes or the parties subject to arbitration cannot be imposed by a court or by an arbitrator. See AT&T Mobility LLC v. Concepcion, 131 S.Ct. 1740, 1752-53 (2011). Hence the New York Convention provides a defense that the arbitration award "deals with a difference not contemplated by or not falling with the terms of the submission to arbitration, or it contains decisions on matters beyond the scope of the submission to arbitration." Art. V.1(c). This defense, however, often becomes entangled with the merits of the claim submitted to arbitration, as it was in *Parsons & Whittemore*. The losing party contended that the contract claim at issue did not extend to "liability for loss of production" because of an explicit exclusion in the contract itself. The arbitration panel considered this exclusion as a limitation on its jurisdiction, but then rejected it. In the enforcement proceedings, the court then deferred to the panel's decision. What was left, then, of the contractual limitations on the panel's authority?

Most courts answer this question by relying on the principle that "ambiguities in the language of the agreement should be resolved in favor of arbitration." EEOC v. Waffle House, Inc., 534 U.S. 279, 294 (2002). Awards clearly beyond the scope of the agreement to arbitrate cannot be enforced. Or, as an early case on labor arbitration framed the principle, an award is "legitimate only so long as it draws its essence from the collective bargaining agreement." United Steelworkers v. Enterprise Wheel & Car Corp., 363 U.S. 593, 597 (1960). The courts resolve the tension between freedom of contract—giving effect to contractual limits on the arbitrator's power—and the presumption in favor of arbitration—deferring to the arbitrator's interpretation of the contract—by deciding themselves whether the parties have validly agreed to arbitrate their dispute. They might give more or less deference to the arbitrator's decision of the same issue, but they review awards in any case for violation of clear limits on the scope of arbitration. Applying that approach, how clear was the purported limit on arbitration in the contract in *Parsons & Whittemore*? Was the clause in question a limit on arbitration at all?

5. *Parsons & Whittemore* also considered the defense that the losing party in arbitration did not have a fair opportunity to be heard. Under the New York Convention, the party who "was not given proper notice" or "was otherwise unable to present his case" can argue against enforcement of the award on those grounds. Art. V.1(b). This defense recognizes a fundamental principle of due process, which applies regardless of the procedures specified in the parties' agreement or by the law of the place of arbitration. Violation of those procedures constitutes a separate defense under the Convention, Art. V.1(d), and denial of due process encompasses grounds independent of those procedures. How much does it add in practice, however?

As with the "public policy" defense, the due process defense is broad in theory but narrow in application. No widely recognized procedures for arbitration allow systematic denial of notice and the opportunity to be heard. The due process defense adds rhetorical force to what might appear to be technical violations of procedural rules, and it might reach a few cases of procedural unfairness not covered by the rules themselves. Apart from that, however, it has only a limited range of operation. The particular objection advanced in *Parsons & Whittemore* was not particularly convincing. The losing party objected that the arbitration panel failed to delay a hearing in order to accommodate the speaking schedule of one of the party's witnesses. If the witness could not give priority to the hearing on his own schedule, why should the arbitration panel have given priority to him? Shouldn't this have been a problem that the witness and the party ought to have worked out for themselves in order to make the arbitration proceed smoothly? In any event, the panel did consider an affidavit by the witness that covered most of the ground that his live testimony would have covered.

6. Interim relief, whether ordered by a court or by an arbitrator, raises a wide range of different issues. These revolve around two questions: (1) How to protect the jurisdiction and process of arbitration, and (2) how to prevent deterioration of the status quo to the detriment of one of the parties? Both questions can be addressed by either a court or the arbitrator, but as they more closely approach the merits of the case, they tend to be given initially to the arbitrator, subject only to judicial review in enforcement proceedings.

Protecting the jurisdiction and process of arbitration begins with a court order requiring arbitration and staying judicial proceedings. That decision precludes further litigation of the merits of the claim in the rendering state. Its effect in other nations depends upon the recognition of the judgment there, as discussed in Chapter 8, or the possibility of obtaining an antisuit injunction in the rendering state, as discussed in Chapter 5. Assuming recognition of the judgment elsewhere—which is likely in states that are parties to the New York Convention or other treaties promoting arbitration—there is usually little need to invoke the cumbersome process of an antisuit injunction—which might well offend the courts of another nation. We consider this possibility in Section D, below.

American courts are divided on their power under the New York Convention to order interim relief to preserve the status quo. The leading decision denying such relief viewed it as a thinly veiled attempt to litigate the merits of the claim rather than sending them to arbitration. McCreary Tire & Rubber Co. v. CEAT S.p.A., 501 F.2d 1032 (3d Cir. 1974). Some courts have therefore distinguished *McCreary* on this ground and ordered interim relief where it was plainly in aid of, rather than a substitute for, arbitration. E.g., Carolina Power & Light Co. v. Uranex, 451 F. Supp. 1044 (N.D. Cal. 1977). Judicially ordered relief might be especially appropriate where the arbitration process has not yet begun (because, for instance, the arbitrator has not yet been selected), and the parties have, as yet, no effective recourse to arbitration.

Interim relief ordered by the arbitrator does not extend to enjoining litigation, since it appears to contradict the basic principle that arbitrators have no coercive power themselves, but must depend upon the courts to enforce their awards. Nevertheless, arbitrators do have the power to compel compliance with the arbitration procedures established by contract or by the law of the place of arbitration. They can do so, if by no other means, simply by altering the final award to the disadvantage of the offending party.

Interim decisions by arbitrators to preserve the status quo typically involve orders requiring a party to post security for the payment of any resulting award or to prevent action by one party that would cause irreparable injury to another during the pendency of the arbitration proceedings. When such orders are specifically authorized by the arbitration agreement or by the law of the place of arbitration, they raise few questions. In the absence of explicit authorization (or explicit prohibition), arbitrators usually find that they have the power to preserve the status quo, but they require progressively stronger showings for more extensive forms of relief. Born, *supra*, at 831-39. Upon entry of an award of interim relief, the prevailing party can then seek enforcement under the standards generally applicable to final awards, as discussed in cases like *Parsons & Whittemore.*

Baxter International, Inc. v. Abbott Laboratories

United States Court of Appeals, Seventh Circuit, 2003.
315 F.3d 829.

EASTERBROOK, CIRCUIT JUDGE.

Baxter International invented sevoflurane in the 1960s. This substance, a gas at room temperature, has good anesthetic properties. But it was too difficult and costly to produce commercially until the early 1980s, when Baxter devised an efficient process for its manufacture. Baxter obtained two process patents, the latter of which expires in December 2005. But the anesthetic gas still could not be sold in the United States unless it first received the FDA's approval, and Baxter was not willing to bear the costs of the required medical testing. So in 1988 it granted to Maruishi Pharmaceutical Company, of Japan, an exclusive worldwide license to practice the sevoflurane process patents Baxter owned or was pursuing. Maruishi obtained approval to sell the anesthetic in Japan, where it was a great success, as it has become in other nations since. This suggested that it would be worth obtaining the FDA's approval to sell in the United States. Abbott Laboratories took a sublicense from Maruishi in 1992, obtained the FDA's approval after spending approximately $60 million on testing, and in 1995 began selling sevoflurane in the United States. Maruishi remains the sole manufacturer under the Baxter patents; Abbott resells sevoflurane that it purchases from Maruishi, which pays Baxter a royalty based on its total sales. Today sevoflurane is the best-selling gas used for anesthesia in the United States, with approximately 58% of sales. * * *

Sevoflurane's success gave rivals an incentive to invent around Baxter's process patents. Ohio Medical Associates (now known as Ohmeda) set out in 1997 to do just this. In 1999 Ohmeda obtained a patent for a new way of making sevoflurane, distinct from Baxter's process but equivalently cheap and effective. It planned to introduce a rival sevoflurane anesthetic, which it could do by filing a "me too" application with the FDA. Ohmeda could receive approval without costly tests just by showing that the finished product is identical to Abbott's.

Before Ohmeda could bring sevoflurane to market, it was acquired (in 1998) by Baxter—which decided to proceed with Ohmeda's plans and compete with the sevoflurane made by Maruishi and sold in the United States by Abbott. Baxter concluded that it would make more from selling Ohmeda-process sevoflurane than it would lose in reduced royalties from Maruishi for Baxter-process sevoflurane. Abbott, which contends that it has spent more than $1 billion to commercialize sevoflurane (including distribution of equipment for administering the drug and marketing to alert anesthesiologists to its benefits) did not welcome competition before the expiration of the Baxter patents. Abbott initiated arbitration under the Baxter-Maruishi agreement (to which it had become a party in 1992) and the Convention on the Recognition and Enforcement of Foreign Arbitral Awards, [1970] 21 U.S.T. 2517, T.I.A.S. No. 6997, implemented by 9 U.S.C. §§ 201-08. The agreement specifies a multi-national tribunal, which consisted of a U.S. attorney, a Spanish attorney, and a Japanese law professor.

Abbott contended that Baxter's sale of Ohmeda-process sevoflurane before the Baxter patents expired would violate the exclusivity term of the license; Baxter replied, first, that the license does not explicitly forbid Baxter itself from competing with Maruishi (in other words, that exclusivity means only that Baxter cannot issue any other licenses), and, second, that if the license does forbid Baxter from competing, then it violates U.S. antitrust law, particularly § 1 of the Sherman Act, 15 U.S.C. § 1, and is unenforceable. The arbitrators ruled against Baxter on both issues. The tribunal held that the license is exclusive in the strong sense and that any reduction in competition is attributable to Baxter's decision to purchase the competing Ohmeda process while bound by this promise not to compete with its licensee. On cross-suits filed by Abbott and Baxter, the district judge then directed Baxter to comply with the award, rejecting its contention that the license, as construed by the tribunal, violates the Sherman Act or the public policy of the United States. * * *

Baxter argues at length in this court that the Baxter-Maruishi license, construed to keep Ohmeda-process sevoflurane off the U.S. market until 2006, is a territorial allocation unlawful *per se* under § 1 of the Sherman Act. But the initial question is whether Baxter is entitled to reargue an issue that was resolved by the arbitral tribunal. We think not; a mistake of law is not a ground on which to set aside an award. Section 207 says that "[t]he court shall confirm the award unless it finds one of the grounds for refusal or deferral of recognition or enforcement of the award specified in the said Convention." Legal errors are not among the grounds that the Convention gives for refusing to enforce international awards. Under domestic law, as well as under the Convention, arbitrators "have completely free rein to decide the law as well as the facts and are not subject to appellate review." *Commonwealth Coatings Corp. v. Continental Casualty Co.,* 393 U.S. 145, 149 (1968). "Courts thus do not sit to hear claims of factual or legal error by an arbitrator". *United Paperworkers v. Misco, Inc.,* 484 U.S. 29, 38 (1987).

Arbitrators regularly handle claims under federal statutes. * * * We do not see any reason why things should be otherwise for antitrust issues—nor, more importantly, does the Supreme Court, which held in *Mitsubishi Motors Corp. v. Soler Chrysler-Plymouth, Inc.,* 473 U.S. 614 (1985), that international arbitration of antitrust disputes is appropriate.

Mitsubishi did not contemplate that, once arbitration was over, the federal courts would throw the result in the waste basket and litigate the antitrust issues anew. That would just be another way of saying that antitrust matters are not arbitrable. Yet this is Baxter's position. It wants us to disregard the panel's award and make our own decision. The Supreme Court's approach in *Mitsubishi* was different. It observed (473 U.S. at 639 n. 21):

"The utility of the Convention in promoting the process of international commercial arbitration depends upon the willingness of national courts to let go of matters they normally would think of as their own. Doubtless, Congress may specify categories of claims it wishes to reserve for decision by our own courts without contravening this Nation's obligations under the Convention. But we decline to subvert the spirit of the United States' accession to the Convention by recognizing subject-matter exceptions where Congress has not expressly directed the courts to do so."

Starting from scratch in court, as Baxter proposes, would subvert the promises the United States made by acceding to the Convention.

According to Baxter, there is a difference between arbitrating an antitrust issue (the subject of *Mitsubishi*) and *creating* one—which it accuses these arbitrators of doing. If the tribunal had construed the Baxter-Maruishi agreement differently, there would have been no antitrust problem. Baxter relies on the observation * * * that arbitrators are not allowed to command the parties to violate rules of positive law. That's true enough, but *whether* the tribunal's construction of the Baxter-Maruishi agreement has that effect was a question put to, and resolved by, the arbitrators. They answered no, and as between Baxter and Abbott their answer is conclusive. This is a point anticipated in *Mitsubishi,* which observed (*id.* at 638): "While the efficacy of the arbitral process requires that substantive review at the award-enforcement stage remain minimal, it would not require intrusive inquiry to ascertain that the tribunal took cognizance of the antitrust claims and actually decided them." The arbitral tribunal in this case "took cognizance of the antitrust claims and actually decided them." Ensuring this is as far as our review legitimately goes.

Treating Baxter as bound (*vis-à-vis* Abbott) by the tribunal's conclusion that the license (as construed to provide strong exclusivity) is lawful does not condemn the public to tolerate a monopoly. If the three-corner arrangement among Baxter, Maruishi, and Abbott really does offend the Sherman Act, then the United States, the FTC, or any purchaser of sevoflurane is free to sue and obtain relief. None of them would be bound by the award. As far as we can see, however, only Baxter is distressed by the award—and Baxter, as a producer, is a poor champion of consumers.

What relief the Antitrust Division, the FTC, or a consumer would obtain, if there is an antitrust problem, is an interesting question. * * * At the time Baxter acquired Ohmeda it was obliged by contract to refrain from producing sevoflurane until 2006. (This is how the tribunal understood the Baxter-Maruishi agreement, and a court must accept this interpretation.) So if there is an antitrust problem, it lies in the acquisition—and the remedy would be divestiture of the Ohmeda process patent. Baxter can achieve that outcome on its own. Baxter, which can solve unilaterally any antitrust problem, is in no position to insist that the burden of solution fall on Abbott by depriving it of the benefit of the exclusive Baxter-Maruishi license. Why should a decision Baxter made in 1998 reduce the rights Abbott enjoys under a promise Baxter made to Maruishi in 1988? But it is unnecessary to pursue this line of argument. All that matters today is that the arbitrators have concluded that the antitrust laws (and Baxter's related arguments, which we need not address) do not diminish Abbott's contractual rights—and that decision is conclusive between these parties.

AFFIRMED.

CUDAHY, CIRCUIT JUDGE, dissenting.

* * *

The majority upholds the arbitration award here by declaring that, once the arbitrators have spoken to the antitrust issues and in effect commanded the parties to violate the Sherman Act, the courts have no business intervening. Of course, the doctrine that requires extreme deference by the courts to arbitration awards is based on the theory that the parties to a contract may cede broad, almost unlimited, power to an arbitration panel to interpret their agreement. All this rests on the proposition that the parties are free to adjust rights and liabilities *among themselves* as they see fit and through the instrumentality of arbitration to follow wherever the situation may demand. In this bilateral context a commitment to deference cannot be questioned.

But other considerations enter the mix when the issue becomes a matter of the arbitrators', in interpreting a statute, commanding the parties to break the law or to violate clearly established norms of public policy. In the case before us, the arbitrators have instructed Abbott and Baxter (by imposing on Baxter a broad covenant not to compete with respect to sales of sevoflurane itself) to effect a horizontal allocation of markets, a clear violation of the Sherman Act. Under the arbitral decision, Abbott is granted a monopoly[2] in the sale of sevoflurane in the United States. * * *

The present case is a good example of the extent to which arbitration has come to pervade the legal culture. First, the parties here constructed an elaborate, pre-dispute arbitration agreement that not only served to regulate the licensing agreement itself, but also, in an extraordinary spasm of creativity during the arbitration, generated a new and seemingly boundless cause of action, entirely separate from the license itself, under which the parties could presumably proceed. Then, during the arbitral process, Baxter submitted to the arbitrators the supplemental argument[3] that, if the arbitrators pursued what eventually did become their line of decision, they would be commanding unlawful conduct

---

[2] There is no dispute that Baxter's Ohmeda is the only generic competitor in the sevoflurane market for the foreseeable future, nor is there a dispute that the arbitral decision's prohibition on the sale of generic sevoflurane by Baxter preserves monopoly prices and levels of output of Abbott's sevoflurane product.

[3] It is an important distinction that this rather meta-juridical antitrust claim "decided" by the arbitrators was not a simple claim by Baxter against Abbott, but rather a request by Baxter that the arbitrators step back and consider the larger implications of their underlying decision. This distinction becomes clear when one recognizes that this issue could simply have been ignored by the arbitrators and considered for the first time in the district court—the arbitrators' interpretation of the license and the DRA did not involve antitrust issues. But, if Baxter had not raised the antitrust issue during arbitration, it would have risked being met with a defense of waiver to consideration of the issue here. Yet, on the other hand, Baxter's position here might well have been strengthened if it had chosen not to bring the question forward during arbitration and thereby armed Abbott with the (dispositive, as it turns out) argument for deference to the arbitration award.

under the Sherman Act. And finally, neither Baxter nor Abbott contend that arbitration was inappropriate for resolution of the antitrust claim.

Now, the majority has taken the process one giant step further and has found that *Mitsubishi* not only allows submission of statutory and antitrust claims to arbitration, but denies our prerogative to refuse to enforce awards that command unlawful conduct. The deciding circumstance, according to the majority, is that the question was put to, and decided by, the arbitrators themselves. Therefore, under the majority's analysis, the rule that unlawful conduct cannot be commanded by arbitrators is consumed by the exception that, if the arbitrators themselves say that what they have commanded is not unlawful, then "their answer is conclusive."

This cannot be correct. While *Mitsubishi* and its progeny make clear that the choice of the arbitral forum is to be respected, they do not confer on the arbitrators a prerogative to preemptively review their own decisions and receive deference on that review in subsequent judicial evaluations. The majority is way off-base when it says that Baxter seeks merely to have us disregard the panel's decision and "throw the result in the waste basket." Instead, we are performing exactly the traditional function of judicial review properly assigned only to us.

Therefore, I do not think we can simply note the arbitration panel's resolution of the antitrust issue and consider our work done. Instead, we must fulfill our judicial responsibilities and examine the effect of the outcome commanded by the arbitral award. This means that we have to determine whether, going forward, the horizontal restraint on Baxter's competing with Abbott in the sevoflurane market violates the Sherman Act. * * *

It is, of course, not the interests of the parties themselves that are primarily at stake in the outcome of this arbitration. Instead the interest of the consuming public is at stake. That public faces higher prices and a constrained supply of sevoflurane as a result of Abbott's monopoly, conferred by the arbitrators. When public rights are at stake, there is good reason to be more reluctant to defer totally to the arbitrators, since they are acting as delegates of the private parties, not of the consuming public. Too deferential an attitude by the courts when the rights of the consuming public are at stake can severely undermine the foundations of our economy. For there can be little doubt that granting Abbott a monopoly to produce sevoflurane in the United States will raise prices and restrict supply. And applying the analysis of the majority to arbitration awards yet to come will open a royal detour around the antitrust laws. * * *

It is not my role to critique the arbitration decision—however flawed— except in this case to object to its anti-competitive outcome, which orders the parties to violate the antitrust laws. The interest of consumers was not represented on the arbitration panel and the panel's decision ignored consumer interests. Defense of public interests is sometimes better fulfilled by courts than by arbitration panels.

Nor am I much reassured by the substitute antitrust enforcement possibilities mentioned by the majority. It is conceivable that the Federal Trade Commission or the Justice Department might attack Abbott's monopoly conferred by the arbitrators or that another competitor might surface to provide competition from a generic sevoflurane manufactured by some process yet to be invented, but these possible sources of law enforcement or of competition are all hypothetical. I know of no authority for the theory that the existence of hypothetical sources of antitrust enforcement or of competition can be a defense to an agreement violative of the antitrust laws or to an arbitration award imposing such an agreement.

So while I agree with the majority that antitrust claims are arbitrable, and I also agree that the grounds for refusing to enforce an arbitration award are limited, I do not agree that there is support in the law for the majority's excision of antitrust arbitration from the general framework of judicial review that prohibits an arbitration panel's award from commanding illegal conduct. And in the case before us, the arbitration panel's ruling granting Abbott a monopoly in the United States sevoflurane market commands illegal conduct on the part both of Baxter and Abbott and is unenforceable.

I would remand with instructions not to enforce the arbitral award, and I therefore respectfully DISSENT.

NOTES AND QUESTIONS FOR DISCUSSION

1. *Baxter International* contains elements of both enforcement of arbitral awards as well as arbitrability of certain issues—the latter being a topic associated with the issues presented in Section B, above. How far does *Baxter International* take the trend in favor of arbitration beyond *Vimar Seguros* and *Parsons & Whittemore*? In ordering arbitration in *Vimar Seguros*, the Supreme Court reserved the question of enforcing the resulting arbitration award. In *Parsons & Whittemore*, the Second Circuit found no impediment in American law or policy to prevent enforcement of an award on a contractual claim. In *Baxter International*, the Seventh Circuit defers to the arbitrators' resolution of an antitrust defense to enforcement of a patent licensing agreement. As the court states the standard: "The arbitral tribunal in this case 'took cognizance of the antitrust claims and actually decided them.'" Does this standard meet the dissent's argument that the arbitrators might have erroneously permitted Abbott to compel compliance with the agreement and violate the antitrust laws?

In the last two paragraphs of its opinion, the court expresses doubts that the agreement "really does offend the Sherman Act" and that Baxter really has an interest in invalidating it on behalf of consumers. The essence of Baxter's defense, after all, was that Abbott had violated the antitrust laws through its agreement with Baxter itself. How persuasive can such an argument be if Baxter has not kept its own hands clean? Does this feature of the case diminish the degree of deference that the court actually gave to the arbitrators' award? The court also notes that third parties, such as government enforcement agencies and consumers, are not bound by the results of the arbitration and that they could bring their own antitrust claims. How likely are they to do so? Or does that return the analysis to the merits of the antitrust claim?

2. Suppose that the agreement had resulted in monopolization of the market for anesthetics, without any semblance of legitimacy under the patent laws. Would that have made the arbitration award "contrary to public policy" or "in manifest disregard of the law"? How blatant does the inconsistency have to be between the arbitration award and otherwise applicable law?   On the facts of *Baxter International* itself, the patent over Sevoflurane gave Baxter a legitimate monopoly over the sale of this anesthetic, which it then proceeded to license to Maruishi which then issued a sublicense to Abbott Laboratories.   Both the license and the sublicense were exclusive—for Maruishi to manufacture Sevoflurane and for Abbott Laboratories to market it in the United States.   The patent conferred a degree of legitimacy on the agreements that they otherwise would have lacked and that led the arbitration panel to enforce the agreements despite Baxter's arguments that they violated the antitrust laws.   Did the plausibility of the arbitration decision effectively render it immune from judicial review?   If so, do the decisions of private arbitrators effectively receive more deference than those of public judges?   At least on questions of law, the decisions of trial judges are subject to de novo appellate review.

For an example of a rare instance in which a court denied enforcement of an arbitration award on the ground that it was against public policy, see Laminoirs-Trefileries-Cableries de Lens, S.A. v. Southwire Co., 484 F. Supp. 1063 (N.D. Ga. 1980).   In that case, the arbitration panel followed French law and imposed an interest on the amount awarded that rose by 5% automatically after two months, resulting in a total interest rate as high as 15%.   The court refused to enforce this part of the award, finding that it contradicted the usury laws of the state of Georgia law, where enforcement was sought.   The clear terms of the award under French law violated the equally clear ceiling on interest rates under Georgia.   It was accordingly in violation of public policy, despite the reasoning of the arbitration panel that French law alone applied to the award.   Decisions such as this confirm both the narrowness of the public policy exception to enforcement and the limits that it places on deference to the arbitrator's decisions.   As with the other defenses to enforcement considered—and rejected—in *Parsons & Whittemore*, public policy succeeds in overcoming the deference generally accorded to arbitrators only when their decisions violate clear limits imposed by applicable law.

3.   The judicial process differs from the arbitration process in more than the standards for appellate review.   It also differs in the degree of publicity and accountability that judicial decisions receive.   They are matters of public record, published or readily available online and subject to media coverage and political criticism.   Arbitration decisions need not be publicized at all, unless the parties agree to make them public and engage in litigation over their enforcement.   Does this raise the possibility that the law applied by arbitrators might diverge by gradual and imperceptible steps from the law by judges?   No one decision might be so clearly wrong that it is denied enforcement, but the cumulative effect of a series of decisions might take the arbitration process far from the results that the judicial process might have reached.   Are the gains from private dispute resolution worth the risk that it might diverge from public adjudication?

In the international context, arbitration typically involves claims between business firms repeatedly involved in commercial and financial transactions and in disputes over them.   The presence of such sophisticated parties diminishes the risk, found in many domestic cases, of one-sided agreements involving consumers or employees who cannot protect themselves by bargaining to alter the terms of arbitration. Small businesses dealing with multinational corporations might face the same imbalance in bargaining power, but they are more likely to be on either side of a transaction—as buyers in some cases, and sellers in others; as debtors and creditors; and more generally, as parties seeking or avoiding arbitration. All the parties in *Baxter International*, for instance, were major drug companies perfectly capable of protecting themselves in contract negotiations and in the arbitration process. If the presence of such parties justifies more deferential review of arbitration awards, would the absence of sophisticated parties justify more stringent review? The latter situation might arise in a variant on the facts of *Vimar Seguros*, in which the shipper, who owned the cargo, asserted a claim against the carrier, who owned the vessel. What if the shipper only occasionally engaged in international trade? Should that have made a difference in enforcing any resulting arbitration award? How could it under *Parsons & Whittemore* and *Baxter International*?

D. ANTISUIT INJUNCTIONS IN AID OF ARBITRATION

Suppose a party to an arbitration agreement decides to file suit over a dispute arguably covered by the arbitration agreement rather than to arbitrate the dispute. One possibility for the party who would prefer to arbitrate would be to ask the court in which suit has been filed to stay its proceedings and to order arbitration. As discussed in *Vimar Seguros, supra,* section 3 of the FAA ordinarily requires U.S. courts to stay their own proceedings and enforce arbitration agreements covered by the Act. See 9 U.S.C. § 3. (And when no judicial proceedings have been filed but a party wishes to enforce an arbitration clause, section 4 of the FAA provides for obtaining a judicial order to compel arbitration. See 9 U.S.C. § 4.) But what if a lawsuit in arguable derogation of an arbitration clause is filed in a foreign forum in which it might be difficult, for one reason or another, to obtain an order to arbitrate or to obtain such an order in an expeditious manner. Would it be possible for the party who wishes to vindicate the arbitration agreement to seek an antisuit injunction from a second court, enjoining the party who has filed suit from further litigation, and to compel arbitration? How should the basic principles respecting antisuit injunctions (discussed in Chapter 5) be applied in the arbitration setting? In this section, we offer the response of a U.S. court and the response of the European Court of Justice to such requests.

Paramedics Electromedicina Comercial, Ltda. v. GE Medical Systems Information Technologies, Inc.

United States Court of Appeals, Second Circuit, 2004.

369 F.3d 645.

JACOBS, CIRCUIT JUDGE.

Paramedics Electromedicina Comercial, Ltda. (known as "Tecnimed") was a distributor in Brazil for products of GE Medical Systems Information

Technologies, Inc. ("GEMS-IT"), under agreements containing broad arbitration clauses. GEMS-IT invoked the arbitration process in April 2002; Tecnimed soon thereafter commenced a lawsuit in Porto Alegre, Brazil (the "Porto Alegre action") against GEMS-IT and a related company, General Electric do Brasil ("GE Brasil"), and petitioned in New York State court for a permanent stay of the arbitration. GEMS-IT removed the petition to federal court, and counterclaimed for an order to compel arbitration and for an anti-suit injunction to halt the Porto Alegre action.

On June 4, 2003, the [federal] district court * * * issued an order compelling arbitration and directing Tecnimed to "immediately take all steps necessary to cause dismissal of the" Porto Alegre suit. Instead, according to Tecnimed, it requested the Brazilian court to put the case on a "suspense" calendar. Not satisfied, the district court directed Tecnimed to sign a Joint Petition to Dismiss by a certain date, which Tecnimed failed to do. [The district court held Tecnimed and Technimed's president, Werlang, in civil contempt, and ordered Tecnimed and Werlang, jointly and severally, to pay GEMS-IT $1,000 until September 3, 2003, and $5,000 thereafter for each day of continued intransigence.]

Tecnimed argues that the district court erred in enjoining the Porto Alegre action and in holding Tecnimed and Werlang in civil contempt. We conclude (i) that the anti-suit injunction was an appropriate measure to enforce and protect the judgment compelling arbitration; [and] (ii) that the district court did not abuse its discretion in holding Tecnimed and Werlang in civil contempt; * * *.

BACKGROUND

GEMS-IT is a Wisconsin corporation that manufactures and distributes medical equipment. Tecnimed is a Brazilian corporation that markets and sells medical equipment, and has distributed GEMS-IT's products (and those of its predecessor companies) in Brazil since 1995.

In 1999, Tecnimed and GEMS-IT executed two agreements to govern their relationship, a Sales and Service Agreement and a Distribution Agreement (collectively, "the Agreements"). Unlike prior contracts between Tecnimed and predecessors of GEMS-IT, the 1999 Agreements did not grant Tecnimed exclusive distribution rights. Each Agreement contained an arbitration clause. The Sales and Service Agreement provided, in relevant part, that thirty days following notice given by one party to the other of "any controversy, claim or dispute between the Parties arising out of or relating in any way to this Agreement which the Parties are unable to resolve by mutual negotiation" or mediation, "either Party shall be entitled to have such controversy, claim or dispute finally settled by arbitration, in accordance with the [then-effective] rules of the Inter-American Commercial Arbitration Commission" ("IACAC"). The Distribution Agreement contained a clause to the same effect.

By early 2001, controversies had arisen: according to GEMS-IT, Tecnimed owed approximately $1.2 million on unpaid invoices; according to Tecnimed, GEMS-IT sold products directly into the Brazilian market, bypassing Tecnimed in violation of certain licenses. On March 18, 2002, after fruitless negotiations, GEMS-IT wrote to Tecnimed initiating the arbitration process outlined in the

Agreements. Ten days later, Tecnimed advised GEMS-IT that it had commenced legal action in the Tenth Civil Circuit Court of Porto Alegre, Brazil.

On April 22, 2002, GEMS-IT filed a notice and request for arbitration with the IACAC. After further fruitless negotiations, Tecnimed advised the IACAC that the Commission lacked jurisdiction to consider GEMS-IT's claims, and that Tecnimed would not be participating in the arbitration. The IACAC nonetheless appointed a panel, consisting of one arbitrator from Brazil, one from the United States, and one from Canada.

On May 23, 2002, Tecnimed filed its complaint with the Porto Alegre court, naming as defendants GEMS-IT and GE Brasil, and alleging, inter alia: (i) that the Agreements lacked "contractual equilibrium" and were unenforceable under Brazilian law; (ii) that Tecnimed was not required to arbitrate its dispute with GEMS-IT because the Agreements had expired; (iii) that GEMS-IT wrongfully terminated the Agreements, causing a loss of profits to Tecnimed; (iv) that GEMS-IT illegally imported three pieces of equipment into Brazil without Tecnimed's authorization, causing Tecnimed to suffer "moral" damages; (v) that GEMS-IT breached the Agreements by failing to pay Tecnimed sales commissions for certain products; (vi) that Tecnimed was entitled to exclusive distributorship of GEMS-IT products in Brazil; and (vii) that Tecnimed was entitled to a declaration of non-existence of debt to GEMS-IT for equipment purchased by Tecnimed under the Agreements.

GEMS-IT moved on both fronts; it answered the Porto Alegre complaint, and filed a statement of claim with the IACAC arbitral panel. In response, Tecnimed filed a petition in New York State court seeking a permanent stay of the arbitration (the "New York action"). GEMS-IT removed the petition to the United States District Court for the Southern District of New York, and asserted counterclaims for an order compelling arbitration and for an anti-suit injunction to bar Tecnimed from prosecuting the Porto Alegre action.

In April 2003 (while Tecnimed's petition for a stay of arbitration was pending in the [federal] district court), the IACAC panel rejected Tecnimed's challenge to arbitral jurisdiction, ruling that the arbitration clauses were valid and binding; that the claims GEMS-IT had submitted to the panel were within the scope of the arbitration clauses, as were the claims Tecnimed was asserting in Porto Alegre; and that the panel would consider the issues in the Porto Alegre action to the extent deemed necessary.

On June 4, 2003, the district court * * * ruled that the arbitration clauses were valid and that all of GEMS-IT's claims, as well as all of Tecnimed's claims asserted in the Porto Alegre action, were arbitrable. The court thereupon granted GEMS-IT's motion to compel arbitration, rejected Tecnimed's request for a stay, entered an anti-suit injunction, and ordered Tecnimed to "immediately take all steps necessary to cause dismissal of the [Porto Alegre] Action." If the suit in Porto Alegre was not dismissed by June 17, 2003, Tecnimed had until June 20, 2003 to explain why.

On June 17, 2003, Tecnimed filed a notice with the Porto Alegre court requesting that its case be placed on the "suspense" calendar. According to GEMS-IT's expert on Brazilian law, placement on the suspense calendar would halt the case for no more than six months. In any event, the Porto Alegre court notified GEMS-IT on June 30, 2003 that it was required to file a "manifestation" (the Brazilian equivalent of a sur-reply) to Tecnimed's reply to GEMS-IT's answer to the complaint.

Apprised of these developments, the district court directed GEMS-IT to draft a Joint Petition to Dismiss (the "Petition") pursuant to Brazilian law by July 1, 2003, and ordered Tecnimed either to sign it by July 8, 2003, or to register objections to the draft by that date. Tecnimed's counsel refused to sign the Petition on the grounds that it did not protect Tecnimed from the running of the applicable statute of limitations and that, under Brazilian law, Tecnimed would have to pay a large "honorarium" fee of 10-20% of the value of the claim as a consequence of dismissing the case.

On July 14, 2003, GEMS-IT filed a motion [in the federal district court] to hold Tecnimed and its president, Paulo Werlang, in civil contempt for failing to dismiss the Porto Alegre action. GEMS-IT argued: that Tecnimed's notice of suspension to the Porto Alegre court was defective because it failed to furnish a Portuguese translation of the district court's order; that the honorarium fee—based on the stated value of the claim—would be nominal; and that under Brazilian law the statute of limitations would be tolled automatically pending arbitration.

On July 21, 2003, the district court ordered the parties to amend the Petition to provide expressly that the statute of limitations would be tolled pending the arbitration, ordered Tecnimed to sign the modified Petition by July 24, 2003, and warned that noncompliance would trigger sanctions. Tecnimed did not sign. Instead, it moved for a stay of the injunction pending appeal and for postponement of the scheduled July 31 hearing. The district court denied the postponement, found that Tecnimed had violated its July 21 order to sign the Petition[.] [The district court then held Tecnimed in civil contempt, ordering it to pay a sum to the court of $1,000 per day for each day of noncompliance with its orders.]

This Court consolidated Tecnimed's separate appeals of the district court's grant of an anti-suit injunction and its contempt ruling.

DISCUSSION

I

The standard of review for the grant of a permanent injunction, including an anti-suit injunction, is abuse of discretion. *S.C. Johnson & Son, Inc. v. Clorox Co.*, 241 F.3d 232, 237 (2d Cir. 2001); *see also China Trade & Dev. Corp. v. M.V. Choong Yong,* 837 F.2d 33, 37 (2d Cir.1987).

It is beyond question that a federal court may enjoin a party before it from pursuing litigation in a foreign forum. *China Trade,* 837 F.2d at 35. But principles of comity counsel that injunctions restraining foreign litigation be "used sparingly" and "granted only with care and great restraint." *Id.* at 36 (internal quotation marks and citations omitted); *see also Gen. Elec. Co. v. Deutz AG,* 270 F.3d 144, 160 (3d Cir. 2001).

An anti-suit injunction against parallel litigation may be imposed only if: (A) the parties are the same in both matters, and (B) resolution of the case before the enjoining court is dispositive of the action to be enjoined. *China Trade,* 837 F.2d at 35. Once past this threshold, courts are directed to consider a number of additional factors, including whether the foreign action threatens the jurisdiction or the strong public policies of the enjoining forum. *Id.* at 36. Tecnimed contends that neither threshold requirement has been satisfied, and that comity considerations render the injunction inappropriate.

A.

Tecnimed asserts that the parties in the two matters are not identical because GE Brasil, which Tecnimed named as a defendant in the Porto Alegre action, is not a party in the New York action. The record supports the district court's finding of substantial similarity and affiliation between GEMS-IT and GE Brasil. * * *

B.

Under *China Trade,* an anti-suit injunction may be proper if "resolution of the case before the enjoining court would be dispositive of the enjoined action." 837 F.2d at 36. The case before the enjoining court here concerns the arbitrability of the parties' claims; therefore the question under *China Trade* is whether the ruling on arbitrability is dispositive of the Porto Alegre litigation, even though the underlying disputes are confided to the arbitral panel and will not be decided by the enjoining court.[3] In short, the district court's judgment disposes of the Porto Alegre action because the Porto Alegre litigation concerns issues that, by virtue of the district court's judgment, are reserved to arbitration.

Tecnimed argues that its Brazilian claim for "moral damages" stemming from GEMS-IT's alleged violation of Brazil's import and licensing laws is a tort claim unique to Brazilian law that cannot be resolved through arbitration because "an arbitration in the United States will result in a misunderstanding of Brazilian import and registration law by the IACAC arbitrators." Perhaps this is true, though the panel assigned by the IACAC includes one arbitrator from Brazil; however, to the extent that the claim is arbitrable, the district court's ruling is dispositive even if the claim is unique to Brazil.

As to arbitrability, Tecnimed argues that this claim is not "based upon the sale of GEMS-IT's products by Tecnimed pursuant to the terms of the . . .

---

[3] Compare the cases in which the domestic court speaks to the merits of a controversy under domestic law while an analogous claim under foreign law is pending in a foreign forum, and in which resolution of one action may not dispose of the other. *See Sperry Rand Corp. v. Sunbeam Corp.,* 285 F.2d 542, 545 (7th Cir. 1960) (disposition of trademark action in Illinois would not necessarily resolve subsequently trademark suit filed in Germany under German law by plaintiff's German licensee, which "involv[ed] specific foreign rights arising under and enforceable only through the laws of" Germany); *Rauland Borg Corp. v. TCS Mgmt. Group, Inc.,* 1995 WL 31569 (N.D.Ill. Jan. 25, 1995), 1995 U.S. Dist. LEXIS 893, at *9–*12 (American trademark action implicated a different set of laws—and raised a potentially unique set of defenses—from a Canadian trademark action involving the same parties and issues).

Agreements," i.e., that it falls outside the purview of the arbitration clauses.[4] We review *de novo* a district court's determination that a claim is arbitrable. *Vera v. Saks & Co.,* 335 F.3d 109, 116 (2d Cir. 2003).

Federal policy strongly favors the enforcement of arbitration agreements. *See* 9 U.S.C. § 2; *Moses H. Cone Mem'l Hosp. v. Mercury Constr. Corp.,* 460 U.S. 1, 24-25 (1983). Therefore, "the existence of any broad agreement to arbitrate creates a presumption of arbitrability which is only overcome if it may be said with positive assurance that the arbitration clause is not susceptible of an interpretation that covers the asserted dispute. Doubts should be resolved in favor of coverage." *Smith/Enron Cogeneration Ltd. P'ship v. Smith Cogeneration Int'l Inc.,* 198 F.3d 88, 99 (2d Cir. 1999) (quoting *WorldCrisa Corp. v. Armstrong,* 129 F.3d 71, 74 (2d Cir. 1997)); * * *. The arbitration agreement here, covering as it does "any controversy, claim or dispute" arising out of the Agreements, is of the broad type. "If the allegations underlying the claims 'touch matters' covered by the parties' . . . agreements, then those claims must be arbitrated." *Smith/Enron,* 198 F.3d at 99 (citation omitted).

Tecnimed's claim for moral damages alleges that GEMS-IT circumvented Tecnimed as the distribution agent for certain products that were imported into Brazil. This claim "touches matters" covered by the Agreements, which govern the relationship between the companies regarding the distribution, sale, and service of GEMS-IT's products in Brazil. Certainly, the arbitration agreements here are "susceptible of an interpretation that covers the asserted dispute." *Id.* The district court committed no error in ruling that the claim for moral damages is arbitrable, and that such ruling is dispositive of the claim.

C.

Beyond the threshold criteria of *China Trade,* other considerations include whether the foreign proceeding threatens a strong public policy or the jurisdiction of the domestic forum. *See China Trade,* 837 F.2d at 36-37. Both considerations are salient in this case.

As the D.C. Circuit has noted, "an anti-suit injunction will issue to preclude participation in the litigation only when the strongest equitable factors favor its use," and the granting of an injunction depends in part on the "importance to the forum of the law allegedly evaded." *Laker Airways Ltd. v. Sabena, Belgian World Airlines,* 731 F.2d 909, 931-32 (D.C. Cir. 1984); *see also Gau Shan Co. v. Bankers Trust Co.,* 956 F.2d 1349, 1358 (6th Cir. 1992) ("only the evasion of the most compelling public policies of the forum will support the issuance of an antisuit injunction").

The federal policy favoring the liberal enforcement of arbitration clauses (as discussed above) applies with particular force in international disputes. *See Mitsubishi Motors Corp. v. Soler Chrysler-Plymouth, Inc.,* 473 U.S. 614, 638-40 (1985); *Smith/Enron,* 198 F.3d at 92. The Porto Alegre action, filed 31 days after

---

[4] Tecnimed's claims on appeal are limited to the district court's grant of an anti-suit injunction and its contempt finding; there is no clear appeal of the district court's determination that all the claims are arbitrable. However, certain language in Tecnimed's brief can nonetheless be liberally construed to raise this argument, and we will therefore consider it.

GEMS-IT filed a notice and request for arbitration with the IACAC, was a tactic to evade arbitration. As Mr. Werlang, Tecnimed's president, stated in his affidavit, Tecnimed initiated the Porto Alegre action "to avoid being dragged into an arbitration process that GE had no right to force upon it."

We need not decide categorically whether an attempt to sidestep arbitration is alone sufficient to support a foreign anti-suit injunction, because "[t]here is less justification for permitting a second action," as here, "after a prior court has reached a judgment on the same issues." *Laker Airways,* 731 F.2d at 928 n. 53. An anti-suit injunction may be needed to protect the court's jurisdiction once a judgment has been rendered. The doctrine of res judicata, where applied, may obviate injunctive relief against re-litigation in a second forum; but a foreign court might not give res judicata effect to a United States judgment, particularly since United States courts "may choose to give res judicata effect to foreign judgments on the basis of comity," but "are not obliged" to do so. *Mezitis Diorinou v. Mezitis,* 237 F.3d 133, 140 (2d Cir. 2001) (internal quotation marks and citation omitted).

Principles of comity weigh heavily in the decision to impose a foreign anti-suit injunction; while such an injunction in terms is leveled against the party bringing the suit, it nonetheless "effectively restricts the jurisdiction of the court of a foreign sovereign." *China Trade,* 837 F.2d at 35. So courts that contemplate this extreme measure often must reconcile the protection of their own jurisdiction with respect for the foreign forum. But where one court has already reached a judgment—on the same issues, involving the same parties—considerations of comity have diminished force.

II

[The Court of Appeals also upheld the contempt sanctions that the district court had ordered for noncompliance with its orders.]

CONCLUSION

For the foregoing reasons, we affirm the district court's judgment * * *.

NOTES AND QUESTIONS FOR DISCUSSION

1. In ruling on the propriety of the antisuit injunction in aid of arbitration, the Court of Appeals in *Paramedics Electromedicina* refers primarily to decisional law respecting antisuit injunctions outside the arbitral setting. How relevant are those decisions or their presumptions respecting the availablility of intercourt injunctive relief in the *non*arbitral setting to the availability of such relief in the arbitral setting? After all, in the nonarbitral setting, some court will hear the dispute, the primary question being "Which one?" But the point of arbitration is that no court should be hearing the dispute at all. Does that make the argument for enjoining litigation in the arbitral setting a stronger one than in the nonarbitral setting? Under what circumstances?

2. Consider what is at stake in the ordinary setting of antisuit injunctions, as discussed above in Chapter 5, Section C. On the one hand, there are comity concerns based on respect for foreign country judicial proceedings, particularly if they are already well underway and can promptly vindicate the rights of the parties with relative convenience and efficiency. Although federal courts have articulated different views respecting the ease with which such injunctions may be obtained against the maintenance of foreign litigation, even the narrower view appears to allow for such injunctions when their jurisdiction is fundamentally threatened. Is a similar principle at work when a party seeks an injunction from one court against proceedings in another court, at least when the dispute is one that is properly subject to arbitration? In other words, could such an antisuit injunction arguably be in aid of the jurisdiction of the arbitral tribunal, and if so, under what circumstances?

3. The FAA does not itself speak specifically of the possibility of antisuit injunctions to enforce or vindicate arbitration. What it does provide is for the court in which litigation may have been brought to stay its proceedings in favor of arbitration of properly arbitrable disputes (which includes international arbitration clauses under the New York Convention). See 9 U.S.C. § 3 (providing for stay) and 9 U.S.C. §§ 201-208 (incorporating New York Convention and various procedures). See also id. at § 4 (providing for parties to seek an order in a federal court to compel arbitration if subject matter jurisdiction otherwise exists). Is this sufficient authorization for a U.S. court to enjoin foreign litigation that has been brought in derogation of arbitration (as in *Paramedics Electromedicina*)? Or do antisuit injunctions, as a general matter, not need any specific authorization? See Born, *supra,* at 268-80 (discussing different courts' willingness (or unwillingness) to grant such injunctions).

4. As set out in Chapter 5, within its scope of application, the current Brussels Regulation (44/2001) does not permit parallel litigation of the same issue(s) in multiple courts at the same time. The Regulation espouses, instead, a strict priority (first-come-first-served) principle. See also Appendix D. According to that principle, once a party has initiated legal proceedings before a court within a Member State of the European Union, no other court within the EU may exercise jurisdiction over the same dispute. Even though the Regulation explicitly states that it does not apply to arbitration (see Article 1(2)(d)), the priority principle has nevertheless been held to apply in cases in which a party resorted to a national court despite an arbitration clause pursuant to which the parties had originally agreed to submit their disputes to arbitration. The European Court of Justice famously so held in the decision that follows:

Allianz SpA, and Generali Assicurazioni Generali SpA v. West Tankers Inc.

Court of Justice of the European Communities, 2009.

Case C-185/07, 2009 E.C.R. I-00663

* * *

9. In August 2000 the *Front Comor*, a vessel owned by West Tankers and chartered by Erg Petroli SpA ('Erg'), collided in Syracuse (Italy) with a jetty owned by Erg and caused damage. The charterparty was governed by English law and contained a clause providing for arbitration in London (United Kingdom).

10. Erg claimed compensation from its insurers Allianz and Generali up to the limit of its insurance cover and commenced arbitration proceedings in London against West Tankers for the excess. West Tankers denied liability for the damage caused by the collision.

11. Having paid Erg compensation under the insurance policies for the loss it had suffered, Allianz and Generali brought proceedings on 30 July 2003 against West Tankers before the Tribunale di Siracusa (Italy) in order to recover the sums they had paid to Erg. The action was based on their statutory right of subrogation to Erg's claims, in accordance with Article 1916 of the Italian Civil Code. West Tankers raised an objection of lack of jurisdiction on the basis of the existence of the arbitration agreement.

12. In parallel, West Tankers brought proceedings, on 10 September 2004, before the High Court of Justice of England and Wales, Queens Bench Division (Commercial Court), seeking a declaration that the dispute between itself, on the one hand, and Allianz and Generali, on the other, was to be settled by arbitration pursuant to the arbitration agreement. West Tankers also sought an injunction restraining Allianz and Generali from pursuing any proceedings other than arbitration and requiring them to discontinue the proceedings commenced before the Tribunale di Siracusa ('the anti-suit injunction').

13. By judgment of 21 March 2005, the High Court of Justice of England and Wales, Queens Bench Division (Commercial Court), upheld West Tankers' claims and granted the anti-suit injunction sought against Allianz and Generali. The latter appealed against that judgment to the House of Lords. They argued that the grant of such an injunction is contrary to Regulation No 44/2001.

14. The House of Lords first referred to the judgments in Case C-116/02 *Gasser* [2003] ECR I-14693 and Case C-159/02 *Turner* [2004] ECR I-3565 [See Chapter 5, Section C, excerpting *Turner*—eds.] which decided in substance that an injunction restraining a party from commencing or continuing proceedings in a court of a Member State cannot be compatible with the system established by Regulation No 44/2001, even where it is granted by the court having jurisdiction under that regulation. That is because the regulation provides a complete set of uniform rules on the allocation of jurisdiction between the courts of the Member States which must trust each other to apply those rules correctly.

15. However, that principle cannot, in the view of the House of Lords, be extended to arbitration, which is completely excluded from the scope of Regulation No 44/2001 by virtue of Article 1(2)(d) thereof. In that field, there is no set of uniform Community rules, which is a necessary condition in order that mutual trust between the courts of the Member States may be established and applied. Moreover, it is clear from the judgment in Case C-190/89 *Rich* [1991] ECR I-3855 that the exclusion in Article 1(2)(d) of Regulation No 44/2001 applies not only to arbitration proceedings as such, but also to legal proceedings the subject-matter of which is arbitration. The judgment in Case C-391/95 *Van Uden* [1998] ECR I-7091 stated that arbitration is the subject-matter of proceedings where they serve to protect the right to determine the dispute by arbitration, which is the case in the main proceedings.

16. The House of Lords adds that since all arbitration matters fall outside the scope of Regulation No 44/2001, an injunction addressed to Allianz and Generali restraining them from having recourse to proceedings other than arbitration and from continuing proceedings before the Tribunale di Siracusa cannot infringe the regulation.

17. Finally, the House of Lords points out that the courts of the United Kingdom have for many years used anti-suit injunctions. That practice is, in its view, a valuable tool for the court of the seat of arbitration, exercising supervisory jurisdiction over the arbitration, as it promotes legal certainty and reduces the possibility of conflict between the arbitration award and the judgment of a national court. Furthermore, if the practice were also adopted by the courts in other Member States it would make the European Community more competitive vis-à-vis international arbitration centres such as New York, Bermuda and Singapore.

18. In those circumstances, the House of Lords decided to stay its proceedings and to refer the following question to the Court for a preliminary ruling:

> 'Is it consistent with Regulation No 44/2001 for a court of a Member State to make an order to restrain a person from commencing or continuing proceedings in another Member State on the ground that such proceedings are in breach of an arbitration agreement?'

The question referred for a preliminary ruling

19. By its question, the House of Lords asks, essentially, whether it is incompatible with Regulation No 44/2001 for a court of a Member State to make an order to restrain a person from commencing or continuing proceedings before the courts of another Member State on the ground that such proceedings would be contrary to an arbitration agreement, even though Article 1(2)(d) of the regulation excludes arbitration from the scope thereof.

20. An anti-suit injunction, such as that in the main proceedings, may be directed against actual or potential claimants in proceedings abroad. * * *

22. * * * [I]t must be borne in mind that, in order to determine whether a dispute falls within the scope of Regulation No 44/2001, reference must be made solely to the subject-matter of the proceedings. More specifically, its place in the scope of Regulation No 44/2001 is determined by the nature of the rights which the proceedings in question serve to protect.

23. Proceedings, such as those in the main proceedings, which lead to the making of an anti-suit injunction, cannot, therefore, come within the scope of Regulation No 44/2001.

24. However, even though proceedings do not come within the scope of Regulation No 44/2001, they may nevertheless have consequences which undermine its effectiveness, namely preventing the attainment of the objectives of unification of the rules of conflict of jurisdiction in civil and commercial matters and the free movement of decisions in those matters. This is so, inter alia, where such proceedings prevent a court of another Member State from exercising the jurisdiction conferred on it by Regulation No 44/2001.

25. It is therefore appropriate to consider whether the proceedings brought by Allianz and Generali against West Tankers before the Tribunale di Siracusa

themselves come within the scope of Regulation No 44/2001 and then to ascertain the effects of the anti-suit injunction on those proceedings.

26. In that regard, the Court finds, * * * that, if, because of the subject-matter of the dispute, that is, the nature of the rights to be protected in proceedings, such as a claim for damages, those proceedings come within the scope of Regulation No 44/2001, a preliminary issue concerning the applicability of an arbitration agreement, including in particular its validity, also comes within its scope of application. * * *

27. It follows that the objection of lack of jurisdiction raised by West Tankers before the Tribunale di Siracusa on the basis of the existence of an arbitration agreement, including the question of the validity of that agreement, comes within the scope of Regulation No 44/2001 and that it is therefore exclusively for that court to rule on that objection and on its own jurisdiction, pursuant to Articles 1(2)(d) and 5(3) of that regulation.

28. Accordingly, the use of an anti-suit injunction to prevent a court of a Member State, which normally has jurisdiction to resolve a dispute under Article 5(3) of Regulation No 44/2001, from ruling, in accordance with Article 1(2)(d) of that regulation, on the very applicability of the regulation to the dispute brought before it necessarily amounts to stripping that court of the power to rule on its own jurisdiction under Regulation No 44/2001.

29. It follows, first, * * * that an anti-suit injunction, such as that in the main proceedings, is contrary to the general principle which emerges from the case-law of the Court on the Brussels Convention, that every court seised itself determines, under the rules applicable to it, whether it has jurisdiction to resolve the dispute before it * * *. It should be borne in mind in that regard that Regulation No 44/2001, apart from a few limited exceptions which are not relevant to the main proceedings, does not authorise the jurisdiction of a court of a Member State to be reviewed by a court in another Member State. That jurisdiction is determined directly by the rules laid down by that regulation, including those relating to its scope of application. Thus in no case is a court of one Member State in a better position to determine whether the court of another Member State has jurisdiction.

30. Further, in obstructing the court of another Member State in the exercise of the powers conferred on it by Regulation No 44/2001, namely to decide, on the basis of the rules defining the material scope of that regulation, including Article 1(2)(d) thereof, whether that regulation is applicable, such an anti-suit injunction also runs counter to the trust which the Member States accord to one another's legal systems and judicial institutions and on which the system of jurisdiction under Regulation No 44/2001 is based (see, to that effect, *Turner*, paragraph 24). * * *

32. Consequently, an anti-suit injunction, such as that in the main proceedings, is not compatible with Regulation No 44/2001.

33. This finding is supported by Article II(3) of the New York Convention, according to which it is the court of a Contracting State, when seised of an action in a matter in respect of which the parties have made an arbitration agreement, that will, at the request of one of the parties, refer the parties to arbitration,

unless it finds that the said agreement is null and void, inoperative or incapable of being performed.

34. In the light of the foregoing considerations, the answer to the question referred is that it is incompatible with Regulation No 44/2001 for a court of a Member State to make an order to restrain a person from commencing or continuing proceedings before the courts of another Member State on the ground that such proceedings would be contrary to an arbitration agreement.

NOTES AND QUESTIONS FOR DISCUSSION

1. Given that Article 1(2)(d) of the Regulation explicitly provides that the Regulation does not apply to arbitration, why should the English courts be prevented from issuing an antisuit injunction? What exactly is the ECJ's reasoning in this respect? Is it persuasive?

2. In paragraph 33 of its decision, the Court noted that its finding is supported by Article II.3 of the New York Convention. See Appendix E. According to this provision, a party must apply to the court where the litigation is pending in order to end that litigation if it was initiated in breach of a valid arbitration agreement. Considering the length of court proceedings in some member states, such as Italy (see the discussion of the so-called "torpedo" suits, in Chapter 5, Section B), does it make sense to have such a requirement?

3. Consider whether it should it be possible to obtain alternative remedies from subsequent arbitration proceedings, such as damages for having breached the arbitration agreement. The English High Court of Justice ruled in the affirmative. In the 2012 decision of West Tankers Inc. v. Allianz SpA & Generali Assicurazioni Generali SpA, [2012] EWHC 854 (Comm), it held that the earlier *West Tankers* decision, excerpted above, did not preclude the arbitral tribunal from awarding damages for the breach of an arbitration agreement by having instituted judicial proceedings in the Italian court. Specifically, the Court held that "arbitration falls outside the Regulation and an arbitral tribunal is not bound to give effect to the principle of effective judicial protection. It follows that the tribunal was wrong to conclude that it did not have jurisdiction to make an award of damages for breach of the obligation to arbitrate or for an indemnity." Id. at para. 68.

4. Note that under the revised version of the Brussels Regulation, which will apply as of January 10, 2015 (see Chapter 1, Section G; Chapter 5, Section B), arbitration continues to remain outside the scope of the Regulation. However, Recital 12 of the revised Regulation signals a shift away from the *West Tankers* adherence to the strict priority principle and strengthens the status of arbitration. Among other things, Recital 12 provides:

> A ruling given by a court of a Member State as to whether or not an arbitration agreement is null and void, inoperative or incapable of being performed should not be subject to the rules of recognition and enforcement laid down in this Regulation, regardless of whether the court decided on this as a principal issue or as an incidental question.
>
> On the other hand, where a court of a Member State, exercising jurisdiction under this Regulation or under national law, has determined

that an arbitration agreement is null and void, inoperative or incapable of being performed, this should not preclude that court's judgment on the substance of the matter from being recognised or, as the case may be, enforced in accordance with this Regulation. This should be without prejudice to the competence of the courts of the Member States to decide on the recognition and enforcement of arbitral awards in accordance with the Convention on the Recognition and Enforcement of Foreign Arbitral Awards, done at New York on 10 June 1958 ('the 1958 New York Convention'), which takes precedence over this Regulation.

Thus, the decision of a member state court that an arbitration clause is invalid neither prevents the courts of another member state, nor the arbitrators, from concluding that the clause is valid and enforceable and that the arbitration should proceed. Without addressing the issue of antisuit injunctions, the Recital therefore legislatively overturns the core holding of the *West Tankers* decision. What is more, the revised Regulation explicitly vests the New York Convention with primacy over the Brussels Regulation. Not all consequences of these revisions are clear, however. In particular, there is uncertainty as to how to solve a conflict between a court decision invalidating the arbitration clause and a diverging (affirmative) decision in another member state by a court or an arbitral tribunal.

Appendices

A. THE HAGUE SERVICE CONVENTION

CONVENTION ON THE SERVICE ABROAD OF JUDICIAL AND EXTRAJUDICIAL DOCUMENTS IN CIVIL OR COMMERCIAL MATTERS

(Concluded 15 November 1965)

The States signatory to the present Convention,

Desiring to create appropriate means to ensure that judicial and extrajudicial documents to be served abroad shall be brought to the notice of the addressee in sufficient time,

Desiring to improve the organisation of mutual judicial assistance for that purpose by simplifying and expediting the procedure,

Have resolved to conclude a Convention to this effect and have agreed upon the following provisions:

Article 1

The present Convention shall apply in all cases, in civil or commercial matters, where there is occasion to transmit a judicial or extrajudicial document for service abroad.

This Convention shall not apply where the address of the person to be served with the document is not known.

CHAPTER I—JUDICIAL DOCUMENTS

Article 2

Each Contracting State shall designate a Central Authority which will undertake to receive requests for service coming from other Contracting States and to proceed in conformity with the provisions of Articles 3 to 6.

Each State shall organise the Central Authority in conformity with its own law.

Article 3

The authority or judicial officer competent under the law of the State in which the documents originate shall forward to the Central Authority of the State addressed a request conforming to the model annexed to the present Convention, without any requirement of legalisation or other equivalent formality.

The document to be served or a copy thereof shall be annexed to the request. The request and the document shall both be furnished in duplicate.

Article 4

If the Central Authority considers that the request does not comply with the provisions of the present Convention it shall promptly inform the applicant and specify its objections to the request.

Article 5

The Central Authority of the State addressed shall itself serve the document or shall arrange to have it served by an appropriate agency, either -

> *(a)* by a method prescribed by its internal law for the service of documents in domestic actions upon persons who are within its territory, or

> *(b)* by a particular method requested by the applicant, unless such a method is incompatible with the law of the State addressed.

Subject to sub-paragraph *(b)* of the first paragraph of this Article, the document may always be served by delivery to an addressee who accepts it voluntarily.

If the document is to be served under the first paragraph above, the Central Authority may require the document to be written in, or translated into, the official language or one of the official languages of the State addressed.

That part of the request, in the form attached to the present Convention, which contains a summary of the document to be served, shall be served with the document.

Article 6

The Central Authority of the State addressed or any authority which it may have designated for that purpose, shall complete a certificate in the form of the model annexed to the present Convention.

The certificate shall state that the document has been served and shall include the method, the place and the date of service and the person to whom the document was delivered. If the document has not been served, the certificate shall set out the reasons which have prevented service.

The applicant may require that a certificate not completed by a Central Authority or by a judicial authority shall be countersigned by one of these authorities.

The certificate shall be forwarded directly to the applicant.

Article 7

The standard terms in the model annexed to the present Convention shall in all cases be written either in French or in English. They may also be written in the official language, or in one of the official languages, of the State in which the documents originate.

The corresponding blanks shall be completed either in the language of the State addressed or in French or in English.

Article 8

Each Contracting State shall be free to effect service of judicial documents upon persons abroad, without application of any compulsion, directly through its diplomatic or consular agents.

Any State may declare that it is opposed to such service within its territory, unless the document is to be served upon a national of the State in which the documents originate.

Article 9

Each Contracting State shall be free, in addition, to use consular channels to forward documents, for the purpose of service, to those authorities of another Contracting State which are designated by the latter for this purpose.

Each Contracting State may, if exceptional circumstances so require, use diplomatic channels for the same purpose.

Article 10

Provided the State of destination does not object, the present Convention shall not interfere with -

(a) the freedom to send judicial documents, by postal channels, directly to persons abroad,

(b) the freedom of judicial officers, officials or other competent persons of the State of origin to effect service of judicial documents directly through the judicial officers, officials or other competent persons of the State of destination,

(c) the freedom of any person interested in a judicial proceeding to effect service of judicial documents directly through the judicial officers, officials or other competent persons of the State of destination.

Article 11

The present Convention shall not prevent two or more Contracting States from agreeing to permit, for the purpose of service of judicial documents, channels of transmission other than those provided for in the preceding Articles and, in particular, direct communication between their respective authorities.

* * *

Article 13

Where a request for service complies with the terms of the present Convention, the State addressed may refuse to comply therewith only if it deems that compliance would infringe its sovereignty or security.

It may not refuse to comply solely on the ground that, under its internal law, it claims exclusive jurisdiction over the subject-matter of the action or that its internal law would not permit the action upon which the application is based.

The Central Authority shall, in case of refusal, promptly inform the applicant and state the reasons for the refusal.

* * *

Article 15

Where a writ of summons or an equivalent document had to be transmitted abroad for the purpose of service, under the provisions of the present Convention, and the defendant has not appeared, judgment shall not be given until it is established that -

(a) the document was served by a method prescribed by the internal law of the State addressed for the service of documents in domestic actions upon persons who are within its territory, or

(b) the document was actually delivered to the defendant or to his residence by another method provided for by this Convention,

and that in either of these cases the service or the delivery was effected in sufficient time to enable the defendant to defend.

Each Contracting State shall be free to declare that the judge, notwithstanding the provisions of the first paragraph of this Article, may give judgment even if no certificate of service or delivery has been received, if all the following conditions are fulfilled -

(a) the document was transmitted by one of the methods provided for in this Convention,

(b) a period of time of not less than six months, considered adequate by the judge in the particular case, has elapsed since the date of the transmission of the document,

(c) no certificate of any kind has been received, even though every reasonable effort has been made to obtain it through the competent authorities of the State addressed.

Notwithstanding the provisions of the preceding paragraphs the judge may order, in case of urgency, any provisional or protective measures.

Article 16

When a writ of summons or an equivalent document had to be transmitted abroad for the purpose of service, under the provisions of the present Convention, and a judgment has been entered against a defendant who has not appeared, the judge shall have the power to relieve the defendant from the effects of the expiration of the time for appeal from the judgment if the following conditions are fulfilled -

(a) the defendant, without any fault on his part, did not have knowledge of the document in sufficient time to defend, or knowledge of the judgment in sufficient time to appeal, and

(b) the defendant has disclosed a *prima facie* defence to the action on the merits.

An application for relief may be filed only within a reasonable time after the defendant has knowledge of the judgment.

Each Contracting State may declare that the application will not be entertained if it is filed after the expiration of a time to be stated in the declaration, but which shall in no case be less than one year following the date of the judgment.

This Article shall not apply to judgments concerning status or capacity of persons.

CHAPTER II—EXTRAJUDICIAL DOCUMENTS

Article 17

Extrajudicial documents emanating from authorities and judicial officers of a Contracting State may be transmitted for the purpose of service in another Contracting State by the methods and under the provisions of the present Convention.

CHAPTER III—GENERAL CLAUSES

Article 18

Each Contracting State may designate other authorities in addition to the Central Authority and shall determine the extent of their competence.

The applicant shall, however, in all cases, have the right to address a request directly to the Central Authority.

Federal States shall be free to designate more than one Central Authority.

Article 19

To the extent that the internal law of a Contracting State permits methods of transmission, other than those provided for in the preceding Articles, of documents coming from abroad, for service within its territory, the present Convention shall not affect such provisions.

Article 20

The present Convention shall not prevent an agreement between any two or more Contracting States to dispense with -

(a) the necessity for duplicate copies of transmitted documents as required by the second paragraph of Article 3,

(b) the language requirements of the third paragraph of Article 5 and Article 7,

(c) the provisions of the fourth paragraph of Article 5,

(d) the provisions of the second paragraph of Article 12.

* * *

B. THE HAGUE EVIDENCE CONVENTION

CONVENTION ON THE TAKING OF EVIDENCE ABROAD IN CIVIL OR COMMERCIAL MATTERS
(Concluded 18 March 1970)

The States signatory to the present Convention,

Desiring to facilitate the transmission and execution of Letters of Request and to further the accommodation of the different methods which they use for this purpose,

Desiring to improve mutual judicial co-operation in civil or commercial matters,

Have resolved to conclude a Convention to this effect and have agreed upon the following provisions -

CHAPTER I—LETTERS OF REQUEST
Article 1

In civil or commercial matters a judicial authority of a Contracting State may, in accordance with the provisions of the law of that State, request the competent authority of another Contracting State, by means of a Letter of Request, to obtain evidence, or to perform some other judicial act.

A Letter shall not be used to obtain evidence which is not intended for use in judicial proceedings, commenced or contemplated.

The expression "other judicial act" does not cover the service of judicial documents or the issuance of any process by which judgments or orders are executed or enforced, or orders for provisional or protective measures.

Article 2

A Contracting State shall designate a Central Authority which will undertake to receive Letters of Request coming from a judicial authority of another Contracting State and to transmit them to the authority competent to execute them. Each State shall organise the Central Authority in accordance with its own law.

Letters shall be sent to the Central Authority of the State of execution without being transmitted through any other authority of that State.

Article 3

A Letter of Request shall specify -

   (a) the authority requesting its execution and the authority requested to execute it, if known to the requesting authority;

   (b) the names and addresses of the parties to the proceedings and their representatives, if any;

   (c) the nature of the proceedings for which the evidence is required, giving all necessary information in regard thereto;

(d) the evidence to be obtained or other judicial act to be performed.

Where appropriate, the Letter shall specify, *inter alia* -

(e) the names and addresses of the persons to be examined;

(f) the questions to be put to the persons to be examined or a statement of the subject-matter about which they are to be examined;

(g) the documents or other property, real or personal, to be inspected;

(h) any requirement that the evidence is to be given on oath or affirmation, and any special form to be used;

(i) any special method or procedure to be followed under Article 9.

A Letter may also mention any information necessary for the application of Article 11.

No legalisation or other like formality may be required.

Article 4

A Letter of Request shall be in the language of the authority requested to execute it or be accompanied by a translation into that language.

Nevertheless, a Contracting State shall accept a Letter in either English or French, or a translation into one of these languages, unless it has made the reservation authorised by Article 33.

A Contracting State which has more than one official language and cannot, for reasons of internal law, accept Letters in one of these languages for the whole of its territory, shall, by declaration, specify the language in which the Letter or translation thereof shall be expressed for execution in the specified parts of its territory. In case of failure to comply with this declaration, without justifiable excuse, the costs of translation into the required language shall be borne by the State of origin.

A Contracting State may, by declaration, specify the language or languages other than those referred to in the preceding paragraphs, in which a Letter may be sent to its Central Authority.

Any translation accompanying a Letter shall be certified as correct, either by a diplomatic officer or consular agent or by a sworn translator or by any other person so authorised in either State.

Article 5

If the Central Authority considers that the request does not comply with the provisions of the present Convention, it shall promptly inform the authority of the State of origin which transmitted the Letter of Request, specifying the objections to the Letter.

Article 6

If the authority to whom a Letter of Request has been transmitted is not competent to execute it, the Letter shall be sent forthwith to the authority in the same State which is competent to execute it in accordance with the provisions of its own law.

Article 7

The requesting authority shall, if it so desires, be informed of the time when, and the place where, the proceedings will take place, in order that the parties concerned, and their representatives, if any, may be present. This information shall be sent directly to the parties or their representatives when the authority of the State of origin so requests.

Article 8

A Contracting State may declare that members of the judicial personnel of the requesting authority of another Contracting State may be present at the execution of a Letter of Request. Prior authorisation by the competent authority designated by the declaring State may be required.

Article 9

The judicial authority which executes a Letter of Request shall apply its own law as to the methods and procedures to be followed.

However, it will follow a request of the requesting authority that a special method or procedure be followed, unless this is incompatible with the internal law of the State of execution or is impossible of performance by reason of its internal practice and procedure or by reason of practical difficulties.

A Letter of Request shall be executed expeditiously.

Article 10

In executing a Letter of Request the requested authority shall apply the appropriate measures of compulsion in the instances and to the same extent as are provided by its internal law for the execution of orders issued by the authorities of its own country or of requests made by parties in internal proceedings.

Article 11

In the execution of a Letter of Request the person concerned may refuse to give evidence in so far as he has a privilege or duty to refuse to give the evidence -

> *(a)* under the law of the State of execution; or

> *(b)* under the law of the State of origin, and the privilege or duty has been specified in the Letter, or, at the instance of the requested authority, has been otherwise confirmed to that authority by the requesting authority.

A Contracting State may declare that, in addition, it will respect privileges and duties existing under the law of States other than the State of origin and the State of execution, to the extent specified in that declaration.

Article 12

The execution of a Letter of Request may be refused only to the extent that -

> *(a)* in the State of execution the execution of the Letter does not fall within the functions of the judiciary; or

> *(b)* the State addressed considers that its sovereignty or security would be prejudiced thereby.

Execution may not be refused solely on the ground that under its internal law the State of execution claims exclusive jurisdiction over the subject-matter of the action or that its internal law would not admit a right of action on it.

Article 13

The documents establishing the execution of the Letter of Request shall be sent by the requested authority to the requesting authority by the same channel which was used by the latter.

In every instance where the Letter is not executed in whole or in part, the requesting authority shall be informed immediately through the same channel and advised of the reasons.

* * *

CHAPTER II—TAKING OF EVIDENCE BY DIPLOMATIC OFFICERS, CONSULAR AGENTS AND COMMISSIONERS

Article 15

In a civil or commercial matter, a diplomatic officer or consular agent of a Contracting State may, in the territory of another Contracting State and within the area where he exercises his functions, take the evidence without compulsion of nationals of a State which he represents in aid of proceedings commenced in the courts of a State which he represents.

A Contracting State may declare that evidence may be taken by a diplomatic officer or consular agent only if permission to that effect is given upon application made by him or on his behalf to the appropriate authority designated by the declaring State.

Article 16

A diplomatic officer or consular agent of a Contracting State may, in the territory of another Contracting State and within the area where he exercises his functions, also take the evidence, without compulsion, of nationals of the State in which he exercises his functions or of a third State, in aid of proceedings commenced in the courts of a State which he represents, if -

(a) a competent authority designated by the State in which he exercises his functions has given its permission either generally or in the particular case, and

(b) he complies with the conditions which the competent authority has specified in the permission.

A Contracting State may declare that evidence may be taken under this Article without its prior permission.

Article 17

In a civil or commercial matter, a person duly appointed as a commissioner for the purpose may, without compulsion, take evidence in the territory of a Contracting State in aid of proceedings commenced in the courts of another Contracting State if -

(a) a competent authority designated by the State where the evidence is to be taken has given its permission either generally or in the particular case; and

(b) he complies with the conditions which the competent authority has specified in the permission.

A Contracting State may declare that evidence may be taken under this Article without its prior permission.

Article 18

A Contracting State may declare that a diplomatic officer, consular agent or commissioner authorised to take evidence under Articles 15, 16 or 17, may apply to the competent authority designated by the declaring State for appropriate assistance to obtain the evidence by compulsion. The declaration may contain such conditions as the declaring State may see fit to impose.

If the authority grants the application it shall apply any measures of compulsion which are appropriate and are prescribed by its law for use in internal proceedings.

Article 19

The competent authority, in giving the permission referred to in Articles 15, 16 or 17, or in granting the application referred to in Article 18, may lay down such conditions as it deems fit, *inter alia*, as to the time and place of the taking of the evidence. Similarly it may require that it be given reasonable advance notice of the time, date and place of the taking of the evidence; in such a case a representative of the authority shall be entitled to be present at the taking of the evidence.

Article 20

In the taking of evidence under any Article of this Chapter persons concerned may be legally represented.

Article 21

Where a diplomatic officer, consular agent or commissioner is authorised under Articles 15, 16 or 17 to take evidence -

(a) he may take all kinds of evidence which are not incompatible with the law of the State where the evidence is taken or contrary to any permission granted pursuant to the above Articles, and shall have power within such limits to administer an oath or take an affirmation;

(b) a request to a person to appear or to give evidence shall, unless the recipient is a national of the State where the action is pending, be drawn up in the language of the place where the evidence is taken or be accompanied by a translation into such language;

(c) the request shall inform the person that he may be legally represented and, in any State that has not filed a declaration under Article 18, shall also inform him that he is not compelled to appear or to give evidence;

(d) the evidence may be taken in the manner provided by the law applicable to the court in which the action is pending provided that such manner is not forbidden by the law of the State where the evidence is taken;

(e) a person requested to give evidence may invoke the privileges and duties to refuse to give the evidence contained in Article 11.

Article 22

The fact that an attempt to take evidence under the procedure laid down in this Chapter has failed, owing to the refusal of a person to give evidence, shall not prevent an application being subsequently made to take the evidence in accordance with Chapter I.

CHAPTER III—GENERAL CLAUSES

Article 23

A Contracting State may at the time of signature, ratification or accession, declare that it will not execute Letters of Request issued for the purpose of obtaining pre-trial discovery of documents as known in Common Law countries.

* * *

Article 27

The provisions of the present Convention shall not prevent a Contracting State from -

(a) declaring that Letters of Request may be transmitted to its judicial authorities through channels other than those provided for in Article 2;

(b) permitting, by internal law or practice, any act provided for in this Convention to be performed upon less restrictive conditions;

(c) permitting, by internal law or practice, methods of taking evidence other than those provided for in this Convention.

* * *

Article 33

A State may, at the time of signature, ratification or accession exclude, in whole or in part, the application of the provisions of paragraph 2 of Article 4 and of Chapter II. No other reservation shall be permitted.

Each Contracting State may at any time withdraw a reservation it has made; the reservation shall cease to have effect on the sixtieth day after notification of the withdrawal.

When a State has made a reservation, any other State affected thereby may apply the same rule against the reserving State.

* * *

C. THE HAGUE CHOICE OF COURT CONVENTION

CONVENTION ON CHOICE OF COURT AGREEMENTS
(Concluded 30 June 2005)

The States Parties to the present Convention,

Desiring to promote international trade and investment through enhanced judicial co-operation,

Believing that such co-operation can be enhanced by uniform rules on jurisdiction and on recognition and enforcement of foreign judgments in civil or commercial matters,

Believing that such enhanced co-operation requires in particular an international legal regime that provides certainty and ensures the effectiveness of exclusive choice of court agreements between parties to commercial transactions and that governs the recognition and enforcement of judgments resulting from proceedings based on such agreements,

Have resolved to conclude this Convention and have agreed upon the following provisions -

CHAPTER I—SCOPE AND DEFINITIONS
Article 1
Scope

(1) This Convention shall apply in international cases to exclusive choice of court agreements concluded in civil or commercial matters.

(2) For the purposes of Chapter II, a case is international unless the parties are resident in the same Contracting State and the relationship of the parties and all other elements relevant to the dispute, regardless of the location of the chosen court, are connected only with that State.

(3) For the purposes of Chapter III, a case is international where recognition or enforcement of a foreign judgment is sought.

Article 2
Exclusions from scope

(1) This Convention shall not apply to exclusive choice of court agreements -

(a) to which a natural person acting primarily for personal, family or household purposes (a consumer) is a party;

(b) relating to contracts of employment, including collective agreements.

(2) This Convention shall not apply to the following matters -

(a) the status and legal capacity of natural persons;

(b) maintenance obligations;

(c) other family law matters, including matrimonial property regimes and other rights or obligations arising out of marriage or similar relationships;

(d) wills and succession;

(e) insolvency, composition and analogous matters;

(f) the carriage of passengers and goods;

(g) marine pollution, limitation of liability for maritime claims, general average, and emergency towage and salvage;

(h) anti-trust (competition) matters;

(i) liability for nuclear damage;

(j) claims for personal injury brought by or on behalf of natural persons;

(k) tort or delict claims for damage to tangible property that do not arise from a contractual relationship;

(l) rights *in rem* in immovable property, and tenancies of immovable property;

(m) the validity, nullity, or dissolution of legal persons, and the validity of decisions of their organs;

(n) the validity of intellectual property rights other than copyright and related rights;

(o) infringement of intellectual property rights other than copyright and related rights, except where infringement proceedings are brought for breach of a contract between the parties relating to such rights, or could have been brought for breach of that contract;

(p) the validity of entries in public registers.

(3) Notwithstanding paragraph 2, proceedings are not excluded from the scope of this Convention where a matter excluded under that paragraph arises merely as a preliminary question and not as an object of the proceedings. In particular, the mere fact that a matter excluded under paragraph 2 arises by way of defence does not exclude proceedings from the Convention, if that matter is not an object of the proceedings.

(4) This Convention shall not apply to arbitration and related proceedings.

(5) Proceedings are not excluded from the scope of this Convention by the mere fact that a State, including a government, a governmental agency or any person acting for a State, is a party thereto.

(6) Nothing in this Convention shall affect privileges and immunities of States or of international organisations, in respect of themselves and of their property.

Article 3
Exclusive choice of court agreements

For the purposes of this Convention –

(a) "exclusive choice of court agreement" means an agreement concluded by two or more parties that meets the requirements of paragraph *(c)* and designates, for the purpose of deciding disputes which have arisen or may arise in connection with a particular legal relationship, the courts of one Contracting State or one or more specific courts of one Contracting State to the exclusion of the jurisdiction of any other courts;

(b) a choice of court agreement which designates the courts of one Contracting State or one or more specific courts of one Contracting State shall

be deemed to be exclusive unless the parties have expressly provided otherwise;

(c) an exclusive choice of court agreement must be concluded or documented -

(i) in writing; or

(ii) by any other means of communication which renders information accessible so as to be usable for subsequent reference;

(d) an exclusive choice of court agreement that forms part of a contract shall be treated as an agreement independent of the other terms of the contract. The validity of the exclusive choice of court agreement cannot be contested solely on the ground that the contract is not valid.

Article 4
Other definitions

(1) In this Convention, "judgment" means any decision on the merits given by a court, whatever it may be called, including a decree or order, and a determination of costs or expenses by the court (including an officer of the court), provided that the determination relates to a decision on the merits which may be recognised or enforced under this Convention. An interim measure of protection is not a judgment.

(2) For the purposes of this Convention, an entity or person other than a natural person shall be considered to be resident in the State -

(a) where it has its statutory seat;

(b) under whose law it was incorporated or formed;

(c) where it has its central administration; or

(d) where it has its principal place of business.

CHAPTER II—JURISDICTION
Article 5
Jurisdiction of the chosen court

(1) The court or courts of a Contracting State designated in an exclusive choice of court agreement shall have jurisdiction to decide a dispute to which the agreement applies, unless the agreement is null and void under the law of that State.

(2) A court that has jurisdiction under paragraph 1 shall not decline to exercise jurisdiction on the ground that the dispute should be decided in a court of another State.

(3) The preceding paragraphs shall not affect rules –

(a) on jurisdiction related to subject matter or to the value of the claim;

(b) on the internal allocation of jurisdiction among the courts of a Contracting State. However, where the chosen court has discretion as to whether to transfer a case, due consideration should be given to the choice of the parties.

Article 6
Obligations of a court not chosen

A court of a Contracting State other than that of the chosen court shall suspend or dismiss proceedings to which an exclusive choice of court agreement applies unless -

(a) the agreement is null and void under the law of the State of the chosen court;

(b) a party lacked the capacity to conclude the agreement under the law of the State of the court seised;

(c) giving effect to the agreement would lead to a manifest injustice or would be manifestly contrary to the public policy of the State of the court seised;

(d) for exceptional reasons beyond the control of the parties, the agreement cannot reasonably be performed; or

(e) the chosen court has decided not to hear the case.

Article 7
Interim measures of protection

Interim measures of protection are not governed by this Convention. This Convention neither requires nor precludes the grant, refusal or termination of interim measures of protection by a court of a Contracting State and does not affect whether or not a party may request or a court should grant, refuse or terminate such measures.

CHAPTER III—RECOGNITION AND ENFORCEMENT
Article 8
Recognition and enforcement

(1) A judgment given by a court of a Contracting State designated in an exclusive choice of court agreement shall be recognised and enforced in other Contracting States in accordance with this Chapter. Recognition or enforcement may be refused only on the grounds specified in this Convention.

(2) Without prejudice to such review as is necessary for the application of the provisions of this Chapter, there shall be no review of the merits of the judgment given by the court of origin. The court addressed shall be bound by the findings of fact on which the court of origin based its jurisdiction, unless the judgment was given by default.

(3) A judgment shall be recognised only if it has effect in the State of origin, and shall be enforced only if it is enforceable in the State of origin.

(4) Recognition or enforcement may be postponed or refused if the judgment is the subject of review in the State of origin or if the time limit for seeking ordinary review has not expired. A refusal does not prevent a subsequent application for recognition or enforcement of the judgment.

(5) This Article shall also apply to a judgment given by a court of a Contracting State pursuant to a transfer of the case from the chosen court in that Contracting State as permitted by Article 5, paragraph 3. However, where the chosen court

had discretion as to whether to transfer the case to another court, recognition or enforcement of the judgment may be refused against a party who objected to the transfer in a timely manner in the State of origin.

Article 9
Refusal of recognition or enforcement

Recognition or enforcement may be refused if -

(a) the agreement was null and void under the law of the State of the chosen court, unless the chosen court has determined that the agreement is valid;

(b) a party lacked the capacity to conclude the agreement under the law of the requested State;

(c) the document which instituted the proceedings or an equivalent document, including the essential elements of the claim,

(i) was not notified to the defendant in sufficient time and in such a way as to enable him to arrange for his defence, unless the defendant entered an appearance and presented his case without contesting notification in the court of origin, provided that the law of the State of origin permitted notification to be contested; or

(ii) was notified to the defendant in the requested State in a manner that is incompatible with fundamental principles of the requested State concerning service of documents;

(d) the judgment was obtained by fraud in connection with a matter of procedure;

(e) recognition or enforcement would be manifestly incompatible with the public policy of the requested State, including situations where the specific proceedings leading to the judgment were incompatible with fundamental principles of procedural fairness of that State;

(f) the judgment is inconsistent with a judgment given in the requested State in a dispute between the same parties; or

(g) the judgment is inconsistent with an earlier judgment given in another State between the same parties on the same cause of action, provided that the earlier judgment fulfils the conditions necessary for its recognition in the requested State.

Article 10
Preliminary questions

(1) Where a matter excluded under Article 2, paragraph 2, or under Article 21, arose as a preliminary question, the ruling on that question shall not be recognised or enforced under this Convention.

(2) Recognition or enforcement of a judgment may be refused if, and to the extent that, the judgment was based on a ruling on a matter excluded under Article 2, paragraph 2.

(3) However, in the case of a ruling on the validity of an intellectual property right other than copyright or a related right, recognition or enforcement of a

judgment may be refused or postponed under the preceding paragraph only where –

(a) that ruling is inconsistent with a judgment or a decision of a competent authority on that matter given in the State under the law of which the intellectual property right arose; or

(b) proceedings concerning the validity of the intellectual property right are pending in that State.

(4) Recognition or enforcement of a judgment may be refused if, and to the extent that, the judgment was based on a ruling on a matter excluded pursuant to a declaration made by the requested State under Article 21.

Article 11
Damages

(1) Recognition or enforcement of a judgment may be refused if, and to the extent that, the judgment awards damages, including exemplary or punitive damages, that do not compensate a party for actual loss or harm suffered.

(2) The court addressed shall take into account whether and to what extent the damages awarded by the court of origin serve to cover costs and expenses relating to the proceedings.

Article 12
Judicial settlements (*transactions judiciaires*)

Judicial settlements (*transactions judiciaires*) which a court of a Contracting State designated in an exclusive choice of court agreement has approved, or which have been concluded before that court in the course of proceedings, and which are enforceable in the same manner as a judgment in the State of origin, shall be enforced under this Convention in the same manner as a judgment.

Article 13
Documents to be produced

(1) The party seeking recognition or applying for enforcement shall produce –

(a) a complete and certified copy of the judgment;

(b) the exclusive choice of court agreement, a certified copy thereof, or other evidence of its existence;

(c) if the judgment was given by default, the original or a certified copy of a document establishing that the document which instituted the proceedings or an equivalent document was notified to the defaulting party;

(d) any documents necessary to establish that the judgment has effect or, where applicable, is enforceable in the State of origin;

(e) in the case referred to in Article 12, a certificate of a court of the State of origin that the judicial settlement or a part of it is enforceable in the same manner as a judgment in the State of origin.

(2) If the terms of the judgment do not permit the court addressed to verify whether the conditions of this Chapter have been complied with, that court may require any necessary documents.

(3) An application for recognition or enforcement may be accompanied by a document, issued by a court (including an officer of the court) of the State of origin, in the form recommended and published by the Hague Conference on Private International Law.

(4) If the documents referred to in this Article are not in an official language of the requested State, they shall be accompanied by a certified translation into an official language, unless the law of the requested State provides otherwise.

Article 14
Procedure

The procedure for recognition, declaration of enforceability or registration for enforcement, and the enforcement of the judgment, are governed by the law of the requested State unless this Convention provides otherwise. The court addressed shall act expeditiously.

Article 15
Severability

Recognition or enforcement of a severable part of a judgment shall be granted where recognition or enforcement of that part is applied for, or only part of the judgment is capable of being recognised or enforced under this Convention.

CHAPTER IV—GENERAL CLAUSES

Article 16
Transitional provisions

(1) This Convention shall apply to exclusive choice of court agreements concluded after its entry into force for the State of the chosen court.

(2) This Convention shall not apply to proceedings instituted before its entry into force for the State of the court seised.

* * *

Article 19
Declarations limiting jurisdiction

A State may declare that its courts may refuse to determine disputes to which an exclusive choice of court agreement applies if, except for the location of the chosen court, there is no connection between that State and the parties or the dispute.

Article 20
Declarations limiting recognition and enforcement

A State may declare that its courts may refuse to recognise or enforce a judgment given by a court of another Contracting State if the parties were resident in the requested State, and the relationship of the parties and all other elements relevant to the dispute, other than the location of the chosen court, were connected only with the requested State.

Article 21
Declarations with respect to specific matters

(1) Where a State has a strong interest in not applying this Convention to a specific matter, that State may declare that it will not apply the Convention to that

matter. The State making such a declaration shall ensure that the declaration is no broader than necessary and that the specific matter excluded is clearly and precisely defined.

(2) With regard to that matter, the Convention shall not apply –

(a) in the Contracting State that made the declaration;

(b) in other Contracting States, where an exclusive choice of court agreement designates the courts, or one or more specific courts, of the State that made the declaration.

Article 22
Reciprocal declarations on non-exclusive choice of court agreements

(1) A Contracting State may declare that its courts will recognise and enforce judgments given by courts of other Contracting States designated in a choice of court agreement concluded by two or more parties that meets the requirements of Article 3, paragraph *(c)*, and designates, for the purpose of deciding disputes which have arisen or may arise in connection with a particular legal relationship, a court or courts of one or more Contracting States (a non-exclusive choice of court agreement).

(2) Where recognition or enforcement of a judgment given in a Contracting State that has made such a declaration is sought in another Contracting State that has made such a declaration, the judgment shall be recognised and enforced under this Convention, if –

> *(a)* the court of origin was designated in a non-exclusive choice of court agreement;

> *(b)* there exists neither a judgment given by any other court before which proceedings could be brought in accordance with the non-exclusive choice of court agreement, nor a proceeding pending between the same parties in any other such court on the same cause of action; and

> *(c)* the court of origin was the court first seised.

Article 23
Uniform interpretation

In the interpretation of this Convention, regard shall be had to its international character and to the need to promote uniformity in its application.

* * *

Article 25
Non-unified legal systems

(1) In relation to a Contracting State in which two or more systems of law apply in different territorial units with regard to any matter dealt with in this Convention -

> *(a)* any reference to the law or procedure of a State shall be construed as referring, where appropriate, to the law or procedure in force in the relevant territorial unit;

> *(b)* any reference to residence in a State shall be construed as referring, where appropriate, to residence in the relevant territorial unit;

(c) any reference to the court or courts of a State shall be construed as referring, where appropriate, to the court or courts in the relevant territorial unit;

(d) any reference to a connection with a State shall be construed as referring, where appropriate, to a connection with the relevant territorial unit.

(2) Notwithstanding the preceding paragraph, a Contracting State with two or more territorial units in which different systems of law apply shall not be bound to apply this Convention to situations which involve solely such different territorial units.

(3) A court in a territorial unit of a Contracting State with two or more territorial units in which different systems of law apply shall not be bound to recognise or enforce a judgment from another Contracting State solely because the judgment has been recognised or enforced in another territorial unit of the same Contracting State under this Convention.

(4) This Article shall not apply to a Regional Economic Integration Organisation.

Article 26
Relationship with other international instruments

(1) This Convention shall be interpreted so far as possible to be compatible with other treaties in force for Contracting States, whether concluded before or after this Convention.

(2) This Convention shall not affect the application by a Contracting State of a treaty, whether concluded before or after this Convention, in cases where none of the parties is resident in a Contracting State that is not a Party to the treaty.

(3) This Convention shall not affect the application by a Contracting State of a treaty that was concluded before this Convention entered into force for that Contracting State, if applying this Convention would be inconsistent with the obligations of that Contracting State to any non-Contracting State. This paragraph shall also apply to treaties that revise or replace a treaty concluded before this Convention entered into force for that Contracting State, except to the extent that the revision or replacement creates new inconsistencies with this Convention.

(4) This Convention shall not affect the application by a Contracting State of a treaty, whether concluded before or after this Convention, for the purposes of obtaining recognition or enforcement of a judgment given by a court of a Contracting State that is also a Party to that treaty. However, the judgment shall not be recognised or enforced to a lesser extent than under this Convention.

(5) This Convention shall not affect the application by a Contracting State of a treaty which, in relation to a specific matter, governs jurisdiction or the recognition or enforcement of judgments, even if concluded after this Convention and even if all States concerned are Parties to this Convention. This paragraph shall apply only if the Contracting State has made a declaration in respect of the treaty under this paragraph. In the case of such a declaration, other Contracting States shall not be obliged to apply this Convention to that specific matter to the extent of any inconsistency, where an exclusive choice of court agreement des-

ignates the courts, or one or more specific courts, of the Contracting State that made the declaration.

(6) This Convention shall not affect the application of the rules of a Regional Economic Integration Organisation that is a Party to this Convention, whether adopted before or after this Convention –

(a) where none of the parties is resident in a Contracting State that is not a Member State of the Regional Economic Integration Organisation;

(b) as concerns the recognition or enforcement of judgments as between Member States of the Regional Economic Integration Organisation.

CHAPTER V—FINAL CLAUSES

* * *

Article 31
Entry into force

(1) This Convention shall enter into force on the first day of the month following the expiration of three months after the deposit of the second instrument of ratification, acceptance, approval or accession referred to in Article 27.

(2) Thereafter this Convention shall enter into force -

> *(a)* for each State or Regional Economic Integration Organisation subsequently ratifying, accepting, approving or acceding to it, on the first day of the month following the expiration of three months after the deposit of its instrument of ratification, acceptance, approval or accession;

> *(b)* for a territorial unit to which this Convention has been extended in accordance with Article 28, paragraph 1, on the first day of the month following the expiration of three months after the notification of the declaration referred to in that Article.

* * *

D. THE BRUSSELS REGULATION (E.C. REGULATION 44/2001)

[On Dec. 6, 2012, the Council of the EU Justice Ministers adopted a recast version of this Regulation. (*Regulation (EU) 1215/2012 of the European Parliament and of the Council of 12 December 2012 on jurisdiction and the recognition and enforcement of judgments in civil and commercial matters (recast).* Official Journal, OJ 20 December 2012, L 351/1). Although the new Regulation became effective as of Jan. 10, 2013, it will not apply until Jan. 20, 2015. The newest Regulation will make generally modest substantive changes to the current Regulation set out below.]

Council Regulation (EC) No 44/2001 of 22 December 2000
On Jurisdiction and the Recognition and Enforcement of Judgments in Civil and Commercial Matters

CHAPTER I
SCOPE

Article 1

1. This Regulation shall apply in civil and commercial matters whatever the nature of the court or tribunal. It shall not extend, in particular, to revenue, customs or administrative matters.

2. The Regulation shall not apply to:

> (a) the status or legal capacity of natural persons, rights in property arising out of a matrimonial relationship, wills and succession;

> (b) bankruptcy, proceedings relating to the winding-up of insolvent companies or other legal persons, judicial arrangements, compositions and analogous proceedings;

> (c) social security;

> (d) arbitration.

3. In this Regulation, the term "Member State" shall mean Member States with the exception of Denmark.

CHAPTER II
JURISDICTION

Section 1
General provisions

Article 2

1. Subject to this Regulation, persons domiciled in a Member State shall, whatever their nationality, be sued in the courts of that Member State.

2. Persons who are not nationals of the Member State in which they are domiciled shall be governed by the rules of jurisdiction applicable to nationals of that State.

Article 3

1. Persons domiciled in a Member State may be sued in the courts of another Member State only by virtue of the rules set out in Sections 2 to 7 of this Chapter.

2. In particular the rules of national jurisdiction set out in Annex I shall not be applicable as against them.

Article 4

1. If the defendant is not domiciled in a Member State, the jurisdiction of the courts of each Member State shall, subject to Articles 22 and 23, be determined by the law of that Member State.

2. As against such a defendant, any person domiciled in a Member State may, whatever his nationality, avail himself in that State of the rules of jurisdiction there in force, and in particular those specified in Annex I, in the same way as the nationals of that State.

Section 2
Special jurisdiction

Article 5

A person domiciled in a Member State may, in another Member State, be sued:

1.   (a) in matters relating to a contract, in the courts for the place of performance of the obligation in question;

(b) for the purpose of this provision and unless otherwise agreed, the place of performance of the obligation in question shall be:

- in the case of the sale of goods, the place in a Member State where, under the contract, the goods were delivered or should have been delivered,

- in the case of the provision of services, the place in a Member State where, under the contract, the services were provided or should have been provided,

(c) if subparagraph (b) does not apply then subparagraph (a) applies;

2. in matters relating to maintenance, in the courts for the place where the maintenance creditor is domiciled or habitually resident or, if the matter is ancillary to proceedings concerning the status of a person, in the court which, according to its own law, has jurisdiction to entertain those proceedings, unless that jurisdiction is based solely on the nationality of one of the parties;

3. in matters relating to tort, delict or quasi-delict, in the courts for the place where the harmful event occurred or may occur;

4. as regards a civil claim for damages or restitution which is based on an act giving rise to criminal proceedings, in the court seised of those proceedings, to the extent that that court has jurisdiction under its own law to entertain civil proceedings;

5. as regards a dispute arising out of the operations of a branch, agency or other establishment, in the courts for the place in which the branch, agency or other establishment is situated;

6. as settlor, trustee or beneficiary of a trust created by the operation of a statute, or by a written instrument, or created orally and evidenced in writing, in the courts of the Member State in which the trust is domiciled;

7. as regards a dispute concerning the payment of remuneration claimed in respect of the salvage of a cargo or freight, in the court under the authority of which the cargo or freight in question:

> (a) has been arrested to secure such payment, or

> (b) could have been so arrested, but bail or other security has been given;

provided that this provision shall apply only if it is claimed that the defendant has an interest in the cargo or freight or had such an interest at the time of salvage.

Article 6

A person domiciled in a Member State may also be sued:

1. where he is one of a number of defendants, in the courts for the place where any one of them is domiciled, provided the claims are so closely connected that it is expedient to hear and determine them together to avoid the risk of irreconcilable judgments resulting from separate proceedings;

2. as a third party in an action on a warranty or guarantee or in any other third party proceedings, in the court seised of the original proceedings, unless these were instituted solely with the object of removing him from the jurisdiction of the court which would be competent in his case;

3. on a counter-claim arising from the same contract or facts on which the original claim was based, in the court in which the original claim is pending;

4. in matters relating to a contract, if the action may be combined with an action against the same defendant in matters relating to rights in rem in immovable property, in the court of the Member State in which the property is situated.

Article 7

Where by virtue of this Regulation a court of a Member State has jurisdiction in actions relating to liability from the use or operation of a ship, that court, or any other court substituted for this purpose by the internal law of that Member State, shall also have jurisdiction over claims for limitation of such liability.

Section 3
Jurisdiction in matters relating to insurance

Article 8

In matters relating to insurance, jurisdiction shall be determined by this Section, without prejudice to Article 4 and point 5 of Article 5.

Article 9

1. An insurer domiciled in a Member State may be sued:

(a) in the courts of the Member State where he is domiciled, or

(b) in another Member State, in the case of actions brought by the policyholder, the insured or a beneficiary, in the courts for the place where the plaintiff is domiciled,

(c) if he is a co-insurer, in the courts of a Member State in which proceedings are brought against the leading insurer.

2. An insurer who is not domiciled in a Member State but has a branch, agency or other establishment in one of the Member States shall, in disputes arising out of the operations of the branch, agency or establishment, be deemed to be domiciled in that Member State.

Article 10

In respect of liability insurance or insurance of immovable property, the insurer may in addition be sued in the courts for the place where the harmful event occurred. The same applies if movable and immovable property are covered by the same insurance policy and both are adversely affected by the same contingency.

Article 11

1. In respect of liability insurance, the insurer may also, if the law of the court permits it, be joined in proceedings which the injured party has brought against the insured.

2. Articles 8, 9 and 10 shall apply to actions brought by the injured party directly against the insurer, where such direct actions are permitted.

3. If the law governing such direct actions provides that the policyholder or the insured may be joined as a party to the action, the same court shall have jurisdiction over them.

Article 12

1. Without prejudice to Article 11(3), an insurer may bring proceedings only in the courts of the Member State in which the defendant is domiciled, irrespective of whether he is the policyholder, the insured or a beneficiary.

2. The provisions of this Section shall not affect the right to bring a counterclaim in the court in which, in accordance with this Section, the original claim is pending.

Article 13

The provisions of this Section may be departed from only by an agreement:

1. which is entered into after the dispute has arisen, or

2. which allows the policyholder, the insured or a beneficiary to bring proceedings in courts other than those indicated in this Section, or

3. which is concluded between a policyholder and an insurer, both of whom are at the time of conclusion of the contract domiciled or habitually resident in the same Member State, and which has the effect of conferring jurisdiction on the courts of that State even if the harmful event were to occur abroad, provided that such an agreement is not contrary to the law of that State, or

4. which is concluded with a policyholder who is not domiciled in a Member State, except in so far as the insurance is compulsory or relates to immovable property in a Member State, or

5. which relates to a contract of insurance in so far as it covers one or more of the risks set out in Article 14.

Article 14

The following are the risks referred to in Article 13(5):

1. any loss of or damage to:

(a) seagoing ships, installations situated offshore or on the high seas, or aircraft, arising from perils which relate to their use for commercial purposes;

(b) goods in transit other than passengers' baggage where the transit consists of or includes carriage by such ships or aircraft;

2. any liability, other than for bodily injury to passengers or loss of or damage to their baggage:

(a) arising out of the use or operation of ships, installations or aircraft as referred to in point 1(a) in so far as, in respect of the latter, the law of the Member State in which such aircraft are registered does not prohibit agreements on jurisdiction regarding insurance of such risks;

(b) for loss or damage caused by goods in transit as described in point 1(b);

3. any financial loss connected with the use or operation of ships, installations or aircraft as referred to in point 1(a), in particular loss of freight or charter-hire;

4. any risk or interest connected with any of those referred to in points 1 to 3;

5. notwithstanding points 1 to 4, all "large risks" as defined in Council Directive 73/239/EEC(7), as amended by Council Directives 88/357/EEC(8) and 90/618/EEC(9), as they may be amended.

Section 4
Jurisdiction over consumer contracts

Article 15

1. In matters relating to a contract concluded by a person, the consumer, for a purpose which can be regarded as being outside his trade or profession, jurisdiction shall be determined by this Section, without prejudice to Article 4 and point 5 of Article 5, if:

(a) it is a contract for the sale of goods on instalment credit terms; or

(b) it is a contract for a loan repayable by instalments, or for any other form of credit, made to finance the sale of goods; or

(c) in all other cases, the contract has been concluded with a person who pursues commercial or professional activities in the Member State of the consumer's domicile or, by any means, directs such activities to that Member State or to several States including that Member State, and the contract falls within the scope of such activities.

2. Where a consumer enters into a contract with a party who is not domiciled in the Member State but has a branch, agency or other establishment in one of the Member States, that party shall, in disputes arising out of the operations of the branch, agency or establishment, be deemed to be domiciled in that State.

3. This Section shall not apply to a contract of transport other than a contract which, for an inclusive price, provides for a combination of travel and accommodation.

Article 16

1. A consumer may bring proceedings against the other party to a contract either in the courts of the Member State in which that party is domiciled or in the courts for the place where the consumer is domiciled.

2. Proceedings may be brought against a consumer by the other party to the contract only in the courts of the Member State in which the consumer is domiciled.

3. This Article shall not affect the right to bring a counter-claim in the court in which, in accordance with this Section, the original claim is pending.

Article 17

The provisions of this Section may be departed from only by an agreement:

1. which is entered into after the dispute has arisen; or

2. which allows the consumer to bring proceedings in courts other than those indicated in this Section; or

3. which is entered into by the consumer and the other party to the contract, both of whom are at the time of conclusion of the contract domiciled or habitually resident in the same Member State, and which confers jurisdiction on the courts of that Member State, provided that such an agreement is not contrary to the law of that Member State.

Section 5
Jurisdiction over individual contracts of employment

Article 18

1. In matters relating to individual contracts of employment, jurisdiction shall be determined by this Section, without prejudice to Article 4 and point 5 of Article 5.

2. Where an employee enters into an individual contract of employment with an employer who is not domiciled in a Member State but has a branch, agency or other establishment in one of the Member States, the employer shall, in disputes arising out of the operations of the branch, agency or establishment, be deemed to be domiciled in that Member State.

Article 19

An employer domiciled in a Member State may be sued:

1. in the courts of the Member State where he is domiciled; or

2. in another Member State:

> (a) in the courts for the place where the employee habitually carries out his work or in the courts for the last place where he did so, or

> (b) if the employee does not or did not habitually carry out his work in any one country, in the courts for the place where the business which engaged the employee is or was situated.

Article 20

1. An employer may bring proceedings only in the courts of the Member State in which the employee is domiciled.

2. The provisions of this Section shall not affect the right to bring a counterclaim in the court in which, in accordance with this Section, the original claim is pending.

Article 21

The provisions of this Section may be departed from only by an agreement on jurisdiction:

1. which is entered into after the dispute has arisen; or

2. which allows the employee to bring proceedings in courts other than those indicated in this Section.

Section 6
Exclusive jurisdiction

Article 22

The following courts shall have exclusive jurisdiction, regardless of domicile:

1. in proceedings which have as their object rights in rem in immovable property or tenancies of immovable property, the courts of the Member State in which the property is situated.

However, in proceedings which have as their object tenancies of immovable property concluded for temporary private use for a maximum period of six consecutive months, the courts of the Member State in which the defendant is domiciled shall also have jurisdiction, provided that the tenant is a natural person and that the landlord and the tenant are domiciled in the same Member State;

2. in proceedings which have as their object the validity of the constitution, the nullity or the dissolution of companies or other legal persons or associations of natural or legal persons, or of the validity of the decisions of their organs, the courts of the Member State in which the company, legal person or association has its seat. In order to determine that seat, the court shall apply its rules of private international law;

3. in proceedings which have as their object the validity of entries in public registers, the courts of the Member State in which the register is kept;

4. in proceedings concerned with the registration or validity of patents, trade marks, designs, or other similar rights required to be deposited or registered, the courts of the Member State in which the deposit or registration has been applied for, has taken place or is under the terms of a Community instrument or an international convention deemed to have taken place.

Without prejudice to the jurisdiction of the European Patent Office under the Convention on the Grant of European Patents, signed at Munich on 5 October 1973, the courts of each Member State shall have exclusive jurisdiction, regardless of domicile, in proceedings concerned with the registration or validity of any European patent granted for that State;

5. in proceedings concerned with the enforcement of judgments, the courts of the Member State in which the judgment has been or is to be enforced.

Section 7
Prorogation of jurisdiction

Article 23

1. If the parties, one or more of whom is domiciled in a Member State, have agreed that a court or the courts of a Member State are to have jurisdiction to settle any disputes which have arisen or which may arise in connection with a particular legal relationship, that court or those courts shall have jurisdiction. Such jurisdiction shall be exclusive unless the parties have agreed otherwise. Such an agreement conferring jurisdiction shall be either:

(a) in writing or evidenced in writing; or

(b) in a form which accords with practices which the parties have established between themselves; or

(c) in international trade or commerce, in a form which accords with a usage of which the parties are or ought to have been aware and which in such trade or commerce is widely known to, and regularly observed by, parties to contracts of the type involved in the particular trade or commerce concerned.

2. Any communication by electronic means which provides a durable record of the agreement shall be equivalent to "writing".

3. Where such an agreement is concluded by parties, none of whom is domiciled in a Member State, the courts of other Member States shall have no jurisdiction over their disputes unless the court or courts chosen have declined jurisdiction.

4. The court or courts of a Member State on which a trust instrument has conferred jurisdiction shall have exclusive jurisdiction in any proceedings brought against a settlor, trustee or beneficiary, if relations between these persons or their rights or obligations under the trust are involved.

5. Agreements or provisions of a trust instrument conferring jurisdiction shall have no legal force if they are contrary to Articles 13, 17 or 21, or if the courts whose jurisdiction they purport to exclude have exclusive jurisdiction by virtue of Article 22.

Article 24

Apart from jurisdiction derived from other provisions of this Regulation, a court of a Member State before which a defendant enters an appearance shall have jurisdiction. This rule shall not apply where appearance was entered to contest the jurisdiction, or where another court has exclusive jurisdiction by virtue of Article 22.

Section 8
Examination as to jurisdiction and admissibility

Article 25

Where a court of a Member State is seised of a claim which is principally concerned with a matter over which the courts of another Member State have exclusive jurisdiction by virtue of Article 22, it shall declare of its own motion that it has no jurisdiction.

Article 26

1. Where a defendant domiciled in one Member State is sued in a court of another Member State and does not enter an appearance, the court shall declare of its own motion that it has no jurisdiction unless its jurisdiction is derived from the provisions of this Regulation.

2. The court shall stay the proceedings so long as it is not shown that the defendant has been able to receive the document instituting the proceedings or an equivalent document in sufficient time to enable him to arrange for his defence, or that all necessary steps have been taken to this end.

3. Article 19 of Council Regulation (EC) No 1348/2000 of 29 May 2000 on the service in the Member States of judicial and extrajudicial documents in civil or commercial matters(10) shall apply instead of the provisions of paragraph 2 if the document instituting the proceedings or an equivalent document had to be transmitted from one Member State to another pursuant to this Regulation.

4. Where the provisions of Regulation (EC) No 1348/2000 are not applicable, Article 15 of the Hague Convention of 15 November 1965 on the Service Abroad of Judicial and Extrajudicial Documents in Civil or Commercial Matters shall apply if the document instituting the proceedings or an equivalent document had to be transmitted pursuant to that Convention.

Section 9
Lis pendens—related actions

Article 27

1. Where proceedings involving the same cause of action and between the same parties are brought in the courts of different Member States, any court other than the court first seised shall of its own motion stay its proceedings until such time as the jurisdiction of the court first seised is established.

2. Where the jurisdiction of the court first seised is established, any court other than the court first seised shall decline jurisdiction in favour of that court.

Article 28

1. Where related actions are pending in the courts of different Member States, any court other than the court first seised may stay its proceedings.

2. Where these actions are pending at first instance, any court other than the court first seised may also, on the application of one of the parties, decline jurisdiction if the court first seised has jurisdiction over the actions in question and its law permits the consolidation thereof.

3. For the purposes of this Article, actions are deemed to be related where they are so closely connected that it is expedient to hear and determine them together to avoid the risk of irreconcilable judgments resulting from separate proceedings.

Article 29

Where actions come within the exclusive jurisdiction of several courts, any court other than the court first seised shall decline jurisdiction in favour of that court.

Article 30

For the purposes of this Section, a court shall be deemed to be seised:

1. at the time when the document instituting the proceedings or an equivalent document is lodged with the court, provided that the plaintiff has not subsequently failed to take the steps he was required to take to have service effected on the defendant, or

2. if the document has to be served before being lodged with the court, at the time when it is received by the authority responsible for service, provided that the plaintiff has not subsequently failed to take the steps he was required to take to have the document lodged with the court.

Section 10
Provisional, including protective, measures

Article 31

Application may be made to the courts of a Member State for such provisional, including protective, measures as may be available under the law of that State, even if, under this Regulation, the courts of another Member State have jurisdiction as to the substance of the matter.

CHAPTER III
RECOGNITION AND ENFORCEMENT

Article 32

For the purposes of this Regulation, "judgment" means any judgment given by a court or tribunal of a Member State, whatever the judgment may be called, including a decree, order, decision or writ of execution, as well as the determination of costs or expenses by an officer of the court.

Section 1
Recognition

Article 33

1. A judgment given in a Member State shall be recognised in the other Member States without any special procedure being required.

2. Any interested party who raises the recognition of a judgment as the principal issue in a dispute may, in accordance with the procedures provided for in Sections 2 and 3 of this Chapter, apply for a decision that the judgment be recognised.

3. If the outcome of proceedings in a court of a Member State depends on the determination of an incidental question of recognition that court shall have jurisdiction over that question.

Article 34

A judgment shall not be recognised:

1. if such recognition is manifestly contrary to public policy in the Member State in which recognition is sought;

2. where it was given in default of appearance, if the defendant was not served with the document which instituted the proceedings or with an equivalent document in sufficient time and in such a way as to enable him to arrange for his defence, unless the defendant failed to commence proceedings to challenge the judgment when it was possible for him to do so;

3. if it is irreconcilable with a judgment given in a dispute between the same parties in the Member State in which recognition is sought;

4. if it is irreconcilable with an earlier judgment given in another Member State or in a third State involving the same cause of action and between the same parties, provided that the earlier judgment fulfils the conditions necessary for its recognition in the Member State addressed.

Article 35

1. Moreover, a judgment shall not be recognised if it conflicts with Sections 3, 4 or 6 of Chapter II, or in a case provided for in Article 72.

2. In its examination of the grounds of jurisdiction referred to in the foregoing paragraph, the court or authority applied to shall be bound by the findings of fact on which the court of the Member State of origin based its jurisdiction.

3. Subject to the paragraph 1, the jurisdiction of the court of the Member State of origin may not be reviewed. The test of public policy referred to in point 1 of Article 34 may not be applied to the rules relating to jurisdiction.

Article 36

Under no circumstances may a foreign judgment be reviewed as to its substance.

Article 37

1. A court of a Member State in which recognition is sought of a judgment given in another Member State may stay the proceedings if an ordinary appeal against the judgment has been lodged.

2. A court of a Member State in which recognition is sought of a judgment given in Ireland or the United Kingdom may stay the proceedings if enforcement is suspended in the State of origin, by reason of an appeal.

Section 2
Enforcement

Article 38

1. A judgment given in a Member State and enforceable in that State shall be enforced in another Member State when, on the application of any interested party, it has been declared enforceable there. * * *

* * *

Article 41

The judgment shall be declared enforceable immediately on completion of the formalities in Article 53 without any review under Articles 34 and 35. The party against whom enforcement is sought shall not at this stage of the proceedings be entitled to make any submissions on the application.

* * *

Article 43

1. The decision on the application for a declaration of enforceability may be appealed against by either party. * * *

Section 3
Common provisions

Article 53

1. A party seeking recognition or applying for a declaration of enforceability shall produce a copy of the judgment which satisfies the conditions necessary to establish its authenticity.

2. A party applying for a declaration of enforceability shall also produce the certificate referred to in Article 54, without prejudice to Article 55.

Article 54

The court or competent authority of a Member State where a judgment was given shall issue, at the request of any interested party, a certificate using the standard form in Annex V to this Regulation.

* * *

CHAPTER V
GENERAL PROVISIONS

Article 59

1. In order to determine whether a party is domiciled in the Member State whose courts are seised of a matter, the court shall apply its internal law.

2. If a party is not domiciled in the Member State whose courts are seised of the matter, then, in order to determine whether the party is domiciled in another Member State, the court shall apply the law of that Member State.

Article 60

1. For the purposes of this Regulation, a company or other legal person or association of natural or legal persons is domiciled at the place where it has its:

(a) statutory seat, or

(b) central administration, or

(c) principal place of business.

2. For the purposes of the United Kingdom and Ireland "statutory seat" means the registered office or, where there is no such office anywhere, the place of incorporation or, where there is no such place anywhere, the place under the law of which the formation took place.

3. In order to determine whether a trust is domiciled in the Member State whose courts are seised of the matter, the court shall apply its rules of private international law. * * *

CHAPTER VI
TRANSITIONAL PROVISIONS

Article 66

1. This Regulation shall apply only to legal proceedings instituted and to documents formally drawn up or registered as authentic instruments after the entry into force thereof.

2. However, if the proceedings in the Member State of origin were instituted before the entry into force of this Regulation, judgments given after that date shall be recognised and enforced in accordance with Chapter III,

(a) if the proceedings in the Member State of origin were instituted after the entry into force of the Brussels or the Lugano Convention both in the Member State or origin and in the Member State addressed;

(b) in all other cases, if jurisdiction was founded upon rules which accorded with those provided for either in Chapter II or in a convention concluded between the Member State of origin and the Member State addressed which was in force when the proceedings were instituted.

* * *

CHAPTER VIII
FINAL PROVISIONS
* * *

Article 76

This Regulation shall enter into force on 1 March 2002.

This Regulation is binding in its entirety and directly applicable in the Member States in accordance with the Treaty establishing the European Community.

E. THE NEW YORK ARBITRATION CONVENTION

UNITED NATIONS CONVENTION ON THE RECOGNITION AND ENFORCEMENT OF FOREIGN ARBITRAL AWARDS

(New York, 10 June 1958)

Article I

1. This Convention shall apply to the recognition and enforcement of arbitral awards made in the territory of a State other than the State where the recognition and enforcement of such awards are sought, and arising out of differences between persons, whether physical or legal. It shall also apply to arbitral awards not considered as domestic awards in the State where their recognition and enforcement are sought.

2. The term "arbitral awards" shall include not only awards made by arbitrators appointed for each case but also those made by permanent arbitral bodies to which the parties have submitted.

3. When signing, ratifying or acceding to this Convention, or notifying extension under article X hereof, any State may on the basis of reciprocity declare that it will apply the Convention to the recognition and enforcement of awards made only in the territory of another Contracting State. It may also declare that it will apply the Convention only to differences arising out of legal relationships, whether contractual or not, which are considered as commercial under the national law of the State making such declaration.

Article II

1. Each Contracting State shall recognize an agreement in writing under which the parties undertake to submit to arbitration all or any differences which have arisen or which may arise between them in respect of a defined legal relationship, whether contractual or not, concerning a subject matter capable of settlement by arbitration.

2. The term "agreement in writing" shall include an arbitral clause in a contract or an arbitration agreement, signed by the parties or contained in an exchange of letters or telegrams.

3. The court of a Contracting State, when seized of an action in a matter in respect of which the parties have made an agreement within the meaning of this article, shall, at the request of one of the parties, refer the parties to arbitration, unless it finds that the said agreement is null and void, inoperative or incapable of being performed.

Article III

Each Contracting State shall recognize arbitral awards as binding and enforce them in accordance with the rules of procedure of the territory where the award is relied upon, under the conditions laid down in the following articles. There shall not be imposed substantially more onerous conditions or higher fees or charges on the recognition or enforcement of arbitral awards to which this Convention applies than are imposed on the recognition or enforcement of domestic arbitral awards.

Article IV

1. To obtain the recognition and enforcement mentioned in the preceding article, the party applying for recognition and enforcement shall, at the time of the application, supply:

(a) The duly authenticated original award or a duly certified copy thereof;

(b) The original agreement referred to in article II or a duly certified copy thereof.

2. If the said award or agreement is not made in an official language of the country in which the award is relied upon, the party applying for recognition and enforcement of the award shall produce a translation of these documents into such language. The translation shall be certified by an official or sworn translator or by a diplomatic or consular agent.

Article V

1. Recognition and enforcement of the award may be refused, at the request of the party against whom it is invoked, only if that party furnishes to the competent authority where the recognition and enforcement is sought, proof that:

(a) The parties to the agreement referred to in article II were, under the law applicable to them, under some incapacity, or the said agreement is not valid under the law to which the parties have subjected it or, failing any indication thereon, under the law of the country where the award was made; or

(b) The party against whom the award is invoked was not given proper notice of the appointment of the arbitrator or of the arbitration proceedings or was otherwise unable to present his case; or

(c) The award deals with a difference not contemplated by or not falling within the terms of the submission to arbitration, or it contains decisions on matters beyond the scope of the submission to arbitration, provided that, if the decisions on matters submitted to arbitration can be separated from those not so submitted, that part of the award which contains decisions on matters submitted to arbitration may be recognized and enforced; or

(d) The composition of the arbitral authority or the arbitral procedure was not in accordance with the agreement of the parties, or, failing such agreement, was not in accordance with the law of the country where the arbitration took place; or

(e) The award has not yet become binding on the parties, or has been set aside or suspended by a competent authority of the country in which, or under the law of which, that award was made.

2. Recognition and enforcement of an arbitral award may also be refused if the competent authority in the country where recognition and enforcement is sought finds that:

(a) The subject matter of the difference is not capable of settlement by arbitration under the law of that country; or

(b) The recognition or enforcement of the award would be contrary to the public policy of that country.

Article VI

If an application for the setting aside or suspension of the award has been made to a competent authority referred to in article V (1) (e), the authority before which the award is sought to be relied upon may, if it considers it proper, adjourn the decision on the enforcement of the award and may also, on the application of the party claiming enforcement of the award, order the other party to give suitable security.

Article VII

1. The provisions of the present Convention shall not affect the validity of multilateral or bilateral agreements concerning the recognition and enforcement of arbitral awards entered into by the Contracting States nor deprive any interested party of any right he may have to avail himself of an arbitral award in the manner and to the extent allowed by the law or the treaties of the country where such award is sought to be relied upon.

2. The Geneva Protocol on Arbitration Clauses of 1923 and the Geneva Convention on the Execution of Foreign Arbitral Awards of 1927 shall cease to have effect between Contracting States on their becoming bound and to the extent that they become bound, by this Convention.

Article VIII

1. This Convention shall be open until 31 December 1958 for signature on behalf of any Member of the United Nations and also on behalf of any other State which is or hereafter becomes a member of any specialized agency of the United Nations, or which is or hereafter becomes a party to the Statute of the International Court of Justice, or any other State to which an invitation has been addressed by the General Assembly of the United Nations.

2. This Convention shall be ratified and the instrument of ratification shall be deposited with the Secretary-General of the United Nations.

Article IX

1. This Convention shall be open for accession to all States referred to in article VIII.

2. Accession shall be effected by the deposit of an instrument of accession with the Secretary-General of the United Nations.

Article X

1. Any State may, at the time of signature, ratification or accession, declare that this Convention shall extend to all or any of the territories for the international relations of which it is responsible. Such a declaration shall take effect when the Convention enters into force for the State concerned.

2. At any time thereafter any such extension shall be made by notification addressed to the Secretary-General of the United Nations and shall take effect as from the ninetieth day after the day of receipt by the Secretary-General of the

United Nations of this notification, or as from the date of entry into force of the Convention for the State concerned, whichever is the later.

3. With respect to those territories to which this Convention is not extended at the time of signature, ratification or accession, each State concerned shall consider the possibility of taking the necessary steps in order to extend the application of this Convention to such territories, subject, where necessary for constitutional reasons, to the consent of the Governments of such territories.

Article XI

In the case of a federal or non-unitary State, the following provisions shall apply:

(a) With respect to those articles of this Convention that come within the legislative jurisdiction of the federal authority, the obligations of the federal Government shall to this extent be the same as those of Contracting States which are not federal States;

(b) With respect to those articles of this Convention that come within the legislative jurisdiction of constituent states or provinces which are not, under the constitutional system of the federation, bound to take legislative action, the federal Government shall bring such articles with a favourable recommendation to the notice of the appropriate authorities of constituent states or provinces at the earliest possible moment;

(c) A federal State Party to this Convention shall, at the request of any other Contracting State transmitted through the Secretary-General of the United Nations, supply a statement of the law and practice of the federation and its constituent units in regard to any particular provision of this Convention, showing the extent to which effect has been given to that provision by legislative or other action.

Article XII

1. This Convention shall come into force on the ninetieth day following the date of deposit of the third instrument of ratification or accession.

2. For each State ratifying or acceding to this Convention after the deposit of the third instrument of ratification or accession, this Convention shall enter into force on the ninetieth day after deposit by such State of its instrument of ratification or accession.

Article XIII

1. Any Contracting State may denounce this Convention by a written notification to the Secretary-General of the United Nations. Denunciation shall take effect one year after the date of receipt of the notification by the Secretary-General.

2. Any State which has made a declaration or notification under article X may, at any time thereafter, by notification to the Secretary-General of the United Nations, declare that this Convention shall cease to extend to the territory concerned one year after the date of the receipt of the notification by the Secretary-General.

3. This Convention shall continue to be applicable to arbitral awards in respect of which recognition and enforcement proceedings have been instituted before the denunciation takes effect.

Article XIV

A Contracting State shall not be entitled to avail itself of the present Convention against other Contracting States except to the extent that it is itself bound to apply the Convention.

Article XV

The Secretary-General of the United Nations shall notify the States contemplated in article VIII of the following:

(a) Signatures and ratifications in accordance with article VIII;

(b) Accessions in accordance with article IX;

(c) Declarations and notifications under articles I, X and XI;

(d) The date upon which this Convention enters into force in accordance with article XII;

(e) Denunciations and notifications in accordance with article XIII.

Article XVI

1. This Convention, of which the Chinese, English, French, Russian and Spanish texts shall be equally authentic, shall be deposited in the archives of the United Nations.

2. The Secretary-General of the United Nations shall transmit a certified copy of this Convention to the States contemplated in article VIII.

Reservations and declarations *[Omitted]*

F. THE FOREIGN SOVEREIGN IMMUNITIES ACT OF 1976
28 U.S.C. § ____.

Sec. 1602. Findings and declaration of purpose

The Congress finds that the determination by United States courts of the claims of foreign states to immunity from the jurisdiction of such courts would serve the interests of justice and would protect the rights of both foreign states and litigants in United States courts. Under international law, states are not immune from the jurisdiction of foreign courts insofar as their commercial activities are concerned, and their commercial property may be levied upon for the satisfaction of judgments rendered against them in connection with their commercial activities. Claims of foreign states to immunity should henceforth be decided by courts of the United States and of the States in conformity with the principles set forth in this chapter.

Sec. 1603. Definitions

For purposes of this chapter—

(a) A "foreign state", except as used in section 1608 of this title, includes a political subdivision of a foreign state or an agency or instrumentality of a foreign state as defined in subsection (b).

(b) An "agency or instrumentality of a foreign state" means any entity—

(1) which is a separate legal person, corporate or otherwise, and

(2) which is an organ of a foreign state or political subdivision thereof, or a majority of whose shares or other   ownership interest is owned by a foreign state or political subdivision thereof, and

(3) which is neither a citizen of a State of the United States as defined in section 1332 (c) and (e) of this title, nor created under the laws of any third country.

(c) The "United States" includes all territory and waters, continental or insular, subject to the jurisdiction of the United States.

(d) A "commercial activity" means either a regular course of commercial conduct or a particular commercial transaction or act. The commercial character of an activity shall be determined by reference to the nature of the course of conduct or particular transaction or act, rather than by reference to its purpose.

(e) A "commercial activity carried on in the United States by a foreign state" means commercial activity carried on by such state and having substantial contact with the United States.

Sec. 1604. Immunity of a foreign state from jurisdiction

Subject to existing international agreements to which the United States is a party at the time of enactment of this Act a foreign state shall be immune from the jurisdiction of the courts of the United States and of the States except as provided in sections 1605 to 1607 of this chapter.

Sec. 1605. General exceptions to the jurisdictional immunity of a foreign state

(a) A foreign state shall not be immune from the jurisdiction of courts of the United States or of the States in any case—

(1) in which the foreign state has waived its immunity either explicitly or by implication, notwithstanding any withdrawal of the waiver which the foreign state may purport to effect except in accordance with the terms of the waiver;

(2) in which the action is based upon a commercial activity carried on in the United States by the foreign state; or upon an act performed in the United States in connection with a commercial activity of the foreign state elsewhere; or upon an act outside the territory of the United States in connection with a commercial activity of the foreign state elsewhere and that act causes a direct effect in the United States;

(3) in which rights in property taken in violation of international law are in issue and that property or any property exchanged for such property is present in the United States in connection with a commercial activity carried on in the United States by the foreign state; or that property or any property exchanged for such property is owned or operated by an agency or instrumentality of the foreign state and that agency or instrumentality is engaged in a commercial activity in the United States;

(4) in which rights in property in the United States acquired by succession or gift or rights in immovable property situated in the United States are in issue;

(5) not otherwise encompassed in paragraph (2) above, in which money damages are sought against a foreign state for personal injury or death, or damage to or loss of property, occurring in the United States and caused by the tortious act or omission of that foreign state or of any official or employee of that foreign state while acting within the scope of his office or employment; except this paragraph shall not apply to—

(A) any claim based upon the exercise or performance or the failure to exercise or perform a discretionary function regardless of whether the discretion be abused, or

(B) any claim arising out of malicious prosecution, abuse of process, libel, slander, misrepresentation, deceit, or interference with contract rights; or

(6) in which the action is brought, either to enforce an agreement made by the foreign state with or for the benefit of a private party to submit to arbitration all or any differences which have arisen or which may arise between the parties with respect to a defined legal relationship, whether contractual or not, concerning a subject matter capable of settlement by arbitration under the laws of the United States, or to confirm an award made pursuant to such an agreement to arbitrate, if (A) the arbitration takes place or is intended to take place in the United States, (B) the agreement

or award is or may be governed by a treaty or other international agreement in force for the United States calling for the recognition and enforcement of arbitral awards, (C) the underlying claim, save for the agreement to arbitrate, could have been brought in a United States court under this section or section 1607, or (D) paragraph (1) of this subsection is otherwise applicable.

(b) A foreign state shall not be immune from the jurisdiction of the courts of the United States in any case in which a suit in admiralty is brought to enforce a maritime lien against a vessel or cargo of the foreign state, which maritime lien is based upon a commercial activity of the foreign state: Provided, That

(1) notice of the suit is given by delivery of a copy of the summons and of the complaint to the person, or his agent, having possession of the vessel or cargo against which the maritime lien is asserted; and if the vessel or cargo is arrested pursuant to process obtained on behalf of the party bringing the suit, the service of process of arrest shall be deemed to constitute valid delivery of such notice, but the party bringing the suit shall be liable for any damages sustained by the foreign state as a result of the arrest if the party bringing the suit had actual or constructive knowledge that the vessel or cargo of a foreign state was involved; and

(2) notice to the foreign state of the commencement of suit as provided in section 1608 of this title is initiated within ten days either of the delivery of notice as provided in paragraph (1) of this subsection or, in the case of a party who was unaware that the vessel or cargo of a foreign state was involved, of the date such party determined the existence of the foreign state's interest.

(c) Whenever notice is delivered under subsection (b)(1), the suit to enforce a maritime lien shall thereafter proceed and shall be heard and determined according to the principles of law and rules of practice of suits in rem whenever it appears that, had the vessel been privately owned and possessed, a suit in rem might have been maintained. A decree against the foreign state may include costs of the suit and, if the decree is for a money judgment, interest as ordered by the court, except that the court may not award judgment against the foreign state in an amount greater than the value of the vessel or cargo upon which the maritime lien arose. Such value shall be determined as of the time notice is served under subsection (b)(1). Decrees shall be subject to appeal and revision as provided in other cases of admiralty and maritime jurisdiction. Nothing shall preclude the plaintiff in any proper case from seeking relief in personam in the same action brought to enforce a maritime lien as provided in this section.

(d) A foreign state shall not be immune from the jurisdiction of the courts of the United States in any action brought to foreclose a preferred mortgage, as defined in section 31301 of title 46. Such action shall be brought, heard, and determined in accordance with the provisions of chapter 313 of title 46 and in accordance with the principles of law and rules of practice of suits in rem, whenever it appears that had the vessel been privately owned and possessed a suit in rem might have been maintained.

* * *

Sec. 1605A. Terrorism exception to the jurisdictional immunity of a foreign state

(a) In general.—

(1) No immunity.—A foreign state shall not be immune from the jurisdiction of courts of the United States or of the States in any case not otherwise covered by this chapter in which money damages are sought against a foreign state for personal injury or death that was caused by an act of torture, extrajudicial killing, aircraft sabotage, hostage taking, or the provision of material support or resources for such an act if such act or provision of material support or resources is engaged in by an official, employee, or agent of such foreign state while acting within the scope of his or her office, employment, or agency.

(2) Claim heard.—The court shall hear a claim under this section if—

(A)(i)(I) the foreign state was designated as a state sponsor of terrorism at the time the act described in paragraph (1) occurred, or was so designated as a result of such act, and, subject to subclause (II), either remains so designated when the claim is filed under this section or was so designated within the 6-month period before the claim is filed under this section; or

(II) in the case of an action that is refiled under this section by reason of section 1083(c)(2)(A) of the National Defense Authorization Act for Fiscal Year 2008 or is filed under this section by reason of section 1083(c)(3) of that Act, the foreign state was designated as a state sponsor of terrorism when the original action or the related action under section 1605(a)(7) (as in effect before the enactment of this section) or section 589 of the Foreign Operations, Export Financing, and Related Programs Appropriations Act, 1997 (as contained in section 101(c) of division A of Public Law 104-208) was filed;

(ii) the claimant or the victim was, at the time the act described in paragraph (1) occurred—

(I) a national of the United States;

(II) a member of the armed forces; or

(III) otherwise an employee of the Government of the United States, or of an individual performing a contract awarded by the United States Government, acting within the scope of the employee's employment; and

(iii) in a case in which the act occurred in the foreign state against which the claim has been brought, the claimant has afforded the foreign state a reasonable opportunity to arbitrate the claim in accordance with the accepted international rules of arbitration; or

(B) the act described in paragraph (1) is related to Case Number 1:00CV03110 (EGS) in the United States District Court for the District of Columbia.

(b) Limitations.—An action may be brought or maintained under this section if the action is commenced, or a related action was commenced under section 1605(a)(7) (before the date of the enactment of this section) or section 589 of the Foreign Operations, Export Financing, and Related Programs Appropriations Act, 1997 (as contained in section 101(c) of division A of Public Law 104-208) not later than the latter of—

(1) 10 years after April 24, 1996; or

(2) 10 years after the date on which the cause of action arose.

(c) Private right of action.—A foreign state that is or was a state sponsor of terrorism as described in subsection (a)(2)(A)(i), and any official, employee, or agent of that foreign state while acting within the scope of his or her office, employment, or agency, shall be liable to—

(1) a national of the United States,

(2) a member of the armed forces,

(3) an employee of the Government of the United States, or of an individual performing a contract awarded by the United States Government, acting within the scope of the employee's employment, or

(4) the legal representative of a person described in paragraph (1), (2), or (3),

for personal injury or death caused by acts described in subsection (a)(1) of that foreign state, or of an official, employee, or agent of that foreign state, for which the courts of the United States may maintain jurisdiction under this section for money damages. In any such action, damages may include economic damages, solatium, pain and suffering, and punitive damages. In any such action, a foreign state shall be vicariously liable for the acts of its officials, employees, or agents.

* * *

Sec. 1606. Extent of liability

As to any claim for relief with respect to which a foreign state is not entitled to immunity under section 1605 or 1607 of this chapter, the foreign state shall be liable in the same manner and to the same extent as a private individual under like circumstances; but a foreign state except for an agency or instrumentality thereof shall not be liable for punitive damages; if, however, in any case wherein death was caused, the law of the place where the action or omission occurred provides, or has been construed to provide, for damages only punitive in nature, the foreign state shall be liable for actual or compensatory damages measured by the pecuniary injuries resulting from such death which were incurred by the persons for whose benefit the action was brought. * * *

Sec. 1607. Counterclaims

In any action brought by a foreign state, or in which a foreign state intervenes, in a court of the United States or of a State, the foreign state shall not be accorded immunity with respect to any counterclaim—

(a) for which a foreign state would not be entitled to immunity under section 1605 or 1605A of this chapter had such claim been brought in a separate action against the foreign state; or

(b) arising out of the transaction or occurrence that is the subject matter of the claim of the foreign state; or

(c) to the extent that the counterclaim does not seek relief exceeding in amount or differing in kind from that sought by the foreign state.

Sec. 1608. Service; time to answer; default

(a) Service in the courts of the United States and of the States shall be made upon a foreign state or political subdivision of a foreign state:

(1) by delivery of a copy of the summons and complaint in accordance with any special arrangement for service between the plaintiff and the foreign state or political subdivision; or

(2) if no special arrangement exists, by delivery of a copy of the summons and complaint in accordance with an applicable international convention on service of judicial documents; or

(3) if service cannot be made under paragraphs (1) or (2), by sending a copy of the summons and complaint and a notice of suit, together with a translation of each into the official language of the foreign state, by any form of mail requiring a signed receipt, to be addressed and dispatched by the clerk of the court to the head of the ministry of foreign affairs of the foreign state concerned, or

(4) if service cannot be made within 30 days under paragraph (3), by sending two copies of the summons and complaint and a notice of suit, together with a translation of each into the official language of the foreign state, by any form of mail requiring a signed receipt, to be addressed and dispatched by the clerk of the court to the Secretary of State in Washington, District of Columbia, to the attention of the Director of Special Consular Services—and the Secretary shall transmit one copy of the papers through diplomatic channels to the foreign state and shall send to the clerk of the court a certified copy of the diplomatic note indicating when the papers were transmitted.

As used in this subsection, a "notice of suit" shall mean a notice addressed to a foreign state and in a form prescribed by the Secretary of State by regulation.

(b) Service in the courts of the United States and of the States shall be made upon an agency or instrumentality of a foreign state:

(1) by delivery of a copy of the summons and complaint in   accordance with any special arrangement for service between the plaintiff and the agency or instrumentality; or

(2) if no special arrangement exists, by delivery of a copy of the summons and complaint either to an officer, a managing or general agent, or to any other agent authorized by appointment or by law to receive service of process in the United States; or in accordance with an applicable international convention on service of judicial documents; or

(3) if service cannot be made under paragraphs (1) or (2), and if reasonably calculated to give actual notice, by delivery of a copy of the summons

and complaint, together with a translation of each into the official language of the foreign state—

(A) as directed by an authority of the foreign state or political subdivision in response to a letter rogatory or request or

(B) by any form of mail requiring a signed receipt, to be addressed and dispatched by the clerk of the court to the agency or instrumentality to be served, or

(C) as directed by order of the court consistent with the law of the place where service is to be made.

(c) Service shall be deemed to have been made—

(1) in the case of service under subsection (a)(4), as of the date of transmittal indicated in the certified copy of the diplomatic note; and

(2) in any other case under this section, as of the date of receipt indicated in the certification, signed and returned postal receipt, or other proof of service applicable to the method of service employed.

(d) In any action brought in a court of the United States or of a State, a foreign state, a political subdivision thereof, or an agency or instrumentality of a foreign state shall serve an answer or other responsive pleading to the complaint within sixty days after service has been made under this section.

(e) No judgment by default shall be entered by a court of the United States or of a State against a foreign state, a political subdivision thereof, or an agency or instrumentality of a foreign state, unless the claimant establishes his claim or right to relief by evidence satisfactory to the court. A copy of any such default judgment shall be sent to the foreign state or political subdivision in the manner prescribed for service in this section.

Sec. 1609. Immunity from attachment and execution of property of a foreign state

Subject to existing international agreements to which the United States is a party at the time of enactment of this Act the property in the United States of a foreign state shall be immune from attachment arrest and execution except as provided in sections 1610 and 1611 of this chapter.

Sec. 1610. Exceptions to the immunity from attachment or execution

(a) The property in the United States of a foreign state, as defined in section 1603(a) of this chapter, used for a commercial activity in the United States, shall not be immune from attachment in aid of execution, or from execution, upon a judgment entered by a court of the United States or of a State after the effective date of this Act, if—

(1) the foreign state has waived its immunity from attachment in aid of execution or from execution either explicitly or by implication, notwithstanding any withdrawal of the waiver the foreign state may purport to effect except in accordance with the terms of the waiver, or

(2) the property is or was used for the commercial activity upon which the claim is based, or

(3) the execution relates to a judgment establishing rights in property which has been taken in violation of international law or which has been exchanged for property taken in violation of international law, or

(4) the execution relates to a judgment establishing rights in property—

(A) which is acquired by succession or gift, or

(B) which is immovable and situated in the United States: *Provided*, That such property is not used for purposes of maintaining a diplomatic or consular mission or the residence of the Chief of such mission, or

 (5) the property consists of any contractual obligation or any proceeds from such a contractual obligation to indemnify or hold harmless the foreign state or its employees under a policy of automobile or other liability or casualty insurance covering the claim which merged into the judgment, or

(6) the judgment is based on an order confirming an arbitral award rendered against the foreign state, provided that attachment in aid of execution, or execution, would not be inconsistent with any provision in the arbitral agreement, or

(7) the judgment relates to a claim for which the foreign state is not immune under section 1605A, or section 1605(a)(7) (as such section was in effect on January 27, 2008), regardless of whether the property is or was involved with the act upon which the claim is based.

 (b) In addition to subsection (a), any property in the United States of an agency or instrumentality of a foreign state engaged in commercial activity in the United States shall not be immune from attachment in aid of execution, or from execution, upon a judgment entered by a court of the United States or of a State after the effective date of this Act, if—

(1) the agency or instrumentality has waived its immunity from attachment in aid of execution or from execution either explicitly or implicitly, notwithstanding any withdrawal of the waiver the agency or instrumentality may purport to effect except in accordance with the terms of the waiver, or

(2) the judgment relates to a claim for which the agency or instrumentality is not immune by virtue of section 1605(a) (2), (3), or (5), 1605(b), or 1605A of this chapter, regardless of whether the property is or was involved in the act upon which the claim is based.

(3) the judgment relates to a claim for which the agency or instrumentality is not immune by virtue of section 1605A of this chapter or section 1605(a)(7) of this chapter (as such section was in effect on January 27, 2008), regardlesss of whether the property is or was involved in the act upon which the claim is based.

 (c) No attachment or execution referred to in subsections (a) and (b) of this section shall be permitted until the court has ordered such attachment and execution after having determined that a reasonable period of time has elapsed following the entry of judgment and the giving of any notice required under section 1608(e) of this chapter.

(d) The property of a foreign state, as defined in section 1603(a) of this chapter, used for a commercial activity in the United States, shall not be immune from attachment prior to the entry of judgment in any action brought in a court of the United States or of a State, or prior to the elapse of the period of time provided in subsection (c) of this section, if—

(1) the foreign state has explicitly waived its immunity from attachment prior to judgment, notwithstanding any withdrawal of the waiver the foreign state may purport to effect except in accordance with the terms of the waiver, and

(2) the purpose of the attachment is to secure satisfaction of a judgment that has been or may ultimately be entered against the foreign state, and not to obtain jurisdiction.

(e) The vessels of a foreign state shall not be immune from arrest in rem, interlocutory sale, and execution in actions brought to foreclose a preferred mortgage as provided in section 1605(d).

(f)(1)(A) Notwithstanding any other provision of law, including but not limited to section 208(f) of the Foreign Missions Act (22 U.S.C. 4308(f)), and except as provided in subparagraph (B), any property with respect to which financial transactions are prohibited or regulated pursuant to section 5(b) of the Trading with the Enemy Act (50 U.S.C. App. 5(b)), section 620(a) of the Foreign Assistance Act of 1961 (22 U.S.C. 2370(a)), sections 202 and 203 of the International Emergency Economic Powers Act (50 U.S.C. 1701-1702), or any other proclamation, order, regulation, or license issued pursuant thereto, shall be subject to execution or attachment in aid of execution of any judgment relating to a claim for which a foreign state (including any agency or instrumentality or such state) claiming such property is not immune under section 1605(a)(7) (as in effect before the enactment of section 1605A) or section 1605A.

(B) Subparagraph (A) shall not apply if, at the time the property is expropriated or seized by the foreign state, the property has been held in title by a natural person or, if held in trust, has been held for the benefit of a natural person or persons.

(2)(A) At the request of any party in whose favor a judgment has been issued with respect to a claim for which the foreign state is not immune under section 1605(a)(7) (as in effect before the enactment of section 1605A) or section 1605A, the Secretary of the Treasury and the Secretary of State should make every effort to fully, promptly, and effectively assist any judgment creditor or any court that has issued any such judgment in identifying, locating, and executing against the property of that foreign state or any agency or instrumentality of such state.

(B) In providing such assistance, the Secretaries—

(i) may provide such information to the court under seal; and

(ii) should make every effort to provide the information in a manner sufficient to allow the court to direct the United States Marshall's office to promptly and effectively execute against that property.

(3) Waiver.–The President may waive any provision of paragraph (1) in the interest of national security.

(g) Property in certain actions.—

(1) In general.—Subject to paragraph (3), the property of a foreign state against which a judgment is entered under section 1605A, and the property of an agency or instrumentality of such a state, including property that is a separate juridical entity or is an interest held directly or indirectly in a separate juridical entity, is subject to attachment in aid of execution, and execution, upon that judgment as provided in this section, regardless of—

(A) the level of economic control over the property by the government of the foreign state;

(B) whether the profits of the property go to that government;

(C) the degree to which officials of that government manage the property or otherwise control its daily affairs;

(D) whether that government is the sole beneficiary in interest of the property; or

(E) whether establishing the property as a separate entity would entitle the foreign state to benefits in United States courts while avoiding its obligations.

(2) United states sovereign immunity inapplicable.—Any property of a foreign state, or agency or instrumentality of a foreign state, to which paragraph (1) applies shall not be immune from attachment in aid of execution, or execution, upon a judgment entered under section 1605A because the property is regulated by the United States Government by reason of action taken against that foreign state under the Trading With the Enemy Act or the International Emergency Economic Powers Act.

(3) Third-party joint property holders.—Nothing in this subsection shall be construed to supersede the authority of a court to prevent appropriately the impairment of an interest held by a person who is not liable in the action giving rise to a judgment in property subject to attachment in aid of execution, or execution, upon such judgment.

Sec. 1611. Certain types of property immune from execution

(a) Notwithstanding the provisions of section 1610 of this chapter, the property of those organizations designated by the President as being entitled to enjoy the privileges, exemptions, and immunities provided by the International Organizations Immunities Act shall not be subject to attachment or any other judicial process impeding the disbursement of funds to, or on the order of, a foreign state as the result of an action brought in the courts of the United States or of the States.

(b) Notwithstanding the provisions of section 1610 of this chapter, the property of a foreign state shall be immune from attachment and from execution, if—

(1) the property is that of a foreign central bank or monetary authority held for its own account, unless such bank or authority, or its parent foreign government, has explicitly waived its immunity from attachment in aid of execution, or from execution, notwithstanding any withdrawal of the waiver which the bank, authority or government may purport to effect except in accordance with the terms of the waiver; or

(2) the property is, or is intended to be, used in connection with a military activity and

(A) is of a military character, or

(B) is under the control of a military authority or defense agency.

(c) Notwithstanding the provisions of section 1610 of this chapter, the property of a foreign state shall be immune from attachment and from execution in an action brought under section 302 of the Cuban Liberty and Democratic Solidarity (LIBERTAD) Act of 1996 to the extent that the property is a facility or installation used by an accredited diplomatic mission for official purposes.

INDEX

References are to Pages

ABSTENTION

Generally, 398 et seq.

See also Lis Pendens, this index

Act of state doctrine, 315

Federal court abstention doctrines, 401

Political questions, 308

ACT OF STATE DOCTRINE

Generally, 291 et seq.

Abstention, 315

Bernstein exception, 294

Bernstein letters, 303

Bribery claims, 313

Choice of law analysis of doctrine, 316

Comity aspects of doctrine, 314

Commercial vs governmental acts, 306

Erie doctrine, 295

Expropriations, 291, 304

Foreign Sovereign Immunities Act, this index

Formal and informal acts, 308

Hickenlooper Amendment, 302, 312

Human rights litigation, 317

International law claims, 197, 297, 319

International relations law, 197

Locus of challenged acts, 311

Police power exercises, 317

Public vs private acts, 306

Recognition of judgments analysis of doctrine, 316

Refusals to act, 309

Separation of powers, 295

Situs of challenged acts, 311

Treaty enforcement, 301

ADMIRALTY LAW

Arbitration in admiralty, 703

Attachment, 101

Authority of federal courts to create, 178

Forum selection clauses, 124

General maritime law, 178

Jurisdiction, 162

ALI JUDGMENT RECOGNITION PROPOSAL

See Recognition and Enforcement of Judgments, this index

ALIEN TORT STATUTE (ATS)

Generally, 163 et seq.

Abduction claim, 167

Causes of action, 167

Color of law, 192

Corporations, claims against, 196

Federal jurisdiction, 163 et seq.

Foreign Sovereign Immunities Act applicability, 235, 238

Foreign Sovereign Immunities Act limitations, 181

Human rights litigation, 283

International law claims, 164, 186

Parties, 181, 187

Service of process, 193

Sovereign defendants, 181

State action requirement, 188

Torture claims, 164

Torture Victim Protection Act distinguished, 193

Torture Victim Protection Act harmonization, 183

Treaty enforcement, 205

ALIENAGE JURISDICTION

See Subject Matter Jurisdiction, this index

ALIENS

Domicile, 218

Foreign Sovereign Immunities Act claims, 231

Permanent Resident Aliens, this index

Venue in actions against. See Venue, this index

ANTI-INJUNCTION ACT

Generally, 400

Exceptions, 432

ANTISUIT INJUNCTIONS

Generally, 415 et seq.

Airline disaster, foreign courts, 437

Antitrust litigation, 431

Comity considerations

Generally, 417

Arbitration, injunctions in aid of, 729

Counter injunctions, 431

787

Discovery issues underlying international parallel proceedings, 423

English Courts, 437, 446

European courts, international injunctions, 432 et seq.

Federal-state parallel litigation

    Generally, 400

    Exceptions, 432

Foreign-US parallel litigation

    International injunctions by European courts, 432 et seq.

    International injunctions by US courts, 415 et seq.

Forum selection clause enforcement, 415

Lis pendens contrasted, 399

Personal jurisdiction, 431

Quasi in rem proceedings, 422

Reciprocity concerns, 419

Securities litigation, 423

Standard of review of preliminary injunctions, 424

State-state parallel litigation, 402

US courts, international injunctions, 415 et seq.

ANTI-TERRORISM ACT OF 1990

    Generally, 184

Color of law, 184

Parties, 183

ANTITRUST LAWS

Antisuit injunctions, 431

Arbitrability of claims, 716

Choice of law contract provision conflicts, 545

Claw-back policy of UK, 572

European Union's extraterritorial antitrust laws, 590

Extraterritoriality of US statutes, this index

Foreign Trade Antitrust Improvement Act, 586

Forum non conveniens challenges to federal statutory claims, 393

ARBITRATION

    Generally, 693 et seq.

Ad hoc

    Institutional arbitration distinguished, 694

    UNCITRAL rules, 694

Admiralty law claims, 703

Antisuit injunctions in aid of arbitration

    Generally, 723 et seq.

    European Court of Justice, 723, 730

Antitrust law claims, 716

Awards

    Enforcement of awards, below

    Judicial review standards, 722

Bills of lading clauses, 695

Brussels Regulation priority principle applied in aid of arbitration

    Generally, 730

    Revision effective in 2015, 734

Carriage of Goods by Sea claims, arbitrability, 695

Choice of law

    Arbitrability determinations, 703

    Enforcement determinations

       Generally, 704

       Public policy defenses, 713

Claims subject to arbitration

    Generally, 695 et seq.

    Choice of law as to determination, 703

    Enforcement stage arbitrability challenges, 708, 713

    Jurisdiction to determine arbitrability, 703

    Liberal federal policy favoring arbitration, 702

Comity, antisuit injunctions in aid of arbitration, 729

Confidentiality advantages, 693

Contract clauses

    Adhesive contracts, 722

    Bills of lading, 695

    Damages for breach, 734

    Interpretation rules, 714

    Procedural rules specifications, 702

Defenses to enforcement of awards, 706

Due process challenges to awards, 714

Enforcement advantages, 693

Enforcement of awards

    Generally, 704 et seq.

    Antitrust law claim awards, 716

    Arbitrability challenges at enforcement stage, 708

    Burden of proof, 706

    Choice of law as to enforcement of awards, above

    Defenses, 706

    Due process challenges, 714

    Federal Arbitration Act defenses, 711

    Interim relief, 715

    Judicial review standards, 722

    Jurisdiction challenges, 709

Manifest disregard of law defense, 710

New York Convention defenses, 711

Public policy defenses to enforcement of awards, below

Reciprocity considerations, 707

Scope of award exceeding contract, 713

European Court of Justice, antisuit injunctions in aid of arbitration, 723, 730

Federal Arbitration Act, this index

Finality advantages, 693

Institutional, ad hoc arbitration distinguished, 694

Inter-American Convention (or Panama Convention) on International

Commercial Arbitration, 694

Interim relief enforcement of awards, 715

Interpretation of arbitration clauses, 714

Judicial review of awards, 722

Jurisdiction challenges to enforcement of awards, 709

Jurisdiction to determine arbitrability, 703

Manifest disregard of law defense to enforcement of awards, 710

New York Convention, this index

Orders compelling arbitration, Federal Arbitration Act, 723

Procedural flexibility

Generally, 694

Contractual procedure rules, 702

Public policy defenses to enforcement of awards

Generally, 707

Choice of law as to relevant public policy, 713

Usury laws, award violating, 722

Public records of awards, 722

Reciprocity considerations in enforcement of awards, 707

Scope. Claims subject to arbitration, above

Seat of arbitration, 704

Securities law claims arbitrability, 702

Stay orders to enforce, 723, 730

UNCITRAL ad hoc arbitration rules, 694

Usury laws, award violating, 722

ATTACHMENT

See Pre-Trial Attachment, this index

BERNSTEIN EXCEPTION

Act of state doctrine, 294

BERNSTEIN LETTERS

Act of state doctrine, 303

BIVENS CLAIMS

Federal common law, 178

BLOCKING STATUTES

See Hague Evidence Convention, this index

BRUSSELS CONVENTION

Parallel proceedings, 439

Personal jurisdiction, 79 et seq.

Recognition and enforcement of judgments, 684

BRUSSELS REGULATION

Arbitration, this index

Forum non conveniens, 396

Forum selection clauses, 138

Fundamental rights principle, 690

Lis pendens, 414, 432

Personal jurisdiction, 689

Priority principle applied in aid of arbitration

Generally, 730

Revision effective in 2015, 734

Provisional remedies, 113

Recognition and enforcement of judgments, 684

Text of, 758-770

BURDEN OF PROOF

Arbitration award enforcement, 706

Choice of law issues, 525

Hague Evidence Convention

Blocking statutes, good faith attempts to secure waivers, 493

Demonstrating of need to utilize, 479

Hague Evidence Convention employment, burden of demonstrating need, 479

Personal jurisdiction establishment, 20, 35

CARRIAGE OF GOODS BY SEA

Arbitrability of claims, 695

CENTRAL AUTHORITIES

Hague Evidence Convention, 453

Hague Service Convention, this index

CHARMING BETSY CANON

Generally, 233

CHOICE OF FORUM

See Forum Selection, this index

CHOICE OF LAW

Generally, 511 et seq.

Act of state doctrine, choice of law analysis, 316

Antitrust law, contract provision conflicts, 545

Arbitration, this index

Burden of proof as to choice of law issues, 525

Characterization issues, 512

Civil law regimes, 554

Comity

Generally, 319

Domestic law, 514

Conflicts resolution, 514

Constitutional limits in US courts, 526

Contract provisions

Generally, 533 et seq.

Antitrust law conflicts, 545

Enforceability, 535

Forum selection clause interrelationships, 546 et seq.

Forum selection clauses compared, 534

Forum selection clauses distinguished, 123

Interpretation of choice of law clauses, below

Non-contractual claims applicability, 535

Public policy challenges, 538

Regulatory statute conflicts, 544

Restatement (2d) of Conflicts of Laws, 535, 542

Securities laws, 72

Validation, 534

Depecage, 515

Domestic, 511 et seq.

Due process, 526

European Union

Generally, 554 et seq.

Rome II Convention, 560

Extraterritoriality of US statutes, this index

Federal common law, state law conflicts, 199

Federalism issues facing foreign parties in US courts, 526

Forum non conveniens

Dismissal effects, 375

Transfer of venue distinguished, 377

Forum selection and choice of law clauses distinguished, 123

Full faith and credit standard, 514, 527

Governmental interests analysis, 514

Governmental interests test, 375

International choice of law in US courts, 518 et seq.

Interpretation of choice of law clauses

Generally, 534

Choice of interpretation law, 535

Jurisdiction selecting rules, 512

Jurisdictional requirements, recognition and enforcement of judgments, 636

Lex loci contractus, 512

Lex loci delicti, 511

Localization issues, 512

Notice of intent to assert foreign law, 526

Party expectations, Restatement (2d) of Conflicts of Laws, 525

Proving of foreign law, 526

Public policy conflicts

Contractual choice of law, 538

Domestic, 514, 522

Foreign, 530

Recognition and enforcement of judgments, jurisdictional requirements, 636

Regulatory statutes, contractual choice of law conflicts, 544

Renvoi doctrine, 513

Restatement (2d) of Conflicts of Laws

Generally, 516

Contractual choice of law, 535, 542

Party expectations, 525

Rome I Convention, 559

Rome II Convention, 560

Service of process requirements, 351

Situs of real property, 512

State laws, federal common law conflicts, 199

State vs state domestic law, 511 et seq.

Statutory provisions, 555

Traditional rules, 511

Transfer of venue, effect on choice

Generally, 372

Forum non conveniens distinguished, 377

Treaty interpretations, 340

US choice of law

Domestic setting, 511 et seq.

Federal court applications of state court rules, 519

International setting, 518 et seq.

CITIZENS
Dual citizenship, alienage jurisdiction, 148, 153

CIVIL LAW REGIMES
Choice of law, 554
Service of process requirements, 351

COLOR OF LAW
Generally, 192
Actual or apparent, 193
Alien Tort Statute, 192
Anti-Terrorism Act of 1990, 184
Torture Victim Protection Act, 183
Torture Victims Protection Act, 193

COMITY
Generally, 575
Act of state doctrine, 314
Act of state doctrine, comity aspects of doctrine, 319
Antisuit injunctions, comity considerations
Generally, 417
Arbitration, injunctions in aid of, 729
Attachment, public policy limitations, 113
Bankruptcy cases, comity dismissals of parallel litigation, 405
Choice of law, domestic, 514
Choice of law affects, 319
Extraterritoriality of US statutes, this index
International comity abstention, 405
Lis pendens, 403
Lis pendens, international comity considerations, 410
Pre-trial attachment, public policy limitations, 113
Public policy conflicts, 113, 432
Reciprocity principles and, 428
Recognition and Enforcement of Judgments, this index
Rule of practice vs rule of law, 629

COMMON LAW
Generally, 178
Federal Common law, this index
Judgment recognition, 630

CONCURRENT JURISDICTION
See Parallel Litigation, this index

CONFISCATION
See Expropriations, this index

CONFLICT OF LAWS
Generally, 511 et seq.
See also Choice of Law, this index

CONSTITUTIONAL LAW
Choice of law rules, constitutional limits, 526
Due Process, this index
Federal common law causes of action, 178
First Amendment protections, enforceability of foreign judgments infringing. See SPEECH Act of 2010, this index
Foreign Sovereign Immunities Act challenge
Generally, 225
Due process, 261
Full Faith and Credit, this index

CORPORATIONS
Alien Torts Statute claims against, 196
Foreign Corporations, this index
Foreign Sovereign Immunities Act, corporations as instrumentalities of foreign states, 245
Human rights violations liability, 195
Parent and subsidiaries
Agency test, 54
Single enterprise theory, 44, 49
Personal Jurisdiction, this index

DAMAGES
Antitrust laws, treble damages, 564
Arbitration clauses, damages for breach, 734
Punitive Damages, this index
Warsaw Convention, damages claims, 216

DEFAMATION
See SPEECH Act of 2010, this index

DEPECAGE
Choice of law, 515

DISCOVERY
Foreign and US discovery principles distinguished, 449, 453
Foreign utilization of US discovery
Generally, 496 et seq.
Court orders, 496
Discretion of US courts, 506, 510
European Commission, 497
Letters rogatory, 496
Privileges, 497, 507, 510
Statutory requirements, 497

Tailored discovery orders, 508

Forum non conveniens, discovery
adequacy of alternative forum, 383

US discovery abroad

Generally, 471

Antisuit injunctions in aid of US
discovery rights, 423

Bank records, 483

Burden of demonstrating need for
Hague Evidence Convention
utilization, 479

Foreign government sanctions
enforcing blocking statutes,
491

Foreign sovereign compulsion
doctrine, 493

Hague Evidence Convention, this
index

Jurisdictional discovery, 473

Letters of request, Hague Evidence
Convention, 456

Letters rogatory compared, 430

Nonparty witnesses, 473

Personal jurisdiction, 473

Restatement (3rd) of Foreign
Relations Law, 488

Secrecy laws conflicts

Generally, 424, 484

State secrecy claims, 494

US discovery rights

Antisuit injunctions in aid of, 423

Secrecy laws of foreign jurisdictions
conflicting, 424

DIVERSITY JURISDICTION

See Subject Matter Jurisdiction, this
index

DOING BUSINESS

See Personal Jurisdiction, this index

DOMICILE

Aliens, 218

Change or loss of domicile, 153

Diversity jurisdiction, national vs state
domiciliaries, 146

Federal common law, 146

Permanent Resident Aliens, this index

Personal Jurisdiction, this index

Subject Matter Jurisdiction, this index

Venue, this index

DUE PROCESS

Arbitration awards challenges, 714

Choice of law, 526

Extraterritoriality of US statutes, 531

Foreign Sovereign Immunities Act
challenge, 261

Full faith and credit standards
compared, 533

International due process, 671

Personal Jurisdiction, this index

Quasi in rem jurisdiction, 100

Recognition and Enforcement of
Judgments, this index

Service of process limitations, 62

ENFORCEMENT OF JUDGMENTS

See Recognition and Enforcement of
Judgments, this index

ERIE DOCTRINE

Act of state doctrine, 295

Attachment as substantive right for
purposes of doctrine, 112

Federal Common Law, this index

Forum selection clauses, 124

International law issues, 199

Recognition and enforcement of
judgments, 630

EUROPEAN COMMISSION

Lis pendens reform proposal, 413

US discovery utilization, 497

**EUROPEAN COURT OF JUSTICE
(ECJ)**

Antisuit injunctions, 432

Antisuit injunctions in aid of arbitration,
723, 730

Brussels Regulation priority principle

Generally, 730

Revision effective in 2015, 734

EUROPEAN UNION

Choice of Law, this index

Evidence gathering, US system
compared, 452

Extraterritorial antitrust laws, 590

Forum non conveniens, 395

Forum selection clauses, 138

Lis pendens, 412, 432

Personal Jurisdiction, this index

Recognition and Enforcement of
Judgments, this index

Service of documents, 350

Service of process, 350

Taking evidence abroad, 452

EVIDENCE AND WITNESSES

Discovery, this index

Forum non conveniens, witness and
evidence availability in alternative
forum, 379

Hague Evidence Convention, this index

Letters Rogatory, this index

Nonparty witnesses, US discovery abroad, 473

Taking Evidence Abroad, this index

EXPROPRIATIONS

Act of state doctrine, 291, 304

Foreign Sovereign Immunities Act exception, 285

Human rights violations distinguished, 304

EXTRATERRITORIALITY OF US STATUTES

Generally, 563 et seq.

Antitrust laws

Generally, 564 et seq.

Claw-back policy of UK, 572

Comity limitation, 578, 595

Direct and substantial effect on US, 568

Effects doctrine, 481

European Union's extraterritorial antitrust laws, 590

Foreign Trade Antitrust Improvement Act, 586

Treaties modifying extraterritoriality, 588

Treble damages, 564

Tripartite analysis of extraterritoriality, 574

Universality principle, 567

Attachment, 111

Choice of law clause conflicts, 544

Comity complaints of foreign parties, 574

Comity limitation, 578, 595

Conduct-and-effects test, 604, 615

Congressional intent, securities laws, 604

Direct and substantial effect on US, 568

Due process challenges, 531

Effects doctrine, 481

F-cubed transactions, 615

Globalization impacts, 563, 571

Human rights litigation, 284

Jurisdiction principles and, 563

Pre-trial attachment, 111

Regulatory vs private enforcement of securities laws, 615

Restatement (3rd) of Foreign Relations Law, 576

Securities laws

Generally, 603 et seq.

Conduct-and-effects test, 604, 615

Congressional intent, 604

F-cubed transactions, 615

Regulatory vs private enforcement, 615

SPEECH Act, quasi-extraterritorial effect, 663

Treaties modifying extraterritoriality, 588

Tripartite analysis of antitrust laws extraterritoriality, 574

Universal jurisdiction, 205

Universality principle, 567

FEDERAL ARBITRATION ACT

Defenses to enforcement of awards, 711

Liberal federal policy favoring arbitration, 702

New York Convention, FAA harmonization amendments, 694

Orders compelling arbitration, 723, 730

FEDERAL COMMON LAW

Authority to create, 178, 303

Bivens claims, 178

Choice of forum clauses, 553

Civil rights litigation, 254

Constitutional rights claims, 178

Discovered and made, 178

Domicile, 146

Erie doctrine mandate, 178, 554

Foreign Sovereign Immunities Act, 234

Forum non conveniens, 393

Forum selection clauses, 124

International law as, 164

Made and discovered, 178

Recognition and enforcement of judgments, 631

Separation of powers issue, 180

State law conflicts, 199

FEDERAL QUESTION JURISDICTION

Generally, 141

See Subject Matter Jurisdiction, this index

Alien Tort Statute, 163 et seq.

Anti-Terrorism Act of 1990, this index

Foreign policy concerns, litigation impacting, 197

Removal, 162

Sequencing of jurisdictional and related objections, 221

State law claims implicating foreign relations interests, 200, 203

Torture Victim Protection Act, this index

Treaty Enforcement, this index

Universal Jurisdiction, this index

Well-pleaded complaint rule, 162, 198

FEDERALISM

Anti-Injunction Act

Generally, 400

Exceptions, 432

Choice of law issues facing foreign parties in US courts, 526

Federal-state parallel proceedings conflicts, 410

International law claims in federal courts, 165

SPEECH Act, 663

FOREIGN AND US JURISPRUDENCE COMPARED

Discovery, 449, 453

Doing business as basis for personal jurisdiction, 57

Evidence gathering, 452

Lis pendens, 412

Mareva injunctions, 113

Personal jurisdiction

Generally, 28

European Union market integration, 79 et seq.

Products liability, 372, 381

Punitive damages, 11

Transient jurisdiction, 62, 337

FOREIGN CORPORATIONS

Diversity jurisdiction, 160

Personal jurisdiction in federal courts, 64

Service of process on agents, 349

Service of process on domestic affiliates, 326

Venue, 218

FOREIGN RELATIONS INTERESTS

Choice of law, public policy conflicts, 530

Federal question jurisdiction

Litigation involving foreign policy, 197

State law claims implicating, 200, 203

FOREIGN SOVEREIGN IMMUNITIES ACT

Generally, 223

Absolute vs restrictive immunity, 267

Act of state doctrine compared

Generally, 312, 318

Commercial exception, 310

Alien Tort Statute claims, 181, 235, 238

Aliens' claims, 231

Commercial activities exception

Generally, 224, 255, 264

Act of state doctrine compared, 310

Carried on in US, 270

Substantial connection with US, 272

Congressional intent, 251

Constitutionality

Generally, 225

Due process, 261

Corporations as instrumentalities of foreign states, 245

Direct effects in US, 260

Exceptions

Generally, 239, 255 et seq.

Commercial activities exception, above

Expropriation exception, 285

Federal common law, 234

Flatow Amendment, 279

Human rights litigation, 242, 275

Jurisdiction

Generally, 224

Protective jurisdiction, 232

Public vs private acts of sovereigns, 267

Punitive damages

Generally, 250

Flatow Amendment, 279

Restrictive vs absolute immunity, 224, 267

Retroactive application, 244

Service of process on foreign states, agencies and instrumentalities, 361, 369

State court litigation, 369

State Department suggestions of immunity

Generally, 223

Tate letters, 224, 303

Terrorism exception, 276

Text of, 776-786

FOREIGN TRADE ANTITRUST IMPROVEMENT ACT

Generally, 586

FORUM NON CONVENIENS

Generally, 371 et seq.

Abstention in federal courts distinguished, 410

Alien defendants, 220

Alternative forum considerations

Discovery mechanisms adequacy, 383

Institutional adequacy, 381
Jurisdiction in, 373
Related litigation in, 389
Remedial adequacy, 382
Waivers of procedural defenses, 374
Balancing test, 373
Brussels Regulation, 396
Choice of forum clauses, 392
Choice of law implications
Generally, 375
Transfer of venue distinguished, 377
Discretion of trial court, 391
Domestic and international, 220
European Union, 395
Federal common law, 393
Federal statutory claims, 393
Foreign alternative forums, 374
Foreign incident litigation
Foreign plaintiffs, 372, 391
US plaintiffs, 385, 391
Home forum of plaintiffs, 388
Inconsistent verdict risks, 374
Presumption favoring plaintiff's choice, 378
Products liability litigation in US, 372, 381
Public and private factors, 220
Public and private interest factors, 380
Related litigation in alternative forum, 389
Sequencing of jurisdictional and related objections, 221
State courts, 393
Transfer of venue distinguished
Generally, 220, 372
Appellate review, 394
Choice of law considerations, 377
Witness and evidence availability, 379

FORUM SELECTION
Generally, 1 et seq.
See also Personal Jurisdiction, this index
Antisuit Injunctions, this index
Arbitration, this index
Contract provisions
Generally, 114 et seq.
Admiralty law, 124
Antisuit injunctions to enforce, 415
Antiwaiver statutory provision conflicts, 126, 134
Appellate review of enforceability challenges, 135

Arbitration, this index
Balance of convenience, 121
Brussels Regulation, 138
Choice of law clause interrelationships, 546 et seq.
Choice of law clauses compared, 534
Choice of law clauses distinguished, 123
Consumer vs commercial transactions, 123
Domestic vs foreign clauses, 122
Enforceability
Generally, 114
Appellate review, 135
Erie doctrine applicability, 124
European Union, 138
Federal common law, 124, 553
Forum non conveniens challenges, 392
Fraud or duress challenges, 123
Hague Choice of Court Convention, 414
Inconvenience challenges, 119, 122
Judicial hostility, 123
Lis pendens conflicts, 413
Model Choice of Forum Act, 123
Negotiated provisions, 121
Public policy challenges, 414
Reasonableness, 120, 122
Scope of clause, 125
Securities laws, 72
Statutory antiwaiver provision conflicts, 126, 134
Venue transfer conflicts, 134
Forum Non Conveniens, this index
Hague Choice of Court Convention, 414
Judgment enforcement considerations. See Recognition and Enforcement of Judgments, this index
Parallel Litigation, this index
Transfer of Venue, this index

FORUM SHOPPING
Generally, 395

FREEDOM OF SPEECH
See SPEECH Act of 2010, this index

FULL FAITH AND CREDIT
Choice of law standard, 514, 527
Due process standards compared, 533
Foreign judgments not entitled to, 422
Recognition and Enforcement of Judgments, this index

GENERAL JURISDICTION

See also Personal Jurisdiction, this index

Personal and subject matter general jurisdiction distinguished, 63

GERMAN CODE OF CIVIL PROCEDURE (ZPO)

Punitive damages, 352

Recognition and Enforcement of Judgments, this index

Service of process, 356

GLOBALIZATION

Extraterritorial application of US statutes, 563, 571

Internet Activities, this index

Personal jurisdiction jurisprudence, globalization impacts, 19

HAGUE CONVENTION ON CHOICE OF COURTS

Generally, 124

Forum selection clauses, 414

Recognition and enforcement of judgments, 620

Scope of Convention, 137

Text of 748-757

HAGUE EVIDENCE CONVENTION

Generally, 453 et seq.

Blocking statutes

Generally, 481 et seq.

Amicus briefs of foreign governments, 494

Foreign government sanctions enforcing, 491

Foreign sovereign compulsion doctrine, 493

Good faith attempts to secure waivers

Generally, 487, 489

Burden of proof, 493

Injunctive enforcement, 495

Lax enforcement, 493

Products liability litigation, 458

Secrecy laws, 483

US courts' rejection, 482

Burden of demonstrating need, US discovery abroad, 479

Central authorities, 453

Letters of request, 456

Mandatory vs optional employment, 469, 481

Personal jurisdiction, 473

Privileges, 454

Products liability litigation, blocking statutes, 458

Secrecy laws, blocking statutes, 483

Supremacy Clause, 481

Text of, 742-747

US courts' rejection of blocking statutes, 482

US discovery abroad

Generally, 471

Burden of demonstrating need, 479

Three-prong test, 474

HAGUE SERVICE CONVENTION

Generally, 321

Applicability

Generally, 338

Trigger of applicability, 348

Central authority for service, 324

Diplomatic service utilization for service of process, 326

Document service, 324, 356

Domestic vs service abroad, 345

Drafting history as interpretive aid, 340, 347

European Union procedure compared, 350

Federal rules coordination, 325

Mandatory and optional provisions, 344

Notice standards, 341

Objectives of treaty, interpretation to effect, 342

Postal channels utilization, 325, 338

Punitive damages claims, 353

Sovereignty and security, compliance infringing, 353

Text of, 737-741

Trigger of applicability, 348

HICKENLOOPER AMENDMENT

Act of state doctrine, 302, 312

HUMAN RIGHTS LITIGATION

Act of state doctrine, 317

Alien Tort Statute, 283

Corporations, claims against, 195

Domestic civil rights litigation compared, 254, 318

Expropriations and human rights violations distinguished, 304

Extraterritoriality, 284

Flatow Amendment, 282

Foreign Sovereign Immunities Act, 242, 275

International law, 166

Torture Victims Protection Act, 283

Transient jurisdiction, 61

Universal scope, 284

IMMUNITY

Foreign Sovereign Immunities Act, this index

Status and conduct immunity distinguished, 254

INJUNCTIONS

Antisuit Injunctions, this index

Hague Evidence Convention, blocking statutes enforcement, 495

Mareva Injunctions, this index

INTER-AMERICAN CONVENTION (OR PANAMA CONVENTION) ON INTERNATIONAL COMMERCIAL ARBITRATION

Generally, 694

INTER-AMERICAN SERVICE CONVENTION ON LETTERS ROGATORY

Generally, 350

INTERIM RELIEF

See Provisional Remedies, this index

INTERNATIONAL LAW

Act of State Doctrine, this index

Alien Tort Statute claims

Generally, 186

Jurisdiction, 164

Brussels Convention, this index

Erie doctrine applicability, 199

Federal common law treatment, 164

Federalism issues, 165

Human rights norms, 166

Individual liability, Restatement (3rd) of Foreign Relations Law, 187

Operationalization as federal law, 165

Revisionist position, 165

Service of process provisions, construction in accord with, 352, 360

State actor doctrine, 194

State interpretations, 199

Universal jurisdiction, 236

INTERNATIONAL SHOE DOCTRINE

Personal Jurisdiction, this index

Quasi in rem jurisdiction, 100

INTERNET ACTIVITIES

See also SPEECH Act of 2010, this index

Personal jurisdiction, 96, 99

Recognition and enforcement of judgments, 664

ITALIAN TORPEDO

Lis pendens, forum selection clause conflicts, 413

JUDGMENTS

Preclusive effect, 617

Recognition and Enforcement of Judgments, this index

Restatement (2d) of Judgments, 643

JURISDICTION

Adjudicatory and legislative jurisdiction distinguished, 242

Alienage jurisdiction. See Subject Matter Jurisdiction, this index

Anticipating jurisdictional issues, 2

Arbitration

Jurisdiction challenges to enforcement of awards, 709

Jurisdiction to determine arbitrability, 703

Choice of law, jurisdiction selecting rules, 512

Discovery, jurisdictional, 473

Discretion of court to decline jurisdiction, 2

Doing business. See Personal Jurisdiction, this index

Extraterritoriality and, 563

Federal Question Jurisdiction, this index

Foreign Sovereign Immunities Act

Generally, 224

Protective jurisdiction, 232

Forum non conveniens, jurisdiction in alternative forum, 373

General

See also Personal Jurisdiction, this index

Personal and subject matter general jurisdiction distinguished, 63

Judgments, jurisdictional validity. See Recognition and Enforcement of Judgments, this index

Legislative and adjudicatory jurisdiction distinguished, 242

Mareva Injunctions, this index

Parallel Litigation, this index

Personal Jurisdiction, this index

Quasi in Rem Jurisdiction, this index

Sequencing of jurisdictional and related objections, 221

Service of Process, this index

Specific vs general. See Personal Jurisdiction, this index

Subject Matter Jurisdiction, this index

Transient jurisdiction. See Personal
Jurisdiction, this index

Treaty Enforcement, this index

Universal Jurisdiction, this index

JUSTICIABILITY

Separation of powers, 193

LAW OF NATIONS

See International Law, this index

LETTERS OF REQUEST

Hague Evidence Convention, 456

LETTERS ROGATORY

Discovery compared, 430

Inter-American Service Convention on
Letters Rogatory, 350

US discovery for foreign tribunals, 496

LIBEL

See SPEECH Act of 2010, this index

LIS PENDENS

Generally, 398 et seq.

Antisuit injunctions contrasted, 399

Bankruptcy cases, parallel litigation, 405

Brussels Regulation, 414, 432

Comity

Generally, 403

International comity abstention, 405

International comity considerations,
410

Comparative law, 412

Domestic parallel litigation, 399

European Commission reform proposal,
413

European Union, 412, 432

Federal court abstention doctrines, 401

Federal courts, comity dismissals

Generally, 403

Relevant factors, 411

Federal-federal parallel litigation, 402

Federal-state parallel litigation

Generally, 399

Anti-Injunction Act, this index

Federalism concerns, 410

First in time rule

Federal-federal parallel litigation,
402

International parallel litigation, 432

Forum non conveniens, abstention in
federal courts distinguished, 410

Forum selection clause conflicts, 413

State-state parallel litigation, 402

Virtual unflagging obligation of federal
courts to exercise jurisdiction, 400,
403

LONG ARM STATUTES

Generally, 2

Defamation judgment creditors, 39

Doing business, 56

Federal court recourse to state statute,
66

Jurisdictional challenges to resulting
judgments, 642

Specific jurisdiction, 31, 48

Substituted service, 343

MAREVA INJUNCTIONS

Generally, 102, 105

Foreign vs US jurisprudence, 113

MINIMUM CONTACTS ANALYSIS

See Personal Jurisdiction, this index

MODEL CHOICE OF FORUM ACT

Generally, 123

**MONTREAL CONVENTION (AIR
TRANSPORTATION)**

Treaty enforcement, 214

**NEW YORK CONVENTION
(ARBITRATION)**

Generally, 693

Defenses to enforcement of arbitration
awards, 711

Federal Arbitration Act harmonization
amendments, 694

Interim relief, 715

Liberal policy favoring arbitration, 702

Manifest disregard of law defense to
enforcement of awards, 710

Party signatories, 693

Purposes, 693

Text of, 771-777

ORDRE PUBLIC

Generally, 354

See also Public Policy, this index

PARALLEL LITIGATION

Generally, 371 et seq.

Alternative forum and single forum
cases distinguished, 442, 446

Antisuit Injunctions, this index

Brussels Convention, 439

Brussels Regulation, 396,413,432,437

Concurrent jurisdiction, 399

Consolidation of federal court cases, 402

First in time rule

Federal-federal conflicts, 402

International parallel litigation, 432

Forum Non Conveniens, this index

Forum shopping, 395

Inconsistent verdict risks, forum non conveniens to remedy, 374

Lis Pendens, this index

Removal to resolve, 399

Transfer of Venue, this index

PARTIES

Alien Tort Statute, 181, 187

Anti-Terrorism Act of 1990, 183

Torture Victim Protection Act, 183

PERMANENT RESIDENT ALIENS

Diversity jurisdiction, 145, 155

Venue, 218

PERSONAL JURISDICTION

Generally, 1 et seq.

Agency test, parent and subsidiary corporations, 54

Antisuit injunctions, 431

Appellate review of personal jurisdiction issues, 79

Brussels Convention, 79 et seq.

Brussels Regulation, 689

Burden of proof of establishment, 20, 35

Certainty issues presented by US jurisprudence, 28

Coerced presence in jurisdiction, transient jurisdiction, 61

Consent, acquisition by, 16

Contacts-related activities, specific jurisdiction, 38

Continuous contacts, general jurisdiction, 44

Contracts law litigation

Minimum contacts established by, 40

Specific jurisdiction, 40

Contractual forum selection. See Forum Selection, this index

Corporations

General jurisdiction, 50

Parent and subsidiary corporations, below

Transient jurisdiction, 61

Defamation judgment creditors

See also SPEECH Act of 2010, this index

Long-arm statutes reaching, 39

Specific jurisdiction, 36

Discovery, jurisdictional, 473

Doing business as basis of general jurisdiction, 55, 395

Domicile as basis

Generally, 16

General jurisdiction, 50

Due process limitations

Generally, 2, 5, 46

Transient jurisdiction, 58

Effects test, intentional torts, 32, 36

European Union, 79 et seq.

European vs US jurisprudence, 28

Fair play and substantial justice, 3

Fairness calculus, specific jurisdiction, 28

Federal courts

National contacts, 71

Recourse to state long-arm statutes, 66

Federal vs state court general jurisdiction, 53

Foreign corporations, personal jurisdiction in federal courts, 64

Foreign parent corporation's US subsidiary, 53

Foreign subsidiary of US parent corporation, 44

Foreign vs domestic defendants, specific jurisdiction, 10, 18, 22

Foreseeability of litigation in forum state, 5, 9

General jurisdiction

Generally, 43 et seq.

Corporations, 50

Federal courts, 72

Federal vs state court reach, 53

International Shoe doctrine, 44, 46

Specific jurisdiction distinguished, 44

Globalization and personal jurisdiction, 19

Hague Evidence Convention, 473

Human rights litigation, transient jurisdiction, 61

Intentional torts, effects test, 32, 36

International Shoe doctrine

General jurisdiction, 44, 46

Specific jurisdiction, 3, 23

Transient jurisdiction, 59

Internet activities litigation, 96, 99

Isolated occurrences in forum state, 8

Judgment enforcement, jurisdictional challenges. See Recognition and Enforcement of Judgments, this index

Legitimate interests of forum state, specific jurisdiction, 7

Litigating personal jurisdiction
Generally, 73
Sequencing of jurisdictional and related objections, 221

Long Arm Statutes, this index

Mail contacts, 41

Minimum contacts
Generally, 3, 10
Contracts establishing, 40
Judgment challenges, 641
Mail and wire contacts, 41
Subsidiary corporation's, 42

National contacts, federal courts, 71

Parent and subsidiary corporations
Agency test, 54
Contacts of subsidiary, 42
Foreign parent's US subsidiary, 53
Foreign subsidiary of US parent corporation, 44
General jurisdiction, 44
Single enterprise theory, 44, 49

Predictability issues presented by US jurisprudence, 28

Presence, acquisition by, 16

Process. See Service of Process, this index

Products liability claims against foreign manufacturers, 3, 14, 27

Property liability claims, 44

Purposeful action directed to forum state, 6

Purposeful availment analysis, 8, 10, 16

Quasi in Rem Jurisdiction, this index

Reasonableness calculus, specific jurisdiction, 28

Sequencing of jurisdictional and related objections, 221

Service of Process, this index

Single enterprise theory, parent and subsidiary corporations, 44, 49

Special appearance to challenge jurisdiction, 78

Specific jurisdiction
Generally, 3 et seq.
Contracts law litigation, 40
Defamation judgment creditors, 36
Federal courts, 72
Foreign vs domestic defendants, 22
General jurisdiction distinguished, 44
Long-arm statutes, 31, 48

SPEECH Act of 2010, this index

Stipulated jurisdiction
Generally, 114 et seq.
See also Forum Selection, this index

Stream of commerce analysis, 5, 16

Stream of commerce metaphor, general jurisdiction, 47

Subject matter jurisdiction distinguished, 1, 76

Systematic contacts, general jurisdiction, 44

Transient ("tag") jurisdiction
Generally, 58
Coerced presence in jurisdiction, 61
Corporations, 61
Due process challenges, 58
Foreign vs US jurisprudence, 62, 337
Forum non convenience, 61
Human rights litigation, 61
International Shoe doctrine, 59
Service of process, 337

US discovery abroad, 473

Waiver of defects, 77

Waiver of jurisdictional issues in trial court and enforcement of resulting judgment, 643

Wire contacts, 41

POLITICAL QUESTION DOCTRINE

Abstention, 308

Separation of powers, 193

PREEMPTION

Generally, 204

Human rights litigation, 284

Removal of cases to federal court, 214

Treaty enforcement, preemption of state law claims, 217

PRE-TRIAL ATTACHMENT

Generally, 99 et seq.
See also Quasi in Rem Jurisdiction, this index

Admiralty law, 101

Comity, public policy limitations on doctrine, 113

Erie doctrine, attachment as substantive right, 112

Extraterritorial, 111

Mareva Injunctions, this index

PROCESS

See Service of Process, this index

PRODUCTS LIABILITY

Foreign vs US jurisprudence, 372, 381

Hague Evidence Convention blocking statutes, 458

Personal jurisdiction, claims against foreign manufacturers, 3, 14, 27

Service of process on foreign manufacturers, 326

US suits, international forum non conveniens motions, 372, 381

PROTECTIVE JURISDICTION

Foreign Sovereign Immunities Act, 232

PROVING OF FOREIGN LAW

Generally, 526

See also Choice of Law, this index

PROVISIONAL REMEDIES

Arbitrations, interim relief, 715

Brussels Regulation, 113

Mareva Injunctions, this index

Pre-Trial Attachment, this index

PUBLIC POLICY

Choice of Law, this index

Comity conflicts, 432

Comity limitations, attachment, 113

Forum selection clause challenges, 414

Recognition and Enforcement of Judgments, this index

Service of process challenges, 354

PUNITIVE DAMAGES

Foreign Sovereign Immunities Act

Generally, 250

Flatow Amendment, 279

Foreign vs US jurisprudence, 11

German Code of Civil Procedure, 352

Hague Service Convention conflict, 353

Montreal Convention (air transportation), 215

Recognition and enforcement of judgments, 353, 620

State court awards based on out-of-forum activities, 95

PURPOSEFUL AVAILMENT ANALYSIS

See Personal Jurisdiction, this index

QUASI IN REM JURISDICTION

Generally, 99 et seq.

Antisuit injunctions, 422

Due process, 100

International Shoe doctrine, 100

RECIPROCITY

Antisuit injunctions, reciprocity concerns, 419

Arbitration awards enforcement considerations, 707

Comity and, 428

Recognition and Enforcement of Judgments, this index

RECOGNITION AND ENFORCEMENT OF ARBITRAL AWARDS

Arbitration, this index

Federal Arbitration Act, this index

New York Convention, this index

RECOGNITION AND ENFORCEMENT OF JUDGMENTS

Generally, 617 et seq.

Act of state doctrine, recognition of judgments analysis, 316

ALI judgment recognition proposal

Generally, 631

Default judgments, 651

Bilateral treaties, 673

Brussels Convention, 684 et seq.

Brussels Regulation

Fundamental rights principle, 690

Public policy, 687

Choice of law as to jurisdiction requirements, 636

Comity

Foreign judgment in US, 621

Full faith and credit principle compared, 626

Rule of practice or rule of law, 629

Common law of judgment recognition, 630

Declaratory judgments, foreign judgements in US, 642

Defamation judgments, public policy challenges, 656

Default judgments

ALI judgment recognition proposal, 651

Foreign judgments in US courts, 643

Due process

Foreign judgment in US, 666

International due process, 671

Personal jurisdiction requirement in US courts, minimum contacts standard, 641

Uniform Foreign Country Money Judgments Recognition Act, 666

Erie Doctrine, 630

European Union
   Generally, 684 et seq.
   Brussels Regulation, above
   Full faith and credit, 684

Federal common law, 631

First Amendment protections of US
   citizens, 656

Foreign country vs state judgments,
   public policy challenges, 651

Foreign judgment in US
   Generally, 621 et seq.
   ALI judgment recognition proposal,
      above
   Comity, 621
   Declaratory judgments, 642
   Defamation judgments, public policy
      challenges, 656
   Default judgments, 643
   Due process, 666
   Erie Doctrine, 630
   Federal common law, 631
   First Amendment protections of US
      citizens, 656
   Personal jurisdiction requirement in
      US courts, below
   Reciprocity, 624, 626
   Res judicata applicability to
      jurisdictional issues, 643
   Restatement (3rd) of Foreign
      Relations Law, 630
   Source of law, 627 et seq.
   SPEECH Act of 2010, this index
   State law, 632
   Tax and penal judgments, 623, 672
   Traditional approaches, 621
   Uniform Foreign Country Money
      Judgments Recognition Act,
      633
   US judgments abroad contrasted,
      618

Forum selection issues related, 617

Full faith and credit
   Generally, 618
   Comity principle compared, 626
   European Union, 684

Fundamental rights principle, Brussels
   Regulation, 690

German Code of Civil Procedure
   Generally, 674
   Punitive damages, 680, 682

Hague Convention on Choice of Courts,
   620

Internet-related litigation, 664

Personal jurisdiction requirement in US
   courts
   Generally, 1, 636 et seq.
   Choice of law issues, 636
   Declaratory judgments, 642
   Default judgments, 643
   Due process minimum contacts
      standard, 641
   Forum selection considerations, 618
   Jurisdictional validity, 1
   Res judicata applicability, 643
   Uniform Foreign Country Money
      Judgments Recognition Act,
      641
   Waiver of jurisdictional issues in
      trial court, 643

Preclusive effect of judgments, 617

Procedural fairness, public policy
   challenges to judgments, 666

Public policy challenges to judgments
   Generally, 618
   Brussels Regulation, 687
   Defamation judgments, 656
   Domestic public policy concerns, 651
      et seq.
   First Amendment protections of US
      citizens, 656
   Foreign country vs state judgments,
      651
   Foreign public policy concerns, 673
      et seq.
   Ordre Public, this index
   Procedural fairness, 666
   Punitive damages awards, foreign
      enforcement, 680, 682
   SPEECH Act of 2010, this index
   Substantive laws, 651
   Uniform Foreign Country Money
      Judgments Recognition Act,
      651

Reciprocity, 624, 626

Res judicata applicability to
   jurisdictional issues, 643

Restatement (3rd) of Foreign Relations
   Law
   Generally, 630
   Tax and penal judgments, 672

Service of process failures, 337

Service of process violating foreign law,
   351

SPEECH Act of 2010, this index

State law, foreign judgment in US, 632

State-state enforcement, 617

Substantive laws, public policy challenges to judgments, 651

Transient jurisdiction based judgments, 62

Treaties

Generally, 619

Bilateral treaties, 673

Brussels Convention, 674, 684 et seq.

Uniform Foreign Country Money Judgments Recognition Act

Generally, 633

Due process, 666

Personal jurisdiction requirement in US courts, 641

Public policy challenges to judgments, 651

US judgments abroad

Generally, 673 et seq.

Foreign judgment in US contrasted, 618

German Code of Civil Procedure, above

Punitive damages, 620

REGULATORY STATUTES

Antitrust Laws, this index

Carriage of Goods by Sea claims, arbitrability, 695

Choice of law, contract provision conflicts, 544

Extraterritoriality of US statutes, this index

Forum non conveniens applicability to claims, 393

Securities Laws, this index

REMOVAL TO FEDERAL COURT

Generally, 142, 161, 399

Procedural requirements, 162

RENVOI DOCTRINE

Choice of law, 513

RESTATEMENT (2D) OF CONFLICT OF LAWS

See Choice of Law, this index

RESTATEMENT (2D) OF JUDGMENTS

Enforcement of judgments, jurisdictional defects, 643

RESTATEMENT (3RD) OF FOREIGN RELATIONS LAW

Extraterritorial application of US statutes, 576

International law violations, individual liability, 187

Recognition and Enforcement of Judgments, this index

Service of process, 351

Universal jurisdiction, 204

US discovery abroad, 488

REVENUE LAWS

Pre-trial attachment, 104

Recognition and Enforcement of Judgments, this index

ROME CONVENTIONS

See Choice of Law, this index

RULE 4, FEDERAL RULES OF CIVIL PROCEDURE

Long arm statutes, 2, 65

Personal jurisdiction, 53, 62

Service of process, 321 et seq.

SECRECY LAWS

US discovery abroad conflicts

Generally, 484

State secrecy claims, 494

US discovery rights conflicts

Generally, 424

SECURITIES LAWS

Antisuit injunctions in securities litigation, 423

Antiwaiver provisions, 126

Arbitration of claims, 702

Choice of forum and choice of law clauses, 72

Extraterritoriality of US statutes, this index

F-cubed transaction, 615

Forum non conveniens challenges to federal statutory claims, 393

Service of process, nationwide service, 72

SEPARATION OF POWERS

Act of state doctrine, 295

Federal common law raising issues of, 180

Justiciability, 193

Political question doctrine, 193

SERVICE OF DOCUMENTS

European Union, 350

Hague Service Convention, this index

SERVICE OF PROCESS

Generally, 58 et seq., 321 et seq.

Actual notice standard, service on foreign states, agencies and instrumentalities, 361

Agent, service on under state law, 349

Alien Tort Statute, 193

Choice of law as to service requirements, 351

Civil law service requirements, 351

Commercial enterprises as foreign instrumentalities for purposes of service on, 365

Corporation agents, service on under state laws, 349

Costs, 321

Court approval for service on foreign defendants, 333

Criminal proscriptions of foreign laws, 351

Diplomatic service, Hague Convention, 326

Domestic affiliate of foreign corporation, 326

Domestic agent for service of process of foreign defendant, 338

Due process limitations, 62

Email service, 333

Enforcement of judgment requirements, 337

European Union, 350

Federal courts, nationwide service, 62, 72

Federal Rules of Civil Procedure

    Generally, 321

    Foreign law, service violating, 351, 359

    Hague convention coordination, 325

    Mail service to foreign defendants, 329

Foreign defendants, service under federal rules, 321

Foreign law, service violating

    Generally, 350 et seq.

    Civil law service requirements, 351

    Criminal proscriptions, 351

    Enforcement of judgment challenges, 351

    Federal Rules of Civil Procedure, 351, 359

    German Code of Civil Procedure, 356

    Public policy challenges, 354

    Public service, 356

    Quashal of service in foreign courts, 351

    Swiss law, 358

Foreign states, agencies and instrumentalities, service on

    Generally, 361 et seq.

    Actual notice standard, 361

    Commercial enterprises, 365

Core functions analysis, 364

    Foreign Sovereign Immunities Act, 361, 369

German Code of Civil Procedure, 356

Hague Service Convention, this index

Immunity from service, 193

Inter-American Service Convention on Letters Rogatory, 350

International law, construction of service provisions to accord to, 352, 360

Judgment challenges based on service failures, 337

Long arm statutes providing for substituted service, 343

Mail service to foreign defendants

    Federal Rules of Civil Procedure, 329

    Hague Convention, 325

    State Department guidelines, 332

Notice purposes, 321

Notice standards, service on foreign states, agencies and instrumentalities, 361

Public policy challenges to service, 354

Public service, 356

Publication, 333

Quashal of service in foreign courts, 351

Requests for waivers, 321

Restatement (3rd) of Foreign Relations Law, 351

Securities laws, nationwide service, 72

SPEECH Act, 40

State Department guidelines, mail service to foreign defendants, 332

Substituted service under long arm statutes, 343

Swiss law, 358

Tag jurisdiction service, 337

Telex, 333

Torture Victims Protection Act, 193

Translation of documents served abroad, 326, 337

Waivers of service

    Costs assessments on failure to waive, 335

    Foreign defendants, 334

    Requests for waivers, 321

SOVEREIGNS

Act of State Doctrine, this index

Foreign Sovereign Immunities Act, this index

Service of Process, this index

SPECIFIC JURISDICTION

See Personal Jurisdiction, this index

SPEECH ACT OF 2010

Congressional intent, 663

Federalism, 663

Personal jurisdiction over defamation judgment creditors, 40

Quasi-extraterritorial effect, 663

Service of process, 40

Subject matter jurisdiction, 665

STATE ACTION REQUIREMENT

Alien Tort Statute, 188

Torture Victim Protection Act, 184, 188

STATE ACTOR DOCTRINE

International laws, 194

STATE DEPARTMENT

Foreign Sovereign Immunities Act, this index

Mail service to foreign defendants, State Department guidelines, 332

STATE LAWS

Anti-Injunction Act, this index

Antisuit injunctions, state-state parallel litigation, 402

Enforcement of judgments in another state, 617

Federal common law conflicts, 199

Federal question jurisdiction, state law claims implicating foreign relations interests, 200, 203

Federalism, this index

Forum non conveniens, 393

Lis pendens, federal-state parallel litigation, 399

Long Arm Statutes, this index

Personal Jurisdiction, this index

Recognition and enforcement of foreign judgments, 632

Service of process, agents for, 349

Subject matter jurisdiction, state- vs federal-court limitations, 2, 141

Treaty enforcement, 217

STATUTES

Extraterritoriality of US Statutes, this index

Regulatory Statutes, this index

STREAM OF COMMERCE METAPHOR

See Personal Jurisdiction, this index

SUBJECT MATTER JURISDICTION

Generally, 141 et seq.

Admiralty law, 162

Alienage jurisdiction

Generally, 142

Complete diversity, 153

Dual citizenship, 148, 153

Permanent Resident Aliens, this index

Purposes, 152

Statutory exceptions, 154

Venue, this index

Americans domiciled abroad, diversity jurisdiction, 146

Constitutional limitations on federal courts, 141

Diversity jurisdiction

Generally, 142 et seq.

Americans domiciled abroad, 146

Complete diversity, 153

Foreign corporations, 160

Incomplete diversity, 162

National vs state domiciliaries, 146

Permanent Resident Aliens, this index

Purposes, 152

Removal to Federal Courts, this index

Domicile, this index

Dual citizenship, alienage jurisdiction, 148, 153

Federal Question Jurisdiction, this index

Federal vs state courts, 141

Foreign corporations, diversity jurisdiction, 160

General jurisdiction, personal and subject matter distinguished, 63

Limited jurisdiction of federal courts, 141

National vs state domiciliaries, diversity jurisdiction, 146

Personal jurisdiction distinguished, 1, 76

Purposes of diversity and alienage jurisdiction, 152

Removal to Federal Courts, this index

Sequencing of jurisdictional and related objections, 221

SPEECH Act, 665

State- vs federal-court limitations, 2

Statutory limitations on federal courts, 141

Waiver of jurisdictional issues in trial court and enforcement of resulting judgment, 643

SUPREMACY CLAUSE

Treaty enforcement, 205

Treaty interpretation, 481

SWISS LAW

Service of process, 358

TAG JURISDICTION

See Personal Jurisdiction, this index

TAKING EVIDENCE ABROAD

Generally, 449 et seq.

Discovery, this index

European Union, 452

Hague Evidence Convention, this index

US and foreign methods of obtaining
evidence compared, 452

TATE LETTERS

See Foreign Sovereign Immunities Act,
this index

TERRORISM

Anti-Terrorism Act of 1990, this index

Foreign Sovereign Immunities Act,
terrorism exception, 276

TORTURE

Alien Tort Statute, this index

Human Rights Litigation, this index

Torture Victim Protection Act, this index

**TORTURE VICTIM PROTECTION
ACT (TVPA)**

Generally, 182

Alien Tort Statute distinguished, 193

Alien Tort Statute harmonization, 183

Color of law requirement, 183, 193

Extrajudicial killing, 182

Human rights litigation, 283

Parties, 183

Service of process, 193

State action requirement, 184, 188

TRANSFER OF VENUE

Alien defendants, 219

Choice of law implications

Generally, 372

Forum non conveniens
distinguished, 377

Federal court system, 371

Forum non conveniens distinguished

Generally, 220, 372

Appellate review, 394

Choice of law considerations, 377

Forum selection clauses, venue transfer
conflicts, 134

TRANSIENT JURISDICTION

See Personal Jurisdiction, this index

TREATY ENFORCEMENT

Generally, 205 et seq.

Alien Tort Statute, 205

Bilateral judgment recognition and
enforcement treaties, 673

Choice of law in interpretation of
treaties, 340

Concurrent jurisdiction of state courts,
217

Interpretation of treaties, 339

Judgment recognition and enforcement
treaties

Generally, 619

Bilateral treaties, 673

Montreal Convention (air
transportation), 214

Objectives of treaty, interpretation to
effect, 342

Preemption of state law claims, 217

Recognition and enforcement of
judgments treaties

Generally, 619

Bilateral treaties, 673

Self-executing status questions, 205, 216

State courts, concurrent jurisdiction, 217

Supremacy Clause, 205

Warsaw Convention (air transportation)

Generally, 206

Baggage claims, 217

Death damages, 216

UNCITRAL

Arbitration, this index

New York Convention development, 693

UNCONSCIONABILITY

Forum selection clauses, fraud or duress
challenges, 123

**UNIFORM FOREIGN COUNTRY
MONEY JUDGMENTS
RECOGNITION ACT**

See Recognition and Enforcement of
Judgments, this index

UNIVERSAL JURISDICTION

Generally, 204

Extraterritoriality principles, 205

International law, 236

Restatement (3rd) of Foreign Relations
Law, 204

VENUE

Generally, 218

Alien defendants

Domicile, 218

Fall-back venue, 219

Foreign corporations, 218

Forum non conveniens, 220

Transfer of Venue, this index

Domicile

Alien defendants, 218

Fall-back venue, 219

Foreign corporations, 218

Forum Non Conveniens, this index

Forum selection clauses, venue transfer
conflicts, 134

Permanent resident aliens, 218

Transfer of Venue, this index

Transient jurisdiction, 61

WAIVER OF SERVICE

See Service of Process, this index

**WARSAW CONVENTION (AIR
TRANSPORTATION)**

Generally, 206

Baggage claims, 217

Death damages, 216

WITNESSES

See Evidence and Witnesses, this index